BRIEF GUIDE TO TOPICS

FUNDAMENTALS OF INVESTING
Fourth Edition

FUNDAMENTALS OF INVESTING

Fourth Edition

LAWRENCE J. GITMAN
San Diego State University

MICHAEL D. JOEHNK
Arizona State University

1817

HARPER & ROW, PUBLISHERS, New York

Cambridge, Philadelphia, San Francisco, Washington,
London, Mexico City, São Paulo, Singapore, Sydney

To our wives, Robin and Charlene

Sponsoring Editor: John Greenman
Development Editor: Ann Torbert
Project Coordination, Text and Cover Design: York Production Services
Production Manager: Jeanie Berke
Printer and Binder: R. R. Donnelley & Sons Company

Fundamentals of Investing, Fourth Edition
Copyright © 1990 by Lawrence J. Gitman and Michael D. Joehnk

Library of Congress Cataloging in Publication Data

Gitman, Lawrence J.
    Fundamentals of Investing / Lawrence J. Gitman, Michael D. Joehnk.—4th ed.
        p.   cm.
    Includes bibliographical references.
    ISBN 0-06-042362-5
    1. Investments   I. Joehnk, Michael D.   II. Title
HG4521.G547   1990
332.6′78—dc20

89-26683
CIP

90 91 92 93 9 8 7 6 5 4 3 2 1

Contents in Brief

Contents in Detail

Preface

Fundamentals of Investing is designed to serve investors who are (or will be) actively developing and monitoring their own investment portfolios. It may be used with good results in the first course in investments offered at colleges and universities, junior and community colleges, trade and technical schools, professional certification programs, and continuing education courses. The book describes techniques, vehicles, and strategies for implementing investment goals in a portfolio context and in light of risk-return trade-offs. It is written in an informal, conversational tone wherever possible and liberally uses examples to demonstrate important investment concepts, strategies, and techniques. A variety of headings and visual devices enhance the presentation, and great care has been taken to ensure a consistent reading level throughout the book. Clearly, the benefits of readability accrue not only to students, but also to instructors, whose job of teaching is made easier.

CHANGES IN THE FOURTH EDITION

Much has happened in the practice of investing over the past few years—some good, some bad. The stock market achieved new highs throughout much of the 1980s, and on October 19, 1987, it also experienced a new low as it recorded the biggest crash in history. Since then, the market has made a strong recovery, although its relatively high volatility continues to challenge many investors. In addition, tax revision occurred; numerous mega mergers, leveraged buyouts, and corporate restructuring continued to take place; new investment vehicles and strategies were developed and marketed; computer models yielded sophisticated new trading strategies; and a number of investment professionals were indicted for ''insider trading'' activities.

These economic and market changes, along with the ever-present time constraints placed on instructors in investments, have necessitated this significantly revised fourth edition. Using information gathered from both academicians and practicing investment professionals, feedback from adopters, colleagues, and students, and observations gained from using the text ourselves, we developed a detailed revision plan for this edition. We decided that the role of the personal computer in the investment process, deregulation of the financial marketplace, and the

financial services revolution should continue to receive major attention in this edition. The development of investment strategies, with specific attention to liquidity and the need to consider taxes, are also stressed throughout. The major revisions in this edition are of two types: general changes and content changes.

General Changes

Three major general changes were made to retain the text's up-to-date coverage and organization and to enhance its state-of-the-art pedagogy.

Timely Topics. A number of ongoing as well as post-crash issues and developments are reshaping the financial markets and investment vehicles, strategies, and techniques. In order to retain the text's state-of-the-art coverage, all important developments have been carefully integrated throughout the text. Included are discussions of globalization of the financial markets; ethics and insider trading; event risk; buybacks, buyouts, and LBOs; program trading; and asset allocation schemes. These discussions should provide students with a realistic understanding of the investment arena, thereby allowing them to develop and implement relevant and effective investment strategies.

Relevant Investor Insights. Investor insights boxes, relating real-life stories or events to the text discussions, continue to be included in this edition. Each of the two boxes included in every chapter is now referred to in the related textual discussions. About two-thirds of the boxes are new to this edition. Linking the boxes to the text should greatly enrich the students' total learning experience by allowing them to more clearly understand the boxes' relevance to the textual discussion.

New Running Glossary. Throughout the text, key terms and their definitions appear in the text margin when they are first introduced. The running glossary replaces the end of chapter lists of key terms included in earlier editions. For convenience the text continues to include a separate end-of-book glossary. The running glossary will allow students to quickly recognize and understand new terminology when first introduced, and the end-of-book glossary will continue to provide them with a quick reference to key term definitions.

Content Changes

A number of other important but less sweeping changes have also been made:

1. Coverage of globalization of financial markets and the question of ethics, including a discussion of insider trading, has been added to Chapter 1.
2. Chapter 2, on investment markets and transactions, now includes discussion of arbitration procedures for disputes between investors and brokers and also describes the wrap account—a new type of brokerage account.
3. *Money* magazine's Small Investor Index is now described in Chapter 3 on sources of investment information and advice; also, the section describing the role of the personal computer in investments has been thoroughly revised to

include brief descriptions of the major investments software currently available from Dow Jones.

4. Chapter 4, on developing investment strategies, has been thoroughly updated and now includes discussions of variable life insurance, central asset accounts, and brokered CDs.

5. Interest-on-interest, the critical assumption underlying yield, is now explained in Chapter 5, on measuring investment return and risk. In addition, a discussion of event risk is now included in this chapter.

6. Extensive coverage of the market crash of October 1987 was added to Chapter 6, along with data and discussion of historical total return performance in the stock market over the past 40 years.

7. Discussion of the statement of cash flows, now a required element in the annual reports of publicly traded companies, was added to Chapter 7.

8. Chapter 8, on stock valuation, now includes a major new section dealing with corporate takeovers, LBOs, and program trading, and their impact on the market.

9. Material on securitization and asset-based securities was added to Chapter 9, on bonds; in addition, to put matters into perspective, total return performance over the past 40 years is also included for debt securities.

10. Chapter 10 now includes discussions on PIK-preferreds, the preferred stock equivalent of junk bonds.

11. Chapter 11 was updated, as appropriate, to account for new options vehicles.

12. In Chapter 12 some new material was added on index arbitrage program trading.

13. There is expanded coverage of the mutual fund selection process in Chapter 13, along with more material on mutual fund loads, charges, and fees.

14. Chapter 15, on tax shelters and limited partnerships, has been thoroughly updated to reflect the latest tax law revisions and interpretations; in addition, the discussion of single-premium life insurance has been revised to reflect its legislatively reduced tax-shelter appeal.

15. The procedures for building a portfolio using asset allocation schemes are now carefully explained and demonstrated in Chapter 16 on portfolio management.

PEDAGOGICAL FEATURES

The text includes numerous useful pedagogical aids. Among them are a comprehensive yet flexible organization, learning objectives, running glossary, numerous examples, high-interest boxes, varied end-of-chapter materials, computer-based investment management sections, and a number of useful appendixes. In addition, there is available (upon request from the publisher) a *Valuation Supplement* to accompany this book; written by David J. McLaughlin of Chase Investment Counsel, it provides broader coverage of a number of major valuation concepts introduced in the text.

Comprehensive Yet Flexible Organization

This text is organized in a logical sequence. Beginning with a description of the investment environment that includes the concepts of return and risk, it then exam-

ines each popular investment vehicle—common stocks, fixed-income securities, speculative investments, real estate, and tax shelters. The final section includes two chapters on investment administration that interrelates all the investment vehicles. Although the first and last parts of the text are best covered at the start and end of the course, respectively, coverage of particular investment vehicles may be sequenced according to the instructor's preference.

In organizing each chapter we tried to maintain a decision-making perspective. By pointing out the pros and cons of various strategies and vehicles, we have provided useful information but have left it to individual investors to select the actions that are consistent with their objectives. In addition, we've tried to illustrate each of the vehicles and strategies so that the student is not left with just an abstract definition but truly senses the decision-making implications and consequences of each contemplated investment action. The comprehensive yet flexible nature of the book makes it adaptable to a variety of course structures and teaching objectives.

Learning Objectives

Each chapter begins with six learning objectives that clearly state the concepts and materials to be covered. We have found that these objectives help guide students through the chapter's content.

Running Glossary

New terms are set in boldface type and defined when first introduced. In addition, each of those terms and its definition appears in the text margin in order to enhance student understanding and ease of review. All of the running glossary terms also appear in a separate end-of-book glossary.

Numerous Examples

The text contains a wealth of examples and illustrations to help clarify potentially troublesome concepts.

High-Interest Boxes

Each chapter includes two boxed essays, called ''Investor Insights,'' that describe real-life situations or events. The boxes, which demonstrate text concepts and enliven the text, are linked to related text discussions.

End-of-Chapter Materials

A number of important elements are included at the end of each chapter in order to provide students with a mechanism for reviewing and reinforcing the concepts, tools, and techniques described within the chapter.

Summary.   Each chapter is summarized with a list of key concepts and ideas.

Review Questions and Problems.   A comprehensive set of 20 or so review questions and problems is included at the end of each chapter for student practice. As in the previous edition, we continue to include as many problem-type questions as possible, while still maintaining a balance with essay-type questions.

Case Problems. Each chapter ends with two distinct case problems. These brief accounts encourage the student to apply techniques presented in the chapter and make recommendations on how an investor might solve a specific problem.

Selected Readings. A list of selected readings directs the student to recent articles from such publications as *Barron's, Changing Times, Financial World, Forbes, Money,* and *The Wall Street Journal.* These timely references enable students to gain further investment insights from the popular press.

Computer-Based Investment Management Sections

At the end of each of the six parts of the text, a "Computer-Based Investment Management" section is included. Each of these sections includes an introductory discussion of software applications and an annotated list of some popular investment software relevant to the material covered in the part. This material should help students become familiar with the computer software available for performing various types of investment analysis and management.

Useful Appendixes

In addition, the text includes three appendixes. Appendix A contains a detailed list of sources of financial information as well as a list of leading mutual funds. Included within the mutual fund list are the major families of funds. The material provided in this appendix should help students obtain useful information about specific securities and track down mutual fund investment opportunities. Appendix B includes a full set of financial tables that may be used in making investment calculations. Appendix C includes a guide to professional certification programs, including the major professional certifications, requirements for obtaining them, and mailing addresses for obtaining further information.

SUPPLEMENTAL MATERIALS

A number of additional materials are available to aid and enrich the learning and teaching process.

Study Guide

The student review manual, *Study Guide to Accompany Fundamentals of Investing,* Fourth Edition, prepared by Elizabeth Hennigar of the University of San Diego, has been completely revised. Each chapter of the study guide contains a chapter summary, a chapter outline, a programmed self-test, true-false and multiple-choice questions, and problems with detailed solutions.

The Investment Management Disk

The Investment Management Disk (IMD) was revised and improved for this fourth edition by Donald G. Crawford of DGC Consulting, Phoenix, AZ, along with the assistance of the text authors. The purpose of the disk is to perform the calculations of virtually all of the formulas, ratios, and valuation procedures presented in the

book. The disk is user-friendly, fully interactive, and is more than a problem solver; it is also written to enhance the student's understanding of the investment process. The disk's use is keyed to all applicable text discussions and end-of-chapter and ancillary materials with a computer disk symbol (▉). The IMD is available free to adopters and is prepared to run on the IBM PC, as well as on most compatibles.

Instructor's Manual

Written by the text authors, the manual contains chapter outlines, a list of major topics discussed in each chapter, detailed chapter reviews, answers to all review questions and problems, solutions to the cases, and outside projects. Instructions for the outside projects are printed on separate sheets in order to make duplication for classroom distribution a simple task.

Test Bank

Revised by Elizabeth Hennigar, the new test bank contains 10 to 15 true-false questions, 40 (or more) multiple-choice questions, and 5 problems and short essay questions for each chapter. The test bank went through a major revision for this edition, including the addition of a substantial number of new questions and refinements to the older ones. It is available on Harper Test, a highly acclaimed microcomputerized test-generating system with full word-processing capabilities. It produces customized tests and allows instructors to scramble questions and/or add new ones. Harper Test is available for Apple, IBM, and some compatibles.

Acetate Transparencies

A set of 75 transparency acetates developed with the assistance of Thomas M. Krueger of the University of Wisconsin at LaCrosse is available free to adopters. The acetates include key text exhibits and problem and case solutions.

ACKNOWLEDGMENTS

Many people gave us their generous assistance during the initial development and revisions of *Fundamentals of Investing*. The expertise, classroom experience, and general advice of both colleagues and practitioners were invaluable. Reactions and suggestions from students throughout the country—which we especially enjoy receiving—sustained our belief in the need for a fresh, informative, and teachable investments text.

A few individuals provided significant subject matter expertise in the initial development of this text. They are Terry S. Maness of Baylor University, Arthur L. Schwartz, Jr., of the University of South Florida at St. Petersburg, and Gary W. Eldred. Their contributions are greatly appreciated. In addition, Harper & Row obtained the experienced advice of a large group of reviewers. We appreciate their many suggestions and criticisms, which have had a strong influence on various aspects of this volume. Our special thanks go to the following people who reviewed all or part of the manuscripts for this and the previous three editions of the book.

Gary Baker

Harisha Batra

Cecil C. Bigelow

Richard B. Bellinfante

A. David Brummett

Gary P. Cain

Daniel J. Cartell

P.R. Chandy

David M. Cordell

Timothy Cowling

Robert M. Crowe

Clifford A. Diebold

James Dunn

Betty Marie Dyatt

Steven J. Elbert

Frank J. Fabozzi

Robert A. Ford

Harry P. Guenther

Elizabeth Hennigar

Robert D. Hollinger

Roland Hudson, Jr.

A. James Ifflander

Donald W. Johnson

Daniel J. Kaufmann, Jr.

David S. Kidwell

Sheri Kole

Thomas M. Krueger

Robert T. LeClair

Weston A. McCormac

David J. McLaughlin

Keith Manko

Kathy Milligan

Warren E. Moeller

Homer Mohr

Joseph Newhouse

Joseph F. Ollivier

John Park

Stephen W. Pruitt

William A. Richard

William A. Rini

Roy A. Roberson

Edward Rozalewicz

William J. Ruckstuhl

Gary G. Schlarbaum

Keith V. Smith

Harold W. Stevenson

Nancy E. Strickler

Glenn T. Sweeny

Phillip D. Taylor

Robert C. Tueting

Allan J. Twark

John R. Weigel

Glenn A. Wilt, Jr.

John C. Woods

Richard H. Yanow

Because of the wide variety of topics covered in this edition, we called upon many experts for advice. We'd like to thank them and their firms for allowing us to draw on their insights and awareness of recent developments in order to ensure that the text is as current as possible. In particular, we want to mention Russell L. Block, San Diego, California; N. Arthur Hulick, Investment Planning and Management, Scottsdale, Arizona; Bill Kane, Kane Financial Service, Dayton, Ohio; Stanley J. Katz, Prudential-Bache Securities, Dayton, Ohio; Robert L. Hauser, Valley National Bank, Phoenix, Arizona; Linda H. Taufen, Northern Trust Bank, Tucson, Arizona; David J. McLaughlin, Chase Investment Counsel Corp., Charlottesville, Virginia; Jack Landis, Landis and Associates Insurance, Englewood, Ohio; Robert Moore, Paine Webber, Sedona, Arizona; Edwin P. Morrow, Confidential Planning Services, Inc., Middletown, Ohio; Michael R. Murphy, Sceptre Investment Counsel, Toronto, Ontario, Canada; Ronald S. Pretekin, Coolidge, Wall Co., LPA, Dayton, Ohio; John Richardson, Harris Trust Co. of Arizona, Scottsdale, Arizona; Pat Rupp, IDS, Inc., Dayton, Ohio; R. Daniel Sadlier, Bank One, Dayton, Ohio; and Fred Weaver, Great Western Bank, Phoenix, Arizona.

A number of colleagues have lent us expertise, encouragement, and support. They include Peter W. Bacon, Daniel J. Kaufman, Jr., Richard E. Williams, and M. Fall Ainina, Wright State University and George Gallinger and Glenn Wilt of Arizona State University. Special thanks go to tax experts Russell H. Hereth and John C. Talbott of Wright State University for their help in revising and updating the many tax discussions, to Dick Yanow of North Adams State College for the superb work he did in preparing the material on ''The Changing Face of the Market'', and William J. Ruckstuhl of the American College for his many helpful suggestions. We would also like to thank Elizabeth Hennigar of the University of San Diego for her useful feedback, as well as for authoring the *Study Guide* and helping with the *Test Bank*. Our thanks also go to Don Crawford for developing the new *Investment Management Disk* and to Thomas M. Krueger of the University of Wisconsin at LaCrosse for his help in selecting transparency acetates. Finally, we want to thank Robert J. Doyle, Jr., and Jane Dawson, both of The American College for developing and revising Appendix A on ''Sources of Financial Information'' and, of course, we are grateful for the research assistance provided by Mary Beth Kaminski and Roger Oldenkamp, and the clerical assistance of Tammy Johns and Hope Klassen.

The staff of Harper & Row, particularly John Greenman and Suzy Spivey, contributed their creativity, enthusiasm, and commitment to this text. Freelance development editor, Ann Torbert, and project editor, Susan Bogle of York Production Services, deserve a special word of thanks for shepherding the manuscript through the development and production stages. Without their care and concern the text would not have evolved into the teachable and interesting text we believe it to be.

Finally our wives, Robin and Charlene, and our children, Jessica and Zachary, and Chris and Terry, have played important parts by providing support and understanding during the book's development, revision, and production. We are forever grateful to them and hope that this edition will justify the sacrifices required during the many hours we were away from them working on this book.

Lawrence J. Gitman
Michael D. Joehnk

ONE

THE INVESTMENT ENVIRONMENT

THE INVESTMENT ENVIRONMENT

INVESTMENT ADMINISTRATION

INVESTING IN COMMON STOCK	INVESTING IN FIXED-INCOME SECURITIES
SPECULATIVE INVESTMENT VEHICLES	OTHER POPULAR INVESTMENT VEHICLES

1

THE ROLE AND SCOPE OF INVESTMENTS

After studying this chapter you should be able to:

● Grasp the meaning of the term *investments* and understand the factors commonly used to differentiate between various types of investments.

● Describe the structure of and participants in the investment process, the types of investors, and the rewards from investing.

● Gain an understanding of the steps involved in investing, as well as some of the recent developments in investing.

● Discuss the principal types of investment vehicles, including short-term securities, common stocks, and fixed-income securities, such as bonds, preferred stocks, and convertibles.

● Describe other kinds of popular investments, such as options, commodities and financial futures, tangibles, mutual funds, real estate, tax shelters, and limited partnerships.

● Summarize the content and organizational model around which this text is structured.

How would you like to make a million, own an expensive house and car, and travel the world in your own private jet? Sounds good, doesn't it? Well, the odds are probably against your achieving such financial success. Unless you inherit a large sum of money, win a lottery, or find yourself ''in the right place at the right time,'' you will probably never make a million. But would you be unhappy with half that amount? Probably not! Studying this book may not enable you to make a million, but it can help you make the most of your available financial resources. Our text provides the understanding needed to establish and fulfill investment goals by creating a *portfolio* containing a variety of investment vehicles that will produce an acceptable return for an acceptable level of risk. Familiarity with the organizations, vehicles, procedures, costs, characteristics, and strengths and weaknesses of various investment alternatives, plus a set of well-developed investment plans, should greatly increase your chance of achieving a reasonable degree of financial success. This chapter sets the stage for an in-depth look at the essential concepts, tools, and techniques of investing that are presented throughout the text.

THE ROLE OF INVESTMENTS

The word investments can be used in a variety of ways. It can mean stocks or bonds purchased to fulfill certain financial goals; it can also mean tangible assets such as machines acquired to produce and sell a product. In the broadest sense, investments provide the mechanism needed to finance the growth and development of our economy. To give you a general idea of the role of investments, we begin by looking at the key definitions, the structure of the investment process, the participants, and the types of investors.

Investment Defined

investment
a vehicle for funds, expected to maintain or increase its value and/or generate positive returns.

Simply stated, an **investment** is any vehicle into which funds can be placed with the expectation that they will be preserved or increase in value and/or generate positive returns. Idle cash is not an investment, since its value is likely to be eroded by inflation and since it fails to provide any type of return. The same cash placed in a bank savings account would be considered an investment, since the account provides a positive return. The various types of investment can be differentiated on the basis of a number of factors, such as whether the investment is a security or property; direct or indirect; debt, equity, or options; low or high risk; and short or long term.

securities
investments that represent debt, business ownership, or the legal right to acquire or sell a business ownership interest.

Securities and Property

property
investments in real property or in tangible personal property.

Investments that represent evidence of debt, ownership of a business, or the legal right to acquire or sell an ownership interest in a business are called **securities.** The most common types of securities are bonds, stocks, and options. **Property,** on the other hand, is investments in real property or tangible personal property. **Real property** is land, buildings, and that which is permanently affixed to the land; **tangible personal property** includes items such as gold, antiques, art, and other collectibles. Although security investments are quite popular, many people prefer property investments because they feel more comfortable owning something they can see and touch. But because of the existence of organized mechanisms for buy-

real property
land, buildings, and that which is permanently affixed to the land.

tangible personal property
property such as gold, antiques, art, and other collectibles.

direct investment
investment in which an investor directly acquires a claim on a security or property.

indirect investment
investment made in a portfolio or group of securities or properties.

mutual fund
a diversified portfolio of securities.

debt
funds loaned in exchange for the receipt of interest income and the promised repayment of the loan at a given future date.

equity
an ongoing ownership interest in a specific business or property.

stock
securities that give the purchaser an equity interest in a business.

options
securities that provide the investor an opportunity to purchase another security or asset at a specified price over a stated time period.

ing and selling securities and their widespread popularity, we will focus primarily on securities rather than on property investments.

Direct and Indirect

A **direct investment** is one in which an investor directly acquires a claim on a security or property. For example, when a person buys a stock, a bond, a rare coin, or a parcel of real estate in order to preserve value or earn income, that individual has made a direct investment. An **indirect investment** is an investment made in a portfolio or group of securities or properties. For example, an investor may purchase a share of a **mutual fund,** which is a diversified portfolio of securities issued by a variety of firms. By doing so, she will own a claim on a fraction of the entire portfolio rather than on the security of a single firm. It is also possible to invest indirectly in property—for example, by buying an interest in a limited partnership that deals in real estate, oil wells, and the like. Although direct investments are preferred by many investors, indirect investments have certain attributes that make them attractive as well.

Debt, Equity, and Options

Usually, an investment will represent a debt or an equity interest. **Debt**—an intangible investment—represents funds loaned in exchange for the receipt of interest income and the promised repayment of the loan at a given future date. When an investor buys a debt instrument like a *bond,* he in effect lends money to the issuer, who agrees to pay a stated rate of interest over a specified period of time, at the end of which the original sum will be returned. **Equity** represents an ongoing ownership interest in a specific business or property. An equity investment may be held as a security or by title to a specific property. An investor typically obtains an equity interest in a business by purchasing securities known collectively as **stock. Options** are neither debt nor equity; rather, they are securities that provide the investor with an opportunity to purchase another security or asset at a specified price over a stated period of time. An investor may, for example, pay $500 for an option to purchase a 2 percent interest in the Alex Company for $30,000 until December 31, 1993. If a 2 percent interest is currently valued at only $24,000, the person would not now exercise this option. Option investments, although not as common as various types of debt and equity investments, are growing rapidly in popularity.

Low and High Risk

Investments are sometimes differentiated on the basis of risk. As used in finance, *risk* refers to the chance that the value or return on an investment will differ unfavorably from its expected value—in other words, the chance of something undesirable occurring. The broader the range of possible values or returns associated with an investment, the greater its risk, and vice versa. The individual investor is confronted with a continuum ranging from low-risk government securities to high-risk commodities. Although each type of investment vehicle has a basic risk characteristic, the actual level of risk depends on the specific vehicle. For example, even though stocks are generally believed to be more risky than bonds, it is not difficult to find high-risk bonds that are in fact more risky than the stock of a financially sound firm

INVESTOR INSIGHTS

"A High Just-About-Guaranteed Return" Is Probably an Investment Scam!

Somewhere out there is a smooth-talking scam artist who wants to get his hooks into your money. He may be in Denver, Colorado; Salt Lake City, Utah; Miami, Florida; or Newport Beach, California. Those are some of the hot spots for investment fraud. Then again, you might have to look no further than the local branch office of your favorite brokerage firm.

Investment-related fraud is a billion-dollar business that keeps getting bigger. Its victims include affluent business people and professionals as well as less sophisticated investors. Perpetrators, known as "perps" to regulators who try to stop them, range from fast-talking smoothies in thick gold chains and three-ounce pinkie rings to seemingly conservative money managers with fancy diplomas and well-cut suits. Some of their schemes are blatantly criminal activities, like selling nonexistent gold coins over the telephone. Other scammers engage in more sophisticated forms of fraud, which are harder to spot.

Take the penny-stock peddlers. Some firms do a perfectly legal business selling low-priced shares of upstart companies in fields such as oil exploration or fast food franchises. The shares of just about any new company are by nature highly speculative, but can be legitimate investments for investors willing to bite off big risks. However, some fly-by-night companies do a thriving business in penny stocks of companies that aren't worthy of the name. Worse, they manipulate the share prices through sleazy tactics so that investors end up paying outrageous prices for worthless stock. Happens every day.

Out in Utah, they have something aptly called a "blind pool." Promoters of blind pools raise cash—lots of it—for unspecified "investments." Often, the money ends up in the promoters' pockets. But investors keep coming back for more. Sad, ain't it?

Call it the financial supermarket of the damned: investors can buy worthless stocks, phony futures contracts, nonexistent gold bars and coins, diamonds that never were, useless real estate, and worse. And they can buy it all from the comfort of their living rooms, since many scammers operate by telephone or through the mail.

Why would people invest in something they can't see? For some investors, the reason is greed, plain and simple. Why leave the money in Treasury bills earning 6 percent, when this nice man on the telephone tells you that you can make 40 percent a year—just about guaranteed—in oil leases or commodities futures? Sure, there's risk involved. But any investment is risky, right? And if everything goes right on this one, it will be great telling your friends that you made $12,000 by investing in undervalued Alaskan oil leases.

One simple rule can protect you from a wide variety of underhanded schemes: Don't talk to strangers. At the very least, don't invest with them. But that rule won't cover every situation. Some sophisticated investors who wouldn't dream of falling for fast talk over the telephone get taken in person.

It's not always greed that will get you into trouble. Maybe you're a fast tracker busy with your career. You need investment advice; someone to do your investing for you. Or maybe you've inherited a large sum, or made a small fortune in real estate, and you're looking for a place to put the money. That guy you met at your best friend's barbecue party—the one where they roasted a steer out in the backyard—sounded like a smart fellow. Nice guy, too. Why not give him some cash, and see what he can do with it? Turns

out your friend let him handle some money, and did real well. *Real* well. Your friend says go for it.

Whoa, cowboy. Nothing wrong with taking your friend's advice—as long as you check out this guy yourself. Better yet, if he offers you a share in that private partnership he's putting together, have an expert look at the deal. That bears repeating: *Look at the deal.* Too often, investors do nothing of the sort.

You say the guy has a great track record? So did plenty of guys who are doing time now for taking other people's money. Many of the most successful frauds are classic Ponzi schemes: The perp starts out by promising great returns. Once the money starts flowing in from investors, he sends part of it back, claiming that it represents profits from brilliant currency trades or giant pineapple farms on the outskirts of the Sahara. The investors don't much care, as long as the ''profits'' keep coming. And so they do, as long as the perp can keep the cash coming in.

But sooner or later, somebody smells a rat. The regulators move in, and it turns out that there are no currency trades, no pineapples—and no money. The bad guy spent the cash, or hid it, or lost it. He goes to jail—maybe. The investors go home to eat peanut-butter sandwiches and think about meeting their mortgage payments. They shoulda looked at the deal.

Another bit of advice: Once you've hired someone to help you look after your investments, stay in touch. ''Keep track of your investments and meet with your advisor at least every quarter,'' says Edward F. Garcia, a certified financial planner with Dean Witter Reynolds. ''Take responsibility for your money. Don't leave it up to someone else.''

Clients of Los Angeles financial advisor Stephen Henry made that mistake, and they're paying for it. Henry convinced hundreds of people, including many physicians and other professionals, to turn their money over to him. He charged $300 an hour for his advice, and told them he was investing their money in high-yielding certificates of deposit. But clients received no independent confirmation of the transaction; instead, Henry sent them a letter on company stationery describing the investment in detail—right down to the serial numbers on the CDs. When investors asked for confirmation from the bank, he procrastinated. When they asked for their money he stalled, or tried to talk them out of it.

As it turned out, the CDs didn't exist. Henry invested the money in his own bank account. Among the victims were a local television reporter and a number of prominent professionals. His best friend invested close to $400,000. So much for trusting your instincts about a guy.

You say you only do business with reputable firms? That's good, but it's no guarantee against getting bilked. Brokers at established firms have hoodwinked customers by sending them false account statements. According to the statements, the client is making a profit. In reality, the broker has mismanaged or stolen the money in the account. ''Keep an eye on your statements,'' says Chase Adams, a financial consultant with Merrill Lynch in Boca Raton, Florida. ''It's also a good idea to visit your broker, introduce yourself to his boss, and ask the accounting department to show you your statement. That way, you'll have independent corroboration of what your broker tells you about your account.''

You say you're a great judge of people? You'd know a crook if you saw one? These guys are experts. They often seem competent, confident, and caring. In short, the kind of people who wouldn't hurt a fly.

They'd just take its money.

Source: ''Scams, Dupes, Grafts, and Goldbricks,'' *Private Clubs,* November/December 1988, pp. 10–13. Reprinted by permission.

such as IBM or McDonald's. Of course, as noted in the Investor Insights box on pages 6 and 7, the honesty of the issuer, promoter, or seller of an investment vehicle also greatly affects its risk.

Low-risk investments are those considered safe with regard to the receipt of a positive return. **High-risk investments** are considered speculative. The terms *investment* and *speculation* are used to refer to different approaches to the investment process. As already stated, *investment* is viewed as the process of purchasing securities or property for which stability of value and level of expected return are not only positive but somewhat predictable. **Speculation** is the process of buying similar media in which the future value and level of expected earnings are highly uncertain. Simply stated, speculation is on the high-risk end of the investment process. Of course, due to the greater risk, the returns associated with speculation are expected to be greater. In this book we will use the term "investment" for both processes, and we will consider the issue of investment return and risk more closely in Chapter 5.

Short and Long Term

The life of an investment can be described as either short or long term. **Short-term investments** typically mature within one year; **long-term investments** are those with longer maturities or perhaps, like common stock, with no maturity at all. For example, a six-month certificate of deposit (CD) would be a short-term investment, whereas a 20-year bond would be a long-term investment. Of course, by purchasing a long-term investment and selling it after a short period of time, say six months, an investor can use a long-term vehicle to meet a short-term goal. As will become clear later, it is not unusual to find investors matching the maturity of an investment to the period of time over which they wish to invest their funds. For instance, an investor with money that will not be needed for six months could purchase a six-month certificate of deposit, whereas a 40-year-old investor wishing to build a retirement fund may well purchase a 20-year corporate bond. The breakdown of short-term and long term may also be useful for tax purposes. Although currently the tax laws do not distinguish between short-term and long-term gains and losses, it is possible that future tax legislation will reinstate such treatment, which existed prior to passage of the Tax Reform Act of 1986. Tax considerations will be discussed in Chapter 4, and various types of tax-sheltered investments will be described in Chapter 15.

The Structure of the Investment Process

The overall investment process is the mechanism for bringing together suppliers (those having extra funds) with demanders (those who need funds). Suppliers and demanders are most often brought together through a financial institution or a financial market. Occasionally—especially in property transactions such as real estate—buyers and sellers deal directly with one another. **Financial institutions** are organizations such as banks and savings and loan associations that typically accept deposits and then lend them out or invest them. **Financial markets** are forums in which suppliers and demanders of funds are brought together to make transactions, often

---

low-risk investments
investments considered safe with regard to the receipt of a positive return.

high-risk investments
investments considered speculative with regard to the receipt of a positive return.

speculation
the process of buying investment vehicles in which the future value and level of expected earnings are uncertain.

short-term investments
investments that typically mature within one year.

long-term investments
investments with maturities of longer than a year, or with no maturity at all.

financial institutions
organizations that typically accept deposits and then lend or invest them.

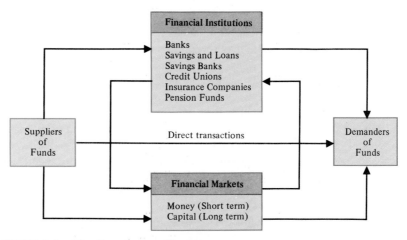

FIGURE 1.1   The Investment Process.
Note that financial institutions participate in the financial markets as well as transfer funds
between suppliers and demanders. Although the arrows go only from suppliers to demanders,
for some investment transactions, such as the sale of a bond, the principal amount borrowed
by the demander from the supplier (the lender) will eventually be returned.

financial markets
*forums in which suppliers and demanders
of funds are brought
together to make
transactions.*

market price
*the point of equilibrium between the
forces of supply and
demand.*

money market
the short-term financial market.

capital market
the long-term financial market, dominated by various securities exchanges.

through intermediaries such as organized securities exchanges. There are a number
of financial markets, such as stock markets, bond markets, and options markets.
Their common feature is that the price of the investment vehicle at any point in time
results from an equilibrium between the forces of supply and demand. And as new
information about returns, risk, inflation, world events, and so on, becomes available, the changes in the forces of supply and/or demand may result in a new
equilibrium or **market price.**

   Figure 1.1 diagrams the investment process. Note that the suppliers of funds may
transfer their resources to demanders through a financial institution, through a financial market, or directly. As the illustration shows, financial institutions can
participate in financial markets as either suppliers or demanders of funds. The
short-term financial market is called the **money market;** the long-term sector is the
capital market, which is dominated by various securities exchanges. The characteristics of these markets will be discussed in greater detail in Chapter 2.

Participants in the Investment Process

Government, business, and individuals are the three key participants in the investment process, and each may act as a supplier or demander of funds.

Government

Each level of government—federal, state, and local—requires vast sums of money
to meet its operating needs. These needs center around capital expenditures, which
are long-term projects related to the construction of public facilities such as schools,
hospitals, housing, and highways. Usually the financing for such projects is ob-

tained through the issuance of various types of long-term debt securities. Another source of demand for funds results from operating needs. The federal government, for example, may spend more than it receives in taxes. Or a city might need operating funds when the tax money it will collect is not due for some time. Usually governments finance these operating needs with short-term debt securities.

Sometimes, governments are also suppliers of funds. If a city has temporarily idle cash, rather than hold these resources in a checking account, it may make a short-term investment to earn a positive return. The financial activities of governments both as demanders and suppliers of funds significantly affect the behavior of financial institutions and financial markets. In general, government is a *net demander* of funds, which means that it demands more funds than it supplies.

Business

Most business firms, no matter what the type, require large sums of money to support operations. Like government, the financial needs of business are both short and long term. On the long-term side, businesses seek funds to build plants, acquire equipment and facilities, and develop products. Short-term needs tend to revolve around the need to finance inventory, accounts receivable, and other operating costs. Businesses issue a wide variety of debt and equity securities to finance these long- and short-term needs. They also supply funds when they have a temporary excess amount of cash. In fact, many large business firms have active and sophisticated cash-management operations and are major purchasers of short-term securities. But like government, business firms in general are *net demanders* of funds.

Individuals

Individuals supply funds through the investment process in a variety of ways. They may place funds in savings accounts, buy debt or equity instruments, buy insurance, or purchase various types of property. Depending upon personal investment goals and objectives, the choice of vehicles in which to place funds is often a difficult one. The key source of demand for funds by individuals typically comes in the form of loans needed to finance the acquisition of property, usually automobiles and homes. Although the demand for such funds seems great, as a group individuals are *net suppliers* of funds; that is, they put more funds into the investment process than they take out. Since both government and business are net demanders of funds, the individual investor's role in providing the funds needed to finance economic growth and development is significant.

Types of Investors

institutional investors
investment professionals paid to manage other people's money.

Investors can be either of two types—institutional investors or individual investors. **Institutional investors** are investment professionals who are paid to manage other people's money. They are employed by financial institutions, such as banks, life insurance companies, mutual funds, and pension funds; large nonfinancial corporations; and, in some cases, by individuals. Financial institutions invest large sums in order to earn a significant return for their customers. For example, a bank trust department must earn an acceptable return on the funds with which it is entrusted,

and a life insurance company must invest its premium receipts in order to earn returns that will permit the payment of contractual cash values or death benefits to policyholders or beneficiaries. Nonfinancial businesses such as manufacturers and distributors often have large sums of money which they invest in order to earn a return on idle funds or to meet future investment and operating needs.

individual investors
investors who manage their own funds.

Individual investors manage their personal funds in order to provide for achievement of their financial goals. The individual investor usually concentrates his or her investment activities on earning a return on idle funds, providing a source of retirement income, or on providing security for one's family. The sole activity of many individual investors involves selecting the investment vehicles to be included in their individual portfolio and/or employer retirement plan. Individuals with large sums of money to invest, or who lack the time or expertise to make investment decisions, often employ an institutional investor such as a bank trust department or a professional investment adviser to manage their money.

The fundamental principles used by both institutional and individual investors are similar, although institutional investors generally invest larger sums of money on behalf of others and therefore are often more sophisticated in both knowledge and methods than individual investors. Thus while the information presented in this text may be adequate for an individual investor, it represents only the first step toward developing the expertise needed to qualify as an institutional investor.

INVESTING

The process of placing funds in selected investment vehicles with the expectation of increasing their value and/or earning a positive return is called **investing.** This activity has broad economic importance, provides rewards, and can be pursued by following a logical progression of steps. Investing has been further enhanced and streamlined by certain recent developments.

The Economic Importance of Investing

investing
the process of placing funds in selected investment vehicles with the expectation of increasing their value and/or earning a positive return.

The functioning and growth of our economy depend on the ready availability of funds to finance the increased needs not only of government and business, but also of individuals. For example, without mortgage loans, very few homes would be purchased. Such a lack of mortgage money would result in fewer persons being employed to build homes as well as to manufacture the needed components (lumber, nails, glass, and so on). The net effect of decreased mortgage financing would thus probably contribute to a general slowdown in economic activity—an undesirable result since the availability of funds to qualified individuals (as well as government and business) is needed to allow the economy to grow and prosper. Because individuals as a group are net suppliers of such funds while government and business are net demanders, the process of investing thus has a profound impact.

The Rewards from Investing

The rewards, or returns, from placing funds in the investment process may be received in either of two basic forms—current income or increased value. For example, money placed in a bank savings account would provide current income in

the form of periodic interest payments, whereas a raw land investment might offer returns in the form of an increase in value between the time of purchase and the time it is sold. In order for those needing funds to attract funds from those having an excess, a reward or return adequate to compensate the suppliers for the risk involved must be provided. Simply stated, funds suppliers must be rewarded and funds demanders must provide these rewards in order for the investment process to function smoothly. The magnitude and form of such rewards depends on factors such as the type of security or property transaction, the length of time involved, and the risks embedded in the transaction.

Steps in Investing

Investing can be conducted in various ways. One approach is to rely on plans carefully developed to achieve specific goals. Another, and diametrically opposite, approach is the haphazard, "seat-of-the-pants" method, in which actions are taken on a strictly intuitive basis. Evidence suggests that the more logical approach usually results in better returns. The serious investor should therefore try to plan, develop, and execute an investment program consistent with the achievement of overall financial goals. Such a program should result in an investment portfolio that possesses the return and risk behavior desired. A brief overview of the steps in investing should help to set the stage for the more detailed discussion of the concepts, tools, and techniques presented throughout the text.

Meeting Investment Prerequisites

Before investing, an individual must make certain that the necessities of life are adequately provided for. Investments are not an alternative to such needs, but rather are the mechanism for using current funds to satisfy future needs. In addition, a minimum savings account (or some form of liquid short-term investment vehicle) should be established to meet emergency cash needs. Another prerequisite would be adequate protection against the losses that could result from loss of life, illness or disability, damage to property, or a negligent act. Protection against such risks can be acquired through life, health, property, and liability insurance. Although some types of insurance possess certain investment attributes, provision for adequate insurance protection is a necessary prerequisite to investing. Planning for adequate retirement income may be viewed as an investment prerequisite, the achievement of which may partially depend on the success of the investment program. At a minimum, the individual needs to establish certain retirement goals prior to setting specific investment goals. Considerations involved in establishing and satisfying investment prerequisites are discussed in Chapter 4.

Establishing Investment Goals

investment goals
statements of the timing, magnitude, form, and risks associated with a desired return.

Once the investor has satisfied the prerequisites and has clearly defined financial goals, he or she must establish **investment goals**—specific statements of the timing, magnitude, form, and risks associated with a desired return. For example, an investment goal might be to accumulate $15,000 for the down payment on a summer home to be purchased in 1994, or to accumulate $250,000 for use at retirement

in 2006. These goals must not only be consistent with overall financial goals, but they must also be realistic. Adequate funds must be available for investment, and an attainable rate of return must be used to achieve them. The development of investment goals as part of the overall personal financial planning process is discussed in Chapter 4.

Evaluating Investment Vehicles

valuation
procedure for estimating the perceived worth of an investment vehicle; includes measures of return, risk, and value.

Before selecting investment vehicles, it is important to evaluate them in terms of investment goals. The evaluation process involves assessing the potential returns and risks offered by each vehicle. This process typically involves **valuation,** which is a procedure for estimating the perceived worth of an investment vehicle. The output of the valuation process includes measures of return, risk, and value for that vehicle. A general discussion of the procedures for measuring these key dimensions of potential investments is included in Chapter 5.

Selecting Suitable Investments

The *selection* of investments is important because it determines a course of action and can significantly affect the investor's success in achieving goals established in the planning process. The best investments may not be those that simply maximize return; other requirements, such as risk and tax considerations, may also be relevant. For example, an investor wishing to receive maximum annual dividends may purchase the common stock with the highest expected earnings. If the firm whose stock was purchased goes bankrupt, the investor could lose the money instead. Careful selection of investment vehicles consistent with established goals and having acceptable levels of return, risk, and value is paramount for the successful management of investments.

Constructing a Diversified Portfolio

portfolio
a collection of investment vehicles assembled to meet one or more investment goals.

An investment **portfolio** is a collection of investment vehicles assembled to meet one or more investment goals. Joan Smith's investment portfolio might contain 20 shares of IBM common stock, $20,000 in government bonds, and 10 shares of IDS Growth mutual fund. Using a variety of available tools and techniques, the investor can combine vehicles in such a way that investment goals can be achieved, and return, risk, and investment values are optimized.

diversification
the inclusion of a number of different investment vehicles in a portfolio, in order to increase returns or be exposed to less risk.

Diversification, which involves the inclusion of a number of different investment vehicles, is fundamental to constructing an effective portfolio. By diversifying, investors are able, on balance, to earn higher returns or be exposed to less risk than if they limit their investments to just one or two vehicles. A portfolio has the surprising quality of possessing a different risk-return characteristic from those of the individual investment vehicles that comprise it. For example, gold and other precious metals are by themselves extremely risky investments—their prices fluctuate constantly and often dramatically in commodity markets. Yet when they are held with securities such as common stock in a diversified portfolio, over time the portfolio exhibits lower risk or a higher return than if only metals or only common stock were held.

**random diversifica-
tion**
*selecting investment
vehicles at random.*

**purposive diversifi-
cation**
*selecting investment
vehicles to achieve a
stated portfolio ob-
jective.*

There are two types of diversification technique—random and purposive. **Random diversification** takes place when investment vehicles are selected at random, such as by drawing names from a hat. This may hardly seem like a sound investment strategy, but it can work. Portfolios constructed this way have sometimes performed better than those designed by professionals. **Purposive diversification** is the process of selecting vehicles to achieve a stated portfolio objective. For example, an investor might observe that whenever the new car industry is depressed and its sales and profits are low, the car replacement parts industry is in just the reverse situation. By diversifying between firms in each industry, it might be possible to reduce risk exposure while maintaining a return equal to what could be earned by investing in only one of the two industries. Purposive diversification is usually done with more technically efficient methods than the one in the example here. We will examine these other approaches in Chapter 16.

Managing the Portfolio

Once a portfolio has been constructed, the investor must measure and evaluate its actual behavior in relation to expected performance. If, for example, the investment return, risk, or value is not consistent with the investor's objectives or expectations, corrective action may be required. Such action usually involves selling certain investments and using the proceeds to acquire other vehicles for the portfolio. Portfolio management therefore involves not only selecting a compatible group of investments that meet the investor's goals, but also monitoring and restructuring the portfolio as dictated by the actual behavior of the investments. Chapter 17 is devoted to monitoring the investment portfolio.

Recent Developments in Investing

A few developments have recently taken place in the field of investments that are likely to have a profound impact on investors. The first of these is the widespread use of the *personal computer (PC);* the second is the growing trend toward servicing investors' total financial needs through one company—the *financial supermarket;* and third is the *globalization* of the financial markets.

The Personal Computer (PC)

The process of evaluating and selecting securities, and then managing the resulting investment portfolio, requires considerable time and research. Historically, the individual investor's solution to this problem has been to select a stockbroker or institutional investor and then follow his or her advice. Many investors still operate this way and will continue to do so in the future. However, a growing number are choosing instead to do their own research and make their own decisions. They are aided considerably in this effort by the **personal computer (PC)**—a relatively inexpensive but powerful home computer. Rapidly expanding PC technology has made available both very sophisticated *hardware* (the physical parts of a computer system, such as a console, a processor, and a printer) and *software* (programs designed to tell the computer what functions to perform).

**personal computer
(PC)**
*a relatively inexpen-
sive but powerful
home computer.*

Equally important, investors now have computer access to a variety of *data bases*

that are needed for research. For example, Dow Jones (the publisher of *The Wall Street Journal* and *Barron's* newspapers) offers a variety of news/retrieval services, ranging from current price quotations on stocks, bonds, options, and most other securities to detailed financial statistics on over 5,400 companies. It even offers transcripts from a popular TV show on investments, *Wall Street Week*. Along with news/retrieval, Dow Jones (as well as others) has software programs that perform analytical functions on the data available through news/retrieval. An investor can thus do fundamental or technical analyses (these two basic approaches to security evaluation will be explained in Chapters 7 and 8) of the market as a whole or of specific securities with the aid of a PC.

Despite falling prices, PC systems are still too expensive for many individual investors, both in acquisition and maintenance costs and in charges for data retrieval. But these costs must be tempered by (1) the possible savings in commissions if the investor uses a discount, rather than a full-service, broker; and (2) the fact that the costs of purchasing and operating the PC are tax-deductible to the extent that it is used for investment or other income-producing activities. In addition, one would typically not limit use of a PC solely to investment activities, since it can do so much more.

Some observers believe PCs will bring about important changes in the investments area. Since it will be relatively simple for both private individuals and professionals to have access to data and analytical models, less emphasis will be placed on specific security selection and more on integrating the investment process into a person's or a family's total financial plan. This plan includes not only investing, but also other activities such as cash management, insurance, estate planning, credit management, tax shelters, and tax strategies.

Financial Supermarkets

financial super-market
a financial institution at which customers can obtain a full array of financial services.

Within the past 10 years major changes have taken place in the structure of financial institutions. The first of these was an innovation introduced by Merrill Lynch that combined an investor's banking and stockbrokerage activities into one account called a Cash Management Account (CMA). This proved enormously successful, attracting billions of dollars in deposits for Merrill Lynch and prompting most other brokerage firms to follow suit. But the CMA was only the beginning; it was followed by passage of the Depository Institutions Deregulation and Monetary Control Act of 1980 (DIDMCA), which signaled the beginning of the "financial services revolution" that continues to change the nature of financial institutions. What is now evolving is the **financial supermarket,** at which a customer can obtain a full array of financial services such as checking, savings, brokerage, insurance, retirement, and estate planning. The acquisition by Prudential Insurance of Bache and by American Express of Shearson, Lehman, and Hutton, both brokerage firms, is testimony to this revolution. Most notable, however, is Sears Roebuck and Company's "Sears Financial Network." In addition to its credit and insurance (Allstate) and home mortgage (Sears Mortgage) operations, Sears owns a major stockbrokerage firm (Dean Witter), a national real estate brokerage firm (Coldwell Banker), and a West Coast savings and loan (Allstate Savings and Loan). And

furthermore, it offers all these financial services in a growing number of "Financial Network Centers" housed within its retail stores.

The thrust of such numerous and important financial mergers has been to create a marketing system and a mix of products for comprehensive financial servicing. If an agent is meeting with a client to discuss insurance needs, he or she can at the same time offer an investments package integrated within the insurance plan to create a total savings-investments-insurance plan. Illustrative of this total approach is Prudential-Bache's Total Financial Planning Program, which includes over 65 financial alternatives. It seems clear that in years to come investors will be likely to choose a single financial service organization rather than a stockbroker, an insurance company, a bank, and so forth.

Globalization of the Financial Markets

globalization (financial markets)
the access of investors to financial markets around the world.

In recent years, improved access to the securities of foreign companies has greatly expanded the choices available to American investors; at the same time, foreign investors have become an important factor in U.S. markets by heavily investing in American stocks and bonds. In short, we are witnessing a true **globalization** of the financial market system, whereby U.S. investors have wider access to foreign markets, just as foreign investors have to the U.S. markets. Enhanced communications and the elimination of regulatory barriers have, in effect, *"globalized"* the financial marketplace—allowing investors here and abroad to conveniently make transactions in the securities of major foreign companies. For example, although the NYSE is open from 9:30 am to 4:00 pm, the fact is that many U.S. stocks are traded literally around the clock on foreign stock exchanges throughout the world, including the world's largest—Japan's Tokyo Stock Exchange. And it's just as easy for American investors to buy foreign securities because many of them are denominated in dollars and hundreds more are traded in the United States as a derivative dollar-denominated security, known as an *American Depositary Receipt (ADR)*—more on these in Chapters 2 and 6. American investors can also buy foreign securities through scores of mutual funds that invest in well-balanced portfolios of foreign securities. In addition to international (or global) stock funds, there are also international bond funds and even global money market funds.

A key by-product of the globalization process is that U.S. securities markets are no longer viewed in isolation, but rather, the returns in U.S. markets are measured relative to those in other major markets around the world. U.S. money and capital markets are now facing stiff competition from organized markets in Tokyo, London, Frankfurt, Hong Kong, Sydney, and Toronto, among others. The major institutional investors around the world (the *really* big players) invest their money where they feel they can get the best return for the amount of risk involved. If that's in the United States, fine; if it's in Tokyo or London, that's OK, too. Foreign investors have become a major force in the U.S. market; they've invested hundreds of billions of dollars in the stocks and bonds of American corporations, as well as in U.S. government securities. To continue to attract such capital, the United States will have to continue to offer safe, competitive returns to investors—a prospect that will

benefit not only foreign investors, but U.S. investors, too. Clearly, today's globalized financial markets offer investors new challenges, as well as expanded opportunities.

The Question of Ethics

Following the stock market crash of October 19, 1987, a great deal of public as well as private attention focused on uncovering its causes and establishing regulations that would help to avoid a future collapse of securities prices and investor confidence. As a result of these investigations and studies, as well as pre-crash publicity generated by the "insider-trading" conviction of Ivan Boesky, a great deal of attention began to be focused on ethical issues surrounding the activities of other major market participants. Most notable is the insider-trading practices of Michael Milken—the "Junk Bond King"—and his employer, Drexel Burnham Lambert Inc. **Insider trading** involves using *inside information,* which is private (non-public) information about a company's plans, performance, or discoveries that is obtained from an officer, director, major stockholder, banker, or investment banker, to make profitable securities transactions. *Insider trading in securities is illegal as well as unethical.*

insider trading
the illegal use of non-public information about a company to make profitable securities transactions.

ethics
standards of conduct or moral judgment.

The Boesky, Milken, and many other insider-trading cases have raised the question of **ethics**—standards of conduct or moral judgment. Today the financial community is involved in developing and enforcing ethical standards that will motivate market participants to adhere to laws and regulations concerned with the unfair use of inside information as well as other documented abuses by brokers, investment bankers, corporations and their officers, and government officials. The publicity surrounding major insider-trading cases has generated significant dialogue that is expected to result in better regulation and control of ethical standards as well as greater awareness of the consequences of legal prosecution for this and other ethical violations. Although it is indeed difficult to enforce ethical standards, it appears that opportunities for abuses in the financial markets will be reduced, thereby providing a more level playing field in which market participants will have less likelihood of becoming victims of ethical violations.

INVESTMENT VEHICLES

A broad range of investment vehicles is available to individual investors. Some are securities; others are not. And there are many different types of securities, each type offering vehicles having different lives, costs, return and risk characteristics, and tax considerations. The same is true of property investments. The guidelines in the Investor Insights box should be followed before selecting any type of investment vehicle. We will devote the bulk of this book—Chapters 6 through 15—to describing the characteristics, special features, returns and risks, and possible investment strategies that can be used with vehicles available to the individual investor. Here we will introduce the various investment outlets and give a brief description of each. The introduction is broken down by general types: short-term vehicles, common stock, fixed-income securities, speculative investment vehicles, and other popular investment vehicles.

INVESTOR INSIGHTS

Some Basics for the Beginning Investor

Many people have a mental block when it comes to investments. To the neophyte, the investment world often seems ominous, full of pitfalls for the uninitiated. This need not be the case, for the basics of investing can be learned by anyone.

Investment means managing your resources so that you can preserve your money's buying power, generate more money and obtain income. Once you decide to put money to work by investing, you will need a procedure for making sense of the multitude of financial options available to you.

IDENTIFYING GOALS

You can begin by clarifying what your investment goals are. Ask yourself the following:

Where am I now financially?
Where do I want to be in five years?
Ten years?
Twenty years?

You will have to take a financial inventory to assess where you are now. Ideally, this should be done when you are not under pressure.

Once you have carefully made this inventory, taking into account your liquid assets, fixed assets and obligations, you should be ready to identify where you want to be at the end of a specific period. Keep in mind that your goals will vary at different times in your life. For example, if you were to marry or to receive an inheritance your financial plan would change.

CONSULTING PROFESSIONALS

A guide and mentor helps. His or her selection should be done with care. If you pick an investment broker, choose someone from a reputable brokerage house, where the research is of the highest quality.

A good way to begin your search for an adviser might be to introduce yourself to the manager of a local brokerage firm. Let the manager recommend one or two brokers for you to interview.

Look for a personal rapport. Beware of a high pressure salesman, someone who is not

Short-Term Vehicles

short-term vehicles
savings instruments that usually have lives of one year or less.

Short-term vehicles include savings instruments that usually have lives of one year or less. The most important of these are savings and NOW accounts, money market deposit accounts and mutual funds, certificates of deposit, commercial paper, U.S. Treasury bills (T-bills), central asset accounts, and even Series EE savings bonds. Often such instruments are used to "warehouse" idle funds and earn a return while suitable long-term vehicles are being evaluated; that is, they serve as a liquid re-

willing to spend time with you, nor willing to admit a mistake. Ask your prospective broker how much time you can expect him or her to give you. He should feel free to call you with recommendations, and you should feel free to come to him with your questions.

WHO AM I?

Once you have selected an individual with whom you feel comfortable, he should help you evaluate your financial situation and identify your investment goals. You will also want to explore such issues as:

Am I a speculator?
Do I feel more comfortable with stocks, or would I prefer a highly rated municipal bond?
Should I look at tax-sheltered investments?
Which investments provide income exempt from federal and state taxes?

Together, you and your broker should review the many financial options available to you, such as corporate and municipal bonds, common and preferred stocks, listed options, tax shelters, or fixed-income trusts, to name a few. Your broker will help you to understand each of them and can point out which will best fulfill your objectives.

If, for instance, current income from investments is of paramount importance, you will want regular dividends, an attractive rate of return, safety of principal, plus good liquidity, should you need funds on short notice.

EDUCATING YOURSELF

As you work with your investment broker, make every effort to become as knowledgeable as possible about financial markets. This will help both you and your broker. Read *The Wall Street Journal* and the financial section of your local newspaper. You may even want to scan periodicals, such as, *Barron's, Forbes* and *Business Week.*

In short, you as an investor should learn all you can, so that you can be a full partner with your carefully chosen investment broker in planning and executing a flexible, responsive investment portfolio that conforms to your investment goals. The more time and attention you are willing to devote to this undertaking, the more you will accomplish. Study and experience, along with timely information transactions, are the keys. The rewards of successful investment can be worth the effort.

Source: Howard E. Kramer, ''Initial Investments,'' *New Accountant,* January 1987, pp. 40–41.

serve. Because these vehicles generally carry little or no risk, they tend to be popular among those wishing to earn something on temporarily idle funds, and also among conservative investors who may use short-term vehicles as a primary investment outlet.

In addition to the ''warehousing'' function served by short-term vehicles, they are also important in their own right because they round out an investor's portfolio by meeting liquidity needs, which are an important part of any financial plan. As a

rule of thumb, financial planners often suggest that anywhere from three to six months of after-tax income should be held in short-term vehicles to meet unexpected needs. A serious illness or loss of a job could create a need for immediate cash, and this might come at a time when longer-term security prices are low. Being forced to sell the long-term securities at such a time can result in substantial losses and possible financial embarrassment. A closer look at meeting liquidity needs is provided in Chapter 4.

Common Stock

common stock
equity investment representing ownership in a corporation; each share represents a fractional ownership interest in the firm.

Common stock is an equity investment that represents ownership in a corporation. Each share of common stock represents a fractional ownership interest in the firm. For example, one share of common stock in a corporation that has 10,000 shares outstanding would represent 1/10,000 ownership interest. The return on common stock investment comes from either of two sources—the periodic receipt of **dividends,** which are payments made by the firm to its shareholders, and increases in value, or **capital gains,** which result from selling the stock at a price above that originally paid. For example, imagine you purchased a single share of M and N Industries common stock for $40 per share. During the first year you owned it you received $2.50 per share in cash dividends, and at the end of the year you sold the stock for $44 per share. If we ignore the costs associated with buying and selling the stock, you would have earned $2.50 in dividends and $4 in capital gains ($44 sale price − $40 purchase price). Next to short-term vehicles and home ownership, common stock, which offers a broad range of return-risk combinations, is the most popular form of investment vehicle. Because of the widespread popularity of common stock, three chapters—6, 7, and 8—are devoted to the study of this investment vehicle.

dividends
periodic payments made by firms to their stockholders.

capital gains
the profit realized from selling stock at a price above that paid for it.

Fixed-Income Securities

fixed-income securities
investment vehicles that offer a fixed periodic return.

Fixed-income securities are a group of investment vehicles that offer a fixed periodic return. Some forms offer contractually guaranteed returns; others have specified, but not guaranteed, returns. Due to their fixed returns, fixed-income securities tend to experience their greatest popularity during periods of high interest rates, such as those during the late 1970s and early 1980s. The key forms of fixed-income securities are bonds, preferred stock, and convertible securities.

Bonds

bonds
long-term securities that offer a known interest return plus the return of the face value at maturity.

Bonds are the IOUs of corporations and governments. A bondholder receives a known interest return, typically paid semiannually, plus the return of the face value of the bond (say $1,000) at maturity (typically 20 to 40 years). If you purchased a $1,000 bond paying 9 percent interest in semiannual installments, you would expect to be paid $45 (that is, ½ year × 9% × $1,000) every six months, and at maturity you would receive the $1,000 face value of the bond. Of course, an investor may be able to buy or sell a bond prior to maturity at a price different from its face value. As with common stock, a wide range of return-risk combinations is available to the bond investor. We will examine bond investments in detail in Chapter 9.

Preferred Stock

preferred stock
ownership interest in a firm, giving a stated dividend rate, payment of which is given preference over dividends to holders of the firm's common stock.

Like common stock, **preferred stock** represents an ownership interest in a corporation. Unlike common stock, preferred has a stated dividend rate, payment of which is given preference over dividends to holders of common stock of the same firm. Preferred stock has no maturity date. Investors typically purchase it for the dividends, but it may also provide capital gains. The key aspects of preferred stock are described in Chapter 10.

Convertible Securities

convertible security
a fixed-income obligation with a feature permitting conversion into a specified number of shares of common stock.

A **convertible security** is a special type of fixed-income obligation (bond or preferred stock) that possesses a conversion feature permitting the investor to convert it into a specified number of shares of common stock. Convertible bonds and convertible preferreds are attractive investment vehicles because they provide the fixed-income benefit of a bond (interest) or preferred stock (dividends), while offering the price-appreciation (capital gain) potential of common stock. A detailed discussion of this behavior of convertibles, along with other important characteristics of the vehicle, appears in Chapter 10.

Speculative Investment Vehicles

speculative investment vehicles
investment vehicles with high levels of risk.

Speculative investment vehicles are those generally possessing high levels of risk. They usually have nonexistent or imperfect records of success, uncertain earnings, and unstable market values. Because of their above-average risk, these vehicles also have high levels of expected return. The key speculative vehicles are options, commodities and financial futures, and tangibles.

Options: Rights, Warrants, Puts and Calls

options
securities that allow the investor to sell or buy another security at a specified price over a given time period.

Securities that provide the investor with an opportunity to sell or buy another security or asset at a specified price over a given period of time are called **options.** These are acquired and used by investors in a variety of ways and for a variety of reasons. Most often options are purchased in order to take advantage of an anticipated decrease or increase in the price of common stock. However, since these circumstances are speculative, the purchaser of an option is not guaranteed any return and could lose the entire amount invested, either because the option never becomes attractive enough to use or because the life of the option expires. Aside from their speculative use, options are sometimes used to protect existing investment positions against losses.

right
an option for a short period of time to buy a fraction of a share of an issue of common stock at a price below the current market price.

warrant
an option for a long period of time to buy one or more shares of common stock at a price initially above the market price.

The three basic types of options are rights, warrants, and puts and calls (these are discussed in detail in Chapter 11). A **right** is an option to buy a *fraction of a share* of a new issue of common stock at a price *below* the current market price over a *short period* of time—generally one or two months. For example, one might obtain rights entitling the holder to buy one share of stock, with a current market price of $55 per share, at $50 per share for every 10 rights held (that is, each right is good for one-tenth of a share of common stock). A **warrant** is similar to a right but gives its holder an opportunity to purchase *one or more shares* of common stock at a price

that is initially *above* the market price over a *long period* of time—typically 2 to 10 years or more. For example, a General Manufacturing warrant might allow its holder to purchase three shares of its stock currently selling for $70 per share at $80 per share at any time prior to December 31, 1997.

Puts and calls are types of options that have gained great popularity over the past 15 years. A **put** is an option to sell 100 shares of common stock on or before some future date at a specified price. A **call** is an option to buy 100 shares on or before some future date at a specified price. Most puts and calls have lives of 1 to 9 months and occasionally a year. The exercise or striking price of both puts and calls is set close to the market price at the time they are issued. Investors tend to purchase puts when they anticipate price declines and calls when they expect prices to rise. An example of a call option might be a six-month call to buy 100 shares of Stable Industries at $30 per share. The holder of such an option could, anytime before its expiration, buy 100 shares of Stable at $30 per share regardless of the actual market price of the stock. As we will see in Chapter 11, although put and call options are generally viewed as speculative investments, they can also be used to protect an investor's position against loss.

put
an option to sell 100 shares of common stock at a specified price on or before some future date.

call
an option to buy 100 shares of common stock at a specified price on or before some future date.

Commodities and Financial Futures, and Tangibles

commodities and financial futures contracts
obligations that the sellers of the contracts will make delivery and the buyers will take delivery of a specified commodity foreign currency, or financial instrument at some specific date in the future.

tangibles
investment assets, other than real estate, that can be seen or touched.

Two other types of speculative investment vehicles are commodities and financial futures, and tangibles. **Commodities and financial futures contracts** are legally binding obligations that the sellers of such contracts will *make delivery* and the buyers of the contracts will *take delivery* of a specified commodity (for example, soybeans, pork bellies, cocoa), foreign currency, or financial instrument (a specific security or its cash equivalent) at some specific date in the future. Trading in commodities and financial futures is generally a highly specialized, high-risk proposition since the opportunity to make a profit depends on a variety of uncontrollable factors tied to world events and economic activity. **Tangibles,** in contrast, are investment assets, other than real estate, that can be seen or touched. They include gold and other precious metals, diamonds, and collectibles such as stamps, coins, art, and antiques. These speculative vehicles are purchased as investments in anticipation of price increases; during the ownership period some may also provide the investor with psychological or esthetic enjoyment. An expanded discussion of commodities and financial futures and tangibles is presented in Chapter 12.

Other Popular Investment Vehicles

Various other investment vehicles are also widely used by investors. The most common are mutual funds, real estate, and tax shelters and limited partnerships.

Mutual Funds

mutual fund
a company that invests in a diversified portfolio of securities and sells shares to investors who thus obtain an interest in the portfolio.

A company that invests in a diversified portfolio of securities is called a **mutual fund.** The fund sells shares to investors, who thus obtain an interest in the portfolio of securities owned by the fund. Most mutual funds issue and repurchase shares as demanded at a price reflecting the proportionate value of the portfolio at the time the transaction is made. Chapter 13 is devoted to the study of this popular investment vehicle.

Real Estate

real estate
property such as residential homes, raw land, and income property (warehouses, apartment buildings, cooperatives, and condominiums).

The term **real estate** includes investment in such entities as owner-occupied homes, raw land, and a variety of forms of income property, such as warehouses, apartment buildings, cooperatives (co-ops), and condominiums. As a result of generally increasing values and favorable tax treatments, real estate has over the past 15 years become a popular vehicle. Its appeal stems from the fact that real estate investments offer returns in the form of rental income, depreciation write-offs, and capital gains that are not available from alternative investment vehicles. A detailed look at the role real estate can play in the investment portfolio is presented in Chapter 14.

Tax Shelters and Limited Partnerships

tax shelters
investments structured to take advantage of existing tax laws.

limited partnerships
a form of passive investment offering partners limited liability, active professional management, and the resulting profit or loss.

Due to provisions in the federal tax law, some investments offer certain tax advantages over others. As an example, interest received on most municipal bonds is not taxed at all, and income from Individual Retirement Accounts (IRAs) is deferred from taxes until the money is actually taken out of the account. Since the income tax rate for an individual can be as high as 33 percent, many investors find that their after-tax rates of return can be far higher from **tax shelters**—investments structured to take advantage of existing tax laws—than from conventional investments. **Limited partnerships** may be attractive to those wishing to passively invest with limited liability, receiving the benefit of active professional management, and applying the resulting profit or loss (under certain conditions) when calculating their tax liability. Various types of tax-sheltered investments, often structured as limited partnerships, were severely impacted by the Tax Reform Act of 1986; a comprehensive review of the more common tax shelters and limited partnerships is presented in Chapter 15.

AN OVERVIEW OF THE TEXT

The text contains 17 chapters divided into six major parts.

Part One: The Investment Environment
Part Two: Investing in Common Stock
Part Three: Investing in Fixed-Income Securities
Part Four: Speculative Investment Vehicles
Part Five: Other Popular Investment Vehicles
Part Six: Investment Administration

Each part, which is introduced with a listing of its chapters as well as its relationship to the overall investment process, explains an important aspect of investing. This plan of organization links the investor's activities in developing, implementing, and monitoring investment plans. It is intended to provide the understanding needed to establish an investment portfolio that provides an acceptable return for an acceptable level of risk.

To enhance the topical coverage and practical utility of the text, the computer has been introduced, where appropriate, as an investment decision-making aid. Keyed to various parts of the text is the *Investment Management Disk (IMD),* a menu-driven computer disk compatible with most personal computers that can be used as

```
+-----------------------------------------------+
|                  PART ONE                     |
|          The Investment Environment           |
|  +-----------------------------------------+  |
|  |                PART SIX                 |  |
|  |         Investment Administration       |  |
|  |  +-----------------+-----------------+  |  |
|  |  |    PART TWO     |   PART THREE    |  |  |
|  |  |    Investing    |    Investing    |  |  |
|  |  |       in        |       in        |  |  |
|  |  |     Common      |  Fixed-Income   |  |  |
|  |  |     Stock       |   Securities    |  |  |
|  |  +-----------------+-----------------+  |  |
|  |  |   PART FOUR     |   PART FIVE     |  |  |
|  |  |  Speculative    | Other Popular  |  |  |
|  |  |  Investment     |  Investment    |  |  |
|  |  |   Vehicles      |   Vehicles     |  |  |
|  |  +-----------------+-----------------+  |  |
|  |                                         |  |
|  +-----------------------------------------+  |
|                                               |
+-----------------------------------------------+
```

FIGURE 1.2 An Overview of the Major Parts of the Text.
The text approaches the individual investment process in a logical fashion, beginning with an overview of the investment environment (Part One). This is followed with a description of the key aspects of the most popular investment vehicles (Parts Two through Five). The text concludes with a discussion of investment administration (Part Six).

an aid in performing many of the routine investment calculations and procedures presented. Appendix D describes this evaluation and decision aid, which for convenience is keyed to text discussions and end-of-chapter review questions and problems and cases that can be solved with it. These items are clearly denoted by a disk symbol: ▪. In addition, each of the six parts of the book ends with a section called *Computer-Based Investment Management*. Each of these opens with a brief discussion of how the computer can be used in a given aspect of investing (for example, when investing in common stock, or fixed-income securities), and then several popular computer programs are described, including cost, major functions performed, and other noteworthy features.

Brief descriptions of Parts One through Six are given below. These descriptions are summarized in Figure 1.2, which relates each part of the text to the investment process.

Part One: The Investment Environment

Before investing takes place, the investor should be familiar with the way security markets operate, how transactions are made, and the role of brokerage firms in executing transactions. In addition, the investor must become acquainted with the available sources of investment information and advice, procedures for developing investment strategies, and the concepts and procedures used to measure investment return and risk.

Part Two: Investing in Common Stock

One of the most popular forms of investing—common stock—is discussed in detail in Part Two. The fundamental characteristics of common stock and the procedures

available for analyzing potential investments are presented, along with some of the technical aspects of common stock, such as valuation, technical analysis, and efficient markets.

Part Three: Investing in Fixed-Income Securities

Another popular type of investment vehicle is fixed-income securities, which includes bonds, preferred stock, and convertibles. Part Three covers the key characteristics, types, and suitability of each of these forms, with special emphasis on the role each can play in the individual's investment portfolio.

Part Four: Speculative Investment Vehicles

For those investors willing to accept the increased risks, speculative investments provide opportunities to earn high returns. Part Four discusses several kinds of speculative securities—options: rights, warrants, puts and calls; commodities and financial futures; and tangibles—that are readily available to investors.

Part Five: Other Popular Investment Vehicles

This part of the text takes a look at several other forms of widely used investment vehicles, including mutual funds, real estate, and tax shelters and limited partnerships. The discussion of tax shelters specifically emphasizes effective tax strategies under the Tax Reform Act of 1986 and various types of annuities. The key characteristics and suitability of each of these vehicles are evaluated.

Part Six: Investment Administration

The final part of the text is concerned with the administration process, which provides a basis for linking the many concepts, tools, and techniques presented in the earlier parts of the text. This linkage is provided by the development of the technical and applied aspects of portfolio management. In addition, this part of the text discusses the ongoing process of monitoring the investment portfolio.

SUMMARY

- An investment is any vehicle into which funds can be placed in order to earn an expected positive return. Some vehicles are forms of property; others are securities. Some investments are made directly, others indirectly.

- An investment can be a debt, an equity, or an option. It can possess risk ranging from very low to extremely high. An individual can invest in either short-term or long-term vehicles.

- The investment process is structured around financial institutions and financial markets that bring together suppliers and demanders of funds. The participants are government, business, and individuals; of these groups, only individuals are net fund suppliers.

- Investors can be either institutional investors or individual investors. Investing is important since it makes available funds needed to permit our economy to

function and grow. The rewards for investing can be received either as current income or increased value.

- The steps in investing involve the following: meeting investment prerequisites; establishing investment goals; evaluating investment vehicles; selecting suitable investments; constructing a diversified portfolio; and managing the portfolio. Recent developments in investing include use of the personal computer, financial supermarkets, and the globalization of financial markets.

- A broad range of investment vehicles is available. Short-term vehicles have low risk and are used to earn a return on temporarily idle funds, or as the primary investment of conservative investors. Common stocks offer dividends and capital gains. Fixed-income securities—bonds, preferred stock, and convertibles—offer fixed periodic returns with some potential for gain in value.

- Speculative investment outlets are high-risk vehicles such as options (rights, warrants, puts and calls), commodities and financial futures, and tangibles that offer above-average expected returns. Other popular vehicles include mutual funds, real estate, and tax shelters and limited partnerships.

- The text is divided into six major parts containing 17 chapters. A simple model is used to link each part to the investment process.

REVIEW QUESTIONS AND PROBLEMS

1. Define the term *investments* and explain why individuals invest. What alternatives exist for investing idle funds?

2. Differentiate between security and property investments. Which form of investment is more popular among individual investors?

3. What is the difference between direct and indirect investments? Cite an example of each.

4. Differentiate among debt, equity, and option investments, and give an example of each.

5. Describe how the term *risk* is used to depict the behavior of certain investments. Differentiate between low-risk and high-risk investments.

6. Describe the structure of the overall investment process. Define and explain the role played by financial institutions and financial markets.

7. Classify the role of: (a) government, (b) business, and (c) individuals as net suppliers or net demanders of funds. Discuss the impact of each on the investment process.

8. Define and differentiate between institutional investors and individual investors. Which group tends to be more sophisticated? Why?

9. Briefly discuss the economic importance of investing, and describe the rewards available to those placing funds in the investment process.

10. List and discuss the six steps involved in the personal investment process.

11. Describe a personal computer (PC) and the role it can play in the personal investment process.

12. What is a financial supermarket? Do you feel your investment needs could be served by one? Explain.

13. What is *insider trading?* Explain how it has acted as a catalyst in raising ethical issues related to securities markets and transactions.

14. Discuss the role of short-term investment vehicles in an individual's investment plans and portfolio.

15. How much would an investor earn on a stock purchased one year ago for $63 if it paid an annual cash dividend of $3.75 and had just been sold for $67.50? Did the investor experience a capital gain? Explain.

16. Briefly define and differentiate the following fixed-income securities:

    a. Bonds.
    b. Preferred stocks.
    c. Convertible securities.

17. Explain the nature of an option and describe the opportunity for profit offered by this type of investment vehicle.

18. Describe the similarities and differences between rights and warrants.

19. What is the difference between a put and a call? If you did not own shares of a company's stock but felt that its price would decline significantly in the near future, would you be likely to buy a put or a call? Explain.

20. Briefly describe each of the following types of investments, and indicate which factors are likely to affect the returns on each:

    a. Commodities and financial futures.
    b. Tangibles.

21. Briefly describe each of the following popular investment vehicles:

    a. Mutual funds.
    b. Real estate.
    c. Tax shelters.
    d. Limited partnerships.

CASE PROBLEMS

1.1 Investments or Racquetball?

Judd Read and Judi Todd are senior accounting majors at a large midwestern university. They have been good friends since high school and look forward to their graduation at the end of next semester. Each has already found a job, which will begin upon graduation. Judd has accepted a position as an internal auditor in a medium-sized manufacturing firm; Judi will be working for one of the major public accounting firms. Each is looking forward to the challenge of a new career and to the prospect of achieving success both professionally and financially.

Judd and Judi are preparing to register for their final semester. Each has one free elective to select. Judd is considering taking a racquetball course offered by the physical education department, while Judi is planning to take a basic investments course. Judi has been trying to convince Judd to take investments instead of racquetball. Judd believes he doesn't need to

take investments, since he already knows what common stock is. He believes that whenever he has accumulated excess funds, he can invest in the stock of a company that is doing well. Judi argues that there is much more to it than simply choosing common stock. She feels an exposure to the field of investments would certainly be more beneficial than learning how to play racquetball.

Questions
1. Explain to Judd the structure of the investment process and the economic importance of investing.
2. Describe to Judd the steps in investing and emphasize the importance of this process to his overall financial success.
3. List and discuss the other types of investment vehicles with which Judd is apparently unfamiliar.
4. Assuming Judd is in good physical condition, what arguments would you give to convince Judd to take investments rather than racquetball?

1.2 Evaluating Molly Porter's Investment Plan

Molly Porter's husband, Vance, was recently killed in an airplane crash. Fortunately, he had a sizable amount of life insurance, the proceeds of which should provide Molly with adequate income for a number of years. Molly is 33 years old and has two children, David and Phyllis, who are 6 and 7 years old, respectively. Although Molly does not rule out the possibility of marrying again, she feels it is best not to consider this when making her financial plans. In order to provide adequate funds to finance her children's college education as well as for her own retirement, Molly has estimated that she needs to accumulate $230,000 within the next 15 years. If she continues to teach school, she believes sufficient excess funds will be available each year (salary plus insurance proceeds minus expenses) to permit achievement of this goal. She plans to make annual deposits of these excess funds into her money market deposit account, which currently pays 7 percent interest.

Questions
1. In view of Molly's long-term investment goals, assess her choice of a money market deposit account as the appropriate investment vehicle.
2. What alternative investment vehicles might you recommend that Molly consider prior to committing her money to the money market deposit account?
3. If you were Molly, given your limited knowledge of investments, in what vehicles would you invest the excess funds? Explain.

SELECTED READINGS

Egan, Jack. "Investors' Wish List for Washington." *U.S. News & World Report,* February 13, 1989, p. 83.

Fierman, Jaclyn. "What It Takes to Be Rich in America." *Fortune,* April 13, 1987, pp. 22–28.

Goode, Erica E. "On the Delicate Subject of Money." *U.S. News & World Report,* March 7, 1988, pp. 68–69.

Jacobs, Sanford L. "Investment City." *The Wall Street Journal,* December 2, 1988, pp. R9–R10.

Kehrer, Daniel M. "Five Population Trends Every Investor Should Know." *Changing Times,* September 1988, pp. 58–64.

Lynch, Peter. "One Up on Wall Street." *Money,* January 1989, pp. 128–43.
Reid, Jeanne L. "Twelve Steps to Financial Security." *Money,* January 1988, pp. 66–74.
Schiffres, Manuel. "Outlook Investing." *Changing Times,* January 1989, pp. 40–46.
"Ten Steps to Financial Freedom." *Changing Times,* September 1988, pp. 23–37.
"Your Finances." *Money Extra,* 1988, pp. 95–115.

2

INVESTMENT MARKETS AND TRANSACTIONS

After studying this chapter you should be able to:

● Describe the basic types of securities markets and the characteristics of both organized exchanges and the over-the-counter market.

● Discuss regulation of the securities markets as well as the general market conditions that have prevailed over the last fifty or so years.

● Explain the role of the stockbroker and describe the basic types of orders and costs involved in making securities transactions.

● Understand the economic motives and procedures for making margin transactions.

● Summarize the various margin requirements and discuss the popular uses of margin trading.

● Describe the motives for short selling, the procedures used by short sellers, and the popular applications of this trading technique.

In general, it is difficult to play a game, whatever it may be, without fully understanding the rules. In spite of the fact that you may possess potential and skill for playing the game, without adequate knowledge you will probably be unable to play well. The same type of logic applies to investing. For although investing is far more than a game, it does have a number of important rules you need to know. Regardless of how well prepared you might be to select the best vehicle for achieving your particular investment goals, you cannot make that selection if you do not understand the workings of the market in which that vehicle is bought and sold, if you do not know how to find and enter the market, and if you do not understand the basic types of transactions required. In this chapter we will look at key aspects of the investment environment so that you will know which market to enter for your purposes, how to enter it, and which basic types of transactions to make.

securities markets
markets allowing suppliers and demanders of funds to make transactions; may provide trading in either money or capital.

SECURITIES MARKETS

Securities markets are the mechanism that allows suppliers and demanders of funds to make transactions. These markets play a key role in the purchase and sales activities of investors. Not only do they provide the mechanism through which purchasers and sellers can make transactions, but they permit such transactions to be made *quickly* and at a fair price. Before describing the methods used to enter these markets, let us look at the various types of markets, their organization, their regulation, and their general behavior.

money market
market in which short-term securities are bought and sold.

Types of Markets

The securities markets may be classified as either money markets or capital markets. The **money market** is where short-term securities are bought and sold. The **capital market** is where transactions are made in longer-term securities such as stocks and bonds. Because the money market is concerned with short-term securities and because the size of these transactions is generally larger than the scope of the average investor's resources (usually $100,000 or more), we will devote most of our attention in this book to the capital market, which is made up of different kinds of securities exchanges through which stock, bond, options, and futures investments can be made. Capital markets can be classified as either primary or secondary.

capital market
market in which long-term securities such as stocks and bonds are bought and sold.

primary market
market in which new issues of securities are brought to the public.

Primary Markets

The market in which new issues of securities are brought to the public is the **primary market.** When a company offers a new security, a number of institutions are likely to be involved in the selling process. The corporation issuing the security will probably use the services of an **investment banking firm,** an organization that specializes in selling new security issues. The investment banker's activities are often described as **underwriting,** or guaranteeing to the issuer that it will receive a specified minimum amount for the issue. Not only does the investment banking firm sell new security issues on behalf of issuers, it also provides the issuing corporation with advice about pricing and other important aspects of the issue. In the case of very large security issues, the banking firm will bring in other firms as partners to

investment banking firm
organization that specializes in selling new security issues.

underwriting
the guarantee of an investment banker that a firm issuing a new security will receive a specified minimum amount for the issue.

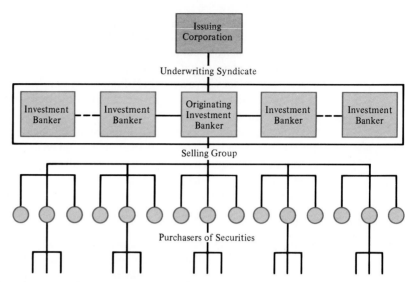

FIGURE 2.1 The New Security Selling Process.
The investment banker hired by the issuing corporation may form an underwriting syndicate, which then establishes a selling group to sell the new security issue in the primary market.

underwriting syndicate
a group formed to spread the financial risk associated with the selling of new securities.

selling group
a large number of brokerage firms that join to accept responsibility for selling a certain portion of the issue of a new security.

form an **underwriting syndicate** in order to spread the financial risk associated with the selling of the new securities. The originating investment banker with the assistance of the syndicate members puts together a **selling group,** normally made up of a large number of brokerage firms, each of which accepts the responsibility for selling a certain portion of the issue. The selling process for a new security issue is depicted in Figure 2.1. The relationships among the participants in this process can also be seen in the announcement of the offering of a new security issue, shown in Figure 2.2. The role of the various firms participating in the selling process can be differentiated on the basis of the layout of the announcement. Isolated firm names (or in many cases, a larger typeface) reflect the importance of the firm in the sale process (the key participants in the offering are labeled in the margin at the right).

Compensation for underwriting and selling services typically comes in the form of a discount from the sale price of the securities. For example, an investment banker may pay the issuer $24 per share for stock to be sold for $25 per share. The investment banker may then sell the shares to members of the selling group for $24.75 per share. In this case, the original investment banker earns $0.75 per share ($24.75 sale price less $24 purchase price), and the members of the selling group earn $0.25 for each share they sell ($25 sale price less $24.75 purchase price). Although some primary security offerings are sold directly by the issuer, the majority of new issues are sold through the mechanism just described.

Secondary Markets

secondary market
the market in which securities are traded after they have been issued; also called the aftermarket.

The market in which securities are traded after they have been issued is the **secondary market** or the aftermarket. The secondary market exists because after a security

This advertisement is neither an offer to sell nor a solicitation of an offer to buy any of these securities. The offering is made only by the Prospectus.

April 14, 1989

1,350,000 Shares

Bytex

Common Stock

Price $8.00 Per Share

Copies of the Prospectus may be obtained from such of the Underwriters as may legally offer these securities in compliance with the securities laws of the respective states.

Investment Banking Syndicate

Alex. Brown & Sons
Incorporated

Volpe & Covington

Selling Group

Bear, Stearns & Co. Inc.	**The First Boston Corporation**	**Dillon, Read & Co. Inc.**
Donaldson, Lufkin & Jenrette Securities Corporation	**Drexel Burnham Lambert** Incorporated	**Goldman, Sachs & Co.**
Hambrecht & Quist Incorporated	**Kidder, Peabody & Co.** Incorporated	**Lazard Frères & Co.**
Merrill Lynch Capital Markets	**Montgomery Securities**	**Morgan Stanley & Co.** Incorporated
PaineWebber Incorporated	**Prudential-Bache Capital Funding**	**Robertson, Stephens & Company**
Salomon Brothers Inc	**Shearson Lehman Hutton Inc.**	**Smith Barney, Harris Upham & Co.** Incorporated
Wertheim Schroder & Co. Incorporated	**Dean Witter Reynolds Inc.**	**Adams, Harkness & Hill, Inc.**
William Blair & Company	**Dain Bosworth** Incorporated	**A. G. Edwards & Sons, Inc.**
Oppenheimer & Co., Inc.	**Piper, Jaffray & Hopwood** Incorporated	**The Robinson-Humphrey Company, Inc.**
Thomson McKinnon Securities Inc.		**Wheat, First Securities, Inc.**

Robert W. Baird & Co. Incorporated	**Blunt Ellis & Loewi** Incorporated	**R. G. Dickinson & Co.**	**McDonald & Company** Securities, Inc.
The Ohio Company	**Stifel, Nicolaus & Company** Incorporated		**Wessels, Arnold & Henderson**

FIGURE 2.2   An Offering Announcement.
This form of an offering announcement is commonly referred to as a ''tombstone,'' apparently because of its close resemblance to such markings. The participants in both the investment banking syndicate and the selling group established to sell the common stock of Bytex are clearly noted on the tombstone. (*Source: The Wall Street Journal,* April 14, 1989, p. C17.)

organized securities exchanges
centralized institutions in which transactions are made in already outstanding securities.

has been issued, some purchasers may wish to sell their shares, and others may wish to buy them. Included among secondary markets are the various organized securities exchanges and the over-the-counter market. **Organized securities exchanges** are centralized institutions in which the forces of supply and demand for certain securities are brought together. They are secondary markets in which transactions are made in already outstanding securities. The **over-the-counter (OTC) market,** on the other hand, is a widely scattered telecommunications network through which buyers and sellers of certain securities can be brought together. In addition to creating a secondary market for securities, the over-the-counter market is a primary market in which public issues—including those listed on organized exchanges—are sold. Because so many different kinds of popular investment vehicles are traded on both the organized securities exchanges and over-the-counter markets, the individual investor will probably make transactions in both of these markets.

Organized Securities Exchanges

over-the-counter (OTC) market
widely scattered telecommunications network through which buyers and sellers of certain securities can be brought together; also the primary market in which public issues are sold.

"Listed" securities are traded on organized securities exchanges and account for about two-thirds of the total volume of domestic shares traded. All trading at a given exchange is carried out in one place (such as the New York Stock Exchange on Wall Street) and under a broad set of rules by persons who are members of that exchange. The best known exchanges on which stock and bond transactions are made are the New York Stock Exchange (NYSE) and the American Stock Exchange (AMEX), both located in New York City and accounting for approximately 85 and 5 percent, respectively, of the total annual dollar volume of shares traded on organized U.S. exchanges. Other domestic exchanges include the Midwest Stock Exchange, the Pacific Stock Exchange, the Philadelphia Stock Exchange, and the Boston Stock Exchange; these are known as *regional exchanges,* and together, they account for about 10 percent of the annual dollar share volume on organized U.S. exchanges. There are 13 regional exchanges, and each deals primarily in securities with local or regional appeal. In addition, foreign stock exchanges list and trade shares of firms in their own foreign markets. Separate domestic exchanges exist for options trading and trading in commodities and financial futures. Let us now consider the basic structure, rules, and operations of each of these organized securities exchanges.

The New York Stock Exchange

Since most organized securities exchanges are modeled after the New York Stock Exchange (NYSE), a description of its membership, listing policies, and trading activity will provide a basis for discussing other exchanges.

Membership. Membership in the New York Stock Exchange is expensive. In order to be a member, an individual or firm must own or lease a "seat" on the exchange. The word *seat* is used only figuratively, since members trade securities standing up. There are a total of 1,366 seats on the NYSE. Seats on the exchange have sold for as much as $1,250,000 (in 1987) and as little as $4,000 (in 1876 and 1878). The majority of seat holders are brokerage firms, each typically owning more than one seat. (The largest brokerage firm, Merrill Lynch Pierce Fenner &

TABLE 2.1 NYSE Member Activities

Type of Member	Approximate % Total Membership*	Primary Activities
A. Make Transactions for Customers		
Commission brokers	52%	Make stock and bond purchase and sale transactions as requested by customers.
Bond brokers	2	Commission brokers who only make bond transactions for customers.
B. Make Transactions for Other Members		
Floor brokers (Two-dollar brokers)	10	Execute orders for other brokers who are unable to do so due to excessive market activity.
Specialists	29	Make a continuous, fair, and orderly market in the 6 to 15 issues assigned to them. They also make odd-lot purchase and sale transactions for members of the exchange.
C. Make Transactions for Their Own Account		
Registered traders	4	Purchase and sell securities for their own account. Must abide by certain regulations established to protect the public.

*Because approximately 3 percent of the members are inactive, the percentages given total to only 97 percent.

Smith Inc., owns over 20 seats.) Firms such as Merrill Lynch designate officers to occupy seats, and only such designated individuals are permitted to make transactions on the floor of the exchange. Membership is often divided into broad classes based on the members' activities. Although the majority of members make purchase and sale transactions on behalf of their customers, some members make transactions for other members or for their own account. Table 2.1 classifies and briefly describes member activities. It should be clear that commission brokers and specialists perform the majority of the activities on the exchange.

Listing Policies. To become listed on an organized stock exchange, a firm must file an application. Some firms are listed on more than one exchange; when this occurs, the firm's shares are said to have **dual listing.** The New York Stock Exchange has the most stringent listing requirements. Currently over 1,600 firms, accounting for over 2,200 stocks and over 3,300 bonds, are listed on the NYSE. In order to be eligible for listing on the NYSE, a firm must have at least 2,000 stockholders owning 100 or more shares. It must have a minimum of 1.1 million shares of publicly held stock, a demonstrated earning power of $2.5 million before taxes at the time of the listing and $2 million before taxes for each of the preceding two

dual listing
a listing of a firm's shares on more than one exchange.

years, net tangible assets of $16 million, a total of $18 million in market value of publicly traded shares, and it must pay a listing fee. Once a firm's securities have been accepted for listing, it must meet the requirements of the federal Securities and Exchange Commission (SEC), which regulates certain aspects of listed securities. If listed firms do not continue to meet specified requirements, they may be **de-listed** from the exchange.

de-listed
to be removed from one's listing on an organized stock exchange for failure to meet specified listing requirements.

Trading Activity. Trading is carried out on the floor of an exchange. The floor of the NYSE is an area about the size of a football field. On the floor are 18 trading posts, and around the perimeter are telephones and telegraph equipment which are used to transmit buy-and-sell orders from brokers' offices to the exchange floor and back again once an order has been executed. Certain stocks are traded at each of the trading posts. Bonds and less active stocks are traded in an annex. All trades are made on the floor of the exchange by members of the exchange. Trades are made in **round lots** (usually lots of 100 shares), and not in **odd lots** (less than 100 shares). The **specialists,** members who specialize in one or more stocks, make odd-lot transactions for members desiring this service.

round lots
100-share units of stock or multiples thereof.

odd lots
less than 100 shares of stock.

specialists
stock exchange members who specialize in one or more stocks and make odd-lot transactions for exchange members.

All transactions on the floor of the exchange are made through an auction process. The goal is to fill all buy orders at the lowest price and to fill all sell orders at the highest price, thereby giving both purchasers and sellers the best possible advantage. The actual auction takes place at a post on the floor of the exchange where the particular security is traded. Members interested in purchasing a given security publicly negotiate a transaction with members interested in selling that security. The specialist's job in such a transaction is to provide for a continuous and orderly market in the security. The specialist performs this job by offering to buy or sell (at specified prices) whenever there is a lack of continuity or order in the market for the security.

The American Stock Exchange

The American Stock Exchange (AMEX) is the second largest organized U.S. security exchange in terms of the number of listed companies, but in terms of dollar volume of trading, the AMEX is actually smaller than the two largest regional exchanges—the Midwest and the Pacific. Its organization and procedures are quite similar to those of the New York Stock Exchange, except that its listing requirements are not as stringent as those of the NYSE. There are approximately 660 seats on the AMEX, with over 950 listed stocks and 325 listed bonds.

Regional Stock Exchanges

The number of companies having securities listed on each of the regional exchanges is typically in the range of 100 to 500. As a group these exchanges handle about 10 percent of the dollar volume of all shares traded on organized U.S. exchanges. Nine of the 13 American regional exchanges are registered with an agency of the federal government; the other four are not large enough to require registration. Table 2.2 lists the regional stock exchanges. Of these the Midwest, Pacific, Philadelphia, and Boston are the dominant ones. Most regional exchanges are modeled after the

---

TABLE 2.2   Regional Stock Exchanges—Registered (R), Unregistered (U)

Boston Stock Exchange (R)	Pacific Stock Exchange (R)
Cincinnati Stock Exchange (R)	Philadelphia Stock Exchange (R)
Colorado Stock Exchange (U)	Pittsburgh Stock Exchange (R)
Detroit Stock Exchange (U)	Richmond Stock Exchange (U)
Honolulu Stock Exchange (R)	Spokane Stock Exchange (R)
Intermountain Stock Exchange (R)	Wheeling Stock Exchange (U)
Midwest Stock Exchange (R)	

NYSE, but their membership and listing requirements are considerably more lenient than the latter. It is not uncommon for the regional exchanges to list securities that are also listed on the NYSE or AMEX. This dual listing is often done to enhance a security's trading activity. In addition, a number of the regional exchanges, along with the NYSE, AMEX, and the over-the-counter market, are linked together through an electronic communications network—the *Intermarket Trading System (ITS)*—which allows brokers and other traders to make transactions at the best prices.

Foreign Stock Exchanges

In addition to the domestic stock exchanges there are a number of foreign stock exchanges. In Canada, the Toronto Stock Exchange and the Montreal Stock Exchange are the dominant exchanges. On a worldwide basis the Tokyo Stock Exchange and the London Stock Exchange are first and third in dollar volume, respectively; the New York Stock Exchange is second. Other important foreign exchanges include the Zurich Stock Exchange (Switzerland), Sydney Stock Exchange (Australia), Paris Stock Exchange (France), Frankfurt Stock Exchange (West Germany), Hong Kong Stock Exchange (China), and South African Exchange. The foreign exchanges are organized in a fashion similar to those in the United States and create a marketplace in which the securities of companies based in the given country are traded. Often these companies are foreign subsidiaries of American companies.

Investors wishing to make transactions in the stock of foreign companies have available two basic options. The first is to purchase the foreign security through a foreign broker or the foreign branch office of a U.S. broker. This approach is somewhat difficult due to possible administrative, tax, and transfer problems. Thus a second and more popular approach is for the investor to purchase the stock of the firm directly on a major U.S. security exchange or in the over-the-counter market. Shares of certain foreign securities are traded in the form of **American Depositary Receipts (ADRs),** which are negotiable receipts for the stock of the company that is held in trust in a foreign branch of a U.S. bank. Two forms of ADRs are available. **Company-sponsored ADRs** meet certain government registration requirements and are listed and traded on the New York or American Stock Exchange. Shares of foreign firms, such as British Petroleum (Great Britain) and Sony Corporation (Japan), are company-sponsored ADRs. **Unsponsored ADRs** lack registration and

American Depositary Receipts (ADRs) *negotiable receipts for the stock of a company which are held in trust in a foreign branch of a U.S. bank; may be company sponsored or unsponsored.*

company-sponsored ADRs *ADRs that meet certain government registration requirements and are listed and traded on the New York or American stock exchange.*

unsponsored ADRs *ADRs that are not registered with the U.S. government and therefore are traded over the counter.*

therefore are traded on an over-the-counter basis. Popular unsponsored ADRs include DeBeers Mines (South Africa) and Canon (Japan). Regardless of whether they are sponsored or unsponsored, investors can conveniently make transactions in ADRs with the assistance of their brokers. (ADRs are further discussed in Chapter 6.)

Options Exchanges

Options, which allow the holder to purchase or sell a financial asset at a specified price over a stated period of time, are listed and traded on the Chicago Board Options Exchange (CBOE), as well as on the American Stock Exchange, the New York Stock Exchange, the Pacific Stock Exchange, and the Philadelphia Stock Exchange. The dominant options exchange is the CBOE, which was established in 1973. The CBOE, like other exchanges, has membership, listing, and trading requirements. Usually an option for the purchase (a call) or sale (a put) of a given financial asset is listed on only one of the options exchanges, although dual listing does sometimes occur. Options exchanges deal only in security options; options to purchase or sell property are not traded in this marketplace.

Futures Exchanges

Futures, which are contracts guaranteeing the future delivery of some commodity, foreign currency, or financial instrument at a given future date, are purchased and sold on a variety of exchanges. The dominant exchange on which commodity and financial futures are traded is the Chicago Board of Trade (CBT). It provides an organized forum in which members can make transactions in any of the listed commodity and financial futures contracts. There are a number of other futures exchanges, some of which specialize in certain commodities rather than the broad spectrum listed on the CBT. The larger of these exchanges include the Chicago Mercantile Exchange, the Chicago Rice & Cotton Exchange, the Commodity Exchange of New York, the International Petroleum Exchange, the Kansas City Board of Trade, the Mid America Commodity Exchange, the Minneapolis Grain Exchange, the New York Coffee, Sugar, and Cocoa Exchange, the New York Cotton Exchange, the New York Futures Exchange (a NYSE subsidiary), the New York Mercantile Exchange, the Philadelphia Board of Trade, and the Winnipeg Commodity Exchange.

The Over-the-Counter Market

The over-the-counter market is not a specific institution; rather, it is another way of trading securities. It accounts for about one-third of *all* shares traded. Securities traded in this market are sometimes called *unlisted securities*. The over-the-counter (OTC) market is the result of an intangible relationship among purchasers and sellers of securities. The active traders in this market are linked by a sophisticated telecommunications network, and the prices at which securities are traded are determined by both competitive bids and negotiation. The actual process depends on the general activity of the security. A numerical majority of stocks are traded over the counter, as are most government and corporate bonds. Of the over 30,000 issues

traded over the counter, about 5,000 have an active market in which frequent transactions take place. A numerical majority of all corporate bonds, some of which are also listed on the NYSE, are traded in the OTC market.

New Issues and Secondary Distributions

In order to create a continuous market for unlisted securities, the OTC market also provides a forum in which new public issues, both listed and unlisted, are sold. If they are listed, subsequent transactions will be made on the appropriate organized securities exchange; unlisted securities will continue to trade in the OTC market. *Secondary distributions* involve the sale of large blocks of securities by major shareholders and are also often made in the OTC market rather than on the appropriate organized exchange. This is done to minimize the potentially negative effects of such transactions on the price of listed securities.

The Role of Dealers

The market price of OTC securities results from a matching of the forces of supply and demand for the security by traders known as **dealers.** Each makes markets in certain securities by offering to buy or sell at stated prices. Thus, unlike the organized exchanges (where the buyer and seller of a security are brought together by a broker), these dealers are always the second party to a transaction. For example, a dealer making a market in Raco Enterprises might offer to buy shares from investors at $29.50 and sell shares to other investors at $31. The **bid price** is the highest price offered by the dealer to purchase a given security; the **ask price** is the lowest price at which the dealer is willing to sell the security. As an investor, a person could *sell* stock in Raco Enterprises at the (lower) bid price of $29.50; or he could *buy* it at the (higher) ask price of $31. The dealer makes a profit from the spread between the bid and the ask price.

NASDAQ

OTC dealers are linked with the purchasers and sellers of securities through the **National Association of Securities Dealers Automated Quotation (NASDAQ) System,** an automated system that provides up-to-date bid and ask prices on over 5,100 selected, highly active OTC securities. NASDAQ has provided a great deal of continuity in the OTC market because it allows buyers and sellers to locate one another easily. To trade in securities not quoted on NASDAQ, purchasers and sellers must find each other through references or through known dealers in the securities. About 2,900 of the NASDAQ stocks meeting the qualification standards relative to financial size, performance, and trading activity are included in the **NASDAQ/National Market System (NASDAQ/NMS).** Transactions in stocks on this list are carefully tracked, and their more detailed quotations are therefore isolated from other OTC stocks when published in the financial press.

Third and Fourth Markets

The **third market** is the name give to over-the-counter transactions made in securities listed on the NYSE, AMEX, or one of the other organized exchanges. It exists

dealers
traders who make markets by offering to buy or sell certain over-the-counter securities at stated prices.

bid price
the highest price offered by a dealer to purchase a given security.

ask price
the lowest price at which a dealer is willing to sell a given security.

National Association of Securities Dealers Automated Quotation (NASDAQ) System
an automated system that provides up-to-date bid and ask prices on certain selected, highly active OTC securities.

NASDAQ/National Market System (NASDAQ/NMS)
a list of NASDAQ stocks meeting certain qualification standards relative to financial size, performance, and trading activity.

third market
over-the-counter transactions made in securities listed on the NYSE, AMEX, or other organized exchanges.

INVESTOR INSIGHTS

Electronic 24-Hour Trading on the NYSE: Will It Happen?

The New York Stock Exchange, in a drive to keep up with rival exchanges and the explosion of 24-hour trading, is considering trading its stocks electronically during the hours its exchange floor is closed.

A move to so-called off-hours trading would be an historic development for the 198-year-old Big Board, the world's No. 2 stock exchange behind the Tokyo Stock Exchange. Until now, the Big Board has shunned efforts by other stock and commodity exchanges in the U.S. and abroad that have made markets around the clock in stocks, futures and other financial instruments, either through electronic systems or live trading.

"We've got a timeframe of probably six to 24 months before we sketch out and share with the customer community on a much broader base our model for off-hours trading," Richard Grasso, Big Board president and chief operating officer, said in an interview. "To the extent that a customer has a need in the off-hours, this institution has a commitment to meet that need."

. . .

Mr. Grasso said it would be premature for him to describe details of a possible Big Board electronic trading system. But the exchange is already receiving overtures from the Chicago exchanges, who want to link their systems with the Big Board.

. . .

With advanced computers capable of handling daily trading of hundreds of millions of shares, the Big Board could design its own 24-hour trading system. Some New York securities firms, however, fear that competitors will wind up dictating the Big Board's off-hours system if the exchange doesn't move quickly on its own. "The Big Board is becoming increasingly sensitive about the competition for off-hours trading," said an official at Salomon Brothers Inc.

The Big Board's consideration of off-hours trading comes as exchanges around the world are starting to explore the use of technology to match buyers and sellers of a wide range of securities.

Order-matching technology has existed for years, and has been used successfully by airlines, banks, and other industries with heavy volumes of fast-paced transactions. But most of the world's stock, futures and options exchanges, where traders stand on a floor and help to match buyers and sellers, have adamantly resisted automating that process. By

to serve the needs of large institutional investors, such as mutual funds, pension funds, and life insurance companies, by allowing them to make large transactions at a reduced cost. These transactions are typically handled by firms or dealers that are not members of an organized securities exchange. For bringing together large buyers and sellers, these firms charge commissions below those charged for making similar transactions on the associated securities exchange. Institutional investors are thus often able to realize sizable savings in brokerage commissions as well as to

contrast, traders who deal in foreign-exchange and bonds already use electronic links instead of an exchange trading floor.

Exchanges' resistance is easing, however, thanks to the explosion of international links between markets that has placed exchanges increasingly in competition with each other. The links have forced the exchanges to start regarding themselves as nodes on an international trading network—not as self-contained islands.

While the Big Board has lost only a small percentage of its total business to trading overseas when the exchange is closed between 4 p.m. and 9:30 a.m. EST, some members worry that the volume of lost business could grow, particularly in a bull market.

. . .

In the face of tough markets, which have continued since the crash, Big Board officials have been scrambling to find new revenue sources, floor traders say. Big Wall Street firms and money managers, facing their own revenue crunch, continue to press the exchange's market makers—known as specialists—for commission cuts.

But a move to 24-hour trading, which would almost certainly involve a market of competing dealers—rather than the Big Board's own specialist system—would be controversial. Even in hours when the exchange floor is closed, such a step would threaten to erode the power of dozens of specialists, each of whom makes markets in a handful of stocks to insure that the rise and fall of prices is orderly.

. . .

The specialists note with some glee that those electronic trading systems now in use do very little business. The biggest problem with electronic trading is that money managers and other big traders are reluctant to enter large buy or sell orders into a computer system that would allow the entire market to know what they intend to do before they do it. On the other hand, computer experts say they can design electronic trading systems that minimize this problem.

Should a money manager advertise over a computer the fact that he needs to buy 100,000 shares of American Express Co., for example, the price of American Express stock could rise sharply before he ever gets to buy a single share as other traders buy ahead of his order. The Big Board floor provides an element of secrecy: floor traders canvass cautiously looking for buy and sell opportunities for their clients without tipping their hand. The specialist, as a market maker, often acts like a matchmaker, bringing together buyers and sellers without divulging the position of either. . . .

Source: Matthew Winkler, Michael W. Miller, and Steve Swartz, ''Big Board Considers Trading Electronically During Off-Hours,'' *The Wall Street Journal,* April 21, 1989, p. C1.

have minimal impact on the price of the transaction. Since the introduction of negotiated commissions on the organized exchanges in 1975, the importance of this market has been somewhat reduced.

fourth market
transactions made directly between large institutional buyers and sellers.

The **fourth market** is the name given to transactions made directly between large institutional buyers and sellers. Unlike the third market, fourth-market transactions bypass the dealer. But in order to find a suitable seller or buyer, an institution may hire a firm to facilitate the transaction.

Regulation of Securities Markets

As a result of various abuses and misrepresentations, a number of state and federal laws have been enacted to provide for adequate and accurate disclosure of information to potential and existing investors. Such laws also regulate the activities of various participants in the securities markets. State laws, which regulate the sale of securities within state borders, are commonly called "blue sky laws" because they are intended to prevent investors from being sold nothing but "blue sky." These laws typically establish procedures for regulating both security issues and sellers of securities doing business within the state. As part of this process, most states have a regulatory body, such as a state securities commission, that is charged with the enforcement of the related state statutes. But the most important securities laws are those enacted by the federal government.

Securities Act of 1933

This act was passed by Congress to ensure full disclosure of information with respect to new security issues and prevent a stock market collapse similar to that which occurred in 1929–1932. It requires the issuer of a new security to file a registration statement containing information with respect to the new issue with the Securities and Exchange Commission (SEC). The firm cannot sell the security until the SEC approves the registration statement, a process that usually takes about 20 days.

prospectus
the summary of data in a security registration statement.

red herring
a preliminary statement available to prospective investors after a registration statement has been filed but before its approval.

One portion of the registration statement, called the **prospectus,** summarizes the registration data. During the waiting period between filing the statement and its approval, a **red herring,** which is a preliminary statement indicating the tentative nature of the offer, is made available to prospective investors; it is so named because, printed in red on the front of the prospectus, it states that the information contained therein is preliminary and subject to change. Once the statement has been approved, the new security issue can be offered for sale if the prospectus is made available to all interested parties. If the registration statement is found to be fraudulent, the SEC will reject the issue and may also sue the directors and others responsible for the misrepresentation. *Approval of the registration statement by the SEC does not mean the security is a good investment; it merely indicates that the facts presented in the statement appear to reflect the firm's true position.*

Securities Exchange Act of 1934

This act expanded the scope of federal regulation and formally established the SEC as the agency in charge of the administration of federal securities laws. The act established the SEC's power to regulate the organized securities exchanges and over-the-counter markets by extending disclosure requirements to outstanding securities. It required the stock exchanges as well as the stocks traded on them to be registered with the SEC.

As a result of this act, the regulatory power of the SEC became all-encompassing; it covered exchanges and the OTC market, their members, brokers and dealers, and the securities traded in these markets. Each of these participants is required to

file registration statements and additional financial data with the SEC and must periodically update such data. The act has been instrumental in providing adequate disclosure of facts on outstanding issues that are traded in the secondary markets. The 1934 act, which has been amended several times over the years, and the Securities Act of 1933, remain the key pieces of legislation that protect participants in the securities markets.

Maloney Act of 1938

This act, which was in fact an amendment to the Securities Exchange Act of 1934, provided for the establishment of trade associations for the purpose of self-regulation within the securities industry. The act required such associations to register with the SEC. Since its passage, only one such trade association, the National Association of Securities Dealers (NASD), has been formed. NASD members include nearly all of the nation's securities firms that do business with the public. Membership in NASD is a must for most firms, since it allows member firms to make transactions with other member firms at rates below those charged to nonmembers. Today any securities firms that are not members of NASD must agree to be supervised directly by the SEC. Because the SEC has the power to revoke NASD's registration, its power over this organization is the same as over the exchanges. In addition to its self-regulatory role, NASD has greatly streamlined the functioning of the over-the-counter market by creating NASDAQ. From the viewpoint of the individual investor, the establishment of the NASD has created a convenient mechanism that makes transactions as well as price quotations in OTC securities readily available.

Investment Company Act of 1940

This act was passed to protect those purchasing investment company shares. An investment company is one that obtains funds by selling its shares to numerous investors and uses the proceeds to purchase securities. By buying investment company shares, an investor is indirectly investing in a wide variety of securities. There are two types of investment companies: **closed-end companies,** in which the number of shares sold is limited, and **open-end companies,** in which there is no limit on the number of shares outstanding. The dominant type of investment company, the open-end, or mutual fund, is discussed in detail in Chapter 13.

closed-end companies
investment companies in which the number of shares sold is limited.

open-end companies
investment companies, such as mutual funds, in which there is no limit on the number of shares outstanding.

The Investment Company Act of 1940 established rules and regulations for investment companies and formally authorized the SEC to regulate their practices and procedures. It required the investment companies to register with the SEC and to fulfill certain disclosure requirements. The act was amended in 1970 to prohibit investment companies from paying excessive fees to their advisors as well as from charging excessive commissions to purchasers of company shares. From the point of view of the individual investor, this act provides protection against inadequate or inaccurate disclosure of information, and against being charged excessive fees indirectly by the fund's advisors, and directly through the commissions paid to purchase company shares.

Investment Advisors Act of 1940

This act was passed to protect investors against potential abuses by investment advisors, who are persons hired by investors to advise them about security investments. It was passed to make sure that advisors disclose all relevant information about their backgrounds, conflicts of interest, and so on, as well as about any investments they recommend. The act requires advisors to register and file periodic reports with the SEC. A 1960 amendment extended the SEC's powers to permit inspection of the records of investment advisors and revocation of the registration of advisors who violate the act's provisions. *This act does not provide any guarantee of competence on the part of advisors; it merely helps to protect the investor against fraudulent and unethical practices by the advisor.*

Securities Acts Amendments of 1975

In 1975 Congress amended the securities acts to require the SEC and the securities industry to develop a competitive national system for trading securities. Although the charge to the securities industry was vague, the SEC as a first step abolished fixed commission schedules in 1975, thereby providing for negotiated commissions. A second action was the establishment of the Intermarket Trading System (ITS) in 1978. Today this electronic communications network links eight markets, including the NYSE, AMEX, and the OTC market, and trades over 1,500 eligible issues. Unquestionably the Securities Acts Amendments have been highly effective in initiating the evaluation and deliberation of a national market system. However, because many institutional and organizational barriers remain to be overcome before a truly competitive national market system can be established, it is difficult to predict when the goals of such a system will ultimately be reached.

General Market Conditions: Bull or Bear

Conditions in the securities markets are commonly classified as "bull" or "bear," depending on whether the general level of prices is rising (a bull market) or falling (a bear market). Changing market conditions generally stem from changes in investor attitudes, changes in economic activity, and government actions aimed at stimulating or slowing down the level of economic activity. **Bull markets** are favorable markets normally associated with investor optimism, economic recovery, and governmental stimulus; **bear markets** are unfavorable markets normally associated with investor pessimism, economic slowdowns, and government restraint. Over the past fifty or so years, the behavior of the stock market has been generally bullish, reflecting the growth and prosperity of the economy. Figure 2.3 shows that there have been five major bull markets since World War II, the longest of which lasted *97 months*—from June 1949 to July 1957. The most notorious of the five was surely the latest one, which started in August of 1982 and peaked out in August of 1987, for it is the one that's associated with the big market crash of October 19, 1987. Actually, the market had started dropping in late August of 1987 and by mid-October, the Dow Jones Industrial Average had already fallen about 15 percent. Then came "black Monday," when the market experienced its biggest and hardest crash

bull markets *favorable markets associated with investor optimism, economic recovery, and governmental stimulus.*

bear markets *unfavorable markets associated with investor pessimism, economic slowdowns, and government restraint.*

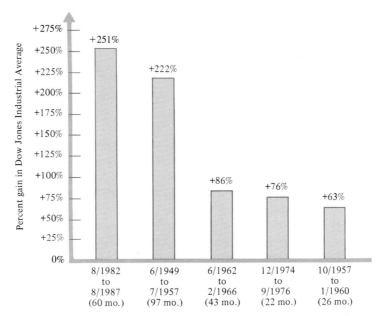

FIGURE 2.3 The Five Biggest Bull Markets Since World War II.
Based on changes in the Dow Jones Industrial Average, the biggest bull market since World War II was the one that ended in August 1987. Generally the prices of most stocks go up in a bull market and as such, it's difficult to lose money, though not impossible, since not all stocks will appreciate in value during bull markets.

in history: in *one day* the Dow fell nearly 23 percent, and the market lost roughly half a *trillion* dollars in value. The bear market initiated with this decline was primarily the result of major budget deficits and unfavorable trade balances.

In general, the investor experiences higher (or positive) returns on common stock investments during a bull market. However, it is not unusual to find securities that are bullish in a bear market or bearish in a bull market. Of course, during bear markets many investors will invest in vehicles other than securities to obtain higher and less risky returns. Market conditions are difficult to predict and usually can be identified only after they exist. The actual assessment of market conditions and the use of this information by the investor is described in Chapter 3.

MAKING SECURITY TRANSACTIONS

Understanding the structure and functioning of the securities markets is just the first step in developing a sound investment program; an investor must also be able to enter these markets to make transactions. The individual investor must understand the procedures required to make transactions as well as the various types of orders that can be placed. It is also important to have an appreciation of the costs associated with making investment transactions.

Stockbrokers

stockbrokers
*individuals licensed
by stock exchanges
to enable investors to
buy and sell securi-
ties; also called* ac-
count executives.

Stockbrokers, or account executives, as they are sometimes called, enable investors to purchase and sell securities. They must be licensed by the exchanges on
which they place orders and must abide by the ethical guidelines of the exchanges
and the SEC. Stockbrokers work for the brokerage firms that own seats on the
organized securities exchanges. Members of the securities exchange actually execute orders transmitted to them by the brokers in the various sales offices. For
example, the largest U.S. brokerage firm, Merrill Lynch Pierce Fenner & Smith,
has offices in most major cities throughout the country. Orders from these offices
are transmitted to the main office of Merrill Lynch and then to the floor of the stock
exchange (NYSE, AMEX), or to the OTC market, where they are executed. Confirmation of the order is sent back to the broker placing the order, who then relays it
to the customer. This process, which can be carried out in a matter of minutes with
the use of sophisticated telecommunications networks, is illustrated in Figure 2.4.
Currently, orders are transacted during normal business hours but, as the Investor
Insights box on pages 40 and 41 indicates, due to mounting competitive pressure,
24-hour trading will soon be ushered in.

Orders for over-the-counter securities must be executed through *market makers,*
who are dealers specializing in that security. The NASDAQ system, along with the
available information on who makes markets in certain securities, allows the brokers to execute orders in OTC securities. Normally, OTC transactions can be executed rapidly, since market makers maintain inventories of the securities in which
they deal. Although the procedure for executing orders on organized exchanges may
differ from that in the OTC market, an investor always places orders with his or her
broker in the same manner, regardless of the market in which the security is traded.

Brokerage Services

The primary activity of stockbrokers involves making the purchase and sale transactions requested by clients. Account executives do not actually buy or sell securities;
they only execute their clients' transactions at the best possible price. Brokerage
firms will hold the client's security certificates for safekeeping. The stocks kept by
the firm in this manner are said to be held in "street name," since the broker can
liquidate them for the client without having to obtain the latter's signature. In
addition, stockbrokers offer clients a variety of other services. For example, the
stockbrokerage firm normally provides a wide variety of free information ranging
from stock and bond guides that summarize the activity of securities to research
reports on specific securities or industries. Quite often the firm will have a research
staff that periodically issues analyses of economic, market, industry, or company
behavior and relates these reports to recommendations it makes to buy or sell certain
securities. It is the job of the stockbroker to provide the client with the type of
information most relevant to the client's investment goals. As a client of a large
brokerage firm, you can expect to receive regularly bulletins discussing market
activity and possibly including a recommended investment list. You will also receive a statement describing all your transactions for the month and showing com-

1. The account executive discusses a customer's order and will convey it to the stock exchange via a telecommunications terminal.

2. The firm's commission broker executes this sale on the floor of the exchange.

3. The confirmation is wired back to the account executive.

4. The account executive notifies the customer that the transaction has been made.

FIGURE 2.4 **How Stocks Are Bought and Sold on the New York Stock Exchange.**
(Sources: Photos 1, 3, and 4 courtesy of Prudential-Bache, Inc.; photo 2 courtesy of The New York Stock Exchange.)

mission charges, interest charges, dividends received, interest received, and your account balance.

Today, most brokerage firms will invest surplus cash left in a customer's account in a money market fund, allowing the customer to earn a reasonable rate of interest on these balances. Such arrangements help the investor to manage cash effectively and earn as much as possible on temporarily idle funds. Additionally, for a fee, some brokers will assist the investor in finding and working with a professional money manager. Most brokerage offices also have electronic equipment of some sort that provides up-to-the-minute stock price quotations and world news. Price information can be obtained from the quotation board (a large screen that electronically displays all NYSE and AMEX security transactions within minutes after they take place) or by keying into the telequote system, which relies on a computer terminal to provide a capsulized description of almost all securities and their prices. World news, which can significantly affect the stock market, is obtained from a wire service subscribed to by the brokerage office. Moreover, most offices have a reference library available for use by the firm's clients.

Investor Protection: SIPC and Arbitration

As a client, you are protected against the loss of the securities or cash held by your broker. The **Securities Investor Protection Corporation (SIPC),** an agency of the federal government, was established by the Securities Investor Protection Act of 1970 to protect customer accounts against the consequences of financial failure of the brokerage firm. It insures each customer's account for up to $500,000, except that claims for cash are limited to $100,000 per customer. Note, however, that SIPC insurance *does not* guarantee that the dollar value of the securities will be recovered; it guarantees only that the securities themselves will be returned. Some brokerage firms insure certain customer accounts for amounts in excess of the required $500,000 of SIPC insurance. Certainly, in light of the diversity and quality of services available among brokerage houses, careful consideration should be given not only to the selection of an individual broker (the *person* you deal with), but also to the choice of a *firm*.

SIPC provides protection in case your brokerage firm fails. But what happens if your broker gave you bad advice and as a result, you lost a lot of money on an investment? SIPC won't help; it's not intended to insure you against bad investment advice. Instead, if you have a dispute with your broker, the first thing you should do is discuss the situation with the managing officer at the branch where you do your business. If that doesn't do any good, then write or talk to the firm's compliance officer, and contact the securities commission in your home state.

If you still don't get any satisfaction, you may have no choice but to take the case to **arbitration,** a process whereby you and your broker present the two sides of the argument before an arbitration panel, which then makes a decision about how the case shall be resolved. If it's *binding* arbitration, and it usually is, you have no choice but to accept the decision—you *can't* go to court to appeal your case. To make matters even worse, many brokerage firms require you to resolve disputes by binding arbitration—in which case, you don't even have the option to sue. Thus,

Securities Investor Protection Corporation (SIPC)
an agency of the federal government that insures each brokerage customer's account for up to $500,000.

arbitration
a dispute process in which a broker and customer present their cases before a panel which then makes a decision to resolve the dispute.

before you open an account, check the brokerage agreement; it may contain a binding arbitration clause. Binding arbitration wouldn't be so bad if the track record was a lot more evenly balanced. But the fact is that the decisions handed down in the past have been heavily stacked in favor of brokers. But that may be about to change, as the SEC has recently handed down changes aimed at reforming the arbitration process. Even so, probably the best thing you can do to avoid such a situation is to use care when selecting a broker, and then carefully evaluate the advice he or she offers.

Selecting a Stockbroker

It is of primary importance to select a stockbroker who understands your investment goals and who can effectively assist you in pursuing these goals. If you choose a broker whose own disposition toward investing is quite similar to yours, you should be able to avoid conflict and establish a solid working relationship. It is probably best to ask friends or business associates to recommend a broker. However, it is not important—and often not even advisable—to know your stockbroker personally! A strictly business relationship eliminates the possibility that social concerns will interfere with the achievement of your investment goals. This does not mean, of course, that your broker's sole interest should be commissions. Responsible brokers make a concerted effort to establish a long-term broker-client relationship; they do not "churn accounts"—that is, attempt to have their clients make many transactions simply in order to generate numerous and sizable commissions. In addition, consideration should be given to the cost and types of services available from the firm with which the broker is affiliated. Often, significant differences can be found among firms. The broker you select should be the person you believe best understands your investment goals and who will provide the best service at the lowest possible cost to you.

Investors who wish merely to make transactions and are not interested in obtaining the full array of brokerage services mentioned above should probably consider using a **discount broker.** These brokers merely make transactions for customers— they provide little or no research information or investment advice. Transactions are initiated by calling a toll-free number; the discount broker then confirms the transaction by return mail. The rapidly growing volume of business done by discount brokers attests to their success, which has served as an incentive for other financial institutions, such as banks and insurance companies, to enter the brokerage business. Many banks and savings institutions, in fact, are making discount brokerage services available to their customers/depositors and, as noted in Chapter 1, the financial markets appear to be heading toward a supermarket style in which an investor's total financial needs will be met in one place.

discount broker
brokers who make transactions for customers but provide little or no research information or advice.

Opening an Account

To open an account, the broker will ask the customer to fill out various documents that establish a legal relationship between the customer and the brokerage firm. By filling out and signing a signature card and a personal data card, the client provides the information needed to identify his or her account. The stockbroker must also

have a reasonable understanding of a client's personal financial situation in order to assess his or her investment goals and also to be sure that the client can pay for the securities purchased. In addition to personal information, instructions relating to the transfer and custody of securities must also be given to the broker. If the customer wishes to borrow money in order to make transactions, a *margin account* will have to be established (described below). If the customer is acting as a trustee or an executor, or is a corporation, additional documents will be necessary to establish the account. No laws or rules prohibit an investor from establishing accounts with more than one stockbroker. Many investors establish accounts at different firms in order to obtain the benefit and opinions of a diverse group of brokers.

Types of Accounts

A number of different types of accounts can be established with a stockbroker. We will now briefly consider several of the more popular types.

custodial account
the brokerage account of a minor, in which a parent or guardian is part of all transactions.

Single or Joint. A brokerage account may be either single or joint. Joint accounts are most common between husband and wife or parent and child. The account of a minor (a person less than 18 years of age) is a **custodial account,** in which a parent or guardian must be part of all transactions. Sometimes a married couple will have two or more accounts—each spouse will have a single account and together they will have a joint account. Regardless of which form of account is maintained, the name(s) of the account holder(s), along with an account number, is used to identify the account.

cash account
a brokerage account in which a customer can make only cash transactions.

margin account
a brokerage account in which the customer has borrowing privileges.

Cash or margin. A **cash account,** the most common type, is one in which the customer can make only cash transactions. Customers can initiate transactions via the phone, even though they may not have sufficient cash in their account to cover the cost of the transaction. They are given five business days in which to get the cash to the brokerage firm; the firm is likewise given five business days in which to deposit the proceeds from the sale of securities in the customer's account. A **margin account** is an account in which the customer has been extended borrowing privileges by the brokerage firm. By leaving securities with the firm to be held as collateral, the customer is permitted to borrow a prespecified proportion of the purchase price. Prior to opening a margin account, the brokerage firm will assess the creditworthiness of the customer, and it will of course charge the customer a specified rate of interest on borrowings. (A more detailed discussion of margin trading is included later in this chapter.)

discretionary account
an account in which a broker can use his or her discretion to buy or sell stock on behalf of the customer.

Discretionary. Occasionally a customer will establish a discretionary account with a broker. A **discretionary account** is one in which the *broker* can use his or her discretion to make purchase and sale transactions on behalf of the customer. The organized exchanges are generally against this practice and permit it only when an officer of the brokerage firm is involved in the supervision of such an account. A more limited type of discretionary account permits a broker to buy or sell a stated amount of a given security (as specified by the customer) at a time or price the

broker believes to be in the customer's best interest. The decision to extend discretionary privileges to the broker depends on a customer's confidence in that particular individual as well as the amount of time the customer has to devote to trading. Such accounts are usually established by wealthy investors rather than by investors of more moderate means.

wrap account
an account in which customers with large portfolios pay to a brokerage firm a flat annual fee that covers the cost of a money manager's services and the cost of commissions.

Wrap. The **wrap account** is a relatively new type of account being marketed to brokerage customers with portfolios of $100,000 or more. These accounts allow the wealthy investor to conveniently shift the burden of stock-selection decisions to a professional—either in-house or independent—money manager. In return for paying a flat annual fee equal to between 2 and 3 percent of the portfolio's total asset value, the brokerage firm helps the investor select a money manager, pays the manager's fee, and executes the money manager's trades. Of course the investor's overall goals are initially communicated to the manager. Wrap accounts are appealing for a number of reasons other than convenience. Because the annual fee in most cases covers commissions on *all* trades, the chance that the broker will churn the account is virtually eliminated. In addition, the broker monitors the manager's performance and provides the investor with detailed reports, typically quarterly.

Odd-Lot or Round-Lot Transactions

Security transactions can be made in either odd or round lots. An *odd lot* consists of less than 100 shares of a security, while a *round lot* is a 100-share unit or multiple thereof. Thus, you would be dealing in an odd lot if you bought, say, 25 shares of stock, but a round lot if you bought 200 shares; a trade of 225 shares would be a combination of an odd and two round lots. Because the purchase or sale of odd lots requires additional processing and the assistance of a specialist, an added fee—known as an *odd-lot differential*—is tacked on to the normal commission charge, driving up the costs of these small trades. Small investors in the early stages of their investment programs are primarily responsible for odd-lot transactions.

Basic Types of Orders

Different types of orders are used in making security transactions. The type placed normally depends on the investor's goals and expectations with respect to the given transaction. The three basic types of orders are the market order, the limit order, and the stop-loss order.

Market Order

market order
an order to buy or sell stock at the best price available at the time the order is placed.

An order to buy or sell stock at the best price available at the time the order is placed is a **market order.** It is usually the quickest way to have orders filled, since market orders are usually executed as soon as they reach the exchange floor or are received by the market maker. The process by which these orders are transacted was described earlier and shown in Figure 2.4 . Because of the speed with which market orders are executed, the buyer or seller of a security can be sure that the price at which the order is transacted will be very close to the market price prevailing at the time the order was placed.

Limit Order

An order to buy at a specified price or lower, or sell at or above a specified price, is known as a **limit order.** When a limit order is placed, the broker transmits it to a specialist dealing in the security on the floor of the exchange. The specialist makes a notation in his or her book, indicating the number of shares and price of the limit order. The order is executed as soon as the specified market price (or better) exists and all other orders with precedence (similar orders received earlier, or buy orders at a higher specified price, or sell orders at a lower specified price) have been satisfied. The order can be placed as: (1) a **fill-or-kill order** that if not immediately executed is cancelled; (2) a **day order** that if not executed is automatically cancelled at the end of the day; or (3) a **good-'til-cancelled (GTC) order** that generally remains in effect for six months unless executed, cancelled, or renewed.

Assume, by way of example, that you place a limit order to buy 100 shares of a stock currently selling at 30½ (security market terminology for $30.50) at a limit price of $30. Once the specialist has cleared all similar orders received before yours, and once the market price of the stock has fallen to $30 or less, the order is executed. It is possible, of course, that your order might expire (if it is not a GTC order) before the stock price drops to $30. Although a limit order can be quite effective, it can also keep you from making a transaction. If, for instance, you wish to buy at $30 or less and the stock price moves from its current $30.50 price to $42 while you are waiting, your limit order has caused you to forgo the opportunity to make a profit of $11.50 per share ($42 − $30.50). Had you placed a market order to buy at the best available price ($30.50), this profit of $11.50 would have been yours. Limit orders for the sale of a stock are also disadvantageous when the stock price closely approaches but does not attain the minimum sale price limit before dropping substantially. Generally speaking, limit orders are most effective when the price of a stock is known to fluctuate greatly, since there is then a better chance that the order will be executed.

Stop-Loss Order

An order to sell a stock when its market price reaches or drops below a specified level is called a **stop-loss** or **stop order.** Stop-loss orders are *suspended orders* that are placed on stocks when and if a certain price is reached. The stop-loss order is placed on the specialist's book and becomes active once the stop price has been reached. When activated, the stop order becomes a *market order* to sell the security at the best price available. Because of this, it is possible that the actual price at which the sale is made could be well below the price at which the stop was initiated. These orders are used to protect the investor against the adverse effects of a rapid decline in share price. For example, assume you own 100 shares of Ballard Industries, which is currently selling for $35 per share. Because you believe the stock price could decline rapidly at any time, you place a stop order to sell at $30. If the stock price does in fact drop to $30, the specialist will sell the 100 shares of Ballard at the best price available at that time. But if the market price declines to $28 by the time your stop-loss order comes up, you will receive less than $30 per share. Of

course, if the market price stays above $30 per share you will have lost nothing as a result of placing the order, as the stop order will never be initiated. Often investors will raise the level of the stop as the price of the stock rises; such action helps to lock in a higher profit when the price is increasing.

Stop orders can also be placed to *buy* a stock, although they are far less common than sell orders. For example, an investor may place a stop order to buy 100 shares of MJ Enterprises, currently selling for $70 per share, once its price rises to, say, $75—the stop price. These orders are commonly used to limit losses on short sales (discussed later) and to get into a stock as its price supposedly starts to rise.

To avoid the risk of the market moving against you when your stop order becomes a market order, you can place a *stop-limit* order, rather than a plain stop order. It is an order to buy or sell stock at a given price once a stipulated stop price has been met. For example, in the Ballard Industries illustration above, had a stop-limit order been in effect, once the market price of Ballard dropped to $30, the broker would have entered a limit order to sell your 100 shares at $30 a share, *or better*. Thus, there would be no risk of you getting less than $30 a share for your stock—*unless the price of the stock kept right on falling*. Then, like any limit order, you might miss the market altogether and end up with stock worth much less than $30. Even though the stop order to sell was triggered (at $30), the stock will *not* be sold, with a limit order, if it keeps falling in price.

Transaction Costs

There are normally certain costs associated with making investment transactions. Such costs are usually levied on both the purchase and the sale of securities. Transaction costs must be paid by the investor to compensate the broker for executing the transaction. It is difficult, if not impossible, for an investor wishing to buy or sell a given investment vehicle to find a suitable counterpart, on his own, with which to negotiate a transaction. Thus rather than going through the trouble of direct negotiation, investors make transactions through brokers or dealers. The structure and magnitude of transaction costs need to be considered when making investment decisions, since they affect returns.

fixed-commission schedules
fixed brokerage charges applicable to small transactions.

negotiated commissions
competitive brokerage charges offered institutional or other large investors.

With the passage of the Securities Acts Amendments of 1975, brokers have been permitted to charge whatever commission they deem appropriate. Most firms have established **fixed-commission schedules** that are applicable to small transactions, which are the ones most often made by individual investors. On large institutional transactions, **negotiated commissions** are usually used. Brokerage firms can thus compete not only on the basis of services offered, but also on a cost basis. Negotiated commissions are also available to individual investors who maintain sizable accounts—typically in the range of $25,000 or more.

The basic commission structure varies depending upon the type of security. (The basic commission structures for various types of securities are described in subsequent chapters as part of the detailed discussion of the given security.) For example, the suggested fee schedule used by one large full-service brokerage firm to set commissions on *common stock* transactions is given in Table 2.3. Although this schedule does not specifically levy a premium on odd-lot transactions, the fixed-

TABLE 2.3 Suggested Broker Commissions on Common Stock Transactions

Value of Transaction	Fees for an Odd or Round Lot	Surcharge
Up to $800	$8.43 + 2.7% of the value of the transaction	
$800 to $2,500	$16.85 + 1.7% of the value of the transaction	+3.15¢/share
$2,500 to $5,000	$29.50 + 1.3% of the value of the transaction	+3.15¢/share

Source: A major stockbrokerage firm.

cost fee component does tend to raise the per-share cost of odd-lot transactions. (In addition to the fees shown in the schedule, *some* brokerage firms will charge an *odd-lot differential* of 12½ cents per share on odd-lot transactions.) Using this fee schedule to calculate brokerage fees on the purchase of 80 shares of XYZ stock at $30 per share, we see that the total value of the transaction would be $2,400 (80 shares × $30/share) and the brokerage fee would therefore be:

$$\$16.85 + (1.7\% \times \$2,400) + (\$0.0315 \times 80 \text{ shares}) = \$16.85 + \$40.80 + \$2.52$$

$$= \underline{\underline{\$60.17}}.$$

The $60.17 brokerage fee amounts to about 2.5 percent of the $2,400 transaction value. A common rule of thumb is that brokerage fees on a round lot of common stock will amount to between 1 and 3 percent of the transaction value.

A discount broker would charge substantially less for the same transaction. Most discounters charge a minimum fee to discourage small orders. For example, Charles Schwab and Company, the nation's largest discounter, charges a minimum fee of $39 for any stock transaction. Depending on the size and type of transaction, the discount broker can typically save investors between 30 and 80 percent of the commission charged by the full-service broker. The savings from the discounter are substantial; however, investors must weigh the added commissions they pay a full-service broker against the value of the advice they receive, since that is the only major difference between the discount and the full-service broker.

BASIC TYPES OF TRANSACTIONS

An investor can make a number of basic types of security transactions. Each type is available to those who meet certain requirements established by various government agencies as well as by brokerage firms. Although the various types of transactions

can be used in a number of ways to meet investment objectives, only the most popular use of each transaction is described here. The three most common types of transaction are the long purchase, margin trading, and short selling.

Long Purchase

long purchase
a transaction in which investors buy securities in the hope that they will increase in value and can be sold for profit at a later date.

The **long purchase** refers to the most common type of transaction, in which investors buy securities in the hope that they will increase in value and can be sold at a later date for profit. The object, then, is to buy low and sell high. Each of the basic types of orders described above can be used with long transactions. Because investors generally expect the price of the security to rise over the period of time they plan to hold it, their return comes from any dividends or interest received during the ownership period, plus the difference between the price at which they sell the security and the price paid to purchase it (capital gains). This return, of course, would be reduced by the brokerage fees paid to purchase and sell the securities.

Ignoring any dividends (or interest) and brokerage fees, the long purchase can be illustrated by a simple example. After studying various aspects of Varner Manufacturing, Inc., Fae Johnson is convinced that its common stock, which currently sells for $20 per share, will increase in value over the next few years. Based on her analysis, Fae expects the stock price to rise to $30 per share within two years. She places a limit order and buys a round lot (100 shares) of Varner for $20. If the stock price rises to, say, $40 per share, Fae will profit from her long purchase; if it drops below $20 per share, she will experience a loss on the transaction. It should be clear that one of the major motivating factors in making a long transaction is an expected rise in the price of the security. Of course, the impact of dividends or interest on these transactions is also an important consideration; this effect will be discussed in greater detail in Chapter 5.

Margin Trading

margin trading
the use of borrowed funds to purchase securities; magnifies returns by reducing the amount of capital that must be put up by the investor.

Most security purchases do not have to be made on a cash basis; borrowed funds can be used instead. This activity is referred to as **margin trading,** and it is used for one basic reason: to magnify returns. This is possible because the use of borrowed funds reduces the amount of capital that must be put up by the investor. As peculiar as it may sound, the term *margin* itself refers to the amount of *equity* in an investment, or the amount that is not borrowed. If an investor uses 75 percent margin, for example, it means that 75 percent of the investment position is being financed with the person's own capital and the balance (25 percent) with borrowed money. The Federal Reserve Board (popularly called "the Fed"), which governs our banking system, sets the requirements that specify how much of the dollar price of a security must be the purchaser's own funds. By raising or lowering margin requirements, the Fed can depress or stimulate activity in the securities markets. Margin purchases must be approved by a broker. The brokerage firm then lends the purchaser the needed funds and retains the purchased securities as collateral. Some brokerage firms have in-house margin requirements that are stricter than those of the Fed. Margin requirements for stocks have been at 50 percent for some time. It is important to recognize that margin purchasers must pay a specified rate of interest on what

they borrow. This rate is usually 1 to 3 percent above the **prime rate**—the lowest rate charged the best business borrowers—or at the prime rate for large accounts.

A simple example will help to clarify the basic margin transaction. Jeffrey Lawrence wishes to purchase 70 shares of Universal Fiber common stock, which is currently selling for $63.50 per share. Since the prevailing margin requirement is 50 percent, Jeffrey must put up only 50 percent of the total purchase price of $4,445 ($63.50 per share × 70 shares), or $2,222.50, in cash. The remaining $2,222.50 will be lent to Jeffrey by his brokerage firm. Jeffrey will, of course, have to pay interest on the $2,222.50 he borrows, along with the applicable brokerage fees. It should be clear that with the use of margin an investor can purchase more securities than he or she could afford on a strictly cash basis and in this way can magnify his or her returns.

Essentials of Margin Trading

Margin trading can be used with most kinds of securities; it is regularly used, for example, with both common and preferred stocks, most types of bonds, warrants, commodities, financial futures, and mutual funds. It is not normally used with tax-exempt municipal bonds since the interest paid on such margin loans is not deductible for income tax purposes. (Note: The Tax Reform Act of 1986 provides that in 1990 individuals can deduct $1,000 more in investment interest expense than the investment income they receive. Under the law, the excess amount is scheduled to drop to $0 after 1990.) For simplicity we will use common stock as the vehicle in our discussion of margin trading, and assume that the stock selection process has been completed (that is, that the securities have already been analyzed along the lines to be discussed in Chapters 7 and 8). In essence we are assuming that the investor has uncovered a security that promises to increase in value in the near future, so the major concern here is whether or not to use margin in the investment transaction. Although margin trading normally leads to increased returns, there are also some substantial risks to be considered. One of the biggest is that the issue will not perform as expected. If this in fact occurs, no amount of margin trading can correct matters. For margin trading can only *magnify* returns, not *produce* them. Because the security being margined is always the ultimate source of return, *the security selection process is critical to this trading strategy.*

Magnified Profits and Losses. Using an investor's equity as a base, the idea of margin trading is to employ financial leverage, or debt, in order to magnify returns. Here is how it works. Suppose you have $5,000 to invest and are considering the purchase of 100 shares of stock (at $50 per share) because you feel the stock in question will go up in price. If you do not margin, you can buy outright (ignoring brokerage commissions) 100 shares of the stock. However, if you margin the transaction—for example, at 50 percent—you could acquire the same $5,000 position with only $2,500 of your own money. This would leave you with $2,500 to use for other investments, or to buy another 100 shares of the same stock. Either way, you will reap greater benefits from the stock's price appreciation by margining.

The concept of margin trading is more fully illustrated in Table 2.4. An unmar-

TABLE 2.4 The Effect of Margin Trading on Security Returns

	Without Margin (100% Equity)	With Margins of		
		80%	**65%**	**50%**
Number of $50 shares purchased	100	100	100	100
Cost of investment	$5,000	$5,000	$5,000	$5,000
Less: borrowed money	0	1,000	1,750	2,500
Equity in investment	$5,000	$4,000	$3,250	$2,500

A. Investor's Position if Price Rises by $30 to $80/Share

Value of stock	$8,000	$8,000	$8,000	$8,000
Less: cost of investment	5,000	5,000	5,000	5,000
Capital gain	$3,000	$3,000	$3,000	$3,000
Return on investor's equity (capital gain/equity in investment)	60%	75%	92.3%	120%

B. Investor's Position if Price Falls by $30 to $20/Share

Value of stock	$2,000	$2,000	$2,000	$2,000
Less: cost of investment	5,000	5,000	5,000	5,000
Capital *loss*	$3,000	$3,000	$3,000	$3,000
Return on investor's equity (capital loss/equity in investment)*	(60%)	(75%)	(92.3%)	(120%)

*With a capital loss, return on investor's equity is *negative*.

gined (100 percent equity) transaction is depicted along with the same transaction using various margins. Remember that the margin rates (such as 65 percent) indicate the equity in the investment, or the amount of capital the investor must put up. When the investment is unmargined and the price of the stock goes up by $30 per share, the investor enjoys a very respectable 60 percent rate of return. However, observe what happens when margin is used: The rate of return shoots up to as high as 120 percent, depending on the amount of equity in the investment. This is so because the gain is the same ($3,000) *regardless of how the transaction is financed*. Clearly, as the investor's equity in the investment *declines* (with lower margins), rate of return *increases* accordingly.

Three facets of margin trading become obvious from the table: (1) the price of the stock will move in one way or another regardless of how the position is financed; (2) the lower the amount of the investor's equity in the position, the greater the rate of return the investor will enjoy when the price of the security rises; and (3) the risk of loss is also magnified (by the same rate) when the price of the security falls.

Advantages and Disadvantages. As already stated, a magnified return is the

TABLE 2.5   The Return Potential of Margin Trading

Percentage Change in Price of Security	Percentage Change in Return on Investor's Money with Margins of				
	90%	75%	50%	25%	10%
20%	22.2%	26.6%	40%	80%	200%
50	55.6	66.7	100	200	500
75	83.3	100.0	150	300	750
100	111.1	133.3	200	400	1,000
200	222.2	266.6	400	800	2,000

major advantage of margin trading. Table 2.5 reveals how important this benefit can be. The table demonstrates that the size of the magnified return will depend on both the price behavior of the security being margined and the amount of margin being used. For example, with a 90 percent margin, a 50 percent change in the price of the security results in a return of 55.6 percent to the investor; with a 50 percent margin, the 50 percent change in the security price results in a 100 percent return. Another, more modest benefit of margin trading is that it allows for greater diversification of security holdings, since investors can spread their capital over a greater number of investments.

The major disadvantage of this trading strategy, of course, is that the security being margined may not behave in the desired fashion, resulting in magnified losses rather than gains. Another disadvantage is the cost of the margin loans themselves. A **margin loan** is the official vehicle through which the borrowed funds are made available in a margin transaction; such loans are used with all types of margin transactions except short sales, commodities, and financial futures. All margin loans are made at a stated interest rate, the amount of which depends on prevailing market rates and the amount of money being borrowed. This cost, which must be absorbed by the investor, will mount daily, reducing the level of profits (or magnifying losses) accordingly.

margin loan
vehicle through which borrowed funds are made available, at a stated interest rate, in a margin transaction.

Making Margin Transactions

To execute a margin transaction, it is necessary to establish a *margin account*. This is a special type of account set up at a broker's office to handle all types of margin transactions, regardless of the type of security being margined. It is opened with a minimum of $2,000 in equity, either in the form of cash or by depositing securities. Margin transactions are executed like any others; they can be used with any type of order and are subject to normal commissions and transfer taxes. Of course, once margin transactions have been made, interest begins to accumulate on any margin loans taken out, and the broker will retain any securities purchased on margin as collateral for the loan. Margin credit can be obtained from a broker or a banker, although due to its convenience nearly all margin trading is done through brokers.

TABLE 2.6 Initial Margin Requirements for Various Types of Securities (May 1989)

Security	Minimum Initial Margin (Equity) Required
Listed common and preferred stock	50%
OTC stocks traded on NASDAQ/NMS	50
Convertible bonds	50
Corporate bonds	30
U.S. Treasury bills, notes, and bonds	8% of principal
Other federal government issues	10% of principal
Federal government guaranteed issues	15% of principal

Margin Requirements

Margin requirements are established by the Federal Reserve Board; these requirements establish the minimum amount of equity for margin transactions. This does not mean, of course, that investors must execute all margin transactions by using exactly the minimum amount of margin; they can use more than the minimum if they wish. For example, if the minimum margin requirement on stock were 50 percent, an investor could buy the shares by using a 75 percent margin instead. Moreover, it is not unusual for brokerage houses and the major exchanges to establish their own margin requirements, which are more restrictive than those of the Federal Reserve. This is done to curb trading excesses and to provide added credit protection for the brokers. There are basically two types of margin requirements: initial margin and maintenance margin.

initial margin
the minimum amount of money (or equity) that must be provided by a margin investor at the time of purchase.

Initial Margin. **Initial margin** is used to prevent overtrading and excessive speculation; it stipulates the minimum amount of money (or equity) that must be provided by the investor *at the time of purchase*. Generally, it is this margin requirement that investors refer to when discussing margin trading. Any security that can be margined has a specific initial requirement, although these can be changed by the authorities from time to time. As Table 2.6 shows, initial margin requirements vary by type of security. The more stable investment vehicles, such as Treasury issues, generally enjoy substantially lower margin requirements and therefore offer greater magnification opportunities. Note in Table 2.6 that OTC stocks traded on the NASDAQ/NMS can be margined like listed securities; about 2,900 OTC stocks qualify, including those of most of the "major" firms traded over-the-counter (issues of banks, insurance companies, industrial and retail firms, and so on). All other OTC stocks are considered to have *no* collateral value and therefore *cannot* be margined.

Initial margin requirements also provide a check on the current status of an investor's margin account. As long as the margin, or collateral, in the account remains at a level equal to or greater than prevailing initial requirements, the inves-

tor is free to use the account in any way he or she sees fit. Should the value of the investor's holdings decline, the margin in his or her account will also drop, and this can lead to what is known as a **restricted account.** A restricted account is one that carries a margin level less than prevailing initial margin requirements. For example, if initial margin requirements are, say, 50 percent, an account would become restricted when its margin falls to 49 percent or less. A restricted account does not mean that the investor must put up additional cash or equity. However, one of the important restrictions placed on the account is that should the investor sell securities while the account is restricted, the amount that can be withdrawn is limited until the account is brought back up to initial margin levels.

Maintenance Margin. Maintenance margin is used to protect the creditors in margin transactions—the brokerage houses and banks doing the lending. It specifies a minimum amount of equity that investors must carry in their margin accounts at all times. It is the absolute minimum amount of margin an account must contain before the broker is authorized to sell enough of the investor's securities to bring the account back up to standard. As we will see below, when an insufficient amount of margin exists, an investor will receive a *margin call* to remedy the situation. In this way, brokers avoid having to absorb excessive investor losses, and investors avoid being wiped out. The maintenance margin on equity securities is currently at 25 percent and rarely changes, although it is often set slightly higher by brokerage houses for the added protection of both brokers and their customers. For straight debt securities like Treasury bonds, there is no official maintenance margin except that set by the brokerage houses themselves.

As explained in the preceding section, a margin account is considered restricted as long as its equity remains below the initial margin requirement; it will remain restricted until it finally falls below the maintenance level. At that point the account will become **undermargined,** leaving the investor only one course of action: to bring the equity back up to the maintenance margin level, or to an even higher level as required by the brokerage firm (either of which could involve substantial sums of money). Whenever an account becomes undermargined, the investor receives what is known as a **margin call.** This gives the investor a short period of time (perhaps 72 hours) to find some means of bringing the equity up to the required level. If this is not done, the broker has no alternative but to sell enough of the investor's margined holdings to bring the equity in the account up to this level.

The Basic Margin Formula

The amount of margin in a transaction (or account) is always measured in terms of its relative amount of equity, which is considered the investor's collateral. A simple formula can be used with all types of long transactions to determine the amount of margin in a transaction (or account) at any given point. (As we will see below, a different formula is used for margins in short sale transactions.) Basically, only two pieces of information are required: (1) the prevailing market value of the securities being margined, and (2) the amount of money being borrowed, or the size of the

---

restricted account *a margin account whose equity is less than the initial margin requirement and from which the amount that can be withdrawn is restricted until the account is restored to initial margin levels.*

maintenance margin *the minimum amount of equity that investors must carry in their margin accounts at all times.*

undermargined *the condition of a margin account whose equity is less than the maintenance margin level.*

margin call *notification of the need to bring the equity of an undermargined account up to the required level or have margined holdings sold to reach this point.*

debit balance
*the amount of money
being borrowed; the
size of a margin
loan.*

margin loan, which is known as the **debit balance.** Given this information, we can
compute margin according to the following equation:

$$\text{margin (\%)} = \frac{\text{value of securities} - \text{debit balance}}{\text{value of securities}}$$

$$= \frac{V - D}{V}$$

To illustrate its use, consider the following example. Assume an investor wants
to purchase 100 shares of stock at $40 per share, using a 70 percent initial margin.
First we must determine how this $4,000 transaction will be financed. Since we
know that 70 percent of it (the stated prevailing initial margin requirement) must be
financed with equity, the balance (30 percent) can be financed with a margin loan.
Therefore the investor will borrow $1,200 ($4,000 × .30 = $1,200); this, of
course, is the debit balance. The remainder ($2,800) represents the investor's equity
in the transaction; this is measured as the difference between the value of the securities being margined ($4,000) and the amount being borrowed ($1,200). In other
words, *equity* is represented by the numerator $(V - D)$ in the margin formula. If
over time the price of the stock moves to $65, the margin would then be:

$$\text{margin (\%)} = \frac{V - D}{V} = \frac{\$6,500 - \$1,200}{\$6,500} = \underline{81.5\%}$$

Notice that while the "value of securities" in the equation changes with the
market price of the stock ($V = \$65 \times 100 = \$6,500$), the size of the debit balance
does not and will not change *unless* the investor pays off or takes out more margin
loans. Also note that the margin (equity) in this investment position has now risen to
81.5 percent. This results from the fact that when the price of the stock goes up, the
investor's margin also increases. When the price of the security goes down, so does
the amount of margin. For instance, if the price of the stock in our illustration drops
to $30 per share, the new margin would equal only 60 percent—in which case we
would be dealing with a restricted account, since the margin level has dropped
below the prevailing initial margin. Finally, note that although our discussion has
been couched mostly in terms of individual transactions, the same margin formula is
used with *margin accounts*. The only difference is that we would be dealing with
input that applies to the account as a whole. To find the prevailing margin in an
account, simply determine the value of all securities held in the account and the total
amount of margin loans, and use this information in the basic margin formula.

Return on Invested Capital

Most investors who trade on margin do so by using fairly short investment periods;
the lengths of such transactions are usually measured in months and seldom exceed
a year. Because of these short holding periods, investment yield is usually measured
in terms of holding period return (described in Chapter 5). With margin transactions, however, it is necessary to take into account the fact that the individual puts
up only part of the funds, the balance being provided by borrowed money. Therefore, in assessing return, we are concerned with the rate of profit earned *on only that*

portion of the funds provided by the investor. Using both current income received from dividends or interest and total interest paid on the margin loan, we can determine *return on invested capital* in a margin transaction as follows:

$$\begin{array}{c} \text{return on} \\ \text{invested} \\ \text{capital} \end{array} = \frac{\begin{array}{c}\text{total current} \\ \text{income} \\ \text{received}\end{array} - \begin{array}{c}\text{total interest} \\ \text{paid on} \\ \text{margin loan}\end{array} + \begin{array}{c}\text{market value} \\ \text{of securities} \\ \text{at sale}\end{array} - \begin{array}{c}\text{market value} \\ \text{of securities} \\ \text{at purchase}\end{array}}{\text{amount of equity invested}}$$

This form of the equation can be used to compute the expected or actual return from a margin transaction. To illustrate: consider an investor who wants to buy 100 shares of stock at $50 per share because she feels it will rise to $75 within six months. The stock pays $2 per share in annual dividends (though with the six-month holding period, the investor will receive only half of that amount, or $1 per share); in addition, the investor is going to buy the stock with 50 percent margin and pay 10 percent interest on the margin loan. Thus, our investor is going to put up $2,500 equity to buy $5,000 worth of stock that she hopes will increase to $7,500 in six months. Since the investor will have a $2,500 margin loan outstanding at 10 percent for six months, she will pay $125 in total interest costs ($2,500 × .10 × ⁶/₁₂ = $125). Using this information, we can compute the expected return on invested capital for this transaction as follows:

$$\begin{array}{c}\text{return on} \\ \text{invested capital}\end{array} = \frac{\$100 - \$125 + \$7,500 - \$5,000}{\$2,500} = \frac{\$2,475}{\$2,500} = \underline{\underline{99\%}}$$

Keep in mind that the 99 percent figure calculated above represents the rate of return earned over a six-month holding period. If we wanted to compare this rate of return to other investment opportunities, we could determine the transaction's *annualized* rate of return by multiplying by 2—the number of six-month periods in a year. This would amount to 198 percent (99% × 2 = 198%).

Uses of Margin Trading

Margin trading is most often used in one of two ways. As we have already seen, one of its uses is to magnify transaction returns. Another major margin tactic is called pyramiding, which takes the concept of magnified returns to its limits. In general, margin trading is simple, but it is also risky. It should therefore be used only by investors who fully understand its operation and appreciate its pitfalls.

Magnifying Transaction Returns. This strategy is relatively straightforward and is perhaps the most basic use of margin trading. The investor seeking to increase capital gains from a specific transaction finds a security that offers promising price appreciation and then margins it at (or above) the prevailing initial margin level in order to stretch his or her investment resources as far as they will go. For example, assume that Blair Barnes has $4,000 of available capital and the prevailing initial margin requirement for common stock is 50 percent. She has uncovered a stock that presently trades at $20 per share, though she is convinced it will move to $30 within six months. Because she feels so strongly about the appreciation potential of this

TABLE 2.7 Margin Trading to Magnify Transaction Returns

Invested capital (equity)	$4,000
Borrowed funds (margin loan)	4,000
Total investment (to purchase 400 shares)	$8,000
Cost to *buy* 400 shares (at $20/share)	$8,000
6 months later—stock *sold* at $30/share: proceeds at sale	12,000
Gross profit from transaction	$4,000
Less: interest cost* on borrowed funds	200
Net profit	$3,800
Return on invested capital	
(net profit/invested capital = $3,800/$4,000)	95%
Annualized rate of return (95% × ^{12}⁄₆)	190%

*The investor is assumed to pay 10% interest on borrowed funds; thus her interest cost for 6 months = .10 × 4,000 × ⁶⁄₁₂ = $200.

stock, Blair decides to margin it at the limit—the prevailing initial margin. Her capital is limited to $4,000, but she can borrow another $4,000 on margin and increase the size of her investment to $8,000.

Ignoring dividends and brokerage commissions, Table 2.7 summarizes what happens in this transaction if, in fact the price of the stock does go to $30 within six months. Note that the $12,000 received at sale is divided three ways: (1) Blair recovered her initial capital ($4,000); (2) the margin loan ($4,000) and interest costs ($200) were paid off; and (3) Blair took her net profit ($3,800). Compared to the 50 percent return Blair Barnes would have earned had she not used margin, the 95 percent return on invested capital is indeed an improvement.

Pyramiding Profits. The aim of pyramiding is to use the margin account to build up investment holdings. When investors hold securities that go up in value, they earn what are known as *paper profits*. This means the investor has made money on the transactions but has not sold the securities, so any profit is still only on paper. **Pyramiding** uses the paper profits in margin accounts to partly or fully finance the acquisition of additional securities. This allows such transactions to be made at margins below prevailing initial margin levels, and sometimes substantially so. In fact, with this technique, it is even possible to buy securities with no new cash at all; rather, they can all be financed entirely with margin loans. This is because the paper profits in the account lead to **excess margin,** which means there is more equity in the account than necessary. For instance, if a margin account holds $60,000 worth of securities and has a debit balance of $20,000, it is at a margin level of 66⅔ percent. Thus this account would hold a substantial amount of excess margin if the prevailing initial margin requirement were only 50 percent. The principle of pyramiding is to use the excess margin in the account to purchase additional securities.

pyramiding
the technique of using paper profits in margin accounts to partly or fully finance the acquisition of additional securities.

excess margin
more equity than is required in a margin account.

The only constraint, and the key to pyramiding, is that after the additional securities are purchased, the investor's margin account must remain at or above the prevailing required initial margin level. For it is the account, and not the individual transactions, that must meet the minimum standards. If the account has excess margin, the investor is free to use it to build up security holdings.

As an example of how pyramiding works, let us continue the illustration we began in Table 2.7 (ignoring any dividends received, brokerage commissions, and interest paid) and suppose that the stock actually does rise to $30 per share. Our investor, Blair Barnes, wants to continue to ride with this stock but has just recently uncovered another issue she feels is also ready to take off. Naturally she would like to buy some, but unfortunately she has just about exhausted her investment capital. Blair is in luck, however, since she can use the excess margin that now exists in her account to purchase shares of the new stock—in effect, she can start pyramiding her paper profits. Assume that while the old stock is trading at $30, the second issue is trading at $10. Table 2.8 summarizes what happens when the investor uses pyramiding to buy the additional shares of stock. Notice that at step B, because of paper profits, the account held excess margin—66⅔ percent versus the prevailing initial margin of only 50 percent. And even after the second transaction was completely financed with margin loans (see step C, which shows that *no* new capital was used), the margin account still carried the required level of 50 percent (as shown in step D). This type of pyramiding can continue as long as there are additional paper profits in the margin account and as long as the margin level exceeds the prevailing initial requirement. The tactic is somewhat complex but also profitable, especially in light of the fact that it minimizes the amount of new capital required in the investor's account.

Short Selling

Short selling is used when a decline in security prices is anticipated. This technique enables investors to profit from falling security prices; however, as we shall see, it can also be used to *protect* investors from falling security prices. Almost any type of security can be "shorted"—common and preferred stocks, all types of bonds, convertible securities, warrants, puts and calls, and listed mutual funds can all be sold short. Although the list is fairly extensive, the short selling activities of most investors are limited almost exclusively to common stock and puts and calls. Because short sales, like long and margin transactions, require the investor to work through a broker, it is important to consider the tips for finding the right stockbroker given in the accompanying Investor Insights box on pages 66 and 67. The material that follows reviews the short selling tactic and discusses some of the essential ingredients of this trading technique. We will then look at short sale procedures, and examine some of the popular uses of short selling.

short selling
the sale of borrowed securities, their eventual repurchase by the short seller at a hopefully lower price, and their return to the lender.

Essentials of Short Selling

Short selling has been defined as the practice of selling borrowed property, and that is exactly what it is. For short sales start when securities that have been borrowed from a broker are sold in the marketplace. Later, when the price of the issue has

TABLE 2.8 Building a Margin Pyramid

Step A:
The Original Margin Transaction

400 shares purchased at $20 per share using 50% initial margin (first transaction)	Value of securities	$8,000
	Debit balance	4,000
	Equity	4,000

Step B:
Some Time Later

Price of the 400 shares rises to $30 per share	Value of securities	$12,000
	Debit balance	4,000
	Equity	8,000

$$\text{New margin} = \frac{V - D}{V} = \frac{\$12,000 - \$4,000}{\$12,000} = \underline{\underline{66\tfrac{2}{3}\%}}$$

Step C:
The Investor Pyramids Her Margin Account

400 shares of *another* stock purchased at $10 per share (second transaction)	Value of securities	$4,000
	Debit balance	4,000
	New capital (equity)	0

Step D:
The New Margin Account

Total of the two transactions *after* the pyramiding	Value of securities	$16,000*
	Debit balance	8,000**
	Equity	8,000

$$\text{New margin} = \frac{\$16,000 - \$8,000}{\$16,000} = \underline{\underline{50\%}}$$

*400 shares at $30 per share (first transaction) *plus* another 400 shares at $10 per share (second transaction) = $12,000 + $4,000 = $16,000.

**Debit balance from first transaction *plus* debit balance from second transaction = $4,000 + $4,000 = $8,000.

hopefully declined, the short seller buys back the securities, which are then returned to the lender. Of foremost concern in a short sale transaction is that the lenders of the securities being shorted be provided total and constant protection.

Making Money When Prices Fall.   Although the idea may seem un-American, making money when security prices fall is what short selling is all about. Like their colleagues in the rest of the investment world, short sellers are also trying to make money by buying low and selling high. The only difference is that they reverse the investment process by starting the transaction with a sale and ending it with a purchase. An investor becomes a short seller when, working through a broker, he or

Some Tips for Finding the Right Stockbroker

First-time investors often walk into a brokerage asking for any available stockbroker. They are likely to be introduced to the broker of the day, "the broker who, that day, gets all the walk-ins and phone-ins of new clients," said Bob Edwards, director of education for the American Association of Individual Investors, a non-profit educational group based in Chicago.

And remember: Stockbrokers are primarily salespeople. If that stockbroker has an avid interest in options, he probably will try to sell you options, even though you may feel more comfortable investing in bonds.

"While that broker may be theoretically qualified to help you purchase bonds, he's going to put his time and energy into options," Edwards said. "You just are not going to be at the top of the priority list."

But brokers say any individual with at least $10,000 should consider hiring a professional to oversee their finances. The way to avoid getting tangled in this system is to screen your prospective brokers. Ask the brokerage's office manager for the names of those brokers whose investment philosophies most closely match your own, then interview them about their experience.

. . .

If you walk into the brokerage office off the street, you will need to select the brokers in that office you would like to interview. Ask for the office manager, who oversees the brokers in the office, David H. Rambeau, a Florida stockbroker, said. Explain to the manager the types of investments you are interested in and ask to be introduced to a broker with an interest in those securities. If your interests are very broad, ask for a broker who is a generalist, he said.

Of course, you must decide—before interviewing brokers—what kind of investments you want. You may have to do some research beforehand if this is the first time you have opened an account. "You should not, in general, rely on the broker to perform a teaching function. They would rather be dealing with knowledgeable investors they don't have to hand hold through every step," Edwards said.

Once you are sitting across the desk from the candidates you have chosen, you should interview them extensively. Your questions should include:

- How long have you been in the business? Rambeau said investors should look for a broker with at least three years of experience. That is long enough, he said, to winnow out the brokers who find they don't like the job and those who find they can't do the job.

  Edwards said the best brokers usually are those who have weathered a bear mar-

she sells *borrowed* securities. At some later time the investor covers the short sale by buying back the necessary shares and closing out (ending) the transaction. At this point the borrowed securities are returned to their original owners. Table 2.9 shows how a short sale works and how investors can profit from such transactions. In the illustration, we assume the investor has found a stock he feels will drop from its

ket, or who at least have stayed in the business through the market crash of 1987. Newer brokers, however, generally have smaller customer lists and therefore can devote more attention to each client.

- What is your educational background? All stockbrokers must pass the so-called Series 7 exam, administered by the NASD, to earn a broker's license, but Edwards recommended that you look for a broker who has an economic and financial education. The Series 7 classes teach brokers the mechanics of the market, but not the theories behind the valuation of investments, Edwards said.

- What is your investment philosophy? Do you prefer to buy and hold investments or trade quickly as the value rises? What is your opinion about stocks (bonds, options, futures or other investments) as an investment? Why do you like or dislike that type of investment? What kind of stocks (bonds, options, futures and other investments) do you recommend, and what makes the investment attractive? There are no right or wrong answers to these questions, the experts say, but their answers should agree with yours.

- May I have the names of three to five satisfied customers? Financial professionals differ on whether investors should ask prospective brokers about past performance, because, Edwards pointed out, past performance is no indicator of future performance. On the other hand, it may give you an idea of how that broker performs during bear markets.

They also differ on whether you should ask the broker about his own portfolio. Many investors feel more comfortable with someone who invests in the securities he recommends to others, but Rambeau said he would not discuss his personal investments with a customer. "I don't have the capital to invest in everything that comes along the pipe that I think is marvelous," he said.

You should not be the only one doing the interviewing, however. If the broker does not bother to ask you about your annual household income, or how much you paid in income taxes last year, he will not be interested enough in your account to make proper and profitable recommendations, Rambeau said.

· · ·

All brokers must register with the NASD to trade securities, and the NASD keeps a record of their conduct on the job. To learn if your prospective broker has ever been disciplined by the NASD, the SEC, one of the stock exchanges or a state government, or if he has ever been convicted on criminal charges, write or call the NASD.

· · ·

Finally, though, "it has to boil down to a gut reaction," Rambeau said. "You know when you sit down with somebody there's that chemistry."

Source: Lisa M. Keefe, of the *Orlando Sentinel,* "Going for Brokers: Check it Out," reprinted in *Dayton, Inc.* of the *Dayton Daily News,* February 9, 1989, p. 12.

present level of $50 per share to about $25. As a result, it has all the ingredients of a profitable short sale. It is evident from the table that the amount of profit or loss generated in a short sale is dependent on the price at which the short seller can buy back the stock. Short sellers make money only when the proceeds from the sale of the stock are greater than the cost of buying the stock back.

TABLE 2.9   The Mechanics of a Short Sale

1. 100 shares of stock are *sold* at $50/share:
     Proceeds from sale to investor $5,000
2. Later, 100 shares of the stock are *purchased* at $25/share:
     Cost to investor   2,500
         Net profit $2,500

High Risk, Limited Return.   A fact of many short sale transactions is that the investor must settle for high-risk exposure in the face of limited return opportunities. This is so since the price of a security can fall only so far (to a value of or near zero), yet there is really no limit to how far such securities can rise in price. (Remember, when a security goes up in price, a short seller loses.) For example, notice in Table 2.9 that the stock in question cannot possibly fall by more than $50, yet who is to say how high it can go in price?

Another less serious disadvantage is that short sellers never earn dividends (or interest income). In fact, short sellers are actually responsible for making up the dividends (or interest) that are paid while the transaction is outstanding. That is, if a dividend is paid during the course of a short sale transaction, the *short seller* must pay an equal amount to the lender of the stock (the mechanics of which are taken care of automatically by the short seller's broker). The major *advantage* of selling short is, of course, the chance to convert a price decline into a profit-making situation. In addition, the technique can be used by investors to protect profits that have already been earned and to defer the taxes on such profits. And as we will see, when used in this manner, short selling becomes a highly conservative investment strategy.

Short Sale Procedures

Slightly less than four billion shares of stock were sold short on the NYSE in 1987, accounting for about 8.3 percent of total share volume. Although most short selling is done by exchange specialists and other floor members, short sales by individual investors did amount to about 934,000,000 shares in 1987—and this was on the New York Stock Exchange alone. In addition to NYSE stock, virtually any type of security (listed or OTC) can be shorted, and such transactions can be executed in both odd and round lots. Moreover, they are subject to the same commissions and transaction costs as any other type of transaction. In fact, about the only difference is that a short sale transaction must be identified as such on the broker's order-execution form. The reason for this is that these transactions are stringently regulated by the SEC and can be executed only when the price of a stock has gone up.

The Basic Rules.   Extensive regulation of short selling was required in order to curb the many abuses and misuses of this tactic that occurred prior to the great crash of 1929. Today a short sale can be executed only when the price of a security rises

or is unchanged, when the prior change was an increase. This is known as an **uptick** and indicates that the price of an issue has gone up since its last transaction. For example, a stock can be sold short at 51⅛ if the transaction just before was at 51; but it cannot be shorted at a price of 50⅞, since this would be less than the preceding price of 51. The latter situation is known as a **downtick** and indicates that the price of the security is off from its last transaction. As as investor, you can place a short sell order at any time, but your broker will not be able to execute it until the issue undergoes an uptick.

One point that is often the cause of much misunderstanding on the part of uninitiated short sellers concerns the amount of investment capital required to make such transactions. Many people seem to think that since the transactions start with a sale, there is no need for the investor to put up any money. This is simply not true. Certain (minimal) amounts of equity capital must be put up by the short seller in order to initiate a short sale transaction. The investment necessary to execute a short sale is defined by an initial margin requirement that designates the amount of cash (or equity) the investor must deposit with a broker. This requirement is currently 50 percent for equity securities like common stock. Thus if an investor wishes to short $5,000 worth of stock at a time when the prevailing short sale margin requirement is 50 percent, he or she must deposit $2,500 with a broker.

Who Lends the Securities?   Acting through their brokers, who earn commissions on short sale transactions, short sellers obtain securities from brokerage houses or from other investors. Of the two, brokers are the principle source of borrowed securities. As a service to their customers they lend securities held in their own (the brokers') portfolios, or in what are known as **street name** accounts. Street name securities are those held by brokers for their customers; the stock certificates are issued in the brokerage house's name but held in trust for the account of their clients. This is actually a common way of buying securities, since many investors do not want to be bothered with handling and safeguarding stock certificates. In such cases, the certificates are issued in the street name of the broker, who then records the details of the transaction and keeps track of these investments through a series of bookkeeping entries. When dividends, notices, and so on, are received by the broker, they are automatically forwarded to the proper owner of the securities. It is important to recognize that the broker lends the short seller the securities of other investors, and the short seller sells these borrowed securities with the expectation that she can later purchase them at a lower price and return them to the lender.

Uses of Short Selling

Investors short sell for one of two reasons: to seek speculative profits when the price of a security is expected to drop, or to protect a profit and defer taxes by hedging their position. The first use is more common and represents the standard short sale transaction. The hedge tactic, in contrast, is a conservative use of short selling and is employed to lock in a given profit level. All shorts are executed on margin, so it seems appropriate to begin our discussion of investor uses of short selling by looking at how margin fits into a short sale and affects returns.

Shorting on Margin. There is an old saying on Wall Street: ''Bulls pay interest, bears do not.'' This has to do with margin trading and the fact that margins are used with both long and short transactions. However, there are no borrowed funds with margined short sales. With short selling, the term ''margin'' simply indicates the size of the equity deposit the investor must make in order to initiate the transaction. The absence of borrowing means there will be no interest. Margined short sales are executed in the same margin account as margined long transactions. They are subject to initial margin requirements; have maintenance margin levels; and if the price of the security being shorted goes *up* too much, the account can become restricted or even subject to a margin call. In fact, the only thing that we do not have to be concerned about with a margined short sale is the account's debit balance. Margining a short sale, then, is much like margining a long transaction; many of the investment principles, margin features, and behavioral characteristics we discussed previously apply equally here.

The margin on a short sale, however, is figured with a different formula than that used with long transactions. Specifically, the margin position of a short sale account is determined as follows:

$$\text{margin } (\%) = \left(\frac{\text{sales proceeds} + \text{equity deposit}}{\text{value of securities}} \right) - 1$$

$$= \left(\frac{SP + ED}{V} \right) - 1$$

The sales proceeds (*SP*) represent the net amount realized from the sale of the securities when the short transaction was established; the equity deposit (*ED*) denotes the required initial margin that was deposited by the short seller at the time of the transaction; and the value of securities (*V*) represents the prevailing market value (price) of the securities being shorted. Note that the values for ''sales proceeds'' and ''equity deposit'' never change for a given margin transaction; instead, as with long transactions, the only item that is subject to change in the equation is *V* (value of securities), and that changes only as the market price of the securities being shorted changes.

To see how this margin formula works, consider the following hypothetical investment situation: Assume an investor wants to short 100 shares of stock at $60 per share by using the prevailing 70 percent initial margin. In this instance, the value of the securities (*V*) amounts to $6,000 (100 × $60), and so too do the sales proceeds (*SP*), as this is the amount of money that would be realized by selling 100 shares of stock at $60 per share. The size of the equity deposit (*ED*) is $4,200 and is easily found by taking the amount of the transaction relative to the prevailing initial margin requirement ($6,000 × .70). Now let us see what happens when the price of the stock rises $10 to $70 per share. Using our short sale margin formula, we discover that the margin amounts to only 46 percent:

$$\text{margin } (\%) = \left(\frac{SP + ED}{V} \right) - 1 = \left(\frac{\$6,000 + \$4,200}{\$7,000} \right) - 1 = 46\%$$

The sales proceeds and equity deposit remain unchanged at $6,000 and $4,200, respectively; only the value of the collateral changes (and this has gone up to $7,000). But notice what is happening: As the price of the stock goes up, the amount of margin in the position drops. This is because the investor loses money in a short position when the price of the stock goes up, and as a result the amount of his or her equity drops accordingly. Because (at 46 percent) the amount of margin has dropped below the initial margin requirement (70 percent), the investor would be faced with a restricted account. The reverse would happen if, instead of rising, the price of the stock falls $10 to $50 per share. In this case, the amount of margin would rise to 104 percent ($[(\$6,000 + \$4,200)/\$5,000] - 1$), providing excess equity which could then be used for pyramiding.

Return on Invested Capital. Because short sales are executed on margin, the amount of invested capital is limited to the investor's equity deposit. This is all the investor puts up in the transaction and therefore is the basis for figuring the rate of return. The only complication in this return measure is that any dividends paid by the short seller to the lender of the securities must be netted out of the profit. Other than that, no dividends are received by the short seller and no interest is paid, so this return formula is fairly straightforward:

$$\text{return on invested capital from a short sale} = \frac{\text{proceeds from sale} - \text{purchase cost of securities} - \text{dividends paid by short seller}}{\text{equity deposit}}$$

To illustrate, assume an investor uses 70 percent initial margin to short a stock at $60 per share he feels will drop to $40 within a six-month period. Because the company pays annual dividends of $2 per share, the short seller estimates he will probably be liable for about $1 per share over the expected six-month holding period. Computing the return on a per-share basis (this figure will be the same regardless of how many shares are actually involved in the transaction), we see that the expected return on invested capital for this short sale will equal 45 percent:

$$\text{return on invested capital from a short sale} = \frac{\$60 - \$40 - \$1}{\$42} = \frac{\$19}{\$42} = \underline{\underline{45\%}}$$

This hefty profit rate is made possible not only because of the profit earned when the price of the stock drops, but also because of the limited amount of capital put up by the investor (the equity deposit equaled only 70 percent of the transaction amount).

Speculating with Short Sales. Selling short for speculative purposes is perhaps the most basic use of this technique. Because the short seller is betting against the market, this approach is highly speculative and subject to a considerable amount of risk exposure. It works like this: Assume an investor has uncovered a stock that she feels is about to tumble over the next eight months from its present level of $50 per share to somewhere around $30. She therefore decides to short sell 300 shares of the

TABLE 2.10   Speculating with a Short Sale

Short sale initiated: 300 shares of the stock sold at $50/share	$15,000
Short sale covered: 300 shares of the stock bought back at $30/share	9,000
Net profit	$ 6,000
Equity deposit (.50 × $15,000)	$ 7,500

$$\text{Return on invested capital*} = \frac{\$15,000 - \$9,000}{\$7,500} = \frac{\$6,000}{\$7,500} = 80\%$$

*Assume the stock pays no dividends and therefore the short seller has no dividend liability.

stock at $50 by using 50 percent margin (the prevailing initial margin requirement). Table 2.10 shows the basics of this hypothetical transaction. Note that the transaction generates a profit of $6,000 to the investor (ignoring dividends and brokerage commissions) and, since it can be executed with an equity deposit of only $7,500, should yield a return on invested capital of 80 percent. Understandably, if the market moves against the short seller, all or most of her $7,500 investment could be lost.

Shorting-Against-the-Box.   This exotic-sounding term describes a conservative technique to protect existing security profits. Like insurance, the purpose of this hedge is to minimize or eliminate exposure to loss. **Shorting-against-the-box** is done after an investor has generated a profit through an earlier long transaction by following it with a short sale. An investor who already owns 100 shares of stock (the long transaction) would short an equal number of shares of stock in the same company. By doing this, he or she is able to protect the profit already made in the long transaction: and, as a by-product, can defer the taxes on this profit until the next taxable year.

shorting-against-
the-box
*a conservative tech-
nique to protect ex-
isting security profits
by following a profit-
able long transaction
with a short sale.*

Here is how it works. Suppose that early last year you bought 100 shares of NuLox, Inc., at $20 per share, and have since watched the price of NuLox rise to $50. You presently have a $3,000 capital gain. Although you do not want to sell the stock right now, you do not want to lose any of your profit either. In essence, you would like to ride things out for a while and still protect the profit you have earned up to now. A simple short sale against the box will allow you to do this—just short 100 shares of NuLox at $50 per share, and you have "locked in" your profit of $3,000. For no matter what happens to the price of the stock, you are guaranteed a profit of $3,000. You now have two positions—one long and one short—but both involve an equal number of shares. Table 2.11 summarizes this tactic and demonstrates how the profit becomes locked in. Note, however, that while this short sale transaction is executed with borrowed securities, it is not necessary to put up an equity deposit because your current holdings of the stock serve this purpose. Thus,

TABLE 2.11   Shorting-Against-the-Box (Hedging with a Short Sale)

Transaction 1: Purchase 100 shares of stock at $20		$2,000
Price of Stock Rises to $50/Share		
Current profit in transaction:		
Current value of stock		$5,000
Cost of transaction		⟨2,000⟩
Net profit		$3,000
Transaction 2: Short sell 100 shares at $50		
A. Now Price of Stock Rises to $80/Share		
Current profit in *both* transactions:		
Value of stocks owned (trans. 1)		$8,000
Cost of transaction		⟨2,000⟩
Profit		$6,000
Less loss on short sale:		
Short sale initiated	$5,000	
Short sale covered	⟨8,000⟩	⟨3,000⟩
Net profit		$3,000
B. Price of Stock Falls to $30/Share		
Current profit in *both* transactions:		
Value of stock owned (trans. 1)		$3,000
Cost of transaction		⟨2,000⟩
Profit		$1,000
Plus profit from short sale:		
Short sale initiated	$5,000	
Short sale covered	⟨3,000⟩	2,000
Net profit		$3,000

the cost of shorting-against-the-box is reasonably low and involves only the brokerage commissions associated with initiating and covering the short sale.

SUMMARY

- Short-term investment vehicles are traded in the money market, whereas longer-term securities, such as stocks and bonds, are traded in the capital market. New securities are sold in the primary market, and outstanding securities are traded in the secondary market.
- The key organized securities exchanges are the New York Stock Exchange (NYSE) and the American Stock Exchange (AMEX). In addition, there are 13 regional stock exchanges, a few Canadian exchanges, a number of foreign stock exchanges, and other specialized exchanges. The over-the-counter (OTC) market is an intangible relationship between purchasers and sellers of securities that is linked together by the National Association of Securities Dealers Automated Quotation (NASDAQ) System.

- The securities markets are regulated by a federal commission, the Securities and Exchange Commission (SEC), as well as by state commissions. The key federal laws regulating the securities industry are the Securities Act of 1933; Securities Exchange Act of 1934; Maloney Act of 1938; Investment Company Act of 1940; Investment Advisors Act of 1940; and the Securities Acts Amendments of 1975.

- Stockbrokers (full-service or discount), by executing clients' purchase and sale transactions, provide the key link between the individual investor and the markets. In addition, full-service brokers offer a variety of services to customers. The Securities Investor Protection Corporation (SIPC) insures customers' brokerage accounts for up to a stated amount.

- A variety of types of brokerage accounts, such as single, joint, custodial, cash, margin, discretionary, and wrap, may be established. An investor can make odd-lot and round-lot transactions using the market order, the limit order, or the stop-loss order. The costs associated with making investment transactions vary. On small transactions most brokers have fixed-commission schedules; on larger transactions they will negotiate commissions.

- Most investors make long purchases in expectation of price increases. Many investors establish margin accounts in order to use borrowed funds to enhance their buying power. Short sale transactions are much less common, although they provide opportunities for financial gain when a decline in share price is anticipated.

- When stock is bought on margin, the investor puts up cash or securities equal to a portion of the purchase price and borrows the rest from a brokerage house or a commercial bank. If a stock purchased on margin increases in price, the investor's rate of return on funds is larger than it would have been on a straight cash purchase. If the stock declines, however, exactly the reverse is true. Margin is commonly used to increase transaction returns, or as a way to pyramid profits.

- The Federal Reserve Board (popularly called "the Fed") sets the minimum down payment (initial margin) required to purchase securities. If the security declines in price, reducing its collateral value below the minimum initial margin, the account becomes restricted. Should prices continue to decline and the account equity drop below the maintenance level, the investor receives a margin call and must deposit additional funds with the lender.

- The logic of short selling is to sell borrowed securities currently at a high price with the expectation that they can be repurchased at a lower price in the future, thus extracting a profit. To execute a short sale, the investor establishes a margin account and borrows the necessary shares through a broker or other investor. The original owner of the shares loses voting rights but retains all other important benefits of ownership, such as the receipt of dividends.

- If the price of shorted securities rises, the short seller may be required to deposit additional margin or may even incur an outright loss if the shares are eventually

repurchased at a higher price. A short seller is exposed to potentially unlimited losses, while gains are limited to the amount of the short sale price. Short selling may be used for speculative purposes by shorting stocks in anticipation of a share price decline; alternatively, it can be used to protect earned profits and defer the associated taxes by shorting-against-the-box.

REVIEW QUESTIONS AND PROBLEMS

1. Define and differentiate between each of the following pairs of words:

   a. Money market and capital market.
   b. Primary market and secondary market.
   c. Organized securities exchanges and over-the-counter (OTC) market.

2. Briefly describe the following aspects of the New York Stock Exchange (NYSE):

   a. Membership.
   b. Listing policies.
   c. Trading activity.

3. For each of the items in the left-hand column match the most appropriate item in the right-hand column. Explain the relationship between the items matched.

a. AMEX.	1. Unlisted securities are traded.
b. CBT.	2. Futures exchange.
c. Boston Stock Exchange.	3. Options exchange.
d. CBOE.	4. Foreign securities are traded.
e. OTC.	5. Second largest security exchange.
f. ADR.	6. Regional stock exchange.

4. Describe the over-the-counter market, and explain how it works. Be sure to mention dealers, bid and ask prices, NASDAQ, and the NASDAQ/NMS. What role do new issues and secondary distributions play in this market?

5. Briefly describe the key rules and regulations resulting from each of the following securities acts:

   a. Securities Act of 1933.
   b. Securities Exchange Act of 1934.
   c. Maloney Act of 1938.
   d. Investment Company Act of 1940.
   e. Investment Advisors Act of 1940.
   f. Securities Acts Amendments of 1975.

6. What role does the stockbroker play in the overall investment process? Describe the types of services offered by brokerage firms, and discuss the criteria for selecting a suitable stockbroker.

7. What must one do in order to open a brokerage account? Briefly differentiate among the following types of brokerage accounts:

   a. Single or joint.   d. Margin.
   b. Custodial.   e. Discretionary.
   c. Cash.   f. Wrap.

8.   Albert Cromwell places a market order to buy a round lot of Thomas, Inc., common stock, which is traded on the NYSE and is currently quoted at $50 per share. Ignoring brokerage commissions, how much money would Cromwell likely have to pay? If he had placed a market order to sell, how much money would he receive? Explain.

9.   Imagine that you have placed a limit order to buy 100 shares of Sallisaw Tool at a price of $38, though the stock is currently selling for $41. Discuss the consequences, if any, of each of the following:

   a. The stock price drops to $39 per share two months prior to cancellation of the limit order.
   b. The stock price drops to $38 per share.
   c. The minimum stock price achieved prior to cancellation of the limit order was $38.50, and when canceled the stock was selling for $47.50 per share.

10.   Explain the rationale for using a stop-loss order. If you place a stop-loss order to sell at $23 on a stock currently selling for $26.50 per share, what is likely to be the minimum loss you will experience on 50 shares if the stock price rapidly declines to $20.50 per share? Explain. What if you had placed a stop-limit order to sell at $23, and the stock price tumbles to $20.50?

11.   Using the brokerage commission schedule given in Table 2.3, along with the odd-lot differential (if applicable), calculate the brokerage commissions on the following common stock transactions:

   a. Purchase 70 shares of ABC for $60 per share.
   b. Sell 100 shares of DEF for $7.50 per share.

12.   Elmo Inc.'s stock is currently selling at $60 per share. For each of the following situations (ignoring brokerage commissions), calculate the gain or loss realized by Maureen Katz if she makes a round-lot transaction.

   a. She sells short and repurchases the borrowed shares at $70 per share.
   b. She takes a long position and sells the stock at $75 per share.
   c. She sells short and repurchases the borrowed shares at $45 per share.
   d. She takes a long position and sells the stock at $60 per share.

13.   Describe margin trading, and explain how profits (and losses) are magnified with margin trading.

14.   Assume an investor buys 100 shares of stock at $50 per share, putting up a 70 percent margin.

   a. What would be the debit balance in this transaction?
   b. How much equity capital would the investor have to provide in order to make this margin transaction?
   c. If the stock rises to $80 per share, what would be the investor's new margin position?

15.   Ms. Jerri Kingston bought 100 shares of stock at $80 per share using an initial margin of 60 percent. Given a maintenance margin of 25 percent, how far does the stock have to drop before Ms. Kingston faces a margin call? (Assume there are no other securities in the margin account.)

16.   What advantages and disadvantages does margin trading hold for the individual investor?

17.   An investor buys 200 shares of stock selling for $80 per share, using a margin of 60 percent; if the stock pays *annual* dividends of $1 per share and a margin loan can be obtained at an

annual interest cost of 8 percent, determine the return on invested capital the investor would realize if the price of the stock increases to $104 within six months. What is the annualized rate of return on this transaction?

18. Not long ago Dave Edwards bought 200 shares of Almost Anything, Inc., at $45 per share; he bought the stock on margin of 60 percent. The stock is now trading at $60 per share, and the Federal Reserve has recently lowered initial margin requirements to 50 percent. Dave now wants to do a little pyramiding and buy another 300 shares of the stock. What's the minimum amount of equity he'll have to put up in this transaction?

19. Describe the process of short selling; note how profits are made in such transactions. Be sure to explain how margin is used in a short sale transaction.

20. Assume an investor short sells 100 shares of stock at $50 per share, putting up a 70 percent margin.

   a. How much cash will the investor have to deposit in order to execute this short sale transaction?
   b. What is the new margin for this transaction if the price of the stock falls to $20 per share?

21. A well-heeled investor, Mr. Oliver Stanley, recently purchased 1,000 shares of stock at $48 per share. They have since risen to $55 per share, and while Mr. Stanley wants to sell out, he hesitates to do so because it is so near the end of the year and he wants to defer the tax liability until next year. As a result, Oliver decides to short-against-the-box; he does this by shorting 1,000 shares of the stock at its current price of $55. What total profit will Mr. Stanley make if the price of the stock continues to rise to $60 per share? How much of this will come from the long transaction and how much from the short sale?

22. What are the advantages and disadvantages of short selling? What is shorting-against-the-box, and how does it differ from a regular short sale?

23. Bob Barloe recently short sold 200 shares of stock at $72 per share, using 50 percent margin.

   a. Determine the size of the initial margin deposit required to make this transaction.
   b. What would the new margin (in percent) be if the stock price drops to $50 a share?
   c. What kind of profit (in dollars) and return on invested capital would Bob realize if he covered this short sale at $50 a share?
   d. What would the new margin position (in percent) be if, instead of dropping, the price of the stock *rose* to $86.50 a share? Given a 25 percent maintenance margin, would this account be subject to a margin call?

CASE PROBLEMS

2.1 Dara's Dilemma: Hold, Sell, Or?

As a result of her recent divorce, Dara Simmons—a 40-year-old mother of two teenage children—received 400 shares of Casinos International common stock. The stock is currently selling for $54 per share. After a long discussion with a friend, who is an economist with a major commercial bank, Dara believes that the economy is turning down and a bear market is likely. She has researched, with the aid of her stockbroker, Casinos International's current financial situation and finds that the future success of the company may hinge on the outcome of pending court proceedings relative to the firm's application to open a new gambling casino in Pacific City. If the permit is granted, it seems likely that the firm's stock will experience a

rapid increase in value, regardless of economic conditions. On the other hand, if the permit is not granted, the stock value is likely to be adversely affected.

Dara felt that, based upon the available information, the price of Casinos was likely to fluctuate a great deal over the near future. Her first reaction was to sell the stock and invest the money in a safer security, such as a high-rated corporate bond. At the same time, she felt that she might be overly pessimistic due to her semidepressed emotional state resulting from the recent divorce. She realized that if Casinos had their Pacific City application granted, she would make a killing on the stock. As a final check before making any decision, Dara talked with her accountant, who suggested that for tax purposes it would be best to delay the sale of the stock for an additional four months. After making a variety of calculations, the accountant indicated that the consequences of selling the stock now at $54 per share would be approximately equivalent to receiving $48 per share anytime after the four-month period had elapsed.

Dara felt the following four alternatives were open to her:

Alternative 1. Sell now at $54 per share and use the proceeds to buy high-rated corporate bonds.

Alternative 2. Keep the stock and place a limit order to sell the stock at $60 per share.

Alternative 3. Keep the stock and place a stop-loss order to sell at $45 per share.

Alternative 4. Hold the stock for an additional four months prior to making any decision.

Questions
1. Evaluate each of these alternatives, and based on the limited information presented, recommend what you feel is best.
2. If the stock price rises to $60, what will happen under alternatives 2 and 3? Evaluate the pros and cons of these outcomes.
3. If the stock price drops to $45, what will happen under alternatives 2 and 3? Evaluate the pros and cons of these outcomes.
4. In light of the rapid fluctuations anticipated in the price of Casinos' stock, how might a stop-limit order to sell be used by Dara to reduce the risk associated with the stock? What is the cost of such a strategy? Explain.

2.2 Ravi Dumar's High-Flying Margin Account

Ravi Dumar is a stockbroker who lives with his wife Sasha and their five children in Milwaukee, Wisconsin. Ravi likes to practice what he preaches; specifically, he firmly believes that the only way to make money in the market is to follow an aggressive investment posture—for example, to use margin trading. In fact, Ravi himself has built a substantial margin account over the years. He presently holds $75,000 worth of stock in his margin account, though the debit balance in the account amounts to only $30,000. Recently Ravi uncovered a stock which, based on extensive analysis, he feels is about to take off in a big way. The stock, Running Shoes (RS), currently trades at $20 per share. Ravi feels it should soar to at least $50 within a year. RS pays no dividends, the prevailing initial margin requirement is 50 percent, and margin loans are now carrying an annual interest charge of 10 percent. Because Ravi feels so strongly about RS, he wants to do some pyramiding by using his margin account to purchase 1,000 shares of the stock.

Questions
1. Discuss the concept of pyramiding as it applies to this investment situation.

2. What is the present margin position (in percent) of Ravi's account?

3. Ravi buys the 1,000 shares of RS through his margin account (bear in mind that this is a $20,000 transaction). Now:

   a. What would the margin position of the account be *after* the RS transaction if Ravi followed the prevailing initial margin (50 percent) and used $10,000 of his money to buy the stock?

   b. What if he uses only $2,500 equity and obtains a margin loan for the balance ($17,500)?

   c. How do you explain the fact that the stock can be purchased with only 12.5 percent margin when the prevailing initial margin requirement equals 50 percent?

4. Assume that Ravi buys 1,000 shares of RS stock at $20 per share with a minimum cash investment of $2,500, and that the stock does take off by moving to $40 per share in a year.

   a. What is the return on invested capital for this transaction?

   b. What return would Ravi have earned had he bought the stock without margin—if he had used all of his own money?

5. What do you think of Ravi's idea to pyramid? What are the risks and rewards of this strategy?

SELECTED READINGS

Boland, John C. "Selling Short." *Sylvia Porter's Personal Finance,* July–August 1986, pp. 86–87.

Edgerton, Jerry. "Let's Get Serious About Reform." *Money,* October 1988, pp. 60–61.

Ellis, Junius. "Money's All-Pro Stockbrokers." *Money,* October 1988, pp. 105–112.

Giese, William. "Broker's Statements: Close, But No Cigar." *Changing Times,* March 1989, pp. 47–51.

———. "Stockbrokers: When Discounts Don't Count." *Changing Times,* February 1989, pp. 50–56.

Jakus, Judy, and P.R. Chandy. "After Your Order: The Saga of a Stock Transaction." *AAII Journal,* March 1989, pp. 11–14.

Jamieson, Dan. "Margin for Profit." *Personal Investor,* July 1986, pp. 40–45.

Kosnett, Jeff. "How to Start Investing." *Changing Times,* April 1987, pp. 22–28.

Newport, John Paul, Jr. "Little Guys Face A New Market Era." *Fortune,* September 26, 1988, pp. 117–120.

Weil, Henry. "Uncovering the Pearls in the Pink Sheets." *Money,* November 1988, pp. 123–128.

3

SOURCES OF INVESTMENT INFORMATION AND ADVICE

After studying this chapter you should be able to:

● Identify the benefits and costs, types, and uses of investment information.

● Summarize some of the major sources of economic and current event information.

● Specify the various sources of information available to investors for assessing the performance of specific industries and companies.

● Discuss sources of information on security prices, and explain the characteristics, interpretation, and uses of commonly cited market averages and indexes.

● Describe the regulation of, types, costs, and effective uses of the services provided by investment advisors, and the features of investment clubs.

● Understand the role of the personal computer (PC) both as a tool in evaluating investments and as a source of data bases.

Generally speaking, *it takes more than money to be a successful investor!* Indeed, an understanding of where to find useful investment information and sound investment advice is vital to the whole investment process. Although there are people who have made a lot of money by investing without such understanding, the investor who understands the state of the economy, the market, and the specific company will normally be more effective than those operating solely on the basis of intuition. Some individuals will buy stock like McDonald's fast foods because they like the product and have noticed large crowds at their local retail establishment. Such observations, while helpful, are clearly insufficient for decision-making purposes because they leave unanswered numerous relevant questions, such as: How will the economy change? What behavior is the stock market expected to exhibit over the near term? Is McDonald's a profitable company, and will it continue so? Others shy away from security investments because they feel uncertain about the future behavior of the national economy, the market, and therefore about security investments in general.

By gaining familiarity with the key sources of investment information and advice the investor should be able to not only expand the scope of acceptable investments, but also do a better job of investing his or her money. For the payoff of an informed approach to investing is both an improved chance of gain and a reduced risk of loss. As such, the informed investor will probably earn better and safer returns than the uninformed investor, regardless of whether the latter makes decisions solely by intuition or merely by avoiding risky investments. In addition, with the increasing availability of personal computers and compatible investor-oriented software and data bases, it is important that the investor understand the role these new technologies can play in developing, monitoring, and managing a portfolio.

descriptive information
factual data on the past behavior of the economy, the stock market, or a given investment vehicle.

GETTING AND STAYING IN TOUCH WITH THE INVESTMENT WORLD

Investment information and advice can be considered either descriptive or analytical. **Descriptive information** presents factual data on the past behavior of the economy, the market, or a given investment vehicle; **analytical information** presents available current data, and includes projections and recommendations about potential investments. The sample page from *Value Line* included in Figure 3.1 provides both descriptive and analytical information on Eastman Kodak Company. Items that are primarily descriptive are keyed with a *D;* analytical items are noted with an *A*.

analytical information
available current data in conjunction with projections and recommendations about potential investments.

Some forms of investment information are free, while others must be purchased individually or by annual subscription. Although it is difficult to assess the quality and accuracy of investment information, there are certain benefits, costs, and economic considerations involved in the choice process.

Benefits and Costs of Information

One important benefit of the use of investment information is that it provides a basis for allowing the investor to formulate expectations of the risk-return behavior of potential investments. With better estimates of risk and return, investors should be

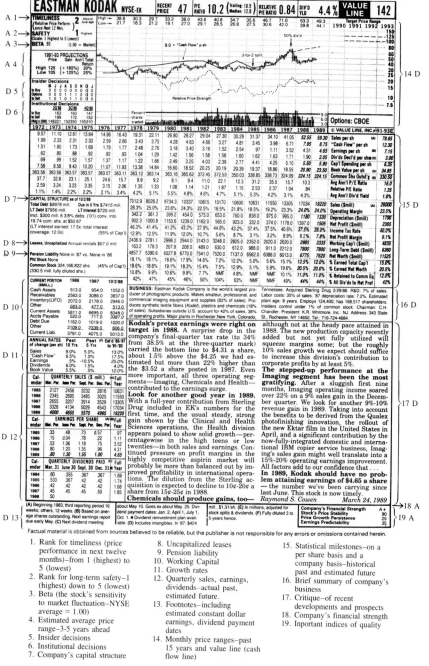

1. Rank for timeliness (price performance in next twelve months)–from 1 (highest) to 5 (lowest)
2. Rank for long-term safety–1 (highest) down to 5 (lowest)
3. Beta (the stock's sensitivity to market fluctuation–NYSE average = 1.00)
4. Estimated average price range–3-5 years ahead
5. Insider decisions
6. Institutional decisions
7. Company's capital structure

8. Uncapitalized leases
9. Pension liability
10. Working Capital
11. Growth rates
12. Quarterly sales, earnings, dividends–actual past, estimated future.
13. Footnotes–including estimated constant dollar earnings, dividend payment dates
14. Monthly price ranges–past 15 years and value line (cash flow line)

15. Statistical milestones–on a per share basis and a company basis–historical past and estimated future
16. Brief summary of company's business
17. Critique–of recent developments and prospects
18. Company's financial strength
19. Inportant indices of quality

FIGURE 3.1 A Report Containing Descriptive and Analytical Information: *Value Line* **Full-Page Report (Eastman Kodak Company, March 24, 1989).** This report contains both descriptive (noted D) and analytical (noted A) information. Examples of descriptive information are ''company's capital structure'' and ''monthly price ranges—past 15 years''; examples of analytical information are ''rank for timeliness'' and ''estimated average price range—3 to 5 years ahead.'' (*Source:* Adapted from Arnold Bernhard and Co., *The Value Line Investment Survey, Ratings and Reports*, Edition 1, March 24, 1989, p. 142. © Value Line, Inc.)

able to select vehicles exhibiting behaviors consistent with their goals. Although the use of investment information to formulate risk-return expectations does not ensure success, it should help in making more informed and intelligent judgments. A second benefit of investment information is that it may help the investor avoid the undesirable consequences that could result from a misrepresentation of facts by the issuer and/or seller of a vehicle. In spite of accepted accounting practices, as well as a variety of federal and state laws, factual misrepresentations do occur. To avoid the potentially devastating consequences of such misrepresentations, it is often helpful to obtain and evaluate information provided by an independent source before making a decision.

Free information can be obtained from newspapers, magazines, and brokerage firms, and more can be found in public, university, and brokerage firm libraries. Alternatively, an investor can subscribe to services that provide clients with periodic reports summarizing the investment outlook and recommending certain actions. Such services will cost the investor money, but obtaining, reading, and analyzing free information all cost time. So it is necessary to calculate the worth of potential information in terms of one's investment program. For example, spending 15 hours locating or paying $40 for information or advice that increases one's return by $27 would not be economically sound; had the cost been 2 hours or $10, such action would have made more economic sense. The larger an individual's investment portfolio, the easier it is to justify information purchases, since their benefit can usually be applied to a number of investments.

In addition to quantity there is also the question of the quality of investment information. As is true for most products and services, some investment information and advice is good and some is not. Often cost and quality of investment information and advice are not consistent.

Types and Uses of Information

Investment information can be conveniently classed into five types, each concerned with an important aspect of the investment process. (1) Economic and current event information provide background as well as forecast data related to economic, political, and social trends on a domestic as well as worldwide basis. Such information is useful to all investors, since it provides a basis for assessing the environment in which decisions are made. (2) Industry and company information provides background as well as forecast data on specific industries and companies. This type of information is used by investors to assess the outlook in a given industry and/or specific company. Due to its company orientation, it is most relevant to stock, bond, or options investments. (3) Information on alternative investment vehicles provides background and predictive data for securities other than stocks, bonds, and options, as well as for various forms of property investment. (4) Price information contains current price quotations on certain investment vehicles, particularly securities. These quotations are commonly accompanied by statistics on the recent price behavior of the vehicle. (5) Information on personal investment strategies provides recommendations on investment strategies and/or specific purchase or sale actions. In general this information tends to be educational or analytical rather than descriptive.

Sources of Information

A complete listing of the sources of each type of investment information is beyond the scope of this book; we can consider only the basic forms of investment information here. For those desiring expanded source information, Appendix A provides an annotated listing. Detailed descriptions of relevant information sources as well as demonstrations of their use are included in the discussions of specific investment vehicles and strategies presented in Chapters 6 through 17. The discussion here is concerned with the most common sources of information on economic and current events, industries and companies, and prices.

Economic and Current Event Information

It is clearly important for all investors to stay abreast of major economic and current events. An awareness of such events, coupled with the ability to relate them to the behavior of various investment vehicles, should translate into better decisions. The more popular sources of economic and current event information include the financial journals, general newspapers, institutional news, business periodicals, and special subscription services.

The Wall Street Journal
a daily newspaper, published regionally by Dow Jones; the most popular source of financial news.

Financial Journals. *The Wall Street Journal* is the most popular source of financial news. It is published daily and has a circulation of around 2 million. In order to provide regionally based articles and timely distribution, it is published in a number of locations around the country. In addition to giving daily price quotations on thousands of investment vehicles, it reports world, national, regional, and corporate news. An excerpt from one such article describing an unusual stock offering is given in the Investor Insights box. The first page of the third section of the *Journal* usually contains a column ''Your Money Matters,'' which addresses topics that deal directly with personal finance issues.

Barron's
a weekly publication by Dow Jones; the second most popular source of financial news.

A second popular source of financial news is **Barron's,** which is published weekly by Dow Jones, the same company that publishes *The Wall Street Journal.* Articles in *Barron's* tend to be directed more at strictly financial types of issues than those in the *Journal. Barron's* generally offers lengthier articles on a variety of topics of interest to individual investors. Probably the most popular column in *Barron's* is Alan Abelson's ''Up and Down Wall Street,'' which provides a critical, and often humorous, assessment of major developments affecting the stock market as well as specific industries and companies. In addition, current price quotations as well as a summary of statistics on a wide range of investment vehicles are included in each issue.

Investor's Daily, a third national business newspaper is published daily Monday through Friday and has a paid circulation of about 100,000. It is similar to *The Wall Street Journal* but contains more detailed price and market data. Other sources of financial news are the *Commerical and Financial Chronicle,* the *Media General Financial Weekly,* and the *Journal of Commerce.*

General Newspapers. Another popular source of financial news is *USA Today*—the dominant national newspaper published Monday through Friday and read by

INVESTOR INSIGHTS

Psst, You Wanna Buy Shares in a Brothel?

Thousands of investors who are eager to buy a piece of the first publicly traded brothel [in mid 1989] are taking cold showers instead.

Despite widespread lust for the much publicized $23.3 million initial public offering of Mustang Ranch—one of Nevada's largest legal bordellos—only 10 states are allowing their residents to participate. Many other investors are shut out because their brokers aren't in the underwriting group, Mustang Ranch officials said.

Consequently, the underwriters said they have had to turn away numerous orders and are about $5 million short of their target, as the May 10 deadline for the offering approaches. Mustang Ranch officials said they haven't decided whether they will restructure the offering or settle for a smaller offering.

"We have tremendous investor interest, but we're only 75% subscribed," said Eric Walloga, president of Mustang Ranch's lead underwriter, America Wallstreet Securities of Tampa, Fla.

. . .

Mustang Ranch is headed for the Nasdaq over-the-counter market and plans to trade under the symbol MARI. The offering of 1,165,000 shares at $20 a share has a 40-member selling group, made up mostly of independent brokers, rather than Wall Street's big securities firms, Mr. Walloga said.

Peter Perry, Mustang Ranch's chief executive officer, believes that the big securities firms don't want their names attached to the initial public offering and are waiting for public trading to begin before processing the orders they have been receiving.

But some firms dispute that. "They sent us a prospectus, but it wasn't something we felt our clients would be interested in," said Alexander Daignault, a managing director at Alex, Brown & Sons in Baltimore. "We haven't had any calls from our branches saying there's interest in the stock."

It's clear that not everyone is titillated by the prospect of buying shares in a brothel. "Some people have told me God will condemn me for this," said Mr. Walloga, who isn't fazed by such talk. He said Mustang Ranch plans to diversify into sidelines such as T-shirt sales and maybe even a television show, and added: "Who's to say Mustang Ranch won't be something entirely different in the future?"

Also, Mr. Walloga contends that investors are attracted by Mustang Ranch's financial prospects. The company earned $917,000 on revenue of $5.3 million in 1987. Results for 1988 haven't been released.

Of course, many investors may be seduced by the unique investment opportunity. As added enticement, some investors also will receive signed prints of an original LeRoy Neiman painting of Mustang Ranch scenes. "Mustang Ranch (attracts) both the sophisticated and the novelty investor," said Mr. Walloga. "We don't have many who ask about price-to-earnings ratios."

[P.S. The offering was unsuccessful and remained $5 million short at the May 10 deadline. The underwriter—American Wallstreet Securities—negotiated an extension of the sale until October 31, 1989, to restructure the offer.]

Source: Sonja Steptoe, "Investors Eager to Buy Shares in Brothel are Being Turned Away in Many States," *The Wall Street Journal*, May 1, 1989, p. C1.

over 5 million people daily. Each issue contains a "Money" section devoted to business and personal financial news in addition to including current security price quotations and summary statistics.

Local newspapers provide still another convenient source of financial news. In most cities with populations in excess of 200,000, the daily newspaper devotes two or more pages to financial and business news. Major metropolitan newspapers such as *The New York Times* and *The Los Angeles Times* provide investors with a wealth of financial information. Most major newspapers contain stock price quotations for major exchanges, price quotations on stocks of local interest, and a summary of the major stock market averages and indexes. Reading the financial pages of the local newspaper is an inexpensive way of staying abreast of key financial developments.

Institutional News. The monthly economic letters of the nation's leading banks, such as Bank of America (San Francisco), Citibank (New York), and Harris Trust (Chicago), provide useful economic information. To keep customers abreast of important news developments, most brokerage firms subscribe to a number of wire services such as the Dow Jones, AP (Associated Press), and UPI (United Press International) services.

Business Periodicals. Business periodicals range in scope from those presenting general business and economic articles, to those covering securities markets and related topics, to those devoted solely to specific industries or property investments. Regardless of the subject matter, most financial periodicals present descriptive information, although some also include analytical information. However, they rarely offer recommendations.

General business and economic articles are presented in periodicals such as *Newsweek* ("Business" section), *Time* ("Economy and Business" section), and *U.S. News and World Report* ("Business" section). A number of strictly business and finance-oriented periodicals are also available. These include *Business Week, Fortune, Business Month,* and *Nation's Business.* Other sources of general business and economic articles are government publications such as the *Federal Reserve Bulletin* and the *Survey of Current Business.*

Securities and marketplace articles can be found in a number of financial periodicals. The most basic, commonsense articles appear in *Forbes, Changing Times,* and *Money. Forbes,* which is published every two weeks, is the most investment oriented. Each January it publishes an "Annual Report on American Industry," which compares the growth and performance of key industries over the past five years. In August of each year *Forbes* also publishes a comparative evaluation of mutual funds. *Changing Times* and *Money* are published monthly and contain a variety of articles on managing personal finances. Each issue also contains investments articles.

Popular periodicals aimed at the more sophisticated investor include *Financial World, Personal Investor,* and *The Wall Street Transcript. Financial World* is published every two weeks and presents articles on the market and specific industries and companies. Subscribers periodically receive statistical data on listed stocks, both common and preferred, and on mutual funds. (An annual reference book to

leading stocks is also provided.) *Personal Investor* is a monthly publication that is aimed at the general investing public and contains articles dealing with all sorts of investment vehicles and strategies. *The Wall Street Transcript* is similar to *Financial World* in that it also provides both investment information and analyses. Even more professionally oriented are the *Financial Analyst's Journal, The Money Manager, The Institutional Investor, Pension and Investment Age, Journal of Portfolio Management,* and *AAII Journal.* Each of these periodicals offers technical analyses and information useful to professional and sophisticated individual investors.

Special Subscription Services.   In addition to the broad range of financial news and business periodicals, special subscription services are available for those who want additional insights into business and economic conditions. These reports tend to include business and economic forecasts and give notice of new government policies, union plans and tactics, taxes, prices, wages, and so on. One of the more popular services is the *Kiplinger Washington Letter,* a weekly publication that costs about $60 per year. It provides a wealth of economic information and analyses. Other special subscription services that concentrate on the economy in general are McGraw-Hill's *Personal Finance Letter, Babson's Reports,* and the *Wellington Financial Letter.*

Industry and Company Information

Of special interest to security investors is information on particular industries and companies. Often, after choosing an industry in which to invest, the investor will proceed to analyze specific companies in order to select a suitable investment. General articles related to the activities of specific industries can be found in trade publications such as *Chemical Week, American Banker, Computer, Public Utilities Fortnightly,* and *Brewers Digest.* More specific popular sources of industry and company information include stockholder's reports, subscription services, brokerage reports, and investment letters.

stockholder's (annual) report
a report published yearly by every publicly held firm; contains a wide range of information including financial statements for the most recent fiscal year.

Form 10-K
a statement filed with the SEC by all firms listed on a securities exchange or traded in the national OTC market.

Stockholder's Reports.   An excellent source of recent operating data on an individual business firm is its **stockholder's** or **annual report,** published yearly by publicly held corporations. These contain a wide range of information, including financial statements for the most recent period of operation, along with summarized statements for several prior years. A sample page from the Eastman Kodak Company's 1988 Stockholder's Report is shown in Figure 3.2. These reports are free and provide a useful source of investment information on publicly held companies. In addition to the stockholder's report, many serious investors will review a company's **Form 10-K,** which is a statement that firms having securities listed on an organized exchange or traded in the national OTC market must file with the SEC.

Subscription Services.   A variety of subscription services provide information on specific industries and companies. Generally, a subscriber pays a basic fee that entitles him or her to certain information published and periodically updated by the service. In addition to the basic service, a subscriber can purchase other services that provide information of greater depth or range. The major subscription services

Summary of the Year in Figures

Eastman Kodak Company and Subsidiary Companies

(Dollar amounts and shares in millions, except per share figures)	1988*	1987	Change
Sales	$ 17,034	$ 13,305	+28%
Earnings from operations	2,938	2,111	+39%
Net earnings	1,397	1,178	+19%
−percent of sales	8.2%	8.9%	
−per common share	$ 4.31	$ 3.52	
Cash dividends declared	$ 616	$ 572	
−per common share	$ 1.90	$ 1.71	
Average number of common shares outstanding	324.2	334.7	
Shareowners at close of year	174,110	168,517	
Total net assets (shareowners' equity)	$ 6,780	$ 6,013	+13%
Additions to properties	$ 1,914	$ 1,652	+16%
Depreciation	$ 1,057	$ 962	+10%
Wages, salaries, and employee benefits	$ 5,469	$ 4,645	+18%
Employees at the close of year			
−in the United States	87,900	81,800	+ 7%
−worldwide	145,300	124,400	+17%

*Sales, earnings, assets, and employment data include Sterling Drug Inc. since the date of acquisition (February 23, 1988).

Contents

FIGURE 3.2   A Page from a Stockholder's Report (Eastman Kodak Company, 1988).
The inside of the front cover of Eastman Kodak Company's report quickly acquaints the investor with the key aspects of the firm's operations over the past year as well as the report's contents. (*Source:* Eastman Kodak Company, 1988 Stockholder's Report. Rochester, New York: Eastman Kodak Company, 1988. Reprinted courtesy of Eastman Kodak Company.)

provide both descriptive and analytical information; but they generally do not make recommendations. Subscribers to these services include corporations, banks, insurance companies, brokerage firms, libraries, and individuals. Most investors, rather than subscribing to these services, gain access to them through their stockbroker or at a large public or university library. The dominant subscription services are those offered by Standard & Poor's Corporation, Moody's Investor Services, and the *Value Line Investment Survey.*

Standard & Poor's
Corp. (S&P)
publisher of a variety
of financial reports
and services, includ-
ing Corporation Rec-
ords *and* Stock Re-
ports.

Standard & Poor's Corporation (S&P) offers approximately 25 different financial reports and services. One major service, *Corporation Records*, provides detailed descriptions of issues of publicly traded securities. A second major service, *Stock Reports*, contains up-to-date reports on firms. Each report presents a concise summary of the firm's financial history, its current finances, and its future prospects (for selected companies only). A sample report (dated November 16, 1988) for Eastman Kodak, is presented in Figure 3.3. Standard & Poor's Trade and Securities Service provides background information on business in general, as well as past, present, and future assessments of specific industries. The *Stock Guide* and *Bond Guide* are additional S&P publications. These guides, published monthly, contain statistical information on the major stocks and bonds and include descriptive data along with an analytical ranking of investment desirability. Figure 3.4 shows a sample two-page spread from the March 1989 S&P *Stock Guide*. Eastman Kodak has an A⁻ rating, indicating that it is in one of the highest-rated groups. One other S&P publication worthy of note is its weekly magazine, *Outlook*, which includes analytical articles providing investment advice about the market and about specific industries and/or securities.

Moody's Investors
Services
publisher of a variety
of financial reference
manuals, including
Moody's Manuals.

Moody's Investors Services publishes a variety of useful materials. They key publications are reference manuals (*Moody's Manuals*), which are similar to S&P's *Corporation Records*. Each of the six reference manuals contains a wealth of historical and current financial, organizational, and operational data on all major firms within certain business groupings. In order to keep these manuals up to date, frequent supplements are made available to subscribers. Other publications are the *Handbook of Common Stocks*, which provides much financial information on over 1,000 stocks; *Dividend Record*, which provides recent dividend announcements and payments by thousands of companies; *Bond Survey*, a weekly publication that assesses market conditions and new offerings; and *Bond Record*, a monthly publication reporting the price and interest rate behavior of thousands of bonds.

Value Line Invest-
ment Survey
a weekly subscription
service covering
about 1,700 of the
most widely held
stocks and their in-
dustries; popular
among individual
investors.

The **Value Line Investment Survey** is one of the most popular subscription services used by individual investors. It is published weekly and covers approximately 1,700 of the most widely held stocks and their industries. Ratings of "timeliness," "safety," and "financial strength" are included for each company. In exchange for an annual subscription fee of about $500, three basic services are provided *Value Line* subscribers. The "Summary and Index" is a weekly update showing the current ratings for each stock. "Ratings and Reports" is also updated weekly and contains a full-page analysis for each of about 130 stocks. (One example of such a report for Eastman Kodak Company was included earlier in Figure 3.1.) The third service, "Selection and Opinion," is a weekly section containing a

Eastman Kodak 802

NYSE Symbol EK Options on CBOE(Jan-Apr-Jul-Oct) In S&P 500

Price	Range	P-E Ratio	Dividend	Yield	S&P Ranking	Beta
Nov. 8'88	1988					
45½	53¼-39⅛	11	2.00	4.4%	A-	0.88

Summary

Eastman Kodak is the world's largest maker of photographic products, and also manufactures synthetic fibers, plastics and chemicals. In February, 1988 EK acquired Sterling Drug Inc., substantially expanding its presence in the health care area. A patent infringement suit brought by Polaroid Corp. could result in EK paying a large damage award or settlement in the future.

Current Outlook

Earnings for 1989 are estimated at $4.65 a share, up from the $4.25 expected for 1988. Estimates exclude a potentially large damage award or settlement related to the Polaroid patent infringement suit.

The dividend was raised 11%, to $0.50 quarterly from $0.45, with the October 1988 payment.

Revenue and operating profit growth is expected in all three of EK's business segments in 1989. Interest expense is likely to be higher and the Sterling Drug acquisition is expected to again be dilutive to profits. Earnings growth in 1988 has been helped by a lower tax rate.

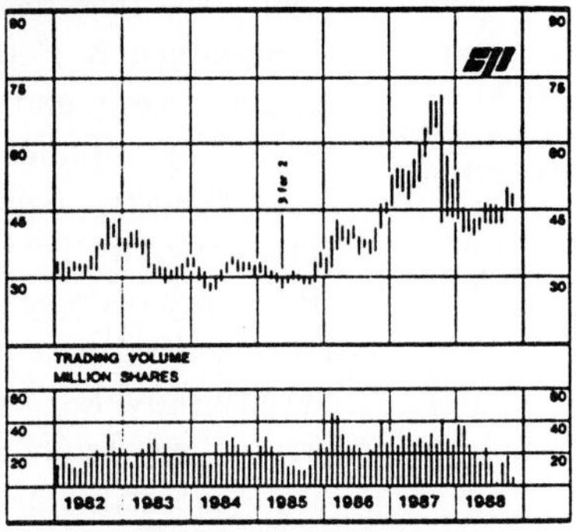

Sales (Billion $)

Period:	1988	1987	1986	1985
12 Wks. Mar.	3.33	2.66	2.35	2.13
12 Wks. Jun.	4.13	3.21	2.69	2.46
16 Wks. Sep.	5.03	3.91	3.48	3.23
12 Wks. Dec.	---	3.53	3.03	2.82
	---	13.31	11.55	10.63

Sales for the 40 weeks ended October 2, 1988 increased 28%, year to year. Pretax income rose 7.0%, and after taxes at 38.5%, versus 43.2%, net income was up 16%, to $3.35 a share (on 4.0% fewer shares) from $2.77.

Common Share Earnings ($)

Period:	1988	1987	1986	1985
12 Wks. Mar.	0.80	0.53	0.15	0.33
12 Wks. Jun.	1.20	1.07	d0.04	0.48
16 Wks. Sep.	1.35	1.18	0.78	0.73
12 Wks. Dec.	E0.90	0.75	0.22	d0.57
	E4.25	3.52	1.11	0.97

Important Developments

Nov. '88— In the 1988 third quarter sales of Eastman Kodak's imaging segment (about 62% of sales) rose 8.2%, year to year, and operating profit was up 9.3%. Results of EK's U.S. photofinishing business were not included following their contribution to a joint venture (of which EK owns 49%) in late March. Chemical sales (19%) were up 18% in the quarter and segment profits rose 34%. Health segment sales (22%) more than tripled, mostly due to the February, 1988 acquisition of Sterling Drug Inc., and profit more than tripled. EK's total operating profit in the quarter was up 31%, but most of the rise was offset by higher interest expense, largely acquisition-related. About 40% of the company's total third quarter sales were outside the U.S.

Next earnings report expected mid-February.

Per Share Data ($)

Yr. End Dec. 31	1987	1986	1985	[1]1984	1983	1982	1981	1980	1979	1978
Book Value	17.23	17.71	18.85	20.37	20.18	20.25	18.37	16.58	14.83	13.35
Earnings	3.52	1.11	0.97	2.54	1.51	3.17	3.41	3.18	2.75	2.49
Dividends	1.71	1.62¾	1.62¼	1.60	1.57⅞	1.57⅞	1.55½	1.42¼	1.28⅞	1.03½
Payout Ratio	47%	147%	166%	61%	104%	51%	46%	45%	47%	42%
Prices—High	71	46¾	35½	34¾	40¾	43⅝	37⅞	33¼	29¾	30⅜
Low	41⅞	30½	27⅜	26¾	28½	29	26⅞	19	21¼	18⅜
P/E Ratio—	20-12	42-28	37-28	14-11	27-19	14-9	11-8	10-6	11-8	12-7

Data as orig. reptd. Adj. for stk. div(s). of 50% Oct. 1987. 50% May 1985. 1. Reflects merger or acquisition. d-Deficit. E-Estimated.

Standard NYSE Stock Reports
Vol. 55/No. 222/Sec. 8

November 16, 1988

Copyright © 1988 Standard & Poor's Corp. All Rights Reserved

Standard & Poor's Corp.
25 Broadway, NY, NY 10004

FIGURE 3.3 Standard & Poor's Standard NYSE Stock Report for Eastman Kodak Company (November 16, 1988).

Standard & Poor's stock reports present in a concise fashion both descriptive and analytical information on thousands of companies whose shares are traded on the NYSE, AMEX, or OTC. (*Source:* Standard & Poor's Corporation, *Standard NYSE Stock Reports*. New York: Standard & Poor's Corporation, November 16, 1988.)

Eastman Kodak Company

Income Data (Million $)

Year Ended Dec. 31	Revs.	Oper. Inc.	% Oper. Inc. of Revs.	Cap. Exp.	Depr.	Int. Exp.	[1]Net Bef. Taxes	Eff. Tax Rate	Net Inc.	% Net Inc. of Revs.
1987	13,305	3,073	23.1	1,652	962	230	1,984	40.6%	[2]1,178	8.9
1986	11,550	2,200	19.0	1,438	956	235	598	37.5%	374	3.2
1985	10,631	1,955	18.4	1,495	831	183	530	37.4%	332	3.1
[3]1984	10,600	2,305	21.7	970	758	114	1,624	43.2%	923	8.7
1983	10,170	1,679	16.5	889	652	117	1,020	44.6%	565	5.6
1982	10,815	2,435	22.5	1,500	575	89	1,872	37.9%	1,162	10.7
1981	10,337	2,512	24.3	1,190	452	64	2,183	43.2%	1,239	12.0
1980	9,734	2,296	23.6	902	399	46	1,963	41.2%	1,154	11.9
1979	8,028	2,012	25.1	603	363	25	1,707	41.4%	1,001	12.5
1978	7,013	1,989	28.4	442	344	19	1,681	46.3%	902	12.9

Balance Sheet Data (Million $)

Dec. 31	Cash	Assets	Curr. Liab.	Ratio	Total Assets	Ret. On Assets	Long Term Debt	Common Equity	Total Cap.	% LT Debt of Cap.	Ret. On Equity
1987	954	6,695	4,075	1.6	14,451	8.8%	2,212	6,013	9,633	23.0	19.4%
1986	613	5,811	3,791	1.5	12,902	3.0%	911	6,388	8,508	10.7	5.8%
1985	813	5,677	3,325	1.7	12,142	2.9%	988	6,562	8,598	11.5	4.9%
1984	1,011	5,131	2,306	2.2	10,778	8.8%	409	7,137	8,269	4.9	13.0%
1983	1,562	5,420	2,172	2.5	10,928	5.2%	416	7,520	8,542	4.9	7.5%
1982	1,018	5,289	2,146	2.5	10,622	11.5%	350	7,541	8,337	4.2	16.1%
1981	1,122	5,063	2,119	2.4	9,446	13.6%	93	6,770	7,212	1.3	19.3%
1980	1,585	5,246	2,247	2.3	8,754	14.1%	79	6,028	6,378	1.2	20.2%
1979	1,541	4,522	1,741	2.6	7,554	13.9%	76	5,391	5,703	1.3	19.5%
1978	1,379	4,000	1,563	2.6	6,801	14.2%	76	4,858	5,144	1.5	19.6%

Data as orig. reptd. 1. Incl. equity in earns. of nonconsol. subs. 2. Reflects accounting change. 3. Reflects merger or acquisition.

Business Summary

Eastman Kodak is the largest producer of photographic products in the world, and is an important manufacturer of chemicals, fibers and plastics. In February 1988, EK acquired Sterling Drug Inc., whose products include prescription and over-the-counter medicines and other consumer products. Prior to 1988, health care-related results were included in EK's imaging segment. Industry segment contributions in 1987:

	Sales	Profits
Imaging	82%	82%
Chemicals	18%	18%

Sales to customers outside the U.S. accounted for 40% of sales in 1987.

EK manufactures a wide variety of imaging products, including cameras, projectors, films, processing services, photographic papers, photofinishing equipment, audiovisual equipment, and office copy, microfilm and other business equipment. Also, EK's Verbatim unit provides flexible magnetic media for small computers. Recent product introductions include the VR line of 35-millimeter cameras and two new lines of batteries (Supralife alkaline and Ultralife lithium).

EK's chemical products are used primarily by manufacturers, including their use by EK in the manufacture of photographic products. Principal chemical product areas are olefin (ethylene and propylene), acetyl, polyester and specialty chemicals. Areas in which EK products are used include textiles and plastics packaging.

Dividend Data

Dividends have been paid since 1902. A dividend reinvestment plan is available.

Amt. of Divd. $	Date Decl.	Ex-divd. Date	Stock of Record	Payment Date
0.45	Sep. 11	Nov. 24	Dec. 1	Jan. 4'88
0.45	Feb. 12	Feb. 24	Mar. 1	Apr. 1'88
0.45	May 11	May 25	Jun. 1	Jul. 1'88
0.50	Aug. 12	Aug. 26	Sep. 1	Oct. 3'88

Next dividend meeting: Nov. 11 '88.

Finances

In October, 1986 the U.S. Supreme Court denied a petition by EK appealing Polaroid's lower court victories in a patent infringement suit.

Capitalization

Long Term Debt: $7,440,000,000.

Common Stock: 324,154,364 shs. ($2.50 par).
Institutions hold about 48%.
Shareholders of record: 168,517.

Office 343 State St., Rochester, N.Y. 14650. Tel—(716) 724-4000. Chrmn & CEO—C. H. Chandler. Pres—K. R. Whitmore. Secy—A. P. Donovan. Treas—C. M. Hamilton. Investor Contact—G. A. Steenberge (716) 724-4365. Dirs—R. E. Anderson, J. F. Burlingame, C. H. Chandler, K. M. Cole, M. L. Collins, C. T. Duncan, W. A. Fallon, J. M. Kreps, C. D. Quillen, Jr., T. F. Reid, J. P. Semper, D. S. Saxon, P. L. Smith, W. L. Sutton, K. R. Whitmore. Transfer Agents & Registrars—Chase Lincoln First Bank of Rochester, N.Y.; First Jersey National Bank, Jersey City. Incorporated in New Jersey in 1901. Empl—124,400.

Information has been obtained from sources believed to be reliable, but its accuracy and completeness are not guaranteed.   Tom Graves, CFA

FIGURE 3.3 (*continued*)

74 DUQ-EAT

Standard & Poor's Corporation

Index (¶S&P 500, •Options)	Ticker Symbol	Name of Issue (Call Price of Pfd. Stocks)	Market	Com. Rank. & Pfd. Rating	Par Val.	Inst. Hold Cos	Inst. Hold Shs. (000)	Principal Business	Price Range 1971-87 High	1971-87 Low	1988 High	1988 Low	1989 High	1989 Low	Feb. Sales in 100s	February, 1989 Last Sale Or Bid High	Low	Last	%Div Yield	P-E Ratio
1	DQU	Duquesne Light	NY,B,C,M,P,Ph	B+	1	93	14530	Electric utility-Pittsburgh	26¾	10⅝	18⅞	11¾	18¾	17⅞	30686	18⅝	18	18⅝	6.9	10
2	Pr A	$2.10 cm Pfd(51.84)	NY(10)	BBB−	50	..	...	& parts of Allegheny &	32¾	14	23	19	22¾	21½	26	22½	21⅞	22¼B	9.4	..
3	Pr J	$2.315 cm Pref([51]25.90)	NY(10)	BB+	1	1	31	Beaver counties,Penna	28	13¾	24	21⅝	23⅝	22½	788	23½	22¾	22¾	10.2	..
4	Pr K	$2.10 cm Pref([52]25.70)	NY	BB+	1	..	...	Fueled:82% coal,18% nuclear	26¼	12½	23	19⅜	21⅞	20¼	319	21⅞	20¼	20½	10.2	..
5	DUQN	Duquesne Systems[53]	OTC	B+	No	57	4111	Mkts IBM-compatible softw	33¼	2½	22¼	15¾	24	21	7687	24	21½	23¼B	...	21
6	DRKN	Durakon Industries	OTC	B−	No	22	1699	Mfr plastic truckbed liners	18	5⅝	14¼	6¼	9¾	6⅛	4025	9¾	6⅛	7¾B	...	39
7	DRMD	Duramed Pharmaceutical	OTC	NR	1¢	5	92	Generic prescription drugs	24½	1¾	8½	2	8½	3⅞	8613	8½	6⅛	7¼B	...	d
8	DRTK	Duratek Corp	OTC	NR	1¢	4	32	Radioactive wtr treat sys	6⅜	2⅜	3⅞	1⅞	3⅛	2½	1645	3⅛	2½	3B	...	75
9	DUCO	Durham Corp	OTC	B	5	21	1928	Insur hldg:broadcast'g	34	2¾	36¾	21½	33¾	30	1396	33	30	32½B	2.8	34
10	DURI	Duriron Co	OTC	B−	1¼	67	5045	Corrosion resist process eq	18⅝	1 13/16	25⅝	13¼	25⅝	21⅞	10494	25⅝	23¼	23¾B	2.9	12
11	DUFM	Durr-Fillauer Medic	OTC	A+	50¢	43	3660	Dstr medical-surg eq,drugs	18	11/16	18½	8½	19⅞	18⅛	5673	19⅞	18⅝	18¾B	1.0	20
12	DWG	DWG Corp	AS,B,P	B−	10¢	26	3176	LPG dstr:subsid util,apparel	7⅝	⅜	9¼	5¾	8¼	5⅜	52022	8¼	5⅜	7½	...	5
13	DYAN	Dyansen Corp	OTC	NR	1¢	9	642	Mkts fine art & related prod	3	¾	3¼	1 7/16	2 5/16	1⅞	3821	2¼	1⅞	2B	...	17
14	DYTR	Dyatron Corp	OTC	B−	66⅔¢	13	1025	Auto dealer computer serv	15¼	1⅛	15¼	10¾	15¼	12¾	1846	15¼	13¼	13½B	...	9
15	DYCO	Dycom Indus	OTC	NR	33⅓¢	27	889	Telecommunication svcs	16	⅝	21	9¼	25	19¼	6196	24½	19¼	19⅝B	...	15
16	DYA	Dynamics Corp Amer	NY,M	B+	10¢	30	2213	Appliances,metal fab,power	33¼	¼	23⅞	16⅞	24⅜	22⅞	524	24⅜	22⅞	22⅞	0.9	12
17	DRCO	Dynamics Research	OTC,B	B+	10¢	17	1271	Mfr encoders: computer svs	11¼	1/16	11	6½	9	6½	1584	9	7⅛	8¾B	...	11
18	DYNA	Dynascan Corp	OTC	B	33⅓¢	31	2606	Consumer & ind'l electronics	23½	⅜	9⅞	6	10⅛	9	3329	9½	9	9B	...	8
19	DYTC	Dynatech Corp	OTC	B+	20¢	91	6272	Communic&med'l pr,sci instr	43½	5/16	24	16½	19¼	18	13679	19	18½	18¾B	...	9
20	DYNI	Dynatrend Inc[58]	OTC	NR	5¢	2	190	Plann'g,engineer'g,mgmt svcs	4¾	⅛	2	1⅛	2⅛	2	118	2⅛	2 1/16	2⅛B	...	16
¶21•1	ESY	E-Systems	NY,B,M,P,Ph	↑A	1	178	14723	Electronic sys & eq-defense	44¾	13/16	33½	25½	31¼	28⅝	18313	31⅛	28⅞	29¾	1.7	12
22	EBMI	E & B Marine Inc	OTC,B	C	1¢	9	90	Dstr of marine supplies	25	5½	6½	2	2⅝	1⅞	3024	2¼	1⅞	2⅛B	...	d
23	EZEM	E-Z-EM Inc	OTC	B+	10¢	31	1562	Mfr diagnostic imag'g prod	18⅞	5⅝	14¾	9¼	14	12	657	13	12¼	12¼B	...	14
24	EACO	EA Engr Science/Tech	OTC	NR	1¢	8	506	Environmental consult'g svcs	10½	3½	7	4⅜	7¼	5¾	363	7	6⅝	6⅝B	...	18
25	EAC	EAC Indus	AS	C	10¢	7	148	Mfrd housing,hardware	17⅝	13/16	8⅜	4⅞	8¼	6⅞	1305	8¼	6⅞	7⅝	...	28
26	EGL	Eagle Clothes	AS	C	1	13	1120	Mfrs menswear:retail svcs	16¾	¼	1⅝	5/16	1⅛	¾	1040	1	¾	13/16	...	d
27	EAG	Eagle Financial	AS	NR	1¢	10	377	Savings&loan,Connecticut	14½	7⅜	11¼	7¾	10⅛	8⅛	519	10⅛	9¼	9½	5.3	10
28	EPI	Eagle-Picher Indus	NY,C,M	↓C	1¼	101	6208	Ind'l pr: mchy&auto parts	53	5⅞	33¼	12⅝	17½	15⅛	7033	17½	15⅛	15⅜	...	d
29	EGLA	Eagle Telephonics	OTC	NR	1¢	7	425	Mfr telephone keysets/eqp	5¾	½	1⅜	5/16	7/16	5/16	1809	⅜	5/16	5/16B	...	d
30	ETCO	Earth Technology	OTC	NR	10¢	13	446	Enviro/tech consult'g svcs	9⅝	2⅝	5⅜	3¼	6¼	4⅜	2958	6¼	4½	5¼B	...	13
31	TOOL	Easco Hand Tools	OTC	NR	1¢	43	3392	Mfrs specialized hand tools	13	5¾	13½	6¾	8⅞	7½	1512	8¾	7½	7¾B	...	10
32	ESTO	Eastco Industrial Safety	OTC	B−	1¢	2	48	Mfr protective cloth'g/equip	2 9/16	1/16	6⅞	¾	7¾	5½	2597	7¾	6¼	6½B	...	14
33	EALPrD	Eastern Air[60]11.36%Dep[61]Pfd	AS	NR	1	21	2540	Subsid of Texas Air	23⅞	12¼	18	12⅛	16½	14⅜	13469	16⅜	14⅞	16	17.8	..
34	Pr E	$2.72[62]cm Pfd (25)	AS	NR	1	2	158		23½	6½	15	7	7½	6½	2555	7	6½	6⅝	41.1	..
35	Pr F	$3.24[65]cm Pfd (21.625)	AS	NR	1	12	1219		26¼	8⅛	15¾	6½	7⅝	6⅝	3336	7⅜	6⅝	7¼	44.7	..
36	Pr G	$3.12[66]cm Jr Pfd(25)	AS	NR	1	3	239		22½	7¼	16⅛	6¾	7¾	6½	2618	7⅛	6½	6¾	46.2	..
37	EML	Eastern Co.	AS,M	B	5	16	575	Mine roof supports:metal fab	18⅜	3⅜	19¼	12¼	14⅞	13	187	14⅞	13	14⅞	3.8	11
38	EESI	East'n Environmental Svc	OTC	NR	1¢	7	151	Asbestos removal/abatement	12¼	4⅜	6⅜	3	5⅛	3¾	3410	4⅞	3¾	3¾B	...	14
¶39•2	EFU	East'n Gas & Fuel	NY,B,C,M,P,Ph	B−	1	133	16240	Coal, river barg'g: Boston Gas	33¼	5½	26¾	21¾	25¾	22¾	7953	25¾	24	24⅛	5.8	11
40	EUA	Eastern Util Assoc	NY,B,M,P	A−	5	99	6933	Util hldg co: Mass & RI elec	40½	8	33⅛	21⅛	32⅞	31¼	5694	32⅝	32	32¼	7.4	11
41	EGP	EastGroup Properties SBI	AS	NR	1	15	614	Real estate investment trust	40	3⅝	25¼	20¼	24⅛	21⅜	450	24⅛	22¼	22½	11.6	..
→ ¶42•3	EK	Eastman Kodak	NY,B,C,M,P,Ph	A−	2½	956	160774	Photograph apparatus,chem	71	18¼	53¼	39⅛	49¼	44⅛	187415	49¼	46⅛	46⅛	4.3	11 ←
43	KDU	East Kodak,Americus(Unit[69])	AS,M	NR	No	4	1107	Unit Trust For Eastman Kodak	104½	71¼	78⅛	60¼	73½	69½	10	73½	69½	70B	4.2	..
44	KDS	Score	AS,M	NR	No	7	368	Capital appreciation	46⅜	14½	19	6⅛	10¾	5½	2535	10¾	9⅛	9⅛	...	..
45	KDP	Prime	AS,M	NR	No	22	736	divd income pay'g component	67	50½	64⅞	48	64¼	61	109	64¼	63	63½	4.6	..
¶46•3	ETN	Eaton Corp	NY,B,M,P,Ph	B	50¢	312	22443	Electronic/electric sys,eqp:	71⅞	8	57⅜	44⅜	59¾	54¾	15343	59⅛	57	58⅜	3.4	9

Uniform Footnote Explanations-See Page 1. Other: [1]P:Cycle 2. [2]Ph:Cycle 1. [3]CBOE:Cycle 1. [51]To 3-31-91,then $25.25. [52]To 3-31-92,then $25. [53]Plan comb w/Morino Inc,1 shr. [54]Δ$0.21,'86. [55]®$0.87,'88. [56]®$1.11,'88. [57]Excl 2M Cl'B'(Cv at 100 to 1). [58]EG&G plans acq, $2.20. [59]®$0.65,'87. [60]Cm:Div in cash or Dep Pfd thru'90,then cash. [61]Dep for1/100 shr of 11.36% Jr Pfd:callable $25. [62]Divd in cash or $2.72Pfd thru'90,then cash. [63]0.0375 Pfd shrs. [64]Incl 0.075 Pfd shrs. [65]Divd in cash or $3.24Pfd stk thru'90,then cash. [66]Divd in cash or $3.12Pfd stk thru'90,then cash. [67]Subsid Pfd in M$. [68]Fiscal Nov'87 & prior. [69]Represents 1.5 Eastman Kodak com shrs. [70]®$4.67,'87.

Common and Preferred Stocks

DUQ-EAT 75

Index (Splits •)	Cash Divs. Ea. Yr. Since	Dividends Latest Payment Period $	Date	Ex. Div.	Total $ So Far 1989	Ind. Rate	Paid 1988	Financial Position Mil-$ Cash& Equiv.	Curr. Assets	Curr. Liab.	Balance Sheet Date	Capitalization Lg Trm Debt Mil-$	Shs. 000 Pfd.	Com.	Earnings $ Per Shr. Years End	1984	1985	1986	1987	1988	Last 12 Mos.	Interim Earnings Period	$ per Shr. 1987	1988	Index
1	1913	Q0.32	1-1-89	11-30	0.32	1.28	1.20	212	437	353	9-30-88	11697	5069	60242	Dc	2.21	2.26	1.79	1.81	P1.86	1.86				1
2	1955	Q0.525	4-1-89	3-6	1.05	2.10	2.10	....	...	...		....	160	...	Dc	b1.98	b2.04	b1.88	b2.22	....	....				2
3	1976	Q0.57⅞	4-1-89	3-6	1.15¾	2.315	2.31½	....	...	...		....	1200	...	Dc	b1.98	b2.04	b1.88	b2.22	....	....				3
4	1977	Q0.525	4-1-89	3-6	1.05	2.10	2.10	....	...	...		....	1200	...	Dc	b1.98	b2.04	b1.88	b2.22	....	....				4
5•	....	None Since Public			....	Nil	....	28.4	44.0	7.19	12-31-88	....	...	10661	Sp	p0.19	0.27	0.52	0.75	1.02	1.10	3 Mo Dec	0.25	0.33	5
6•	....	None Since Public			....	Nil	....	2.41	43.5	11.4	9-30-88	36.0	...	6159	Dc	0.60	0.73	0.71	0.93	P0.20	0.20				6
7	....	None Since Public			....	Nil	....	0.11	10.9	15.9	9-30-88	5.35	...	3423	Dc	d0.92	d0.94	*Δ0.37	d1.87	Pd0.38	d0.38				7
8	....	None Since Public			....	Nil	....	1.87	4.28	0.50	9-30-88	....	...	3940	Dc	pd1.06	pd1.07	d0.12	*0.13	....	0.04	9 Mo Sep	*0.08	d0.01	8
9•	1918	Q0.23	3-14-89	2-22	0.23	0.92	0.92	Equity per shr $26.23			9-30-88	....	...	8433	Dc	Δ3.46	Δ2.43	Δ1.99	Δ1.17	PΔ0.96	0.96				9
10•	1935	Q0.17¼	3-3-89	2-14	0.17¼	0.69	0.59	23.4	113	38.4	9-30-88	38.5	...	7895	Dc	d0.32	0.85	Δ[64]0.29	0.88	*P1.95	1.95				10
11•	1937	Q0.04½	3-10-89	2-23	0.04½	0.18	0.17¾	10.0	137	58.6	9-30-88	37.9	...	7472	Dc	0.73	0.78	0.82	0.87	P[66]0.92	0.92				11
12•	....	5%Stk	4-25-86	3-25	....	Nil	....	59.9	356	146	10-31-88	456	1656	16448	Ap	*0.12	*0.29	□d0.50	*0.72	[56]1.58	1.49	6 Mo Oct	0.37	*0.28	12
13	....	None Since Public			....	Nil	....	0.13	12.2	8.27	9-30-88	3.10	...	5291	Dc	0.11	*0.09	0.15	Δ0.24	....	0.12	9 Mo Sep	0.20	0.08	13
14	....	0.06	4-17-81	3-16	....	Nil	....	0.12	11.7	6.15	9-30-88	2.39	300	[57]2817	Dc	0.07	*0.12	*0.40	1.11	P1.44	1.44				14
15•	....	5%Stk	12-21-87	12-1	....	Nil	....	4.64	34.7	20.2	10-31-88	3.36	...	4575	Jl	*0.13	*0.30	*0.53	0.71	1.01	1.27	6 Mo JanΔ	0.43	0.69	15
16	1978	S0.10	3-1-89	2-7	0.10	0.20	0.20	24.9	88.6	39.2	9-30-88	19.0	...	±4041	Dc	2.02	3.66	Δ0.11	*0.89	....	1.97	9 Mo Sep	*0.67	1.75	16
17•	....	s0.012	4-13-84	3-26	....	Nil	....	n/a	30.8	17.7	9-03-88	....	...	5040	Dc	0.30	0.03	0.49	0.74	P0.81	0.81				17
18•	....	3%Stk	6-1-84	5-8	....	Nil	....	3.50	93.8	25.4	9-30-88	34.7	...	6730	Dc	d2.35	0.02	0.85	1.13	....	1.18	9 Mo Sep	0.59	0.64	18
19•	....	None Since Public			....	Nil	....	22.6	187	52.4	12-31-88	35.7	...	12400	Mr	1.96	1.95	2.10	2.08	....	2.07	9 Mo Dec	1.51	1.50	19
20	....	None Paid			....	Nil	....	0.06	2.44	0.73	9-25-88	0.01	...	3120	Je	d0.38	*0.01	*0.03	*0.09	*0.13	0.13	3 Mo Sep	*0.03	*0.03	20
21	1966	Q0.12½	4-5-89	3-13	0.25	0.50	0.50	6.30	509	146	9-30-88	103	...	30879	Dc	2.02	1.47	2.00	1.95	P2.40	2.40				21
22	....	None Since Public			....	Nil	....	1.29	26.1	23.4	7-03-88	15.8	...	1993	Dc	0.85	0.63	d0.84	d2.47	....	d1.97	9 Mo Sep	d0.63	d0.13	22
23•	....	None Since Public			....	Nil	....	21.0	44.5	7.86	12-03-88	....	...	7981	My	0.65	0.70	0.87	[58]0.67	0.86	0.88	6 Mo Nov	0.44	0.46	23
24	....	None Since Public			....	Nil	....	3.19	18.8	10.8	11-30-88	0.22	...	2450	Au	*0.15	0.07	0.53	0.23	0.34	0.37	3 Mo Nov	0.11	0.14	24
25	....	0.10	12-15-86	11-7	....	Nil	....	1.26	24.4	9.56	10-31-88	14.5	...	1947	Ja	d0.07	0.03	d0.50	d1.05	....	0.27	9 Mo Oct	d0.42	0.90	25
26	....	0.03	9-30-70	9-15	....	Nil	....	0.44	43.1	24.4	10-29-88	5.09	...	p9214	Jl	*□0.24	*0.08	*d0.27	*0.04	Δd0.75	d0.77	3 Mo Oct	*d0.04	Δd0.06	26
27	1987	Q0.12½	3-1-89	2-9	0.12½	0.50	0.37½	Book Value $16.54			9-30-88	37.0	...	2688	Sp	...	...	...	....	0.68	0.92	3 Mo Dec	0.14	0.38	27
28	1936	0.28	9-9-88	8-15	....	Nil	0.84	15.7	338	277	11-30-88	94.3	...	10679	Nv	2.91	d12.52	3.80	3.70	d43.54	d43.54				28
29	....	None Since Public			....	Nil	....	0.26	23.8	14.7	7-31-88	0.26	...	15244	Oc	d0.44	d0.34	*0.08	*0.09	....	d0.04	9 Mo Jul	*0.08	d0.05	29
30	....	None Since Public			....	Nil	....	4.37	15.4	5.73	11-25-88	0.48	...	2856	Au	0.06	0.11	0.31	0.52	0.41	0.42	3 Mo Nov	0.09	0.10	30
31	....	None Since Public			....	Nil	....	69.0	154	33.6	10-01-88	103	...	13392	Dc	...	...	...	p0.70	P0.79	0.79				31
32•	....	None Paid			....	Nil	....	0.05	13.2	10.4	12-31-88	0.25	...	2455	Je	d0.10	Nil	*Nil	*0.02	0.26	0.46	6 Mo Dec	0.06	0.26	32
33	1987	Q0.71	2-28-89	2-1	0.71	2.84	2.84	387	1024	1134	9-30-88	2296	±1102	72519		0.00	...	...	b0.31	....	....	SF fr Nv'92 thru'97,$25			33
34	1987	[63]....	2-15-89	2-1	[63]....	2.72	[64]1.36	....	...	...		....	2153	...		...	...	...	b0.31	....	....	SF 4% fr Nov'90-'94,$25			34
35	1987	[63]....	2-15-89	2-1	[63]....	3.24	[64]1.62	....	...	...		....	4820	...		...	...	...	b0.31	....	....	SF3%fr Nov'90-99,$21.625			35
36	1987	[63]....	2-15-89	2-1	[63]....	3.12	[64]1.56	....	...	...		....	2153	...		...	...	...	b0.31	....	....	SF 3% fr Nov'90-'99,$25			36
37•	1940	Q0.14	12-15-88	11-18	....	0.56	0.54½	1.80	23.6	8.39	10-01-88	5.23	...	1857	Dc	1.42	1.18	0.88	1.46	P1.38	1.38				37
38	....	None Since Public			....	Nil	....	4.08	9.24	2.25	9-30-88	....	...	±4260	Je	±0.03	±0.01	±0.12	±0.34	±Δ0.36	0.26	6 Mo Dec	±0.27	±0.17	38
39	1974	Q0.35	4-3-89	2-28	0.67½	1.40	1.30	100	246	118	9-30-88	270	...	23164	Dc	0.73	d1.61	0.82	2.05	P2.18	2.18				39
40	1928	Q0.60	2-15-89	1-26	0.60	2.40	2.37½	25.1	102	123	9-30-88	534	[67]50	13276	Dc	2.85	2.67	2.82	3.46	P2.85	2.85				40
41	1978	Q0.65	1-25-89	12-30	0.65	2.60	2.60	Equity per shr $19.75			9-30-88	17.2	...	2538	Dc	9.68	4.40	3.10	[68]2.51	....	....	9 Mo Sep		3.89	41
→ 42•	1902	Q0.50	4-3-89	2-23	1.00	2.00	1.85	1052	8348	5013	10-02-88	7956	...	324167	Dc	2.54	■0.97	■1.10	3.52	P4.31	4.31				42 ←
43	1987	Q0.73¾	4-12-89	2-23	1.47½	2.95	2.72½	Net Asset Val $73.50			12-31-87	....	...	2252	Dc	...	...	...	§73.50	....	....	Expires 4-15-92			43
44	....	None Since Public			....	Nil	....	....	...	...		....	...	...	Dc	...	...	...	....	....	....				44
45	1987	Q0.73¾	4-12-89	2-23	1.47½	2.95	2.72½	Termination claim $92				....	...	...	Dc	...	...	...	....	....	....				45
46•	1923	Q0.50	2-24-89	1-31	0.50	2.00	1.666	130	1224	643	9-30-88	643	...	37102	Dc	5.23	4.67	2.86	[70]4.77	P□6.17	6.17				46

•Stock Splits & Divs By Line Reference Index [5]2-for-1,'86,'87. [6]3-for-2,'86. [9]2-for-1,'84:3-for-2,'87. [10]To split 3-for-2,ex Mar 21. [11]5-for-4,'85. [12]Adj to 5%,'86. [15]2-for-1,'86:Adj to 5%,'87. [17]Adj for 5%,'84:5-for-4,'84,'86,twice,'87. [18]Adj for 3%,'84:3-for-2,'87. [19]3-for-2,'84. [23]3-for-2,'86. [32]3-for-1,'88. [37]2-for-1,'88. [42]3-for-2,'85,'87. [46]3-for-2,'88.

FIGURE 3.4 A Two-Page Spread from Standard & Poor's Stock Guide (March 1989).

In Standard & Poor's *Stock Guide,* common stocks are ranked relative to the growth and stability of earnings and dividends, whereas preferred stocks are ranked relative to the issuer's capacity and willingness to make scheduled dividend payments. From the data on line 42 you can see that Eastman Kodak Company, having an A− rating, falls within one of the highest-rated groups of common stock. (*Source:* Standard & Poor's Corporation, *Stock Guide*. New York: Standard & Poor's Corporation, March 1989, pp. 74–75.)

detailed analysis of an especially recommended stock plus a large amount of investment background information.

Brokerage Reports. Another popular source of investment information is brokerage firms. In addition to making available reports from various subscription services, brokerage firms provide clients with prospectuses for new security issues and back-office research reports. A **prospectus** is a document describing in detail the key aspects of the issuer, its management and financial position, and the security to be issued. It contains a wealth of information that should be useful in evaluating the investment suitability of a new issue. The cover of the 54-page prospectus describing the 1989 stock issue of Silk Greenhouse, Inc., is shown in Figure 3.5. **Back-office research reports** are published by and made available to clients of brokerage firms. They include analyses of and recommendations on current and future prospects for the securities markets, specific industries, and/or specific securities. Usually a brokerage firm will publish lists of securities classified as either "buy" or "sell," depending upon the research staff's analysis of their anticipated price behavior. Brokerage research reports are available at no cost to existing as well as potential customers.

Investment Letters. **Investment letters** provide, on a subscription basis, the analyses, conclusions, and recommendations of various experts in different aspects of securities investment. The cost as well as general thrust of these letters varies. Some concentrate on specific types of securities, whereas others are concerned solely with assessing the economy and/or security markets. Among the more popular investment letters are *Dick Davis Digest, The Dines Letter, Granville Market Letter, Growth Stock Outlook, Holt Investment Advisory, Prudent Speculator, Professional Tape Reader, Wellington Letter,* and *The Zweig Forecast.* The more popular ones, which are generally issued weekly or monthly, usually range in cost from $75 to $300 a year. Advertisements for many of these investment letters can be found in *Barron's.*

Price Information

Price information about various types of securities is contained in their **quotations,** which include current price data along with statistics on recent price behavior. Price quotations are readily available for actively traded securities and provide a picture of the securities' behavior in the marketplace. The most up-to-date quotations can be obtained from a stockbroker. Some brokerage offices have equipment that allows customers to key into a computer terminal and obtain quotations. Another automated quotation device found in most brokerage offices in the *ticker,* a lighted screen on which stock transactions made on the floor of the exchange are reported immediately as they occur. The ticker symbols for some well-known companies are included in Table 3.1. Today more sophisticated computer terminals are rapidly displacing the ticker as the major source of up-to-the-minute stock price information. Access to price information via personal computers is now available on a fee basis for use by professional and active individual investors.

prospectus
a document detailing the key aspects of new security issues, the issuer, and its management and financial position.

back-office research reports
analyses of and recommendations on current and future investment opportunities; published by and made available to clients of brokerage firms.

investment letters
provide, on a subscription basis, the analyses, conclusions, and recommendations of various experts in different aspects of securities investment.

quotations
price information about various types of securities, including current price data and statistics on recent price behavior.

SILK GREENHOUSE®

1,700,000 Shares

Common Stock

Of the 1,700,000 shares of Common Stock offered, 1,400,000 are being sold by Silk Greenhouse, Inc. (the "Company") and 300,000 are being sold by certain Selling Shareholders. See "Principal and Selling Shareholders." The Company will not receive any proceeds from the shares being sold by the Selling Shareholders.

The Common Stock of the Company is traded in the over-the-counter market. On February 1, 1989, the closing price as reported on the NASDAQ National Market System was $17.25 per share. See "Price Range of Common Stock."

See "Certain Factors" for a discussion of risks that should be considered by prospective investors.

THESE SECURITIES HAVE NOT BEEN APPROVED OR DISAPPROVED BY THE SECURITIES AND EXCHANGE COMMISSION NOR HAS THE COMMISSION PASSED UPON THE ACCURACY OR ADEQUACY OF THIS PROSPECTUS. ANY REPRESENTATION TO THE CONTRARY IS A CRIMINAL OFFENSE.

	Price to Public	Underwriting Discounts and Commissions(1)	Proceeds to Company(2)	Proceeds to Selling Shareholders(2)
Per Share	$17.25	$1.04	$16.21	$16.21
Total(3)	$29,325,000	$1,768,000	$22,694,000	$4,863,000

(1) The Company and the Selling Shareholders have agreed to indemnify the Underwriters against certain civil liabilities, including liabilities under the Securities Act of 1933. See "Underwriting."

(2) Before deducting expenses of this offering payable by the Company estimated at $185,000 and by the Selling Shareholders estimated at $15,000.

(3) The Company and certain of the Selling Shareholders have granted to the Underwriters a 30-day option to purchase up to 85,000 and 170,000 additional shares of Common Stock, respectively, solely to cover over-allotments, if any. To the extent the option is exercised, the Underwriters will offer the additional shares at the Price to Public shown above. If the option is exercised in full, the total Price to Public will be $33,723,750, total Underwriting Discounts and Commissions will be $2,033,200, total Proceeds to Company will be $24,071,850 and total Proceeds to Selling Shareholders will be $7,618,700. See "Underwriting."

The shares of Common Stock are being offered by the several Underwriters named herein, subject to prior sale, when, as and if delivered to and accepted by them, and subject to the right of the Underwriters to reject any order in whole or in part. It is expected that delivery of the shares will be made at the offices of Alex. Brown & Sons Incorporated, Baltimore, Maryland, on or about February 8, 1989.

Alex. Brown & Sons
Incorporated

Robertson, Colman & Stephens

The date of this Prospectus is February 1, 1989.

FIGURE 3.5 Cover of a Prospectus for a Stock Issue.
Some of the key factors relative to the 1989 stock issue by Silk Greenhouse, Inc., are summarized on the cover of its 54-page prospectus. (*Source:* Silk Greenhouse, Inc., February 1, 1989, p. 1.)

TABLE 3.1 Ticker Symbols for Some Well-Known Companies

Company	Symbol
Aluminum Co. of America	AA
American Telephone & Telegraph	T
Coca-Cola	KO
Eastman Kodak	EK
Ford Motor	F
General Electric	GE
General Motors	GM
International Business Machines	IBM
Minnesota Mining and Manufacturing	MMM
Mobil Corporation	MOB
Occidental Petroleum	OXY
Pan American Corporation	PN
Polaroid Corporation	PRD
Procter & Gamble	PG
Quaker Oats	OAT
Sears, Roebuck	S
Sherwin-Williams	SHW
Texas Instruments	TXN
Wendy's International	WEN
Xerox Corporation	XRX

An investor can easily find security price quotations in the published news media, both nonfinancial and financial. Most big city newspapers report daily activity on the major exchanges, but such quotations are typically limited to stocks. Local newspaper quotations often highlight certain stocks of local interest in addition to reporting major exchange transactions. The major source of security price quotations is *The Wall Street Journal,* which is published every business day and presents quotations for each previous business day's activities in all major markets. It contains quotations on stocks, bonds, listed options, commodities and financial futures, mutual funds, and other popular forms of investment. As noted earlier, *Barron's* and *Investor's Daily* also provide a wealth of security price quotations. (Actual price quotations will be demonstrated and discussed as part of the coverage of specific investment vehicles in later chapters.)

MARKET AVERAGES AND INDEXES

Investors also need to monitor and keep abreast of the behavior of securities *markets*. The ability to interpret various market measures should help an investor to select and *time* investment actions. Just as it is important to understand when the economy is moving up (expansion) or down (recession), it is also important to know whether market behavior is favorable or unfavorable. Market behavior is, of course, affected by the economy, and as a result it is difficult to view each independently. Yet it is in a given security—rather than the economy—that an investor places

money, and therefore it is important that the investor understand how to measure the general behavior of the market. A widely used way to assess the behavior of securities markets is to study the performance of market averages and indexes. Key measures of stock and bond market activity and the small investor's portfolio are discussed here; discussion of averages and indexes associated with other forms of investments is deferred to the chapters devoted to each vehicle.

Stock Market Averages and Indexes

averages
numbers used to measure the general behavior of stock prices by reflecting the arithmetic average price behavior of a representative group of stocks at a given point in time.

indexes
numbers used to measure the general behavior of stock prices by measuring the current price behavior of a representative group of stocks in relation to a base value set at an earlier point in time.

Dow Jones Industrial Average (DJIA)
a stock average made up of 30 high-quality industrial stocks selected for total market value and broad public ownership and believed to reflect overall market activity.

Stock market averages and indexes are used to measure the general behavior of stock prices over time. Although the terms "average" and "index" tend to be used interchangeably when discussing market behavior, technically they are different types of measures. **Averages** reflect the arithmetic average price behavior of a representative group of stocks at a given point in time; **indexes** measure the current price behavior of a representative group of stocks in relation to a base value set at an earlier point in time. Many investors compare averages (or indexes) at differing points in time in order to assess the relative strength or weakness of the market. When the averages (or indexes) reflect an upward trend in prices, a *bull market* is said to exist; in contrast, a downward trend is reflective of a *bear market*. Because they provide a convenient method of capturing the general mood of the market, an understanding of the major averages is important. Current and recent values of the key averages are quoted daily in the financial news; most local newspapers and many radio and television news programs also quote the prevailing values of such averages. Let us take a brief look at the key averages (or indexes).

The Dow Jones Averages

Dow Jones, publisher of *The Wall Street Journal,* prepares four stock averages. The most popular is the **Dow Jones Industrial Average (DJIA),** which is made up of 30 stocks selected for total market value and broad public ownership. The group consists of high-quality industrial stocks whose activities are believed to reflect overall market activity. The box within Figure 3.6 lists the stocks currently included in the DJIA. Occasionally a merger, a bankruptcy, or extreme lack of activity causes a particular stock to be dropped from the average; in such a case a new stock is added, and the average is readjusted so that it continues to behave in a way consistent with the immediate past. The actual value of the DJIA is meaningful only when compared to earlier values. For example, the DJIA on April 27, 1989, closed at 2418.99; this value in and of itself becomes meaningful only when compared to the day-earlier closing value of 2389.11. Many people mistakenly believe that one DJIA "point" equals $1 in the value of an average share; actually one point currently translates into about 2.27 cents in share value. Figure 3.6 shows the DJIA over the period October 28, 1988, to April 27, 1989. It can be seen that beginning in mid-November of 1988, the DJIA showed a steady increase through April of 1989. As the most commonly cited stock market average, the DJIA is quoted daily in the news media.

The three other Dow Jones averages are the transportation, the utilities, and the composite. The Dow Jones transportation average is based on 20 stocks, including

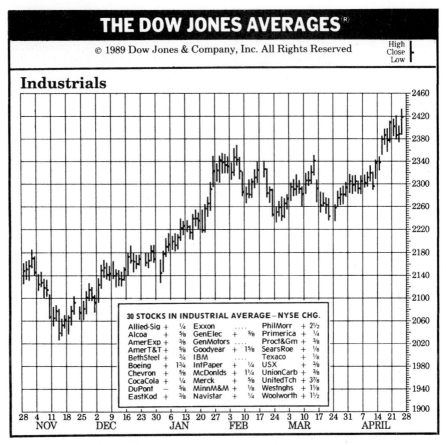

FIGURE 3.6   The DJIA from October 28, 1988, to April 27, 1989.
As can be seen, in late 1988 through early 1989 the stock market was bullish; indeed, the stock market as measured by the DJIA moved from 2100 to 2400, for a gain of over 14 percent (and all within 180 days). (*Source: The Wall Street Journal,* April 28, 1989, p. C3. Reprinted by permission of *The Wall Street Journal,* © Dow Jones & Comapny, Inc. 1989. All rights reserved.)

railroads, airlines, freight forwarders, and mixed transportation companies. The Dow Jones utilities average is computed using 15 public utility stocks. The Dow Jones 65 stocks composite average is made up of the 30 industrials, the 20 transportations, and the 15 utilities. Like the DJIA, each of the other Dow Jones averages is calculated in a fashion that allows for continuity of the average over time. The transportation, utilities, and 65 stocks composite average are often cited in the financial news along with the DJIA.

Standard & Poor's (S&P's) Indexes

Standard & Poor's indexes
true indexes that measure the current price of a group of stocks relative to a base established for the 1941–1943 period, which has an index value of 10.

Standard & Poor's Corporation, another major financial publisher, publishes five common stock indexes. Unlike the Dow Jones averages, **Standard & Poor's in-**

dexes are true indexes. They relate the current price of a group of stocks to a base established for the 1941–1943 period, which has an index value of 10. In other words, if an S&P index is currently 100, this means the average share prices of stock in the index has increased by the factor of 10 (100 ÷ 10) since the 1941–1943 period. A second way in which the S&P indexes differ from the Dow Jones averages is that whereas the Dow Jones averages weight each stock by its price, the S&P indexes consider the relative importance of each share in the marketplace. S&P accomplishes this by weighting each company's share price in its index by the *number of shares outstanding*. Although the Dow Jones averages are the most popular, many professional investors prefer S&P's indexes, since they are felt to reflect more accurately the price behavior of the market overall.

The five common stock indexes published by Standard & Poor's are the industrials, transportation, utilities, financials, and composite. The industrials index is made up of the common stock of 400 industrial firms; the transportation index includes the stock of 20 transportation companies; the utilities index is made up of 40 public utility stocks; the financials index contains 40 financial stocks; and the composite index consists of the total of 500 stocks included in the industrials, transportation, utilities, and financials indexes. Like the Dow, the S&P indexes are frequently quoted in the financial news.

Although the Dow Jones Averages and S&P's indexes tend to behave in a similar fashion over time, their day-to-day magnitude and even direction (up or down) can differ from one another significantly, since the Dows are averages and the S&P's are indexes. Take the industrials, for example: On April 26, 1989, the DJIA was 2389.11, and the S&P 400 was 353.98. Although the DJIA increased 29.88 points the following day, the S&P 400 increased only 2.84 points. However, the magnitude of these changes is brought into perspective when viewed in relation to the absolute size of the average or index. For example, on April 27, 1989, the DJIA increased by 1.24 percent (29.88 ÷ 2389.11), and the S&P 400 increased by 0.80 percent (2.84 ÷ 353.98).

NYSE, AMEX, and NASDAQ Indexes

Three exchange-based indexes are the New York Stock Exchange (NYSE), the American Stock Exchange (AMEX), and the National Association of Securities Dealers Automated Quotation (NASDAQ). The **NYSE index** includes all of the over 2,200 stocks listed on the "big board" (another name for the New York Stock Exchange). It is calculated in a way similar to that used for the S&P indexes. The base of 50 reflects the December 31, 1965, value of stocks listed on the NYSE. In addition to the composite index, the NYSE also publishes indexes for industrials, utilities, transportation, and finance subgroups. The behavior of the NYSE industrial index will normally be quite similar to that of the DJIA and the S&P 400 indexes.

The **AMEX index** reflects the price of shares on the American Stock Exchange relative to a base of 100, which is set at August 31, 1973. The AMEX index is based on all stocks trading on the exchange and is calculated by a method similar to that used for the S&P indexes. Although it may not always closely follow the S&P

NYSE index
measure of the current price behavior of the stocks listed on the NYSE in relation to a base of 50, set 12/31/65.

AMEX index
measure of the current price behavior of stocks listed on the AMEX, relative to a base of 100, set 8/31/73.

or NYSE indexes, the AMEX index does tend to behave in a fashion similar to those mentioned earlier. Like the NYSE indexes, the AMEX index is often cited in the financial news.

NASDAQ indexes
measures of current price behavior of securities sold OTC.

The **NASDAQ indexes,** which reflect over-the-counter market activity, are calculated like the S&P, NYSE, and AMEX indexes. They are based on a value of 100 set February 5, 1971. The most comprehensive of the NASDAQ indexes is the OTC composite index, which is calculated using more than 4,200 domestic common stocks traded on the NASDAQ system. The other five commonly quoted NASDAQ indexes are the industrials, the insurance, the banks, the national market composite, and the national market industrials. Although their degrees of responsiveness may vary, the NASDAQ indexes tend to move in the same direction at the same time as the other major indexes.

Value Line Averages

Value Line composite average
a stock average, published by Value Line, that reflects the percentage changes in share price of about 1,700 stocks traded on the NYSE, AMEX, and OTC market relative to a base of 100, set 6/30/61.

Value Line publishes a number of stock averages constructed by equally weighting the prices of each stock included within them. This is accomplished by considering only the percentage changes in stock prices. This approach is appealing since it eliminates the effects of differing market price and total market value on the relative importance of each stock included in the average. Instead the average captures only the effects of *changes* in share prices. The **Value Line composite average** includes the approximately 1,700 stocks in the *Value Line Investment Survey* and traded on the NYSE, AMEX, and OTC market. The base of 100 reflects the June 30, 1961, average of the stocks. In addition to its composite average, Value Line publishes averages for industrials, rails, and utilities. These averages are especially appealing to individual investors because they include stocks that are likely to be held in their portfolios.

Other Averages and Indexes

Wilshire 5000 Index
measure of the total dollar value (in billions) of 5,000 actively traded stocks, including all those on the NYSE and the AMEX, plus active OTC stocks.

In addition to the major indexes just described, a number of others are available. The **Wilshire 5000 Index,** published by Wilshire Associates, Inc., is reported daily in *The Wall Street Journal*. It represents the total dollar value (in billions of dollars) of 5,000 actively traded stocks, including all those on the NYSE and AMEX in addition to active OTC stocks. *Barron's* publishes a 50-Stock Average and a Low-Price Stock Index. *The New York Times* publishes its own average, which is quite similar to the Dow Jones averages. And Moody's Investors Services prepares market indicators for a variety of groupings of common stock. Each of these averages and indexes, like the major ones, reflects the general behavior of all the securities markets or a specific segment of them.

Bond Market Indicators

A number of bond market indicators are available for assessing the general behavior of these markets. However, because the individual investor is less likely to trade bonds in the same way as stocks, there are not nearly as many indicators of overall bond market behavior. The key measures are bond yields, the Dow Jones bond averages, and the New York Stock Exchange bond statistics.

Bond Yields

Bond yields indicate the behavior of market interest rates and represent a type of summary measure of the return an investor would receive on a bond if it were held to maturity. They are reported as an annual rate of return; for example, a bond with a yield of 9.50 percent will provide its owner with a return in the form of periodic interest *and* capital gain or loss that would be equivalent to a 9.50 percent annual rate of earnings on the amount invested, if held to maturity. Typically, bond yields are quoted for a group of bonds that are similar with respect to type and quality of issuer, bond maturity, and so on. For example, *Barron's* quotes the average yields for the Dow Jones 10 utilities, 10 industrials, 20 bond composites, as well as for other groups of Treasury and municipal bonds. The yields quoted by *Barron's* for the week ended April 28, 1989, were 10.03 percent for utilities, 10.13 percent for industrials, and 10.08 percent for the composite. Similar bond yield data are also available from S&P, Moody's, and the Federal Reserve. Like stock market averages and indexes, bond yield data are especially useful when viewed over time; studying the trend in bond yields can help the investor time purchases and sales effectively.

Dow Jones Bond Averages

The **Dow Jones bond averages** include a utility, industrial, and a composite bond average. Each average reflects the simple mathematical average of the closing prices rather than yields for each group of bonds included. The utility bond average is based on the closing prices of 10 utility bonds; the industrial bond average is based on the closing prices of 10 industrial bonds; and the composite bond average is based on the closing prices of 10 utility and 10 industrial bonds. Like bond price quotations, the bond averages are presented in terms of the percentage of face value at which the bond sells. For example, the April 28, 1989, Dow Jones composite bond average of 89.02 indicates that, on average, bonds were, on the day reported, selling for 89.02 percent of their face or maturity value; for a $1,000 bond that means the average price of an issue would equal about $890.20. The Dow Jones bond averages are published daily in *The Wall Street Journal* and are summarized on a weekly basis in *Barron's*.

New York Stock Exchange Bond Statistics

The New York Stock Exchange is the dominant organized exchange on which bonds are traded, so certain summary statistics on daily bond-trading activity on the NYSE provide useful insight into the behavior of the bond markets in general. These statistics include the number of issues traded; the number that advanced, declined, or remained unchanged; the number of new highs and new lows; and total sales volume in dollars. For example, on April 28, 1989, 629 domestic issues were traded; 285 advanced; 198 declined; and 146 remained unchanged. Of the issues traded, 16 achieved new price highs for the year, and 16 fell to the new price lows. Total sales volume was $30,900,000. NYSE bond statistics are published daily in *The Wall Street Journal,* and a weekly summary can be found in *Barron's*.

TABLE 3.2   Investments Included in *Money*'s Small Investor Index

Type of Investment	Percent of Portfolio
NYSE stocks	21.3%
AMEX/OTC stocks	6.7
Stock mutual funds	3.3
Taxable bonds	13.3
Municipal bonds	5.8
Bond mutual funds	4.1
Certificates of deposit	28.0
Money market funds	16.0
Real estate (excludes residences)	.9
Gold	.6
Total Portfolio	100.0%

Small Investor's Portfolio Index

Small Investor Index
a index that measures gains and losses of the average investor relative to a base of 100 set on 12/31/87; based on a portfolio including types of investments held by average small investors.

Money magazine's **Small Investor Index** can be used to measure the average investor's gains and losses. The index is based on a value of 100 set on December 31, 1987, and is reported weekly each Monday in *USA Today* and monthly as part of *Money's* "Investor's Scorecard." The small investor index is based on a portfolio that includes ten types of investments held in proportions consistent with Federal Reserve data on what the average household owns. The investments included and their proportions in the small investor's portfolio are shown in Table 3.2.

The value of the index on March 31, 1989 was 112.80, which reflected a 0.60% gain for the month and an 8.77% gain over a year earlier. Although this index is not widely used on Wall Street, its importance lies in the fact that it provides the individual investor with a standard against which he or she can assess both the composition and performance of his or her portfolio.

INVESTMENT ADVISORS

In spite of the fact that there are numerous sources of financial information available, many investors have neither the time nor the expertise to analyze this information and make decisions on their own. Instead, they use some type of investment advisor. **Investment advisors** are individuals or firms that provide investment advice—typically for a fee—to clients. They provide services ranging from recommendations on investment vehicles and strategies to complete money management, which might include financial planning, tax return preparation, and so on.

investment advisors
individuals or firms that provide investment advice, usually for a fee.

The Advisor's Product

The "product" provided by investment advisors ranges from broad general advice to specific detailed analyses and recommendations. The most general form of ad-

vice is a newsletter published by the advisor and provided to clients. These letters offer general advice on the economy, current events, market behavior, and specific securities. Investment advisors also provide complete investment evaluation, recommendation, and management services. For a fee they will evaluate an investor's objectives, financial resources, and current investment portfolio, and suggest a recommended course of action. In some cases the advisor is given total discretion over the client's portfolio.

Regulation of Advisors

As we pointed out in Chapter 2, the Investment Advisors Act of 1940 was passed in order to ensure that investment advisors make full disclosure of information about their backgrounds, conflicts of interest, and so on. The act requires professional advisors to register and file periodic reports with the SEC. A 1960 amendment extended the SEC's powers to permit it to inspect the records of investment advisors and to revoke the registration of those who violate the act's provisions. Persons such as financial planners, stockbrokers, bankers, and accountants, who provide investment advice in addition to their main professional activity, are not regulated by the act.

As additional protection many states have passed similar legislation requiring investment advisors to register and abide by the guidelines established by the state law. The federal and state laws regulating the activities of professional investment advisors do not guarantee *competence;* rather, they are intended to protect the investor against fraudulent and unethical practices. It is important to recognize that, at present, *no* law or regulatory body controls entrance into the field. Therefore investment advisors can range from the highly informed professional to the totally incompetent amateur. Advisors possessing a professional designation such as CFA (Chartered Financial Analyst), CIC (Chartered Investment Counselor), CFP (Certified Financial Planner), ChFC (Chartered Financial Consultant), CLU (Chartered Life Underwriter), or CPA (Certified Public Accountant) are usually preferred because they have completed academic courses in areas directly or peripherally related to the investment process. Appendix C provides a guide to these professional certification programs; for each program it describes the certification, the enrollment prerequisites, and the required course of study, and it includes contact information.

Types of Advisors

Investment advisors come from the ranks of financial planners, stockbrokers, bankers, subscription services, and individual advisors and advisory firms.

Financial Planners

financial planner
a professional advisor who works with a client to develop a financial plan or strategy.

A **financial planner** works with an individual client to develop a financial plan or strategy. **Personal financial planning** is the process by which all of a person's assets, liabilities, and sources of income are so arranged as to maximize the achievement of his or her financial goals and objectives. The financial planner identifies the client's financial objectives, collects and assesses all relevant data, develops a written plan, assists in implementing it, and periodically reviews and

personal financial planning
the process by which a person's assets, liabilities, and sources of income are so arranged as to maximize the achievement of their financial goals and objectives.

revises the plan as conditions warrant. For these services the planner receives specific fees for services rendered and/or a commission on products, such as insurance, investments, and legal services, provided by or through them. Today most professional financial planners possess either the CFP or ChFC designation or both.

Stockbrokers

The primary role of the stockbroker is to make purchase and sale transactions on behalf of clients. In exchange for this service, brokers are paid a commission that is their primary source of income. Stockbrokers also provide clients with information and advice. Many brokers will analyze a client's portfolio and make recommendations as to how the portfolio might be changed to better conform with the investor's goals. Although information provided to clients is generally free, portfolio analysis and advice are often provided on a fee basis. As noted in Chapter 2, a *wrap account* can be established with a stockbroker to shift the burden of stock selection to a professional money manager. These accounts typically require minimum portfolios of $100,000 and charge a flat annual fee of between 2 and 3 percent of the portfolio's total asset value to cover the cost of commissions on all trades in addition to professional management.

Bankers

Bankers, like stockbrokers, commonly provide investment advice to their customers. Such advice generally comes from trust officers, whose activities involve investing funds held in trust for customers. The degree of involvement of the bank may range from strict bookkeeping, in which the bank may act as custodian for the investor's securities, to managing (often as part of a trust agreement) an individual's investments.

Typically, if the bank is to become involved in keeping records, advising, or actually managing an individual's investments, a minimum portfolio of $40,000 to $50,000 is required. Because banks tend to recommend higher-quality investments, their advice and management activities tend to be rather conservative. Over the past few years more and more banks seem to have established investment advisory departments, which for a fee will manage the investment portfolio of the small investor. A similar trend seems to be occurring in brokerage firms as well.

Subscription Services

Publishers of subscription services and investment letters offer advisory assistance to subscribers ranging from general advice on the economy, markets, or specific securities to periodic portfolio reviews and even active management of a subscriber's portfolio. For active management, an additional fee is charged. The amount of personal advice available as part of a subscription service or investment letter is clearly stated in advance, as are services available on a fee basis.

Individual Advisors and Advisory Firms

For a fee individual advisors will manage the investment portfolios of clients. These people are paid to stay abreast of tax laws and market developments and to use this

knowledge to fulfill their clients' investment goals. Individual advisors usually do not accept many clients and are therefore quite selective. They will sometimes agree to manage a client's portfolio only on a *discretionary basis,* which means that they are given complete control of the portfolio; more often, however, they will provide advice and recommendations directly to clients as developments unfold or opportunities arise.

On a larger scale, investment advisory firms deal primarily in the sale of advisory services. These operations have staffs of researchers and advisors, many of whom hold the CFA designation, each specializing in certain types of portfolios. Some advisors may be specialists in managing large, growth-oriented portfolios; others may concentrate on more conservative, income-oriented portfolios. Often these firms will use computer-based models and other sophisticated investment strategies. Clients are assigned to staff members on the basis of the size and objectives of their portfolios. Although these firms prefer to manage portfolios on a discretionary basis, clients can arrange to have final approval of any changes. Advisory firms, like individual advisors, tend to accept accounts with total funds of $100,000 or more, and unlike financial planners, tend to deal strictly in investment matters.

The Cost of Investment Advice

Professional investment advice typically costs between ¼ of 1 percent and 2 percent annually of the amount of money being managed. For large portfolios, the fee is typically in the range of ¼ to ¾ percent. For small portfolios (less than $100,000) an annual fee ranging from 1 to 2 percent of the amount of funds managed would not be unusual. These fees generally cover complete management of a client's money, excluding, of course, any purchase or sale commissions; the cost of periodic investment advice not provided as part of a subscription service could be based on a fixed-fee schedule or quoted as an hourly charge for consultation.

Effective Use of Investment Advice

Like most services, some investment advisory services are better than others. In many cases a less expensive service may provide better advice than a more expensive one. It is best to study carefully the "track record" and overall reputation of an investment advisor prior to purchasing its services. Not only should the advisor have a good performance record, but it is important that he or she be responsive to the investor's personal goals. A careful assessment of the costs and potential benefits of professional investment advice should be made and, if it appears to be economically justified, the investor should purchase the best quality advice available per dollar of cost.

Investment Clubs

In order to gain both investment advice and experience in constructing and managing a portfolio, many investors—especially those of moderate means—join an investment club. The **investment club** is a legal partnership binding a group of investors (partners) to a specified organizational structure, operating procedures, and purpose. The goal of most clubs is making investments in vehicles of moderate risk

investment club
a legal partnership through which a group of investors is bound to an organizational structure, operating procedures, and purpose—typically making moderate-risk investments to earn favorable long-run returns.

to earn favorable long-run returns; only rarely are investment clubs formed to make speculative investments.

Investment clubs are usually formed by a group of individuals having similar goals and wishing to pool their knowledge and money to create a jointly owned portfolio. The clubs are structured so that certain members are responsible for obtaining and analyzing data relative to a specific investment vehicle or strategy. At periodic meetings the members present their findings and recommendations, which are discussed and further analyzed by the membership which, as a group, decides whether or not the proposed vehicle or strategy should be pursued. Most clubs require members to make scheduled contributions to the club's treasury, thereby providing for periodic increases in the pool of investable funds. Although most clubs concentrate on investments in stocks and bonds, they are occasionally formed to invest in options, commodities, and real estate.

Membership in an investment club provides an excellent way for the new investor to learn the key aspects of portfolio construction and investment management, while (one hopes) earning a favorable return on funds. The National Association of Investors Corporation, which has about 7,000 affiliated clubs, publishes a variety of useful materials and also sponsors regional and national meetings providing information on club organization and activities as well as on emerging investment techniques and strategies. Most stockbrokers can provide information and assistance to those wishing to form or join an investment club. Moreover, with more investors turning to personal computers (our next topic) to assist them in making decisions, the investment club is an excellent arrangement for sharing common costs. A $500 software program may be too expensive for a single investor, but shared by 10 or more members of an investment club, the reduced cost per user makes it affordable. The Investor Insights box provides additional information on the benefit of investment club membership and the basic procedures for joining or starting one.

THE ROLE OF THE PERSONAL COMPUTER IN INVESTMENTS

The widespread availability of personal computers (PCs) and their use in the investment process was mentioned in Chapter 1. In this section we will briefly discuss the use of the PC in investment management and present detailed information about hardware, software, news/retrieval and databases, and the cost of using a PC.

A PC offers many personal, financial, and entertainment applications in addition to investing. It can be used in family budgeting, insurance planning, paying bills and monitoring checking accounts, storing data, playing video games, and more. Thus in deciding whether a PC is a worthwhile expenditure, one must also consider the value of these additional functions.

Using the PC in Investment Management

The use of personal computers in investment management both by institutional and individual investors is rapidly expanding. This recent growth is attributable to the widespread acceptance of PCs, declining hardware (equipment) costs, and the availability of numerous new and useful software (programs). Today software can be

INVESTOR INSIGHTS

Joining—or Starting—an Investment Club

. . . You might want to consider joining—or even starting—an investment club. Generally organized by 15 or so friends in the form of a partnership, the clubs offer a way to pool investment money and knowledge while at the same time lessening the anxiety level.

The benefits of membership are not restricted to stock picking, either. "Although the main purpose of our club is to become better educated on the stock market, we regularly invite speakers on other financial topics," said Ellen Quest, vice president of the 20/20 Investment Club in Denver. "That helps us to make better-informed decisions on financial matters beyond our club activities." For instance, a recent speaker reported on overall financial planning considerations.

"In a club atmosphere, you gain from other people's experience and investment ideas," said Ms. Quest, whose club is two years old.

And many of the clubs offer a social dividend as well. For example, the Minneapolis/St. Paul Council, a group representing investment clubs in that area, invites all the regional members each year to a wine and cheese party.

For all these reasons, club membership has held steady since Black Monday even as many individual investors quit the market, according to the National Association of Investors Corporation, a nonprofit group of investment clubs and individual investors. It estimates that there are nearly 29,000 investor clubs in the country, approximately one-fourth of which belong to the association.

The average club is more than nine years old and has an investment portfolio of nearly $110,000, the association says. The typical family income of members exceeds $61,000, and 84 percent of the members have a college education. About 25 percent are under 40 years of age and 29 percent are over 60; nearly two-thirds are men.

The association provides an informational package without charge on how to start a club. (Write to NAIC, 1515 East Eleven Mile Road, Royal Oak, Mich. 48067, or call 313 543-0612.) Membership in the association is not required to receive the materials. Should your club decide to join the group, there is a fee of $30 a year for the club plus $8 for each

purchased for use in maintaining investment records, evaluating companies and investment vehicles, accessing market data, selecting securities, monitoring security price and market movements, creating and managing portfolios, and applying a variety of investment trading strategies.

The potential benefit of the PC to investment management is its capacity to analyze and manipulate large amounts of data and immediately print or project results on a screen in the form of charts, tables, or graphs. This enables the investor to save valuable time while evaluating buying opportunities or selling situations quickly, graphically, and generally more accurately than with calculations performed by hand. Furthermore, the computer can be programmed to monitor the price and trading volume of stocks, and, based on these and other variables, apply

club member. Membership entitles the club to the monthly publication "Better Investing," a $25,000 fidelity bond and access to educational materials and programs.

   . . .

When starting a club, it is important to clearly define the responsibility of each club member and to select a time and place for regular meetings. The members also should develop a speakers' program, establish rules for entering and leaving the club, set methods and dates for portfolio valuation and agree on a policy for dividend distributions.

The club also needs to address the safeguarding of stocks and whether to register them in the club's name, the name of a bonded officer or in "street name" with the club's broker.

The club broker must be able to provide the level of service and information you desire at competitive commission rates. In addition, the Federal Government requires each club to obtain a tax identification number and file the appropriate tax forms. If the club is a partnership, the members must report their share of profits or losses on individual tax returns.

Perhaps most important, an overall investment philosophy should be agreed upon in advance to prevent major disagreements down the road.

The 20-member Break Even Plus Club uses the committee approach to keep the club running efficiently. Half the membership belongs to the stock selection committee, which decides on new purchases, while the other half is the portfolio committee, which monitors stock holdings to decide when to sell or buy more.

"We keep the interest up by keeping everyone involved in the investment process," said Mr. Ronallo. The National Association of Investors "helped us with a lot of investment ideas to form a solid base to do investigation on our own."

   . . .

Viewed from a long-term perspective, the steady, conservative approach of investment clubs appears to make sense.

"Over the past 25 years, investment clubs have outperformed the pros nearly 80 percent of the time," said Mark J. Appleman, an investor relations consultant based in New York.

The even-keel strategy of the clubs, and their heavy reliance on dollar cost averaging, pays off during all but consistent bull markets, when the pros have a performance edge.

Source: Richard T. Maturi, "Taking Stock of Investment Clubs," *The New York Times,* January 1, 1988, p. F-7.

program trading
use of a computer to monitor price and trading volume of stocks and to apply various rules to initiate trades and create or revise portfolios.

various rules to initiate trades and create or revise a portfolio consistent with specified objectives. This practice, known as **program trading,** has been used with increasing frequency by institutional investors in recent years. Clearly the use of a PC can add consistency to the investment management activity while allowing application of better and more sophisticated analyses and strategies quickly, and at a cost justifiable by the time saved and higher expected returns.

Hardware

hardware
the mechanical components of a computer system.

Hardware refers to the physical, or mechanical, components of a PC system. A critical question about hardware is the amount of memory the unit has—it must be enough to permit the investment applications the user has in mind. Smaller and less

TABLE 3.3   Retail Hardware Costs for a Complete and Reasonably Sophisticated PC System for Use in Investments (May 1989)

Hardware	Retail Cost
Computer unit (processor, keyboard, monitor, hard disk, 640K of internal memory)	$1,800
Printer (high quality with graphics capability)	400
Modem (allows connection to phone line)	200
Other (surge protector and 10 disks)	50
Total retail cost	$2,450

expensive PCs usually lack sufficient memory and therefore are not suitable. Before purchasing any system, one must determine how it will be used, both immediately and in the more distant future. One firm specializing in this area suggests the hardware and retail costs noted in Table 3.3 as appropriate to a complete and reasonably sophisticated system that will do investment applications adequately. These costs were based on competitive prices as of May 1989. This system would be capable of utilizing most of the software available at this time, and could be used to obtain security price quotes and other information from the Dow Jones News/Retrieval Service and to communicate with computer networks or on-line data bases.

Software

software
the programs that instruct a computer which functions to perform.

Without adequate software the computer is useless. **Software** consists of the programs that instruct the computer which functions it is to perform. With the increased use of PCs has come a proliferation of software programs catering to the specialized approaches used to evaluate individual securities and the market in general. Moreover, as PCs have become more "user friendly" (easier to understand and operate) investors are better able to design their own programs, which can perfectly match their evaluation models.

As of this writing, Dow Jones publishes a number of software programs that deal with common investment problems. Other companies also offer software. The three Dow Jones programs explained below illustrate the kinds of functions PCs perform. Although all the terms used may not be familiar to you yet, they indicate the very impressive capabilities of PCs. (You may wish to return to this discussion later in the course.)

Dow Jones Market Analyzer PLUS™

Dow Jones in its advertising describes this program as follows: "A technical analysis program [see Chapter 8] that collects up to 15 years of historical price and volume data from News/Retrieval to construct charts that reveal underlying trends

for individual stocks and the entire market. Has sorting and screening, user-assignable function keys, automated run, spreadsheet interface, portfolio management, and extensive charting capabilities.'' The suggested retail price of this program is $449.

Dow Jones Market Manager PLUS 2.0™

Dow Jones developed this program for three different levels of investors. The 2.0 version was developed for investment professionals and individual investors. Dow Jones advertisements describe it this way: ''For anyone who maintains one or more portfolios. It enables users to minimize tax liability, track commissions, monitor dividends, display reports, and access News/Retrieval. Includes tax-lot accounting and automatic price updating. Handles up to 256 portfolios and 1500 securities.'' The suggested retail price of the program (2.0) is $299. The less sophisticated version (1.0) costs $249, and the more sophisticated version (Professional) costs $499.

Dow Jones Spreadsheet Link™

This program is described as follows: ''Enables corporate planners, investors, researchers, and competitive analysts to extract data from News/Retrieval for extensive analysis with Lotus 1-2-3, Symphony, Multiplan, or VisiCalc. Increases the value of spreadsheets by linking them with key financial data. The program automatically logs on, collects specified data, and enters it into the spreadsheet for further analysis.'' The suggested retail price of this program is $249.

News/Retrieval and Databases

databases
organized collections of information, both historical and current.

Just as hardware is useless without software, PCs are not as useful without news/retrieval capabilities and **databases**—organized collections of historical as well as current information. Investment analyses, as will be demonstrated in Chapters 7 and 8, require considerable amounts of economic and financial information, and the more current it is, the better. (As you will notice when you become involved in the investment process, securities prices react quickly to unexpected news.)

Professional investors are in constant contact with many news sources, and they buy and/or sell securities almost automatically when important events take place. In addition to having access to current news, the PC owner can use this same news to update his or her database. Notice in the description of the Dow Jones Market Analyzer PLUS that it automatically collects historical price and volume data and uses it to update technical graphs and charts. As hardware and software become more available, so will news/retrieval systems. Currently Dow Jones is the undisputed leader in investment news/retrieval software. Table 3.4 summarizes the key investor information services available on Dow Jones News/Retrieval. The costs of these services depend on whether news is retrieved during prime or nonprime time. For instance, the Dow Jones Quotes cost $1.00 a minute in prime time and $0.20 a minute in nonprime time; the per-minute costs of most of the Business and Investor Services are $1.30 and $0.80, respectively. In addition, for individual subscribers there currently is a $30 one-time fee plus an annual service fee of $18, which is

TABLE 3.4   Summary of Key Investor Services Available on Dow Jones News/Retrieval

Business News

//DJNEWS   Dow Jones[SM] News
- Stories from the Dow Jones News Service® wire and selected, condensed stories from *The Wall Street Journal* and *Barron's*.
- As recent as 90 seconds and as far back as 90 days. Searched easily by company, industry or category.

//BUSINESS   Business and Finance Report
- Continuously updated business and financial news culled from *The Wall Street Journal,* Dow Jones News Service® and other newswires.
- The latest news on domestic and international economies.
- Cross referenced to related information in Dow Jones News/Retrieval.

//CMR   Capital Markets and Financial Futures Report[SM]
- Newswire providing current, comprehensive coverage of fixed-income and financial futures markets around the world.

//TEXT   Text-Search Services[SM]
- **The Wall Street Journal:** Full text of articles that appeared or were scheduled to appear in *The Wall Street Journal* since January 1984.
- **Dow Jones News:** Selected Dow Jones News Service wire stories and selected, condensed stories from *The Wall Street Journal* and *Barron's* since June 1979.
- **Barron's:** Full text of articles in *Barron's* since January 1987.
- **The Washington Post:** Full text of selected articles from *The Washington Post* since January 1984.
- **The Business Library:** Full text of selected articles from *Forbes, Fortune, Money, Inc., American Demographics, Financial World*, the full text of the PR Newswire and the Japan Economic Newswire since January 1985.
- **Business Dateline:** Full text of selected articles from more than 140 regional business journals since January 1985.
- **DataTimes:** Full text of articles from 13 regional newspapers, two Associated Press wires, *The Congressional Quarterly,* Gannett News Service and *USA Today*. (DataTimes is not included in the //TEXT ALL Command.)

//KYODO   Japan Economic Daily
- Same-day coverage of major Japanese business, financial and political news from the Kyodo News Service in Japan.

General News

//NEWS   News/Retrieval World Report[SM]
- Continuously updated national and international news from the Associated Press, Dow Jones News Service and broadcast media.

//SPORTS   News/Retrieval Sports Report[SM]
- Continuously updated stories, scores, stats, standings and schedules for most major sports.

//WTHR   News/Retrieval Weather Report[SM]
- Three day Accu-Weather® forecasts for more than 100 U.S. and foreign cities.

Company and Industry Statistics and Forecasts

//DSCLO   Disclosure® Online
- 10-K extracts, company profiles and other detailed data on over 12,000 publicly held companies from reports filed with the SEC and other sources.

//EPS   Zacks Corporate Earnings Estimator[SM]
- Consensus earnings-per-share estimates and P/E ratio forecasts for over 4,800 companies. Industry earnings estimates and lists of stocks outperforming or underperforming analysts' forecasts.

//INSIDER   Insider Trading Monitor
- Insider trading information on transactions of 100 shares or more for over 6,500 publicly held companies and nearly 60,000 individuals (corporate directors, officers or shareholders with more than 10% ownership).

//INVEST   Investext
- Full text of more than 20,000 research reports from top brokers, investment bankers and other analysts.
- Covers more than 4,000 U.S. and Canadian companies and 52 industries.
- Historical, current and forecasted marketing and financial information.

//MG   Media General Financial Services
- Detailed financial information on 5,400 companies and 180 industries.
- Major categories include: revenue, earnings, dividends, volume, ratio, shareholdings, and price changes.
- Compare 2 different companies, company versus industry or industry versus industry data on the same screen.

//MMS   MMS Weekly Market Analysis[SM]
- Weekly survey of U.S. money market and foreign exchange trends.
- Median forecasts of monetary and economic indicators.
- Weekly analyses of debt, currency and equity markets.

//SP   Standard & Poor's Online®
- Concise profiles of 4,700 companies containing

TABLE 3.4 *(continued)*

earnings, dividends and market figures for the past four years.
• Corporate overviews plus S&P earnings estimates for most major companies.

Company Profiles and Reports

//QUICK   **Dow Jones**[SM] **QuickSearch**
• One command will generate a complete corporate report drawing information from multiple Dow Jones News/Retrieval sources.

//TRACK   **Tracking Service**[SM]
• Create customized portfolios of up to 125 companies and industries and automatically track news and quotes.

Quotes and Market Averages

//CQE   **Enhanced Current Quotes**
Minimum 15-minute delay during market hours)
• Quotes on common stocks (with **News Alert** feature).
• Preferred stocks, warrants, corporate and foreign bonds, mutual funds, U.S. Treasury issues and options.

//HQ   **Historical Quotes**
• Daily high, low, close and volume for stock prices and composites.
• Monthly stock price summaries back to 1979; quarterly summaries back to 1978.

//FUTURES   **Futures Quotes**
• Current (10-30 minute delay) and historical quotes for more than 80 commodities from the major North American exchanges updated continuously during market hours.
• Daily open, high, low, last and settlement prices.
• Daily volume and open interest, lifetime high and low.

//DJA   **Historical Dow Jones Averages**®
• Historical averages including daily high, low, close and volume available for the last trading year for industrials, transportation, utilities, and 65-stock composite indexes.

//FIDELITY   **Fidelity Investor's Express**
• Place trades online for listed securities with Fidelity discount brokerage.
• Organize your portfolios and monitor your investments with a Fidelity Investor's Express account.

Business Services

//OAG   **Official Airline Guide**®
• Airline schedules and fares for 600 airlines worldwide.
• Hotel and motel information.

//MCI   **MCI Mail**®
• Electronic mail service for sending printed and electronic communications next door or worldwide.

//WSW   **Wall $treet Week**[SM] **Online**
• Four most recent transcripts of the popular PBS television program Wall $treet Week.

General Services

//STORE   **Comp-u-store Online**®
• An electronic shopping service with more than 250,000 discounted brand-name products ranging from appliances and sporting goods to gourmet foods.

//ENCYC   **Academic American Encyclopedia**®
• More than 32,000 carefully researched and concisely written articles covering industry and finance as well as academic subject areas.
• Updated quarterly.

//SCHOOL   **Peterson's College Selection Service**[SM]
• Peterson's Guide to two- and four-year colleges and universities.
• Search by size, entrance difficulty, location, cost, financial aid and majors.

//MOVIES   **Cineman Movie Reviews**
• Reviews of the latest releases as well as thousands of movies dating back to 1926.

//BOOKS   **Magill Book Reviews**
• Reviews of recent fiction and non-fiction works with new titles added weekly.

Online Reference Tools

//FYI   **For Your Information**
• **Free** online newsletter for News/Retrieval members.
• New database announcements, enhancements, rate changes, free-time offers, online user's agreement and other important information.

//MENU   **Master Menu**
• A complete listing of the information contained in the service, along with instructions on how to access each database.

//SYMBOL   **News/Retrieval Symbols Directory**[SM]
• A comprehensive online listing of the symbols and codes used to access Dow Jones News/Retrieval services.
• Updated daily.

//DEFINE   **Words of Wall Street**[SM]
• Definitions of over 2,000 business and financial terms used by professional investors.

Source: Dow Jones News/Retrieval *Summary of Information Services,* May 1989.

waived in the first year. (Note that Dow Jones makes special rates available to academic institutions.)

In addition to the software discussed here, there are a variety of other investment-oriented computer programs reviewed at the end of each of the six parts of this book (see, for example, pages 211–213). Entitled *Computer-Based Investment Management,* these sections provide brief overviews of ways computers can be used in the management of investments and descriptions of some popular investment software.

Annual Cost of Using a PC

If we take the cost estimate for hardware given in Table 3.3 and assume the three Dow Jones software programs described above are purchased, along with a subscription to the News/Retrieval service, a user's total investment would be $2,450 + $1,027 = $3,477. As a rough estimate of the annual cost, we might assume the hardware would last five years and may be worth, say, $600 at the end of that period. Annual depreciation can then be estimated at about $370 ($1,850 ÷ 5). Assuming software has a perpetual life (this might be unrealistic if better programs become available), and allowing an interest rate of, say, 10 percent, would add an annual opportunity cost (what could be earned on the money in a similar-risk alternative investment) of about $350 (0.10 × $3,477). Finally, assuming news/retrieval costs are $280 a year, the estimated annual cost before taxes for the system would be as follows:

Item	Annual cost
Depreciation	$ 370
Opportunity cost	350
News/retrieval	280
Total annual cost	$1,000

Is the system worth this annual cost? That depends, of course, on whether or not the investor can increase his or her annual dollar return by an amount greater than this cost. This, in turn, depends on the size of the investor's portfolio. If the total amount in the portfolio is relatively small—for example, $5,000—it would seem almost impossible to justify an annual cost of $1,000. On the other hand, if the portfolio has, say, $50,000 to $100,000 of securities, the PC system may well be worthwhile. However, remember that services of a professional investment advisor can be purchased for an annual fee of 1 to 2 percent of the portfolio value. Assuming a 2 percent fee, at about $50,000 ($1,000 ÷ .02), the investor would incur an equal annual cost with either the PC or the professional investment advisor—*as long as* the investor, aided by the PC, can do as well as the professional. If his or her performance is below the professional's, then that must be considered an added cost of using the PC. Of course it is also possible that the investor might do better than the professional; and if the hardware has additional uses, this should also be considered in the decision. Furthermore, all available tax benefits accruing from

either alternative—use of a PC for managing investments or use of a professional investment advisor—should be considered when comparing annual costs.

SUMMARY

- Investment information can be descriptive or analytical, and it is likely to vary in quality. Investment information can be classified as economic and current events; industry and company; alternative investment vehicles; price information; and personal investment strategies.

- The key sources of economic and current event information include the financial journals such as *The Wall Street Journal* and general newspapers such as *USA Today,* business periodicals such as *Business Week* and *Forbes,* and special subscription services such as the *Kiplinger Washington Letter.*

- Industry and company information can be found in trade publications, stockholder's reports, and subscription services. The major subscription services are published by Standard and Poor's Corporation, Moody's Investors Services, and the *Value Line Investment Survey.* The costs of these services vary; many can be used at no charge at a brokerage firm or public or university library.

- Brokerage firms provide prospectuses as well as back-office research reports at no cost to clients. Investment letters, which provide analytical data along with the conclusions and recommendations of experts, are also available on a subscription basis.

- Information on specific security prices and returns can be obtained from a variety of sources. Price quotations can be obtained from a stockbroker or from the financial news. The most comprehensive and up-to-date quotations are published in *The Wall Street Journal, Barron's,* and *Investor's Daily.*

- Investors commonly rely on stock market averages and indexes to stay abreast of market behavior. The most cited averages are the Dow Jones, which includes the Dow Jones Industrial Average (DJIA). Other popular averages and indexes are Standard & Poor's, the New York Stock Exchange index, the American Stock Exchange index, the NASDAQ indexes, and the Value Line averages.

- Bond market indicators are most often reported in terms of average bond yields and average prices. The Dow Jones bond averages are among the most popular. Both stock and bond market statistics are published daily in *The Wall Street Journal* and summarized weekly in *Barron's.*

- *Money* magazine's Small Investor Index, published weekly in *USA Today* and in each issue of *Money,* provides the individual investor with a standard that can be used to assess the composition and performance of his or her portfolio.

- Investment advisors are usually financial planners, stockbrokers, bankers, subscription services, individual advisors, or advisory firms. They may charge an annual fee ranging from ¼ of 1 percent to 2 percent of the amount being

managed and often are regulated by federal and state law. Investment clubs are used by individual investors to obtain investment advice and experience.

- Personal computers (PCs) can be effectively used in investment management. PC systems consist of hardware, software, and news/retrieval and data bases. Dow Jones publishes a number of software programs dealing with common investment problems. The effective use of a PC may permit the investor to perform the functions of an investment advisor at a reduced cost.

REVIEW QUESTIONS AND PROBLEMS

1. Define and differentiate between the following types of information:
    a. Descriptive.
    b. Analytical.

2. Explain how one might logically assess whether or not the acquisition of investment information or advice is economically justified. Be sure to discuss the following as part of your answer:
    a. Benefits.
    b. Costs.
    c. Quality of information.

3. List and briefly discuss a few of the more popular financial business periodicals providing
    a. Financial news.
    b. General news.
    c. Business news.

4. Describe the role played by special subscription services in providing insight into general business and economic conditions.

5. Briefly describe the following sources of company information. Indicate the types of information available from each source.
    a. Stockholder's report.
    b. Form 10-K.
    c. Standard & Poor's *Stock Reports*.
    d. Moody's *Handbook of Common Stocks*.

6. List and briefly describe the subscription services available from
    a. Standard & Poor's Corporation.
    b. Moody's Investors Services.
    c. *Value Line Investment Survey*.

7. Describe the type of information and associated cost available from
    a. Prospectuses.
    b. Back-office brokerage research.
    c. Investment letters.

8. What are security quotations? Describe the various sources of security quotations available to the individual investor.

9. Describe the basic philosophy and use of stock market averages and indexes. Explain how the

behavior of an average or index can be used to classify general market conditions as bull or bear.

10. List each of the major averages or indexes prepared by (1) Dow Jones and Company and (2) Standard & Poor's Corporation. Indicate the number and source of the securities used in calculating each average or index. Where are these averages and indexes most easily found? Explain.

11. Briefly describe the composition and general thrust of each of the following indexes:

    a. New York Stock Exchange indexes.
    b. American Stock Exchange index.
    c. NASDAQ indexes.
    d. Value Line composite average.

12. Discuss each of the following as they relate to assessing bond market conditions:

    a. Bond yields.
    b. Dow Jones bond averages.
    c. New York Stock Exchange bond statistics.

13. Briefly describe *Money's* Small Investor Index. How might an individual investor use this index to evaluate his or her portfolio?

14. What is personal financial planning? What is a financial planner? What role might he or she play in providing investment advice?

15. Discuss the role of each of the following in providing investment advice:

    a. Stockbrokers.
    b. Bankers.
    c. Subscription services.
    d. Individual advisors and advisory firms.

16. What is the range of cost for investment advice, and what type of minimum portfolio sizes do professional investment advisors require? How should the decision to purchase investment advice be made? Explain.

17. What is an investment club? What benefits does it offer the small investor?

18. What has caused the rapid growth in the use of personal computers (PCs) in investment management in recent years? How are PCs used by investors? What are program trades?

19. Explain how hardware, software, and news/retrieval and databases are used in personal computer (PC) systems. What factors need to be considered before you invest in a PC system? Would you advise the purchase of a PC for an investor managing a $5,000 portfolio? Discuss.

CASE PROBLEMS

3.1 A Reading Program for Harry

Harry Mack recently graduated from a large West Coast university with a degree in communications and has accepted a job with Allen Brothers, a large San Francisco advertising agency. During his senior year, at the advice of a close friend, Harry took an elective course called ''Basic Investments.'' He found the course, which was taught by Alex Krok, a multi-

millionaire who only 20 years earlier had come to the United States as a poor Russian immigrant, most enlightening. Harry hoped that, like Professor Krok, he too could some day make a great fortune in the securities markets.

Now that he has settled into his new job, Harry wishes to gain practical experience in monitoring economic and current events as well as following the general behavior of the securities markets. He plans to spend the next two to three years gaining general familiarity with economic and market activity prior to attempting to choose the best securities in which to invest. Harry feels that such familiarity will help him choose securities when he has actually accumulated sufficient funds to make investments. Although he knows that the odds are against his achieving great wealth through security investments, Harry strongly believes that by gaining economic and market familiarity over the next few years, he will enhance his chances of success. Harry's plans center around reading economic and business articles and following various indicators of market activity. The only constraints facing Harry are a budget of $250 per year and about 12 hours per week of reading time.

Questions
1. List and describe the major sources of financial news available to Harry.
2. List and describe the key periodicals Harry may wish to consider, assuming he is interested only in stock and bond investments.
3. Explain to Harry how each of the following might be used to stay abreast of the stock and bond markets and the small investor's portfolio. Recommend specific averages and indexes he might want to watch. Explain.
    a. Stock market averages and indexes.
    b. Bond market indicators.
    c. Money's *Small Investor Index*.
4. In light of Harry's objective, and given his budget and time constraints, recommend a regular reading program. Mention specific publications and point out the parts of them Harry should read. Be sure to explain why you are making such recommendations.

3.2   A Rich Uncle—The Perezes' Good Fortune

Angel and Marie Perez own a small pool hall located in southern New Jersey. They enjoy running the business, which they have owned for nearly three years. Angel, a retired professional pool shooter, saved for nearly 10 years to buy this business, which he and his wife own free and clear. The income from the pool hall is adequate to allow Angel, Marie, and their two children, Mary (age 10) and José (age 4), to live comfortably. Although lacking any formal education beyond the tenth grade, Angel has become an avid reader. He enjoys reading about current events and consumer affairs. He especially likes *Consumer Reports*, from which he has gained numerous insights for making various purchase transactions. Because of the long hours required to run the business, Angel can devote three to four hours a day (on the job) to reading.

Recently Angel and Marie were notified that Marie's uncle had died and left them a portfolio of stocks and bonds having a current market value of $300,000. They were elated to learn of their good fortune, but decided it would be best not to change their life style as a result of this inheritance. Instead, they wanted their new-found wealth to provide for their children's college education as well as their own retirement. They decided that like their uncle, they would keep these funds invested in stocks and bonds. Angel felt that in view of this, he needed to acquaint himself with the securities currently in the portfolio. He knew that if he were to manage the portfolio himself, he would have to stay abreast of the securities markets as well as the economy in general. He also realized he would need to follow each

security in the portfolio and continuously evaluate possible alternative securities which could be substituted as conditions warranted. Because Angel had plenty of time in which to follow the market, he strongly believed that with proper information, he could manage the portfolio. Because of the amount of money involved, Angel was not too concerned with the information costs; rather, he wanted the best information he could get at a reasonable price.

Questions

1. Explain what role *The Wall Street Journal* and/or *Barron's* might play in fulfilling Angel's needs. What other general sources of economic and current event information might you recommend to Angel? Explain.

2. How might Angel be able to use the services of Standard & Poor's Corporation, Moody's Investors Services, and/or *Value Line Investment Survey* in order to acquaint himself with securities in the portfolio? Indicate which, if any, of these services you would recommend, and why.

3. Explain to Angel the need to find a good stockbroker and the role the stockbroker could play in providing information and advice.

4. Describe the services and sources of investment advice available to Angel. Would you recommend that he hire an advisor to manage the portfolio for him? Explain the potential costs and benefits of such an alternative.

5. Give Angel a summary prescription for obtaining information and advice that will help to ensure the preservation and growth of Marie's and his new-found wealth.

SELECTED READINGS

American Association of Individual Investors. *The Individual Investor's Microcomputer Resource Guide,* 6th edition. Chicago: International Publishing Corporation, 1988.

Geise, William. "The 'Club' for Do-It-Yourself Investors." *Changing Times,* December 1988, pp. 73–77.

Kichen, Steve. "Investing by the Numbers." *Forbes,* June 27, 1988, pp. 196–198.

Lesko, Matthew. *The Investor's Information Sourcebook.* New York: Harper & Row, Publishers, 1988.

Paulson, Morton C. "You Know All About the Dow. But Did You Know It's One of the Least Useful Indexes?" *Changing Times,* December 1988, p. 19.

Peers, Alexandra. "Keep Registration for Small Advisers, Critics of SEC Say." *The Wall Street Journal,* February 1, 1989, p. C1.

Schiffres, Manuel. "How to Know What the Pros Know." *Changing Times,* October 1988, p. 107.

Smith, Priscilla Ann. "Gearing Up: More Small Investors Turn to Computers for Assistance." *The Wall Street Journal,* June 25, 1987, p. 27.

Updegrave, Walter L. "How to Launch an Investment Club." *Money,* May 1989, pp. 117–25.

Walbert, Laura R. "Shopping For Advice." *Forbes,* June 27, 1988, pp. 260–62.

4

DEVELOPING INVESTMENT STRATEGIES

After studying this chapter you should be able to:

● Describe common investment goals and the role of life insurance in the investment program.

● Explain the methods used to establish an investment program and note how the process of investing changes in different economic environments and over the life cycle.

● Summarize the basic sources of taxation, the types of taxable income, and the potential impact of each on the investor.

● Understand the role of liquidity and the basic considerations surrounding the selection of short-term securities to meet liquidity needs.

● Identify the respective merits and suitability of popular short-term investments, including their availability, safety, liquidity, and yields.

● Discuss the role of retirement planning and the basic types of retirement programs, including self-directed Keoghs and IRAs.

A ship at sea can be directed toward its desired destination only with appropriate navigational aids and expertise. Correspondingly, the achievement of your financial goals in life can be reached only through the use of carefully selected investment strategies and techniques. First, attention must be given to providing for various contingencies through life insurance and through an understanding of the effects of a changing economic environment and life cycle. In addition, the investor must have a knowledge of various taxes and their potential impact on investment returns. Maintaining an adequate level of liquidity and planning for retirement are also important to the development of a successful investment program. Investors need some degree of liquidity to keep their options open and to meet unforeseen emergencies; at the same time, a part of the portfolio should be set aside to provide income for retirement. In order to develop investment strategies, investors must establish goals and plans in light of tax laws, liquidity needs, and retirement goals. We begin this chapter by examining investment goals and plans.

INVESTMENT GOALS AND PLANS

investment plan
a written document describing investment goals, how funds will be invested, the target date for the accomplishment of goals, and the amount of tolerable risk.

Establishing investment goals consistent with overall financial objectives is important. Once such goals have been established, an **investment plan,** a written document describing how funds will be invested, should be developed. For each goal, the target date for its achievement and the amount of tolerable risk must be specified. Generally the more important the financial objective, the less the risk that should be assumed. Investment plans must be developed in a manner that considers taxes, and with adequate provision for life insurance coverage and liquidity. Here we discuss investment goals, life insurance needs, the investment program, and economic and life cycle considerations.

Investment Goals

investment plan
a written document describing investment goals, how funds will be invested, the target date for the accomplishment of goals, and the amount of tolerable risk.

Investment goals are the financial objectives that one wishes to achieve by investing in any of a wide range of potential investment vehicles. Clearly your investment goals will determine the types of investments you will make. Common investment goals include (1) enhancing current income; (2) saving for major expenditures; (3) accumulating retirement funds; and (4) sheltering income from taxes.

Current Income

The ability of an investment to enhance current income depends on the amount of income, usually dividends or interest, that it can bring in. Retired individuals frequently choose investments offering *high current income at low risk,* since their other sources of retirement income probably total less than their level of pre-retirement income. The idea of a retired person ''clipping coupons'' from high-yield bonds is a fair description of what most senior citizens *should* be doing at that point in their lives.

Another common reason for seeking supplemental current income is the need for extended, costly medical care. Even after insurance, such recurring costs can burden a family budget heavily unless the latter is supplemented by additional income.

Major Expenditures

Families often put money aside over the years in order to accumulate the funds necessary for making a few major expenditures. The most common of these are (1) the down payment on a home; (2) college education for one's children; (3) an expensive, perhaps "once-in-a-lifetime," vacation; (4) building up enough capital to start one's own business; and (5) the purchase of a very special item (perhaps jewelry or an antique). Once the amount of money needed is known, the appropriate types of investment vehicles can be selected. For example, a low-risk approach would be to make a single lump-sum investment in a bond that matures in the year in which the funds are needed. Alternatively, a more risky plan would call for investing a specific amount over time in, say, a growth-oriented mutual fund, where there is little or no assurance of what the future value of the investment will be. For purposes such as the down payment on a home or a child's education much *less* risk should be tolerated than for other goals, since the attainment of such basic goals should not, if possible, be placed in jeopardy.

Retirement

Accumulating funds for retirement is *the single most important reason for investing*. Too often, however, retirement planning occupies only a small amount of a person's time, since many people tend to rely heavily on social security and employers for this provision. It is of the utmost importance to review the amounts that can realistically be expected from these sources and decide, based on your retirement goals, *whether or not they will be adequate to meet your needs*. If they are not, such sources must be supplemented through your own investment program. The earlier in life an assessment of retirement needs is made, the greater the chance of success in accumulating the needed funds. (Retirement plans will be discussed in greater detail in the final section of this chapter.)

Shelter from Taxes

As will be explained later in this chapter, federal income tax law does not treat all sources of income equally. For example, if you own and actively participate in the management of rental real estate, you may be able to take depreciation deductions against certain other sources of income, thereby reducing the amount of final taxable income. This tax write-off feature can make real estate an attractive investment *for some investors,* even though its pretax rate of return may not appear very high. Sheltering income from taxes has been made considerably more difficult by the Tax Reform Act of 1986; even so, this goal for some investors still goes hand-in-hand with saving for a major outlay or retirement. Obviously if a person can avoid (or defer) paying taxes on the income from an investment, he or she will, all other things considered, have more funds left for reinvestment.

Meeting Life Insurance Needs

Insurance is an important prerequisite to investment planning for two reasons: (1) it provides protection against consequences that can adversely affect finances and (2) it can provide certain long-run cash benefits. An **insurance policy** is a contract

insurance policy
a contract between the insured and the insurer that requires the insured to make periodic premium payments in exchange for the insurer's promise to pay for losses according to specified terms.

between the insured (you) and the insurer (an insurance company) that requires the insured to make periodic premium payments in exchange for the insurer's promise to pay for losses according to specified terms. Decisions regarding insurance purchases may affect the amount of funds available for investment. It is therefore important that you select insurance carefully, because costs and benefits can vary widely from one company to another. Although insurance is a necessary expenditure, its cost can consume funds that might otherwise be productively invested in any of a wide variety of alternative investment vehicles.

Fundamentals of Insurance

The many different types of insurance available can be broken down into three basic forms: life insurance, health insurance, and property and liability insurance. Although each form provides a different type of protection, all have certain characteristics in common; these include risk, the mechanism through which insurance coverage is provided, and the characteristics of an insurable risk.

risk
in insurance, the uncertainty related to economic loss.

Risk in Insurance. **Risk,** as used in discussing insurance, is defined as the uncertainty related to economic loss. Because the consequences of economic loss are never favorable, one way to avoid such loss is to purchase insurance.

insurance
a mechanism that allows people to reduce financial risk by sharing in the losses associated with the occurrence of uncertain events.

The Insurance Mechanism. **Insurance** is a mechanism that allows people to reduce financial risk by sharing in the losses associated with the occurrence of uncertain events. Insurers combine the experience of a large group of people and apply certain statistics in order to predict the losses that might occur. Using these predictions, they establish ratings as well as an associated fee structure. Each insured individual pays a small premium (relative to the amount of coverage) to the insurance company in exchange for the promise that he or she will be reimbursed for losses up to a specified limit. Because of its reliance on the "law of large numbers," the insurer can predict reasonably well the amount of losses it will have to pay over a given period. The insured benefits from the ability to *transfer risk* to the insurer. In turn the insurer, if it accurately predicts actual loss experience, gains from the profit that has been built into the premiums charged the insured.

Characteristics of an Insurable Risk. For a risk to be insurable, it must display certain characteristics: (1) there must be a large group of persons with similar loss exposure; (2) the loss exposure must be one that results from unintentional and unexpected causes; (3) the cost of the insurance must be relatively low; and (4) the risk should not have the potential for a widespread catastrophe, such as war or nuclear explosion. Here we focus on life insurance because obtaining adequate life insurance coverage is a prerequisite to the implementation of an investment program.

life insurance
a mechanism that can provide financial protection for a family if the primary breadwinner or other family member dies prematurely.

Types of Life Insurance

Life insurance provides a mechanism that can be used to provide financial protection for a family in the event that the primary breadwinner or any other family member dies prematurely. Some types of life insurance provide only death benefits;

others also allow for the accumulation of savings. We will look at four basic types of life insurance: term, whole life, universal life, and variable life.

Term Insurance.   A **term life insurance** policy is one in which the insurance company is obligated to pay a specified amount if the insured dies within the policy period. *Term is the least expensive form of life insurance.* It provides protection but does not contain the savings features of the three other types of life insurance. A number of types of term insurance are available. These include straight term, renewable term, convertible term, decreasing term, and group term.

A *straight term policy* is written for a fixed number of years. A *renewable term policy* guarantees that it can be renewed at the option of the insured for another term of equal length. *Convertible term* provides that the policy can be converted to a whole life (or other specified type of policy) at the insured's option. Although straight term is the least expensive of all types of life insurance, its cost does rise with the insured's age, and it can be very expensive for persons 60 years of age or older. An alternative, *decreasing term,* maintains a level premium throughout all periods of coverage, while the amount of protection decreases. Renewable term costs slightly more, but it does ensure the continued insurability of the insured. Despite its slightly higher cost, renewable term—straight or decreasing—may be a good choice for those needing life insurance protection.

Term life insurance can also be designed to meet an insured's debt obligations at death. *Mortgage life insurance,* for example, is a form of decreasing term that will pay off the outstanding principal balance of the insured's home loan should he or she die. *Credit life insurance,* a similar form of decreasing term insurance, will pay off the insured's installment loan balances at his or her demise. Term life insurance of this type should be selected very carefully, because some life insurance companies charge extremely high premiums for it. Occasionally mortgage life and credit life are sold via high-pressure tactics and by unscrupulous insurance agents. Indeed, it may be best to avoid this type of insurance altogether. If you believe you need term life insurance protection to meet a debt, a decreasing term policy may be a much better buy.

Many employers offer free and/or low-cost *group term insurance* protection for their employees. Very frequently this benefit is the least expensive way to obtain life insurance. If you need to increase your term life insurance, you may be able to purchase additional amounts at low cost through group insurance. Keep in mind that many of these plans are not transportable, however. That means that you can't take your term protection with you if you leave your job for some reason or another.

Whole Life.   As the name implies, **whole life insurance** provides insurance coverage over the entire life of an insured. In addition, it also offers a savings benefit commonly called the **cash value.** The cash value is the amount of money set aside by the insurer to provide for the payment of the death benefit. Since the insurer's earnings and premium receipts increase over time, the cash value also increases as the age of the insured increases. From the insurer's view, increased cash values are necessary since as the insured gets older the probability of death increases. Either

term life insurance
form of life insurance in which the insurer agrees to pay a specified amount if the insured dies within the policy period; the least expensive form of life insurance.

whole life insurance
form of life insurance that provides coverage over the entire life of the insured; offers a savings benefit.

cash value
the amount of money set aside by an insurer to provide for the payment of a death benefit.

the beneficiaries of the insured will receive the amount of the death benefit upon the death of the insured, or the policyholder at some predetermined time can terminate the policy and receive its cash value. Like term insurance, whole life policies may contain a variety of options and features.

Most people acquire whole life insurance by paying a level premium each year until they die or terminate the policy (*continuous-premium whole life*). As an alternative, whole life policies can be purchased either by making level payments over a specified number of years at the end of which the policy is paid up (*limited-payment whole life*) or by making a single cash payment (*single-premium whole life*). Although single-premium policies have little usefulness in the life insurance programs of most families, they may have some appeal as a tax-sheltered investment vehicle (as discussed in Chapter 15).

Compared to term insurance, whole life insurance is advantageous in the sense that the premium payments contribute toward the tax-sheltered accumulation of value regardless of whether the insured lives or dies. It also provides insurance protection at a given premium rate over the whole life of the insured. On the other hand, more death protection per premium dollar can be obtained by purchasing term insurance, and the actual cash value accumulation of a whole life policy reflects an annual earnings rate of approximately 5 to 8 percent, frequently *below* what could be earned on alternative investments. For this reason some financial advisors recommend purchasing the cheaper term insurance and investing the premium savings.

universal life insurance

form of life insurance that retains the savings features of whole life but provides a higher return on the cash value portion of the policy than most whole life policies; combines term insurance with a tax sheltered savings/investment account that pays interest at competitive rates.

Universal Life. **Universal life insurance** is a popular form of life insurance that retains the savings features of whole life but provides a higher return on the cash value portion of the policy than most whole life policies. Basically, universal life combines *term* insurance, which provides the death benefits, with a tax-sheltered savings/investment account that pays interest at *competitive money market rates.* Universal life has many other progressive features that distinguish it from whole life, including full disclosure of all buyer-paid costs; higher yields on cash value than whole life; flexibility in level of coverage and premium costs; and greater policyholder flexibility.

One notable advantage of universal life over whole life is that the purchaser is more aware of what he or she is buying than the whole life policyholder. In contrast to whole life, universal life insurance carries a detailed breakdown of policy costs as well as all benefits. All charges for costs, such as sales commissions, insurance company service fees, and actual insurance protection, are explicitly listed. Most whole life policies do not explicitly provide information about such items as sales commissions, the true cost of insurance, and other policy costs. (Usually whole life sellers quote the premium amount and little else.)

When a universal life policy is purchased, premiums are deposited in a fund called the policy's *accumulation account,* which is similar to the *cash value* of a whole life policy. Then, the insurance company issuing the policy deducts from this account the cost of insurance as well as commissions and service charges. After these deductions, the account balance earns interest at a *current rate* that generally varies with market yields, but is guaranteed to be at least equal to a stated *minimum*

rate (generally 4 to 5 percent). Most issuers of universal life pay higher interest rates on account balances than those paid on whole life policies. In early 1989, for example, universal life policyholders were earning 8 to 10 percent annual returns on their cash values. But there's more, for in a fashion similar to whole life, all or most of the investment earnings on a universal life policy accumulate tax free; thus, they are viewed by many as a form of *tax-sheltered investment.*

The accumulation account buildup in a universal life policy can be partially withdrawn or borrowed against at the policyholder's option, although there may be penalties, in addition to taxes, on withdrawals. In contrast, whole life policies generally have no withdrawal provisions. The universal policyholder can also borrow from the insurance company an amount up to the policy's accumulation account balance. (This is similar to whole life policy provisions.) The interest rate charged on these borrowings is usually fairly low, often around 8 percent. Many companies net this interest cost out against (that is, subtract it from) the minimum rate applicable to the accumulated balance and thus effectively charge only about 2 to 4 percent on such borrowing.

Another advantageous feature of universal life is that many policies allow a buyer to skip or reduce a premium payment if the policy's accumulation account balance is sufficient to pay the monthly cost of insurance protection. The universal life policy itself will not lapse unless the accumulation account has been exhausted. Most whole life policies, in contrast, have a more rigid premium payment schedule. A further plus factor for universal life is that the buyer pays only for actual insurance protection—the difference between the face amount and the accumulation account balance. Whole life premiums are usually based strictly on the policy's face amount.

Table 4.1 presents a summary comparison of some key features of the three principal forms of life insurance—term insurance, whole life insurance, and universal life. Overall, universal life appears to be a competitive alternative to whole life insurance. It retains the general investment features of whole life while providing a higher return on cash value. Universal life is more expensive than term life insurance; however, term insurance has no savings feature. If you want life insurance that has a savings feature, universal life merits consideration.

variable life insurance
form of life insurance that offers insurance coverage with a savings feature that allows the insured to decide how the cash value is invested; the amount of insurance coverage varies with the policy's investment returns.

Variable Life. **Variable life insurance** is like whole life and universal life in that it combines insurance coverage with a savings account; it differs from them in two respects—(1) it allows the policyholder to decide how the money in the savings account (cash value or accumulation account balance) is invested, and (2) it does *not* specify a guaranteed minimum return. Variable life offers the highest and most attractive level of investment returns. And, as its name implies, the amount of insurance coverage provided will *vary* with the profit (*and losses*) being generated in the investment (savings) account. Thus, in variable life insurance, the amount of death benefit payable is, for the most part, related to the policy's investment returns. (*Note:* The level of insurance coverage can never fall below the policy's stated *minimum death benefit.*)

Variable life insurance investment accounts are set up just like mutual funds, and

TABLE 4.1   Key Features of the Principal Forms of Life Insurance

Feature	Term Insurance	Whole Life	Universal Life
Premium	Increases on preset schedule	Constant	Flexible
Company-fee portion of premium	Undisclosed	Undisclosed	Disclosed
Protection	Fixed	Fixed	Flexible
Savings (cash value or accumulation account balance)	None usually	Increases on preset schedule	Variable, competitive rates
Tax-sheltered accumulation of earnings	No	Yes	Yes

Source: *Consumer Reports*, January 1982, p. 43

most insurers let the policyholder choose from a full menu of different types of funds, ranging from money market and bond funds to aggressively managed stock funds. Policyholders can have their money placed in one or more funds *and* can freely move money from one fund to another as market conditions warrant. Like all life insurance, the investment earnings can grow within the policy free of any current taxation, and the policy's death benefit passes tax-free to beneficiaries. Of course with the prospect of higher investment returns comes the risk of reduced insurance coverage—investments can lose money, which can lead to lower cash value and reduced insurance coverage. Because variable life is really an *investment vehicle* wrapped in an insurance policy (in order to achieve favorable tax benefits), it is *probably best used as a tax-sheltered investment vehicle* rather than a source of primary life insurance coverage.

Estimating Life Insurance Needs

Any of a number of possible techniques can be used to estimate a person's life insurance needs. One can assess the individual's financial situation to determine how much protection is required in order to leave his or her dependents (or beneficiaries) in a desired financial position. Or one can look at the individual's projected earnings and convert them into a present value that would represent the amount of needed insurance protection. A form providing a simplified demonstration of the procedures used to estimate life insurance needs is given in the Investor Insights box. Another approach is to use a multiple of earnings. For example, assume that the appropriate multiple for a 25-year-old wishing to obtain enough insurance to replace 75 percent of his or her income, which is currently $23,500 per year, is 6.5. Multiplying the $23,500 by 6.5 indicates that this person needs $152,750 of life insurance coverage. Regardless of which technique is used, logical bases for determining the appropriate amount of life insurance coverage are available.

INVESTOR INSIGHTS

Life Insurance: How Much Do You Really Need?

Every year or two, people who need life insurance should recalculate whether they have enough. This worksheet eases the task and takes you through it with a real family, the Gordons. . . . The reason they need more than minimal insurance is the usual one: children. They have a son, 2, and another child on the way.

You can work out all the entries for yourself except Social Security payments. Those amounts are based on a parent's age at death—you should assume that it occurs this year—and on his earnings history. Your nearest Social Security office can find out for you what your survivors would get. Ask for your maximum monthly benefit per survivor and your maximum family benefit. Multiply these amounts by 12 to get annual income and enter the results on lines 14a and 14b of the worksheet.

To determine the years of eligibility for various levels of survivors' benefits, start with line 14c, 14f, or 14i, depending on your family size, and fill in each subsequent blank. The Gordons counted Mrs. Gordon as a Social Security beneficiary for only six years because after that she would go back to work. But while she stayed home, three survivors would be eligible, so the Gordons started computing Social Security on line 14c. Both children would remain eligible for 10 more years (line 14g). The younger child, then 16, would collect for a final two years (line 14j).

	MICHAEL GORDON	YOU
Funds Needed		
1. Annual contribution to household	$_____16,000	$_____
2. Remaining years of child rearing	×_____18	×_____
3. Multiply line 1 by line 2	$_____288,000	$_____
4. College contribution per child	$_____40,000	$_____
5. Number of children	×_____2	×_____
6. Multiply line 4 by line 5	$_____80,000	$_____
7. Funeral and estate costs and debts (excluding mortgage)	$_____20,000	$_____
8. Total needed now: add lines 3, 6, and 7	$_____388,000	$_____

Obtaining Life Insurance Coverage

Once the desired amount of life insurance coverage has been estimated, the form(s) of insurance used to meet this need must be determined. The form selected will depend on the age of the family (or individual), their financial position, and their ability and/or desire to save or invest. Generally, young families need large amounts of death protection whereas older individuals and maturing families tend to need more moderate amounts of protection. For the young family with a limited budget, term insurance would probably best fulfill its needs; more mature families might prefer whole life policies. Families (or individuals) more concerned with the

	MICHAEL GORDON	YOU
Existing Resources		
9. Life insurance	$ 85,000	$
10. Savings and investments	$ 2,000	$
11. Wife's earning power per year	$ 12,000	$
12. Years she'd work during child rearing	× 10	×
13. Multiply line 11 by line 12	$ 120,000	$
14. Social Security (per year):		
14a. Benefit for each survivor	$ 3,912	$
14b. Maximum family benefit	$ 9,720	$
14c. Benefit for three or more survivors: enter amount on line 14b	$ 9,720	$
14d. Years of eligibility	× 6	×
14e. Multiply line 14c by line 14d	$ 58,320	$
14f. Benefit for two survivors: multiply line 14a by 2	$ 7,824	$
14g. Years of eligibility	× 10	×
14h. Multiply line 14f by line 14g	$ 78,240	$
14i. Benefit for one survivor: enter amount on line 14a	$ 3,912	$
14j. Years of eligibility	× 2	×
14k. Multiply line 14i by line 14j	$ 7,824	$
15. Total resources: add lines 9, 10, 13, 14e, 14h, and 14k	$ 351,384	$
Insurance Needed		
16. Subtract line 15 from line 8	$ 36,616	$

Source: Malcolm N. Carter, "How Much Do You Really Need?" *Money*, April 1982, p. 134.

tax-sheltered accumulation of savings than with the acquisition of death protection might find a variable life insurance policy best suited to their needs. Those who feel comfortable with their ability to save and invest and who do not need the forced savings of whole life or universal life would probably do best with term insurance. If you wish life insurance with an attractive savings feature, universal life could be the best alternative. When evaluating life insurance, the choice seems to be either term insurance or universal life. If you want inexpensive life insurance with no savings feature, look for a term policy. If you want life insurance with a competitive savings feature, then consider universal life. An individual should acquire an

amount of life insurance protection that adequately protects his or her financial position and that provides a death benefit and savings accumulation mix with which he or she feels comfortable.

Quantifying Investment Goals

The procedures for quantifying investment goals begin with established long-run personal financial goals, which include retirement goals. Generally, any long-run financial goal specifying the creation of an annual cash flow stream or the accumulation of a lump sum at some future date must be viewed as an investment goal, since it is through some type of investment that such a goal can be achieved. In spite of the fact that individuals may receive certain benefits from the government and/or employers may contribute toward achievement of the goal, the goal must be stated and therefore established as a target toward which financial activities will be directed.

A series of supporting investment goals can be developed for each long-run goal. For example, if one long-run goal is to accumulate $80,000 in cash at the end of 10 years, it clearly can be treated as an investment goal. In this case one must specify the desired return, acceptable risk, and relevant tax considerations associated with this goal. Our example could be more precisely stated as an investment goal to accumulate $80,000 in cash by investing in a portfolio evenly divided between blue chip and speculative stocks providing a total return of 10 percent per year split between 20 percent current income and 80 percent deferred capital gains. By stating an investment goal in this fashion, return (10 percent per year), risk (half blue chip and half speculative stock), and taxes (20 percent current income and 80 percent deferred capital gains) have all been specified. The more specific you can be in the statement of investment goals, the easier it will be to establish an investment plan consistent with your goals.

When quantifying investment goals and looking at ways to meet them, personal computers can help. A well-programmed personal computer can aid in the evaluation of investment alternatives and in analyzing your tax situation. The personal computer can also provide alternative ideas based on the data you input. Of course, as pointed out in Chapter 3, the cost of the PC must be justified by the benefits it provides its user.

The Investment Program

Once goals have been specified, a program must be developed. The backbone of the program is the *investment plan,* which makes the investment goals operational. The plan indicates the general strategy that will be used to achieve each goal. Since some portion of the goals may be achieved through government and/or employer pension programs outside the individual's control, any contribution of such plans toward goal achievement must be recognized. For example, in the case of achieving the $80,000 goal mentioned in the preceding section, assume the individual will have a fully vested $30,000 in a retirement plan at the end of the 10-year period. If the retirement plan permits a cash lump-sum withdrawal upon vesting, a portion of the individual's investment plan would already be provided. Primary emphasis

diversification
*the use of a variety
of investments in
order to minimize
risk.*

would therefore center on the accumulation of the remaining $50,000. The overriding consideration that should be incorporated in the plan to accumulate $50,000 is **diversification.** This concept emphasizes the need to hold a variety of investment vehicles in order to minimize the risk that one bad investment will hinder the goal of accumulating a specified amount. A well-balanced portfolio lessens such risk.

Considering available resources and projected budget surpluses, a plan that will provide for the accumulation of $50,000 by investing in an equal mix of blue chip and speculative stocks providing a total return of 10 percent per year, of which 20 percent is current income and 80 percent is deferred capital gains, must be developed. If we assume the investor feels she can earn a 10 percent total return in the desired form by investing in the specified mix of blue chip and speculative common stock, we must isolate the source of investment capital that will ultimately provide for the $50,000 accumulation. The source can be current investable balances not committed to the achievement of an investment goal and/or an allocation of income earned over future years. Let's assume that our investor currently has available $10,000 that can be used in achieving this goal. By investing this money in the desired types of vehicles earning a 10 percent return over the 10-year period, a future sum of about $26,000 (calculated using time value techniques that are described in Chapter 5) would be accumulated. Subtracting this amount from the $50,000 leaves $24,000 that must be obtained from the investment of current income over the period. At a 10 percent rate approximately $1,500 per year must be invested at the end of each of the next 10 years in order to accumulate this sum. (This was also found using time value techniques that are explained in Chapter 5.) If our investor believes that $1,500 a year in each of the next 10 years can be allocated to this activity, specific securities can be selected for investment. On the other hand, if an allocation of $1,500 annually does not seem feasible, her goals must be revised accordingly.

As any investment program progresses, checkpoints should be established at various time intervals to allow for assessment of progress. Adjustments in both goals and plans may be required as new information is received; goals may be too lax or too restrictive, or plans unrealistic. By monitoring actual outcomes and making needed adjustments, an investor should be better able to establish and achieve realistic financial goals over the long run.

Investing in Different Economic Environments

The first rule of investing is to know *where* to put your money; the second is to know *when* to make your moves. The first question is easier to deal with because it basically involves matching your risk and return objectives with the available investment alternatives. For example, if you're a seasoned investor who can tolerate the risk, then speculative stocks may be right for you; on the other hand, if you're a novice who wants a fair return on your capital, then maybe you should consider a good growth-oriented mutual fund. Unfortunately, although stocks or growth funds may do well when the economy is expanding, they can turn out to be disasters at other times. This leads us to our second, and more difficult question, that of *when* to invest.

A healthy investment outlook would probably suggest a course of action quite different from the one you would follow if you thought the market was headed for trouble. The question of when to invest is difficult because it deals with *market timing*. The fact is that most investors, even professional money managers, *cannot* predict the peaks and troughs in the market with much consistency! In contrast, it's a lot easier to get a handle on the *current state* of the economy/market. That is, knowing whether the economy/market is in a state of expansion or decline is considerably different from being able to pinpoint when it's about to change course. Thus for our purposes we can define market timing as *the process through which we identify the current state of the economy/market, and assess the likelihood of its continuing on its present course.*

As an investor, it's probably best to confine your assessment of the market to three distinct conditions: (1) the economy/market is in a state of *recovery/expansion;* (2) it's in a state of *decline/recession;* or (3) you're *uncertain* as to the direction in which it's going to move. These different stages are illustrated in Figure 4.1. It's easy to see when things are moving up (recovery/expansion) or when they're moving down (decline/recession); the difficulty comes with the peaks and troughs. That is why these are shown in the shaded areas, depicting *uncertainty*.

If you're totally *uncertain* as to which direction the market's going to take, then your best course of action is to "sit it out on the sidelines." If you have new money to invest, hold off until you get a better handle on the future course of the market. Under these conditions the best thing you can do is to temporarily put your money into some form of savings account or money market fund. Then, when things start to clear up, move your money to a more permanent investment vehicle (stocks, bonds, mutual funds, or such). In a like fashion, if you already have money invested in stocks or bonds, then stay put! Don't move out of your investments until you're satisfied that the market has indeed changed course or is almost certainly about to do so. That still leaves the two other market conditions (expansion and decline) to deal with. How you will respond to these conditions depends on whether you're in stocks, bonds, or tangible investments.

Stocks and the Business Cycle

Common stocks and other equity-related securities (such as stock mutual funds, convertible securities, stock options, and stock index futures) are highly responsive to conditions in the economy, which are described generically as "the business cycle." The business cycle reflects the current status of a variety of economic variables, including GNP (gross national product), industrial production, personal disposable income, unemployment rates, and more. When the economy is strong, it's reflected in a strong, expanding business cycle; and when business is good and profits are up, stocks react accordingly. Thus it makes sense to be in stocks during such times. Growth-oriented and speculative stocks tend to do especially well in such markets as, to a lesser extent, do blue chip and income-oriented stocks. In contrast, when the business cycle is declining the returns on common stocks tend to be off as well.

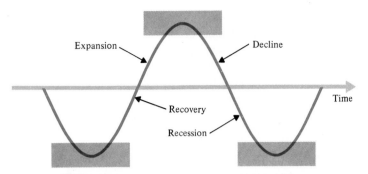

FIGURE 4.1 Different Stages of an Economic/Market Cycle.
The economic/market cycle exhibits three distinct conditions: (1) the economy/market is in a state of recovery/expansion; (2) it's in a state of decline/recession; and (3) uncertainty exists as to the direction in which the economy/market is going to move (noted by the shaded areas at peak and troughs).

Bonds and Interest Rates

Bonds and other forms of fixed-income securities, such as preferred stocks and bond funds, are highly sensitive to movements in interest rates. In fact, interest rates are the single most important variable in determining bond price behavior and returns to investors. Because interest rates and bond prices move in *opposite* directions, it follows that rising interest rates are *unfavorable* for bonds. If you feel that interest rates will *continue to rise*, then hold off buying long-term bonds. By doing so you'll benefit in two ways: First, you'll avoid the *loss* that is guaranteed to occur when rates increase; and second, by waiting you'll be able to capture even higher bond yields. Thus as long as interest rates are heading upward, the best course of action is to hold *short-term money market investments* (such as money market deposit accounts or money funds); this will enable you to preserve your capital and generate higher long-run returns. On the other hand, when rates start heading down, then that's the time to start *buying long-term bonds* as the way to lock in high current yields and/or generate attractive capital gains.

Tangible Investments and Inflation

Tangible investments include things like real estate, commodities, and gold. These vehicles are generally responsive more to the *rate of inflation* than to anything else. The cost of housing, along with commodities like coffee, oil, meat, corn, and sugar, goes into making up the consumer price index (CPI); and *when prices start rising the returns on these tangible asset investments start going up as well*. Consider what happened over the 14-year period from 1977 to 1990. In the first five years of that period inflation was running high, hitting 15 percent and more; at the same time investments in real estate, commodities, and other tangible assets were generating correspondingly high rates of return and, indeed, outperforming all other forms of investments. But when inflation was brought back down to more normal

levels, beginning around 1982, returns on tangible investments plummeted. Certainly if inflation becomes a serious problem again, the demand for tangible investments will likely pick up and so, too, will their returns. However, except for isolated pockets of performance here and there, as long as inflation remains under control, these investments are likely to provide substandard rates of return. Thus you'll probably do better over the long haul putting your money elsewhere (for example, in stocks, bonds, and other investment vehicles that benefit from lower inflation).

Investing Over the Life Cycle

Just as investors take different courses of action as they move through different stages of an economic/market cycle, they also tend to follow different investment philosophies as they move through different stages of the life cycle. Generally speaking, most investors tend to be more aggressive when they're young and more conservative as they grow older. In general, investors tend to move through the following investment stages:

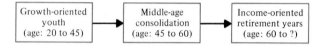

Most young investors (those in their twenties and thirties) tend to prefer growth-oriented investments that stress *capital gains* rather than current income. Often young investors don't have much in the way of investable funds, so capital gains are viewed as the quickest (if not necessarily the surest) way to build up investment capital. Such investors are inclined to favor speculative and growth-oriented common stocks and mutual funds, convertible securities, and other investment vehicles (like puts and calls, and stock index options) that offer substantial price appreciation within relatively short time periods.

As investors approach the middle-age consolidation stage of life (the mid-forties), family demands and responsibilities take a big change and so does the approach to investing. While growth-oriented securities are still employed, investing is far *less* speculative. *Quality-growth* vehicles are used, and more attention is given to *current income* as an important source of return. Thus the whole portfolio goes through a transition to higher-quality securities, and at the same time the foundation is being set for the retirement years. Blue chip growth and income stocks, preferred stocks, convertibles, high-grade bonds, and mutual funds are all widely used at this point in life. And because taxes are likely becoming a bigger burden (with a rising income and standard of living), tax-free municipal bonds and tax-sheltered investments assume a more prominent role.

Finally, the investor moves into his or her retirement years, wherein *preservation of capital and current income* are the principal concerns. A *secure, high level of income* is now paramount, and capital gains are viewed as merely a pleasant occasional by-product of investing. The investment portfolio has become *highly conser-*

vative, as it now consists of blue chip income stocks, high-yielding government bonds, quality corporate bonds, bank certificates of deposit (CDs), and other money market investments. In fact along with much higher quality securities, the portfolio has probably also become a lot "shorter," as more money is being placed into various (short-term) savings accounts and money market funds. The objective at this point is to live as comfortably as you can off of your investments, for it's here that you should be able to really reap the rewards of a lifetime of saving and investing.

PERSONAL TAXES

The tax consequences associated with various investment vehicles and strategies must be considered when establishing an investment program. Since tax considerations affect nearly all investment decisions, a knowledge of the tax laws should help you to employ strategies that result in the reduction of taxes, thereby increasing the amount of after-tax dollars available for achieving your investment goals. Because tax laws are complicated and subject to frequent revision, here we will present only the key concepts and their applications to basic investment transactions.

Basic Sources of Taxation

The two major types of taxes are those levied by the federal government and by state and local governments. The major federal tax is the income tax, which is also the major source of personal taxation. It is levied on a "pay-as-you-go" basis, since employers withhold a portion of each employee's wages each pay period and send these withheld taxes to the federal government. Self-employed persons as well as individuals who are not employees (consultants, attorneys) are required to make estimated tax payments, generally on a quarterly basis. At the end of the year, each taxpayer files a return that reconciles the payments made with what is owed. Unlike federal taxes, state and local taxes vary from area to area. Some states have income taxes that may range as high as 15 percent or more of income. Some cities, especially large East Coast cities, also have local income taxes that typically range between 1 and 5 percent of income. Most state and local income taxes are also on a pay-as-you-go basis. In addition to income taxes, state and local governments rely heavily on sales and property taxes as a source of revenue. Although sales taxes vary from state to state, most are in the 3 to 6 percent range. Property taxes, which are levied on real estate and personal property, such as furniture and automobiles, are the primary source of revenue for local communities and school districts. These taxes vary from community to community; in some states a portion of this tax goes to the state.

State and local taxes, especially income and property taxes, are important in the overall investment planning process. Income taxes have the greatest impact on security investments, while property taxes could have a sizable impact on real estate and other forms of property investment. Although primary emphasis here is on the federal income tax, individuals should acquaint themselves with the potential impact state and local taxes can have on alternative investment vehicles and strategies.

Types of Income and Tax Rates

The income of individuals used to be classified simply as either ordinary or capital gain (or loss). Under the Tax Reform Act of 1986, that's no longer the case. For one of the major revisions of the sweeping 1986 tax legislation was the creation of *three basic categories of income*. Devised as a way to curtail the amount of write-offs that could be taken in tax-sheltered investments, they consist of the following: (1) active (ordinary "earned") income; (2) portfolio (investment) income; and (3) passive income. *Active income* is the broadest category and consists of every-thing from wages and salaries to bonuses, tips, pension income, and alimony. It is made up of income earned on the job as well as most other forms of *noninvestment* income. *Portfolio income,* in contrast, is comprised of the earnings generated from various types of investment holdings—in fact, this category of income covers *most* (but not all) types of investments, from stocks, bonds, savings accounts, and mutual funds to stock options and commodities. For the most part, portfolio income con-sists of interest, dividends, and capital gains (i.e., the profit on the sale of an investment). Finally, there is *passive income,* a special category of income that is comprised chiefly of income derived from real estate, limited partnerships, and other forms of tax shelters.

The key feature of these categories is that they limit the amount of deductions and write-offs that can be taken, particularly with regard to portfolio and passive income. Specifically, the amount of allowable, deductible expenses associated with portfolio and passive income *is limited to the amount of income derived from these two sources*. For example, if you had a total of $380 in portfolio income for the year, you could write off no more than $380 in investment-related interest expense. Note, however, that if you have more investment expenses than portfolio income, you can "accumulate" the difference and write it off in later years (when you have sufficient portfolio income) or when you finally sell the investment. Likewise, the same rules generally apply to passive income and related expenses (with a few notable exceptions, some of which will be discussed later in the book). Thus, if you own limited partnerships that generate no income, you can *not* write off the losses from those partnerships (at least not in the year in which they occur—as with investment expenses, you can "accumulate" these losses and write them off later).

It is important to understand that for deduction purposes, the portfolio and pas-sive income categories cannot be mixed and/or combined with each other or with active income. *Investment-related expenses can be used only with portfolio income,* and with a few exceptions, *passive investment expenses can be used only to offset the income from passive investments*. [*Note:* Since such limitations did *not* exist prior to the Tax Reform Act of 1986, a five-year phase-in was established for the portfolio and passive income provisions to ease the transition to the new standards. Thus, regardless of the level of portfolio and passive income, up to 40 percent of the write-offs from these investments could be deducted from other (active) income in 1988, with the amount dropping to 20 percent in 1989, and finally to 10 percent in 1990, making the law fully operational by 1991.]

TABLE 4.2 Tax Rates and Income Brackets for Individual and Joint Returns (1990)

	Taxable Income	
Tax Rates	**Individual Returns**	**Joint Returns**
15%	$ 0 to $17,850	$ 0 to $29,750
28%	$17,851 to $43,150	$29,751 to $71,900
33%	$43,151 to $89,560*	$71,901 to $149,250*
28%	over $89,560*	over $149,250*

Note: In order to phase out exemptions, an additional amount equal to the lesser of (1) 5% of income in *excess of* $89,560 (for individual returns) or $149,250 (for joint returns) or (2) $546 multiplied by the number of exemptions claimed must be included in taxes due.

Ordinary Income

Regardless of whether it's classified as active, portfolio, or passive, such income—after certain computations—is taxed at one of three rates: either 15, 28, or 33 percent. There is one structure of tax rates for taxpayers filing *individual* returns and another for those filing *joint* returns. Table 4.2 shows the tax rates and income brackets for these two major filing categories. Notice that the rates are somewhat progressive since individuals with taxable income above a specified amount are usually taxed at a higher rate.

Consider, for example, the Ellis sisters, Joni and Charlyn. They are single, and Joni's taxable income is $17,500. Charlyn's is $35,000. Using Table 4.2, their taxes are calculated as follows:

Joni:
$(.15 \times \$17,500) = \underline{\$2,625}$

Charlyn:
$(.15 \times \$17,850) + (.28 \times (\$35,000 - \$17,850)) = \$2,678 + \$4,802 = \underline{\$7,480}$

The average tax rate is calculated by dividing the tax liability by the amount of taxable income. For Joni it is 15 percent ($2,625 in taxes ÷ $17,500 taxable income); and for Charlyn it is 21.4 percent ($7,480 in taxes ÷ $35,000 taxable income). The progressive nature of the federal income tax structure can be seen by the fact that although Charlyn's taxable income is twice that of Joni ($35,000 versus $17,500), her income tax is nearly three times Joni's ($7,480 versus $2,625).

capital asset
property owned and used by the taxpayer for personal reasons, pleasure, or investment.

Capital Gains and Losses

A **capital asset** is property owned and used by the taxpayer for personal reasons, pleasure, or investment. The most common types are securities and real estate, including one's home. A **capital gain** represents the amount by which the proceeds from the sale of a capital asset exceed its original purchase price. Prior to the passage of the Tax Reform Act of 1986 capital gains were taxed at much lower rates

capital gain
the amount by which the proceeds from the sale of a capital asset exceed its original purchase price.

than other types of income; however, under the new act they are treated *no differently* from any other kind of income. In other words, the amount of any capital gains realized is added to other sources of income and the total is taxed at the rates given in Table 4.2. This can be illustrated by a simple example. Imagine that James McFail, a single person who has other taxable income totaling $40,000, sold at $12 per share 500 shares of stock originally purchased for $10 per share. The total capital gain on this transaction was $1,000 (500 shares × ($12/share − $10/share)). Thus McFail's taxable income would total $41,000, which should be subject to the tax rates in Table 4.2. His total tax would be $9,160 [(.15 × $17,850) + (.28 × ($41,000 − $17,850))].

unrealized gain
a capital gain not realized—and not taxable—until the capital asset is sold; also called paper gain.

In spite of the fact that all types of income are taxed at the same rate, capital gains are appealing since *they are not taxed until actually realized*. For example, if you own a stock originally purchased for $50 per share and at the end of the tax year having a market price of $60 per share, you have a "paper gain" of $10 per share ($60 per share − $50 per share). This paper or **unrealized gain** is not taxable since you still own the stock. Only **realized gains** are taxed; if you sold the stock for $60 per share during the tax year you would have a realized, and therefore taxable, gain of $10 per share. Since investors can, unlike in the case of interest and dividend receipts, control when capital gains are realized, an opportunity exists to defer taxes by carefully timing the sale of assets on which capital gains exist. This strategy is addressed in greater detail in Chapter 15.

realized gain
a capital gain realized upon the sale of a capital asset.

capital loss
the amount by which the proceeds from the sale of a capital asset are less than its original purchase price.

Capital losses result when a capital asset is sold for less than its original purchase price. Before taxes are calculated, all gains and losses must be netted out. Up to $3,000 of **net losses** can be applied against ordinary (active) income. Losses that cannot be applied in the current year may be carried forward and used to offset future income, subject to certain conditions.

net losses
amount by which capital losses exceed capital gains; up to $3,000 can be applied against ordinary (active) income.

Because capital losses can be used to reduce taxable income, the IRS has established certain regulations to prevent the abuse of the capital loss deduction. The regulations prohibit what are commonly called **wash sales**, selling securities on which capital losses can be realized and then immediately buying them back. The IRS requires that any loss on the sale of a security that is offset by a purchase of the same security within 30 days before or after the sale cannot be claimed as a loss for tax purposes. Instead, the purchase and sale are "washed out," and for tax purposes the sale is considered not to have occurred. A way of avoiding this law is to use a **tax swap,** which involves replacing the security sold at a loss with a *similar,* though not identical, security. In this case the rule has not been violated, but the desired result has been obtained. Many brokerage firms provide lists of securities and suitable replacements for use in tax swaps. As one might expect, these swaps are most prevalent at year-end. The IRS also has regulations governing transactions made between relatives to capitalize on certain tax benefits that might be achieved from realizing a capital gain or loss.

wash sales
the practice of selling securities on which capital losses can be realized and then buying them right back; not allowed under IRS regulations.

tax swap
replacing a security sold at a loss with a similar but not identical security as a way of avoiding IRS regulations against wash sales.

Investments and Taxes

From an investor's point of view, the key dimensions of taxes revolve around current (ordinary) income, capital gains, tax shelters, and tax planning. Persons

investing in vehicles providing current income tend to be those in the lower (15 or 28 percent) tax brackets—especially retirees. The predominant form of current investment income is interest and dividends; another source of current income is rental income from various types of real estate investment. Strictly from a tax point of view, capital gains resulting from the appreciation in the value of an investment is still very appealing to many investors. The fact that these gains are not taxed until actually realized allows the investor to defer as well as control the timing of the tax payments on them. Of course since capital gains are taxed as ordinary income they do not provide any *tax rate* advantage.

Due to the generally higher risk associated with capital gain income versus current investment income, the choice of investment vehicles cannot be made solely on the basis of the timing of tax payments. The levels of return and risk need to be viewed in light of their tax effects. Clearly, *it is the after-tax return and associated risk* that should be considered.

Tax Shelters

tax shelters
investments that make use of available tax writeoffs to reduce taxable income; the writeoffs are deductions from income that do not involve a current outlay of cash.

Tax shelters are certain forms of investment that capitalize on available "tax write-offs." Prior to passage of the Tax Reform Act of 1986 tax shelters were especially popular among individuals in high tax brackets. Today some real estate (income-generating property) and natural resource (oil and gas drilling) investments still provide these desirable deductions, but only under the very restrictive conditions outlined in the Tax Reform Act of 1986. The writeoffs come in the form of deductions from income that do not involve any current outlay of cash by the investor. Since an investor may be able to reduce taxable income by the amount of such noncash expenditures, these deductions may be effectively used to lower tax liability. For example, assume an individual who owns and manages an apartment building in the given year generates $4,000 of income before depreciation and taxes and is eligible for a depreciation writeoff on the building (deduction from income) of $14,000. What this means is that the $4,000 of income is completely "sheltered," and an additional $10,000 ($14,000 − $4,000) can (subject to certain limitations) be deducted from *other* sources of income. In other words, $10,000 of income from other sources, such as wages, salaries, interest, dividends, and capital gains, can be "sheltered." No taxes will be due on this sheltered income. Chapter 15 presents detailed discussions and illustrations of the basic mechanics of tax-sheltered investments.

Tax Planning

tax planning
the formulation of strategies that will defer and minimize an individual's level of taxes.

Due to the opportunities and challenges created by the tax laws, tax planning is important in the investment process. **Tax planning** involves looking at an individual's current and projected earnings and developing strategies that will defer and minimize the level of taxes. The tax plan should guide an investor's activities in such a way that over the long run he or she will achieve maximum after-tax returns for an acceptable level of risk.

Tax plans should also reflect the desired form in which returns are to be received—current income, capital gains, or tax-sheltered income. One common strategy is to

claim losses as soon as they occur and to delay profit taking. Such an approach allows you to benefit from the tax deductibility of a loss and to delay having to claim income from gains. Although the use of tax planning, which is commonly done in coordination with an accountant, tax expert, or tax attorney, is most common among individuals with high levels of income ($75,000 or more annually), sizable savings can result for investors with lower incomes as well.

MEETING LIQUIDITY NEEDS: INVESTING IN SHORT-TERM SECURITIES

liquidity
the ability to convert an investment into cash quickly and with little or no loss in value.

Investment goals and plans should be developed in a fashion that provides the investor with adequate liquidity. **Liquidity** as used here refers to the ability to convert an investment into cash quickly and without loss. Highly liquid assets can be converted to cash easily and with little or no loss in value. A checking account is highly liquid, whereas stocks and bonds are not because there is no definite assurance of being able to sell the securities at a price equal to or greater than their purchase price. Over the past fifteen years, particularly since the Depository Institutions Deregulation and Monetary Control Act of 1980, the number and variety of investment vehicles serving liquidity needs has increased significantly. Although all these vehicles meet the same basic needs to one degree or another, they are different in terms of how they pay interest and the relative ease with which they can be converted into cash. It is important to recognize these differences and to understand why *liquid assets* are held in the first place.

Role of Short-Term Securities

discount basis
a method of earning interest on short-term investments by purchasing a security at a price below its redemption value, the difference being the interest earned.

Short-term securities are an important part of most savings and investment programs. Although they do generate income—which can be quite high during periods of high interest rates—their primary savings function is to provide a pool of reserves that can be used for emergencies, or simply to accumulate funds for some specific purpose, such as buying a home or a car. When viewed as part of an investment portfolio, short-term securities are usually held as a temporary, highly liquid investment outlet until something better comes along, or as a more suitable form of investment by individuals who like the yields they offer and/or are more comfortable with these kinds of investment vehicles. In fact, this approach has had considerable merit during periods of economic (and investment) instability, such as those experienced during the 1970s and early 1980s. Whatever the reasons for holding them, short-term securities should be evaluated in terms of their risk and return.

Determining Interest on Short-Term Securities

Short-term investments earn interest in one of two ways. First, some investments, such as a savings account, pay a stated rate of interest. In this case the interest rate is generally easily obtained by the investor—it's the stated rate on the account. Another way interest is earned on short-term investments is on a **discount basis.** This means that the security is purchased at a price below its redemption value, the difference being the interest earned. Treasury bills (T-bills), for example, are issued

on a discount basis. This return can be expressed as an annual rate, using the following equation:

$$\text{annual rate of return on a discount security} = \left[\dfrac{360}{\text{number of days to maturity}} \right] \times \left[\dfrac{\text{redemption} \quad \text{purchase}}{\text{value} \quad - \quad \text{price}} \right]$$

$$= [360/n] \times \left[\dfrac{R - P}{P} \right]$$

To illustrate, suppose you buy a T-bill for $9,700 that can be redeemed for $10,000 at the end of 90 days. The total interest on this security is $300 (redemption value − purchase price), and its annual rate of return is:

$$\text{annual rate of return} = (360/90) \times \left(\dfrac{\$10,000 - \$9,700}{\$9,700} \right)$$

$$= (4.000) \times (.0309) = \underline{\underline{.1236, \text{ or } 12.36\%}}$$

Risk Characteristics

Short-term investments are generally considered low in risk. The primary risk results from the loss of potential purchasing power that occurs when the rate of return on these investments falls short of the inflation rate. Unfortunately this has often been the case with deposits such as passbook savings accounts; most other short-term investments have averaged, over long periods of time, rates of return that are about equal to, or maybe even slightly higher than, the average inflation rate.

The risk of default (nonpayment) is virtually nonexistent with short-term investment vehicles. The principal reason for this is that the primary issuers of most money market securities are highly reputable institutions, such as the U.S. Treasury, large money center banks, and major corporations. Furthermore, deposits in federally regulated commercial banks, savings banks, savings and loans, and credit unions are insured for up to $100,000 per account by agencies of the federal government. Most savings institutions that do not have federal insurance have other deposit insurance arrangements. Finally, because the value of short-term investments does not change much in response to changing interest rates, exposure to capital loss is correspondingly low. This is so because these securities have such short maturities (often measured in days and never exceeding a year), and the shorter the maturity of an issue, the less volatile its market price. This is perhaps most evident with six-month Treasury bills; their yields may vary over a wide range, but their prices change relatively little.

Advantages and Disadvantages of Short-Term Investments

As we have already discussed, among the major advantages of short-term investments is the fact that they are highly liquid, and low in risk. Most are available from local financial institutions and can be readily converted to cash with minimal inconvenience. Finally, since the returns on most short-term investments vary with inflation and market interest rates, investors can readily capture the higher returns as

rates move up. Of course on the negative side, when interest rates go down returns to short-term investors drop as well.

Although a decline in market rates has undesirable effects on most short-term vehicles, perhaps their biggest disadvantage is their relatively low return. Because these securities are generally so low in risk, and because low risk is usually translated into low return, you can expect the returns on short-term investments to generally average less than the returns on long-term investments. As an investor you must decide whether higher return is sufficient compensation for holding, say, riskier corporate bonds. If it is, then you should hold only a minimum amount of short-term securities and place your extra investment funds in long-term securities.

Popular Short-Term Investment Vehicles

Over the past 10 to 15 years there has been a tremendous proliferation of savings and short-term investment vehicles, particularly for the individual investor of modest means. Saving and investing in short-term securities is no longer the easy task it once was, when the decision for most people amounted to whether funds should be placed in a passbook savings account or in Series E bonds. Today even checking accounts pay interest on idle balances. The variety of savings and short-term investment vehicles from which investors can now choose includes passbook savings accounts, NOW accounts, money market deposit accounts and mutual funds, central asset accounts, certificates of deposit (CDs), commercial paper, U.S. Treasury bills, and Series EE savings bonds. Along with the dramatic increase in investment alternatives has come greater sophistication in short-term investment management. Short-term vehicles can be used as secure investment outlets for the long haul, or as a place to hold cash until the market becomes stronger and a more permanent outlet for the funds can be found. To gain the most from short-term investment funds, you must fully understand the range of alternatives. In the material that follows we will examine each of the major savings and short-term investment deposits and vehicles; later we will look at several ways in which these deposits/securities can be used in an investment portfolio. (Note that all the *deposit* accounts discussed below are issued by commercial banks, savings and loans [S&Ls], savings banks, and credit unions; very often we will simply use the term "bank" to refer to any one or all of these financial institutions and not necessarily to commercial banks alone.)

Passbook Savings Accounts

passbook savings account
a savings vehicle, offered by banks and other thrift institutions that generally pays a low rate of interest, has no minimum balance, and few or no restrictions on withdrawal.

The **passbook savings account** has been the traditional savings vehicle for many Americans. The term "passbook" arises from the fact that activity in the account is often recorded in a passbook, although bank statement report forms are rapidly replacing the old passbooks. Generally there are no minimum balances on these accounts, and you can make as many withdrawals as you choose, though there would be a slight fee for some of the withdrawals. (For example, there often is a charge if withdrawals exceed a predetermined number in a month or quarter.) These accounts are offered by banks and other thrift institutions. In spite of the fact that effective April 1, 1986, interest rate ceilings on these accounts were eliminated,

these accounts continue to pay a relatively low rate of interest, typically between 4 and 6 percent. Passbook savings accounts are used primarily by depositors who like the convenience of maintaining a savings account at their local bank, who lack sufficient resources to invest in other short-term vehicles, or who are simply unaware of the availability of higher-yielding, equally safe outlets. Passbook accounts are generally viewed as a convenient savings vehicle (appropriate perhaps for the accumulation of emergency funds) but have little or no role in an investment program.

NOW Accounts

NOW (Negotiated Order of With-drawal) account
a checking account that pays interest; has no legal minimum balance but many banks impose their own.

A **NOW (Negotiated Order of Withdrawal) account** is simply a checking account that pays interest at whatever rate the financial institution chooses. There is no legal minimum for a NOW, but many banks impose their own requirement, often between $500 and $1,000. Some banks have no minimum and pay interest on any balance in the account. Many banks pay interest at a higher rate on all balances over a specified amount, such as $2,500.

NOW accounts should be viewed primarily as checking accounts that are also potentially attractive savings vehicles. Since NOWs are in fact checking accounts, investors can earn interest on balances that must be kept for transaction purposes anyway; thus an individual can earn a profit on what would otherwise be idle money. In most cases service charges on NOWs, if any, are no greater than those on regular checking accounts. However, despite the apparent appeal of NOWs, alternatives should be examined closely. The key is how the rates on a NOW account compare with the rates you might earn by investing in other short-term vehicles. If alternative rates are much higher than the NOW rates, it may be to your advantage to invest any excess funds in some other outlet.

Money Market Deposit Accounts

money market deposit accounts (MMDAs)
a federally insured bank account with features similar to money market mutual funds; has no legal minimum balance but many banks impose their own.

Money market deposit accounts (MMDAs) were introduced in December 1982 and were extremely popular with depositors almost at once. They were created as a way of giving banks and thrift institutions a vehicle with which to compete with money market mutual funds (discussed below). Although MMDAs do not legally require a minimum balance, banks commonly set a minimum of around $2,500. Most banks pay interest rates on these accounts that are 2 to 3 percent below those offered by money market mutual funds. MMDAs are popular with savers and investors due to their convenience and safety; the deposits, unlike those in money funds, are *federally insured*. Depositors have access to their MMDAs through checkwriting privileges or through automated teller machines; a total of six transfers (only three by check) is allowed each month, after which a penalty is charged for additional withdrawals. This feature reduces the flexibility of these accounts and makes them less attractive than NOWs. However, most banks offer higher rates on MMDAs than on NOWs, which enhances their appeal. And since most depositors apparently look upon MMDAs as a savings outlet rather than a convenience account, the limited-access feature has not been a serious obstacle to investing in them.

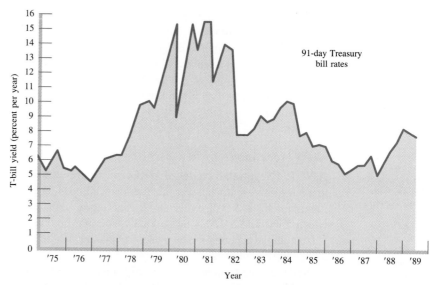

FIGURE 4.2 The Behavior of Short-Term Market Rates over Time.
The yields on marketable short-term securities (like those on Treasury bills) are highly unstable and as such, have a dramatic effect on returns to investors in money funds and other short-term vehicles (like MMDAs).

Money Market Mutual Funds

money market mutual fund (MMMF) *a mutual fund that pools the capital of a large number of investors and uses it to invest in high-yielding, short-term securities.*

A **money market mutual fund (MMMF)** is simply a mutual fund that pools the capital of a great number of investors and uses it to invest exclusively in high-yielding, short-term securities, such as Treasury bills, corporate commercial paper, jumbo certificates of deposit, and the like. Since these securities are sold in denominations of $10,000 to $1 million (or more), most small investors cannot purchase them individually, yet they very often offer the highest short-term yields. The MMMF makes these rates available to even small investors. Shares of MMMFs can be purchased (through brokers, investment dealers, and so on) with initial investments as low as $500 to $1,000 (although $1,000 to $5,000 is a more typical amount). Almost every major brokerage firm has a money fund of its own, and there are another 300 or so that are unaffiliated with a specific brokerage house and are sold primarily as no-load funds (see Chapter 13). The Investor Insights box on pages 144 and 145 provides some historical insights into the creation of money market funds by Bruce Bent in 1969 and their meteoric growth beginning in 1973.

The returns on money funds amount to what fund managers are able to earn from their investment activity in various short-term securities; as such, the returns rise and fall with money market interest rates. As Figure 4.2 shows, these are *highly volatile rates* that cause investor yields to vary accordingly. The returns on MMMFs are closely followed in the financial media and, in fact, the current yields on about 450 of the largest funds are regularly reported in *The Wall Street Journal* and other major newspapers (see Figure 4.3). Note in this case that not only are yields re-

MONEY MARKET MUTUAL FUNDS

The following quotations, collected by the National Association of Securities Dealers Inc., represent the average of annualized yields and dollar-weighted portfolio maturities ending Wednesday, May 10, 1989. Yields are based on actual dividends to shareholders.

Fund	Avg. Mat.	7Day Yld.	e7Day Yld.	Assets
AALMny	34	8.99	9.40	148
AARP	32	8.80	9.14	303
AMA TrP	1	8.67	9.05	18
AMA PrP	47	9.24	9.67	125
AMEV	30	8.94	9.35	76
ASO Pr	42	9.45	9.90	287
ASO US	32	8.86	9.26	109
ActAsGv	38	9.04	9.46	231
ActAsMny	50	9.38	9.82	2854
AlexBwn	29	9.47	9.92	1072
AlxBGvt	22	8.98	9.38	215
AlgerMM	31	9.97	10.48	55
AlliaCpRs	53	9.00	9.42	1435
AlliaGvRs	27	8.65	9.03	465
AlliMny	36	9.18	9.61	482
AlturaPr	22	9.33	9.77	233
AlturUS	33	9.17	9.59	42
AmCRs a	23	9.39	9.84	493
AmNatl	23	8.66	9.04	16
ArchFd	27	9.47	9.92	438

Fund	Avg. Mat.	7Day Yld.	e7Day Yld.	Assets
FIDSPM	32	10.15	10.68	1619
FidTrLP	11	8.40	8.76	100
FidUS Tr	7	9.35	9.80	361
FidelUS	7	9.04	9.46	1540
FinDlInc	22	9.26	9.70	361
FnclRsv	22	9.35	9.80	460
FstAmer	28	9.46	9.92	162
FtBost	35	9.57	10.03	131
FtInvCs f	17	9.14	9.53	266
FtLkMM	14	9.26	9.69	202
FtLkGv	9	8.81	9.20	164
FtVarG f	19	8.88	9.28	357
FlexFd	42	9.60	10.07	200
FtWash	32	9.19	9.62	60
Founders	20	8.82	9.22	51
FountSq	33	8.96	9.37	118
FrkMny a	17	9.05	9.46	1677
FrkFdl b	1	8.57	8.94	129
FrnkGvt	7	9.90	....	111
FrnkIFT	17	9.65	....	145
FremntMM	16	9.22	9.65	33
FdGvtInv	18	8.80	9.19	654
FdSrce	29	9.12	9.54	117
FdSMony	29	9.36	9.80	126
FSWash	43	9.27	9.70	126
Gab OC DP	23	9.57	10.03	186
GalaxyGv	14	9.28	9.72	285
GalxyMM	28	9.44	9.89	310
GnGvSec	52	8.72	9.10	284

Fund	Avg. Mat.	7Day Yld.	e7Day Yld.	Assets
MetLfStMM	28	9.29	9.69	73
MdIncTrGvt	29	8.69	9.07	109
MdInInst	13	9.41	9.85	98
Mon&ManPr	18	8.96	9.37	110
MonManGvt	5	8.98	9.39	17
MonMMgt f	39	9.04	9.45	199
MonMkTrst	37	9.50	....	1576
MonitorGov	40	9.18	9.61	74
MonitorMM	27	9.49	9.95	281
MutlOmah	34	8.87	9.27	186
MutlOmahC	37	8.62	9.00	48
NLR Cash	31	9.35	9.79	1508
NLR Gvt	20	8.73	9.12	94
NatlCash	23	9.19	9.66	59
NatwMM	38	9.31	9.76	476
NeubCsh	33	9.38	9.82	203
NeubGvt	54	8.18	8.52	134
NEMMkt	38	9.37	9.81	949
NEUSGvt	23	8.66	9.04	58
Newton	29	9.41	9.86	99
Nicholas	38	9.22	9.65	56
OppMoney	20	9.20	9.63	862
PSB Gov	20	8.99	9.40	56
PcHrzGvt	32	8.90	9.30	1234
PcHzMMP	38	9.32	9.76	863
PW Cash	36	9.37	9.81	4410
PW MstrM b	25	8.75	9.14	53
ParkPr	20	9.28	9.72	487
ParkUS	34	8.89	9.29	185

FIGURE 4.3   Published Yield Information on Major Money Market Mutual Funds.

Data on money funds is widely quoted in the financial press; here we see that the information includes the portfolios' average maturity (in days), the seven-day average of the yield currently available, the seven-day effective yield (noted "e7Day") that would have been earned over the prior seven-day period, and the total assets in the portfolio measured in millions of dollars. (*Source: The Wall Street Journal*, May 11, 1989, p. C21. Reprinted by permission of *The Wall Street Journal*, © Dow Jones & Company, Inc., 1989. All rights reserved.)

ported, but so are average maturities. MMMFs provide convenient and easy access to funds through checkwriting privileges, although the checks often have to be written for a stipulated minimum amount (usually $500); the nice feature of this privilege is that you continue to earn interest while the check is being cleared through the banking system. In addition, the larger funds often allow investors to transfer money from their MMMF to other funds they manage.

We will describe mutual funds more fully in Chapter 13, which is devoted exclusively to such securities; however, several characteristics of money funds should be noted here. One concern of many investors revolves around the question of safety. Since they are not federally insured, one could argue that MMMFs will always be less secure than deposits in federally insured institutions; banks underscored this theme when they introduced their NOWs and MMDAs. However, the fact is that the history of MMMFs has been virtually free of even the threat of failure. Default risk is almost zero, since the securities the funds purchase are very low in risk to

INVESTOR INSIGHTS

Bruce Bent: He Invented the Money Market Fund

To Bruce Bent, the creator of the money market fund, the description has become a cliché: ''It's so elegant, so simple,'' he hears yet another observer say.

Yes, the money market fund is elegant and simple. It turned banking on its ear and helped end regulated, low interest rates and usher in interest-bearing checking accounts. But Bent's inspiration was 99% perspiration.

He was 32 in 1969, and the bulk of his experience lay in investing premiums paid to Teachers Insurance and Annuity Association, his employer, where they would earn the greatest and safest return. That meant CDs and commercial paper. He like the challenge of short-term investing. He just didn't like doing it for someone else.

Restless, he teamed up with his ex-boss at Teachers, Henry B.R. Brown, and went looking for money to manage for investors wanting good yields from short-term instruments. ''We asked ourselves: 'Where is there a service need that isn't being met?' ''

BRIGHT IDEA

They found their niche when interest rates on CDs and commercial paper hit 8% and 9%. Compare that to the federally regulated bank and S&L rates of 4% to 5% and you could see where smart people ought to have put their money.

The trouble was, only the big players, such as Teachers, with the financial wherewithal to buy six-figure CDs could enjoy the higher rate. Anyone else was stuck in line at the bank.

Bent and Brown spent months looking for a bank that wasn't subject to Regulation Q, the federal law that capped bank and S&L interest rates for small investors. They didn't find one.

Then inspiration struck: Why not a mutual fund? But instead of trading stocks, their fund would trade in . . . money. Investors with as little as $1,000 could get in on the action. What's more, Brown and Bent would stagger maturities so that the fund would be liquid enough to pay off shareholders on demand. The icing on the cake was the form those withdrawals would take: Shareholders could simply write a check. Bent was creating a floating-rate, interest-bearing checking account.

---

tax-exempt money fund
a money market mutual fund that limits its investments to tax-exempt municipal securities with very short maturities.

begin with, and diversification by the funds lowers risk even more. Despite this remarkable record of safety, it is impossible to say with certainty that MMMFs are *as* risk-free as federally insured deposits—and in the event of a massive financial crisis, they probably are not. On the other hand, the amount of extra risk might be viewed as so minimal as to be easily offset by a slightly higher yield. This is a choice the individual investor must make within his or her own risk-return framework.

In addition to the standard money market mutual fund, there are tax-exempt money funds and government securities money funds. The **tax-exempt money fund** limits its investments to tax-exempt municipal securities with very short (30 to

It was a revolutionary idea in 1969. But it just sat there. Corporations and their chief financial officers, to whom Bent directed sales pitches, weren't interested. The Securities and Exchange Commission, from which they would need permission to operate, sat on their application for months.

At the time, Bent was living on $11,000 a year to support a wife and two sons, and his venture was $250,000 in debt. At the close of 1972, the Reserve Fund, with just $300,000 in deposits, appeared stillborn. Bent offered 80% of the business to a Virginia investor just to settle the debt. The man balked, wanting a better deal.

Then, on January 7, 1973, the *New York Times* reported on the Reserve Fund. "A mutual find for overnight money," the headline read. A hundred calls came in the next day, and Bent answered many of them himself. In a month the fund had $1.9 million in deposits; in three months, $10 million; in a year, $100 million. The guy in Virginia probably wanted to kill himself.

BACK ON TOP

Money market funds are taken for granted these days. More than 524 now exist, managing more than $338 billion. *The Wall Street Journal* has ranked the money market fund among the ten most significant innovations in finance. Bent's Reserve funds (there are five, including tax-exempt funds for New York and Connecticut) have assets over $3 billion.

But his invention was nearly a victim of its own success. Money market funds became so popular that banks were clamoring to compete. Regulation Q was fading out in 1982, and banks were soon offering rates just attractive enough (although rarely equal) to woo depositors away. Bent had suffered a similar calamity in 1977, when rates on CDs fell and made yields on his funds unattractive. Each time, rates rose again and he got back on top.

Bent smiles with satisfaction, making a final question almost irrelevant: Does he have any other good ideas? The smile broadens, the ice-blue eyes crinkle. The son of a mailman, the guy who put himself through night school at St. John's University and New York University for an MBA, shoots his arms up to cradle the back of his head. His silver cuff links gleam in the sunlight of a corner office. He leans into a view of Manhattan from the Hudson River to Central Park. "Do I need any?" he asks.

Source: Dan Moreau, "Changing Agents: Money-Market Funds Didn't Seem Such a Great Idea in 1970," *Changing Times,* March 1989, p. 132

government securities money fund
a money market mutual fund that limits its investments to Treasury bills and other short-term securities of the U.S. government and its agencies.

90 days) maturities. Except for this feature they are like the standard money market funds, being highly liquid, offering checkwriting privileges, and so on. Since their income is free from federal (and some state) income tax, they yield less than standard, fully taxable money funds. They appeal predominantly to investors in the higher tax bracket for whom the lower tax-free yield is better than the *after-tax* return they could earn on standard money funds. **Government securities money funds** were established as a way to meet investor concerns for safety. In essence these funds effectively eliminate any risk of default by confining their investments to Treasury bills and other short-term securities of the U.S. government and its agencies (like the Federal National Mortgage Association). They are like standard

MMMFs in all other respects except for their slightly lower yields (which is the price you pay for the higher quality). As one might expect, the closest competitor today for the MMMF (in terms of yield and liquidity) is the money market deposit account offered by banks and other financial institutions.

Central Asset Accounts

central asset account
a comprehensive deposit account that combines checking, investing, and borrowing activities and automatically sweeps excess balances into short-term investments.

The **central asset account** was first introduced in 1977 as the ''cash management account'' or ''CMA'' by the Wall Street brokerage firm of Merrrill Lynch. The account is not a separate investment vehicle, but rather a comprehensive deposit account that combines checking, investing, and borrowing activities. These accounts are offered by banks, other depository institutions, brokerage houses, mutual funds, and insurance companies. Their distinguishing feature is that they automatically ''sweep'' excess balances into short-term investments. For example, a bank central asset account might be set up to combine a NOW and an MMDA. At the end of each day, if the NOW account balance exceeds $500, the excess is automatically swept into the higher-yielding MMDA. Merrill Lynch's CMA automatically sweeps the account holder's funds into its money market mutual fund, and if securities are purchased for an amount greater than the current balance, the needed funds are supplied automatically through a loan. Central asset accounts are exceptionally popular with investors. However, stipulated minimum balance requirements ranging from $5,000 to $20,000—the CMA, for example, requires an initial balance of $20,000 in cash or securities—limit the availability of central asset accounts to those with greater savings.

Certificates of Deposit (CDs)

certificates of deposit (CDs)
savings instruments in which funds must remain on deposit for a specified period; premature withdrawals incur interest penalties.

Certificates of deposit (CDs) differ from the savings instruments discussed above in that funds must remain on deposit for a specified period, which can range from seven days to a year or more. Although it is possible to withdraw funds prior to maturity, an interest penalty (of 31 to 90 days of interest, depending on the original maturity of the CD) usually makes withdrawal somewhat costly. Banks and S&Ls today are free to offer any rate and maturity on these securities. Some institutions will even allow you to specify the maturity date (for example, on a birthday or anniversary). A wide variety of CDs is offered by most banks and thrift institutions, and these go by an equally wide variety of names. CDs are convenient to buy and hold, and all offer attractive and highly competitive returns plus federal insurance protection. The critical factor in deciding whether to invest in one of these or in, say, MMDAs or MMMFs, is the willingness to tie up funds for a certain time period. If you think interest rates will be falling and that the return on your MMDA or MMMF might go much below what is now available on CDs, then you should choose CDs; if you believe interest rates will rise, the MMDA or MMMF may be the better choice.

brokered CDs
certificates of deposit sold by stockbrokers; offer slightly higher yields than other CDs and no penalty for sale prior to maturity.

In addition to CDs purchased directly from the issuer, they also can be purchased from stockbrokers. **Brokered CDs** are simply bank certificates of deposit sold by stockbrokers. The brokerage house looks around the country for the best deal—highest yield—it can get and then sells these CDs to its customers. In essence, a

bank or S&L issues the CDs, and the brokerage house merely sells (or places) them with the investing public. The minimum denomination is usually only $1,000, so they are affordable, and there's usually no commission to pay since the broker earns its commission from the issuing bank or S&L. Brokered CDs are attractive for two reasons: *First,* you can sell them prior to maturity without incurring a penalty, since the brokerage firms maintain active secondary markets; therefore, you can improve your liquidity. But remember, there are no guarantees here—the market prevails, so if rates go up, the relative value of your CD falls, and you don't end up earning the rate you started out with. *Second,* you may be able to get higher yields from brokered CDs than from your local bank or thrift institution. Frequently, you can gain ¼ to ¾ of a percent by dealing with a broker. But be careful. The broker can always get higher yields by selling CDs issued by troubled financial institutions. Therefore, *never buy a brokered CD unless it's from a federally insured institution—* ask your broker, just to be sure.

Commercial Paper

commercial paper
short-term, unse-cured promissory notes issued by cor-porations with very high credit stand-ings.

Commercial paper is short-term, unsecured promissory notes (IOUs) issued by corporations with very high credit standings. These notes are typically sold by firms in need of short-term loans to other businesses, banks, brokerage firms, money market mutual funds, and individuals wishing to invest funds for a short period of time. Although it is sometimes issued in denominations as small as $25,000 or $50,000, most commercial paper is initially sold in multiples of $100,000. Typical maturities range from a few days up to 270 days, the maximum maturity that does not require registration with the Securities and Exchange Commission (SEC). The secondary market for commercial paper is very limited, and therefore most inves-tors hold commercial paper to maturity. Commercial paper is rated as to its quality by independent agencies. Its yield is comparable to the rate of return earned on large-denomination CDs.

Due to its large denominations, typically only larger institutions deal directly in commercial paper. Most individual investors obtain commercial paper from a bank or broker, who will "break down" the paper and sell the investor a small portion, such as $10,000 of the paper at a slightly lower yield in order to cover administra-tive costs. MMMFs, who generally buy large quantities of paper to be included in their portfolios, probably provide the best method for the small investor to invest in commercial paper. Individual investors can generally earn returns competitive with commercial paper by purchasing CDs, which, like commercial paper, have a fixed maturity but in addition have federal insurance protection. Investors buying com-mercial paper should buy only high-rated paper with a maturity closely matched to their desired investment horizon.

U.S. Treasury Bills

U.S. Treasury bills (T-bills)
obligations of the U.S. Treasury, sold on a discount basis, and having varying short-term maturities and virtually no risk.

Prior to the many changes that have taken place in the financial markets in recent years, **U.S. Treasury bills** were the key short-term investment for most people who had sufficient funds to meet their rather high minimum investment requirement. T-bills are obligations of the U.S. Treasury issued as part of its ongoing process of

funding the national debt. T-bills are sold on a discount basis in minimum denominations of $10,000, with $5,000 increments above that. Treasury bills are issued with 3-month (13-week), 6-month (26-week), and 1-year maturities. The 3- and 6-month bills are auctioned off every Monday (for delivery on the following Thursday), and there is an auction for 1-year bills approximately every four weeks. An individual investor can purchase T-bills directly (through participation in the weekly Treasury auctions) or indirectly through local commercial banks or security dealers who buy bills for investors on a commission basis. Outstanding Treasury bills can also be purchased in the secondary market through banks or brokers. The biggest advantage of this approach is that the investor has a much wider selection of maturities to choose from, ranging from less than a week to as long as a year. It is actually relatively simple to buy T-bills directly. All one need do is submit a tender to the nearest Federal Reserve Bank, or branch, specifying both the amount and maturity desired (tender forms are short and can be obtained by writing the Bureau of Public Debt, Securities Transaction Branch; Main Treasury Building; Washington, D.C. 20239; or by calling 202-287-4113). The Treasury tries to accommodate individual investors through its noncompetitive bidding system, which most individual investors use because of its simplicity. In essence, all noncompetitive tender offers are awarded T-bills at a price equal to the average of all the accepted competitive bids. Thus, the investor is assured of buying bills in the quantity desired, while obtaining the benefits of an open auction system—all without going through the hassle of a competitive bid. But be careful: T-bills bought directly through noncompetitive bidding are meant to be held to maturity; they should *not* be purchased by investors who may want to trade them since it's a difficult and time-consuming process to sell them in the after-market.

Treasury bill rates are quoted daily in *The Wall Street Journal* and other major financial media. A particularly attractive feature of T-bills is that they are *exempt from state and local income taxes,* which in some areas can be as high as 20 percent—and like CDs and commercial paper, there are *no* (federal) taxes due until the interest is actually received at maturity. Because they are issued by the U.S. Treasury, T-bills are regarded as the safest but generally lowest-yielding of all investments. Furthermore there is a highly active secondary market for Treasury bills, so they can easily be sold if the investor needs the cash.

Series EE Savings Bonds

Series EE savings bonds are the well-known savings bonds that have been available for decades. (First issued in 1941, these used to be called Series E bonds.) EE bonds are often purchased through payroll deduction plans. Although issued by the U.S. Treasury, they are quite different from T-bills; in fact, perhaps their only similarity to the latter is that they are sold on a discount basis and are also exempt from state and local income taxes. These bonds are **accrual-type securities,** which means that interest is paid when the bond is cashed, on or before maturity, rather than periodically over the life of the bond. (The government does make Series HH bonds available; these can be obtained only through the exchange of Series E or Series EE bonds, have a 10-year maturity, and are available in denominations of $500 to

Series EE savings bonds
savings bonds issued by the U.S. Treasury and sold at banks and through payroll deduction plans, in varying denominations, at 50% of face value; pay a variable rate of interest depending on the length of time held.

accrual-type securities
securities for which interest is paid when the bond is cashed, on or before maturity, rather than periodically over the life of the bond.

$10,000. Unlike EE bonds, HH bonds are issued at their full face value and pay interest semiannually at the current fixed rate of 6 percent.) Series EE bonds are backed by the full faith and credit of the U.S. government, and can be replaced without charge in case of loss, theft, or destruction. They can be purchased at banks or other thrift institutions, or through payroll deduction plans. They are issued in denominations of $50 through $10,000, with the purchase price of all denominations being 50 percent of the face amount (thus a $100 bond will cost $50 and be worth $100 at maturity).

The actual maturity date on EE bonds is unspecified, since the issues pay a variable rate of interest. The higher the rate of interest being earned, the shorter the period of time it takes for the bond to accrue from its discounted purchase price to its maturity value. In an effort to make these securities more attractive to investors, all EE bonds held five years or longer currently receive interest at the higher of 6 percent or 85 percent of the average return on five-year Treasury securities, as calculated every six months in May and November. The yield, therefore, changes every six months in accordance with prevailing Treasury security yields, although it can never drop below a guaranteed minimum rate of 6 percent. The rate being quoted in late-1989 was 6.98 percent. Current rates on Series EE bonds can be obtained from your bank or simply by calling 1-800-872-6637 (1-800-U.S. BONDS). EEs held for less than five years (they can be redeemed any time after the first six months) earn interest according to a fixed, graduated scale beginning at 4.16 percent for bonds held six months and rising gradually to not less than the 6 percent guaranteed minimum rate at five years.

In addition to being exempt from state and local taxes, Series EE bonds provide their holders with an appealing tax twist. *Investors need not report the interest earned on federal tax returns until the bonds are redeemed.* Although interest can be reported annually (this might be done, for example, if the bonds are held in the name of a child who has limited interest income), most investors choose to defer it. In effect, this means the funds are being reinvested at an after-tax rate of no less than the guaranteed minimum rate of 6 percent. What's more, it is even possible to defer the tax shelter *beyond* the redemption date of your Series EE bond. For you can extend your tax shelter if, instead of cashing in the bonds, you exchange them for Series HH bonds. The accumulated interest on the Series EE bonds remains free of federal income tax for a while longer, since you will not have to pay the tax on those interest earnings until the HH bonds reach maturity (10 years) or until you cash *them* in. Thus in contrast to their predecessors, not only do today's Series EE bonds represent a safe and secure form of investment, but they also provide highly competitive yields and offer attractive tax incentives. Another attractive tax feature allows complete tax avoidance of EE bond earnings when proceeds are used to pay education expenses, such as college, by married couples with less than $60,000 of adjusted gross income, $40,000 or less for single filers.

Investment Suitability

The accounts and securities discussed above are widely used by individuals as both savings and investment vehicles. They are used to build up or maintain a desired

level of *savings* to meet unforeseen emergencies and/or for major expenditures that will or are likely to occur in the future; some people may also use their savings to take advantage of the unexpected opportunities that sometimes materialize. Whatever the reason, savings are viewed chiefly as a means of accumulating funds that will be readily available when and if the need arises—in essence, to provide safety and security. In this case high yield is less important than safety, liquidity, and convenience. Passbook savings accounts, NOW accounts, and Series EE savings bonds are popular savings vehicles as, to a lesser extent, are money market deposit accounts, money funds, central asset accounts, CDs, commercial paper, and T-bills.

When used for *investment* purposes, yield is often just as important as these vehicles' liquidity characteristics. However, because the objective is different the securities tend to be used much more aggressively than in savings programs. Most investors will hold at least a part of their portfolio in short-term, highly liquid securities, if for no other reason than to be able to act on unanticipated investment opportunities. Some investors, in fact, may as a matter of practice devote all or most of their portfolios to such securities in the belief that these investments provide attractive rates of return for the risk, because they are unfamiliar with other investment vehicles, or simply because they do not wish to devote the time necessary to managing their portfolios. One of the most common uses of short-term securities as investment vehicles is to employ them as temporary investment outlets. This is done for two reasons: either until an attractive permanent investment can be found, or as a temporary holding place in times of unsettled or undesirable market conditions. For example, an investor who has just sold some stock and who does not have a suitable long-term investment alternative, might place the proceeds in a money fund until he finds a more permanent use for them. Or, an investor who feels that interest rates are about to rise sharply sells her long-term bonds and uses the proceeds to buy T-bills. The high-yielding securities—like MMDAs, money funds, CDs, and commercial paper—are generally preferred for use as part of an investment program, as are the central asset accounts at major brokerage houses.

Deciding which securities are most appropriate for a particular situation requires consideration of such issue characteristics as availability, safety, liquidity, and yield. Although all the investments we have discussed satisfy the basic liquidity demand, they do so to varying degrees. A NOW account is unquestionably the most liquid of all, since you can write as many checks as you wish and for any amount. A certificate of deposit, on the other hand, is not as liquid, since early redemption involves an interest penalty. Table 4.3 summarizes the key characteristics for most of the short-term investments discussed here. The letter grade assigned the investments for each characteristic reflects an estimate of the investment's quality in that area. For example, MMMFs received only a B+ on liquidity, since withdrawals usually require a minimum of $500; MMDAs, on the other hand, are judged somewhat better in this respect, since a withdrawal can be for any amount and is also available through automated teller machines. Yields are in the main self-explanatory, although you should note that as an investment scores lower on availability, safety, or liquidity, it will generally offer a higher yield.

TABLE 4.3   A Scorecard for Short-Term Accounts and Securities

Savings or Investment Vehicle	Availability	Safety	Liquidity	Yield (Average Rate)*
Passbook savings account	A+	A+	A	F (4.0%)
NOW account	A−	A+	A+	C− (4.8)
Money market deposit account (MMDA)	B	A+	A	B− (6.2)
Money market mutual fund (MMMF): standard and government security funds	B	A/A+	B+	A (9.3)
Central asset account	B−	A	A+	B− (6.2)
Certificate of deposit (3-month, large denomination)	B	A+	C	A (9.8)
Commercial paper (90-day)	B−	A−	C	A (9.6)
U.S. Treasury Bill (91-day)	B−	A++	A−	A− (8.4)
Series EE savings bond	A+	A++	C−	B+ (7.8)

*The average rates reflect representative or typical rates that existed in mid-1989.

MEETING RETIREMENT NEEDS: PLANNING FOR THE LONG HAUL

When we are young, retirement is often viewed as far away; it is a bit difficult to get excited about an event that may not take place for another 40 or 45 years. In some respects this is unfortunate, because the sooner one plans for retirement the better the chances that he or she will be able to put together a successful program. This is so for several reasons. First, retirement requires careful planning, both in terms of having the financial resources to sustain us when we no longer produce income and also with respect to determining what our needs will be during the retirement years. Second, the sooner you invest to accumulate a retirement nest egg, the more productive your funds will be. This is a simple matter of the power of compound interest, or of how money grows over time. For example, if you invest $1,000 today for, say 30 years, you will amass $17,449, assuming you can achieve a 10 percent rate of return during the entire 30-year period. But if you can invest the same $1,000 for 10 years longer, your investment would grow to a whopping $45,258—over 2.5 times more ! (The method used to find these future values is described in Chapter 5.) Of course you may not realize a 10 percent rate of return over the full life of your investment; and even if you do, inflation will probably account for a good part of it. Nevertheless the crucial point is that the sooner you invest for retirement, the *progressively greater* amount you will accumulate, regardless of the reinvestment rate.

Retirement Planning

Planning begins by considering retirement as one part of your overall investment program. In drawing up your retirement plans, you need to consider how much income you can logically expect from the principal sources of retirement income—

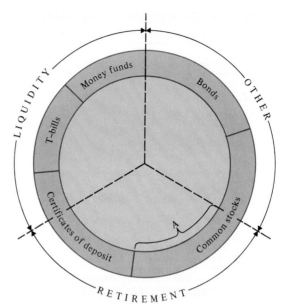

FIGURE 4.4 Retirement Planning Within an Overall Investment Program.
There are many parts to an investment portfolio, and retirement investments are certainly one of them; in fact, the securities held for retirement should be viewed as an integral part of the total portfolio, and actively managed as such.

social security and employer-sponsored programs. If these fall short of your income requirements, you will have to supplement them with your own self-directed program. In addition to developing such a program, you will need to determine how it will be funded. These are topics we now briefly consider.

Role of Retirement in an Investment Program

As we have noted throughout this chapter, investment activity is usually best undertaken to accomplish specific goals. This same matching of investments to objectives is necessary for retirement planning. This is true even if the investing is done for you; that is, if most of your retirement income (other than social security) will be derived from an employer-sponsored program. To illustrate this, consider the diagram in Figure 4.4. Here, total investment requirements are divided into three areas—liquidity, retirement, and other needs, each of which is represented by an equal slice of the circle. (Remember this is just an illustration; we are not suggesting these needs are all equal.) Now, suppose you believe that a portion of your retirement assets should be in common stock, say, the amount designated A; if your employer-sponsored program does not provide for common stock investments, the only way to meet your goal is to do it yourself, by investing amount A in stocks. On the other hand, if your employer-sponsored program is heavily invested in stocks, you may want to put less of your own retirement portfolio into stocks and more into other securities, such as bonds or other fixed-income securities. The important point

TABLE 4.4 A Retirement Plan for Roy and Sue Sloane

	Current Dollars	Inflation Factor	Future Needs
Estimated Expenditures			
Housing and utilities	$ 5,600		
Food—at home and dining out	6,000		
Transportation	2,200		
Travel and entertainment	5,200		
Medical	2,000		
All other	7,000		
Total expenditures	$28,000 × 4.322*	=	$121,016
Estimated Income			
Social security	$12,000 × 4.322*	=	$ 51,864
Employer retirement plan	7,000 × 5.743**	=	40,201
Subtotal	$19,000		$ 92,065
Additional required income	9,000		28,951
Total income	$28,000		$121,016
Asset Requirement			
Anticipated return on assets held during retirement			0.10
Assets required ($28,951/.10)			$289,510

*Inflation rate (or growth rate) of 5% per year for 30 years.
**Growth rate of 6% per year for 30 years.

is that meeting retirement needs should be an integral part of every investment program, and the assets or investments held for retirement purposes should be just as actively managed as all other parts of the portfolio. The ultimate target is to derive a final portfolio that meets all of one's needs within a level of risk considered appropriate for the expected return.

Determining Future Needs and Income

To illustrate the process of coordinating future needs and income, let us consider the Roy and Sue Sloane family. The Sloanes are in their mid-thirties, have two children, and an annual income of about $45,000 before taxes. They have given little thought to retirement, but now believe that even though it is still some 30 years away, they should review their situation to see if they will be able to pursue a life-style in retirement that appeals to them. Table 4.4 shows how the Sloanes have estimated their retirement income and how they must accumulate investment assets of roughly $289,510 to meet their retirement objectives. Let's see how they did this.

Roy and Sue Sloane began their calculations by determining their expenditures on the assumption that retirement would take place *immediately;* this allowed them

to think in terms of today's dollar. They determined that it would take $28,000 a year to attain their retirement life-style. The next step was to see how much their retirement income would be, given retirement today. The Sloanes believe social security will provide $12,000, and Roy's retirement plan would add another $7,000; unfortunately, the total of $19,000 was $9,000 short of their estimated expenditures. But this shortfall is in today's dollars and not in the dollars that will exist when the Sloanes' retirement will actually take place. Thus Roy and Sue face the difficult task of estimating future values. They believe that inflation will average 5 percent over the next 30 years (when their retirement will begin). This means that the $28,000 of expenditures will grow to $121,016; this number is calculated using the future value techniques that are described in Chapter 5. Roy and Sue also believe that social security increases will match the inflation rate; based on past performance, they think their retirement plan should do a little better and grow by 6 percent. Given these assumptions about future income growth, the Sloanes would have a total annual income of $92,065 (see Table 4.4), which means their annual shortfall in future dollars is $28,951 ($121,016 − $92,065).

The next step is to estimate the rate of return the Sloanes think they will be able to earn on their investments *after* they retire. This will tell them how big their nest egg must be *by retirement* in order to eliminate the expected annual shortfall of $28,951. Let's assume this return is estimated to be 10 percent, in which case the Sloanes must accumulate $289,510 by retirement. That figure is found by determining the principal sum needed, at a 10 percent rate of return, to earn $28,951 annually; this value is found by dividing the annual amount by the rate of return: $28,951/.10 = $289,510. Such a nest egg will yield $28,951 a year, given that a 10 percent rate of return can be earned ($289,510 × .10 = $28,951). And as long as the capital ($289,510) remains untouched, it will generate the same annual amount throughout the Sloanes' lifetime and can eventually become a part of their estate.

Now that the Sloanes know how big their nest egg has to be, the final question is how are they going to accumulate that amount by the time they retire? For most people this means setting up a *systematic savings plan* that involves putting away a certain amount each year. To find out how much must be saved annually to achieve a targeted sum, future value calculations, which are discussed in Chapter 5, would be applied. Assuming they can earn a 10 percent rate of return, applying future value techniques indicates the Sloanes will have to save $1,760 each year for the next 30 years in order to accumulate $289,510 by retirement. But there's more to be taken into account. For our calculations, we've assumed the Sloanes will in fact be able to achieve a 10 percent rate of return on their investments. Failure to do so will mean they won't achieve their targeted nest egg. For example, if they can earn only 8 percent on their investments, they will have only $199,376 by retirement. While this means the Sloanes will have accumulated an investment pool of nearly $200,000 (certainly not a paltry sum), the fact remains that they will be about $90,000 short of their target by retirement, and hence will either have to reduce their standard of living in retirement or start tapping their capital earlier than expected. Similar results will occur if they fail to put aside the needed amount each year—for example, if the best they can do is save $1,200 per year (but still achieve

TABLE 4.5 Financing the Sloans' First Three Years of Retirement

	Years		
	1	2	3
Expenditures*	$121,016	$127,067	$133,420
Income			
Social security*	$ 51,864	$ 54,457	$ 57,180
Employer retirement plan	40,201	40,201	40,201
Supplemental income	28,951	28,951	28,605
Total income	$121,016	$123,609	$125,986
Budget deficit	$ 0	$ 3,458	$ 7,434
Retirement assets at end of year	$289,510	$286,052	$278,618

*Assumes a rate of growth of 5% for years 2 and 3.

a 10 percent rate of return on their investments), the Sloanes' nest egg will grow to only $197,389.

Actually, we have simplified the Sloanes' retirement plan a bit, for there are other complications to consider: First, inflation will probably continue after their retirement. Although social security income will probably continue to grow at or near the annual rate of inflation, the benefits from Roy's retirement plan will not, and neither will the income from their investment assets. This means that each retirement year would require a drawing down of these assets to sustain their lifestyle. Table 4.5 illustrates this process for the first three years. The question now is how long these assets will last if they are constantly being depleted. Naturally one cannot answer that unless an assumption is made about how long Roy and Sue live beyond the onset of retirement. Planning retirement income, then, is no easy task. In the Sloanes' case $289,510 probably should be sufficient for their retirement years, but their estate will decrease as time passes. To provide a hedge against this type of uncertainty, the Sloanes might want to increase the size of their annual retirement contribution to $2,000 or $2,500 to build up a bigger nest egg. A second simplification in the Sloane example is that we have ignored the impact of federal income taxes. Under current social security law (discussed below), a portion of their social security income may be taxable. Depending on how Roy's retirement plan is structured, a portion or all of their retirement income may also be taxable. And in all likelihood, all their investment income will be taxable. Holding everything else the same but adding in taxes means that the additional required income would have to be greater than $9,000 a year, and that the required retirement assets would need to be more than $289,510.

Retirement Programs

There are three basic sources of retirement income: (1) social security; (2) employer-sponsored retirement programs, both basic and supplemental; and (3) individual self-directed retirement programs, specifically Keoghs and IRAs. Although

most people still rely on social security and employer-sponsored programs to supply the bulk of their retirement income, certain tax-advantaged, self-directed plans are available. These plans are of the greatest importance to students of investments, since they must be established and managed by the individual. We will examine all three retirement programs below, but our emphasis will be on the self-directed plans.

Social Security

social security
federal government income program for retired or disabled persons, to which individuals contribute over their working lifetimes, and with benefits and conditions set by law.

Virtually all Americans are affected by **social security.** With recent congressional changes in the law, if your income was $20,000 in 1989, the social security tax withheld from your wage annually would have been $1,502; at the maximum, you would have paid $3,605 annually. Someone who retired in 1988 at age 65, and who had earned the maximum amount of earnings used to determine benefits, would now receive about $840 *monthly* from social security. If this person is a man who is married, his wife would also be eligible to receive social security benefits, the exact amount of which would depend on whether or not she had also been employed and had paid into social security. At the minimum, she would be eligible to receive half of her husband's benefits, so their combined social security benefits should amount to about $1,260 per month. Of course the actual amount of benefit received depends on a formula used by the Social Security Administration (SSA). This formula is so complex that the SSA no longer publishes tables that fit all situations. Moreover, cost-of-living adjustments (COLAs) also affect future benefits. Due to the complexity of the benefit estimation process, in 1988 the SSA introduced a computerized benefits estimation service. Using this program, a person fills out a brief questionnaire (obtained by calling 1-800-937-2000) and sends it to the SSA, which returns a *Personal Earnings and Benefit Estimate Statement* that lists expected benefits under three popular retirement scenarios. If actual retirement is far in the future, however, current benefits may be altered substantially by the time retirement age is reached—which, by the way, was also lengthened from 65 to 66 years of age (by 2009) and to age 67 (by 2027).

Social security benefits *may be subject to income tax.* A retiree must add half of his or her benefits to adjusted gross income, and if this total exceeds $25,000 for an individual and $32,000 for a couple filing a joint return, up to half of the benefits are subject to tax, based on a graduated scale. Moreover, the retiree must include tax-free income in determining the base amount. A rough current rule of thumb is that an average retired, married wage earner can expect social security benefits of between 40 and 60 percent of his or her wages in the year before retirement. (If your income was much above the average—as was the case for the Sloane family—the percentage is less.) Clearly individuals with higher incomes will have to rely less on social security—particularly when potential additional income taxes are considered—and more on other sources of retirement income.

Employer-Sponsored Programs—Basic Plans

Many employers provide retirement programs as part of the total compensation package offered employees. These programs are popular for several reasons: First,

most retirees find that social security benefits are inadequate to sustain their retirement life-styles. Second, having contributions provided by an employer in many cases means they escape federal income taxation, both when they are withheld and initially invested, and as their earnings are subsequently reinvested. If you had to provide your own retirement funds and no individual tax relief were available, you could do so only with after-tax dollars. If you are in the 28 percent tax bracket, this means for every $72 you put into retirement on your own, you could have $100 invested through an employer plan. A difference this large compounded over many years leads to an incredibly large difference in total dollars at retirement.

noncontributory plan
retirement plan completely funded by the employer.

contributory plan
retirement plan partially funded by the employee, whose contributions usually amount to 3–10 percent of wages.

vested (benefits)
benefits, accumulated under a pension plan, that have become the employee's nonforfeitable rights.

defined benefit plan
retirement plan that links benefits to a formula that is generally based on level of earnings and length of service.

defined contribution plan
retirement plan that defines precisely the amounts employer and employee contribute to the plan, but does not specify the retirement income.

401(k) plan
a retirement plan that allows employees to divert a portion of salary to a company-sponsored tax-sheltered savings account, thus deferring taxes until retirement.

Employer plans are **noncontributory** if the employer bears all the cost, and **contributory** if you share in the cost, which usually amounts to 3 to 10 percent of your total wages. Although most corporate pension plans are noncontributory, a growing number of them are switching to the contributory type. Benefits accumulated from employer contributions under a pension plan at some point in time become your nonforfeitable right; they are then described as **vested.** Prior to the Employee Retirement Income Security Act (ERISA) of 1974, there was considerable variation, and occasional abuse, of vesting. ERISA as modified by the Tax Reform Act of 1986 establishes minimum vesting requirements so that full vesting must take place after only 5 to 7 years of employment depending upon which of two vesting schedules the company is using. Of course, employers can (and often do) shorten these vesting periods, thereby offering more favorable vesting terms.

Every retirement program must explain how your retirement benefits will be determined. Two basic methods are used to make such determinations. A **defined benefit plan** indicates exactly what your benefits will be by linking them to a formula that generally includes factors for level of earnings and length of service with the employer. A typical plan might pay 1 percent of your average annual salary for the last three years of employment for each year of your employment. For example, if you averaged $45,000 a year over the last three years of service and had 20 years of employment, your annual retirement income would be $9,000 (0.01 × $45,000 × 20). A **defined contribution plan** does not spell out your retirement income, but defines precisely the amounts your employer and you contribute to the plan. Your actual retirement income then depends on how much is accumulated for you at retirement. Obviously, the amount cannot be known with certainty until the retirement date. A defined contribution plan requires more effort in planning your retirement income and managing your overall investment portfolio than does the defined benefit plan. (As explained earlier, these retirement assets should be considered a part of your portfolio.)

Employer-Sponsored Programs—Supplemental Plans

In addition to a basic retirement plan, many employers offer supplemental plans. Most medium- to large-sized firms have adopted a *salary reduction plan,* or the so-called **401(k) plan.** While quite popular from their inception in 1978, changes introduced by the Tax Reform Act of 1986 significantly impacted the funding capabilities of these plans. (While our discussion here will center on 401(k) plans, similar programs are also available for employees of public, nonprofit organiza-

tions; known as 403(b) plans, they offer many of the same features and tax shelter provisions as 401(k) plans.)

Basically, a 401(k) plan gives you, as an employee, the option to divert a portion of your salary to a company-sponsored tax-sheltered savings account. In this way the earnings placed in the savings plan accumulate tax-free. Taxes will have to be paid on these funds eventually, but not until you start drawing down the account at retirement and presumably are in a lower tax bracket. In 1989, an individual employee could put as much as $7,627 (depending on his or her salary) into a tax-deferred 401(k) plan—the annual dollar cap increases yearly, since it is indexed to the rate of inflation. (The contribution limits for 403(b) plans are currently set at a maximum of $9,500 per year, and that amount won't be indexed to inflation until 401(k) contributions attain parity with these plans.) To encourage savings for retirement, such contributions are "locked up" until the employee turns 59½ or leaves the company; a major exception to this rule lets employees tap their accounts, without penalties, in the event of any of a number of clearly defined "financial hardships."

To see how such tax-deferred plans work, consider an individual who earned, say, $45,000 in 1989, and who would like to contribute the maximum allowable— $7,627—to the 401(k) plan where she works. Doing so would reduce her taxable income to $37,373 and enable her to lower her federal tax bill by nearly $2,136 (i.e., .28 × $7,627). Such tax savings will offset a good portion of her contribution to the 401(k) savings plan; that is, it will fund about 28 percent of her contribution. In effect, she will add $7,627 to her retirement program with only $5,491 of her own money; the rest will come from the IRS via a reduced tax bill. What's more, all the *earnings* on her savings account will accumulate tax free as well. A special attraction of most 401(k) plans is that the firms offering them often "sweeten the pot" by matching all or part of an employee's contribution (up to a set limit). Presently, about 85 percent of the companies that offer 401(k) plans have some type of matching contribution program, often putting up 50 cents (or more) for each dollar contributed by the employee. Such matching programs provide both tax and savings incentives to individuals and clearly enhance the appeal of 401(k) plans.

Self-Directed Retirement Programs—Keogh Plans

Keogh plan

a retirement plan that allows self-employed individuals to establish tax-deferred retirement plans for themselves and their employees.

Keogh plans go back to 1962, when they were introduced as part of the Self-Employment Individuals Retirement Act—HR10, or simply the Keogh Act. They allow self-employed individuals to establish tax-deferred retirement plans for themselves and their employees. Like contributions to 401(k) plans, payments to Keogh accounts may be taken as deductions from taxable income. As a result they reduce the tax bill of self-employed individuals. The maximum contribution to this tax-deferred retirement plan is $30,000 per year or 20 percent of earned income, whichever is less. Any individual who is self-employed, either full- or part-time, is eligible to set up a Keogh account. Not only can the self-employed businessman or professional use Keoghs, they can also be used by individuals who hold full-time jobs *and* who "moon-light" on a part-time basis—for example, the engineer who has a small consulting business on the side, or the accountant who does tax returns

in the evenings and on weekends. Take the engineer for example; if he earns $10,000 a year from his part-time consulting business, he can contribute 20 percent of that income ($2,000) to his Keogh account and in so doing reduce both his taxable income and the amount he pays in taxes. And he is still eligible to receive full retirement benefits from his full-time job. The only catch to Keogh accounts is that the individual has to be self-employed—that is, the income must be derived from the net earnings (after all expenses except taxes and retirement contributions) of a self-employed person.

Keogh accounts can be opened at banks, insurance companies, brokerage houses, mutual funds, and other financial institutions. Annual contributions must be made at the time the respective tax return is filed, or by April 15 of the following calendar year (e.g., you have until April 15, 1990, to make the contribution to your Keogh for 1989). While a designated financial institution acts as custodian of all the funds held in a Keogh account, *the actual investments held in the account are under the complete direction of the individual contributor.* For unlike 401(k) plans, these are self-directed retirement programs and as such, the *individual* decides which investments to buy and sell (subject to a few basic restrictions). The income earned from the investments must be plowed back into the account and it, too, accrues tax-free. All Keogh contributions and investment earnings must remain in the account until the individual turns 59½, unless the individual becomes seriously ill or disabled. However, you are *not required* to start withdrawing the funds at age 59½; rather, they can stay in the account and continue to earn tax-free income until you turn 70½, at which time you have 10 years to clean out the account. In fact, as long as the self-employment income continues, an individual can continue to make tax-deferred contributions to a Keogh account up to the maximum age of 70½. Of course once an individual starts withdrawing funds from a Keogh account (when or after he or she is 59½), all such withdrawals are treated as active income and are subject to the payment of ordinary income taxes. Thus the taxes on all contributions to and earnings from a Keogh account are eventually going to have to be paid, a characteristic of any tax-*deferred* (as opposed to a tax-*free*) program. [*Note:* A program that's similar in many respects to the Keogh account is something called a *Simplified Employee Pension Plan (SEP–IRA).* It's aimed at small business owners, particularly those with *no employees,* who want a plan that is simple to set up and administer. SEP–IRAs *can be used in place of Keoghs* and although they are simpler to administer and have the same annual dollar contribution cap ($30,000), their contribution *rate* is less generous: you can put in only 15% of earned income for a SEP–IRA, versus 20% for a Keogh.]

individual retirement account (IRA) *a self-directed, tax-deferred retirement plan, in which gainfully employed persons may contribute annually up to $2,000 per individual or $2,250 for an individual and nonworking spouse; tax-deductibility of contributions depends on conditions relative to coverage by company-sponsored pension plans and the level of adjusted gross income.*

Self-Directed Retirement Programs—Individual Retirement Accounts (IRAs)

Some people mistakenly believe that an IRA is a specialized type of investment. It is not. An **individual retirement account (IRA)** is virtually the same as any other investment account you open with a bank, savings and loan, credit union, stockbroker, mutual fund, or insurance company—except that an IRA is a tax-deferred retirement program that is available to any gainfully employed individual. The form

you complete designates the account as an IRA and makes the institution its trustee. The maximum annual IRA contribution is $2,000 for an individual and $2,250 for an individual and a nonworking spouse. If both spouses work, each can contribute up to $2,000 to his or her own IRA. The Tax Reform Act of 1986 placed limits on the tax deductibility of IRA contributions. Specifically, in order to be able to use your annual IRA contributions as a tax deduction, *one* of the following two conditions has to be met: (1) neither you nor your spouse (if filing a joint return) can be covered by a company-sponsored pension plan, or (2) your adjusted gross income has to be less than $40,000 (for married couples) or $25,000 (for singles). Translated, this means your IRA contributions *would fully qualify* as a tax deduction if you were covered by a company-sponsored pension plan but your adjusted gross income fell below the specified amounts (of $40,000 for joint filers or $25,000 for singles), *or* if you (or your spouse) weren't covered by a company-sponsored pension plan, no matter how much your adjusted gross income was. [Note that the income ceilings are phased out, so that people with adjusted gross incomes of $40,000 to $50,000 (or $25,000 to $35,000) who are covered by employer pension plans, are still entitled to prorated *partial deductions*.] If the contributions qualify as tax deductions (as per the two conditions noted above), then the amount of the IRA contributions can be shown on the tax return as a deduction from taxable income—which, of course, will also reduce the amount of taxes that have to be paid. Even if you don't qualify for a tax deduction, you can *still contribute up to the maximum of $2,000 a year to an IRA account;* the big difference is that these nondeductible contributions will have to be made with after-tax income. As with Keoghs and 401(k) programs, the taxes on all the *earnings* from an IRA account are deferred until you start drawing down the funds, and this provision applies regardless of your income or whether you're already covered by a pension plan at your place of employment.

Even if your IRA contributions don't qualify for tax shelter, *you can still make annual contributions with after-tax dollars, and the earnings you generate from the investments you hold in your IRA account are tax sheltered to the extent that they can accumulate in a tax-free manner.* You can deposit as much or as little as you want up to the applicable limit, and there are no percentage-of-income contribution limitations; if your earned income is, say, only $1,800 then you can contribute *all* of it to your IRA. IRAs are *self-directed accounts* (that is, you are free, within limits, to make whatever investment decisions you wish with the capital held or deposited in your IRA). Of course, your investment options are limited by the types of products offered by competing financial institutions. Banks and thrift institutions push their savings vehicles, insurance companies have their annuities, and brokerage houses offer everything from mutual funds to stocks, bonds, and annuities. IRAs are the simplest and most flexible of all self-directed retirement plans to start and maintain. There are, however, restrictions on withdrawing funds. Except for serious illness, any withdrawals from an IRA prior to age 59½ are subject to a 10 percent penalty on top of the regular tax on the withdrawal itself.

Bear in mind that IRAs, along with all other retirement plans permitting contributions on a pretax basis, *defer* but do not *eliminate* taxes. When you receive the

TABLE 4.6   Accumulated Funds from a $1,000-a-Year Investment in an IRA and from a Fully Taxable (Non-IRA) Account*

Years Held	IRA	Non-IRA
1	$ 1,080	$ 762
5	6,335	4,272
10	15,645	9,926
15	29,323	17,405
20	49,421	27,359
25	78,951	40,471
30	122,341	57,821
35	186,097	80,778
40	279,774	111,153
45	417,417	159,502

*Contributions and earnings are taxed at 28 percent in the non-IRA account but are tax-free in the IRA; a rate of return of 8 percent is assumed in both cases.

income (contributions and investment earnings) in retirement, it is then taxed, at the then-prevailing tax rates. Even so, the impact of tax deferral is substantial. As Table 4.6 indicates, after about 25 years accumulated funds under an IRA are about twice as great as for a non-IRA; after 45 years the funds are nearly 2.6 times as great ($417,417 versus $159,502). This example assumes that you invest $1,000 of earned income each year. If you choose an IRA, you shelter from taxes both the $1,000 initial investment and its subsequent earnings, so that at the end of the first year, for example, you have accumulated $1,080. If you select the same investment vehicle but do not make it an IRA, you must first pay $280 in taxes (assuming a 28 percent tax rate), leaving only $720 to invest; the subsequent earnings of $58 ($0.08 × 720) are also taxed at 28 percent, leaving after-tax income of only $42 [$58 − 0.28($58)] = $58 − $16 = 42). Thus the first-year accumulation is just $762.

Many other regulations for IRAs should be understood before you open one. Some of the more important are these:

- You do not have to stay with the same IRA every year. In fact, you may have as many different IRAs as you wish.
- You can switch from one IRA account to another—either by having the trustee make the transfer or by withdrawing the funds yourself and depositing them in the new account subject to certain rules.
- After age 59½ you can withdraw funds as you see fit, including one lump sum, although this may not be practical from a tax point of view.

- You *must* begin withdrawing by age 70½.
- You cannot borrow from or against your IRA account.

Clearly, if you qualify for fully deductible IRA contributions, you should seriously consider depositing the maximum amount allowable.

Funding Keoghs and IRAs

As with any investment, an individual can be conservative or aggressive in choosing securities for a Keogh or IRA, though the nature of these retirement programs generally favors a more conservative approach. In fact, conventional wisdom favors funding your Keogh and IRA with *income-producing assets;* this would also suggest that if you are looking for capital gains, it is best to do so *outside* of your retirement account. The reasons for this are twofold: (1) Growth-oriented securities are by nature *more risky* and (2) you cannot write off losses from the sale of securities held in a Keogh or IRA account. This does *not* mean it would be altogether inappropriate to place a good-quality growth stock or mutual fund in a Keogh or IRA—in fact, many advisors contend that growth investments should *always* have a place in your retirement account. The reason is their *performance:* Such investments may pay off handsomely, since they can appreciate totally free of taxes. In the end, *it is how much you have in your retirement account that matters rather than how your earnings were made along the way.*

Although very few types of investment are prohibited outright, there are some that should be avoided simply because they are inappropriate for such accounts (for example tax-free municipal securities, because the tax shelter from a Keogh or IRA would be redundant since their income is tax exempt anyway). In addition to most long-term securities, money market accounts—both bank deposits (MMDAs) and mutual funds (MMMFs)—also appeal to Keogh and IRA investors, especially to those who view short-term securities as one way to capture volatile market rates. Not surprisingly, as the size of an account begins to build up an investor will often use more than one kind of security, which makes sense from a portfolio-diversification point of view. For remember, although Keoghs and IRAs offer attractive tax shelter incentives, they in no way affect the underlying risks of the securities held in these accounts. Also, regardless of what types of investment vehicles are used, keep in mind that once money is put into a Keogh or IRA, it's meant to stay there for the long haul.

Most IRA accounts were set up initially with banks and other thrifts. Later, investors began looking more toward brokerage firms, insurance companies, and mutual funds as a source of IRA investments. You can expect wide variations in the charges each of these levies to open and administer your account. Brokerage firms appear to be the most expensive, with initial fees of $25 to $50 not uncommon, and annual maintenance fees of about the same. Banks, thrifts, and mutual funds are generally lower. Before you open an account, by all means inquire about what the costs will be.

SUMMARY

- Investment goals determine the types of investments made. Common investment goals include (1) enhancing current income; (2) saving for major expenditures; (3) accumulating retirement funds; and (4) sheltering income from taxes.

- Provision for adequate life insurance is an important prerequisite to investment planning. Life insurance, which provides financial protection in the event of premature death, may be bought in any of four basic forms: term; whole life; universal; and variable life insurance. A variety of techniques are available for estimating life insurance needs and obtaining the best form of coverage.

- Investment goals are quantified beginning with established long-run financial goals, which include retirement goals. The plan for goal achievement should first consider any known benefits as well as available funds to determine the level of annual investment required to meet each goal. The actual investment vehicles selected will be affected by both economic/market cycles and the investor's stage in his or her life cycle.

- Tax consequences associated with various investment vehicles and strategies must be considered when establishing an investment program. An individual's income can be classified as active (ordinary "earned"), portfolio (investment), or passive; regardless of its classification, income can be ordinary or capital gains—both subject to the same tax rate. From an individual investor's point of view, the key tax dimensions to consider are ordinary income, capital gains and losses, tax shelters, and tax planning.

- Investment goals and plans should provide adequate liquidity, which can be met by holding a variety of short-term securities. In addition to providing liquidity, such vehicles earn interest, which occasionally is higher than that available on long-term securities.

- Short-term investments can earn interest in one of two ways: Either they are sold on a discount basis, or interest is paid at a stated rate. They carry a low risk; the primary risk results from a potential loss in purchasing power.

- Most saving and short-term investing is done with the following: passbook savings accounts; NOW accounts; money market deposit accounts and mutual funds; central asset accounts; certificates of deposit; commercial paper; U.S. Treasury bills; and Series EE savings bonds. The suitability of any of these for the individual investor depends on the latter's attitude toward availability, safety, liquidity, and yield.

- Retirement planning should be started early in life as part of one's overall investment program. Retirement strategy includes reviewing needs for the retirement years, estimating how much retirement income will be necessary to support those needs, and investing to provide needed funding in addition to that provided by existing government benefits and employer plans.

- Social security is the cornerstone of most retirement plans. Employer-spon-

sored retirement programs include (1) basic plans provided by most employers, and (2) supplemental plans—401(k) plans—that allow employees to reduce their wages in favor of additional retirement contributions.

- A Keogh plan is a self-directed retirement plan available to self-employed individuals. An individual retirement account (IRA), in contrast, is a self-directed retirement plan available to most people. Both Keoghs and IRAs are easy to open and administer, provide for tax-deferred earnings accumulation (and possibly tax-deductible contributions), and can be funded with almost any type of investment vehicle.

REVIEW QUESTIONS AND PROBLEMS

1. What are investment goals? Briefly describe each of the following commonly cited investment goals:
   a. Enhancing current income.
   b. Saving for major expenditures.
   c. Accumulating retirement funds.
   d. Sheltering income from taxes.

2. Define insurance, and discuss the basic characteristics of an insurable risk.

3. Briefly define and differentiate among the following types of life insurance. Describe the basic motives that should underlie the use of each of these forms.
   a. Term insurance.
   b. Whole life insurance.
   c. Universal life insurance.
   d. Variable life insurance.

4. Explain why term insurance and universal life insurance would most likely be the best forms to choose in fulfilling life insurance needs.

5. Explain how one should go about preparing an investment plan that provides for achievement of a given investment goal. Be sure to explain how existing investments or retirement benefits and current investable balances can be important factors to consider when estimating the amount of annual income that must be invested to achieve the goal. Comment on the role that monitoring an investment plan plays in the total investment program.

6. Describe the four stages of the economic/market cycle, and discuss the impact of this cycle on each of the following forms of investment:
   a. Stocks.
   b. Bonds.
   c. Tangible investments.

7. Describe the differing investment philosophies typically observed during each of the following stages of an investor's life cycle:
   a. Youth (age 20 to 45).
   b. Middle-age (age 45 to 60).
   c. Retirement years (age 60 to ?).

8. Define, differentiate, and explain federal income taxes as they relate to the following forms of income:

   a. Active (ordinary "earned") income.
   b. Portfolio (investment) and passive income.
   c. Capital gains.
   d. Capital loss.
      (1) On a wash sale.
      (2) On a tax swap.

9. Briefly define and discuss the role of tax shelters and tax planning in one's investment program.

10. What makes an asset liquid? Why would you want to hold liquid assets? Would 100 shares of IBM stock be considered a liquid investment? Explain.

11. Suppose you can purchase a 90-day T-bill with a $10,000 redemption value for $9,500; calculate the annual rate of return on this investment, assuming you hold the bill to maturity.

12. Explain the characteristics of short-term investments with respect to both purchasing power and default risk.

13. Complete the following table for the short-term investments listed. You will have to make assumptions about their yields.

Investment	Insured	Yield	Minimum Balance	Method and Ease of Withdrawing Funds
a. Passbook savings account	Yes	4.0%	None	In person or through teller machines; very easy
b. NOW account				Unlimited check-writing privileges
c. Money market deposit account (MMDA)				
d. Money market mutual fund (MMMF)				
e. Central asset account				
f. Certificate of deposit (CD)				
g. Commercial paper				
h. U.S. Treasury bill		8.5%		
i. Series EE savings bond			Virtually none	

14. Is retirement planning a part of—or distinct from—an overall investment program? Explain why it is important to begin planning for retirement early in your career.

15. Explain the impact of inflation on a retirement plan. (Cover retirement income as well as retirement expenditures.)

16. Describe and discuss the steps involved in coordinating future needs and income in order to develop a retirement plan. Be sure to explain how existing retirement programs are considered in this process.

17. Describe the basic features of social security retirement benefits. Roughly what percent of pre-retirement wages will social security provide to the average wage earner?

18. Distinguish between a defined benefit plan and a defined contribution plan; indicate how retirement benefits might be determined under a typical defined benefit plan.

19. What is a 401(k) plan? In what way(s) might it serve your supplemental retirement program?

20. Briefly describe Keoghs and IRAs, and compare their relative advantages and disadvantages. Which investment vehicles might be suitable for funding a Keogh or an IRA? Explain.

CASE PROBLEMS

4.1 The Chungs' Dilemma Over How to Save

Allen and Linda Chung are a recently married couple. Each has just begun a professional career and earns about $25,000 a year before taxes. (With a combined *gross* income of $50,000 per year, they're in the 28 percent tax bracket.) In spite of their income, Al and Linda have not yet accumulated many investment assets. Their net worth is about $15,000, and most of it is the difference between the market values of their two cars—$14,000—and the installment loan balances still due on them—$5,000. They have about $1,100 in a passbook savings account, and the average balance in their checking account (a regular account, not a NOW) is about $800. Other than the installment loans on their cars, the Chungs have virtually no liabilities except $100 in unpaid charge accounts. Both Al and Linda have very good retirement plans where they work.

Not long ago, Al and Linda set a goal for themselves of trying to save $7,000 a year for the next five to eight years, and they now need to decide how to invest the savings they are starting to accumulate. Al is of the opinion that most of the money—if not all of it—should go into speculative growth stocks. He reasons that now is the time to take risks, and you might as well "make it or break it." Linda is not in complete agreement with this view. For one thing, she is disturbed by how low their liquid reserves are; an accident or a layoff could play havoc with their budget, not to mention that it might force them to sell one of the cars to pay off their loans. Besides, Linda doesn't think they are currently managing their liquid assets very well. They very often let the checking account balance get too high before they transfer funds to the savings account. Because they are kept busy with their careers, they really don't have the time to go to the bank as often as they should. Linda thinks all their extra savings should go into 36-month CDs; she would even withdraw the $1,100 from the passbook account and put it in CDs as well. Al believes Linda worries too much about catastrophes that probably will never happen. He agrees that they manage their cash poorly, but if he has his way, their checking account would never get too high because he would systematically buy shares in a mutual fund investing in small-sized, high-technology firms.

Questions

1. Do you think the Chungs have sufficient liquid assets? Explain your position.

2. Provide details for a liquid asset plan for the Chungs, pinpointing how much you think

should be invested in short-term accounts or securities and the specific ones they should use.

3. The Chungs are in a high tax bracket (28 percent); do you think it would be advantageous for them to make IRAs a part of their savings plan? Explain.

4.2   Preparing Carolyn Bowen's Investment Plan

Carolyn Bowen, who just turned 55, is a widow currently employed as a receptionist for the Xcon Corporation, where she has worked for the past 20 years. She is in good health, lives alone, and has two grown children. A few months ago her husband, who was an alcoholic, died of liver disease. Although at one time a highly successful automobile dealer, Carolyn's husband has left her with only their home and the proceeds from a $30,000 life insurance policy. After paying medical and funeral expenses, $20,000 of the life insurance proceeds remained. In addition to the life insurance proceeds, Carolyn has $15,000 in a savings account, which she had secretly built over the past 10 years. Recognizing that she is within 10 years of retirement, Carolyn wishes to use her limited resources to develop an investment program that will allow her to live comfortably once she retires.

Carolyn is quite superstitious. After consulting with a number of psychics and studying her family tree, she feels certain she will not live past 80. She plans to retire at either 62 or 65, whichever will better allow her to meet her long-run financial goals. After talking with a number of knowledgable individuals—including, of course, the psychics—Carolyn estimates that to live comfortably, she will need $20,000 per year before taxes once she retires. This amount will be required annually for each of 18 years if she retires at 62 or for each of 15 years if she retires at 65. As part of her financial plans, Carolyn intends to sell her home at retirement and rent an apartment. She has estimated that she will net $37,000 if she sells the house at 62 and $41,000 if she sells it at 65. Carolyn has no financial dependents and is not concerned about leaving a sizable estate to her heirs.

If Carolyn retires at age 62, she will receive from social security and an employer-sponsored pension plan a total of $604 per month ($7,248 annually); if she waits until age 65 to retire, her total retirement income would be $750 per month ($9,000 annually). For convenience, Carolyn has already decided that in order to convert all her assets at the time of retirement into a stream of annual income, she will at that time purchase an annuity by paying a single premium. The annuity will have a life just equal to the number of years remaining until her eightieth birthday. Because Carolyn is uncertain as to the actual age at which she will retire, she obtained the following interest factors from her insurance agent in order to estimate the annual annuity benefit provided for a given purchase price.

Life of Annuity	Interest Factor
15 years	11.118
18 years	12.659

By dividing the factors into the purchase price, the yearly annuity benefit can be calculated. Carolyn plans to place any funds currently available into a savings account paying 6 percent compounded annually until retirement. She does not expect to be able to save or invest any additional funds between now and retirement. In order to calculate the future value of her savings, she will need to multiply the amount of money currently available to her by one of the following factors, depending upon the retirement age being considered.

Retirement Age	Time to Retirement	Future-Value Interest Factor
62	7 years	1.504
65	10 years	1.791

Questions

1. By placing currently available funds in the savings account, determine the amount of money Carolyn will have available at retirement once she sells her house if she retires at (a) age 62 and (b) age 65.

2. Using the results from question 1 and the interest factors given above, determine the level of annual income that will be provided to Carolyn through purchase of an annuity at (a) age 62 and (b) age 65.

3. With the results found in the preceding questions, determine the total annual retirement income Carolyn will have if she retires at (a) age 62 and (b) age 65.

4. From your findings, do you think Carolyn will be able to achieve her long-run financial goal by retiring at (a) age 62 and (b) age 65? Explain.

5. Evaluate Carolyn's investment plan in terms of her use of a savings account and an annuity rather than some other investment vehicles. Comment on the risk and return characteristics of her plan. What recommendations might you offer Carolyn? Be specific.

SELECTED READINGS

Boroson, Warren. "The Myths and Facts About Money Market Funds." *Sylvia Porter's Personal Finance,* March 1988, pp. 68–75.

Dentzer, Susan. "Social Security's Big Fix." *U.S. News & World Report,* December 26, 1988/January 2, 1989, pp. 27–30.

Kosnott, Jeff. "Taking the Plunge: How to Start Investing." *Changing Times,* April 1987, pp. 22–28.

Pratt, James W., Jane O. Burns, and William N. Kulsrud. *Federal Taxation,* annual edition. Homewood, IL: annual.

Rejda, George E. *Principles of Insurance,* 3rd edition. Glenview, IL: Scott, Foresman & Co., 1989.

Schurenberg, Eric. "Firm Footing for Your Retirement." *Money,* January 1988, pp. 102–111.

Smith, Marguerite T. "Why You Might Go For a Cash-Value Policy." *Money,* December 1988, pp. 153–61.

Towle, Lisa H. "Lining Up a First-Rate Preparer." *Money,* January 1989, pp. 64–65.

Willis, Clint. "Retiring Soonest with the Mostest." *Money,* November 1988, pp. 78–87.

White, James A. "Be Your Own Pension Manager?" *The Wall Street Journal,* January 16, 1989, p. C1,ff.

5

MEASURING INVESTMENT RETURN AND RISK

After studying this chapter you should be able to:

● Understand the concept, components, and importance of return and the forces that affect the level of return realized by an investor.

● Discuss the time value of money and the calculations involved in finding the future value of various types of cash flows.

● Explain the concept of present value, the procedures for calculating present values, and the use of present value in determining a satisfactory investment.

● Describe the computation and application of holding period return, yield (internal rate of return), and approximate yield.

● Discuss the concept of risk, its relationship to return, and the major sources of risk.

● Gain an appreciation of beta and the capital asset pricing model (CAPM), and the structure they provide for evaluating the risk-return characteristics of alternative investment vehicles.

When buying goods and services, most people have preconceived notions of value that they use in deciding whether or not to acquire an item. For relatively inexpensive goods and services individuals will pay the "marked" or "quoted" price; in the purchase of more expensive items considerations of value and price become more important. The value of a good or service to individuals largely depends on the satisfaction they expect to receive from it. Because price and value are not necessarily the same, an economically rational individual would endeavor never to pay a price in excess of value. When making investment decisions the same logic should apply in an even stricter sense.

An investment can be viewed as a financial commodity, the price of which results from the interaction of supply and demand. While an investment's lack of physical qualities tends to complicate the valuation process, keep in mind that just as a physical commodity, such as an automobile, has certain characteristics (age, mileage, condition), so does an investment vehicle. The key characteristics of investments are return and risk. An understanding of these dimensions and their measurement is a vital prerequisite to making wise decisions. Let us look first at the concept of return.

THE CONCEPT OF RETURN

return
the expected level of profit from an investment; the reward for investing.

Although a return on an investment is not necessarily guaranteed, it is the expected return that motivates people to invest in a given vehicle. **Return** can be seen as the reward for investing. Suppose, for example, you have $1,000 in a savings account paying 5 percent annual interest, and a business associate has asked you to lend her that much money. If you lend her the money for one year, at the end of which she pays you back, your return would depend on the amount of interest you charged. If you made an interest-free loan, your return would be zero. If you charged 5 percent interest, your return would be $50 (.05 × $1,000). Since prior to making the loan you were earning a safe 5 percent on the $1,000, it seems clear that you should charge your associate a minimum of 5 percent interest.

Every investment vehicle does not guarantee a return. For example, the $1,000 deposited in a savings account at a large bank can be viewed as a certain return, whereas the $1,000 loan might be less so. In other words, what is your return in the event that the person to whom you lent the $1,000 runs into financial difficulty? Assume that at the end of one year you are able to recover only $950. In this case, your return would be minus $50 ($950 − $1,000) or minus 5 percent ($50 ÷ $1,000). Thus the size of the expected return is one important factor in choosing a suitable investment.

Components of Return

The return on an investment may be made up of more than one source of income. The most common source is periodic payments such as interest or dividends. The other source of return results from appreciation in value—the ability to sell an investment vehicle for more than its original purchase price. We will call these sources of return current income and capital gains (or losses).

TABLE 5.1   Profiles of Two Investments

	Investment	
	A	**B**
Purchase price (beginning of year)	$1,000	$1,000
Cash received		
1st quarter	$ 10	$ 0
2nd quarter	20	0
3rd quarter	20	0
4th quarter	30	120
Total (for year)	$ 80	$ 120
Sale price (end of year)	$1,100	$ 960

Current Income

Current income, which is received periodically, may take the form of interest received on bonds, dividends from stocks, rent received from real estate, and so on. To be considered income, it must be received in the form of cash or be readily convertible into cash. For our purposes **current income** will be defined as cash or near-cash that is periodically received as a result of owning an investment.

current income
cash or near-cash that is periodically received as a result of owning an investment.

Using the data in Table 5.1 we can calculate the current income from investments A and B—both purchased for $1,000—over a one-year period of ownership. By investing in A, a person would have received current income of $80; investment B would have provided a $120 return. On the basis of the current income received over the one-year period it appears that investment B would be preferred. Of course, because the total return on each of these investments must include some consideration of what happened to the invested funds, it would be premature to draw conclusions as to which investment is better.

Capital Gains (or Losses)

The second dimension of return is concerned with the change, if any, in the market value of an investment. Investors pay a certain amount for an investment from which they expect to receive not only current income, but also the return of the invested funds sometime in the future. In the case of a bond, the return of invested funds will occur at maturity, or the investor can sell the bond prior to maturity. Since stocks and other investment vehicles may not have a specific maturity date, the amount of invested funds that will be returned in the future is generally not known with certainty. As noted in Chapter 4, the amount by which the proceeds from the sale of an investment exceed the original purchase price is called a *capital gain*. If an investment is sold for less than its original purchase price, a *capital loss* results.

The calculation of a capital gain or loss can again be illustrated by Table 5.1. For investment A, a capital gain of $100 ($1,100 sale price − $1,000 purchase price) is realized over the one-year period. In the case of investment B, a $40 capital loss

total return
the sum of the current income and the capital gains (or losses) earned on an investment over a specified period of time.

($960 sale price − $1,000 purchase price) results. Combining the capital gains with the current income calculated in the preceding section gives the **total return** on each investment:

	Investment	
Return	A	B
Current income	$ 80	$120
Capital gain (loss)	100	(40)
Total return	$180	$ 80

It should be clear that in terms of the total return earned on the $1,000 investment over the one-year period, investment A is superior to investment B. Stated as a percentage of the initial investment, an 18 percent return ($180 ÷ $1,000) was earned on investment A, whereas B yielded only an 8 percent return ($80 ÷ $1,000). Although at this point investment A appears preferable, consideration of differences in risk as well as certain tax factors might cause some investors to prefer B. (We will see why later in the chapter.)

Why Return Is Important

Return is a key variable in the investment decision because this measure allows us to compare the amount of actual or expected gain provided by various investments. Return can be measured in a historical sense, or used to formulate future expectations. By using historical data in combination with other environmental factors, expected returns can be estimated and utilized in making the investment decision.

Historical Performance

Although most people recognize that the future is not necessarily a reflection of the past, they would agree that past data often provide a meaningful basis for formulating future expectations. A common practice in the investment world is to look closely at the historical performance of a given vehicle when formulating expectations about its future performance. Because interest rates and other financial return measures are most often cited on an annual basis, evaluation of past investment returns is typically done on the same basis. Consider the data presented in Table 5.2. Two aspects of this historical return data are important: First, we can determine the average level of return generated by this investment over the past 10 years; second, the trend in this return can be analyzed. As a percentage, the average total return (column 6) over the past 10 years was 8.10 percent. Looking at the yearly returns, we can see that after the negative return in 1981 four years of positive and generally increasing returns occurred before the negative return was repeated in 1986. From 1987 through 1990 positive and increasing returns were again realized.

Expected Return

Return can be used more directly in the investment decision process in terms of expected rather than historical behavior. In the final analysis, it's the *future* that

TABLE 5.2 Historical Investment Data for a Hypothetical Investment

Year	(1) Income	Market Value (Price)			Total Return	
		(2) Beginning of the Year	(3) End of the Year	(4) (3) − (2) Capital Gain	(5) (1) + (4) ($)	(6) (5) ÷ (2) (%)*
1981	$4.00	$100	$ 95	−$ 5.00	−$ 1.00	− 1.00%
1982	3.00	95	99	4.00	7.00	7.37
1983	4.00	99	105	6.00	10.00	10.10
1984	5.00	105	115	10.00	15.00	14.29
1985	5.00	115	125	10.00	15.00	12.00
1986	3.00	125	120	− 5.00	− 2.00	− 1.60
1987	3.00	120	122	2.00	5.00	4.17
1988	4.00	122	130	8.00	12.00	9.84
1989	5.00	130	140	10.00	15.00	11.54
1990	5.00	140	155	15.00	20.00	14.29
Average	$4.10			$ 5.50	$ 9.60	8.10%

*Percent return on beginning-of-year market value of investment.

matters and as such, *expected return* is a vital measure of performance. It's what you think the stock or bonds will earn in the future (in terms of dividend/interest receipts and capital gains) that determines what an investor should be willing to pay for a security. To see how, let's return to the data in Table 5.2. Looking at the historical return figures in the table, an investor would note the increasing trend in returns from 1987 through 1990. But to project returns for 1991, 1992, and so on, insights into the prospects for the investment are needed. If continuation of the trend in returns seems likely, an expected return in the range of 12 to 15 percent for 1991 or 1992 would seem reasonable. On the other hand, if future prospects seem poor, or if the investment is believed to exhibit a cyclical behavior pattern, an expected return of 8 to 9 percent may be a more reasonable estimate. Because over the past 10 years the returns have cycled from one poor year (1981 and 1986) to four years of increasing return (1982–1985 and 1987–1990), we might expect low returns in 1991 to be followed by increasing returns in the 1992–1995 period.

Level of Return

The level of return achieved or expected from an investment will depend on a variety of factors. The key forces are internal characteristics, external forces, and inflation.

Internal Characteristics

Certain characteristics such as the type of investment vehicle, the quality of management, the way the investment is financed, the customer base of the issuer, and so on, all affect the level of return. The common stock of a large, well-managed,

completely equity-financed steel manufacturer whose major customer is General Motors would be expected to provide a level of return different from that of a small, poorly managed, largely debt-financed, clothing manufacturer whose customers are small specialty stores. As we will see in later chapters, an assessment of internal factors and their impact on the return offered by a specific investment vehicle is one important step in the process of analyzing potential investments.

External Forces

External forces such as war, shortages, price controls, Federal Reserve actions, and political events, which are not under the control of the issuer of the investment vehicle, may also affect the level of return. Because different investment vehicles are affected differently by these forces, it is not unusual to find two vehicles with similar internal characteristics offering significantly different returns. Thus as a result of the same external force the expected return from one vehicle may increase, whereas that of another may be reduced.

Inflation

Inflation, which has been relatively common in the U.S. economy for many years, tends to have a favorable impact on certain types of investment vehicles, such as real estate, and a negative one on others, such as stocks and fixed-income securities. Rising interest rates, which normally accompany increasing rates of inflation, can significantly affect returns. Depending upon which, if any, actions are taken by the federal government to control inflation, its presence can increase, decrease, or have no effect on investment returns. Furthermore, the return on each *type* of investment vehicle exhibits its own unique response to inflation.

THE TIME VALUE OF MONEY

Imagine that at age 25 you begin making annual cash deposits of $1,000 into a savings account that pays 5 percent annual interest. After 40 years, at age 65, you would have made deposits totaling $40,000 (40 years × $1,000 per year). Assuming you have made no withdrawals, what do you think your account balance would be then—$50,000? $75,000? $100,000? The answer is none of the above; for your $40,000 would have grown to nearly $121,000! Why? Because the time value of money allowed the deposits to earn interest that was compounded over the 40 years.

time value of money
the principle that as long as an opportunity exists to earn interest, the value of money is affected by the point in time when it is expected to be received.

Time value of money refers to the fact that as long as an opportunity exists to earn interest, the value of money is affected by the point in time when it is expected to be received.

Because opportunities to earn interest on funds are readily available, *the sooner one receives a return on a given investment the better*. For example, two investments each requiring a $1,000 outlay and each expected to return $100 over a two-year holding period are *not* necessarily equally desirable. Assuming the base value of each investment remains at $1,000, if the first investment returns $100 at the end of the first year while the second investment returns the $100 at the end of the second, the first investment is preferable. This is so because the $100 interest earned by investment number 1 could be *reinvested to earn more interest* while the

initial $100 from investment number 2 is still accruing. Thus time-value concepts should be considered when making investment decisions.

Interest: The Basic Return to Savers

A savings account at a financial institution is one of the most basic forms of investment. The saver receives interest in exchange for placing idle funds in an account. The interest received is clearly current income; but the saver will experience neither a capital gain nor loss, since the value of the investment (the initial deposit) will change only by the amount of interest earned. For the saver the interest earned over a given timeframe is that period's current income. In other words, total return comes from the current income provided through interest.

Simple Interest

simple interest
interest paid only on the actual balance for the actual amount of time it is on deposit.

The income paid on such vehicles as certificates of deposit (CDs), bonds, and other forms of investment that pay interest is most often calculated using the **simple interest** method. Interest is paid only on the actual balance for the actual amount of time it is on deposit. If you have $100 on deposit in an account paying 6 percent interest for 1½ years, you would earn $9 in interest (1½ × .06 × $100) over this period. Had you withdrawn $50 at the end of half a year, the total interest earned over the 1½ years would be $6, since you would earn $3 interest on $100 for the first half year (½ × .06 × $100) and $3 interest on $50 for the next full year (1 × .06 × $50).

Using the simple interest method, the stated rate of interest is the *true rate of interest (or return)*—which is that rate of interest earned on the actual balance for the actual amount of time it is on deposit. In the example above, the true rate of interest would be 6 percent. Because the interest rate reflects the rate at which current income is earned regardless of the size of the deposit, it is a useful measure of current income.

Compound Interest

compound interest
interest paid not only on the initial deposit but also on any interest accumulated from one period to the next.

Compound interest is paid not only on the initial deposit but also on any interest accumulated from one period to the next. This is the method usually used by savings institutions. The Investor Insights box emphasizes the magical power and other interesting characteristics of compound interest. When interest is compounded annually, compound and simple interest calculations would provide similar results; in this case the stated interest rate and the true interest rate would be equal. The data in Table 5.3 can be used to illustrate compound interest. In this case the interest earned each year is left on deposit rather than withdrawn. The $50 of interest earned on the $1,000 on deposit during 1989 becomes part of the balance on which interest is paid in 1990, and so on. *Note that the simple interest method is used in the compounding process;* that is, interest is paid only on the actual balance for the actual amount of time it is on deposit.

When compound interest is used, the stated and true interest rates are equal *only* when interest is compounded annually. In general, *the more frequently interest is compounded at a stated rate, the higher will be the true rate of interest.* The interest

INVESTOR INSIGHTS

The Magic of Compound Interest

John Maynard Keynes supposedly called it magic. One of the Rothschilds is said to have proclaimed it the eighth wonder of the world. Today people continue to extol its wonder and its glory.

The object of their affection: compound interest, a subject that bores or confuses as many people as it impresses.

Yet understanding compound interest can help people calculate the return on savings and investments, as well as the cost of borrowing. These calculations apply to almost any financial decision, from the reinvestment of dividends to the purchase of a zero-coupon bond for an individual retirement account.

Simply stated, compound interest is "interest on interest." Interest earned after a given period, for example, a year, is added to the principal amount and included in the next period's interest calculation. . . .

"With all the time you spend working, saving, borrowing and investing," says Richard P. Brief, a New York University business professor, "one could argue that the calculations (of compound interest) ought to be understood by most people. And it is within reach of most people."

The power of compound interest has intrigued people for years. Early in the last century, an English astronomer, Francis Baily, figured that a British penny invested at an annual compound interest of 5% at the birth of Christ would have yielded enough gold by 1810 to fill 357 million earths. Benjamin Franklin was more practical. At his death in 1790, he left 1,000 pounds each to the cities of Boston and Philadelphia on the condition they wouldn't touch the money for 100 years. Boston's bequest, which was equivalent to about $4,600, ballooned to $332,000 by 1890.

But savers and investors don't have to live to 100 to reap its benefits.

Consider an investment with a current value of $10,000 earning annual interest of 8%. After a year the investment grows to $10,800 (1.08 times $10,000). After the second year it's worth $11,664 (1.08 times $10,800). After three more years, the investment grows to $14,693.

The same concept applies to consumer borrowing. A $10,000 loan, with an 8% interest charge compounded annually, would cost $14,693 to repay in a lump sum after five years. . . .

Investors and savers can also take a rule-of-thumb shortcut to determine how long it would take to double a sum of money at a given interest rate with annual compounding: Divide 72 by the rate. For example, the $10,000 investment yielding 8% a year would double in about nine years (72 divided by eight).

But people should be aware that inflation compounds, too. Unless inflation disappears, that projected $20,000 investment nine years from now will be worth something less than that in today's dollars.

Source: Adapted from Robert L. Rose, "Compounding: It's Boring but a Wonder," *The Wall Street Journal,* June 17, 1985, p. 21. Reprinted by permission of *The Wall Street Journal,* © Dow Jones & Company, 1985. All rights reserved.

**TABLE 5.3   Savings Account Balance Data
(5% Interest Compounded Annually)**

Date	(1) Deposit or (Withdrawal)	(2) Beginning Account Balance	(3) 0.05 × (2) Interest for Year	(4) (2) + (3) Ending Account Balance
1/1/89	$1,000	$1,000.00	$50.00	$1,050.00
1/1/90	(300)	750.00	37.50	787.50
1/1/91	1,000	1,787.50	89.38	1,876.88

calculations for the deposit data in Table 5.3, assuming that interest is compounded semiannually (twice a year), are included in Table 5.4. The interest for each six-month period is found by multiplying the balance for the six months by half of the stated 5 percent interest rate (see column 3 of Table 5.4). Comparing the end of 1991 account balance of $1,876.88 calculated in Table 5.3 at 5 percent compounded annually with the end of 1991 account balance of $1,879.19 calculated in Table 5.4 at 5 percent compounded semiannually, we can see that larger returns are associated with more frequent compounding. Clearly, with semiannual compounding the true rate of interest is greater than the 5 percent rate associated with annual compounding. Using techniques beyond the scope of this text, the true interest rate for the deposit shown in Table 5.4 is 5.063 percent. A summary of the true rates of interest associated with a 5 percent stated rate and various compounding periods is given in Table 5.5.

continuous compounding
interest calculation in which interest is compounded over the smallest interval of time possible; results in the maximum rate of return that can be achieved with a stated interest rate.

    Continuous compounding, which is compounding over the smallest interval of time possible, results in the maximum rate of return that can be achieved with a stated rate of interest. It should be clear from the data in Table 5.5 that the more frequently interest is compounded, the higher the true rate of interest. Due to the impact that differences in compounding periods have on return, an investor should evaluate the true rate of interest associated with various alternatives prior to making a deposit.

**TABLE 5.4   Savings Account Balance Data
(5% Interest Compounded Semiannually)**

Date	(1) Deposit or (Withdrawal)	(2) Beginning Account Balance	(3) 0.05 × ½ × (2) Interest for Period (6 mo.)	(4) (2) + (3) Ending Account Balance
1/1/89	$1,000	$1,000.00	$25.00	$1,025.00
7/1/89		1,025.00	25.63	1,050.63
1/1/90	(300)	750.63	18.77	769.40
7/1/90		769.40	19.24	788.64
1/1/91	1,000	1,788.64	44.72	1,833.36
7/1/91		1,833.36	45.83	1,879.19

TABLE 5.5   True Rate of Interest for Various Compounding Periods (5% Stated Rate of Interest)

Compounding Period	True Rate of Interest
Annually	5.000%
Semiannually	5.063
Quarterly	5.094
Monthly	5.120
Weekly	5.125
Continuously	5.127

Future Value: An Extension of Compounding

future value
the amount to which a current deposit will grow over a period of time when it is placed in an account paying compound interest.

Future value is the amount to which a current deposit will grow over a period of time when it is placed in an account paying compound interest. Take a deposit of $1,000 that is earning 8 percent compounded annually. In order to find the future value of this deposit at the end of one year, the following calculation would be made:

$$\text{amount of money at end of year 1} = \$1,000 \times (1 + .08)$$
$$= \underline{\underline{\$1,080}}$$

If the money were left on deposit for another year, 8 percent interest would be paid on the account balance of $1,080. Thus at the end of the second year there would be $1,166.40 in the account. This $1,166.40 would represent the beginning-of-year balance of $1,080 plus 8 percent of the $1,080 ($86.40) in interest. The future value at the end of the second year is calculated as follows:

$$\text{amount of money at end of year 2} = \$1,080 \times (1 + .08)$$
$$= \underline{\underline{\$1,166.40}}$$

In order to find the future value of the $1,000 at the end of year *n*, the procedures illustrated above would have to be repeated *n* times. Because this process can be quite tedious, tables of future-value interest factors are available. A complete set of these tables is included in Appendix B, Table B.1. A portion of Table B.1 is shown in Table 5.6. The factors in the table represent the amount to which an initial $1 deposit would grow for various combinations of years and interest rates. For example, a dollar deposited in an account paying 8 percent interest and left there for two years would accumulate to $1.166. Using the future-value interest factor for 8 percent and 2 years (1.166), the future value of an investment (deposit) that can earn 8 percent over 2 years is found by *multiplying* the amount invested (or deposited) by the appropriate interest factor, from Appendix B, Table B.1 (or Table 5.6). In the case of $1,000 left on deposit for 2 years at 8 percent, the resulting future value is $1,166 (1.166 × $1,000), which agrees (except for a slight rounding difference) with the value calculated earlier.

TABLE 5.6   Future-Value Interest Factors for One Dollar

Year	\multicolumn{6}{c}{Interest Rate}
	5%	6%	7%	8% ↓	9%	10%
1	1.050	1.060	1.070	1.080	1.090	1.100
→2	1.102	1.124	1.145	1.166	1.188	1.210
3	1.158	1.191	1.225	1.260	1.295	1.331
4	1.216	1.262	1.311	1.360	1.412	1.464
5	1.276	1.338	1.403	1.469	1.539	1.611
6	1.340	1.419	1.501	1.587	1.677	1.772
7	1.407	1.504	1.606	1.714	1.828	1.949
8	1.477	1.594	1.718	1.851	1.993	2.144
9	1.551	1.689	1.838	1.999	2.172	2.358
10	1.629	1.791	1.967	2.159	2.367	2.594

Note: All table values have been rounded to the nearest one-thousandth; thus calculated values may differ slightly from the table values.

A few points with respect to the future-value table should be highlighted. First, values in the table represent factors for determining the future value of one dollar at the end of the given year. Second, as the interest rate increases for any given year, the future-value interest factor also increases. Thus the higher the interest rate, the greater the future value. Finally, note that for a given interest rate the future value of a dollar increases with the passage of time. It is also important to recognize that the future-value interest factor is always greater than 1; only if the interest rate were zero would this factor equal 1 and the future value therefore equal the initial deposit.

Future Value of an Annuity

annuity
a stream of equal cash flows that occur in equal intervals over time.

An **annuity** is a stream of equal cash flows that occur in equal intervals over time. To receive $1,000 per year at the end of each of the next 10 years is an example of an annuity. The cash flows can be *inflows* of returns earned from an investment or *outflows* of funds invested (deposited) in order to earn future returns. Investors are sometimes interested in finding the future value of an annuity. Their concern is typically with what's called an "ordinary annuity"—one for which the cash flows occur at the *end* of each year. (We likewise will concern ourselves only with this type of annuity.) Future value can be determined mathematically, using a financial calculator or computer, or using appropriate financial tables. Here we use tables of future-value interest factors for an annuity. A complete set of future-value interest tables for an annuity is included in Appendix B, Table B.2. A sample part of Table B.2 is shown in Table 5.7. The factors in the table represent the amount to which annual end-of-year deposits of $1 would grow for various combinations of years and interest rates. For example, a dollar deposited at the end of each year for eight years into an account paying 6 percent interest would accumulate to $9.897. Using the future-value interest factor for an 8-year annuity earning 6 percent (9.897), the future value of this cash flow is found by *multiplying* the annual investment (deposit) by

TABLE 5.7 Future-Value Interest Factors for a One-Dollar Annuity

Year	Interest Rate					
	5%	6% ↓	7%	8%	9%	10%
1	1.000	1.000	1.000	1.000	1.000	1.000
2	2.050	2.060	2.070	2.080	2.090	2.100
3	3.152	3.184	3.215	3.246	3.278	3.310
4	4.310	4.375	4.440	4.506	4.573	4.641
5	5.526	5.637	5.751	5.867	5.985	6.105
6	6.802	6.975	7.153	7.336	7.523	7.716
7	8.142	8.394	8.654	8.923	9.200	9.487
→8	9.549	9.897	10.260	10.637	11.028	11.436
9	11.027	11.491	11.978	12.488	13.021	13.579
10	12.578	13.181	13.816	14.487	15.193	15.937

Note: All table values have been rounded to the nearest one-thousandth; thus calculated values may differ slightly from the table values.

the appropriate interest factor. In the case of $1,000 deposited at the end of each year for 8 years at 6 percent, the resulting future value is $9,897 (9.897 × $1,000).

Present Value: An Extension of Future Value

present value
the current value of a future sum; the inverse of future value.

discount rate
the annual rate of return that could be earned currently on a similar investment; used when finding present value; also called opportunity cost.

Present value is the inverse of future value. That is, rather than measuring the value of a present amount at some future date, **present value** is concerned with finding the current value of a future sum. By applying present value techniques, the value today of a sum to be received at some future date can be calculated.

When determining the present value of a future sum, the basic question being answered is: How much would have to be deposited today into an account paying *y* percent interest in order to equal a specified sum to be received so many years in the future? The applicable interest rate when finding present value is commonly called the **discount rate** (or *opportunity cost*). It represents the annual rate of return that could be earned currently on a similar investment. The basic present value calculation is best illustrated using a simple example. Imagine that you are offered an opportunity that will provide you with exactly $1,000 one year from today. If you could earn 8 percent on similar types of investments, how much is the most you would pay for this opportunity? In other words, what is the present value of $1,000 to be received one year from now discounted at 8 percent? Letting *X* equal the present value, the following equation can be used to describe this situation:

$$X \times (1 + .08) = \$1,000$$

Solving the equation for *X*, we get:

$$X = \frac{\$1,000}{(1 + .08)} = \underline{\underline{\$925.93}}$$

It should be clear from this result that the present value of $1,000 to be received one

TABLE 5.8   Present-Value Interest Factors for One Dollar

Year	5%	6% ↓	7%	8% ↓	9%	10%
→1	.952	.943	.935	.926	.917	.909
2	.907	.890	.873	.857	.842	.826
3	.864	.840	.816	.794	.772	.751
4	.823	.792	.763	.735	.708	.683
5	.784	.747	.713	.681	.650	.621
6	.746	.705	.666	.630	.596	.564
→7	.711	.665	.623	.583	.547	.513
8	.677	.627	.582	.540	.502	.467
9	.645	.592	.544	.500	.460	.424
10	.614	.558	.508	.463	.422	.386

Discount (Interest) Rate spans columns 5%–10%.

year from now, discounted at 8 percent, is $925.93. In other words, $925.93 deposited today into an account paying 8 percent interest will accumulate to $1,000 in one year. To check this conclusion, *multiply* the future-value interest factor for 8 percent and one year, or 1.080 (from Table 5.6), by $925.93. This yields a future value of $1,000 (1.080 × $925.93).

Because the calculations involved in finding the present value of sums to be received in the distant future are more complex than for a one-year investment, the use of present value tables is highly recommended. A complete set of these tables is included in Appendix B, Table B.3; a sample portion is given in Table 5.8. The factors in the table represent the present value of $1 associated with various combinations of years and discount rates. For example, the present value of $1 to be received one year from now discounted at 8 percent is $.926. Using this factor (.926), the present value of $1,000 to be received one year from now at an 8 percent discount rate can be found by *multiplying* it by $1,000. The resulting present value of $926 (.926 × $1,000) agrees (except for a slight rounding difference) with the value calculated earlier.

Another example may help clarify the use of present value tables. The present value of $500 to be received seven years from now, discounted at 6 percent, would be calculated as follows:

$$present\ value = .665 \times \$500 = \underline{\$332.50}$$

The .665 represents the present-value interest factor for seven years discounted at 6 percent.

A few points with respect to present value tables should be highlighted. First, the present-value interest factor for a single sum is always less than 1; only if the discount rate were zero would this factor equal 1. Second, the higher the discount rate for a given year, the smaller the present-value interest factor. In other words, the greater your opportunity cost, the less you have to invest today in order to have a given amount in the future. Finally, the further in the future a sum is to be received,

TABLE 5.9   Mixed and Annuity Return Streams

	Returns	
Year	Mixed Stream	Annuity
1990	$30	$50
1991	40	50
1992	50	50
1993	60	50
1994	70	50

the less it is worth presently. It is also important to note that given a discount rate of 0 percent the present-value interest factor always equals 1, and therefore in such a case the future value of a sum equals its present value.

The Present Value of a Stream of Income

mixed stream
a stream of returns that, unlike an annuity, exhibits no special pattern.

In the material above we illustrated the technique for finding the present value of a single sum to be received at some future date. Because the returns from a given investment are likely to be received at various future dates rather than as a single lump sum, the ability to find the present value of a stream of returns is needed. A stream of returns can be viewed as a package of single-sum returns and may be classified as a mixed stream or an annuity. A **mixed stream** of returns is one that exhibits no special pattern; as noted earlier, an *annuity* is a pattern of equal returns. Table 5.9 illustrates each of these types of return patterns. In order to find the present value of each of these streams (measured at the beginning of 1990), the total of the present values of all component returns must be calculated. Because certain shortcuts can be used in the case of an annuity, the calculation of the present value of each type of return stream will be illustrated separately.

Mixed Stream

In order to find the present value of the mixed stream of returns given in Table 5.9, the present value of all of the returns must be found and then totaled. Assuming a 9 percent discount rate, the calculation of the present value of the mixed stream is illustrated in Table 5.10. The resulting present value of $187.77 represents the amount today (beginning of 1990) invested at 9 percent that would provide the same cash flows as the stream of returns in column 1 of Table 5.10. Once the present value of each return is found, the values can be added, since each is measured at the same point in time.

Annuity

The present value of an annuity can be found in the same way as the present value of a mixed stream, but fortunately there is also a simpler approach. Financial tables of present-value interest factors for annuities are available. A complete set of present-value interest factors for an annuity is included in Appendix B, Table B.4; a sample

TABLE 5.10   Mixed-Stream Present-Value Calculation

Year	(1) Return	(2) 9% Present-Value Interest Factor	(3) (1) × (2) Present Value
1990	$30	.917	$ 27.51
1991	40	.842	33.68
1992	50	.772	38.60
1993	60	.708	42.48
1994	70	.650	45.50
		Present value of stream	$187.77

Note: Column (1) values are from Table 5.9. Column (2) values are from Table 5.8 for 9 percent discount rate and 1 through 5 years.

portion is given in Table 5.11. The factors in the table represent the present value of a one-dollar annuity associated with various combinations of years and discount rates. For example, the present value of $1 to be received each year for the next five years discounted at 9 percent is $3.890. Using this factor, the present value of the $50, five-year annuity (given in Table 5.9) at a 9 percent discount rate can be found by *multiplying* the annual return by the appropriate interest factor. The resulting present value is $194.50 (3.890 × $50).

Determining a Satisfactory Investment

The present-value concept can be used to determine an acceptable investment. Ignoring risk at this point, a satisfactory investment would be one in which the present value of benefits (discounted at the appropriate rate) equals or exceeds the present value of costs. Since the cost (or purchase price) of the investment would be

TABLE 5.11   Present-Value Interest Factors for a One-Dollar Annuity

Year	5%	6%	7%	8%	9% ↓	10%
1	.952	.943	.935	.926	.917	.909
2	1.859	1.833	1.808	1.783	1.759	1.736
3	2.723	2.673	2.624	2.577	2.531	2.487
4	3.546	3.465	3.387	3.312	3.240	3.170
→5	4.329	4.212	4.100	3.993	3.890	3.791
6	5.076	4.917	4.767	4.623	4.486	4.355
7	5.786	5.582	5.389	5.206	5.033	4.868
8	6.463	6.210	5.971	5.747	5.535	5.335
9	7.108	6.802	6.515	6.247	5.995	5.759
10	7.722	7.360	7.024	6.710	6.418	6.145

Discount (Interest) Rate

TABLE 5.12   Present Value Applied to an Investment

Year	(1) Benefits	(2) 8% Present-Value Interest Factor	(3) (1) × (2) Present Value
1990	$ 90	.926	$ 83.34
1991	100	.857	85.70
1992	110	.794	87.34
1993	120	.735	88.20
1994	100	.681	68.10
1995	100	.630	63.00
1996	1,200	.583	699.60
		Present value of benefits	$1,175.28

incurred initially (at time zero), the cost and its present value are viewed as one and the same. If the present value of the benefits just equals the cost, an investor would earn a rate of return equal to the discount rate. If the present value of benefits exceeds the cost, the investor would earn more than the discount rate; and if the present value of benefits were less than the cost, the investor would earn less than the discount rate. It should be clear that an investor would therefore prefer only those investments for which the present value of benefits equals or exceeds cost; in these cases the return would be equal to or greater than the discount rate.

The information in Table 5.12 can be used to illustrate the application of present value to investment decision making. Assuming an 8 percent discount rate to be appropriate, we can see that the present value of the benefits to be received over the assumed seven-year period (1990–1996) is $1,175.28. If the cost of the investment were any amount less than or equal to $1,175.28, it would be acceptable; at a cost above $1,175.28, the investment would not be acceptable. At a cost of less than or equal to the $1,175.28 present value of benefits, a return equal to at least 8 percent would be earned; at a cost greater than $1,175.28, the return would be less than 8 percent.

MEASURING RETURN

Thus far we have discussed the concept of return in terms of its components (current income and capital gains), its importance, and the key forces affecting the level of return (internal characteristics, external forces, and inflation). These discussions intentionally oversimplified the computations usually involved in determining the historical or expected return. In order to compare returns from different investment vehicles, we need to apply a consistent measure. Such a measure must somehow incorporate time value of money concepts that explicitly consider differences in the timing of investment income and/or capital gains (or losses). Such an approach will also allow us to place a current value on future benefits. Here we will look at several measures that allow us to assess alternative investment outlets effectively: first we will consider holding period return and then discuss yield, a conceptually more appealing return measure.

Holding Period Return

The returns to a saver are a function of the amount of current income (interest) earned on a given deposit. However, the amount on deposit in a savings account is not subject to change in value, as it is for investments such as stocks, bonds, and real estate. Because we are concerned with a broad range of investment vehicles, most of which have some degree of marketability, we need a measure of return that captures *both* periodic benefits and changes in value. One such measure is called *holding period return.* The **holding period** is the relevant period of time over which one wishes to measure the return on any investment vehicle. When making return comparisons, the use of holding periods of the same length of time adds further objectivity to the analysis. For example, comparison of the return on a stock over a six-month period ended December 31, 1989, with the return on a bond over a one-year holding period ended June 30, 1989, could result in a poor investment decision. To avoid this type of situation, the holding period should be defined and consistently applied or annualized to create a standard; and similar periods *in* time should be used when comparing the returns from alternative investment vehicles.

holding period
the relevant period of time over which one wishes to measure the return on any investment vehicle.

Understanding Return Components

Earlier in this chapter we isolated the two components of investment return: current income and capital gains (or losses). The portion of return considered current income is a **realized return,** since it is generally received by the investor during the period. Returns in the form of capital gains may not be realized; they may merely be **paper returns.** Capital gain returns are realized only when the investment vehicle is actually sold at the end of the holding period. For example, the capital gain return on an investment that experiences an increase in market value from $50 to $70 during a year is $20. To be realized, the investor would have had to have purchased the investment at the beginning of the year for $50 and sold it for $70 at the end of that year. The investor who purchased the same investment three years earlier but plans to hold it for another three years would also have experienced the $20 capital gain return during the year specified; although he or she would not have realized the gain in terms of cash flow. *In spite of the fact that the capital gain return may not be realized during the period over which the total return is measured, it must be included in the return calculation.*

realized return
return received by an investor during the period.

paper return
a capital gain return that has been achieved, but not yet realized from the sale of an investment vehicle.

A second point to recognize about returns is that *both* the current income and the capital gain component can have a negative value. Occasionally an investment may have negative current income, which means that the investor may be required to pay out cash in order to meet certain obligations. This situation is most likely to occur in various types of property investments. For example, an investor may purchase an apartment complex, and due to poor occupancy the rental income may be inadequate to meet the payments associated with its operation. In such a case the investor would have to pay the deficit in operating costs, and such a payment would represent negative current income. A capital loss can be experienced by *any* investment vehicle. Stocks, bonds, options, commodities, gold, mutual funds, and real estate all behave in such a way that their market value can decline over a given holding period.

TABLE 5.13   Key Financial Variables for Four Investment Vehicles

	Investment Vehicle			
	Savings Account	Common Stock	Bond	Real Estate
Cash received				
1st quarter	$15	$10	$ 0	$0
2nd quarter	15	10	50	0
3rd quarter	15	10	0	0
4th quarter	15	15	50	0
(1) Total current income	$60	$45	$100	$0
Investment value				
End-of-year	$1,000	$2,100	$ 970	$3,200
(2) Beginning-of-year	1,000	2,000	1,000	3,000
(3) Capital gain (loss)	$ 0	$ 100	($ 30)	$ 200
(4) Total return [(1) + (3)]	$ 60	$ 145	$ 70	$ 200
(5) Holding period return [(4) ÷ (2)]	6.00%	7.25%	7.00%	6.67%

Computing the Holding Period Return (HPR)

The **holding period return (HPR)** is the total return earned from holding an investment for a specified period of time (the holding period). It represents the sum of current income and capital gains (or losses) achieved over the holding period, divided by the beginning investment value; *it is customarily used with holding periods of one year or less.* The equation for HPR is as follows:

$$HPR = \frac{\text{current income} + \text{capital gain (or loss)}}{\text{beginning investment value}}$$

where

$$\begin{array}{l} \text{ending investment value} \\ - \text{ beginning investment value} \\ \hline = \text{capital gain (or loss)} \end{array}$$

The HPR equation provides a convenient method for measuring the total return realized or expected on a given investment. Table 5.13 summarizes the key financial variables for four investment vehicles over the past year. The total current income and capital gain or loss for each during the one-year holding period is given in the lines labeled (1) and (3), respectively. By adding these two sources of return, the total return over the year is calculated as shown in line (4). Dividing the total return value [line (4)] by the beginning-of-year investment value [line (2)], we find the holding period return, given in line (5). Over the one-year holding period the common stock had the highest HPR, 7.25 percent, and the savings account had the

lowest, 6 percent. It should be clear from these calculations that in order to find the HPR, all that is needed are beginning- and end-of-period investment values, along with the value of current income received by the investor during the period. Note that the HPR values calculated in line (5) of Table 5.13 would be the *same* regardless of whether the holding period were less or greater than one year. Had the same data been drawn from a six-month rather than a one-year period, the resulting HPRs would still be valid.

Using the HPR in Investment Decisions

The holding period return provides an easy-to-calculate mechanism for use in making investment decisions. Because it considers both current income and capital gains relative to the beginning investment value, it tends to overcome any problems that might be associated with comparing investments of different size. If we look at the total returns [line (4)] calculated for each of the four investments presented in Table 5.13, it would appear that the real estate investment is best since it has the highest total return. However, on further investigation it becomes clear that the real estate investment would require the largest dollar outlay ($3,000). By dividing the total return by the amount of the investment (beginning-of-year investment value), a relative comparison can be made. In order to choose the investment alternative providing the highest total return, a simple comparison of HPRs provides the needed information; in line (5) of Table 5.13 the common stock's HPR of 7.25 percent is the highest. Since the return per invested dollar tends to reflect the efficiency of the investment, the HPR provides a logical method for evaluating and comparing the investment returns.

The HPR can assume negative as well as positive values. The presence of negative returns should not cause any problem when using the HPR to assess alternative investments. HPRs can be calculated using either historical (as in the preceding example) or forecast data. Regardless of whether historical or forecast data are used, the HPR formula presented earlier is still applicable.

Yield: The Internal Rate of Return

yield
the actual rate of return earned by a long-term investment; it considers the time value of money; also called the internal rate of return.

An alternative way to define a satisfactory investment is in terms of the annual rate of return it earns. The actual rate of return earned by a long-term investment is often referred to as its **yield** (or **internal rate of return**). While the holding period return (HPR) is useful with investments held for one year or less, it is generally inappropriate for longer holding periods. Because HPR fails to consider the time value of money, a present-value-based measure of yield is used to determine the annual rate of return on investments held for more than a year. As such, the yield on an investment can be defined as the discount rate that produces a present value of benefits that is just equal to its cost. The yield approach answers the question: What is the true rate of return earned on a given investment? Once the yield has been determined, acceptability can be decided. If the yield on an investment is equal to or greater than the appropriate discount rate, the investment would be acceptable. An investment having a yield below the appropriate discount rate would be unacceptable since it fails to provide a satisfactory rate of return. The yield on an investment

providing a single future cash flow is relatively easy to calculate, whereas the yield on an investment providing a stream of future cash flows generally involves more time-consuming calculations. Note that many hand-held calculators as well as computer software programs are available for simplifying these otherwise difficult and time-consuming calculations.

For a Single Cash Flow

The yield for an investment expected to provide a single future cash flow can be estimated using either future-value or present-value interest factors. Here we will use the present-value interest factors given in Appendix B, Table B.3. To illustrate the yield calculation, assume an investor wishes to find the yield on an investment requiring $1,000 today and expected to be worth $1,400 at the end of a five-year holding period. We can find the yield on this investment by solving for the discount rate that causes the $1,400 to be received five years from now to equal the initial investment of $1,000. The first step involves dividing the present value ($1,000) by the future value ($1,400), which results in a value of .714 ($1,000 ÷ $1,400). The second step is to find in the table of present-value interest factors the *five-year* factor that is closest to .714. Referring to the abbreviated present-value table (see Table 5.8), we find that for five years the factor closest to .714 is .713, which occurs at a 7 percent discount rate. Therefore the yield on this investment is approximately 7 percent. If the investor requires only a 6 percent return, this investment would be acceptable since the 7 percent yield exceeds the 6 percent minimum required return. (As we'll see in Chapter 9, this method is the best—and easiest—way to find the yield on a so-called "zero coupon bond.")

For a Stream of Income

The yield for a stream of income is much more difficult to estimate. The most accurate approach is based on searching for the discount rate that produces a present value of benefits just equal to the cost of the investment. If we use the investment given earlier in Table 5.12 and assume that its cost is $1,100, it should be clear that the yield must be greater than 8 percent, since at an 8 percent discount rate the present value of benefits is greater than the cost ($1,175.28 vs. $1,100). The present values at both 9 percent and 10 percent discount rates are calculated in Table 5.14. If we look at the present value of benefits calculated at the 9 and 10 percent rates ($1,117.61 and $1,063.08, respectively), we see that the yield on the investment must be somewhere between 9 and 10 percent, because it's clear that somewhere between 9 and 10 percent we'll end up with a present value of $1,100 (note at 9 percent, the present value is too high and at 10 percent it's too low). The discount rate that causes the present value of benefits to be closest to the $1,100 cost is 9 percent, since it is only $17.61 away from $1,100 ($1,117.61 − $1,100). At the 10 percent rate the present value of benefits is $36.92 away from $1,100 ($1,100 − $1,063.08). Thus if the investor requires an 8 percent return on this investment it is clearly acceptable, since the yield of approximately 9 percent is greater than this minimum.

TABLE 5.14   Yield Calculation for a $1,100 Investment

Year	(1) Benefits	(2) 9% Present-Value Interest Factor	(3) (1) × (2) Present Value at 9%	(4) 10% Present-Value Interest Factor	(5) (1) × (4) Present Value at 10%
1990	$ 90	.917	$ 82.53	.909	$ 81.81
1991	100	.842	84.20	.826	82.60
1992	110	.772	84.92	.751	82.61
1993	120	.708	84.96	.683	81.96
1994	100	.650	65.00	.621	62.10
1995	100	.596	59.60	.564	56.40
1996	1,200	.547	656.40	.513	615.60
	Present value of benefits		$1,117.61		$1,063.08

Interest-on-Interest: The Critical Assumption

The critical assumption underlying the use of yield as a return measure is an ability to earn a return equal to the calculated yield on all income received from the investment during the holding period. This concept can be best illustrated using a simple example. Suppose you buy a $1,000 U.S. Treasury bond that pays 8 percent annual interest ($80) over its 20-year maturity. Each year you receive $80 and at maturity the $1,000 in principal is repaid. There is no loss in capital, no default; all payments are made right on time. But if you are unable to reinvest the $80 annual interest receipts you could end up earning only 5 percent—rather than 8 percent—on this investment. Figure 5.1, which shows the elements of return on this investment, can be used to demonstrate this behavior. If you *don't reinvest* the interest income of $80 per year, you'll end up on the 5 percent line; you'll have $2,600—the $1,000 principal plus $1,600 interest income (i.e., $80/year x 20 years)—at the end of 20 years. (The yield on a single cash flow of $1,000 today that will be worth $2,600 in 20 years is 5 percent.) In order to move to the 8 percent line you have to earn 8 percent on the annual interest receipts. If you do, you'll have $4,661—the $1,000 principal plus the $3,661 future value of the 20-year $80 annuity of interest receipts invested at 8 percent [i.e., $80/year x 45.762 (the 8%, 20-year factor from Table B.2)]—at the end of 20 years. (The yield on a single cash flow of $1,000 today that will be worth $4,661 in 20 years is 8 percent.) By earning interest-on-interest the future value of the investment will be $2,061 greater (i.e., $4,661 − $2,600) than it would be without reinvestment of the interest receipts.

From the preceding illustration it should be clear that since you started out with an 8 percent investment, 8 percent is the rate of return you have to earn when reinvesting your income. The rate of return you start with, in effect, is the required, or minimum, reinvestment rate. By putting your current income to work at this rate you'll earn the rate of return you set out to; fail to do so, and your return will decline accordingly. Keep in mind that even though a bond was used in this illustration, the

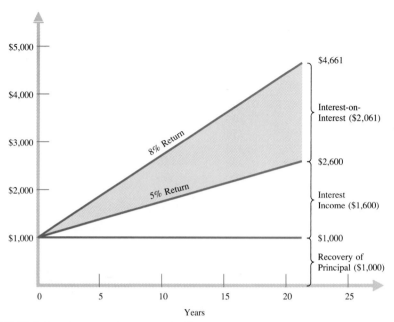

FIGURE 5.1   **Earning Interest-on-Interest.**

An investor in a $1,000, 20-year bond with an 8 percent coupon would, if he or she did not reinvest the $80 annual interest receipts, have only $2,600 at the end of 20 years—a 5 percent rate of return. If the interest receipts were, instead, reinvested at the 8 percent bond interest rate, the investor would have $4,661 at the end of 20 years—an 8 percent return. In order to achieve the calculated yield of 8 percent, the investor must therefore be able to earn interest-on-interest at that rate.

same principle applies to any type of investment vehicle. It's just as relevant to common stocks, mutual funds, or T-bills as it is to long-term bonds. The notion of earning interest-on-interest is what the market refers to as a *fully compounded rate of return.* It's an important concept because you can't start reaping the full potential from your investments until you start earning a fully compounded return on your money.

As long as periodic investment income is involved, the reinvestment of that income and interest-on-interest are matters that have to be dealt with. In fact, *interest-on-interest is a particularly important element of return for investment programs that involve a lot of current income.* The reason is that, in contrast to capital gains, current income has to be reinvested by the individual investor. (With capital gains, the investment vehicle itself is doing the reinvesting, all automatically.) It follows, therefore, that for investment programs that lean toward income-oriented securities, interest-on-interest—and the continued reinvestment of income—plays an important role in defining the amount of investment success achieved.

Approximate Yield

For a given investment the *present value and yield will provide the same conclusion with respect to acceptability*. It is clearly simpler to calculate present value as opposed to the yield, although many calculators provide the capability to find yields quickly. Even without a calculator it is possible to estimate the yield on an investment if the annual benefits are not radically different on a year-to-year basis. This estimate is made using the following *approximate yield formula:*

$$\text{approximate yield} = \cfrac{\text{average annual benefit} + \cfrac{\substack{\text{future price} \\ \text{of investment}} - \substack{\text{current price} \\ \text{of investment}}}{\text{number of years in investment horizon}}}{\cfrac{\substack{\text{future price} \\ \text{of investment}} + \substack{\text{current price} \\ \text{of investment}}}{2}}$$

This formula can be applied to estimate the yield for both single cash flows and streams of income.

Single Cash Flow

Using our earlier example of the $1,000 investment that will be worth $1,400 in five years, we can demonstrate application of the approximate yield formula to a single cash flow. Since the investment involves a single future cash flow the average annual benefit is zero. Substituting this value along with a future price of $1,400, current price of $1,000, and an investment horizon of 5 years in the approximate yield formula we get

$$\text{approximate yield} = \cfrac{\$0 + \cfrac{\$1,400 - \$1,000}{5}}{\cfrac{\$1,400 + \$1,000}{2}} = \frac{\$0 + \$80}{\$1,200} = \frac{\$80}{\$1,200}$$

$$= \underline{0.0667, \text{ or } 6.67\%}$$

The approximate yield of 6.67 percent is reasonably close to the actual yield of 7 percent calculated earlier.

Stream of Income

We can use the data in Table 5.12 to illustrate the application of the approximate yield formula to a stream of income. Suppose that in the year 1996 the $1,000 investment is sold for the future price of $1,200, shown in the table, and that it is the only benefit in that year. Assume further that the current price of the investment is $1,175.28. (*Note:* Setting up the investment this way should lead to an exact 8 percent yield, since that is the rate used to discount the benefits in Table 5.12 to obtain the $1,175.28 value.) The average annual benefit is calculated by dividing the $620 of total annual benefits from 1990 through 1995 ($90 + $100 + $110 +

$120 + \$100 + \$100$) by 7—the number of years in the investment horizon. An average annual benefit of \$88.57 (\$620 ÷ 7) results. Substituting the data into the approximate yield formula results in the following calculations:

$$\text{approximate yield} = \frac{\$88.57 + \dfrac{\$1{,}200 - \$1{,}175.28}{7}}{\dfrac{\$1{,}200 + \$1{,}175.28}{2}}$$

$$= \frac{\$88.57 + \$3.53}{\$1{,}187.64} = \frac{\$92.10}{\$1{,}187.64}$$

$$= \underline{0.0776, \text{ or } 7.76\%}$$

The approximate yield of 7.76 percent is reasonably close to the true yield of 8 percent. The approximate yield formula will be used at numerous points throughout the text to simplify what would otherwise be tedious yield calculations.

RISK: THE OTHER SIDE OF THE COIN

risk
the chance that the actual return from an investment may differ from what is expected; the more variable, or broader, the range of possible returns, the greater the risk, and vice versa.

Thus far the primary concern of this chapter has been return. This important investment dimension cannot be considered without also looking at **risk,** the chance that the actual return from an investment may differ from what is expected. In general, the more variable, or broader, the range of possible return values associated with a given investment, the greater its risk, and vice versa. To get a feel for your risk-taking orientation, you can take the Farley Test included in the accompanying Investor Insights box. In this part of the chapter we will examine the risk-return tradeoff; sources of risk; beta, a modern measure of risk; and the capital asset pricing model (CAPM), which uses beta to estimate return. Then we will discuss how to evaluate the risk associated with a potential investment.

The Risk-Return Tradeoff

risk-return tradeoff
the relationship between risk and return, in which investments with more risk should provide higher returns, and vice versa.

The risk associated with a given investment is directly related to its expected return— or put another way, riskier investments should provide a higher level of return. Otherwise, what incentive is there for an investor to risk his or her capital? In general, an investor will attempt to minimize risk for a given level of return or maximize return for a given level of risk. This relationship between risk and return, called the **risk-return tradeoff,** will be discussed later in this chapter.

Sources of Risk

The total risk associated with a given investment vehicle may result from a combination of any of a variety of possible sources. Because a number of these sources are interrelated, it would be virtually impossible to measure the risk resulting from each one. The major sources of risk include business risk, financial risk, purchasing power risk, interest rate risk, liquidity risk, market risk, and event risk.

INVESTOR INSIGHTS

Are You a Risk-Taker? . . . Find Out with the Farley Test

Answer yes or no to each item as it applies to you
(check your answer).

1. I would take the risk of starting my own business rather than work for someone else. [YES] (NO)

2. I would never take a job that requires lots of traveling. [YES] (NO)

3. If I were to gamble, I would never make small bets. [YES] (NO)

4. I like to improve on ideas. (YES) [NO]

5. I would never give up my job before I was certain I had another one. [YES] [NO]

6. I would never invest in highly speculative stocks. (YES) [NO]

7. To broaden my horizons, I would be willing to take risks. [YES] (NO)

8. Thinking of investing in stocks does not excite me. [YES] (NO)

9. I would consider working strictly on a commission basis. [YES] (NO)

10. Knowing that any particular new business can fail, I would avoid investing in one even if the potential payoff was high. [YES] (NO)

11. I would like to experience as much of life as possible. [YES] [NO]

12. I don't feel that I have a strong need for excitement. [YES] (NO)

13. I am high in energy. [YES] (NO)

14. I can easily generate lots of money-making ideas. [YES] (NO)

15. I would never bet more money than I had at the time. [YES] (NO)

16. I enjoy proposing new ideas or concepts when the reactions of others—my boss, for example—are unknown or uncertain. [YES] [NO]

17. I have never written checks without having sufficient funds in the bank to cover them. [YES] (NO)

18. Business deals that are relatively certain are the only ones I would engage in. [YES] (NO)

19. A less secure job with a large income is more to my liking than a more secure job with an average income. [YES] (NO)

20. I am not very independent-minded. [YES] (NO)

If you answered yes on the Farley Fisc-Risk Scale to questions 1, 3, 4, 7, 9, 11, 13, 14, 16, 19, give 1 point for each answer. If you answered no to items 2, 5, 6, 8, 10, 12, 15, 17, 18, 20, give 1 point for each answer.

If your total score was 17 or 18 or higher, this might suggest financial-risk-taking potential. However, this questionnaire is a sample and is not definitive. Scores may vary from person to person and from time to time because of many factors.

Test used with permission of Frank Farley.

Source: "Risk Takers," *U.S. News & World Report,* January 26, 1987, p. 64.

Business Risk

It is possible for a business firm or property to experience poor earnings and fail as a result. In this case, business and/or property owners might receive no return when earnings are not adequate to meet obligations. Debtholders, on the other hand, are likely to receive some—but not necessarily all—of the amount owed them, due to the preferential treatment they are legally afforded. Bankruptcy is the most severe outcome. In general **business risk** is concerned with the degree of uncertainty associated with an investment's earnings and the investment's ability to pay investors interest, principal, dividends, and any other returns owed them.

business risk
the degree of uncertainty associated with an investment's earnings and the investment's ability to pay investors the returns owed them.

Much of the business risk associated with a given investment vehicle is related to the kind of business. For example, the business risk associated with the common stock of a public utility differs from that associated with a high-fashion clothing manufacturer or a parcel of commercial real estate. It is generally believed that investments in similar types of firms or properties have similar business risk, although differences in management, costs, and location can cause similar businesses or properties to have considerably varying levels of risk.

Financial Risk

The risk associated with the mix of debt and equity used to finance a firm or property is called **financial risk.** The larger the proportion of debt used to finance a firm or property, the greater its financial risk. The increased risk results from the fact that debt financing means obligations to make interest payments as well as to repay the debts. These fixed-payment obligations must be met prior to distributing any earnings to the owners of such firms or properties. Inability to meet obligations associated with the use of debt could result in failure, and in losses for bondholders as well as stockholders and owners.

financial risk
the degree of uncertainty associated with the mix of debt and equity used to finance a firm or property; the larger the proportion of debt used the greater the financial risk.

Purchasing Power Risk

The possibility of changes in price levels within the economy also results in risk. In periods of rising prices, known as **inflation,** the **purchasing power** of the dollar will decline. This means that a smaller quantity of some commodity can be purchased with a given number of dollars than could have been purchased in the past. For example, if last year a dollar would buy five candy bars, an increase in the price of a candy bar to 25 cents would mean that only four candy bars could be bought with the same dollar today. In periods of declining price levels, the purchasing power of the dollar will increase. In general, investments whose values move with general price levels are most profitable during periods of rising prices, whereas those providing fixed returns are preferred during periods of declining price levels or low inflation. The returns on property investments, for example, tend to move with the general price level, whereas returns from savings accounts and bonds do not.

inflation
a period of rising price levels.

purchasing power
the amount of some commodity that can be bought with a given amount of a currency, such as one dollar.

Interest Rate Risk

interest rate risk
the degree of uncertainty in the prices of securities associated with changes in interest rates; as interest rates rise, the prices of securities— particularly fixed- income securities— decline, and vice versa.

Securities that offer purchasers a fixed periodic return are especially affected by **interest rate risk.** As interest rates change, the prices of these securities fluctuate, decreasing with increasing interest rates and increasing with decreasing interest rates. As we will see in greater detail in Chapters 9 and 10, the prices of fixed-income securities drop when interest rates rise in order to provide purchasers with the same rate of return that would be available at prevailing rates. Increases in price due to declining interest rates result from the fact that the return on a fixed-income security is adjusted downward to a competitive level by an upward adjustment in its market price. The actual interest rate changes causing the market price adjustments result from changes in the general relationship between the supply and demand for money. All investment vehicles are actually subject to interest rate risk. Although fixed-income securities are most directly affected by interest rate movements, other vehicles such as common stock and property are also influenced by them. Generally the higher the interest rate the lower the value, and vice versa.

Liquidity Risk

liquidity risk
the risk of not being able to liquidate an investment conveniently and at a reasonable price.

The risk of not being able to liquidate an investment conveniently and at a reasonable price is called **liquidity risk.** The liquidity of a given investment vehicle is an important consideration for an investor who wishes to maintain flexibility in his or her portfolio. In general, investment vehicles traded in *thin markets,* where demand and supply are small, tend to be less liquid than those traded in *broad markets.* However, to be liquid an investment must be easily sold at a reasonable price. One can generally sell an investment vehicle merely by significantly cutting its price. For example, a security recently purchased for $1,000 would not be viewed as highly liquid if it can be quickly sold only at a greatly reduced price, such as $500. Vehicles such as bonds and stocks of major companies listed on the New York Stock Exchange are generally highly liquid, whereas others, such as an isolated parcel of raw land located in rural Georgia, are not.

Market Risk

market risk
risk of changes in investment returns that result from factors independent of the given security or property investment, such as political, economic, and social events, or changes in investor tastes and preferences.

Changes in the level of returns on an investment vehicle often result from **market risk.** The risk tends to be caused by factors independent of the given security or property investment, such as political, economic, and social events, or changes in investor tastes and preferences. For example, in spite of the fact that a real estate investment is well managed, a major shift in consumer housing preferences could adversely affect its market value and therefore the actual return realized. The impact of these market factors on investment returns is not uniform; the degree as well as the direction of change in return resulting from a change in some market factor differs among investment vehicles. A threat of war in the oil-rich Middle East may result in a significant increase in the value (and therefore return) of a military aircraft manufacturer's stock, whereas the stock value and return from an oil company might significantly decline. Essentially, market risk is reflected in the *price*

volatility of a security—the more volatile the price of a security, the greater its perceived market risk.

Event Risk

More than just a buzz word used in the financial media, **event risk** occurs when something substantial happens to a company or property and that event, in itself, has a sudden impact on its financial condition. Event risk goes beyond business and financial risk, can have a direct and dramatic impact on return, and does not neces-sarily mean the company or market is doing poorly. Instead, it involves an event that is largely (or totally) unexpected, and which has a significant and usually immediate effect on the underlying value of an investment. Two good examples of event risk are corporate takeovers and so-called "leveraged buyouts." Both of these events usually involve the use of enormous amounts of debt financing, and as a result, they present a genuine risk for conservative bond investors. Consider, for example, the celebrated 1989 buyout of *RJR Nabisco* by Kohlberg Kravis Roberts & Company. Here was a situation where the debt piled on in the buyout transformed high-quality bonds into low-quality ones overnight. In spite of the fact that this buyout had a positive effect on stock prices, the impact on bondholders was *devas-tating*—the market value of RJR bonds plunged nearly 20 percent in just two days. Event risk can take many forms and affect all types of investment vehicles, though, fortunately, its impact tends to be isolated in most cases, affecting only certain companies or properties. For instance, in the RJR Nabisco deal, the buyout affected the bonds of only one company.

Beta: A Modern Measure of Risk

Over approximately the past 25 years much theoretical work has been done on the measurement of risk and its use in assessing returns. The two key components of this theory are *beta*, which is a measure of risk, and the *capital asset pricing model (CAPM)*, which relates the risk measured by beta to the level of required (or ex-pected) return. Before discussing how beta is interpreted and applied, in the follow-ing section we will explain what is meant by diversifiable and nondiversifiable risk.

Basic Types of Risk

The *total risk* of an investment consists of two components: diversifiable and nondiversifiable risk. **Diversifiable risk,** which is sometimes called **unsystematic risk,** represents the portion of an investment's risk that can be eliminated through diversification. It results from uncontrollable or random events, such as labor strikes, lawsuits, and regulatory actions, and affects various investment vehicles differently. **Nondiversifiable risk,** which is also called **systematic risk,** is attrib-uted to forces, like war, inflation, and political events, that affect all investments and are therefore not unique to a given vehicle. The relationship between total risk, diversifiable risk, and nondiversifiable risk is given by the equation below.

$$\text{total risk} = \text{diversifiable risk} + \text{nondiversifiable risk}$$

systematic risk
same as nondiversifiable risk.

Because any intelligent investor can eliminate diversifiable risk by holding a diversified portfolio of securities, *the only relevant risk is nondiversifiable risk.* Studies have shown that by carefully selecting 8 to 15 securities to be included in a portfolio, diversifiable risk can be eliminated, or almost completely so. Nondiversifiable (or systematic) risk, which is like the market risk discussed earlier, is inescapable. Each security possesses its own unique level of nondiversifiable risk, which we can measure with beta.

Interpreting Beta

beta
a measure of nondiversifiable risk, which shows how the price of a security responds to market forces; found by relating the historical returns on a security with the historical returns for the market in general the higher the beta, the riskier the security.

market return
the average return on all, or a large sample of, stocks, such as those in the Standard & Poor's 500 stock composite index.

Beta is a measure of nondiversifiable, or market, risk; that is, it shows how the price of a security responds to market forces—the more responsive the price of a security is to changes in the market, the higher will be that security's beta. It is found by relating the historical returns on a security with the historical returns for the market. **Market return** is typically measured by the average return of all (or a large sample of) stocks. The average return on all stocks in the Standard & Poor's 500 stock composite index or some other broad stock index is commonly used to measure market return. The beta for the overall market is equal to 1; all other betas are viewed in relation to this value. Table 5.15 shows some selected beta values and their associated interpretations. As can be seen, betas can be positive or negative, though nearly all betas are positive and most stocks have betas that fall between 0.5 and 1.75. Listed below, for illustrative purposes, are the betas for some popular stocks; note these are real betas as reported by *Value Line* in mid 1989:

Stock	Beta	Stock	Beta
American Greetings	.95	Eastman Kodak	.90
Atlas Corporation	.75	Ford Motor	1.20
Bank of Boston	1.20	B.F. Goodrich	1.35
Briggs & Stratton	1.00	Greyhound Corporation	1.00
Champion International	1.25	Hawaiian Electric	.65
Cincinnati Bell	.85	Lotus Development	1.55
Compaq Computer	1.50	Maytag Corporation	1.05
Digital Equipment	1.20	United Brands	.70
Disney	1.20	United Telecom	.85
Dow Chemical	1.20	Winnebago Industries	1.45

Many large brokerage firms as well as subscription services (like *Value Line*) publish betas for a broad range of securities. The ready availability of security betas has enhanced their use in assessing investment risks. In general the higher the beta, the riskier the security. The positive or negative sign preceding the beta number merely indicates whether the stock's return changes in the same direction as the general market (positive beta) or in the opposite direction (negative beta). The importance of beta in developing and monitoring portfolios of securities will be discussed in greater detail in Chapter 16.

TABLE 5.15 **Selected Betas and Associated Interpretations**

Beta	Comment	Interpretation*
2.0	Move in same direction	Twice as responsive as the market.
1.0	as market.	Same response or risk as the market.
0.5		Only half as responsive as the market.
0		Unaffected by market movement
−0.5	Move in opposite	Only half as responsive as the market.
−1.0	direction to market.	Same response or risk as the market.
−2.0		Twice as responsive as the market.

*A stock that is twice as responsive as the market will experience a 2 percent change in its return for each 1 percent change in the return of the market portfolio; the return of a stock that is half as responsive as the market will change by ½ of 1 percent for each 1 percent change in the return of the market portfolio.

Understanding Beta

The individual investor will find beta useful in assessing market risk and understanding the impact the market can have on the return expected from a share of stock. Beta reveals the type of response a security has to market forces. For example, if the market is expected to experience a 10 percent increase in its rate of return over the next period, then a stock having a beta of 1.50 would be expected to experience an increase in return of approximately 15 percent (1.50 × 10%) over the same period. (Because the beta of this particular stock is greater than 1, it is more volatile than the market as a whole.)

For stocks having positive betas, increases in market returns result in increases in security returns. Unfortunately decreases in market returns are likewise translated into decreasing security returns—and this is where the risk lies. In the preceding example, if the market is expected to experience a 10 percent decline in its return, then the stock with a beta of 1.50 should experience a 15 percent decrease in its return. Because the stock has a beta of greater than 1, it is more responsive than the market, experiencing a 15 percent decline in its return as compared to the 10 percent decline in the market return. Stocks having betas of less than 1 will of course be less responsive to changing returns in the market, and therefore are considered less risky. For example, a stock having a beta of 0.50 will experience an increase or decrease in its return of about half that in the market as a whole; thus as the market goes down by 8 percent, such a stock will probably experience only about a 4 percent decline.

Here are some important points to remember about beta:

1. Beta measures the nondiversifiable, or market, risk of a security.
2. The beta for the market is 1.
3. Stocks may have positive or negative betas; nearly all are positive.
4. Stocks with betas of greater than 1 are more responsive to changes in market

return—and therefore more risky—than the market; stocks with betas of less than 1, are less risky than the market.

5. Due to its greater risk, the higher a stock's beta, the greater should be its level of expected return, and vice versa.

CAPM: Using Beta to Estimate Return

capital asset pricing model (CAPM) *model that helps investors evaluate risk-return tradeoffs in investment decisions; uses beta and market return to find required return for securities.*

The **capital asset pricing model (CAPM)** uses beta to link together formally the notions of risk and return. CAPM was developed to explain the behavior of security prices and provide a mechanism whereby investors can assess the impact of a proposed security investment on their portfolio's risk and return. We can use CAPM to understand the basic risk-return tradeoffs involved in various types of investment decisions. CAPM can be viewed both as an equation and, graphically, as the security market line (SML).

 The Equation

Using beta as the measure of nondiversifiable risk, the capital asset pricing model (CAPM) is used to define the required return on an investment according to the following equation:

$$\text{required return} = \text{risk-free rate} + \left[\text{beta} \times \left(\begin{matrix} \text{market} \\ \text{return} \end{matrix} - \begin{matrix} \text{risk-free} \\ \text{rate} \end{matrix} \right) \right]$$

where

required return = the return required on the investment given its risk as measured by beta

risk-free rate = the return that can be earned on a risk-free investment, commonly measured by the return on a U.S. Treasury bill

market return = the average return on all securities (typically measured by the average return on all securities in the Standard & Poor's 500 stock composite index or some other broad stock index)

It can be seen that the required return for a given security increases with increases in its beta.

Application of the CAPM can be demonstrated with the following example. Assume a security with a beta of 1.25 is being considered at a time when the risk-free rate is 6 percent and the market return is 10 percent. Substituting these data into the CAPM equation, we get

$$\text{required return} = 6\% + [1.25 \times (10\% - 6\%)] = 6\% + [1.25 \times 4\%]$$
$$= 6\% + 5\% = \underline{11\%}$$

The investor should therefore expect—indeed, require—an 11 percent return on this investment as compensation for the risk she has to assume, given the security's beta of 1.25. If the beta were lower, say 1.00, the required return would be 10 percent [6% + [1.00 × (10% − 6%)]], and if the beta had been higher, say 1.50, the required return would be 12 percent [6% + [1.50 × (10% − 6%)]]. Clearly

CAPM reflects the positive mathematical relationship between risk and return, since the higher the risk (beta) the higher the required return.

The Graph: The Security Market Line (SML)

security market line
(SML)
*the graphic depiction
of the capital asset
pricing model; re-
flects for each level
of nondiversifiable
risk, measured by
beta, the investor's
required return.*

When the capital asset pricing model (CAPM) is depicted graphically, it is called the **security market line (SML).** Plotting CAPM, we would find that the SML will, in fact, be a straight line. It reflects for each level of nondiversifiable risk (beta), the required return the investor should earn in the marketplace. The CAPM can be plotted by simply calculating the required return for a variety of betas—holding the risk-free rate and market return constant. For example, as we saw above, using a 6 percent risk-free rate and a 10 percent market return, the required return is 11 percent when beta is 1.25. Increase the beta to 2.0, and the required return equals 14 percent [6% + [2.0 × (10% − 6%)]]. In a similar fashion we can find the required return for a number of betas and end up with the following combinations of risk (beta) and required return:

Risk (beta)	Required return (percent)
0.0	6
0.5	8
1.0	10
1.5	12
2.0	14
2.5	16

Plotting these values on a graph (with beta on the horizontal axis and required returns on the vertical axis), we would have a straight line like the one in Figure 5.2. It is clear from the SML that as risk (beta) increases so does the required return, and vice versa.

Evaluating Risk

Although a variety of techniques are available for quantifying the risk of a given investment vehicle, investors must somehow relate the risk perceived in a given vehicle not only to the expected return but also to their own dispositions toward risk. Thus the evaluation process is not one in which a calculated value of risk is compared to a maximum risk level associated with an investment offering a given return. Rather the individual investor typically tends to seek answers to these questions: "Is the amount of perceived risk worth taking in order to get the expected return?" "Can I get a higher return for the same level of risk or a lower risk for the same level of return?" A look at the general risk-return characteristics of alternative investment vehicles, the question of an acceptable level of risk, and the decision process will help shed light on the nature of risk evaluations.

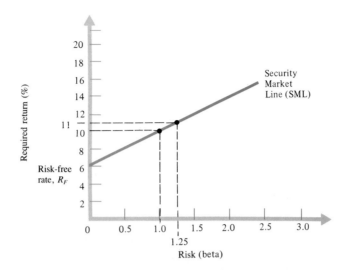

FIGURE 5.2 The Security Market Line (SML).
The security market line (SML) clearly depicts the tradeoff between risk and return. At a beta of 0, the required return is the risk-free rate of 6 percent, and at a beta of 1.0, the market return is 10 percent. Given this data, the required return on an investment with a beta of 1.25 is 11 percent.

Risk-Return Characteristics of Alternative Investment Vehicles

A wide variety of risk-return behaviors is associated with each type of investment vehicle. Some common stocks offer low returns and low risk; others exhibit high returns and high risk. In general the risk-return characteristics of each of the major investment vehicles can be depicted on a set of risk-return axes, as shown in Figure 5.3. Although the locations on the risk-return axes are only approximate, it should be clear that an investor can select from a wide variety of vehicles, each having certain characteristic risk-return behaviors. Of course, for each type, or category, of investment vehicle a broad range of risk-return behaviors exists for specific investments. In other words, once the appropriate type of vehicle has been selected, the decision as to which specific security or property to acquire must still be made.

An Acceptable Level of Risk

Because of differing investor preferences, it is impossible to specify a general acceptable level of risk. The three basic risk-preference behaviors—risk-indifferent, risk-averse, and risk-taking—are depicted graphically in Figure 5.4. From the graph it can be seen that as risk goes from x_1 to x_2, for the **risk-indifferent** investor the required return does not change. In essence, no change in return would be required as compensation for the increase in risk. For the **risk-averse** investor the required return increases for an increase in risk. And for the **risk-taking** investor the

risk-indifferent
describes an investor who does not require greater return in exchange for greater risk

risk-averse
describes an investor who requires greater return in exchange for greater risk.

risk-taking
describes an investor who will accept a lower return in exchange for greater risk.

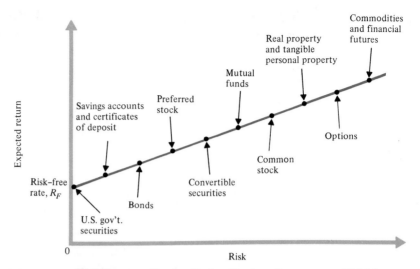

FIGURE 5.3 Risk-Return Tradeoffs for Various Investment Vehicles.
A risk-return tradeoff exists such that for a higher risk one expects a higher return, and vice versa. Low-risk–low-return investment vehicles are U.S. government securities, savings accounts, and so on; high-risk–high-return vehicles include real property and tangible personal property, options, and commodities and financial futures.

required return decreases for an increase in risk. *Most investors are risk-averse, since for a given increase in risk they require an increase in return.* Of course, the amount of return required by each investor for a given increase in risk will differ depending upon the investor's degree of risk aversion (reflected in the slope of the line). Although in theory the risk disposition of each investor can be measured, in practice individual investors tend to accept only those risks with which they feel comfortable. Moreover, investors generally tend to be conservative rather than aggressive when accepting risk.

The Decision Process

In the decision process investors should take the following steps when selecting from among alternative investments:

1. Using historical or projected return data, estimate the expected return over a given holding period. Use yield (or present value) techniques to make sure that the time value of money is given adequate consideration.
2. Using historical or projected return data, assess the risk associated with the investment. The use of subjective risk assessment of past returns and beta (for securities) are the primary approaches available to the individual investor.
3. Evaluate the risk-return behavior of each alternative investment to make sure that the return expected is "reasonable" given its level of risk. If other vehicles

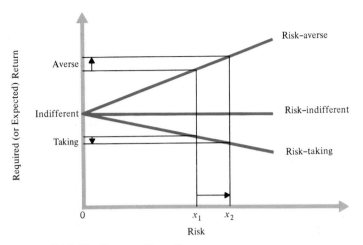

FIGURE 5.4 Risk Preference Functions.
The risk-indifferent investor requires no change in return for a given increase in risk, while the risk-averse investor requires an increase in return for a given risk increase, and the risk-taking investor gives up some return for a given increase in risk. The majority of investors are risk-averse.

   with equal or lower levels of risk provide equal or greater returns, the investment would not be deemed acceptable.

4. Select the investment vehicles that offer the highest returns associated with the level of risk the investor is willing to take. Since most investors are risk-averse they will acquire lower-risk vehicles, thereby receiving lower investment returns. As long as they get the highest return for the acceptable level of risk, they have made a "good investment."

   Probably the most difficult step in this process is assessing risk. Aside from risk and return considerations, other factors such as taxes, liquidity, and portfolio considerations will affect the investment decision. We will look at these in later chapters.

SUMMARY

- Returns can be viewed as the reward for investing. The total return provided by an investment includes current income and capital gains (or losses). Return is commonly calculated on a historical basis and then used to project expected returns.

- The level of return provided by a given investment vehicle depends on internal characteristics, such as the type of investment vehicle, and external forces such as war, shortages, and so on. In addition, the impact of inflation on interest rates can significantly affect investment returns.

- The time value of money is an important concept that must be considered when evaluating investment returns. The opportunity to earn interest, which is the basic return to savers, provides the basis for using time value to measure investment returns.

- Interest can be applied using either the simple interest method, under which the stated interest rate will equal the true interest rate, or the compound method, under which for annual compounding the stated interest rate and true interest are also equal. The more frequently interest is compounded at a stated rate, the higher the true rate of interest.

- The future value of a current sum can be found using compound interest concepts. In addition, these concepts can be used to find the future value of an annuity, which is a stream of equal cash flows.

- The present value of a future sum is the amount deposited today into an account earning at a given rate that would accumulate to the specified future sum. The present value of streams of future returns can be found by adding the individual return present values. A satisfactory investment is one for which the present value of benefits exceeds the present value of costs.

- The holding period is the relevant period of time over which one measures an investment's past or expected return. The holding period return (HPR) is the return earned over a specified period of time. It is frequently used to compare returns earned in periods of one year or less.

- Yield (or internal rate of return) is the actual rate of return earned on a long-term investment. If the yield is greater than or equal to the appropriate discount rate, the investment would be acceptable. Implicit in the use of yield is an ability to earn a return equal to the calculated yield on all income received from the investment during the holding period. The yield on an investment can be estimated using the approximate yield formula.

- Risk is the chance that the actual investment return will differ from what is expected. There is a tradeoff between risk and return. Total risk derives from a variety of sources such as business risk, financial risk, purchasing power risk, interest rate risk, liquidity risk, market risk, and event risk.

- Beta can be used to measure the nondiversifiable, or market, risk associated with a security investment. The capital asset pricing model (CAPM), which can be depicted graphically as the security market line (SML), relates risk (as measured by beta) to return. CAPM reflects increasing required returns for increasing risk.

- Generally, each type of investment vehicle displays certain risk-return characteristics. Most investors are risk-averse, which means that in exchange for a given increase in risk they require an increase in return. The investment decision will ultimately be made by combining the investor's risk preference with the expected return and risk data for a given investment.

REVIEW QUESTIONS AND PROBLEMS

1.   Define what is meant by the return on an investment. Explain why a person wishing to invest should be able to earn a positive return.

2.   Define and differentiate between current income and capital gains (or losses); if you purchased a share of stock for $50 one year ago and sold it today for $60, and during the year received three dividend payments totaling $2.70, calculate:

   a. Current income.
   b. Capital gain (or loss).
   c. Total return.

3.   Given the historical data below:

   a. Calculate the total return (in dollars) for each year.
   b. Indicate the level of return you would expect in 1991 and 1992.
   c. Comment on your forecast.

| | | Market Value (Price) | |
Year	Income	Beginning	Ending
1986	$1.00	$30.00	$32.50
1987	1.20	32.50	35.00
1988	1.30	35.00	33.00
1989	1.60	33.00	40.00
1990	1.75	40.00	45.00

4.   Define, discuss, and contrast the following terms:

   a. Interest.
   b. Simple interest.
   c. Compound interest.

5.   For the following savings account transactions, calculate:

   a. End-of-year account balance (assume that the account balance at December 31, 1989, is zero).
   b. Annual interest, using 6 percent simple interest and assuming all interest is withdrawn from the account as it is earned.
   c. True rate of interest, and compare it to the stated rate of interest. Discuss your finding.

Date	Deposit or (Withdrawal)
1/1/90	$5,000
1/1/91	(4,000)
1/1/92	2,000
1/1/93	3,000

6.   Describe, compare, and contrast the concepts of future value and present value. Explain the role of the discount rate (or opportunity cost) in the present-value calculation.

7. Using the appropriate table of interest factors found in Appendix B, calculate:

    a. The future value of a $300 deposit left in a account paying 7 percent annual interest for 12 years.

    b. The future value at the end of 6 years of an $800 annual end-of-year deposit into an account paying 7 percent annual interest.

8. Using the appropriate table of interest factors found in Appendix B, calculate:

    a. The present value of $500 to be received four years from now, using an 11 percent discount rate.

    b. The present value of the following end-of-year benefit streams, using a 9 percent discount rate and assuming it is now the beginning of 1991.

Year	Stream A	Stream B
1991	$80	$140
1992	80	120
1993	80	100
1994	80	80
1995	80	60
1996	80	40
1997	80	20

9. Define what is meant by the holding period, and explain why it is advisable to use equal-length holding periods (covering the same period in time) when comparing alternative investment vehicles.

10. Calculate the holding period return (HPR) for the following two investment alternatives. Which, if any, of the return components is likely *not* to be realized if you continue to hold each of the investments beyond one year? Which vehicle would you prefer, assuming they are of equal risk? Explain.

	Investment Vehicle	
	X	Y
Cash received		
1st quarter	$ 1.00	$ 0
2nd quarter	1.20	0
3rd quarter	0	0
4th quarter	2.30	2.00
Investment value		
End-of-year	$29.00	$56.00
Beginning-of-year	30.00	50.00

11. Assume that you invest $5,000 today in an investment vehicle that promises to return to you $9,000 in exactly 10 years.

    a. Use the present-value technique to estimate the yield on this investment.

b. Apply the approximate yield formula in order to estimate the yield on this investment.

c. If a minimum return of 9 percent is required, would you recommend this investment?

12. Explain why you must earn 10 percent on all income received from an investment during its holding period in order for its yield actually to equal the 10 percent value you've calculated.

13. Assume the investment-generating benefit stream B in question 8 can be purchased at the beginning of 1991 for $1,000 and sold at the end of 1997 for $1,200. Calculate the approximate yield for this investment. If a minimum return of 9 percent is required, would you recommend this investment? Explain.

14. Explain how either the present value or the yield measure can be used to find a satisfactory investment. Given the following data, indicate which, if any, of the following investments is acceptable. Explain your findings.

	Investment		
	A	**B**	**C**
Cost	$200	$160	$500
Appropriate discount rate	7%	10%	9%
Present value of returns	—	$150	—
Yield	8%	—	8%

15. Define risk. Explain what is meant by the risk-return tradeoff. What happens to the required return as risk increases? Explain.

16. Define and briefly discuss each of the following sources of risk:

a. Business risk.   e. Liquidity risk.
b. Financial risk.   f. Market risk.
c. Purchasing power risk.   g. Event risk.
d. Interest rate risk.

17. Explain what is meant by beta. Name and describe the two components of total risk. What is the relevant risk measured by beta? Explain.

18. Explain what is meant by the market return. Where is it obtained? What range of values does beta typically exhibit? Are positive or negative betas more common? Explain.

19. Assume the betas for securities A, B, and C are as given below:

Security	Beta
A	1.40
B	.80
C	− .90

a. Calculate the change in return for each security if the market experiences an increase in its rate of return of 13.2 percent over the next period.

b. Calculate the change in returns for each security if the market experiences a decrease in its rate of return of 10.8 percent over the next period.

c. Rank and discuss the relative risk of each security based on your findings. Which security might perform best during an economic downturn? Explain.

 20. The risk-free rate is currently 7 percent and the market return is 12 percent. Assume you are considering the following investment vehicles with the betas noted below:

Investment Vehicle	Beta
A	1.50
B	1.00
C	.75
D	0
E	2.00

a. Which vehicle is most risky? Least risky?
b. Use the capital asset pricing model (CAPM) to find the required return on each of the investment vehicles.
c. Draw the security market line (SML) using your findings above.
d. Based on your findings, what relationship exists between risk and return? Explain.

21. Differentiate among the three basic risk preferences—risk-indifferent, risk-averse, and risk-taking. Which of these behaviors best describes most investors? Explain. How does an investor's risk preference typically enter the investment decision process?

22. Describe the basic steps involved in the investment decision process. Be sure to mention how returns and risks can be measured and used to determine the group of acceptable or "reasonable" investments from which the final selection can be made.

CASE PROBLEMS

5.1 (Dave) Solomon Says: A or B?

Dave Solomon, a 23-year-old mathematics teacher at Xavier High School, recently received a tax refund of $1,100. Because Dave doesn't currently have any need for this money, he decided to make a long-term investment. After surveying a large number of alternative investments costing no more than $1,100, Dave isolated two that seemed most suitable to his needs. Each of the investments cost $1,050 and was expected to provide benefits over a 10-year period. Investment A provided a relatively certain stream of benefits, while Dave was a little less certain of the benefits provided by investment B. From his search for suitable alternatives, Dave found that the appropriate discount rate for a relatively certain investment was 12 percent. Because he felt a bit uncomfortable with an investment such as B, he estimated that such an investment would have to provide a return at least 4 percent *higher* than investment A. Although Dave planned to reinvest funds returned from the investments in other vehicles providing similar returns, he wished to keep the extra $50 ($1,100 − $1,050) invested for the full 10 years in a savings account paying 8 percent interest compounded annually. In order to make his investment decision, Dave has asked for your help in answering the questions which follow the expected return data for each investment.

| | Expected Returns | |
Year	A	B
1991	$ 150	$100
1992	150	150
1993	150	200
1994	150	250
1995	150	300
1996	150	350
1997	150	300
1998	150	250
1999	150	200
2000	1,150	150

Questions

1. Assuming investments A and B are equally risky, using the 12 percent discount rate apply the present-value technique to assess the acceptability of each investment as well as the preferred investment. Explain your findings.

2. Recognizing the fact that investment B is more risky than investment A, reassess the two alternatives applying a 16 percent discount rate to investment B. Compare your findings relative to acceptability and preference to those found for question 1.

3. From your findings in questions 1 and 2, indicate whether the yield for investment A is above or below 12 percent and for investment B above or below 16 percent. Approximately what is the yield for investment B? Explain.

4. From the information given, which, if either, of the two investments would you recommend Dave make? Explain your answer.

5. Indicate to Dave how much money the extra $50 will have grown to by the end of 2000, given that he makes no withdrawals from the savings account.

5.2 The Risk-Return Tradeoff: Molly O'Rourke's Stock Purchase Decision

Over the past 10 years Molly O'Rourke has slowly built a diversified portfolio of common stock. Currently her portfolio includes 20 different common stock issues and has a total market value of $82,500. Molly is presently considering the addition of 50 shares of one of two common stock issues—X or Y. In order to assess the return and risk of each of these issues, she has gathered dividend income and share price data for both over each of the last 10 years (1981 through 1990). Molly's investigation of the outlook for these issues suggests that each will, on average, tend to behave in the future just as it has in the past. She therefore believes that the expected return can be estimated by finding the average holding period return (HPR) over the past 10 years for each of the stocks.

Molly plans to use betas to assess the risk and required return of each stock. Her broker, Jim McDaniel, indicated that the betas for stocks X and Y are 1.60 and 1.10, respectively. In addition, currently the risk-free rate is 7 percent and the market return is 10 percent. The historical dividend income and stock price data collected by Molly are given below.

| | Stock X | | | Stock Y | | |
| Year | Dividend Income | Share Price | | Dividend Income | Share Price | |
		Beginning	Ending		Beginning	Ending
1981	$1.00	$20.00	$22.00	$1.50	$20.00	$20.00
1982	1.50	22.00	21.00	1.60	20.00	20.00
1983	1.40	21.00	24.00	1.70	20.00	21.00
1984	1.70	24.00	22.00	1.80	21.00	21.00
1985	1.90	22.00	23.00	1.90	21.00	22.00
1986	1.60	23.00	26.00	2.00	22.00	23.00
1987	1.70	26.00	25.00	2.10	23.00	23.00
1988	2.00	25.00	24.00	2.20	23.00	24.00
1989	2.10	24.00	27.00	2.30	24.00	25.00
1990	2.20	27.00	30.00	2.40	25.00	25.00

Questions

1. Determine the holding period return (HPR) for each stock in each of the preceding 10 years. Find the expected return for each stock using the approach specified by Molly.
2. Subjectively evaluate and discuss the return and risk associated with stocks X and Y. Which stock seems preferable? Explain.

3. Use the capital asset pricing model (CAPM) to find the required return for each stock. Compare this value with the average HPRs calculated in question 1.
4. Compare and contrast your findings in questions 2 and 3. What recommendation would you give Molly in light of the investment decision currently under consideration? Explain why Molly is better off using beta rather than a strictly subjective approach to assess investment risk.

SELECTED READINGS

Frailey, Fred W. "How to Tell How You're Doing," *Changing Times*, January 1988, pp. 37–42.

Fromson, Brett Duval. "A Low-Risk Path to Profits." *Fortune 1989 Investor's Guide*, pp. 14–22.

Gitman, Lawrence J. *Principles of Managerial Finance*, 5th ed. New York: Harper & Row, Publishers, 1988, Chapter 7.

Gurney, Kathleen. "Your Money Personality." *New Accountant*, March 1989, pp. 38–40.

Josen, Georgette. "Compounding Is Key to Investment Yields." *The Wall Street Journal*, April 20, 1989, pp. C1, C16.

Paulson, Morton C. "How to Cut the Risk When You Invest." *Changing Times*, December 1988, pp. 85–90.

Updegrove, Walter L. "Capital Gains: The Twisting Path to Appreciation." *Money*, December 1988, pp. 83–88.

Weberman, Ben. "Risks Without Rewards." *Forbes*, May 30, 1988. p. 319.

Willis, Clint. "Mastering the Math Behind Your Money." *Money*, May 1989, pp. 129–38.

Zarowin, Stanley. "Winners & Losers." *Sylvia Porter's Personal Finance*, July–August 1987, pp. 50–55.

PART ONE

COMPUTER-BASED INVESTMENT MANAGEMENT: STRATEGIES AND TRANSACTIONS

The investment environment presents an almost overwhelming number of alternatives. Puts and calls, rights and warrants, tax deferral and tax avoidance, securities or commodities, and a great deal more. Furthermore, the increasingly sophisticated capabilities of telecommunications permit investment transactions to occur worldwide within a matter of minutes. These factors make the investment environment more dynamic and probably more efficient, which in turn should maximize the effectiveness and value of the various markets. But if an individual investor cannot access information and follow market activities in a timely and consistent fashion, he or she will be at a disadvantage when making investment decisions. Fortunately there are many software packages that have been specifically written to enhance the effectiveness and efficiency of the individual investor. Some of the more popular programs currently available are listed below.

- *Disclosure Database* (Disclosure Incorporated, 5161 River Road, Bethesda, MD 20816; (301)951-1300; price varies by vendor; any computer with modem and communications software.) A database containing financial and textual data from SEC documents on over 1,200 companies. For each company over 250 variables such as company name, address, phone number, financial statements, financial ratios, weekly prices, etc. are included. Also available on CD.
- Dow Jones & Company Programs (Dow Jones & Co., P.O. Box 300, Princeton, NJ 08540; (609) 520-4000 or (800) 257-5114). Available programs and databases and their associated prices are described in Chapter 3.
- *Investment Record* (Claude E. Cleeton, 122–109th Avenue S.E., Bellevue, WA 98004; (206) 451-0293; $62.50; IBM PCs and compatibles.) An investment organizer that can track up to 10 accounts, each having up to 150 total investments in 10 categories. Produces two reports: (1) a capital asset statement

providing detailed information on all investment assets owned and (2) a personal income statement giving a detailed description of the investor's financial performance—both actual and estimated—for the year including yield and tax status.

- *Lotus 1-2-3* (Lotus Development Corp., 55 Cambridge Parkway, P.O. Box 9123, Cambridge, MA 02139-9123; (617) 577-8500 or (800) 343-5414; $495; IBM PC/XT/AT/Jr. and compatibles.) This is a spreadsheet program with built-in financial calculations. Bond buyers can calculate the value of securities; internal rate of return for cash flows can be approximated. User can do cash flow projections, alphabetize tables, keep track of cash flow for a portfolio of selected securities, track rental income, expenses, debt service, and perform various rate-of-return evaluations. Data tables may be evaluated and sorted with user-defined default values. Groups of stocks can be pulled from spreadsheet and sorted according to dollar value or number of shares owned per issue. Graphing feature automatically updates bar graphs and trend lines when portions of the program's data are changed.

- *Managing Your Money, Version 4.0* (MECA Ventures, Inc., 355 Riverside Avenue, Westport, CT 06880; (203) 226-2400; $219.98; IBM PC/XT/AT/Jr. and compatibles and Macintosh; simplified Apple II version available for $149.95.) A personal financial management program that includes a full-featured word processor. The program includes checkbook management, tax planning, insurance and retirement planning, portfolio management, home banking, accounts payable and receivable, five-year budget and tax forecasting, and many more personal financial planning models and conveniences.

- *Modern Jazz* (Lotus Development Corp., 55 Cambridge Parkway, P.O. Box 9123, Cambridge, MA 02139-1923; (617) 577-8500 or (800) 343-5414; $395; MacIntosh.) This is a multifunction program (word processing, worksheet, graphics, database, and communications.) Capabilities include letter, memo, and report writing; forecasting; monitoring files and records; communicating with other computers. "Hot View" feature enables user to incorporate graphs and tables directly into documents.

- *Symphony* (Lotus Development Corp., 55 Cambridge Parkway, P.O. Box 9123, Cambridge, MA 02139-1923; (617) 577-8500 or (800) 343-5414; $695; IBM PC and compatibles.) This program is for the investor seeking multiple function software. It builds on *Lotus' 1-2-3* spreadsheet program with integrated word processing, telecommunications, and a programmable command language. Can communicate over phone lines with any financial database or electronic network; automatically dials into a data service and retrieves and stores requested data. User can define macros. Includes eight graph styles.

- *Turbo Tax Personal 1040* (ChipSoft, Inc., 5045 Shoreham Place, Suite 100, San Diego, CA 92122; (619) 453-8722; $75 plus $37.50 for each annual update; IBM PC/XT/AT and compatibles.) A tax preparation, planning, and record-keeping program. Set up similar to a spreadsheet that provides facsimile tax forms that make data entry simple and easy to learn. Prepares over 30

forms, schedules, and worksheets and prints forms to IRS specifications. Companion programs are available for preparing state tax returns for 26 states.

NOTE: The above list of programs should be viewed as illustrative in nature, and *not* interpreted as an endorsement or recommendation. Listed prices and phone numbers are the latest available and are, of course, subject to change without notice.

TWO

INVESTING IN COMMON STOCK

Part Two includes:

THE INVESTMENT ENVIRONMENT

INVESTMENT ADMINISTRATION

INVESTING IN COMMON STOCK	INVESTING IN FIXED-INCOME SECURITIES
SPECULATIVE INVESTMENT VEHICLES	OTHER POPULAR INVESTMENT VEHICLES

6

COMMON STOCK INVESTMENTS

After studying this chapter you should be able to:

● Explain the investment appeal of common stocks.

● Describe stock returns from an historical perspective and in so doing, gain an appreciation of how current returns measure up to historical standards of performance.

● Discuss the basic features of common stocks, including issue characteristics, voting rights, transaction costs, and stock quotations.

● Gain an understanding of the different kinds of common stock values and the ability of common stocks to serve as an inflation hedge.

● Discuss common stock dividends, including how dividend decisions are made, types of dividends, and dividend policies.

● Describe various types of common stocks, and note the different ways that they can be used as investment vehicles.

Common stocks appeal to investors for a variety of reasons. To some, investing in stocks is a way to "hit it big" if the issues shoot up in price; to others, it's the level of current income they offer. Given the size and diversity of the stock market, it's safe to say that no matter what the investment objective, there are common stocks to fit the bill. This is the first of three chapters on common stock investing. Here we will be concerned with some of the basic principles of investing in common stock. The next two chapters will look at how stocks can be valued and how to judge whether or not an issue might make an acceptable investment vehicle.

THE INVESTMENT APPEAL OF COMMON STOCKS

residual owners
owners/stockholders of a firm, who are entitled to dividend income and a prorated share of the firm's earnings only after all the firm's other obligations have been met.

The basic investment attribute of common stocks is that they enable investors to participate in the profits of the firm. Every shareholder is, in effect, a part owner of the firm and as such, is entitled to a piece of the firm's profit. But this claim on income is not without its limitations, for common stockholders are really the **residual owners** of the company. That is, they are entitled to dividend income and a prorated share of the company's earnings only after all the firm's other obligations have been met. Equally important, as residual owners, holders of common stock have *no* guarantee that they will ever receive any return on their investment. The challenge, of course, is to find stocks that will provide the kind of return you're looking for—no easy task, given that there are between 20 and 30 *thousand* publicly traded listed and OTC stocks to choose from. Now many of these are, of course, closely held companies with very thin (or even nonexistent) secondary markets. But with this many stocks available, how do you select the handful that will provide the type of investment performance you seek? This is a problem investors grapple with every day. Unfortunately, because investing is not an exact science, there are no hard and fast answers to this question.

What Stocks Have to Offer

Common stocks are a highly popular form of investing, used by literally millions of individual and institutional investors. Their popularity stems in large part from the fact that they offer investors the opportunity to tailor their investment programs to meet individual needs and preferences. For retired people and others living off their investment holdings, stocks provide an excellent way of earning a steady stream of current income (from the dividends that they produce). For other investors (less concerned about current income), common stocks can serve as the basis for long-run wealth accumulation programs, wherein stocks are used very much like a savings account. That is, investors will buy stock for the long haul as a way to earn not only dividends, but also a steady flow of capital gains. These investors recognize that stocks have a tendency to go up in price over time, and they simply position themselves to take advantage of that fact. Indeed, it is this potential for capital gains that is the real draw for most investors. For whereas dividends provide a nice, steady stream of income, the big returns come from capital gains! And few securities can match common stocks when it comes to capital gains.

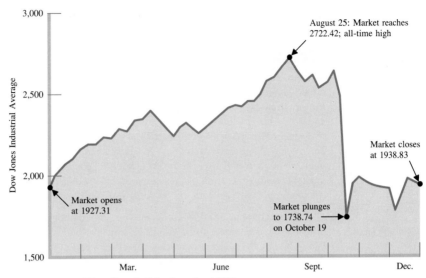

FIGURE 6.1 **The Stock Market in 1987.**

A not-so-funny thing happened to the stock market in October of 1987. The stock market "crashed"; it experienced a "major correction"; it went through a "melt down." No matter how you describe it, the events in October certainly weren't very pleasant! The incredible bull market that had begun some 5 years earlier was over. It was now the bears' turn to have the run of Wall Street.

Putting Stock Returns into Perspective

Given the underlying nature of common stocks, when the market is strong, investors can generally expect to benefit in the form of steady price appreciation; when the market falters, so do investor returns. Although the stock market can perform beautifully—like it did in 1986, when it went up by nearly 23 percent—it can also behave like a dog! There's no better example of the latter than the year 1987. As seen in Figure 6.1, stock prices shot up in the first part of the year (incredibly, the market had gone up almost 30 percent by mid-summer), only to experience a terrible market crash on October 19th, when stock prices, as measured by the Dow Jones Industrial Average, fell 508 points on volume of over 600 million shares. Make no mistake about it: October 19, 1987, was not just another bad day in the market—it was history! The 508 point drop easily set a record, as did the one-day volume of 600 million shares; and the percentage decline of 23 percent was almost twice the previous single-day record. To give you a feel for what that day was like on Wall Street, take a look at the accompanying Investor Insights box, as it traces the events of that fateful day.

The reasons for the crash are still being debated and likely will continue to be for years to come. Some would argue that it was the government's inability to do anything about the enormous budget and trade deficits facing this country; others

INVESTOR INSIGHTS

Meltdown Monday: The Day the Market Crashed

Starting in August 1982, the stock market took off on a five-year ascent that eventually turned into a flight of fancy. The value of shares on the New York Stock Exchange nearly tripled, from $1.1 trillion to $2.8 trillion. One of every three adult Americans climbed aboard for the ride, directly participating in the market. Millions of others had a stake in its fortunes through pension funds, IRA accounts, insurance policies, savings programs. Then came "Meltdown Monday." It would change both the mood and shape of our financial markets and force major shifts in U.S. economic policy. Even if we managed to avert a crippling recession, many experts claimed that neither our money markets nor our country would ever be quite the same again. Here's what happened:

Friday, October 16, 1987. "When you go home tonight," advises John Gavin, an official of a Wall Street firm, "walk close to the buildings"—referring, of course, to falling bodies. As trading approaches the closing bell, a trader in stock-index options on the American Stock Exchange shrieks, "It's the end of the world!"

Not quite. But the Dow Jones Industrial Average closes down a record 108.35 points to 2246.74, on record volume of 338.5 million shares. What began some two months ago as a tame decline in stock prices has degenerated into a terrifying rout. The value of New York Stock Exchange common stock has slumped about $220 billion over the week—more than eight percent.

8 p.m. At Harry's bar, a Wall Street watering hole, hordes of yuppie brokers and traders are preoccupied with getting dates for the evening. "They've never seen a sick market before," says an over-the-counter stock trader. "They think it's going back up a hundred points on Monday." But Robert L. Pelz, Jr., 33, a grain broker in Leawood, Kan., goes home Friday night and says to his wife, "I think the world as you and I know it has changed."

A New York real-estate attorney notes: "I've got a nine-month-old daughter and I'm buying a house. A volatile stock market is no place for me." He had planted much of his savings in stocks. Worried, on this day he has begun to sell.

There were 44.1 million individuals in the stock market at the beginning of 1987—and a record 50.7 million at the end of August. Now, in October, the number has shrunk to 45.1 million.

Investors have been growing gloomier because of signs that inflation is advancing, interest rates are edging higher and the dollar is weakening. Two leading banks have increased their prime lending rate, jolting some investors. Foreign investors are worried by the worsening U.S. trade deficit. A frenzied sell-off the week before by small and large investors as well as arbitragers—professionals who hedge their trading by buying in one market and selling in another—has cracked the market's foundations.

The snowballing has begun.

Sunday, October 18, 1987. At a party in Dallas, Richard W. Fisher, who manages about $200 million for a group of wealthy investors, finds his suspicions confirmed. After dinner, one of the guests goes to a phone to check on markets in Asia. She returns and says they are tumbling. The guest is Margaret Thatcher, the British prime minister, and the dinner is at the Dallas home of her son, Mark.

Monday, October 19, 1987. Troubling news: an Iranian oil platform in the Persian Gulf has been bombed by U.S. warships. John Phelan, chairman of the New York Stock Exchange, arrives at work expecting a tough day. He will be startled by what actually happens.

9 a.m. In the 34th-floor trading room of the Donaldson, Lufkin & Jenrette (DLJ) brokerage firm on Wall Street, corporate officials, deluged by sell orders, know a difficult day is ahead. The firm's brokers are perspiring at their telephone consoles, staring at banks of blinking buttons. Dudley Eppel, a managing director, delivers a grim pep talk: "Well, here we go. Let's keep our cool and maybe we'll all get through this thing alive. Let's go get 'em!"

9:30 a.m. Right from the opening bell, a tidal wave of sell orders swamps the exchange. The ticker shows that IBM might trade as low as $125, down ten points from Friday. But actual trading can't take place unless some buyers show up, and there aren't any.

At the bell, the Dow is off 200 points. "We're going underwater!" shouts DLJ trader John Sesko as he pops candies into his dry mouth. "Fifty-five thousand Pepsi's to sell!" barks one trader. "Sixty thousand GM to sell!" yells another. Long before lunchtime, a trader shouts, "Hamburgers to go in six figures!" He wants to peddle 100,000 shares of McDonald's.

10 a.m. The men who run Wall Street's leading brokerage houses pour into the exchange. Phelan wants to assess firsthand how they are handling the strains. He has spoken to David S. Ruder, chairman of the Securities and Exchange Commission, and decided they have to "tough it out." Even a brief closing might give the impression that the system is falling apart. "Everybody in the world is watching," he says. "You have to prove the system is holding together."

10:30 a.m. The Dow has sunk 93 points, to 2153.55.

In Los Angeles, where it is 7:30 a.m., physician Richard Weiss listens to radio reports as he drives to work. He pulls off the freeway and phones his broker to sell his entire portfolio. The broker ticks off plummeting quotes: "There's Disney going 56, 55, 54. We're making history here!" Says Weiss: "Yes, but we're doing it with my money!" He loses $100,000.

Investors crowd the sidewalk outside a Fidelity Investments office on the corner of Park Avenue and 51st Street in New York, watching the stock postings in horrified fascination. A young, well-dressed woman says simply, "The sky is falling."

Small investors are becoming increasingly nervous. Robert C. McCollum, an elementary-school principal in Galena Park, Texas, says, "For someone on my salary to lose $10,000 or $15,000 in a few days, you know it hurts. I'd jump out of the window, but it's a first-story window and I'd only skin my knee."

10:40 a.m. The SEC's Ruder arrives at the Mayflower Hotel in Washington to deliver a speech before a conference of the American Stock Exchange. But during a break, the room empties out into the lobby, where people huddle around a Quotron machine for market data. Some race back and forth to a bank of pay phones to call their offices.

The market has plunged more than 200 points when one person bursts from the phones shouting, "The buy programs have kicked in!" The computer-assisted trading rooms of the major firms have started issuing orders to buy stock. The market starts to improve.

11:30 a.m. Ruder emerges from his speech and is engulfed by reporters. He is asked what actions could be taken against a market collapse, and he lists several, including one calling for a brief trading halt. When the statement reaches the financial markets, it is interpreted to mean that such a halt is in the works. Far from calming the markets, it further roils them, and the SEC chief spends the day trying to clarify his remarks.

Noon. The Dow is at 2103. Lines of people form in the NYSE's visitors' gallery. One young woman wonders if the plunging market means she will never be a mother. "Even in good times, men are scared of getting married," she says.

Brokers across the United States keep phones pressed to both ears. "This is going to make '29 look like a kiddie party," shouts a trader on the Los Angeles floor of the Pacific Stock Exchange.

1 p.m. A number of small investors conclude it is too late to bail out. "I'm scared to death, but I'm going to leave it there," says Jerry Nasello, a salesman at Global Imports, Inc., an Atlanta BMW dealership, who says he is "about 90 percent" invested in the market.

2 p.m. The Dow Jones average crashes through the 2000 barrier, down about 250 points from Friday's close. Volume sweeps past 400 million shares, a record, with two hours still remaining.

The exchange witnesses its first insolvency. A small firm called H.B. Shaine & Co. in Grand Rapids, Mich., is sucked under. According to a New York Stock Exchange press release, this firm has fallen below minimum financial requirements and reports that it can no longer do business as a member firm. Within days, five more firms will be declared insolvent.

A mob gathers outside the New York Stock Exchange, clogging the sidewalk and spilling out to Broad Street. The heart of the financial district has become a combination carnival and tent revival, replete with gaping bystanders, hawkers, pickpockets, prophets, hymn-singing religious groups, and comedians.

"The end is near!" yells a wraithlike man with a drooping mustache. "It's all over for the yuppies!"

Needing money for a new truck, a forestry consultant in Marietta, Ga., sells the mutual funds in which he has invested most of his savings. Their value is down about 30 percent. Never again, he says, will he put money in a mutual fund.

2:44 p.m. The ticker tape is two hours late. Nobody knows where the market is, but it doesn't matter. People are selling at any price.

Del Barrows, a Johnson, Vt., clothing manufacturer, is a conservative investor who has always favored blue-chip stocks. Even so, Barrows's portfolio loses 25 to 30 percent of its value. "Every day seems to erase more of my gains," he laments.

3:40 p.m. White House Chief of Staff Howard Baker has been on the telephone with Wall Street to get market reports. Twenty minutes before the close of trading, he gives

say that it was caused by inflation fears and sharply rising interest rates; and there is a large group of investors who feel very strongly that while both of the above-noted causes probably played a role, the extent of the market drop was grossly magnified by a relatively small handful of institutional traders using fancy computer-driven techniques (like "program trading" and "portfolio insurance") that ultimately

President Reagan a status report. But prices are tumbling too rapidly for anyone to keep track.

A couple who own a photo-reproduction business in New York City say they have three-quarters of their assets in the stock market. ''We've lost more than $200,000,'' the wife observes. But they have made a decision to hold fast. ''We're praying a lot,'' she adds, ''but it's not working.''

In the final half-hour, the average falls another 130 points.

4 p.m. The New York Stock Exchange closes. But there is no sense of relief, because harried traders and clerks now have to face the damage. Many stand around and just stare at each other. For the first time, people use the word ''crash.''

The Dow Jones Industrial Average has plunged 508 points, or an incredible 22.6 percent, to close at 1738.74. The eventual paper loss will total some $560 *billion,* a sum roughly equal to the gross national product of France. Volume on the New York exchange reached 604.8 million shares, nearly doubling the all-time record. Brokers can find only one word to describe the rout, a word long out of fashion: panic.

The drop far exceeds the 12.8 percent decline on October 28, 1929, one of the first—and worst—days of the stock-market crash that marked the beginning of the Great Depression. The decline today and last week totals 743.47 points, or 30 percent. By comparison, the total drop on October 28 and October 29, 1929, was 68.90 points, or 23.1 percent.

4:30 p.m. From Maine to California, the news causes consumers to reassess their plans.

In Atlanta a secretary at an engineering firm and her husband decide to put off buying a new car: ''We figure people will be desperate to sell cars, furniture, houses. If we wait awhile, maybe we can get a better price.''

In Berwyn, Pa., a real-estate agent and her husband drop plans to buy a second home as an investment. ''This shake-up convinces us that we have to be more liquid,'' she explains.

Although the turmoil on Wall Street has been the focus of intense national and international attention, plenty of Americans don't see it as a crisis. Some even see a certain justice in the market's collapse, especially in the farm and rust belts, where thousands of people have suffered through bankruptcies and factory closings.

Donald Sutter, a farmer in Pleasantville, Iowa, thinks it was ''good the way those rich people were getting hit just as us poor guys have been.'' But as he watches grain, hog and cattle prices follow stocks down, he becomes concerned. And on Wall Street that night, Harry's bar is as packed and boisterous as ever. The pizza is still free, but a bartender jokes that credit cards are no longer accepted.

Source: ''Meltdown Monday—The Day the Market Crashed,'' *Reader's Digest,* February 1988, pp. 86–92.

drove prices down *much farther* than they would otherwise have gone. Whatever the reason, the crash did occur, and it's likely to have a long-lasting effect on the market, to the extent that it won't be something that investors will easily forget.

Fortunately, the October 19ths of this world are the rare exception, rather than the rule. As a result, the stock market is not all risk and wild price volatility. There

are also some pretty attractive rewards. Consider the fact that even though the last quarter of 1987 was a wild and woolly one, the market still ended the year on the plus side—if up by only a meager 2 percent; and in 1988, the market went up another 12 percent. Indeed, if you look at the six-plus years from August 1982 (which is generally regarded as the beginning of the 1982–87 bull market) through December 1988, you'll find the market went up roughly 180 percent—and that's *after* factoring in the impact of the October crash. Clearly, it's this kind of performance that explains the appeal of common stocks.

A Look at the Record: 1949 to 1988

What would you consider to be an acceptable rate of return on common stocks? It's difficult to know what's good or bad, or high or low, unless you have some understanding of the kind of returns common stocks are capable of producing. The best way to develop a feel for the market is to look at the market's past. Table 6.1 provides such a standard of performance, as it uses the DJIA to show average market returns over the 40 year period from 1949 through 1988. In addition to total annual returns, market performance is also broken out between the two basic sources of return: dividends and capital gains. These figures, of course, are meant to reflect the *general behavior of the market as a whole,* and not necessarily that of *individual* stocks—think of them as the return behavior on a well-balanced portfolio of common stocks.

The numbers show a market that has provided total returns ranging from a high of 48.28 percent (in 1954) to a low of −21.45 percent (in 1974). Breaking out the returns between dividends and capital gains, it's clear where the big returns (or losses) come from: *capital gains.* And in that regard, note that prices went up far more often than they went down (as a point of reference, the DJIA moved from just under 100 in January 1949 to nearly 2200 by the end of 1988). Overall, *stocks provided average annual returns of around 11 percent over the full forty-year period.* And if you look at just the last 10 to 15 years, you'll find *average returns have been more like 13 to 15 percent!* Keep in mind that these are market averages and that *individual stocks* can, and often do, perform a lot differently. But at least the averages provide us with a benchmark against which we can assess stock returns and our expectations. For example, if a return of 12 to 14 percent can be considered a good mid-point, then *sustained* returns of 18 to 20 percent, or more, should probably be viewed as fairly attractive, or even extraordinary. (These returns are possible, of course, but if you want the higher returns, you're probably going to have to take on more risks.) Likewise, long-run returns of only 6 to 8 percent should definitely be viewed as being on the low side—if that's the best you think you can do, then stick with bonds or CDs. Actually, returns of 12 percent or so are not all that bad, as the bottom panel of Table 6.1 shows what a $10,000 investment would have grown to over various holding periods within the 1949–88 time frame.

Advantages and Disadvantages of Stock Ownership

One reason stocks are so appealing to investors is the substantial return opportunities they offer. Indeed, as we just saw, stocks generally do provide attractive, highly

TABLE 6.1 **Historical Returns in the Stock Market—1949 to 1988**

(Returns based on performance of the DJIA)

I. Annual Returns

Year	Rate of Return from Dividends	Rate of Return from Capital Gains	Total Rate of Return
1988	3.67%	11.85%	15.52%
1987	3.67	2.26	5.93
1986	3.54	22.58	26.12
1985	4.01	27.66	31.67
1984	5.00	−3.74	1.26
1983	4.47	20.27	24.74
1982	5.17	19.60	24.77
1981	6.42	−9.23	−2.81
1980	5.64	14.93	20.57
1979	6.08	4.19	10.27
1978	6.03	−3.15	2.88
1977	5.51	−17.27	−11.76
1976	4.12	17.86	21.98
1975	4.39	38.32	42.71
1974	6.12	−27.57	−21.45
1973	4.15	−16.58	−12.43
1972	3.16	14.58	17.74
1971	3.47	6.11	9.58
1970	3.76	4.82	8.58
1969	4.24	−15.19	−10.95
1968	3.32	4.27	7.59
1967	3.33	15.20	18.53
1966	4.06	−18.94	−14.88
1965	2.95	10.88	13.83
1964	3.57	14.57	18.14
1963	3.07	17.00	20.07
1962	3.57	−10.81	−7.24
1961	3.11	18.71	21.82
1960	3.47	−9.34	−5.87
1959	3.05	16.40	19.45
1958	3.43	33.96	37.39
1957	4.96	−12.77	−7.81
1956	4.60	2.27	6.87
1955	4.42	20.77	25.19
1954	4.32	43.96	48.28
1953	5.73	−3.77	1.96
1952	5.29	8.42	13.71
1951	6.07	14.37	20.44
1950	6.85	17.63	24.48
1949	6.39	12.88	19.27

(Continued)

TABLE 6.1 (*Continued*)

II. Holding Period Returns

Holding Periods	Avg. Annual Total Returns	Cumulative Total Returns	Amount to Which a $10,000 Investment Will Grow over Holding Period
5 yrs: 1984–88	15.53%	105.77%	$20,577
10 yrs: 1979–88	15.25	313.83	41,383
15 yrs: 1974–88	11.53	413.69	51,369
20 yrs: 1969–88	8.93	461.18	56,118
25 yrs: 1964–88	8.05	719.19	81,919
30 yrs: 1959–88	8.78	1,149.72	124,972
40 yrs: 1949–88	11.01	6,410.13	651,013

Note: Total return and average annual total return figures are fully compounded returns and are based on dividend income *and* capital gains (or losses); all figures compiled from DJIA performance information, as obtained from *Barron's*.

competitive returns over the long haul. This is so because, as equity securities, stockholders are entitled to participate fully in the residual profits of the firm. The market price of a share of stock ordinarily reflects the profit potential of the firm, so that when the company prospers, so do investors. These increasing profits, in turn, translate into rising share prices (capital gains) and are a critical part of stock returns.

Investors are also drawn to common stocks for the current income they offer in the form of dividends, especially now that the Tax Reform Act of 1986 has effectively *lowered* taxes on dividends and *raised* them on capital gains. But stocks offer other benefits as well. One of these is that they are both highly liquid and easily transferable. Common stocks are easy to buy and sell, and the transaction costs are modest; moreover, price and market information is widely disseminated in the news and financial media. A final advantage of stock ownership is that the unit cost of a share of common is usually fairly low and well within the reach of most individual savers and investors. Unlike bonds, which carry minimum denominations of at least $1,000, and some mutual funds that have fairly hefty minimum requirements, common stocks present no such investment hurdles. Instead, most stocks today are priced at less than $50 per share—and any number of shares, no matter how few, can be bought or sold.

There are also some *disadvantages* to investing in common stock. The risky nature of the security is perhaps the most significant disadvantage. Stocks are subject to a number of different types of risk, including business and financial risk, purchasing power risk, market risk and possibly event risk—all of which can adversely affect a stock's earnings and dividends, its price appreciation, and, of course, the rate of return earned by the investor. Even the best of stocks possess elements of risk that are difficult to overcome. A major reason for this is that

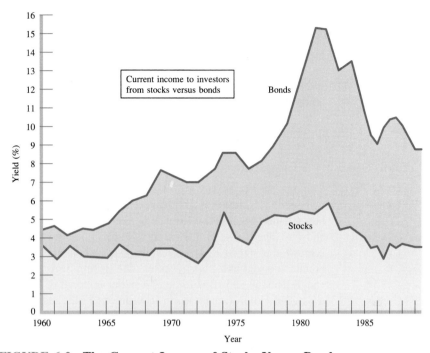

Current income to investors
from stocks versus bonds

Bonds

Stocks

FIGURE 6.2 The Current Income of Stocks Versus Bonds.
Clearly, current income (dividends) to stockholders has failed to keep pace with the amount
of interest income paid to bondholders.

common stock represents residual ownership of a company whose earnings are
subject to many factors, including government control and regulation, foreign competition, and the state of the economy. Because such factors can affect sales and
profits, they can also affect the price behavior of the stock and possibly even dividends. This leads to another disadvantage: Since the earnings and general performance of stocks are subject to such wide swings, it is extremely difficult to value
common stocks and consistently select top performers. The selection process is
difficult and complex because so many elements go into formulating expectations of
how the price of the stock should perform in the future. In other words, not only is
the future outcome of the company and its stock uncertain, but the evaluation and
selection process itself is far from perfect. A final disadvantage is the sacrifice in
current income. Several types of investments—bonds for instance—not only pay
higher levels of income, but do so with much greater certainty. Figure 6.2, which
compares the dividend yield of common stocks with the coupon yield of bonds,
shows how the spread in current income has behaved over time and reveals the kind
of sacrifice common stock investors make. Although the spread has improved
lately, common stocks still have a long way to go before they catch up with the
current income levels available from some investment vehicles.

BASIC CHARACTERISTICS OF COMMON STOCK

Each share of common stock represents an equal part ownership position in a corporation. For example, if a company had 1,000 shares outstanding, every share would symbolize an identical 1/1000 ownership position. Every share would entitle the holder to equal participation in the corporation's earnings and dividends, an equal vote, and an equal voice in management. A typical share of common stock is illustrated in Figure 6.3.

Common Stock as a Corporate Security

equity capital
evidence of ownership position in a firm, in the form of shares of common stock.

publicly traded issues
shares of stock readily available to the general public, which are bought and sold in the open market.

Common stocks are a form of **equity capital,** such shares being evidence of an ownership position in a company. The shares of many corporations, however, are never traded because the firms are either too small or are strictly family controlled and run. The stocks of interest to us in this book are the so-called **publicly traded issues**—the shares that are readily available to the general public and that are bought and sold in the open market. The issuing firms range from giants like American Telephone and IBM to much smaller regional or local firms, whose securities are traded either over-the-counter or on one of the regional exchanges. The dimensions of the market for publicly traded stocks are immense; for example, the market value of all actively traded listed and OTC stocks in early 1989 was over $3 *trillion.* Let's now look more closely at common stocks—at the basic nature and investment merits of this popular form of security.

Kinds of Issues

Just about every facet of American industry is represented in the stock market. You can buy shares in public utilities, manufacturing firms, airlines, mining concerns, and retail organizations, or in financial institutions like banks and insurance companies. The number of shares issued by a firm depends on the size of the corporation and its financial needs. Common stock has no maturity date and as a result, remains outstanding indefinitely.

public offering
an offering to sell to the investing public a set number of shares of a firm's stock at a specified price.

rights offering
an offering of a new issue of stock to existing stockholders who may purchase new shares in proportion to their current ownership position.

Shares of common stock can be issued in one of several ways. One popular method is a **public offering.** The corporation, working with its underwriter, simply offers the investing public a certain number of shares of its stock at a certain price. Figure 6.4 depicts an announcement for such an offering. Note that Chambers Development Company is issuing nearly 3 million shares of common stock at a price of $25 a share. When issued, the new shares of stock will be co-mingled with the outstanding shares, and the net result will be an increase in the number of shares outstanding. A **rights offering** is another popular way of issuing common stock. Such offerings are compulsory in states which require that existing stockholders be given first crack at the new issue and be allowed to purchase new shares in proportion to their current ownership position. For instance, if a stockholder currently owns 1 percent of a firm's stock and the firm issues 10,000 additional shares, that stockholder will be given the opportunity (via a rights offering) to purchase 1 percent (or 100 shares) of the new issue.

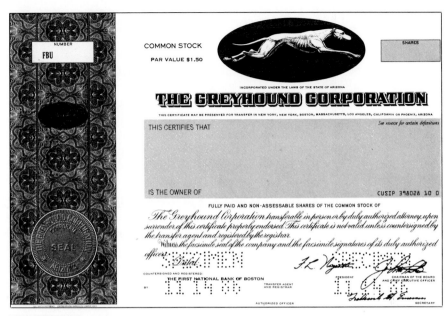

FIGURE 6.3 A Common Stock Certificate.
This certificate is evidence that the shareholder owns shares of the stock and is entitled to all the rights and privileges of ownership. Note the stock carries a par value of $1.50 a share. (*Source:* The Greyhound Corporation.)

deferred equity securities
securities initially issued in one form (warrants or convertibles) and later redeemed or converted into shares of common stock.

Still another way to issue common stock is through the use of **deferred equity securities.** Warrants and convertible securities are issued to enable holders to buy a stipulated number of shares of common stock at a stipulated price within a stipulated time period (as in the case of warrants), or to exchange them for a certain number of shares of common stock (as in the case of convertibles). Either way, the securities are initially issued in one form and then later redeemed or converted into shares of common stock. The net result is the same as with a public offering or a rights offering: The firm ends up with more equity in its capital structure, and the number of shares outstanding increases.

Stock Splits

stock split
a maneuver in which a company increases the number of shares outstanding by exchanging a specified number of new shares of stock for each outstanding share.

Companies can also increase the number of shares outstanding by executing what is known as a **stock split.** In declaring a split, a firm merely announces its intention to increase the number of shares outstanding by exchanging a specified number of new shares for each outstanding share of stock. For example, in a 2 for 1 stock split, two new shares of stock are exchanged for each old share; in a 3 for 2 split, three new shares are exchanged for every two shares outstanding. Thus, a stockholder who owned 200 shares of stock before a 2 for 1 split automatically becomes the owner of 400 shares, while the same investor would hold 300 shares if there had been a 3 for 2 split.

Stock splits are used whenever a firm, believing the price of its stock is too high,

---

2,850,000 Shares

Chambers Development Company, Inc.

Class A Common Stock

Price $25 Per Share

Copies of the Prospectus may be obtained from any of the several Underwriters
only in states in which such Underwriters are qualified to act as dealers
in securities and in which the Prospectus may be legally distributed.

Dean Witter Reynolds Inc.

Kidder, Peabody & Co.
Incorporated

First Analysis Securities
Corporation

Bear, Stearns & Co. Inc.	**The First Boston Corporation** *Incorporated*	**Alex. Brown & Sons** *Incorporated*
Dillon, Read & Co. Inc.	**Donaldson, Lufkin & Jenrette** *Securities Corporation*	**Drexel Burnham Lambert** *Incorporated*
Goldman, Sachs & Co.	**Lazard Frères & Co.**	**Merrill Lynch Capital Markets**

PaineWebber Incorporated   **Prudential-Bache Capital Funding**

Salomon Brothers Inc   **Shearson Lehman Hutton Inc.**

Smith Barney, Harris Upham & Co.   **Wertheim Schroder & Co.**
Incorporated   *Incorporated*

Bateman Eichler, Hill Richards   **Sutro & Co.**
Incorporated   *Incorporated*

April 25, 1989

FIGURE 6.4 An Announcement of a New Common Stock Issue.
The company is issuing 2,850,000 shares of common stock at a price of $25 per share; for the
Chambers Development Co., that means over $71 million of new capital. (*Source: The Wall
Street Journal,* April 25, 1989.)

wants to enhance the stock's trading appeal by lowering its market price. In fact, unless the stock split is accompanied by a big increase in the level of dividends, it is normal market behavior for the price of the stock to fall in close relation to the terms of the split. Thus, using the ratio of the number of old shares to new, we can expect a $100 stock, for example, to trade at or close to $50 after a 2 for 1 split; specifically, dividing the original price of $100 a share by the ratio of new shares to old (2/1), we have: $100 ÷ 2/1 = $100 ÷ 2 = $50. That same $100 stock would trade at about $67 with a 3 for 2 split ($100 ÷ 3/2 = $100 ÷ 1.5 = $67). Most stock splits are executed in order to increase the number of shares outstanding. Sometimes, however, a **reverse stock split** is declared; such splits serve to reduce the number of shares outstanding and increase the share price of the stock by exchanging less than one share of new stock for each outstanding share. For example, in a 1 for 2 reverse split one new share of stock is exchanged for two old shares. Reverse splits are also used to enhance the trading appeal of the stock by boosting the price of a stock to a more respectable range. (A popular variation of the stock split, known as a *stock dividend,* will be discussed later in this chapter.)

reverse stock split
a maneuver in which a company reduces the number of shares outstanding by exchanging a fractional amount of a new share for each outstanding share of stock.

Treasury Stock

Corporations sometimes find it desirable to reduce the number of shares in the hands of the investing public, and they do this by buying back their own stock. These *buy-backs,* as they're called, have become very popular with corporations since 1983, and have contributed in large part to the whopping *35 percent* reduction in the number of common shares trading in the market. Generally speaking, firms repurchase their own stocks when they view them as undervalued (i.e., underpriced) in the marketplace. When that happens, the company's own stock becomes an attractive investment candidate, and those firms that can afford it will begin acquiring their stock in the open market by becoming an investor like any other individual or institution. When these shares are acquired, they become known as **treasury stock.** Technically, treasury stocks are simply shares of stock that have been issued and subsequently repurchased by the issuing firm. Treasury stocks are retained by the corporation and can be used by it for purposes of mergers and acquisitions, to meet employee stock option plans, or as a means of paying stock dividends—or they can simply be held in treasury for an indefinite period of time. The impact of share repurchases from the investor's point of view will, of course, vary with the number of shares repurchased. If the stock buy-back plan is substantial, the stockholder's equity position and claim on income will increase, which, in turn, is likely to benefit stockholders to the extent that such action has a positive effect on the market price of the stock.

treasury stock
shares of stock that have been issued and subsequently repurchased (and held) by the issuing firm.

Classified Common Stock

For the most part, all the stockholders in a corporation enjoy the same benefits of ownership. Occasionally, however, a company will issue different classes of common stock, each of which entitles the holder to different privileges and benefits. These issues are known as **classified common stock,** and it's estimated that well over 300 publicly traded firms have created such stock classes. Even though offered

classified common stock
common stock issued in different classes, each of which offers different privileges and benefits to its holders.

by the same company, each class of common stock is different and has its own value. Classified common stock is customarily used to denote either different voting rights and/or different dividend obligations. For instance, class A could be used to designate nonvoting shares, and class B would carry normal voting rights; or the class A stock could receive *no* dividends, whereas class B receives regular cash dividends. A variation of this concept, used by some public utility firms, is to automatically reinvest the dividend income into additional company shares for the class A stock and pay out dividends (in cash) for the class B stock. Some firms *combine* voting rights and dividend privileges in their classification systems. Class A stock may have no voting rights but receive extra-large dividends; class B may have extra voting rights but receive lower-than-normal dividends; and class C stock may have normal voting rights and dividend privileges.

Notable for its use of classified stock is the Ford Motor Company, which has two classes of stock outstanding: class A stock is owned by the investing public, and class B stock is owned by the Ford family and their trusts or corporations. The two classes of stock share equally in the dividends but whereas class A stock has one vote per share, the voting rights of the class B stock are structured to give the Ford family a 40-percent absolute control of the company. Similar stock classes are used at the Washington Post, General Media, Dow Jones & Co., and the Adolph Coors Company. General Motors also issues classified stock, but does it with an unusual twist. That is, in addition to GM common, the company also has GM-E and GM-H stock outstanding. The class E and class H stocks were issued in conjunction with mergers that the company undertook: The class E stock was issued when GM purchased Electronic Data Systems Corp., and the class H was issued when the firm purchased Hughes Aircraft. Class E and class H stock both have reduced voting rights, and their dividends are linked to the earnings of their respective operating divisions. For example, GM pays out 25 percent of the earnings of Hughes Aircraft to shareholders of GM-H stock, so if Hughes' earnings go up, so too do GM-H dividends. Regardless of the specifics, whenever there is more than one class of common stock outstanding, investors should always be sure to determine the privileges, benefits, and limitations of each class *before* buying stock in the company.

Buying and Selling Stocks

Whether buying or selling stocks, an investor should be familiar with the way stocks are quoted, and with the costs of executing common stock transactions. Certainly, staying abreast of current prices is an essential element in the buy-and-sell decisions of investors—in essence, it's the link in the decision process that tells the investor whether the stock is underpriced (and therefore a viable *buy*) or overpriced (and therefore a good candidate to *sell*). In a similar fashion, transaction costs are important because of the impact they can have on investment returns. Indeed, sometimes just the costs of executing stock transactions can consume most or all of the profits from an investment; as a result, these costs should not be taken lightly.

Stock Quotes

Investors in the stock market have come to rely on a highly efficient information system that quickly disseminates market prices to the public. The stock quotes that

appear daily in the financial press are a vital part of that information system. To see how price quotations work and what they mean, consider the quotes that appear daily (Monday through Friday) in *The Wall Street Journal.* As we'll see, these quotations give not only the most recent prices of each stock, but a great deal of additional information as well.

Some NYSE stock quotes are presented below—let's use the *Walt Disney* quotations for purposes of illustration. These quotes were published in *The Wall Street Journal* on Thursday, January 26, 1989, and describe the trading activity that occurred the day before, on January 25, 1989. A glance at the quotations shows that stock prices are expressed in eighths of a dollar—with each eighth of a point worth 12½ cents. The first two columns, labeled "Hi" and "Lo," contain the highest and lowest prices at which the stock sold during the past 52 weeks; note that Disney traded between 54 and 71⅞ during the 52-week period ending January 25. By the way, note the arrow pointing up (↑) in the margin: It means the stock just set a new high for the year. Listed to the right of the company's name is its *stock symbol* (Disney goes by the three-letter abbreviation **DIS**); these stock symbols are the abbreviations used on the *market tapes* seen in brokerage offices and on FNN television to identify specific companies. The figure listed right after the stock

Disney Stock ⟶

	52 Weeks					Yld		Vol				Net
	Hi	Lo	Stock	Sym	Div	%	PE	100s	Hi	Lo	Close	Chg
	8⅜	4	DianaCp	DNA		...	...	10	5	4⅞	4⅞−	⅛
	48	34	Diebold	DBD	1.40	3.4	15	409	41⅛	40½	40⅞+	⅛
	38	16½	DigitalComm	DCA		...	13	1355	25	23⅞	24½−	½
	127⅜	86⅜	DigitalEqp	DEC		...	12	17032	111¾	109½	111⅝+	3
	21¼	12	DimeSvgNY	DME	.60	4.8	5	1425	12⅞	12¼	12⅜−	⅜
↑	71⅞	54	Disney	DIS	.40	.6	19	7936	72½	71¾	72 +	½
	29⅝	23½	DivrsEngies	DEI	1.52	6.3	11	219	24	23¾	24	...
	6⅛	3½	Divrsind	DMC		...	...	37	6⅛	6	6⅛	...
	47¼	40⅞	DominRes	D	3.20	7.5	9	502	42⅝	42⅜	42½	...
	13⅝	9⅝	Domtar	DTC	.50	...	...	1828	13½	13⅜	13½+	⅛
s	25¾	17¾	Donaldson	DCI	.38	1.8	11	48	20⅞	20⅝	20¾+	⅛
	38¾	30⅝	Donelley	DNY	.78	2.1	15	1559	36⅞	36¼	36⅞+	¼
s	36⅝	26⅝	Dover	DOV	.68	2.3	13	637	29⅝	29⅛	29½+	⅛
	93	76¾	DowChem	DOW	2.80	3.0	8	9083	92½	91⅝	92½+	1
	36½	27¾	DowJones	DJ	.72	2.3	13	1488	31½	30¾	31¼+	⅜
	19⅝	13¼	DowneySL	DSL	.40	2.3	10	34	17⅝	17⅜	17⅝+	¼
	17⅜	11⅝	Dravo	DRV		...	29	784	17	16⅞	17 +	⅛
	35⅝	24⅜	Dresserind	DI	.80	2.6	14	1372	30⅞	30½	30½	...
	10½	5	Dresher	DSR	.16	2.8	11	143	5¾	5½	5⅝−	⅜
	30½	24¼	Dreyfus	DRY	.52	1.9	12	636	28½	27¾	28 −	⅜
	10½	9⅜	DreyfusMuni	LEO	.78a	7.5	...	246	10½	10⅜	10⅛	...
n	12	10⅜	DreyfStrGvfd	DSI	1.20	10.9	...	107	11	10⅞	11 +	⅛
↑	96⅜	77⅜	DuPont	DD	3.80	3.9	11	13495	98½	95½	98½+	2⅛
	57	49¾	DuPont pf		4.50	8.9	...	14	50¾	50¾	50¾−	¼
x	9⅜	7¾	DuffPhelps	DNP	.72a	8.6	...	x2558	8½	8¼	8⅜−	⅛
	49	42¼	DukePwr	DUK	2.96	6.4	9	447	46⅝	46¼	46⅜+	⅛
	97½	88	DukePwr pf		8.70	9.5	...	z100	92	92	92 +	½
	90½	82	DukePwr pf		8.20	9.4	...	z7540	88	87¼	87¼+	¼

Source: *The Wall Street Journal,* January 26, 1989.

symbol is the annual cash dividend paid on each share of stock. This is followed by the stock's dividend yield and its price/earnings (P/E) ratio. The daily volume follows the P/E ratio; the sales numbers are listed in lots of 100 shares, so the figure 7936 means that there were actually 793,600 shares of Disney stock traded on January 25. The next three entries, in the ''Hi,'' ''Lo,'' and ''Close'' columns, contain the highest, lowest, and last (closing) prices at which the stock sold on the day in question. Finally, as the last (Net Change) column shows, Disney closed up half a point on January 25, which means that the stock closed ½ a point higher than it did the day before (put another way, it closed at 71½ a day earlier).

The same basic quotation system is used for AMEX stocks and for *some* OTC stocks. Actually, for quotation purposes, OTC stocks can be divided into two groups: NASDAQ National Market issues and other OTC stocks. The National Market stocks are those of major, actively traded companies; *they are quoted just like NYSE issues*. All other OTC stocks—and that's the vast majority of over-the-counter stocks—are listed on the basis of their *bid* and *ask* prices. (Recall the bid price is what the investor can *sell* a stock for, whereas the ask price is what the investor would pay to *buy* the stock.) An example from *The Wall Street Journal* of a ''NASDAQ Bid & Asked Quote'' is provided below:

| | Sales | | | Net |
Stock & Div.	(100s)	Bid	Asked	Chg
CrownAm .40	115	12¼	13	−¼

The name of the company and the amount of cash dividends paid are indicated, as is the sales volume in round lots (115 = 11,500 shares of stock traded). Then, the *highest* bid price for the day is listed along with the *lowest* ask price; finally, the change shown represents the change in the ask price of the stock. In addition to these quoted OTC stocks, there are thousands of small, thinly traded stocks whose prices are *not* regularly reported in the financial press. These are the so-called *pink sheet* stocks, and the only way to find their prices is to call your broker.

Transaction Costs

round lot
a 100-unit share of stock, or multiple thereof.

odd lot
fewer than 100 shares of stock.

negotiated commissions
transactions costs for the sale and purchase of securities that are negotiated between brokers and institutional investors or individuals with large accounts.

Common stock can be bought in round or odd lots. A **round lot** is 100 shares of stock, or multiples thereof; an **odd lot** denotes transactions involving less than 100 shares. The sale of 400 shares of stock would be considered a round lot transaction, but the purchase of 75 shares would be an odd lot transaction; trading 250 shares of stock would involve a combination of two round lots and an odd lot. The cost of executing common stock transactions has risen dramatically since the introduction— on May 1, 1975—of negotiated commissions. **Negotiated commissions** mean, in effect, that brokerage fees are not fixed. In practice, however, most brokerage firms have fixed fee schedules that are applied to small transactions. As a result, although negotiated commissions are fine for large institutional investors and individuals of substantial capital, they have not proved so beneficial for investors of more modest means.

Basically, an investor incurs two types of transaction costs when buying or

TABLE 6.2 A Schedule of Brokerage Commissions Paid in Common Stock Transactions

Share Price	Number of Shares						
	5	10	25	50	100	200	500
$ 1	$35.00	$35.00	$35.00	$35.00	$35.00	$ 35.00	$ 59.81
5	35.00	35.00	35.00	35.00	35.00	44.90	101.13
10	35.00	35.00	35.00	35.00	35.92	66.77	129.73
25	35.00	35.00	35.00	37.52	58.71	103.63	225.03
35	35.00	35.00	35.00	45.79	70.15	132.11	284.83
50	35.00	35.00	37.26	58.18	84.77	168.00	354.60
75	35.00	35.00	47:58	72.48	88.52	175.97	434.33
100	35.00	35.00	57.91	84.23	88.52	175.97	438.33
125	35.00	37.10	65.06	87.99	88.52	175.97	438.33
150	35.00	41.22	72.21	87.99	88.52	175.97	438.33

Source: A major full-service brokerage house. (*Note:* These commissions are, of course, subject to change; also, some brokers/dealers may charge more than the indicated commission, others less.)

selling stock. The major component is, of course, the brokerage fee paid at the time of transaction. As a rule, brokerage fees equal between 1 and 5 percent of most transactions—though they can go much higher, particularly for very small trades. Table 6.2 shows a commission schedule used by one major brokerage house. Not surprisingly, the amount of commission increases as the number and price of the shares traded increases. Thus, the cost of selling 50 shares of stock trading at $10 per share amounts to $35, whereas the cost of trading 200 shares of a $75 stock is $175.97. Although the dollar cost obviously increases with the size of the transaction, on a relative basis it actually declines. For instance, in the examples above, the brokerage fees for the 50-share transaction amount to 7 percent of the transaction, whereas those for the 200-share trade represent a cost of only 1.1 percent. Clearly, dealing in odd lots quickly adds to the cost of a stock transaction. This is so because all transactions made on the floors of the major stock exchanges are in *round* lots and, as such, the purchase or sale of odd lots requires the assistance of a specialist, known as an odd-lot dealer. This usually results in an *odd lot differential* of 12.5 to 25 cents per share, which is tacked on to the normal commission charge, driving up the costs of these small trades. Indeed, the relatively high cost of an odd-lot trade makes it better to deal in round lots whenever possible. The other components of the transaction cost are the transfer fees and taxes levied on the *seller* of the securities. Fortunately, these charges are modest compared to the brokerage commission.

discount brokers *security brokers who execute orders for clients at substantially reduced commissions.*

The commission schedule in Table 6.2 is that used by a full-service brokerage firm. Security transactions can also be made through **discount brokers.** Discounters are basically in business to execute orders for their customers at *substantially reduced commissions.* Listed on the following page are some of the major discount and full-service brokerage houses:

- *Discount Brokers*
    Brown & Company
    Bull & Bear Securities
    Charles Schwab
    Fidelity Brokerage Services
    Muriel Siebert & Company
    Quick & Reilly
    Rose & Company
    Vanguard Discount Brokers
- *Full-Service Brokers*
    A.G. Edwards & Sons
    Dean Witter
    Kidder, Peabody
    Merrill Lynch
    Paine Webber
    Prudential-Bache Securities
    Shearson Lehman Hutton
    Smith Barney, Harris Upham

As a rule, discount brokers are best suited to active traders who deal in round lots and who are not all that interested in obtaining other broker services. Discount brokers tend to have low overhead operations and offer little or nothing in the way of customer services. Transactions are initiated by calling a toll-free number and placing the desired buy or sell order; the order is then executed by the broker at the best possible price, with details of the transaction confirmed shortly thereafter by mail. In order to discourage small orders, most discounters charge a minimum transaction fee of $25 to $40. Normally, depending on the size of the transaction, discount brokers can save investors from 30 to 80 percent of the commissions charged by full-service brokers. A brief comparison of full-service versus discount brokerage commissions is provided in Table 6.3.

Voting Rights and Procedures

annual
stockholders'
meeting
yearly meeting of a firm's stockholders at which time the annual report is presented, board members are elected, and other special business transacted.

As a rule, the holders of common stock are entitled to vote on matters affecting general corporate operations. The principle at work here is that since stockholders are owners, they should have some input on important issues that have a bearing on earnings and dividends. Of course, stockholders do not vote on every minor company decision; instead, selected major items are placed on an agenda, and voting takes place at the **annual stockholders' meeting.** These meetings are generally held at or near the headquarters of the corporation, and all stockholders are welcome, regardless of the number of shares owned. At this meeting company executives present and discuss the annual report and future prospects, members of the board of directors are elected, and other special issues are voted on. Unless the company has different classes of stock outstanding, each shareholder is entitled to cast one vote for each share of stock held. If a stockholder cannot attend the meeting, he or she may cast votes in absentia by means of a proxy. A *proxy* is a signed form that assigns the stockholder's voting rights to another party, usually a member

TABLE 6.3 Comparative Commissions: Full-Service Brokers versus Discounters

Type of Broker	Size of Stock Transaction				
	$3,000 (100 shs. at $30)	$5,000 (500 shs. at $10)	$10,000 (1,000 shs. at $10)	$15,000 (300 shs. at $50)	$25,000 (500 shs. at $50)
Typical full-service broker	$65	$130	$240	$235	$355
Typical discount broker	$40	$60	$ 80	$ 60	$ 80
Discount Broker Commissions as Percent of Full-Service Broker Commissions	61%	46%	33%	25%	22%

of the board of directors, who is then bound to cast the vote as indicated by the stockholder. Figure 6.5 depicts a typical proxy statement. In order for it to be valid, it must be signed and dated by the stockholder and returned prior to the date of the annual meeting.

Majority or Cumulative Voting

majority voting
the most common system of stockholder voting, in which each shareholder is entitled to one vote per share of stock owned and may cast that number of votes for each position on the board.

There are two ways in which a stockholder can cast votes when electing members of the board of directors. The most common stystem is known as **majority voting.** Each stockholder is entitled to one vote per share of stock owned, and he or she may cast that number of votes for each position on the board. Thus, if you hold 100 shares of stock and three directors are being elected, you can cast 100 votes for *each* of your three candidates. (Those receiving the majority of votes are elected.) Under this system, it is impossible for minority interests to elect board members by themselves. An alternative system, devised to overcome or at least minimize this problem, is **cumulative voting.** (A handful of states require cumulative voting, and all others permit its use.) This system allows shareholders to cast all their *combined votes* in any manner they wish. In the example above, in which an investor held 100 shares of stock and was voting on the election of three directors, all 300 votes could be cast for *one* director. The advantage of this system is that it provides minority shareholders the opportunity to elect at least one or two directors and thereby have at least some representation on the board.

cumulative voting
a system of stockholder voting in which shareholders cast all their combined votes in any manner they wish.

Common Stock Values

The worth of a share of common stock can be described in a number of ways. Terms such as par value, book value, liquidation value, market value, and investment value are all found in the financial media, and each designates some accounting, investment, or monetary attribute of the stock in question.

Par Value

par value
the stated, or face, value of a stock.

The term **par value** denotes the stated, or face, value of a stock. It is not really a measure of anything and so, except for accounting purposes, is relatively useless. In

---

PROXY

THE GREYHOUND CORPORATION
418 GREYHOUND TOWER, PHOENIX, ARIZONA 85077

The undersigned hereby appoints John H. Johnson, Dennis C. Stanfill and John W. Teets, and each of them, to have all the powers hereunder, including full power of substitution, as Proxies for the undersigned to vote as indicated below at the Annual Meeting of Shareholders of The Greyhound Corporation to be held on Tuesday, May 9, 1989, and at any adjournment thereof, all shares of stock which the undersigned is entitled to vote, with all voting rights the undersigned would have if personally present.

The Board of Directors recommends a vote FOR:

1. Election of the class of directors whose term expires in 1992:

      ☐ FOR all nominees listed below (except as indicated to the   ☐ WITHHOLD AUTHORITY to vote for all nominees
      contrary below)   listed below
            Jess Hay   John H. Johnson   Allen E. Paulson

      (INSTRUCTION: To withhold authority to vote for any of the above nominees write that nominee's name in the space below.)

      _____

2. ☐ FOR   ☐ AGAINST   ☐ ABSTAIN   Ratification of the appointment of Touche Ross & Co. as the independent public
                                          accountants of the Company for 1989

The Board of Directors recommends a vote AGAINST:

3. ☐ FOR   ☐ AGAINST   ☐ ABSTAIN   Shareholder proposal regarding animal testing of consumer products

      PLEASE SIGN AND DATE ON REVERSE SIDE AND RETURN PROMPTLY IN THE ENCLOSED ENVELOPE

64247

4. In their discretion, the Proxies are authorized to vote upon such other business as may properly come before the meeting and to vote cumulatively in the election of directors unless contrary directions are given.

This proxy when properly executed will be voted in the manner directed herein by the undersigned shareholder. If no direction is given, this proxy will be voted FOR proposals 1 and 2 and AGAINST proposal 3.

Dated _____, 1989

_____
Signature

_____
Signature if held jointly

Please sign exactly as name appears above. When shares are held by joint tenants, both should sign. When signing as attorney, executor, administrator, trustee or guardian, please give full title as such. If a corporation, please sign in full corporate name by president or other authorized officer. If a partnership, please sign in partnership name by authorized person.

THIS PROXY IS SOLICITED ON BEHALF OF THE BOARD OF DIRECTORS

FIGURE 6.5   A Typical Proxy Statement.

This proxy statement, not valid until signed by the shareholder, enables stockholders to vote without actually being present at the meeting—in this case, to cast their votes for members of the board, to approve the appointment of Touche Ross as the company's auditor/accountant, to vote on a shareholder proposal regarding animal testing, and to vote on other matters that require stockholders' approval. (*Source:* The Greyhound Corporation.)

book value
the amount of stockholders' equity in a firm; equals the amount of the firm's assets minus the firm's liabilities and preferred stock.

many ways, it is a throwback to the early days of corporate law, when par value was used as a basis for assessing the extent of a stockholder's legal liability. Since the term holds little or no significance for investors, many stocks today are issued as no par or low par stocks.

Book Value

Book value represents the amount of stockholders' equity in the firm. It is an accounting measure which, as we will see in the next chapter, is widely used in

security analysis and stock valuation. Book value is determined by subtracting the firm's liabilities and preferred stock from the amount of the firm's assets. It indicates the amount of stockholder funds used to finance the firm. Let's assume that a corporation has $10 million in assets, owes $5 million in various forms of short- and long-term debt, and has $1 million worth of preferred stock outstanding. The book value of this firm would be $4 million. This amount can be converted to a per share basis—*book value per share*—by simply dividing it by the number of shares outstanding. For example, if this firm has 100,000 shares of common stock outstanding, then its book value per share would be $40. As a rule, you'd expect most stocks to have market prices that are above their book values.

Liquidation Value

Liquidation value is an indication of what a firm would bring on the auction block, were it to cease operations. After the assets are sold or auctioned off at the best possible price, and the liabilities and preferred stockholders paid off, what is left is known as the **liquidation value** of the firm. Obviously, if and until liquidation actually occurs, this measure is no more than an estimate of what the firm would be worth under such circumstances. While this measure is vital to high stakes LBO and take-over artists, it is *very difficult* to arrive at and is generally of little interest to the typical individual investor who tends to view the firm as a "going concern."

liquidation value
the amount left if a firm's assets were sold or auctioned off and the liabilities and preferred stockholders paid off.

Market Value

This value is one of the easiest to determine, since **market value** is simply the prevailing market price of an issue. In essence, market value is an indication of how the market participants as a whole have assessed the worth of a share of stock. By multiplying the market price of the stock by the number of shares outstanding, we can also obtain the market value of the firm itself. For example, if a firm has 1 million shares outstanding and its stock is trading at $50 per share, the firm has a market value of $50 million. Because investors are always interested in an issue's market price, the market value of a share of stock is generally of considerable importance to most stockholders; it is obviously something an investor wants to know when formulating investment policies and programs.

market value
the prevailing market price of a security.

Investment Value

Investment value is probably the most important measure for a stockholder, for it is an indication of the worth investors place on the stock—in effect, it is what they think the stock should be trading for. Determining a security's investment worth is a fairly complex process, but in essence it is based on expectations of the return and risk behavior of a stock. Any stock has two potential sources of return: annual dividend payments and the capital gains that arise from appreciation in market price. In establishing investment value, investors try to determine how much money they will make from these two sources, and then use such estimated information as the basis for formulating the return potential of the stock. At the same time, they try to assess the amount of risk to which they will be exposed by holding the stock. Together, such return and risk information helps them place an investment value on

investment value
the amount that investors believe a security should be trading for, or what they think it's worth.

the stock. This is represented by a *maximum* price they would be willing to pay for the issue (and is the major topic of discussion in Chapter 8).

Stocks as an Inflation Hedge

For many years, conventional wisdom held that common stocks were the ideal inflation hedge. This line of reasoning followed from the belief that common stocks, on average, could provide rates of return that were large enough to cover the annual rate of inflation and still leave additional profits for the stockholder—or, stated another way, that stocks could be counted on to provide rates of return that consistently exceeded the annual inflation rate. Through the mid-1960s, stocks did indeed perform as inflationary hedges. But then inflation in this country rose alarmingly, and most stocks simply could not keep up. Instead, many other investment vehicles, such as fixed income securities and even short-term Treasury bills, began to outperform common stocks. With the quality of earnings declining in an inflationary economy, stock prices reacted predictably: They began to stagnate. The net result, as seen in Figure 6.6, was a DJIA that literally went nowhere from 1965 to 1982. Even more alarming was the effect inflation had on the "real" value of stocks. Note that two lines appear in Figure 6.6; the upper line indicates the actual reported behavior of the Dow, and the other, lower, line shows what happens when the DJIA is adjusted for inflation. In real terms, *the Dow fell almost without interruption for 17 years*. Clearly, during this period, stocks were anything but an inflation hedge! However, in 1982 a major bull market began, and as inflation subsided, stocks once again became a viable inflation hedge. While the average rate of return on stocks since 1982 has far outstripped inflation, the market still has a way to go to make up for lost ground, as the Dow in 1989 would have to rise to *over 3000* just to match its "real" value in the mid-1960s.

COMMON STOCK DIVIDENDS

In 1988, corporations paid out some $104 billion in dividends—nearly twice the amount paid in 1980. Yet, in spite of these numbers, there are still a lot of investors who look down their noses at dividends and view them as an insignificant dimension of investment return. That's unfortunate, since the tax code, as revised in 1986, definitely *favors* dividends as a form of income. The preferential treatment of long-term capital gains has been eliminated, so that capital gains are now taxed at the *same* rate as dividends. Thus dividends have become more valuable, since not only is the amount you can keep *after taxes* the same as capital gains, but dividends are far *less risky* than the capital gains that may or may not occur some time in the future. Capital gains are certainly important, and they do represent the principal vehicle through which the really big returns are realized; but the new tax code throws a whole new (and far more favorable) light on dividends! We will now look more closely at this important source of income and examine several procedural aspects of the corporate dividend decision.

The Dividend Decision

Companies often share the profits they earn with their stockholders by paying out dividends, typically on a quarterly basis. Actually, the question of how much to pay

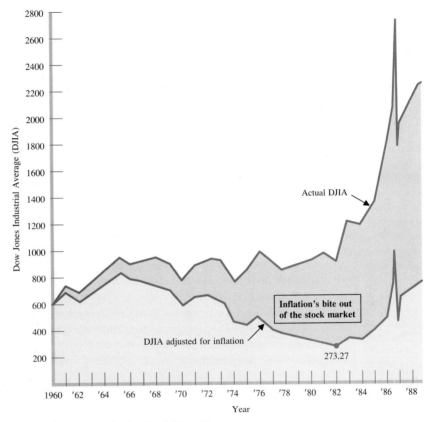

FIGURE 6.6 Stocks in Real Terms.
From 1965 to 1982, stocks were losing ground to inflation; finally, in 1982 the returns from the stock market were once again greater than the rate of inflation and as such, the inflation-adjusted DJIA began to rise sharply.

in dividends is decided by a firm's board of directors. The directors evaluate the firm's operating results and financial condition to determine whether or not, and in what amount, dividends should be paid. If it is decided that a payment of dividends is in order, several important payment dates are also established by the board. But before dealing with those dates, let's take a look at the corporate and market factors that go into the decision to pay dividends, since this type of insight is helpful in assessing the dividend potential of a stock.

Corporate Versus Market Factors

When the board of directors assembles for a regular dividend meeting, it will weigh a variety of factors in determining the size of forthcoming dividend payments. First, the board will look at the firm's earnings. For even though a company doesn't have to show a profit to pay dividends, profits are still considered a vital link to the dividend decision, as a bright profit picture enhances the outlook for dividends. With stocks, the annual earnings of a firm are usually measured and reported in

earnings per share (EPS)
the amount of annual earnings available to common stockholders, as stated on a per share basis.

terms of **earnings per share (EPS).** Basically, EPS translates total corporate profits into profits on a per share basis and provides a convenient measure of the amount of earnings available to stockholders. Earnings per share is found by using the following simple formula:

$$EPS = \frac{\frac{net\ profit}{after\ taxes} - preferred\ dividends}{\begin{array}{c} number\ of\ shares\ of \\ common\ stock\ outstanding \end{array}}$$

For example, if a firm reports a net profit of $1.25 million, pays $250,000 in dividends to preferred stockholders, and has 500,000 shares of common outstanding, it would have an EPS of $2 [($1,250,000 − $250,000)/500,000]. Note that preferred dividends are *subtracted* from profits, since they have to be paid before any monies can be made available to common stockholders.

Dividends are actually charged against the firm's *retained earnings,* which represents the amount of past and current earnings not paid out as dividends, but left to accumulate in the firm to finance the company's operations. Of course, any cash that has to be paid will come from the firm's cash resources, since retained earnings is only a bookkeeping entry and does *not* represent a pool of cash. While profit and retained earnings are being assessed, the board will also look at the firm's growth prospects. Very likely, some of the firm's present earnings will be needed for investment purposes and to finance expected growth partly. Then the firm's cash position will be examined to make sure there is sufficient liquidity to meet a cash dividend of a given size. Finally, the board will want to assure itself that it is meeting all legal and contractual constraints. (For example, the firm may be subject to a loan agreement that legally limits the amount of dividends it can pay.)

After having looked at internal matters, the board will consider certain market effects and responses. The market generally places a high value on dividends. Moreover, most investors feel that if a company is going to retain earnings rather than pay them out in dividends, it should exhibit proportionately higher growth and profit levels. The market's message is clear: If the firm is investing the money wisely and at a high rate of return, fine; otherwise, pay a larger portion of earnings out in the form of dividends. Moreover, to the extent that different types of investors tend to be attracted to certain types of firms, the board must make every effort to meet the dividend expectations of its shareholders. For example, income-oriented investors are attracted to firms that generally pay high dividends; failure to meet these expectations can lead to disastrous results in the marketplace.

Some Important Dates

When the directors declare a dividend, they also indicate the payment times and other important dates associated with the dividend. Normally, the directors issue a statement to the press indicating their dividend decision, along with the pertinent dividend payment dates. These statements are widely quoted in the financial media; typical of such releases are the dividend news captions depicted in Figure 6.7. Three dates are particularly important to the stockholder: date of record, ex-dividend date,

CORPORATE DIVIDEND NEWS

Diamond Shamrock to Cut Quarterly Payout in 1990

DALLAS—**Diamond Shamrock Offshore Partners** said it expects to slash its quarterly distribution of 70 cents a unit in 1990.

The oil and gas partnership said the actual distribution paid will depend on oil and gas prices, but it said distributions probably will be "substantially below" the current $2.80 a unit annual rate.

The company said its cash available for distributions in 1988 after working capital costs and capital expenditures was only about one-third of the actual distributions. **Maxus Energy** Corp., the managing partner of Diamond Shamrock Offshore, made up the balance by purchasing additional Diamond Shamrock units.

Maxus has said it doesn't plan to support the distribution by buying additional units after this year.

* * *

Dividends Reported March 31

Company	Period	Amount	Payable date	Record date
REGULAR				
Ampal-Am Israel clA	S	.04	5–26–89	4–21
Ampco-Pittsburgh	Q	.07½	4–28–89	4–12
AmVestors Finl	Q	.05	5– 1–89	4–14
Amwest Insur Grp	Q	.05	4–15–89	4– 7
BIC Corp	Q	.25	5– 1–89	4–14
Brady(WH)Co clA	Q	.07	4–30–89	4–14
Carnival Cruise	Q	.10	6–14–89	5–31
Consumers Finl	A	.12	5– 1–89	4–14

Company	Period	Amount	Payable date	Record date
IntlMobiMach$2.50pf	S	1.25	6– 1–89	4–14
Productn Operators	Q	.04	5–15–89	4–14
Sierra Pacific Res	Q	.45	5– 1–89	4–14
United Savers Bncp	Q	.18	4–28–89	4–14
Werner Enterp	Q	.02	4–24–89	4–10

FUNDS · REITS · INVESTMENT COS · LPS

Company	Period	Amount	Payable date	Record date
Amer Rlty Tr	Q	.18	4–28–89	4–14
Drexel Burnham Fd	Q	h.27	4–10–89	3–31
DrexelSerTrBdDeb	M	h.07	4–10–89	3–31
DrexelSerTrConvert	Q	h.10	4–10–89	3–31
Drexel Ser Tr Govt	M	h.05½	4–10–89	3–31
DrexelSerTrGrwth	Q	h.05	4–10–89	3–31
DrexelSerTrLtdGvt	M	h.05	4–10–89	3–31
DrexelSerTrOptInco	M	h.03	4–10–89	3–31
Equity Portfol Inco	M	h.06	4–17–89	3–31
Fenimore Intl	Q	h.20	4–10–89	3–31
Franklin AGE	M	.036	4–14–89	4– 3
FranklinCalTxFr	M	.043	4–14–89	4– 3
Franklin Corp Cash	M	.15	4–14–89	4– 3
FranklinFedTxFr	M	.071	4–14–89	4– 3
Franklin Inv Grade	M	.066	4–14–89	4– 3
Franklin NY TxFr	M	.066	4–14–89	4– 3
Franklin Option	–	v.16	4–14–89	4– 3

v-Payment consists of 12 cents from capital gains and four cents from income.

Company	Period	Amount	Payable date	Record date
FranklinRisingDiv	Q	.09	4–14–89	4– 3
Franklin US Gvt	M	.058	4–14–89	4– 3
KemperHighIncoTr	M	.11½	4–28–89	4–14
KemperIntermedGvt	M	.0834	4–28–89	4–14
Kemper Multi Mkt	M	.117	4–28–89	4–14
KemperMuniInco	M	.07¼	4–28–89	4–14
KleinwrtBenAusInco	Q	h.28½	4–21–89	4–13
Worldwide Value	–	n.40	4–24–89	4–11

n-Payment consists of four cents from capital gains and 36 cents from income.

EXTRA

Company	Period	Amount	Payable date	Record date
Werner Enterp	–	.01	4–24–89	4–10

STOCK

Company	Period	Amount	Payable date	Record date
AmVestors Finl	–	w	5– 1–89	4–21

w-Five-for-four stock split.

Company	Period	Amount	Payable date	Record date
Servotronics Inc	–	10%	5–16–89	4–21
Teletimer Int'l	–	p	0– 0–	3–31

p-One-for-ten reverse stock split.

INCREASED

Company	Period	New	Old	Payable date	Record date
		--Amounts--			
Avery Intl	Q	.14	.12	6–21–89	6– 7
Southwestern Bell	Q	.65	.62	5– 1–89	4–10

SPECIAL

Company	Period	Amount	Payable date	Record date
VirginiaBeachFedl	–	.25	4–14–89	4– 6
WstrnFedSvgsBk PR	–	.10	4–21–89	3–31

A-Annual; Ac-Accumulation; b-Payable in Canadian funds; F-Final; G-Interim; h-From Income; k-From capital gains; M-Monthly; Q-Quarterly; S-Semi-annual.

* * *

Stocks Ex-Dividend April 4

Company	Amount	Company	Amount
AmerHrtgLifeInves	.09	Ill Power 7.56%pf	.94½
Augat Inc	.10	Ill Power 8%pf	1.00
Bell Atlantic	1.10	IllinoisPwr8%pf'86	2.00
BellSouth Corp	.63	Ill Power 8.24%pf	1.03
Boston Edison Co	.45½	IllinoisPwr8.52%pf	1.06½
Boston Ed 8.88%pf	2.22	Ill Power 8.94%pf	1.11¾
Campbell Soup Co	.23	Ill Pwr 11.75%pf	1.46⅞
Carolina Pwr & Lt	.71	Ill Pwr adj pfA	.75
Central Hudson G&E	.44	Illinois PwradjpfB	.97½
Centrl Maine Power	.38	Inland Steel pfC	.90⅝
Crown Crtl Pet pfA	.48	Iowa Resources	.41½
CrownCntrlPetropfB	.56¼	Lincoln National	.62
Dreyfus Strat Muni	.06½	Medtronic Inc	.30
Du Pont $3.50pf	.87½	Montana Power	.69
Du Pont $4.50pf	1.12½	Ohio Art Co	.06
General Mills Inc	.47	Oklahoma Gas & El	.59½
Hotel Invstrs Tr	.25	Penney (JC) Co	.56
Illinois Power Co	.66	Southwestern Bell	.65
Ill Power 4.08%pf	.51	Standard Products	.23
Ill Power 4.20%pf	.52½	Superior IndusIntl	.08
Ill Power 4.26%pf	.53¼	TCBY Enterprises	.02
Ill Power 4.42%pf	.55¼	Unocal Corp	.25
Ill Power 4.70%pf	.58¾	Wash Gas Light	.49

FIGURE 6.7 **Important Dates and Data About Dividends.**

The dividend actions of corporations are big news in the financial community; this news release, taken from *The Wall Street Journal,* provides timely imformation about cash and stock dividends, as well as stocks that have gone ex-dividend. (*Source: The Wall Street Journal,* April 3, 1989.)

date of record
the date on which an investor must be a registered shareholder of a firm to be entitled to receive a dividend.

ex-dividend date
the date four business days before the date of record, which determines whether one is an official shareholder of a firm and thus eligible to receive a declared dividend.

and payment date. The **date of record** is the date on which the investor must be a registered shareholder of the firm to be entitled to receive a dividend; these stockholders are often referred to as *holders of record*. When the board specifies the date of record, it means that all investors who are official stockholders of the firm as of the close of business on that date will receive the dividends that have just been declared.

Because of the time needed to make bookkeeping entries when a stock is traded, the stock will sell on an ex-dividend basis for four business days prior to the date of record. Thus, the **ex-dividend date** will dictate whether or not you were an official shareholder and therefore are eligible to receive the declared dividend. If you sell a stock after the ex-dividend date, you receive the dividend; if you sell before, the new shareholder will receive the recently declared dividend. The *payment date* is also set by the board of directors and generally follows the date of record by a few weeks. It is the actual date on which the company will mail dividend checks to holders of record—for example, if you owned 200 shares of a stock that just paid a quarterly cash dividend of 50 cents a share, you'd receive a check in the mail for $100.

Types of Dividends

cash dividend
payment of a dividend in the form of cash.

stock dividend
payment of a dividend in the form of additional shares of stock.

Normally, companies pay dividends in the form of cash, though sometimes they do so by issuing additional shares of stock. The first type of distribution is known as a **cash dividend;** the latter is called a **stock dividend.** Occasionally dividends will be paid in still other forms. For example, the firm might pay what is known as a *spinoff dividend*. This is like a stock dividend, except that the company pays its stockholders in shares *other than its own*. Generally, these are shares in subsidiary companies that the corporation owns and in which, for one reason or another, it is reducing (or eliminating) its investment. Some public utility firms use what are known as *return of capital dividends*. These are cash dividends, but because they are not charged to retained earnings (they are charged against "original paid-in capital") they are different from normal cash dividends. As such they are highly valued by knowledgeable income-oriented investors because they are *not* subject to income tax. But dividends in the form of either cash or stock remain by far the most popular, so let's take a closer look at these.

 Cash or Stock

dividend yield
a measure that relates dividends to share price and in so doing, puts common stock dividends on a relative (percent) rather than absolute (dollar) basis.

More firms use cash dividends than any other type of dividend payment procedure. A nice by-product of cash dividends is that *they tend to increase over time,* with the average annual increase amounting to around 5 to 7 percent. Such a tendency holds a real appeal for investors since a steady stream of dividends—even better, a *steadily increasing* stream of dividends—acts to shore up stock returns in soft markets.

A convenient (and popular) way of assessing the amount of dividends received is to measure the stock's **dividend yield.** Basically, dividend yield is a measure of common stock dividends on a relative (percent) rather than absolute (dollar) basis—that is, the dollar amount of dividends received is related to the market price of the

stock. Dividend yield, in effect, indicates the rate of current income earned on the investment dollar. It is computed as follows:

$$\text{dividend yield} = \frac{\text{annual dividends received per share}}{\text{current market price of the stock}}$$

Thus, a company that annually pays $2 per share in dividends to its stockholders, and whose stock is trading at $25, has a dividend yield of 8 percent.

Occasionally, a firm may declare a stock dividend instead of a cash dividend. A stock dividend simply means that the dividend is paid in additional shares of stock. For instance, if the board declares a 10 percent stock dividend, each shareholder will receive 1 new share of stock for each 10 shares currently owned. If you own 200 shares of stock, you will receive 20 new shares under such an arrangement. Although they seem to satisfy the needs of some investors, *stock dividends really have no value* because they represent the receipt of something already owned. The market will respond to such dividends by simply adjusting share prices according to the terms of the stock dividend. Thus, in the example above, we would normally find that a 10 percent stock dividend will lead to decline of around 10 percent in the share price of the stock. As a result, if the market value of your shareholdings amounted to, say, $10,000 before a stock dividend, it is likely that the same total market value will prevail after the stock dividend (you may have more shares, but each will carry a lower market price). There is, however, one bright spot in all this and that is, unlike cash dividends, at least you don't have to pay taxes on these dividends *until the stocks are actually sold.*

Dividend Reinvestment Plans

dividend reinvest-
ment plans (DRPs)
*plans in which
shareholders have
cash dividends auto-
matically reinvested
in additional shares
of the firm's common
stock.*

In recent years, a growing number of firms have established **dividend reinvestment plans (DRPs),** whereby shareholders can have their cash dividends automatically reinvested into additional shares of the company's common stock. The basic investment philosophy at work here is that *if the company is good enough to invest in, it's good enough to reinvest in.* As Table 6.4 demonstrates, such an approach can have a tremendous impact on your investment position over time. Today, about 1,000 companies (including most major corporations) offer dividend reinvestment plans, and each one provides investors with a convenient and inexpensive way to accumulate capital. Stocks in most DRPs are acquired free of any brokerage commissions, and some plans even sell stocks to their DRP investors at below-market prices— often at discounts of 3 to 5 percent. In addition, most plans will credit fractional shares to the investor's account.

Shareholders can join these plans by simply sending in a completed authorization form to the company (generally, it takes about 30–45 days for all the paper work to be processed). Once the shareholder is enrolled in the plan, the number of shares held will begin to accumulate with each dividend date. There is one important catch, however: Even though these dividends take the form of additional shares of stock, taxes must be paid on them as though they were cash dividends. Don't confuse these dividends with stock dividends—*reinvested dividends are taxable, in*

TABLE 6.4   Cash or Reinvested Dividends?

Situation: Buy 100 shares of stock at $25 a share (total investment $2,500); stock currently pays $1 a share in annual dividends. Price of the stock increases at 8% per year; dividends grow at 5% per year.

Investment Period	Number of Shares Held	Market Value of Stock Holdings	Total Cash Dividends Received
TAKE DIVIDENDS IN CASH			
5 years	100	$ 3,672	$ 552
10 years	100	5,397	1,258
15 years	100	7,930	2,158
20 years	100	11,652	3,307
PARTICIPATE IN DIVIDEND REINVESTMENT PLAN			
5 years	115.59	$ 4,245	$0
10 years	135.66	7,322	0
15 years	155.92	12,364	0
20 years	176.00	20,508	0

the year they're received, as ordinary income, just as if they had been received in cash.

Dividend Policies

On average, companies that pay dividends tend to pay out about half of their earnings, although the specific amount can vary all over the map: from as little as 5 to 10 percent of earnings to as much as 95 or 100 percent. Most companies decide how much to pay in accordance with a stated or implied *dividend policy*. The policy is usually established with an eye toward the financing requirements of the firm and the needs of its stockholders. Because they can affect the level and consistency of dividend payments, these policies are of concern to investors. Let's look now at three of the most widely used dividend policies.

Regular Dividends

Perhaps the most common type of dividend policy, the *regular dividend* approach, is based on the payment of a relatively fixed dollar dividend each quarter. The idea is to keep the level of dividends as regular and consistent as possible. Firms that follow this policy go to almost any extent to avoid missing payments or decreasing the level of dividends. On the other hand, the amount of per-share dividends paid over time will usually undergo a gradual increase as the firm's profit level increases. A firm, therefore, may have an annual dividend rate of, say, $2 per share and hold that level for several years or more, until *earnings* have moved to a new and higher plateau. Then, the level of dividends will be increased to, say, $2.50 per share. The

TABLE 6.5   A Regular-Extra Dividend Policy in Action

Year	Earnings per Share	Regular Dividend per Share	Extra Dividend per Share	Total Dividend per Share
1978	$2.50	$1.00		$1.00
1979	2.63	1.00		1.00
1980	2.98	1.30		1.30
1981	3.46	1.30	$.60	1.90
1982	2.99	1.30		1.30
1983	3.61	1.60		1.60
1984	4.92	1.60	1.00	2.60
1985	4.68	1.60	.40	2.00
1986	5.01	2.00		2.00
1987	4.85	2.00		2.00
1988	5.11	2.25		2.25
1989	5.76	2.25	.65	2.90

object of this policy is to minimize the uncertainty of the dividend flows to stockholders, whose faith in regular dividends is severely tried when a firm fails to maintain payments.

Extra Dividends

extra dividends
additional dividend declared when the level of earnings is higher than expected; usually paid in the final quarter of the year.

Some firms will periodically declare **extra dividends** whenever the level of earnings is higher than normal and the firm has an extra-large pool of funds from which to pay dividends. Extra dividends are usually, but not always, paid in the final quarter of the year and are designated as "extra" in order to avoid giving stockholders the impression that a new level of regular dividends is about to be established. Table 6.5 shows how extra dividends are combined with a regular dividend policy. Note that the level of regular dividends is kept fairly stable for two or three years at a time, and the extra dividends are dispersed only when corporate earnings are especially high.

Fixed Payout Ratio

fixed payout ratio
dividend policy that pays owners a percentage of each dollar earned in the form of a cash dividend.

The dividend policy that gives most attention to the firm, and that some would argue gives too little weight to the needs of stockholders, is the **fixed payout ratio.** It is used by a number of firms, particularly newer ones or those experiencing high growth rates. By definition, a payout ratio describes the percentage of each dollar earned that is distributed to the owners in the form of cash dividends. Little attention is given to the dollar level of dividends, as the thrust of this policy is to keep the ratio of the amount paid out as constant as possible. As a result, if earnings fluctuate, then so (obviously) do dividends; Table 6.6 illustrates this policy in action. In this example, we assume that the firm uses a constant 25 percent payout ratio. The amount of dividends paid per share is determined by multiplying the earnings per

TABLE 6.6   A Fixed Dividend Payout Ratio Policy in Action

Year	Earnings per Share	Payout Ratio	Annual Dividends Paid per Share
1978	$2.50	25%	$ .62½
1979	2.63	25	.66
1980	2.98	25	.74½
1981	3.46	25	.86½
1982	2.99	25	.75
1983	3.61	25	.90
1984	4.92	25	1.23
1985	4.68	25	1.17
1986	5.01	25	1.25
1987	4.85	25	1.21
1988	5.11	25	1.28
1989	5.76	25	1.44

share by the payout ratio (e.g., for 1979: $2.50 × .25 = $.62½). Note that the biggest drawback of this policy is that the instability of dividends often leads to erratic and sometimes depressed market prices of the common stock.

TYPES AND USES OF COMMON STOCK

Common stocks appeal to investors because they are simple and relatively straightforward investment vehicles. Their sources of return are relatively easy to identify, and they offer the potential for everything from current income and stability of capital to attractive capital gains. The market contains a wide range of stock, from the most conservative to the highly speculative. Generally, the kinds of stock sought by investors will depend on their investment objectives and their investment program. We will examine several of the more popular kinds of common stock here, as well as the various ways such securities can be used in different types of investment programs.

Kinds of Stock

It is helpful to understand the market system used to classify common stock, because a stock's general classification denotes not only its fundamental source of return, but also the quality of the company's earnings, the issue's susceptibility to market risks, the nature and stability of its earnings and dividends, and even the susceptibility of the stock to adverse economic conditions. Such insight is useful in selecting stocks that best fit one's overall investment objectives. Among the many different types of stock, blue chips, income stocks, growth stocks, speculative stocks, cyclical stocks, and defensive stocks are the most common. We will now

look at these and several other types of stocks to see not only what they are, but also how they might be used.

Blue Chips

These are the cream of the crop; *blue chips* are stocks that are unsurpassed in quality and have a long and stable record of earnings and dividends. They are issued by large, well-established firms that have impeccable financial credentials. The companies hold important, if not leading, positions in their industries and frequently determine the standards by which other firms are measured. Not all blue chips are alike, however. Some provide consistently high dividend yields, whereas others are more growth oriented. Good examples of blue chip growth firms are McDonalds, Abbott Labs, H.J. Heinz, Dun & Bradstreet, and Merck (shown here); some high-yielding blue chips include PNC Financial, American Brands, Centel, Norstar Bancorp, and Northern States Power. Blue chips are particularly attractive to investors who seek quality investment outlets offering respectable dividend yields and modest growth potential. Many use them for long-term investment purposes, and because of their relatively low risk exposure, as a way of obtaining modest but dependable rates of return on their investment dollars. They are popular with a large segment of the investing public and as a result, are often relatively high in price, especially when the market is unsettled and investors become more quality-conscious.

Merck & Co.

NYSE Symbol MRK   Options on CBOE (Jan-Apr-Jul-Oct)   In S&P 500

Price	Range	P-E Ratio	Dividend	Yield	S&P Ranking	Beta
Jun. 9'89	1989					
71⅜	72⅞–56¼	22	1.64	2.3%	A+	0.80

SUMMARY: This company is the world's largest ethical drug manufacturer, producing a wide range of human and animal pharmaceuticals as well as specialty chemical and environmental products. With nearly half of sales derived from foreign subsidiaries, earnings are often significantly affected by currency exchange fluctuations. Anticipated contributions from new drug products hold much promise for future growth.

Source: Standard & Poor's *NYSE Stock Reports,* June 19, 1989.

Income Stocks

Some stocks are appealing simply because of their attractive dividend yields. This is the case with *income stocks,* issues that have a long and sustained record of regularly paying higher than average dividends. Income shares are ideally suited for individuals who seek a relatively safe and high level of current income from their investment capital. But there's more. Holders of income stocks can expect the

amount of dividends they receive to increase regularly over time, unlike bonds and preferred stocks. Take Potomac Electric Power, for example: it paid dividends of 68 cents a share in 1979; 10 years later, in 1988, it was paying $1.38 a share. That's a big jump in dividends—nearly 103 percent—and it's something that can have quite an impact on total return! On the downside, the major disadvantage of these securities is that some of the firms may be paying the high dividends because of limited growth potential. Indeed, it's not unusual for income shares to exhibit only low or modest rates of growth in earnings. This does not mean that such firms are unprofitable or lack future prospects; quite the contrary, most firms whose stocks qualify as income shares are highly profitable organizations and have excellent future prospects. A number of income stocks are among the giants of American industry, and many are also classified as quality blue chips. Most public utilities, such as Alleghany Power, Brooklyn Union Gas, and SCEcorp (shown here) are found in this group, as are selected industrial and financial issues like General Motors, Imperial Chemical, Bank of New York, and Security Pacific. By their nature, income stocks are not exposed to a great deal of business and market risk but instead are subject to a fair amount of interest rate risk.

SCEcorp

NYSE Symbol SCE Options on Pacific (Jan-Apr-Jul-Oct) in S&P 500

Price	Range	P-E Ratio	Dividend	Yield	S&P Ranking	Beta
Aug. 10'89	1989					
37	37⅞–31	11	2.56	6.9%	A	0.37

SUMMARY: This utility holding company was formed in July, 1988 by Southern California Edison in a corporate restructuring. On November 30, 1988 SCE and San Diego Gas & Electric approved a definitive merger agreement, and shareholders of both companies approved the plan in April, 1989. The merger may be completed by late 1990. The two companies jointly own assets throughout the Southwest. SCE's Southern California Edison serves a diversified industrial and commercial economy, while San Diego Gas & Electric provides service to one of the nation's fastest growing residential communities.

Source: Standard & Poor's *NYSE Stock Reports,* August 18, 1989.

Growth Stocks

Shares that have experienced, and are expected to continue experiencing, consistently high rates of growth in operations and earnings are known as *growth stocks*. A good growth stock might exhibit a *sustained* rate of growth in earnings of 15 to 18 percent over a period when common stocks, on average, are experiencing growth rates of only 5 to 6 percent. Wal-Mart Stores (shown here), Capital Cities/ABC, Gannett, Rubber-Maid, and Marriott are all prime examples of growth stock. As this list suggests, some growth stocks also rate as blue chips and provide quality growth, whereas others possess higher levels of speculation. Growth stocks normally pay little or no dividends, and their payout ratios seldom exceed 25 to 30

percent of earnings, as all or most of the profits are reinvested in the company and used to at least partially finance rapid growth. Thus the major source of return to investors is price appreciation. Growth shares generally appeal to investors who are looking for attractive capital gains rather than dividends, and who are willing to assume a higher element of risk (an outgrowth of the uncertain nature of the investment payoff). Most growth stock investors, however, view this added risk as completely acceptable in light of the relatively high potential return these securities offer.

Wal-Mart Stores

NYSE Symbol WMT   Options on CBOE (Mar-Jun-Sep-Dec)   In S&P 500

Price	Range	P-E Ratio	Dividend	Yield	S&P Ranking	Beta
May 24'89 38½	1989 37⅞–30	25	0.22	0.6%	A+	1.28

SUMMARY: Wal-Mart operates a chain of discount department stores in an area spanning the Sunbelt and the Midwest, with locations generally in smaller communities. Strong base expansion and an aggressive pricing posture should facilitate market share gains in the Wal-Mart division, while improving profitability of the wholesale clubs and contributions from new hypermarkets—combination supermarket/discount merchandisers—and other new store prototypes enhance longer-term prospects.

Source: Standard & Poor's *NYSE Stock Reports*, June 2, 1989.

Speculative Stocks

Shares that lack sustained records of success but still offer the potential for substantial price appreciation are known as *speculative stocks*. Perhaps it's a new management team taking over a troubled company or the introduction of a promising new product that spurs investors' hopes. Other times, it's the possibility that some new information, discovery, or production technique will come along, favorably affect the growth prospects of the firm, and inflate the price of the stock. Speculative stocks are a special breed of securities, and they enjoy a wide following, particularly when the market is bullish. Generally speaking, their earnings are uncertain and highly unstable; they are subject to wide swings in price; and they usually pay little or nothing in dividends. On the plus side, speculative stocks like Microsoft (shown here), Home Depot, Arbor Drugs, ConAgra, and Carter Wallace offer the prospects for growth and the chance to "hit it big" in the market. But to be successful, an investor has to identify the big-money winners before the rest of the market does, and before the price of the stock is driven up. Speculative stocks, then, are highly risky and require not only a strong stomach, but considerable investor know-how as well. They are used to seek capital gains, and investors will often aggressively trade in and out of these securities as the situation demands.

Microsoft Corp.

NASDAQ Symbol MSFT   (Incl. in Nat'l Market) Options on ASE & Pacific (Jan-Apr-Jul-Oct)

Price	Range	P-E Ratio	Dividend	Yield	S&P Ranking	Beta
Dec. 16'88	1988					
49¾	70½–45¼	20	None	None	NR	NA

SUMMARY: Microsoft develops and markets a diverse line of systems and applications microcomputer software—including its MS-DOS operating system, the most widely used operating system for the IBM PC and IBM-compatible microcomputers. The company has introduced MS OS/2, a long-awaited operating system designed to harness the capabilities of personal computers based on the Intel 80286 and 80386 microprocessors. Results for fiscal 1989 should benefit from continued strong computer shipments and the depth of the company's product line.

Source: Standard & Poor's *OTC Stock Reports,* December 23, 1988.

Cyclical Stocks

Cyclical stocks are issued by companies whose earnings are closely linked to the general level of business activity. They tend to reflect the general state of the economy and move up and down as the business cycle moves through its peaks and troughs. Companies that serve markets tied to capital equipment spending on the part of business, or consumer spending for big-ticket durable items like houses and cars, typically head the list of cyclical stocks. These would include companies like Dow Chemical, Alcoa, Georgia Gulf, INCO, and Worthington Industries (shown here). For obvious reasons, these stocks have the most appeal when the economic outlook is strong and are perhaps best avoided when the economy begins to weaken. Because their prices have a tendency to move with the level of economic activity, they are probably more suitable for investors who are willing to trade in and out of these issues as the economic outlook dictates, and who can tolerate the accompanying exposure to risk.

Worthington Industries

NASDAQ Symbol WTHG   (Incl. in Nat'l Market; marginable)   In S&P 500

Price	Range	P-E Ratio	Dividend	Yield	S&P Ranking	Beta
Jan. 25'89	1988–9					
23⅛	24¾–16¾	15	0.44	1.9%	A	1.41

SUMMARY: This processor of close-tolerance steel also manufactures steel castings, pipe fittings, pressure cylinders and custom plastic and precision metal parts. Since 1982, sales, earnings and dividends of this highly efficient manufacturer have risen without interruption. Higher sales together with some improvement in margins and a small decline in the tax rate should result in higher earnings in fiscal 1989.

Source: Standard & Poor's *OTC Stock Reports,* February 3, 1989.

Defensive Stocks

Sometimes it is possible to find stocks whose prices will remain stable, or even prosper, when general economic activity is tapering off. These securities are known as *defensive stocks,* and they tend to be less affected by downswings in the business cycle than the average issue. Examples of defensive stocks include the shares of many public utilities, as well as industrial and consumer goods companies that produce or market such staples as beverages, foods, and drugs. An excellent example of a defensive stock is Bandag (shown here); this recession-resistant company is the world's leading manufacturer of rubber used to retread tires. Another example is Loctite, the producers of super glue. But perhaps the best known of all defensive stocks, particularly in inflationary periods, are gold mining shares; these stocks literally flourish when inflation becomes a serious problem. Defensive shares are commonly used by the more aggressive investors. For the most part, such investors tend to ``park'' their funds temporarily in defensive stocks while the market and/or economy is off (and until the investment atmosphere improves).

Bandag, Inc.

NYSE Symbol BDG

Price	Range	P-E Ratio	Dividend	Yield	S&P Ranking	Beta
Apr. 25'89 72	1989 72⅝–64¼	15	0.90	1.3%	A+	0.97

SUMMARY: This company is a leading manufacturer of tread rubber, equipment and supplies used in a patented "cold" bonding process for the recapping of truck and bus tires. Sales and earnings have been in an uptrend over the past decade, and dividends have been increased in each year since their initiation in 1976. Foreign operations accounted for 37% of sales and 26% of operating earnings in 1988. The Carver family controls about 72% of the voting power.

Source: Standard & Poor's *NYSE Stock Reports,* May 3, 1989.

Other Types of Stocks

American Depositary Receipts (ADRs)
the security through which foreign stocks are traded in American markets, these negotiable instruments are like common stock, as each one represents a specific number of shares in a specific foreign company; traded on the NYSE, AMEX, and OTC markets.

The issues described above represent the major, mainline categories of stocks. In addition to these, there are several other types of stocks that, although not as popular as blue chips or income stocks, do appeal to many of the more seasoned investors. While this ``other'' category includes everything from neglected stocks to so-called *pink sheet stocks* (described in the *Investor Insights* box on pages 256–257), it also embraces foreign stocks, small company stocks, and initial public offerings.

If an investor is willing to put up with all the expense and red tape, one way of investing in foreign stocks is to buy shares listed on foreign stock exchanges. However, a better and far simpler way of investing in foreign stocks is to buy **American Depositary Receipts (ADRs).** Basically, ADRs are negotiable instruments, issued by American banks, with each ADR representing a specific number of shares in a specific foreign company. For example, each Hitachi ADR represents ownership of

10 shares of Hitachi stock. Although Hitachi's stock is not listed on any American exchange, its ADRs are listed on the NYSE, where each ADR trades like a regular share of stock. In essence, an ADR is treated like, and trades like, a share of American stock—and as with any American stock, the holder of an ADR is entitled to all the dividends and capital gains accruing to the underlying foreign stock. There are over 700 ADRs traded on the NYSE, AMEX, and OTC markets. In addition to Hitachi, other foreign stocks that can be purchased on American exchanges as ADRs include British Petroleum, Cannon, NEC, Volvo, Unilever, and Jaguar (shown here). Because ADRs are denominated in dollars, the quoted prices will vary with changes in the latest currency exchange rates.

Jaguar plc

NASDAQ Symbol JAGRY (Incl. in Nat'l Market; marginable)

Price	Range	P-E Ratio	Dividend	Yield	S&P Ranking	Beta
Sep. 6'88	1988					
4¼	6⅛–4	9	¹0.214	¹5.0%	NR	NA

SUMMARY: This British manufacturer of luxury motor cars, sold under the Jaguar and Daimler names, introduced its new Jaguar XJ6 sedan in October, 1986. Earnings for 1987 were restricted by expenses related to the startup of full production of the XJ6 and unfavorable currency fluctuations. (The company's stock trades as ADR's on the NASDAQ; each Jaguar ADR represents one ordinary share.)

Source: Standard & Poor's *NYSE Stock Reports,* September 14, 1988.

Some investors consider *small companies* to be in a class by themselves. They believe the stocks of these firms hold especially attractive capital gains opportunities in strong markets, which in many cases, has turned out to be correct. So-called "small cap" companies generally have sales of less than $250 million, and because of their size, spurts of growth can have dramatic effects on their earnings and stock prices. Bolar Pharmaceuticals, A.T. Cross, Minnetonka, FHP International, Blockbuster Entertainment, and TCBY Enterprises are just a few examples of some well-known small company stocks. Because many of these companies are small and don't have a lot of stock outstanding, their shares are often not widely traded; in addition, small company stocks have a tendency to be "here today and gone tomorrow." While some of these stocks may hold the potential for high returns, investors should also be aware of the very high risk exposure.

initial public offering (IPO)
a special category of common stocks issued by (relatively) new firms going public for the first time.

A special category of small company stock is the so-called **initial public offering.** These IPOs, as they are known, are basically small, relatively new companies that are going public for the first time. There were 830 companies that went public in 1987 and 1988. (Prior to their public offering, these stocks were privately held and *not* publicly traded.) Like small company issues, these stocks are attractive because of the substantial—sometimes phenomenal—capital gains that can be earned by investors. For example, Entertainment Marketing came out in 1985 at an

initial price of $2 a share and six months later was trading at $6.50, providing early investors a 222 percent return. Unfortunately, not all IPOs end up like this. As an illustration, Pizza Transit Authority also came out in 1985, at an initial price of $2.75 a share; by the end of the year it was trading at just $1 a share. Without question, IPOs are extremely high risk investments, with the odds of making the big hit clearly stacked against the investor. Since there's no market record to rely on, these stocks should be used only by investors who know what to look for in the company and who can tolerate the immense exposure to risk. If you are buying IPOs, by all means, diversify; don't put all your money on one long shot. IPOs tend to flourish when the market heats up, and the market is faddish, often dominated by trendy retail chains, food chains, and high-tech firms. Among the promising IPOs that came out in 1987 and 1988 were Octel Communications, System Software, The Sharper Image, FileNet, and Staples, Inc.

Alternative Investment Strategies

Basically, investors use common stocks (1) as a "warehouse" of value, (2) to accumulate capital, and/or (3) as a source of income. Storage of value is important to all investors, since nobody likes to lose money. However, some investors are more concerned about it than others and therefore put safety of principal first in their stock selection process. These investors are more quality-conscious and tend to gravitate toward blue chips and other nonspeculative shares. Accumulation of capital, in contrast, is generally an important goal to individuals with long-term investment horizons. They use the capital gains and/or dividends that stocks provide to build up their wealth. Some use growth stocks for such purposes; others do it with income shares; still others use a little of both. Finally, some people use stocks as a source of income; to them, a dependable flow of dividends is essential. High-yield, good-quality income shares are usually the preferred investment vehicle for these individuals.

Investors can use a number of different *investment strategies* to reach one or more of these investment goals. These include buy-and-hold, high income, quality long-term growth, aggressive stock management, and speculation and short-term trading. The first three strategies would probably appeal to investors who consider storage of value important. Depending on the temperament of the investor and the time he or she has to devote to an investment program, any one of the strategies just mentioned might be used to accumulate capital; the high-income strategy is the most logical choice for those using stocks as a source of income.

Buy-and-Hold

This is the most basic, and certainly one of the most conservative, of all investment strategies; the objective is to place money in a secure investment outlet (safety of principal is vital) and watch it grow over time. High-quality stocks that offer attractive current income and/or capital gains are selected and held for extended periods— perhaps as long as 15 or 20 years. This strategy is often used to finance future retirement plans, to meet the educational needs of children, or simply as a convenient way of accumulating capital over the long haul. Generally, investors will pick

INVESTOR INSIGHTS

Pink Sheets: The Hidden Stock Market

Where can you find a hot stock these days?

Some would say in the same place as always—the brash and risky, rags-to-riches pink sheets market.

Even in the heady days before October 1987's Crash, leading gainers in the listed and over-the-counter national markets were hard-pressed to match the performances of a few obscure issues in the pink sheets.

Investors hailed Merrill Lynch when that venerable full-service brokerage recommended Reuters ADR (OTC) near $50 around the first of the year and the stock rose to more than $90. But how many followed the advice of New York-based Mostel & Taylor at about the same time and bought Cellular America (OTC: CELM) at 37½ cents?

Not many, judging by the fact that the stock never attracted major Wall Street attention, even though it soared in value to $2.43. . . .

So it goes in the pink sheets market, a seedbed for tender young growth stocks and a happy hunting ground for investors seeking diamonds in the rough. Before you buy, however, consider how investing differs in the riskier and low-priced, less well-known pink sheet securities.

Though investment advisers usually equate the pinks with penny stocks and start-up companies, there's nothing new or small about the market.

"Practically every big-name company you see trading in New York and on the OTC market today was at one time a pink sheets stock," says Randall Roeing, investment consultant at *Dow Theory Forecasts,* an advisory service that specializes in low-priced stocks. . . .

Apple Computer, LyphoMed, Liz Claiborne, Seagate Technology, and all your favorite NASDAQ issues are on the pinks as well as the National Association of Securities Dealers' Automated Quotation system (NASDAQ).

There are also about 12,000 issues of firms unable, or unwilling, to meet the Securities and Exchange Commission's financial-reporting requirements. As a result, they are not listed on any exchange or NASD's market system.

Some are well-known: Rand McNally, Hoffmann-LaRoche, Manischewitz, and Churchill Downs are businesses you might expect to find on the Big Board. They prefer instead to remain in the pinks because they're closely held or don't want the publicity that comes with active stock trading.

out a few good stocks and then invest in them on a regular basis for long periods of time; they will stick with these securities until either the investment climate or corporate results change dramatically. Not only do investors regularly add fresh capital to their portfolios (many treat it like a savings plan), but most of the income from annual dividends is also plowed back into the portfolio and reinvested in additional shares (these investors often participate in dividend reinvestment plan). Long popular with so-called *value-oriented investors,* this approach is used by

Founded in 1913, the pink sheets market is one of the oldest in the U.S. Two Wall Street pioneers, Roger Babson and Arthur Elliott, saw the need to disseminate stock-price information and organized the National Quotation Bureau. Runners were sent to brokerage houses to collect sheets of paper on which traders listed prices for the stocks they were willing to buy or sell.

Babson and Elliott consolidated the information, and in the 1930s started printing it on pink sheets for hand delivery to brokerage offices. That process has changed little in the half century since. Today a desk-thumping 400 pages thick and still printed on pink paper, the pink sheets are hand-carried five days a week to brokerages in the financial districts of major cities and shipped overnight to trading offices elsewhere.

One concession to the quickly changing nature of securities trading was made in 1986, when a pink sheets data base was offered over the Quotron computer network to which most brokerage firms subscribe. That means some OTC brokers can look up a pink sheets stock by turning to a desktop terminal.

The information your broker sees displayed may be out of date, however. Trades are not reported, and the bid and offering prices on the system are updated only at the request of traders who make the markets in pink sheet stocks. . . .

Most dealing is still done by telephone. If you ask your broker for a quote on a little-known pink, and the firm doesn't happen to own the stock at the time, your broker has to call a market maker—a broker who does hold the issue—to learn the latest price.

Change is under way, however. On October 1, the NASD began publishing information resulting from a new SEC requirement that market makers report significant trading.

For the first time, reports will indicate the volume of activity in the nonregulated pink sheets, notes Bob Ferri, a NASD spokesman.

There's a chance, too, that a NASD-sponsored electronic bulletin board for a faster and more complete reporting of pink sheet prices may be put in operation before the end of 1988, Ferri says. . . .

[In spite of all these changes, this is still a highly segmented market. Not surprisingly, therefore, bids] and offers recorded on the pink sheets should be regarded as nothing more than indications of what the true prices might be. Spreads between them can be surprising. It's not unusual to see a pink sheet bid at 50 cents and offered at $1.50, and there's no such thing as an "inside" market, or best price.

While your broker should be willing to sell you a pink sheet stock at $1.50 if that's the offered price, he or she isn't obligated to. "Remember that you enjoy none of the safeguards that come with trading a stock listed on an exchange," notes Jacobson.

Source: Dan Ruck, "The Hidden Stock Market," *Money Maker,* December/January 1989, pp. 46–48.

quality-conscious individuals who are looking for highly competitive returns over the long haul.

High Income

Investors often use common stocks to seek high levels of current income. Common stocks are viewed as desirable outlets for such purposes not only because of their current yields, but also because their *dividend levels tend to increase over time.*

Safety of principal and stability of income are vital, and capital gains are of secondary importance. Quality income shares are the popular investment medium for this kind of strategy. Because of the high yields available from many income shares, a number of investors are adopting this strategy simply as a way of earning high (and relatively safe) returns on their investment capital. More often than not, however, high-income strategies are used by those trying to supplement their income and who plan to use the added income for consumption purposes, such as a retired couple supplementing their social security benefits with income from stocks.

Quality Long-Term Growth

This strategy is *less* conservative than either of the first two in that it seeks capital gains as the primary source of return. There is a fair amount of trading with this approach, although most of it is confined to quality growth stocks offering attractive growth prospects and the chance for considerable price appreciation. That doesn't mean, however, that dividends are just ignored, for there are a number of growth stocks that also pay dividends. As such, many growth-oriented investors look on dividends as *an added source of return*. But even with dividend-paying growth stocks, this strategy still emphasizes capital gains as the principal way of earning the bigger returns. The approach definitely involves a greater element of risk and, so, a good deal of diversification is often used. Long-term accumulation of capital is the most common reason for using this approach; but in contrast to the buy-and-hold tactic, the investor aggressively seeks a bigger payoff by doing considerably more trading and assuming more market risk.

Aggressive Stock Management

Aggressive stock management is also based on the principle of using quality issues, but this time to seek attractive rates of return through a fully managed portfolio—that is, one in which the investor aggressively trades in and out of various stocks in order to achieve handsome yields from both current income (dividends) and capital gains. Blue chips, income shares, growth stocks, and cyclical issues are the primary investment vehicles. Income, cyclical, and/or growth stocks would probably be the major investments during bull markets, and defensive securities, cash, or some short-term debt instrument would likely be used when the market is off. This approach is somewhat similar to the quality long-term growth strategy, but it involves considerably more trading, and the investment horizon is generally much shorter. For example, rather than waiting two or three years for a stock to move, an aggressive stock trader would go after the same investment payoff in six months to a year. Timing security transactions and turning investment capital over more rapidly are both key elements of this strategy. It has obvious and substantial risks, and it also places real demands on the individual's time and investment skills. But the rewards can be equally substantial.

Speculation and Short-Term Trading

Speculation and short-term trading is the least conservative of all investment strategies, especially when carried to its extreme. The sole investment objective is capital

gains; and if it can be achieved in two weeks, all the better. Although such investors confine most of their attention to speculative common stocks, they are not averse to using other forms of common stock if they offer attractive short-term capital gains opportunities. Many speculators find that information about the industry or company is much less important in this kind of strategy than market psychology or the general tone of the market itself. Getting out as quickly as possible with substantial capital gains is what this strategy is all about. It is a process of constantly switching from one position to another as new investment opportunities unfold. Because the strategy involves so much risk, many transactions end up with little or no profit, or even substantial losses. The hope is, of course, that when one does hit, it will be in a big way and as such, returns will be more than sufficient to offset losses; that is, the net result will be a hefty rate of return commensurate with the risk involved. Investing this way obviously requires considerable knowledge, time, and—perhaps most important—the psychological and financial fortitude to withstand the shock of financial losses.

SUMMARY

- Common stocks have long been popular because of the attractive return opportunities they provide investors; from current income to capital gains, there are common stocks available to fit just about any investment need.

- Common stockholders are the residual owners of the business and, as such, are entitled to all the profits left after expenses and creditor claims have been met.

- Historically (over the past 40 years), stocks have provided investors with annual returns of around 10 to 15 percent. These returns consist of both dividends and capital gains and are fairly reflective of what you can expect from stocks over the long haul—of course, higher returns may be possible over shorter periods of time and/or for those willing to assume a greater amount of risk.

- Although they may appear to be relatively inconsequential, the transaction costs of buying and selling common stocks can have a measurable impact on the return from an investment; one way to reduce transaction costs is to use a no-frills discount broker, where commission savings of 30 to 80 percent are possible.

- There are several ways to calculate the value of a share of stock, from book value, which represents accounting value, to market and investment value, which are most important to investors as these latter two represent what the stock is, or should be, worth.

- While common stocks are often referred to as the ideal inflation hedge, the fact is that when inflation really starts heating up, stocks generally do a rather unsatisfactory job of protecting the investor from inflation.

- Cash dividends are one form of return to investors, and they are paid out by companies according to certain policies; sometimes companies declare stock

dividends rather than, or in addition to, cash dividends. Many firms have automatic dividend reinvestment plans, whereby shareholders can have their cash dividends automatically reinvested in the company's stock.

- The type of stock selected depends on an investor's needs and preferences. In today's market the investor has a full range of stocks to choose from, including blue chips, income stocks, growth stocks, speculative issues, cyclicals, defensive shares, foreign stocks, small cap stocks, and initial public offerings.

- Generally speaking, common stocks can be used as a storage of value, to accumulate capital, and/or as a source of income. Different investment strategies can be followed to achieve these objectives, including the buy-and-hold technique, high income, quality long-term growth, aggressive stock management, and speculation and short-term trading.

REVIEW QUESTIONS AND PROBLEMS

1. What is a common stock? What is meant by the statement that holders of common stock are the residual owners of the firm?

2. What are two or three of the major investment attributes of common stocks?

3. What are some of the advantages *and* disadvantages of owning common stock? What are the major types of risk to which stockholders are exposed?

4. Explain the difference between a stock split and a stock dividend.

   a. Assume that Daisy Cole holds 250 shares of Consolidated Everything, Inc. How many shares of stock would she hold after the firm declared a 2 for 1 stock split?
   b. What would happen if the firm declared a 200 percent stock dividend?

5. Dwight Cranston owns some stock in General Refrigeration & Cooling. The stock recently underwent a 5 for 2 stock split. If the stock was trading at $50 per share just before the split, how much would each share likely be selling for right after the split? If Dwight owned 200 shares of the stock before the split, how many shares would he own afterward? Explain how the split affected the market value of his holdings.

6. Look at the record of stock returns in Table 6.1, particularly the return performance during the 1970s and 80s.

   a. How would you characterize the returns during the 70s versus those produced in the 80s?
   b. How important are dividends as a source of return? What about capital gains? Which is more important to total return? Which causes wider swings in total return?
   c. Considering the average annual returns that have been generated over *holding periods* of 5 years or more, what rate of return do you feel is typical for the stock market in general? Is it unreasonable to expect this kind of return, on average, in the future? Does this mean that higher rates of return aren't possible? Explain.

7. Why do firms issue treasury stock? Is treasury stock like classified stock? Are some types of classified stock particularly appealing to certain types of investors?

8. Define and differentiate among each of the following pairs of terms:

a. Par value and liquidation value.
b. Cash dividends and stock dividends.
c. Date of record and payment date.
d. Growth stock and speculative stock.

9. The Kracked Pottery Company has total assets of $2.5 million, total short- and long-term debt of $1.8 million, and $200,000 worth of 8 percent preferred stock outstanding. What is the firm's total book value? What would its book value per share amount to if it had 50,000 shares of common stock outstanding?

10. Are stocks a good inflation hedge? Explain.

11. The W. C. Fields Beverage Company recently reported net profits after taxes of $15.8 million; it has 2.5 million shares of common stock outstanding, and pays preferred dividends of $1 million per year.

a. Compute the firm's earnings per share (EPS).
b. Assuming the stock currently trades at $60 per share, what would the firm's dividend yield be if it paid $2 per share to common stockholders?

12. Angus Hoffmeister owns 200 shares of Consolidated Glue. The company's board of directors recently declared a cash dividend of 50 cents a share payable April 18 (a Wednesday) to shareholders of record on March 22 (a Thursday).

a. How much in dividends, if any, will Angus receive if he *sells* his stock on March 20?
b. Assume Angus decides to hold on to the stock rather than sell it; if he belongs to the company's dividend reinvestment plan, how many new shares of stock will he receive if the stock is presently trading at 40 and the plan offers a 5 percent discount on the share price of the stock? (Assume all of Angus's dividends are diverted to the plan.) Will Angus have to pay any taxes on these dividends, since he's taking them in stock rather than cash?

13. Judy Thompson holds 400 shares of the Fourth National Bank and Trust Company; there are three vacancies on the board of directors that will be voted on at the next stockholders' meeting, which Judy plans to attend. One candidate is Mrs. Lucille Sharp, a woman who would bring excellent credentials to the board; Judy feels that the time is long overdue for a woman to be represented on Fourth National's board. How many votes could Judy cast for Mrs. Sharp if the bank used a majority voting system? If it used a cumulative voting system?

a. Explain the basic difference between these two voting procedures.
b. Which one is designed to help minority stockholders?

14. Discuss the investment merits of each of the following:

a. Blue chips.
b. Income stocks.
c. Defensive stocks.
d. American Depositary Receipts

15. Why do most income stocks offer only limited capital gains potential? Does this mean the outlook for continued profitability is also limited? Explain.

16. What is the difference between a fixed dollar level of dividends and a fixed dividend payout policy? Assume that the Southwest Hamburger Company has the following five-year record of earnings per share:

Year	EPS
1985	$1.40
1986	2.10
1987	1.00
1988	3.25
1989	0.80

Which procedure would provide the greater amount of dividends to stockholders over this five-year period:

a. Paying out dividends at a fixed payout ratio of 40 percent? or
b. Paying out dividends at the fixed regular dividend level of $1 per share?

17. Why is the ex-dividend date so important to stockholders?

18. Briefly define each of the following types of investment programs, and note the kinds of common stock (blue chip, speculative stocks, and so on) that would best fit with each:

a. A buy-and-hold strategy.
b. A high income portfolio.
c. Aggressive stock management.

19. Assume the following quote for the Alpha Beta Corp. (a NYSE stock) was obtained from the Thursday, April 10th issue of *The Wall Street Journal:*

   254   150½   AlphaBet   ALF   6.00   3.2   15   755   194¼   189   189⅛   −3⅞

Given this information, answer the following questions.

a. On what day did the trading activity occur?
b. At what price did the stock sell at the end of the day on Wednesday, April 9?
c. What are the highest and lowest prices at which the stock sold on the day quoted?
d. What is the firm's price/earnings ratio? What does that indicate?
e. What is the last price at which the stock traded on the day quoted?
f. How large a dividend is expected in the current year?
g. What is the highest and lowest price at which the stock traded during the latest 52-week period?
h. How many shares of stock were traded on the day quoted?
i. How much, if any, of a change in stock price took place between the day quoted and the immediately preceding day?

20. Answer the questions below using the following quote for DEF, Inc. (a stock traded in the OTC market):

   DEF   1.10   86   41⅝   42⅛   +¼

a. At what price could you have purchased a share of DEF stock on the day quoted? What is this price called?
b. What is the annual dividend per share on DEF's stock?
c. How many shares of DEF were traded on the day reported above?
d. At what price could you have purchased a share of DEF on *the day preceding* that quoted above? Explain.
e. At what price could the stock be *sold* on the day quoted? What is this price called?

21. Using the resources available at your campus or public library, select *any three* common stocks you like and determine the latest book value per share, earnings per share, and dividend yield for each. (*Note:* Show all your calculations.)

CASE PROBLEMS

6.1 Sara Contemplates the Stock Market

Sara Thomas is a child psychologist who has built up a thriving practice in her hometown of Phoenix, Arizona. Her practice has been so lucrative, in fact, that over the past several years she has been able to accumulate a substantial sum of money, held in several savings accounts, and still have plenty left to live very comfortably. She has worked long and hard to be successful, but she never imagined anything like this. Fortunately, success has not spoiled Sara—still single, she keeps to her old circle of friends. One of her closest friends is Terry Jenkins, who happens to be a stockbroker (and a very successful one at that). Sara sees a lot of Terry, who, among other things, has acted as her financial advisor.

Not long ago, Sara attended a public seminar on the stock market and investing. Like a lot of other people, Sara was beginning to feel that holding all her money in low-yielding savings accounts was a serious mistake. One evening, Sara started talking about investing and confided to Terry that she had been doing some reading lately about the stock market and had found several stocks she thought looked "sort of interesting." She described them as follows:

- *North Atlantic Swimsuit Company:* It's a highly speculative stock and pays no dividends. Although the earnings of NASS have been a bit erratic. Sara feels that its growth prospects have never been brighter—"what with more people than ever going to the beaches the way they are these days."
- *Town and Country Computers:* This is a long-established computer firm that pays a modest dividend yield (of about 5 percent). It's considered a quality growth stock and from one of the stock reports she'd read, Sara understands that it offers excellent long-term growth and capital gains potential.
- *Southeastern Public Utility Company:* An income stock, it pays a nice dividend yield of around 8 percent. Although it's a solid company, it has limited growth prospects because of its location.
- *International Gold Mines, Inc.:* This stock performed quite well several years ago, and Sara feels that if it can do so well in inflationary times, it will do even better in a strong economy. Unfortunately, the stock has experienced wide price swings in the past and pays almost no dividends.

Questions

1. What do you think of the idea of Sara keeping "substantial sums" of money in savings accounts? Would common stocks make better investments than savings accounts?
2. What is your opinion of the four stocks Sara has described; do you think they are suitable for her investment needs?
3. What kind of common stock investment program would you recommend for Sara? What investment objectives do you think she should set for herself, and how can common stocks help her achieve her goals?

6.2.   Butch Goes After Dividend Yield

Butch Peterson is a commercial artist who makes a very good living by doing free lance work—mostly layout and illustration work for local ad agencies and major institutional clients, like large department stores. Butch has been investing in the stock market for some time, buying mostly high-quality growth stocks. He has been seeking long-term growth and capital appreciation and feels that with the limited time he has to devote to his security holdings, high-quality issues are his best bet. He has become a bit perplexed lately with the market, disturbed that some of his growth stocks aren't even doing as well as many good-grade income shares. He therefore decides to have a chat with his broker, Al Fried.

During the course of their conversation, it becomes clear that both Al and Butch are thinking along the same lines. Al points out that dividend yields on income shares are, indeed, way up and, because of the state of the economy, the outlook for growth stocks is not particularly bright. He suggests that Butch seriously consider putting some of his money into income shares to capture some of the high dividend yields that are available—after all, as Al points out, "the bottom line is not so much where the payoff comes from, as how much it amounts to!" They then talk about a high-yield public utility stock, Hydro-Electric Light and Power. Al digs up some forecast information about Hydro-Electric and presents it to Butch for his consideration.

Year	Expected EPS	Expected Dividend Payout Ratio
1990	$3.25	40%
1991	3.40	40
1992	3.90	45
1993	4.40	45
1994	5.00	45

The stock presently trades at $60 per share, and Al thinks that within five years it should be trading at a level of $75 to $80. Butch realizes that in order to buy the Hydro-Electric stock, he will have to sell his holdings of CapCo Industries—a highly regarded growth stock with which Butch has become disenchanted because of recent substandard performance.

Questions
1. How would you describe Butch's present investment program? How do you think it fits him and his investment objectives?
2. Looking at the Hydro-Electric stock:
   a. Determine the amount of annual dividends Hydro-Electric is expected to pay over the years 1990 to 1994.
   b. Compute the total dollar return Butch would make from Hydro-Electric if he invests $6,000 in the stock and all the dividend and price expectations are realized.
3. Would Butch be going to a different investment strategy if he decided to buy shares in Hydro-Electric? If the switch is made, how would you describe his new investment program? What do you think of this new approach, and is it likely to lead to more trading on Butch's behalf? If so, how do you think that stacks up with the limited amount of time he has to devote to his portfolio?

SELECTED READINGS

Donnelly, Barbara. "Even at Discount Brokers, Getting The Real Bargains Isn't Automatic." *The Wall Street Journal,* August 24, 1987, p. 17.

Dorfman, John R. "Study of Industrial Averages Finds Stocks With High Dividends Are Big Winners." *The Wall Street Journal,* August 11, 1988, p. 25.

Egan, Jack. "Dividends Are Dandy, But Earnings Still Provide the Pop!" *U.S. News & World Report,* January 12, 1987, p. 51.

Hector, Gary. "What Makes Stock Prices Move?" *Fortune,* October 10, 1988, pp. 69–76.

Kosnett, Jeff. "Are You Ready For The Next Black Monday?" *Changing Times,* June 1988, pp. 41–46.

Kaplan, Charles H. "Behind the Pink Sheets." *Barron's,* September 28, 1987, pp. 16, 88.

Kehrer, Daniel M. "Make Your Dividends Pay Again and Again." *Changing Times,* November 1988, pp. 73–77.

Ostler, Kevin. "Appetizing ADR's." *Personal Investor,* March 1988, pp. 22–29.

Schiffres, Manuel. "Good Stocks For Uncertain Times." *Changing Times,* August 1988, pp. 39–45.

Sorenseon, Laurel. "Class Warfare: How 'Class B' Stock Weakens Your Rights As An Investor." *Sylvia Porter's Personal Finance,* February 1987, pp. 97–99.

7

COMMON STOCK ANALYSIS

After studying this chapter you should be able to:

- Discuss the security analysis process, including its goals and the functions it performs.

- Gain an appreciation of the purpose and contribution of economic and industry analysis to the stock valuation process.

- Describe the concept of fundamental analysis and note how it is used to assess a company's financial position and operating results.

- Describe the various types of accounting statements and their role in analyzing the fundamental position of a company.

- Calculate a variety of financial ratios and use them to evaluate the historical performance of a company.

- Explain fundamental analysis and show how the insights derived from such analysis form the basic input for the valuation process.

To many individuals, common stocks are synonymous with investments. Stories recounting shrewd market plays seem to fascinate people from all walks of life, as the prospect of seeing a small sum grow into a vast fortune has the same attraction for the homemaker, the service station attendant, or the college professor as it does for the Wall Street tycoon. Consider, for example, the case of Wal-Mart. An investor could have purchased 100 shares of Wal-Mart for $1,650 when it first went public in 1970. Adjusting for stock splits, the value of that investment would have skyrocketed to nearly $820,000 by 1988. Not bad for an 18-year period of time—indeed, that's not bad for a lifetime!

Unfortunately, for every story of great success in the market there are dozens more that don't end nearly so well. Most of the disasters can be traced not only to bad timing, but to greed, poor planning, and failure to use simple common sense in making investment decisions. In this, the first of two chapters dealing with security analysis, we will introduce some of the principles and techniques used to evaluate the investment suitability of common stocks. Although these chapters cannot offer the keys to sudden wealth, they do provide sound principles for formulating a successful long-range investment program. The techniques described are quite traditional; they are the same methods that have been used by millions of investors to achieve attractive rates of return on their capital.

PRINCIPLES OF SECURITY ANALYSIS

security analysis
the process of gathering and organizing information and then using it to determine the value of a share of common stock.

intrinsic value
the underlying or inherent value of a stock, as determined through fundamental analysis.

Security analysis consists of gathering information, organizing it into a logical framework, and then using the information to determine the intrinsic value of a common stock. That is, given a desired rate of return and an assessment of the amount of risk involved in a proposed transaction, **intrinsic value** provides a measure of the underlying worth of a share of stock. It provides a standard for helping an investor judge whether a particular stock is undervalued, fairly priced, or overvalued. The question of value in the field of investments centers around return. In particular, a satisfactory investment candidate is one that offers *a level of expected return that's commensurate with the amount of risk involved.* In other words, there's a *desired or minimum rate of return* that you should be able to earn on an investment, which varies with the amount of risk you have to assume. Thus, not only must an investment candidate be profitable, it must be *sufficiently profitable—* in the sense that you'd expect it to generate a return that's high enough to offset perceived exposure to risk.

The whole concept of security analysis is based on the assumption that investors are capable of formulating reliable estimates of a stock's future behavior. This, of course, is a pretty strong assumption, and there are many who, for one reason or another, just don't accept it. These are the so-called "efficient market" advocates who argue that it is virtually impossible to consistently outperform the market. We will study the ideas and implications of efficient markets in some detail in Chapter 8; for now, however, we will assume that traditional security analysis is useful in identifying attractive equity investments.

If you could have your way, you'd probably like to invest in something that offered preservation of capital, along with a satisfactory level of current income

and/or capital gains. The problem, of course, is finding such a security. One approach is to buy whatever strikes your fancy; a more rational approach is to use security analysis to seek out promising investment candidates. Security analysis addresses the question of *what to buy* by determining what a stock *ought to be worth*. Presumably an investor would consider buying a stock only so long as its prevailing market price does not exceed its worth (its computed intrinsic value). Ultimately, intrinsic value will depend on (1) estimates of the stock's future cash flows (the amount of dividends the investor can expect to receive over the holding period, and the estimated price of the stock at time of sale); (2) the discount rate used to translate these future cash flows into a present value; and (3) the amount of risk embedded in achieving the forecasted level of performance. (All these elements of return were introduced and reviewed in Chapter 5.)

Traditional security analysis usually takes a "top-down" approach that begins with economic analysis, then moves to industry analysis, and finally to fundamental analysis. *Economic analysis* is concerned with assessing the general state of the economy and its potential effects on security returns; *industry analysis* deals with the industry within which a particular company operates and the outlook for that industry; *fundamental analysis* looks in depth at the financial condition of a specific company and the underlying behavior of its common stock.

ECONOMIC ANALYSIS

economic analysis
a study of general economic conditions that is used in the valuation of common stock.

Security analysis begins with a study of general economic conditions. It is important that an investor not only have a grasp of the *underlying nature of the economic environment,* but that he or she also be able to assess the *current state* of the economy and formulate expectations about its *future course*. **Economic analysis** may include a detailed examination of each sector of the economy, or it may be done on a very informal basis. Regardless of how it is performed, the purpose is always the same: to establish a sound foundation for the valuation of common stock. Let's briefly examine the economic analysis process to see how it can be carried out by investors.

If we lived in a world where economic activity had absolutely no effect on the stock market or security prices, we could avoid studying the economy altogether. The fact is, of course, that we do not live in such a world; rather, stock prices are heavily influenced by the state of the economy and by economic events that occur over time. As a rule, stock prices tend to move up when the economy is strong, and they retreat when the economy starts to soften. Of course, it's not a perfect relationship, but still, it is a powerful one. Just look what happens to stock prices when the government announces higher-than-expected inflation rates; the same goes for foreign trade figures, unemployment statistics, interest rates, and so forth. The reason the economy is so important to the market is simple: the overall performance of the economy has a significant bearing on the performance and profitability of the companies that issue common stock. As the fortunes of the issuing firms change with economic conditions, so will the prices of their stocks. But not all stocks are affected in the same way and to the same extent. Some sectors of the economy may be only mildly affected, such as defensive industries like food retailing; others, like the cyclical construction and auto industries, are often hard hit when times get rough.

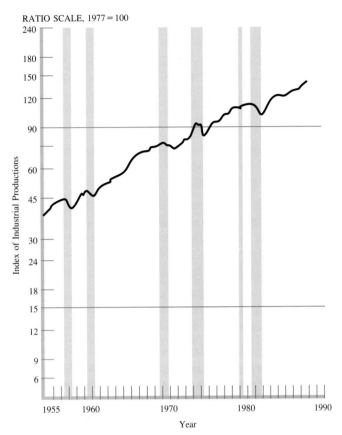

RATIO SCALE, 1977 = 100

FIGURE 7.1 **The Behavior of the Index of Industrial Production over Time.**
The unshaded areas represent periods of prosperity; the shaded areas are recessions. The
index of industrial production is a reflection of the prevailing economic climate. (*Source:*
Federal Reserve Chart Book, 1988.)

Economic Analysis and the Business Cycle

Economic analysis sets the tone for security analysis. If the future looks bleak, then
you can probably expect most stock returns to be equally dismal; if the economy
looks strong, stocks should do well. The behavior of the economy is captured in the
business cycle, which reflects change in total economic activity over time. Two
widely followed measures of the business cycle are gross national product and
industrial production. *Gross national product* (or GNP as it is more commonly
known) represents the market value of all goods and services produced by a country
over the period of a year. *Industrial production,* in contrast, is a measure (actually
it's an index) of the activity/output in the industrial or productive segment of the
economy. Normally, GNP and/or the index of industrial production move up and
down with the business cycle; the nature of this relationship is illustrated in Figure
7.1. Note especially how the index tends to fall off sharply when the economy slips
into a recession (the shaded areas in the graph). One of the major players in this

business cycle

*an indication of the
current state of the
economy, it reflects
change in total eco-
nomic activity over
time.*

INVESTOR INSIGHTS

The Federal Reserve: It Walks Quietly But Carries a Big Economic Stick

When the Federal Reserve raised the discount rate in August [1988], stock prices plunged, interest rates jumped, and the dollar soared in value as foreign investors gobbled up greenbacks. It was a spectacular display of power by a little-understood pillar of government whose influence reaches into our everyday lives. . . .

America's central bank, the Federal Reserve is run by a seven-member board of governors appointed by the President to 14-year terms. One of the governors is designated by the President to serve a four-year term as chairman. Congress could pass legislation requiring the Fed to pursue policies to its liking, but it has never done so.

The discount rate [noted in the opening lines of this article] is the only interest rate controlled directly by the Fed. Each regional Federal Reserve bank stands ready to make temporary loans to any deposit-taking institution that's in a bind and needs the money. The interest charged for such loans is called the *discount rate,* and it can be changed at the Fed's will. A high discount rate tends to discourage borrowing and thus slow the economy down; a low rate tends to encourage borrowing. By boosting this rate . . . the Fed signaled its fear that an overheating economy was threatening to rekindle inflation.

But the Fed's main policy-making body is its Federal Open Market Committee, made up of the seven governors and presidents of five of the 12 regional Federal Reserve banks. Eight times a year it reviews the economy and decides whether to tighten or loosen credit.

Usually the committee relies on subtle and indirect actions. Its favorite tactic is to manipulate the total level of reserves held by banks, s&l's and credit unions. In so doing, the Fed controls the supply of money that financial institutions have for making loans.

A bank with more reserves than it needs can lend some to a bank that's temporarily short of reserves. Borrowing to boost their reserves allows banks to satisfy their customer's cravings for credit; lending out extra reserves lets banks that are flush earn money on their otherwise-idle excess. The interest charged for these overnight loans is called the *federal funds rate.*

economic drama is a small, low-key, but *very powerful* organization known as the Federal Reserve. Even though the Fed, as it's called, is this country's *central bank,* it remains little known and largely misunderstood. The accompanying Investor Insights box sheds some light on this governmental body and briefly explains some of the things it does and why it does them.

Key Economic Factors

Several parts of the economy are especially important because of the impact they normally have on total economic activity. These include:

> *Government fiscal policy*
> > Taxes
> > Government spending

CREATING MONEY

The Fed affects that rate by manipulating the level of reserves via huge purchases or sales of U.S. Treasury securities. The Fed buys from one or more of the 40 banks or brokerage firms that act as primary dealers. It pays by check, and therein lies its power to manipulate the level of reserves available to financial institutions. When the seller's bank presents the check to the Fed for payment, the Fed doesn't fork over any cash; instead, it credits that institution's reserve account at its Federal Reserve bank.

Presto—money has been created. The seller's bank gets additional reserves and increases its lending activity. Thus, with more money available to the economy, the federal funds rate should fall and other short-term interest rates should follow. The reverse occurs if the Fed sells Treasury securities. Reserves at the buyer's bank are marked down to pay for the transaction. The bank makes fewer loans, competition for the available money heats up and short-term rates should rise. . . .

But the impact of the Fed's buying and selling doesn't stop there. In a financial emergency—such as occurred when banks were afraid to lend money to brokerage houses that were squeezed by the stock market's collapse—the Fed can inject almost unlimited amounts of new money into the banking system by buying securities and thus increasing banks' reserves. The mere announcement that it was willing to do so averted a panic last fall.

The Fed has one more weapon in its arsenal. It can raise or lower the amount of cash that deposit-taking institutions must hold in reserve in their vaults or at a regional Fed bank. When the Fed hikes those percentages, financial institutions have less money to lend and interest rates rise. Conversely, when the Fed lowers the reserve requirements, more money is available for loans and rates decline. But altering the *reserve requirement* is administratively awkward and is seldom done.

Source: Manuel Schiffres. "The Federal Reserve Walks Quietly, But it Affects the Economy With a Big Stick," *Changing Times,* October, 1988, p. 16.

> Debt management
> *Monetary policy (actions of the Federal Reserve Board)*
> Money supply
> Interest rates
> *Other factors*
> Inflation
> Consumer spending
> Business investments
> Cost and availability of energy
> Foreign trade and foreign exchange rates

Fiscal policy tends to be *expansive* when it encourages spending—when the government reduces taxes and/or increases the size of the budget; in a similar

fashion, monetary policy is said to be expansive when money is readily available and interest rates are relatively low. An expansive economy also depends on a generous level of spending by consumers and business concerns, as well as an abundant supply of energy that is reasonably priced. These same variables moving in a reverse direction can have a recessionary impact on the economy—for example, when taxes, interest rates, and/or the cost of energy increase, or when spending by consumers and businesses falls off.

The impact of these major forces filters through the system and affects several key dimensions of the economy, the most important of which are industrial production, corporate profits, retail sales, personal income, the unemployment rate, and inflation. For example, a strong economy exists when industrial production, corporate profits, retail sales, and personal income are moving up and unemployment is down. Thus, when conducting economic analysis, an investor will want to keep an eye on fiscal and monetary policies, consumer and business spending, the cost of energy, and foreign trade *for the potential impact they have on the economy*. At the same time, he or she must stay abreast of the level of industrial production, corporate profits, retail sales, personal income, unemployment, and inflation *in order to assess the state of the business cycle*. To help you keep track of the economy, Table 7.1 provides a brief description of some key economic measures. These economic statistics are compiled by government agencies and are widely reported in the financial media (most of the reports are released monthly). By keeping an eye on the behavior of these statistics, you can make your own educated guess as to the current state of the economy and where it's headed.

One final point, as noted in Chapter 6, inflation can have devastating effects on common stocks (and on many other investment vehicles as well). In an inflationary environment, many companies may report higher profits, but the quality of these earnings actually declines as profit margins are "squeezed" and the purchasing power of the dollar deteriorates. Furthermore, the high interest rates that accompany inflation not only contribute to rising costs but also reduce the competitive edge of common stocks. That is, as interest rates rise, the returns to bonds and preferred stock improve and make the investment merits of common stock look less attractive. Because of the serious consequences inflation holds for stock prices, investors should devote special attention to this factor as they analyze the economy and its prospects. By the same token, as we saw in the early to mid-1980s, when inflation slows down, the stock market is often one of the major beneficiaries. Certainly, the bull market that began in 1982 was fueled in large part by a dramatic drop in the rate of inflation, with the economy, corporate profits, and interest rates all benefiting.

Developing an Economic Outlook

Conducting an economic analysis involves studying fiscal and monetary policies, inflationary expectations, consumer and business spending, and the state of the business cycle. Often investors do this on a fairly informal basis; many rely on one or more of the popular published sources (like *The Wall Street Journal, Barron's, Fortune,* and *Business Week*), as well as on periodic reports from major brokerage

TABLE 7.1   Keeping Track of the Economy

To sort out the confusing array of figures that flow almost daily from Washington, and to help you to keep track of what's happening in the economy, here are some of the most important economic measures and reports to watch. . . .

- **Gross national product**—This is the broadest measure of the economy's performance. Issued every three months by the Commerce Department, it is the best estimate of the total dollar value of the nation's output of goods and services. Movements in many areas of the economy are closely related to changes in GNP, making it a good analytic tool. In particular, watch the annual rate of growth or decline in "real" or "constant" dollars. This eliminates the effects of inflation, so that the actual volume of production is measured. Remember, though, that frequent revisions of GNP figures sometimes change the picture of the economy.

- **Industrial production**—Issued monthly by the Federal Reserve Board, this index shows changes in the physical output of America's factories, mines, and electric and gas utilities. The index tends to move in the same direction as the economy, making it a good guide to business conditions between reports on GNP. Detailed breakdowns of the index give a reading on how individual industries are faring.

- **Leading indicators**—This boils down to one number, the movement of a dozen statistics that tend to predict—or "lead"—changes in the GNP. The monthly index, issued by the Commerce Department, includes such things as layoffs of workers, new orders placed by manufacturers, changes in the money supply and the prices of raw materials. If the index moves in the same direction for several months, it's a fair sign that total output will move the same way in the near future.

- **Personal income**—A monthly report from the Commerce Department, this shows the before-tax income received by people in the form of wages and salaries, interest and dividends, rents, and other payments such as Social Security, unemployment, and pensions. As a measure of individuals' spending power, the report helps explain trends in consumer buying habits, a major part of total GNP. When personal income rises, it often means that people will increase their buying. But note a big loophole: Excluded are the billions of dollars that change hands in the so-called underground economy—cash transactions that are never reported to tax or other officials.

- **Retail sales**—The Commerce Department's monthly estimate of total sales at the retail level includes everything from cars to bags of groceries. Based on a sample of retail establishments, the figure gives a rough clue to consumer attitudes. It can also indicate future conditions: A long slowdown in sales can lead to cuts in production.

- **Money supply**—A measure of the amount of money in circulation as reported weekly by the Federal Reserve. Actually, there are *three* measures of the money supply: **M1** (which is basically currency, demand deposits, and NOW accounts), **M2** (the most widely followed measure, it equals M1 plus savings deposits, money market deposit accounts, and money market mutual funds), and **M3** (which is M2 plus large CDs and a few other less significant types of deposits/transactions). It's felt that reasonable growth in the money supply, as measured by M2, is necessary to accommodate an expanding economy. Such growth should have a positive impact on the economy—*unless* the money supply is growing too rapidly.

(Continued)

TABLE 7.1 *(Continued)*

A rapid rate of growth in money is considered to be inflationary; in contrast, a sharp slow-down in the growth rate is viewed as recessionary.

- **Consumer prices**—Issued monthly by the Labor Department, this index shows changes in prices for a fixed market basket of goods and services. The most widely publicized figure is for all urban consumers. A second, used in labor contracts and some government programs, covers urban wage earners and clerical workers. Both are watched as a measure of inflation, but many economists believe that flaws cause them to be wide of the mark.

- **Producer prices**—This is a monthly indicator from the Labor Department showing price changes of goods at various stages of production, from crude materials such as raw cotton, to finished goods like clothing and furniture. An upward surge may mean higher consumer prices later. The index, however, can miss discounts and may exaggerate rising price trends. Watch particularly changes in the prices of finished goods. These do not fluctuate as widely as crude materials and thus are a better measure of inflationary pressures.

- **Employment**—The percentage of the work force that is involuntarily out of work is a broad indicator of economic health. But another monthly figure issued by the Labor Department—the number of payroll jobs—may be better for spotting changes in business. A decreasing number of jobs is a sign that firms are cutting production.

- **Housing starts**—A pickup in the pace of housing starts usually follows an easing of credit conditions—the availability and cost of money—and is an indicator of improvement in economic health. This monthly report from the Commerce Department also includes the number of new building permits issued across the country, an even earlier indicator of the pace of future construction.

houses to form their economic judgments. As Figure 7.2 (on pages 276–277) shows, such sources provide a convenient summary of economic activity and enable investors to develop a general feel for the condition of the economy.

Once a general economic outlook has been developed, the information can be used by the investor in one of two ways. One approach is to construct an economic outlook and then consider where it leads in terms of possible areas for further analysis. For example, suppose that as part of your economic analysis you uncovered information that strongly suggested the outlook for business spending is very positive. Based on such a perspective, you might want to look more closely at capital goods producers, such as machine tool manufacturers, as attractive investment candidates. In a similar fashion, if you uncovered information that suggested that government spending is likely to drop off substantially you might want to avoid the stocks of major defense contractors.

A second way to use information about the economy is to consider specific industries or companies and ask: How will they be affected by expected developments in the economy? Consider, for example, an investor with an interest in ap-

parel stocks. Due to the nature of the business (durable fashion goods), these stocks are susceptible to changing economic conditions. Especially important here is the level of discretionary consumer spending: Normally such spending tends to pick up when the economy is strong and slackens when the economy slows down. In this instance, our imaginary investor would first want to assess the current state of the business cycle and then, using this insight, formulate some expectations about the future.

Let's assume that the economy has just recently entered the recovery stage of the business cycle. Employment is starting to pick up, inflation and interest rates are at "modest" levels, and Congress is putting the finishing touches on a major piece of legislation. More important, because the economy now seems to be in the early stages of a recovery, it should be getting even stronger in the future. The Fed has been cautious about pumping money into the economy, so inflation should not be a problem; and personal income is expected to pick up. This should be good for apparel companies, since a good deal of their sales and an even larger portion of their profits depend on the level of discretionary disposable income. In short, our investor sees an economy that appears to be in good shape and set to become even stronger, the consequences of which are all favorable for apparel stocks. Note that these conclusions were reached by relying on sources no more sophisticated than *Barron's* and *Business Week;* in fact, about the only "special thing" the investor did was to pay careful attention to those economic forces that are important to the apparel industry (like personal income). The economic portion of the analysis, in effect, has set the stage for further evaluation by indicating the type of economic environment to expect in the near future. The next step is to narrow the focus a bit and conduct the industry phase of the analysis.

However, before continuing with our analysis, it is vital to clarify further the relationship between the stock market and the economy. The economic outlook is used to direct investors to developing industry sectors for possible profit, but it is important to note that changes in stock prices normally occur *before* the actual forecasted changes become apparent in the economy. To go a bit further, the current trend of stock prices is frequently used to help *predict* the course of the economy itself. The apparent conflict here can be resolved somewhat by noting that because of this relationship, it is even more important to derive a reliable economic outlook and to be sensitive to underlying economic changes that may mean the current outlook is becoming dated. Investors in the stock market tend to look into the future in order to justify the purchase or sale of stock. If their perception of the future is changing, stock prices will most likely also be changing. Therefore, watching the course of stock prices as well as the course of the general economy can make for more accurate investment forecasting.

INDUSTRY ANALYSIS

An industry is made up of similar firms involved in producing similar goods and services—the oil industry, for example, is made up of firms that produce gasoline and other oil-related products. Companies in an industry may be different in size,

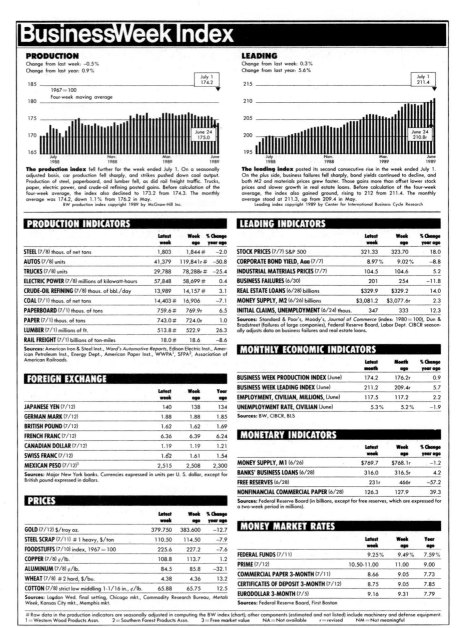

FIGURE 7.2   An Economic Overview.

Reports such as this one and the one on the facing page provide the investor with a convenient overview of the current state of the economy. . .

FORTUNE FORECAST

By Maureen F. Allyn

INFLATION WILL SPEED UP, BUT IT WON'T START RUNNING AWAY

■ Inflation is sneaking back. Given the state of the economy, that is not surprising. More Americans than ever are working, not only in sheer numbers but also as a percent of the adult population—63.6% to be precise. Industrial utilization passed 83% last month, nowhere near a record but a point or two beyond levels where businesses start feeling frisky enough to raise prices.

In the second quarter, inflation rose to 4.7% at an annual rate, up from 3.5% in the first quarter. FORTUNE views this speedup as the beginning of a more inflationary period, though the fourth quarter is likely to show a downward blip. During 1989 we expect inflation will run at a rate of 5.5%. That would be up from 4.4% this year and around 3.5% over the three preceding years. The 5.5% forecast does not assume adoption of a consumption tax in 1989. Were such a tax to take effect during the year, inflation would run even higher for a time. (All these figures refer not to the familiar consumer price index but to the broader fixed-weighted GNP deflator, which tracks prices of an unchanging basket of goods and services.)

Inflation would be moving along faster were it not for several forces restraining it. The Federal Reserve is policing the monetary front. Financial markets are requiring inflation premiums in interest rates. Corporations, whose cost-cutting missions for a while bordered on the kamikaze, are serving as private sector vigilantes. Competitive imports round out the defenses.

Federal Reserve policy is the first thing to look at for clues as to how much inflation will be tolerated. Alan Greenspan's statement that he intended to "err more on the side of restrictiveness" gave a pretty clear signal. Confirming it, the Fed has raised interest rates and slowed money growth.

Investors have provided inflation-fighting help by demanding high real rates on bonds and other interest-bearing securities. For several years earlier in the decade, real rates were higher in the U.S. than in Europe and Japan. That attracted funds to the dollar and pushed it above levels at which U.S. goods were competitive. And that in turn forced American companies to muscle down their costs to protect sales. Even with the dollar's retreat since 1985, the drive to hold down costs goes on.

To judge from past patterns, high interest rates are effective barriers to rapid inflation. Robert Marks of the Siff Oakley & Marks investment counseling firm studied inflation in the U.S. back to 1850 and found no instance in which high real interest rates preceded rapidly accelerating inflation. Inflation liftoffs have followed periods when real rates were very low or negative.

Yet another force restraining inflation is that resolve of business managers to hold down costs. This inevitably includes wages and benefits, which account for two-thirds of aggregate business costs. Until just a year or so ago there was plenty of slack in the labor markets, but that is no longer so and compensation is beginning to reflect this change. Measured by the employment cost index, the best and most comprehensive gauge, compensation has been rising at a rate in excess of 4% this year, after remaining close to 3% since mid-1986. Social Security has been the major culprit, but there has also been some acceleration in wages.

It's not over. As workers realize that they are in short supply, companies will be forced to bid a little higher to fill vacancies. FORTUNE looks for the rate of rise in total compensation to go up more than a percentage point to almost 5.5% by mid-1989 and remain there through the rest of the year. And even at that rate, pay increases will barely keep employees even with inflation.

Aren't employers aware of the squeeze on their staffs? Yes, but employers have been squeezed hard too. Profits have begun to rise again, cash flow margins haven't. Cash flow margins—after-tax profits plus depreciation as a percent of corporate GNP—are crucial not only for pricing but also for evaluation of corporate financial health. So far this year these margins have stayed at 16%. That's the same as in 1987, which had the lowest margins of any year in this recovery.

TRYING to maintain both cash flow margins and competitive position, managers no longer believe they can afford to be responsible for keeping their workers whole against inflation. Recent reports from two leading compensation consultants, the Hay Group and Sibson & Co., show that a rapidly growing percentage of employers are limiting increases in base pay and adopting a variety of nontraditional arrangements that tie part of an employee's compensation to the company's performance. Example: annual bonuses linked to profits.

Small businesses are doing most of the hiring these days and one might expect their wages to reflect the tighter labor markets. Yet they are keeping a firm hold on raises, according to the latest survey by the National Federation of Independent Business. Small companies that expected to give any increases at all were planning on an average of 5.8%, just a smidgen higher than in 1986 and 1987.

Workers seem willing go along with modest increases. Union contracts in the first six months of this heavy bargaining year called for wage raises averaging 2.6% in the first year but just 2.2% a year over the life of the contract. Bonuses, cost-of-living adjustments, and other benefits will boost the rate of increase in total compensation. Even so, it appears that the rise in union pay the rest of this year and next will be moderate. The lack of wage militancy is not confined to union ranks. Non-union compensation has been rising faster, but not by a lot.

Why workers are tamely accepting all this continues to be a bit of a mystery. Regional differences have something to do with it. Most of the manufacturing rebound has taken place in the Midwestern Rust Belt. Even with the resurgence in that region, the unemployment rate in some of the states is still high, and memories of severe joblessness remain frightening.

Baby-boomers, moreover, are not scarce, and that appears to be a major reason for employee docility. People in their 30s and early 40s who have made it into middle management see all too many of their contemporaries vying for the same promotions. The only sound they hear is the talk of continual thinning in middle management. Forget the national employment statistics—for many boomers this is what the Hay Group calls an "era of diminished opportunity." A Hay survey concludes that only 40% of middle managers now feel they have a good chance for advancement, compared with over 70% ten years ago. Thus dispirited, boomers are hardly fired up to stomp into the boss's office and demand a raise.

Younger workers might have a better chance to take advantage of their growing scarcity were it not for the threat of foreign competition. FORTUNE estimates that even aside from oil, imports now account for more than 25% of the goods sold in the U.S. That's a big deterrent to domestic price increases.

The effect of imports in restraining domestic prices may appear to have receded with the big rises in import prices over the past two years. Oil aside, import prices climbed at a rate of nearly 9% a year during that span, more than twice as fast as

OVERVIEW

■ Inflation will rise to 5.5% in 1989, from 4.4% this year.

■ Competition from abroad is serving as a big deterrent to domestic price increases.

■ Employees show remarkable tameness regarding pay.

■ The coming slowdown in growth will be a good thing, helping to restrain inflation.

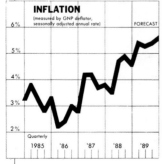

INFLATION
(measured by GNP deflator, seasonally adjusted annual rate)

FORECAST

6% 5% 4% 3% 2%

Quarterly
1985 '86 '87 '88 '89

CHIEF ECONOMIST Todd May Jr.
ASSOCIATE ECONOMIST Vivian Brownstein
STAFF ECONOMIST Maureen F. Allyn
RESEARCH ASSOCIATE Lenore Schiff
FORTUNE's forecast is produced by this magazine's economists using our own economic model.

FIGURE 7.2 Continued

. . . and some observations on where it may be heading. (*Source: Business Week,* July 1989; and *Fortune,* September 26, 1988.

manner of operation, and product lines, but they have similar operating characteristics and are subject to similar socioeconomic forces.

Key Issues

Have you ever thought about buying oil stocks, or autos, or chemicals? How about conglomerates or electric utility stocks? Looking at securities in terms of industry groupings is a popular way of viewing stocks, and is widely used by both individual and professional investors. This is a sensible approach, because stock prices are influenced, at least in part, by industry conditions. The level of demand in an industry and other industry forces set the tone for individual companies; clearly, if the outlook is good for an industry, then the prospects are likely to be strong for the companies that make up that industry.

industry analysis
study of industry groupings, by looking at the competitive position of a particular industry in relation to others and by identifying companies within an industry that hold particular promise.

The first step in **industry analysis** is to establish the competitive position of a particular industry *in relation to others*. For as Figure 7.3 suggests, not all industries perform alike over time. The next step is to identify companies within the industry that hold particular promise. This sets the stage for a more thorough analysis of individual companies and securities. Analyzing an industry means looking at such things as the makeup and basic characteristics of the industry, key economic and operating variables that are important in defining industry performance, and the outlook for the industry. The investor will also want to keep an eye out for specific companies that appear well situated to take advantage of industry conditions.

Normally, an investor can gain valuable insight about an industry by seeking answers to these questions:

1. *What is the nature of the industry?* Is it monopolistic, or are there many competitors; do a few set the trend for the rest?
2. *To what extent is the industry regulated?* Is it regulated (like public utilities) and if so, how "friendly" are the regulatory bodies?
3. *What is the role of "big labor" in the industry?* How important is "big labor"; are there good labor relations within the industry, and when is the next round of contract talks?
4. *How important are technological developments?* Are there any taking place, and what is the likely impact of potential breakthroughs?
5. *Which economic forces are especially important to the industry?* Is demand for the industry's goods and services related to key economic variables, and if so, what is the outlook for those variables? How important is foreign competition to the health of the industry?
6. *What are the important financial and operating considerations?* Is there an adequate supply of labor, material, and capital; and what are the capital spending plans and needs of the industry?

growth cycle
a reflection of the amount of business vitality that occurs within an industry over time.

The above questions can sometimes be answered in terms of an industry's **growth cycle.** The first phase, that of *initial development,* is not one that is usually available to most investors. The industry is new and untried so the risks are very high. The second stage is *rapid expansion,* where product acceptance is spreading

Industry Group	Stock Price Index		Change in Index			1988 EPS	1988 P/E
	12/31/78	12/31/88	10 Year	5 Year	1 Year		
S&P 400 Industrials	$107.12	$321.26	199.9%	83.6%	12.3%	$26.02	12.3
Aerospace	$96.92	$312.90	222.8%	43.2%	21.3%	$36.29	3.1
Airlines	$106.32	$241.36	127.0%	55.6%	33.8%	$34.57	7.0
Automobiles	$76.16	$180.04	136.4%	100.8%	32.9%	$34.68	5.2
Beverages (Alcoholic)	$36.19	$217.14	500.0%	151.9%	2.6%	$18.52	11.7
Beverages	$113.09	$413.25	265.4%	183.8%	19.9%	$27.49	15.0
Broadcast media	$414.17	$3,588.12	766.3%	260.6%	16.6%	$124.17	28.9
Building materials	$56.85	$217.55	282.6%	141.0%	37.8%	$15.00	14.5
Chemicals	$52.84	$145.52	175.4%	108.3%	2.9%	$17.57	8.3
Comm. equip. mfgrs.	$10.19	$30.11	195.4%	−24.2%	−1.3%	$1.70	17.7
Computers/bus. equip.	$110.41	$201.06	82.1%	18.4%	−3.6%	$16.02	12.6
Computer services	$10.16	$64.50	534.8%	110.5%	−13.0%	$3.84	18.5
Conglomerates	$16.74	$50.60	202.2%	76.1%	12.3%	$4.25	11.9
Cosmetics	$65.65	$99.56	51.6%	82.7%	8.3%	$7.12	14.0
Drugs	$160.58	$662.74	312.7%	151.3%	13.1%	$40.19	16.5
Electric utils.	$33.45	$53.87	61.0%	38.5%	8.2%	$5.03	10.7
Electrical equip.	$21.89	$88.18	302.8%	10.5%	−4.7%	$5.32	16.6
Electronics (semicon.)	$19.02	$48.33	154.1%	−0.02%	−17.4%	$3.93	12.3
Entertainment	$146.50	$792.98	441.2%	172.4%	20.6%	$29.57	26.8
Foods	$74.13	$437.38	490.0%	263.3%	33.0%	$26.59	16.4
Homebuilding	$20.35	$43.84	115.4%	−19.6%	18.6%	$3.32	13.2
Hospital management	$10.48	$55.53	429.8%	−18.3%	24.0%	$4.73	11.7
Hospital supplies	$37.05	$112.99	204.9%	49.9%	−7.5%	$8.30	13.6
Hotel-motel	$52.00	$213.13	309.8%	105.5%	17.5%	$14.22	15.0
Household furnish.	$143.49	$423.50	195.1%	39.0%	8.9%	$29.08	14.6
Leisure	$28.84	$196.93	582.8%	102.1%	32.0%	$20.47	9.6
Natural gas	$132.76	$329.97	148.5%	61.4%	4.4%	$18.89	17.5
Oil: domestic	$162.34	$524.22	222.9%	62.2%	12.1%	$40.21	13.0
Oil: international	$75.07	$249.93	232.9%	124.4%	13.4%	$25.10	10.0
Pollution control	$27.80	$212.47	664.2%	218.1%	4.8%	$11.00	19.3
Publishing	$248.78	$1,661.45	567.8%	109.1%	15.8%	$67.84	24.5
Publishing newspapers	$23.10	$102.00	341.5%	64.2%	−5.4%	$7.22	14.1
Retail: dept. stores	$138.25	$737.00	433.0%	119.2%	59.7%	$62.29	11.8
Retail: drug chains	$22.20	$88.26	297.5%	55.6%	−1.5%	$6.42	13.7
Retail: food chains	$55.80	$303.70	444.2%	226.5%	61.1%	$13.36	22.7
Savings and loans	$25.96	$40.84	57.3%	9.8%	1.3%	$4.55	9.0
Telephone	$45.02	$53.32	18.4%	27.0%	20.9%	$8.83	6.0
Textiles apparel mfgrs.	$27.51	$152.93	455.9%	100.2%	10.8%	$12.35	12.4
Textile products	$49.07	$399.64	714.4%	276.4%	82.7%	$27.14	14.7
Tobacco	$73.28	$503.79	587.4%	247.9%	47.4%	$39.15	12.9
Toys	$10.52	$18.81	78.8%	−10.6%	17.7%	−$1.94	—

FIGURE 7.3 A Look at the Stock Performance of Key Industry Groups.
In the search for value in the stock market an early step, even before analyzing one particular industry, is to look at the big picture: *industry group trends*. The data above present a broad overview of 40 key industries from Standard & Poor's list of 87 industry groups; each of these industry groups has its own market index that measures the performance of stocks within that group. As is apparent, some industries have been much better for investors than others. (*Source: 1988 Analyst's Handbook,* Standard & Poor's Corporation.)

and investors can foresee the industry's future more clearly. At this stage, economic variables have little to do with the industry's overall performance, so that investors will be interested in investing almost regardless of the economic climate. This is the phase that is of considerable interest to investors, and a good deal of work is done to find such opportunities. Unfortunately, not all industries experience rapid growth for a very long period of time. Most eventually slip into the category of *mature growth,* which is the third stage and the one most influenced by economic developments. Expansion comes from growth of the economy, a slower source of overall growth than the growth in phase two, which is due to the fact that the product is new and "everybody wants one." In stage three, the long-term nature of the industry becomes apparent. Industries in this category include defensive ones like food and apparel, and cyclical industries like autos and heavy equipment. The last phase is either *stability* or *decline,* in which demand for the industry's products is diminishing, and companies are leaving the industry. In the decline phase, investment opportunities are almost nonexistent, unless the investor is seeking only dividend income. Few companies reach this stage because they try to introduce product changes that will help to continue mature growth. Avoidance of this stage is obviously a major concern to investors.

Developing an Industry Outlook

Industry analysis can be conducted from scratch by investors, or, as is more often the case, with the help of published industry reports such as the popular S&P *Industry Surveys.* These surveys cover all the important economic, market, and financial aspects of an industry, providing commentary as well as vital statistics. Other widely used sources of industry information include brokerage house reports and various writeups in the popular financial media; two popular examples of industry reports are provided in Figure 7.4 (on the facing page and on page 282).

Let's continue the example of the hypothetical investor who is interested in apparel stocks. Recall that his general economic analysis suggested a strong economy for the foreseeable future and one in which the level of personal disposable income would be expanding. Now he is ready to shift his attention to the apparel industry. A logical starting point is to assess the expected industry response to forecasted economic developments. Demand for the product and industry sales would be especially important. The industry is made up of many large and small competitors, and although it is an unregulated industry, it is labor-intensive and big labor is an important force. Thus, our investor may want to look closely at these factors and especially at their potential effect on the industry's cost structure. Also important would be the outlook for imported fashion goods and foreign competition.

Industry analysis provides an understanding of the nature and operating characteristics of an industry, which can then be used to form judgments about the prospects for industry growth. Let's assume that our investor, by using various types of published reports, has examined the key elements of the apparel industry and has concluded that it is indeed well placed to take advantage of the improving economy. Apparel demand should be up, and although profit margins may tighten a bit, the

APPAREL, SHOES AND TEXTILES

5-year average (%)

Return on equity
- 14.0
- 13.9

Sales
- 11.2
- 9.5

Earnings per share
- −2.1
- 3.9

All-industry medians

Fashion and sticker shock. Together they spelled trouble for this volatile industry.

By Gale Eisenstodt

DESPITE THE 10% SALES GROWTH that FORBES shows here, this was a demanding year for apparel manufacturers. In 1988 spending on women's apparel was up only about 4%, after rises of 7% in 1987 and 1986. Who was hurt? For the year, Liz Claiborne's sales grew just 9%, after last year's 30% gain, and earnings per share were off by about 9%. The sluggishness in women's apparel depressed Oxford Industries' bottom line and hurt Leslie Fay through the first half of 1988.

Why the trouble? You can blame any number of economic indicators—consumer debt, recession fears—but fashion and sticker shock were key. Female customers were uncertain about hemlines. The debate between long and short left many confused—and therefore unwilling to buy. High prices compounded the problem, convincing many women that they didn't need that dress after all.

Yardsticks of management performance	% in —segment— sales/profits	Profitability					Growth						Sales
		Return on equity					Sales			Earnings per share			
Company		rank	5-year average	latest 12 months	debt as % of equity	net profit margin	rank	5-year average	latest 12 months	rank	5-year average	latest 12 months	latest 12 mos ($mil)
Apparel													
Liz Claiborne	●/●	1	54.8%	29.8%	3.5%	9.4%	1	46.7%	12.5%	1	51.9%	−5.1%	$1,132
VF	●/●	2	29.4	18.3	30.1	7.1	2	20.8	5.2	5	11.0	8.2	2,531
Russell	●/●	3	17.3	18.0	24.3	10.0	4	11.5	10.0	4	15.9	14.7	512
Kellwood	●/●	4	16.6	19.3	55.0	4.3	11	−1.9	20.2	2	23.3	16.0	712
Oxford Industries	●/●	5	14.3	def	39.0	def	8	3.7	1.9	9	−14.4	P-D	587
Phillips-Van Heusen	●/●	6	14.0	54.8	116.4	4.0	10	1.3	30.2	3	19.0	−12.3	603
Gerber Products	36/18	7	12.5	14.3	41.5	4.7	6	5.2	7.1	8	−13.0	93.4	1,003
Hartmarx	46/80	8	12.5	10.8	40.8	3.3	7	4.3	9.0	7	−1.9	13.1	1,157
Interco	24/7	9	9.3	11.5	24.4	4.9	9	3.5	−1.5	6	4.1	7.5	2,986
Fruit of the Loom	●/●		NA	25.8	395.5	5.0	5	10.2	19.3		NA	107.7	986
Leslie Fay Cos	●/●		NA	21.2	90.3	3.7	3	15.4	10.5		NM	39.3	646
Medians			14.3	18.3	40.8	4.7		5.2	10.0		7.5	13.1	
Shoes													
Reebok International	●/NA	1	200+%[b]	27.7%	1.9%	9.2%	1	254.2%	39.3%	1	200+%	−1.7%	$1,796
NIKE	NA/NA	2	18.6	35.7	7.7	9.3	3	5.4	58.5	2	−8.9	200.0	1,431
US Shoe	34/43	3	12.6	3.1	44.1	0.7	2	11.2	4.6	3	−15.1	−60.4	2,223
Genesco	30/39	4	2.8	12.0	54.1	2.6	4	−8.0	−4.1		NM	−44.0	433
Medians			15.6	19.9	25.9	5.9		8.3	21.9		−12.0	−22.9	
Textiles													
Delta Woodside Inds	●/●	1	200+%[a]	37.8%	34.6%	5.5%	2	35.2%	16.0%		NM	11.3%	$501
Dixie Yarns	●/●	2	15.9	11.1	39.6	3.8	5	14.9	23.0	1	57.8%	−18.7	617
Guilford Mills	●/●	3	15.3	14.3	52.4	4.6	4	16.5	7.2	2	5.1	14.0	585
West Point-Pepperell	44/29	4	10.4	12.3	122.2	4.3	8	9.8	26.3	4	−2.2	29.4	2,151
Springs Industries	42/19	5	8.0	9.0	46.4	2.5	6	14.8	11.5	3	−0.2	−16.8	1,798
DWG	36/36	6	7.1	28.9	362.6	3.3	1	38.5	−1.0		NM	44.6	1,120
Fieldcrest Cannon	NA/NA	7	5.3	def	149.6	def	3	23.1	0.3		NM	P-D	1,355
United Merchants	50/DP	8	def	def	256.4	def	7	10.3	−14.4		NM	D-D	624
Medians			9.2	11.7	87.3	3.5		15.7	9.4		NM	−2.7	
Industry medians			14.0	14.3	44.1	4.3		11.2	10.0		−2.1	8.2	
All-industry medians			13.9	14.1	45.7	4.9		11.2	11.6		−2.1	18.4	

●90% or more. **DD:** Segment deficit, total deficit. **DP:** Segment deficit, total profit. **PD:** Segment profit, total deficit. D-D: Deficit to deficit. D-P: Deficit to profit. P-D: Profit to deficit. def: Deficit. NA: Not available. NE: Negative equity. NM: Not meaningful. a: Three-year average. b: Four-year average. c: Three-year growth. d: Four-year growth. For further explanation, see page 77.

FIGURE 7.4 Two Popular Sources of Industry Information.

Brokerage house reports, like the one shown on the next page, and articles that appear in the popular financial media, like the one above, are just two sources of industry information: they provide easy-to-digest overviews of an industry, its outlook, and vital industry statistics. (*Source: Forbes,* January 9, 1989; and Merrill Lynch Capital Markets, Equity Research Department.)

 **Merrill Lynch**   **Apparel Shares**

July 6, 1989   **Market Performance**

	PRICE 6/30/89	CAL 1989 EPS	P/E E CAL 1989 EPS	E CAL 1990 EPS	P/E E CAL 1990 EPS	PREMIUM/ DISCOUNT vs S&P 400 1989	1990	—% PRICE CHANGE— LATEST QTR	YEAR TO DATE	1 YR TO 12/31/88	BOOK VALUE LATEST QUARTER	PRICE TIMES BOOK	PRICE vs 12 MONTH HIGH	LOW
Bernard Chaus	6 1/4	$0.50	12.5	$0.80	7.8	-2%	-36%	-6%	43%	-5%	$2.59	2.4	-28%	56%
Crystal Brands	31 1/4	$2.80	11.2	$3.30	9.5	-13%	-22%	15%	40%	45%	$24.96	1.3	-7%	44%
Fruit of the Loom	10 3/4	$1.00	10.8	$1.20	9.0	-16%	-26%	21%	69%	28%	$4.27	2.5	-7%	76%
Hartmarx	24 5/8	$1.48	16.6	$2.00	12.3	30%	1%	-11%	2%	3%	$18.71	1.3	-12%	3%
Kellwood Company	30 1/8	$3.05	9.9	$3.40	8.9	-23%	-27%	3%	13%	27%	$16.40	1.8	-9%	14%
Leslie Fay	14 1/2	$1.58	9.2	$1.70	8.5	-28%	-30%	9%	57%	68%	$7.50	1.9	-4%	63%
Liz Claiborne	21 1/4	$1.70	12.5	$2.00	10.6	-2%	-13%	23%	23%	5%	$5.68	3.7	-11%	55%
Oshkosh B'Gosh	32 3/4	$2.10	15.6	$2.40	13.6	22%	11%	31%	47%	-10%	$7.32	4.5	-5%	64%
Oxford	12 1/4	$0.90	13.6	$1.15	10.7	6%	-12%	13%	17%	-5%	$10.74	1.1	-8%	17%
Russ Togs	12 1/2	$0.90	13.9	$1.00	12.5	9%	2%	-6%	-4%	7%	$13.03	1.0	-11%	3%
Russell Corp.	21 5/8	$1.60	13.5	$1.83	11.8	5%	-3%	9%	34%	30%	$8.96	2.4	-7%	38%
Tultex Corp.	9 3/4	$0.75	13.0	$1.03	9.5	2%	-22%	-1%	18%	8%	$4.88	2.0	-11%	26%
V.F. Corp.	31 7/8	$2.80	11.4	$3.05	10.5	-11%	-14%	-4%	11%	17%	$16.29	2.0	-10%	15%
AVE	$259.50	$21.16	12.3	$24.86	10.4	-4%	-14%	7%	24%	14%		2.2	-9%	31%
%CHANGE		41.5%		17.5%										
S&P 500	317.00	$25.54	12.4	$26.93	11.8			8%	14%	12%			-3%	23%
%CHANGE		7.5%		5.4%										
S&P 400	362.60	$28.41	12.8	$29.69	12.2			7%	13%	12%			-3%	23%
%CHANGE		9.2%		4.5%										

Adjusted for stock splits
Fruit of the Loom: From IPO price $9 on 3/3/87.

MARKET PERFORMANCE:

After turning in an exceptionally strong relative performance in the March quarter, our thirteen company Apparel Sample rose 7% in the June quarter, just in line with the S&P 400 index. Year to date, the Group is now up 24% vs 13% for the broader average. Only one issue in our Apparel Sample declined during the first six months and that was Russ Togs, off a modest 4%. Five of the thirteen issues, however, declined in the June quarter led by Hartmarx which was off 11% reflecting sharply lower second quarter earnings due to higher interest costs and weak sales in its retail operations. Consumer resistance to sharply higher prices adversely affected menswear sales. Liz Claiborne registered its entire 23% advance in the June quarter after the market adjusted to the announced retirements of Liz Claiborne and her husband Arthur Ortenberg and started responding to the strong consumer acceptance of the company's lines.

At mid-year, our Apparel Sample sold at an average multiple of 12.3 times estimated 1989 earnings, a modest 4% discount to the S&P 400. We are projecting that profits for our sample will be up by more than 40% this year. If two companies which lost money last year but are expected to make money this year are excluded from the group the increase would be a still healthy 22%. Based on estimated 1990 earnings the Group PE is currently 10.4 times, which represents a more normal 14% discount to the S&P 400.

Merrill Lynch Capital Markets   Brenda J. Gall
Global Securities Research & Economics Group   First Vice President
Fundamental Equity Research Department   212 449-1915

FIGURE 7.4 Continued

level of profits should move up smartly, providing a healthy growth outlook. Several companies within this industry stand out, but one looks particularly attractive: MarCor Industries, a moderately sized but rapidly growing producer of medium- to high-priced apparel for men and women. Everything about the economy and the industry looks favorable, so our hypothetical investor has decided to study MarCor more closely.

FUNDAMENTAL ANALYSIS

fundamental analysis
the in-depth study of the financial condition and operating results of a firm.

Fundamental analysis is the study of the financial affairs of a business, which enables investors to better understand the nature and operating characteristics of the companies that issue common stocks. In this part of the chapter, we will deal with several aspects of fundamental analysis: We will examine the general concept of fundamental analysis, introduce and discuss the several types of financial statements that provide the raw material for this phase of the analytical process, describe the types and explain the rationale for some of the key financial ratios widely used in fundamental analysis, and conclude with a look at the interpretation of financial ratios.

The Concept

Fundamental analysis rests on the belief that *the value of a stock is influenced by the performance of the company that issued the stock.* If a company's prospects look strong, we would expect the market price of its stock to reflect that and be bid up. However, the value of a security depends not only on the return it promises, but also on the amount of its risk exposure. Fundamental analysis captures these dimensions and conveniently incorporates them into the valuation process.

Fundamental analysis begins with an historical analysis of the financial strength of a firm. Using the insights obtained, along with economic and industry figures, an investor can then formulate expectations about the future growth and profitability of a company. In the historical phase of the analysis (which is of primary interest to us at present), the investor would study the financial statements of the firm in order to learn the strengths and weaknesses of the company, identify any underlying trends and developments, evaluate operating efficiency, and gain a general understanding of the nature and operating characteristics of the firm. The following points are of particular interest:

1. The competitive position of the company
2. Its composition and trend in sales
3. Profit margins and company earnings
4. The composition and liquidity of corporate resources (the company's asset mix)
5. The company's capital structure (its financing mix)

The historical phase of fundamental analysis is, in many respects, the most demanding and the most time-consuming. Most investors have neither the time nor the inclination to conduct such an extensive study and, thus, rely on published reports for the needed background material. Investors have many sources to choose from, including the reports and recommendations of major brokerage houses, the

popular financial media, and/or various financial subscription services. These are all valuable sources of information, and the paragraphs that follow are not intended to replace them. Yet, to be an intelligent investor, it is important to understand fully the content and implications of such financial reports, and in the final analysis, to be able to use the information to develop one's own judgments about the company and its stock.

Financial Statements

Financial statements are a vital part of fundamental analysis, since they enable investors to develop an opinion about the operating results and financial condition of a firm. A complete set of financial statements consists of four parts: (1) a balance sheet, (2) an income statement, (3) a statement of cash flows, and (4) a statement of changes in stockholders' equity. The first two statements are essential to carrying out fundamental analysis (in particular, to compute many of the financial ratios), and the third statement—the cash flow report—is of critical importance because it's used to assess the cash/liquidity position of the firm. Company statements are prepared on a quarterly basis (these are *abbreviated* statements compiled for each three-month period of operation) and again at the end of each calendar year or *fiscal year* (a 12-month period the company has defined as its operating year, which may or may not end on December 31). Annual financial statements must be fully verified by independent certified public accountants (CPAs), filed with the U.S. Securities and Exchange Commission, and distributed on a timely basis to all stockholders in the form of annual reports. By themselves, corporate financial statements are a most important source of information to the investor; when used with financial ratios and in fundamental analysis, they become even more powerful. We will now examine each of the four major accounting statements.

The Balance Sheet

balance sheet
a financial summary of a firm's assets, liabilities, and shareholder's equity at a single point in time.

The **balance sheet** is a statement of the company's assets, liabilities, and shareholders' equity. The *assets* represent the resources of the company (the things that belong to the firm), the *liabilities* are its debts, and *equity* is the amount of stockholders' capital in the firm. A balance sheet may be thought of as a summary of the firm's assets balanced against its debt and ownership positions *at a single point in time* (on the last day of the calendar or fiscal year, or at the end of the quarter). In order to balance, the total assets must equal the total amount of liabilities and equity. A typical balance sheet is illustrated in Table 7.2. It shows the comparative 1988–1989 figures for our hypothetical apparel firm, MarCor Industries (note that its fiscal year ends on November 30).

Assets.   The company's assets are listed in the top half of the balance sheet and are broken into two parts: current and long-term assets. *Current assets* consist of cash and other items that will be converted into cash (or in the case of "prepaid expenses," consumed) in one year or less. The four most common current assets are cash and short-term investments, accounts receivable, inventory, and prepaid expenses. The cash account is self-explanatory; accounts receivable represent the

TABLE 7.2 A Corporate Balance Sheet, MarCor Industries ($ in Thousands, Fiscal Year Ending November 30)

	1989	1988	
Current assets	$ 7,846	$ 14,459	Cash and short-term investments
	105,400	102,889	Accounts receivable
	164,356	159,238	Inventories
	1,778	2,111	Prepaid expenses
	$279,380	$278,697	Total current assets
Long-term assets	$ 1,366	$ 1,317	Land
	13,873	13,889	Buildings
	75,717	73,199	Furniture, fixtures, and equipment
	49,412	50,209	Leasehold improvements
	$140,368	$138,614	Gross long-term assets
	(85,203)	(80,865)	Accumulated depreciation
	$ 55,165	$ 57,749	Net long-term assets
	$ 4,075	$ 4,108	Other assets
Total assets	$338,620	$340,554	
Current liabilities	$ 2,000	$ 11,500	Notes payable
	4,831	1,090	Current maturities
	68,849	69,696	Accounts payable and accrued expenses
	3,806	3,119	Taxes on earnings
	5,460	4,550	Other accrued taxes
	$84,946	$89,955	Total current liabilities
Long-term debt	$53,723	$61,807	Long-term debt, less current maturities
Stockholders' equity	$ 21,787	$ 21,777	Common shares, $2.50 par value
	20,068	20,028	Capital surplus
	158,096	146,987	Retained earnings
	$199,951	$188,792	Stockholders' equity
Total liabilities and stockholders' equity	$338,620	$340,554	

amount due the company from customers who purchased goods on credit; inventories are the raw materials used in the production process, work-in-process, and the finished goods ready for shipment to customers; and prepaid expenses represent payments made in advance for such services as utilities and insurance. These assets are the firm's *working capital* and provide the funds for day-to-day operations. Other than the cash account, such assets represent allocations of corporate funds to the resource in question; for example, MarCor had invested more than $105 million in accounts receivable as of November 30, 1989.

The long-term assets of MarCor are represented mostly by land and facilities,

which is typical of most companies. These assets have extended lives (more than one year) and are resources not intended for sale, but for use over and over again in the manufacture, display, warehousing, and transportation of the company's product. The most common long-term assets are land, buildings, plant and equipment, office furnishings, and lease-hold improvements (capital improvements made on property leased by the company). The net amount of long-term assets shown on the balance sheet changes each year because depreciation is charged against these assets. (*Depreciation* is an accounting entry used to systematically account for the wear and tear of an asset, and to cost out a capital asset over time.) The ''accumulated depreciation'' entry reflects the total of past depreciation charged against property still on the books; it is strictly an accounting entry and does *not* represent cash.

Liabilities. The firm's financial structure appears in the lower half of Table 7.2, where the liabilities and stockholders' position are listed. This portion of the balance sheet is divided into three parts: (1) current liabilities, (2) long-term debt, and (3) equity. *Current liabilities* are the debts owed to lenders (notes payable and current maturities), suppliers (trade and accounts payable), employees (accrued expenses), and the government (accrued taxes). Like their counterparts on the asset side of the balance sheet, they are due and payable within a period of one year or less. The current liabilities listed for MarCor Industries are typical of those found on most corporate balance sheets. *Long-term debts* have maturities that extend beyond one year. Note that only the principal amount of current and long-term debt is recorded on the balance sheet; the interest portion appears only on the income statement, as an expense. Long-term liabilities are normally broken into the term portion of the debt and that portion due in one year or less, which is known as *current maturities*. Current maturities are like the next 12 monthly payments on a four-year installment loan. The amount due in the next year would be listed as current maturities, whereas the amount due in years 2 through 4 would be listed as long-term debt.

Equity. In addition to the money the company owes, another type of claim against assets is that of the firm's owners (its stockholders). This is represented by the equity (or net worth) accounts on the balance sheet and is a *residual* position; that is, the claims of all short- and long-term lenders take precedence over those of the owners. The major components of stockholders' equity are the common stock account, capital surplus, and retained earnings. The first two represent paid-in capital and are equal to the proceeds realized by the company from the sale of its stock to the investing public. (The common stock account equals the par or stated value of the stock times the number of shares issued, and capital surplus equals the excess of the net proceeds from the sale of the stock above the stock's par value). Retained earnings, in contrast, are an accumulation of prior earnings that have been retained in the company; they are the earnings left after dividends have been paid. Retained earnings are used to pay off debt, acquire facilities, and invest in receivables, inventories, and the like. They do *not* represent cash or a pool of untapped financ-

TABLE 7.3 A Corporate Income Statement, MarCor Industries ($ in Thousands, Fiscal Year Ended November 30)

1989	1988	
$606,610	$567,986	Net sales
6,792	6,220	Other income
1,504	895	Interest income
$614,906	$575,101	Total revenues
$377,322	$354,424	Cost of goods sold
205,864	194,419	Selling, administrative, and other operating expenses
5,765	5,523	Interest expense
$588,951	$554,366	Total costs and expenses
$ 25,955	$ 20,735	Earnings before taxes
$ 7,950	$ 5,230	Taxes on earnings
$ 18,005	$ 15,505	Net earnings (Net profit after taxes)
$ 2.09	$ 1.80	Earnings per share
8,601	8,601	Number of common shares outstanding (in thousands)

ing, but instead are resources that have been previously allocated to various areas of the firm.

The Income Statement

income statement
a financial summary of the operating results of a firm covering a specified period of time, usually one year.

The **income statement** provides a financial summary of the operating results of the firm. Unlike the balance sheet, the income statement covers activities that have occurred over the course of time, or for a given operating period. Typically, this period extends no longer than a fiscal or calendar year; Table 7.3 shows MarCor Industries' income statements for 1988 and 1989. Note that these annual statements cover operations for a 12-month (fiscal) period ending on November 30, which corresponds to the date of the balance sheet. The income statement indicates how successful the firm has been in using the assets listed on the balance sheet; that is, the amount of success management has in operating the firm is reflected in the profit or loss the company generates during the year.

The income statement is simply a summary of the amount of revenues (sales and income) generated over the period, the cost and expenses incurred over the same period, and the company's profits (which, of course, are obtained by subtracting all costs and expenses, including taxes, from revenues). Note in Table 7.3 that there are four basic types of expenses: *cost of goods sold,* which is often the largest cost item and represents labor, material, and factory overhead expenses: *selling, administrative, and other operating expenses,* representing salaries, advertising and promotion costs, travel and entertainment, office expenses, utilities and insurance, and other costs of operating the firm; *interest expense,* which reflects the cost of borrowing; and *taxes on earnings,* which is the share of profits that goes to various levels of

TABLE 7.4   A Statement of Cash Flows, MarCor Industries ($ in Thousands, Fiscal Year Ended November 30)

1989	1988	
		Cash from Operations
$18,005	$15,505	Net earnings
8,792	8,202	Depreciation and amortization
560	54	Other non-cash charges
(7,296)	(21,696)	Increase in current assets
(1,268)	3,041	Increase (Decrease) in current liabilities
$18,793	$ 5,106	Net cash flow from operations
		Cash from Investment Activities
($ 6,685)	($ 4,686)	Acquisitions of property, plant, and equipment—net
($ 6,685)	($ 4,686)	Net cash flow from investing
		Cash from Financing Activities
—	$ 7,950	Proceeds from long-term borrowing
($11,825)	(1,240)	Reduction in long-term debt, including current maturities and early retirements
(6,896)	(6,220)	Payment of dividends to common stock
($18,721)	$ 490	Net cash flow from financing
($ 6,613)	$ 910	**Net Increase (Decrease) in Cash**
$14,459	$13,549	Cash & short-term investments at beginning of period
$ 7,846	$14,459	Cash & short-term investments at end of period

government. The net earnings of the firm are the "bottom line" of the income statement. If not used to pay common and/or preferred dividends, they go to retained earnings, where they are used to finance growth or repay debt.

Other Statements

statement of cash flows

a financial summary of a firm's cash flow and other events that caused changes in the company's cash position.

Other statements are also made available to investors. One is the **statement of cash flows,** which provides a summary of the firm's cash flow and other events that caused changes in the cash position. A relatively new report, first required in 1988, it is also one of the most useful, as it shows how the company is doing in generating cash. The fact is, a company's reported earnings may have little resemblance to the firm's cash flow. For whereas profits are simply the difference between revenues and the accounting costs that have been charged against them, *cash flow is the amount of money a company takes in as a result of doing business.*

Table 7.4 presents the 1988–1989 statement of cash flows for MarCor Industries. Notice that this report brings together items from *both* the balance sheet and income statement to show how the company obtained its cash and how it used this valuable

liquid resource. The statement is broken into three parts, the most important of which is the first one, labeled "Cash from Operations." It's important because it captures the *net cash flow from operations;* this is what is generally meant by the term *cash flow,* since it represents the amount of cash generated by the company and which was available for investment and financing activities. In the case of MarCor, its 1989 cash flow from operations was nearly $19 million—way up from the year before. However, because the company spent more on its investments and financing activities than it took in, its actual cash position declined by over $6.6 million (note near the bottom of the statement that the company had a net decrease in cash of some $6,613,000). Ideally, you'd like to see a high (and preferably increasing) cash flow, since that would mean the company has plenty of money to pay dividends, service debt, and finance growth. In addition, you'd like to see the firm's cash position increase over time because of the positive impact that has on the company's liquidity and its ability to meet operating needs in a prompt and timely fashion.

statement of changes in stockholders' equity
a financial summary of the amount of profits reinvested in the business, the amount of dividends paid out to investors, and other changes in a firm's equity position.

The fourth and final financial report is the **statement of changes in stockholders' equity,** which recaps the amount of profits reinvested in the business, the amount of dividends paid out to investors, and other changes in the firm's equity position. The company's balance sheet and its income statement are linked in a number of ways, one of which is the tie between net profits and retained earnings. A statement of changes in stockholders' equity shows this relationship and records how profits, dividends, and other transactions affected the stockholders' position. Table 7.5 depicts the 1988–1989 statement for MarCor Industries. Corresponding to the operating periods covered in the other financial statements, it shows how and why retained earnings changed, and what accounted for other changes in this important source of financing.

Key Financial Ratios

To see what accounting statements have to say about the financial condition and operating results of the firm, it's often necessary to turn to *financial ratios.* Such ratios are useful because they provide a different perspective of the financial affairs of the firm—particularly with regard to the balance sheet and income statement— and as such, expand the information content of the company's financial statements. Ratios lie at the very heart of company analysis; indeed, fundamental analysis as a system of information would be incomplete without this key ingredient. **Ratio analysis** is the study of the relationships among and between various financial statement accounts. Each measure relates one item on the balance sheet (or income statement) with another; or as is more often the case, a balance sheet account is related to an operating (or income statement) element. In this way, attention is centered not on the absolute size of the financial statement accounts, but more importantly, on the liquidity, activity, and profitability of the resources, financial structure, and operating results of the firm.

ratio analysis
the study of the relationships among and between various financial statement accounts.

The most significant contribution of financial ratios is that they enable an investor to assess the firm's past and present financial condition and operating results. Ratio mechanics are actually quite simple: Selected information is obtained from annual financial statements and used to compute a set of ratios, that are then com-

TABLE 7.5   A Statement of Changes in Stockholders' Equity, MarCor Industries ($ in Thousands, Fiscal Year Ended November 30)

1989	1988	
$188,792	$179,047	Stockholders' equity—beginning of the fiscal year
$ 18,005	$ 15,505	Plus: Net earnings for the year
(6,896)	(6,220)	Less: Dividends paid to common stock
$ 11,109	$ 9,285	Additions to retained earnings
10	300	Plus: Proceeds from stock issued
40	160	Plus: Excess above par value realized from sale of stock
$199,951	$188,792	Stockholders' equity—end of the year

pared to historical and/or industry standards to evaluate the financial condition and operating results of the company. When historical standards are used, the company's ratios are compared and studied from one year to the next; industry standards, in contrast, involve a comparison of a particular company's ratios to the average performance of other companies in the same line of business.

Financial ratios can be divided into five groups: (1) liquidity; (2) activity; (3) leverage; (4) profitability; and (5) common stock, or market measures. Using the 1989 figures from the MarCor financial statements (Tables 7.2 and 7.3), we will now identify and briefly discuss some of the more widely used measures in each of these five categories.

Measures of Liquidity

liquidity measures *financial ratios concerned with the firm's ability to meet its day-to-day operating expenses and satisfy its short-term obligations as they come due.*

Liquidity is concerned with the firm's ability to meet its day-to-day operating expenses and satisfy its short-term obligations as they come due. Of major concern is whether or not a company has adequate cash and other liquid assets on hand to service its debt and operating needs in a prompt and timely fashion. A general overview of a company's liquidity position can often be obtained with two simple measures: current ratio and net working capital.

Current Ratio. The *current ratio* is one of the most commonly cited of all financial ratios; it is computed as follows:

$$\text{current ratio} = \frac{\text{current assets}}{\text{current liabilities}}$$

In 1989, MarCor Industries had a current ratio of

$$\text{current ratio for MarCor} = \frac{\$279,380}{\$84,946} = 3.29$$

This figure indicates that MarCor had $3.29 in short-term resources to service every dollar of current debt; by most standards, such a current ratio would be considered generous.

Net Working Capital. Though technically not a ratio in the formal sense of the word, net working capital is nonetheless often viewed as such. Actually, *net working capital* is an *absolute* measure of liquidity that indicates the dollar amount of equity in the working capital position of the firm. It is the difference between current assets and current liabilities, and for 1989, the net working capital figure for MarCor Industries equaled:

$$\text{net working capital} = \text{current assets} - \text{current liabilities}$$
$$\text{for MarCor} = \$279{,}380 - \$84{,}946 = \underline{\$194{,}434}$$

A net working capital figure that approaches the $200 million mark is substantial indeed and suggests that the liquidity position of this firm is good—so long as it is not made up of slow-moving and obsolete inventories and/or past due accounts receivable.

Activity Ratios

activity ratios
financial ratios that
are used to measure
how well a firm is
managing its assets.

Measuring general liquidity is only the beginning of the analysis, for we must also assess the composition and underlying liquidity of key current assets, and evaluate how effectively the company is managing its assets. **Activity ratios** compare company sales to various asset categories to measure how well the company is utilizing its assets. Three of the most widely used activity ratios deal with accounts receivable, inventory, and total assets.

Accounts Receivable Turnover. A glance at most financial statements will reveal that the asset side of the balance sheet is dominated by just a few accounts that make up 80 to 90 percent, or even more, of total resources. Certainly, this is the case with MarCor where, as can be seen in Table 7.2, three entries (accounts receivable, inventory, and net long-term assets) accounted for about 95 percent of total assets in 1989. Most firms invest a significant amount of capital in accounts receivable, and for this reason they are viewed as a crucial corporate resource. *Accounts receivable turnover* is a measure of how these resources are being managed and is computed as follows:

$$\text{accounts receivable turnover} = \frac{\text{annual sales}}{\text{accounts receivable}}$$
$$\text{for MarCor} = \frac{\$606{,}610}{\$105{,}400} = \underline{\underline{5.76}}$$

In essence, this turnover figure is an indication of the kind of return the company is getting from its investment in accounts receivable. Other things being equal, the higher the turnover figure, the more favorable it is. Observe that in 1989, MarCor turned its receivables over about 5.8 times; put another way, each dollar invested in receivables supported $5.76 in sales.

Inventory Turnover. Another important corporate resource, and one that requires a considerable amount of management attention, is inventory. Control of inventory

is important to the well-being of a company and is commonly assessed with the *inventory turnover* measure:

$$\text{inventory turnover} = \frac{\text{annual sales}}{\text{inventory}}$$

$$\text{for MarCor} = \frac{\$606,610}{\$164,356} = \underline{\underline{3.69}}$$

Again, the more mileage (sales) the company can get out of its inventory, the better the return on this vital resource. A figure of 3.69 for MarCor reveals its goods were bought and sold out of inventory about 3.7 times a year. Generally, the higher the turnover figure, the less time an item spends in inventory and thus, the better the return the company is able to earn from funds tied up in inventory.

Total Asset Turnover. *Total asset turnover* indicates how efficiently assets are being used to support sales. It is calculated as follows:

$$\text{total asset turnover} = \frac{\text{annual sales}}{\text{total assets}}$$

$$\text{for MarCor} = \frac{\$606,610}{\$338,620} = \underline{\underline{1.79}}$$

Like receivables and inventory, a high (or increasing) total asset turnover figure is viewed as positive because it has a beneficial effect on profitability and return on investment. The principle at work here is much like the return to an individual investor: Earning $100 from a $1,000 investment is far more desirable than earning the same $100 from a $2,000 investment. A high total asset turnover figure suggests that corporate resources are being managed efficiently and that the firm is able to realize a high level of sales (and ultimately, profits) from its asset investments.

 ## *Leverage Measures*

Leverage deals with different types of financing and indicates the amount of debt being used to support the resources and operations of the company. The amount of indebtedness within the financial structure and the ability of the firm to service its debt are major concerns in leverage analysis. There are two widely used leverage ratios: The first, the debt-equity ratio, measures the *amount of debt* being used by the company; the second, times interest earned, assesses how well the company can *service its debt.*

leverage measures *financial ratios that measure the amount of debt being used to support operations, and the ability of the firm to service its debt.*

Debt-Equity Ratio. A measure of leverage, or the relative amount of funds provided by lenders and owners, the *debt-equity ratio* is computed as follows:

$$\text{debt-equity ratio} = \frac{\text{long-term debt}}{\text{stockholders' equity}}$$

$$\text{for MarCor} = \frac{\$53,723}{\$199,951} = \underline{\underline{.27}}$$

Since highly leveraged firms (those using large amounts of debt) run an increased risk of defaulting on their loans, this ratio is particularly helpful in assessing a stock's risk exposure. The 1989 debt-equity ratio for MarCor is *low* (27 percent) and discloses that most of the company's capital comes from its owners; stated another way, this figure means there was only 27 cents of debt in the capital structure for every dollar of equity.

Times Interest Earned. *Times interest earned* is a so-called coverage ratio and measures the ability of the firm to meet its fixed interest payments. It is calculated as follows:

$$\text{times interest earned} = \frac{\text{earnings before interest and taxes}}{\text{interest expense}}$$

$$\text{for MarCor} = \frac{\$25,955 + \$5,765}{\$5,765} = \underline{\underline{5.50}}$$

The ability of the company to meet its interest payments (which, with bonds, are fixed contractual obligations) in a timely and orderly fashion is also an important consideration in evaluating risk exposure. In the case of MarCor Industries, there is about $5.50 available to cover every dollar of interest expense, which is pretty good (as a rule, a coverage ratio of 6 to 7 times earnings is considered strong). On the downside, there's usually little concern until the measure drops to something less than two or three times earnings.

Measures of Profitability

Profitability is a relative measure of success. Each of the various profitability measures relates the returns (profits) of a company to its sales, assets, or equity. There are four widely used profitability measures: operating ratio, net profit margin, return on assets, and return on equity.

profitability measures
financial ratios that measure the returns of a company by relating relative success of a firm through comparison of profits to sales, assets, or equity.

Operating Ratio. The major components of a company's cost structure are captured in its *operating ratio,* a measure that relates total operating expenses to sales:

$$\text{operating ratio} = \frac{\text{cost of goods sold + selling, admin., and other operating expenses}}{\text{annual sales}}$$

$$\text{for MarCor} = \frac{\$377,322 + \$205,864}{\$606,610} = \underline{\underline{96.2\%}}$$

Note that the operating ratio ignores interest, taxes, and other "nonoperating" income and expenses, and deals only with internally generated operating costs incurred in the normal course of business. In essence, this ratio indicates the relative amount of operating expenses used to generate the current level of sales; it provides a measure of the firm's operating efficiency. For MarCor Industries, operating expenses absorbed about 96 percent of sales. Obviously, other things being equal, we'd like to see a low or declining operating ratio, which means higher profit margins and higher earnings.

Net Profit Margin. This is the "bottom line" of operations; *net profit margin* indicates the rate of profit from sales and other revenues. The net profit margin is computed as follows:

$$\text{net profit margin} = \frac{\text{net profit after taxes}}{\text{total revenues}}$$

$$\text{for MarCor} = \frac{\$18,005}{\$614,906} = \underline{\underline{2.9\%}}$$

The net profit margin looks at profits as a percentage of sales, and because it moves with costs, also reveals the type of control management has over the cost structure of the firm. Note that MarCor had a net profit margin of 2.9 percent in 1989—that is, the company's return on sales was roughly 3 cents on the dollar. Although this is a bit below average for American corporations in general, a net profit margin of nearly 3 percent is good (i.e., *above* average) for a fashion apparel firm.

Return on Assets. As a profitability measure, *return on assets* looks at the amount of resources needed to support operations. Return on assets (ROA) reveals management's effectiveness in generating profits from the assets it has available, and is perhaps the single most important measure of return. It is computed as follows:

$$\text{ROA} = \frac{\text{net profit after taxes}}{\text{total assets}}$$

$$\text{for MarCor} = \frac{\$18,005}{\$338,620} = \underline{\underline{5.3\%}}$$

Because both return on sales (net profit margin) and asset productivity (total asset turnover) are embedded in ROA, it provides a clear picture of a company's managerial effectiveness, and the overall profitability of its resource allocation and investment decisions. In the case of MarCor Industries, the company earned 5.3 percent on its asset investments in 1989. As a rule, the higher the ROA, the more profitable the company's going to be.

Return on Equity. A measure of the overall profitability of the firm, *return on equity (ROE)* captures, in a single ratio, the amount of success the firm is having in managing its assets, operations, and capital structure. ROE is closely followed by seasoned investors because of its direct link to the profits, growth, and dividends of the company. Return on equity—or return on investment (ROI), as it's sometimes called—measures the return to the firm's stockholders by relating profits to shareholder equity:

$$\text{return on equity (ROE)} = \frac{\text{net profit after taxes}}{\text{stockholders' equity}}$$

$$\text{for MarCor} = \frac{\$18,005}{\$199,951} = \underline{\underline{9.0\%}}$$

Essentially, ROE is an extension of ROA, as it introduces the company's financing

decisions into the assessment of profitability; that is, it denotes the extent to which leverage can increase return to stockholders. ROE shows the annual payoff to investors, which in the case of MarCor amounts to about 9 cents for every dollar of equity. Generally speaking, look for a high or increasing ROE; in contrast, watch out for a falling ROE, as that could spell trouble later on.

Common Stock Ratios

There are a number of common stock, or so-called market, ratios that convert key bits of information about the company to a per share basis and are used to assess the performance of a company for stock valuation purposes. These ratios tell the investor exactly what portion of total profits, dividends, and equity is allocated to each share of stock. Popular common stock ratios include earnings per share, price/earnings ratio, price-to-sales ratio, dividends per share, dividend yield, payout ratio, and book value per share. We have already examined two of these measures in Chapter 6 (earnings per share and dividend yield); let's look now at the other five.

Price/Earnings Ratio. This measure is an extension of the earnings per share ratio and is used to determine how the market is pricing the company's common stock. The *price/earnings (P/E) ratio* relates the company's earnings per share (EPS) to the market price of its stock:

$$P/E = \frac{\text{market price of common stock}}{\text{EPS}}$$

To compute the P/E ratio, it is necessary first to calculate the stock's EPS; using the *earnings-per-share* equation from the previous chapter, we see that EPS for MarCor Industries in 1989 was

$$EPS = \frac{\text{net profit after taxes} - \text{preferred dividends}}{\text{number of common shares outstanding}}$$

$$\text{for MarCor} = \frac{\$18,005 - \$0}{8,601} = \underline{\$2.09}$$

In this case, the company's profits of $18 million translated into earnings of $2.09 for *each share* of outstanding common stock. Given this EPS figure and the stock's current market price (assume it is currently trading at 31½), we can now determine the P/E ratio for MarCor Industries:

$$P/E = \frac{\$31.50}{\$2.09} = \underline{15.1}$$

In effect, the stock is currently selling at a multiple of about 15 times its 1989 earnings. Price/earnings multiples are widely quoted in the financial press and are an essential part of many stock valuation models.

Price-to-Sales Ratio. Very simply, the *price-to-sales ratio (PSR)* relates sales per share to the market price of the company's stock. This measure has been attracting a

good deal of attention since the early 1980s, as it's been found to do a fairly good job of identifying *overpriced* stocks—or stocks that should be *avoided*. As explained more fully in the accompanying Investor Insights box, the basic principle behind this ratio is that the *lower* the PSR, the *less* likely it is that the stock will be overpriced. PSR is computed as follows:

$$PSR = \frac{\text{market price of common stock}}{\text{annual sales per share}}$$

To find the annual sales (or revenues) per share, just divide the company's annual sales by the number of common shares outstanding; that is:

$$\text{annual sales/shares} = \frac{\text{annual sales}}{\begin{array}{c}\text{number of common} \\ \text{shares outstanding}\end{array}}$$

$$\text{for MarCor} = \frac{\$606,610}{8,601} = \underline{\underline{\$70.53}}$$

Thus, for each share of its common stock, the company is generating $70.53 in sales. We can use this figure, along with the latest market price of the stock, to calculate the price-to-sales ratio as follows:

$$PSR = \frac{\$31.50}{\$70.53} = \underline{\underline{0.45}}$$

At the current market price of $31.50, MarCor's stock is selling at a multiple of less than half its 1989 sales per share. Under most circumstances, this would be viewed as a fairly low price/sales ratio and as such, may be a stock with a lot more play left in it.

Dividends per Share.   The principle here is the same as for EPS: to translate total common stock dividends paid by the company into a per share figure. (Note: If not on the income statement, the amount of dividends paid to common stock can be found on the statement of cash flows—Table 7.4.) *Dividends per share* is measured as follows:

$$\text{dividends per share} = \frac{\text{annual dividends paid to common stock}}{\text{number of common shares outstanding}}$$

$$\text{for MarCor} = \frac{\$6,896}{8,601} = \underline{\underline{\$.80}}$$

For fiscal 1989, MarCor Industries paid out dividends of 80 cents per share—or at a quarterly rate of 20 cents per share. As we saw in the preceding chapter, we can relate dividends per share to the market price of the stock to determine its present *dividend yield:* $0.80/$31.50 = 2.5%.

Payout Ratio.   Another important dividend measure is the dividend *payout ratio;* it provides an indication of the amount of earnings paid out to stockholders in the form of dividends. Well-managed companies have target payout ratios they try to maintain, so if earnings are going up, so will dividends. The payout ratio is calculated according to the equation on page 298.

INVESTOR INSIGHTS

Using the Price-to-Sales Ratio to Identify Stocks to Avoid

New theories on how to evaluate stocks come and go with great regularity. Most of them leave no trail. But one rather simple approach that's showing up in the work of some analysts and money managers is the use of price-to-sales ratios, which they call PSRs. Price/sales ratios are winning particular praise as an aid in screening out bad investments. Because of the relative ease of figuring and applying the ratio, it could be especially well-suited for many individual investors who are as eager for help in avoiding investment disasters as in picking winners. Be forewarned, however, that for the general public the P/S ratio appears not to work as well in figuring which stocks to buy as it does in identifying which to avoid.

P/S ratios are figured like price-to-earnings ratios, except that instead of comparing the per-share price of a company's stock to its per-share earnings for the trailing 12 months, the stock price is compared with the company's sales per share. Proponents say the P/S ratio is especially helpful in evaluating stocks of companies with little or no earnings, or earnings that might not be sustainable. In those cases, price/earnings ratios are often meaningless or misleading, while price/sales ratios paint a valuation picture that's more consistent, even during times of abnormal earnings. Both P/E and P/S ratios measure a stock's popularity. Once investors identify the stocks that already are popular, and those that aren't, they can decide whether to go with the crowd or against it.

One of the most outspoken advocates of the P/S ratio, Kenneth L. Fisher, believes the device works best when it's used by contrarian investors who want to avoid stocks that are already popular and less likely to rise as much as out-of-favor stocks. "Don't waste your time using fundamental analysis on high PSR stocks where there aren't basic opportunities," says Mr. Fisher, who heads Fisher Investments in Burlingame, Calif. Mr. Fisher advises investors to restrict their searches to stocks with low P/S ratios, and then apply fundamental analysis to reach buying decisions. Mr. Fisher classifies stocks with P/S ratios that are too high in three categories: small, growth-oriented or technology companies with P/S ratios of more than 3; concerns with multibillion-dollar sales or small-growth companies with P/S ratios of more than 0.80; and very low-margin companies, such as supermarket operators, with P/S ratios of more than 0.12.

Selecting good buys based on low P/S ratios is a much riskier undertaking, and requires additional analysis. One difficulty is that companies with low P/S ratios sometimes have dangerously high debt levels. Mr. Fisher learned that lesson the hard way in 1984, when two of his recommendations, **Storage Technology** and **Charter Co.,** entered bankruptcy proceedings. Still, portfolio managers who are capable of dissecting companies' balance sheets and other crucial financial data say they've found price/sales ratios useful in making their buying decisions. James M. Gannon of Madison Investment Advisors says P/S ratios help him identify companies that are making profits well below normal on healthy sales. With a low P/S ratio company, "You've often got a sales base to go in there and work on," he says.

Source: Adapted from Dean Rotbart, "Price-to-Sales Ratios Are Gaining Prominence as a Handy Tool to Avoid Poor Investments," *The Wall Street Journal,* November 26, 1984, p. 53.

$$\text{payout ratio} = \frac{\text{dividends per share}}{\text{earnings per share}}$$

$$\text{for MarCor} = \frac{\$.80}{\$2.09} = \underline{\underline{.38}}$$

For MarCor Industries in 1989, dividends accounted for about 38 percent of earnings. This is fairly typical; for most companies that pay dividends tend to pay out somewhere between 40 and 60 percent of earnings.

Book Value Per Share. The last common stock ratio is *book value per share,* a measure that deals with stockholders' equity. Actually, book value is simply another term for equity (or net worth); it represents the difference between total assets and total liabilities. Book value per share is computed as follows:

$$\text{book value per share} = \frac{\text{stockholders' equity}}{\text{number of common shares outstanding}}$$

$$\text{for MarCor} = \frac{\$199,951}{8,601} = \underline{\underline{\$23.25}}$$

Presumably, a stock should sell for *more* than its book value (as MarCor does). If not, it could be an indication that something is seriously wrong with the company's outlook and profitability. A convenient way to relate the book value of a company to the market price of its stock is to compute the *price-to-book-value ratio:*

$$\text{price-to-book-value} = \frac{\text{market price of common stock}}{\text{book value per share}}$$

$$\text{for MarCor} = \frac{\$31.50}{\$23.25} = \underline{\underline{1.35}}$$

Widely used by investors, this ratio shows how aggressively the stock is being priced. As with MarCor, we'd expect most stocks to have a price-to-book-value of more than 1.0 (which simply indicates that the stock is selling for more than its book value). Indeed, in strong bull markets, it's not uncommon to find stocks trading at two or three times their book values; of course, as the markets soften, so do the typical price-to-book-value ratios.

Interpreting Financial Ratios

Rather than compute all the financial ratios themselves, most investors rely on published reports for such information. Many large brokerage houses and a variety of financial services publish such reports, an example of which is given in Figure 7.5. These reports provide a good deal of vital information in a convenient and easy-to-read format, and they relieve investors of the drudgery of computing the financial ratios themselves. However, investors still need to be able to evaluate this information. To see how this is done, consider the case of MarCor Industries, and take a look at Table 7.6 (on page 300), which provides a summary of historical and industry figures for most of the ratios discussed above. To begin with, we can see a modest improvement in an already strong liquidity position, as the current ratio

Hartmarx Corp.

1105

NYSE Symbol HMX In S&P 500

Price	Range	P-E Ratio	Dividend	Yield	S&P Ranking	Beta
May 16'89	1989					
26	28¹/₈-24	13	1.20	4.6%	A	1.11

Summary

This company is a leading manufacturer and retailer of men's and women's apparel under such well-known names as Hart Schaffner & Marx, Henry Grethel and Hickey-Freeman. Continued expansion through acquisitions and store openings, the addition of new lines, and continued efforts to control costs enhance the long-term earnings potential; however, earnings for fiscal 1989 will be hurt by soft retail sales and higher interest charges.

Current Outlook

Earnings for the fiscal year ending November 30, 1989 should decrease to $1.65 a share from fiscal 1988's $2.03.

The quarterly dividend was raised 9.1% to $0.30 from $0.27¹/₂, with the May, 1989 payment.

Net sales for 1989 should advance moderately, reflecting acquisitions, new store openings, and higher apparel manufacturing sales which will offset soft existing store sales. Benefits from cost efficiencies and centralization of retail operations, higher volume of apparel manufacturing sales, and the absence of start-up costs at Henry Grethel may be slightly offset by slower retail sales. Interest charges will be substantially higher.

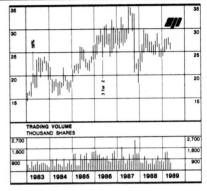

TRADING VOLUME
THOUSAND SHARES

Net Sales (Million $)

Quarter:	1988-9	1987-8	1986-7	1985-6
Feb.	327	302	283	290
May	---	273	248	245
Aug.	---	290	257	253
Nov.	---	310	293	274
	---	1,174	1,080	1,063

Net sales for the three months ended February 28, 1989 rose 8.3%, year to year, reflecting a 10.4% increase in manufacturing sales and a 6.8% rise in retail sales. Margins improved slightly, and pretax income rose 9.9%. After taxes at 38.2%, versus 38.5%, net income rose 10.5%, to $0.50 a share (on 3.9% more shares) from $0.47.

Common Share Earnings ($)

Quarter:	1988-9	1987-8	1986-7	1985-6
Feb.	0.50	0.47	0.54	0.40
May	E0.20	0.44	0.40	0.11
Aug.	E0.20	0.30	0.30	0.18
Nov.	E0.75	0.82	0.77	0.51
	E1.65	2.03	2.01	1.20

Important Developments

May '89— HMX reached an agreement in principle to market apparel under the J.G. Hook Label. In March, 1989 HMX acquired The Biltwell Company, a men's and women's apparel manufacturer, and in December, 1988 it acquired Raleighs, a specialty retailer in Washington, D.C. Meanwhile, in February HMX announced plans to sell its Country Miss division.

Mar. '89— HMX said that it expected higher sales from its existing businesses and acquisitions for the remainder of fiscal 1989. HMX said that fall 1989 advance orders for manufacturing were slightly ahead, year to year, in units, although slower retail sales were affecting current in-stock business. HMX also said that it expected soft retail sales and higher interest charges to adversely affect second-quarter earnings.

Next earnings report expected late June.

Per Share Data ($)

Yr. End Nov. 30	1988	1987	1986	1985	1984	1983	1982	¹1981	1980	1979
Tangible Bk. Val.	**19.21**	18.26	17.59	17.60	16.24	14.80	13.45	12.55	11.69	10.98
Earnings	**2.03**	2.01	1.20	2.25	2.24	2.03	1.67	1.41	1.17	1.09
Dividends	**1.07¹/₂**	0.98	0.90³/₈	0.85³/₈	0.74³/₄	0.60³/₄	0.53⁷/₈	0.48¹/₂	0.43¹/₈	0.39¹/₈
Payout Ratio	**53%**	45%	75%	38%	33%	30%	30%	34%	36%	35%
Prices²—High	**29³/₄**	34³/₄	32	26¹/₂	21⁷/₈	24¹/₈	18¹/₈	10³/₄	7	6⁷/₈
Low	**20³/₄**	18¹/₄	23¹/₂	18³/₄	15³/₄	14¹/₂	8¹/₈	6¹/₄	4³/₈	4³/₈
P/E Ratio—	**15-10**	17-9	27-20	12-8	10-7	12-7	11-5	8-4	6-4	6-4

Data as orig. reptd. Adj. for stk. div(s). of 50% May 1986, & 50% stk. exchange Apr. 1983. 1. Reflects merger or acquisition. 2. Cal. yr. E-Estimated.

Standard NYSE Stock Reports
Vol. 56/No. 100/Sec. 14

May 24, 1989

Standard & Poor's Corp.
25 Broadway, NY, NY 10004

FIGURE 7.5 An Example of a Published Analytical Report with Financial Statistics.

These and similar reports are widely available to investors and play an important part in the security analysis process. (*Source:* Standard & Poor's *NYSE Stock Reports*, May 24, 1989.)

TABLE 7.6   Comparative Historical and Industry Ratios

	Historical Figures for MarCor Industries		1989 Industry Averages for the Apparel Industry
	1988	**1989**	
Liquidity measures			
Current ratio	3.10	3.29	2.87
Net working capital (in millions)	$188.7	$194.4	N.A.
Activity measures			
Receivables turnover	5.52	5.76	8.00
Inventory turnover	3.57	3.69	3.75
Total asset turnover	1.67	1.79	1.42
Leverage measures			
Debt-equity ratio	.33	.27	.49
Times interest earned	4.75	5.50	4.35
Profitability measures			
Operating ratio	96.6%	96.2%	96.9%
Net profit margin	2.7%	2.9%	2.7%
Return on assets	4.6%	5.3%	3.9%
Return on equity	8.2%	9.0%	7.9%
Common stock measures			
Earnings per share	$1.80	$2.09	$1.45
Price/earnings ratio	16.20	15.10	14.00
Price-to-sales ratio	0.44	0.45	0.68
Dividends per share	$0.70	$0.80	$0.40
Dividend yield	2.4%	2.5%	1.9%
Payout ratio	39.0%	38.0%	28.0%
Price-to-book-value	1.33	1.35	1.20

remains well above the industry standard. A look at the activity measures shows that although receivables and inventory turnover are improving, they still remain below industry standards. Accounts receivable turnover appears to be especially out of line and is almost 40 percent below normal. Unless there is an operating or economic explanation for this, it would appear that a lot of excess (nonproductive) resources are being tied up in accounts receivable, which is costing the firm millions of dollars a year in profits. The inventory position, in contrast, has improved and although still a bit below average, it certainly does not appear to be much of a problem. Finally, note that total asset turnover is up from last year and well above average.

The leverage position of MarCor Industries seems well controlled; the company tends to use a lot less debt in its financial structure than the average firm in the apparel industry. The payoff for this judicious use of debt comes in the form of a coverage ratio that is well above average. The profitability picture for MarCor is equally attractive; profit rate, return on assets, and ROE are all improving and remain well above the industry norm. In summary, our analysis suggests that this

firm is, with the possible exception of accounts receivable, fairly well managed and highly profitable. The results of this are reflected in common stock ratios that are consistently equal to or superior to industry figures. Certainly the company has done well in the past and appears to be well managed today. Our major concern at this point (and the topic of the first part of Chapter 9) is whether or not MarCor will continue to be an industry leader and provide above-average returns to investors.

SUMMARY

- While common stocks are popular investment vehicles, success in this market is largely a function of careful security selection and investment timing.

- Security analysis helps the investor make the crucial selection decision by determining the intrinsic value (or underlying worth) of a stock; security analysis consists of economic, industry, and fundamental (company) analyses.

- Economic analysis deals with an evaluation of the general state of the economy and its potential effects on security returns. In essence, economic analysis tries to identify the kind of future economic environment the investor will be facing, and is used to set the tone for the security analysis process.

- In industry analysis, the investor narrows the focus a bit as attention is centered on the activities in one or more industries; again, it is the outlook for the industry that is important.

- Fundamental analysis involves an in-depth study of the financial condition and operating results of the company. Once the historical position of the firm has been established, future expectations can be formulated about the company and its stock.

- Fundamental analysis is conducted on the premise that the value of a share of stock is influenced in part by the performance of the company issuing the stock. Accordingly, the competitive position of the company, its sales and profit margins, asset mix, and capital structure are all important variables.

- Corporate financial statements are an essential part of company analysis and form the raw material of this process; a complete set of financial statements consists of a balance sheet, income statement, a statement of cash flows, and statement of changes in stockholders' equity.

- Financial ratios expand the perspective and information content of financial statements and are an essential part of fundamental analysis. There are five broad categories of financial ratios: liquidity; activity; leverage; profitability; and market (common stock) ratios, all of which involve the study of relationships among and between various financial accounts.

REVIEW QUESTIONS AND PROBLEMS

1. Identify the three major parts of security analysis and discuss why security analysis is so important to the stock selection process. What is intrinsic value, and how does it fit into security analysis?

2. What is a satisfactory investment vehicle? How does security analysis help in identifying such investment candidates?

3. Discuss the general concept of economic analysis. Is this type of analysis really necessary, and can it help the investor make a decision about a stock? Explain.

4. Why is the business cycle so important to economic analysis? Identify each of the following and note how each would probably behave in a strong economy:

   a. Fiscal policy.
   b. Interest rates.
   c. Industrial production.
   d. Retail sales.

5. What is the Federal Reserve and how can it affect the general tone of the economy? What's the difference between the Federal Reserve discount rate and the federal funds rate?

6. Briefly describe each of the following:

   a. Gross national product.
   b. Leading indicators.
   c. Money supply.
   d. Producer prices.

7. What are the alleged causes of inflation? What effect does inflation have on common stocks?

8. Briefly describe the two ways that an economic forecast can be used to help select investments.

9. What is the relationship between the stock market and the economy? How does this relationship affect an economic outlook?

10. What is industry analysis and why is it important? Explain.

11. Identify and briefly discuss several aspects of an industry that are important to its behavior and operating characteristics; note especially how economic issues fit into industry analysis.

12. What are the four stages of an industry's growth cycle? Which of these stages is most influenced by the economic cycle?

13. The Amherst Company has net profits of $10 million, sales of $150 million, and 2.5 million shares of common stock outstanding. It pays $1 per share in common dividends and the stock trades at $20 per share. Given this information, determine:

   a. Amherst's earnings per share (EPS).
   b. Amherst's sales per share.
   c. The firm's price/earnings (P/E) ratio.
   d. Its price-to-sales ratio (PSR).
   e. Its dividend payout ratio.

14. What is fundamental analysis? Does the performance of a company have any bearing on the value of its stock? Explain.

15. Why do investors bother to look at the historical performance of a company when future behavior is what really counts?

16. Identify and briefly discuss the four different types of financial statements companies regularly make available to stockholders.

17. Sunbelt Solar Products produces $2 million in profits from $28 million in sales and has total assets of $15 million; calculate SSP's total asset turnover and compute its net profit margin; also find the company's ROA, ROE, and book value per share, given SSP has a total net worth of $6 million and 500,000 shares of common stock outstanding.

18. What is ratio analysis? Describe the role and contribution of ratio analysis to the study of a company's financial condition and operating results.

19. Match the specific ratios from the left-hand column with the ratio categories listed in the right-hand column:

   a. Inventory turnover.   1. Profitability ratios.
   b. Debt-equity ratio.   2. Activity ratios.
   c. Current ratio.   3. Liquidity ratios.
   d. Net profit margin.   4. Leverage ratios.
   e. Return on assets.   5. Common stock ratios.
   f. Total asset turnover.
   g. Price/earnings ratio.
   h. Price-to-sales ratio.
   i. Times interest earned.
   j. Price-to-book-value.
   k. Payout ratio.

20. The Shasta Flower Firm has total assets of $10 million, an asset turnover of 2.0 times, and a net profit margin of 15 percent. What is Shasta's return on assets? Find Shasta's ROE, given 40 percent of the assets are financed with stockholders' equity.

21. Contrast historical standards of performance with industry standards. Briefly note the role of such standards when analyzing the financial condition and operating results of a company.

22. Find the P/E ratio, PSR, and dividend yield of a company that has 5 million shares of common stock outstanding (the shares trade in the market at $25), earns 10 percent after taxes on annual sales of $150 million, and has a dividend payout ratio of 35 percent.

23. Using the resources available at your campus or public library, select *any* common stock you like and determine as many of the profitability, activity, liquidity, leverage, and market ratios as you can; compute the ratios for the latest available fiscal year. (*Note:* Show your work for all calculations.)

CASE PROBLEMS
7.1 Some Financial Ratios Are Real Eye-Openers

Jack Simms is a resident of Brownfield, Texas, where he is a prosperous rancher and businessman; he has also built up a sizable portfolio of common stock which, he believes, is due to the fact that he thoroughly evaluates each stock he invests in. As Jack says, "Y'all can't be too careful about these things! Anytime I'm fixing to invest in a stock, you can bet I'm gonna learn as much as I can about the company." Jack prefers to compute his own ratios even though he could easily afford to purchase professionally prepared analytical reports or obtain similar types of reports from his broker at no cost. (In fact, Billy Bob Smith, his broker, has been volunteering such services for years.)

Recently, Jack has been keeping an eye on a small chemical issue. This firm, South Plains Chemical Company, is big in the fertilizer business—which, not by coincidence, is some-

thing that Jack knows a lot about. Not long ago, he received a copy of the company's latest financial statements (summarized below) and decided to take a closer look at the company.

Balance Sheet
(Dollars in Thousands)

Cash	$ 1,250		
Accounts receivable	8,000	Current liabilities	$10,000
Inventory	12,000	Long-term debt	8,000
Current assets	$21,250	Stockholders' equity	12,000
Fixed and other assets	8,750		
Total	$30,000	Total	$30,000

Income Statement
(Dollars in Thousands)

Sales	$50,000
Cost of goods sold	25,000
Operating expenses	15,000
Operating profit	$10,000
Interest expense	2,500
Taxes	2,500
Net profit	$ 5,000

Notes: Dividends paid to common (dollars in thousands) — $1,250
Number of common shares outstanding — 5 million
Recent market price of the common stock — $25

Questions

1. Compute the following ratios, using the South Plains Chemical Company figures:

	Latest Industry Averages
Liquidity	
a. Net working capital	N.A.
b. Current ratio	1.95
Activity	
c. Receivables turnover	5.95
d. Inventory turnover	4.50
e. Total asset turnover	2.65
Leverage	
f. Debt-equity ratio	0.45
g. Times interest earned	6.75
Profitability	
h. Operating ratio	85.0%
i. Net profit margin	8.5%

j.	Return on assets	22.5%
k.	ROE	32.2%

Common Stock Ratios

l.	Earnings per share	$2.00
m.	Price/earnings ratio	20.0
n.	Price-to-sales ratio	3.0
o.	Dividends per share	$1.00
p.	Dividend yield	2.5%
q.	Payout ratio	50.0%
r.	Book value per share	$6.25
s.	Price-to-book-value	6.4

2. Compare the company ratios you prepared to the industry figures. What are the company's strengths? What are its weaknesses?
3. What is your overall assessment of South Plains Chemical? Do you think Simms should continue with his evaluation of the stock? Explain.

7.2 Doris Looks at an Auto Issue

Doris Poure is a young career woman; she lives in Chicago, where she owns and operates a highly successful modeling agency. Doris manages her modest but rapidly growing investment portfolio, made up mostly of high-grade common stocks. Because she's young and single, and has no pressing family requirements, Doris has invested primarily in stocks that offer attractive capital gains potential. Her broker recently recommended one of the auto issues and sent her some literature and analytical reports to study. Among the reports was one prepared by the brokerage house she deals with; it provided an up-to-date look at the economy, an extensive study of the auto industry, and an equally extensive review of several auto companies (including the one her broker recommended). She feels very strongly about the merits of security analysis and feels it is important to spend some time studying a stock before making an investment decision.

Questions
1. Doris tries to stay abreast of the economy on a regular basis; at the present time, most economists agree that the economy, now well into the third year of a recovery, is healthy, with industrial activity remaining strong. What other information about the economy do you think Doris would find helpful in evaluating an auto stock? Prepare a list—be specific. Which three items of economic information (from your list) are especially important? Explain.
2. In relation to a study of the auto industry, briefly note the importance of each of the following:
   a. Auto imports.
   b. The United Auto Workers union.
   c. Interest rates.
   d. The price of a gallon of gas.
3. A variety of financial ratios and measures is provided about one of the auto companies and its stock; however, these are a bit incomplete, so some additional information will have to be computed. Specifically, we know that:

Net profit margin is	15%
Total assets are	$250 million
Earnings per share are	$3.00
Total asset turnover is	1.5
Net working capital is	$75 million
Payout ratio is	40%
Current liabilities are	$75 million
Price/earnings ratio is	12.5

Given this information, calculate the following:
a. Sales.
b. Net profits after taxes.
c. Current ratio.
d. Market price of the stock.
e. Dividend yield.

SELECTED READINGS

Dreman, David. "The Glories of Low-P/E Investing." *Forbes,* June 27, 1988, pp. 172–73.

Fredman, Albert J., and Cameron P. Hum. "Reading Small-Cap Companies." *Personal Investor,* March 1986, pp. 50–54.

Harris, Anne. "Looking Beyond P/E Ratios." *Personal Investor,* September 1987, pp. 52–57.

Hector, Gary. "Cute Tricks on the Bottom Line." *Fortune,* April 24, 1989, pp. 193–200.

Hedberg, Augustin. "Oops! Your Stock's in the News." *Money,* June 1988, pp. 119–22.

Nasar, Sylvia. "How to Spot a Recession." *Fortune,* March 28, 1988, pp. 63–68.

Rock, Andrea. "Cash Flow Can Be The Investor's Best Guide to a Stock's True Worth." *Money,* March 1989, pp. 161–62.

Sivy, Michael. "How to Spot a Cheap Stock." *Money,* August 1987, pp. 131–32.

Updegrave, Walter L. "To Keep Profits on a Roll, Stay Tuned to the Business Cycle." *Money,* May 1989, pp. 169–72.

Wiener, Daniel P. "Overlooked and Undervalued." *U.S. News & World Report,* September 12, 1988, pp. 63–64.

8

COMMON STOCK VALUATION, TECHNICAL ANALYSIS, AND EFFICIENT MARKETS

After studying this chapter you should be able to:

- Explain the role that a company's future plays in the stock valuation process, and develop a forecast of a stock's expected cash flow, including future dividends and anticipated price behavior.

- Discuss the concept of intrinsic value and note how it can be used as a standard of performance in judging the investment suitability of a share of common stock.

- Apply a popular and widely used stock valuation model that takes into account both expected return and potential risk.

- Gain an understanding of technical analysis, including its role in the security analysis and stock selection process.

- Discuss the idea of random walks and efficient markets, including the serious challenges these theories hold for the entire stock valuation process.

- Gain an appreciation of some of the major changes taking place in the stock market, including the increasing role of corporate take-overs, leveraged buy-outs, and program trades.

How much would you be willing to pay for a share of stock? That's a tough question and one that investors have been wrestling with for about as long as common stocks have been traded. The answer, of course, depends on the kind of return you expect to receive and the amount of risk involved in the transaction. This chapter looks at the question of a stock's worth in detail as we continue our discussion of the stock valuation process.

In Chapter 7, we dealt with several preliminary aspects of security analysis: economic analysis, industry analysis, and the historical phase of fundamental company analysis. We now need to develop estimates for the future prospects of the company and the expected returns from its stock. Then we can complete the valuation process and finally decide whether a particular stock will make a potentially attractive investment vehicle. This chapter will also examine one of the most serious challenges traditional security analysis has ever faced: that is, as professed by the "efficient market" advocates, that security analysis and all its trappings are largely an exercise in futility.

VALUATION: OBTAINING A STANDARD OF PERFORMANCE

stock valuation
the process by which the underlying value of a stock is established, as based on future risk and return performance of the security.

Obtaining a standard of performance that can be used to judge the investment merits of a share of stock is the underlying purpose of **stock valuation.** A stock's intrinsic value furnishes such a standard since it provides an indication of the future risk and return performance of a security. The question of whether, and to what extent, a stock is undervalued or overvalued is resolved by comparing its current market price to its intrinsic value. At any given point in time, the price of a share of common stock depends on investor expectations about the future behavior of the security. If the outlook for the company and its stock is good, the price will probably be bid up; if conditions deteriorate, the price of the stock can be expected to go down. Let's look now at the single most important issue in the stock valuation process: *the future*.

The Company and Its Future

Thus far, we have examined the historical performance of the company and its stock. It should be clear, however, that it's *not the past* that's important, but rather *the future*. The primary reason for looking at past performance is to gain insight about the future direction of the firm and its profitability. Past performance, in essence, helps us get a handle on the future. Granted, past performance provides no guarantees about future returns, but it can give us a good idea of company strengths and weaknesses. For example, it can tell us how the company's products have done in the marketplace, how the company's fiscal health shapes up, and how management tends to respond to difficult situations. In short, it reveals how well the company has done in the past and perhaps, more importantly, how well it's positioned to take advantage of the things that may occur in the future. Think of it as though we're giving management a grade: if they've done a good job in building the company, dealing with growth, and positioning the firm for the future, we'll give them a

high grade. This is important, because if the company's been successful in the past, then we can be more confident about its prospects in the future.

Because *the value of a stock is a function of its future returns,* the investor's task at hand is to use available historical data to project key financial variables into the future. In this way, the investor can assess the outlook for the company and thereby gain some idea about the benefits to be derived from investing in the stock. We are especially interested in dividends and price behavior. For our purposes here, we will assume that dividends and capital gains are equally important.

Forecasted Sales and Profits

The key to our forecast is, of course, the future behavior of the *company,* and the most important aspects to consider in this regard are the outlook for sales and the trend in the net profit margin. One way to develop a sales forecast is to assume that the company will continue to perform as it has in the past, and simply extend the historical trend. For example, if a firm's sales have been growing at the rate of 10 percent per year, then assume they will continue at that rate of growth. Of course, if there is some evidence about the economy, industry, and/or company that suggests a faster or slower rate of growth, the forecast should be adjusted accordingly. More often than not, this "naive" approach will be just about as effective as other, more complex techniques. Normally, we would expect the sales estimate to cover a period of one to three years; extending it much further would introduce too many uncertainties and jeopardize the validity of our forecasts.

Once the sales forecast has been generated, we can shift our attention to the net profit margin. We want to know what kind of return on sales we can expect from the company. A naive estimate can be obtained simply by using the average profit margin that has prevailed for the past few years; again, this should be adjusted to account for any unusual industry or company developments. For most investors, valuable insight about future revenues and earnings can be obtained from industry and/or company reports put out by brokerage houses, advisory services (like *Value Line*), and the financial media (such as *Forbes*).

Given a satisfactory sales forecast and estimate of the future net profit margin, we can combine these two pieces of information to arrive at future earnings:

$$\text{future after-tax earnings in year } t = \text{estimated sales for year } t \times \text{net profit margin expected in year } t$$

The "year *t*" notation simply denotes a given calendar or fiscal year in the future; it can be next year, the year after that, or any other year in which we happen to be working. Let's say that in the year just completed, a company reported sales of $100 million, and it is estimated that revenues will grow at an 8 percent annual rate, while the net profit margin should amount to about 6 percent. Thus, estimated sales next year will equal $108 million ($100 million × 1.08), and with a 6 percent profit margin, we should see earnings next year of:

$$\text{future after-tax earnings next year} = \$108 \text{ million} \times .06 = \underline{\underline{\$6.5 \text{ million}}}$$

Using this same process, we would then estimate sales and earnings for all other years in our forecast period.

Forecasted Dividends and Prices

At this point, we have an idea of the future earnings performance of the company—assuming, of course, that our expectations and assumptions hold up. We are now ready to evaluate the effects of this performance on returns to common stock investors. Given a corporate earnings forecast, we need three additional pieces of information:

1. An estimate of future dividend payout ratios.
2. The number of common shares that will be outstanding over the forecast period.
3. A future price/earnings (P/E) ratio.

For the first two variables, unless we have evidence to the contrary, we can simply project recent historical experience into the future and assume that these estimates will hold for the forecast period. Payout ratios are usually fairly stable, so there is little risk in using a recent average figure (or, if a company follows a fixed dividend policy, we could use the latest dividend rate in our forecast). At the same time, it is generally safe to assume that the number of common shares outstanding will hold at the latest level.

The only really thorny issue is defining the future P/E ratio. This is an important figure, since it has considerable bearing on the future price of the stock. Generally speaking, the P/E ratio has been shown to be a function of several variables, including: (1) the growth rate in earnings; (2) the general state of the market; (3) the amount of debt in a company's capital structure; and (4) the level of dividends. As a rule, higher ratios can be expected with higher growth rates in earnings, an optimistic market outlook, and lower debt levels (since less debt means less financial risk). We can also argue that a high P/E ratio can be expected with high dividend payouts. In practice, however, most companies with high P/E ratios have *low* dividend payouts due to the fact that earnings growth tends to be more valuable than dividends, especially in companies with high rates of return on equity.

A useful starting point in evaluating the P/E ratio is the *average market multiple,* which is simply the average P/E ratio of stocks in the marketplace. The average market multiple provides insight into the general state of the market and gives the investor an idea of how aggressively the market in general is pricing stocks. (Other things being equal, the higher the P/E, the more optimistic the market.) Table 8.1 lists S&P price/earnings multiples for the past 30 years and shows that market multiples do tend to move over a fairly wide range. With the market multiple as a benchmark, the investor can then evaluate a stock's P/E performance relative to the market—that is, a **relative P/E multiple** can be found by dividing a stock's P/E by the market multiple. For example, if a stock currently has a P/E of 25 while the market multiple is 15, the stock's relative P/E would be $25/15 = 1.67$ *times.* Look-

relative P/E multiple
the measure of how a stock's P/E behaves relative to the average market multiple.

TABLE 8.1   Average Market P/E Multiples 1960–1989

Year	Market Multiples (Avg. S&P P/E Ratio)	Year	Market Multiples (Avg. S&P P/E Ratio)
1960	17.8	1975	11.7
1961	22.4	1976	11.0
1962	17.2	1977	8.8
1963	18.7	1978	8.3
1964	18.6	1979	7.4
1965	17.8	1980	9.1
1966	14.8	1981	8.1
1967	17.7	1982	10.2
1968	18.1	1983	12.4
1969	15.1	1984	10.0
1970	16.7	1985	13.7
1971	18.3	1986	16.3
1972	19.1	1987	15.1
1973	12.2	1988	12.2
1974	7.3	1989	12.8

Source: Average year-end multiples derived from the S&P Index of 500 Stocks, Standard & Poor's *Statistical Service—Security Price Index Record,* various issues; listed P/Es are year-end figures in all cases except 1989, which was obtained at mid-year.

ing at this relative P/E, the investor can quickly get a feel for how aggressively the stock has been priced in the market and what kind of relative P/E is normal for the stock. Other things being equal, a high relative P/E is desirable, since the higher this measure, the higher the stock will be priced in the market; but watch out for the downside: high relative P/E's also mean more price volatility.

Given the above, we can now generate a forecast of what the stock's *future* P/E will be over the anticipated *investment horizon,* the period of time over which we expect to hold the stock. For example, using the existing P/E multiple as a base, an *increase* might be justified if you believe the *market multiple* will increase (as the market tone becomes more bullish) and the *relative P/E* is likely to increase also. Armed with an estimate for the dividend payout ratio, the number of shares outstanding, and the price/earnings multiple, we can now forecast earnings per share:

$$\text{estimated EPS in year } t = \frac{\text{future after-tax earnings in year } t}{\text{number of shares of common stock outstanding in year } t}$$

From here we can estimate dividends per share, as follows:

$$\begin{array}{c}\text{estimated dividends} \\ \text{per share in year } t\end{array} = \begin{array}{c}\text{estimated EPS} \\ \text{in year } t\end{array} \times \begin{array}{c}\text{estimated} \\ \text{payout ratio}\end{array}$$

The last item is the future price of the stock, which can be determined as:

$$\begin{array}{c} \text{estimated share price} \\ \text{at the end of year } t \end{array} = \begin{array}{c} \text{estimated EPS} \\ \text{in year } t \end{array} \times \begin{array}{c} \text{estimated} \\ \text{P/E ratio} \end{array}$$

For example, if the company had 2 million shares of common stock outstanding, and that number was expected to hold in the future, then given the estimated earnings of $6.5 million which we computed earlier, the firm should generate earnings per share (EPS) next year of:

$$\begin{array}{c} \text{estimated EPS} \\ \text{next year} \end{array} = \frac{\$6.5 \text{ million}}{2 \text{ million}} = \underline{\underline{\$3.25}}$$

Using this EPS of $3.25, along with an estimated payout ratio of 40 percent, we see that dividends per share next year should equal:

$$\begin{array}{c} \text{estimated dividends} \\ \text{per share next year} \end{array} = \$3.25 \times .40 = \underline{\underline{\$1.30}}$$

Of course, if the firm adheres to a *fixed dividend policy,* this estimate may have to be adjusted to reflect the level of dividends being paid. For example, if the company has been paying annual dividends at the rate of $1.25 per share, *and is expected to continue doing so for the near future,* then estimated dividends should be adjusted accordingly—that is, use $1.25/share. Finally, if it has been estimated that the stock should sell at 17.5 times earnings, then a share of stock in this company should be trading at a price of about 56⅞ by the *end* of next year:

$$\begin{array}{c} \text{estimated share price} \\ \text{at the end of next year} \end{array} = \$3.25 \times 17.5 = \underline{\underline{\$56.88}}$$

Actually, we are interested in the price of the stock at the end of our anticipated investment horizon. Thus, if we had a one-year horizon, the 56⅞ figure would be appropriate. However, if we had a three-year holding period, we would have to extend the EPS figure for two more years and repeat our calculations with the new data. As we shall see, estimated share price is important because it has embedded in it the capital gains portion of the stock's total return.

Developing an Estimate of Future Behavior

Before illustrating the forecast procedure with a concrete example, let's quickly review the steps involved:

1. Estimate future sales.
2. Estimate a future net profit margin.
3. Derive future after-tax earnings (per first equation).
4. Estimate a future payout ratio (or fixed dividend rate).
5. Estimate the number of common shares outstanding in the future.
6. Estimate a future price/earnings (P/E) ratio.
7. Derive a future EPS figure (per second equation).
8. Derive future dividends per share (per third equation).

9. Derive a future share price (per fourth equation).
10. Repeat the process for each year in the forecast period.

Much of the required forecast data can be obtained from published sources or analytical reports prepared by major brokerage firms. However, investors still have to interject their own judgments and opinions about the future course of a company and its stock, and as a result, *cannot* rely solely on published reports. We either agree or disagree with the published reports. If we agree, then we are inferring that our expectations are compatible with those embodied in the published reports; if we disagree, then we must adjust the forecasts to come up with our own figures.

Now, using the hypothetical firm of MarCor Industries, we can illustrate this forecasting process. Recall from Chapter 7 that an assessment of the economy and the apparel industry was positive, and that the company's operating results and financial condition looked strong, both historically and relative to industry standards. Because everything looks favorable for MarCor, we decide to take a look at the future of the company and its stock. Assume we have chosen a three-year investment horizon, based on our belief (formulated from earlier studies of economic and industry factors) that the economy and the market for apparel stocks should start running out of steam sometime near the end of 1992 or early 1993.

Selected historical financial data are provided in Table 8.2; they cover an eight-year period (ending with the latest 1989 fiscal year) and will provide the basis for much of our forecast. An assessment of Table 8.2 reveals that except for 1983 and 1984 (which were "off" years for MarCor), the company has performed at a fairly stable pace and has been able to maintain a respectable rate of growth. Our economic analysis suggests that things are beginning to pick up. And based on earlier studies, we feel the industry and company are well situated to take advantage of the upswing. Therefore, we conclude that the rate of growth in sales should pick up in 1990 to about 9.5 percent; then, once a modest amount of pent-up demand is worked off, the rate of growth in sales should drop to about 9 percent in 1991 and stay there through 1992.

Since various published industry and company reports suggest a comfortable improvement in earnings, we decide to use a profit margin of 3.0 percent in 1990, followed by an even better 3.2 percent in 1991; finally, because of some capacity problems prominently mentioned in one of the reports, we show a drop in the margin in 1992 back to 3.0 percent. Assume also that our assessment indicates the company will be able to handle the growth in assets and meet financing needs without issuing any additional equity (new common stock). Moreover, assume the dividend payout ratio will hold at about 40 percent of earnings, as it has for most of the recent past—with the notable exceptions of 1983 and 1984. The last element is the forecasted P/E ratio. Based primarily on an outlook for a strong market, coupled with the expectations of improved growth in revenues and earnings, we are projecting a multiple that will rise from its present 15.1 to 17 times earnings by 1992.

The essential elements of the financial forecast for 1990, 1991, and 1992 are provided in Table 8.3. Also included is the sequence involved in arriving at fore-

TABLE 8.2 Selected Historical Financial Data, MarCor Industries (for Fiscal Years Ending November 30)

	1982	1983	1984	1985	1986	1987	1988	1989
Total assets (millions)	$262.8	$254.2	$220.9	$240.7	$274.3	$318.2	$340.5	$338.6
Debt-equity ratio	31%	37%	31%	29%	30%	33%	33%	27%
Total asset turnover	1.73×	1.66×	1.72×	1.81×	1.75×	1.65×	1.67×	1.79×
Net sales (millions)	$454.7	$422.0	$397.9	$435.6	$480.0	$525.0	$568.0	$606.6
Annual rate of growth in sales*	—	−7.2%	−5.7%	9.5%	10.2%	9.4%	8.2%	6.8%
Interest and other income (millions)	$ 6.8	$ 6.5	$ 6.3	$ 6.0	$ 6.8	$ 7.7	$ 7.1	$ 8.3
Net profit margin	2.6%	0.6%	1.1%	2.0%	3.6%	3.0%	2.7%	2.9%
Payout ratio	36.0%	83.0%	97.0%	38.0%	40.0%	40.0%	39.0%	38.0%
Price/earnings ratio	14.5×	6.2×	8.3×	12.8×	9.5×	13.6×	16.2×	15.1×
Number of common shares outstanding (millions)	7.0	7.0	7.1	7.1	8.5	8.6	8.6	8.6

*Annual rate of growth in sales = change in sales from one year to the next divided by the level of sales in the base (or earliest) year; for 1985, the annual rate of growth in sales equaled 9.5% = (1985 sales − 1984 sales)/1984 sales = ($435.6 − $397.9)/$397.9 = .095.

casted dividends and price behavior. Note that the company dimensions of the forecast are handled first, and that after-tax earnings are derived according to the procedure described earlier in this chapter; then per-share data are estimated following the procedures established earlier. The bottom line of the forecast is, of course, the dividend and capital gains returns the investor can expect from a share of MarCor stock, given that the assumptions about net sales, profit margins, earnings per share, and so forth, hold up. We see in Table 8.3 that dividends should go up by about 30 cents per share over the next three years and that the price of a share of stock should undergo a better than 50 percent appreciation in value, rising from its latest price of $31.50 to $47.60. We now have the needed figures on expected shareholder return and are in a position to establish an intrinsic value for MarCor Industries stock.

A STOCK VALUATION FRAMEWORK

At any point in time, a stock is worth just what investors are willing to pay for it. To some, the prevailing market price may seem too high; to others, it may appear to be a bargain. Here we will look at popular stock valuation models and examine the mechanics of the valuation process more closely, using MarCor Industries and the forecast data in Table 8.3 as a basis of illustration.

TABLE 8.3   Summary Forecast Statistics, MarCor Industries

	Latest Actual Figures (Fiscal 1989)	Average for the Past 5 Years (1985–1989)	Forecasted Figures		
			1990	1991	1992
Annual rate of growth in sales	6.8%	8.8%	9.5%	9.0%	9.0%
Net sales (millions)	$606.6	N.A.*	$664.2**	$724.0**	$789.2**
+ Interest and other income (millions)	$ 8.3	$ 7.2	$ 7.2	$ 7.2	$ 7.2
= Total revenue (millions)	$614.9	N.A.	$671.4	$731.2	$796.4
× Net profit margin	2.9%	2.8%	3.0%	3.2%	3.0%
= Net after-tax earnings (millions)	$ 18.0	N.A.	$ 20.1	$ 23.4	$ 24.0
÷ Common shares outstanding (millions)	8.6	8.3	8.6	8.6	8.6
= Earnings per share	$ 2.09	N.A.	$ 2.34	$ 2.72	$ 2.80
× Payout ratio	38.0%	39.0%	40.0%	40.0%	40.0%
= Dividends per share	$ 0.80	$ 0.71	$ 0.95	$ 1.10	$ 1.12
Earnings per share	$ 2.09	N.A.	$ 2.34	$ 2.72	$ 2.80
× P/E ratio	15.10	13.45	15.50	16.00	17.00
= Share price at year end	$ 31.50	N.A.	$ 36.25	$ 43.50	$ 47.60

*N.A. = Not applicable.

**Forecasted sales figures: Sales from *preceding* year × growth rate in sales = growth in sales; then: growth in sales + sales from *preceding* year = forecast sales for the year. For example, for 1991: $664.2 × .09 = $59.8 + $664.2 = $724.0 million.

The Valuation Process

valuation
process by which an investor determines the worth of a security using risk and return concepts.

Valuation is a process by which an investor determines the worth of a security using the risk and return concepts we introduced in Chapter 5. It is a process that can be applied to any asset that produces a stream of cash flow, be it a share of stock, a bond, a piece of real estate, or an oil well. In order to establish the value of an asset, certain key inputs have to be determined, including the amount of future cash flows, the timing of these cash flows, and the rate of return required on the investment. (In security analysis it makes a difference as to not only *how much* cash is received, but also *when* it's received.)

In terms of common stock, the essence of valuation is to determine what the stock *ought to be worth,* given estimated returns to stockholders (future dividends and price behavior) and the amount of potential risk exposure. Stock valuation models determine either an expected rate of return or the intrinsic worth of a share of stock, which in effect represents the stock's "justified price." In this way, we can obtain a standard of performance, based on *future* stock behavior, that can be

used to judge the investment merits of a particular security. Clearly, if the computed rate of return exceeds the yield the investor feels is warranted, or if the justified price (intrinsic worth) is in excess of the current market price, the stock under consideration should be considered a worthwhile investment candidate.

Basically, our analysis of MarCor Industries up to now has been directed toward defining what the future cash flow of the investment is likely to be. This was summarized in Table 8.3, where the forecasted cash flow stream for MarCor was listed in terms of the *amount* of the expected cash flow as well as the *timing* of the receipts (from 95¢ in dividends in the first year to $1.12 + $47.60 in dividends and share price in the third and final year). The only element still missing is the required rate of return, which provides the mechanism whereby the investor can be compensated for the amount of risk incurred in an investment. Since we don't know for sure what the *future* cash flows will be, we should expect to earn a rate of return that reflects this uncertainty. Thus, the greater the risk, the more return we should expect to earn. The *required rate of return* is a part of the valuation process: It is the rate used, along with expected cash flows, to derive the intrinsic value of an investment.

Valuation Models

Certain valuation models, such as the so-called Graham and Dodd model, emphasize appropriate price/earnings multiples as a key element in the valuation process. Another approach that's popular with investors—and which is discussed in more detail in the Investor Insights box on pages 318–319—is the use of book value as a principal factor in finding undervalued stocks. In addition to these, there are still other models that use such variables as dividend yield, price/sales ratios, abnormally low P/E multiples, company size, and so on, as key elements in the decision-making process. Our discussion here will center on a model that is not only popular with a large segment of the investing public but also theoretically sound. It is derived from a procedure known as the dividend valuation model.

The Dividend Valuation Model

In the valuation process the intrinsic value of any investment equals the present value of the expected cash flow benefits. For common stock, this amounts to the cash dividends received each year plus the future sale price of the stock. Another way to view the cash flow benefits from common stock is to assume that the dividends will be received over an infinite time horizon—an assumption that is appropriate so long as the firm is considered a "going concern." Seen from this perspective, *the value of a share of stock is equal to the present value of all the future dividends it is expected to provide over an infinite time horizon.* Although by selling stock at a price above that originally paid, a stockholder can earn capital gains in addition to dividends, from a strictly theoretical point of view, what is really sold is the right to all remaining future dividends. Thus, just as the *current* value of a share of stock is a function of future dividends, the *future* price of the stock is also a function of future dividends. In this framework, the future price of the stock will rise or fall as the outlook for dividends (and the required rate of return) changes.

dividend valuation model
a model that values a share of stock on the basis of the future dividend stream it is expected to produce.

This approach, which holds that the value of a share of stock is a function of its future dividends, has come to be known as the **dividend valuation model.**

The simplest way to picture the dividend valuation model is to assume that you're dealing with a stock that has a fixed stream of dividends—in other words, dividends stay the same year-in, year-out, and they're expected to stay that way in the future. Under such conditions, the value of a zero-growth stock is simply *the capitalized value of its annual dividends.* To find the capitalized value, just divide annual dividends by the required rate of return, which, in effect, acts as the capitalization rate. For example, if a stock paid a (constant) dividend of $3 a share and you wanted to earn 10 percent on your investment, you would value the stock at $30 a share (i.e., $3/.10 = $30). As you can see, the only cash flow variable that's used in this valuation model is the fixed annual dividend. Since the annual dividend on this stock never changes, does that mean the price of the stock will never change? Absolutely not! For as the capitalization rate changes, so will the price of the stock. If the capitalization rate goes up (to, say, 15 percent), the price of the stock will fall to $20 ($3/.15). Although this may be a very simplified view of the valuation model, it's actually not as far-fetched as it may appear—for as we'll see in Chapter 10, this is basically the procedure used to price *preferred stocks* in the marketplace.

Rather than use no growth in dividends, the standard and more widely recognized version of the dividend valuation model assumes that dividends will grow over time at a specified rate. Under this variation of the model, the value of a share of stock is still considered to be a function of its future dividends, except that in this case, such dividends are expected to grow forever (to infinity) at a *constant* rate of growth, *g*. Accordingly, the value of a share of stock can be found as follows:

$$\text{value of a share of stock} = \frac{\text{next year's dividends}}{\text{required rate of return} - \text{constant rate of growth in divs.}}$$

$$= \frac{D_1}{k - g}$$

where:

D_1 = annual dividends expected to be paid *next* year (the first year in the forecast period).

k = the discount rate, or capitalization rate (which defines the required rate of return on the investment).

g = the annual rate of growth in dividends, which is expected to hold constant to infinity.

This model succinctly captures the essence of stock valuation: *Increase* the cash flow (through *D* or *g*) and/or *decrease* the required rate of return (*k*), and the value of the stock will *increase.* (This is precisely what happened in the big bull market of 1982–87, as profits rose and the required rate of return dropped with lower inflation.) As far as the cash flow is concerned, all that's required is some basic information about the stock's *current* level of dividends. For once a dividend growth rate, *g*, has been determined, we can find D_1 as: $D_0 (1 + g)$, where D_0 equals the actual

INVESTOR INSIGHTS

Picking Stocks by the Book

Investment fads come and go, but many successful investors still swear by one of the oldest and easiest ways to buy stocks.

Year in and year out, in bull markets and bear markets, they say, the best way to find undervalued companies and possible takeover candidates is to buy stocks that are selling below their book value.

"If I had to limit my stock selection to only one thing, I'd choose book value," says Charles Allmon, manager of Growth Stock Outlook Trust, Chevy Chase, Md. "I don't care if a company is selling dirty diapers or clean diapers. If the price is right, I'll buy it."

Book value is generally defined as a company's . . . assets minus its liabilities. Those who use the buy-below-book strategy typically focus on "tangible" book value. This excludes such intangibles as patents and good will, which is a monetary value commonly placed on things such as a reputation when one company acquires another.

A company's book value is usually less than its actual "breakup value," or what the company would bring if its assets were sold off separately. That's because for tax purposes "companies hire the smartest accountants to deflate assets and increase liabilities," says Mr. Allmon. . . .

But while buying below book has proved to be a successful strategy over the long term, it can also be a trap. Some stocks sell below book merely because they are out of favor, but others may be genuinely troubled. For example, [in November 1988] 227 of 1,550 New York Stock Exchange companies [were] selling below book, but many of these were selling at less than $5 a share and were having serious difficulties.

"A price below book value is a beginning tool in the hunt for bargain stocks, not an end in itself," says Mark Keller, vice president of securities research at A. G. Edwards. For example, he says, "If you buy a company that sells below book value yet has a high debt, it may never recover."

Some of the biggest proponents of buying below book are followers of Benjamin Graham, the late Columbia University professor generally considered the father of modern portfolio analysis. Successful investors such as Warren Buffet, chairman of Berkshire Hathaway Inc., and William Ruane of Sequoia Fund have credited much of their good fortune to the value investing advocated by Mr. Graham.

(current) level of dividends. Let's say that in the latest year Sweatmore Industries paid $5 a share in dividends; if we expect these dividends to grow at the rate of 10 percent a year, we can find next year's dividends as follows: $D_1 = D_0 (1 + g) = \$5 (1 + .10) = \$5 (1.10) = \$5.50$. The only other information we need is the capitalization rate, or required rate of return, k. Suffice it to say here that the less certain the cash flows and/or future growth rates (that is, the more risk involved), the higher the required rate of return should be. (Note also in the constant growth model that k must be greater than g in order for the model to be mathematically operative.) Many investors, particularly institutional ones, like to use this model, or a variation thereof, as the means of valuing shares of common stock.

In Mr. Graham's view, investors should concentrate on buying stocks below or close to their book value, or no more than 30% above that figure. "The greater the premium above the book value, the less certain the basis for determining intrinsic value, and the more this value depends on the changing moods and measurements of the stock market," Mr. Graham wrote in his 1949 book, "The Intelligent Investor."

Historically, the book value approach has worked out well. A prime example was steel company stocks in 1986. Battered by Japanese competition, Bethlehem Steel and Inland Steel appeared to have a gloomy future. Their stock prices plunged way below book. Analysts couldn't foresee how a change in their cost structure and a decline in the value of the dollar could make them competitive once again. Today they trade over book [and investors] who bought them when they were below book have done well. . . .

Investors who want to try the buy-below-book approach while confining themselves to large, well-capitalized companies have only a limited choice these days. Geraldine Weiss, editor of Investment Quality Trends, a La Jolla, Calif., newsletter, follows 350 blue-chip stocks that, among other things, pay dividends and have a credit rating of single-A or better from S&P. Recently, she found only 25 selling below book. In 1982, before the stock market exploded, Mrs. Weiss says, 50% of the companies in her service were priced below book; in 1974, at the bottom of the bear market, the vast majority were selling below book. . . .

Nonetheless, depending on the daily price fluctuations, such household name stocks as Merrill Lynch & Co., Aetna Life & Casualty, Chase Manhattan Corp., General Motors Corp., ITT Corp., McDonnell Douglas Corp. and Chrysler Corp. have recently [sold] below their book values. Several big utilities also end up on most lists.

"These stocks have a certain commonality," says Mr. Medcalf. "They are [all] in a mature industry with cyclical earnings like the auto industry, or they have a mediocre track record." . . .

Some auto stocks are selling below book because many analysts believe auto companies have passed the peak of their business and that their good years are behind them. . . . Insurance companies have been battered, too, even though their fundamentals look good. But to book value investors, all these "stories" add up to just one thing: the opportunity to earn a nice return on their money!

Source: Adapted from Earl C. Gottschalk, Jr. "Picking Stocks by the Book Is a Standby Some Swear By," *The Wall Street Journal*, November 3, 1988, pg. C1.

To see this dividend valuation model at work, let's consider a stock that currently pays an annual dividend of $1.75 a share. If, after some deliberation, you feel that dividends should grow at the rate of 8 percent a year and that the investment should carry a required rate of return of 12 percent, then we can use the dividend valuation model to price the stock. That is, given $D_0 = \$1.75$, $g = .08$, and $k = .12$, it follows that:

$$\frac{\text{value of a}}{\text{share of stock}} = \frac{D_0\,(1 + g)}{k - g} = \frac{\$1.75\,(1.08)}{.12 - .08} = \frac{\$1.89}{.04} = \underline{\underline{\$47.25}}$$

If the investor wants to earn 12 percent return on this investment, then according to

the constant growth dividend valuation model, she should pay no more than $47.25 a share for the stock.

Note that with this version of the dividend valuation model, *the price of the stock will increase over time* so long as k and g don't change. This occurs because the cash flow from the investment will increase with time as dividends grow. To see how this can happen, let's carry our example further; recall that $D_0 = \$1.75$, $g = 8\%$, $k = 12\%$, and based on this information we found the current value of the stock to be $47.25. Now look what happens to the price of this stock if k and g don't change:

Year	Dividend	Stock Price*
(Current Year) 0	$1.75	$47.25
1	$1.89	$51.00
2	$2.04	$55.00
3	$2.20	$59.50
4	$2.38	$64.25
5	$2.57	$69.50

*As determined by the dividend valuation model, given $g = .08$,
  $k = .12$, and D_0 = dividend level for any given year.

As can be seen in the above illustration, the price of the stock *in the future* can also be found by using the standard dividend valuation model; to do this, we simply redefine the appropriate level of dividends. For example, to find the price of the stock in year 3, we use the expected dividend in the third year, $2.20, and increase it by the factor $(1 + g)$; thus, the stock price in year $3 = D_3(1 + g)/k - g = \$2.20(1 + .08)/.12 - .08 = \$2.38/.04 = \$59.50$. Of course, if future expectations about k and/or g change, the *future price* of the stock will change accordingly; should that occur, an investor could then use this new information to decide whether or not to continue to hold the stock.

Although the constant growth dividend valuation model as presented above has many advantages, it also has some shortcomings, one of the most obvious of which is the fact that it does not allow for any changes in expected growth rates. To compensate for this, there are forms of the model that allow for *variable rates of growth* over time. Generally, these are two- or three-stage models that base the value of a stock on the present value of future cash flow streams. Essentially, a *variable growth dividend valuation model* derives a present value based on future dividends and the future price of the stock (which price is a function of all future dividends to infinity, and is found by using the constant growth dividend valuation model).

The variable growth approach to stock valuation is more compatible with the way most people invest. That is, unlike the underlying assumptions in the standard dividend valuation model (which employs an infinite holding period), most investors have a *finite* holding period that seldom exceeds 5 to 7 years. Under such circumstances, *the relevant cash flows are future dividends and the future selling price of the stock*. The valuation model we will employ below not only is based on

the present value of future dividends and other cash flows, but also is relatively easy to use, primarily because it assumes a *finite* holding period. In spite of the differences in holding period assumptions, this model is little more than an extension of the basic dividend valuation model. In fact, it can be shown mathematically that if you use the same basic assumptions, the present-value model will yield the *same* stock value as the constant growth dividend valuation model. The major advantage of the present-value model is that it is more flexible and a bit easier to understand and apply. There are four main elements to the model: (1) the stock's present market price, (2) its future price, (3) the level of future dividends, and (4) the required return on the investment. As we will see, the model gains much of its strength from the fact that it considers both risk and return in a convenient format, and recognizes the time value of money. If an investor has a short investment horizon—of one year or less—then holding period return should be used to assess the value of a stock; if a longer investment horizon is used, then the present-value–based model is appropriate. In *both* cases, value is based on the expected cash flows of the stock (dividends and future price) over a specified investment horizon.

 ## *Holding Period Return*

Holding period return (HPR) was first introduced in Chapter 5 and was shown to be useful whenever the investment horizon is one year or less. It is computed as follows:

$$HPR = \frac{\begin{array}{c}\text{future dividend}\\\text{receipts}\end{array} + \begin{array}{c}\text{future sale}\\\text{price of the stock}\end{array} - \begin{array}{c}\text{current purchase}\\\text{price of the stock}\end{array}}{\text{current purchase price of the stock}}$$

Holding period return provides a measure of the yield that will be realized *if* the actual performance of the stock lives up to its expectations. The holding period return for MarCor Industries, assuming that the stock can be purchased at its current market price of $31.50 and sold one year later at a price of $36.25, would be as follows:

$$HPR = \frac{\$.95 + \$36.25 - \$31.50}{\$31.50} = \frac{\$.95 + \$4.75}{\$31.50} = \underline{\underline{18.1\%}}$$

Note that although we do not use capital gains specifically in the valuation model, it is embedded in the formula and appears as the difference between the future selling price of the stock and its current purchase price; as it turns out. MarCor Industries should provide a capital gain of around $4.75 a share in the first year.

Required Rate of Return

required (or desired) rate of return
the return necessary to compensate an investor for the risk that's involved in an investment.

In the preceding example, we saw that if an investor had a one-year investment horizon, the holding period return on MarCor Industries would be 18.1 percent. That expected yield is, in effect, our standard of performance. To decide whether that is acceptable or not, it is necessary to formulate a **required (or desired) rate of return.** Generally speaking, the amount of return required by an investor should be related to the level of risk that must be assumed in order to generate that return. The

higher the amount of perceived risk, the greater the return potential that should be offered by the investment. As we saw in Chapter 5, this is basically the notion behind the *capital asset pricing model* (CAPM).

Recall that using the CAPM, we can define a stock's required return as:

$$\text{required rate of return} = \frac{\text{risk-free}}{\text{rate}} + \left[\frac{\text{stock's}}{\text{beta}} \times \left(\frac{\text{market}}{\text{return}} - \frac{\text{risk-free}}{\text{rate}} \right) \right]$$

The required input is readily available, as you can obtain a stock's beta from *Value Line* or S&P's *Stock Reports;* the risk-free rate is basically the average return on Treasury bills for the past year or so; and a good proxy for the market return is the average stock returns over the past 10 to 15 years (like the data reported in Table 6.1). In CAPM, it's felt that the risk of a stock is captured by its beta—for that reason, the required return on a stock will increase (or decrease) with increases (or decreases) in its beta. As an illustration of CAPM at work, consider a stock that has a beta of 1.50; given the risk-free rate is, say 6 percent and the market return is 15 percent, this stock would have a required return of:

$$\text{required return} = 6\% + [1.50 \times (15\% - 6\%)] = \underline{\underline{19.5\%}}$$

This return (let's call it 20%) can now be used in a stock valuation model to assess the investment merits of a share of stock.

As an alternative, or in conjunction with CAPM, we could take a more subjective approach to finding required return. For example, if our assessment of the historical performance of the company had uncovered wide swings in sales and earnings, we could conclude that MarCor's stock is subject to a good deal of business risk. Also important is market risk, as measured by a stock's beta. In a similar fashion, a valuable reference point in arriving at a measure of risk is the rate of return available on less risky, but competitive, investment vehicles. For example, if the rate of return on long-term Treasury bonds or high-grade corporate issues is at a certain level, we can use that benchmark as a starting point in defining our desired rate of return. That is, starting with yields on long-term, low-risk bonds, we can adjust such returns for the levels of business and market risks to which we believe the common stock is exposed.

To see how these elements make up the desired rate of return, consider once again the case of MarCor Industries. Assume it is now early 1990 and rates on high-grade corporate bonds are hovering around 10 percent. Given that our analysis thus far has indicated that the apparel industry and MarCor Industries in particular are subject to a substantial amount of business risk, we would want to adjust that figure upward—probably by around 4 or 5 points. In addition, with its beta of 1.50, we can conclude that the stock carries a good deal of market risk, and that we should increase our base rate of return even more—say, by another 5 points. Given our base (high-grade corporate bond) rate, along with our assessment of the stock's business and market risks, we conclude that an appropriate (desired) rate of return should be around 20 percent for an investment in MarCor Industries common stock. That is, starting from a base of 10 percent, we tack on 5 percent for the company's

added business risk and another 5 percent for the stock's market risk. Note that this figure (of 20 percent) is close to what we obtained with the CAPM, which shouldn't be all that surprising—for if they're carefully (and honestly) done, you'd expect the two procedures (CAPM and the subjective approach) to yield similar results. Using this 20 percent required rate of return, it is clear that a holding period return of 18.1 percent (as computed in the preceding section) is an *insufficient* yield. Although something close to 18 percent may not seem like a bad return—and indeed for many securities it may be more than sufficient—because of the perceived risk exposure, such a level of return is simply an inadequate reward in this case.

Deriving a Justified Price

Although holding period return is effective for assessing the investment merits of securities held for a period of one year or less, HPR should *not* be used with investment horizons that extend for longer periods. Lengthy holding periods mean that we have to introduce the time value of money and deal in terms of present value. A stock valuation model has been developed that conveniently captures the essential elements of expected risk and return, and does so in a present value context. The model is as follows:

$$\begin{array}{l}\text{present value of} \\ \text{a share of stock}\end{array} = \begin{array}{l}\text{present value of} \\ \text{future dividends}\end{array} + \begin{array}{l}\text{present value of the price of the} \\ \text{stock at date of sale}\end{array}$$

$$= (D_1 \times PVIF_1) + (D_2 \times PVIF_2) + \cdots + (D_N \times PVIF_N) + (SP_N \times PVIF_N)$$

where:

D_t = future annual dividend in year t

$PVIF_t$ = present-value interest factor, specified at the desired rate of return for the given year t (use the appropriate interest factor from the "single cash flow" table, Appendix B, Table B.3)

SP_N = estimated share price of the stock at date of sale, year N

N = number of years in the investment horizon

When used in this form, the present-value-based stock valuation model generates a *justified price* based on estimated returns to stockholders (future dividends and share-price behavior). Basically, this stock valuation model is derived from the variable growth dividend valuation model we discussed above. Note that the desired rate of return (and therefore risk) is built right into the model as it is included in the present-value interest factor. The equation above produces the present value of the stock, which represents the elusive intrinsic value we have been seeking. This intrinsic value represents the price we should be willing to pay for the stock given its expected dividend and price behavior, and assuming we want to realize a return that is equal to or greater than our required rate of return, as found by using CAPM or some other more subjective approach.

To see how this procedure works, consider once again the case of MarCor Industries. Let's return to our original three-year investment horizon. Given the forecasted annual dividends and share price from Table 8.3, along with a 20 percent

desired rate of return, we can see from the computations below that the present
value of MarCor is:

$$\begin{array}{ll}
\text{present value of a} \\
\text{share of MarCor stock}
\end{array} = \begin{array}{l}
(\$0.95 \times .833) + (\$1.10 \times .694) + (\$1.12 \times .579) \\
+(\$47.60 \times .579)
\end{array}$$

$$= \$0.79 + \$0.76 + \$0.65 + \$27.56$$

$$= \underline{\underline{\$29.76}}$$

In this case, a present value of $29.76 means that with the projected dividend and
share price behavior, we would realize our desired rate of return *only* if we were
able to buy the stock at around $29.75. Because MarCor Industries is currently
trading at $31.50, we would have to conclude that it is *not* (at the present time at
least) an attractive investment vehicle. For if we pay $31.50 for the stock—and our
dividend and price expectations hold up—we would fail to generate our desired rate
of return. MarCor Industries might look relatively appealing, but it simply does not
provide sufficient returns to enable us to realize a yield commensurate with our
perceived risk exposure.

Determining Approximate Yield

Sometimes investors find it more convenient to deal in terms of expected yield
rather than present worth or justified price. Fortunately, this is no problem, nor is it
necessary to sacrifice the present value dimension of the stock valuation model to
achieve such an end. For the approximate yield measure enables investors to find a
present-value-based rate of return from long-term transactions. This version of the
stock valuation model uses forecasted dividend and price behavior, along with the
current market price of the stock, to arrive at an approximate yield. This measure of
return, first introduced in Chapter 5, is determined as follows:

$$\begin{array}{l}
\text{approximate} \\
\text{yield}
\end{array} = \frac{\begin{array}{l}
\text{average} \\
\text{annual dividend} +
\end{array} \dfrac{\begin{array}{l}\text{future sale} \\ \text{price of the stock}\end{array} - \begin{array}{l}\text{current purchase} \\ \text{price of the stock}\end{array}}{\text{number of years in investment horizon}}}{\dfrac{\text{sales price of the stock} + \text{purchase price of the stock}}{2}}$$

The approximate yield formula is an indication of the fully compounded rate of
return available from a long-term investment. To see how it works, let's look once
more at MarCor Industries:

$$\text{approximate yield} = \frac{\$1.06 + \dfrac{\$47.60 - \$31.50}{3}}{\dfrac{\$47.60 + \$31.50}{2}}$$

$$= \frac{\$1.06 + \$5.37}{\$39.55} = \underline{\underline{16.3\%}}$$

We see that MarCor can be expected to yield an annual return of around 16.3
percent, assuming that the stock can be bought at $31.50, is held for three years

(during which time annual dividends will average out at about $1.06 per share), and then sold for $47.60 per share. Note that in this version of the stock valuation model, it is the *average* annual dividend that is used rather than the specific dividends. For MarCor Industries, dividends will average $1.06 per share over each of the next three years: ($0.95 + $1.10 + $1.12)/3 = $1.06. When compared to the 20 percent required rate of return, the 16.3 percent yield this investment offers is clearly inadequate!

Using Stock Valuation Measures in the Investment Decision

The security analysis process begins with economic and industry analysis and culminates in the determination of a stock's value according to one of the valuation models reviewed above. We can deal in expected yield, as in the case of holding period return and approximate yield measures, or in justified price, as in the case of the present worth of the stock. In any case, the standard of performance obtained can be used in the decision-making process to determine the investment merits of a particular stock.

If yield is used as the standard, it is compared to a desired rate of return to determine investment suitability: so long as the approximate yield (or HPR) is *equal to or greater than* the required rate of return, the stock should be considered worthwhile. This is so because the particular security promises to meet or exceed the minimum rate that has been stipulated, and in so doing will provide adequate compensation for the risk exposure embedded in the investment. Note especially that a security is considered acceptable even if its yield simply *equals* the required rate of return; this is rational to the extent that the security has met the minimum standards established.

If we determine the present worth of a stock, we will compare the computed justified price with its actual market price. So long as the actual market price of the issue is *equal to or less than* the justified price, it would be considered a worthwhile investment. Again, this is so because only under these conditions would we be able to realize the required rate of return we have stipulated for this particular security. But remember that although valuation models play an important part in the investment process, there is *absolutely no assurance* that the actual outcome will be even remotely similar to the forecasted behavior. The stock is still subject to economic, industry, company, and market risks that could well negate all the assumptions about the future. Security analysis and stock valuation models are used not to guarantee success, but to help investors better understand the return and risk dimensions of a proposed transaction.

TECHNICAL ANALYSIS

How many times have you turned on the TV and in the course of the day's news heard a reporter say, "The market was up 17½ points today" or "The market remained sluggish in a fairly light day of trading"? Such comments reflect the importance of the stock market itself. And rightly so; for as we will see, the market *is important* because of the role it plays in determining the price behavior of common stocks. In fact, some experts believe the market is so important that studying it

technical analysis
the study of the various forces at work in the marketplace and their effect on stock prices.

should be the major, if not the only, ingredient in the stock selection process. These experts argue that much of what is done in security analysis is useless because it is the market that matters and not individual companies. Others would argue that studying the stock market is only one element in the security analysis process and is useful in helping the investor time decisions. Analyzing the stock market is known as **technical analysis,** and it involves a study of the various forces at work in the marketplace itself. Here we will examine the major principles and components of technical analysis, as well as some of the techniques used to assess market behavior.

Principles of Market Analysis

Analyzing market behavior dates back to the 1800s, when there was no such thing as industry or company analysis. Detailed financial information simply was not made available to stockholders, let alone the general public. There were no industry figures, balance sheets, or income statements to study, no sales forecasts to make, and no earnings-per-share data or price/earnings multiples. About the only thing investors could study was the market itself. Some analysts used detailed charts in an attempt to monitor what large market operators were doing. These charts were intended to show when major buyers were moving into or out of particular stocks and to provide information that could be used to make profitable buy-and-sell decisions. The charts centered on stock price movements, because it was believed that these movements produced certain ''formations'' that indicated when the time was right to buy or sell a particular stock. The same principle is still applied today: Technical analysts argue that internal market factors, such as trading volume and price movements, often reveal the market's future direction before the cause is evident in financial statistics.

If the behavior of stock prices were completely independent of movements in the market, then market studies and technical analysis would be useless. But we have ample evidence that this is simply not the case; in fact, stock prices do tend to move with the market. Studies of stock betas have shown that, as a rule, anywhere from 20 to 50 percent of the price behavior of a stock can be traced to market forces. When the market is bullish, stock prices in general can be expected to behave accordingly; in contrast, when market participants turn bearish, most issues will feel the brunt to one extent or another. Stock prices, in essence, react to various supply and demand forces that are at work in the market: after all, it's the *demand* for securities and the *supply* of funds in the market that determines a bull or a bear market. So long as a given supply and demand relationship holds, the market will remain strong (or weak); when the balance begins to shift, however, future prices can be expected to change as the market itself changes. More than anything, technical analysis is intended to monitor the pulse of the supply and demand forces in the market, and to detect any shifts in this important relationship.

Measuring the Market

If assessing the market is a worthwhile endeavor, it follows that some sort of tool or measure is needed to do it. Charts are popular with some investors because they

provide a convenient visual summary of the behavior of the market and the price movements of individual stocks. An alternative approach involves the use of various types of market statistics. We will now examine some of the tools of technical analysis, by first considering some basic approaches to technical analysis, including technical indicators and the use of technical analysis, and then addressing the concept of charting.

Approaches to Technical Analysis

Technical analysis addresses those factors in the marketplace that operate in such a way as to have an effect on the price movements of stocks in general. Investment services, major brokerage houses, and popular financial media (like *Barron's*) provide technical information at little or no cost. Of the many approaches to technical analysis, several are particularly noteworthy: (1) the Dow theory, (2) trading action, (3) bellwether stocks, and (4) the technical condition of the market. Let's look at each in turn.

Dow theory
a technical approach that's based on the idea that the market's performance can be described by the long-term price trend in the DJIA, as confirmed by the Dow transportation averages.

The Dow Theory.   The **Dow theory** is based on the idea that it is the price trend in the overall market as a whole that is important. Named after Charles H. Dow, one of the founders of Dow Jones, this approach is supposed to signal the end of both bull and bear markets. Note that the theory does not indicate when a reversal will occur; rather, it is strictly an after-the-fact verification of what has already happened. It concentrates on the long-term trend in market behavior (known as the *primary trend*) and largely ignores day-to-day fluctuations or secondary movements. The Dow Jones industrial *and* transportation averages are used to assess the position of the market. Once a primary trend in the Dow Jones industrial average has been established, the market tends to move in that direction until the trend is canceled out by both the industrial and transportation averages. Known as *confirmation,* this crucial part of the Dow theory occurs when secondary movements in the industrial average are confirmed by secondary movements in the transportation average. When confirmation occurs, the market has changed from bull to bear, or vice versa, and a new primary trend is established. The key elements of the Dow theory are captured in Figure 8.1, on page 328. Observe that in this case, the bull market comes to an end at the point of confirmation—when *both* the industrial and transportation averages are dropping. The biggest drawbacks of the Dow theory are that it is an after-the-fact measure with *no* predictive power, and that the investor really does not know at any given point whether an existing primary trend has a long way to go or is just about to end.

Trading Action.   This approach to technical analysis concentrates on minor trading characteristics in the market. Daily trading activity over long periods of time (sometimes extending back a quarter century or more) is examined in detail to determine whether or not certain characteristics occur with a high degree of frequency. The results of such statistical analysis are a series of trading rules, some of which are a bit bizarre. For example, did you know that if the year starts out strong (that is, if January is a good month for the market), the chances are that it is going to

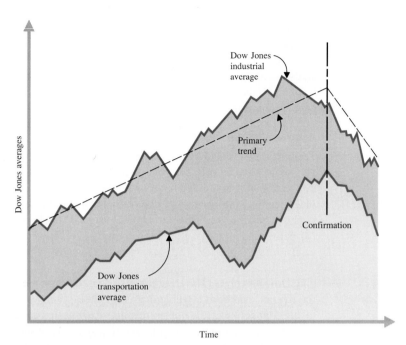

FIGURE 8.1 The Dow Theory in Operation.
Secondary movements (the sharp, short fluctuations in the Dow Jones industrial and transportation lines) are largely unimportant with the Dow theory; however, the primary trend in the DJIA, which is seen to remain on the upswing until a reversal is confirmed by the transportation average, is of key importance.

be a good year as well; that if the party in power wins the presidential election, it is also going to be a good year for the market; and that it is best to buy air conditioning stocks in October and sell the following March (this buy-and-sell strategy was found to be significantly more profitable over the long haul than buy-and-hold). A most unusual but *highly successful* market adage holds that if a team from the NFC (or one that was originally in the NFL, like Indianapolis or Pittsburgh) wins the Super Bowl, the market's in for a good year. Don't laugh; for whatever the reason—which no one seems to know—it's been correct for 20 out of the last 21 Super Bowls! Clearly, the trading action approach is based on the simple assumption that the market moves in cycles that have a tendency to repeat themselves. As a result, the contention is that what has happened in the past will probably happen repeatedly in the future.

bellwether stocks
stocks that are be-lieved to consistently reflect the state of the market; watched by technical analysts for shifts in market behavior.

Bellwether Stocks. There is a saying that "as GM goes, so goes the nation." Whether or not this is true today remains debatable, but to advocates of bellwether stocks, such an idea makes a lot of sense. That's because the stock of General Motors and a handful of others, like IBM, AT&T, and Procter & Gamble, are all considered **bellwether stocks**—stocks that are believed to consistently reflect the current state of the market. Actually, stocks that qualify as bellwether issues tend to slowly change over time—indeed, even today, there's a growing number of inves-

tors who feel IBM is no longer the bellwether issue it once was. Although the prices of bellwether stocks tend to move in a pattern that's close to the Dow, or some other major market index, the bellwether procedure itself is much more than a simple reflection of the current state of affairs in the market. For it is believed that bellwether stocks can also be used to determine shifts in market behavior. In particular, bellwether advocates hold that in a bull market, when a bellwether stock fails to hit a new yearly high for three or four months in a row, a market top is at hand; in a bear market, when the selected stock fails to hit a new low for three or four months, a market bottom is coming. Although there are many skeptics on Wall Street, the bellwether approach does seem to have some merit with respect to appraising the current state of the market.

Technical Condition of the Market. This approach is based on assessing several key elements of market behavior. For example, market prices are affected by such variables as the volume of trading, the amount of short selling, the buying and selling patterns of small investors (known as *odd-lot transactions*), and similar market forces. Normally, several of these indicators would be used together to assess the technical condition of the market. They may be used in an informal way, or more formally as a series of complex ratios and measures—like 200-day moving averages or buy-sell ratios. This is one of the more popular approaches to technical analysis and is often used with some other approach, such as trading action and/or bellwether stocks. We'll now examine several of the more popular technical indicators.

Technical Indicators

Technical indicators are used to assess the current state of the market, as well as the possibility of changes in direction. The idea is to stay abreast of those aspects that reflect supply and demand conditions, underlying price pressures, and the general state of the market. In essence, the premise is that the forces of supply and demand will be reflected in various price and volume patterns. Although there are many technical indicators, we will confine our discussion to several of the more popular and closely followed measures: (1) market volume; (2) breadth of the market; (3) short interest; (4) odd-lot trading; and (5) the confidence index.

Market Volume. Market volume is an obvious indicator of the amount of investor interest. Volume is a function of the supply of and demand for stocks and is indicative of underlying market strengths and weaknesses. The market is considered to be *strong* when volume goes up in a rising market or drops during market declines; in contrast, it is considered *weak* when volume rises during a decline or drops off during rallies. For instance, it would be considered strong if the Dow Jones industrial average went up by, say, 48 points while market volume was very heavy. Investor eagerness to buy or sell is felt to be captured by market volume figures. The financial press regularly publishes volume data, so investors can conveniently stay abreast of this important technical indicator; an example of this and other vital market information is given in Figure 8.2.

BARRON'S / **MARKET WEEK**

MARKET LABORATORY/STOCKS

World Stock Markets Indexes

	6/9/89 Close	Week's Change	– 1988 – '89 High	Low
Australia All-Ord.	1543.60	+ 19.20	1,657.80	1,117.70
Belgium Cash	6128.48	+ 24.50	6,128.48	3,608.35
Canada Composite	3802.41	+ 83.47	3,718.94	2,977.90
France Agefi	417.01	+ 1.70	417.846	251.30
Hong Kong Hang Seng	2268.00	– 407.38	3,285.10	2,223.56
Italy Milan	1062.00	+ 30.00	1,229.00	874.00
Japan Nikkei 225	33,639.98	– 27.44	34,191.62	21,217.04
Netherlands CBS-Shares	192.90	+ 2.10	N.A.	N.A.
Singapore Straits	1241.21	– 64.00	1310.02	833.60
Spain Madrid	314.52	+ 4.17	312.36	225.50
Sweden AffGen	1192.70	+ 13.80	1,178.90	N.A.
Switzerland CrSuisse	593.30	+ 21.30	591.80	466.60
U.K. FinTimes	1,775.70	– 326.90	2,103.40	1,349.00
W. Germany DAX	1,437.29	+ 17.58	1,419.71	931.18

Indexes are based on local currencies.

NYSE Half-Hourly Volume

Daily	Jun 5	6	7	8	9
9:30-10:00	22,490	29,390	31,200	30,410	30,370
10:00-10:30	16,500	15,280	21,510	20,430	17,790
10:30-11:00	13,100	14,210	18,970	17,910	18,530
11:00-11:30	12,260	12,920	16,760	18,120	16,430
11:30-12:00	11,660	13,640	13,760	14,080	10,630
12:00-12:30	9,880	10,510	16,120	25,510	9,390
12:30- 1:00	7,110	8,730	11,990	10,620	10,710
1:00- 1:30	6,370	11,880	11,520	9,820	8,030
1:30- 2:00	8,070	15,540	9,250	10,290	7,210
2:00- 2:30	9,120	13,070	11,580	11,960	9,220
2:30- 3:00	15,290	10,500	17,820	10,860	9,160
3:00- 3:30	10,230	10,920	13,960	15,300	11,560
3:30- 4:00	21,340	20,980	19,270	17,000	14,210

IFC Emerging Market Price Indexes*

Monthly Summary Report
April 1989
(Dec. 1984 = 100)

	Latest Month	Previous Month	% Chg. Last Mo.	% Chg. Year Ago
Latin Amer.	245.20	189.58	29.34	91.20
Argentina	155.81	171.09	–8.93	17.05
Brazil	198.30	134.25	47.71	125.47
Chile	542.07	509.16	6.46	48.75
Mexico	387.89	358.08	8.33	48.74
Asia	379.44	370.33	2.46	59.24
Korea	491.58	525.57	–6.47	53.77
Malaysia	128.45	119.08	7.87	28.51
Taiwan	1,049.84	987.09	6.36	84.63
Thailand	260.64	237.65	9.67	8.34

IFC Emerging Market Price Indexes*

Weekly Summary Report
June 2, 1989
(Dec. 1984 = 100)

	Latest Week	Previous Week	% Chg. Last Wk.	% Chg. 12/88
Latin Amer.	252.97	240.82	5.0	65.5
Argentina	230.52	188.82	22.1	29.6
Brazil	186.47	174.75	6.7	102.0
Chile	600.81	616.19	–2.5	31.5
Mexico	458.66	445.77	2.9	32.0
Asia	434.15	425.88	1.9	49.9
Korea	478.11	487.74	–2.0	–0.8
Malaysia	133.18	128.32	3.8	22.3
Taiwan	1,326.55	1,285.57	3.2	99.3
Thailand	282.82	267.33	5.8	29.6

*Calculated in U.S. $ to permit comparison using a sample of actively traded stocks in each market. Source: IFC-Emerging Markets Data Base, World Bank, Washington, D.C.

Shearson Lehman Hutton Auction-Rate Preferred Index

	Last Week	Prev. Week	Yr. Ago Week
Total Index	7.693	7.778	5.705
Bank	7.511	7.594	5.682
Industrial	7.593	7.671	5.577
Insurance	7.438	7.514	5.553
Financial	7.491	7.596	5.730
Thrift	8.145	8.223	5.809
Utility	7.575	7.675	5.709

Weighted average of last week's auctions: 7.472

The dividend rates on auction-preferred issues are set by auction each week, with each issue's reset every seven weeks. The dividends in the index are the weighted average yield of all public issues rated A or better.

Trading Activity

All numbers in thousands save percentages

	Last Week	Prev. Week	Year Ago
NYSE	950,677	766,971	1,022,080
30 Dow Inds	107,030	145,749	108,725
20 Dow Trans	20,755	18,528	21,600
15 Dow Utils	19,077	15,705	163,410
65 Dow Stks	146,862	179,982	293,735
Amex	71,280	53,030	65,100
OTC	736,782	539,151	695,031
NYSE 15 Most Active			
Average Price	54.68	49.73	34.23
% Tot Vol	12.57	12.40	25.23
Stock Offer ($000)	161,000	403,000	1,348,000
Barron's Low Price			
Stock Index	345.66	334.27	284.34
Vol (000)	9,015.0	5,513.6	2,682.4
% DJI Vol	6.70	4.74	2.47

Daily	Jun 5	6	7	8	9
NYSE 15 Most Active					
% Tot Vol	10.98	13.14	17.84	20.73	14.16
Avg. Price	40.12	44.89	49.71	47.88	54.16

Daily Stock Volume

	Jun 5	6	7	8	9
NYSE	163,420	187,570	213,710	249,769	173,240
30 Inds	18,807.6	21,523.6	20,965.4	25,427.7	20,306.2
20 Trans	3,273.6	4,473.1	3,761.8	4,472.5	4,774.2
15 Utils	2,702.9	3,942.9	4,055.2	4,407.1	3,968.8
65 Stks	24,784.1	29,939.6	28,782.4	34,307.3	29,049.2
Amex	12,590	13,500	17,030	15,100	13,060
OTC-NMS	101,802	106,729	115,667	115,350	95,085

Market Advance/Decline Volumes

	Jun 5	6	7	8	9
NY Up	38,346	120,904	140,286	108,080	74,230
NY Down	107,564	43,037	49,376	82,178	74,419
% (QCHA)	–.33	+.44	+.46	+.34	+.10
Amex Up	3,048	7,966	11,085	7,957	5,790
Amex Down	7,318	2,493	3,112	3,962	5,194
% (QACH)	–.17	+.25	+.63	+.32	+.33
OTC Up	33,519	56,414	82,120	64,052	50,463
OTC Down	66,574	44,033	34,880	51,081	46,844

Supplied by Quotron, "QCHA" is the average percentage movement for all exchange listed stocks each day on an unweighted basis.

NYSE Odd-Lot Trading

Shares in thousands

Daily	Jun 2	5	6	7	8
Purchases	483.8	353.4	433.9	463.8	338.6
Short Sales, z	32,309	47,233	56,226	10,193	47,240
Other sales	596.1	538.4	607.1	565.4	552.2
Total Sales	628.4	585.6	663.4	575.6	599.4

z-Actual sales.

Closing Tick

Daily	June 5	June 6	June 7	June 8	June 9
NYSE	–462	+ 414	+ 116	+ 138	+ 195
Amex	–91	+ 29	+ 24	+ 33	+ 41
DJIA	–6	+ 18	+ 18	+ 8	+ 16

The tick shows the number of stocks whose last change in price was an increase, less the number whose last change was a downtick. It is computed for the NYSE, the American Stock Exchange and for the stocks in the Dow Jones Industrial Average. High positive figures indicate a strong market near the close, while negative ones indicate a weak one.

Arms Index

Daily	June 5	6	7	8	9
NYSE	1.81	.57	.64	.98	.98
AMEX	2.09	.37	.42	.62	.86
NASDAQ	1.33	.72	.61	.90	.80

The Arms index, also known as the short term trading index, is the average volume of declining issues divided by the average volume of advancing issues. It is computed separately for the NYSE, the American Stock Exchange and Nasdaq. A figure of less than 1.0 indicates more action in rising stocks.

Weekly Volume By Markets In NYSE-Listed Stocks

Shares in thousands

	Last Week	Prev. Week	Year Ago
NYSE	950,677	766,971	1,022,080
Midwest	60,346	45,332	60,383
Pacific	36,508	27,164	28,336
NASDAQ	37,275	28,811	20,597
Phila.	16,866	12,406	13,994
Boston	18,985	14,329	11,575
Cincinnati	4,879	3,335	7,509
Instinet	1,774	1,216	1,317
Total	1,127,310	899,564	1,165,791

Large Block Transaction Summary

These are single trades of 100,000 shares and over, and 50,000 to 99,999 shares made each day. An uptick is at a price higher than the last previous trade. A downtick is at a price lower than the last previous trade.

NYSE		Up Ticks	Down Ticks	No Chg.	Totals
100,000 Shares and Over	June 5	23	30	28	81
	June 6	38	31	56	125
	June 7	38	29	68	135
	June 8	31	43	67	141
	June 9	15	25	33	73

		Up Ticks	Down Ticks	No Chg.	Totals
50,000-99,999 Shares	June 5	52	70	90	212
	June 6	56	58	135	249
	June 7	89	64	140	293
	June 8	70	69	148	287
	June 9	65	61	102	228

Other Market Indexes

Daily	Jun 5	6	7	8	9
NYSE Comp.	179.89	180.93	182.34	182.39	182.37
Ind.	215.90	217.19	218.59	218.54	218.57
Util.	87.17	87.83	89.99	88.88	88.65
Tran.	170.88	170.63	172.12	172.72	173.80
Fin.	153.54	154.02	155.31	155.98	156.14
Amex Index	359.58	360.84	364.41	366.00	366.16
S&P500Index	322.03	324.24	326.95	326.75	326.69
Ind.	368.52	371.10	373.82	373.52	373.53
Trans.	265.38	265.09	266.67	266.49	267.98
Utils.	132.45	133.56	135.53	135.18	134.78
Fins.	30.75	30.93	31.22	31.34	31.35
OTCComp.	447.84	447.96	452.20	453.99	453.65
Ind.	441.80	441.37	443.93	444.67	444.35
Insur.	494.78	495.92	501.42	506.61	508.26
Banks	474.63	475.34	476.63	479.20	478.31
NMSComp.	195.48	195.54	197.87	198.21	198.05
Ind.	172.96	172.78	173.78	174.05	173.91
ValueLine(A)	286.02	286.81	288.50	289.31	289.22
ValueLine(G)	264.61	265.25	266.74	267.44	267.31
Wilshire5000	3131.28	3197.95	3221.44	3227.26	3225.92
Russell1000	170.84	171.77	173.26	173.30	173.22
Russell2000	172.37	172.17	172.95	173.23	173.37
Russell3000	183.51	184.42	185.96	186.01	185.95
IMIADRIndex	300.30	299.64	302.11	302.04	298.02

(A)-Arithmetic Index. (G)-Geometric Index.

Market and Volume Reports

All numbers in thousands save percentages and ratios

New York Stock Exchange

	Week May 26	Prev. Week	Year-Ago Week
TOTAL VOLUME			
Weekly	852,327.8	969,064.9	680,552.7
Average Daily	170,465.5	193,813.0	136,110.5
MEMBER ACTIVITY			
Specialists Buys (#†)	79,096.0	86,010.3	53,106.6
Specialists Sales (#†)	78,941.6	86,929.8	54,790.7
Floor Traders Buys	14.0	12.2	44.9
Floor Traders Sales	19.5	22.2	31.9
Other Member Buys (#)	133,801.9	151,592.0	89,353.4
Other Member Sales (#)	118,664.5	146,712.0	98,790.8
Total Member Buys	212,911.9	237,614.5	142,505.0
Total Member Sales	197,625.6	233,664.0	153,613.4
Net Member Buy/Sell	+15,286.3	+3,950.4	–11,108.4
Member volume as % of total	24.08	24.32	21.76
SHORT SALES			
Total	55,240.2	73,459.0	50,435.2
Public	20,354.8	23,350.5	16,168.4
Members Total	34,885.4	50,108.5	34,266.7
Specialists	23,078.4	31,477.3	16,566.2
Floor Traders	9.5	5.0	0
Other Members	11,797.6	18,626.2	17,700.5
Specialists/Public Short Ratio	1.1	1.3	1.0
Members/Public Short Ratio	1.7	2.1	2.1

Customers Odd-Lot Activity

NYSE	Week May 26	Prev. Week	Year-Ago Week
Purchases, shares	2,762.2	3,213.4	1,315.0
Purchases $	114,579.7	132,300.5	45,154.1
Sales, shares	3,929.8	4,419.8	3,223.0
Sales $	154,076.1	172,498.1	125,719.6
Short Sales, shares	60.3	66.0	224.3
Short Sales $	2,559.1	2,848.4	8,455.6

American Stock Exchange

	Week May 26	Prev. Week	Year-Ago Week
TOTAL VOLUME			
Weekly	58,720.2	63,720.1	38,720.7
Average Daily	11,744.0	12,744.0	7,744.1
MEMBER ACTIVITY			
Specialists Buys (#†)	6,272.8	7,108.7	4,205.1
Specialists Sales (#†)	6,651.1	7,381.5	4,467.5
Floor Traders Buys	102.1	89.1	43.7
Floor Traders Sales	94.6	86.2	48.5
Other Member Buys (#)	4,428.4	2,984.5	2,301.7
Other Member Sales (#)	4,509.8	4,487.3	2,813.2
Total Member Buys	10,803.3	10,182.3	6,550.8
Total Member Sales	11,255.5	11,955.0	7,329.3
Net Member Buy/Sell	–425.2	–1,772.7	–778.5
Member volume as % of total	18.78	17.37	17.92
SHORT SALES			
Total	1,199.1	1,252.0	866.3
Public	621.7	712.6	455.8
Member Total	577.3	539.4	410.5
Specialists	56.9	80.6	41.1
Floor Traders	50.4	51.9	16.6
Other Members	470.0	406.9	352.8
Specialists/Public Short Ratio	0.1	0.1	0.1
Members/Public Short Ratio	0.9	0.8	0.9

Customers Odd-Lot Activity

AMEX	Week May 26	Prev. Week	Year-Ago Week
Purchases, shares	93.0	101.2	60.3
Sales, shares	179.8	201.3	119.2

#Includes transactions effected by members acting as Registered Competitive Market-Makers. †Including offsetting round-lot transactions arising from odd-lot dealer activity by specialists and other members. w-Shares and warrants.

FIGURE 8.2 Some Market Statistics.
A variety of information is available about market volume, odd-lot trading, price/earning ratios, the confidence index, and market averages. (*Source: Barron's,* June 12, 1989.)

Breadth of the Market. Each trading day, some stocks go up in price and others go down; in market terminology, some stocks *advance* and others *decline*. The breadth of the market indicator deals with these advances and declines. The idea behind it is actually quite simple: so long as the number of stocks that advance in price on a given day exceeds the number that decline, the market is considered strong. Of course, the extent of that strength depends on the spread between the number of advances and declines. For example, if the spread narrows such that the number of declines starts to approach the number of advances, market strength is said to be deteriorating. In a similar fashion, the market is considered weak when the number of declines repeatedly exceeds the number of advances. The principle behind this indicator is that the number of advances and declines reflects the under-lying sentiment of investors; when the mood is optimistic, for example, look for advances to outnumber declines. Again, information on advances and declines is published daily in the financial press.

Short Interest. Investors will sometimes sell a stock short—that is, they will sell borrowed stock in anticipation of a market decline. The number of stocks sold short in the market at any given point in time is known as the **short interest;** the more stocks that are sold short, the higher the short interest. Since all short sales must eventually be "covered" (the borrowed shares must be returned), a short sale in effect ensures future demand for the stock. Thus, when the level of short interest becomes relatively high by historical standards, the situation is viewed optimistic-ally. The logic is that as shares are bought back to cover outstanding short sales, the additional demand will push prices up. The amount of short interest on the NYSE, AMEX, and NASDAQ's National Market is published monthly in *The Wall Street Journal* and *Barron's*. Keeping track of the level of short interest can indicate future market demand, but it can also reveal *present* market optimism or pessimism. Short selling is usually done by knowledgeable investors, and it is felt that a significant buildup or decline in the level of short interest may reveal the sentiment of suppos-edly sophisticated investors about the current state of the market. For example, a significant shift upward in short interest has pessimistic overtones concerning the *current* state of the market, even though it may be an optimistic signal with regard to *future* levels of demand.

short interest
the number of stocks sold short in the market at any given time; a technical in-dicator believed to indicate future mar-ket demand.

Odd-Lot Trading. There is a rather cynical saying on Wall Street that suggests that the best thing to do is just the opposite of whatever the small investor is doing. The reasoning behind this is that the small investor is notoriously wrong and does a horrible job of timing investment decisions: The investing public usually does not come into the market in force until after a bull market has pretty much run its course, and does not get out until late in a bear market. Whether or not this view is valid is debatable, but it is the premise behind a widely followed technical indicator and is the basis for the **theory of contrary opinion.** This theory uses the amount and type of odd-lot trading as an indicator of the current state of the market and pending changes. Because many individual investors deal in small transactions of less than 100 shares, the combined sentiments of this type of investor are suppos-edly captured in the odd-lot figures. The idea is to see what odd-lot investors are

theory of contrary opinion
a technical indicator that uses the amount and type of odd-lot trading as an indica-tor of the current state of the market and pending changes.

doing "on balance." So long as there is little or no difference in the spread between the volume of odd-lot purchases and sales, we can conclude that the market will probably continue pretty much along its current line (either up or down). But when the balance of odd-lot purchases and sales begins to change dramatically, it may be a signal that a bull or bear market is about to end. For example, if the amount of odd-lot purchases starts to exceed odd-lot sales by an ever-widening margin, it may suggest that speculation on the part of small investors is starting to get out of control—an ominous signal that the final stages of a bull market may be at hand.

confidence index
a ratio of the average yield on high-grade corporate bonds to the average yield on low-grade corporate bonds; a technical indicator based on the theory that market trends usually appear in the bond market before they do in the stock market.

Confidence Index. Another measure that attempts to capture the sentiment of market participants is the **confidence index,** which, unlike other technical measures of the stock market, deals with *bond* returns. Computed and published weekly in *Barron's,* the confidence index is a ratio of the average yield on high-grade corporate bonds to the average yield on low-grade corporate bonds. The theory is that the trend of "smart money" is usually revealed in the bond market before it shows up in the stock market. Although low-rated bonds provide higher yields than high-grade issues, the logic is that the spread in yields between these two types of obligations will change over time as the amount of optimism or pessimism in the market outlook changes. Thus, a sustained rise in the confidence index suggests an increase in investor confidence and a stronger stock market; a drop in the index portends a softer tone.

Using Technical Analysis

Investors have a wide range of choices with respect to technical analysis. They can use the charts and complex ratios of the technical analysts or follow a more informal approach and use technical analysis just to get a general sense of the market. Presumably, in the latter case, it's not market behavior *per se* that is important as much as the implications such market behavior can have on the price performance of a particular common stock. Thus, technical analysis might be used in conjunction with fundamental analysis to determine the proper time to add a particular investment candidate to one's portfolio. Some investors and professional money managers, in fact, look at the technical side of a stock *before* doing any fundamental analysis. If the stock is found to be technically sound, then they'll spend the time to look at its fundamentals; if not, they'll look for another stock. For these investors, the concerns of technical analysis are still the same: *Do the technical factors indicate that this might be a good stock to buy?*

charting
the activity of charting price behavior and other market information, and then using the patterns that these charts form to make investment decisions.

Most investors rely on published sources, such as that depicted in Figure 8.3, to obtain necessary technical insights, and they often find it helpful to use several different approaches. For example, an investor might follow a favorite bellwether stock, such as IBM or AT&T, and at the same time keep track of information on market volume and breadth of the market. This is information that is readily available and is a low-cost way of staying abreast of the market.

Charting

Charting is perhaps the best-known activity of the technical analyst. Technicians—analysts who believe supply-and-demand forces establish stock prices—use various

Donald Kimsey, First Vice President, Senior Market Analyst
Market Analysis Group

The Strategist

One might well ask what the stock market can do for an encore after rising some 26% in calendar 1985. Over the past 40 months, the New York Stock Exchange Composite has risen better than 100% and most market pundits are projecting higher levels to come. We would like to join in the seasonal game of yearly forecasting, but we confess a lack of strong conviction as to how far the various indexes can go. While the advance begun early last October exceeded most market seers' expectations, our own included, there are no serious signs that uptrend has fully run its course.

Gauging from the price action of last year's leading groups, there is the potential for rotation that could well lead to choppy movement of the broader based indexes during the first quarter. We expect to see funds shifted from extended areas such as drugs, insurance, publishing and specialty retailers into laggard cyclicals such as housing, as well as the still-slothful brokerage stocks and semiconductors. As strong as the market has been, it has been quite selective in its emphasis. Secondary stocks continue to lag, but are showing signs of revival. In order for the lower tier to fully emerge, however, public investors and traders need to become more enthusiastic. We would expect some pickup in public participation during the normal reinvestment period of early January.

Tactically, we continue to stress individual laggards, while establishing at least partial profits in extended issues. For that reason, our Group Review on pages 6 & 7 looks at six housing stocks with technical appeal. In addition, Avnet (AVT 34) was added to the Model Portfolio. Other issues on that list that are still in buy areas are: Allied Signal (ALD 47), Baxter Travenol (BAX 15⅝), Colgate (CL 32), IT&T (ITT 38), Motorola (MOT 38½) and Nalco Chemical (NLC 26).

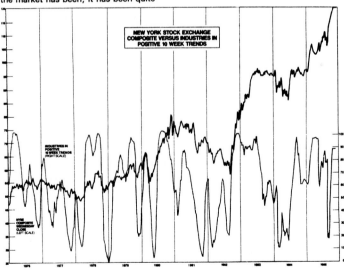

FIGURE 8.3 A Technical Report About the Market.
Technical reports, like this one, are often prepared weekly and contain valuable information about the market in general, as well as insights about stocks or stock groups that hold promise in the emerging market environment. (*Source:* Dean Witter Reynolds.)

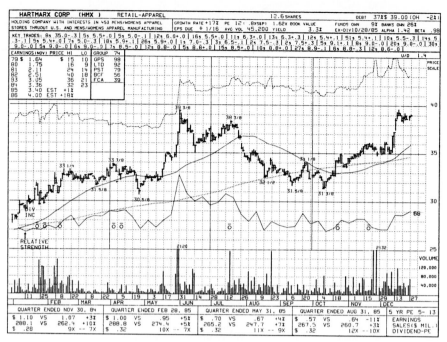

FIGURE 8.4   A Stock Chart.
This chart for Hartmarx Corporation contains information about the daily price behavior of
the stock, a popular technical measure (the 200-day moving average) that shows the long-
range trend in price, the stock's relative strength, its trading volume, and several other pieces
of supplementary data. (*Source:* William O'Neil & Co., Inc., *NYSE/OTC Daily Graphs.*)

types of charts to plot the behavior of everything from the Dow Jones industrial
average to the share-price movements of individual listed and OTC stocks. Also,
just about every kind of technical indicator is charted in one form or another. Figure
8.4 shows a typical stock chart; in this case the price behavior of Hartmarx Corp.
(formerly Hart Schaffner & Marx) has been plotted, along with a variety of supplementary information. Charts are popular because they provide a visual summary of
activity over time, and perhaps more important, because, in the eyes of technicians
at least, they contain valuable information about developing trends and the future
behavior of the market and/or individual stocks. Chartists believe price patterns
evolve into *chart formations* that provide signals about the future course of the
market or a stock. We will now briefly review the practice of charting, including
popular types of charts, chart formations, and investor uses of charts.

bar chart
the simplest kind of
chart on which share
price is plotted on
the vertical axis and
time on the horizon-
tal axis; stock prices
are recorded as ver-
tical bars showing
high, low, and clos-
ing prices.

Bar Charts

The simplest and probably most widely used type of chart is the **bar chart.** Market
or share prices are plotted on the vertical axis, and time on the horizontal axis. This
type of chart derives its name from the fact that prices are recorded as vertical bars
that depict high, low, and closing prices. A typical bar chart is illustrated in Figure

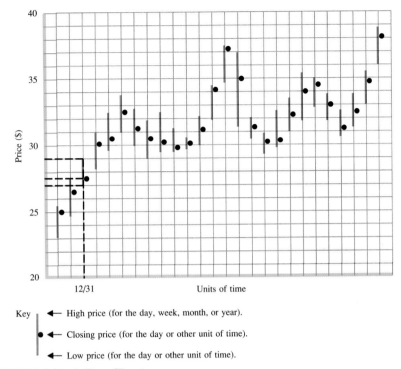

Key

◄— High price (for the day, week, month, or year).

◄— Closing price (for the day or other unit of time).

◄— Low price (for the day or other unit of time).

FIGURE 8.5 A Bar Chart.
Bar charts are widely used to track stock prices, market averages, and numerous other technical measures.

8.5; note that on 12/31, this particular stock had a high price of 29, a low of 27, and closed at 27½. Because these charts contain a time element, technicians will frequently plot a variety of other pertinent information on them; for example, volume is often put at the base of most bar charts (see the Hartmarx chart in Figure 8.4).

Point-and-Figure Charts

point-and-figure charts
charts used to keep track of emerging price patterns by plotting significant price changes with Xs and Os but with no time dimension used.

These charts are used strictly to keep track of emerging price patterns. Because there is no time dimension on **point-and-figure charts,** they are *not* used for plotting technical measures. In addition to the time feature, point-and-figure charts are unique in two other ways: first, only *significant* price changes are recorded on these charts (that is, prices have to move by a certain minimum amount—usually at least a point or two—before a new price level is recognized); and second, price reversals show up only after a predetermined change in direction occurs. Usually only closing prices are charted, though some point-and-figure charts use all price changes during the day. An *X* is used to denote an increase in price, and an *O* a decrease. Figure 8.6 shows a common point-and-figure chart; in this case, the chart employs a 2-point box, which means that the stock must move by a minimum of 2 points before any changes are recorded. The chart could cover a span of one year or less (if the stock

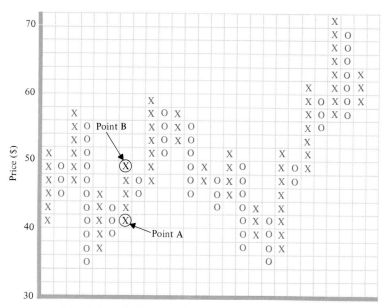

FIGURE 8.6 A Point-and-Figure Chart.
Point-and-figure charts are unusual because they have no time dimension; rather, a column of
Xs is used to reflect a general upward drift in prices and a column of Os is used when prices
are drifting downward.

is highly active), or it could cover a number of years (if the stock is not very active,
the chart could reflect price movements over, say, the past three to five years). As a
rule, low-priced stocks will be charted with 1-point boxes, moderately priced shares
will use increments of 2 to 3 points, and high-priced securities will appear on charts
with 3- to 5-point boxes.

Here is how they work. Suppose we are at point A on the chart in Figure 8.6,
where the stock has been hovering around the $40–$41 mark for some time. Assume, however, that it just closed at 42⅛; because the minimum 2-point movement
has been met, the chartist would place an X in the box immediately *above* point A.
The chartist would remain with this new box as long as the price moved (up or
down) within the 2-point range of 42 to 43⅞. Thus, although the chartist follows
daily prices, a new entry is made on the chart only after the price has changed by a
certain minimum amount and moved into a new 2-point box. We see that from point
A, the price generally moved up over time to nearly $50 a share. At that point
(indicated as point B on the chart), things began to change as a reversal set in. That
is, the price of the stock began to drift downward and in time moved out of the
48–50 box. This reversal prompts the chartist to change columns and symbols: He
moves one column to the right and records the new price level with an O in the
46–48 box. The chartist will continue to use the O as long as the stock continues to
close on a generally lower note.

Chart Formations

The information that charts supposedly contain about the future course of the market (or a stock) is revealed in *chart formations*. That is, in response to certain supply and demand forces, chartists believe that emerging price patterns will result in various types of formations which historically have indicated that certain types of behavior are imminent. If you know how to interpret charts (which, by the way, is no easy task), you can see formations building and will know how to recognize buy and sell signals. As the following list reveals, chart formations are often given some pretty exotic names:

Head-and-shoulders	Broadening top
Double top	Dormant bottom
Triple bottom	Ascending triangle
Diamond	Exhaustion gap
Falling wedge	Island reversal
Pennant	Trend channel
Scallop and saucer	Complex top

Figure 8.7, on the following page, shows six popular formations. The patterns form "support levels" and "resistance lines" that, when combined with the basic formations, yield buy and sell signals. Panel A is an example of a *buy* signal, which occurs when prices break out above a resistance line after a particular pattern has been formed; in contrast, when prices break out below a support level, as they do at the end of the formation in panel B, a *sell* signal is said to occur. Supposedly, a sell signal means everything is in place for a major drop in the market (or in the price of a share of stock), and a buy signal indicates that the opposite is about to occur. Unfortunately, one of the major problems of charting is that the formations rarely appear as neatly and cleanly as those in Figure 8.7; rather, their identification and interpretation often require considerable imagination on the part of the chartist.

Investor Uses

Charts are nothing more than tools used by market analysts and technicians to assess conditions in the market and/or the price behavior of individual stocks. Unlike other types of technical measures, charting is seldom done on an informal basis; you either chart because you believe in its value, or you don't use it at all. A chart by itself tells you little more than where the market or a stock has been. But to a chartist, those price patterns yield formations that, along with things like resistance lines, support levels, and breakouts, tell him or her what to expect in the future. Chartists believe that history repeats itself, so they study the historical reactions of stocks (or the market) to various formations and devise trading rules based on these observations. It makes no difference to chartists whether they are following the market or an individual stock, because it is the formation that matters, not the issue being plotted. The value of charts lies in knowing how to "read" them and how to respond to the signals they supposedly give about the future. There is a long-stand-

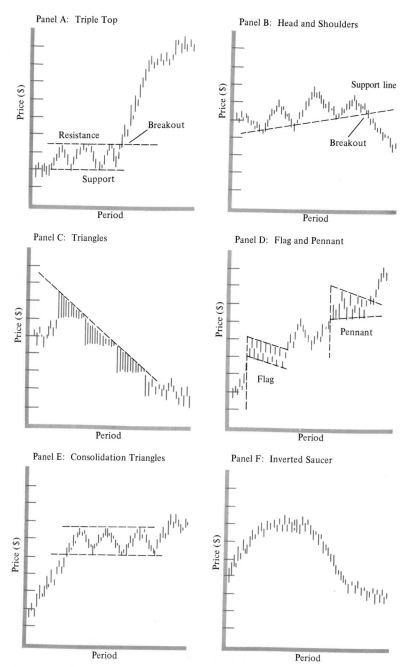

FIGURE 8.7 Some Popular Chart Formations.
To chartists, each of these formations has meaning about the future course of events.

ing debate on Wall Street (some would call it a feud) regarding the merits of charting; although it may be scoffed at by a large segment of those following the market, to avid chartists, charting is no laughing matter.

One Final Point About Investing in Stocks

Keeping track of your investment holdings is an essential part of investing in stocks. For just as you need investment objectives to provide direction to your stock selections, so too do you need to keep track of your stock holdings in order to monitor their performance. We'll discuss the issue of monitoring your investments in detail in Chapter 17; suffice it to say at this point that you can't just buy stocks and then put everything on automatic pilot—most equity investments are simply too risky for that sort of thing. Instead, you have to keep close tabs on how your investments have performed over time, and whether or not they've lived up to expectations. After all, investments sometimes fail to perform the way you'd like them to, in which case, it may be time to *sell* the securities and put the money elsewhere. We have said a lot about *buying* stocks, about how fundamental and technical analysis can be used to find attractive investment candidates, but the fact is, knowing when to sell and when to hold can also have a significant impact on the amount of return you're able to generate from your capital. Indeed, with most securities, it's just as important to know when to say ''bye'' as it is to say ''buy.'' The Investor Insights box, on pages 340–341, provides some suggestions on how to determine whether the time is right for selling a stock.

RANDOM WALKS AND EFFICIENT MARKETS

random walk hypothesis
the theory that stock price movements are unpredictable and, thus, there's really little way of knowing where future prices are headed.

If a drunk were abandoned in an open field at night, where would you begin to search for him the next morning? The answer, of course, is the spot where the drunk was left the night before. To some analysts, stock prices seem to wander about in a similar fashion. Observations of such erratic movements have led to a body of evidence called the **random walk hypothesis.** Its followers believe that price movements are unpredictable and that as a result, security analysis will not help to predict future behavior. This obviously has serious implications for much of what we have discussed in the last two chapters.

A Brief Historical Overview

efficient markets
the theory that the market price of securities always fully reflects available information and therefore it is difficult, if not impossible, to consistently outperform the market by picking ''undervalued'' stocks.

To describe stock prices as a random walk suggests that price movements cannot be expected to follow any type of pattern; or put another way, that price movements are independent of one another. In order to find a theory for such behavior, researchers developed the concept of **efficient markets.** Basically, the idea behind an efficient market is that the market price of securities always fully reflects available information and therefore it is difficult, if not impossible, to consistently outperform the market by picking ''undervalued'' stocks.

Random Walks

The first evidence of random price movements dates back to the early 1900s. During that period, statisticians interested in random processes noted that commodity

INVESTOR INSIGHTS

When to Sell a Stock

Knowing when to sell a stock (or any other investment for that matter) is one of the toughest parts of investing. Too often an investor loses sight of the fact that what is bought will probably also have to be sold at some time in the future—and if things don't work out as planned, the time to sell might be sooner than expected. Sell too soon and you may miss profits; sell too late and you may watch your profits disappear. The decision to sell is seldom an easy one. In contrast, the refusal to sell—be it due to greed, stubbornness, fear, or inattention—is often the undoing of many an investor.

Obviously, you shouldn't cash in every time your stock moves a few points: commissions and taxes can eat you alive. Nor should you panic in the face of a sharp market drop and sell everything. Rather, the best course of action is to pay attention to your stock and to the events that can affect it. Judge each company in which you *hold* stock just as carefully as you would judge a company in which you are considering investing. Based on current prices, earnings, and prospects, would you buy the shares you now own? If the answer is no, you probably should consider selling! As a general rule, *you should continue to hold a stock as long as you can't earn a better risk-adjusted rate of return by putting your money somewhere else.*

Most investment professionals recommend preplanned strategies for taking profits and cutting losses. Unfortunately, the question of when to sell a stock often comes down to an investor's emotional stamina and investment horizon. Most individual investors just aren't disciplined enough to set up a strategy and stick with it in good *and* bad markets. To help you make that tough decision about when to sell a stock, you should keep track of the stock's fundamentals, watch dividends, and set a target.

- *Follow the Fundamentals.* Whether you own stock in IBM, a major utility or an obscure over-the-counter venture, you need to follow the corporation's prospects, its earnings progress, and its business success as reflected in market share, sales growth, and profit margin. These and other basics are called *fundamentals*. How do you keep abreast of such matters? Company documents, news stories, research updates from

prices seemed to follow a "fair game" pattern; that is, prices seemed to move up and down randomly, giving no advantage to any particular trading strategy. Although a few studies appeared in the 1930s, thorough examination of the randomness in stock prices did not begin in earnest until 1959. From that point on, particularly through the decade of the 1960s, the random walk issue has become one of the most keenly debated topics in stock market literature. Some rather ingenious tests, aided by the development of high-speed computers, have compiled convincing evidence that stock prices do come very close to a random walk.

Efficient Markets

Given the extensive random walk evidence, market researchers were faced with another question: What sort of market would produce prices that seem to fluctuate

brokerage houses, and investment newsletters are obvious sources. Your job is to pay close enough attention to be aware of developments that could bode ill for your investment. If the fundamentals start to weaken, it's time to review your position in the stock.

- *Watch the Dividend.* Whether or not you're investing in a company for current income, the security of its dividends is important to any stock's prospects. A dividend cut or signs that the dividend is "in trouble"—meaning that analysts or creditors are quoted somewhere as saying they don't think the company can maintain its payout to shareholders—can undermine the stock price. Although the most dramatic examples of that are found among electric companies that courted financial ruin with bungled nuclear plants, such as General Public Utilities, dividend cuts in troubled heavy industries have also delivered a double whammy to shareholders: less income and falling stock prices.

- *Set a Target.* Many investors find it helpful to set specific price targets. Such guidelines can prompt you to clinch gains before they wither or to dump losers before the damage becomes unmanageable. If you're basically a buy-and-hold investor and your key concern is loss prevention, you don't have to get involved with the intricacies of the technicians' trade. You can take the simpler step of setting a "mental sell level." Watch the quotations daily if you can, and sell any stock that hits your mental sell level. One logical place to set this, given the market's propensity to make higher highs followed by higher lows, is at or near the place where the stock peaked prior to the drop that preceded the rise you're currently enjoying. Your broker can provide a chart mapping the stock's trading trend. Once you've reached your objective, take the money and run. If your price target is met, you ought to sell some or all of your stock. If the goals you've set for your stock are ultraconservative, you may miss some gains, but that's better than holding on too long and falling victim to the Wall Street axiom, "Bulls make money, bears make money, pigs get slaughtered."

Source: Reprinted with permission of *Changing Times* Magazine, © Kiplinger Washington Editors, Inc., "When to *Sell* That Stock," April 1986.

randomly? Such behavior could be the result of investors who are irrational and make investment decisions on whim. But it has been argued much more convincingly that investors are not irrational at all; rather, random price movements simply reflect *a highly competitive market.* Investors, searching for stock market profits, compete vigorously for new information and do extremely thorough analysis. This very competition holds security prices close to their correct level. It is not random behavior on the part of investors, but *random events,* such as labor strikes, shifts in the economy, and changes in product demand, that cause stock prices to change in response to the new information. Swift reaction by investors to this new information causes prices to adjust quickly, and in a manner that reflects the randomness of the arrival of new information. It is, in fact, keen competition among investors and the rapid evaluation of new information that causes stock prices to shift to new levels.

Possible Implications

The concept of an efficient market holds serious implications for investors. In particular, it could have considerable bearing on traditional security analysis and stock valuation procedures, and on the way stocks are selected for investment. There are, in fact, some who contend that rather than trying to beat the market, investors should spend less time analyzing securities and more time on such matters as the reduction of taxes and transaction costs, the elimination of unnecessary risk, and the construction of a widely diversified portfolio that is compatible with the investor's risk temperament. Make no mistake about it, *even in an efficient market there are all sorts of return opportunities available*. But to proponents of efficient markets, the only way to increase returns is to invest in a portfolio of higher-risk securities.

For Technical Analysis

The most serious challenge the random walk evidence presents is to technical analysis. If price fluctuations are purely random, charts of past prices are not likely to produce significant trading profits. In a highly efficient market, shifts in supply and demand occur so rapidly that technical indicators simply measure after-the-fact events, with no implications for the future. If markets are less than perfectly efficient, however, information may be absorbed slowly, producing gradual shifts in supply and demand conditions and therefore profit opportunities for those who recognize the shifts early. Although the great bulk of evidence supports a random walk, many investors follow a technical approach because they believe it improves their investment results.

For Fundamental Analysis

Many strict fundamental analysts were at first pleased by the random walk attack on technical analysis. Further development of the efficient markets concept, however, was not so well received. For in an efficient market, it's argued that prices react so quickly to new information that not even security analysis will enable investors to realize consistently superior returns on their investments. Because of the extreme competition among investors, security prices are seldom far above or below their justified levels, and fundamental analysis thus loses much of its value. The challenge is not that fundamental analysis is poorly done; to the contrary, it is done all too well! As a result, so many investors, competing so vigorously for profit opportunities, simply eliminate the opportunities before other investors can capitalize upon them.

So Who Is Right?

Some type of fundamental analysis probably has a role in the stock selection process. For even in an efficient market, there is no question that stock prices reflect a company's profit performance. Some companies are fundamentally strong and others are fundamentally weak, and investors must be able to distinguish between the two. Thus, some time can profitably be spent in evaluating a company and its stock to determine not if it is undervalued, but whether it is fundamentally strong.

The level of investor return, however, is more than a function of the fundamental

condition of the company; the level of risk exposure is also important. We saw earlier that fundamental analysis can be helpful in assessing potential risk exposure and in identifying securities that possess risk commensurate with the return they offer. The extent to which the markets are efficient is still subject to considerable debate—at present, there seems to be a growing consensus that while the markets may not be *perfectly* efficient, the evidence certainly seems to suggest that they are, at the least, *reasonably* efficient. As such, in the final analysis, it is the individual investor who must decide on the merits of fundamental and technical analysis. Certainly, a large segment of the investing public believes in security analysis, even in a market that may be efficient. What is more, the principles of stock valuation (that promised return should be commensurate with exposure to risk) are valid in any type of market setting.

The Changing Face of the Market

Before leaving stocks, we should say a few things about some major changes that have occurred recently in the marketplace itself. In effect, we're seeing some significant changes in the major players which, in turn, are causing some big changes in the way stocks are bought and sold. Indeed, it would be difficult for one to grasp fully the dynamics of today's market without some understanding of these recent developments and how they have impacted stock prices and valuation, as well as trading and price volatility. Consider, for example, the *globalization of the stock and bond markets*. The fact is that U.S. financial markets and investors no longer dominate world markets and trading—there are now a lot of other big players and their influence on our own markets is significant.

For proof, you need look no further than the great bull market of 1982–1987, and see the extent to which it was influenced by heavy foreign buying of U.S. stocks. The Japanese, in particular, have long had a love affair with U.S. consumer products, and they have a similar taste in stocks. They were heavy buyers of blue chip, ''brand name'' stocks such as G.E., Eastman Kodak, McDonald's, Merck, and Philip Morris—all components of the DJIA. Such buying helped to push up that widely publicized index which, in turn, had the ripple effect of stimulating buying of stocks across the board.

And it's not just stock prices that are subject to global influence. If anything, the U.S. bond market is even more sensitive to foreign decisions. The U.S. Treasury is forced to sell massive amounts of bonds to finance the staggering U.S. budget deficit. The Japanese and others are major buyers, and their willingness to accept or reject the Treasury's interest rate is an important determinant of just what that rate will be. The foreign influence on interest rates, and thus on bond prices, also directly affects *stock prices,* as nervous institutional stock traders often take their cues from how the bond market is doing.

Dominance of Institutional Investors

In addition to foreign investors, another major force in today's market is the *large institutional investor*—that is, the money managers representing the deep-pocketed pension funds, insurance companies, mutual funds, bank trust departments, and

college endowment funds. These investors represent firms with billions of dollars to invest, and as such, their presence is felt throughout the market. And it's been magnified even more since the market crash of 1987, as individual investors, shaken to the core, left the market in droves, putting their funds into risk-free T-bills, CDs, and money market funds. Those who did slowly return tended to invest in equities through the purchase of mutual funds rather than individual stocks. As a result, it is estimated that as much as 70–80 percent of the share volume on the NYSE is now due to institutional trading. Thus, the bulk of buying and selling today is the result not of thousands of individual's investment decisions, but rather of a much smaller number of professional money managers. The effects of this phenomenon and the implications for the individual investor are as follows.

Short-term Orientation. Institutional money managers have a very short investment horizon. They are under intense pressure to "perform"—which means to achieve a higher return than the "averages" (e.g., the S&P 500). To do this, they are quick to sell any stock whose earnings are below analysts' expectations. There is hardly any interest in long-term considerations or any loyalty to a given stock. Indeed it's a bit ironic that the pressure on the money managers to outperform the market comes from the pension fund manager of the very same corporate client who then bemoans the short-term orientation of the market as it affects his stock! Regardless of the absurdity of this situation, it results in a sharp increase in price volatility, exacerbated by the sheer size of institutional buy and sell orders. Blocks of 25,000 to 50,000 shares are common, with many trades of over 100,000 shares. The individual investor, by taking a somewhat longer-term view, can often do quite well by buying a stock temporarily driven down in price by an overreaction to short-term factors.

Herd Mentality. Institutional investors tend to act in concert. They often buy and sell the same stocks at the same time. And unlike the cold-eyed professional one would expect to be managing huge sums of money, they are surprisingly emotional in their trading decisions. Although there are many exceptions, there is simply a dearth of independent thought among these big institutions. Perhaps there is simply too much fear of not outperforming everyone else. The knowledgeable investor can be more nimble and more creative and has the important luxury of a longer time horizon in which to "perform."

program trading
the use of computers to make large-scale trading decisions; widely used by brokerage houses and other Wall Street firms to make money when the futures and stock markets get out of balance, a practice that has led to violent swings in stock prices.

Program Trading. Perhaps the major factor behind the sharp increase in market volatility (sharp increases or decreases in individual share prices) in recent years is the use of computer-assisted trading by institutional investors. Actually, **program trading,** as it is called, involves two separate trading strategies. The first is *index arbitrage*. Here program traders—large institutional investors as well as brokerage firms trading for their own account—monitor the price spread between a stock index *futures contract* trading in Chicago (contracts based on the S&P 500 or 100 index are popular) and the actual stocks trading on the New York Stock Exchange. When the spread widens beyond a "normal" range (generally around 3 points),

then action is called for. For example, a *buy program* might work this way: Assume that optimism about stock prices caused heavy buying in the S&P 100 futures contract (perhaps there was good news on the inflation/interest rate front), causing it to rise sharply and increasing the price spread between it and the S&P index (based on the actual prices of the 100 stocks in the index) to above "normal." Program traders would then sell the suddenly "overvalued" futures contract and *buy* huge baskets of 15 or more stocks that serve as proxies for the stock index upon which the futures contract is based, thus locking up a profit. This heavy, concentrated buying—usually in a matter of minutes—serves to immediately increase the prices of all those big stocks and, with them, the Dow Jones average.

A *sell program* works in reverse. When the futures contract is undervalued compared to the actual stock index, the traders will buy the futures and simultaneously *sell* the actual stocks. Then stock prices—and the Dow Jones average—will fall sharply. From out of nowhere, waves of selling hit the stocks of America's greatest corporations, sometimes knocking their prices down by 5 percent or more in a few minutes. And although the initial sell programs are on the big stocks, the psychological ripple effect often triggers heavy selling in all stocks. Besides the actual price damage done to stocks, program selling can have a pronounced effect on an investor's psyche. Many would argue, in fact, that the extreme price volatility caused by program selling has done more to drive the individual investor from the stock market than any other factor.

The other type of program trading is used *to liquidate or buy large portfolios of stocks*. On the sell side, it is, in effect, a massive computer-based stop-loss strategy. The computer is programmed to sell a stock when its price drops to a target level (or *buy* when its price *rises* to a certain price). Research following the '87 crash shows that these computerized sell programs undertaken on behalf of major institutional investors greatly exacerbated the downward slide in stock prices. Under such circumstances, the whole thing becomes self-fulfilling. Prices drop to target levels, the computer spits out sell orders, prices drop further, triggering more sell orders—and so on, to ground zero. This type of program trading, along with something called *portfolio insurance* (a strategy that quickly fell from favor after the market crash) may well have been *the* leading causes of the crash, transforming a sharp decline in stock prices into a frightening debacle.

Takeovers and Buyouts

Although foreign and institutional investors contributed significantly to the market's liquidity and price volatility, probably the biggest development in the past five years or so has been the growing role of the *corporation* as a major player in the secondary markets. Traditionally, corporations have been little more than the issuers of common stocks and other forms of securities; they never played much of a role in the aftermarkets—at least not until corporate takeovers and leveraged buyouts became a major driving force in the stock market. Today, stock prices can jump 50 to 100 percent almost overnight as one company (or group) announces its intention to acquire the stock of another company at highly inflated prices. Corporations, in short, are now having a direct and significant impact on the stock valuation process

and stock prices. Indeed, some would argue that nothing has so contributed to the changing face of the market in the *late 1980s* as the explosion in mergers, take-overs, and buyouts. The sheer number of these deals and the value of the transactions are staggering. In 1988, for example, the total dollar value of acquisitions, restructurings, and stock buybacks on *Fortune*'s list of just the 50 largest deals was $112 billion. And that did not include the biggest deal in history (as of this writing), the $27 billion buyout of RJR Nabisco, which was not completed until early 1989. In fact, during the five years from 1984 to 1988, the dollar value of mergers, takeovers, and buyouts in this country totalled roughly 1¼ *trillion* dollars! Look at the list below; it includes some of the companies that have been taken over by other firms or that have been taken private:

RJR Nabisco	Lucky Stores
Kraft Foods	Macmillan Publishing
Federated Dept. Stores	Beatrice Cos.
Sterling Drug	RCA
Homestake Mining	Harper & Row
Media General	American Standard
GAF Corp.	Borg Warner
Koppers	R.H. Macy
Safeway Stores	Celanese
Firestone Tire & Rubber	American Motors

Clearly, these are big-name companies, most of which are household words. These companies all have one thing in common: You can no longer buy stock in them, because their stock is no longer publicly traded.

How Mergers and Takeovers Work.   As a rule, mergers and takeovers are done either for cash, cash and stock (and/or bonds), or as stock swaps. Cash deals are most common and are usually most favorable to the investor (though stock swaps have the advantage of not requiring payment of taxes on any gain until/unless the investor sells the acquiring company's stock). Once acquired, the target company ceases to exist as an independent company and becomes either a division or subsidiary of the acquirer, or is simply merged into one of its divisions. The investor surrenders his/her stock and receives payment. Almost without exception the price paid for the target company represents a *substantial premium* to its market price, often 50 percent or more. The price of the *acquiring company* (if it's a company rather than a raider or private investment group) usually either stays the same or actually declines. The reason is that the premium price paid to the target company will almost always reflect a higher price-earnings multiple than its own stock sells for, thus automatically diluting its earnings per share.

   It's important to distinguish between two distinct types of acquisitions, in terms of the acquirer's motivation: *financially motivated acquisitions,* such as the RJR Nabisco LBO (which we'll examine below) and *strategic, structural acquisitions,* where the acquirer is seeking to gain market share or expand product lines. The

Philip Morris acquisition of Kraft is a classic example of a strategic acquisition, as are GE's acquisition of Roper Co. (appliances) and American Home Products' purchase of A.H. Robbins (Chapstick).

To gain a better appreciation of how these acquisitions work, consider the purchase of Champion Products by the Sara Lee Corp. In late 1988, Champion Products stock sold for $35. In March 1989, Champion was acquired by the giant Sara Lee Corp. for $77/share. What did Sara Lee see in this manufacturer of casual/exercise clothing? For openers, a strong, quality brand name in a market with good growth characteristics. But in addition, it saw the opportunity to integrate Champion into its own sizable apparel division and through its much greater financial and distribution clout, generate a more rapid growth in sales and earnings than the smaller Champion could do on its own. For this, Sara Lee was willing to pay a premium price reflecting 19 times Champion's 1988 EPS.

Why So Many Takeovers?   The impetus for the surge in mergers and takeovers stems from a number of factors. First, *many companies are simply not well-run* and present tempting targets to the aggressive acquirer. Grand Met's acquisition of Pillsbury—a well-known company with good brands but lagging financial returns—is an example. Second, *many stocks are undervalued* in relation to their real or intrinsic value. Another reason is the *availability of huge pools of money and credit* to finance these deals. And finally, many argue that the amount of investment banking fees involved is *the* major reason for the explosion in merger activities. Investment banking fees average ½ to 1 percent of the size of the deal. The sums are simply staggering. In the RJR Nabisco deal, for example, the fees paid to such firms as Drexel Burnham and Shearson Lehman Hutton amounted to close to $300 million. And the Wall Street law firms who are always an integral part of these deals don't exactly work for the minimum wage either! When the U.S. Attorney brought racketeering charges against Michael Milken of Drexel Burham in 1989, the disclosure that he had earned $500 million in 1988 startled even the most jaded of Wall Street observers.

Leveraged Buyouts (LBOs)

Essentially, leveraged buyouts are used to take companies private—to buy up all of the outstanding shares in the hands of the investing public. Unlike a merger or takeover, LBOs do not involve the acquisition of one company by another. Instead, the stock of the company may be acquired by the company itself (a group of the firm's senior managers) or by an investment firm that specializes in buyouts. The LBO, in a sense, is the vehicle through which the buyout is carried out. Why would a company go private in the first place? Usually, because it's felt, for one reason or another, that the company's stock is not being fairly valued in the marketplace—in other words, its stock doesn't carry as high a price as the buyout group feels it should. From rather meager beginnings in the early 1980s, LBOs are now being used to underwrite the takeovers of scores of companies, ranging from the huge $27 billion acquisition of RJR Nabisco by Kohlberg Kravis Roberts (KKR, a leading buyout firm) to the $9 million LBO of tiny Schwab Safe Co. (an Indiana manufac-

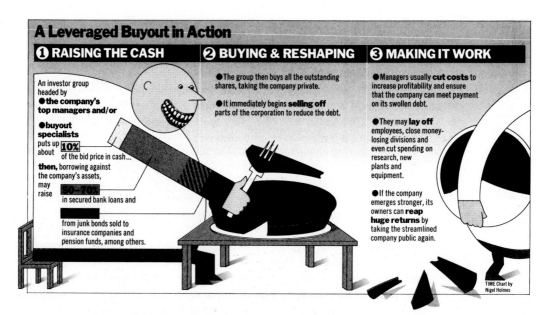

FIGURE 8.8 A Leveraged Buyout in Action.
In an LBO, the buyout group raises the cash to acquire a firm primarily through bank loans and junk bonds, and then uses the acquired company's cash flow to service and eventually pay off the huge debt load. (*Source: Time,* December 5, 1988, p. 68.)

turer of fireproof safes) by its senior management. Besides the sale of entire firms, many large companies are divesting underperforming divisions and selling them to their own managers via LBOs.

The mechanics are fairly simple. The key distinction between an LBO and the traditional cash or stock swap merger is the *heavy use of debt,* hence the term *leveraged.* Perhaps 90 percent or more of the purchase is done with borrowed money. That means that the new owners gain control of the business in return for putting up 10 percent or less of the money. Following the LBO, the company then begins to focus almost exclusively on generating sufficient cash flow to service this massive debt. This usually requires selling off assets and drastically cutting costs.

Initial financing of LBOs comes from the big buyout firms like KKR, who get their capital from the big pension funds, from huge bank loans (with the banks getting maybe 1½ to 2 percent more interest on these loans than on conventional loans), and from the sale of high-yield, high-risk "junk bonds." The whole process is graphically depicted in Figure 8.8, which shows how an LBO is put together and what makes it work. Clearly, LBOs are strictly *financially motivated,* and they're intended really to do just one thing: make the parties to the buyout group *wealthy,* and in some cases, enormously so! Not surprisingly, the companies that make the best LBO candidates are those with strong, consistent cash flows, relatively modest capital spending requirements, and plenty of unused debt capacity (i.e., firms that haven't done a lot of borrowing). In this way, the company itself can not only

provide the needed debt capacity to raise the funds for the LBO, but it can also serve as a source of cash flow to pay off the debt. Popular LBO industries are food, textiles, and retailing—where many companies possess strong cash flows and are relatively insensitive to a recession.

Do LBOs make companies stronger? It's hard to say. Certainly the increased emphasis on cash flow to service the debt forces management to eliminate waste and become more productive—but they should have been doing that all along. And cutting budgets in research and development and in advertising—two prime targets of the cost cutters—could easily do the company more harm than good in the long run.

Are there any losers in LBOs? Yes; besides all the employees who are actually spun-off to increase cash flow, *every* employee goes through months of gut-wrenching uncertainty as to his or her future status. It's no fun being a small piece in a giant game of financial *Monopoly*. The human toll of merger-mania cannot be quantified, but it's clearly immense. Communities, too, suffer, as employees are laid off or plants are sold to new owners with fewer ties to the area and, therefore, less commitment to community support and philanthropy. Finally, the current bondholders lose because by taking on massive new debt, the company finds its ratings on *existing bonds* downgraded and their prices fall in the bond market. This *event risk* is a new risk area for bond investors and a subject of intense debate. It is likely that this problem will be resolved by institutional bond investors demanding that protective covenants be built into bond agreements—and/or a demand for higher interest rates.

SUMMARY

- The final phase of security analysis involves an assessment of the investment merits of a specific company and its stock, and is ultimately aimed at formulating expectations about the company's future prospects and the potential risk and return behavior of the stock.

- Information such as projected sales, forecasted earnings, and estimated dividends is important in establishing the intrinsic worth of a stock—which is a measure of what the stock ought to be worth, based on expected return performance and risk exposure.

- There are a number of stock valuation procedures in use today, including the so-called dividend valuation model, which derives the value of a share of stock from the stock's future growth in dividends and the appropriate market capitalization rate.

- Another popular valuation procedure is the present value approach, whereby an investor can determine the justified price of a security, or the fully compounded yield it offers, given expected security returns (dividends and future price behavior) over a specific investment horizon.

- Using one of the stock valuation models, we can consider a stock to be a viable investment candidate so long as its computed yield is equal to or greater than

the required rate of return, or its computed justified price is equal to or greater than the stock's current market price.

- In order to determine whether a given stock would make a worthwhile investment, the investor must stipulate the required (or desired) rate of return he or she wishes to earn from the investment. This is the minimum rate of return that the investor should earn in order to be fully compensated for the risk involved, and it is found in any well-developed stock valuation model.

- Technical analysis is another phase of the analytical process; it deals with the behavior of the stock market and the various economic forces at work in the marketplace. Many investors use technical analysis to help them time their investment decisions.

- There are a number of approaches to technical analysis, including the use of bellwether stocks and/or following several key elements of market behavior, such as market volume, breadth of the market, short interest positions, odd-lot trading, and the confidence index. Probably the best known tool of the technical analyst is charting. Some people believe that price patterns evolve into chart formations that provide signals about what to expect in the future for a stock, or for the whole market.

- In recent years, the whole notion of both technical and fundamental analysis has been seriously challenged by the random walk and efficient market hypotheses; indeed, there is considerable evidence to indicate that stock prices do move in a random fashion.

- The efficient market hypothesis is an attempt to explain *why* prices behave randomly; the idea behind an efficient market is that available information about the company and/or its stock is always fully reflected in the price of securities, and therefore investors should *not* expect to consistently outperform the market. While few investors believe the market is *perfectly* efficient, there is a good deal of evidence to suggest that it is, at the least, *reasonably* efficient.

- Some major changes have occurred in the stock market in the past few years which have led to big changes in stock price volatility and the way stocks are traded. Paramount among these events is the fact that we've seen institutions and corporations grab a bigger piece of the market, as corporate takeovers, leveraged buy outs, and program trades have become almost commonplace.

REVIEW QUESTIONS AND PROBLEMS

1. Are the expected future earnings of the firm important in determining a stock's investment suitability? Discuss how these and other future estimates fit into the stock valuation framework.

 2. An investor estimates that next year's sales for Gilt Edge Products should amount to about $75 million; the company has 2.5 million shares outstanding, generates a net profit margin of about 5 percent, and has a payout ratio of 50 percent—all figures are expected to hold for next year. Given this information, compute:

   a. Estimated net earnings for next year.

   b. Next year's dividends per share.

   c. The expected price of the stock (assuming the P/E ratio is 12.5 times earnings).

3. Briefly discuss some procedures that might be used by investors to forecast the following types of information about a company and its stock:

   a. Sales.

   b. Net profit margin.

   c. Price/earnings ratio.

4. Can the growth prospects of a company affect its price/earnings multiple? Explain. How about the amount of debt that a firm uses? Are there other variables that affect the level of a firm's P/E ratio? What is the market multiple, and how can it help in evaluating a stock's P/E? Is a stock's relative P/E the same thing as the market multiple? Explain.

5. Briefly describe the dividend valuation model. What is the difference between the constant growth model and the variable growth model?

6. Charlene Lewis is thinking about buying some shares of Education, Inc., at $50 per share; she expects the price of the stock to rise to $75 over the next three years, during which time she also expects to receive annual dividends of $5 per share.

   a. What is the intrinsic worth of this stock, given a 10 percent required rate of return?

   b. What is its approximate yield?

7. Amalgamated Something-or-Other, Inc. is expected to pay a dividend of $1.50 in the coming year. The required rate of return is 16 percent and dividends are expected to grow at 7 percent per year. Using the dividend valuation model, find the intrinsic value of the company's common shares.

8. Assume you've generated the following information about the stock of Bufford's Burger Barns: The company's latest dividends of $4 a share are expected to grow to $4.32 next year, $4.67 the year after that, and $5.04 in year 3; in addition, the price of the stock is expected to rise to $77.75 in 3 years.

   a. Use the present value model and a required rate of return of 15 percent to find the value of the stock.

   b. Given that dividends are expected to grow indefinitely at 8 percent, use a 15 percent required rate of return and the dividend valuation model to find the value of the stock.

   c. Assume dividends in year 3 actually amount to $5.04, the dividend growth rate stays at 8 percent, and the required rate of return stays at 15 percent; use the dividend valuation model to find the price of the stock at the end of year 3. Hint: In this case, the value of the stock will depend on D_4, which equals $D_3 (1 + g)$. Do you note any similarity between your answer here and the forecasted price of the stock ($77.75) given in the problem? Explain.

9. Let's assume that you're thinking about buying some stock in Uniden Electronics. So far in your analysis, you've uncovered the following information: the stock pays annual dividends of $2.50 a share (and that's not expected to change within the next few years—nor are any of the other variables); it trades at a P/E of 12 times earnings and has a beta of 1.15; in addition, you plan on using a risk-free rate of 7½ percent in the CAPM, along with a market return of 14 percent. You would like to hold the stock for 3 years, at the end of which time you think EPS will peak out at about $7 a share. Given that the stock presently trades at $55, use the

approximate yield formula to find this security's expected return. Now use the present value model to put a price on this stock. Does this look like a good investment? Explain.

10. Identify and briefly discuss three different ways of determining (or assessing) a stock's investment value. Note how such information is used in the investment decision-making process.

11. The price of Consolidated Everything is now $75; the company pays no dividends, and Mr. Bossard expects the price three years from now to be $100 per share. Should Mr. B. buy Consolidated E. if he desires a 10 percent rate of return? Explain.

12. Discuss the concept of a required (or desired) rate of return; explain its role in the valuation process.

13. Explain how risk fits into the stock valuation process. (Note especially its relationship to the investment return of a security.)

14. Drabble Company's stock sells at a P/E ratio of 14 times earnings; it is expected to pay dividends of $2 per share in each of the next five years and generate an EPS of $5 per share in year 5. Using the present value model and a 12 percent discount rate, compute the stock's justified price.

15. A particular company currently has sales of $250 million; these are expected to grow by 20 percent next year (year 1). For the year after next (year 2), the growth rate in sales is expected to equal 10 percent. Over each of the next two years the company is expected to have a net profit margin of 8 percent, a payout ratio of 50 percent, and to maintain the number of shares of common stock outstanding at 15 million shares; the stock always trades at a P/E ratio of 15 times earnings, and the investor has a required rate of return of 20 percent. Given this information:

   a. Find the stock's intrinsic value (its justified price).
   b. Determine its approximate yield, given the stock is presently trading at $15 per share.
   c. Find the holding period returns for year 1 and for year 2.

16. What is the purpose of technical analysis? Explain how and why it is used by technicians; note how it can be helpful in timing investment decisions.

17. Can the market really have a measurable effect on the price behavior of individual securities? Explain.

18. Briefly define each of the following, and note the conditions which would suggest that the market is technically strong:

   a. Breadth of the market.
   b. Dow theory.
   c. Bellwether stocks.
   d. Theory of contrary opinion.
   e. Head-and-shoulders.

19. What is a stock chart? What kind of information can be put on charts, and what is the purpose of charting?

   a. What is the difference between a bar chart and a point-and-figure chart?
   b. What are chart formations, and why are they important?

20. What is the random walk hypothesis, and how does it apply to stocks? What is an efficient market; how can a market be efficient if its prices behave in a random fashion?

21. Explain why it is difficult, if not impossible, to consistently outperform an efficient market.

    a. Does that mean that high rates of return are not available in the stock market?
    b. Explain how an investor can earn a high rate of return in an efficient market.

22. What are the implications of random walks and efficient markets for technical analysis? For fundamental analysis? Do random walks and efficient markets mean that technical and fundamental analysis are useless? Explain.

23. Indicate the various ways *foreign investors* can impact the U.S. stock and bond markets. On balance, are they a positive or negative influence? Explain. Define *institutional investors*. In what ways do they influence the stock market? Briefly describe the growing role of *corporations* as major players in the stock market. Can they really have much of an effect on stock prices in the secondary market? Explain.

24. What's the difference between a corporate takeover and an LBO? Briefly explain how these events can affect the market price of a stock. Briefly describe program trading; does it have any impact on the volatility of market prices? Do you feel things like takeovers, buyouts, and program trading make the stock market stronger or weaker? Explain.

CASE PROBLEMS

8.1 Chris Looks for a Way to Invest His New Found Wealth

Chris Norton is a young Hollywood writer who is well on his way to television superstardom. After writing several successful television specials, he was recently named the head writer for the top rated TV sitcom, "The Awesome Years." Chris fully realizes that his business is a fickle one, and on the advice of his dad and manager, has decided to set up an investment program. Chris will earn about half a million dollars this year, and because of his age, income level, and desire to get as big a bang as possible from his investment dollars, he has decided to invest in speculative, high-growth stocks.

He's presently working with a respected and highly regarded Beverly Hills broker and is in the process of building up a diversified portfolio of speculative stocks. His broker recently sent him information on this hot new issue and suggested Chris study the numbers and if he likes them, to buy as many as 1,000 shares of the stock. In particular, the broker forecasts corporate sales for the next three years at:

Year	Sales (in millions)
1	$22.5
2	35.0
3	50.0

The firm has 1.2 million shares of common outstanding (they are currently being traded at 62½ and pay no dividends), it has been running a phenomenal net profit rate of 20 percent, and its stock has been trading at a P/E ratio of around 25 times earnings (which is a bit on the high side). All these operating characteristics are expected to hold in the future.

Questions

1. Looking first at the stock:
   a. Compute the company's net profits and EPS for each of the next three years.
   b. Compute the price of the stock three years from now.

c. Assuming all expectations hold up and that Chris buys the stock at 62½, determine the approximate yield he can expect from this investment.

d. What risks is he facing by buying this stock? Be specific.

e. Should he consider the stock to be a worthwhile investment candidate? Explain.

2. Now, looking at his investment program in general:

    a. What do you think of his investment program? What do you see as its strengths and weaknesses?

    b. Are there any suggestions you would make?

8.2 An Analysis of a High-Flying Stock

Glenn Wilt is a recent university graduate and a security analyst with the Kansas City brokerage firm of Lippman, Brickbats, and Shaft. Wilt has been following one of the hottest issues on Wall Street, C&I Construction Supplies, a company that has turned in an outstanding performance lately and, even more important, has exhibited excellent growth potential. It has 5 million shares outstanding and pays a nominal annual dividend of 25 cents per share. Wilt has decided to take a close look at C&I to see whether or not it still has any investment play left. Assume the company's sales for the *past* five years have been:

Year	Sales (in millions)
1985	$10.0
1986	12.5
1987	16.2
1988	22.0
1989	28.5

Wilt is concerned with the future prospects of the company, not its past; as a result, he pores over the numbers laboriously and generates the following estimates of future performance:

Expected net profit margin	12½%
Estimated annual dividends per share	25¢
Number of common shares outstanding	No change
P/E ratio at the end of 1990	35
P/E ratio at the end of 1991	50

Questions

1. Determine the average annual rate of growth in sales over the past five years.

    a. Use this average growth rate to forecast revenues for next year (1990) and the year after that (1991).

    b. Now determine the company's net earnings and EPS for each of the next two years (1990 and 1991).

    c. Finally, determine the expected future price of the stock at the end of this two-year period.

2. Because of several intrinsic and market factors, Wilt feels that 20 percent is a viable figure to use for a desired rate of return.

    a. Using the 20 percent rate of return and the forecasted figures you came up with above, compute the stock's justified price.

    b. If C&I is presently trading at $25 per share, should Wilt consider the stock a worthwhile investment candidate? Explain.

3. The stock is actively traded on the AMEX and enjoys considerable market interest. Recent closing prices are listed below.
    a. Prepare a point-and-figure chart of these prices (use a 1-point system—i.e., make each box worth $1).
    b. Discuss how these and similar charts are used by technical analysts.
    c. Cite several other types of technical indicators, and note how they might be used in the analysis of this stock.

Recent Price Behavior: C&I Construction Supplies

14 ← (8/15/89)	18½	20	17½
14¼	17½	20¼	18½
14⅞	17½	20¼	19¾
15½	17¼	20⅛	19½
16	17	20	19¼
16	16¾	20¼	20
16½	16½	20½	20⅞
17	16½	20¾	21
17¼	16⅛	20½	21¾
17½	16¾	20	22½
18	17⅛	20¼	23¼
18 ← (9/30/89)	17¼	20	24
18½	17¼	19½	24¼
18½	17¼14 ← (10/31/89)	19¼	24⅛
18¾	17¾	18¼ ← (11/30/89)	24¾
19	18¼	17½	25
19⅛	19¼	16¾	25½
18⅞	20½	17	25½ ← (12/31/89)

SELECTED READINGS

Cullen, Robert. "Patterns For Profit." *Personal Investor*, November 1987, pp. 53–62.

Donnelly, Barbara. "Finding the Common Denominator of Winning Stocks." *The Wall Street Journal*, January 11, 1989, p. C1.

Farrell, James L., Jr. "The Dividend Discount Model: A Primer." *Financial Analysts Journal*, November/December 1985, pp. 16–25.

Fielitz, Bruce D., and F. L. Mullen. "A Simplified Approach to Common Stock Valuation." *Financial Analysts Journal*, November/December 1985, pp. 35–41.

Fredman, Albert J. "The January Effect." *Personal Investor*, January 1988, pp. 40–45.

Morgenson, Gretchen. "A Checklist for Stock Market Prognosticators," *Forbes*, May 4, 1987, pp. 110–14.

Schiffres, Manuel. "How To Tell If The Bear Is Back." *Changing Times*, November 1987, pp. 67–72.

———. "Unloved Stocks You Can Buy At A Discount." *Changing Times*, November 1988, pp. 97–102.

Serwer, Andrew E. "Spotting Takeover Stocks Before The Buyout Bids Are Made." *Fortune*, November 21, 1988, pp. 49–50.

Smith, James R. "Underperforming Assets: Guidelines for When to Sell." *AAII Journal*, September 1988, pp. 5–6.

COMPUTER-BASED INVESTMENT MANAGEMENT: COMMON STOCK

At a recent investment seminar, a top analyst from a major brokerage house was asked what he considered to be the single most important factor in finding undervalued stocks. "A computer," he responded. For as he explained: "It's virtually impossible to screen through the thousands of actively traded stocks without the aid of the computer. With access to a database of information and a computer, you can quickly sift the wheat from the chaff and identify those opportunities that best meet your investment objectives." For years, professional money managers have relied on computers to sort through financial records in search of stocks that are undervalued from a fundamental-analysis perspective. Now, individual investors have this same capability.

As a rule, common stock investors can use computers to perform any one of four different functions: (1) to *screen stocks*—that is, to use programs and databases that quickly and easily screen thousands of stocks for the handful that meet predetermined investment criteria; (2) to conduct *fundamental analysis and stock valuation*—that is, to use the computer to analyze the financial conditions and operating results of the firm, as well as put an intrinsic value on a stock; (3) to perform in-depth *technical analysis* of stocks and markets, which can involve anything from point-and-figure charting to generating all sorts of technical market measures (moving averages, advance-decline ratios, and so on); and (4) for purposes of *portfolio management*—that is, to keep track of the risk-return performance of individual stocks, as well as whole portfolios of stocks. (See Part Six—pages 765–766—for a discussion of computer-based portfolio management.) Many of the real advances in computer-based investment management can be traced to the introduction and development of *computerized databases* that literally convert home computers to on-line libraries of investment information—indeed, many of the stock screening, analytical, and valuation programs (noted above) rely very heavily on such databases for sources of information. Essentially, these database programs enable users to

obtain immediate access to vast amounts of historical and up-to-the-minute information on thousands of companies and securities—everything from financial statement information and ratios to market yields and prices.

While there are hundreds of reasonably priced computer programs to choose from, the following list provides a brief description of some of the more popular equity-oriented software currently available to the investing public:

- *Value/Screen* (Value Line Inc., 711 Third Avenue, New York, NY 10017; 800/654-0508; $232 to $495 a year, depending on frequency of updates; Macintosh series, IBM PCs and compatibles.) This program permits you to quickly and easily screen a 1700-stock database for those issues that meet your personal investment criteria. Periodically, the user receives an updated diskette providing 32 key investment measures (including the stock's beta, P/E ratio, growth rates, dividend yield, and so on) for each stock in the database. These 32 variables are divided into valuation measures, market data, historical performance, and estimates and projections. To screen the database, you simply fill out an on-screen form, listing each variable you want to screen for. Value/Screen then reports the number of stocks that satisfy your requirements and allows you to print out the list of screened stocks. Thus, in a matter of minutes, an investor can generate a manageable list of stocks for further analysis.
- *CompuServe* (CompuServe Information Services, 5000 Arlington Centre Blvd., Columbus, OH 43220; 800/848-8990, $70 plus usage charge of $6 to $12.50/hours; any computer with a modem.) CompuServe is easy to learn and requests are filled almost instantaneously. The service functions as a conduit to other resources and as a result, makes available to subscribers such databases as Value Line and Standard & Poor's (each of which provides extensive financial and market information on a multitude of companies and securities), earnings *projections* for more than 2,400 companies from the Institutional Brokers' Estimate System, detailed financial statements filed with the Securities and Exchange Commission (SEC) by over 10,000 companies, and more. As a subscriber, you have immediate access to any and all of this information—just indicate what you want to see and it will show up almost instantaneously on your home computer screen. Subscribers can also trade stocks, bonds, and options electronically through a hook-up with a major New York–based discount brokerage firm.
- *Market Analyzer Plus* (Dow Jones & Co., P.O. Box 300, Princeton, NJ 08540; 800/257-5114; IBM PC, XT, AT and compatibles.) Market Analyzer Plus uses historical stock quotes collected automatically from Dow Jones News/Retrieval to chart stocks and perform a variety of technical analysis functions. This program not only plots bar and point-and-figure charts for just about any stock you can think of but also calculates and displays a variety of technical measures, including on-balance volume, moving averages, accumulation/distribution figures, and more; with this program, you can even define and chart your own custom indicators.

- *Compustock* (A. S. Gibson & Sons, 1412 E. Vineyard Drive, Bountiful, UT 84010; 801/298-4578; $59 to $64; IBM PCs and compatibles.) This is basically a fundamental analysis and stock valuation program that uses historical data to predict prices, earnings, dividends, and total returns; in addition, the program analyzes and predicts the future financial soundness of companies under review. Uses graphics to show trends and developing strengths and weaknesses; investor/user selects data to be analyzed, which can be input manually or by subscribing to monthly stock database, containing information on over a thousand widely traded stocks.

- *Fundamental Investor* (Savant Corp., P.O. Box 440278, Houston, TX 77244; 800/231-9000; $395; IBM PCs and compatibles.) This program not only conducts in-depth fundamental analysis but also enables the user to maintain a fundamental database of over 35 parameters on up to 2,000 stocks (per floppy disk); data can be entered and edited manually or by modem. Analysis program calculates an array of financial and market ratios from basic financial information (using spreadsheet-like functions); allows screening of all securities in database according to preselected parameters; and can sort stocks on the basis of single or weighted-average parameters.

- *Technical Investor* (Another program of the Savant Corp.—see above; $395; IBM PCs and compatibles.) This is a technical analysis package that combines charting with a far-reaching database of technical measures. The database is capable of storing up to 40 years of daily high, low, close, and volume information on up to 2,500 securities; information on market indexes is also available. Charts include price and volume bar charts; high, low, and close price lines; point-and-figure charts; positive/negative volume indicators; relative strength lines; and much more. Multiple stocks can be displayed on the same screen, or split screens can be used to compare charts of different securities. This is a program that's obviously aimed at the serious chartist.

NOTE: The above list of programs should be viewed as illustrative in nature, and *not* interpreted as an endorsement or recommendation. Listed prices and phone numbers are the latest available and are, of course, subject to change without notice.

THREE

INVESTING IN FIXED-INCOME SECURITIES

Part Three Includes:

Chapter 9   Bond Investments

Chapter 10   Preferred Stock and Convertible Securities

THE INVESTMENT ENVIRONMENT

INVESTMENT ADMINISTRATION

INVESTING IN COMMON STOCK	INVESTING IN FIXED-INCOME SECURITIES
SPECULATIVE INVESTMENT VEHICLES	OTHER POPULAR INVESTMENT VEHICLES

9

BOND INVESTMENTS

After studying this chapter you should be able to:

- Explain the basic investment attributes of bonds and discuss the appeal that these securities hold as investment vehicles.

- Describe the essential features of a bond and the principles of bond price behavior.

- Discuss the advantages and disadvantages of investing in bonds, including the types of risks to which investors are exposed.

- Identify the different types of bonds and the kinds of investment objectives these fixed-income securities can fulfill.

- Gain a fundamental appreciation of the bond valuation process, including basic measures of return.

- Describe various types of bond investment strategies and the different ways these securities can be used by investors.

bonds

publicly traded long-term debt securities, whereby the issuer agrees to pay a fixed amount of interest over a specified period of time and to repay a fixed amount of principal at maturity.

For many years, bonds were viewed as rather dull investments that produced current income and little else. No longer is this true; bonds today are viewed as highly competitive investment vehicles that offer the potential for attractive returns through current income and/or capital gains. **Bonds** are publicly traded long-term debt securities; they are issued in convenient denominations and by a variety of borrowing organizations, including the U.S. Treasury, various agencies of the U.S. government, state and municipal governments, and corporations, as well as institutions such as private nonprofit hospitals and church-related schools. Bonds are often referred to as *fixed-income securities* because the debt-service obligations of the issues are fixed—that is, the issuing organization agrees to pay a fixed amount of interest periodically and to repay a fixed amount of principal at maturity. This is the first of two chapters dealing with various types of fixed-income securities; in this chapter we will examine bonds, and in the next, preferred stocks and convertible securities. Let's begin this chapter by looking at some important issue characteristics, including the sources of return to investors, different types of bond features, and types of issues.

WHY INVEST IN BONDS?

Most people would not buy an expensive piece of property sight unseen, as there are just too many costly pitfalls to such a course of action. Similarly, we would not expect rational investors to spend money on securities they know nothing about. Bonds are no exception; in fact, it is especially important to know what you are getting into with bonds since, as we will see shortly, *many seemingly insignificant features can have dramatic effects on the behavior of an issue and its investment return*.

Like any other type of investment vehicle, bonds provide investors with two kinds of income: (1) They provide a generous amount of current income; and (2) they can often be used to generate substantial amounts of capital gains. The current income, of course, is derived from the interest payments received over the life of the issue. Capital gains, in contrast, are earned whenever market interest rates fall. A basic trading rule in the bond market is that *interest rates and bond prices move in opposite directions*. When interest rates rise, bond prices fall; and when rates drop, bond prices move up. Thus, it is possible to buy bonds at one price and, if interest rate conditions are right, to sell them later at a higher price. Of course, it is also possible to incur a capital loss should market rates move against the investor. Taken together, the current income and capital gains earned from bonds can lead to attractive and highly competitive investor yields.

In addition to their yields, bonds are also a versatile investment outlet. They can be used conservatively by those who primarily (or exclusively) seek high current income. (Indeed, the Tax Reform Act of 1986 has increased the appeal of income-oriented securities, like bonds, as the sharply reduced taxes on interest income means higher after-tax returns.) Alternatively, fixed-income securities can be used aggressively, by those who go after capital gains. Bonds have long been considered excellent investments for those seeking current income, but it has only been since the advent of high and volatile interest rates that they have also become recognized

as excellent trading vehicles. This is so because, given the relation of bond prices to interest rates, investors found that the number of profitable trading opportunities increased substantially as wider and more frequent swings in interest rates began to occur. Finally, due to the generally high quality of many bond issues, they can also be used for the preservation and long-term accumulation of capital. With quality issues, not only do investors have a high degree of assurance that they'll get their money back at maturity, but the stream of interest income is also highly dependable. Granted, investors do have to contend with occasional swings in bond prices, but if they're in for the long haul (and don't have to sell on short notice), such price swings shouldn't be a cause for alarm, since they really don't affect the bond's stream of income.

Putting Bond Market Performance in Perspective

The bond market is driven by interest rates. In fact, the behavior of interest rates is the single most important force in the bond market. These rates determine not only the amount of current income investors will make, but also the amount of capital gains (or losses) that bondholders will incur. It's not surprising, therefore, that interest rates are so closely followed by market participants, and that bond market performance is generally portrayed in terms of market interest rates. Figure 9.1 provides a look at bond interest rates over the 27-year period from 1961 to early 1989. It shows that from a state of relative stability, interest rates took off in 1965, and over the course of the next 15 years the rates paid on high-grade bonds almost tripled! Indeed, interest rates rose from the 4 to 5 percent range in the early sixties to over 16 percent by 1982. But then things began to change, as rates dropped sharply, and by 1986 they were back to the single-digit range once again. Thus, after a protracted bear market (the bond market is considered *bearish* when market interest rates are high or rising), bonds abruptly reversed course, and we experienced one of the strongest bull markets on record from 1982 to early 1987 (the bond market is considered *bullish* when rates are low or falling). And even though interest rates did move up again in 1987–88, they quickly dropped back in '89 to levels we hadn't seen with much regularity since the early seventies.

Just like stocks, *total returns* in the bond market are also made up of current income and capital gains (or losses). Not surprisingly, because rising rates mean falling prices, the drawn-out bear market in bonds meant depressing returns for bondholders. Granted, for investors just entering the market, the higher market yields were welcomed, because they signified higher levels of interest income; *but for those already holding bonds,* the implications were much different, as returns fell way *below* expectations and in many cases, resulted in outright losses! Take a look at Table 9.1; it shows total annual returns (and year-end market yields) for high-grade corporate bonds for the 40-year period from 1949 through 1988. Note how bond returns started to slip in 1965, as market rates began to climb; indeed, from 1965 to 1981, there were no fewer than 8 years when average returns were in the red. It's interesting to compare the market yield column to the total return column. For example, in 1980, market yields went way up, but total returns fell to

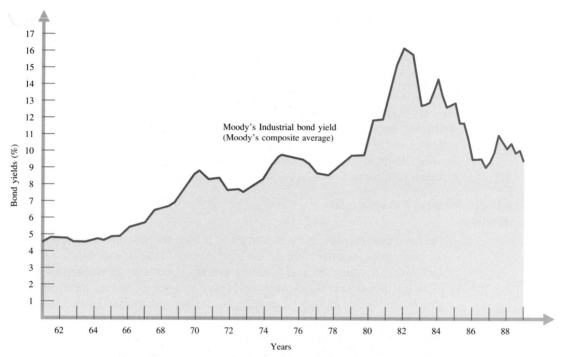

FIGURE 9.1 The Behavior of Interest Rates over Time.
From an era of relative stability, bond interest rates not only rose dramatically, but also became far more volatile. The net result was that bond yields not only became highly compet-itive with the returns offered by other securities, they also provided investors with attractive capital gains opportunities.

−2.62 percent. In contrast, two years later, in 1982, it was market yields that plunged, and as a result, total returns were a whopping 43.8 percent. That year was also the start of the bull market, and it shows in the returns that existed from 1982 to 1986: In that 5-year period of time, high-grade corporate bonds *nearly tripled in value*—a standard of performance that holds up well even against stocks!

In addition to annual returns, Table 9.1 also contains return performance over various *holding periods* of 5 to 40 years. These figures demonstrate the type of long-term returns possible from bonds (clearly, 1982–1986 was more the exception than the rule), and they show that *average annual returns of around 8 to 10 percent on high-grade issues are not out of the question.* Although such performance may lag behind stocks (which it should in light of the reduced exposure to risk), it really isn't all that bad. For if you could earn, say, 9 percent on a $10,000 investment, in 15 years you'd end up with an investment worth more than $36,000.

Essential Features of a Bond Issue

A *bond* is a negotiable, long-term debt instrument that carries certain obligations on the part of the issuer. Unlike the holders of common stock, bondholders have no

TABLE 9.1 Historical Yields and Returns in the Bond Market: 1949–1988
(Yields and returns based on performance of high-grade corporate bonds)

I. Annual Yields and Returns

Year	Year-end Bond Yields[a]	Total Rates of Return[b]
1988	9.81%	10.70%
1987	10.33	− 0.27
1986	9.02	19.85
1985	10.63	30.90
1984	12.05	16.39
1983	12.76	4.70
1982	11.55	43.80
1981	14.98	− 0.96
1980	13.15	− 2.62
1979	10.87	− 4.18
1978	9.32	− 0.07
1977	8.50	1.71
1976	8.14	18.65
1975	8.97	14.64
1974	8.89	− 3.06
1973	7.79	1.14
1972	7.41	7.26
1971	6.48	11.01
1970	6.85	18.37
1969	7.83	− 8.09
1968	6.62	2.57
1967	6.30	− 4.95
1966	5.55	0.20
1965	4.79	− 0.46
1964	4.46	4.77
1963	4.46	2.19
1962	4.34	7.95
1961	4.56	4.82
1960	4.52	9.07
1959	4.68	− 0.97
1958	4.19	− 2.22
1957	4.07	8.71
1956	3.90	− 6.81
1955	3.24	0.48
1954	2.95	5.39
1953	3.20	3.41
1952	3.05	3.52
1951	3.07	− 2.69
1950	2.73	2.12
1949	2.67	3.31

(Continued)

TABLE 9.1   *(Continued)*

II. Holding Period Returns

Holding Periods	Average Annual Total Returns[b]	Cumulative Total Returns	Amount to Which a $10,000 Investment Will Grow Over Holding Period
5 yrs: 1984–88	15.05%	101.59%	$20,159
10 yrs: 1979–88	10.86	180.48	28,048
15 yrs: 1974–88	9.23	275.90	37,590
20 yrs: 1969–88	8.30	392.49	49,249
25 yrs: 1964–88	6.66	401.73	50,173
30 yrs: 1959–88	6.31	526.64	62,664
40 yrs: 1949–88	5.07	622.40	72,240

[a] Year-end bond yields are for (S&P) AA-rated corporate (industrial and utility) bonds.

[b] Total return and average annual holding period return figures are fully compounded returns and are based on interest income as well as capital gains (or losses).

Source: Annual yields obtained from Standard & Poor's *S&P Trade and Security Statistics;* total return figures from Ibbotson and Sinquefield, *Stocks, Bonds, Bills, and Inflation: Historical Returns (1926–1987).*

ownership or equity position in the firm or organization that issues the bond. This is so because bonds are debt and because, in a roundabout way, bondholders are only lending money to the issuer; as such they are not entitled to an ownership position or any of the rights and privileges that go along with it.

Bond Interest and Principal

coupon
the feature on a bond that defines the amount of annual interest income.

principal
on a bond, the amount of capital that must be paid at maturity.

denominations
standard principal amounts into which a bond issue is broken to facilitate its sale to the public.

Bond issues are viewed as fixed-income securities because, in the absence of any trading, an investor's return is limited to fixed interest and principal payments. In essence, bonds involve a fixed claim on the issuer's income (as defined by the size of the periodic interest payments) and a fixed claim on the assets of the issuer (equal to the repayment of principal). As a rule, bonds pay interest every six months. There are exceptions, however; some issues carry interest payment intervals as short as a month, and a few as long as a year. The amount of interest due is a function of the **coupon,** which defines the annual interest income that will be paid by the issuer to the bondholder. For instance, a $1,000 bond with an 8 percent coupon would pay $80 in interest annually—generally in the form of two $40 semiannual payments. The **principal** amount of a bond, also known as an issue's *par value,* specifies the amount of capital that must be repaid at maturity. For example, there is $1,000 of principal in a $1,000 bond.

To facilitate the marketing of bonds, the issues are broken into standard principal amounts, known as **denominations.** Of course, debt securities regularly trade at market prices that differ from their principal (or par) values. This occurs whenever

an issue's coupon differs from the prevailing market rate of interest. The price of the issue will change inversely with interest rates until its yield is compatible with the prevailing market yield. Such behavior explains why a 7 percent issue will carry a market price of only $825 in a 9 percent market. The drop in price (from its par value of $1,000) is necessary to raise the yield on this bond from 7 to 9 percent—part of this new, higher yield will come from annual coupons and the rest from capital gains, as the price of the issue moves from $825 back to $1,000 at maturity. Issues with market values lower than par are known as *discount bonds* and carry coupons that are less than those on new issues. In contrast, issues with market values in excess of par are called *premium bonds* and have coupons greater than those currently being offered on new issues.

Maturity Date

maturity date
the date on which a bond matures and the principal must be repaid.

Unlike common stock, all debt securities have limited lives and expire on a given date, the issue's **maturity date.** Although a bond carries a series of specific interest payment dates, the principal is repaid only once: on or before maturity. Because the maturity date is fixed (and never changes), it not only defines the life of a new issue, but also denotes the amount of time remaining for older, outstanding bonds as well. Such a life span is known as an issue's *term to maturity*. A new issue may come out as a 25-year bond, but 5 years later, it'll have only 20 years remaining to maturity. Two types of bonds can be distinguished on the basis of maturity: term and serial. A **term bond** has a single, fairly lengthy maturity date and is the most common type of issue. A **serial bond,** in contrast, has a series of different maturity dates, perhaps as many as fifteen or twenty, within a single issue. For example, a 20-year term bond issued in 1989 would have a single maturity date of 2009, but that same issue as a serial bond might have twenty annual maturity dates that extend from 1990 through 2009. At each of these annual maturity dates, a certain portion of the issue would come due and be paid off. In addition, maturity is also used to distinguish a *note* from a *bond*. That is, a debt security that's originally issued with a maturity of 2 to 10 years is known as a **note,** whereas a *bond* technically has an initial term to maturity of *more than 10 years*. In practice, notes are often issued with maturities of 5 to 7 years, whereas bonds will normally carry maturities of 20 to 30 years, or more.

term bond
a bond that has a single, fairly lengthy maturity date.

serial bond
a bond that has a series of different maturity dates.

note
a debt security originally issued with a maturity of from 2 to 10 years.

Call Features—Let the Buyer Beware!

call feature
feature that specifies whether, and under what conditions, the issuer can retire a bond prior to maturity.

Consider the following situation: you've just made an investment in a great, high-yielding, 25-year bond. Now all you have to do is sit back and let the cash flow in, right? Well, perhaps. Certainly, that'll happen for the first several years. But if market interest rates drop off, it's also very likely that you'll be hit with a notice from the issuer that the bond is being *called*. This means that the issue is being retired before its time, and there's really nothing you can do but turn in your bond and invest your money elsewhere. How can this happen? Well, so long as the bond is a *callable*, it can be prematurely retired. It's all perfectly legal because every

call premium
the amount added to a bond's par value and paid to investors when a bond is retired prematurely.

call price
the price the issuer must pay to retire a bond prematurely; equal to par value plus the call premium.

refunding provision
a provision similar to a call feature except that it prohibits the premature retirement of an issue from the proceeds of a lower-coupon refunding bond.

sinking fund
a provision that stipulates the amount of principal that will be retired annually over the life of a bond.

senior bonds
secured debt obligations, backed by a legal claim on specific property of the issuer.

mortgage bonds
senior bonds secured by real estate.

collateral trust bonds
senior bonds backed by securities owned by the issuer but held in trust by a third party.

equipment trust certificates
senior bonds secured by specific pieces of equipment; popular with railroads, airlines, and other transportation companies.

bond is issued with a **call feature,** which stipulates whether or not, and under what conditions a bond can be called in for retirement prior to maturity. Basically, there are three types of call features:

1. A bond can be *freely callable,* which means that the issuer can prematurely retire the bond at any time.
2. It can be *noncallable,* meaning that the issuer is prohibited from retiring the bond prior to maturity.
3. The issue could carry a *deferred call,* which means that the issue cannot be called until after a certain length of time has passed from the date of issue—in essence, the issue is noncallable during the deferment period and then becomes freely callable.

Obviously, in our illustration above, the high-yielding bond had to be either freely callable or, at best, it carried a relatively short deferred call provision.

Call features are placed on bonds for the benefit of the issuers. They're used most often to replace an issue with one that carries a lower coupon; the issuer benefits by being able to realize a reduction in annual interest cost. Thus, when market interest rates undergo a sharp decline, as they did in 1982–1986, bond issuers (especially corporate and municipal issuers) will retire their high-yielding bonds (by calling them in) and replace them with lower-yielding obligations. *The net result is that the investor is left with a much lower rate of return than anticipated.*

In a half-hearted attempt to compensate investors who find their bonds called out from under them, a **call premium** is tacked onto a bond and paid to investors, along with the issue's par value, at the time the bond is called. The sum of these two (par value plus call premium) represents the issue's **call price** and amounts to the price the issuer must pay to retire the bond prematurely. As a general rule, such call premiums usually equal about one year's interest at the earliest date of call, and they become systematically smaller as the issue nears maturity. Using this rule, the initial call price of a 9 percent bond would be around $1,090, with $90 representing the call premium. In place of call features, some bonds may contain a specific **refunding provision,** which is exactly like a call feature except that it prohibits just one thing: the premature retirement of an issue from the proceeds of a lower-coupon refunding bond. This distinction is important, since it means that a ''nonrefunding'' or ''deferred refunding'' issue *can still be called and prematurely retired for any reason other than refunding.* Thus, an investor could face a call on a high-yielding (nonrefundable) issue if the issuer has the cash to prematurely retire the bond.

Sinking Funds

Another provision that's important to investors is the **sinking fund,** which stipulates how a bond will be paid off over time. This provision, of course, applies only to term bonds, since serial issues already have a predetermined method of repayment. Not all (term) bonds have sinking fund requirements, but for those that do, a sinking fund specifies the annual repayment schedule that will be used to pay off the issue; it indicates how much principal will be retired each year. Sinking fund requirements

generally begin one to five years after the date of issue, and continue annually thereafter until all or most of the issue is paid off. Any amount not repaid by maturity (this might equal 10 to 25 percent of the issue) would then be retired with a single ''balloon'' payment. Like a call provision, the sinking fund feature also carries a call premium, although it is generally nominal and amounts to perhaps 1 percent or less of the principal being retired.

Types of Issues

first and refunding bonds
a bond that's secured in part with both first and second mortgages.

junior bonds
debt obligations backed only by the promise of the issuer to pay interest and principal on a timely basis.

debenture
an unsecured (junior) bond.

subordinated debentures
unsecured bonds that have a claim that's secondary to other debentures.

income bonds
unsecured bonds that require that interest be paid only if a specified amount of income is earned.

registered bonds
bonds issued to specific owners, whose names are formally registered with the issuer.

bearer bonds
bonds whose holders are considered to be their owners; there is no official record of ownership kept by the issuer.

A single issuer may have many different bonds outstanding at any given point in time. In addition to coupon and maturity, one bond can be differentiated from another by the type of collateral behind the issue. Issues can be either junior or senior. **Senior bonds** are secured obligations, since they are backed by a legal claim on some specific property of the issuer. Such issues would include **mortgage bonds,** which are secured by real estate; **collateral trust bonds,** which are backed by *securities* owned by the issuer but held in trust by a third party; **equipment trust certificates,** which are secured by specific pieces of equipment (like boxcars and airplanes) and are popular with railroads and airlines; and **first and refunding bonds,** which are basically a *combination* of first mortgage and junior lien bonds (i.e., the bonds are secured in part by a first mortgage on some of the issuer's property and in part by second, or third, mortgages on other properties—these issues are *less secure* than, and should *not* be confused with, straight first-mortgage bonds).

   Junior bonds, on the other hand, are backed by only the promise of the issuer to pay interest and principal on a timely basis. There are several classes of unsecured bonds, the most popular of which is known as a **debenture.** Figure 9.2 shows the announcement of a debenture bond that was issued in 1989. Note that even though there was no collateral backing up this obligation, the issuer—GTE Corporation—was able to sell $300 million worth of these 30-year bonds. In addition, **subordinated debentures** are also used; these issues have a claim on income secondary to other debenture bonds. **Income bonds,** probably the most junior of all, are unsecured debts which require that interest be paid only after a certain amount of income is earned; there is no legally binding requirement to meet interest payments on a timely or regular basis so long as a specified amount of income has not been earned. These issues are similar in many respects to *revenue bonds* found in the municipal market.

   Regardless of the type of collateral or kind of issue, a bond may either be registered or issued in bearer form. **Registered bonds** are issued to specific owners, and the names of all bondholders are formally registered with the issuer, who keeps a running account of ownership and automatically pays interest to the owners of record by check. In contrast, the holders, or possessors, of **bearer bonds** are considered to be their owners, and the issuing organization keeps no official record of ownership. Interest is received by ''clipping coupons'' and sending them in for payment. Bearer bonds were the most prevalent type of issue, but they are destined to become obsolete, as Congress has mandated that effective July 1983, all bonds must be issued in registered form. This was done to prevent bondholders from

This announcement is not an offer to sell or a solicitation of an offer to buy any of these securities. The offering is made only by the Prospectus and the related Prospectus Supplement, copies of which may be obtained in any State in which this announcement is circulated only from underwriters qualified to act as dealers in securities in such State.

NEW ISSUE

April 27, 1989

$300,000,000

GTE Corporation

10¼% Debentures Due 2019

———

Price 99.45%
Plus accrued interest from May 1, 1989

———

PaineWebber Incorporated

Goldman, Sachs & Co.

Salomon Brothers Inc

The First Boston Corporation   Merrill Lynch Capital Markets   Morgan Stanley & Co.
                                                                  Incorporated
Shearson Lehman Hutton Inc.   UBS Securities Inc.

Bear, Stearns & Co. Inc.   Daiwa Securities America Inc.   Deutsche Bank Capital
                                                             Corporation
Dillon, Read & Co. Inc.   Donaldson, Lufkin & Jenrette   Drexel Burnham Lambert
                                Securities Corporation   Incorporated
Grigsby Brandford Powell Inc.   Kidder, Peabody & Co.   Lazard Frères & Co.
                                     Incorporated
The Nikko Securities Co.   Nomura Securities International, Inc.
     International, Inc.
Paribas Corporation   Prudential–Bache Capital Funding

Smith Barney, Harris Upham & Co.   Sogen Securities Corporation
          Incorporated
SBCI Swiss Bank Corporation Investment banking   Wertheim Schroder & Co.
                                                         Incorporated
Dean Witter Reynolds Inc.   Yamaichi International (America), Inc.

FIGURE 9.2   The Announcement of a New Corporate Debenture Bond.
This bond was issued by GTE Corporation and is secured with nothing more than the good name of the company. The bond will not mature until 2019, and each year the company will pay $30.8 million in interest; over the full 30-year life of the bond, and in the absence of any refunding or sinking fund payments, the company will pay nearly a billion dollars in interest. (*Source: The Wall Street Journal,* April 27, 1989.)

TABLE 9.2 Economic Dimensions of the Bond Market

	Year-End Amounts Outstanding (in billions)				
Type of Issuer*	1950	1960	1970	1980	1988
U.S. Treasury	$138.7	$149.5	$159.8	$ 427.0	$1,410.2
U.S. agencies	1.1	8.8	17.6	276.1	1,025.7
States and municipalities	24.0	66.5	144.4	322.3	753.8
Corporations	93.8	105.4	181.0	421.7	835.1
Total	$257.6	$330.2	$502.8	$1,447.1	$4,024.8

*Excludes institutional issues, as such data are not available.
Source: Federal Reserve Bulletin, U.S. Treasury Bulletin, and *Survey of Current Business.*

cheating on their taxes (that is, since there's no record of ownership with bearer bonds, some people simply would not report the interest income they received on their tax returns).

THE BOND MARKET

Thus far, our discussion has dealt with basic bond features; we now shift our attention to a review of the market in which these securities are traded. The bond market is chiefly over-the-counter in nature, since listed bonds represent only a small portion of total outstanding obligations. In comparison to the stock market, the bond market is more price stable. Granted, interest rates (and therefore bond prices) do move up and down and have become a bit volatile in recent times, but when bond price activity is measured on a daily basis, it is remarkably stable. Table 9.2 lists the amount of bonds outstanding at selected yearly intervals. A glance at the table reveals not only the rapid growth of the market but also its enormous size. For example, by year-end 1988, the amount of bonds outstanding in this country had mushroomed to some $4 *trillion,* which was nearly a threefold increase from the level that had existed just 8 years earlier (in 1980). We will now examine this important and increasingly popular segment of the market by looking at available investment vehicles, the market's widespread use of bond ratings, the structure and behavior of interest rates, and several other aspects of investment behavior that are important to bond investors.

Available Vehicles

There are issues available in today's bond market to meet almost any type of investment objective and to suit just about any investor, no matter how conservative or aggressive. As a matter of convenience, the bond market is normally separated into five segments, according to type of issuer: Treasury, agency, municipal, corporate, and institutional. As we will see below, each sector has developed its own issue and operating features, as well as trading characteristics.

Treasury Bonds

"Treasuries" (or "governments" as they are sometimes called) are a dominant force in the fixed-income market, and if not the most popular type of bond, they certainly are the best known. The U.S. Treasury issues bonds, notes, and other types of debt securities (such as Treasury bills) as a way of meeting the ever-increasing needs of our federal government. All Treasury obligations are of the highest quality (they are backed by the full faith and credit of the U.S. government) and this feature, along with their liquidity, makes them very popular with individuals and institutions. **Treasury notes** carry maturities of 10 years or less, whereas **Treasury bonds** have maturities as long as 25 years or more. Treasury bonds and notes are generally sold in denominations of $1,000 and $5,000, and are issued in registered form. Interest income is subject to normal federal income tax but *is exempt from state and local taxes.*

Government bonds are either noncallable or issued with very lengthy deferred call features that are measured in relation to the maturity date of the obligation rather than the date of issue. Deferment features that expire 5 years before final maturity seem to be most common. Moreover, these deferred call features are a specific part of the bond listing system; for example, the 10 percent issue of 2005–10 signifies that this Treasury bond has a maturity date of 2010 and a deferred call feature that extends through 2005. Another unique feature is the unusual capital gains opportunity some of these bonds offer. That is, a number of older government bonds can be used, at par, to pay federal estate taxes. It is possible, in effect, to purchase a Treasury issue at a discount and shortly thereafter use it at par to pay estate taxes. Of course, the initial (purchase) transaction has to take place prior to death and the provision is beneficial only to the heirs (and only to the extent that there is a federal estate tax liability). Such bonds have been nicknamed **flower bonds.** Although the Treasury no longer issues new flower bonds, there still are a few of these bonds available in the market, most of which carry 2¾ to 4½ percent coupons and have maturities that range as far out as 1999. The supply of flower bonds is rapidly declining, and when they're gone (which will probably occur within the next several years), that'll be it for these issues.

Agency Bonds

Agency bonds are debt securities issued by various agencies and organizations of the U.S. government—like the Resolution Funding Corp., the Tennessee Valley Authority, and the Financing Corp. (FICO). They are *not* obligations of the U.S. Treasury and, technically, should not be considered the same as a Treasury bond. An important feature of agencies is that they customarily provide yields that are comfortably above the market rates for Treasuries; as such, they offer investors a way to increase returns with little or no real difference in risk. There are two types of agency issues: government-sponsored and federal agencies. Although there are only six government-sponsored organizations, the number of federal agencies exceed two dozen. To overcome some of the problems in the marketing of many relatively small federal agency securities, Congress established the Federal Financ-

---

Treasury notes *debt securities issued by the U.S. Treasury which are issued with maturities of 10 years or less.*

Treasury bonds *U.S. Treasury debt securities which are issued with maturities of more than 10 years—usually 25 years or more.*

flower bonds *older government bonds issued at a discount and used at par to pay federal estate taxes.*

Agency bonds *debt securities issued by various agencies and organizations of the U.S. government, like the Tennessee Valley Authority.*

TABLE 9.3   Characteristics of Popular Agency Issues

Type of Issue	Minimum Denomination	Initial Maturity	Tax Status* Federal	State	Local
Federal Farm Credit Banks	$ 1,000	13 months to 15 years	T	E	E
Federal Intermediate Credit Banks	5,000	9 months to 4 years	T	E	E
Federal Home Loan Bank	10,000	1 to 20 years	T	E	E
Federal Land Banks	1,000	1 to 10 years	T	E	E
Farmers Home Administration	25,000	1 to 25 years	T	T	T
Federal Housing Administration	50,000	1 to 40 years	T	T	T
Federal Home Loan Mortgage Corp.** ("Freddie Macs")	25,000	18 to 30 years	T	T	T
Federal National Mortgage Association** ("Fannie Maes")	25,000	1 to 30 years	T	T	T
Government National Mortgage Association** (GNMA— "Ginnie Maes")	25,000	12 to 40 years	T	T	T
Student Loan Marketing Association	10,000	3 to 10 years	T	E	E
Tennessee Valley Authority (TVA)	1,000	5 to 25 years	T	E	E
U.S. Postal Service	10,000	25 years	T	E	E
Federal Financing Bank	1,000	1 to 20 years	T	E	E

*T = taxable; E = tax-exempt
**Mortgage-backed securities.

---

ing Bank to consolidate the financing activities of all federal agencies. (As a rule, the generic term "agency" is used to denote both government-sponsored and federal agency obligations.)

Selected characteristics of some of the more popular agency bonds are presented in Table 9.3. Although these issues are not direct liabilities of the U.S. government, a few of them actually do carry government guarantees and therefore effectively represent the full faith and credit of the U.S. Treasury. But even those issues that don't carry such guarantees are still highly regarded in the marketplace, since they're all viewed as *moral obligations* of the U.S. government—meaning that it's highly unlikely that Congress would ever allow one to default. Also, like Treasury securities, agency issues are normally non-callable or carry lengthy call deferment features. One final point: Since 1986 *all new agency (and Treasury) securities* have been issued in *book entry* form. This means that there is no certificate of ownership issued to the buyer of the bonds; rather, the buyer receives a "confirmation" of the transaction and then his or her name is entered on a computerized log book, where it remains as long as the security is owned. Many experts believe that in the not-to-distant future all security transactions will be handled in this way.

Municipal Bonds

Municipal bonds are the issues of states, counties, cities, and other political subdivisions, such as school districts and water and sewer districts. They are generally issued as serial obligations, meaning that the issue is broken into a series of smaller bonds, each with its own maturity date and coupon. Municipal bonds—or "munis," as they're often called—are brought to the market as either general obligation or revenue bonds. **General obligation bonds** are backed by the full faith and credit (and taxing power) of the issuer; **revenue bonds,** in contrast, are serviced by the income generated from specific income-producing projects (for example, toll roads). Although general obligations dominated the municipal market prior to the mid-1970s, today the vast majority of munis come out as revenue bonds (accounting for about 65 to 70 percent of the new issue volume). The distinction between a general obligation and a revenue bond is an important one, since the issuer of a revenue bond is obligated to pay principal and interest *only if a sufficient level of revenue is generated*. (If the funds aren't there, the issuer does *not* have to make payment on the bond!) This is not the case with general obligation bonds, however, as these issues are required to be serviced in a prompt and timely fashion irrespective of the level of tax income generated by the municipality. For reasons that should be fairly obvious, revenue bonds involve a lot more risk than general obligations, and because of that, they provide higher yields. Regardless of the type, municipal bonds are customarily issued in $5,000 denominations. Figure 9.3 shows a typical municipal bond issue and illustrates many of the characteristics customarily found with such obligations, including the serial nature of these issues.

A somewhat unusual aspect of municipal bonds is the widespread use of **municipal bond guarantees.** These guarantees provide the bondholder with the assurance of a party other than the issuer that principal and interest payments will be made in a prompt and timely manner. As a result, bond quality is improved. The third party, in essence, provides an additional source of collateral in the form of insurance placed on the bond, at the date of issue, which is nonrevocable over the life of the obligation. Several states and five private organizations provide municipal bond guarantees. The five private insurers are the Municipal Bond Insurance Association (MBIA), the American Municipal Bond Assurance Corporation (AMBAC), Bond Investors Guaranty Insurance Company (BIG), the Financial Guaranty Investment Corporation (FGIC), and Capital Guaranty Insurance Company. All five of the private guarantors will insure any general obligation or revenue bond as long as it carries an S&P rating of triple-B or better. Municipal bond insurance results in higher ratings (up to triple-A) and improved liquidity, as these bonds are generally more actively traded in the secondary markets. Guaranteed municipal bonds are especially common in the revenue market and, as such, put a whole new light on these issues. That is, whereas an uninsured revenue bond lacks certainty of payment, a guaranteed issue is very much like a general obligation bond in that you know principal and interest payments will be made on time. [A variation of the municipal bond insurance concept that's becoming increasingly popular is the use of a bank *letter of credit* (or *LOC*); in essence, an LOC from a major commercial bank is added as collateral to the municipal bond, and the quality of the bond and its

---

municipal bonds
debt securities issued by states, counties, cities, and other political subdivisions, like school districts; most of these bonds are tax-exempt, meaning there's no federal income tax on interest income.

general obligation bonds
municipal bonds backed by the full faith and credit, and taxing power, of the issuer.

revenue bonds
municipal bonds backed by the revenue-generating capacity of the issuer; requires that principal and interest be paid only if a sufficient level of revenue is generated.

municipal bond guarantees
guarantees from a party other than the issuer that principal and interest payments will be made in a prompt and timely manner.

In the opinion of Co-Bond Counsel, based on existing statutes, regulations, rulings and court decisions, and assuming compliance with certain covenants described in the Official Statement, the interest on the Bonds is excuded from gross income for federal income tax purposes and is not an item of tax preference for purposes of the federal individual and corporate alternative minimum tax, although it is included in adjusted book income and adjusted current earnings in calculating corporate alternative minimum taxable income. In the opinion of Co-Bond Counsel, the interest on the Bonds is exempt from State of California personal income taxes.

New Issue

$209,835,000

City of Oakland, California

Special Refunding Revenue Bonds
(Pension Financing) 1988 Series A

Dated: December 1, 1988   Due: August 1, as shown below

The Bonds are issuable in fully registered form in denominations of $5,000 or any integral multiple thereof. Interest on the Bonds will be payable each February 1 and August 1, commencing February 1, 1989. The Bonds are subject to optional and mandatory redemption prior to maturity as described in the Official Statement.

The Bond proceeds are being used by the City of Oakland to prepay the City's lease payments to the Redevelopment Agency of the City under a master lease agreement between the City and the Agency. The Agency will apply such prepayment to the defeasance of the Agency's Certificates of Participation, 1985 Series A.

The Bonds are limited obligations of the City and do not constitute an indebtedness of or a charge against the general credit or the taxing power of the City or the State of California. The Bonds are payable solely from and secured solely by a pledge of the Revenues described in the Indenture, derived from certain payments to the City from the Police and Fire Retirement System pursuant to the First Supplement Annuity Deposit Agreement, described in the Official Statement.

Amount	Maturity	Interest Rate	Price	Amount	Maturity	Interest Rate	Price or Yield	Amount	Maturity	Interest Rate	Price or Yield
$6,515,000	1993	6½ %	100%	$8,485,000	1997	6.90%	100%	$8,305,000	2000	7.20%	100%
6,400,000	1994	6.60	100	8,440,000	1998	7	100	8,235,000	2001	7.30	100
6,245,000	1995	6.70	100	8,380,000	1999	7	7.10	8,140,000	2002	7.40	100
8,515,000	1996	6.80	100					8,035,000	2003	7.35	7.45

$124,140,000 7.60% Term Bonds due August 1, 2021 @ 99.50%
(Accrued Interest to be added)

Bonds of particular maturities may or may not be available from the undersigned or others at the above prices on and after the date of this announcement.

The Bonds are offered when, as and if issued by the City and received by the Underwriters, subject to the approval of validity by Morrison & Foerster, San Francisco, California, and Alexander, Millner & McGee, Oakland, California, Co-Bond Counsel. Certain legal matters will be passed upon for the Underwriters by Ballard, Spahr, Andrews & Ingersoll, Washington, D.C. and Hunter & Anderson, Oakland, California. The offering of the Bonds is made only by the Official Statement, copies of which may be obtained in any state from such of the undersigned as may lawfully offer these securities in such state.

Goldman, Sachs & Co.

Grigsby, Brandford & Co., Inc.

Pryor, Govan, Counts & Co., Inc.

December 22, 1988

FIGURE 9.3   The Announcement for a New Municipal Bond Issue.
This issue is a $209 million revenue bond that matures serially. Note that about 40 percent of the issue is retired annually from 1993 through 2003, and the balance (of nearly $125 million) is due in one large balloon payment some 34 years after the date of issue. Also, note that, as is customary with municipal bonds, the coupon increases with maturity. (*Source: The Wall Street Journal*, December 23, 1988.)

TABLE 9.4 How the States Tax Interest Income from Municipal Bonds

State	Interest on Own Bonds	Interest on Bonds Issued by Other States	State	Interest on Own Bonds	Interest on Bonds Issued by Other States
Alabama (5%)	Exempt	Taxable	Mississippi (5%)	Exempt	Taxable
Alaska (0)	No state income tax		Missouri (6%)	Exempt	Taxable
Arizona (8%)	Exempt	Taxable	Montana (12.1%)	Exempt	Taxable
Arkansas (7%)	Exempt	Taxable	Nebraska (5.9%)	Exempt	Taxable
California (9.3%)	Exempt	Taxable	Nevada (0)	No state income tax	
Colorado (5%)	Exempt (exceptions)	Taxable	New Hampshire (5%)	Exempt	Taxable
			New Jersey (3.5%)	Exempt	Taxable
Connecticut (12%)	Exempt	Taxable	New Mexico (8.5%)	Exempt	Exempt
Delaware (7.7%)	Exempt	Taxable	New York (7.9%)	Exempt	Taxable
D.C. (9.5%)	Exempt	Exempt	North Carolina (7%)	Exempt	Taxable
Florida (0)	No state income tax		North Dakota (12%)	Exempt	Taxable
Georgia (6%)	Exempt	Taxable	Ohio (6.9%)	Exempt	Taxable
Hawaii (10%)	Exempt	Taxable	Oklahoma (6%)	Taxable (limited exceptions)	Taxable
Idaho (8.2%)	Exempt	Taxable			
Illinois (2.5%)	Taxable (limited exceptions)	Taxable	Oregon (9%)	Exempt	Taxable
			Pennsylvania (2.1%)	Exempt	Taxable
Indiana (3.4%)	Exempt	Exempt	Rhode Island (7.6%)	Exempt	Taxable
Iowa (10%)	Taxable (limited exceptions)	Taxable	South Carolina (7%)	Exempt	Taxable
			South Dakota (0)	No state income tax	
Kansas (6.1%)	Exempt (bonds issued after '87)	Taxable	Tennessee (6%)	Exempt	Taxable
			Texas (0)	No state income tax	
Kentucky (6%)	Exempt	Taxable	Utah (7.4%)	Exempt	Exempt
Louisiana (6%)	Exempt	Taxable	Vermont (8.2%)	Exempt	Taxable
Maine (8%)	Exempt	Taxable	Virginia (5.8%)	Exempt	Taxable
Maryland (5%)	Exempt	Taxable	Washington (0)	No state income tax	
Massachusetts (10%)	Exempt	Taxable	West Virginia (6.5%)	Exempt	Taxable
Michigan (4.6%)	Exempt	Taxable	Wisconsin (6.9%)	Taxable	Taxable
Minnesota (8.5%)	Exempt	Taxable	Wyoming (0)	No state income tax	

Note: Percentage figures after state name is the top state tax rate that applies to bond interest income.

agency rating are improved accordingly. An LOC is a lot like a bond guarantee in that the bank stands ready to make principal and interest payments in case the municipality falters.]

Without a doubt, the thing that makes municipal securities unique is the fact that in most cases, their interest income is immune from federal income taxes (which is why these issues are known as tax-free, or tax-exempt, bonds). Note, however, that in contrast to interest income, *capital gains are subject to the usual federal taxes.* Normally, the obligations are also exempt from state and local taxes *in the state in which they were issued.* For example, a California issue would be free of California tax if the bondholder lived in California, but its interest income would be subject to state tax if the investor resided in Connecticut. Table 9.4 provides a complete rundown of the exposure of municipal bond interest income to *state* income taxes;

TABLE 9.5   Taxable Equivalent Yields for Various Tax-Exempt Returns

Taxable Income*			Tax-Free Yield								
Joint Returns ($000)	Individual Returns ($000)	Tax Bracket	5%	6%	7%	8%	9%	10%	12%	14%
$ 0 −$ 30.9	$ 0 −$ 18.5	15%	5.88	7.06	8.24	9.41	10.59	11.76	14.12	16.47
$30.9−$ 74.8	$18.5−$ 44.9	28	6.94	8.33	9.72	11.11	12.50	13.89	16.67	19.44
$74.8−$177.7**	$44.9−$104.3**	33	7.46	8.96	10.45	11.94	13.43	14.92	17.91	20.90

*Taxable income and tax rates effective January 1, 1989.

**Income over these amounts may be taxed at the 28 percent rate.

note that in all but a few cases, the interest income is exempt from state taxes *only if it's an in-state bond.*

Individual investors are today the biggest buyers of municipal bonds, and tax-free yield is certainly a major draw. To put this yield in perspective, Table 9.5 shows what a taxable bond would have to yield to equal the net yield of a tax-free bond. *It demonstrates how the yield attractiveness of municipals varies with an investor's income level;* clearly, the higher the individual's tax bracket, the more attractive municipal bonds become. Generally speaking, an investor has to be in one of the higher tax brackets (i.e., 28 or 33 percent) before municipal bonds offer yields that are competitive with fully taxable issues. This is because municipal yields are substantially lower than the returns available from fully taxable issues (such as corporates), and unless the *tax effect* is sufficient to raise the yield on a municipal to a figure that equals or surpasses taxable rates, it obviously doesn't make much sense to buy municipal bonds.

We can determine the kind of return a fully taxable bond would have to provide in order to match the after-tax return of a lower-yielding, tax-free issue by computing what is known as a municipal's **fully taxable equivalent yield.** This measure can be calculated according to the following simple formula:

fully taxable equivalent yield *the return a fully taxable bond would have to provide to match the after-tax return of a lower-yielding, tax-free municipal bond.*

$$\text{fully taxable equivalent yield} = \frac{\text{yield of municipal bond}}{1 - \text{federal tax rate}}$$

For example, if a certain municipal offered a yield of 6.5 percent, then an individual in the 33 percent tax bracket would have to find a fully taxable bond with a yield of 9.7 percent—6.5 percent/.67 = 9.7 percent—in order to reap the same after-tax returns as the municipal. [Note that since this calculation considers only *federal taxes,* the computed yield would apply only to out-of-state bonds (or to states that have no income tax). But if an investor held an in-state bond, that issue would also provide shelter from *state income taxes.* Such a situation would have the effect of *slightly increasing* (by perhaps ¼ to ½ a percentage point) the yield required on a fully taxable issue; for example, if the individual in our illustration above lived in a state with, say, a 5 or 6 percent state tax, the fully taxable equivalent yield would have to be *adjusted up* from 9.7 percent to about 10 percent, or so. That's roughly

the fully taxable yield that would be necessary to match the 6.5 percent return on this *in-state* bond.]

A word of caution regarding the tax-exempt status of municipal bonds: *Not all municipal bonds are exempt from federal income tax*. One of the provisions of the sweeping tax reform bill of 1986 was to restrict the types of bonds that qualify as tax-exempt issues. Specifically, if the bonds are used to finance projects considered "nonessential," the interest on such obligations is *not* tax exempt. Thus, a whole new breed of municipal bonds was created. Known as **taxable munis,** these issues are expected to eventually account for perhaps 20 to 25 percent of the municipal bond market within a short period of time. As the name implies, the interest income on these bonds is *fully taxable* (at least as far as federal income taxes are concerned). The after-tax yields of taxable municipals generally do *not* measure up to those on tax-free munies, but taxables do have some redeeming qualities of their own. For one thing, these issues offer yields that are considerably higher than those from Treasury bonds; furthermore, taxable munies are usually *noncallable*, thereby allowing investors to lock in the high yields for a number of years.

taxable munis
municipal bonds, used to finance projects considered nonessential, whose interest income is fully taxable by the federal government.

Corporate Bonds

The major nongovernmental issuers of bonds are corporations. The market for *corporate bonds* is customarily subdivided into several segments, which include industrials (the most diverse of the groups); public utilities (the dominant group in terms of volume of new issues); rail and transportation bonds; and financial issues (banks, finance companies, and so forth). Not only is there a full range of bond quality available in the corporate market, but there's also the widest assortment of different types of bonds, ranging from first mortgage obligations to convertible bonds (which we'll examine in the next chapter), debentures, subordinated deben- tures, senior subordinated issues, capital notes (which are a type of unsecured debt issued by banks and other financial institutions), and income bonds. Inter- est on corporate bonds is paid semiannually, and sinking funds are popular. The bonds usually come in $1,000 denominations and are issued on a term basis with a single maturity date. Maturities usually range from 25 to 40 years, and nearly all corporates carry call deferment provisions that prohibit prepayment for the first 5 to 10 years. Corporate issues are popular with individuals because of their relatively attractive yields.

Although most corporates fit the general description above, one that does not is the *equipment trust certificate,* which is issued by railroads, airlines, and other transportation concerns. The proceeds from equipment trust certificates are used to purchase equipment, such as freight cars and railroad engines, which in turn serve as the collateral for the issue. They are usually issued in *serial form* and carry uniform annual installments throughout. These bonds normally carry maturities that range from 1 year to a maximum that seldom exceeds 15 to 17 years. An attractive feature of equipment trust certificates is that in spite of a near-perfect payment record that dates back to predepression days, these issues offer yields to investors that are well above average.

Institutional Bonds

By far the smallest segment of the bond market, *institutional bonds* are marketed (usually in $1,000 denominations) by a variety of private, nonprofit institutions such as schools, hospitals, and churches. Many of the issuers are affiliated with religious orders, and hospitals have been dominant. The bonds are sometimes called *heart bonds* because of their emotional appeal. (Some investors actually view investing in these bonds as a charitable activity.) Even though there's been a relatively small number of defaults, institutional bonds regularly provide returns that are 1 to 2 percentage points *above* comparably-rated corporates. They do so because the secondary market for these issues is almost nonexistent. However, because these bonds are issued on a serial basis, with relatively short maximum maturities (seldom exceeding 15 to 18 years), an investor can overcome this deficiency by purchasing maturities that are in line with portfolio needs—thereby reducing (or even eliminating) the need for subsequent trading.

Specialty Issues

variable-rate note
a specialty bond issue with two unique features: (1) after a specified period of time (6–18 months), the coupon "floats" at a certain amount above T-bill or T-note rates, and (2) every year, or so, the notes are redeemable at par, at the bondholder's option.

put bond
a type of specialty bond that gives the holder the right to redeem the bonds at certain specified times before maturity.

extendable notes
a specialty issue, typically with short maturities (1–5 years), which can be redeemed or renewed for the same period at a new interest rate.

In addition to the basic bond vehicles described above, investors can also choose from a growing number of *specialty issues*—bonds that possess unusual issue characteristics. For the most part, these bonds have coupon or repayment provisions that are out-of-the-ordinary. Most are issued by corporations, although they are being used increasingly by other issuers as well. Probably the oldest type of specialty issue is the **variable-rate note.** First issued in this country in 1974, it has two unique features: (1) after the first 6 to 18 months of an issue's life, the coupon "floats" so that every 6 to 12 months it is pegged at a certain amount above prevailing Treasury bill or Treasury note rates; and (2) every year, the notes are redeemable at par and at the *bondholder's* option. Thus, variable-rate notes represent long-term commitments on the part of borrowers (they're usually issued with 15- to 25-year maturities), yet they provide investors with all the advantages (especially price stability) of short-term obligations. Another specialty issue, similar in some respects to a variable-rate note, is the **put bond.** Such an issue gives the holder the right to redeem the bonds before they mature—usually, 3 to 5 years after the date of issue, and then every 1 to 5 years thereafter. In return for the right to periodically "put the bond" for redemption, the investor receives a lower yield (but it is fixed for the life of the issue). And there are also **extendable notes,** which are actually short-term securities, typically with 1 to 5 year maturities, which can be redeemed or renewed for the same period at a new interest rate. For example, an issue might come out as a series of 3-year renewable notes, over a period of 15 years; every 3 years those notes are extendable for another 3 years, but at a new yield (coupon) comparable to the market interest rates that prevail at the time of renewal.

Specialty issues are often among the more popular bonds on Wall Street. In fact, three of the hottest issues today are securities that are out-of-the-ordinary in one way or another, each having unusual features that distinguish them from the rest of the crowd. The three issues are: zero coupon bonds, mortgage-backed securities, and junk bonds.

Zero-Coupon Bonds

zero-coupon bonds
a bond with no coupons that's sold at a deep discount from par value; they increase in value over time at a compound rate of return so that at maturity they are worth considerably more than their initial cost.

As the name implies, **zero-coupon bonds** have no coupons. Rather, these securities are sold at a deep discount from their par values, and then increase in value over time at a compound rate of return so that at maturity, they are worth much more than their initial investment. Other things being equal, the cheaper the bond, the greater the return you can earn (for example, whereas a 7 percent bond might cost $360, an issue with a 15 percent yield will cost only $123). Because they don't have coupons, these bonds do not pay interest semiannually; in fact they pay *nothing* to the investor until the issue matures. As strange as it might seem, this is the main attraction of zero coupon bonds; that is, since there are no interest payments, investors do not have to worry about reinvesting coupon income twice a year. Instead, the fully compounded rate of return on a zero coupon bond is virtually guaranteed at the stated rate that existed when the issue was purchased. For example, in early 1989, good grade zero-coupon bonds with 20-year maturities were available at yields of around 9 to 10 percent; thus, for just $150 you could buy a bond that would be worth nearly seven times that amount, or $1,000, at maturity in 20 years. Best of all, in the absence of any default, you would be *locking in* a 10 percent compound rate of return on your investment for the full 20-year life of the issue.

The foregoing advantages notwithstanding, there are also some serious disadvantages to zeros. One is that if rates do move up over time, you won't be able to participate in the higher return (since you'll have no coupon income to reinvest). In addition, zero-coupon bonds are subject to tremendous price volatility; thus, if market rates climb, you'll experience a sizable capital loss as the prices of zero coupons plunge! (Of course, if interest rates *drop*, you'll reap enormous capital gains if you hold long-term zeros; indeed, such issues are unsurpassed in capital gains potential.) Finally, the IRS has ruled that zero-coupon bondholders must report interest on an accrual basis, even though no interest is actually received—not a very good deal! For this reason, most fully taxable zero-coupon bonds should either be used in tax-sheltered investments, like individual retirement accounts (IRAs), or be held by minor children, who are 14 or older and likely to be taxed at the lowest rate, if at all. Zeros are issued by corporations, municipalities, federal agencies, and the U.S. Treasury; in addition, many major brokerage houses package U.S. Treasury securities as zeros and sell them to the investing public in the form of investment trusts, which are marketed under such names as TIGRS, CATS, and LIONS.

Mortgage-Backed Securities

mortgage-backed bond
a debt issue secured by a pool of home mortgages; issued primarily by federal agencies.

Simply put, a **mortgage-backed bond** is a debt issue that is secured by a pool of mortgages. An issuer, such as the Government National Mortgage Association (GNMA), puts together a pool of mortgages and then issues securities in the amount of the total mortgage pool. These securities, known as *pass-through securities,* or *participation certificates,* are usually sold in minimum denominations of $25,000. Though their maturities can go out as far as 25 to 30 years, the average life of one of these issues is generally much shorter (perhaps as short as 10 to 12 years), because so many pooled mortgages are paid off early. As an investor in one of these securities, you hold an undivided interest in the pool of mortgages. Thus, when a home-

TABLE 9.6   Major Agency Issuers of Mortgage-Backed Securities.

Agency	Nickname	Description
Government National Mortgage Association (GNMA)	Ginnie Mae	The largest pass-through issuer; packager and sells pools of FHA and VA insured mortgages.
Federal Home Loan Mortgage Association (FHLMC)	Freddie Mac	Second largest. First to offer pools containing conventional mortgages; the major issuer of Participation Certificates (PCs). Government-sponsored but no government guarantees.
Federal National Mortgage Association (FNMA)	Fannie Mae	The oldest of the crowd, offers a pass-through security similar to Participation Certificates. Privately owned corporation with government sponsorship but no government guarantees. Leader in the purchase of "older" mortgages with low coupon rates.

owner makes a monthly mortgage payment, that payment is essentially passed through to you, the bondholder, to pay off the mortgage-backed bond that you hold. Although these securities come with normal coupons, the interest is paid monthly rather than semiannually. Actually, the monthly payments received by bondholders are, like mortgage payments, made up of *both* principal and interest. Since the principal portion of the payment represents return of capital, it is considered tax-free; not so with interest income, however, as it is subject to ordinary state and federal income taxes.

Mortgage-backed securities are issued primarily by three federal agencies. Although there are some state and private issuers—mainly big banks and S&Ls—agency issues dominate the market and account for 90 to 95 percent of the activity. The major agency issuers of pass-through securities are shown and described in Table 9.6.

One of the problems with mortgage-backed securities is that they are *self-liqui-dating,* since a portion of the monthly cash flow to the investor is the principal originally invested in the issue. Thus, the investor is always receiving back part of the original investment capital, so that at maturity there is *no* big principal payment that will be received. (Instead, the principal has been paid back in little chunks over the life of the bond.) Indeed, some uninformed investors are shocked to find there's nothing (or very little) left of their original capital. To counter this problem, a number of *mutual funds* were formed that invest in mortgage-backed securities *but* which automatically and continually reinvest the capital/principal portion of the cash flows. The mutual fund investors therefore receive only the interest from their investment and as such, are able to preserve their capital.

Loan prepayments are another problem with mortgage-backed securities. In fact,

it was in part an effort to defuse some of the prepayment uncertainty in standard mortgage-backed securities that led to the creation of **collateralized mortgage obligations,** or **CMOs.** Normally, as pooled mortgages are prepaid, *all* bondholders receive a prorated share of the prepayments, and as a result the net effect is to sharply reduce the life of the bond. A CMO, in contrast, divides investors into classes (formally called "tranches"), depending on whether they want a short-term, intermediate-term, or long-term investment. Now, while interest is paid to all bondholders, *all principal payments* go first to the shortest class, until it is fully retired; then, the next class (tranche) in the sequence becomes the sole recipient of principal, and so on until the last tranche is retired. Thus in a CMO, only one class of bond at a time receives principal. Actually, nearly all mortgage-backed securities today are sold to the public either as CMOs or as REMICs (*R*eal *E*state *M*ortgage *I*nvestment *C*onduits)—all these really amount to are different ways of packaging mortgages and standard pass-through securities for resale to the investing public.

Generally speaking (with the possible exception of something called a *pass-through residual*), mortgage-backed securities are a safe form of investment, and they offer highly competitive, attractive returns. What's more, there's a well-developed after-market, so it's relatively easy to buy and sell these bonds in the open market. However, these are long-term debt securities and, like any long-term bond, they are subject to wide price swings when interest rates shoot up or down. Just because they're secured with a pool of mortgages doesn't make them immune to price volatility. These securities have been a big hit in the market, as they have been enthusiastically received by both individual and institutional investors. (By 1988, there was over 3/4 of a *trillion* dollars of mortgage-backed securities outstanding.) Such acceptance has led to the development of a new market technology—that is, the process of **securitization,** whereby various types of bank lending vehicles are transformed into marketable securities, much like a mortgage-backed security. Investment bankers are now selling billions of dollars worth of pass-through securities, known as *asset-backed securities,* which are backed by pools of auto loans, credit card bills, and loans on mobile homes and recreational vehicles. For example, GMAC—the financing arm of General Motors—is a regular issuer of collateralized auto loan securities; in a similar fashion, MasterCard and Visa receivables are regularly used as collateral on credit-card–backed securities. These obligations are just like mortgage-backed securities, except they have much shorter maturities (generally less than 3 years) and they're backed by a pool of auto loans or credit card receivables, rather than home mortgages. Figure 9.4 shows an announcement of a newly issued debt security that's backed by credit card receivables.

Junk Bonds

Junk bonds, or "high-yield bonds" as they're also called, are highly speculative securities that have received low ratings (e.g., Ba or B) from such organizations as Moody's and Standard & Poor's. Despite the derogatory terminology, such bonds are a popular investment vehicle (or at least they were until some highly-publicized defaults occurred). Many investors find them attractive because of the very high returns they offer; in early 1989, for example, returns of 16 percent, or more, were not uncommon. However, *such returns were available only because of the very*

This announcement is neither an offer to sell nor a solicitation of offers to buy any of these securities. The offering is made only by the Prospectus.

NEW ISSUE

February 16, 1989

$750,000,000

National Credit Card Trust 1989-2

9.85% Credit Card Participation Certificates

Citibank (South Dakota), N.A.
Seller and Servicer

Citibank (Nevada), National Association
Seller

The 9.85% Credit Card Participation Certificates (the "Certificates") evidence fractional undivided interests in certain assets of the National Credit Card Trust 1989-2 (the "Trust") to be created pursuant to a Pooling and Servicing Agreement among Citibank (South Dakota), N.A. and Citibank (Nevada), National Association, as sellers (collectively, the "Banks"), Citibank (South Dakota), N.A., as servicer, and Bankers Trust Company, as trustee. The Trust assets will include receivables (the "Receivables") generated from time to time in a portfolio of consumer revolving credit card accounts, collections thereon and the benefits of a limited letter of credit all as described in the Prospectus. Certain assets of the Trust will be allocated to Certificateholders, including the right to receive a varying percentage of each month's collections with respect to the Receivables at the times and in the manner described in the Prospectus. The Banks will own the remaining interest in the Trust and Citibank (South Dakota), N.A. will continue to service the Receivables.

The Certificates represent Beneficial Interests in the Trust only and do not represent interests in or obligations of the Banks, Citibank, N.A., Citicorp or any affiliate thereof. Neither the Certificates nor the underlying accounts or Receivables are insured or guaranteed by the Federal Deposit Insurance Corporation or any other governmental agency.

Price 99.8125% Per Certificate

plus accrued interest, if any, from March 1, 1989

Copies of the Prospectus may be obtained in any State in which this announcement is circulated only from such of the undersigned as may legally offer these securities in such State.

The First Boston Corporation

Goldman, Sachs & Co.

Salomon Brothers Inc

Merrill Lynch Capital Markets

UBS Securities Inc.

J. P. Morgan Securities Inc.

FIGURE 9.4 An Asset-Backed Security.

This $750 million, 3-year issue is backed by a pool of credit card receivables. In effect, rather than the bank carrying these assets, it sells them to investors; and it's a *great* deal for the bank: how many credit cards do you know of that charge only 9.85% interest? (*Source: The Wall Street Journal,* February 16, 1989.)

high risk exposure involved. As a result, most experts agree that the safest way to invest in junk bonds is through a diversified portfolio of these securities—preferably in something like a *junk bond mutual fund.*

Junk bonds are issued primarily by corporations, and increasingly, by municipalities as well. Traditionally, the term was applied to the issues of *troubled companies;* these securities might have been well rated when first issued, only to slide to low ratings through corporate mismanagement, heavy competition, or other factors. In the past few years, however, the vast majority of junk bonds have originated *not* with troubled companies, but rather with a growing number of mature (fairly well known) firms that use *enormous* amounts of this form of debt to finance corporate takeovers and leveraged buy-outs. An excellent example of this is the $27 billion LBO of RJR Nabisco, a major chunk of which was financed with low-rated junk bonds. Now, even though RJR Nabisco and other firms like them may not be considered troubled companies in the normal sense of the word (Wall Street refers to them as ''Fallen Angels''), investors should keep in mind that these issues are still low-rated debt that carry with them *a high risk of default!* Like all junk bonds, they should be used only by investors who are thoroughly familiar with the risks and, equally important, who are comfortable with such risk exposure.

Bond Ratings

bond ratings
letter grades that designate investment quality, assigned to a bond issue on the basis of extensive financial analysis.

Bond ratings are like grades; a letter grade is assigned to a bond issue on the basis of extensive, professionally conducted, financial analysis that designates its investment quality. Ratings are widely used and are an important part of the municipal, corporate, and institutional markets, where issues are regularly evaluated and rated by one or more of the rating agencies. Even some agency issues, like the Tennessee Valley Authority (TVA), are rated, although they always receive ratings that confirm the obvious—that the issues are prime grade. The two largest and best-known rating agencies are Moody's and Standard & Poor's.

How Ratings Work

Every time a large new issue comes to the market, it is analyzed by a staff of professional bond analysts to determine default risk exposure and investment quality. The financial records of the issuing organization are thoroughly worked over and its future prospects assessed. Although the specifics of the actual credit analysis conducted by the rating agencies change with each issue, several major factors enter into most bond ratings. For example, with a corporate issue, these factors would include an analysis of the issue's indenture provisions, an in-depth study of the firm's earning power (including the stability of its earnings), a look at the company's liquidity and how it is managed, a study of the company's relative debt burden, and an in-depth exploration of its coverage ratios to determine how well it can service both existing debt and any new bonds that are being contemplated or proposed. (A fee that usually ranges from $500 to $15,000 is charged for rating each corporate bond and is paid by the issuer or the underwriter of the securities being rated.) The product of all this is a bond rating assigned at the time of issue that indicates the ability of the issuing organization to service its debt in a prompt and timely fashion.

TABLE 9.7 Bond Ratings

Moody's	S&P	Definition
Aaa	AAA	*High-grade investment bonds.* The highest rating assigned, denoting extremely strong capacity to pay principal and interest. Often called "gilt edge" securities.
Aa	AA	*High-grade investment bonds.* High quality by all standards, but rated lower primarily because the margins of protection are not quite as strong.
A	A	*Medium-grade investment bonds.* Many favorable investment attributes, but elements may be present which suggest susceptibility to adverse economic changes.
Baa	BBB	*Medium-grade investment bonds.* Adequate capacity to pay principal and interest but possibly lacking certain protective elements against adverse economic conditions.
Ba	BB	*Speculative issues.* Only moderate protection of principal and interest in varied economic times. (This is one of the ratings carried by *junk bonds.*)
B	B	*Speculative issues.* Generally lacking desirable characteristics of investment bonds. Assurance of principal and interest may be small; this is another *junk bond* rating.
Caa	CCC	*Default.* Poor-quality issues that may be in default or in danger of default.
Ca	CC	*Default.* Highly speculative issues, often in default or possessing other market shortcomings.
C		*Default.* These issues may be regarded as extremely poor in investment quality.
	C	*Default.* Rating given to income bonds on which no interest is paid.
	D	*Default.* Issues actually in default, with principal or interest in arrears.

Source: Moody's *Bond Record* and Standard & Poor's *Bond Guide.*

Table 9.7 lists the various ratings assigned to bonds by each of the two major services. In addition to the standard rating categories as denoted in the table, Moody's uses numerical modifiers (1, 2, or 3) on bonds rated double A to B, and S&P uses plus (+) or minus (−) signs on the same rating classes to show relative standing within a major rating category—for example, an A+ (or A1) means a strong, high A rating, but an A− (or A3) indicates the issue is on the low end of the scale. Except for slight variations in designations (Aaa vs. AAA), the meanings and interpretations are basically the same. Most of the time, Moody's and S&P assign identical ratings. Sometimes, however, an issue will carry two different ratings: these are known as **split ratings** and are viewed simply as "shading" the quality of an issue one way or another. For example, an issue might be Aa rated by Moody's, but A or A+ by S&P. Older, outstanding issues are also regularly reviewed to

split ratings
different ratings given to a bond issue by the two major rating agencies.

ensure that the assigned rating is still valid. Most issues will carry a single rating to maturity, but it is not uncommon for some ratings to be revised up or down during the life of the issue. As you might expect, the market responds to rating revisions by adjusting bond yields accordingly—for example, an upward revision (from, say, A to AA) will cause the market yield on the bond to drop, as a reflection of the bond's improved quality. Finally, although it may appear that the firm is receiving the rating, it is actually the *issue* that receives it. As a result, a firm can have different ratings assigned to its issues; the senior securities, for example, might carry one rating and the junior issues another, lower rating.

What Ratings Mean

Most bond investors pay careful attention to agency ratings since they can affect not only potential market behavior, but comparative market yields as well. Specifically, the higher the rating, the lower the yield of an obligation, other things being equal. Thus, whereas an A-rated bond might offer a 10 percent yield, a comparable triple-A issue would probably yield something like 9½ to 9¾ percent. Furthermore, investment-grade securities (those that receive one of the top four ratings) are more interest-sensitive and tend to exhibit more uniform price behavior than lower-rated (speculative-grade) issues. Bond ratings serve to relieve individual investors from the drudgery of evaluating the investment quality of an issue on their own. Large institutional investors often have their own staff of credit analysts who independently assess the creditworthiness of various corporate and municipal issuers; individual investors, in contrast, have very little if anything to gain from conducting their own credit analysis. After all, the credit analysis process is time-consuming, costly, and involves a good deal more expertise than the average individual investor possesses. Most important, the ratings are closely adhered to by a large segment of the bond investment community, in large part because it's been shown that the rating agencies themselves do a remarkably good job of assessing bond quality. Thus, individual investors can depend on assigned agency ratings as a viable measure of the creditworthiness of the issuer and an issue's risk of default. A word of caution is in order, however: Bear in mind that bond ratings are intended as a measure of an issue's *default risk* only, all of which has no bearing whatsoever on an issue's exposure to *market risk*. Thus, if interest rates increase, then even the highest-quality issues can (and will) go down in price, subjecting investors to capital loss and market risk.

Market Interest Rates

The behavior of market interest rates *has significant impact on bond yields and prices,* and as such is closely followed by both conservative and aggressive investors. Interest rates are important to conservative investors, since one of their major objectives is to lock in high yields. Aggressive traders also have a stake in interest rates because their investment programs are built on the capital gains opportunities that accompany major swings in rates.

Just as there is no single bond market, but a series of different market sectors, so too there is no single interest rate applicable to all segments of the market. Rather, each segment has its own, somewhat unique, level of interest rates. Granted, the

yield spreads
*differences in interest
rates that exist in
various sections of
the market.*

various rates do tend to drift in the same direction over time and to follow the same general pattern of behavior, but it's also common for **yield spreads** (or interest-rate differentials) to exist in the various market sectors. We can summarize some of the more important market yields and yield spreads as follows:

1. Municipal bonds usually carry the lowest market rates because of the tax-exempt feature of these obligations; as a rule, their market yields are about two-thirds those of corporates. In the taxable sector, governments have the lowest yields (because they have the least risk), followed by agencies, corporates, and finally, institutional obligations, which provide the highest returns.

2. Those issues that normally carry agency ratings (such as municipals or corporates) generally display the same behavior: The lower the agency rating, the higher the yield.

3. There is generally, a direct relationship between the coupon an issue carries and its yield—discount (low-coupon) bonds yield the least, and premium (high-coupon) bonds the most.

4. In the municipal sector, revenues yield more than general obligations.

5. Bonds that are freely callable generally provide the highest returns, at least at date of issue; these are followed by deferred call obligations, with noncallable bonds yielding the least.

6. As a rule, bonds with long maturities tend to yield more than short issues; however, this rule does not hold all the time, since there are periods, such as in early 1989, for example, when short-term yields exceeded the yields on long-term bonds.

The preceding list can be used as a general guide to the higher-yielding segments of the bond market. For example, income-oriented municipal bond investors might do well to consider certain high-quality revenue bonds as a way to increase yields; and agency bonds, rather than Treasuries, might be selected for the same reason by investors who like to stick to high-quality issues.

Investors should pay close attention to interest rates and yield spreads and try to stay abreast not only of the current state of the market, but also of *the future direction in market rates*. If a conservative (income-oriented) bond investor thinks, for example, that rates have just about peaked, that should be a clue to try to lock in the prevailing high yields with some form of call protection (such as buying bonds—like Treasuries or double A rated utilities—that still have lengthy call deferments). In contrast, if an aggressive bond trader thinks rates have peaked (and are about to drop), that should be a signal to buy bonds that offer maximum price appreciation potential—like low-coupon bonds that still have a long time to go before they mature. Clearly, in either case, *the future direction of interest rates is important!*

But how does a bond investor formulate such expectations? Unless the investor has considerable training in economics, he or she will have to rely on various published sources. Fortunately, there is a wealth of such information available. One's broker is an excellent source for such reports, as are investor services such as Moody's and Standard & Poor's; finally, there are widely circulated business and

CREDIT MARKETS

New 52-Week T-Bills Are Extremely Popular; Bonds Stage Biggest One-Day Rally of the Year

By TOM HERMAN
And RICK STINE
Staff Reporters of THE WALL STREET JOURNAL

NEW YORK—The Treasury's new one-year bills sold yesterday proved to be exceptionally popular.

Treasury officials received a huge volume of bids for the bills from individuals and institutions. The average discount rate was 8.45%, which translates into a bond-equivalent yield of 9.16%.

With short-term rates so high, many investors have concluded that this is a good time to play it safe. The volume of bids from individual investors at yesterday's auction was nearly three times as large as at the previous auction of one-year bills last month.

Moreover, one-year T-bills offer even higher yields than 30-year government bonds, which were quoted late yesterday at 8.98%. "If I can get 9% on a one-year Treasury bill, that allows me time to wait and see how things unfold," said James R. Capra, senior vice president at Shearson Lehman Government Securities Inc.

Meanwhile, the dollar's recent strength in the currency markets helped bolster bonds yesterday. Prices of long-term Treasury issues, which had hardly budged all week, rose about ¾ point, or $7.50 for each $1,000 face amount, the biggest one-day rally in about three weeks.

Trading volume was brisk. "It's by far the busiest retail day we've had" this year, said William Pike, a managing director at Manufacturers Hanover Securities Corp. He said the dollar's stability "emboldened some foreigners to buy more [Treasury bonds] than they would have."

Mr. Pike and several other dealers also attributed the bond rally partly to short-covering, in which dealers scrambled to buy back securities they previously had borrowed and sold. Some dealers also pointed to strong buying in the Chicago futures markets.

Rumors that a government report this morning will show unexpectedly low inflation last month helped fuel the rally, traders said. They said there was speculation that the producer price index for December will show a rise of only 0.2% or 0.3%. That would be lower than the average estimate of a 0.4% increase in a survey of a dozen analysts by Dow Jones Capital Markets Report.

Treasury Securities

The Treasury received a record volume of bids from individual investors at its sale of $9.04 billion of new 52-week bills yesterday.

The Treasury received $1.57 billion of "noncompetitive tenders," mostly from individuals. That was up from $534 million at

record was $886 million at an auction of 52-week bills in September 1983.

The average return of 8.45% was down slightly from 8.49% at the previous 52-week bill auction.

In the bond market, trading was quiet early in the day but prices began to advance in the afternoon. The Treasury's 30-year bonds climbed to 100 5/32 from 99 14/32, while the yield fell to 8.98% from 9.05%. The latest 10-year notes rose to 98 6/32 from 97 22/32, and the yield fell to 9.15%

Money Growth vs. the Fed's Targets
Monthly averages, Seasonally adjusted

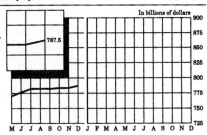

M1 Checking deposits plus cash held by the public. The Fed didn't set a target for M1 growth this year or last year. The inset shows the latest period.

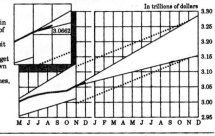

M2 Includes everything in M1 plus most types of savings, including money market deposit accounts. The Fed's tentative growth target for this year, as shown by the large cone as well as the dotted lines, is 3%-to-7% growth, compared with 4%-to-8% last year.

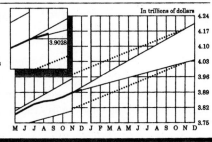

M3 Includes M2 plus some investments such as large certificates of deposit and money market funds sold to institutions. The Fed's tentative target this year is 3.5%-to-7.5% growth, down from 4%-to-8% last year.

High price (Rate) 91.476 (8.43%)
Low price (Rate) 91.446 (8.46%)
Coupon equivalent 9.16%
The bills are dated Jan. 19 and mature Jan. 18, 1990

Corporate Issues

Corporate bond prices finished ⅛ to ½ point higher in light trading.

Only one new issue came to market yesterday and that was a $100 million offering of 10-year notes from **McDonald's** Corp. Underwriters said the issue sold out quickly.

Syndicate officials noted that the issue

FIGURE 9.5 A Popular Source of Information About Interest Rates and the Credit Markets.

The "Credit Markets" column appears every day in *The Wall Street Journal* and provides a capsule view of current conditions and future prospects in the bond market. Note on this particular day that a good deal of the article was devoted to various measures of the money supply and the growth in these measures. (*Source: The Wall Street Journal*, January 13, 1989, p. C12.)

financial publications—like *The Wall Street Journal, Forbes, Business Week,* and *Fortune*—that regularly address the current state and future direction of market interest rates (one of the best of these is illustrated in Figure 9.5). Make no mistake, it's not an easy task! And even worse, it's next to impossible to consistently predict the future direction of interest rates with a high degree of precision. However, by taking the time to regularly and carefully read some of these publications and reports, investors can readily keep track of the behavior of interest rates and at least get a handle on what is likely to occur in the near future (say over the next 6 to 12 months, perhaps longer).

What Causes Interest Rates to Move?

Although the subject of interest rates is a complex economic issue, we do know that certain forces are especially important in influencing the general behavior of market rates. As bond investors, it's in our best interests to become familiar with the major determinants of interest rates and to try to monitor these variables—at least in an informal fashion. Perhaps no variable is more important in this regard than *inflation*. Changes in the inflation rate (or even expectations about the future course of inflation) have had a direct and pronounced effect on market interest rates, and have been a leading cause of the wide swings in interest rates. Clearly, if expectations are for inflation to slow down (that is, to enter a period of "disinflation"), then market interest rates should fall as well. To gain an appreciation of the extent to which interest rates are linked to inflation, refer to Figure 9.6 on page 390; note that as inflation drifts up, so too do interest rates, and that a drop in inflation is matched by a similar decline in interest rates. In addition to inflation, other variables that have an effect on interest rates include: (1) changes in the money supply; (2) the amount of "red ink" in the federal budget (the size of the federal deficit); (3) the demand for loanable funds; and (4) the level of economic activity. An increase or big jump in any one of these will put upward pressure on interest rates. Finally, there are the actions of the Federal Reserve—notably, the level at which it sets its discount rate.

Bond Yield Curves

yield curve
graphic representation of the relationship between a bond's term to maturity and its yield at a given point in time.

Although many factors affect the behavior of market interest rates, one of the most popular and widely studied is *bond maturity.* As noted above, we would normally expect yields to increase as bond maturities are lengthened. The relationship between yield and maturity is often captured in a **yield curve,** which graphically relates term to maturity to a bond's yield at a given point in time. Two different kinds of yield curves are illustrated in Figure 9.7 on page 391. By far, the most common type is *upward sloping,* like curve 1. It shows that yields tend to increase with longer maturities and that higher returns are available to those willing to buy the longer, riskier bonds (because price volatility and the risk of loss increases with bonds that have lengthy maturities). Should the slope of this yield curve start rising *sharply,* that's usually a sign that inflation is starting to heat up and as a result, interest rates are likely to go up, too. Under such conditions, most seasoned bond investors will turn to short or intermediate (3–5 years) maturities, which provide

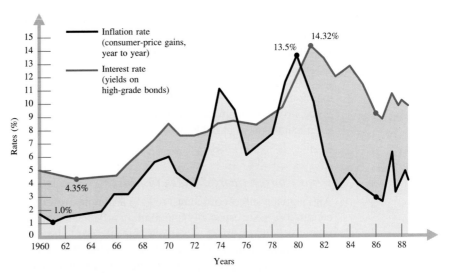

FIGURE 9.6 The Impact of Inflation on the Behavior of Interest Rates.
The behavior of interest rates has always been closely tied to movements in the rate of inflation. What changed in the early 1980s, however, was the spread between inflation and interest rates—whereas a spread of roughly 3 points was common in the past, it has held at about 6 percentage points since 1982.

reasonable returns with minimum exposure to capital loss. Rather than upward sloping, the yield curve may occasionally take on an inverted or downward-sloping shape, like curve 2. This occurs when the Fed pushes short-term rates way up (in an attempt to cool inflation), and it is widely viewed by knowledgeable investors as an almost sure sign that rates have peaked and are about to fall. Accordingly, while inverted yield curves usually don't last long, their appearance is generally felt to present an unusual investment opportunity for investors with available cash.

Yield curves are constructed by plotting the yields for a group of bonds that are similar in all respects except maturity; treasury bonds, for example, are homogeneous with respect to quality and issue characteristics, and their yield curves enjoy widespread publicity in the financial media. A particular yield curve exists for only a short period of time; as market conditions change, so does its shape and location. Information about *changes* in the shape and location of yield curves is helpful in formulating ideas about what interest rates should do in the future and about how they can affect price behavior and comparative returns. The Investor Insights box on pages 392–393 shows how yield curves are constructed and how they can be used.

Investing in the Bond Market

In many respects, dealing in bonds is unlike investing in any other type of security. For one thing, the size of the minimum denominations on these issues is much larger than most. In addition, investors need to have a good understanding of a lot of technical factors—like call features and refunding provisions, yield spreads, and

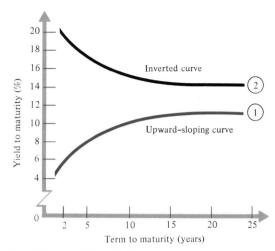

FIGURE 9.7 Two Kinds of Yield Curves.
A yield curve relates term to maturity to yield to maturity at a given point in time; while yield curves come in many shapes and forms, the most common is the upward-sloping, which shows that investor returns (yields) increase with the longer maturities.

the general pricing mechanisms used in the bond market. So, before we examine the various ways that bonds can be used, we need to look at the principles of bond pricing, bond quotes, and basic transaction costs, as well as the advantages and disadvantages of bond ownership.

Principles of Bond Price Behavior

The price of a bond is a function of its coupon, maturity, and the movement of market interest rates. When interest rates go down, bond prices go up, and vice versa. The relationship of bond prices to market rates is captured in Figure 9.8. Basically, the graph serves to reinforce the *inverse* relationship between bond prices and market interest rates: Note that *lower* rates lead to *higher* bond prices. Figure 9.8 also shows the difference between premium and discount bonds. A **premium bond** is one that sells for more than its par value, which occurs whenever market interest rates drop below the coupon rate on the bond; a **discount bond,** in contrast, sells for less than par, and is the result of market rates being greater than the issue's coupon rate. Thus, the 10 percent bond in our illustration traded as a premium bond when market rates were at 8 percent, but as a discount bond when rates stood at 12 percent.

When a bond is first issued, it is usually sold to the public at a price that equals, or is very close to, its par value. Likewise, when the bond matures—some 15, 20, or 30 years later—it will once again be priced at its par value. But what happens to the price of the bond in between is of considerable concern to most bond investors. In this regard, we know that the extent to which bond prices move depends not only on the *direction* of change in interest rates, but also on the *magnitude* of such

premium bond
a bond that has a market value in excess of par; occurs when interest rates drop below the coupon rate.

discount bond
a bond with a market value lower than par; occurs when market rates are greater than the coupon rate.

INVESTOR INSIGHTS

Plotting Your Own Curves

Drawing a yield curve is the financial version of ''connect the dots,'' where lines are drawn to form a picture. Here, the picture that you create shows the yield relationship on any one day for a set of similar debt securities. Maturities, ranging from three months to 30 years, are plotted against available percentage returns resulting in the yield curve. Treasury debt securities (bills, notes, and bonds) are generally used when creating a yield curve. This is because their yields are easily obtainable and differential risk is not a factor. But, municipal bonds, corporate bonds and even bank certificates of deposit can be used to create their own yield curves.

Three yield curves are plotted in the accompanying example—for June 4, 1985, and also for one month and six months prior to that date. To draw your own yield curve all you need is a pen, a sheet of graph paper, and the financial (quotation) tables from your local newspaper or *The Wall Street Journal*. We have reproduced a portion of the Treasury quotes from the June 5, 1985, edition of the *Journal*.

To make the curve, the first step is to obtain the yields for the Treasury issues maturing in approximately three months, six months, one year, two years, five years, 10 years, 20 years, and 30 years. It is not critical that you get securities that expire exactly on these dates, but try to get as close as possible. The securities we used are highlighted. More points could be included, but they would not appreciably change the shape of the curve. The next step is to plot the points on a piece of graph paper, using the horizontal axis as the time to maturity (in years) and the vertical axis as the yield (in percent). Now simply connect the plotted points with straight lines (the artistically inclined can try to make a smoother curve by free-handing it). The result is a yield curve that will graphically illustrate the yield/maturity relationship between the different Treasury securities. It might also help you see patterns that can be used to predict future interest rates. While it may not be as perfectly accurate as the ones the pros use, it should be more than adequate for most investors—and it didn't cost thousands of dollars for computer hardware and programming!

The question now is how can an investor use such yield curves to his or her advantage? To see how, let's look at the first and second curves, for December and May, respectively. The mild drop in long-term rates versus the sharper drop in short-term rates is fairly obvious. Thus one could easily anticipate that long-term rates would likely come down to narrow the spread. The incentive therefore was to invest in instruments with longer maturities.

Examining the middle curve closely, note that the spread in yields from 10 years to 20 years is 32 basis points, and the spread between 10 years and 30 years narrows to only 16 basis points. Not much is gained, therefore, by moving out beyond 10 years in terms of yield, and the risk for the 10-year notes is lower than for the securities with longer maturities. Does a large spread between short- and long-term rates generally indicate an investment opportunity? Probably, but some experts argue that the spread has permanently widened. The dilemma appears to be whether the opportunity to capitalize on the large spread is worth the additional risk of purchasing longer-term securities. The answer lies in one's estimation of the future direction of interest rates. While the yield curve

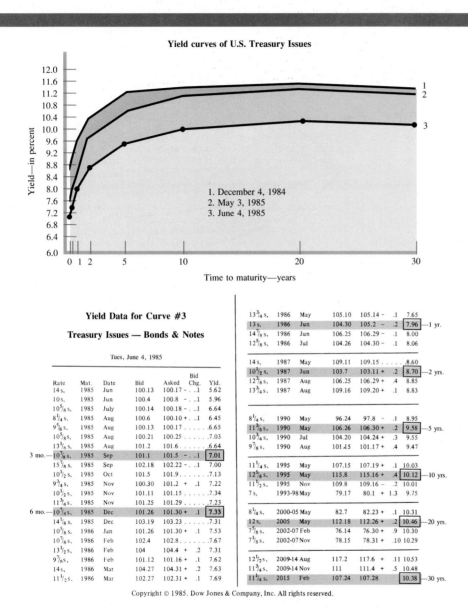

Yield curves of U.S. Treasury Issues

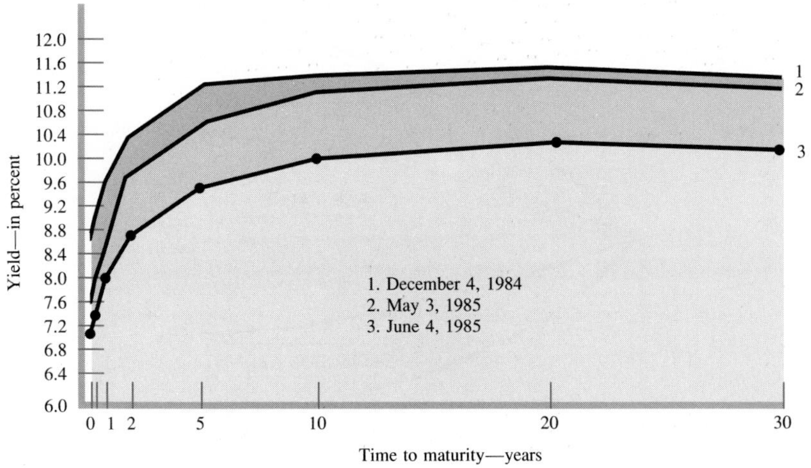
12.0
11.6
11.2
10.8
10.4
10.0
9.6
9.2
8.8
8.4
8.0
7.6
7.2
6.8
6.4
6.0
Yield—in percent
0 1 2 5 10 20 30
Time to maturity—years
1
2
3
1. December 4, 1984
2. May 3, 1985
3. June 4, 1985

Yield Data for Curve #3

Treasury Issues — Bonds & Notes

Tues, June 4, 1985

	Rate	Mat.	Date	Bid	Asked	Bid Chg.	Yld.	
	14 s,	1985	Jun	100.13	100.17	- . ..1	5.62	
	10 s,	1985	Jun	100.4	100.8	- . ..1	5.96	
	$10\frac{5}{8}$ s,	1985	July	100.14	100.18	- . ..1	6.64	
	$8\frac{1}{4}$ s,	1985	Aug	100.6	100.10	+ . ..1	6.45	
	$9\frac{5}{8}$ s,	1985	Aug	100.13	100.17	......	6.65	
	$10\frac{5}{8}$ s,	1985	Aug	100.21	100.25	......	7.03	
	$13\frac{1}{8}$ s,	1985	Aug	101.2	101.6	......	6.64	
3 mo.—	$10\frac{7}{8}$ s,	1985	Sep	101.1	101.5	- . ..1	7.01	
	$15\frac{7}{8}$ s,	1985	Sep	102.18	102.22	- . ..1	7.00	
	$10\frac{1}{2}$ s,	1985	Oct	101.5	101.9	......	7.13	
	$9\frac{3}{4}$ s,	1985	Nov	100.30	101.2	+ .1	7.22	
	$10\frac{1}{2}$ s,	1985	Nov	101.11	101.15	......	7.34	
	$11\frac{3}{4}$ s,	1985	Nov	101.25	101.29	......	7.23	
6 mo.—	$10\frac{7}{8}$ s,	1985	Dec	101.26	101.30	+ .1	7.33	
	$14\frac{1}{8}$ s,	1985	Dec	103.19	103.23	......	7.31	
	$10\frac{5}{8}$ s,	1986	Jan	101.26	101.30	+ .1	7.53	
	$10\frac{7}{8}$ s,	1986	Feb	102.4	102.8	......	7.67	
	$13\frac{1}{2}$ s,	1986	Feb	104	104.4	+ .2	7.31	
	$9\frac{7}{8}$ s,	1986	Feb	101.12	101.16	+ .1	7.62	
	14 s,	1986	Mar	104.27	104.31	+ .2	7.63	
	$11\frac{1}{2}$ s,	1986	Mar	102.27	102.31	+ .1	7.69	
	$13\frac{3}{4}$ s,	1986	May	105.10	105.14	- .1	7.65	
	13 s,	1986	Jun	104.30	105.2	- .2	7.96	—1 yr.
	$14\frac{7}{8}$ s,	1986	Jun	106.25	106.29	- .1	8.00	
	$12\frac{5}{8}$ s,	1986	Jul	104.26	104.30	- .1	8.06	
	14 s,	1987	May	109.11	109.15	.....	8.60	
	$10\frac{1}{2}$ s,	1987	Jun	103.7	103.11	+ .2	8.70	—2 yrs.
	$12\frac{3}{8}$ s,	1987	Aug	106.25	106.29	+ .4	8.85	
	$13\frac{3}{4}$ s,	1987	Aug	109.16	109.20	+ .1	8.83	
	$8\frac{1}{4}$ s,	1990	May	96.24	97.8	- .1	8.95	
	$11\frac{3}{8}$ s,	1990	May	106.26	106.30	+ .2	9.58	—5 yrs.
	$10\frac{3}{4}$ s,	1990	Jul	104.20	104.24	+ .3	9.55	
	$9\frac{7}{8}$ s,	1990	Aug	101.15	101.17	+ .4	9.47	
	$11\frac{1}{4}$ s,	1995	May	107.15	107.19	+ .1	10.03	
	$12\frac{5}{8}$ s,	1995	May	115.8	115.16	+ .4	10.12	—10 yrs.
	$11\frac{1}{2}$ s,	1995	Nov	109.8	109.16	- .2	10.01	
	7 s,	1993-98	May	79.17	80.1	+ 1.3	9.75	
	$8\frac{1}{4}$ s,	2000-05	May	82.7	82.23	+ .1	10.31	
	12 s,	2005	May	112.18	112.26	+ .2	10.46	—20 yrs.
	$7\frac{5}{8}$ s,	2002-07	Feb	76.14	76.30	+ .9	10.30	
	$7\frac{1}{8}$ s,	2002-07	Nov	78.15	78.31	+ .10	10.29	
	$12\frac{1}{2}$ s,	2009-14	Aug	117.2	117.6	+ .11	10.53	
	$11\frac{3}{4}$ s,	2009-14	Nov	111	111.4	+ .5	10.48	
	$11\frac{1}{4}$ s,	2015	Feb	107.24	107.28		10.38	—30 yrs.

cannot answer this question with certainty, it does help you recognize the opportunities available in the fixed-income securities market.

Source: Adapted from Leonard Stern. ''Plotting Your Own Course.'' *Personal Investor,* August 1985, pp. 52–53.

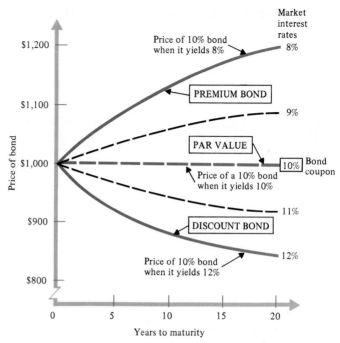

FIGURE 9.8 Price Behavior of a Bond with a 10 Percent Coupon.
A bond will sell at its par value so long as the prevailing market interest rate remains the same
as the bond's coupon (for example, when both coupon and market rates equal 10 percent).
However, when market rates drop, bond prices rise; and as a bond approaches its maturity,
the price of the issue will move toward its par value *regardless* of the level of prevailing
market interest rates.

changes; for the greater the moves in interest rates, the greater the swings in bond
prices. However, bond prices are far more complex than that; for bond price volatility will also vary according to the coupon and maturity of an issue. That is, bonds
with lower coupons and/or longer maturities will respond more vigorously to
changes in market rates and will therefore undergo sharper price swings. (Note in
Figure 9.8 that for a given change in interest rates—for example, from 10 percent to
8 percent—the largest change in price occurs when the bond has the greatest number of years to maturity.) It should be obvious, therefore, that if a *decline* in interest
rates is anticipated, an investor should seek lower coupons and longer maturities
(since this would produce maximum amounts of capital gains). When interest rates
move *up,* the investor should do just the opposite by seeking high coupons with
short maturities; this will cause minimal price variation and act to preserve as much
capital as possible.

Actually, of the two variables, the *maturity* of an issue has the bigger impact on
price volatility. For example, look what happens to the price of an 8 percent bond
when market interest rates rise by 1, 2, or 3 percentage points.

Bond Maturity	Change in the price of an 8% bond when interest rates rise by:		
	1 percentage pt.	2 percentage pts.	3 percentage pts.
5 years	− 4.0%	− 7.7%	−12.5%
25 years	−10.9	−18.2	−33.7

Clearly, the shorter (5-year) bond offers a lot more price stability. Such a behavioral trait is universal with all fixed-income securities. It is important because it means that if you want to reduce your exposure to capital loss, or more to the point, if you want to lower the amount of price volatility in your bond holdings, then just *shorten your maturities*.

Reading the Quotes

One thing you quickly learn in the bond market is that transactions are not always as easy to conduct as they may seem. In the first place, many bonds have relatively "thin" markets; that is, some issues may trade only five or ten bonds a week, and many may have no secondary market at all. There are, of course, numerous high-volume issues, but even so, particularly close attention should be paid to an issue's trading volume—especially if an investor is looking for lots of price action and needs prompt order executions. In addition, there is the problem of the lack of market information. For except for Treasury, agency, and some corporate bonds, it is difficult to readily and conveniently obtain current information on bond prices and other market developments. Finally, investors often have to look to both brokers and bankers to complete transactions. This is so because most brokerage houses tend to confine their activities to new issues and to secondary market transactions of listed Treasury obligations, agency issues, and corporate bonds; commercial banks, in contrast, are still the major dealers in municipal bonds and are fairly active in government securities as well.

Except for municipal issues (which are usually quoted in terms of the yield they offer), all other bonds are quoted on the basis of their dollar prices. Such quotes are always interpreted as a *percent of par;* thus a quote of 97½ does not mean $97.50, but instead that the issue is trading at 97.5 percent of the par value of the obligation. If a bond has a par value of $1,000, then a quote of 97½ translates into a dollar price of $975; a par value of $5,000, in contrast, means a dollar price of $4,875. As can be seen in the bond quotes in Figure 9.9 on page 396, there is one quotation system for corporate bonds and another for governments. (Treasuries and agencies are quoted the same.)

To understand the system used with corporate bonds, look at the Alabama Power (AlaP) issue in Figure 9.9. The group of numbers immediately following the abbreviated company name gives the coupon and the year in which the bond matures; the "9⅝ 08" means that this particular bond carries a 9⅝ percent annual coupon and will mature sometime in the year 2008. The next column, labeled "Curr Yld," provides the *current yield* being offered by the issue at its *current market price*. (As we'll see later, current yield is found by dividing annual coupon by the closing price of the issue.) The "Vol" column shows the *number* of bonds traded on this day.

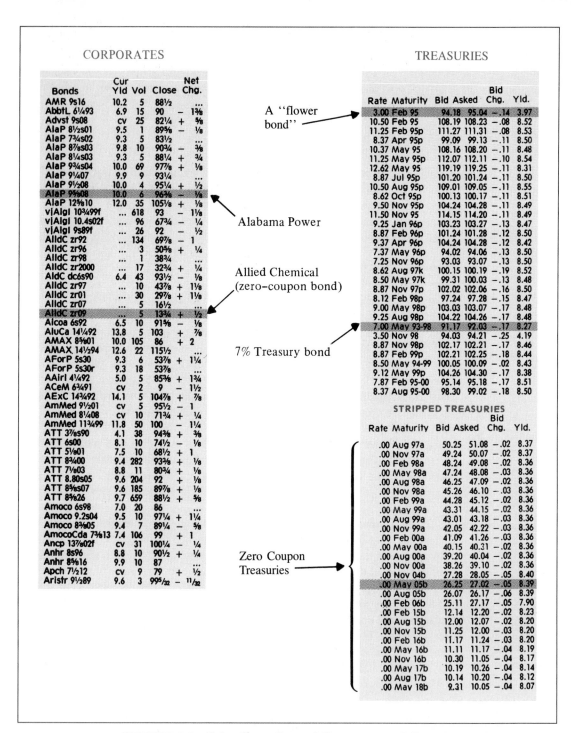

FIGURE 9.9 **Price Quotations of Corporate and Government Bonds.**

Source: The Wall Street Journal.

While both corporate and treasury bonds are quoted in terms (as a percent) of their par values, note that corporates are quoted in eighths of a point, whereas treasuries are quoted in 32's; also observe that both coupon and maturity play vital roles in the quotation system.

The last two columns provide the bond's closing price for the day and the net change in the closing price. Note that corporate bonds are usually quoted in fractions of one-eighths of a point (96⅜). In contrast, government bonds (Treasuries and agencies) are listed in thirty-seconds of a point. With governments, the figures to the right of the decimal point indicate the number of thirty-seconds in the fractional bid or ask price. For example, look at the bid price of the 7 percent Treasury issue; observe that it's being quoted at 91.17 (bid). Translated, that means the bond's being quoted at 91¹⁷/₃₂, or 91.53 percent of par. Thus, an investor who wants to buy $15,000 of this issue can expect to pay $13,729.50 (that is, $15,000 × .9153).

Treasury (and agency) bond quotes include not only the coupon (as per the 7 percent figure in the first column of the Treasury quote), but also the year and *month* of maturity. (Note this 7 percent Treasury bond matures in May of 1998.) When there's more than one date in the maturity column (for example, 1993–98), it's the *second* figure that indicates the issue's maturity date—the first one (1993) reveals when the bond becomes freely callable. Thus, our 7 percent bond matures in 1998 and carries a call deferment provision that extends through 1993. Unlike corporates, these bonds are quoted in bid/ask terms, where the *bid* price signifies what the bond dealers are willing to pay for the securities (which is how much you can *sell* them for) and the *ask* price is what the dealers will sell the bonds for (which is what you have to pay to *buy* them). Finally, note that the "Yld" column is *not* the current yield of the issue, but instead it's the bond's *promised yield-to-maturity,* which is basically a fully compounded measure of return that captures both current income and capital gains, or losses. (We examine yield-to-maturity below.)

The government quotes also include several "flower bonds"; for example, the 3 percent issue of February 1995 is a flower bond. They're easy to pick out: just look in the "Yld" column for bonds with abnormally *low* yields. Note this bond has a yield of less than 4 percent, when most of the other issues are trading at around 8½ percent. Also highlighted in both the corporate and Treasury quotes are some zero-coupon bonds. Look at Allied Chemical ("AlldC") in the corporate column; it has a number of zero-coupon issues outstanding. Such bonds are easy to spot since they have a "zr" in place of their coupons—for instance, with the Allied bonds, the "zr09" means that the issue is a zero-coupon bond that matures in 2009. Zeros are even easier to pick out in the Treasury quotes, as they're all listed under the heading, **stripped Treasuries.** Notice that all these securities have zero (".00") coupon rates. Basically the U.S. Treasury creates these securities by "stripping" the coupons from their bond issues and selling them separately from the principal. By doing so, the principal and interest *cash flows* can be sold on their own, and as such, they appear and perform like any other zero-coupon security. (Look at the stripped Treasury quotes: a small "a" behind the maturity date means the issue is made up of coupon/interest cash flow, whereas a small "b" means it is made up of bond principal.) Regardless of whether they're corporates or stripped Treasuries, the prices of most zeros are quite low compared to regular coupon bonds—this is particularly the case with longer maturities. Thus, the quote of 13¾ for the Allied Chemical issue is *not* a misprint; rather it means that you could buy this bond for $137.50 (13.75 percent of par) and in the year 2009, receive $1,000 in return.

stripped Treasuries
zero-coupon bonds sold by the U.S. Treasury; created by stripping the coupons from a Treasury bond and selling them separately from the principal.

TABLE 9.8   Representative Bond Transaction Costs—Brokerage Fees

CORPORATES AND AGENCIES

	Brokerage Fee
First 5 bonds, or $5,000 par value	$10 each bond, or per $1,000 of par value
Next 20 bonds, or $20,000 par value	$7.50 each bond, or per $1,000 of par value
For everything above 25 bonds, or $25,000 par value	$5 each bond, or per $1,000 of par value

TREASURIES

For transactions involving par value of $50,000 or less	Net bid or ask price* plus $20 oddlot charge (per trade)
For transactions involving par value of $50,000 or more	Net bid or ask price*

*The "net" bid or ask price differs from published bid or ask price quotations by the amount of the brokerage fee charged on the transaction.

Source: A major brokerage house. (Note: These fees are, of course, subject to change. Also, some dealers/brokers may charge more than the indicated fees, others less.)

Likewise, you could buy the May 05 stripped Treasury for just $270.62 (27²/₃₂ percent of par) and in 2005, receive a payment of $1,000 on your investment.

Transaction Costs

Aside from transfer and sales taxes, which are fairly minimal, the major expense in bond transactions is the brokerage fee paid when bonds are bought and sold. The advent of negotiated commission has done away with standard commission tables, but we can indicate *representative* transaction costs that are likely to be incurred when buying or selling bonds (see Table 9.8). The cost of executing small transactions is fairly expensive, but as the size of the transaction increases, the relative cost declines quickly. Consider, for example, the cost of acquiring 40 corporate bonds:

For the first 5 bonds	5 × $10.00 =	$ 50.00
For the next 20 bonds	20 × 7.50 =	150.00
For the next 15 bonds	15 × 5.00 =	75.00
Total commissions		$275.00

In relation to the $40,000 worth of bonds being purchased, commission costs amount to *less* than 1 percent. In fact, compared to most other types of securities, bond transaction costs are relatively low.

Advantages and Disadvantages of Bond Ownership

One of the *advantages* of investing in bonds is the high and competitive rates of return available from these securities, even with nominal amounts of trading and minimal risk exposure. Another advantage is the occasional opportunity to realize substantial capital gains. Also attractive to some are the tax shields that can be obtained with certain types of issues; municipal obligations are perhaps the best

known in this regard, but there are also some unusual tax advantages to Treasury and agency issues as well.

On the other hand, there are some *disadvantages* to investing in bonds. For the individual investor, one of the biggest is the relatively large denominations of the issues. Another is that the coupons are usually fixed for the life of the issue and, therefore, cannot move up over time in response to higher levels of inflation; thus, whereas 5 percent coupons may have looked good in the early 1960s, they are not very competitive today. In fact, inflation is probably the biggest worry for bond investors. Not only does it erode the purchasing power of the principal portion of a bond, but it also has a strong influence on the behavior of interest rates. And as we noted earlier, violent swings in interest rates will lead to violent swings in bond prices, all of which can cause substantial capital losses. In addition to inflation and interest rate risk, certain segments of the bond market have also become exposed to big amounts of *event risk*. Certainly, this has become a major problem in the corporate market, where waves of corporate takeovers and LBOs can quickly turn investment-grade bonds into junk—and that means just one thing for investors who hold the down-graded issues: *big* price declines! No one would disagree that the big losers in the takeover/LBO game so far have been the *bondholders* (ironically, the ones with the most secure position). Indeed, the situation became so bad that in July, 1989, Standard & Poor's began a *new rating system* designed to assess the extent to which investors are protected against event risk via provisions contained in the bond's covenants (*E-1* is the best "E-rating" a bond can get and indicates "strong" protection). A final disadvantage of bonds is the often inactive secondary market, which tends to limit the amount of trading and speculation that can take place.

BOND VALUATION AND TRADING

Thus far most of our discussion has dealt with the technical side of bonds—what they are and how they operate. We now shift our attention to the bond valuation process and bond trading strategies; here we try to establish what the various bonds are actually worth and how they can be used. Bond investors are basically concerned with two measures of performance: bond yields and bond prices. When evaluated along with interest rate expectations and an issue's technical dimensions (such as call feature and sinking fund), these measures provide information for making intelligent decisions and formulating sound investment strategies.

Bond Yields and Prices

current yield
the measure of the amount of current income a bond provides relative to its prevailing market price.

Yield is the single most important measure in the bond market, and it is used in a variety of ways. It serves to track the behavior of the market in general, as well as to measure the return of a single issue. There are basically three types of yield: current yield, promised yield, and realized yield.

Current and Promised Yields

Current yield is the simplest of all return measures and has the most limited application. It indicates the amount of current income a bond provides relative to its prevailing market price:

$$\text{current yield} = \frac{\text{annual interest income}}{\text{current market price of the bond}}$$

For example, an 8 percent bond would pay $80 per year in interest for every $1,000 of principal; however, if the bond were currently priced at $800, it would have a current yield of 10 percent ($80/$800 = .10). Current yield is a measure of a bond's annual coupon income and as such would be of interest to investors seeking high levels of current income.

promised yield
*considers both inter-
est income and price
appreciation, it mea-
sures the fully com-
pounded rate of re-
turn, assuming a
bond is held to matu-
rity.*

yield to maturity
*another name for
promised yield,
above.*

Promised yield, the most important and widely used bond valuation measure, evaluates both interest income and price appreciation, and considers total cash flow received over the life of an issue. Also known as **yield to maturity,** it indicates the fully compounded rate of return available to an investor, assuming the bond is held to maturity. Promised yield provides valuable insight about an issue's investment merits and is used to assess the attractiveness of alternative vehicles. Other things being equal, the higher the promised yield of an issue, the more attractive it is.

Although there are several ways to compute promised yield, the simplest is to use a procedure first introduced in Chapter 5, known as the *approximate yield method:*

$$\text{promised yield} = \frac{\text{annual interest income} + \dfrac{\$1,000 - \text{current market price}}{\text{years remaining till maturity}}}{\dfrac{\$1,000 + \text{current market price}}{2}}$$

$$= \frac{1 + \dfrac{\$1,000 - P}{N}}{\dfrac{\$1,000 + P}{2}}$$

As an example, consider the following hypothetical situation: Assume a $7\frac{1}{2}$ percent bond with a par value of $1,000 has 18 years remaining to maturity and is currently priced at $825. Using this information, we see that the (approximate) promised yield of this bond is:

$$\text{promised yield} = \frac{\$75 + \dfrac{\$1,000 - \$825}{18}}{\dfrac{\$1,000 + \$825}{2}} = \frac{\$75 + \$9.72}{\$912.50} = \underline{\underline{9.28\%}}$$

This same approximate yield formula can also be used to find the promised yield of a zero-coupon bond—the only variation is that the coupon income portion of the equation can be ignored since it will, of course, equal zero. However, a much better (and easier) way to find the promised yield of a zero-coupon issue is to use a present-value table. All you have to do is *divide the current market price of the bond by $1,000;* then, look for the computed factor in the present-value Table B.3 (in Appendix B). To illustrate, consider a 15-year zero-coupon issue that can be purchased for $160. Dividing this amount by the bond's par value of $1,000, we obtain a factor of $160/$1,000 = .160. Now in Appendix B, Table B.3 (the table of present-value interest factors for single cash flows), go down the first column to

year 15 and then look across that row until you find an interest factor that equals (or is very close to) .160. Once you've found the factor, look up the column to the "interest rate" heading and you've got the promised yield of the issue. Using this approach, we see the bond in our example has a promised yield of 13%, since that's the rate that gives us the interest factor we're looking for.

The promised yield figure, whether approximate or not, is based on the concept of present value; as a result, it has important reinvestment implications. For as discussed in Chapter 5 (see the material dealing with interest-on-interest), the promised yield figure itself is the minimum required reinvestment rate the investor must subsequently earn on each of the interim coupon receipts to actually generate a return equal to or greater than promised yield. In essence, the calculated yield-to-maturity figure is only the return "promised" so long as the issuer meets all interest and principal obligations on a timely basis, *and* the investor reinvests all coupon income (from the date of receipt to maturity) at an average rate equal to or greater than the computed promised yield. In our first example above, the investor would have to reinvest (to maturity) each of the coupons received over the next 18 years at a rate of about 9¼ percent. Failure to do so would result in a realized yield of less than the 9.28 percent promised. In fact, if the worst did occur and the investor made no attempt to reinvest any of the coupons, he or she would earn a realized yield over the 18-year investment horizon of only 6 percent. Clearly, unless it's a zero-coupon bond, a significant portion of a bond's total return over time is derived from the *reinvestment of coupons*.

Realized Yield

realized yield
the rate of return earned by an investor over a period of time that's less than the life of the issue.

Rather than buying an issue and holding it to maturity (as presumed in the promised yield formula), many investors will trade in and out of a bond long before it matures. These investors obviously need a measure of return to assess the investment appeal of any bonds they intend to trade. If the anticipated investment horizon is one year or less, it would be appropriate to use the simple holding period return measure described in Chapter 5. When the holding period extends much beyond a year, as many do, **realized yield** should be used to compare the expected payoff of alternative investment vehicles. It is computed as follows:

$$\text{realized yield} = \frac{\begin{array}{c}\text{annual} \\ \text{interest income}\end{array} + \dfrac{\text{expected future price} - \text{current market price}}{\text{years in holding period}}}{\dfrac{\text{expected future price} + \text{current market price}}{2}}$$

$$= \frac{1 + \dfrac{FP - P}{n}}{\dfrac{FP + P}{2}}$$

This measure is really nothing more than a slightly altered version of the standard *approximate yield formula* (the same formula we used above to compute promised

yield). In fact, if you contrast this measure to the promised yield formula above, you'll see that all we did was change two variables to come up with the (approximate) realized yield equation: That is, the *expected future price* of the bond is used in place of par value ($1,000), and the length of the *holding period* is used in place of term to maturity. The *future price* of the bond has to be determined when computing expected realized yield; this is done by the standard bond price formula explained below. The most difficult part of deriving a reliable future price is, of course, coming up with future market interest rates that you feel will exist when the bond is sold. Based on an informal analysis of market interest rates (per the discussion above), *the investor estimates a promised yield that the issue is expected to carry at the date of sale, and then uses that yield to figure the bond's future price.*

To illustrate, let's take another look at our 7½ percent, 18-year bond. This time assume that we anticipate holding the bond for only 3 years and that we have estimated interest rates will change in the future so that the bond's price will move to about $950 from its present level of $825. (Actually, we did this by assuming interest rates *would fall to 8 percent in 3 years;* we then used the standard bond price formula to find the value of a 7½ percent, 15-year obligation, which is how many years to maturity an 18-year bond would have at the end of a 3-year holding period.) Thus, we are assuming that an investor will buy the bond today at a market price of $825 and sell the issue 3 years later—after interest rates have declined to about 8 percent—at a price of $950. Given these assumptions, the realized yield of this bond would be:

$$\text{realized yield} = \frac{\$75 + \dfrac{\$950 - \$825}{3}}{\dfrac{\$950 + \$825}{2}} = \underline{\underline{13.15\%}}$$

The better than 13 percent approximate yield of this investment is fairly substantial, but keep in mind that this is a measure of *expected* yield only. It is, of course, subject to variation if things do not pan out as anticipated, particularly with regard to the market yield expected to prevail at the end of the holding period. There is another—perhaps more sophisticated—way of looking at the impact of price volatility on yield, and that is to measure a bond's *duration*. As more fully explained in the Investor Insights box below (pages 404–405), duration shows how market yields, bond prices, and reinvested income all combine together to produce bond returns over time.

Bond Prices

Although yield is an important measure of return, it is occasionally necessary to deal in bond prices. For example, as we saw above, the determination of a bond's future price is an essential ingredient in measuring realized yield. Also, some issues (municipals, for example) are regularly quoted on a yield basis and have to be converted to dollar prices. Unlike comparative yield measures, price data cannot be used alone as a basis for making investment decisions, since *bond prices are not an indication of return.* A basic present-value model is used to compute bond price. Along with a table of present-value interest factors (see Appendix B, Tables B.3 and

B.4), the following information is needed to determine the price of a bond: (1) the annual coupon payment, (2) par value, and (3) the number of years remaining to maturity. The prevailing market yield (or an estimate of future market rates) is then used to compute bond price as follows:

$$\text{bond price} = \text{present value of the annunity of annual interest income} + \text{present value of the bond's par value}$$

$$= (I \times PVIFA) + (PV \times PVIF)$$

where:

$$I = \text{amount of annual interest income}$$
$$PVIFA = \text{present-value interest factor for an annuity (Appendix B, Table B.4)}$$
$$PV = \text{par value of the bond}$$
$$PVIF = \text{present-value interest factor for a single cash flow (Appendix B, Table B.3)}$$

Information on the prevailing (or forecasted) market interest rate is obtained or estimated by the bond investor and represents the issue's current or expected promised yield. Such yield data, along with the bond's remaining years to maturity, are used to specify *the appropriate present-value interest factor*. To illustrate the bond price formula in action, let us return to the realized yield problem above and compute the future price of the bond used in that illustration. Recall we were considering the purchase of an 18-year, 7½ percent obligation priced at $825. We expect the market rate to drop in 3 years to 8 percent and therefore the price of the bond to increase by the anticipated date of sale. Our task at hand is to find the price of this bond 3 years hence, when it will be a 15-year issue trading at a yield of 8 percent. Using this maturity and interest rate information, we can find the appropriate present-value interest factors (in Appendix B, Tables B.3 and B.4) and compute the expected bond price as follows:

$$\text{bond price} = (\$75 \times \text{present-value interest factor for an annuity at } 8\% \text{ for 15 years}) + (\$1{,}000 \times \text{present-value interest factor for a single cash flow at } 8\% \text{ in 15 years})$$

$$= (\$75 \times 8.560) + (\$1{,}000 \times .315) = \underline{\underline{\$957.00}}$$

We now have a price that can be used in the realized yield measure. The important thing to remember is that it is the issue's current (or expected) promised yield that is used to determine its price.

Valuing a Bond

Depending on investor objectives, the value of a bond can be determined by either its promised or expected (realized) yield. Conservative, income-oriented investors will employ *promised yield* as the way to value bonds. Coupon income over extended periods of time is the principal objective of these investors, and promised yield provides a viable measure of return under these circumstances. More aggressive bond traders, on the other hand, will use *expected realized yield* to value bonds. The capital gains that can be earned by buying and selling bonds over relatively short holding periods is a chief concern of these investors and as such, realized yield is more important to them than the promised yield that exists at the time the bond is

INVESTOR INSIGHTS

A Bond's "Duration" Is Much More Than Its Maturity

Investors who bought long-term bonds in the early 1980s have seen the value of those issues skyrocket. In 1985, for instance, scores of bonds appreciated 20% to 25% or more. But beneath the hoopla and celebrating is a gremlin waiting to strike—and few bondholders even know it exists. This prankster is reinvestment risk, and it can play mischievous tricks on a portfolio.

Yield-to-maturity (YTM), the most popular measurement of a bond's rate of return, assumes that you can reinvest the bond's periodic coupon payments at the same rate over time. But if you reinvest this interest income at a lower rate or spend it, your real return will be much lower than that anticipated by YTM. The assumption that interest rates will remain constant is a key weakness of YTM.

Another flaw with YTM is that it assumes the issuer will make all payments on time and won't call the bonds before maturity, as often happens when interest rates drop. For bonds that aren't held to maturity, prices will reflect prevailing interest rates, which will likely differ from YTM. If rates have moved up since a bond was purchased, the bond will sell at a discount. If interest rates have dropped, it will sell at a premium. The sales price will obviously have a big impact on the total return earned.

What's needed is a yardstick that includes both reinvestment risk and price, or market, risk. That yardstick is provided by a measure known as "duration." Because duration gauges the price volatility of a bond, it gives you a better idea of how likely you are to earn the return (YTM) you expect. That, in turn, will help you tailor your holdings to match your expectations of interest-rate movements.

If you have watched the value of your bond holdings rise as interest rates have fallen, you might be tempted to cash out and take some gains. In fact, selling before maturity is the only way to take advantage of falling interest rates, since a bond will pay its par value at maturity regardless of prevailing interest rates. The problem is that as interest rates fall, so too do opportunities to invest at high rates. So think twice before selling a bond yielding 13% at a large gain. You might be able to reinvest the proceeds at only 8% or so.

Reinvestment risk doesn't apply just to the proceeds from a bond sale. To earn your expected YTM, you have to reinvest each coupon payment at the same rate. When interest rates fall, this isn't always possible without taking on more risk. *The result is that the YTM actually earned might be considerably less than what you expected when you bought the bond.*

In a sense, duration measures reinvestment risk and price risk much like credit ratings size up default risk. You can evaluate default risk—the danger of not receiving interest and principal payments—by looking at a bond's credit rating. Rating agencies such as

purchased. In either case, promised or realized yield provides a *measure of return* that can be used to determine the relative attractiveness of fixed-income securities. To do so, the appropriate measure of return should be evaluated in light of the amount of *risk* involved in the investment. For bonds are no different than stocks to the extent that the amount of expected return should be sufficient to cover the

Standard & Poor's and Moody's analyze many qualitative and quantitative factors about a bond and wrap them up into alphanumeric ratings that are easily compared against one another. To a large extent, duration does the same. It converts price risk and reinvestment risk (collectively known as interest-rate risk) into a single number, expressed in years, that can be used to evaluate different bonds.

The concept of duration is hardly new. It was first outlined by actuary Frederick Macaulay in 1938 to help insurance companies match their cash inflows with payments. When applied to bonds, duration recognizes that the amount and frequency of the interest payments, the YTM and the time to maturity all affect the "time dimension" of a bond. The time to maturity is important because it influences how much a bond's price rises or falls as interest rates change. In general, bonds with longer maturities fluctuate more than shorter-term issues when rates move.

However, maturity alone isn't a sufficient measure of the time dimension of bonds. Maturity only tells you when the last payment will be made. It doesn't say anything about interim payments. The amount of reinvestment risk is also directly related to the size of a bond's coupons. Bonds paying high coupons have greater reinvestment risk simply because there's more to reinvest.

Any change in interest rates will cause price risk and reinvestment risk to push and pull bonds in opposite directions. An increase in rates will produce a drop in price but will lessen reinvestment risk by making it easier to reinvest coupon payments at or above the YTM rate. Declining rates, in contrast, will boost prices but increase reinvestment risk. At some point in time, these two forces should exactly offset each other. *That point in time is the bond's duration.*

In general, bond duration possesses the following properties:

- Higher coupons result in *shorter* durations.
- Longer maturities mean *longer* durations.
- Higher yields (YTMs) lead to *shorter* durations.

Together, a bond's coupon, maturity, and yield interact with one another to produce the issue's measure of duration. Knowing a bond's duration is helpful because it combines price and reinvestment risks in such a way that it captures the underlying *volatility* of a bond. A *bond's duration and volatility are directly related* so that the shorter the duration, the less volatility a bond has. When combined with a bond's agency rating, duration provides a useful evaluation of the "risk" half of the risk-return equation. Viewing all three elements together provides a clearer picture of a bond or bond portfolio.

Source: Albert J. Fredman and Cameron P. Hum, "The Waiting Game," *Personal Investor,* November 1986, pp. 54–56.

investor's exposure to risk. Thus, the greater the amount of perceived risk, the greater the amount of return that the bond should generate. If the bond meets this hurdle, it can then be compared to other potential investment outlets. If you find it difficult to do better (in a risk-return sense), then the bond under evaluation should be given serious consideration as an investment outlet.

Investment Strategies

Generally, bond investors tend to follow one of three kinds of investment programs. First, we have the individual who lives off the income—the conservative, quality-conscious, income-oriented investor who seeks to maximize current income. In contrast, the speculator, or bond trader, has a considerably different investment objective: to maximize capital gains, often within a short time span. This highly speculative investment approach requires considerable expertise, as it is based almost entirely on estimates of the future course of interest rates. Finally, there is the serious long-term investor, whose objectives are to maximize total income—to maximize both current income and capital gains over fairly long holding periods.

In order to achieve the objectives of any one of these three programs, an investor needs to adopt a strategy that will be compatible with his or her goals. Professional money managers use a variety of techniques to manage the multimillion-dollar bond portfolios under their direction. These vary from passive approaches, to semi-active strategies (that employ elaborate procedures with equally exotic names like ''immunization'' and ''dedicated portfolios''), to active, fully managed strategies using interest-rate forecasting and yield-spread analysis. Most of these strategies are fairly complex and require substantial computer support. Not surprisingly, the individual investor has considerably different needs and resources than the large institutional investors. As a general rule, the following bond investment strategies are popular with individuals (of course, they're also used by institutional investors—but on a more sophisticated/analytical basis): the buy-and-hold strategy, bond trading based on forecasted interest rate behavior, and bond swaps.

The Buy-and-Hold Technique

This is the simplest strategy and is obviously not a technique unique to bonds. The *buy-and-hold approach* is based on finding an issue with desired quality, coupon, maturity, and indenture provisions (such as call feature), and then holding it for an extended period—often to maturity. The buy-and-hold strategy involves little trading; rather, it seeks modest returns and minimal risk exposure, frequently by doing little more than collecting coupon income. One approach that's popular with many of these investors is the use of so-called **bond ladders,** wherein an equal amount is invested in a series of bonds with staggered maturities. Here's how a bond ladder works: suppose an individual wants to confine her investing to fixed-income securities with maturities of 10 years or less; she could set up the *ladder* by investing in (roughly) equal amounts of, say, 3-, 5-, 7-, and 10-year issues. Then, when the 3-year issue matures, the money from it (along with any new capital) would be put into a *new* 10-year note. The process would continue rolling over like this so that eventually, the investor would hold a full ladder of staggered 10-year notes. By rolling into new 10-year issues every two or three years, the investor can do a kind of dollar-cost averaging and thereby lessen the impact of swings in market rates. Actually, the laddered approach is a safe, simple, and almost automatic way of investing for the long haul—indeed, once the ladder is set up, it's followed in a fairly routine manner. A key ingredient of this or any buy-and-hold strategy is, of

bond ladders
a bond investment strategy wherein an equal amount of money is invested in a series of bonds with staggered maturities—for example, an equal amount is invested in notes and bonds with maturities of 3, 6, 9, 12, and 15 years.

course, the use of high-quality investment vehicles that possess attractive features, maturities, and yields.

Trading on Forecasted Interest Rate Behavior

The *forecasted interest rate behavior* approach is highly risky, as it relies heavily on the imperfect forecast of future interest rates. It seeks attractive capital gains when interest rates are expected to decline, and the preservation of capital when an increase in interest rates is anticipated. An unusual feature of this tactic is that most of the trading is done with *investment grade securities,* since a high degree of interest sensitivity is required to capture the maximum amount of price behavior. Once interest rate expectations have been specified, this strategy rests largely on technical matters. For example, when a decline in rates is anticipated, aggressive bond investors will often seek long-maturity and low-coupon (discount) issues because this is the best and quickest way of earning capital gains during such periods (indeed, long-term zero-coupon bonds are ideal for such purposes). These interest swings are usually short-lived, so bond traders try to earn as much as possible in as short a time as possible. Margin trading (the use of borrowed money to buy bonds) is also used as a way of magnifying returns. When rates start to level off and move up, these investors begin to shift their money out of long, discounted bonds and into high-yielding issues with short maturities; in other words, they do a complete reversal. During these periods, when bond prices are dropping, investors try to earn high yields and protect their money from capital losses. Thus, they tend to use such high-yield, short-term obligations as Treasury bills, certificates of deposit, money funds, or even variable-rate notes.

Bond Swaps

bond swap
an investment strategy wherein an investor liquidates one of his current bond holdings and simultaneously buys a different issue in its place.

In a **bond swap,** an investor simply liquidates one position and simultaneously buys a different issue in its place; in essence, this is nothing more than the replacement of one bond with another. Swaps can be executed to increase current yield or yield to maturity, to take advantage of shifts in interest rates, to improve the quality of a portfolio, or for tax purposes. Although some swaps are highly sophisticated, most are fairly simple transactions. They go by a variety of colorful names, such as "profit takeout," "substitution swap," and "tax swap," but they are all used for one basic reason: *to seek portfolio improvement.* We will briefly review two types of bond swaps that are fairly simple and hold considerable appeal for investors: the yield pickup swap and the tax swap.

yield pickup swap
replacement of a low-coupon bond for a comparable higher-coupon bond in order to realize an increase in current yield and yield to maturity.

In a **yield pickup swap** an investor switches out of a low-coupon bond into a comparable higher-coupon issue in order to realize an automatic and instantaneous pickup of current yield and yield to maturity. For example, you would be executing a yield pickup swap if you sold the 20-year, A-rated 6½ percent bonds you held (which were yielding 8 percent at the time) and replaced them with an equal amount of 20-year, A-rated, 7 percent bonds that were priced to yield 8½ percent. By executing the swap, you would improve your current yield (by moving from coupon income of $65 a year to $70 a year), as well as your yield to maturity (from 8

percent to 8½ percent). Basically, such swap opportunities arise because of the *yield spreads* that normally exist between, say, industrial and public utility bonds. The mechanics are fairly simple, and any investor can execute such swaps by simply watching for swap candidates and/or by asking your broker to do so. In fact, the only thing you have to be careful of is that commissions and transaction costs do not eat up all the profits.

tax swap

replacement of a bond that has a capital loss for a similar security; used to offset a gain generated in another part of an investor's portfolio, the net result being the elimination or reduction of a capital gains tax liability.

The other type of swap that's popular with many investors is the **tax swap,** which is also relatively simple and involves few risks. The technique would be used whenever an investor has a substantial tax liability that has come about as a result of selling some security holdings at a profit; the objective is to execute a bond swap in such a way that the tax liability which accompanies the capital gains *can be eliminated or substantially reduced.* This is done by selling an issue that has undergone a capital *loss* and replacing it with a comparable obligation. For example, assume that an investor had $10,000 worth of corporate bonds that she sold (in the current year) for $15,000, resulting in a capital gain of $5,000. The investor can eliminate the tax liability accompanying the capital gain by selling securities that have capital losses of $5,000. Let's assume the investor finds she holds a 20-year, 4¾ percent municipal bond that (strictly by coincidence of course) has undergone the needed $5,000 drop in value. The investor has the needed tax shield in her portfolio, so now all she has to do is find a viable swap candidate. Suppose she finds a comparable 20-year, 5 percent municipal issue currently trading at about the same price as the issue being sold. By selling the 4¾s and simultaneously buying a comparable amount of the 5s, the investor will not only increase her tax-free yield (from 4¾ to 5 percent), but she'll also eliminate the capital gains tax liability. The only caution that should be kept in mind is that *identical issues cannot be used* in such swap transactions, since the IRS would consider this a "wash sale" (see Chapter 4) and therefore disallow the loss. Moreover, it should be clear that the capital loss must occur in the same taxable year as the capital gain. These are the only limitations and explain why this technique is so popular with knowledgeable investors, particularly at year end, when tax loss sales (and tax swaps) multiply as investors hurry to establish capital losses.

SUMMARY

- A bond is basically a publicly traded debt security that represents a loan between the issuer and an investor; the bondholder receives periodic interest payments and repayment of principal at maturity.

- Bonds provide investors with two types of income: (1) they provide a generous amount of current income; and (2) they can be used to generate substantial amounts of capital gains. Current income, of course, is derived from the coupon (interest) payments received over the life of the issue, whereas capital gains can be earned whenever market interest rates fall.

- Investor interest in bonds has increased substantially in recent years as higher

and more volatile interest rates have attracted both income- and capital-gains-oriented investors to the bond market.

- The behavior of *interest rates* is the single most important force in the bond market, as it determines not only the amount of current income an investor will receive but also the amount of capital gains (or losses) that an investor will earn—indeed, changes in market interest rates can have a dramatic impact on the *total annual returns* actually obtained from bonds over time. Also, whereas current income investors prefer high interest rates, those who go after capital gains would rather see them fall.

- Bonds can be issued either with a single maturity date (a term bond) or with a series of maturities (as in a serial bond). Every bond is issued with some type of call feature, be it freely callable, noncallable, or deferred feature; in addition, bonds can be issued with sinking fund provisions, which specify how an issue will be paid off over time.

- Due to their senior position, bonds are relatively secure investments and are usually viewed as relatively default-free securities. There is price risk, however, as even the highest grade bonds will fall in price when interest rates begin to move up; in effect, since the provisions of a bond are fixed at the time of issue, changes in market conditions will cause the price of the bond to change.

- Basically, the bond market is divided into five segments: treasuries; agencies; municipals; corporates; and institutional issues. Treasury (or government) bonds are issued by the U.S. Treasury and are considered to be virtually default-free. Agency bonds are issued by various political subdivisions of the U.S. government and make up an increasingly important segment of the bond market. Municipal bonds are issued by state and local governments in the form of either general obligation or revenue bonds. (Most municipal bonds are tax exempt, but there's a growing market for taxable munis.) Corporate bonds make up the major nongovernment sector of the market and are backed by the assets and profitability of the issuing companies.

- Municipal and corporate issues are regularly rated for bond quality by independent rating agencies. A rating of Aaa indicates an impeccable record; lower ratings, such as A or Baa, indicate less protection for the investor; as with all investments, the returns required of lower-quality instruments generally are higher than those required of high-quality bonds.

- The price behavior of a bond depends on the issue's coupon and maturity and on the movement in market interest rates. When interest rates go down, bond prices go up, and vice versa; however, the extent to which bond prices move up or down depends on the coupon and maturity of an issue. Bonds with lower coupons and/or longer maturities generate larger price swings.

- There are basically three types of yields that are important to investors: current yield, promised yield, and realized yield. Promised yield (also known as yield to maturity) is the most important and widely used bond valuation measure, and

captures both the current income and price appreciation of an issue. Realized yield, in contrast, is a valuation measure that's used by aggressive bond traders to show the total return that can be earned from trading in and out of a bond long before it matures.

● As investment vehicles, bonds can be used as a source of income, as a way to seek capital gains by speculating on the movement in interest rates, or as a way of achieving attractive long-term returns. To achieve these objectives, investors will usually employ one or more of the following bond investment strategies: the buy-and-hold strategy, bond trading based on forecasted interest rate behavior, and bond swaps.

REVIEW QUESTIONS AND PROBLEMS

1. Note some of the major advantages and disadvantages of investing in: (a) Treasury bonds, (b) agency issues, (c) municipal issues, (d) corporate bonds, and (e) institutional obligations.

2. Do issue characteristics (such as coupon and call features) affect the yield and price behavior of bonds? Explain.

3. Using Table 9.1 as a basis of discussion, how would you describe the behavior of bond returns over the past 10 to 15 years? What do you think would be a fair rate of return to expect from an investment in bonds? Do swings in market interest rates have any bearing on bond returns? Explain.

4. A 6 percent, 15-year bond has 3 years remaining on a deferred call feature (call premium is equal to 1 year's interest); the bond is currently priced in the market at $850. What is the issue's current yield and promised yield?

5. Is there a single market rate of interest applicable to all segments of the bond market, or is there a series of market yields that exists? Explain and note the investment implications of such a market environment.

6. Why is the reinvestment of interest income so important to bond investors?

7. An investor is in the 28 percent tax bracket. He is trying to decide which of two bonds to purchase: one is a 7½ percent corporate bond which is selling at par; the other is a municipal bond with a 5¼ percent coupon, which is also selling at par. If all other features of these two bonds are comparable, which should the investor select? Why? Would your answer change if this were an *in-state* municipal bond and the investor lived in a place with high state income taxes? Explain.

8. Why is interest sensitivity so important to bond speculators? Does the need for interest sensitivity explain why active bond traders tend to use high-grade issues? Explain.

9. Two bonds have par values of $1,000; one is a 5 percent, 15-year bond priced to yield 8 percent, and the other is a 7½ percent, 20-year bond priced to yield 6 percent. Which of these two has the lower price?

10. Treasury securities are guaranteed by the U.S. government; therefore, there is no risk in ownership of such bonds. Briefly discuss the wisdom (or folly) of this statement.

11. Briefly define each of the following and note how they might be used by fixed-income investors: (a) zero-coupon bonds; (b) CMOs; (c) taxable munis; and (d) junk bonds.

12. Is risk of default important in the bond evaluation and selection process? Is event risk important? Explain.

13. Why should an investor be concerned with the trading volume of a particular issue?

14. Compute the current yield of a 10 percent, 25-year bond that is currently priced in the market at $1,200.

15. What are the unusual tax features of: (1) Treasury issues; (2) agency obligations; and (3) municipal bonds?

16. A 25-year, zero-coupon bond was recently being quoted at 11⅝. Find the current yield *and* promised yield of this issue, given the bond has a par value of $1,000. How much would an investor have to pay for this bond if it were priced to yield 12 percent?

17. What three attributes are most important in determining an issue's price volatility? Explain.

18. Assume that an investor pays $800 for a long-term bond that carries an 8 percent coupon; in three years she hopes to sell the issue for $850. If her hopes come true, what realized yield would this investor earn? What would her holding period return be if she is able to sell the bond (at $850) after only six months?

19. Explain why interest rates are important to both conservative and aggressive bond investors. What causes interest rates to move, and how can individual investors monitor such movements?

20. What is a tax swap, and why are such transactions so popular with individual investors?

21. Arlene Darling is an aggressive bond trader who likes to speculate on interest rate swings. Market interest rates are presently at 9 percent, but they're expected to fall to 7 percent within a year. As a result Arlene is thinking about buying one of the following issues: *either* a 25-year, zero-coupon bond, *or* a 20-year, 7½ percent bond (both bonds have $1,000 par values and carry the same agency rating). Assuming Arlene wants to maximize capital gains, which one of the two issues should she select? What if she wants to maximize the total return (interest income and capital gains) from her investment? Why did one issue provide better capital gains than the other?

22. What is a bond ladder? Set up an example of a bond ladder and note how (and why) it would be used by an investor.

23. An investor is considering the purchase of a 7 percent, 20-year bond that is presently priced to yield 10 percent. Based on extensive analysis of market interest rates, he thinks rates will fall so that over the course of the next two years the market yield on this issue will drop to 8 percent. If his expectations are correct, what kind of realized yield will the investor earn on this bond? What is the major risk of this investment?

24. Using the resources available at your campus or public library, select *any six* bonds you like, consisting of *two* Treasury bonds, *two* corporate bonds, and *two* agency issues; then determine the latest current yield and promised yield for each. (Note: Show your work for all calculations.)

25. Obtain a copy of last week's *Wall Street Journal* or *Barron's;* using one of these as a source of data, construct a *yield curve* consisting of Treasury bond yields. To do so, select one Treasury issue for each of the following maturities: 1 year to maturity; 3 years; 5 years; 10 years; 15 years; and 20 years to maturity. Use the reported yield for each bond selected to

graph your yield curve, putting term to maturity on the horizontal axis of your graph and yield to maturity on the vertical axis. Briefly discuss the general shape of your yield curve.

CASE PROBLEMS

9.1   Lenny and Lucille Leftsinger Develop a Bond Investment Program

Lenny and Lucille Leftsinger, along with their two teenage sons, Lou and Lamar, live in Jenks, Oklahoma. Lenny works as an electronics salesman, and Lucille is a personnel officer at a local bank; together, they earn an annual income of around $50,000. Lenny has just learned that his recently departed rich uncle has named him in his will to the tune of some $150,000, after taxes. Needless to say, Lenny, Lucille, Lou, and Lamar are elated. Lenny intends to spend $50,000 of his inheritance on a number of long-overdue family items (like some badly needed remodeling of their kitchen and family room, a new Nissan 300ZX, and braces to correct Lamar's overbite); he wants to invest the remaining $100,000 in various types of fixed income securities. Lenny and Lucille have no unusual income requirements, health problems, or the like. Their only investment objectives are that they want to achieve some capital appreciation, and they want to keep their funds invested for a period of at least 20 years; they do not intend to rely on their investments as a source of additional current income.

Questions

1. What type of bond investment program do you think would be best suited to the needs of Lenny and Lucille? Explain.
2. Would you recommend they follow a "buy-and-hold" investment strategy, or that they use some other approach? Do you think they should consider the use of a bond ladder? Explain.
3. List several different types of issues you would recommend, and briefly indicate why you selected each.
4. How big would their investment account be after five years if they were lucky enough to consistently earn an average (after tax) rate of return of 10 percent? How big would it be if they earned 10 percent, but regularly withdrew $10,000 a year for living purposes?

9.2   The Bond Investment Decisions of George Jock

George and Penelope Jock live in the Boston area, where he has a successful orthodontics practice. The Jocks have built up a sizable investment portfolio and have always had a major portion of their investments in fixed-income securities. They adhere to a fairly aggressive investment posture and actively go after both attractive current income and substantial capital gains. Assume that it is now 1990 and George is currently evaluating two investment decisions: one involves an addition to their portfolio, and the other a revision to it.

The Jocks' first investment decision involves a short-term trading opportunity. In particular, George has a chance to buy a 7½ percent, 25-year bond that is currently priced at $852 to yield 9 percent; he feels that in two years the promised yield of the issue should drop to 8 percent.

The second is a bond swap; the Jocks hold some Beta Corporation 7 percent, 2008 bonds that are currently priced at $785. They want to improve both current income and yield to maturity, and are considering one of three issues as a possible swap candidate: (a) Dental Floss, Inc., 7¼ percent, 2008, currently priced at $780; (b) Root Canal Products of America, 6½ percent, 2006, selling at $885; and (c) Kansas City Dental Insurance, 8 percent, 2010,

priced at $950. All of the swap candidates are of comparable quality and have comparable issue characteristics.

Questions

1. Regarding the short-term trading opportunity:
   a. What basic trading principle is involved in this situation?
   b. If George's expectations are correct, what will the price of this bond be in two years?
   c. What is the expected realized yield of this investment?
   d. Should this investment be made? Why?

2. Regarding the bond swap opportunity:
   a. Compute the current and promised yields of the bond the Jocks currently hold and each of the three swap candidates.
   b. Do any of the three swap candidates provide better current income and/or current yield than the Beta Corporation bond the Jocks currently hold? Which one(s)?
   c. Do you see any reason why George should switch from his present bond holding into one of the other three issues? If so, which swap candidate would be the best choice? Why?

SELECTED READINGS

"If You Think There's Nothing in a Zero, You May Miss a Real Winner." *Money,* November 1988, pp. 9–10.

Markese, John. "U.S. Government Securities: Buying Direct from the Factory." *AAII Journal,* August 1988, pp. 31–34.

———. "Interest Rate Changes and Their Effect on Bond Prices." *AAII Journal,* November 1987, pp. 29–31.

Myers, David W. "The Ups and Downs of Bond Investing." *Personal Investor,* September 1987, pp. 72–75.

Schifrin, Matthew. "Zombie Bonds." *Forbes,* April 3, 1989, p. 70.

Slater, Karen. "Investors Playing the Bond Game Should Watch Out for Bad Calls." *The Wall Street Journal,* April 28, 1989, pp. C1, C19.

Sloan, Allan. "The Rape of the Bondholder." *Forbes,* January 23, 1989, pp. 67–69.

Smith, Marguerite T. "Curves That Yield the Shape of Things to Come." *Money,* December 1988, pp. 179–80.

Veale, Stuart R., and Russ Wiles. "The Basics of Bond Swaps." *Personal Investor,* May 1987, pp. 63–66.

Weberman, Ben. "Insuring Success." *Forbes,* October 17, 1988, p. 179.

10

PREFERRED STOCK AND CONVERTIBLE SECURITIES

After studying this chapter you should be able to:

● Describe the basic features of preferred stock, including sources of value and exposure to risk.

● Discuss the rights and claims of preferred stockholders, and note some of the popular issue characteristics that are often found with these securities.

● Develop an understanding of the various measures of investment worth, and identify several investment strategies that can be used with preferred stocks.

● Identify the fundamental characteristics of convertible securities, and explain the nature of the underlying conversion privilege.

● Describe the advantages and disadvantages of investing in convertible securities, including the risk and return attributes of these investment vehicles.

● Measure the value of a convertible security, and explain how these securities can be used to meet different investment objectives.

Preferred stocks and convertible securities are corporate issues that hold a position of seniority to the company's common stock. Although preferreds are actually a form of equity ownership, they, along with convertibles, are considered to be *fixed-income securities* because their level of current income is fixed. Convertible securities, usually issued as bonds, are subsequently convertible into shares of the issuing firm's common stock. Indeed, the investment merits of these securities are based principally on the *equity kicker* they provide; that is, the tendency is for the market price of these issues to behave much like the common stock into which they can be converted. Preferred stocks, in contrast, are issued and remain as equity. However, like bonds, they too produce a fixed-income. In fact, preferred stocks derive their name in part from the *preferred claim* on income they hold: All preferred dividends must be paid before any payment can be made to holders of common stock. In many respects, these two issues represent types of *hybrid securities* since there is a bit of debt and equity in both of them. Let's now take a closer look at each, starting with preferred stocks.

PREFERRED STOCKS

preferred stock
a stock that has a prior claim (ahead of common) on the income and assets of the issuing firm.

A **preferred stock** carries a fixed dividend that is paid quarterly and is expressed either in dollar terms or as a percentage of the stock's par (or stated) value. There are today about a thousand OTC and listed preferred stocks outstanding, most of which are issued by public utilities (although the number of industrial, financial, and insurance issues is rapidly increasing). Preferreds are available in a wide range of quality ratings, from investment-grade issues to highly speculative stocks. Table 10.1 provides a representative sample of some actively traded preferred stocks and illustrates the types of annual dividends and dividend yields these securities were producing in early 1989. Note especially the variety of different types of issuers, and how the market price of a preferred tends to vary with the size of the annual dividend. Moreover, observe that the higher yields are generally associated with the lower-rated issues, which is as you'd expect to the extent that higher risk should lead to higher return.

Preferred Stocks as Investment Vehicles

For many years, the preferred stock market was dominated by institutional and corporate investors. However, things changed dramatically in the early 1970s, when preferred stocks became increasingly popular with individual investors. Corporate issuers responded by making preferreds more attractive to individuals, principally by reducing the par value on new issues to the $10 to $25 range and by pushing annual dividend levels to new heights. As a result, fixed-income investments were finally made available to individual investors at both reasonable unit prices and attractive current yields.

Preferred stocks are considered hybrid securities because they possess features of both common stocks and corporate bonds. They are like common stock in that they pay dividends, which may be suspended, or "passed," when corporate earnings fall below certain levels. Moreover, preferreds are a form of equity ownership and are issued without stated maturity dates. On the other hand, preferreds are like bonds in

TABLE 10.1   A Sample of Some High-Yielding Preferred Stock

S&P Rating	Issuer	Annual Dividend	Market Price (May 1989)	Dividend Yield
BBB+	American Brands	$2.75	$27.75	9.91%
AA−	Capital Holdings	7.60	83.00	9.16
BBB+	Chase Manhattan Bank	6.75	68.75	9.82
A+	Citicorp	7.00	76.37	9.17
CCC	Control Data	4.50	39.00	11.54
AA	Dupont Chemical	3.50	39.75	8.81
AA−	General Motors	3.75	42.00	8.93
A−	GTE	2.48	26.25	9.45
B	Gulf States Utilities	3.85	31.62	12.17
BBB−	Illinois Power	3.78	33.50	11.28
BBB	Occidental Petroleum	14.00	125.50	11.16
BB+	Philadelphia Electric	1.42	12.00	11.79
A−	San Diego Gas & Electric	7.80	87.50	8.91
AA	Wisconsin Power and Light	4.50	46.87	9.60

Note: All of these issues are straight (nonconvertible) preferred stocks traded on the NYSE.

that they provide investors with prior claims on income and assets, and the level of current income is usually fixed for the life of the issue. Furthermore, preferred stocks can carry call features and sinking fund provisions, and a firm can have more than one issue of preferred outstanding at any point in time. Most important, perhaps, because these securities usually trade on the basis of their yield, they are in fact priced in the marketplace like fixed-income obligations and, as a result, are considered by many investors to be competitive with bonds.

Advantages and Disadvantages

Investors are attracted to preferred stocks because of the current income they provide. Moreover, such dividend income is highly predictable, even though it lacks legal backing and can, under certain circumstances, be passed. Figure 10.1 illustrates the yields that have been available from preferred stocks and shows how they compare to high-grade bond returns. Note the tendency for preferreds to yield returns that are slightly *less* than those on high-grade bonds. This is due to the fact that 70 percent of the preferred dividends *received by a corporation* are exempt from federal income taxes. Safety is another desirable feature of preferreds. For despite a few well-publicized incidents (such as the passing of preferred dividends by Consolidated Edison in 1974), *high-grade* preferred stocks have an excellent record of meeting dividend payments in a prompt and timely manner. A final advantage of preferred stocks is the low unit cost of many of the issues, which enables even small investors to participate actively in preferreds.

A major disadvantage of preferred stocks is, of course, their susceptibility to inflation and high interest rates. For like many fixed-income securities, preferred

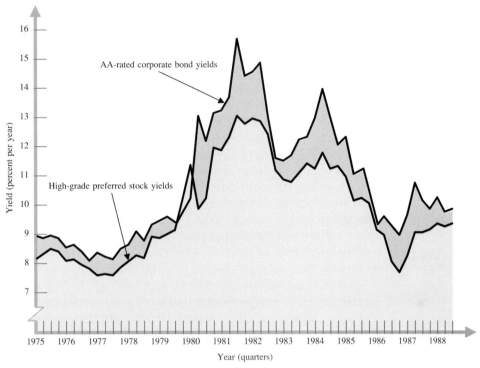

FIGURE 10.1 **Average High-Grade Preferred Stock Yields versus Average Market Yields on AA-Rated Corporate Bonds.**
Note how preferred stock yields tend to move in concert with the market behavior of bond returns—and how they tend to stay *below* bond yields. (*Source:* Standard & Poor's *Trade and Securities Statistics.*)

stocks simply have not proved to be satisfactory long-term hedges against inflation. Another disadvantage is that most preferreds lack substantial capital gains potential. Although it is possible to enjoy fairly attractive capital gains from preferred stocks when interest rates decline dramatically, these amounts generally do not match the price performances of common stocks. Perhaps the biggest disadvantage of preferred stocks is the *yield give-up* they incur relative to bonds. In essence, there is virtually nothing a preferred has to offer that can't be obtained from a comparably rated corporate bond—and *at less risk and more return than can be earned from a preferred.*

Sources of Value

With the exception of convertible preferreds, the value of high-grade preferred stocks is a function of the dividend yield they provide to investors. More specifically, the value (or market price) of a preferred stock is closely related to prevailing market rates. Thus as the general level of interest rates move up, so too do the yields of preferreds, and as such, their prices decline; when interest rates drift downward,

so will the yields on preferreds, as their prices rise. *The price behavior of a high-grade preferred stock, therefore, is inversely related to market interest rates.* More-over, its price is directly linked to the issue's level of income; that is, other things being equal, the higher the dividend payment, the higher the market price of an issue. As such, the price of a preferred can be defined as follows:

$$price = \frac{annual\ dividend\ income}{prevailing\ market\ yield}$$

This equation is simply a variation of the standard dividend yield formula, but here we solve for the price of the issue (you might also detect a similarity between this formula and the constant dividend version of the dividend valuation model intro-duced in Chapter 8). The formula described above is used to price preferred stocks and to compute the future price of a preferred, given an estimate of expected market interest rates. For example, a $2.50 preferred stock (which implies that the stock pays a dividend of $2.50 per year) would be priced at $20.83 if the prevailing market yield were 12 percent:

$$price = \frac{\$2.50}{.12} = \underline{\underline{\$20.83}}$$

Note that higher prices are obtained with this formula by increasing the dividend level and/or decreasing market yield.

   In addition to yield, the value of a preferred stock is also a function of the issue's quality; that is, the lower the quality of a preferred, the higher its yield. Such behavior is, of course, compatible with the risk-return tradeoffs that usually exist in the marketplace. Fortunately, the quality of preferred stocks is also rated, much like bonds, by Moody's and by Standard & Poor's. Finally, the value of a preferred is affected by issue characteristics such as call features and sinking fund provisions. For example, freely callable preferreds will normally provide higher yields to inves-tors than noncallable issues, due to the greater call risk inherent in the former type of security. Quality and issue features, however, have only slight effects on price behavior over time, and certainly do not compare in importance with the movement of market yields.

Risk Exposure

Preferred stock investors are exposed to business and interest rate risks. Business risk is important with preferreds, since they are a form of equity ownership and lack many of the legal protections available with bonds. Annual operating costs and corporate financial strength, therefore, are of concern to preferred stockholders. Moody's and S&P preferred stock ratings (which are discussed later in this chapter) can be used to assess the amount of business risk embedded in an issue—that is, higher-quality/higher-rated issues are believed to possess less business risk. Interest rate risk is also important because of the fixed income nature of preferred stocks. In fact, because of the effects that interest rates have on the prices of investment-qual-ity preferreds, this is generally viewed as the most important type of risk. Certainly

it can be the most damaging, should interest rates move against the investor. Unlike corporate bonds, there's not a lot of event risk in the preferred market simply because there aren't many (nonconvertible) industrial preferreds outstanding.

Transaction Costs

Preferred stocks are subject to the same transaction costs as shares of common stock: Brokerage fees and transfer taxes are identical. In addition, preferred investors use the same types of orders (market, limit, or stop-loss) and operate under the same margin requirements. Even the quotes of preferred stock are intermingled with those of common. Fortunately, preferreds are easy to pick out in the financial pages; simply look for the letters *pf* or *pr* after the name of the company (technically, the *pf* denotes *regular preferred* stock, and the *pr* stands for *prior preferred* stock—the differences will be explained below).

The quotes are interpreted exactly like those for common stock, except that the price/earnings ratios are not listed. Note also that the preferreds are always listed right after the company's common stock. In the quotes in Figure 10.2, we see that there are six issues of preferred stocks listed for Pennsylvania Power & Light (PennP&L)—actually, the company could have other issues outstanding, but if they didn't trade on the day of the quotes, they wouldn't be listed. These preferreds pay annual dividends of anywhere from $4.40 per share to $9.24 (note that the higher the annual dividend, the higher the price of the stock). At quoted market prices, these preferreds were providing current yields of around 9 to 10 percent. Observe also the relatively low unit cost of the stock, as two of the preferreds are priced at less than $50 a share and the other four are moderately priced within the $80 to $100 range. As an aside, note the small letter *z* in the volume (or sales) column; this symbol has important meaning to serious preferred stock traders since it signifies *the actual number of shares traded,* rather than the normal round lot volume. For example, the *"z10"* listed with the $8.60 preferred doesn't mean there were 10 round lots (1,000 shares) traded; rather, it means *there were only 10 shares* of the $8.60 preferreds that changed hands on this day.

Issue Characteristics

Preferred stocks possess features that not only distinguish them from other types of securities, but also help differentiate one preferred from another. For example, preferred stocks may be issued as convertible or nonconvertible, although the ma-

conversion feature
allows the holder of a convertible preferred to convert to a specified number of shares of the issuing company's common stock; a feature that's more commonly found on bonds (as in convertible bonds).

jority fall into the nonconvertible category. A **conversion feature** allows the holder to convert the preferred stock into a specified number of shares of the issuing company's common stock. Because convertible preferreds are, for all intents and purposes, very much like convertible bonds, a thorough examination of this vehicle will be deferred to later in the chapter; at this point we'll concentrate on *nonconvertible issues,* although many of the features and measures of investment merit we are about to discuss are equally applicable to convertible preferreds.

In addition to convertibility, there are several other important preferred stock features that investors should be aware of; they include the rights of preferred

52 Weeks		Stock	Sym	Div	Yld %	PE	Vol 100s	Hi	Lo	Close	Net Chg
Hi	Lo										
$15\frac{3}{4}$	$14\frac{1}{8}$	PacAmShrs	PAI	1.54a	10.4	...	42	$14\frac{7}{8}$	$14\frac{5}{8}$	$14\frac{3}{4}$	...
$49\frac{1}{2}$	$35\frac{5}{8}$	PacEnt	PET	3.48	8.0	13	559	$43\frac{1}{2}$	$42\frac{7}{8}$	$43\frac{1}{2}$	$+\frac{1}{2}$
↑ $19\frac{5}{8}$	14	PacGE	PCG	1.40	7.1	12	5342	$19\frac{7}{8}$	$19\frac{3}{8}$	$19\frac{5}{8}$	$+\frac{1}{4}$
$18\frac{1}{2}$	9	PacScientif	PSX	...	...		105	$12\frac{3}{8}$	$11\frac{7}{8}$	$12\frac{1}{4}$	$+\frac{1}{2}$
↑ $40\frac{1}{4}$	$27\frac{3}{4}$	PacTelesis	PAC	1.88	4.6	14	4776	$40\frac{3}{4}$	$39\frac{7}{8}$	$40\frac{5}{8}$	$+\frac{3}{4}$
↑ $38\frac{1}{2}$	$33\frac{1}{8}$	PacifiCp	PPW	2.64	6.9	11	4142	$39\frac{7}{8}$	$38\frac{1}{4}$	$38\frac{3}{8}$	$-\frac{1}{8}$
$19\frac{7}{8}$	$14\frac{3}{4}$	PaineWebber	PWJ	.52	2.7	90	2083	$19\frac{1}{4}$	$18\frac{5}{8}$	19	$+\frac{1}{4}$
$16\frac{3}{4}$	14	PaineWebber pf		1.37	8.3	...	54	$16\frac{1}{2}$	$16\frac{1}{2}$	$16\frac{1}{2}$	...
$5\frac{1}{8}$	$2\frac{1}{4}$	PanAm	PN	...	...		6375	$4\frac{5}{8}$	$4\frac{1}{2}$	$4\frac{1}{2}$	$-\frac{1}{8}$
$1\frac{1}{4}$	$^{11}/_{32}$	PanAm wt		...	...		42	$1\frac{1}{8}$	1	1	...
$27\frac{1}{8}$	$20\frac{1}{2}$	PanhdlEast	PEL	2.00	9.1	...	2408	$21\frac{7}{8}$	$21\frac{5}{8}$	$21\frac{7}{8}$	$+\frac{1}{4}$
$12\frac{1}{8}$	5	PannillKnit	PKC	...		37	6	$11\frac{1}{2}$	$11\frac{1}{2}$	$11\frac{1}{2}$	...
↑ $17\frac{7}{8}$	$11\frac{1}{2}$	PansophSys	PNS	.16	.9	18	198	18	$17\frac{3}{4}$	$17\frac{3}{4}$	...
$18\frac{1}{2}$	$7\frac{7}{8}$	ParPharma	PRX	.04	.4	11	552	$10\frac{1}{4}$	$9\frac{5}{8}$	$10\frac{1}{8}$	$+\frac{3}{8}$
$10\frac{1}{4}$	6	ParTech	PTC	...		47	4	$7\frac{5}{8}$	$7\frac{1}{2}$	$7\frac{1}{2}$	...
$20\frac{1}{2}$	$14\frac{3}{4}$	ParkElchm	PKE	.32	2.1	11	15	$15\frac{3}{8}$	$15\frac{3}{8}$	$15\frac{3}{8}$	$-\frac{1}{8}$
$6\frac{7}{8}$	$3\frac{1}{2}$	ParkerDrl	PKD		.2	3	581	$6\frac{5}{8}$	$6\frac{1}{2}$	$6\frac{5}{8}$	$+\frac{1}{8}$
$36\frac{7}{8}$	$26\frac{1}{4}$	ParkerHan	PH	.84	3.0	13	788	$28\frac{1}{2}$	28	$28\frac{3}{8}$	...
$5\frac{1}{2}$	3	**PatheComm PCC**		...	...		537	$4\frac{5}{8}$	$4\frac{3}{8}$	$4\frac{5}{8}$	$+\frac{3}{8}$
6	$3\frac{1}{2}$	PatrickPete	PPC	...		49	82	5	$4\frac{7}{8}$	$4\frac{7}{8}$	...
n $10\frac{1}{8}$	9	PatrPremDivFd	PDF	1.20	12.5	...	456	$9\frac{3}{4}$	$9\frac{5}{8}$	$9\frac{5}{8}$	...
6	$2\frac{3}{4}$	Patten	PAT	.12	4.4	4	461	$2\frac{7}{8}$	$2\frac{3}{4}$	$2\frac{3}{4}$	...
$25\frac{3}{8}$	21	PennCentral	PC	.40	1.6	10	1676	$25\frac{1}{8}$	$24\frac{7}{8}$	$24\frac{7}{8}$	...
60	$43\frac{1}{2}$	Penney JC	JCP	2.24	3.8	10	4546	59	$58\frac{1}{2}$	59	$+\frac{1}{4}$
$37\frac{1}{2}$	$33\frac{3}{4}$	PennP&L	PPL	2.86	7.7	10	1732	$37\frac{1}{4}$	$36\frac{3}{4}$	$37\frac{1}{4}$	$+\frac{3}{8}$
$49\frac{1}{2}$	44	PennP&L pf		4.40	9.7	...	z80	$45\frac{1}{4}$	$45\frac{1}{4}$	$45\frac{1}{4}$	$-\frac{3}{4}$
$49\frac{3}{4}$	$44\frac{3}{4}$	PennP&L pf		4.50	9.9	...	z20	$45\frac{1}{4}$	$45\frac{1}{4}$	$45\frac{1}{4}$	$+\frac{1}{4}$
89	$83\frac{5}{8}$	PennP&L pf		8.60	9.8	...	z10	$87\frac{1}{2}$	$87\frac{1}{2}$	$87\frac{1}{2}$	$+1\frac{1}{2}$
$88\frac{1}{2}$	81	PennP&L pr		8.40	10.1	...	z430	84	$83\frac{1}{4}$	$83\frac{1}{4}$	$-\frac{3}{4}$
$103\frac{1}{2}$	$98\frac{3}{8}$	PennP&L pf		9.24	9.2	...	z100	$100\frac{3}{4}$	$100\frac{3}{4}$	$100\frac{3}{4}$	-1
$84\frac{1}{2}$	$79\frac{1}{2}$	PennP&L pr		8.00	10.0	...	z100	$81\frac{1}{2}$	$80\frac{1}{4}$	$80\frac{1}{4}$	...
$130\frac{1}{2}$	$60\frac{1}{8}$	Pennwalt	PSM	2.40	1.9	20	1362	128	125	$125\frac{3}{4}$	$-2\frac{1}{2}$
86	$69\frac{3}{4}$	Pennzoil	PZL	3.00	3.6	...	327	$83\frac{1}{2}$	$82\frac{7}{8}$	$83\frac{1}{4}$	$-\frac{1}{4}$
$23\frac{1}{8}$	$17\frac{3}{4}$	PeopEngy	PGL	1.60	7.4	10	532	$21\frac{3}{4}$	$21\frac{3}{8}$	$21\frac{3}{4}$	$+\frac{1}{4}$
↑ $15\frac{5}{8}$	$10\frac{3}{8}$	PepBoys	PBY	.11	.7	23	1144	$15\frac{3}{4}$	$15\frac{1}{4}$	$15\frac{3}{4}$	$+\frac{3}{8}$
↑ $52\frac{3}{4}$	$32\frac{3}{4}$	PepsiCo	PEP	1.00	1.9	17	9468	$54\frac{1}{4}$	$52\frac{1}{4}$	$53\frac{3}{4}$	$+1\frac{5}{8}$
12	$9\frac{1}{2}$	PerkFamR	PFR	1.20e	10.5	12	157	$11\frac{1}{2}$	$11\frac{1}{8}$	$11\frac{3}{8}$	$+\frac{1}{8}$
$26\frac{5}{8}$	$20\frac{1}{2}$	PerkElmer	PKN	.68	2.7	...	1308	$25\frac{1}{4}$	25	$25\frac{1}{8}$	$+\frac{1}{8}$

FIGURE 10.2   Published Stock Quotes Showing Quotes for Preferred Issues.
Preferred stock quotes are listed right along with the company's common stock, and they're identified by the 2-letter initials *pf* or *pr* that appear after the name of the company. *Source: The Wall Street Journal.*

stockholders; the provisions for cumulative and participating dividends; call features; and sinking fund provisions.

Rights of Preferred Stockholders

The contractual agreement of a preferred stock specifies the rights and privileges of a preferred stockholder. The most important of these deal with the level of annual dividends, the claim on income, voting rights, and the claim on assets. The issuing company agrees that it will pay preferred stockholders a (minimum) fixed level of quarterly dividends and that such payments will take priority over common stock dividends. The only condition is that the firm generate income sufficient to meet the preferred dividend requirements. The firm, however, is not legally bound to honor the dividend obligation. Of course, the company cannot pass dividends on preferred stocks and then turn around and pay dividends on common stock, as this would clearly violate the preferreds' prior claim on income. Although most preferred stocks are issued with dividend rates that remain fixed for the life of the issue, in the early 1980s some began to appear with floating dividend rates. Known as **adjustable** (or **floating**) **rate preferreds,** the dividends on these issues are adjusted quarterly in line with yields on specific Treasury issues, although a minimum and maximum dividend rate is usually established as a safeguard.

Even though they hold an ownership position in the firm, preferred stockholders normally have no voting rights. If, however, conditions deteriorate to the point that the firm needs to pass one or more consecutive quarterly dividends, preferred shareholders are usually given the right to elect a certain number of corporate directors so that their views can be represented. And if liquidation becomes necessary, the holders of preferreds are given a prior claim on assets. These preferred claims, limited to the par or stated value of the stock, must be satisfied before those of the common stockholders. Of course, this does not always mean that the full par or stated value of the preferred will be recovered, since the claims of senior securities, like bonds, must be met first. When a company has more than one issue of preferred stock outstanding, it will sometimes issue **preference** (or **prior preferred**) **stocks.** Essentially, these stocks have seniority over other preferred stock in their right to receive dividends and in their claim on assets in the event of liquidation. As such, preference stocks should be viewed as *senior preferreds;* they're usually easy to pick out in the financial pages as they use the letters *pr* instead of *pf* in their quotes. (For example, if you refer back to the preferred quotes in Figure 10.2, you'll notice Pennsylvania P&L has two preference stocks listed along with their ''regular'' preferred stock issues).

Cumulative Provisions

Most preferred stocks are issued on a **cumulative** basis. This means that any preferred dividends that have been passed must be made up in full before dividends can be restored to common stockholders. Thus, as long as the dividends on preferred stocks remain **in arrears** (which denotes that there are outstanding unfulfilled preferred dividend obligations), a corporation will not be able to make dividend payments on common shares. Assume, for example, that a firm normally pays a $1

adjustable rate preferreds
preferred stock whose dividends are adjusted periodically in line with yields on Treasury issues; also called floating rate preferreds.

preference preferreds
a type of preferred that has seniority over other preferred stock in its right to receive dividends and in its claim on assets; also called prior preferred stock.

cumulative provision
a provision on preferred stock requiring that any preferred dividends that have been passed must be paid in full before dividends can be restored to common stockholders.

in arrears
having outstanding unfulfilled preferred-dividend obligations.

quarterly dividend on its preferred stock, but has missed the dividend for three quarterly payments. In this case, the firm has preferred dividends in arrears of $3 a share, which it is obligated to meet along with the next quarterly dividend payment before dividends can be paid to common shareholders. It could fulfill this obligation by paying, say, $2 per share to the preferred stockholders at the next quarterly dividend date, and $3 per share at the following one (with the $3 covering the remaining $2 arrears and the current $1 quarterly payment). If the preferred stock had carried a **noncumulative provision**—and some do—the issuing company would have no obligation to make up any of the passed dividends. Of course, the firm could not make dividend payments on common stock either; but all it would have to do to resume such payments would be to meet the next quarterly preferred dividend. Other things being equal, a cumulative preferred stock should be more highly valued than an issue without such a provision—that is, it should increase the price (and in so doing, lower the yield) of these issues.

noncumulative provision
a provision found on some preferred stocks excusing the issuing firm from having to make up any passed dividends.

Participating Preferreds

Most preferred stocks do *not* carry participating provisions. Occasionally, however, a preferred is issued on a **participating** basis, which means that the preferred stockholder can enjoy additional dividends if payments to common stockholders exceed a certain amount. This type of security not only specifies the annual preferred dividend, but also sets a maximum dividend that common stockholders can receive each year. Once that maximum has been met, any additional dividends to common stockholders must be shared on a specified basis (perhaps 50–50) with preferred stockholders. For example, assume the maximum common stock dividend is $2 per share and the participation provision calls for equal participation. Under these conditions, if the firm wanted to pay another $1 per share to common stockholders, it would also have to pay an equal amount ($1 per share) to the participating preferred stockholders. And unless the provision is subsequently amended, the company would have to continue to pay participating dividends to preferred stockholders for as long as the amount of dividends to common shareholders exceeded the maximum. Obviously, with the tendency for common stock dividends to increase over time, the participating provision has considerable appeal to preferred stockholders and, other things being equal, increases the value of these issues.

participating provision
a provision on some preferred stocks giving preferred stockholders additional dividends when and if payments to common stockholders exceed a certain amount.

Call Features

Beginning in the early 1970s, it became increasingly popular to issue preferred stocks with call features. Today, a large number of preferreds carry this provision, which gives the firm the right to call the preferred for retirement. Callable preferreds are usually issued on a deferred-call basis, meaning that they cannot be retired for a certain number of years after the date of issue. After the deferral period, which often extends for five to seven years, the preferreds become freely callable. Of course, such issues are then susceptible to call if the market rate for preferreds declines dramatically, which explains why the yields on freely callable preferreds should be higher than those on noncallable issues. As with bonds, the call price of a preferred is made up of the par value of the issue and a call premium that generally amounts to approximately one year's dividends.

Sinking Fund Provisions

Another preferred stock feature that has become popular in the past 10 years or so is the *sinking fund provision,* which denotes how (all or a part of) an issue will be amortized, or paid off, over time. Such sinking fund preferreds actually have implied maturity dates. They are used by firms to reduce the cost of financing (sinking fund issues generally have *lower* yields than nonsinking fund preferreds). A typical sinking fund preferred might require the firm to retire half the issue over a 10-year period by retiring, say, 5 percent of the issue each year. Unfortunately, the investor has no control over which shares are called for sinking fund purposes.

Putting a Value on Preferreds

Evaluating the investment suitability of preferreds involves an assessment of comparative return opportunities. Let's look now at some of the return measures that are important to preferred stockholders, as well as at the role that agency ratings play in the valuation process.

 ### Dividend Yield: A Critical Measure of Value

Dividend yield is the key variable in determining the price and return behavior of most preferred stocks. It is computed according to the following simple formula:

$$\text{dividend yield} = \frac{\text{annual dividend income}}{\text{preferred stock price}}$$

dividend yield
a measure of the amount of return earned on dividend income; equals annual dividend income divided by the price of the stock.

Dividend yield is a reflection of an issue's current yield and is the basis upon which comparative preferred investment opportunities are evaluated. Here is how it works: Suppose an 8 percent preferred stock has a par value of $25 and is currently trading at a price of $20 per share. The annual dividend of this stock is $2—for preferreds whose dividends are denoted as a percent of par (or stated) value, the dollar value of the annual dividend is found by multiplying the dividend rate (8 percent) by the par value ($25). The dividend yield in this example is:

$$\text{dividend yield} = \frac{\$2}{\$20} = \underline{\underline{10\%}}$$

The 10 percent figure represents the ''promised'' yield of this particular preferred issue. In practice, we would expect investors to compute, or have available, a current dividend yield measure for each preferred under consideration, and then to make a decision by assessing the yields offered by alternative preferreds—relative, of course, to the risk and issue characteristics of each.

As we saw earlier, preferred stock prices are determined by using a variation of this basic dividend yield formula (that is, preferred stock prices = annual dividend income divided by dividend yield). Long-term investors consider dividend yield to be a critical factor in their investment decisions; short-term traders, in contrast, generally center their attention on anticipated price behavior and the expected return from buying and selling an issue over a short period of time. Thus, the expected future price of a preferred is important to short-term traders. It is found by first forecasting future market interest rates and then using this information to determine expected future price. To illustrate, suppose a preferred stock pays $3 in dividends

and its yield is expected to decline to 6 percent within the next two years. If such market rates prevail, then two years from now the issue would have a market price of $50 (annual dividend ÷ yield = $3 ÷ .06 = $50). This forecasted price, along with the current market price and level of annual dividends, would then be used to compute the expected realized yield from the transaction.

To continue the example, if the stock were currently priced at $28 a share, the expected realized yield of this stock over the two-year investment horizon would be a very attractive 35.9 percent:

$$\text{realized yield} = \frac{\text{annual dividend} + \dfrac{\text{expected future selling price} - \text{current market price}}{\text{years in holding period}}}{\dfrac{\text{expected future selling price} + \text{current market price}}{2}}$$

$$= \frac{\$3 + \dfrac{\$50 - \$28}{2}}{\dfrac{\$50 + \$28}{2}} = \frac{\$3 + \$11}{\$39} = \underline{\underline{35.9\%}}$$

Such information is used to judge the relative attractiveness of preferred stock. In general, the higher the expected realized yield figure, the more appealing the investment. Now, as the *Investor Insights* box on pages 426–427 reveals, although yield, in one form or another, may be important to most preferred stocks, there's a new breed of preferreds—known as *PIK preferreds*—that gives a whole new meaning to the word "yield." Essentially, these are the preferred stock equivalent of junk bonds, and in more ways than one, there's a good deal of uncertainty surrounding the stocks' payment of dividends.

Book Value

book value
a measure of the amount of debt-free assets supporting each share of preferred stock; equals the total assets of a firm minus its liabilities; also called net asset value.

The **book value** (or **net asset value**) of a preferred stock is simply a measure of the amount of debt-free assets supporting each share of preferred stock. Book value per share is found by subtracting all the liabilities of the firm from its total assets and dividing the difference by the number of preferred shares outstanding. It reflects the quality of an issue with regard to the preferred's *claim on assets*. Obviously, a preferred with a book (or net asset) value of $150 per share enjoys generous asset support, and more than adequately secures a par value of, say, $25 a share. Net asset value is most relevant when it is used relative to an issue's par, or stated, value; other things being equal, *the quality of an issue improves as the margin by which book value exceeds par value increases.*

Fixed Charge Coverage

fixed charge coverage
a measure of how well a firm is able to cover its preferred stock dividends.

Fixed charge coverage is a measure of how well a firm is able to cover its preferred dividends; attention is on the firm's ability to service its preferred stock and live up to the preferred's preferential *claim on income*. As such, fixed charge coverage is an important ingredient in determining the quality of a preferred issue. Fixed charge coverage is computed as follows:

$$\text{fixed charge coverage} = \frac{\text{earnings before interest and taxes (or EBIT)}}{\text{interest expense} + \dfrac{\text{preferred dividends}}{.66}}$$

The preferred dividends are adjusted by a factor of .66, which is equivalent to multiplying dividends by 1.5, to take into account the (maximum) 34 percent corporate tax rate and to place preferred dividends on the same base as interest paid on bonds. (Recall that bond interest is tax deductible, whereas preferred dividends are not.) Normally, the higher the fixed charge coverage, the greater the margin of safety. A ratio of 1.0 means the company is generating just enough earnings to meet its preferred dividend payments—certainly not a very healthy situation. A coverage ratio of 0.5 would suggest the potential for some real problems, whereas a coverage of, say, 5.0 would indicate that the preferred dividends are fairly secure.

Agency Ratings

Standard & Poor's has long rated the investment quality of preferred stocks, and since 1973, so has Moody's. S&P uses basically the same rating system as with bonds; Moody's uses a slightly different system. Figure 10.3 on page 428 shows Moody's system and indicates why the various ratings are assigned. These agencies evaluate and assign ratings largely on the basis of their judgment regarding the relative safety of dividends. The greater the likelihood that the issuer will be able to service the preferred in a prompt and timely fashion, the higher the rating. Much like bonds, the top four ratings are used to designate *investment-grade* (highest quality) preferreds. Although preferreds come with a full range of agency ratings, most tend to fall in the medium-grade categories (a and baa), or lower; generally speaking, higher agency ratings reduce the market yield of an issue and increase its interest sensitivity. Agency ratings are important to serious, long-term investors as well as to those who use preferreds for short-term trading. Not only do they eliminate much of the need for fundamental analysis, but they also reveal the yield and potential price behavior of an issue.

Investment Strategies

There are several investment strategies that can be followed by preferred stockholders. Each is useful in meeting a different investment objective, and each one offers a different level of return and exposure to risk.

Using Preferreds to Obtain Attractive Yields

This strategy is perhaps the most popular use of preferred stocks and is ideally suited for serious long-term investors. High current income is the objective here, and the procedure basically involves seeking out those preferreds with the most attractive yields. Of course, consideration must also be given to such features as the quality of the issue, the cumulative/participating nature of dividends, and the issue's call feature. This approach to investing got a big boost when Congress passed the Tax Reform Act of 1986, thereby sharply reducing tax rates. *The reason: investors gain more from income-oriented securities, like preferred stocks, when tax rates are lowered.*

INVESTOR INSIGHTS
PIK-Preferreds: More Stock than Dividends

Individual investors looking for high yields may soon be hearing a lot about an unfamiliar type of security. As part of its takeover of RJR Nabisco Inc., Kohlberg Kravis Roberts & Co. plans to issue $4.1 billion of a special kind of preferred stock that promises initial dividends of as much as 16⅝%. Yields like that don't come without risk, however, and the security KKR plans to issue can be especially dicey. The security is *pay-in-kind preferred stock,* known among Wall Street pros as *"PIK preferred."*

As the name suggests, PIK preferreds *usually don't pay cash dividends.* Instead, investors get more preferred stock, which pays dividends in even more preferred stock. This printing-press financing goes on for five or six years, after which time most such preferreds are supposed to begin cash dividends, or give holders a chance to swap them for another, more traditional security.

PIK preferred was first launched in 1986. Up to now, most of it has been bought by junk-bond funds and aggressive money managers. But individual investors are likely to be hearing from their brokers about the huge RJR offering. Raymond Minella, co-head of merchant banking at Merrill Lynch & Co., predicts it "will draw investors to the high-yield market that have never bought" such securities before.

To attract investors, PIK-preferred stocks usually carry plump dividend rates of 12% to 18% at the outset. But even that often isn't enough to overcome qualms about the leveraged acquisitions the shares typically help finance. If the company runs into trouble, holders may end up with worthless paper, little chance of ever seeing cash dividends, and scant legal recourse. As a result, the trading charts on many PIK preferreds look like miniature versions of the Black Monday crash.

Certainty of income and safety are important in this strategy, since yields are attractive only as long as dividends are paid. Some investors may never buy anything but the highest-quality preferreds. Others may sacrifice quality in return for higher yields when the economy is strong, and use higher-quality issues only during periods of economic distress. But whenever you leave one of the top four agency ratings, you must recognize the speculative position you are assuming and the implications it holds for your investment portfolio. This is especially so with preferreds, since their dividends lack legal enforcement. Individual investors should keep in mind, however, that this investment strategy generally involves a *yield give-up* relative to what could be obtained from comparably rated corporate bonds. For as we saw in Figure 10.1, preferreds usually generate somewhat lower yields than bonds, even though they are less secure and may be subject to a bit more risk.

Trading on Interest Rate Swings
Rather than assuming a "safe" buy-and-hold position, the investor who trades on movements in interest rates adopts an aggressive short-term trading posture. This is done for one major reason: *capital gains.* Of course, although a high level of return

RJR's preferred would dwarf all the PIK preferred issued by every other company to date. The planned preferred could either pay cash or preferred-stock dividends for its first six years. (Odds are, it will pay out stock to conserve cash.) For the first year or two, its dividend rate will be 5.5 percentage points above the yield on Treasury securities, within a band of 12⅝% to 16⅝%. After that, investment bankers will reset the dividend rate so the tobacco and food company's issue trades at par, or full face value. . . . "We think it's an extremely strong piece of paper," says Robert Lovejoy, an investment banker at Lazard Freres & Co., which is advising RJR Nabisco. If the offering does well, investment bankers say, it's likely that PIK preferred will become a much more common investment choice.

Not everyone is as upbeat as Mr. Lovejoy. Takeover-stock speculators, or risk arbitragers, who own a lot of RJR's stock, think the PIK preferred may sink 25% to 40% once it starts trading. . . . The preferred's market value will be tested early next year. KKR has agreed to pay $109 a share to RJR holders for 74% of their stock, with the remaining payment in PIK preferred and debentures. . . .

If a selling rush plunges the RJR issue to a big discount, some investors say they would love to own it. "I'd value it at 89 cents on the dollar," says a high-yield money manager in Los Angeles. Financial projections suggest RJR will remain healthy despite its big new debt load, he adds. . . . Still, should RJR . . . run into financial trouble, there isn't much that PIK preferred holders can do. Unlike senior lenders, they can't force a company into bankruptcy proceedings or make any claims on its assets. Their only power is that if RJR omits dividends on its preferred stock for *six quarters,* they can elect two directors to the company's board.

Sources: Adapted from George Anders. "Picking a Peck of PIK-Preferred Can Be Precarious." *The Wall Street Journal,* December 9, 1988, p. C1.

may be possible with this approach, it is not without the burden of higher risk exposure. Because preferreds are fixed-income securities, the market behavior of investment-grade issues is closely linked to the movements in interest rates. If market interest rates are expected to decline substantially, attractive capital gains opportunities may be realized from preferred stocks. Indeed, this is precisely what happened in the mid-80s, when market interest rates dropped sharply—during this period, it was not uncommon to find preferreds generating *annual* returns of 20 to 30 percent, or more! As is probably clear by now, this strategy is identical to that used by bond investors; in fact, many of the same principles used with bonds apply equally well to preferred stocks. For example, it is important to select high-grade preferred stocks, since interest sensitivity is an essential ingredient of this investment configuration. Moreover, margin trading is often used as a way of magnifying short-term holding period returns. A basic difference is that the very high leverage rates of bonds are not available with preferreds, since they fall under the same (less generous) margin requirements as common stocks. The investment selection process is simplified somewhat as well, since neither maturity nor the size of the annual preferred dividend (which is comparable to a bond's coupon) has an effect on the

Rating Symbol	Definition
aaa	Indicates a "top quality" issue which provides good asset protection and the least risk of dividend impairment.
aa	A "high grade" issue with reasonable assurance that earnings will be relatively well-protected in the near future.
a	"Upper medium grade." Somewhat greater risk than *aa* and *aaa*, but dividends are still considered adequately protected.
baa	"Lower medium grade." Earnings protection adequate at present, but may be questionable in the future.
ba	A "speculative" type issue, its future earnings may be moderate and not well safeguarded. Uncertainty of position is common for this class.
b	Generally lacking in desirable investment quality, this class may have little assurance of future dividends.
caa–c	Likely to already be in arrears on dividend payments. These categories are reserved for securities that offer little or no likelihood of eventual payment.

Note: Preferred stock ratings should not be compared with bond ratings as they are not equivalent; preferreds occupy a position junior to the bonds.

FIGURE 10.3 Moody's Preferred Stock Ratings.
These agency ratings are intended to provide an indication of the quality of the issue and are based largely on an assessment of the firm's ability to pay preferred dividends in a prompt and timely fashion. (*Source:* Moody's Investor's Service, Inc.)

rate of price volatility; that is, a $2 preferred will appreciate just as much (in terms of percentage) as an $8 preferred for a given change in market yields.

Speculating on Turnarounds

This speculative investment strategy can prove profitable, but it can be followed only rarely. The idea is to find preferred stocks whose dividends have gone into arrears and whose rating has tumbled to one of the speculative categories. The price of the issue, of course, would be depressed to reflect the corporate problems of the issuer. There is more to this strategy, however, than simply finding a speculative-grade preferred stock. The difficult part is to uncover a speculative issue whose fortunes, for one reason or another, are about to undergo a substantial *turnaround*. This requires sound fundamental analysis of the corporate issuer, as well as the ability to predict such situations before they are widely recognized in the market-place. The tactic is obviously highly risky and is in many respects akin to investing in speculative common stock. In essence, the investor is assuming that the firm will undergo a turnaround and will once again be able to service its preferred dividend obligations easily. Unfortunately, although the rewards from this kind of investing can be substantial, they are somewhat limited. For example, if the turnaround can-

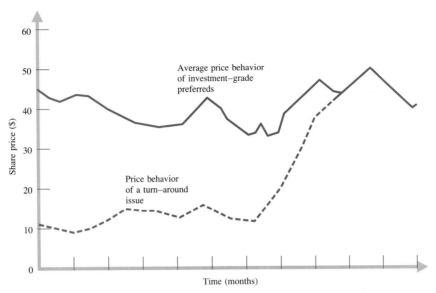

FIGURE 10.4 **Illustrative Price Pattern of a Hypothetical Preferred "Turn-around" Candidate.**
Although the turnaround issue will seek the price level of other preferreds of comparable quality and dividend payout, this level also acts as a type of price cap and clearly limits capital appreciation.

didate is expected to recover to a single-a rating, we would expect its capital gains potential to be limited by the price level of other a-rated preferreds. This condition is depicted in Figure 10.4. As can be seen, while price performance may be somewhat limited, it is still substantial and can readily amount to holding period returns of 100 percent or more. However, in view of the substantial risks involved, such returns are certainly not out of line.

Investing in Convertible and Participating Preferreds

The investor following this strategy uses certain preferred stock features to go after speculative opportunities and the chance for attractive returns. The use of convertible preferreds is based on the equity kicker of the issue (that is, its link to the company's common stock) and the belief that it will provide generous price appreciation. Convertibles will be reviewed in detail below; at this point, suffice it to say that as the price of the underlying common stock appreciates in value, so will the market price of a convertible preferred. This strategy can offer handsome returns, but remember that investors who employ it are actually speculating on the common stock dimension of the security, and therefore it is the equity position of the issue that should be subjected to scrutiny. In essence, the investor seeks equity situations that hold considerable promise for appreciation, and then, rather than buying the common stock of the firm, purchases its convertible preferred instead.

Participating preferreds are fairly rare, but the use of such issues can sometimes

prove rewarding so long as the issuing firm is enjoying prosperity and is likely to be in a position to declare participating dividends to preferred stockholders. It works like this: If the investor believes strongly that the fortunes of the firm are such that the likelihood of a declared participating dividend is fairly high, the purchase of that preferred may be appropriate. Of course, the investor would want to see to it that the market has not already discounted such a possibility. This can be done by making sure that the issue is not trading at a yield well below comparable preferreds (which would happen if the price of the preferred were forced up by the likelihood of a participating dividend). Assuming this is not the case, given the manner in which preferred stocks are priced, a participating dividend very likely would lead to an increase in the price of the stock. For example, consider a $4 preferred stock that is priced to yield 6 percent; this issue would be trading at about $67. If the firm declared a participating dividend of, say, $1 per share, the price of the stock should jump to about $83 so long as it continues to yield 6 percent. The catch, of course, is to identify a participating preferred before it actually begins to participate, and also to have some assurance that *the firm will continue to pay this level of participating dividend for the foreseeable future.*

CONVERTIBLE SECURITIES

convertible securities
fixed-income obligations, with a feature permitting the holder to convert the security into a specified number of shares of the issuing company's common stock.

Convertible securities, more popularly known simply as "convertibles," represent still another type of fixed-income security. Usually issued as bonds, convertibles are subsequently convertible into shares of the issuing firm's common stock. A convertible is also a type of hybrid security and, although possessing the features and performance characteristics of both a fixed-income security and equity, it should be viewed primarily as a form of equity. Most investors commit their capital to such obligations not because of the attractive yields they provide, but because of the potential price performance that the stock side of the issue offers. In fact, it is always a good idea *to determine whether a corporation has convertible issues outstanding whenever you are considering a common stock investment,* for there may well be circumstances in which the convertible will be a better investment than the firm's common stock.

Convertibles as Investment Outlets

equity kicker
the tendency for the market price of convertible issues to behave much like the common stock into which they can be converted.

deferred equity
securities issued in one form and later redeemed or converted into shares of common stock.

Convertible securities are popular with individual investors because of the **equity kicker** they provide. They are issued by all types of corporations, and in 1989 there were over 1,000 convertible bonds and several hundred convertible preferreds outstanding. They are usually viewed as a form of **deferred equity** because they are intended to be converted eventually into shares of the company's common stock. Not surprisingly, whenever the stock market is strong, convertibles tend to be strong; when the market softens, so does interest in convertibles. Convertible bonds and convertible preferreds are both linked to the equity position of the firm and are therefore usually considered interchangeable for investment purposes. Except for a few peculiarities, such as the fact that preferreds pay dividends rather than interest, and do so on a quarterly basis rather than semiannually, convertible bonds and convertible preferreds are evaluated similarly. Our discussion therefore will be

mostly in terms of bonds, but the information and implications apply equally well to convertible preferreds.

Convertible Bonds

Convertible bonds are usually issued as debentures (long-term, unsecured corporate debt), but carry the provision that within a stipulated time period *the bond may be converted into a certain number of shares of the issuing company's common stock.* Generally there is little or no cash involved at the time of conversion, since the investor merely trades in the convertible bond for a stipulated number of shares of common stock. Figure 10.5 provides the details of a convertible bond recently issued by The Home Depot. Note that this obligation originally came out as a 6¾ percent subordinated debenture bond, but in time each $1,000 bond can be converted into Home Depot stock at $49 per share. Thus, *regardless of what happens to the market price of the stock,* the convertible bond investor can redeem each $1,000 bond for 20.41 shares of stock—that is, $1,000/$49 = 20.41 shares. If at the time of conversion the stocks are trading in the market at $100 a share, then the investor would have just converted a $1,000 bond into $2,041 worth of stocks (20.41 × $100)!

forced conversion
the calling in of convertible bonds by the issuing firm.

The *bondholder* is the one who has the right to convert the bond at any time, but more commonly, the issuing firm will initiate conversion by calling the bonds—a practice known as **forced conversion.** To provide the corporation with the flexibility to retire the debt and force conversion, most convertibles come out as freely callable issues, or they carry *very short* call deferment periods. To force conversion, the corporation would call for the retirement of the bond and give the bondholder one of two options: to convert the bond into common stock, or to redeem the bond for cash at the stipulated call price (which, in the case of convertibles, contains very little call premium). So long as the convertible is called when the market value of the stock exceeds the call price of the issue, seasoned investors would never choose the second option. Instead, they would opt to convert the bond, as the firm wants them to. After the conversion is complete, the bonds no longer exist; instead, there is additional common stock in their place.

Conversion Privilege

conversion privilege
the conditions and specific nature (such as timing and price) of the conversion feature of convertible securities.

conversion period
the time period during which a convertible issue can be converted.

The key element of any convertible is its **conversion privilege,** which stipulates the conditions and specific nature of the conversion feature. To begin with, it states exactly when the debenture can be converted. Generally, there will be an initial waiting period of six months to perhaps two years after the date of issue, during which time the security cannot be converted. The **conversion period** then begins, after which the issue can be converted at any time. Although the conversion period typically extends for the remaining life of the debenture, it may exist for only a certain number of years. This is done to provide the issuing firm with more control over its capital structure. If the issue has not been converted by the end of its conversion period, it then reverts to a straight debt issue with *no* conversion privileges.

From the investor's point of view, the most important piece of information is the

NEW ISSUE   May 12, 1989

$225,000,000

The Home Depot, Inc.

6¾% Convertible Subordinated Debentures Due 2014

The Debentures are convertible into Common Stock of the Company at any
time on or before May 15, 2014, unless previously redeemed, at a conver-
sion price of $49 per share, subject to adjustment in certain events.

Price 100%

plus accrued interest, if any, from May 18, 1989

Copies of the Prospectus may be obtained in any State in which this announcement is circulated
only from such of the undersigned as may legally offer these securities in such State.
These securities are redeemable prior to maturity as set forth in the Prospectus.

The First Boston Corporation   Invemed Associates, Inc.

FIGURE 10.5   A New Convertible Bond Issue.
Holders of this Home Depot bond can convert it into the company's common stock at the
stated price of $49 per share and, as a result, receive 20.41 shares of stock for each $1,000
convertible bond they own. Prior to conversion, the bondholder will receive annual interest
income of $67.50 for each bond. (*Source: The Wall Street Journal,* May 12, 1989.)

conversion ratio
the number of shares
of common stock into
which a convertible
issue can be con-
verted.

conversion price
the stated price per
share at which com-
mon stock will be
delivered to the in-
vestor in exchange
for a convertible
issue.

conversion price, or conversion ratio. These terms are used interchangeably and
specify the number of shares into which the bond can be converted. **Conversion
ratio** denotes the number of common shares into which the bond can be converted;
conversion price indicates the stated value per share at which the common stock
will be delivered to the investor in exchange for the bond. For example, a $1,000
convertible bond might stipulate a conversion ratio of 20, meaning that the bond can
be converted into 20 shares of common stock. This same privilege could also be
stated in terms of a conversion price—that the $1,000 bond may be used to acquire
stock in the corporation at a "price" of $50 per share. Note that the Home Depot
convertible depicted in Figure 10.5 uses the conversion price (of $49 a share) to
describe its conversion feature. (One basic difference between a convertible debenture and a convertible preferred is that whereas the conversion ratio of a debenture
generally deals with large multiples of common stock, such as 15, 20, or 30 shares,

TABLE 10.2 **Features of Some Actively Traded Convertible Securities**

Issue	S&P Rating	Size of Issue (millions)	Conversion Ratio	Mkt. Pr. of Conv. (Early '89)	Yield*	Conversion Premium
Convertible Bonds						
CBI Industries 7 (2011)	BB+	$ 75	29.42	$ 958.80	7.4%	+19%
Champion 6½ (2011)	BBB−	150	28.78	1035.00	6.2	+9
Chubb Corp. 5½ (1993)	AA	200	11.72	930.00	7.3	+24
Dana Corp. 5⅞ (2006)	A−	150	19.83	892.50	7.0	+17
Eastman Kodak 6⅜ (2011)	BBB+	300	19.74	1055.00	5.7	+16
Federal Realty 5¼ (2002)	BBB	100	32.66	930.00	6.0	+24
IBM 7⅞ (2004)	AAA	1,285	6.51	1005.00	7.8	+26
McKesson Inc. 9¾ (2006)	A−	80	45.70	1431.30	5.7	+2
NBD Bancorp 8¼ (2010)	AA−	100	34.88	1328.80	5.6	−1
Potlatch 5¾ (2012)	BBB	75	22.07	870.00	6.9	+20
Convertible Preferreds						
Arkla $3.00 pfd.	A−	$ 130	1.75	$ 41.38	7.3%	+11%
Baxter Travenol $3.50 pfd.	BBB−	550	2.98	63.38	5.5	+14
Cameron Iron $3.50 pfd.	BB+	75	2.17	46.25	7.6	+22
Cyprus Minerals $3.75 pfd.	BB+	175	1.34	59.00	6.4	+14
First Exec $1.56 pfd.	A	225	1.11	17.50	8.9	+15
BF Goodrich $3.50 pfd.	BB+	100	0.91	50.63	6.9	0
Int'l Mineral $3.75 pfd.	BBB−	125	1.22	52.00	7.2	+8
Potlatch $3.75 pfd.	BBB	50	1.89	60.88	6.2	−1
Unisys $3.75 pfd.	BBB	1,200	1.67	52.38	7.2	+9
USF&G $4.10 pfd.	A	200	1.09	42.63	9.6	+25

*Yield-to-maturity for convertible bonds; current yield for convertible preferreds.

the conversion ratio of a preferred is generally very small, often less than 1 share of common and seldom exceeds more than 2 or 3 shares.)

The conversion ratio is generally fixed over the conversion period, although some convertibles are issued with variable ratios/prices. In such cases, the conversion ratio decreases (while the conversion price increases) over the life of the conversion period to reflect the supposedly higher value of the equity. The conversion ratio is also normally adjusted for stock splits and significant stock dividends to maintain the conversion rights of the investor. As a result, if a firm declares, say, a 2-for-1 stock split, the conversion ratio of any of its outstanding convertible issues would also double. When the ratio includes a fraction, such as 33⅓ shares of common, the conversion privilege will specify how any fractional shares are to be handled: usually, either the investor can put up the additional funds necessary to purchase another full share of stock at the conversion price, or receive the cash equivalent of the fractional share (at the conversion price). Table 10.2 lists some basic features of a number of actively traded convertible bonds and preferreds, and reveals a variety of conversion privileges.

Sources of Value

Because convertibles are fixed-income securities linked to the equity position of the firm, they are normally valued in terms of both the bond and the stock dimensions of the issue. In fact, it is ultimately the stock and the bond dimensions of the convertible that give the security its value. This, of course, explains why it is so important to analyze the underlying common stock *and* to formulate interest rate expectations when considering convertibles as an investment outlet. Let's look first at the stock dimension.

Convertible securities will trade much like common stock—in effect, they derive their value from the common stock—whenever the market price of the stock is equal to or greater than the stated conversion price. This means that whenever a convertible trades at or above its par value ($1,000), it will exhibit price behavior that closely matches that of the underlying common stock: If the stock goes up in price, so will the convertible, and vice versa. In fact, the price change of the convertible will *exceed* that of the common, since the conversion ratio will define the convertible's rate of price change. For example, if a convertible carries a conversion ratio of, say, 20, then for every point the common stock goes up (or down) in price, the price of the convertible will move in the *same direction by a multiple of 20*. In essence, whenever a convertible trades as a stock, its market price will approximate a multiple of the share price of the common, with the size of the multiple being defined by the conversion ratio.

When the price of the common is depressed, so that its trading price is well below the conversion price, the convertible will lose its ties to the underlying common stock and begin to trade as a bond. The issue should then trade according to prevailing bond yields, which would prompt an investor to focus major concern on market rates of interest. However, because of the equity kicker and their relatively low agency ratings, convertibles generally do not possess high interest rate sensitivity. Gaining more than a rough idea of what the prevailing yield of the convertible obligation ought to be is often difficult. For example, if the issue is rated Baa by Moody's, and if the market rate for this quality range is 9 percent, the convertible should be priced to yield *something around* 9 percent, plus or minus perhaps as much as half a percentage point or so. The bond feature will also establish a *price floor* for the convertible. This price floor tends to parallel interest rates, and it exists independently of the depressed behavior of the common share prices. When convertible securities are viewed in this light, it's not surprising that the market of 1985–1986 was so good to convertible bondholders. For these investors were able to experience the best of both worlds: that is, not only did stock prices jump up, but bond interest rates dropped way down! Thus, *both* the stock values of convertibles and their bond price floors were going up together and in so doing, providing investors not only with improved returns, but with reduced exposure to risk as well.

Risk Exposure

The risk exposure of a convertible is a function of the issue's fixed-income and equity characteristics. Due to the vital role equity plays in defining the stock value of a convertible, the investor should evaluate the business, financial, and market

risks to which the underlying common stock is exposed. Likewise, because of the fixed-income nature of convertibles, and because this aspect defines its price floor, purchasing power (inflation) risk and interest rate risk are also important.

Advantages and Disadvantages of Investing in Convertibles

The major advantage of a convertible issue is that it reduces downward risk (via the issue's bond value or price floor) and at the same time provides an upward price potential comparable to that of the firm's common stock. This two-sided feature is critical with convertibles and is impossible to match with straight common or straight debt. Another benefit is that the current income from bond interest normally exceeds the income from dividends that would be paid with a *comparable investment* in the underlying common stock. For example, let's say you had the choice of investing $1,000 in a new 8 percent convertible or the same amount in the company's common stock, presently trading at $42.50 a share (which price as is customary with new convertibles, is a bit *under* the bond's conversion price—of $50 a share). Under these circumstances, the investor could buy *one* convertible, or *23½ shares* of common stock (i.e., $1,000/$42.50 = 23.5). Now, if the stock paid $2 a share in annual dividends, a $1,000 investment in the stocks would yield $47 a year in dividends; in contrast, the investor could collect substantially more by putting the same amount into the company's convertible bond (where the investor would receive $80 a year in interest income). Thus, it is possible with convertibles to reap the advantages of common stock (in the form of potential upward price appreciation) and yet generate improved current income.

On the negative side, there is the conversion premium, or, as it is sometimes called, *water*. Unless the market price of the stock is very high and exceeds the conversion price by a wide margin, a convertible will almost always trade at a price that is above its true value. The amount of this excess price is conversion premium, and it has the unfortunate side effect of diluting the price appreciation potential of a convertible. What is more, an investor who truly wants to hold bonds can almost certainly find better current and promised yields from straight debt obligations, and because of conversion premiums, he or she can probably realize greater capital gains by investing directly in the common stock. So if improved returns are normally available from the direct investment in either straight debt and/or straight equity, why buy a convertible? The answer is simple: Convertibles provide a sound way to achieve attractive risk-return tradeoffs. In particular, by combining the characteristics of both stocks and bonds into one security, convertibles offer some risk protection and at the same time considerable, although perhaps not maximum, upward price potential. Thus, although the return may not be the most in absolute terms, neither is the risk.

Transaction Costs

Convertible bonds are subject to the same brokerage fees and transfer taxes as straight corporate debt; and convertible preferreds trade at the same costs as straight preferreds and common stock. Any type of market or limit order that can be used with bonds or stocks can also be used with convertibles. Convertible debentures are

Bonds	Cur Yld	Vol	Close	Net Chg.
Coastl 11¼96	11.3	30	99⅞	+ 1¼
Coastl 11¾06	12.0	96	98	+ ⅜
Coastl 8.48s91	8.9	33	95½	...
Coastl 11⅛98	11.4	65	97⅞	+ ⅜
ColuG 9⅛95	9.2	5	99½	+ 1⅞
ColuG 8⅜96	8.9	10	93⅞	+ ⅛
CmwE 8s03	9.1	50	88⅜	+ 2⅞
CmwE 9⅜04	9.9	5	94½	+ ½
CmwE 9⅛08	9.9	7	91¾	+ ⅛
CmwE 11⅛10	10.7	13	103¾	+ ½
CmwE 12⅛13	11.2	77	107⅞	+ ⅛
CmwE 10⅝95	10.4	10	102½	+ ¾
CmwE 11¾15	11.2	5	104⅝	− ⅜
Compq 6½13	cv	98	137	+ 1
ConEd 5s90	5.4	10	92½	− ¼
ConEd 9⅜00	9.5	3	98½	− ⅞
ConEd 7.9s01	9.0	5	88	...
ConEd 7.9s02	9.0	15	88⅛	+ ⅝
ConEd 7¾03	9.0	10	86½	+ ¼
ConEd 9⅛04	9.5	36	96	+ ⅝
CnNG 8¼94	8.7	2	94¾	...
CnNG M 8⅜96	9.1	2	92½	− 1
CnNG 8⅛97	8.9	10	91	+ ⅜
CnPw 6⅞98	8.6	10	80	− ⅜
CnPw 7⅝99	9.0	75	85	+ ⅜
CnPw 8⅛01	9.3	10	87	...
CnPw 7½2020	9.3	13	81	+ ½
CnPw 8⅝03	9.7	8	88¾	− ⅛
CnPw 9¾06	10.1	5	97	+ ½

FIGURE 10.6 Listed Quotes for Convertible Bonds.
Convertible bonds are listed along with other corporate issues and are identified by the letters *cv* in the "Cur Yld" column; except for this distinguishing feature, they are quoted like any other corporate bond. *Source: The Wall Street Journal.*

listed along with corporate bonds; they are distinguished from straight debt issues by the "cv" in the "Cur Yld" column of the bond quotes, as illustrated in Figure 10.6. Note that it's not unusual for some convertibles (like the Compaq Computer 6½ percent issue of 2013, for example) to trade at very high prices. These situations are justified by the correspondingly high values attained by the underlying common stock. Convertible preferreds, in contrast, normally are not isolated from other preferreds. They are listed with the "pf" markings, but they carry no other distinguishing symbols. As a result, the investor must turn to some other source to find out whether a preferred is convertible (one national business newspaper that *does* identify convertible preferreds is *Investor's Daily*—it provides a separate list of

preferred stocks traded on the NYSE and AMEX and uses boldface type to highlight the convertible issues).

Measuring the Value of a Convertible

Evaluating the investment merits of convertible securities includes consideration of both the bond and stock dimensions of the issue. Fundamental security analysis of the equity position is, of course, especially important in light of the key role the equity kicker plays in defining the price behavior of a convertible. Agency ratings are helpful and are widely used in evaluating the bond side of the issue. In addition to analyzing the bond and stock dimensions of the issue, it is essential to evaluate the conversion feature itself. The two critical areas in this regard are conversion value and investment value. These measures have a vital bearing on a convertible's price behavior and therefore can have a dramatic effect on an issue's realized holding period return.

Conversion Value

conversion value
an indication of what a convertible issue should trade for if it were priced to sell on the basis of its stock value; equals the conversion ratio of the issue times the current market price of the underlying common stock.

conversion equivalent
the price at which the common stock would have to sell in order to make the convertible security worth its present market price; also called conversion parity.

conversion premium
the amount by which the market price of a convertible exceeds its conversion value.

In essence, **conversion value** is an indication of what a convertible issue should trade for if it were priced to sell on the basis of its stock value. Conversion value is easy to find: Simply multiply the conversion ratio of the issue by the current market price of the underlying common stock. For example, a convertible that carries a conversion ratio of 20 would have a conversion value of $1,200 if the firm's stock traded at a current market price of $60 per share (20 × $60 = $1,200). Sometimes an alternative measure is used and the **conversion equivalent,** or what is also known as **conversion parity,** may be computed. The conversion equivalent indicates the price at which the common stock would have to sell in order to make the convertible security worth its present market price. To find the conversion equivalent, simply divide the current market price of the convertible by its conversion ratio. If, for example, a convertible were trading at $1,400 and it had a conversion ratio of 20, then the conversion equivalent of the common stock would equal $70 per share ($1,400 ÷ 20 = $70). In effect, we would expect the current market price of the common stock in this example to be at or near $70 per share in order to support a convertible trading at $1,400.

Unfortunately, convertible issues *seldom* trade precisely at their conversion values; rather, as noted earlier, they invariably trade at a **conversion premium.** The absolute size of an issue's conversion premium is determined by taking the difference between the convertible's market price and its conversion value. To place the premium on a relative basis, simply divide the dollar amount of the conversion premium by the issue's conversion value. For example, if a convertible trades at $1,400 and its conversion value equals $1,200, it would have a conversion premium of $200 ($1,400 − $1,200 = $200); in relation to what the convertible should be trading at, this differential would amount to a conversion premium of 16.7 percent (the dollar amount of the conversion premium divided by the issue's conversion value, or $200/$1,200). Conversion premiums are common in the market (see Table 10.2, page 433) and can often amount to as much as *25 to 30 percent* (or

more) of an issue's true conversion value; indeed, the average conversion premium in a normal market is around 20 percent.

Investors are willing to pay a conversion premium because of the added current income that a convertible provides relative to the underlying common stock, and so long as the issue possesses promising price potential. An investor can recover the conversion premium from the added income that the convertible provides, and/or by subsequently selling the issue at a premium equal to or greater than that which existed at the time of purchase. Unfortunately, conversion premiums generally diminish as the price of the issue increases. Therefore, if a convertible is bought for its potential price appreciation, all or a major portion of this price premium will disappear as the convertible appreciates and moves closer to its true conversion value. As a result, investors should watch out for abnormally high conversion premiums; indeed, as the accompanying Investor Insights box suggests, the investor should always take care to *fully evaluate a bond's conversion premium before investing in one of these securities*.

Investment Value

*investment value
the price at which a
convertible would
trade if it were non-
convertible and if it
were priced at or
near the prevailing
market yields of
comparable noncon-
vertible issues.*

The price floor of a convertible is defined by its bond properties and is the object of the investment value measure; it's the point within the evaluation process where attention is centered on current and expected market interest rates. **Investment value** is the price at which the bond would trade if it were nonconvertible and if it were priced at (or near) the prevailing market yields of comparable nonconvertible bonds. The same bond price formula given in Chapter 9 is used to compute investment value. Since the coupon and maturity are known, the only additional piece of information needed is the market yield to maturity of comparably rated issues. For example, if comparable nonconvertible bonds are trading at 9 percent yields, and if a particular 20-year convertible carries a 6 percent coupon, its investment value would be $725. (Note: This value was calculated using techniques discussed in Chapter 9.) This figure indicates how far the convertible will have to fall before it hits its price floor and begins trading as a straight debt instrument. Other things being equal, the greater the distance between the current market price of a convertible and its investment value, the further the issue can fall in price before it hits its bond floor, and as a result, the greater the downside risk exposure.

Investment Strategies

Convertible securities offer some unusual, though rewarding, investment opportunities; some investors buy them because of the underlying stock, others because of the attractive yields they offer as fixed-income securities. But before we examine the investment strategies used to capture the benefits of these securities, we need to review the general price and investment behavior of convertibles.

An Overview of Price and Investment Behavior

The price behavior of a convertible security is influenced by both the equity and fixed-income elements of the obligation. The variables that play key roles in defining the market value of a typical convertible therefore include: (1) the potential price behavior of the underlying common stock; and (2) expectations regarding the pat-

Convertible Investors: Watch Out for Those Conversion Premiums!

Rising stocks and falling interest rates are a winning combination for convertibles—bonds that can be swapped for common stock. But picking convertibles is tricky business for newcomers. You have to warm up your calculator and do some figuring to spot good buys. When interest rates are declining and prospects are good for stocks, convertibles offer high current yield plus the chance to participate in the appreciation on the underlying stock. There is also protection: if the stock goes down, the price of the convertible won't fall below what it would fetch if it were simply an ordinary bond. Because convertibles frequently have an income edge over the underlying stock, however, they often sell at premiums over their conversion value. In picking convertibles, the big question is whether the premium on a particular bond is justified. . . .

As a rule of thumb, most professional money managers advise against paying a premium of more than a half year's interest for a convertible that is selling near or above its call price. In any case, you should expect to recover the premium—from the *extra* interest income that you can earn from a convertible—in less than four years. Otherwise, you would probably be better off owning the stock.

Here's why: In a rising stock market, a company's common will generally appreciate faster than any convertible it offers because of the premium. So, you have to figure how much you are paying to get the difference in income. For instance, not long ago, Storer Broadcasting Co.'s common stock fell to a low of 19, while the company's 8½% convertible, due in 2005, sold as low as 73.75. The bonds, which are exchangeable for 25 shares, had a conversion value, based on that price, of 475. An investor who bought the convertible got an 11.53% current yield. Storer common, on the other hand, paid quarterly dividends of 18 cents a share, for a 3.8% current yield. The bond investor, then, paid a whopping 55% premium to get the additional yield. But he will have to hang on to the convertible for almost four years just to make up the premium from the additional interest income. What happened to the appreciation on both securities? Storer common shot up to around $30 a share, for almost a 59% gain. The 8½% convertible, in turn, moved up to 97, for a 31% gain. Thus, while the bond investor gave up the appreciation he could have had on the stock, he enjoyed the extra income and took less risk than the stock buyer.

While examining premiums takes some number crunching, it can prevent you from making bad choices. Take the case of Prime Computer's 10% convertibles, that were due in 2000. At a low of 94, they also looked like a good buy when the company's common shares were selling at about $16. At the time, the bonds were yielding 10.99%, while the common has never paid a dividend. The bonds were exchangeable for 31.58 shares. But at a price of 94, they were selling at an 86% premium over their conversion value. And because the bonds were trading close to their call price, the payback until an investor would recover that premium was considerably more than four years. Since then, Prime Computer's stock more than doubled, but when the bonds recently surged over their 107 call price, the company decided to redeem them. Investors who bought the bonds at 94 were foolish to pay so much of a premium over conversion value for convertibles trading that close to their call price, *since they never came close to recovering such an astronomical premium.*

Source: Adapted from Jill Bettner, "Convertible Bonds May Be Right for the Times, But Do Some Figuring Before You Buy Them." *The Wall Street Journal,* December 13, 1982.

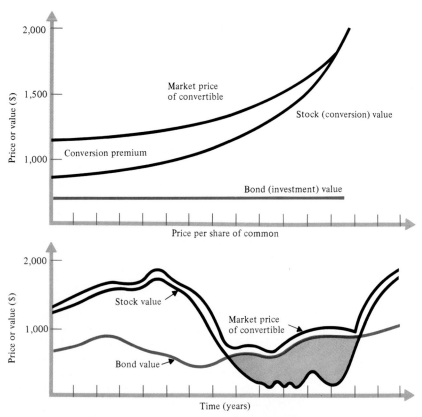

FIGURE 10.7 Typical Price Behavior of a Convertible Issue.
The price behavior of a convertible security is tied to the stock or the bond dimension of the issue—when the price of the underlying stock is up, the convertible will trade much like the stock, whereas the bond value will act as a price floor for the convertible.

tern of future market yields and interest rates. The typical price behavior of a convertible issue is depicted in Figure 10.7. In the top panel are the three market elements of a convertible bond: the bond value, or price floor; the stock (conversion) value of the issue; and the actual market price. The figure reveals the customary relationship between these three important elements, and shows that conversion premium is a common occurrence with these securities. Note especially that the conversion premium tends to diminish as the price of the stock increases. The top panel of Figure 10.7 is somewhat simplified, however, because of the steady price floor (which unrealistically assumes no variation in interest rates) and the steady upswing in the stock's value. The lower panel of the figure relaxes these conditions, although for simplicity, we will ignore conversion premium. The figure illustrates how the market value of a convertible will approximate the price behavior of the underlying stock so long as stock value is greater than bond value. When the stock value drops below the bond value floor, as it does in the shaded area of the illustration, the market value of the convertible becomes linked to the bond value of the

obligation, and it continues to move as a debt security until the price of the underlying stock picks up again and approaches, or equals, this price floor.

Convertibles as Deferred Equity Investments

Convertibles are purchased most often because of the *equity attributes* they offer to investors. As an alternative to a company's common stock, investors may be able to match (or possibly even exceed) the return from the common, but with less exposure to risk; also, relative to stocks, convertibles generally offer improved current income. Convertibles can be profitably used as alternative equity investments whenever it is felt that the underlying stock offers desired capital gains opportunities. In order to achieve maximum price appreciation under such circumstances, the investor would want assurance that the convertible is trading in concert with its stock value, and that it does not have an inordinate amount of conversion premium. If these necessary conditions do in fact exist, investor attention should logically center on the potential market behavior of the underlying stock. To assess such behavior, it is necessary to evaluate both current and expected conversion value.

For example, assume a 7 percent convertible bond carries a conversion ratio of 25 and is presently trading in the market at $900; in addition, assume the stock (which pays no dividends) is currently trading at $32 and the convertible is trading at a conversion premium of $100, or 12.5 percent. The formulation of future interest rates also comes into play with this trading strategy, as the investor will want to assess the bond price floor and the extent of downward risk exposure; using the same technique developed in Chapter 9, future interest rates would be forecast and used to determine the possible bond price behavior of the issue. Generally speaking, a *drop* in interest rates would be viewed positively by convertible bond investors, since such behavior would signal a rise in the price floor of the convertible issue and therefore a reduction in downside risk exposure. That is, should the common stock not perform as expected, the price of the convertible could still go up as the (bond) price floor rises—or at the least, it would reduce any drop in the price of the convertible issue.

But most of the attention is centered not on the bond price floor; rather, it is directed toward the anticipated behavior of the common stock and the conversion premium. To continue our example, assume the investor expects the price of the stock to rise to $60 per share within the next two years. A conversion ratio of 25 would then yield a future conversion value of $1,500. If an expected conversion premium of 6 to 7 percent (or about $100) is added, it follows that the market price of the convertible should rise to about $1,600 by the end of the two-year investment horizon. This expected future price of the convertible, along with its annual coupon payment and current market price, would then be used in the approximate realized yield equation to determine the issue's realized yield. For example,

$$\text{realized yield} = \frac{\$70 + \dfrac{\$1,600 - \$900}{2}}{\dfrac{\$1,600 + \$900}{2}} = \frac{\$70 + \$350}{\$1,250} = \underline{\underline{33.6\%}}$$

The realized yield equation above is identical to the one used with straight bonds and preferred stocks. Although this 33.6 percent rate of return may indeed appear attractive, the investor should be sure of several points before committing capital to this security—in particular, that this approach is in fact superior to a direct investment in the issuer's common stock (at least from a risk-return point of view), and that there is no better rate of return (with commensurate risk exposure) available from some other investment vehicle. To the extent that these conditions are met, investing in a convertible may be a suitable course of action, especially if (1) the price of the underlying common stock is under strong upward pressure; (2) bond interest rates are falling off sharply; and (3) there is little or no conversion premium in the price of the convertible. The first attribute means conversion value should move up, leading to appreciation in the price of the convertible; the second means that the bond value (price floor) should also move up, thereby reducing exposure to risk; and the third feature means the investor should be able to capture all or most of the price appreciation of the underlying common stock rather than lose a chunk of it to the inevitable drop in conversion premium.

Convertibles as High-Yield Fixed-Income Investments

Another common use of convertibles is to buy such issues for the attractive *fixed-income* returns they offer. The key element in this strategy is the issue's bond dimension. Many convertible securities provide current yields and yields to maturity that are safe and highly competitive with straight debt obligations. Care must be taken, however, to make certain that the high yields are not a function of low (speculative) ratings. Normally, such investors would seek discount issues, particularly those that are trading close to their bond price floor; otherwise, the issue would be trading at a premium price, which would certainly involve a yield give-up, and perhaps a substantial one. Most of these investors view convertibles as ideal for locking in high rates of return. Convertibles are not widely used for speculating on interest rates, however, because even investment-grade convertibles often lack the needed interest sensitivity (due to the equity kicker of the issue). Yet for those who use convertibles to seek high, safe yields, the equity kicker can provide an added source of return if the underlying stock does indeed take off. The investor then has a bond that offers a handsome rate of return, and an equity kicker to boot.

SUMMARY

- Preferred stocks and convertible securities play an important role in many sound, well-balanced investment programs. They are hybrid securities (combining features of both debt and equity) that offer investors some interesting and potentially rewarding investment opportunities.

- Preferred stocks provide attractive dividend yields and, when interest rates decline, will produce capital gains as well. Preferreds are considered less risky than common because their shareholders enjoy a senior position with regard to dividend payments and asset claims.

- Except for specialty issues—like floating rate and participating preferreds—most other forms of preferred stocks pay a fixed level of annual dividends, which can be passed if earnings fail to live up to expectations. Although failure to pay preferred dividends does not carry with it the same serious consequences as missing the interest payments on a bond, no common stock dividends can be paid until all preferred obligations are satisfied.

- Preferreds are bought and sold on the various exchanges and in the OTC market in exactly the same manner as common stocks; commissions are the same, and so are price quotations and transaction costs.

- Except for convertible preferreds, the value of a preferred stock is generally linked to the dividend yield it provides to investors. Indeed, the price behavior of a preferred stock generally is inversely related to market interest rates.

- The principal purpose for holding preferreds is their yield; in addition, preferreds can be held for capital gains purposes by investors willing to trade on interest rate behavior or on turnaround situations.

- Convertible securities are initially issued as bonds (or preferreds), but they can subsequently be converted into shares of common stock. As such, these securities are highly attractive because they offer investors a generous stream of fixed income (in the form of annual coupon payments) and an equity kicker to boot.

- Because convertible securities can be converted into common stock, the value of a convertible depends largely on the price behavior of the underlying common. This is captured in the security's conversion value, which represents the worth of a convertible if it were converted into common stock. (Conversion value rises in direct proportion to increases in share prices.)

- Should the price of the common decline, the conversion value will drop as well; but the convertible will drop only so far, since the fixed-income feature of the issue will act as a floor for its market price.

- From an investment perspective, convertibles provide a combination of both good upside potential (from the equity feature of the issue) and good downside protection (through the fixed-income characteristics of the issue); in fact, this risk-return tradeoff, combined with their relatively high current income, is unmatched by any other type of security.

- Investors use convertible securities primarily as a form of deferred equity, when the investment is made as a way to capture the capital gains potential of the underlying common stock. In addition, convertibles are sometimes used as high-yielding fixed-income securities, when the investor principally goes after the high current income of the bond (and the equity kicker is viewed as little more than a pleasant by-product).

REVIEW QUESTIONS AND PROBLEMS

1. Define a preferred stock. What types of prior claims do preferred stockholders enjoy?

2.   In what ways is a preferred stock like equity? like a bond?

3.   Distinguish a cumulative preferred from a callable preferred. Do cumulative and call provisions affect the investment merits of preferred issues? Explain.

4.   Briefly describe each of the following, and note how each differs from a ''regular'' preferred stock:

a. Participating preferred.
b. Floating-rate preferred.
c. Preference preferred.
d. PIK preferred.

5.   Describe some of the advantages and disadvantages of investing in preferreds.

6.   Assume an $8 preferred stock is currently selling at a dividend yield of 9 percent. The company then pays a $2 participating dividend, which is expected to hold in the future. What would the new current yield of this issue be if its market price does not change? What would the new market price of the issue be if the stock's dividend yield holds at 9 percent?

7.   Discuss why dividend yield is critical in evaluating the investment merits of high-grade preferred stocks during periods when market yields are expected to decline.

8.   Briefly discuss several investment uses of preferred stocks. Would preferreds be suitable for both conservative and aggressive investors? Explain.

9.   The Danzer Company has 500,000 shares of $2 preferred stock outstanding; it generates an EBIT of $40,000,000 and has annual interest payments of $2,000,000. Given the above information, determine the fixed charge coverage of the preferred stock.

10. Is it possible for a firm to pass dividends on preferred stocks, even if it earns enough to pay them? Explain. What usually happens when a company passes (misses) a dividend on a (cumulative) preferred stock; are common stock dividends affected in any way?

11. Charlene Weaver likes to speculate with preferred stock by trading on movements in market interest rates. Right now, she thinks the market is poised for a big drop in rates; accordingly, she is seriously thinking about investing in a certain preferred stock that pays $7 in annual dividends and is presently trading at $75 per share. What rate of return would she realize on this investment if the market yield on the preferred drops to $6\frac{1}{2}$ percent within two years?

12. What is a convertible debenture? How does a convertible bond differ from a convertible preferred?

13. Identify the equity kicker of a convertible security, and explain how it affects the value and price behavior of convertibles.

14. Explain why it is necessary to examine both the bond and stock properties of a convertible debenture when determining its investment appeal.

15. What are the investment attributes of convertible debentures? What are the disadvantages of such vehicles?

16. A certain 6 percent convertible bond (maturing in 20 years) is convertible at the holder's option into 20 shares of common stock; the bond is currently trading at $800 and the stock at $35 per share:

a. What is the current yield of the convertible bond?

b. What is the conversion price?

c. What is the conversion ratio?

d. What is the conversion value of this issue? What is its conversion parity?

e. What is the conversion premium, in dollars and as a percentage?

f. What is the approximate yield to maturity of the convertible bond?

g. If comparably rated nonconvertible bonds sell to yield 8 percent, what is the investment value of the convertible?

17. What is the difference between conversion parity and conversion value? What is the bond investment value of a convertible and what does it reveal?

18. An 8 percent convertible bond carries a par value of $1,000 and a conversion ratio of 20. Assume that an investor has $5,000 to invest and that the convertible sells at a price of $1,000 (which includes a 25 percent conversion premium). How much total income (coupon plus capital gains) would this investment offer if, over the course of the next 12 months, the price of the stock moves to $75 per share and the convertible trades at a price which includes a conversion premium of 10 percent? What is the holding period return on this investment? Finally, given the information in the problem, what is the underlying common stock currently selling for?

19. Discuss the various uses of convertible debentures. What are the three major attributes that make for an ideal investment outlet and that investors should look for when using convertibles as deferred equity investments?

20. Assume you just paid $1,200 for a convertible bond that carries a 7½ percent coupon and has 15 years to maturity. The bond can be converted into 24 shares of stock, which are now trading at $50 a share. Find the bond investment value of this issue, given that comparable nonconvertible bonds are presently selling to yield 9 percent.

21. Find the conversion value of a *convertible preferred stock* that carries a conversion ratio of 1.8, given that the market price of the underlying common stock is $40 a share. Would there be any conversion premium if the convertible preferred were selling at $90 a share? If so, how much (in dollar and percentage terms)? Also, explain the concept of conversion parity and then find the conversion parity of this issue, given that the preferred trades at $90 per share.

22. Using the resources available at your campus or public library, find the information requested below. (Note: Be sure to show your work for all calculations.)

a. Select any two *nonconvertible preferred stocks* and determine the current yield of each.

b. Select any two *convertible debentures* and determine the conversion ratio, conversion parity, conversion value, and conversion premium for each.

c. Select any two *convertible preferreds* and determine the conversion ratio, conversion parity, conversion value, and conversion premium of each.

CASE PROBLEMS

10.1 Mary Beth Shows a Preference for Preferreds

Ms. Mary Beth Kaminski is a young career woman who has built up a substantial investment portfolio. Most of her holdings are preferred stocks—a situation she does not want to change. Ms. Kaminski is now considering the purchase of $4,800 worth of LaRamie Mine's $5 preferred, which is currently trading at $48 per share. Mary Beth's stockbroker, Mr. Mike,

has told her that he feels the market yield on preferreds like LaRamie should drop to 8 percent within the new two years, and that these preferreds would make a sound investment. Instead of buying the LaRamie preferred, Mary Beth has an alternate investment (with comparable risk exposure) which she is confident can produce earnings of about 10 percent over each of the next two years.

Questions

1. If preferred yields behave as Mary Beth's stockbroker thinks they will, what will be the price of the LaRamie $5 preferred in two years?
2. What realized yield would this investment offer over the two-year holding period if all the expectations about it come true (particularly with regard to the price it is supposed to reach)? How much profit (in dollars) will Mary Beth make from her investment?
3. Would you recommend that Ms. Kaminski buy the LaRamie preferred? Why?
4. What are the investment merits of this transaction? What are its risks?

10.2 Dave and Marlene Consider Convertibles

Dave and Marlene Normington live in Irvine, California, where she manages a bridal shop and he runs an industrial supply firm. Their annual income is usually in the mid to upper seventies; they have no children and maintain a "comfortable" life style. Recently, they came into a bit of money and are anxious to invest it in some high-yielding fixed-income security. Although not aggressive investors, they like to maximize the return on every investment dollar they have. For this reason, they like the high yields and added equity kicker of convertible bonds, and are presently looking at such an issue as a way to invest their recent windfall. In particular, they have their eyes on the convertible debentures of Maria Pottery, Inc. They have heard that the price of the stock is on the way up, and after some in-depth analysis of their own, they feel the company's prospects are indeed bright. They've also looked at market interest rates, and based on economic reports obtained from their broker, Dave and Marlene expect interest rates to decline sharply.

The details on the convertible they're looking at are as follows: It's a 20-year, $1,000 par value issue that carries a 7½ percent coupon and is presently trading at $800; the issue is convertible into 15 shares of stock and the stock, which pays no dividends, was recently quoted at $49.50 per share.

Questions

1. Ignoring conversion premium, find the price of the convertible if the stock goes up to $66.67 per share; what if it goes up to $75 per share, or $100 per share? Repeat the computations, assuming the convertible will trade at a 5 percent conversion premium.

2. Find the approximate promised yield of the convertible. (*Hint:* Use the same approach as we did with straight bonds in Chapter 9.)
    a. Now find the bond value of the convertible if, within two years, interest rates drop to 8 percent. (Remember: in two years, the security will have only 18 years remaining to maturity.) What if they drop to 6 percent?
    b. What implication does the drop in interest rates hold as far as the investment appeal of the convertible is concerned?

3. Given expected future stock prices and interest rate levels (per above), find the minimum and maximum realized yield that this investment offers over the two-year holding period.
    a. What is the worst return (realized yield) Dave and Marlene can expect over their two-year holding period if the price of the stock drops to $40 per share and interest

rates drop to only 9 percent? What if the price of the stock drops (to $40) and interest rates rise to 11 percent? (Assume a zero conversion premium in both cases.)

4. Should the Normingtons invest in the Maria convertibles? Discuss the pros and cons of the investment.

SELECTED READINGS

Bryant, William C. ''When to Prefer Preferreds.'' *U.S. News & World Report,* September 23, 1985, p. 75.

Curran, John J. ''Playing It Safe With Convertibles.'' *Fortune,* February 1, 1988, pp. 99–100.

Fredman, Albert J., and Cameron P. Hum. ''Investing in Convertibles.'' *Personal Investor,* January 1987, pp. 70–75.

Scharf, Jeffrey R. ''Question of Preference: How Preferreds Stack Up vs. Bonds.'' *Barron's,* September 8, 1986, p. 71.

''Smoother Ride in Convertibles: They're a Neat Hedge Against Higher or Lower Equity Prices.'' *Barron's,* March 6, 1989, pp. 26–27.

''The Preferred Approach.'' *Personal Investor,* June 1985, pp. 50–52.

Thompson, Terri. ''The Reliability of a Bond, The Allure of a Stock.'' *U.S. News & World Report,* May 22, 1989, p. 77.

Weberman, Ben, and Jason Zweig. ''The Mixed Bag—Convertible Bonds and Preferred.'' *Forbes,* June 27, 1988, pp. 222–23.

Wiles, Russ. ''Convertible Crunch.'' *Personal Investor,* November 1988, pp. 53–57.

Willis, Clint. ''Convertible Issues Can Reduce Your Investment Risks.'' *Money,* April 1988, p. 193.

COMPUTER-BASED INVESTMENT MANAGEMENT: FIXED-INCOME SECURITIES

Though at times it may appear deceptively simple, investing in fixed-income securities can be a complex and highly technical matter. Indeed, serious bond investors have to deal with different kinds of yields, call features and sinking funds, yield spreads, future price behavior, conversion features, duration measures, and assorted types of bond swaps. This is precisely where the computer comes into play; for a wide range of software is now available to perform most of the mathematical and analytical functions that fixed-income investors have to face. Generally speaking, fixed-income investors (that is, those who invest in bonds, convertibles, and preferreds) tend to use computers for one or more of the following reasons: (1) to perform basic *valuation* functions—that is, to compute the basic comparative yield/return calculations (like promised yield, duration, future price, and expected/realized yield); (2) to analyze alternative bond swap and other bond *trading strategies;* and (3) to *manage* portfolios of bonds and other fixed-income securities—that is, to help in the construction, monitoring, and revision of the fixed-income portion of securities portfolios (see Part Six—pages 765–766—for a discussion of such uses). Of course, many of these computer-oriented investors have access to database/screening programs which they use primarily to carry out the trading, analysis, and portfolio management functions. Such information bases are usually obtained from either general database/screening programs (like CompuServe or Dow Jones News/Retrieval) which provide, as part of their inventory of information, company and market statistics on a number of fixed-income securities, or by using interfacing software that links up a specific bond analysis program (like the Bond Swap Analyzer, described below) with an on-line database that provides up-to-the-minute quotes and other information on literally thousands of different types of fixed-income securities.

The following is just a small sample of some of the bond/fixed-income computer programs available to the serious investor.

- *Master Brain Bond Calculator* (Decision Programming, 5640 Nicholson Ln., Suite 102, Rockville, MD 20852; 301/231-6393; $175; IBM PCs and compatibles.) This is an all-purpose program that performs an array of basic yield, return, and price computations; it can rapidly (and with a minimum amount of input) calculate current and expected/future bond prices, promised yield, yield-to-call, pre-tax and after-tax yields, realized yields, and other price and yield analyses for various types of fixed-income securities.
- *Yield Calculator* (Technical Data Corp., 330 Congress St., Boston, MA 02210; 617/482-3341; $375; Apples, IBM PCs and compatibles.) A program that works on all different types of fixed-income securities, including government, agency, corporate, and municipal bonds, short-term money market securities, and mortgage backed securities; it calculates duration, annual rates of return, taxable equivalent yields, and various promised and realized yields.
- *CV Evaluator* (Beta Systems Co., P.O. Box 1189, Boston, MA 02205; 617/861-1655; $295/yr.; IBM PCs or compatibles.) Updated database consisting of 500 convertible bonds and preferreds provides market quotes, quality rating, and betas. Calculates and evaluates various yield and conversion values; also projects convertible values based on expected price behavior of underlying common stock and interest rate environments.
- *BondWare* (Davidge Data Systems, 12 White St., New York, NY 10013; 212/226-3335; $450; IBM PCs and compatibles.) This is an integrated fixed-income security analysis package consisting of a yield calculator, portfolio analyzer, and bond swap analyzer. The program makes yield calculations for all types of fixed-income securities, and data may be stored in files for later recall or used with the portfolio or swap-analyzer modules. The portfolio analyzer gives the pre- and after-tax effect of liquidating one bond portfolio and purchasing another. This software is also compatible with Lotus 1-2-3 for graphical analysis. In addition to performing a wide variety of yield, price, duration, and return calculations, the program's capabilities also include access to bond databases, the preparation of amortization tables, and strip-zero coupon yield charts.
- *The Bond Swap Analyzer* (Technical Data Corp., 330 Congress St., Boston, MA 02210; 617/482-3341; $1700 plus annual maintenance fee; Apples, IBM PCs and compatibles.) This program determines the profitability and comparative rates of return from proposed bond swap transactions; works on most types of fixed-income securities. Computes prices/yields, durations, accrued interest, and after-tax returns for each issue in a proposed swap transaction; also finds comparative yields and net advantage to swapping based on user-specified horizon periods and future yields for the alternative bonds in the swap transaction. (Interface software available to link this program with an on-line database that provides market information and price updates on a wide assortment of fixed-income securities.)
- *Mortgage Backed Securities Calculator* (Bond-Tech, Inc., P.O. Box 192, Englewood, OH 45322; 513/836-3991; $250; IBM PCs and compatibles.) A program for serious mortgage-backed bond investors, this software provides a flexible yet powerful tool for analyzing the yield behavior of mortgage-backed

securities under a variety of prepayment assumptions. The program analyzes historical prepayment performance and permits the calculation of yield, semi-annual equivalent yield, and modified duration, using various assumptions concerning future prepayment experiences. This program permits the easy determination of otherwise complex mathematical formulas used to find yield, price, and return performance of mortgage-backed securities.

NOTE: The above list of programs should be viewed as illustrative in nature, and *not* interpreted as an endorsement or recommendation. Listed prices and phone numbers are the latest available and are, of course, subject to change without notice.

FOUR

SPECULATIVE INVESTMENT VEHICLES

Part Four includes:

Chapter 11   **Options: Rights, Warrants, Puts and Calls**

Chapter 12   **Commodities, Financial Futures, and Intangible Investments**

THE INVESTMENT ENVIRONMENT

INVESTMENT ADMINISTRATION

INVESTING IN COMMON STOCK	INVESTING IN FIXED-INCOME SECURITIES
SPECULATIVE INVESTMENT VEHICLES	OTHER POPULAR INVESTMENT VEHICLES

11

OPTIONS: RIGHTS, WARRANTS, PUTS AND CALLS

After studying this chapter you should be able to:

● Describe the basic features and investment merits of stock rights.

● Identify the general attributes and behavioral characteristics of warrants.

● Develop an understanding of the impact that leverage has on the speculative appeal of warrants, and discuss the trading strategies that can be used to gain maximum benefits from this investment vehicle.

● Discuss the basic nature of puts and calls, how these investment vehicles work, and why they are so popular with individual and institutional investors.

● Describe the different kinds of listed options, including puts and calls on stocks, stock indexes, debt securities, and foreign currencies.

● Explain the profit potential of puts and calls, as well as the risk and return behavior of various put and call investment strategies.

When investors buy shares of common or preferred stock, they become the registered owners of the securities and are entitled to all the rights and privileges of ownership. Investors who acquire bonds or convertible issues are also entitled to the benefits of ownership. However, options are another matter, for investors who buy options acquire nothing more than the right to subsequently buy or sell other, related securities. That is, an **option** gives the holder the right to buy or sell a certain amount of an underlying security at a specified price over a specified period of time.

option
a type of security that gives the holder the right to buy or sell a certain amount of an underlying financial asset at a specified price for a specified period of time.

The three basic kinds of options are: (1) rights; (2) warrants; and (3) puts and calls. The first type has little investment appeal for the average investor, but the latter two enjoy considerable popularity today as attractive trading vehicles. All of these securities are a bit unusual, and as such their use requires special investor know-how. The thrust of the present chapter, therefore, is to learn what we can about the essential characteristics and investment merits of these securities, and to see how they can be used in various types of investment programs.

RIGHTS

right
an option to buy shares of a new issue of common stock at a specified price, over a specified (fairly short) period of time.

A **right** is a special type of option that has a short market life; it usually exists for no more than several weeks. Essentially, rights originate when corporations raise money by issuing new shares of common stock. From an investor's perspective, a right enables a stockholder to buy shares of the new issue at a specified price, over a specified (fairly short) time period. Although not specifically designed for speculation or for use as trading vehicles, *they do have value* and as such, they should never be lightly discarded; instead, unwanted rights should be sold in the open market.

Characteristics

Let's say a firm has 1 million shares of common stock outstanding and that it has decided to issue another 250,000 shares. This might well be done through a *rights offering* whereby the firm, rather than directly issuing the new shares of common, would issue stock rights instead. These rights could then be used by their holders to purchase the new issue of stock. This procedure would be followed when existing stockholders are given the right to maintain their proportionate share of ownership in a firm, a privilege known as a **preemptive right.** Since each stockholder receives, without charge, one right for each share of stock currently owned, the company in our example would have to issue one million rights and as a result, it would take *four rights to buy one new share of common.*

preemptive right
the right of existing stockholders to maintain their proportionate share of ownership in a firm.

Rights and Privileges

exercise price
with options, the price at which a new share of common stock will be sold; also called subscription price.

Because most stock rights allow their holders to purchase only a fractional share of the new common stock, two or more rights are usually needed to buy a single new share. The price of the new stock is spelled out in the right. This is known as the **exercise** (or **subscription**) **price,** and it is always set below the prevailing market price of the stock. For each new share of common stock purchased, the investor would be expected to redeem a specified number of rights and pay the stipulated subscription price in cash. Rights not used by their expiration date lose all value and

simply cease to exist. Unfortunately, many investors allow their rights to expire and thereby lose money.

The Value of a Right

rights-on
a condition when a firm's common stock is trading with a stock right attached to it.

rights-off
a condition when a firm's common stock and its rights are trading in separate markets, separate from each other; also called ex-rights.

Technically, the precise measure of a right's value depends on whether the security is trading rights-on or rights-off. **Rights-on** indicates that the common stock is trading with the right attached to it; an investor who buys a share of stock during such a period also receives the attached stock right. When issues are trading **rights-off,** or "ex-rights," the company's stock and its rights are trading in separate markets and distinct from one another. Regardless of how these securities are trading, we can use the following approximation formula to measure the value of a right:

$$\text{value of a right} = \frac{\text{market price of old stock} - \text{subscription price of new stock}}{\text{number of rights needed to buy one new share}}$$

As an example of how the formula works, we will continue the illustration above. Assume the prevailing market price of the old stock is $50 and the new shares carry a subscription price of $40 per share. Remember that it takes four rights and $40 to buy one new share of stock. We thus find the approximate value of a right as follows:

$$\text{value of a right} = \frac{\$50 - \$40}{4} = \frac{\$10}{4} = \$2.50$$

Each right in our hypothetical example will have a market value of about $2.50 (as long as the price of the stock remains at $50).

Investment Merits

The major investment attribute of a stock right is that it allows the holder to acquire stock at a reduced price. It also enables the holder to acquire additional shares of stock *without paying the customary commission fees*. Although the savings may not be enormous, the opportunity to execute commission-free transactions should not be overlooked. However, except for the commission savings, the cost of buying the stock will be the same regardless of whether the shares are bought outright or through the use of rights; that is, the cost of the rights plus the subscription price of the stock should just about equal the market price of the common. Unfortunately, stock rights hold little opportunity for profitable trading. The life of these securities is simply too short and the range of price activity too narrow to allow for any significant trading profits. Thus, the role of stock rights is limited in most individual investor portfolios to selling unwanted rights or to buying/using them to reduce the commissions on subsequent stock transactions.

WARRANTS

A *warrant* is also an option that enables the holder to acquire common stock and, like rights, is found only in the corporate sector of the market. Occasionally, war-

rants can be used to purchase preferred stock or even bonds, but common stock is the leading redemption vehicle.

What Is a Warrant?

warrant

a long-lived option that gives the holder the right to buy stock in a company at a price as specified in the warrant itself.

A **warrant** is a long-lived option. In fact, of the various types of options, warrants have the longest lives, with maturities that extend to 5, 10, or even 20 years or more—indeed, some warrants have no maturity date at all. They have no voting rights, pay no dividends, and have no claim on the assets of the company. All the warrant offers is a chance to participate indirectly in the market behavior of the issuing firm's common stock and in so doing, to generate some capital gains. With warrants, *price behavior and capital appreciation are the only dimensions of return.*

General Attributes

Warrants are created as "sweeteners" to bond issues. That is, as a way to make a bond more attractive, the issuing corporation will sometimes attach warrants, which give the holder the right to purchase a stipulated number of stocks at a stipulated price any time within a stipulated period of time. A single warrant usually allows the holder to buy one full share of stock, although some involve more than one share per warrant and an even fewer number involve fractional shares. The life of a

expiration date

the date at which the life of a warrant expires.

exercise price

the price at which a share of stock can be purchased, as specified on a warrant.

warrant is specified by its **expiration date,** and the stock purchase price stipulated on the warrant is known as the **exercise price.**

Warrants are issued by all types of firms, and by prime-grade as well as highly speculative companies. Because warrants are a type of equity issue, they can be margined at the same rate as common stock. They are purchased through brokers and are subject to commission and transaction costs similar to those for common stock. Warrants are usually listed with the common stock of the issuer, but their quotes are easy to pick out, since the letters *wt* appear next to the name of the company. For example, the quote for the Federal National Mortgage ("FedNMtg") warrant is highlighted in Figure 11.1; notice that the market information for warrants is listed just like any other common stock except, of course, there's no dividend, dividend yield, or price/earnings ratio.

Advantages and Disadvantages

leverage

a concept whereby debt is used to reduce the level of required capital in a given investment position, thereby magnifying returns.

Warrants offer several advantages to investors, one of which is their tendency to exhibit price behavior much like the common stock to which they are linked. This tendency to behave like stocks provides the investor with an alternative way of achieving capital gains from an equity issue. That is, instead of buying the stock, the investor can purchase warrants on the stock; indeed, such a tactic may even be more rewarding than investing directly in the stock. Another advantage is the relatively low unit cost of warrants and the attractive leverage potential that accompanies this low unit cost. The concept of **leverage** rests on the principle of reducing the level of required capital in a given investment position, without affecting the payoff or capital appreciation of that investment. Put another way, an investor can use warrants to obtain a given equity position at a substantially reduced capital

52 Weeks					Yld		Vol				Net
Hi	Lo	Stock	Sym	Div	%	PE	100s	Hi	Lo	Close	Chg
↓ 13	9½	FMC Gold	FGL	.05e	.5	10	106	9⅞	9⅜	9⅜	− ¼
32	28½	FPL Gp	FPL	2.28	7.2	10	1997	31⅝	31⅛	31½	+ ¼
17⅞	9¾	Fairchild	FEN	.20	1.1	27	584	17¾	17⅝	17⅝	...
↓ 42	36½	Fairchild pf		3.60	9.9	...	14	36½	36¼	36½	...
7¾	4⅞	Fairfield	FCI	...	...	35	133	6½	6¼	6⅜	+ ⅛
16	10	FamDollr	FDO	.36	3.2	12	959	11⅛	10⅞	11⅛	+ ⅛
13½	9⅜	Fansteel	FNL	.40	3.4	55	71	11⅞	11⅝	11⅝	− ⅛
11½	7⅜	FarWestFnl	FWF	.40	3.9	7	19	10⅝	10⅜	10⅜	− ⅛
12⅝	7¼	Farah Inc	FRA	...	...	...	213	11⅝	11⅝	11⅝	...
12	7⅞	FaysDrug	FAY	.20b	1.7	16	310	12	11⅝	11⅝	− ¼
17⅝	7⅝	Fedders	FJQ	.40	2.3	16	482	17¼	17	17⅛	− ⅛
56⅜	38⅞	FedlExp	FDX	...	...	12	2282	46⅛	45⅞	45⅞	− ¼
↑ 69⅞	45½	FedlHmLoan pf		...	...	...	11849	70½	68¼	69⅝	+ ⅜
57¼	36¾	FedlMogul	FMO	1.84	3.4	18	330	54¼	54	54¼	+ ⅛
↑ 77⅜	34⅞	FedlNMtg	FNM	1.28	1.6	11	13381	80⅛	76⅞	80⅛	+2¾
↑ 36¼	7⅝	FedlNMtg wt		...	...	...	9192	39½	35¾	39¼	+3
s 28⅛	16⅞	FedlPapBd	FBO	.80	3.2	6	766	25½	25	25¼	+ ¼
52½	39	FedlPapBd pf		2.87	5.9	...	28	48½	48	48½	+ ½
24¼	20	FedlRlty	FRT	1.40	5.9	38	30	24	23⅝	23¾	− ¼
26	15	FedlSgnl	FSS	.84b	3.2	13	90	26	25⅝	25⅞	...
50⅝	29⅝	Ferro	FOE	.84	1.7	14	2959	49⅛	48¼	48¾	+ ¼
n↓ 35⅝	32½	Fiat	FIA	...	...	...	5	32¼	32¼	32¼	− ¼
↓ 21½	21	Fiat pf		...	...	...	5	20¾	20¾	20¾	− ¼
↓ 21⅝	21¼	Fiat pfA		...	...	...	2	21	21	21	− ¼
27½	16¼	Fieldcrst	FLD	.68	2.5	17	490	27	26⅜	27	+ ½
10⅛	6⅞	Filtertek	FTK	.44	5.8	10	248	7⅞	7½	7⅝	− ⅛
18½	11⅞	FnlNewsFd	FIF	.81e	4.4	...	35	18½	18¼	18½	+ ⅛
5⅝	1½	FnlCpSBar	FSB	...	...	...	8	2⅜	2¼	2¼	...
16	12¾	FineHomes	FHI	2.25	14.8	12	48	15⅜	15⅛	15¼	+ ⅛

FIGURE 11.1 Stock Quotations Showing Market Information for a Warrant.
Warrants are listed right along with common stocks, but they're easy to pick out—just look for the letters *wt* behind the company's name. (*Source: The Wall Street Journal.*)

investment, and in so doing *magnify returns,* since the warrant provides basically the same capital appreciation as the more costly common stock. Finally, the low unit cost of warrants also leads to reduced downside risk exposure. In essence, the lower unit cost simply means there is less to lose if the investment goes sour. For example, a $50 stock can drop to $25 if the market becomes depressed, but there is obviously no way the same company's $10 warrants can drop by a comparable amount.

There are, however, some disadvantages. For one, warrants are somewhat unusual and therefore require specialized investor know-how. Another disadvantage is that warrants pay no dividends, which means that investors sacrifice current in-

TABLE 11.1   Selected Features of a Sample of Warrants

Issuer	Market Where Traded	Exercise Price	Expiration Date
AM International	AMEX	$ 5.83	2/97
Assix International	NASDAQ	5.75	7/91
Atlas Corp.	AMEX	15.63	None
British Petroleum (ADR)	NYSE	80.00	1/93
Cell Technology	NASDAQ	8.00	8/92
Fed. Nat'l Mortgage Assoc'n	NYSE	44.25	2/91
Global Marine	NYSE	3.00	2/96
Halsey Drugs	AMEX	1.90	3/91
Hanson plc (ADR)	NYSE	18.00	9/94
Intel	NASDAQ	26.67	5/95
Manville Corp.	NYSE	9.40	6/96
McDermott International	NYSE	25.00	4/90
National Semiconductor	NYSE	22.25	5/92
Navistar International	NYSE	5.00	12/93
Rymer Foods	AMEX	17.50	10/92

Note: All these warrants enable the holder to purchase *one* share of stock (or ADR) at the specified exercise price.

come. And because these issues usually carry an expiration date, there is only a certain period of time during which an investor can capture the type of price behavior sought. Although this may not be much of a problem with long-term warrants, it can prove to be a burden for those issues with fairly short lives (of perhaps one to two years, or less).

Characteristics of Warrants

There are three aspects of warrants that are particularly important to investors: (1) the issue's exercise price; (2) the value of a warrant; and (3) the amount of the premium. These features not only affect the price and return behavior of warrants but also have a bearing on formulating an appropriate investment strategy.

Exercise Price

The exercise price is the stated price the warrant holder will have to pay to acquire a share of the underlying common stock. It is the share price paid to the firm when the warrant is used to buy the stock—that is, when the option is "exercised." Usually, the exercise price remains fixed for the issue's full life, but some warrants may provide for an increase or decrease in exercise price as the security nears its expiration date. In addition, the exercise price of a warrant will automatically be adjusted for stock splits or major stock dividends. Table 11.1 illustrates selected issue features for a sample of warrants traded on the NYSE, AMEX, and NASDAQ National Market—note especially how the exercise price can range anywhere from less than $10 to $50 or more. As we'll see below, the real significance of exercise price is

when it's viewed in relation to the market price of the underlying common stock, for that's what drives value and propels the *market price of the warrant*.

Value

Warrants possess value whenever the market price of the underlying common equals or exceeds the exercise price stated on the warrant. This value is determined as follows:

$$\text{value of a warrant} = (M - E) \times N$$

where

M = prevailing market price of the common stock
E = exercise price
N = number of shares of stock that can be acquired with one warrant (if one warrant entitles the holder to buy one share of stock, $N = 1$; if, however, two warrants are required to buy one share of stock, $N = .5$, etc.)

The formula shows what the market value of a warrant *should be,* given the respective market and exercise prices of the common and the number of shares of stock that can be acquired with one warrant. As an example, consider a warrant that carries an exercise price of $40 per share and enables the holder to purchase one share of stock per warrant; if the common stock has a current market price of $50 a share, then the warrants would be valued at $10 each:

$$\text{value of a warrant} = (\$50 - \$40) \times 1 = (\$10) \times 1 = \$10$$

Obviously the greater the spread between the market and exercise prices, the greater the market value of a warrant. And so long as the market price of the stock equals or exceeds the exercise price, and the redemption provision carries a 1-to-1 ratio (meaning one share of common can be bought with each warrant), the value of a warrant will be directly linked to the price behavior of the common stock. Thus, other things being equal, if the stock goes up (or down) by $2, the warrant should do likewise.

Premium

Our formula indicates how warrants should be valued, but they are seldom priced exactly that way in the marketplace; instead, the market price of a warrant invariably *exceeds* its computed (or true) value. This happens when warrants with negative values trade at prices greater than zero. It also occurs when warrants with positive values trade at even higher market prices (as, for example, when a warrant that's valued at $10 trades at $15). This discrepancy is known as **warrant premium,** and it exists because warrants possess speculative value. As a rule, the amount of premium embedded in the market price of a warrant is directly related to the option's time to expiration and the volatility of the underlying common stock; that is, the longer the time to expiration date and the more volatile the stock, the greater the size of the premium. On the other hand, the amount of premium does tend to diminish as the underlying value of a warrant increases. This can be seen in Figure 11.2, which shows the typical behavior of warrant premiums. Premium is easy to measure: Just take the difference between the value of a warrant (as computed according to the

warrant premium *the difference between the true value of a warrant and its market price.*

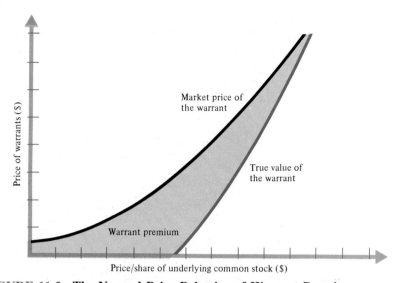

FIGURE 11.2 The Normal Price Behavior of Warrant Premiums.
Observe that as the price of the underlying common stock increases, the amount of premium in the market price of the warrant tends to decrease—though it never totally disappears.

formula above) and its market price. For instance, a warrant has $5 in premium if it has a value of $10 but is trading at $15. We can also put the amount of premium on a relative (percentage) basis by dividing the dollar premium by the warrant's true (computed) value. For example, there is a 50 percent premium embedded in the price of our $15 warrant above; that is, the dollar premium ÷ the value of the warrant = $5 ÷ $10 = .50. Premiums on warrants can at times become fairly substantial; indeed, premiums of 20 to 30 percent, or more, are not all that uncommon.

Trading Strategies

Because their attraction to investors rests primarily with the capital gains opportunities they provide, warrants are used chiefly as alternatives to common stock investments. Let's now look at warrant trading strategies and the basic ways in which these securities can be profitably employed by investors.

The Basic Price Behavior of Warrants

Assume an investor, Olivia Whitehead, has uncovered a company that she feels will experience strong performance in the foreseeable future. Olivia would like to invest in this company and has the ready capital. Being an astute investor, always on the lookout for alternative investment vehicles, she discovers that the firm also has warrants outstanding. Under such conditions, *both* the stock and the warrants should be evaluated before a decision is made. This scenario highlights several important investment ground rules: (1) Investors should always determine whether alternative vehicles exist before a decision is made; and (2) the basic investment use

of a warrant, at least by the nonprofessional individual investor, is as a substitute for common stock.

Since warrants carry relatively low unit costs, they possess much greater price volatility and the potential for generating substantially higher rates of return than a direct investment in the underlying common stock. Consider the following illustration, which involves the common shares and warrants of the same company. Say the price of the common is now $50 per share and the warrant, which carries a one-to-one redemption provision, has a $40 exercise price (we will ignore premium in this illustration). Observe below what happens when the price of the stock increases by $10.

	Common Stock	**Warrant**
Issue price *before* increase	$50	$10
Increase in price of common	$10	—
Issue price *after* increase	$60	$20
Increase in market value	$10	$10
Holding period return (increase in value/beginning issue price)	20%	100%

The fact that the warrants provide a rate of return five times greater than the common is due to the fact that the two issues move parallel to one another, even though the warrant carries a lower unit cost.

As in our illustration above, holding period return would normally be used to assess the payoff when the investment horizon equals one year or less, whereas approximate yield would be used when the investment horizon amounts to more than a year. More specifically, we would measure holding period return (HPR) for warrants as:

$$\text{HPR} = \frac{\text{sale price of warrant} - \text{purchase price of warrant}}{\text{purchase price of warrant}}$$

The holding period return for the warrants in our illustration above, would be:

$$\text{HPR} = \frac{\$20 - \$10}{\$10} = \frac{\$10}{\$10} = 100\%$$

In contrast, if we assumed a three-year investment horizon, the approximate yield on the transaction would amount to:

$$\text{approximate yield} = \frac{\dfrac{\text{sale price of warrant} - \text{purchase price of warrant}}{\text{no. of years in investment horizon}}}{\dfrac{\text{sale price} + \text{purchase price}}{2}}$$

$$= \frac{\dfrac{\$20 - \$10}{3}}{\dfrac{\$20 + \$10}{2}} = \frac{\$3.33}{\$15} = 22.2\%$$

Note that with both HPR and approximate yield we have ignored dividends, as they are not paid to warrant holders.

Trading with Warrants

Warrant trading generally follows one of two approaches: (1) The leverage embedded in warrants is used to magnify dollar returns; or (2) their low unit cost is used to reduce the amount of invested capital and limit losses. The first approach is obviously the more aggressive, whereas the second has considerable merit as a potentially conservative strategy. Our comparative illustration above can be used to demonstrate the first technique, which seeks to magnify returns. Obviously, if an investor wishes to make a $5,000 equity investment and if price appreciation is the main objective, he or she would be better off by committing such a sum to the warrants. The reason is that a $5,000 investment in the common will buy 100 shares of stock ($5,000 ÷ $50 = 100 shares) which will generate only $1,000 in capital gains ($10 profits per share × 100 shares), whereas that same $5,000 invested in the lower-priced warrants will buy 500 of these securities ($5,000 ÷ $10 = 500 warrants) and will result in $5,000 in profits ($10 in profits per warrant × 500 warrants). The common stock thus provides a 20 percent HPR, whereas the warrants yield 100 percent.

The major drawbacks to this approach are that the investor receives no dividends and that price appreciation has to occur before the warrant expires. The biggest risk in this investment is the potential loss exposure. Observe that if the price of the stock in our example decreases by $10, the warrant holder is virtually wiped out, if we assume, in the absence of any warrant premium, that the price of the warrant drops to just above zero. In contrast, the price of the stock drops to "only" $40, and the stockholder would still have $4,000 in capital left.

One way to limit this exposure to loss is to assume a more conservative investment posture (and to follow the second trading approach). This can be done by buying only enough warrants to realize the same level of capital gains as available from the common stock. Referring again to our illustration, since we are dealing with options that carry one-to-one redemption provisions, the investor would need to acquire only 100 warrants to obtain the same price behavior as 100 shares of stock. Thus, rather than buying $5,000 worth of stock, the investor need purchase only $1,000 worth of the warrants to realize the same capital gains. If the stock does perform as expected, the warrant investor will realize a 100 percent holding period return (as computed above) by generating the same amount of capital gains as the stock—$1,000. But since this will be done with substantially less capital, there will not only be greater yield with the warrants, but also less loss exposure. In this case, if the price of the stock does drop by 10 points, the most the warrant holder can lose is $1,000, although this is unlikely because premium will probably keep the price above zero. On the other hand, if the price of the stock drops by *more* than $10 a share, the warrant holder will still lose no more than $1,000, whereas the stockholder can lose a lot more, depending on the extent of the drop in share price.

Security Selection: A Critical Dimension

Regardless of how warrants are used by investors, security selection is a critical dimension in the investment process. So long as the price behavior of the underlying common stock is a key element in defining the price behavior of a warrant, it is important that the investor be satisfied that the *common stock* does indeed have the type of price potential desired. As a technical matter, in order to obtain maximum price behavior, it is also important that the market price of the common be equal to or greater than the exercise price of the warrant. Given that the price potential of the common stock and the exercise price of the warrant have been carefully assessed, the question of stock versus warrant reduces to one of comparative returns, risk exposure, and investor preferences.

Leverage and the Importance of Timing

Thus far we have assumed that the price behavior of a warrant is unaffected by outside variables. This assumption, although convenient, is not altogether true, for both leverage and downside risk protection are functions of the market price of the warrant. In particular, to realize maximum price appreciation, it is generally recommended that lower-priced issues be used. Other things being equal, the lower the price of the warrant, the greater its leverage potential. Not only does the amount of magnified return potential become less and less as the price of the warrant increases, but the risk exposure of a subsequent drop in price also becomes greater. For example, consider a $40 stock and a $5 warrant (the warrant in this case would have an exercise price of $35). If the stock price increases by $40, it will generate a 100 percent rate of return as it moves to its new $80 level; conversely, the warrant will move to $45 and provide an 800 percent rate of return. Note, however, that when the stock is at $160 and then undergoes that same $40 price appreciation (to $200 per share), this performance yields only a 25 percent rate of return. Under such circumstances, our warrant would now have a price of $125 and should move to $165, generating a yield of some 32 percent.

Clearly, as its price increases, *the warrant begins to behave more like its underlying common stock.* With our warrant at $125, it no longer has a low unit cost, its leverage and rate of return are not much different from the underlying common stock, and the risk exposure of a drop in price may now be substantial. Figure 11.3 illustrates how the return behavior of a warrant is related to its price level. The shape of the curve clearly indicates that a warrant's rate of return potential drops dramatically with increases in its market price. Certainly, a low warrant price alone will not guarantee success, but it is obvious that a low warrant price is more desirable than a higher one since the *low unit price allows the investor to capture both increased price volatility and reduced downside risk.*

PUTS AND CALLS

The life span, or maturity, of puts and calls is generally a good deal *longer* than rights, but substantially *shorter* than warrants. As a rule, you'll find put and call

FIGURE 11.3 The Normal Return Behavior of Warrants.
As a rule, higher-priced warrants provide lower rates of return because they offer less leverage than lower-priced warrants.

derivative securities
securities, such as puts & calls and other options, whose value is derived from the price behavior of an underlying financial asset.

maturities typically range from about 30 days to eight months or so in duration, and occasionally to one year. Often referred to as **derivative securities**—because their value is *derived* from the price behavior of some underlying financial asset—options are much like warrants to the extent that they provide attractive speculative outlets, offer appealing leverage potential, and can act as a nice alternative to the direct investment in common stock. Although for years puts and calls were written almost exclusively on common stocks, dramatic changes occurred in this market in the fall of 1981, when trading began in other kinds of options. Today, investors can trade puts and calls on:

- Common stock
- Stock indexes
- Debt instruments
- Foreign currencies
- Commodities and financial futures

As we will see, although the underlying financial assets may vary, the basic features and behavioral characteristics of these securities are much the same.

Definitions and Characteristics

One of the phenomena of the market of the 1970s was the remarkable performance and investment popularity of stock options—puts and calls on common stock. By the early 1980s, the interest in options spilled over to other kinds of financial assets and was a major factor behind the development of interest rate, currency, index, and futures options. Not surprisingly, much of the popularity of the options market

stems from the fact that investors can buy a lot of price action with a limited amount of capital, while nearly always enjoying limited risk exposure.

A Negotiable Instrument

put
a negotiable instrument that enables the holder to sell the underlying security at a specified price over a set period of time.

call
a negotiable instrument that gives the holder the right to buy securities at a stated price within a certain time period.

Puts and calls are negotiable instruments issued in bearer form that allow the holder to buy or sell a specified amount of a specified security at a specified price. (As an example, a put or a call on common stock covers 100 shares of stock in a specific company.) A **put** enables the holder to sell the underlying security at a specified price over a set period of time. A **call,** in contrast, gives the holder the right to buy the securities at a stated price within a certain time period. Puts and calls possess value to the extent that they allow the holder to participate in the price behavior of the underlying financial asset. As with any option, there is no interest or dividend income, no voting rights, and no privileges of ownership.

Puts and calls are traded on listed exchanges and, on a *much smaller* scale, in the over-the-counter market. They provide attractive leverage opportunities because they carry relatively low prices—at least relative to the market price of the underlying financial assets. To illustrate, consider a call on a common stock that gives the holder the right to buy 100 shares of a $50 stock at a price of, say, $45 a share. The stock would be priced at $50, but the call would trade at an effective price of only $5 a share (or the difference between the market price of the common and the price it can be purchased at as specified on the call). However, since a single stock option always involves 100 shares of stock, the actual market price of our $5 call would be $500; i.e., $5 × 100 shares = $500. And in a similar fashion, if the price of the underlying stock went up $10 a share, the value of the stock option would go up 100 times that amount, or $1,000!

Maker versus Purchaser

option maker
the individual or institution that writes put and call options; also called option writer.

Puts and calls are a unique type of security since they are *not* issued by the organizations that issue the underlying stocks and bonds. Instead, puts and calls *are created by investors.* It works like this: Suppose one individual wants to sell to another the right to buy 100 shares of common stock. This individual would *write* a call; the individual or institution writing the option is known as the **option maker** or **writer.** The maker who writes (and sells) an option is entitled to receive the price paid for the put or call (less modest commissions and other transaction costs). The put or call option is now a full-fledged financial asset and trades in the open market much like any other security. Puts and calls are both written (sold) and purchased through security brokers and dealers, and they are actively bought and sold in the secondary market. The writer stands behind the option at all times, regardless of how many times the security has been traded or who the current owners are, for it is the *writer* who must buy or deliver the stocks or other financial assets according to the terms of the option.

Puts and calls are written for a variety of reasons, most of which we will explore below. At this point, however, suffice it to say that writing options can be a viable investment strategy and can be a profitable course of action since, more often than not, *options expire unexercised.* But when options do hit, they usually hit big. As a

result, investors are lured to the buy side of these securities by the profits they offer and the low-cost, speculative nature of the issue. In essence, the buyers of puts and calls are willing to invest their capital in return for the right to participate in the future price performance of the underlying security, and to do so at low unit cost and limited risk exposure.

How Puts and Calls Work

Using the buyer's point of view, let us now briefly examine how puts and calls work, and how they derive their value. To understand the mechanics of puts and calls, it is best to look at their profit-making potential. For example, using stock options as a basis of discussion, consider a stock currently priced at $50 a share; assume we can buy a call on the stock for $500, with the call enabling us to purchase 100 shares of the stock at a fixed price of $50 each. A *rise* in the price of the underlying security (in this case, common stock) is what the investor would hope for. With that in mind, what is the profit from this transaction if the price of the stock does indeed move up to, say, $75 by the expiration date on the call? The answer is that we will earn $25 ($75 − $50) on *each* of the 100 shares of stock in the call—or a total gross profit of some $2,500; and all from a $500 investment! This is so since we can buy 100 shares of the stock—from the option writer—at a price of $50 each and immediately turn around and sell them in the market for $75 a share. We could have made the same profit by investing directly in the common stock, but because we would have had to invest $5,000 (100 shares × $50 per share), our rate of return would have been much lower. Obviously, there is a considerable difference between the profit potential of common stocks and calls; and it is this differential that attracts investors and speculators to calls whenever the price outlook for the underlying financial asset is *upward*. (Note that although our illustration is couched in terms of common stock, this same valuation principle applies to any of the other financial assets that may underlie call options, such as bonds, foreign currencies, or futures contracts.)

A similar situation can also be worked out for puts. Assume that for the same $50 stock we could pay $500 and buy a put to sell 100 shares of the stock at $50 each. Now we, as the buyer of a put, want the price of the stock to *drop,* so that we can use the put as a way to make money. Assume our expectations are correct and the price of the stock does indeed drop, to $25 a share. Here again, we would realize a gross profit of $25 for each of the 100 shares in the put. We can do this by going to the market and buying 100 shares of the stock at a price of $25 a share, and immediately turning around and selling them to the writer of the put at a price of $50 per share. Fortunately, put and call investors do *not* have to exercise these options and make simultaneous buy and sell transactions in order to receive their profit, *since options do have value and can be traded in the secondary market*. In fact, the value of both puts and calls is directly linked to the market price of the underlying financial asset. That is, the value of a *call* increases as the market price of the underlying security *rises,* whereas the value of a *put* increases as the price of the security *declines*. Thus, *investors can get their money out of options by selling them in the open market,* just as with any other security.

Advantages and Disadvantages

The major advantage of investing in puts and calls is the leverage they offer. This feature also carries the advantage of limiting the investor's exposure to risk, since there is only a set amount of money (the purchase price of the option) that can be lost. Also appealing is the fact that puts and calls can be used profitably when the price of the underlying security goes up *or* down.

A major disadvantage of puts and calls is that the holder enjoys no interest or dividend income, nor any other ownership benefit. Moreover, because the instruments have limited lives, the investor has a limited time frame in which to capture desired price behavior. Another disadvantage is the fact that puts and calls themselves are a bit unusual, and many of their trading strategies are complex; thus investors must possess special knowledge and fully understand the subtleties of this trading vehicle.

Options Markets

Although the concept of options can be traced back to the writings of Aristotle, options trading in the United States did not begin until the late 1700s; and until the early 1970s, this market remained fairly small, largely unorganized, and the almost private domain of a handful of specialists and traders. All this changed, however, on April 26, 1973, when a new securities market was created with the launching of the Chicago Board Options Exchange (CBOE).

Conventional Options

Prior to the creation of the CBOE, put and call options trading was conducted in the over-the-counter market through a handful of specialized dealers. Investors who wished to purchase puts and calls dealt with these options dealers via their own brokers, and the dealers would actually find individuals (or institutions) willing to write the options. If the buyer wished to exercise an option, he or she did so with the writer, and no one else—a system that largely prohibited any secondary trading. On the other hand, there were virtually no limits to what could be written, so long as the buyer was willing to pay the price. Put and call options were written on New York and American stocks as well as on regional and over-the-counter securities; and they were written for as short as 30 days and as long as a year. Over-the-counter options,

conventional options
put and call options sold over the counter.

known today as **conventional options,** were hard hit by the CBOE and other options exchanges. The conventional market still exists, although on a greatly reduced scale.

Listed Options

listed options
put and call options listed and traded on organized securities exchanges, such as the CBOE.

The creation of the CBOE marked the first time in American capital market history that stock options were traded on listed exchanges. It signaled the birth of so-called **listed options,** a term used to denote put and call options traded on organized exchanges, as opposed to the conventional options traded in the over-the-counter market. The CBOE created the listed options concept by launching trading in calls on just 16 firms. From these rather humble beginnings, there evolved in a relatively

TABLE 11.2   Some Actively Traded Listed Stock Options

Delta Airlines	Paine Webber	Baxter Internat'l	Amoco
Exxon	Upjohn	Atlantic Richfield	Bank of America
Eastman Kodak	Digital Equipment	General Electric	MCI
IBM	Disney	CBS	Merck
Xerox	McDonald's	AT&T	USX
Boeing	JCPenney	ITT	Phelps Dodge
Chrysler	Borg-Warner	Wendy's	Eli Lilly
Ford	Unocal	Scott Paper	Anheuser Busch
Reebok	Marriott	Duke Power	Compaq
Wal-Mart	Sears	Motorola	du Pont

Note: Both put and call options are available on all these stocks.

short period of time a large and very active market for listed options. Today, trading in all listed options is done in terms of both puts and calls and takes place on five exchanges, the largest of which is the CBOE. Options are also traded on the AMEX, the NYSE, the Philadelphia Exchange, and the Pacific Stock Exchange. Looking at these five exchanges in total, *put and call options are now traded on nearly 650 different stocks;* although most of these are NYSE issues, the list does include several dozen OTC stocks, such as Apple Computer, Intel, Liz Claiborne, and MCI. Table 11.2 provides a short list of some popular and widely traded listed stock options. (In addition to stocks, listed options are also available on stock indexes, debt securities, foreign currencies, and even commodities and financial futures.)

The listed options concept provided not only a convenient market for the trading of puts and calls, but also standardized the expiration dates and the prices specified on the options. The listed options exchanges created a clearinghouse organization that eliminated direct ties between buyers and writers of options and reduced the cost of executing put and call transactions. They also developed an active secondary market, with wide distribution of price information. As a result, it is now as easy to trade a listed option as a listed stock.

Stock Options

The advent of the CBOE and other listed option exchanges had a quick and dramatic impact on the trading volume of puts and calls. As seen in Figure 11.4, the level of activity in listed stock options grew rapidly—so much so, in fact, that it took only eight years for the annual volume of contracts traded to pass the 100 million mark. And although contract volume was off in 1988, it was still holding at nearly 115 million contracts. In terms of stock, such a contract volume translates into 11.5 *billion* shares of stock (since each option contract covers 100 shares of the underlying common stock)—a figure equivalent to roughly 30 percent of all shares traded on the NYSE in 1988!

As a rule, there's far more interest in calls than in puts. As a result about 70 percent of the stock option contract volume is in calls, and the balance, about 30

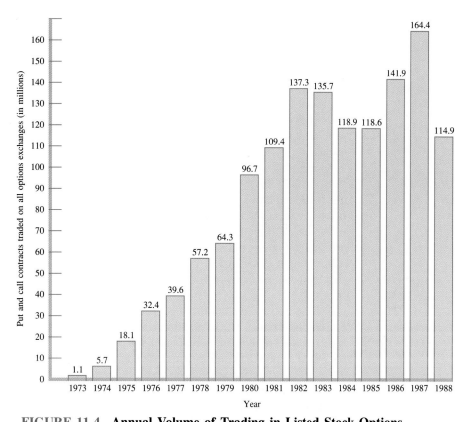

FIGURE 11.4 Annual Volume of Trading in Listed Stock Options.
Clearly, the volume of trading in the puts and calls of listed equity options has increased dramatically since the concept was first introduced in 1973. Although the level of activity is off from its peak (in 1987), it still remains very high as these securities continue to be popular with investors. (*Source: CBOE Market Statistics—1988.*)

percent, is in puts. The creation and continued expansion of listed options exchanges has unquestionably given the field of investments a whole new dimension. However, in order to use these securities properly and avoid serious (and possibly expensive) mistakes, the investor must fully understand the basic features of these securities. In the sections that follow, we will look closely at the investment attributes and trading strategies that can be used with stock options; later we'll explore index, interest rate, and currency options, and then take up futures options in Chapter 12.

Stock Option Provisions

Because of their low unit cost, stock options (or *equity options* as they're also called) are very popular with individual investors. Except for the underlying financial asset, they are like any other type of put or call, subject to the same kinds of contract provisions and market forces. In that regard, there are three aspects of

equity options to which investors should pay particular attention: (1) the price at which the stock can be bought or sold; (2) the amount of time remaining until expiration; and (3) the purchase price of the option itself.

Striking Price.   The **striking price** represents the price contract between the buyer of the option and the writer. For a call, the striking price specifies the price at which each of the 100 shares of stock can be bought. For a put, it represents the price at which the stock can be sold to the writer. (The striking price is also known as the exercise price.) With conventional (OTC) options, there are no constraints on striking price, although it is usually specified at or near the prevailing market price of the stock at the time the option is written. With listed options, however, the striking prices are *standardized* such that stocks selling for less than $25 per share carry striking prices that are set in 2½ dollar increments (that is, $7½, $10, $12½, $15, and so on). The increment then jumps to $5 for stocks selling between $25 and $200 per share. Finally, for stocks that trade at prices in excess of $200 a share, the striking price is set in $10 increments. And of course, the striking price of both conventional and listed options is adjusted for substantial stock dividends and stock splits.

Expiration Date.   The **expiration date** is also an important provision because it specifies the life of the option in much the same way that the maturity date indicates the life of a bond. Expiration dates for options in the conventional market can fall on any working day of the month. In contrast, expiration dates are standardized in the listed options market. The exchanges initially created three expiration cycles for all listed options, and each issue was (and still is) assigned to one of these three cycles. One cycle is January, April, July, and October; another is February, May, August, and November; and the third is March, June, September, and December. This system has been modified a bit to include *both* the current month and the following month, *plus* the next two months in the regular expiration cycle. The exchanges still use *the same three expiration cycles,* but they've been altered so investors will always be able to trade in current month options. Take, for example, the January cycle—you'd find the following options available in January: January, February, April, and July. Thus, we'd have the two current months, plus the next two months in the cycle—though prices are usually reported in the financial media for only the first *three* maturities. Then, in February, the available contracts would be: February, March, April, and July. Finally, come March, there would be across-the-board changes as follows: March, April, July, and October. And so on, as the expiration dates would continue rolling-over like this during the course of the year. Under this system, the longest option contract you can deal in is *eight months* (technically, options can be bought, sold, or written for *any of the four* expiration dates currently outstanding). Given the month of expiration, the actual day of expiration is always the same: the Saturday following the third Friday of each expiration month. Thus, for all practical purposes, listed options always expire on the third Friday of the month of expiration.

The expiration date, in effect, specifies the length of the contract between the

holder and the writer of the option. Thus, if you hold a six-month call on Sears, that option would give you the right to buy 100 shares of Sears common stock at a striking price of, say, $40 per share at any time over the next six months. Now, *no matter what happens to the market price of the stock,* you can use your call option to buy 100 shares of Sears at $40 a share for the next six months. If the price moves up you stand to make money, whereas if it goes down you'll be out the cost of the option.

option premium
the listed purchase price of a put or call option.

Premium. The purchase price of a put or call is known as the **option premium.** With most securities, the term ''premium'' is used to denote that portion of the purchase price that exceeds some predetermined theoretical value. With puts and calls, ''premium'' represents the cost of an option and the price the buyer would have to pay to the writer (or seller) in order to acquire the put or call. The size of the option premium is obviously important to buyers, writers, and sellers. One factor that affects the size of option premiums is the current market price of the underlying stock: The greater the difference between the price of the stock and the striking price on the option, the greater the value of the put or call. Another factor is the length of time until the expiration date of the option; the longer the time until expiration, the greater the size of the premium. Still another is the volatility of the underlying security, which is important to the extent that it enhances (or detracts from) the speculative appeal of the option. Other, less important variables include the dividend yield of the underlying stock, the trading volume of the option, and the exchange on which the option is listed.

Put and Call Transactions

Option traders are subject to commission and transaction costs whenever they buy or sell an option, or when an option is written. The writing of puts and calls is subject to normal options transaction cost, since it effectively represents remuneration to the broker or dealer for *selling* the option. In relation to the number of shares of common stock controlled (100 shares per option), the transaction costs for executing put and call trades is relatively low. However, when the transaction costs are compared to the size of the transaction itself, you'll discover that option transactions are fairly costly—particularly if you're buying or selling only a few options. Table 11.3 illustrates the commission costs on listed options and shows how transaction costs vary with the number and market price of the options (the same commissions apply to both puts and calls). To see how expensive options transactions can get, consider the purchase of a $5 call; note that the cost of buying one $5 option would involve an investment of $500 and a transaction cost of $30.00. Although this may be low compared to what it would take to buy outright 100 shares of the underlying stock, simple arithmetic indicates that it involves a 6 percent charge ($30.00/$500 = .06). This is fairly steep, especially when you consider that this commission might have to be paid again if the option is sold prior to its expiration date. (Of course, there is *no* cost involved if the option is simply allowed to expire.)

Listed options also have their own marketplace and quotation system. Finding the price (or premium) for a listed stock option is fairly easy, as the options quota-

TABLE 11.3   Commission Costs on Listed Options

Option Premium	Number of Options														
	1	2	3	4	5	6	7	8	9	10	11	12	13	14	15
1/16	30.00	30.00	30.00	30.00	30.00	30.00	30.00	30.00	30.00	30.00	30.00	30.00	30.00	30.00	30.00
1/8	30.00	30.00	30.00	30.00	30.00	30.00	30.00	30.00	30.00	30.00	30.00	30.00	30.00	30.00	30.00
3/16	30.00	30.00	30.00	30.00	30.00	30.00	30.00	30.00	30.00	30.00	30.00	30.00	30.00	30.00	31.17
1/4	30.00	30.00	30.00	30.00	30.00	30.00	30.00	30.00	30.00	30.00	30.50	33.17	35.85	38.52	41.20
5/16	30.00	30.00	30.00	30.00	30.00	30.00	30.00	30.00	31.17	34.51	37.86	41.20	44.54	47.88	51.23
3/8	30.00	30.00	30.00	30.00	30.00	30.00	30.00	33.17	37.18	41.20	45.21	49.22	53.23	57.25	61.26
7/16	30.00	30.00	30.00	30.00	30.00	30.00	33.84	38.52	43.21	47.88	52.57	57.25	61.93	66.61	71.29
1/2	30.00	30.00	30.00	30.00	30.00	33.17	38.52	43.87	49.22	54.57	59.92	65.27	70.62	75.97	81.32
9/16	30.00	30.00	30.00	30.00	31.17	37.18	43.21	49.22	55.24	61.26	67.28	73.30	79.32	85.33	91.36
5/8	30.00	30.00	30.00	30.00	34.51	41.20	47.88	54.57	61.26	67.95	74.63	81.32	88.01	94.70	101.38
11/16	30.00	30.00	30.00	30.50	37.86	45.21	52.57	59.92	67.28	74.63	81.99	89.35	96.71	104.06	109.74
3/4	30.00	30.00	30.00	33.17	41.20	49.22	57.25	65.27	73.30	81.32	89.35	97.37	105.40	110.75	114.76
13/16	30.00	30.00	30.00	35.85	44.54	53.23	61.93	70.62	79.32	88.01	96.71	105.40	111.08	115.43	119.78
7/8	30.00	30.00	30.00	38.52	47.88	57.25	66.61	75.97	85.33	94.70	104.06	110.75	115.43	120.11	124.79
15/16	30.00	30.00	31.17	41.20	51.23	61.26	71.29	81.32	91.36	101.12	107.35	113.59	119.78	124.79	129.80
$1	30.00	32.38	40.97	49.56	58.15	66.75	75.34	83.93	95.52	101.12	107.35	113.59	119.83	126.07	132.31
$5	30.00	44.62	59.33	74.04	88.76	101.12	113.47	125.83	138.19	150.55	167.81	178.26	188.73	199.18	209.65
1/8	30.00	45.00	59.91	74.81	89.42	101.92	114.40	126.89	139.38	158.73	169.33	179.92	190.51	201.13	211.72
1/4	30.00	45.39	60.49	75.57	90.08	102.71	115.34	127.95	140.58	160.11	170.86	181.59	192.32	203.05	213.80
3/8	30.00	45.77	61.05	76.34	90.75	103.50	116.26	129.01	141.76	161.51	172.37	183.25	194.12	205.00	215.86
1/2	30.00	46.15	61.63	77.10	91.41	104.29	117.19	130.07	142.96	162.89	173.90	184.91	195.92	206.94	217.95
5/8	30.00	46.53	62.20	77.87	92.06	105.10	118.11	131.13	150.65	164.27	175.42	186.57	197.71	208.87	220.02
3/4	30.00	46.92	62.78	78.63	92.74	105.89	119.04	132.19	151.91	165.65	176.95	188.23	199.52	210.81	222.10
7/8	30.00	47.30	63.34	79.40	93.39	106.68	119.96	133.25	153.15	167.04	178.45	189.89	201.32	212.75	224.18
$9	30.00	56.86	76.75	93.35	109.94	132.24	149.60	166.94	184.30	201.64	216.54	231.42	246.31	261.20	276.09
1/8	30.00	57.25	77.15	93.88	110.61	113.08	150.56	168.05	185.54	203.03	218.06	233.08	348.10	263.15	278.17
1/4	30.00	57.63	77.55	94.41	111.27	113.90	151.53	169.16	186.79	204.41	219.59	234.75	249.91	265.07	280.24
3/8	30.00	58.02	77.94	94.94	111.93	134.73	152.50	170.27	188.03	205.80	221.09	236.41	251.71	267.02	282.31
1/2	30.00	58.39	78.35	95.47	112.60	135.57	153.47	171.37	189.27	207.18	222.62	238.06	253.50	268.96	284.40
5/8	30.00	58.78	78.74	96.00	113.25	136.40	154.44	172.48	190.51	208.56	224.14	239.72	255.30	270.89	286.47
3/4	30.11	59.16	79.14	96.52	113.92	137.23	155.41	173.59	191.78	209.94	225.67	241.39	257.11	272.83	288.55
7/8	30.30	59.55	79.53	97.06	114.58	138.06	156.37	174.70	193.02	211.34	227.18	243.05	258.91	274.77	290.62
$10	30.50	59.92	79.93	97.58	115.24	138.69	157.34	175.80	194.26	212.72	227.71	244.71	260.71	276.70	292.70

Source: A major brokerage firm.

tions in Figure 11.5 indicate. Note that quotes are provided for calls and puts separately; and for each option, there are three expiration dates listed (in this case, May, June, and September). Along with the striking price, such information is the basis for differentiating among various options. For example, there are numerous puts and calls outstanding on the Philip Morris stock, each with its own expiration date and striking price.

The quotes are standardized and are read as follows: The name of the company and the closing price of the underlying stocks are listed first (note Philip Morris's stock closed at 136⅛); the striking price is listed next; then closing prices are quoted

Option & NY Close	Strike Price	Calls—Last			Puts—Last		
		May	Jun	Sep	May	Jun	Sep
Kellog	60	r	8 3/8	10 1/4	r	r	r
69 1/4	65	4 1/8	3 3/4	r	r	r	1 1/8
69 1/4	70	3/16	1	2 3/4	r	r	3
NiagMP	12 1/2	r	r	3/16	r	r	r
PacGE	17 1/2	r	2 1/2	r	r	r	r
19 7/8	20	r	3/8	13/16	r	3/4	r
Pfizer	60	3 1/2	4 5/8	5 5/8	r	3/16	7/8
63 5/8	65	1/16	1	2 3/4	r	2	3
63 5/8	70	r	r	1	r	r	r
Ph Mor	100	s	36 7/8	r	s	r	r
136 1/8	105	r	r	33 3/8	r	1/16	r
136 1/8	110	r	26 3/4	28 3/8	r	r	r
136 1/8	115	r	21 7/8	23 3/4	r	1/16	1/2
136 1/8	120	16 1/4	16 3/4	r	1/16	r	1
136 1/8	125	10 7/8	11 3/4	15	r	3/8	1 7/8
136 1/8	130	6	7 1/4	11 1/8	1/16	1	3
136 1/8	135	1 5/16	3 1/2	8 1/8	1/2	2 9/16	4 3/4
136 1/8	140	s	1 5/8	5 5/8	s	5 5/8	r
PrimeC	12 1/2	s	3 5/8	s	s	3/16	s
15 7/8	15	5/8	1 7/8	2 1/4	1/8	13/16	1 1/8
15 7/8	17 1/2	1/16	5/8	1 1/16	1 3/4	2 1/8	2 3/8
15 7/8	20	r	1/8	3/8	4 1/2	4 1/2	r
QuakSt	15	2 1/8	2 3/8	2 5/8	r	r	r
16 7/8	17 1/2	1/16	3/8	1 3/16	1/2	3/4	1 3/8
SFePac	20	2 1/8	2 3/8	3 5/8	r	r	r
22 1/8	22 1/2	1/16	3/4	1 7/8	3/8	r	r
22 1/8	25	r	1/4	7/8	r	r	r
Seagte	7 1/2	r	6 1/2	r	r	r	r
13 3/4	10	r	3 3/4	4 1/2	r	r	r
13 3/4	12 1/2	1 9/16	1 3/4	2 7/8	r	3/16	5/8
13 3/4	15	r	1/2	1 3/8	1	1 3/16	2
13 3/4	17 1/2	r	r	5/8	r	r	3 1/2

FIGURE 11.5 Listed Options Quotations.
As seen here, the quotes for puts and calls are usually listed side-by-side, and in addition to the closing price of the option, the latest price on the underlying security is also shown along with the strike price on the option. (*Source: The Wall Street Journal.*)

relative to their expiration dates, with the three calls listed first followed by the three puts. Thus, we can see that a Philip Morris *call* with a \$130 striking price and a June expiration date is quoted at 7¼; in contrast, a Philip Morris *put* with a \$130 striking price and a September expiration date is trading at 3. Recall, however, that option premiums are listed on a per-share basis, and so the actual price of the Philip Morris options is a multiple of 100. Therefore, the call would cost \$750 and the put would cost \$300.

Finding the Value of Puts and Calls

The value of a put or call depends on the market behavior of the common stock or other financial asset that underlies the option. Since capital appreciation is the only source of return on options, getting a firm grip on the current and expected future

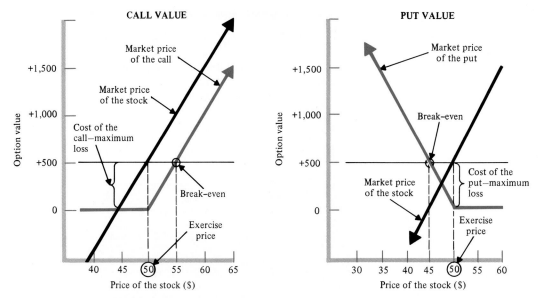

FIGURE 11.6 The Valuation Properties of Put and Call Options.
The value of a put or call is a reflection of the price behavior of its underlying common stock.
As such, once the cost of the option has been recovered (which occurs when the option passes
its break-even point), the profit potential of a put or call is limited only by the price behavior
of its underlying stock.

value of a put or call is extremely important to options traders and investors. Continuing to use stock options as a basis of discussion, let's look now at some of the basic principles of options valuation, starting with a brief review of how profits are derived from puts and calls.

The Profit Potential of Puts and Calls

Although the quoted market price (premium) of a put or call is affected by such factors as time to expiration, stock volatility, market interest rates, and supply and demand conditions, by far the most important variable is *the market price behavior of the underlying common stock*. This is the variable that drives any significant moves in the price of the option and which in turn determines the option's profit (return) potential. Thus, when the underlying stock moves up in price, *calls do well;* and when the price of the stock drops, *puts do well*. Such performance also explains why it's so important to get a good handle on the expected future price behavior of a stock *before* an option is bought or sold (written).

The typical price behavior of an option is illustrated graphically in Figure 11.6. The diagram on the left depicts a call, and the one on the right shows a put. The *call* diagram is constructed assuming you pay $500 for a call that carries an exercise price of $50; likewise, the *put* diagram assumes you can buy a put for $500 and obtain the right to sell the underlying stock at $50 a share. With the call, the diagram shows what happens to the value of the option when the price of the stock

increases; and with the put, it shows what happens when the price of the stock falls. Observe that a call doesn't gain in value until the price of the stock advances past the stated *exercise price* ($50). Also, since it costs $500 to buy the call, the stock has to move up another 5 points (from $50 to $55) in order for the option investor to recover the premium and thereby reach a break-even situation. So long as the stock continues to rise in price, everything from there on out is profit; that is, once the premium is recouped, the profit from the call position is limited only by the extent to which the stock price increases over the remaining life of the contract!

In a similar fashion, the value of a *put* is also derived from the price of the underlying stock, except their respective market prices move in opposite directions. We can see that the value of the put remains constant until the market price of the corresponding stock drops to the exercise price ($50) on the put. Then, as the price of the stock continues to fall the value of the option increases accordingly. And again, note that since the put cost $500, you don't start making money on the investment until the price of the stock drops below the break even point of $45 a share. Beyond that point, the profit from the put is defined by the extent to which the price of the underlying stock continues to fall over the remaining life of the option.

Measuring Value

As we saw above, the value of a put or call depends ultimately on the exercise price stated on the option, as well as on the prevailing market price of the underlying common stock. More specifically, *the value of a call* is determined according to the following simple formula:

$$\text{value of a call} = \left(\begin{array}{ccc} \text{market price of} & & \text{striking price} \\ \text{underlying} & - & \text{on} \\ \text{common stock} & & \text{the call} \end{array} \right) \times 100$$

$$V = (MP - SPC) \times 100$$

In other words, the value of a call is nothing more than the difference between market price and striking price—as implied in the formula, a call has value whenever the market price of the underlying stock (or financial asset) *exceeds* the striking price stipulated on the call. A simple illustration will show that a call carrying a striking price of $50 on a stock presently trading at $60 has a value of $1,000 [($60 − $50) × 100 = $10 × 100]. A put, on the other hand, cannot be valued in the same way, since puts and calls allow the holder to do different things. To find *the value of a put,* simply reverse the order of the equation a bit, so that we have:

$$\text{value of a put} = \left(\begin{array}{ccc} \text{striking price} & & \text{market price of} \\ \text{on the} & - & \text{underlying} \\ \text{put} & & \text{common stock} \end{array} \right) \times 100$$

$$V = (SPP - MP) \times 100$$

In this case, you can see that a put has value so long as the market price of the underlying stock (or financial asset) *is less than* the striking price stipulated on the put.

Put and call values denote what the options *should* be valued and trading at. Unfortunately, this rarely occurs. Instead, these securities almost always trade at prices higher than their true values, especially for options that still have a long time to run. This difference is known as **investment premium,** and it indicates the amount of "excess value" embedded in the quoted price of the put or call. Investment premium can be found as follows:

investment premium
the difference between the market value of an option and its true value; indicates the amount of excess value embedded in the quoted price of a put or call.

$$\text{investment premium} = \frac{\text{option premium} - \text{value of the option}}{\text{value of the option}}$$

$$IP = \frac{OP - V}{V}$$

For example, take another look at the Philip Morris quotes in Figure 11.5 (on page 473). And in particular, look at the June *call* with the $130 striking price. This call is quoted at 7¼ (or $725); however, it should be valued at:

$$(\$136.125 - \$130.00) \times 100 = \underline{\$612.50}$$

Using the formula above, we see that the price of this call contains an investment premium of:

$$(\$725 - \$612.50)/\$612.50 = \underline{18.4\%}$$

This particular Philip Morris call, in essence, is trading at a premium of 18.4 percent, or $112.50 above its true underlying value. Many of the same factors that affect option premium also affect investment premium; for example, investment premium tends to increase for longer options and for those on highly volatile stock. Unless it can be recovered when the investor sells the option, investment premium represents a form of "sunk" cost that is lost for good.

In-the-Money/Out-of-the-Money

in-the-money
a call option with a striking price less than the market price of the underlying security; a put option with striking price greater than the market price of the underlying security.

out-of-the-money
a call option with no real value because the striking price exceeds the market price of the stock; a put option whose market price exceeds the striking price.

When written, options do not necessarily have to carry striking prices at the prevailing market prices of the underlying common stocks. And as an option subsequently trades on the listed exchanges, the price of the option will move in response to moves in the price of the underlying common stock. When a call has a striking price that is less than the market price of the underlying common stock, it has a positive value and is known as an **in-the-money** option. A major portion of the option premium in this case is based on (or derived from) the true value of the call. When the striking price exceeds the market price of the stock, the call has no "real" value and is known as an **out-of-the-money** option. Since the option has no value, its price is made up solely of investment premium. These terms are much more than convenient, exotic names given to options, for as we will see below, they characterize the investment behavior of options and can affect return and risk. A put option, by the way, is "in-the-money" when its striking price is greater than the market price of the stock; it is "out-of-the-money" when the market price of the stock exceeds the striking price.

Trading Strategies

For the most part, stock options can be used in three types of trading strategies: (1) buying puts and calls for speculation; (2) hedging with puts and calls; and (3) option writing and spreading.

Buying for Speculation

Buying for speculation is the simplest and most straightforward use of puts and calls. Basically, it is just like buying stock ("buy low, sell high") and in fact represents an alternative to investing in stock. For example, if an investor feels the market price of a particular stock is going to move up, one way of capturing that price appreciation is to buy a call on the stock. In contrast, if an investor feels the stock is about to drop in price, a put could convert the price decline into a profitable situation. In essence, investors buy options rather than stock whenever the options are likely to yield a greater return. The principle here, of course, is to get the largest return from one's investment dollar—something that can often be done with puts and calls due to the added leverage they offer.

To illustrate the essentials of speculating with options, consider a situation in which you have uncovered a stock you feel will move up in price over the next six months. What you would like to find out at this point is this: What would happen if you were to buy a call on this stock rather than investing directly in the firm's common? To find out, let's see what the numbers show. Assume the price of the stock is now $49, and you anticipate that within six months it will rise to about $65. In order to determine the relative merits of your investment alternatives, you need to determine the expected return associated with each course of action. Because call options have short lives, holding period return can be used to measure yield. Thus, if your expectations about the *stock* are correct, it should go up by $16 and in so doing provide stockholders with a 33 percent holding period return [($65 − $49) ÷ $49 = $16 ÷ $49 = .33]. But there are also some listed options available on this stock, so let's see how they would do. We will use for illustrative purposes two six-month calls that carry $40 and $50 striking prices, respectively. A recap of these two call alternatives, relative to the behavior of the underlying common stock, is summarized in Table 11.4. Clearly either call option represents a superior investment to buying the stock itself. The dollar amount of profit may be a bit more with the stock, but notice that the size of the required investment ($4,900) is *a lot* more, too.

Observe that one of the calls is an in-the-money option (the one with the $40 striking price) and the other is out-of-the-money. The difference in returns generated by these calls is rather typical: that is, investors are usually able to generate better rates of return with lower-priced (out-of-the-money) options and also enjoy less exposure to loss. Of course, the major drawback of out-of-the-money options is that their price is made up solely of investment premium—a sunk cost that will be lost if the stock does not move in price.

To see how investors can speculate in puts, consider the following situation: Assume that the price of your stock is now $51, but this time you anticipate a drop

TABLE 11.4   Speculating with Call Options

	100 Shares of Underlying Common Stock	Six-Month Call Options on the Stock	
		$40 Striking Price	$50 Striking Price
TODAY			
Market value of stock (at $49/sh.)	$4,900		
Market price of calls*		$1,100	$ 400
SIX MONTHS LATER			
Expected value of stock (at $65/sh.)	$6,500		
Expected price of calls*		$2,500	$1,500
Profit	$1,600	$1,400	$1,100
Holding period return	33%	127%	275%

*The price of the calls was computed according to the call valuation formula and includes some investment premium in the purchase price of the calls, but *none* in the expected sales price.

in price to about $35 within the next six months. If that occurs, you could short sell the stock and make a profit of $16 per share (see Chapter 2 for a discussion of short selling). Alternatively, an out-of-the-money put (with a striking price of $50) can be purchased for, say, $300. Again, if the price of the underlying stock does indeed drop, investors will make money with the put. The profit and rate of return on the put are summarized below, along with the comparative returns from short selling the stock:

	BUY 1 PUT	SHORT SELL 100 SHARES OF STOCK
Purchase price (today)	$ 300	
Selling price (6 months later)	1,500	
Short sell (today)		$5,100
Cover (6 months later)		3,500
Profit	$1,200	$1,600
Holding period return	400%	63%*

*Assumes the short sale was made with a required margin deposit of 50 percent.

Once more, in terms of holding period return, the stock option is the superior investment vehicle by a wide margin. Of course, not all option investments end up nearly so well as the ones in our examples, for success in this strategy rests on picking the right underlying common stock. Thus, *security analysis and proper stock selection are critical dimensions of this technique*. It is a highly risky investment strategy, but it may be well suited for the more speculatively inclined investor.

Hedging

hedge

a combination of two or more securities into a single investment position for the purpose of reducing or eliminating risk.

A **hedge** is really nothing more than a combination of two or more securities into a single investment position for the purpose of reducing risk. This strategy might involve, for example, buying a stock and simultaneously buying a put on that same stock; or it might consist of buying stock and then writing a call. There are many types of hedges, some of which are very sophisticated and others very simple; but they all are used as a way to earn or protect a profit without exposing the investor to excessive loss. An options hedge may be appropriate if you have generated a profit from an earlier common stock investment and wish to protect that profit, or if you are about to enter into a common stock investment and wish to protect your money by limiting potential capital loss. If you hold a stock that has gone up in price, the purchase of a put would provide the type of downside protection you need; the purchase of a call, in contrast, would provide protection to a short seller of common stock. Thus, option hedging always involves two transactions—one, the initial common stock position (long or short), and the other, the simultaneous or subsequent purchase of the option.

Let's examine a simple options hedge by seeing how a put can be used to limit capital loss or protect profit. Consider an investor, Boris Hognester, who wants to buy 100 shares of stock. Being a bit apprehensive about the stock's outlook, Boris decides to use an option hedge to protect his capital against loss. He, therefore, simultaneously buys the stock and a put on the stock (which fully covers the 100 shares owned). Preferably, the put would be a low-priced option with a striking price at or near the current market price of the stock. Suppose Mr. Hognester purchases the common at $25 and pays $150 for a put with a $25 striking price. Now, no matter what happens to the price of the stock over the life of the put, Boris can lose no more than $150; at the same time, there's no limit on the gains. If the stock does not move, he will be out the cost of a put; if it drops in price, then whatever is lost on the stock will be made up with the put. However, if the price of the stock goes up (as hoped), the put becomes useless, and Boris rakes in the capital gains from the stock. The essentials of this option hedge are shown in Table 11.5. The $150 paid for the put is sunk cost, and that's lost no matter what happens to the price of the stock; in effect, it is the price paid for the hedge. Moreover, this hedge is good only as long as the investor holds the put. When this put expires, Boris will have to replace it with another put or forget about hedging his capital.

The other basic use of an option hedge involves entering into the options position *after* a profit has already been made on the underlying stock. This could be done because of investment uncertainty, or for tax purposes (to carry over a profit to the next taxable year). For example, if Wanda Willson bought 100 shares of stock at $35 and it moved to $75, there would be a profit of $40 per share to protect. The profit could be protected with an option hedge by buying a put. Assume Wanda buys a three-month put with a $75 striking price at a cost of $250. Now, regardless of what happens to the stock over the life of the put, Ms. Willson is guaranteed a minimum profit of $3,750 (the $4,000 profit in the stock made so far, less the $250 cost of the put). This can be seen in Table 11.6. Notice that if the price of the stock should fall, the worst that can happen is a guaranteed minimum profit of $3,750.

TABLE 11.5   Limiting Capital Loss with a Put Hedge

		Stock	Put*
TODAY			
Purchase price of the stock		$25	
Purchase price of the put			$1½
*Put is purchased simultaneously and carries a striking price of $25			
SOMETIME LATER			
A. Price of common goes *up* to:		$50	
Value of put			$0
Profit:			
100 shares of stock ($50 − $25)	$2,500		
Less: Cost of put	−150		
Profit:	$2,350		
B. Price of common goes *down* to:		$10	
Value of put (see put valuation formula)			$15
Profit:			
100 shares of stock (loss: $10 − $25)	−$1,500		
Value of put (profit)	+ 1,500		
Less: Cost of put	− 150		
Loss:	$ 150		

And there is still *no limit on how much profit can be made;* as long as the stock continues to go up, the investor will reap the benefits. (And note that although this discussion pertains to put hedges, it should be clear that call hedges can also be set up to limit the loss or protect a profit on a short sale. For example, when a stock is sold short, a call can be purchased to protect the short seller against a rise in the price of the stock—with the same basic results as outlined above.)

Option Writing and Spreading

The advent of listed options has led to many intriguing options trading strategies. Yet, in spite of the apparent appeal of these exotic techniques, there is one important point that all the experts agree on: *Such specialized trading strategies should be left to experienced investors who fully understand their subtleties.* Our goal at this point is not to master these specialized strategies, but to learn in general terms what they are and how they operate. There are two types of specialized options strategies: (1) writing options, and (2) spreading options.

Writing Options.   Generally, investors write options because they feel the price of the underlying stock is going to move in their favor; that is, it is not going to rise as

TABLE 11.6 Protecting Profits with a Put Hedge

	Stock	Three-Month Put with a $75 Striking Price
Purchase price of the stock (some time ago)	$35	
TODAY		
Market price of the stock	$75	
Market price of the put		$2½
THREE MONTHS LATER		
A. Price of common goes *up* to:	$100	
Value of put		$0
Profit:		
100 shares of stock ($100 − $35) $6,500		
Less: Cost of put −250		
Profit: $6,250		
B. Price of common goes *down* to:	$50	
Value of put (see put valuation formula)		$25
Profit:		
100 shares of stock ($50 − $35) $1,500		
Value of put (profit) 2,500		
Less: Cost of put − 250		
Profit: $3,750		

much as the buyer of a call expects, or fall as much as the buyer of a put hopes. *And more often than not, the option writer is right;* that is, he or she is going to make money far more often than the buyer of the put or call. Such favorable odds explain, in part, the underlying economic motivation for writing put and call options. Options writing represents an investment transaction to the writers, since they receive the full option premium (less normal transaction costs, of course) in exchange for agreeing to live up to the terms of the option.

naked options
options written on securities not owned by the writer.

Investors can write options in one of two ways. One is to write **naked options,** which are options on stock not owned by the writer. The investor simply writes the put or call, collects the option premium, and hopes that the price of the underlying stock does not move against him. If successful, naked writing can be highly profitable due to the very modest amount of capital required. One thing that should be kept in mind, however, is that *the amount of return to the writer is always limited to the amount of option premium received.* On the other hand, there is really no limit to loss exposure. And that is the catch: The price of the underlying stock can rise or

fall by just about any amount over the life of the option, and in so doing deal a real blow to the naked put or call writer.

covered options
options written against stock owned (or short sold) by the writer.

Such risk exposure can be partially offset by writing **covered options,** which involves writing options against stocks which the investor (writer) already owns or has a position in. An investor, for example, could write a call against stock she owns, or a put against stock she has short sold. In this way the investor can use the long or short position to meet the terms of the option. Such a strategy represents a fairly conservative way to generate attractive rates of return. The object is to write a slightly out-of-the-money option, pocket the option premium, and hope that the price of the underlying stock will move up or down to (but not exceed) the option's striking price. In effect, what an investor is doing is adding option premium to the other usual sources of return that accompany stock ownership or short sales (dividends and/or capital gains). But there's more; for while the option premium adds to the return, it also reduces risk, since it can be used to cushion a loss should the price of the stock move against the investor. There is a hitch to all this, of course, and that is the amount of return the covered option investor can realize is limited. For once the price of the underlying common stock begins to exceed the striking price on the option, the option becomes valuable. And once that happens, the investor starts *losing* money on her options since, from this point on, for every dollar the investor makes on the stock position, she loses an equal amount on the option position. That's a major risk of writing covered call options—if the price of the underlying stock takes off, you'll miss out on the added profits. For more discussion on writing covered call options, take a look at the accompanying Investor Insights box.

options spreading
combining two or more options with different strike prices and/or expiration dates into a single transaction.

Spreading Options.   **Options spreading** is nothing more than combining two or more options into a single transaction. We could create an options spread, for example, by simultaneously buying and writing options on the same underlying stock. These cannot be identical options, however; they must differ with respect to striking price and/or expiration date. Spreads are a very popular use of listed options, and they account for a substantial amount of the trading activity on the listed options exchanges. These spreads go by a variety of exotic names, such as "bull spreads," "bear spreads," "money spreads," "vertical spreads," and "butterfly spreads." Each is different and is constructed to meet a certain type of investment goal. Consider, for example, a vertical spread; this particular type of spread would be set up by *buying* a call at one strike price and then *writing* a call (on the same stock and for the same expiration date) at a different—higher—strike price. A case in point: buy a February call on XYZ at a strike price of, say, 30 *and* simultaneously sell (write) a February call on XYZ at a strike price of 35. As bizarre as it may sound, such a position would generate a hefty return if the price of the underlying XYZ stock goes up by just a few points. Other spreads are used to profit from a falling market, and still others try to make money when the price of the underlying stock goes up *or* down! Whatever the objective, most spreads are created to take advantage of differences in prevailing option premiums. The payoff from spreading is usually substantial, but so is the risk. In fact, some spreads that seem to involve

INVESTOR INSIGHTS

Writing Covered Calls— Is It a Sure Road to Profits?

Most people think of options as one of the headiest gambles on Wall Street. Puts and calls have become the market's $2 window, and traders will tell you that for every plunger who makes money, nine others lose. But they're talking about *buying* options. Selling calls on stocks you already own—known as writing covered calls—is far less hazardous. Indeed, many knowledgeable and cautious investors sell options to squeeze extra income out of their stockholdings, defray part of the cost of buying favored shares, or hedge against large losses.

Covered-call writing is the most conservative of all option techniques. In return for agreeing to sell shares from your portfolio at a prearranged price, you receive income from an investor who wants the right to buy shares from you at that price. Let's say you own 100 shares of Honeywell that you recently bought for $73 each. You decide to sell a call option giving the buyer the right to take the stock off your hands at $80 a share anytime in the next three months. The buyer pays you a fee of $170, called the premium. Because you still own the stock, you keep any dividends that are paid while the option is in force. If the buyer exercises the call and buys the stock, you will have sold your shares for $700 more than you paid for them. You will also have taken in the $170 premium and $47.50 in dividends. Your annualized return: 38% *after* subtracting commissions of $215.

The call buyer hopes that the shares will go up; if they don't, he won't exercise the option and you'll keep your stock plus the $170 premium. Should Honeywell drop below the $73 you paid for it, the option income will defray some of your paper losses. *The risk you take in covered-call writing is that the shares will race ahead of the strike price.* Say Honeywell goes to $85. Then your stock will be called away from you at $80, and you'll have given up a potential $500 profit. To prevent that from happening, you could buy back the option you sold. But you'd have to pay about $600 because the option will have risen in value along with the stock. For this reason, you should not write a covered call if you aren't prepared to sell your shares. Says Drake Lorence, an account executive at Dain Bosworth, a brokerage firm in Minneapolis: "The highest returns—from premiums, dividends and capital gains—come when options are exercised."

Source: Adapted from Gretchen Morgenson, "Options," *Money,* October 1984, p. 69.

almost no risk may end up with devastating results if the market and the "spread" (or difference) between option premiums move against the investor.

option straddle

the simultaneous purchase (or sale) of a put and a call on the same underlying common stock.

A variation of this theme involves an **option straddle,** the simultaneous purchase (or sale) of a put *and* a call on the same underlying common stock. Unlike spreads, straddles will normally involve the same striking price and expiration date. Here, the object is to earn a profit from *either* an increase or decrease in the price of the underlying stock. Otherwise, the principles of straddles are much like those for

spreads: to build an investment position with combinations of options that will enable an investor to capture the benefits of certain types of stock price behavior. But keep in mind that if the prices of the underlying stock and/or the option premiums do not behave in the anticipated manner, the investor loses. *Spreads and straddles are extremely tricky and should not be used by novice investors.*

Stock Index Options

Imagine being able to buy or sell a major stock market index like the S&P 500—and at a reasonable cost! Think of what you could do: If you felt the market was heading up, you could invest in a security that tracks the price behavior of the S&P 500 index and make money when the market goes up. No longer would you have to go through the often haphazard process of selecting specific stocks that you *hope* will capture the market's performance. Rather, you could *play the market as a whole*. Well, that's exactly what investors can do with *stock index options*—puts and calls that are written on major stock market indexes. Even though index options have been around for only a few years (since 1983), they have become immensely popular with both individual and institutional investors. In fact, the volume of trading in index options is about half that of stock options. This volume is quite a feat when you stop to consider that nearly all of the trading in index options is confined to just *six* different contracts, compared to the more than *600* different stock option contracts! Let's now take a closer look at these popular and often highly profitable investment vehicles.

Contract Provisions

stock index option
a put or call option written on a specific stock market index, such as the S&P 500.

Basically, a **stock index option** is nothing more than a put or call option written on a specific stock market index, like the S&P 500. The underlying security in this case is the specific market index; thus, when the market index moves in one direction or another, the value of the index option moves accordingly. Since there are no stocks or other financial assets backing these options, settlement is defined in terms of cash. Specifically the cash value of an *index option* is equal to 100 times the published market index that underlies the option. As such, if the S&P 500 is at 238, the cash value of an S&P 500 index option is: $\$100 \times 238 = \$23,800$; and if the underlying index moves up or down in the market, so will the cash value of the option.

In early 1989, there were nine stock market index options available:

- S&P 500 Index (traded on CBOE)
- S&P 100 Index (CBOE)
- NYSE Index (NYSE)
- Value Line Index (Philadelphia Exchange)
- National OTC Index (Philadelphia Exchange)
- Major Market Index (AMEX)
- Institutional Index (AMEX)
- International Market Index (AMEX)
- Financial News Composite Index (Pacific Exchange)

By far the most popular option is the S&P 100 Index; in fact, this is *the most actively traded* of all listed options. As the above list reveals, the options cover not only the popular S&P and NYSE indexes, but also the Value Line index (of 1,700 stocks tracked by Value Line Investment Service) and an index of 100 large, actively traded OTC stocks. There's even an index based on the 75 stocks that are most favored by institutional investors, and another (the International Market Index) that's based on 50 foreign stocks that trade in the United States as ADRs. And although the most popular index of them all—the Dow Jones Industrial Average—has refused to let itself be the basis of an index option, the AMEX has come up with an index (the Major Market Index) designed to imitate the Dow.

There are both puts and calls available on index options. They are valued and have issue characteristics like any other put or call. That is, a *put* lets a holder profit from a *drop* in the market (when the underlying market index goes down, the value of a put goes up), whereas a *call* enables the holder to profit from a market that's going *up*. As seen in Figure 11.7, these options even have a quotation system that is virtually identical to puts and calls on stocks.

Putting a Value on Stock Index Options

Like equity options, the market price of index options is a function of the difference in the striking price on the option (which is stated in terms of the underlying index) and the latest published stock market index. To illustrate, consider the highly popular S&P 100 Index, traded on the CBOE. As the index option quotes in Figure 11.7 reveal, this index recently closed at 296.91; at the same time, there was a July *call* on this index that carried striking price of 290. Given that a stock index *call* will have a value so long as the underlying index exceeds the index striking price (just the opposite for *puts*), the intrinsic value of this call is $296.91 - 290 = 6.91$. Now, as we can see in the quotes, this call was trading at 14⅛, some 7.21 points above the call's underlying true value; this difference was, of course, investment premium. As a rule, the amount of investment premium in an index option tends to *increase* with *longer* options (note the difference between May and July options) and with *more volatile* market conditions. Returning to our example, if the S&P 100 Index were to go up to 310 by late July (the expiration date on the call), this option would be quoted at $310 - 280 = 30$; now since all index options are valued in multiples of $100, this option would be worth $3,000. If an investor had purchased the option when it was trading at 14⅛, it would have cost $1,412.50 ($14.125 \times 100) and in a little over two months would have generated a profit of $3,000 - $1,412.50 = $1,587.50$. From this example, it should be clear that because they're a form of derivative security, *index options are valued according to how the market/market index performs*. Thus, calls should be more highly valued if the market is expected to go up in the future, whereas puts should be more highly valued in falling markets.

Investment Uses

Although they can, of course, be used in spreads and straddles, index options are used most often for speculating or for hedging. As a speculative vehicle, they

INDEX TRADING

OPTIONS

Chicago Board

S&P 100 INDEX

Strike	Calls–Last			Puts–Last		
Price	May	Jun	Jul	May	Jun	Jul
260	38	39	....	....	3/16	½
265	32¾	34	....	1/16	¼	⅝
270	27	29½	32½	1/16	⅜	1
275	22⅛	23⅝		1/16	⅝	1½
280	17⅛	19¼	22	1/16	1	2⅛
285	12¼	14¾	18	⅛	1⅝	3⅛
290	7⅜	10⅝	14⅛	5/16	2⅝	4¼
295	3⅛	7¼	10¾	1 5/16	4¼	5⅞
300	13/16	4½	7¾	4	6⅞	8
305	⅛	2⅝	5⅜	8¾	9¾	10¼
310	1 7/16	....	3⅝	....	13⅞	13¾

Total call volume 178,364 Total call open int. 330,898
Total put volume 136,154 Total put open int. 516,277
The index: High 297.56; Low 294.56; index close 296.91

S&P 500 INDEX

Strike	Calls–Last			Puts–Last		
Price	May	Jun	Sep	May	Jun	Sep
175	....	141	....	....	1/16	....
260	....	....	....	....	1/16	....
275	....	....	....	....	1/16	1⅛
280	....	39⅛	....	....	⅛	1½
285	32⅜	34¼	....	....	....	....
290	....	....	....	....	⅜	2¼
295	22⅞	....	....	....	9/16	3⅛
300	17⅞	20	....	1/16	13/16	3½
305	12¾	15½	20½	1/16	1⅜	....
310	7½	11½	17⅜	3/16	2 3/16	5⅞
315	3⅝	7¾	14¾	1	3¾	7⅜
320	1	5	12¾	3⅛	5⅞	....
325	3/16	3	....	....	8⅛	....
330	....	1⅝	7¼	....	....	....
350	....	⅛	2⅜	....	32⅝	29

Total call volume 12,457 Total call open int. 236,110
Total put volume 9,918 Total put open int. 230,045
The index: High 317.94; Low 315.11; Close 317.48, +2.20.

American Exchange

MAJOR MARKET INDEX

Strike	Calls–Last			Puts–Last		
Price	May	Jun	Jul	May	Jun	Jul
430	....	55⅞	....	....	⅜	....
435	....	....	....	....	½	....
440	....	....	....	....	9/16	....
445	37⅛	....	....	....	¾	....
450	31⅜	....	....	....	15/16	2 5/16
455	28½	30¾	35½	1/16	1 3/16	3¼
460	23¼	25⅝	....	1/16	1 11/16	3⅝
465	20⅛	22	26	⅛	2⅜	4¾
470	¼	3⅜	5⅝	13	16¼	23⅛
475	8⅝	14¼	21⅜	11/16	4¾	8⅜
480	4¾	11¼	16⅝	1 15/16	6⅜	8¾
485	2⅛	8½	13⅛	4¼	8½	11
490	13/16	6	11¾	6½	10¾	14½
495	5/16	4⅛	7⅞	25	13⅜	17⅜
500	⅛	2⅞	7¼	....	17⅝	21⅜
505	5	2	5¾	....	....	....

Total call volume 35,127 Total call open int. 66,116
Total put volume 28,023 Total put open int. 65,091
The index: High 484.31; Low 479.38; Close 482.90, +3.24.

FIGURE 11.7 Quotations on Index Options.
The quotations system used with index options is very similar to that used with stock options: i.e., the prices for puts and calls are listed relative to their expiration dates (May, June, or July), and to their strike prices; even the latest market value of the index itself is shown—see ''index close''. (*Source: The Wall Street Journal.*)

provide investors with the opportunity to play the market with a relatively small amount of capital. For example, if an investor thinks the market is heading up, she can capitalize on those expectations by buying a call on one of the market indexes. Let's say the S&P 500 index is at 235 and our investor feels confident it'll move up to around 250 within the next couple of months. (She's convinced the tone of the market is such that it's poised for a big advance.) To back up her expectations, she buys three 60-day *calls* on the S&P 500; the options carry striking prices of 235 and are quoted at 2½. Since each call costs $250 (that is, 2½ × $100), our investor is able to speculate on the market with just $750 (the price of three calls). Now if the market does take off and the S&P 500 rises to, say, 248.5 by the expiration date on the calls, the investor will make a profit of $3,300; that is:

Value of each call at expiration (market "price"	
Less strike "price" = 248.5 − 235.0)	13.5
Less: cost of the call	− 2.5
	11.0
Times: cash value	× $100.00
Total profit made on each call	$1,100.00
Times: number of calls held	× 3
Total profit	$3,300.00

Since this profit was made from an investment of just $750 (which, by the way, is also the most that could have been lost in this transaction), the holding period return on the transaction amounts to a very attractive 440 percent—$3,300/$750. Thus, like any other put or call, *index options provide attractive leverage opportunities and at the same time limit the exposure to loss to the price paid for the option.*

Index options are equally effective as a hedging vehicle. For instance, one way to protect a portfolio of common stocks against an adverse market is to buy *puts* on one of the market indexes. If you think the market's heading down and you hold a portfolio of, say, a dozen different stocks, you can protect your capital by selling all your stocks. However, that could become very expensive, especially if you plan on getting back into the market after it drops. One way to "have your cake and eat it, too" is to hedge your stock portfolio with a stock index put. In this way, if the market does go down you'll make money on your puts, which can then be used to buy more stocks at the lower, "bargain" prices. On the other hand, if the market doesn't retreat but continues to go up, you'll be out only the cost of the puts—which could well be recovered from the increased value of your stock holdings. The principles of hedging with index options are exactly the same as those for hedging with stock options (explained earlier in this chapter); the only difference is that with index options, we're trying to protect a *whole portfolio* of stocks rather than *individual* stocks.

There is one important consideration to keep in mind, however. That is, the

INVESTOR INSIGHTS

Using Index Options to Protect a Whole Portfolio of Stocks

When the stock market starts heading down, investors begin to worry about protecting the value of their portfolios. But simply liquidating their stock holdings and putting the proceeds into a money market fund is too drastic a step for most people. Not only would they incur substantial brokerage commissions and capital gains taxes; they also would risk being caught on the sidelines if the market rally regains its breath.

There is, however, a far less drastic—and less costly—way for investors to shield their portfolios from the possibility of a sustained sell-off. Many market specialists say investors should consider buying "insurance" in the form of put options. A put option is a legal contract that gives the holder the right, for a specified period of time, to sell a specified amount of the underlying security at a fixed price, called the exercise price or strike price. Put options gain in value when the underlying security loses value. . . .

Put options are traded on individual issues and on stock indexes, such as the Standard & Poor's 100 or the Major Market Index. Puts based on a stock index offer a simple method of insuring the value of an entire portfolio with a single trade. That can be especially helpful because many issues in an investor's portfolio may not have individual put options traded on them. The four most widely used market index options are the S&P 500, the S&P 100, the Major Market Index, and the NYSE Composite.

Insurance on stock portfolios is in many ways no different from any other kind of insurance. The more protection investors want, and the less risk they are willing to bear, the more the insurance costs. For example, suppose an investor wants to hedge a $100,000 stock portfolio. Also suppose that after examining the characteristics of the major stock indexes, the investor concludes that the S&P 100 comes closest to matching the portfolio. With the S&P 100 index standing at 272, the market value of the S&P 100 index would be $27,200. So the investor would have to buy four puts to approximate the total value of the $100,000 portfolio.

The investor might decide to buy four "May 260" puts, which are puts that expire in May and have a strike price of 260. The price of these puts is about 4. To turn that into

amount of profit you make, or protection you obtain, depends in large part on how closely the behavior of your stock portfolio is matched by the behavior of the index option you employ in the hedge. For there is *no guarantee* that the two will behave in the same way! Care should be taken, therefore, to select an index option that closely reflects the nature of the stocks in your portfolio. If, for example, you hold a number of OTC stocks, you might be well advised to select something like the National OTC Index as the hedging vehicle; or if you hold mostly blue chips, maybe you should go with the Major Market Index. While you'll probably be hard pressed to get dollar-for-dollar portfolio protection, at least you should try to get as close a match as possible. After all, the closer the match the better the hedge, and therefore the greater your chances of offsetting any portfolio losses with gains from the index

dollars, an investor multiplies by 100; the puts would cost about $400 each. That would mean $1,600 for all four—1.6% of the $100,000 value of the portfolio. Now suppose the market retreats 20% from current levels, which would bring the S&P 100 down to about 218. Each of the May 260 puts would be worth a minimum of 42 points (260 minus 218), or $4,200. After paying their cost, the investor would have a profit on the puts of $15,200, offsetting a substantial portion of the $20,000 the portfolio would have lost in a 20% decline.

By purchasing put options with a strike price only 12 points under the current level of the S&P 100 index, the investor effectively insured the portfolio against losses incurred after the first 12 points, or 4.4%, of the index's decline. Had the investor been willing to bear more of the market risk, the cost of the insurance could have been reduced by purchasing puts with a lower strike price. [On the other hand,] an investor who wanted to be fully insured might have bought puts with a higher strike price, but this would have raised the cost of the insurance. May 270 puts, for instance, would have cost 7¼, or $725 each.

Harrison Roth, options strategist at Drexel Burnham Lambert Inc., says the basic question for investors is: "Do you want to hedge against any and all declines, or do you simply want protection against catastrophic moves?" He says he believes that "most investors are in the second camp."

Even with relatively low-cost puts such as the May 260s, the cost of hedging with put options can add up if the insurance goes unused. Buying puts such as these with a three-month lifetime four times a year, for instance, would cost the investor the equivalent of 6.4% of a $100,000 portfolio. One way to reduce the cost is to sell the put options before they expire. Put options lose most of their value in the final six weeks before their expiration if they have strike prices below the current price of the underlying securities.

Mr. Schaeffer of Index Option Advisor suggests that investors only hold their options for a month before selling them and then buying the next month out. In that way they would recover most of the options' value, significantly reducing the cost of the hedge even after considering the higher commissions they would incur.

Source: Stanley W. Angrist, "Put Options Can Help Protect Portfolios," *The Wall Street Journal*, February 28, 1989, p. C1.

options. Another factor that's important in portfolio hedging is the cost of the underlying hedge vehicle itself; this and other considerations are discussed in the accompanying Investor Insights box above, which deals with the use of index options in portfolio hedging.

Given their effectiveness for either speculating or hedging the entire market, it's little wonder that index options have become so popular with investors. But a word of caution is in order: Although trading index options appears simple and seems to provide high rates of return, they are in reality *high-risk* trading vehicles that are subject to considerable price volatility and should *not* be used by amateurs! True, there's only so much you can lose with these options: the trouble is, it's very easy to do just that! Attractive profits are indeed available from these securities, but they're not investments you can buy and then "forget about" until they expire; for with the

wide market swings we're experiencing these days, *these securities have to be closely monitored on a daily basis.*

Other Types of Options

Although options on stocks and stock indexes account for most of the market activity in listed options, put and call options can also be obtained on selected industries, debt instruments, and foreign currencies. These options are used primarily by professional and institutional traders as so-called *risk modifiers*—hedging vehicles used to protect a position in stocks, debt securities, or foreign currencies. For one reason or another, they just haven't caught on widely among individual investors; even so, they do provide some interesting investment opportunities, and as such, we'll now take a brief look at these other kinds of options, starting with industry options.

Industry Options

industry option
a put or call option written on a portfolio of stocks from a specific industry segment of the market; also called a sub-index option.

An industry option is like an index option, except that it's written on a smaller segment of the market. Specifically, an **industry option** (or **sub-index option,** as it's also called) is written on a portfolio of stocks from a specific industry segment of the market. For example, the AMEX has sub-index options (puts and calls) available on computer technology stocks, and another one on oil stocks, while the Philadelphia Exchange lists an index of utility shares. These options are written against a portfolio of stocks that are supposed to reflect the average price performance of all stocks in that industry. Thus, underlying the AMEX's computer technology options is an index that is composed of 30 computer stocks, weighted by their market value. As the index moves up or down—in conjunction with the weighted average market price of the stocks that make up the index—the option premiums move accordingly. When the industry index goes up, the value of a *call* increases; when the index goes down, the value of a *put* goes up. Index options can be used for speculation or for hedging. And although they haven't really caught on as trading vehicles (volume remains low on these options), they do provide investors with the opportunity to invest in a whole industry with a relatively small amount of capital.

Interest Rate Options

interest rate options
put and call options written on fixed-income (debt) securities.

Puts and calls on fixed-income (debt) securities are known as **interest rate options.** Specific Treasury securities (Treasury *notes* and *bonds*) underlie these options, and as their prices go up or down in the market, the puts and calls respond accordingly. A call, for example, enables the holder to buy a certain amount (usually $100,000) of a specific Treasury bond or note at a stipulated (striking) price for a specified period of time (as defined by the option's expiration date); a put, in contrast, gives the holder the right to sell the underlying financial assets under comparable provisions. In 1989, trading in interest rate options was centered on the CBOE and involved four Treasury bonds and three Treasury notes—including, for example, the 8⅞ percent T-bond of 2019 and the 9 percent note of 1993. One noteworthy feature of these options is that as a rule the securities will exist for *only one cycle.*

That is, unless the debt security is considered to be a bellwether issue (one that's closely followed in the marketplace), once the initial three- and six-month options have expired, *there'll be no more puts and calls written on those Treasury securities.* The reason for this is that after the initial life of a T-bond or note, there's just not enough secondary trading in the securities to support an active options market. Thus, new options are constantly coming out on new government security issues. The market for interest rate options never took hold and to this day remains very small; most professional/institutional traders tend to use interest rate futures contracts or options on these futures contracts (both of which we'll examine in Chapter 12). In an effort to beef up volume, the CBOE in mid-1989 introduced two new trading vehicles: an *option on short-term interest rates* and an *option on long-term rates*. The short-term option is based on the yield for the most recently auctioned 13-week T-bill, and the long option is based on the average yield of the most recently auctioned 7- and 10-year T-notes and 30-year T-bonds. Unlike standard interest rate options, these securities are *yield* driven (rather than price driven), meaning that when market interest rates rise, for example, the value of the underlying call option will also rise (the value of the put will fall), and vice versa. In addition, these short- and long-term rate options can be exercised only on the last day of trading. Whether or not these options breathe new life into the interest rate options market remains to be seen. Right now, it's too early to tell; as a result, we'll confine our discussion for the balance of this material to standard interest rate options.

With (''standard'') interest rate options, the price of a call increases when the yield or interest rate on the underlying debt security *decreases*. Just the reverse occurs with puts. This is because such interest rate behavior will cause the underlying debt security to increase or decrease in value. Recall from Chapter 9 that a drop in interest rates results in a rise in the value of a debt security. Since an option should reflect the market behavior of the underlying security, the same valuation principle applies with options as with the securities themselves. If the market yield on Treasury notes and bonds drops, the market value of these securities *and* the price of calls on them will go up together, while the value of puts will decline. Interest rate options are appealing to investors because of their limited exposure to loss, as well as the attractive leverage they offer—which can lead to substantial capital gains and very high rates of return. They also provide a very effective yet inexpensive way to hedge a position in fixed-income securities. For example, a put option on a Treasury bond might be purchased to protect an investor's bond portfolio against a decline in value. This hedge would work just like a stock hedge: If interest rates go up, the value of the put would increase and in so doing, would offset all or part of the decline in the value of the bond portfolio. Actually, interest rate options can be used not only for hedging but also for speculating, for options writing programs, and for spreading purposes; essentially they can be used in just about any way that a stock option can.

Speculating on the behavior of interest rates is a common use of interest rate options. Indeed, an investor who wants to speculate on interest rate movements has two choices: He or she can do so with fixed-income securities (as described in

Chapter 9) or by buying put or call options on debt securities. The basic advantage of the latter choice is that it gives the investor just as much price action, but at reduced risk. For instance, if an investor thinks interest rates are going to *fall* in the near future, she could buy some Treasury bond *calls* at a very modest cost; then, if rates do fall, the value of the calls will shoot up, and she'll be able to enjoy a substantial rate of return on her investment. In contrast, if she thinks market rates are headed *up,* she could buy some *puts* and reap similar benefits. Clearly, the ability to forecast interest rates (which is *not* an easy task) lies at the heart of this trading strategy, for the amount of investment success or failure (profit or loss) is directly linked to how well interest rates are forecast. On the other hand, because of their limited exposure to loss, the use of interest rate options will at least lessen the potential impact of faulty judgment. (In other words, if you are wrong, there's only so much you can lose with calls, which is not the case when you speculate directly in bonds.) Because of the pervasive effects that the underlying debt securities have on the price behavior of interest rate options, it goes without saying that these securities should *only be used by knowledgeable and experienced investors who fully understand the mechanics of interest rates and the behavior of debt securities!*

Currency Options

currency options
put and call options written on foreign currencies.

Foreign exchange options, or **currency options** as they're more commonly called, provide investors with a way to speculate on foreign exchange rates or to hedge foreign currency holdings. Currency options are available on most of the countries we have strong trading ties with. These options are traded on the Philadelphia Exchange, and include the following currencies:

- British pound
- Swiss franc
- West German mark
- Canadian dollar
- Japanese yen
- French franc
- Australian dollar

In essence, puts and calls on these currencies give the holders the right to sell or buy large amounts of the specified foreign currency. However, in contrast to the standardized contracts used with stock and stock index options, the specific unit of trading in this market varies with the particular underlying currency, the details of which are spelled out in Table 11.7. Currency options are traded in full or fractional cents per unit of the underlying currency, relative to the amount of foreign currency involved. Thus, if a put or call on the British pound were quoted at, say, 6.40 (which is read as "6.4 cents"), it would be valued at $2,000, since there are 31,250 British pounds that underlie this option—that is, 31,250 × .064 = $2,000.

The value of a currency option is linked to the exchange rate between the American dollar and the underlying foreign currency. For example, if the Canadian dollar becomes stronger *relative to the American dollar,* causing the exchange rates to go up, the price of a *call* option on the Canadian dollar will increase, and the price of

---

TABLE 11.7   **Foreign Currency Option Contracts on the Philadelphia Exchange**

Underlying Currency*	Size of Contracts
British pound	31,250 pounds
Swiss franc	62,500 francs
West German mark	62,500 marks
Canadian dollar	50,000 dollars
Japanese yen	6,250,000 yen
French franc	125,000 francs
Australian dollar	50,000 dollars

*The British pound, Swiss franc, West German mark, Canadian dollar, and Australian dollar are all quoted in full cents; the French franc in tenths of a cent; and the Japanese yen in one-hundredths of a cent.

---

a *put* will decline. To understand how you can make money with currency options, consider a situation where an investor wants to *speculate* on exchange rates. The striking price of a currency option is stated in terms of *exchange rates*. Thus, a strike price of 150, for example, implies each unit of the foreign currency (such as one British pound) is worth 150 cents, or $1.50, in American money. If an investor held a (150) call on this foreign currency, he would make money if the foreign currency strengthened relative to the U.S. dollar so that the exchange rate rose (to, say, 155); in contrast, if he held a (150) put, he would profit from a decline in the exchange rate (to, say, 145). Let's use a put on the British pound to illustrate what happens. Say we could buy a (150) put at a premium of 1.50; this means the put would cost us $468.75 ($.015 × 31,250). Now, if the exchange rate actually does drop to 145 by expiration, the put would be worth the difference in the prevailing (spot) exchange rate and the exchange rate stipulated in the striking price; in our example, the puts would be trading at 5.00, and each one would be worth $1,562.50 ($.05 × 31,250). For each put we held we would make a profit of $1,562.50 − $468.75 = $1,093.75 and generate a holding period return of ($1,562.50 − $468.75)/$468.75 = 233.3 percent. Success in forecasting movements in foreign exchange rates is obviously essential to a profitable foreign currency options program.

SUMMARY

- Basically, an option is a type of security that gives its holder the right to subsequently buy or sell other securities at a specified price over a specified period of time; there are three kinds of options: (1) rights; (2) warrants; and (3) puts and calls.

- A right is a short-lived financial instrument that enables its holder to purchase a new issue of common stock at a subscription price that's set below the prevail-

ing market price of the existing stock. Only if the shareholder exercises the right or sells it will he or she realize any financial benefits from its issue.

- A warrant is similar to a right but its maturity is much longer. Attached to bond issues as "sweeteners," warrants allow the holder to purchase the corporation's common stock at a set exercise price on or before the stipulated expiration date. The value of a warrant is linked to the market price of the underlying common stock, although warrants frequently trade at premium prices due to their speculative value.

- Warrants offer advantages to their owners in the form of (1) attractive capital gains; (2) low unit cost; and (3) the benefits of leverage (which accompany the low unit cost). In weighing these advantages, the investor must consider the fact that warrants pay no dividends, but they do carry expiration dates.

- While sometimes used as a way to limit exposure to loss, trading in warrants is done primarily as a substitute for common stock investing and is based on the magnified capital gains they offer. The value of a warrant changes directly with and by approximately the same amount as the underlying common stock; but since a warrant's unit cost is often much lower than that of the common stock, the same dollar change in price represents a considerably larger percentage yield.

- Puts and calls are by far the most popular and widely used type of option; these derivative securities offer attractive speculative value and considerable leverage potential.

- A put enables the holder to sell a certain amount of a specified security at a specified price over a specified time period; a call, in contrast, gives the holder the right to buy the same securities at a specified price over a specified period of time. Most puts and calls sell at premium prices, the amount of which depends on the length of the option contract and the speculative appeal of the underlying financial asset.

- The three basic features of puts and calls are (1) striking price; (2) the expiration date; and (3) the purchase price of the option itself. The value of a call is measured by the market price of the underlying security less the striking price designated on the call. The value of a put is its striking price less the market price of the security.

- Since 1973, the Chicago Board Options Exchange (CBOE) has made option trading easy and convenient; contracts have been standardized with regard to striking prices and expiration dates; trading activity has increased; and options trading has become a widely used investment technique. Today, trading in listed options is conducted not only on the CBOE, but also on the AMEX, the NYSE, the Philadelphia Exchange, and the Pacific Stock Exchange.

- Standardized listed put and call options are presently available on over 600 (mostly NYSE) common stocks (equity options); nine stock market indexes, like the S&P 500 (index options); a number of debt securities and foreign currencies (interest rate and currency options); and a small group of industry

indexes (sub-index options). Equity and stock index options are the most popular with investors and account for most of the market activity in puts and calls.

- Put and call options can be used for speculation, as a way to hedge a position,
  or in option writing and spreading programs.

- Aggressive investors will use puts and calls either for speculation or in highly
  specialized writing and spreading programs. One of the reasons that these options are so popular with speculators is that they offer very attractive returns,
  while limiting exposure to loss.

- Conservative investors may be attracted to put and call purchases because of
  their low cost and the limited risk they offer in absolute dollar terms. Often,
  conservative investors will use options in covered call writing programs, or to
  form hedge positions in combination with other securities.

REVIEW QUESTIONS AND PROBLEMS

1. Describe a stock right and note how such rights are tied to the preemptive rights of investors.

2. How would a stock right be used by an investor? Why does it have such limited investment
   appeal?

3. Assume a company has 1 million shares of common stock outstanding and intends to issue
   another 200,000 shares via a rights offering; the rights will carry a subscription price of $48.
   If the current market price of the stock is $53, what is the value of one right?

4. What is a warrant? What is the chief attraction of a warrant?

5. Assume that one warrant gives the holder the right to buy one share of stock at an exercise
   price of $40; what is the value of this warrant if the current market price of the stock is $44?
   At what ($ and %) premium would the warrants be trading if they were quoted in the market
   at a price of $5?

6. Why are warrants often considered viable investment alternatives to common stock?

7. Describe the leverage feature of a warrant and note why leverage is so attractive to investors.

8. A warrant carries an exercise price of $20; assume it takes three warrants to buy one share of
   stock. At what price would the warrant be trading if it sold at a 20 percent premium, while the
   market price of the stock was $35 per share?

9. Why might it be unwise to exercise warrants?

10. What factors are important in determining the investment appeal of warrants? Why is the
    price of the warrant itself so important in the investment decision?

11. Describe put and call options. Are they issued like other corporate securities? Explain.

12. What are listed options, and how do they differ from conventional options? What's the
    difference between option premium and investment premium? What's a derivative security?
    Give an example of one.

13. Assume an investor buys a six-month put for $600; the put has a striking price of $80, and the
    current market price of the underlying stock is $75. How much investment premium is there
    in the put?

14. What are the main investment attractions of put and call options? What are the risks?

15. Briefly discuss the differences and similarities in stock index options and stock options; do the same for interest rate and foreign currency options (relative to stock options).

16. Using the stock option or index option quotations in Figures 11.5 and 11.7, respectively, find the option premium, investment premium, and the stock/index breakeven point for the following puts and calls:

a. The June Prime Computer *put,* with the striking price of 17½.
b. The September Pfizer *call,* with the $60 striking price.
c. The June Major Market *call,* with the striking price of 475.
d. The July S&P 100 *put,* with the striking price of 300.

17. Note the various ways stock options can be used by investors; do the same for index options and interest rate options.

18. A six-month call on a certain common stock carries a striking price of $60; it can be purchased at a cost of $600. Assume that the underlying stock rises to $75 per share by the expiration date of the option. How much profit would this option generate over the six-month holding period, and what is its rate of return?

19. If you felt that interest rates were headed way up over the course of the next six months, would it make sense to buy a *call* on a Treasury bond? Explain. How about a *put?* Briefly explain how you can use interest rate options to profit from a *drop* in interest rates.

20. Dorothy Cappel does a lot of investing in the stock market and is a frequent user of stock index options. She is convinced that the market is about to undergo a broad retreat and has decided to buy a put on the S&P 100 Index. The put carries a striking price of 290 and is quoted in the financial press at 4½. Although the S&P Index of 100 stocks is presently at 286.45, Dorothy thinks it will drop to 265 by the expiration date on the option. How much profit will she make, *and* what will her holding period return be if she is right?

21. Assume an investor holds a well-balanced portfolio of common stocks; under what conditions might he want to use a stock index option to hedge his portfolio?

a. Briefly explain how such options could be used to hedge a portfolio against a drop in the market.
b. Discuss what would happen if the market does in fact go down.
c. What happens if the market goes up instead?

CASE PROBLEMS

11.1   The Slaters' Investment Options

Phil Slater is a highly successful businessman in Atlanta. The box manufacturing firm he and his wife Judy founded several years ago has prospered. Because he is self-employed, he is building his own retirement fund. So far he has accumulated a substantial sum in his investment account, mostly by following an aggressive investment posture; he does this because, as he puts it, ''you never know when the bottom's gonna fall out in this business.'' Phil has been following the stock of Rembrandt Paper Products (RPP) and after conducting extensive analysis, feels the stock is about ready to move. Specifically, he believes that within the next six months, RPP could go to about $80 per share, from its current level of $57.50. The stock pays annual dividends of $2.40 per share, and Phil figures he would receive two quarterly

dividend payments over his six-month investment horizon. In studying the company, Phil has learned that it has some warrants outstanding (they mature in eight years and carry an exercise price of $45); also, it has six-month call options (with $50 and $60 striking prices) listed on the CBOE. Each warrant is good for one share of stock, and they are currently trading at $15; the CBOE calls are quoted at $8 for the options with $50 striking prices, and $5 for the $60 options.

Questions

1. How many alternative investment vehicles does Phil have if he wants to invest in RPP for no more than six months? What if he has a two-year investment horizon?

2. Using a six-month holding period and assuming the stock does indeed rise to $80 over this time frame:
   a. Find the market price of the warrants at the end of the holding period, given that they then trade at a premium of 10 percent.
   b. Find the value of both calls, given that at the end of the holding period neither contains any investment premium.
   c. Determine the holding period rate of return for each of the four investment alternatives open to Mr. Slater.

3. Which course of action would you recommend if Phil simply wants to maximize profit? Would your answer change if other factors (like comparative risk exposure) were considered along with return? Explain.

11.2   Fred's Quandary—To Hedge or Not to Hedge

A little more than ten months ago, Fred Weaver, a mortgage banker in Dallas, bought 300 shares of stock at $40 per share. Since then, the price of the stock has risen to $75 per share. It is now near the end of the year, and the market is starting to weaken; Fred feels there is still plenty of play left in the stock but is afraid the tone of the market will be detrimental to his position. His wife Denise is taking an extension course on the stock market and has just learned about put and call hedges. She suggests that he use puts to hedge his position. Fred is intrigued with the idea, which he discusses with his broker—who advises him that, indeed, the needed puts are available on his stock. Specifically, he can buy three-month puts, with $75 striking prices, at a cost of $550 each (quoted at 5½).

Questions

1. Given the circumstances surrounding Fred's current investment position, what benefits could be derived from using the puts as a hedge device? What would be the major drawback?

2. What would Fred's minimum profit be if he buys three puts at the indicated option premium? How much would he make if he did not hedge but instead sold his stock immediately at a price of $75 per share?

3. Assuming Fred uses three puts to hedge his position, indicate the amount of profit he would generate if the stock moves to $100 by the expiration date of the puts. What if the stock drops to $50 per share?

4. Should he use the puts as a hedge? Explain. Under what conditions would you urge him not to use the puts as a hedge?

SELECTED READINGS

Boland, John C. "Winning with Warrants." *Sylvia Porter's Personal Finance,* October 1987, pp. 88–91.

Carey, David. ''Options: Wall Street's New Siren Song.'' *Financial World,* March 24, 1987, pp. 22–24.

Curran, John J. ''Selling Call Options: A Low-Risk Strategy With Stocks.'' *Fortune,* July 20, 1987, pp. 105–6.

Fredman, Albert J., and R. T. Nishio. ''Warming Up to Debt Options.'' *Personal Investor,* January 1986, pp. 67–72.

Moscovitz, Steven D. ''They Warrant a Look—How Warrants Work as Hedging Devices.'' *Barron's,* December 21, 1987, pp. 28–29.

Rachlin, Jill. ''Racing the Market With Options.'' *U.S. News & World Report,* September 21, 1987, pp. 75–76.

Sachar, Laura. ''Warrants: Less Speculation, More Leverage.'' *Financial World,* February 10, 1987, pp. 24–25.

Scherschel, Patricia M. ''The Zip in Stock-Index Options.'' *U.S. News & World Report,* March 31, 1986, p. 54.

Schiffres, Manuel. ''When Stock Prices Seem to be Going Nowhere, Maybe It's Time For a Call.'' *Changing Times,* November 1988, p. 88.

Zimmerman, Marlene. ''Selling Call Options.'' *Sylvia Porter's Personal Finance,* August 1985, pp. 54–57.

12

COMMODITIES, FINANCIAL FUTURES, AND TANGIBLE INVESTMENTS

After studying this chapter you should be able to:

● Describe the essential features of a futures contract, as well as the basic operating characteristics of the futures market.

● Identify the major commodities exchanges, and explain the role that hedgers and speculators play in these markets, including how profits are made and lost.

● Distinguish between a physical commodity and a financial future, and between a futures contract and an option on a futures contract.

● Gain an appreciation of the different trading techniques that can be used with these securities, and how investment return can be measured.

● Explain the risk-return characteristics of these securities and the various investment strategies that investors can follow when dealing in commodities and financial futures.

● Develop a basic understanding of the investment characteristics and suitability of gold and other tangible investments, such as silver, strategic metals, diamonds, and collectibles.

Psst, wanna buy some copper? Well how about some gold, or pork bellies, or plywood? Maybe the Japanese yen or Swiss franc strikes your fancy. Sound a bit unusual? Perhaps, but all these items have one thing in common: They represent investment vehicles that are popular with millions of investors. This is the more exotic side of investing—the market for commodities and financial futures—and it often involves a considerable amount of speculation. In fact, the risks are enormous; but the payoffs in these markets can at times be nothing short of phenomenal. For example, a $1,500 investment in a gasoline futures contract in January of 1989 would have brought a whopping $7,500 in profits in less than five months. A little bit of luck is obviously helpful in such situations, but equally important is the need for patience and know-how. *These are specialized investment vehicles that require specialized investor skills.* We will now look at these investment outlets to see not only what they are, but how they can be used in various types of investment programs. First, we will examine the futures market itself; then we will look at investing in commodities and financial futures. The chapter concludes with a brief review of the investment features and merits of still another type of specialized investment vehicle: so-called *tangible investments,* such as gold, precious metals and gemstones, stamps, coins, and antiques.

THE FUTURES MARKET

The amount of futures trading in the United States has mushroomed over the past 10 to 15 years as an increasing number of investors have turned to futures trading as a way to earn attractive, highly competitive rates of return. But it's *not* the traditional commodities contracts that have drawn many of these investors; rather, it's the new investment vehicles being offered. A major reason behind the growth in the volume of futures trading has been *the big jump in the number and variety of contracts available for trading.* Thus, today we find that in addition to the traditional primary commodities, such as grains and metals, markets also exist for live animals, processed commodities, crude oil and gasoline, foreign currencies, money market securities, U.S. Treasury notes and bonds, Eurodollar securities, and common stocks (via stock market indexes). Indeed, there are even listed put and call options available on a select but growing list of futures contracts. All these commodities and financial assets are traded in what is known as the futures market.

Market Structure

cash market
a market where a product or commodity changes hands in exchange for a cash price paid at the time the transaction is completed.

futures market
the organized market for the trading of futures contracts.

When a bushel of wheat is sold, the transaction takes place in the **cash market;** in other words, the bushel changes hands in exchange for a cash price paid to the seller. The transaction occurs at that point in time and for all practical purposes is completed then and there. Most traditional securities are traded in this type of market. However, a bushel of wheat could also be sold in the **futures market;** in such cases, the seller would not actually deliver the wheat until some mutually agreed-upon date in the future. As a result, the transaction would not be completed for some time; the seller would receive partial payment for the bushel of wheat at the time the agreement was entered into, and the balance on delivery. The buyer, in turn, would own a highly liquid futures contract that could be held (and presented

for delivery of the bushel of wheat) or traded in the futures market. No matter what the buyer does with the contract, as long as it is outstanding, the seller has a legal and binding *obligation to make delivery* of the stated quantity of wheat on a specified date in the future, and the buyer/holder has a similar *obligation to take delivery* of the underlying commodity.

In many respects futures contracts are closely related to the call options we studied earlier. Both involve the future delivery of an item at an agreed-upon price. But there is *a significant difference* between a futures contract and an options contract. A futures contract *obligates* a person to buy or sell a specified amount of a given commodity at a stated price on or before a stated date, unless the contract is cancelled or liquidated before it expires; in contrast, an option gives the holder the *right* to buy or sell a specific amount of a real or financial asset at a specific price over a specified period of time. Equally important, the risk of loss with an option is limited to the price paid for it, whereas a futures contract has no such limit on exposure to loss.

Major Exchanges

Although futures contracts can be traced back to biblical times, their use on an organized basis in this country did not occur until the mid-1800s. They originated in the agricultural segment of the economy, where individuals who produced, owned, and/or processed foodstuffs sought a way to protect themselves against adverse price movements. Subsequently, futures contracts came to be traded by individuals who wanted to make money with commodities by speculating on their price swings. The first organized commodity exchange in the United States, the Chicago Board of Trade, opened in 1848. Over time additional exchanges came into existence, so that today futures trading is conducted on 13 North American exchanges—12 U.S. and 1 Canadian:

- Chicago Board of Trade
- Chicago Mercantile Exchange
- Chicago Rice & Cotton Exchange
- Commodity Exchange of New York
- International Petroleum Exchange
- Kansas City Board of Trade
- MidAmerica Commodity Exchange
- Minneapolis Grain Exchange
- New York Coffee, Sugar, and Cocoa Exchange
- New York Cotton Exchange
- New York Futures Exchange (a NYSE subsidiary)
- New York Mercantile Exchange
- Winnipeg Commodity Exchange

The Chicago Board of Trade is the biggest exchange, as measured by contract trading volume, followed by the Chicago Mercantile Exchange, the NY Merc, and the Commodity Exchange of New York. These four exchanges account for more than 80 percent of all the trading volume conducted on North American futures

exchanges. All totalled, trading activity on the 13 major exchanges has reached the point where the futures market is today a *trillion-dollar* institution that, in many respects, rivals the stock market!

Each exchange deals in a variety of futures contracts, although some are more limited in their activities than others. For example, in contrast to the New York Cotton Exchange, which deals in just a couple of contracts, the Chicago Mercantile Exchange trades pork bellies, cattle, eggs, lumber, potatoes, turkeys, butter, and gold, as well as a variety of foreign currencies, debt securities, and stock market indexes. Table 12.1, on pages 504 and 505, provides a list of where the major commodities, financial futures, and futures options are traded. Note that most of the exchanges deal in a number of commodities and/or financial assets, and many commodities and financial futures are traded on more than one exchange (for example, gold is traded on three exchanges). Although the exchanges are highly efficient and annual volume has surpassed the trillion-dollar mark, futures trading is still conducted by **open outcry auction;** in other words, as shown in Figure 12.1, on page 506, actual trading on the floors of these exchanges is conducted through a series of shouts, body motions, and hand signals.

open outcry auction
in futures trading, auction in which trading is done through a series of shouts, body motions, and hand signals.

Futures Contracts

futures contract
a commitment to deliver a certain amount of some specified item at some specified date in the future.

A **futures contract** is a commitment to deliver a certain amount of some specified item at some specified date in the future. The seller of the contract agrees to make the specified future delivery, and the buyer agrees to accept it. Each exchange establishes its own contract specifications, which include not only the quantity and quality of the item, but the delivery procedure and delivery month as well. For example, the Chicago Board of Trade specifies that each of its soybean contracts will involve 5,000 bushels of USDA grade No. 2 yellow soybeans; delivery months include January, March, May, July, August, September, and November. The **delivery month** for a futures contract is much like the expiration date used on put and call options; it specifies when the commodity or item must be delivered and thus defines the life of the contract. In addition, *futures contracts have their own trading hours.* Unlike listed stocks and bonds, which begin and end trading at the same time, normal trading hours for commodities and financial futures vary widely. For example, oats trade from 9:30 to 1:15 (Central), live cattle from 9:05 to 12:45, U.S. Treasury bills from 7:20 to 2:00, gold from 8:00 to 1:30, and so forth. It may sound a bit confusing, but it seems to work.

delivery month
the time when a commodity must be delivered; defines the life of a futures contract.

The maximum life of a futures contract is about one year or less, although some (like silver and Treasury bonds) have lives as long as 2½ to 3 years. Table 12.2, on page 507, lists a cross section of 12 different commodities and financial futures and shows that the typical futures contract covers a large quantity of the underlying product or financial instrument. However, although the value of a single contract is normally quite large, the actual amount of investor capital required to deal in these vehicles is relatively small, because all trading in this market is done on a margin basis.

Trading

Basically, the futures market contains two types of traders: hedgers and speculators. The market simply could not exist and operate efficiently without either one. The

hedgers
the producers and processors who use futures contracts as a way to protect their interest in an underlying commodity or financial instrument.

hedgers are the producers and processors (which today include financial institutions and corporate money managers) who use futures contracts as a way to protect their interest in the underlying commodity or financial instrument. For example, if a rancher thinks the price of cattle will drop in the near future, he will act as a hedger and sell a futures contract on cattle in the hope of locking in as high a price as possible for his herd. In effect, the hedgers provide the underlying strength of the futures market and represent the very reason for its existence. *Speculators,* in contrast, give the market liquidity; they are the ones who trade futures contracts not because of a need to protect a position in the underlying commodity, but simply to earn a profit on expected swings in the price of a futures contract. They are the risk takers, the investors who have no inherent interest in the commodity or financial future other than the price action and potential capital gains it can produce.

Trading Mechanics

Once the futures contracts are created by the hedgers and speculators, they can readily be traded in the market. Like common stocks and other traditional investment vehicles, futures contracts are bought and sold through local brokerage offices. Most firms have at least one or two people in each office (more in some cases) who specialize in futures contracts; in addition, a number of commodity firms that deal only in futures contracts stand ready to help individuals with their investment needs. Except for setting up a special commodity trading account, there is really no difference between trading futures and dealing in stocks or bonds. The same types of orders are used, and the use of margin is a standard way of trading futures. Any investor can buy or sell any contract, with any delivery month, and at any time, so long as it is currently being traded on one of the exchanges.

Buying a contract is referred to as taking a *long position,* whereas selling one is termed taking a *short position*. It is exactly like going long or short with stocks and has the same connotation: The investor who is long wants the price to rise, and the short seller wants it to drop. Both long and short positions can be liquidated simply by executing an offsetting transaction; the short seller, for example, would cover his or her position by buying an equal amount of the contract. In general, less than 1 percent of all futures contracts are settled by delivery; the rest are offset prior to the delivery month. All trades are subject to normal transaction costs, which include **round trip commissions** of about $60 to $90 for each contract traded. (A round trip commission includes the commission costs on both ends of the transaction—to buy and sell a contract.) The exact size of the commission depends on the number and type of contracts being traded.

round trip commissions
the commission costs on both ends (buying and selling) of a securities transaction.

Margin Trading

Buying on margin means putting up only a fraction of the total price in cash; margin, in effect, is the amount of equity that goes into the deal. Margin trading plays a crucial role in futures transactions because *all futures contracts are traded on a margin basis*—it is the normal way of trading in this market. The margin required usually ranges from about 2 to 10 percent of the value of the contract which, when compared to the margin required for stocks and most other types of securities, is very low. Furthermore, there is *no borrowing* required on the part of

TABLE 12.1 Where the Active Futures Contracts and Futures Options Are Traded (Mid-year 1989)

	Chicago Board of Trade (CBOT)	Chicago Mercantile Exchange (MERC)	Kansas City Board of Trade (KCBT)	Mid-America Commodities Exchange (MIDAM)	Minneapolis Grain Exchange	Chicago Rice & Cotton Exchange	New York Coffee, Sugar & Cocoa Exchange (NYSCTE)	New York Cotton Exchange	New York Commodities Exchange (COMEX)	New York Futures Exchange (NYFE)	New York Mercantile Exchange (NYMERC)	Winnipeg Commods. Exchange (WPG)
● COMMODITIES												
Barley												F
Canola												F
Cattle		F, O		F								
Cocoa							F, O					
Coffee							F, O					
Copper									F, O			
Corn	F, O			F								
Cotton								F, O				
Crude Oil											F, O	
CRB Index										F		
Flaxseed												F
Gasoline											F, O	
Gold	F			F					F, O			
Heating Oil											F, O	
Hogs/Pork Bellies		F, O		F								
Lumber		F, O										
Oats	F											F
Orange Juice								F				
Palladium											F	
Platinum											F	
Propane											F	
Rice						F						
Rye												F

Silver — F, O

Soybeans — F, O

Soybean Meal, Oil — F, O

Sugar — F, O

Wheat — F, O   F, O   F   F   F   F

• FOREIGN CURRENCY CONTRACTS

Australian Dollar — F, O

British Pound — F, O   F

Canadian Dollar — F, O

W. German Mark — F, O   F

Japanese Yen — F, O   F

Swiss Franc — F, O   F

U.S. Dollar Index — F

• INTEREST RATE CONTRACTS

Eurodollars — F, O

Muni-Bond Index — F, O

U.S. T-Bills — F, O

U.S. T-Notes — F, O

U.S. T-Bonds — F, O   F   F

• STOCK INDEX CONTRACTS

Major Market — F

NYSE Composite — F, O

S&P 500 — F, O   F, O

Value Line — F

Note: F = Futures contracts; O = Options on futures.

In addition to the contracts listed in this table the International Petroleum Exchange (IPE) also trades futures contracts in Gas Oil.

TABLE 12.2   Futures Contract Dimensions

Contract	Size of a Contract*	Recent** Market Value of a Single Contract
Corn	5,000 bu	$ 13,200
Wheat	5,000 bu	20,600
Live cattle	40,000 lb	28,400
Pork bellies	40,000 lb	13,700
Coffee	37,500 lb	50,500
Cotton	50,000 lb	33,500
Gold	100 troy oz	36,400
Copper	25,000 lb	27,300
Japanese yen	12.5 million yen	88,200
Treasury bills	$1 million	918,000
Treasury bonds	$100,000	92,800
S&P 500 Stock Index	500 times the index	160,100

*The size of some contracts may vary by exchange.
**Contract values are representative of those that existed in mid-1989.

margin deposit
amount deposited with a broker to cover any loss in the market value of a futures contract that may result from adverse price movements.

initial deposit
the amount of investor capital that must be deposited with a broker at the time of a commodity transaction.

the investor to finance the balance of the contract, for the margin, or **margin deposit** as it is called with futures, exists simply as a way to guarantee fulfillment of the contract. The margin deposit is not a partial payment for the commodity or financial instrument, nor is it in any way related to the value of the product or item underlying the contract. Rather, it represents security to cover any loss in the market value of the contract that may result from adverse price movements.

The size of the required margin deposit is specified as a dollar amount and varies according to the type of contract and, in some cases, the exchange. Table 12.3 gives the margin requirements for the same 12 commodities and financial instruments listed in Table 12.2, above. In sharp contrast to the size and value of futures contracts, margin requirements are kept very low. The **initial deposit** noted in Table 12.3 specifies the amount of investor capital that must be deposited with the broker at the time the transaction is initiated and represents the amount of money required to make a given investment. After the investment is made, the market value of a contract will, of course, rise and fall as the quoted price of the underlying commodity or financial instrument goes up or down. Such market behavior will cause the

FIGURE 12.1 (Facing Page)   The Auction Market at Work on the Floor of the Chicago Board of Trade.
Traders employ a system of open outcry and hand signals to indicate whether they wish to buy or sell and the price at which they wish to buy or sell. Fingers held vertically indicate the number of contracts a trader wishes to buy or sell. Fingers held horizontally indicate the fraction of a cent above or below the last traded full cent price at which the trader will buy or sell. (*Source:* Chicago Board of Trade, *Action in the Marketplace: Commodity Futures Trading,* 1978.)

TABLE 12.3   Margin Requirements for a Sample of Commodities and Financial Futures*

	Initial Margin Deposit	Maintenance Margin Deposit
Corn	$1,000	$ 750
Wheat	1,500	1,200
Live cattle	1,500	1,200
Pork bellies	1,500	1,200
Coffee	3,500	2,600
Cotton	1,500	1,200
Gold	3,500	2,600
Copper	1,600	1,200
Japanese yen	1,800	1,400
Treasury bills	2,000	1,500
Treasury bonds	2,000	1,500
S&P 500 Stock Index	6,000	4,500

*These margin requirements were specified by a major full-service brokerage firm in mid-1989, and they may exceed the minimums established by the various exchanges. They are meant to be typical of the on-going requirements that customers are expected to live up to. Depending upon the volatility of the market, exchange-minimum margin requirements are changed frequently, and thus the requirements in this table are also subject to change on short notice.

amount of margin on deposit to change. To be sure that an adequate margin is always on hand, investors are required to meet a second type of margin requirement, the **maintenance deposit.** This deposit is slightly less than the initial deposit and establishes the minimum amount of margin that must be kept in the account at all times. For instance, if the initial deposit on a commodity is $1,000 per contract, its maintenance margin might be $750. So long as the market value of the contract does not fall by more than $250 (the difference between the contract's initial and maintenance margins), the investor has no problem. But if the market moves against the investor and the value of the contract drops by more than the allowed amount, the investor will receive a *margin call,* which means he or she must immediately deposit enough cash to bring the position back to the initial margin level. An investor's margin position is checked daily via a procedure known as **mark-to-the-market.** That is, the gain or loss in a contract's value is determined at the end of each session, at which time the broker debits or credits the trader's account accordingly. In a falling market, an investor may receive a number of margin calls and be required to make additional margin payments (perhaps on a daily basis) in order to keep the position above the maintenance margin level. Failure to do so will mean that the broker has no choice but to close out the position.

maintenance deposit
the minimum amount of margin that must be kept in a margin account at all times.

mark-to-the-market
a daily check of an investor's margin position; the gain or loss in a contract's value is determined at the end of each session, at which time the broker debits or credits the account as needed.

COMMODITIES

Physical commodities like grains, metals, wood, and meat make up a major portion of the futures market. They have been actively traded in this country for well over a

TABLE 12.4 Major Classes of Commodities

Grains and Oilseeds	Metals and Petroleum
Corn	Aluminum
Oats	Copper
Soybeans	Gold
Wheat	Platinum
Barley	Silver
Canola	Palladium
Flaxseed	Mercury
Rapeseed	Gasoline
Sorghum	Heating oil
Rye	Crude oil
Rice	Gas oil
	Propane
Livestock and Meat	
Cattle	**Food and Fiber**
Hogs and pork bellies	Cocoa
Broilers	Coffee
Turkeys	Cotton
	Orange juice
Wood	Sugar
Lumber	Eggs
Plywood	Potatoes
Stud lumber	Butter
Other	
Rubber	
Silver coins	
Gold coins	

century, and still account for a good deal of the trading activity. The material that follows focuses on *commodities trading* and begins with a review of the basic characteristics and investment merits of these vehicles.

Basic Characteristics

Various types of physical commodities are found on nearly all of the thirteen North American futures exchanges (in fact, seven of them deal only in commodities). The market for commodity contracts is divided into five major segments: grains and oilseeds, livestock and meat, food and fiber, metals and petroleum, and wood. Such segmentation does not affect trading mechanics and procedures but provides a convenient way of categorizing commodities into groups based on similar underlying characteristics. Table 12.4 shows the diversity of the commodities market and the variety of contracts available. The list seems to increase yearly, but we can see from the table that investors had more than 40 different commodities to choose from in mid-1989, and a number of these (like soybeans and wheat) are available in several different forms or grades.

A Commodities Contract

Every commodity has its own specifications regarding the amounts and quality of the product being traded. Figure 12.2 on the facing page is an excerpt from the "Commodity Futures Prices" section of *The Wall Street Journal* and shows the contract and quotation system used with commodities. Although some commodities (such as wheat and gold, for instance) are traded on more than one exchange, each commodity quote is made up of the same five parts, and all prices are quoted in an identical fashion. In particular, every commodities contract (and quote) specifies: (1) the product; (2) the exchange on which the contract is traded; (3) the size of the contract (in bushels, pounds, tons, or whatever); (4) the method of valuing the contract, or pricing unit (like cents per pound, or dollars per ton); and (5) the delivery month. Using a corn contract as an illustration, we can see each of these parts in the illustration below:

	Open	High	Low	Settle	Change	Lifetime High	Lifetime Low	Open Interest
Corn (CBT)—5,000 bu.; cents per bu.								
May	253½	253¾	252¼	252½	−1¾	286½	230½	42,796
July	258	258	256½	256¾	−1¾	288	233	60,447
Sept.	260	260½	259	259	−1½	263	236	7,760
Dec	263½	264	262½	263	−1¼	267¼	244	41,638
Mar 90	271¾	272	270¼	271	−1¼	276	254¾	11,098
May	277¼	278	276¼	277	−1	281	273¼	1,326

KEY
① the product
② the exchange
③ the size of the contract
④ the pricing unit
⑤ the delivery months

settle price
the closing price (last price of the day) for commodities and financial futures.

open interest
the number of contracts presently outstanding on a commodity or financial future.

The quotation system used for commodities is based on the size of the contract and the pricing unit. The financial media generally report the open, high, low, and closing prices for each delivery month (with commodities, the last price of the day, or the closing price, is known as the **settle price**). Also reported, at least by *The Wall Street Journal,* is the amount of **open interest** in each contract—that is, the number of contracts presently outstanding. Note in the preceding illustration that the settle price for May corn was quoted at 252½. Since the pricing system is cents per bushel, this means that the contract was being traded at $2.52½ per bushel, and that the market value of the contract was $12,625 (since each contract involves 5,000 bushels and each bushel is worth $2.52½, we have 5,000 × $2.525 = $12,625).

Price Behavior

Commodity prices react to a unique set of economic, political, and international pressures—not to mention the weather. Although the explanation of why commodity prices change is beyond the scope of this book, it should be clear that they do

FIGURE 12.2 (Facing Page) Quotations on Actively Traded Commodity Futures Contracts.

These quotes reveal at a glance key information about the various commodities, including the latest high, low and closing ("settle") prices, as well as the lifetime high and low prices for each contract. (*Source: The Wall Street Journal,* May 24, 1989.)

COMMODITY FUTURES PRICES

Open Interest Reflects Previous Trading Day.

	Open	High	Low	Settle	Change	Lifetime High	Lifetime Low	Open Interest

HOGS (CME) 30,000 lbs.; cents per lb.

	Open	High	Low	Settle	Change	Lifetime High	Lifetime Low	Open Interest
June	49.20	49.30	48.55	48.65	– .40	56.25	42.50	9,699
July	49.50	49.50	48.90	49.10	– .02	56.00	45.20	9,415
Aug	47.25	47.40	46.82	47.07	– .10	51.00	43.80	4,760
Oct	43.50	43.75	43.32	43.65	+ .20	47.00	40.80	2,864
Dec	45.50	45.65	45.42	45.52	– .07	47.25	42.52	2,430
Fb90	46.65	46.75	46.55	46.65	+ .10	47.40	43.70	811
Apr	44.40	44.45	44.30	44.45	– .05	45.10	42.77	193

Est vol 8,675; vol Mon 8,100; open int 30,221, –176.

PORK BELLIES (CME) 40,000 lbs.; cents per lb.

	Open	High	Low	Settle	Change	Lifetime High	Lifetime Low	Open Interest
May	36.65	36.65	34.15	34.32	– .47	65.50	30.47	115
July	36.00	36.50	33.80	34.80	+ .25	64.50	30.70	10,951
Aug	36.00	36.20	33.70	34.45	+ .20	58.25	30.45	10,613
Fb90	52.60	54.00	51.35	51.57	– .52	61.60	42.00	2,704

Est vol 10,963; vol Mon 7,021; open int 24,446, +114.

–FOOD & FIBER–

COCOA (CSCE)–10 metric tons; $ per ton.

	Open	High	Low	Settle	Change	Lifetime High	Lifetime Low	Open Interest
July	1,254	1,260	1,224	1,247	– 13	1,985	1,125	10,006
Sept	1,207	1,218	1,191	1,212	+ 4	1,850	1,127	10,292
Dec	1,207	1,220	1,196	1,217	+ 8	1,735	1,133	6,394
Mr90	1,205	1,216	1,189	1,211	+ 6	1,535	1,133	6,103
May	1,195	1,208	1,189	1,208	+ 13	1,465	1,138	5,634
July	1,215	1,215	1,201	1,217	+ 5	1,280	1,154	763
Sept	....	....	....	1,241	+ 6	1,280	1,180	3,023

Est vol 7,231; vol Mon9,110; open int 42,215, +479.

COFFEE (CSCE)–37,500 lbs.; cents per lb.

	Open	High	Low	Settle	Change	Lifetime High	Lifetime Low	Open Interest
July	133.25	134.90	132.75	134.61	– .74	155.25	114.00	10,642
Sept	126.75	128.75	126.55	128.75	+ .16	152.90	114.00	7,400
Dec	122.60	125.00	122.60	124.60	+ .30	149.50	114.75	4,078
Mr90	121.60	123.75	121.60	123.50	....	146.00	114.75	1,374
May	122.00	122.50	122.00	122.88	– 1.05	123.50	116.00	118

Est vol 4,171; vol Mon5,797; open int 23,624, +622.

SUGAR–WORLD (CSCE)–112,000 lbs.; cents per lb.

	Open	High	Low	Settle	Change	Lifetime High	Lifetime Low	Open Interest
July	11.77	11.83	11.53	11.54	– .17	13.40	8.10	46,744
Oct	11.65	11.71	11.45	11.46	– .07	13.30	8.45	71,237
Mr90	11.31	11.36	11.15	11.16	– .09	12.10	8.75	27,884
May	11.32	11.32	11.15	11.15	– .15	12.05	9.20	3,170
July	11.30	11.30	11.15	11.15	– .10	12.00	10.68	311

Est vol 30,528; vol Mon39,780; open int 149,363, –873.

SUGAR–DOMESTIC (CSCE)–112,000 lbs.; cents per lb.

	Open	High	Low	Settle	Change	Lifetime High	Lifetime Low	Open Interest
July	22.42	22.53	22.42	22.51	+ .10	22.60	21.80	2,015
Sept	22.47	22.50	22.47	22.51	+ .04	22.61	21.95	2,625
Nov	22.39	22.40	22.38	22.41	+ .02	22.50	21.62	2,077
Ja90	....	....	....	22.19	+ .01	22.22	21.61	470
Mar	....	....	....	22.18	+ .01	22.22	21.80	341
May	....	....	....	22.22	+ .01	22.25	21.80	508
July	....	....	....	22.26	....	22.28	21.95	176
Sept	....	....	....	22.26	....	22.28	22.10	323

Est vol 306; vol Mon95; open int 8,625, –95.

COTTON (CTN)–50,000 lbs.; cents per lb.

	Open	High	Low	Settle	Change	Lifetime High	Lifetime Low	Open Interest
July	66.90	67.20	66.59	67.10	+ .13	68.53	49.26	16,498
Oct	68.00	68.25	67.90	68.05	....	68.90	50.35	6,274
Dec	68.32	68.74	68.30	68.42	– .11	69.38	50.75	16,460
Mr90	68.80	69.10	68.80	68.93	+ .06	69.70	53.60	2,103
May	69.10	69.60	69.10	69.33	+ .03	69.75	59.75	1,155

Est vol 6,500; vol Mon 5,629; open int 42,653, +150.

ORANGE JUICE (CTN)–15,000 lbs.; cents per lb.

	Open	High	Low	Settle	Change	Lifetime High	Lifetime Low	Open Interest
July	185.75	186.50	182.75	183.00	– 2.50	195.00	132.00	4,156
Sept	180.75	182.25	178.50	178.50	– 2.00	187.75	132.00	2,483
Nov	171.50	172.00	168.50	168.75	– 1.25	176.75	129.00	961
Ja90	166.00	166.25	164.60	164.60	– .40	173.00	127.50	645
Mar	165.00	165.00	163.55	163.55	– .85	171.30	127.75	285

Est vol 1,500; vol Mon 2,773; open int 8,829, +100.

–METALS & PETROLEUM–

COPPER-STANDARD (CMX)–25,000 lbs.; cents per lb.

	Open	High	Low	Settle	Change	Lifetime High	Lifetime Low	Open Interest
May	111.00	112.00	109.00	109.30	– 2.05	146.00	73.15	964
June	....	....	....	110.00	– 2.25	137.70	115.50	123
July	112.00	113.00	109.00	110.60	– 1.95	138.50	76.00	20,279
Sept	111.90	112.50	109.00	109.80	– 2.45	131.50	76.00	5,689
Dec	111.00	111.00	108.50	109.60	– 1.65	126.00	77.45	2,787

Est vol 7,000; vol Mon 10,814; open int 29,842, –462.

GOLD (CMX)–100 troy oz.; $ per troy oz.

	Open	High	Low	Settle	Change	Lifetime High	Lifetime Low	Open Interest
May	....	....	....	363.80	+ .60	384.20	369.50	21
June	365.50	367.50	363.80	364.30	+ .60	570.00	360.60	54,552
Aug	369.00	370.50	367.00	367.20	+ .50	575.00	363.80	35,339
Oct	372.00	373.80	370.90	370.80	+ .50	575.50	367.70	6,512
Dec	375.50	377.50	374.10	374.40	+ .50	514.50	371.00	31,351
Fb90	379.50	379.50	378.10	378.00	+ .50	516.00	375.50	7,987
Apr	383.80	384.50	382.50	381.80	+ .60	525.80	379.00	10,567
June	365.50	389.50	385.50	385.70	+ .70	497.00	382.00	10,987
Aug	391.40	391.40	389.50	389.60	+ .80	487.00	389.50	6,690
Oct	....	....	....	393.60	+ .90	472.00	400.50	2,420
Dec	401.00	401.00	401.00	397.70	+ 1.00	455.00	395.50	7,050
Fb91	404.00	404.00	402.00	401.80	+ 1.10	450.00	397.50	8,444

Est vol 50,000; vol Mon 52,224; open int 181,920, –2,696.

PALLADIUM (NYM) 100 troy oz.; $ per troy oz.

	Open	High	Low	Settle	Change	Lifetime High	Lifetime Low	Open Interest
May	....	....	....	151.45	+ 2.45	163.00	153.50	5
June	150.00	151.25	148.50	149.45	+ .95	184.00	114.00	3,306
Sept	148.75	150.50	147.25	148.65	+ 1.50	180.00	119.00	2,492
Dec	146.00	149.00	146.00	147.15	+ 1.90	177.50	122.25	2,058
Mr90	144.00	147.00	144.00	144.65	+ 1.90	176.00	123.00	721
June	143.00	144.00	143.00	142.65	+ 1.90	175.00	140.75	233

Est vol 1,900; vol Mon 719; open int 8,815, –184.

SILVER (CMX)–5,000 troy oz.; cents per troy oz.

	Open	High	Low	Settle	Change	Lifetime High	Lifetime Low	Open Interest
May	525.0	527.0	525.0	517.3	+ 6.7	965.0	506.0	64
June	....	....	....	518.1	+ 6.7	589.0	525.0	207
July	523.5	535.0	522.0	523.2	+ 6.7	985.0	512.0	49,765
Sept	533.0	545.0	530.0	532.2	+ 6.8	861.0	522.0	11,239
Dec	543.5	558.0	543.0	544.7	+ 6.9	886.0	532.0	13,254
Mr90	561.0	568.5	555.0	557.1	+ 7.0	910.0	547.5	8,136
May	575.0	575.0	567.0	565.7	+ 7.0	910.0	558.0	3,944
July	576.0	583.0	575.0	574.5	+ 7.0	761.5	566.0	2,489
Sept	....	....	....	583.6	+ 7.0	760.0	602.0	780
Dec	....	....	....	596.1	+ 7.0	742.0	582.0	694
Mr91	....	....	....	609.1	+ 7.0	665.0	603.0	333

Est vol 23,000; vol Mon 17,706; open int 90,922, –1,402.

SILVER (CBT)–1,000 troy oz.; cents per troy oz.

	Open	High	Low	Settle	Change	Lifetime High	Lifetime Low	Open Interest
May	527.0	527.0	516.0	516.0	+ 5.0	628.0	510.0	12
June	517.0	530.0	516.0	517.0	+ 5.0	865.0	507.0	3,815
Aug	527.0	538.0	526.5	526.5	+ 3.5	700.0	517.0	1,695
Oct	539.0	548.0	536.0	536.0	+ 5.0	716.0	526.0	159
Dec	544.0	559.0	544.0	546.0	+ 6.0	735.0	535.0	3,853
Fb90	560.0	565.0	555.0	555.5	+ 5.5	694.0	545.0	103

Est vol 1,000; vol Mon 2,996; open int 9,784, +243.

CRUDE OIL, Light Sweet (NYM) 1,000 bbls.; $ per bbl.

	Open	High	Low	Settle	Change	Lifetime High	Lifetime Low	Open Interest
July	18.84	19.30	18.73	19.04	+ .43	20.50	12.65	85,761
Aug	17.98	18.38	17.94	18.16	+ .33	19.63	12.60	50,762
Sept	17.60	17.90	17.57	17.71	+ .23	19.28	12.68	23,139
Oct	17.45	17.63	17.35	17.46	+ .19	18.93	12.75	16,682
Nov	17.30	17.47	17.21	17.28	+ .17	18.67	15.00	12,981
Dec	17.17	17.30	17.10	17.13	+ .15	18.50	12.87	13,116
Ja90	17.00	17.20	17.00	16.98	+ .13	18.10	15.67	6,331
Feb	16.97	17.01	16.92	16.86	+ .12	17.95	15.74	3,938
Mar	16.87	16.93	16.85	16.76	+ .12	17.80	16.10	2,766
Apr	16.77	16.83	16.77	16.67	+ .12	17.65	16.70	624
May	16.70	16.85	16.70	16.58	+ .11	18.17	16.25	1,016
June	16.65	16.65	16.65	16.51	+ .11	17.20	16.60	185

Est vol 98,032; vol Mon 109,312; open int 226,902, –5,206.

HEATING OIL NO. 2 (NYM) 42,000 gal.; $ per gal.

	Open	High	Low	Settle	Change	Lifetime High	Lifetime Low	Open Interest
June	.4740	.4770	.4690	.4750	+ .0052	.5475	.3465	7,622
July	.4590	.4620	.4525	.4570	+ .0005	.5380	.4540	17,984
Aug	.4610	.4660	.4570	.4604	+ .0008	.5400	.3545	10,141
Sept	.4705	.4730	.4660	.4674	+ .0008	.5450	.3640	5,072
Oct	.4760	.4790	.4740	.4744	+ .0008	.5490	.3720	2,127
Nov	.4835	.4875	.4800	.4814	+ .0008	.5550	.3800	2,958
Dec	.4920	.4940	.4885	.4884	+ .0008	.5605	.3785	2,257
Ja90	.4930	.4985	.4905	.4909	+ .0008	.5300	.4660	213

Est vol 23,496; vol Mon 13,250; open int 48,504, +152.

GASOLINE, Unleaded (NYM) 42,000 gal.; $ per gal.

	Open	High	Low	Settle	Change	Lifetime High	Lifetime Low	Open Interest
June	.6430	.6460	.6350	.6424	+ .0034	.7325	.3850	12,160
July	.6115	.6185	.6070	.6135	+ .0052	.6915	.4050	21,705
Aug	.5850	.5920	.5810	.5878	+ .0041	.6510	.4020	18,932
Sept	.5580	.5640	.5550	.5591	+ .0041	.6150	.4000	8,776
Oct	.5205	.5285	.5200	.5237	+ .0067	.5800	.4380	2,955
Nov	.4950	.5040	.4950	.4977	+ .0077	.5550	.4125	2,455
Dec	.4780	.4830	.4780	.4797	+ .0077	.5390	.4675	1,827

Est vol 21,941; vol Mon 19,872; open int 68,833, –201.

GAS OIL (IPE) 100 metric tons; $ per ton

	Open	High	Low	Settle	Change	Lifetime High	Lifetime Low	Open Interest
June	141.00	141.75	140.25	140.75	+ .50	158.25	112.75	19,811
July	138.50	140.00	138.50	138.75	+ .50	158.25	110.75	15,394
Aug	138.75	140.00	138.75	139.00	+ .50	159.00	110.75	50,766
Sept	139.25	140.75	139.00	139.50	+ .50	165.00	136.50	1,414
Oct	141.25	141.75	141.00	141.00	+ .50	168.00	138.00	1,042
Nov	142.50	143.00	141.50	141.50	+ .75	168.00	137.00	1,357
Dec	143.00	143.75	142.00	142.00	– .50	169.00	142.00	1,183

Actual Tues; vol 6,119; open int 45,284, +3,131.

–WOOD–

LUMBER (CME)–150,000 bd. ft.; $ per 1,000 bd. ft.

	Open	High	Low	Settle	Change	Lifetime High	Lifetime Low	Open Interest
July	180.00	181.20	179.50	180.50	– .40	196.00	175.00	3,266
Sept	183.00	183.70	182.20	182.80	– .70	194.70	175.10	1,345
Nov	181.00	181.00	180.00	180.50	– .60	190.60	176.30	1,442
Ja90	185.00	186.00	185.00	185.90	– .60	192.00	181.20	194
Mar	188.70	189.10	188.00	188.90	– .10	192.40	185.00	166
May	192.00	192.00	191.00	191.50	+ .20	193.50	188.00	553

Est vol 1,084; vol Mon 782; open int 7,031, –44.

move up and down just like any other investment vehicle—which is precisely what speculators want. However, because we are dealing in such large trading units (like 5,000 bushels of this or 40,000 pounds of that), even a rather modest price change can have an enormous impact on the market value of a contract, and therefore on investor returns or losses. For example, if the price of corn goes up or down by just 20 cents per bushel, the value of a single contract will change by $1,000. Since a corn contract can be bought with a $1,000 initial margin deposit, it is easy to see the effect this kind of price behavior can have on investor return. But do commodity prices really move all that much? Judge for yourself. If we examine the price change columns in Figure 12.2, we can uncover some excellent examples of sizable price changes that occur from one day to the next. Note, for example, that July orange juice contracts fell $375, September copper dropped $612, and July crude oil rose $430. Now, keep in mind that these are *daily* price swings that occurred on *single* contracts. By themselves, such changes are, indeed, sizable; but when you look at them relative to the (very small) original investment required, they add up to serious returns (or losses) in a hurry! And they occur not because the underlying prices are so volatile, but because of the sheer magnitude of the commodities contracts themselves.

Clearly, such price behavior is one of the magnets that draws investors to commodities. The exchanges recognize the volatile nature of commodities contracts and try to put lids on price fluctuations by imposing daily price limits and maximum daily price ranges (similar limits are also put on financial futures). The **daily price limit** restricts the interday change in the price of the underlying commodity; for example, the price of corn can change by no more than 10 cents per bushel from one day to the next, and the daily limit on copper is 3 cents per pound. Such limits, however, still leave plenty of room to turn a quick profit. For example, the daily limits on corn and copper translate into per day changes of $500 for one corn contract and $750 for a copper contract. The **maximum daily price range,** in contrast, limits the amount the price can change *during* the day and is usually equal to twice the daily limit restrictions. For example, the daily price limit on corn can be 10 cents per bushel and its maximum daily range 20 cents per bushel.

daily price limit
restriction on the day-to-day change in the price of an underlying commodity.

maximum daily price range
the amount a commodity price can change during a day; usually equal to twice the daily price limit.

 ## *Holding Period Return*

Futures contracts have only one source of return: the capital gains that can be earned when prices move in a favorable direction. There is no current income of any kind. The volatile price behavior of futures contracts is one reason high returns are possible with commodities; the other is leverage. That is, the fact that all futures trading is done on margin means that it takes only a small amount of money to control a large investment position and to participate in the large price swings that accompany many futures contracts. Of course, the use of leverage also means that it is possible to be wiped out with just one or two bad days.

return on invested capital
return to investors based on the amount of money actually invested in a security, rather than the value of the contract itself.

Investment return can be measured by calculating **return on invested capital.** This is simply a variation of the standard holding period return formula that bases return to investors on *the amount of money actually invested in the contract* rather than on the value of the contract itself; it is used because of the generous amount of

leverage (margin) used in commodities trading. The return on invested capital for a commodities position can be determined according to the following simple formula:

$$\text{return on invested capital} = \frac{\begin{array}{c}\text{selling price of} \\ \text{commodity contract}\end{array} - \begin{array}{c}\text{purchase price of} \\ \text{commodity contract}\end{array}}{\text{amount of margin deposit}}$$

This formula can be used for both long and short transactions. To see how it works, assume you bought two September corn contracts at 245 ($2.45 per bushel) by depositing the required initial margin of $2,000 (or $1,000 for each contract). Your investment amounts to only $2,000, even though you control 10,000 bushels of corn worth $24,500 at the time they were purchased. Now assume September corn has just closed at 259, so you decide to sell out and take your profit. Your return on invested capital would be as follows:

$$\text{return on invested capital} = \frac{\$25,900 - \$24,500}{\$2,000}$$

$$= \frac{\$1,400}{\$2,000} = \underline{\underline{70.0\%}}$$

Clearly this high rate of return was due not only to an increase in the price of the commodity, but also, and perhaps more important, to the fact that you were using very low margin. (The initial margin in this particular transaction equaled about 6 percent of the underlying value of the contract).

Trading Commodities

Investing in commodities takes one of three forms. The first is *speculating,* which is popular with investors who use commodities as a way to generate capital gains. In essence, they try to capitalize on the wide price swings that are characteristic of so many commodities. Figure 12.3 provides the Commodity Research Bureau's (CRB) composite index of futures prices over the six-year period from mid-1982 through mid-1988, and graphically illustrates the volatile behavior of commodity prices. Although such price movements may be appealing to speculators, they can frighten a lot of other investors. Some of these more cautious investors turn to *spreading,* the second form of commodities investing; they use sophisticated trading techniques intended to capture the benefits of volatile prices but at the same time limit their exposure to loss. Finally, producers and processors use various *hedging* strategies as a way to protect their interests in the underlying commodities. We will briefly examine each of these trading tactics not only to see what they are, but also to gain a better understanding of the various ways commodities can be used as investment vehicles.

Speculating

Speculators are in the market for one reason: They expect the price of a commodity to go up or down, and they hope to capitalize on it by going long or short. To see why a speculator would go long when prices are expected to rise, consider an

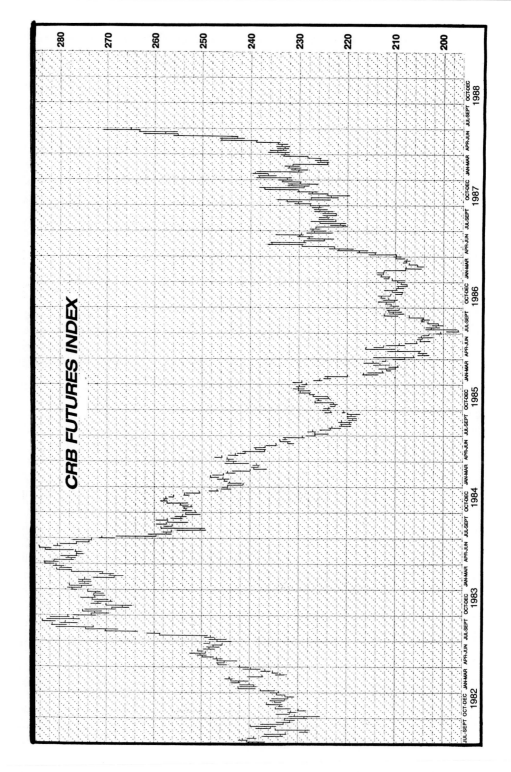

individual who buys a February silver contract at 533½ by depositing the required initial margin of $1,000. Since one silver contract involves 5,000 troy ounces, it has a market value of $26,675. If silver goes up, the investor makes money. Assume it does, and that by January (one month before the contract expires) the price of the contract rises to 552. The speculator then liquidates and makes a profit of 18½ cents per ounce (552 − 533½). That means $925 profit from an investment of just $1,000—which translates into a return on invested capital of 92.5 percent. Of course, instead of rising, the price of silver could have dropped by 18½ cents per ounce. In this case, our investor would have lost just about all of his original investment ($1,000 − $925 leaves only $75, out of which would have to come a round trip commission of $60 or $70). But to the short seller, the drop in price would be just what she was after, for she could profit from such a turn of events. Here's how: She sells (shorts) the February silver at 533½ and buys it back sometime later at 515. Clearly, the difference between her selling price and purchase price is the same 18½ cents, but in this case it is *profit,* since the selling price exceeds the purchase price (see Chapter 2 for a review of short selling).

Spreading

Instead of attempting to speculate on the price behavior of a futures contract, an investor might choose to follow a more conservative tactic, by using a strategy known as spreading. (The principles of spreading futures contracts are much the same as we discussed with put and call options.) The idea is to combine two or more different contracts into one investment position that offers the potential for generating a modest amount of profit while restricting exposure to loss. One very important reason for spreading in the commodities market is that unlike stock options, *there is no limit to the amount of loss that can occur with a futures contract.* An investor will set up a spread by buying one contract and simultaneously selling another. Although one side of the transaction will lead to a loss, the investor obviously hopes that the profit earned from the other side will be more than enough compensation and that the net result will be at least a modest amount of profit. If the investor is wrong, the spread will serve to limit (but not eliminate) any losses.

Here is a simplified version of how a spread might work: Suppose we buy contract A at 533½ and at the same time short sell contract B for 575½. Sometime later we close out our interest in contract A by selling it at 542 and simultaneously cover our short position in B by purchasing a contract at 579. Although we made a profit of 8½ points on the long position, contract A (542 − 533½), we lost 3½ points on the contract that we shorted, B (575½ − 579). The net effect, however, is a profit of 5 points, which, if we were dealing in cents per pound, would mean a profit of $250 on a 5,000-pound contract. All sorts of commodity spreads can be set

---

FIGURE 12.3 (Facing Page) **The Behavior of Commodity Prices over Time (1982–88).**
This graph shows the volatile nature of commodity prices and underscores the need for investor knowhow when dealing in commodities. (*Source:* Courtesy of *Commodity Price Charts,* 219 Parkade, Cedar Falls, IA 50613.)

up for almost any type of investment situation, but most are highly sophisticated and require specialized skills.

Hedging

A hedge is a "technical" approach to commodity trading used by producers and processors to protect a position in a product or commodity. For example, a producer or grower would use a commodity hedge to obtain as *high* a price for the goods he sells as possible; the processor or manufacturer who uses the commodity, however, would employ a hedge to obtain the goods at as *low* a price as possible. A successful hedge, in effect, means added income to producers and lower costs to processors. An example will show how hedging works and why it is done. Suppose a manufacturer uses platinum as a basic raw material in the production of catalytic converters. It is early in the year and platinum is selling for $480 per ounce, but it is expected to shoot up in price and be much more expensive by the end of the year. To protect against future price increases, our manufacturer decides to buy a platinum futures contract, now trading at $505 an ounce. Assume that eight months later, the price of platinum has indeed gone up (to $580 per ounce) but so has the price of the futures contract, which is now trading at $625 an ounce. The manufacturer has made $120 per ounce on the 50-ounce futures contract and is $6,000 ahead on the transaction—a gain that will be used to offset the increase in the cost of platinum. As it turns out, the gain on the futures contract is $1,000 more than the increased cost of 50 ounces of platinum on the open market, since the cost of platinum rose by only $100 per ounce and the cost of 50 ounces of platinum went up by only $5,000. This was a successful hedge for the manufacturer because it kept the cost of this raw material in check, at least for the time being. (Technically, the manufacturer could take delivery of the contracted platinum—at an *effective* cost of $505 per ounce, the price at which the futures contract was purchased—but that is unlikely in this case, since the manufacturer would have to forgo the $1,000 profit in order to do so.)

Commodities and the Individual Investor

For the most part individuals use commodities in one of two ways: for speculation and/or spreading. Commodities appeal to investors because of the high rates of return they offer and their ability to act as inflation hedges during periods of rapidly rising consumer prices. When sustained high rates of inflation become a problem, traditional investment outlets just do not seem to be able to provide the type of return necessary to keep investors ahead of the game. That is, it seems that more often than not, in periods of high inflation, investors lose more in purchasing power than they gain from after-tax returns. Under such circumstances, investors can be expected to seek outlets that provide better protection against inflation, all of which explains why the interest in commodities tends to pick up with inflation.

Commodities can play an important role in a portfolio so long as *the investor understands the risks involved and is well versed in the principles and mechanics of commodities trading*. The fact is, however, that over the long run the average return to commodities investors is *negative*. As such, it should be clear that the quickest

way to lose money in commodities is to jump in without knowing what you are doing. Because there is the potential for a lot of price volatility and because commodity trading is done on a very low margin, the potential for loss is enormous. Accordingly, most experts recommend that only a portion of an individual's investment capital be committed to commodities. The specific amount would, of course, be a function of investor aversion to risk and the amount of resources available. An investor has to be prepared mentally and should be in a position financially to absorb losses—perhaps a number of them. Not only should an adequate cash reserve be kept on hand (to absorb losses and/or meet margin calls), but it is also a good idea to maintain a diversified holding of commodities in order to spread your risks.

Individuals can invest directly in the commodities market, or they can buy put and call *options* on a number of the actively traded futures contracts; alternatively, they can buy *commodities mutual funds,* or they can invest in limited-partnership *commodity pools.* The latter two approaches might be used by individuals who wish to invest in the commodities market but who lack the time and/or expertise to manage their own investments. But remember that although these approaches offer professional management, they by no means guarantee a profit; instead, they only reduce some of the more obvious risks of commodity investing.

FINANCIAL FUTURES

Another dimension of the futures market is **financial futures,** a segment of the market where futures contracts are traded on a variety of financial instruments. Actually, financial futures are little more than an extension of the commodities concept. They were created for much the same reason as commodity futures; they are traded in the same market; their prices behave much like commodities; and they have similar investment merits. Yet, in spite of all these similarities, financial futures are a unique type of investment vehicle. Let's look more closely at these instruments and how they can be used.

The Market

financial futures
a type of futures contract where the underlying "commodity" consists of a certain amount of some type of financial asset, such as debt securities, foreign currencies, or market baskets of common stocks.

Even though the financial futures market has existed for only a little more than 15 years, it is today a dominant force in the whole futures market, and has reached a level of trading that surpasses the traditional commodities market. Indeed, as Figure 12.4 discloses, not only is the best-selling futures contract a financial future (the Chicago Board of Trade's U.S. Treasury bond contract), but 7 of the 12 most actively traded contracts are financial futures. Much of this activity is due, of course, to hedgers and big institutional investors who use financial futures as portfolio- and debt-management tools. But there are still plenty of opportunities here for individual investors. For example, financial futures offer still another way to speculate on the behavior of interest rates; or they can be used by investors who wish to speculate in the stock market. They even offer a convenient way to speculate in the highly specialized, and often highly profitable, foreign currency markets.

The financial futures market was established in response to the economic turmoil the United States had been experiencing during the 1970s. The dollar had become

Rank	Contract	Number of Contracts Traded
1	• Treasury bonds (CBT)	66,841,474
2	• Eurodollar (IMM)	20,416,216
3	• S&P 500 (IOM)	19,044,673
4	Crude oil (NYMEX)	14,581,614
5	Gold (COMEX)	10,239,805
6	Soybeans (CBT)	7,378,760
7	Corn (CBT)	7,253,212
8	• Deutsche mark (IMM)	6,037,048
9	• Japanese yen (IMM)	5,358,556
10	• Swiss franc (IMM)	5,268,276
11	• Treasury notes (CBT)	5,253,791
12	Live cattle (CME)	5,229,294

• Denotes a financial futures contract.

FIGURE 12.4   The Top Dozen: The 12 Most Actively Traded Futures Contracts in 1987.
The major role played by financial futures is readily evident in this exhibit, which shows that seven of the twelve most actively traded contracts were financial futures. Equally impressive is the fact that these seven financial futures accounted for fully 75 percent of the total trading volume generated by the top dozen contracts. (*Source:* ''1987 Volume Is a Record High,'' *Futures,* March 1988, p. 38.)

unstable on the world market and was causing serious problems for multinational firms; closer to home, interest rates had begun to behave in a volatile manner, which caused severe difficulties for corporate treasurers, financial institutions, and money managers in general. All these parties needed a way to protect themselves from the ravages of wide fluctuations in the value of the dollar and interest rates, and so a market for financial futures was born. Hedging provided the economic rationale for the market in financial futures, but speculators were quick to respond as they found the price volatility of these instruments attractive and, at times, highly profitable. At the present time, financial futures are traded on six exchanges: the New York Futures Exchange (NYFE), the Kansas City Board of Trade, the MidAmerica Commodity Exchange, the New York Cotton Exchange (through it's FINEX subsidiary), the Chicago Board of Trade, and the Chicago Merchantile Exchange (including a subsidiary of the CME set up to trade foreign currencies, the International Monetary Market). The three basic types of financial futures include foreign currencies, debt securities, and stock indexes.

Foreign Currencies, Interest Rates, and Stocks

currency futures
futures contracts on foreign currencies, traded much like commodities.

The financial futures market started rather inconspicuously in May 1972 with the listing of a handful of foreign currency contracts. Known as **currency futures,** they have become a major hedging vehicle as international trade (to and from this country) has mushroomed; most of the currency trading today is conducted in the following six foreign currencies:

- British pound
- West German mark
- Swiss franc
- Canadian dollar
- Japanese yen
- Australian dollar

interest rate futures
futures contracts on debt securities, traded much like commodities.

All these currencies involve countries with which the United States has strong international trade and exchange ties. A few years later, in October 1975, the first futures contract on debt securities, or **interest rate futures** as they are more commonly known, was established when trading started in GNMA pass-through certificates (a special type of mortgage-backed bond issued by an agency of the U.S. government). In time, other types of issues were added, so that today trading is carried out in the following kinds of debt securities and interest rates:

- U.S. Treasury bills
- 30-day interest rates
- 90-day Eurodollar deposits
- U.S. Treasury notes
- U.S. Treasury bonds

All of these futures contracts, except the Eurodollar deposits, are based on *domestic* securities. Eurodollar deposits are dollars deposited in interest-bearing accounts in banks outside the United States. Interest rate futures were immediately successful, and their popularity has grown rapidly.

stock index futures
futures contracts written on broad based measures of stock market performance like the S&P 500 Stock Index; traded much like commodities, allowing investors to participate in the general movements of the stock market.

Finally, in February 1982, a new trading vehicle was introduced: the stock index futures contract. **Stock index futures**, as they are called, are contracts pegged to broad-based measures of stock market performance. At the present time, trading is done in just four stock index futures:

- S&P 500 Stock Index
- NYSE Composite Stock Index
- Value Line Composite Stock Index
- Major Market Index

Stock index futures—which are similar to the index options discussed in the preceding chapter—allow investors to participate in the general movements of the entire stock market. These index futures (and other futures contracts) represent a type of *derivative security*, to the extent that they, like options, derive their value from the price behavior of the assets that underlie them. In the case of stock index futures, they are supposed to reflect the general performance of the stock market as a whole, as measured by a particular index like the S&P 500. Thus, when the market, as measured by the S&P 500 goes up, the value of an S&P 500 futures contract should go up as well. Such behavior enables investors to use stock index futures as a way to buy the market—or a reasonable proxy thereof—and thereby participate in broad

INVESTOR INSIGHTS

A Primer on Program Trading

In the postmortems of the October 1987 stock-market Crash, one of the chief villains consistently fingered was *program trading*. And, not surprisingly, for some time after that debacle this trading technique fell into relative disuse. But recently, program trading has returned with a bang and is again causing sharp intraday swings in stock prices. So, that makes this a good time to take another look at program trading, what it is and how it came to be Wall Street's nemesis.

Program trading originated as a means for brokerage firms to buy or sell large baskets of stock for institutions without drastically disturbing share prices. But in April 1982, the introduction of a futures contract linked to the Standard & Poor's 500-stock index created the opportunity for *index arbitrage*, the exploitation of minute differences between the price of the futures and the price of the underlying stocks. . . . Normally, the value of the stock-index futures closely tracks changes in the prices of the underlying shares, but sometimes strays by a few points. *Users of index arbitrage build computer models to monitor both the price of the futures and the related stocks.* If the price difference widens enough, the programs call for automatic placement of orders to sell the more expensive item and buy the cheaper one. By buying or selling *hundreds of thousands* of shares of stock simultaneously, index arbitrage can wring a substantial profit from even the smallest price difference.

Each user of index arbitrage employs his own formula to determine the appropriate spread, or fair value, of futures prices above or below the cash value of the stock portfolio. Calculating fair value, in turn, involves expectations of the direction of the market and the economy, the desired yield of the trading strategy, current interest rates, and the structure of the stock portfolio, including whether stock must be borrowed to execute the trades. Jack Barbanel, a futures expert at Gruntal & Co., says that index arbitrageurs usually seek to capture a yield 1%-1.5% above the Treasury-bill rate.

For example, not long ago, the S&P 500 index closed at 308.69 and the June futures contract closed at 311.40, or a premium of 271 basis points to the cash index (each basis point is one-hundredth of an index point). The next day, the futures trading department at Donaldson Lufkin & Jenrette reckoned that the fair value of the June futures contract was 208 basis points over cash, using a 9.7% interest rate to determine financing costs. Donaldson also figured that buy programs could be triggered if the futures' premium to the cash index rose to 290 basis points, while sell programs could be triggered if the premium fell to 110 basis points.

---

program trading
computer-assisted trading whereby brokerage houses and institutional investors simultaneously buy and sell large quantities of common stocks and stock index futures contracts.

market moves. As explained in the Investor Insights box above, stock index futures contracts are widely used in **program trading**—a kind of computer-assisted trading strategy whereby brokerage houses and institutional investors will simultaneously buy and sell *large* quantities of common stocks and stocks index futures contracts. This particular type of a program trade is known as an *index arbitrage* and has come under a lot of fire because it's felt that such trading leads to wide (and largely unjustified) swings in stock prices. Indeed, some would argue that we've reached

When those buy or sell levels are reached and program trading begins, *the huge order flow can heavily influence the stock market's direction*, at least temporarily. Recent sessions have produced steep hikes and falls in share prices as programmed trades hit the [stock] market. Critics contend that program trading creates opportunities for abuse. For example, non-program traders, knowing the degree to which programs can affect stock prices, may buy stock or liquidate their positions when they see the programs start to run.

In the wake of the Crash, the New York Stock Exchange began requiring member firms to stop using its high-speed order-delivery system for program trades when the DJIA moves 50 points in either direction. But program trading continued, and in the spring of 1988 the market often approached the 50-point barrier but stopped just short of crossing it. In May [1988], responding to an outcry from individual investors and institutions that don't use program trading, the largest brokerage firms using index arbitrage, including Morgan Stanley, Salomon Brothers and Bear Stearns, stopped executing the trades for their own accounts, although some continued to place customers' orders.

Wide disagreement exists on the result of those actions. Supporters of program trading claim that manually executed programs from the large institutions kept program trading at high levels without causing another crash. But trading volatility did in fact slow, and by last summer the markets had calmed to the point that the Big Board claimed the 50-point collar was no longer needed. It instead adopted a plan to shut down for one hour if the Dow Industrials moved 250 points in a single session and for an additional two hours if the move reached 400 points. Trading in the related futures contracts also would be halted. In February [1989], the same firms that had so nobly washed their hands of index arbitrage resumed the practice, led by an announcement from Morgan Stanley. Program trading levels began to rise.

Average daily volume for program trades in March (1989) on the NYSE came to 17.7 million shares, the biggest total since records started being kept last July, and the activity in April showed scant signs of slowing. On April 18, the 41-point gain in the Dow Industrials was provided added impetus by program trading; the rally was kicked off by favorable inflation news. On April 21, *40 million shares traded hands in the final half hour of trading, and the Dow jumped 20 points in the closing minutes.* And Thursday, traders said program trading caused as much as 20 points of a nearly 30-point rally in the Dow average. Just the kind of action that suggests the program traders are back in full force.

Source: Adapted from Edward A. Wyatt, "Program Trading: Gosh, Here It Comes Again," *Barron's*, May 1, 1989, p. 58.

the point where, on far too many occasions, it's the futures contracts that are driving stock prices, rather than the other way around. (Note that in addition to stock market indexes, there are several other types of index-based futures contracts available. For example, there's a futures contract available on an index of *municipal bonds;* another on an index that measures the value of the *U.S. dollar* against 8 key foreign currencies; and even one based on an index of 27 *commodities* futures contracts!)

Contract Specifications

In principle, financial futures contracts are like the commodities contracts that we examined above. They control large sums of the underlying financial instrument and are issued with a variety of delivery months. All this can be seen in Figure 12.5, which lists quotes for several foreign currency, interest rate, and stock index futures contracts. Looking first at currency futures, we see that the contracts entitle the holders to a certain position in a specified foreign currency; in effect, the owner of a currency future holds a claim on a certain amount of foreign money. The precise amount ranges from 62,500 British pounds to 12.5 million Japanese yen. In a similar fashion, holders of interest rate futures have a claim on a certain amount of the underlying debt security. This claim is also quite large, as it amounts to $100,000 worth of Treasury notes and bonds, $1 million worth of Eurodollar deposits and Treasury bills, and $5 million in 30-day bank deposits.

Stock index futures, however, are a bit different, as the seller of one of these contracts is *not* obligated to deliver the *underlying stocks* at expiration date. Instead, ultimate delivery is in the form of cash (which is fortunate, since it would indeed be a task to make delivery of the 1,700 stocks that make up the Value Line Index, or the 500 issues in the S&P index). The commodity underlying stock index futures, therefore, is *cash*; with a few exceptions (like the Major Market Index), the amount of underlying cash is set at 500 times the value of the stock index. For example, if the Value Line Index stood at 320, the amount of cash underlying a single Value Line stock index futures contract would be $500 × 320 = $160,000. Again, the value is substantial. In terms of delivery months, the lives of financial futures contracts run from about 18 months or less for stock index and currency futures to about 3 years or less for interest rate instruments.

Prices and Profits

All currency futures are quoted in dollars or cents per unit of the underlying foreign currency (for instance, in dollars per British pound or cents per Japanese yen). Thus, according to the closing ("settle") prices in Figure 12.5, one December British pound contract was worth $95,800 (62,500 pounds × $1.5328) and a December Japanese yen was valued at $89,875 (since a quote of .7190 cents per yen amounts to less than a cent, we have 12,500,000 yen × $0.007190). Except for the quotes on Treasury bills and other short-term securities, which will be examined below, interest rate futures contracts are priced as a percentage of the par value of the underlying debt instrument (either Treasury notes or Treasury bonds). Since these instruments are quoted in increments of 1/32 of 1 percent, a quote of 92–27 for the settle price on the June Treasury bonds (in Figure 12.5) translates into 92 27/32—which, when you divide 27 by 32, converts finally into a quote of 92.84375 percent of par. Applying this rate to the par value of the underlying securities, we see that a June Treasury bond contract is worth $92,843.75 (i.e., $100,000 × 0.9284375). Stock index futures are quoted in terms of the actual underlying index, but, as noted above, most carry a face value of $500 times the index.

CURRENCY FUTURES

JAPANESE YEN (IMM) 12.5 million yen; $ per yen (.00)

	Open	High	Low	Settle	Change	Lifetime High	Low	Open Interest
June	.7093	.7100	.7046	.7052	− .0018	.8485	.7046	68,966
Sept	.7162	.7172	.7118	.7123	− .0020	.8580	.7118	4,773
Dec	.7220	.7235	.7182	.7190	− .0023	.8635	.7182	741
Mr90	.7285	.7295	.7264	.7254	− .0026	.8357	.7264	188

Est vol 40,365; vol Mon 43,848; open int 74,668, +1,721.

W. GERMAN MARK (IMM) − 125,000 marks; $ per mark

	Open	High	Low	Settle	Change	Lifetime High	Low	Open Interest
June	.4996	.5018	.4973	.4983	....	.5975	.4973	70,230
Sept	.5022	.5042	.4998	.5006	....	.5977	.4998	6,260
Dec	.5045	.5065	.5025	.5028	− .0002	.5895	.5023	780

Est vol 41,111; vol Mon 44,386; open int 77,270, +5,149.

CANADIAN DOLLAR (IMM) − 100,000 dlrs.; $ per Can $

	Open	High	Low	Settle	Change	Lifetime High	Low	Open Interest
June	.8334	.8337	.8308	.8313	+ .0006	.8440	.7670	19,965
Sept	.8285	.8290	.8262	.8267	+ .0004	.8396	.7990	2,310
Dec	.8245	.8252	.8228	.8228	+ .0002	.8370	.7920	679
Mr90	.8193	.8193	.8193	.8193	....	.8322	.7890	100
June	....	....	....	.8161	− .0002	.8272	.8193	554

Est vol 7,727; vol Mon 8,118; open int 23,608, +328.

BRITISH POUND (IMM) − 62,500 pds.; $ per pound

	Open	High	Low	Settle	Change	Lifetime High	Low	Open Interest
June	1.5782	1.5806	1.5570	1.5608	− .0120	1.8370	1.5570	24,750
Sept	1.5636	1.5660	1.5410	1.5458	− .0124	1.8030	1.5410	1,609
Dec	1.5490	1.5500	1.5250	1.5328	− .0130	1.7450	1.5250	186
June	1.5150	1.5270	1.5090	1.5088	− .0130	1.6950	1.5090	151

INTEREST RATE FUTURES

TREASURY BONDS (CBT) − $100,000; pts. 32nds of 100%

	Open	High	Low	Settle	Chg	Yield Settle	Chg	Open Interest
June	93-02	93-15	92-19	92-27	− 10	8.765	+ .035	201,176
Sept	92-31	93-09	92-15	92-23	− 9	8.779	+ .032	95,031
Dec	92-25	93-04	92-12	92-18	− 10	8.797	+ .036	19,538
Mr90	92-21	92-28	92-09	92-14	− 9	8.811	+ .032	6,693
June	92-22	92-22	92-04	92-10	− 8	8.825	+ .028	4,346
Sept	92-15	92-15	91-31	92-05	− 8	8.843	+ .029	1,999
Dec	....	....	....	92-00	− 7	8.861	+ .025	266
Mr91	....	....	....	91-26	− 7	8.882	+ .025	160
June	....	....	....	91-20	− 7	8.904	+ .025	206

Est vol 300,000; vol Mon 371,102; op int 329,435, −6,668.

5 YR TREAS NOTES (CBT) $100,000; pts. 32 of 100%

	Open	High	Low	Settle	Chg	Yield Settle	Chg	Open Interest
June	97-16	97-165	97-08	97-125	− 0.5	8.65	....	39,618
Sept	97-20	97-21	97-12	97-165	− 0.5	8.62	....	7,622

Est vol 9,000; vol Mon 8,113; open int 47,242, −327.

TREASURY BILLS (IMM) − $1 mil.; pts. of 100%

	Open	High	Low	Settle	Chg	Discount Settle	Chg	Open Interest
June	91.88	91.89	91.74	91.80	− .02	8.20	+ .02	10,320
Sept	92.38	92.38	92.23	92.30	+ .04	7.70	− .04	10,622
Dec	92.40	92.41	92.28	92.38	+ .06	7.62	− .06	2,527
Mr90	92.46	92.46	92.40	92.46	+ .03	7.54	− .03	294

Est vol 6,682; vol Mon 9,470; open int 23,815, +2,791.

STOCK INDEX FUTURES

S&P 500 INDEX (CME) 500 times index

	Open	High	Low	Settle	Chg	High	Low	Open Interest
June	322.60	322.85	319.75	320.10	− 3.50	325.00	263.80	123,884
Sept	327.00	327.25	324.15	324.45	− 3.55	329.40	271.50	17,286
Dec	331.40	331.40	328.30	328.65	− 3.60	333.60	298.90	1,295

Est vol 47,059; vol Mon 53,670; open int 142,466, +813.
Indx prelim High 321.98; Low 318.20; Close 318.30−3.66

NYSE COMPOSITE INDEX (NYFE) 500 times index

	Open	High	Low	Settle	Chg	High	Low	Open Interest
June	179.75	179.90	178.35	178.50	− 1.75	181.05	149.60	5,407
Sept	182.15	182.25	180.80	180.85	− 1.80	183.50	153.90	1,342
Dec	184.50	184.50	183.95	183.20	− 1.90	185.70	161.10	415

Est vol 6,890; vol Mon 5,900; open int 7,223, +16.
The index: High 179.34; Low 177.56; Close 177.61 −1.73

MAJOR MKT INDEX (CBT) $250 times index

	Open	High	Low	Settle	Chg	High	Low	Open Interest
June	491.90	492.20	488.00	488.60	− 4.85	496.40	442.50	2,285
July	495.00	495.20	491.50	491.80	− 4.90	499.60	469.10	564

Est vol 4,000; vol Mon 2,472; open int 2,849, −12,563.
The index: High 491.49; Low 485.58; Close 486.14 −5.35

KC VALUE LINE INDEX (KC) 500 times index

	Open	High	Low	Settle	Chg	High	Low	Open Interest
June	283.80	283.85	282.20	282.60	− 1.90	285.60	245.65	1,264
Sept	287.65	287.65	286.60	286.80	− 1.90	289.10	267.40	133

Est vol 105; vol Mon 181; open int 1,400, −1.
The index: High 281.93; Low 280.60; Close 280.67 −1.23

FIGURE 12.5 Quotations on Selected Actively Traded Financial Futures.
The trading exchange, size of the trading unit, pricing unit, and delivery months are all vital pieces of information and are all part of the quotation system used with financial futures. (*Source: The Wall Street Journal.*)

The value of an interest rate futures contract responds to interest rates exactly like the debt instrument that underlies the contract. That is, when interest rates go up, the value of an interest rate futures contract goes down, and vice versa. However, the quote system for interest rate as well as currency and stock index futures is set up to reflect the market value of the contract itself. Thus, when the price or quote of a financial futures contract increases, the investor who is long makes money; in contrast, when the price decreases, the short seller makes money. Price behavior is the only source of return to speculators; for even though stocks and debt securities are involved in some financial futures, such contracts have no claim on the dividend and interest income of the underlying issues. Even so, huge profits (or losses) are possible with financial futures due to the equally large size of the contracts. For instance, if the price of Swiss francs goes up by just 2 cents against the dollar, the investor is ahead $2,500, since one futures contract covers 125,000 Swiss francs; likewise, a 3-point drop in the NYSE Composite Index means a $1,500 loss to an investor (3 × 500). When related to the relatively small initial margin deposit required to make transactions in the financial futures markets, such price activity can mean very high rates of return—or very high risk of a total wipeout.

Pricing Futures on Treasury Bills and Other Short-Term Securities

index price
technique used to price T-bill (and other short-term securities) futures contracts, which reflects the actual price movements of these futures contracts.

Because Treasury bills and other short-term securities are normally traded in the money market on what is known as a "discount" basis, it was necessary to devise a special pricing system that would reflect the actual price movements of these futures contracts. To accomplish this, an **index price** system was developed whereby the yield is subtracted from an index of 100. Thus, a Treasury bill or Eurodollar contract, for example, would be quoted at an index of 94.75 when the yield on the underlying security is 5.25 percent (100.00 − 5.25). Under such a system, when someone buys, say, a T-bill future and the index goes up, that individual has made money; when the index goes down, a short seller has made money. Note also that T-bill and Eurodollar contracts are quoted in **basis points**, where 1 basis point equals 1/100 of 1 percent. Thus, a quote of 92.38 (which was the settle price of the December T-bill contract) translates into a T-bill yield of 7.62 percent (100.00 − 92.38).

basis points
an amount equal to 1/100 of 1 percent, used to quote T-bill and Eurodollar contracts.

The index price system traces only the price behavior of the futures contract; to find the *actual price* or *value* of a 90-day T-bill or Eurodollar contract, we have to use the following formula:

$$\text{price of a 90-day futures contract} = \$1,000,000 - \left(\frac{\text{security's yield} \times 90 \times \$10,000}{360}\right)$$

Notice that this price formula is based not on the quoted price index, but on the yield of the security itself, which can be determined by subtracting the price index quote from 100.00. To see how it works, consider a 90-day T-bill futures contract quoted at 92.38; recall this T-bill futures contract is priced to yield 7.62 percent. Now, using our formula we find that the price (or value) of this futures contract is:

$$\text{price of 90-day (CD)} \atop \text{futures contract} = \$1,000,000 - \left(\frac{7.62 \times 90 \times \$10,000}{360} \right)$$

$$= \$1,000,000 - \$19,050$$

$$= \underline{\underline{\$980,950}}$$

A handy shortcut for *tracking the price behavior* of T-bill or Eurodollar futures contracts is to remember that the price of a 90-day contract will change by $25 for every one basis point change in yield. Thus, when the yield on the underlying 90-day security moves from, say, 7.30 to 7.45 percent, it goes up by 15 basis points and causes the price of the futures contract to drop by 15 × $25 = *$375*. (Note: Although not shown here, a similar type of formula is used to price 30-day interest rate contracts.)

Trading Techniques

Financial futures can be used for purposes of *hedging*. Multinational companies and firms that are active in international trade might at times consider hedging with currency or Eurodollar futures, whereas various types of financial institutions and corporate money managers often use interest rate futures for hedging purposes. In either case the objectives are the same: to lock in the best monetary exchange or interest rate possible. In addition, individual investors and portfolio managers might use stock index futures for hedging purposes in order to protect their security holdings against temporary market declines. Financial futures can also be used for *spreading;* this tactic is popular with investors who often adopt elaborate strategies of simultaneously buying and selling combinations of two or more contracts to form a desired investment position. Finally, financial futures are widely used for *speculation*. As this brief review suggests, although the instruments may differ, the trading techniques used with financial futures are virtually identical to those used with commodities. Although all three techniques are widely employed by investors, we will illustrate the use of financial futures by speculators and hedgers only (see the commodities section above for more discussion of spreading). We will first examine speculating in currency and interest rate futures and then look at hedging with stock index futures.

Speculating in Financial Futures

Speculators are especially interested in financial futures because of the large size of the futures contracts. For instance, in early 1989, Canadian dollar contracts were worth over $82,000, Treasury notes were going for nearly $100,000, and Treasury bill contracts were being quoted at close to a million dollars. With contracts of this size, it obviously does not take much movement in the underlying asset to produce big price swings and therefore big profits. An investor can use currency or interest rate futures for just about any speculative purpose. For example, if an investor expects the dollar to be devalued relative to the German mark, she would buy mark currency futures, since the contracts should go up in value. If a speculator anticipates a rise in interest rates, he might consider going short (selling) interest rate

futures, since they should go down in value. Because margin is used and financial futures have the same source of return as commodities (appreciation in the price of the futures contract), return on invested capital is used to measure the profitability of financial futures.

Let's look at an example of a foreign currency contract. Suppose an individual investor feels that the Japanese yen is about to appreciate in value *relative to the dollar*. As a result, this investor decides to buy three September yen contracts at .6195. Each contract is worth $77,438 (12,500,000 × 0.006195), so the total market value of three contracts would be $232,314. Even so, the investor has to deposit only $5,400 to acquire this position. (Recall from Table 12.3 that the required initial margin for Japanese yen is $1,800 per contract.) If the price of the yen moves up just a fraction (from .6195 to .6700), the value of the three contracts will rise to $251,250, and the investor, in a matter of months, will have made a profit of $18,936. Using the formula for return on invested capital introduced above, such a profit translates into an enormous 351 percent rate of return. Of course, an even smaller fractional change in the other direction would have wiped out this investment, so it should be clear that *these high returns are not without their equally high risks*.

Now consider an investment in an interest rate future. Assume the investor is anticipating a sharp rise in long-term rates. Because a rise in rates means that interest rate futures will drop in value, the investor decides to short sell two December T-bond contracts at 87–22; this quote translates into a price of 87 22/32, or 87.6875 percent of par. The two contracts are worth $175,375 ($100,000 × .876875 × 2), but the amount of money required to make the investment is only $4,000 (as the initial margin deposit is $2,000 per contract). Assume that interest rates do in fact move up and as a result the price on Treasury bond contracts drops to 80. Under such circumstances, the investor would buy back the two December T-bond contracts (in order to cover his short position) and in the process make a profit of $15,375. (Recall that he originally sold the two contracts at $175,375 and then bought them back some time later at $160,000, and that like any investment, the difference between what you pay for a security and what you sell it for is profit.) In this case, the return on invested capital amounts to a whopping 384 percent. Again, however, this kind of return is due in no small part to the *enormous risk of loss* the investor assumes.

Trading Stock Index Futures

Most investors use stock index futures for speculation or hedging. (Stock index futures are similar to the *index options* introduced in Chapter 11 and, as such, much of the discussion that follows also applies to index options.) Whether speculating or hedging, the key to success is *predicting the future course of the stock market*. Because investors are buying the market with stock index futures, it is important to get a handle on the future direction of the market via technical analysis (as discussed in Chapter 8) or some other technique. Once an investor feels she has this, she can formulate a stock index futures trading or hedging strategy. For example, if she feels strongly that the market is headed up, she would want to go long (buy stock

index futures); in contrast, if her analysis of the market suggests a sharp drop in equity values, she could make money by going short (selling stock index futures). Speculating in this way would prove profitable so long as our investor's expectations about the market actually materialize.

Consider, for instance, an investor who believes the market is undervalued and therefore a move up is imminent. He can try to identify one or a handful of stocks that should go up with the market (and assume the stock selection risks that go along with this approach), or he can buy an S&P 500 stock index future presently trading at, say, 324.45. To execute such a transaction the speculator need deposit an initial margin of only $6,000. Now, if his expectations are correct and the market does rise so that the S&P 500 Index moves to 340.95 by the expiration of the futures contract, the investor will earn a profit of $8.250: $(340.95 - 324.45) \times 500 = \$8,250$. Given this amount was earned on a $6,000 investment, his return on invested capital would amount to 138 percent! Of course, keep in mind that if the market drops by only 7 points, the investment will be a *total loss*.

Stock index futures also make excellent hedging vehicles in that they provide investors with a highly effective way of protecting stock holdings in a declining market. Although this tactic is not perfect, it does enable investors to obtain desired protection without disturbing their equity holdings. Here's how a so-called short hedge, which is used to protect an investor's stock portfolio against a decline in the market, would work. Assume an investor holds a total of 1,000 shares of stock in 15 different companies and that the market value of this portfolio is $75,000. If the investor thinks the market is about to undergo a temporary sharp decline, he can sell his shares, short sell all his stock holdings against the box, or buy puts on each of his stocks. Clearly, these alternatives are cumbersome and/or costly, and therefore are undesirable for protecting a widely diversified portfolio. The desired results could be achieved, however, by short selling stock index futures. (Note that basically the same protection can be obtained in this hedging situation by turning to options and buying a *stock index put*.)

Suppose the investor short sells one NYSE stock index future at 145.75. Such a contract would provide a close match to the current value of the investor's portfolio, as it would be valued at approximately $73,000, and yet it would require an initial margin deposit of only $4,500. (Margin deposits are less for hedgers than for speculators.) Now, if the NYSE Composite Index does drop to, say, 125.00, the investor will make a profit from the short sale transaction of some $10,000; that is, since the index fell 20.75 points $(145.75 - 125.00)$, the total profit will be: $20.75 \times \$500 = \$10,375$. Ignoring taxes, this profit can be added to the portfolio (additional shares of stock can be purchased at their new lower prices), with the net result being a new portfolio position that will approximate the one that existed prior to the decline in the market. How well the "before" and "after" portfolio positions match will depend on how far the portfolio dropped in value. If the average price dropped about $10 per share in our example, the positions will closely match. However, this does not always happen; the price of some stocks will change more than others and, as such, the amount of protection provided by this type of short hedge depends on how sensitive the stock portfolio is to movements in the market. Thus, the type of

stocks held in the portfolio is an important consideration in structuring the stock index short hedge. OTC and highly volatile stocks will probably require more protection than stocks that are relatively more price-stable or have betas closer to 1.0. In any event, hedging with stock index futures can be a low-cost yet effective way of obtaining protection against loss in a declining stock market.

Financial Futures and the Individual Investor

Financial futures can play an important role in an investor's portfolio so long as: (1) the individual thoroughly understands these investment vehicles; (2) he or she clearly recognizes the tremendous risk exposure of such vehicles; and (3) he or she is fully prepared (financially and emotionally) to absorb some losses. Financial futures are highly volatile securities that have enormous profit and loss potential. For instance, in the five months from December 1988 through May 1989, the (September) S&P 500 futures contract fluctuated in price from a low of 271.50 to a high of 329.40. This range of nearly 58 points for a single contract translated into a profit, or loss, of nearly $29,000—and all from an initial investment of only $6,000. Investment diversification is obviously essential as a means of reducing the potentially devastating impact of price volatility. Financial futures are exotic investment vehicles, but if properly used they can provide generous returns.

Options on Futures

futures options
options that give the holders the right to buy or sell a single standardized futures contract for a specified period of time at a specified striking price; the ultimate leverage vehicle.

The evolution that began with listed stock options and financial futures in time spread to interest rate options and stock index futures; eventually, this led to the merger of options and futures and to the creation of the ultimate leverage vehicle: options on futures contracts. Known as **futures options**, they represent listed puts and calls on actively traded futures contracts. In essence, they give the holders the right to buy (with calls) or sell (with puts) a single standardized futures contract for a specific period of time at a specified striking price. Table 12.5, on page 530 provides a list of the futures options available in early 1989; note that such options are available on both commodities and financial futures. These puts and calls cover the same amount of assets as the underlying futures contracts—for example, 112,000 pounds of sugar, 100 ounces of gold, 62,500 British pounds, or $100,000 in Treasury bonds. Accordingly, they also involve the same amount of price activity as normally found with commodities and financial futures.

Futures options have the same standardized striking prices, expiration dates, and quotation system as other listed options. Depending on the striking price on the option and the market value of the underlying futures contract, these options can also be in-the-money and out-of-the-money. Futures options are valued like other puts and calls—by the difference between the option's striking price and the market price of the underlying futures contract (see Chapter 11). Moreover, they can also be used like any other listed option; that is, for speculating or hedging, in writing programs, or for spreading.

The biggest difference between a futures option and a futures contract is that *the option limits the loss exposure* to the price of the option. The most you can lose is the price paid for the put or call, whereas there is no real limit to the amount of loss

a futures investor can incur. To see how futures options work, consider an investor who wants to trade some gold contracts. She feels very strongly that the price of gold will increase over the next nine months from its present level of $455 an ounce to around $500 an ounce. She can buy a futures contract at 464.50 by depositing the required initial margin of $3,500, or she can buy a futures call option with a $440 per ounce striking price that is presently being quoted at, say, 20.00 (since the underlying futures contract cover 100 ounces of gold, the total cost of this option would be: $20.00 \times 100 = \$2,000$). Note that the call is an in-the-money option, since the market price of gold exceeds the exercise price on the option. The figures below summarize what happens to both investments if the price of gold reaches $500 per ounce by the expiration date; in addition, it shows what happens if the price of gold drops by $45 to $410 an ounce:

	Futures Contract		Futures Option	
	Dollar Profit (or Loss)	Return on Invested Capital	Dollar Profit (or Loss)	Return on Invested Capital
If price of gold *increases* by $45 an ounce	$3,550	101.4%	$4,000	200.0%
If price of gold *decreases* by $45 an ounce	($5,450)	—	($2,000)	—

Clearly, the futures option provides a much higher rate of return as well as a reduced exposure to loss. Futures options offer interesting investment opportunities, but they should be used only by knowledgeable commodities and financial futures investors.

TANGIBLE INVESTMENTS

tangible investments an investment that has an actual form or substance, such as precious metals, stamps, or works of art; assets which are held, in part, for their investment merits.

A **tangible investment** is one that can be seen and touched and that has an actual form or substance. Examples of tangible investments include real estate, precious metals and stones, stamps, coins, works of art, antiques, and other-so-called *hard assets.* A *financial asset,* in contrast, is a claim on paper evidencing ownership, debt, or an option to acquire an interest in some intangible or tangible asset. Many investors own tangibles because they can be seen and touched; others prefer them for their investment value. During the decade of the 1970s, particularly in 1978 and 1979, tangible investments soared in popularity. There were several reasons for this. First, the 1970s was a period of very high inflation. Double-digit inflation rates, unknown in the United States since the late 1940s, became commonplace. These high inflation rates made investors nervous about holding financial assets, like money, bank accounts, stocks, and bonds. Their nervousness was heightened by the poor returns financial assets offered in those years. As a result, they turned their attention to investments on which they could earn returns that were higher than

TABLE 12.5   Futures Options: Puts and Calls on Futures Contracts

Commodities	Financial Futures
Corn	British pound
Soybeans	West German mark
Soybean meal	Swiss franc
Soybean oil	Japanese yen
Heating oil	Canadian dollar
Gasoline	Australian dollar
Cotton	U.S. dollar index
Sugar	Municipal bond index
Live cattle	Eurodollar deposits
Live hogs	Treasury bills
Feeder cattle	Treasury notes
Pork bellies	Treasury bonds
Lumber	NYSE Composite Index
Cocoa	S&P 500 Stock Index
Coffee	
Wheat	
Copper	
Gold	
Silver	
Crude oil	

inflation—in other words, tangibles. The year 1979 in particular was a period of heavy tangibles investing. During that year, inflation soared, and the expectation was for even worse inflation in the future. Investors began to consider, and in many cases, to buy, tangibles. Other factors that increased the popularity of tangibles included the generally unstable domestic and foreign political conditions of the 1970s—Watergate, the Arab oil boycott, the Soviet Union's invasion of Afghanistan, and the Iranian hostage crisis.

In 1981 and 1982, things began to change, however, as interest in tangibles began to wane and their prices underwent substantial declines. For example, in the 12-month period from June 1981 to June 1982 the price of gold dropped 34 percent, silver plunged 45 percent, and U.S. coins fell almost 30 percent in value. With a few exceptions, the investment returns on tangible investments continued at a substandard pace through the rest of the 1980s. Such performance, of course, is precisely what you would have expected; for just as these investment vehicles tend to perform very nicely during periods of high inflation, they don't do nearly as well when inflation drops off—as it has since 1982. Indeed, as Table 12.6 reveals, the investment performance of tangibles from 1972 to 1982 stands in stark contrast to the returns on these investments over the five-year period from 1983 to 1988. Note especially how stocks and bonds stack up in the latest period compared to the decade of the seventies: There's no doubt financial assets are back and that such investments today are more lucrative than most tangible investments. Even so, since

TABLE 12.6   Comparative Rates of Return for Various Investment Vehicles

10 Years (June 1972–June 1982)	Return*	5 Years (June 1983–June 1988)	Return*
1. Coins	22.5%	Stocks	13.8%
2. Stamps	21.9	Bonds	13.4
3. Gold	18.6	Old Master paintings	12.0
4. Chinese ceramics	15.3	Coins	10.1
5. Silver	13.6	Diamonds	7.5
6. Diamonds	13.3	Chinese ceramics	5.5
7. Housing	9.9	Housing	5.0
8. Old Master paintings	9.0	Gold	2.2
9. Stocks	3.8	Stamps	0.2
10. Bonds	3.6	Silver	−11.6

*Investment returns are measured in terms of *average annual* fully compounded rates of return. As such, they represent the effective *annual* yields from these investments; annual returns do *not* include taxes or transaction costs.

Source: Salomon Bros., Inc., January, 1989.

there's still a lot of interest in tangibles as investment vehicles, let's now take a brief look at this unusual, but at times highly profitable, form of investing.

Tangible Assets as Investment Outlets

Tangibles are real things: You can sit in an antique car, hold a gold coin, or look at a work of art. Some tangibles, such as gold and diamonds, are portable; others, such as land, are not. These differences can affect the price behavior of tangibles. Land, for example, tends to appreciate fairly rapidly during periods of high inflation and relatively stable international conditions. Gold, on the other hand, is preferred during periods of unstable international conditions in part because it is portable. Investors appear to believe that if international conditions deteriorate past the crisis point, at least they can "take their gold and run." The market for tangibles varies widely and therefore so too does the *liquidity* of these investments. On one hand we have gold and silver, which can be purchased in a variety of forms and which are generally viewed as being fairly liquid to the extent that it's relatively easy to buy and sell these metals. (To a degree, platinum also falls into this category, since it's widely traded as a futures contract.) On the other hand, we have *all* the other forms of tangible investments, which are highly *illiquid:* They are bought and sold in rather fragmented markets, where transaction costs are very high and where selling an item is often a time-consuming and laborious process.

Alternative Investment Vehicles

One very popular way of investing in tangible assets is to buy *real estate;* indeed, such investing dwarfs all other tangibles, and because of its importance, we exam-

ine real estate investing separately in Chapter 14. That still leaves a wide range of tangible investment vehicles to choose from. Basically, tangibles are made up of the following types of investments:

- Gold and other precious metals
- Strategic metals
- Gemstones
- Collectibles

Next to real estate, gold is probably the most popular form of tangible investment. But gold is just one of several kinds of *precious metals;* in addition, there is silver and platinum. *Strategic metals* have far less-developed markets than precious metals and include resources with such exotic names as cadmium, selenium, titanium, and vanadium. These are all metals that have, or are expected to have, short supplies coupled with big demands. *Gemstones* include the likes of diamonds, rubies, and emeralds, whereas *collectibles* cover everything from stamps and coins to artworks and antiques. These are the tangibles that are likely to be of interest to so-called collector-investors.

One characteristic all these investments have in common is their relative *scarcity value*. Gold, for example, is a fairly rare metal in the earth's crust. Diamonds, particularly those of investment grade, are very rare as well. A 1933 commemorative stamp has rarity value because only a limited number of such stamps were originally printed and only a fraction of those exist today. The supply of Gauguin paintings is limited because the artist died in 1903. The relative scarcity of tangibles is an investment characteristic that attracts investors.

Investment Merits

The only source of return from a tangible investment comes in the form of *appreciation in value*—capital gains, in other words. There's no current income (dividends or interest) from holding tangible investments; instead, investors may be facing substantial *opportunity costs* (in the form of lost income that could have been earned on the capital) if their tangibles do not appreciate rapidly in value. Another factor to consider is that most tangibles have *storage* and/or *insurance costs* that require regular cash outlays.

The future prices, and therefore potential returns, on tangible investments tend to be affected by one or more of the following three key factors:

- Rate of inflation
- Scarcity (or supply and demand) of the assets
- Domestic and international instability

Because future prices are linked to inflation as well as to the changing supply of these assets, such investments tend to be somewhat risky. A slowdown in inflation or a sizable increase in the supply of the asset can unfavorably affect its market price. On the other hand, increasing inflation and continued scarcity can favorably

influence the return. Another factor that tends to affect the market value—and therefore the return—of tangible investments, especially precious metals and gemstones, is the domestic and/or international political environment. In favorable times, these forms of investing are not especially popular, whereas in times of turmoil, their demand tends to rise due to their tangible nature.

Investing in Tangibles

Investing in tangibles is, to some extent, no different from investing in securities. Selection and timing are important in both cases and play a key role in determining the rate of return on invested capital. Yet, when investing in tangibles, you have to be careful to separate the economics of the decision from the pleasure of owning these assets. Let's face it, many people gain a lot of pleasure from wearing a diamond, driving a rare automobile, or owning a piece of fine art. And there's certainly nothing wrong with that; but when you're buying tangible assets for their investment merits, there's only one thing that matters, and that's the economic payoff from the investment! Thus, as a so-called serious investor, consideration should be given to expected price appreciation, anticipated holding period, and potential sources of risk. In addition, investors should carefully weigh the insurance and storage costs of holding such assets, as well as the potential impact that a lack of a good resale market can have on return. Perhaps most important, *don't start a serious tangibles investment program until you really know what you're doing.* Know what to look for when buying a piece of fine art, a diamond, or a rare coin, and know what separates the good artworks (or diamonds or rare coins) from the rest of the pack. In the material that follows, we look at tangibles strictly as *investment vehicles*.

Gold and Other Precious Metals

Precious metals concentrate a great deal of value in a small amount of weight and volume. In other words, just a small piece of a precious metal is worth a lot of money. There are three kinds of **precious metals** that command the most investor attention: gold, silver, and platinum. Of these three, silver is the cheapest, platinum is the most expensive, and gold is by far the most popular. Thus, we'll use gold here as the principal vehicle to discuss precious metals. For thousands of years, people have been fascinated with gold. Records from the age of the pharaohs in Egypt show a desire to own gold. Today ownership of gold is still regarded as a necessity by many investors, although its price has dropped considerably since the January 1980 peak of $850 per ounce. Actually, Americans are relatively recent gold investors, due to the legal prohibition on gold ownership, except in jewelry form, that existed from the mid-1930s until January 1, 1975. After that date, millions of Americans invested in gold; and despite a recent cooling in the desire to own gold, many Americans are still vitally interested in this metal.

precious metals
tangible assets, like gold, silver, and platinum, that concentrate a great deal of value in a small amount of weight and volume.

Like other forms of precious metals, gold is a highly speculative investment vehicle whose price has fluctuated widely in recent years (see Figure 12.6). Many investors hold at least a part—and at times, a substantial part—of their portfolios in gold as a hedge against inflation and/or a world economic or political disaster. Gold

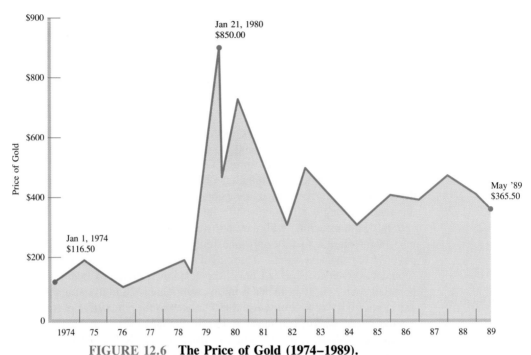

FIGURE 12.6   The Price of Gold (1974–1989).
The price of gold is highly volatile, and can pave the way to big profits or just as easily, subject the investor to enormous losses.

can be purchased as coins, bullion, or jewelry (all of which can be physically held); alternatively, it can be purchased though gold futures (and futures options) contracts, gold mining stocks, mutual funds, and gold certificates. Here's a brief review of the different ways that gold can be held as a form of investing:

> **Gold Coins.** Gold coins have little or no collector value (and thus are referred to as "nonnumismatic gold coins"); rather, their value is determined primarily by the quality and amount of gold in the coins. Popular gold coins include the American Eagle, the Canadian Maple Leaf, the Mexican 50-Peso, and the Chinese Panda.
>
> **Gold Bullion.** Gold bullion is gold in its basic ingot form. Bullion ranges in weight from 5-gram to 400-gram bars, although the kilo bar (which weighs 32.15 troy ounces) is probably the most popular size.
>
> **Gold Jewelry.** Jewelry is a popular way to own gold, but it's not a very good way to *invest* in gold. This is because gold jewelry usually sells for a substantial premium over its underlying gold value (to reflect artisan costs, retail markups, and other factors); moreover, most jewelry is not pure 24-carat gold but a 14- or 18-carat *blend* of gold and other nonprecious metals.
>
> **Gold Futures.** A popular way of investing in the short-term price volatility of gold is through futures contracts or futures options.
>
> **Gold Stocks and Mutual Funds.** Many investors prefer to purchase shares of

gold-mining companies or mutual funds that invest in *gold stocks*. The prices of gold-mining stocks tend to move in direct relationship to the price of gold. Thus, if gold rises in value, these stocks usually move up too. It is also possible to purchase shares in mutual funds that invest primarily in gold-mining stocks. The advantage of this method of investing is a higher measure of diversification than if only one or two stocks were purchased; the shares of gold-oriented mutual funds also tend to fluctuate along with the price of gold.

Gold Certificates. A convenient and safe way to own gold is to purchase a gold certificate through a bank or broker. The certificate represents ownership of a specific quantity of gold that is stored in a bank vault. In this way, the investor does not have to be concerned about the safety that taking physical possession of gold entails; also, by purchasing gold certificates, state sales taxes (which may be imposed on coin or bullion purchases) can be avoided.

Like gold, silver and platinum can also be bought in a variety of forms. Silver can be purchased as bags of silver coins, bars or ingots, futures contracts, futures options, or stock shares. Similarly, platinum can be bought in the form of plates and ingots, coins, futures contracts, and platinum stocks.

Transaction costs in gold and other precious metals vary widely, depending on the investment form chosen. At one extreme, an investor buying one Canadian Maple Leaf coin might pay 5 percent commission, 7 percent dealer markup, and 4 percent gross excise tax (sales tax). In contrast, the purchase of a gold certificate would entail only a 2 percent total commission and markup, with no sales tax. The transactions costs of buying and selling gold are generally a function of the quantity purchased. The greater the amount, the lower the transactions costs on a percentage basis. Storage costs for gold vary as well. Gold coins and bars can easily be stored in a safety deposit box that costs perhaps $20 per year. Gold purchased via gold certificates usually is subject to a storage fee of less than 1 percent per year. Gold coins, bullion, and jewelry are easy for thieves to sell, so it is imperative that these items be safely stored. A safety deposit box at a bank or other depository can alleviate this worry.

Strategic Metals

strategic metals
non-U.S.-mined metals, like cobalt, chromium, and magnesium, vital to the production of many U.S.-made goods.

A number of non-U.S.-mined metals are vital to the production of many U.S.-made goods. The vast American production system would be shut down fairly quickly if manufacturers could no longer import such metals, often called **strategic metals.** These include cobalt, chromium, gallium, germanium, indium, magnesium, rhodium, and titanium. Titanium, for example, is vital in the construction of fighter planes. Rhodium is used in auto catalytic converters to reduce engine emissions. The logic behind strategic metals is simple: Such metals are vital industrial materials (in electronics, telecommunications, aerospace, and other high-tech applications) for which the United States has no significant domestic sources and, therefore, must rely on external suppliers.

Beginning in 1980 and 1981, strategic metals became recognized as an invest-

ment vehicle and were sold to investors as hedges against a crisis-caused cutoff of supplies. Sellers argued that foreign wars, rebellions, and other related problems could leave U.S. manufacturers without these vital raw materials. Should that occur, manufacturers would pay investors almost any price to buy their stored holdings, thus providing huge profits. Although there is some logic to this line of thinking, the predictions of impending strategic metal shortages have not materialized. In fact, most strategic metals investors have earned little if any profits, and many are holding large metal positions that if sold would result in a loss.

Strategic metals are a high-risk investment. High profits are possible, but there are several risk factors to consider. First, the resale markets for these metals are erratic; a position could be very difficult to sell. Commissions and dealer markups are high, and storage costs will be incurred. Finally, and most important, a total cutoff of these metals will probably never occur. Producer countries, such as Zaire and South Africa, generally need the export dollars these metals bring. Overall, the investment characteristics of these metals are such that they probably should be avoided by all investors except wealthy persons who can bear a high risk of loss and the possibility of holding a very illiquid investment vehicle.

Gemstones

gemstones
diamonds and colored precious stones (rubies, sapphires, and emeralds).

By definition, **gemstones** consist of diamonds and the so-called colored stones (rubies, sapphires, and emeralds). Precious stones offer their owners beauty and as such have been purchased by the wealthy (and not-so-wealthy) for psychic and aesthetic pleasure. However, diamonds and colored stones also serve as a viable form of investing. Along with gold, they are among the oldest of investment vehicles, providing a source of real wealth as well as a hedge against political and economic uncertainties. However, diamonds and colored stones are very much a specialist's domain. Generally, standards of value are fully appreciated only by experienced personnel at fine retail stores, dealers, cutters, and an occasional connoisseur-collector. In diamonds, the value depends on the whiteness of the stone and the purity of crystallization. A key factor, therefore, is for the purchaser to understand the determinants of quality. Precious stones will vary enormously in price, depending on how close they come to gem color and purity.

Investment diamonds and colored stones can be purchased through registered gem dealers. Depending on quality and grade, commissions and dealer markups can range from 20 to 100 percent. Due to the difficulty in valuing gemstones, it is imperative that you select only dealers with impeccable reputations. As investment vehicles, colored stones and diamonds offer no current income, but their prices are *highly* susceptible to changing market conditions. For example, the peak price of a one-carat flawless diamond, a popular investment diamond, was about $60,000 in early 1980. By late 1982, this stone was worth only about $20,000—a drop of 67 percent in just over two years. The big difficulty in precious stone investments, aside from the expertise needed in deciding what is in fact gem quality, is the relative *illiquidity* of the stones. As a rule gemstones should be purchased only by investors who can hold them for at least two years: High transaction costs usually prevent profitable resale after shorter periods. Furthermore, gemstones can be diffi-

cult to resell, and sellers often wait a month or more for a sale. Diamonds and colored stones also require secure storage, and there are no payoffs prior to sale.

Collectibles

collectibles
items that have value because of their attractiveness to collectors and because of their relative scarcity and historical significance.

Collectibles represent a broad range of items (from coins and stamps, to cars and posters) that are desirable for any number of reasons, such as beauty, scarcity, and age. A **collectible** has value because of its attractiveness to collectors. During the decade of the seventies, many collectibles shot up in value, but since the early 1980s, most have either fallen in value or have appreciated at a much lower rate than inflation. There are some exceptions, of course, but they remain just that—the exception rather than the rule. Some examples of collectibles that have done well during the eighties include expensive paintings, exotic automobiles and early muscle cars, cartoon celluloids, and baseball cards (as explained in the accompanying Investor Insights box).

In general, collectibles are *not* very liquid. Their resale markets are poor, and transaction costs can be very high. Artwork, for example, commonly has a 100 percent dealer markup, and sales tax is added to the retail price. An investor who wishes to sell artwork quickly may be able to obtain only 50 percent of its retail price. Works sold on consignment to a dealer may incur a 25 percent commission and may take months to sell. In addition, investing in collectibles can be extremely hazardous unless the investor really understands the intricacies of the market. In this area of investing, *one is well advised to become a knowledgeable collector before even attempting to be a serious investor in collectibles.* Despite these obstacles, collectibles can provide highly competitive rates of return and can be good inflation hedges during periods of abnormally high inflation.

An investment-grade collectible is an item that is relatively scarce as well as historically significant within the context of the collectible genre itself, and, preferably, within the larger context of the culture that produced it. Futher, it should be in excellent condition and attractive to display. Although there are almost no bounds to what can be collected (for example, beer cans, fishing tackle, magazines, and sheet music), the major categories of collectibles that tend to offer the greatest investment potential include:

- Rare coins (*numismatics*)
- Rare stamps (*philately*)
- Artwork (the paintings, prints, sculpture, and crafts of recognized artists)
- Antiques (cars, furniture, and so on)
- Baseball cards
- Comic books
- Fantasy art
- Games and toys
- Posters
- Movie memorabilia

Various forms of collecting often provide pleasure and satisfaction as well as attractive returns. However, although certain psychic income may be realized in the

INVESTOR INSIGHTS

Take Me Out to the Baseball Card Swap Meet

Henry Aaron, Mickey Mantle, Willie Mays, Honus Wagner, Reggie Jackson, Rod Carew, George Brett, and Mike Schmidt were not just good ball players, they've also been very good to *baseball card collectors*. Interest in baseball cards has exploded since the late 70's and this year alone [1988], hobbyists, investors, and speculators—not to mention young fans—will buy more than 5 *billion* new and old cards. Total sales will approach $150 million. To serve this market, there are now 10,000 dealers, including 3,500 retail shops, and at least 100 weekly swap meets.

Along with the growing interest in baseball cards has come attractive returns to investors. Cards that cost just a few cents new (or may have even been free) are now selling for hundreds or even thousands of dollars: for example, a Mickey Mantle card can bring as much as $6,000; a Mike Schmidt card is worth $125; and a 1951 Willie Mays will fetch $1,200 or more. Indeed, some vintage cards with unusual histories now sell for huge prices. For instance, a T206 Honus Wagner from a 1909–11 set sold for a record $110,000 this year. Its price is a function of scarcity more than adoration of the Hall of Fame Pittsburgh Pirate shortstop nicknamed The Flying Dutchman; fewer than a hundred of the cards are known to be in existence. There are two explanatory theories. One school holds that Wagner, an ardent nonsmoker, got an injunction prohibiting the card's manufacturer, the American Tobacco Co., from distributing it. Others maintain that Wagner had the cards recalled because he was never paid to appear on them.

Anyone who has not bought baseball cards since childhood might be surprised at the changing nature of this investment. Twenty years ago, a pack cost a nickel. Today, a wrapped group of 15 to 17 cards costs 40 cents to 75 cents. Only Topps Chewing Gum Co. adds its supersweet pink bubble gum as a dividend, and only in some packages. The other card issuers—Donruss, Fleer and Major League Marketing (distributor of Sportflics and Score)—include puzzles, team logo stickers, and trivia cards. A complete annual set of virtually every player who goes to the major league spring training camps contains 700 to 800 cards and runs about $20.

To put matters into perspective, a brief historical review of the baseball card market might be helpful. Baseball cards were first issued during the 1880s by U.S. cigarette companies to promote business. Very few of those early issues remain in salable condition today, because most were printed on cheap cardboard and suffered from poor-quality photography. The extremely small supply and enormous demand for these cards make them highly valued (the Honus Wagner card is a case in point). When World War I led to raw-material shortages, cigarette companies gave up the premiums. After the war, baseball cards were again printed and distributed in mass quantities, this time by candy and gum companies. The new cards were superior in quality to earlier ones and issued in considerably greater quantity, typically tens of millions annually.

One of the most valuable complete sets of baseball cards is Goudey Gum Co.'s 240-card collection from 1933. The set includes Babe Ruth and Lou Gehrig and might command $18,000. It also has one of the priciest cards today—at $9,000—that of another Hall of Famer, Napoleon Lajoie, which is so valuable because its print order was small and was inadvertently delayed until 1934.

The second era of card collecting faded in World War II when paper and rubber shortages limited card and gum production. Bowman Gum Co. resumed the business in 1948. Topps followed in 1951 and today dominates the market with more than half of the total card sales annually. The first complete Topps set, issued in 1952 with 407 cards, now fetches as much as $40,000. The set is highly prized by collectors largely because it contains the Topps rookie cards of Mickey Mantle and Willie Mays, two of baseball's most popular players. For more than two decades after its 1956 acquisition of Bowman, Topps had a virtual monopoly on the card industry. Then in 1980, a U.S. district court ruled that Topps and the major leagues could not prevent other gum companies from issuing cards. A year later, Fleer and Donruss started competing. Sportflics followed in 1986, and Score jumped in this year.

The price of a baseball card is determined, like any other financial asset, by supply and demand. While demand remains attractively high, many of the total annual printing of some 5 million cards per player vanishes within a few years. One reason is that cards are not made to last for more than several years, and creases and bent corners automatically reduce value. Thus few cards issued before World War II have survived in investment-grade condition. The supply of even modern-era baseball cards, especially those issued prior to 1981, is far less than the total number of cards printed, owing to their fragility. Before the cards were viewed as attractive investments, many were thrown away or destroyed (frequently by collectors' mothers).

Various external factors influence the demand for, and consequently the price of, a baseball card. Among them are: the year of issue (in general, older cards and ones from years with many superb rookies are especially valuable); the fortunes of the player on the card; whether it is his rookie card (a rookie card is a major leaguer's first appearance in a regularly issued, nationally distributed card set); the condition of the card; the popularity of the complete set; and whether the card contains a manufacturer's mistake. As a rule, the stronger the combination of these factors, the higher the card's price. For example, a mint 1955 rookie card of Dodger Sandy Koufax can be worth $250; a dog-eared 1960 card of Yankee Duke Carmel, 8 cents. Demand is also highly regional, depending on rooting interests, and produces price variations of as much as 100 percent for comparable players. Met and Yankee cards often sell for twice as much in New York as in Illinois, where cards of former Cubs and White Sox players are treasured.

Source: Adapted from David S. Krause, "Baseball Cards Bat .425," *Money,* June 1988, pp. 140–47.

form of aesthetic pleasure, the financial return, if any, is realized only when the item is sold. While the acquisition of collectibles commonly stems from an individual's personal interest, on a strictly financial basis, items that have a good market and are likely to appreciate in value are the ones to collect. If an item under consideration is expensive, *its value and authenticity should always be confirmed by an expert prior to purchase* (there are many unscrupulous dealers in collectible items). And after purchase, one should make certain to store collectibles in a safe place and adequately insure them against all relevant perils.

SUMMARY

- Commodities and financial futures are traded in the futures market, a market that has its roots in the agricultural segment of our economy. Today there are 13 exchanges that deal in futures contracts, which are commitments to make (or take) delivery of a certain amount of some specified item or commodity at a specified date in the future.

- The futures market is made up of hedgers and speculators who provide both the supply and demand for futures contracts. The hedgers are the producers, processors, and corporate money managers who use futures as a way to protect their position in the underlying commodity or financial instrument. The speculators, in contrast, are the ones who give the market liquidity by trading futures solely for the profit potential they offer.

- From the investor's point of view, the key fact about futures contracts is that they control large amounts of the underlying commodity or financial instrument and, as a result, can produce wide price swings and very attractive rates of return (or very unattractive losses).

- Commodities like grains, metals, meat, and wood make up the traditional segment of the futures market. Recently investors could choose from some 40 different types of physical commodities, and several of these were available in different forms or grades; many were traded on more than one exchange.

- Financial futures are the newcomers to the futures market. Trading in these vehicles did not begin until 1972; but even so, this segment of the market has grown to the point that the volume of trading in financial futures now exceeds that of commodities.

- There are three types of financial futures: currency futures, interest rate futures, and stock index futures. The first type deals in six different kinds of foreign currencies. Interest rate futures, in contrast, involve various types of short- and long-term debt instruments, like Treasury bonds and Treasury bills. Stock index futures are contracts pegged to broad movements in the stock market, as measured by such indexes as the S&P 500 or the Value Line Stock Index.

- The newest, and perhaps the most unusual, futures trading vehicle is the futures options: listed puts and calls on a select but growing number of commodities and financial futures.

- The same trading strategies are used with both commodities and financial futures; that is, they can be used for speculating, spreading, or hedging. Regardless of how they are used, all futures trading is done on margin. The required margin is very low (usually no more than 2 to 10 percent of the market value of the contract) and acts to magnify returns to investors.

- Irrespective of whether investors are in a long or short position, they have only one source of return from commodities and financial futures: that is, appreciation (or depreciation) in the price of the contract. Investors use the rate of return on invested capital to assess the actual or potential profitability of a futures transaction.

- Commodities and financial futures can play an important part in one's portfolio as long as the investor is well versed in the mechanics and pitfalls of futures trading, can afford to take losses, and appreciates the kind of risk exposure he or she is assuming.

- Tangible assets represent a special type of investment vehicle; such investments can be seen and touched, and they have an actual form and substance. Excluding real estate, the four basic types of tangible investments include precious metals (gold, silver, and platinum); strategic metals; gemstones (diamonds and colored stones); and collectibles (coins, stamps, baseball cards, toys, and so on).

- Although tangible investments were able to provide substantial returns over the decade of the seventies, with few exceptions, they haven't done nearly so well over most of the eighties. Capital gains is the only source of return for these investments, and the future price performance of a tangible investment is influenced by three key factors: inflation, scarcity, and political/economic instability.

REVIEW QUESTIONS AND PROBLEMS

1. What is a futures contract? Briefly explain how it is used as an investment vehicle.

2. Discuss the difference between a cash market and a futures market.

   a. Note some of the reasons why the futures market has become so popular.
   b. What effect does inflation have on the futures market?

3. What is the major source of return to commodities speculators? How important are various types of current income like dividends and interest to these investors?

4. Using Figure 12.2, indicate how much profit or loss you would make in the following transactions:

   a. You buy a coffee contract at $1.19 a pound and sell it at $1.54½ a pound.
   b. The price of orange juice goes up 60 cents a pound, and you hold 3 contracts.
   c. You short sell two pork belly contracts at 70 cents a pound, and the price of pork bellies drops to 40 cents a pound.
   d. You recently purchased palladium at $170 an ounce, and the price drops to $150 an ounce.

   e. You short sell four heating oil contracts at 35 cents a gallon, and the price of heating oil
      rises to 48 cents a gallon.

5. Using settle prices from Figure 12.2, find the value of the following commodity contracts:

   a. July coffee.
   b. February ('90) gold.
   c. August crude oil.
   d. November lumber.

6. Why are both hedgers and speculators so important to the efficient operation of a futures
   market?

7. Explain how margin trading is conducted in the futures market.

   a. What is the difference between an initial deposit and a maintenance deposit?
   b. Are investors ever required to put up additional margin? When?
   c. What is the effect of margin trading on an investor's rate of return?

8. Note and briefly define the five essential parts of a commodity contract. Which parts have a
   direct bearing on the price behavior of the contract?

9. Briefly define each of the following:

   a. Settle price.
   b. Daily price limit.
   c. Open interest.
   d. Maximum daily price range.
   e. Delivery month.

10. Kirk O'Malley considers himself to be a shrewd commodities investor. For instance, not long
    ago he bought one July cotton contract at 54 cents a pound and recently sold it at 58 cents a
    pound. How much profit did he make? What was his return on invested capital if he had to
    put up a $1,500 initial deposit?

11. Note several approaches to investing in commodities and explain the investment objectives of
    each.

12. What is the difference between physical commodities and financial futures? What are their
    similarities?

13. Mrs. Shirley Ledbetter is a regular commodities speculator; she is presently considering a
    short position in July oats, which are now trading at 148. Her analysis suggests that July oats
    should be trading at about 140 in a couple of months. Assuming her expectations hold up,
    what kind of return on invested capital would she make if she shorts three July oats contracts
    (with each contract covering 5,000 bushels of oats) by depositing an initial margin of $500
    per contract?

14. Describe a currency future and contrast it with an interest rate future. What is a stock index
    future, and how can it be used by investors?

15. What is program trading? What kind of futures contracts are used in program trading? Does
    program trading have any impact on the price behavior of common stocks? Explain.

16. Explain the index price system used with Treasury bill futures contracts. Also, find the value
    of the following financial futures contracts:

a. September German marks quoted at .5392.

b. December Treasury bonds that settled at 87–22.

c. March 90-day T-bills quoted at 93.55.

d. June S&P 500 index that opened at 362.15.

17. Walt Benaski is thinking about doing some speculating in interest rates; he thinks rates will fall and in so doing, the price of Treasury bond futures should move from 92–15, their present quote, to a level of about 98. Given a required margin deposit of $2,000 per contract, what would Walt's return on invested capital be if prices behave as he expects?

18. Explain why it is so important that an individual be well versed in the behavior and investment characteristics of commodities and financial futures. Why should futures holdings be well diversified?

19. Discuss how stock index futures can be used for purposes of speculation; for purposes of hedging. What advantages are there to speculating with stock index futures rather than specific issues of common stock?

20. Judi Jordan has been an avid stock market investor for years; she manages her portfolio fairly aggressively and likes to short sell whenever the opportunity presents itself. Recently, she has become fascinated with stock index futures, especially the idea of being able to play the market as a whole. At the present time, Judi thinks the market is headed down, and she decides to short sell some Value Line stock index futures. Assume she shorts three contracts at 187.95 and that she has to make a margin deposit of $6,000 for each contract. How much profit will she make, and what will her return on invested capital be if the market does indeed drop so that Value Line contracts are trading at 165.00 by the time they expire?

21. What are futures options? Explain how they can be used by speculators. Why, for example, would an investor want to use an option on an interest rate futures contract rather than the futures contract itself? How much profit would an investor make if he or she bought a call option on gold at 7.20 when gold was trading at $482 an ounce, given the price of gold went up to $525 an ounce by the expiration date on the call? (Note: Assume the call carried a striking price of 480.)

22. Compare and contrast financial assets with tangible assets as investment vehicles.

23. Explain the widespread popularity of tangible investments during the 1970s, and describe the conditions that tend to cause tangibles to rise in price and hence find favor with investors. How have these investments fared in the 1980s? Give some examples of tangible investments that have done well during the eighties; name some that have not done so well.

24. Identify and briefly discuss the four classes of tangible investments; compare and contrast precious metals with strategic metals; do likewise for gemstones and collectibles.

25. Suppose Eastman Kodak has just announced a new film that does not require silver in its manufacture or development. How do you suppose this development will affect silver bullion prices? Silver mining stock prices?

CASE PROBLEMS

12.1 T. J.'s Fast Track Investment Program

T. J. Patrick is a successful industrial designer who enjoys the excitement of commodities speculation. Although only 29 years old, T. J. has been dabbling in commodities since he was

a teenager. He was introduced to it by his dad, who is a grain buyer for one of the leading food processors. T. J. recognizes the enormous risks involved in commodities speculating but feels that since he's still single, now is the perfect time to take chances. And he can well afford it too; for this Vail, Colorado, resident is not only a principal in a thriving design firm, he also holds a substantial interest in several local business ventures. T. J.'s income ranges between $60,000 and $75,000 per year—enough to allow him to enjoy some of the finer things in life (like the slightly used Porsche 911 Turbo he recently purchased). Even so, he does follow a well-disciplined investment program, and annually adds $10,000 to $15,000 to his portfolio.

Recently, T. J. has started playing with financial futures—interest rate futures, to be exact. He admits he is no expert in interest rates, but likes the price action these investment vehicles offer. This all started several months ago when T. J. was at a party and became acquainted with Mr. Vinnie Banano, a broker who specializes in financial futures. T. J. liked what Vinnie had to say (mostly how you couldn't go wrong with interest rate futures), and set up a trading account with Vinnie's firm: Banano's of the Rockies. The other day, Vinnie called T. J. and suggested he get into T-bill futures. As Vinnie saw it, interest rates were going to continue to head up at a brisk pace, and T. J. should short sell some 90-day T-bill futures. In particular, he thinks that rates on T-bills should go up by another half-point (moving from about 8½ up to 9 percent) and recommends that T. J. short four contracts. This would be an $8,000 investment, since each contract requires an initial margin deposit of $2,000.

Questions

1. Assume 90-day T-bill futures are now being quoted at 91.35.

    a. Determine the current price (underlying value) of this T-bill futures contract.
    b. What would this futures contract be quoted at if Vinnie is right and the yield goes up by ½ of 1 percent?

2. Determine how much profit T. J. would make if he shorts four contracts at 91.35, and T-bill yields do go up by ½ of 1 percent—that is, that T. J. covers his short position when T-bill futures contracts are quoted at 90.85. Also, calculate the return on invested capital from this transaction.

3. What happens if rates go down; for example, how much would T. J. make if the yield on T-bill futures goes down by just ¼ of 1 percent?

4. What risks do you see in the recommended short sale transaction? What is your assessment of T. J.'s new interest in financial futures; how do you think it stacks up to his established commodities investment program?

12.2 Jim Parker Tries Hedging with Stock Index Futures

Jim Parker and his wife, Polly, live in Birmingham, Alabama; like many young couples today, the Parkers are a two-income family, as both are graduates of professional schools and hold well-paying jobs. Jim has been an avid investor in the stock market for a number of years and over time has built up a portfolio that is currently worth nearly $75,000. The Parker's portfolio is well balanced: it contains quality growth stocks, some high-income utilities, and a small amount of moderately speculative stock. The Parkers reinvest all dividends and regularly add investment capital to their portfolio; up to now, they have avoided short selling and do only a modest amount of margin trading.

Their portfolio has undergone a substantial amount of capital appreciation in the last 18 months or so, and Jim is anxious to protect the profit they have earned. And that's the

problem! For Jim feels the market has pretty much run its course and is about to enter a period of decline. Parker has studied the market and economic news very carefully, and as a result does not believe the retreat will be of a major magnitude or cover an especially long period of time. He feels fairly certain, however, that most, if not all, of the stocks in his portfolio will be adversely affected by these market conditions—though they certainly won't all be affected to the same degree (some will drop more in price than others). Jim has been following stock index futures since they were first introduced in 1982. He's done some investing in them (with a moderate amount of success) and feels he knows the ins and outs of these securities pretty well. After careful deliberation, Jim decides to use stock index futures—in particular, the NYSE Composite futures contract—as a way to protect (hedge) his portfolio of common stocks.

Questions

1. Explain why Parker would want to use stock index futures to hedge his stock portfolio and note how he would go about setting up such a hedge; be specific.

   a. What alternatives does Jim have to protect the capital value of his portfolio?
   b. What are the benefits and risks of using stock index futures for such purposes (as hedging vehicles)?

 2. Presume NYSE Composite futures contracts are presently being quoted at 165.60. How many contracts would Parker have to buy (or sell) to set up the hedge?

   a. If the value of the Parker portfolio dropped 12 percent over the course of the market retreat, to what price must the stock index futures contract move in order to cover that loss?
   b. Given that a $6,000 margin deposit is required to buy or sell a single NYSE futures contract, what would be the Parkers' return on invested capital if the price of the futures contract changes by the amount computed in part 2(a)?

3. Assume the value of the Parker portfolio declined by $12,000, while the price of a NYSE Composite futures contract moved from 165.60 to 147.60 (assume Jim short sold one futures contract to set up the hedge).

   a. Add the profit from the hedge transaction to the new (depreciated) value of the stock portfolio; how does this compare to the $75,000 portfolio that existed just before the market started its retreat?
   b. Why did the stock index futures hedge fail to give complete protection to the Parker portfolio? Is it possible to obtain *perfect* (dollar-for-dollar) protection from these types of hedges? Explain.

4. What if, instead of hedging with futures contracts, Parker decides to set up the hedge by using *futures options*. Suppose a put on a NYSE Composite futures contract (strike price = 165) is presently quoted at 5.80, while a comparable call is being quoted at 2.35. Use the same portfolio and futures price conditions as set out in question 3 (above) to determine how well the portfolio would be protected. (Hint: Add the net profit from the hedge to the new depreciated value of the stock portfolio.) What are the advantages and disadvantages of using futures options to hedge a stock portfolio, rather than the stock index futures contract itself?

SELECTED READINGS

Bard, Susan M. "Playing the Field With Stock Index Products." *Personal Investor,* May 1985, pp. 56–60.

Dubashi, Jagannath. "Futures and Options." *Financial World,* August 23, 1988, pp. 24–30.

Hager, Bruce. "Commodities: A Shift Away From Traditional Plays." *Financial World,* April 19, 1986, pp. 46–54.

"Interest-Rate Futures: From Birth to Boom." *Financial World,* April 29, 1986, pp. 28–35.

Kerwin, Kathleen. "Is the Tail Wagging the Dog?—Sizing Up the Impact of Stock-Index Futures on the Market." *Barron's,* December 10, 1986, pp. 11, 30–42.

Mandel, Dutch. "Classic Car Prices: Up, Up and Away." *Autoweek,* February 29, 1988, pp. 24–25.

Paulson, Morton C. "Collectibles—What's Hot, What's Not." *Changing Times,* November 1987, pp. 123–28.

Roha, Ronaleen R. "How to Sell Any Collectible." *Changing Times,* March 1988, pp. 62–66.

Ruck, Dan. "Commodities: Profit Plays for Small Investors." *Money Maker,* August/September 1988, pp. 35–38.

Wiles, Russ. "Valuing Gold." *Personal Investor,* July 1987, pp. 43–48.

COMPUTER-BASED INVESTMENT MANAGEMENT: OPTIONS & FUTURES

Options and futures are fairly complex financial instruments, since their value is derived from the behavior of some underlying commodity or financial asset (such as a stock, a market index, some debt security, or a foreign currency); what's more, they're often used in unusual trading strategies (like spreads, straddles, and covered writing). As a result, most options and futures traders who use computers do so for two basic reasons: (1) *for valuation purposes*—that is, to place a value on specific options/futures contracts in order to determine if they're viable investment candidates; and (2) *for trading purposes*—that is, to evaluate assorted trading strategies by determining the relative profit profiles of various combinations of options, futures, and/or some underlying financial asset. Actually, options and futures trading is a lot like technical analysis to the extent that it is highly complex and sophisticated; accordingly, there's a lot of number crunching involved. This is an obvious application for the computer, and it explains in large part why the computer is so widely used by serious options/futures traders. Consider, for example, the problems faced by stock option investors. Generally speaking, such investors tend to employ option strategies that attempt to increase the potential return on invested capital without increasing the risk—indeed, this is the underlying objective of spreading and covered writing programs. Such strategies usually require comparisons of potential profit or loss under a variety of outcomes, for a variety of stock and option investments, in a number of different underlying stocks. Because of all the calculations involved, it is virtually impossible for an individual to do all the work in a timely fashion without the aid of a computer.

The following list provides an indication of the type of options/futures software available to investors.

- *Stock Option Analysis Package (SOAP)* (H&H Scientific, 13507 Pendleton St., Ft. Washington, MD 20744; 301/292-2958; $150; Apples, IBM PCs and com-

patibles.) SOAP calculates the values of put and call options using popular options valuation techniques; program can do a series of ''what if'' computations for a variety of stock options positions. In addition to basic options valuation, this software can also be used to evaluate various kinds of spreads, straddles, and covered options positions. Program provides volatility information and can graph expected profit or loss as a function of the price of the underlying stock. (SOAP is set up to interface with Dow Jones News/Retrieval in order to obtain on-line stock and option prices.)

- *Futuresoft* (CISCO, 327 S. LaSalle St., Suite 1133, Chicago, IL 60604; 312/ 922-3661; $295; IBM PCs and compatibles.) This is a commodities program which analyzes daily and historical prices on foreign currencies, metals, and other futures as well as options. The system calculates a number of technical indicators and displays the results graphically; moreover, its standard output files are compatible with most popular spreadsheet programs. Users have the option to either manually update their database files or automatically update from a variety of data services, and the system is open-ended, which gives users the capability of adding their own analytical/valuation models. The base system includes a data management program, five analysis programs, a trading model, and a plotting program.

- *Commodity Futures Real-Time Charts* (Ensign Software, 7337 Northview, Boise, ID 83704; 208/378-8086; $895; IBM PCs and compatibles.) A program aimed at the very serious commodity/financial futures trader, it provides a full range of complicated technical analysis measures using an on-line telecommunications system. The program is capable of performing dozens of different statistical/technical measures, and it produces the output not only in statistical/ tabular format but also in the form of real-time and historical charts and graphs.

- *Warner Options Database* (Warner Computer Systems, 1 University Plaza, Hackensack, NJ 07601; 800/626-4634; $48 plus usage fee; Apples, IBM PCs and compatibles.) Provides current and historical price information on *all* options traded in the U.S.; database accessible by modem and available 24 hours a day; all quotes up-dated daily.

- *Option Valuator* (Revenge Software, P.O. Box 1073, Huntington, NY 11743; 516/271-9556; $145; Apple II series, IBM PCs and compatibles.) This program predicts fair market options values and calculates volatility ratios and hedge ratios on both put and call options; plots time-dependent graphs of how option value should change as expiration data approaches. Also includes an option writer routine, which computes and displays risk-return data for covered writing strategies.

- *Stock Option Scanner (SOS)* (H&H Scientific, 13507 Pendleton St., Ft. Washington, MD 20744; 301/292-2958; $150; Apples, IBM PCs, and compatibles.) Basically, SOS is an options screening program that scans the on-line price of up to 3,000 stock options and then ranks the top and bottom 50 options according to expected rate of return (program analyzes both put and calls); spreads, straddles, and hedges can also be ranked. Can run analyses for up to five

preselected scanning criteria. (SOS is set up to obtain on-line information from Dow Jones News/Retrieval.)

NOTE: The above list of programs should be viewed as illustrative in nature, and *not* interpreted as an endorsement or recommendation; listed prices and phone numbers are the latest available and are, of course, subject to change without notice.

FIVE

OTHER POPULAR
INVESTMENT VEHICLES

Part Five includes:

THE INVESTMENT ENVIRONMENT

INVESTMENT ADMINISTRATION

INVESTING IN COMMON STOCK	INVESTING IN FIXED-INCOME SECURITIES
SPECULATIVE INVESTMENT VEHICLES	OTHER POPULAR INVESTMENT VEHICLES

13

MUTUAL FUNDS: AN INDIRECT ROUTE TO THE MARKET

After studying this chapter you should be able to:

● Describe the features and basic characteristics of mutual funds, and explain how diversification and professional management are the cornerstones of the industry.

● Explain the advantages and disadvantages of investing in mutual funds.

● Discuss the types of funds available and the variety of investment objectives these funds seek to fulfill.

● Identify and discuss the different kinds of investor services offered by mutual funds, and how these services can fit into an investment program.

● Gain an appreciation of the investor uses of mutual funds, along with ways of assessing and selecting funds that are compatible with investor needs.

● Identify sources of return and compute the rate of return earned on an investment in a mutual fund.

Mutual funds are popular because they offer not only a variety of interesting investment opportunities but also a wide array of services that many investors find appealing. Basically, a mutual fund is a type of financial service organization (an *investment company*) that receives money from its shareholders and then invests those funds on their behalf in a diversified portfolio of securities. An investment in a mutual fund, therefore, represents an *ownership position in a professionally managed portfolio of securities;* when you buy shares in a mutual fund, you become a part owner of a portfolio of securities.

There are mutual funds available to meet just about any type of investment objective. These funds can be used to accumulate wealth, as a storehouse of value, or as a means of seeking high returns. Mutual funds are truly versatile investment vehicles with much to offer investors—and this applies not only to those with limited resources but to well-heeled, seasoned investors as well. We will now take a close look at the operating characteristics, sources of return, uses, and limitations of mutual funds. We begin by looking at the mutual fund concept, and some of the basic characteristics of mutual funds and mutual fund ownership.

THE MUTUAL FUND PHENOMENON

The first mutual fund in this country was started in Boston in 1924; by 1940 there were 68 funds with $448 million in assets and nearly 300,000 shareholder accounts. But that was only the beginning; by 1988, assets under management had grown to well over three-quarters of a *trillion* dollars, as more than 54 *million* investors held shares in over 2,700 publicly traded mutual funds. As Figure 13.1 shows, the mutual fund industry experienced a big jump in growth during the late 1970s, when money market mutual funds became popular and helped to breathe life into an otherwise seriously ill industry, and then again in the early 1980s.

In the 1980s, as the popularity of money funds declined—with falling interest rates and the introduction of money market deposit accounts—two key developments took place to stimulate unprecedented growth in the mutual fund industry: First, there was the introduction/liberalization of self-directed individual retirement accounts (IRAs), which in itself created a strong demand for mutual fund products; and second, the stock and bond markets benefited from a number of factors (including sharply reduced inflation) that led to record-breaking performances. Investors in unprecedented numbers began coming to the market, and the mutual fund industry responded by developing new products and new funds. Not too surprisingly, the industry's rapid growth came to an abrupt halt when the market crashed in October 1987 and mutual fund redemptions soared. But even then, while the overall *rate of growth* dropped dramatically, total assets under management still grew by some $53 billion in 1987, and another $40 billion in 1988. The net result was that in the nine years from 1980 to 1988, the number of mutual fund shareholders increased more than fourfold, while the number of funds in existence grew over the same period from 524 to 2,718 publicly traded mutual funds. Indeed, *there are more mutual funds today than there are stocks on the NYSE*. Mutual fund investors come from all walks of life and all income levels; they range from highly inexperienced to highly

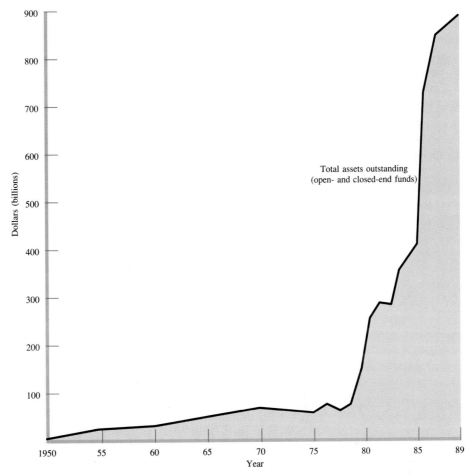

FIGURE 13.1 Growth in Mutual Fund and Investment Company Assets.
The mutual fund industry has mushroomed in the past 15 years and has become one of the leading financial forces in our money and capital markets. (*Source:* Wiesenberger's Investment Company Service and Investment Company Institute.)

experienced investors who all share a common view: Each has decided, for one reason or another, to turn over all or a part of their investment management activities to professionals. The widespread acceptance of the mutual fund concept has, in itself, been something of a phenomenon. From rather meager beginnings only a few decades ago, mutual funds have grown so that they are today a powerful force in the securities markets and a major financial institution in our economy.

An Overview of Mutual Funds

Questions of which stock or bond to select, when to buy, and when to sell have plagued investors for as long as there have been organized capital markets. Such

concerns lie at the very heart of the mutual fund concept and explain, in large part, the growth mutual funds have experienced. Many investors lack the time, the know-how, or the commitment to manage their own portfolios. As a result, they turn to others; more often than not, that means the professional portfolio management of mutual funds.

Pooled Diversification

investment company
a firm, such as a mutual fund, that combines the investment capital of many people with similar investment goals and invests the funds in a wide variety of securities.

The mutual fund concept is based on the simple idea of turning the problems of security selection and portfolio management over to professional money managers. In essence, a mutual fund is of an **investment company** that combines the investment capital of many people with similar investment goals and invests the funds for those individuals in a wide variety of securities. (In an abstract sense, you might think of a mutual fund as the *financial product* that's sold to the public by an investment company; that is, the investment company builds and manages a portfolio of securities, and then sells ownership interests in that portfolio through a vehicle known as a mutual fund.) Investors receive shares of stock in the mutual fund and, through the fund, are able to enjoy much wider investment diversification than they could otherwise achieve. To appreciate the extent of such diversification, one need only look at Figure 13.2, which provides a partial list of the securities actually held in the portfolio of a major mutual fund (actually, this is just one page of an 11-page list of security holdings). Observe that in January 1989, the fund owned anywhere from 600 shares of one company (Amoco Corp.) to over *three million* shares of another (Lloyds Bank); furthermore, note that within each industry segment, the fund diversified its holdings across a number of different stocks. Clearly, except for all but the super-rich, this is far more diversification than most investors could ever hope to attain. Yet each investor who owns shares in this fund is, in effect, a part owner of this diversified portfolio of securities.

pooled diversification
a process used to spread the risk of securities' ownership whereby investors buy into a diversified portfolio of securities; which is held for the collective benefit of the individual investors.

Of course, not all funds are as big or as diversified as the one depicted in Figure 13.2; but even so, as the securities held by a fund move up and down in price, the market value of the mutual fund shares moves accordingly. When dividend and interest payments are received by the fund, they are passed on to the mutual fund shareholders and distributed on the basis of prorated ownership. For example, if you owned 1,000 shares of stock in a mutual fund and that represented 10 percent of all shares outstanding, you would receive 10 percent of the dividends paid by the fund. When a security held by the fund is sold for a profit, this capital gain is also passed on to fund shareholders. The whole mutual fund idea, in fact, rests on the concept of **pooled diversification,** and it works much like the idea of insurance. Individuals pool their resources for the collective benefit of the individual contributors.

Attractions and Drawbacks of Mutual Fund Ownership

The attractions of mutual fund ownership are numerous. One of the most important is something we have touched on above: *diversification*. Diversification has been an underlying theme of this book, and diversification is exactly what the investor obtains with mutual funds. Diversification is beneficial since it reduces the risk

	Shares	Value (Note 1)		Shares	Value (Note 1)
COMMON STOCKS—*continued*					
DURABLES—*continued*			**Banks**—*continued*		
Motor Vehicles—2.7%			Bankers Trust New York Corp.	1,047,572	$ 40,462,468
Americus Trust for Ford Motor Co. (Prime)	47,900	$ 4,059,525	Barclays plc Ord	878,700	7,279,669
Americus Trust for General Motors Corp.			Boatmen's Bancshares, Inc.	296,100	9,068,062
(Prime)	95,800	7,544,250	Chase Manhattan Corp.	1,060,686	33,411,609
Chrysler Corp.	5,200	151,450	Chemical Banking Corp.	697,375	22,577,515
Ford Motor Co.	224,100	12,213,450	Chemical Banking Corp. Class B	27,400	119,875
General Motors Corp.	992,660	90,704,307	Citicorp	2,853,876	78,124,855
Quaker State Corp.	127,000	2,254,250	Citizens & Southern Corp.	670,200	17,257,650
		116,927,232	Comerica, Inc.	260,100	12,419,775
			Continental Bank Corp.	275,850	5,654,925
			First Bank System, Inc.	889,649	17,904,186
			First Chicago Corp.	1,865,042	64,110,818
TOTAL DURABLES . . . . †		120,096,756	First City Bancorporation of Texas, Inc.†	387,100	11,225,900
ENERGY—6.8%			First Fidelity Bancorporation	1,087,197	31,392,813
Energy Services—0.8%			First Interstate Bancorp	158,100	7,430,700
Baker Hughes, Inc.	1,004,700	15,070,500	First Virginia Banks, Inc.	49,000	1,261,750
Halliburton Co.	199,900	5,897,050	Fleet/Norstar Financial Group, Inc.	72,345	1,953,315
McDermott International, Inc.	897,500	15,818,437	Grant Street National Bank	322,620	181,473
		36,785,987	KeyCorp.	417,000	9,017,625
			Lloyds Bank plc	3,152,700	20,817,751
Oil and Gas—6.0%			Manufacturers Hanover Corp.	128,900	3,883,112
Americus Trust for Chevron Corp. (Prime)	94,100	4,234,500	Manufacturers National Corp.	142,739	6,619,521
Americus Trust for Mobil Corp. (Prime) . .	71,200	3,061,600	Mellon Bank Corp.	326,581	9,225,913
Amoco Corp.	600	46,575	Mercantile Bancorporation, Inc.	100,300	2,783,325
Chevron Corp.	96,000	4,752,000	Morgan (J.P.) & Co., Inc.	74,426	2,716,548
Elf Aquitaine	94,800	6,216,636	National City Corp.	428,404	14,030,231
Energy Development Partners Ltd.	150,000	468,750	National Westminster Bank plc	988,900	10,392,350
Freeport-McMoRan, Inc.	1,845,581	62,057,661	Norwest Corp.	412,015	14,832,540
Louisiana Land & Exploration Co.	1,000	32,250	NCNB Corp.	70,795	2,123,850
Mobil Corp.	4,800	232,800	Security Pacific Corp.	2,398,430	91,440,143
Murphy Oil Corp.	147,500	4,720,000	Shawmut National Corp.	902,081	22,439,264
Occidental Petroleum Corp.	907,700	25,415,600	Society Corporation	800	27,600
Pennzoil Co.	1,043,850	82,464,150	Southeast Banking Corp.	1,085,086	25,363,885
Sun Company, Inc.	131,200	4,641,200	United Jersey Banks	400,000	8,500,000
Sun Exploration & Production Co.	135,800	3,921,225			698,888,913
USX Corp.	1,888,600	60,199,125			
Union Exploration Partners, Ltd.	15,911	232,698	**Credit and Other Finance—0.2%**		
		262,696,770	American Express Co.	132,200	4,048,625
			Federal National Mortgage Assn.	1,000	59,750
TOTAL ENERGY		299,482,757	Lomas & Nettleton Financial Corp.	443,600	5,434,100
FINANCE—22.9%			Primerica Corp.	44,500	1,045,750
Banks—15.9%					10,588,225
AmeriTrust Corp.	64,000	1,392,000			
AmSouth Bancorporation	221,600	5,429,200	**Insurance—4.8%**		
Banc One Corp.	15,200	385,700	Aetna Life & Casualty Co.	1,130,196	55,944,702
Banca Nazionale Del Lavoro Risp	120,000	1,034,007	American Bankers Insurance Group, Inc. . .	551,600	6,619,200
Bank of Boston Corp.	1,376,565	35,102,407	American General Corp.	392,500	13,295,937
Bank of Montreal	792,300	19,410,090	Aon Corp.	349,600	9,963,600
Bank of New England Corp.	141,632	3,363,760	Chubb Corp. (The)	54,900	3,328,312
Bank of New York Co., Inc.	685,147	26,720,733	Continental Corp.	245,600	8,442,500
			CIGNA Corp.	320,300	16,695,637

FIGURE 13.2   A Partial List of Portfolio Holdings.
The list of holdings in this one fund alone goes on for 10 more pages, and includes stocks in several hundred different companies. Certainly, this is far more diversification than most investors can ever hope to achieve! (*Source:* Fidelity Investments.)

inherent in any one investment by spreading out holdings to include a wide variety of industries and companies. Table 13.1 illustrates how the notion of diversification is applied to the equity holdings of the country's largest mutual funds, and it shows how security holdings will change over time as the market outlook changes. Another appeal is the full-time professional management that these funds offer, thereby removing much of the day-to-day management and recordkeeping chores from the shoulders of investors. What's more, the fund may be able to provide better investment talents than individual investors have to offer. Still another advantage is that most (but not all) mutual fund investments can be started with a modest capital outlay. Sometimes there is no minimum investment required at all; and after the initial investment has been made, additional shares can usually be purchased in small amounts. The services mutual funds offer also make them appealing to many investors; these include the automatic reinvestment of dividends, withdrawal plans, exchange privileges, checkwriting privileges, and the like. Finally, mutual funds offer convenience; they are relatively easy to acquire, the funds handle the paperwork and recordkeeping, their prices are widely quoted, and it is possible to deal in fractional shares.

There are, of course, some major drawbacks. One of these is the lack of liquidity that characterizes many mutual funds. Most funds are fairly easy to buy, but they are not so easy to sell. That is, selling mutual funds is more often than not a do-it-yourself project that involves selling the shares back to the fund itself. Since there are usually no commissions on sales, brokers tend to be, shall we say, a bit "unenthusiastic" about handling such transactions for investors. All this, of course, assumes that the fund does not offer a *phone switching* service—or that you're not taking advantage of it. This service, which is available from most investment companies, enables you to simply pick up the phone to move money from one fund to another—the only constraint is that the funds must be managed by the same investment company. Most companies charge little or nothing for these shifts, although funds that offer free exchange privileges often place a limit on the number of times you can switch each year. (We'll discuss this service in more detail later in the chapter when we cover *conversion privileges*.) Another, far more important, drawback is that mutual funds in general are fairly costly to acquire. Many funds carry sizable commission charges (or what are known as "load charges"). In addition, a **management fee** is levied annually for the professional services provided, and it is deducted right off the top, regardless of whether it has been a good or bad year.

management fee
a fee levied annually for professional mutual fund services provided; paid regardless of the performance of the portfolio.

Finally, in spite of all the professional management and advice, it seems that mutual fund performance over the long haul is at best about equal to what you would expect from the market as a whole. There are some notable exceptions, of course, but most funds do little more than just keep up with the market. Take a look at Figure 13.3; it shows the investment performance of 15 different types of equity funds over the 5-year period from 1984 through 1988 (which covers most of the 1982–87 bull market, including the October crash). These are fully compounded returns, and assume that all dividends and capital gains distributions are reinvested into additional shares of stock. Note that when compared to the S&P 500, only *three*

TABLE 13.1 Diversification in the Common Stock Holdings of Mutual Funds*

	Market Value 1983	Market Value 1988
Agricultural Equipment	0.40%	0.49%
Aircraft Mfg. & Aerospace	2.16	1.68
Air Transport	1.88	2.09
Auto & Accessories (excl. Tires)	3.21	4.45
Building Materials & Equipment	1.83	0.93
Chemicals	5.63	4.92
Communications (TV, Radio, Motion Pictures) (a)	2.50	7.82
Computer Services	0.72	2.97
Conglomerates	2.59	2.49
Containers	0.80	0.15
Drugs & Cosmetics	5.87	4.77
Elec. Equip. & Electronics (excl. TV & Radio)	13.15	4.47
Financial (incl. Banks & Insurance)	8.69	17.73
Foods and Beverages	2.57	3.07
Hospital Supplies & Services	1.17	1.34
Leisure Time	2.38	2.07
Machinery	1.85	1.8
Metals & Mining	1.85	3.08
Office Equipment	7.13	4.14
Oil	8.92	6.78
Paper	1.99	2.31
Printing & Publishing	1.43	1.57
Public Utilities (incl. Natural Gas) (b)	8.24	5.81
Railroads & Railroad Equipment	1.28	1.21
Retail Trade	5.61	5.39
Rubber (incl. Tires)	0.79	0.35
Steel	0.76	0.58
Textiles	0.72	0.60
Tobacco	1.00	1.49
Miscellaneous	2.88	3.45
Totals	100.00%	100.00%

*Composite industry investments drawn from the portfolios of the largest investment companies as of the end of calendar years 1983 and 1988.

(a) Includes telephone companies in 1988.

(b) Includes telephone companies in 1983.

Source: Mutual Fund Fact Book, 1984 and 1989.

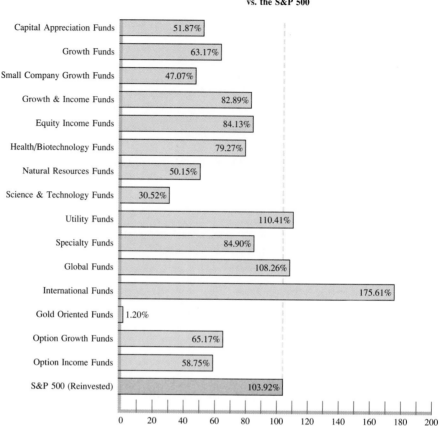

**The Performance of 15 Groups of Equity Funds
From Jan. 1984 to Dec. 1988
vs. the S&P 500**

FIGURE 13.3   The Comparative Performance of Mutual Funds Versus the Market.

As shown here, even with the services of professional money managers, it's tough for mutual funds to outperform the market. In this case, the average performance of 12 out of the 15 fund categories failed to meet the market's standard of return. (*Source: Barron's,* February 13, 1989.)

types of funds outperformed the market, and many others fell far short of the mark. The message is clear: *consistently beating the market is no easy task—not even for professional money managers.* Even though a handful of funds have given investors above-average, and even spectacular, rates of return, most mutual funds simply do not meet this level of performance. This is not to say that the long-term returns from mutual funds are substandard or that they fail to equal what you could achieve by

putting your money in, say, a savings account or some similar risk-free investment outlet. Quite the contrary: The long-term returns from mutual funds have been substantial, but most of this return can be traced to strong market conditions and/or to the reinvestment of dividends and capital gains.

Mutual Fund Regulations

Although securities regulations were discussed in Chapter 2, it might be helpful to briefly review some of the major regulatory provisions that apply to mutual funds. To begin with, the *Securities Act of 1933* requires the filing of full information about the fund with the SEC; this act also requires the fund to provide potential investors with a current prospectus, disclosing the fund's management, its investment policies and objectives, and other essential data. In addition, the purchase and sale of mutual fund shares are subject to the anti-fraud provisions of the *Securities Exchange Act of 1934,* and the *Investment Advisors Act of 1940* regulates the activities of the investment advisors that work for mutual funds. Most important of all, in order to qualify for investment company status, a fund must comply with the provisions of the *Investment Company Act of 1940*. That comprehensive piece of legislation provides the foundation for the regulation of the mutual fund industry and, among other things, establishes standards of income distribution, fee structures, and diversification of assets. Finally, from a tax perspective, a mutual fund can be treated as an essentially tax-exempt organization (and thereby avoid the double taxation of dividends and income) so long as it qualifies under *Subchapter M* of the Internal Revenue Code of 1954. Briefly, to operate as a regulated investment company and enjoy the attending tax benefits, a fund must distribute at least 90 percent of its income each year to its shareholders. That way, the fund will pay *no* taxes on any of its earnings, irrespective of whether they're derived from current income or capital gains.

mutual fund
an open-end investment company that invests its shareholders' money in a diversified portfolio of securities.

Essential Characteristics

Not only are there many types of mutual funds available, there are also significant differences in organization, fees charged to investors, and methods of buying and selling funds. Let us now look at some of these characteristics.

Open-End Investment Companies

open-end investment company
a type of investment company in which investors buy shares from, and sell them back to, the mutual fund itself; there is no limit on the number of shares the fund can issue.

The term **mutual fund** is commonly used to denote an open-end investment company. Mutual funds are the dominant type of investment company and account for well over 90 percent of the assets under management. Many of these funds are fairly large, with some having portfolios that are measured in the *billions* of dollars. In an **open-end investment company,** investors actually buy their shares from, and sell them back to, the mutual fund itself. When the investor buys shares in an open-end fund, the fund issues new shares of stock and fills the purchase order with these new shares. There is no limit to the number of shares the fund can issue; the only restraint on the number of shares issued is investor demand. Furthermore, all open-

end mutual funds stand behind their shares and buy them back when investors decide to sell. Thus, there is never any trading between individuals.

Both buy and sell transactions are carried out at prices based on the current value of all the securities held in the fund's portfolio. This is known as the fund's **net asset value (NAV);** it is calculated at least once a day and represents the underlying value of a share of stock in a particular mutual fund. NAV is found by taking the total market value of all securities held by the fund, less any liabilities, and dividing this amount by the number of fund shares outstanding. For example, if on a given day the market value of all the securities held by the XYZ mutual fund equaled some $10 million, and if XYZ on that particular day had 500,000 shares outstanding, the fund's net asset value per share would amount to $20 ($10,000,000/ 500,000 = $20). This figure, as we'll see below, is then used to derive the price at which the fund shares are bought and sold.

net asset value (NAV)
the underlying value of a share of stock in a particular mutual fund; represents the net market value of the securities held by a mutual fund.

Closed-End Investment Companies

Whereas the term *mutual fund* is supposed to be used only with open-end funds, it is, as a practical matter, regularly used with closed-end investment companies as well. Basically, **closed-end investment companies** operate with a fixed number of shares outstanding and do *not* regularly issue new shares of stock. In effect, they have a capital structure like that of any other corporation, except that the corporation's business happens to be investing in marketable securities. At the end of 1988 there were around 200 publicly traded closed-end funds, whose shares had a combined market value of some $35 billion. Closed-end investment company shares are actively traded in the secondary market, like any other common stock. Most are traded on the New York Stock Exchange, several are on the American Exchange, and some are traded in the OTC market. As seen in Figure 13.4, the shares of closed-end companies are listed right along with other common stocks. In this case ASA Ltd. and Adams Express (two of the larger closed-end investment companies) are quoted on the NYSE.

closed-end investment companies
a type of investment company that operates with a fixed number of shares outstanding.

The share prices of closed-end companies are determined not only by their net asset values, but also by general supply and demand conditions in the stock market. As a result, closed-end companies generally trade at a discount or premium to NAV. For example, if a fund has a net asset value of $10 per share and is trading at $9, it would be selling at a discount of $1; it would be selling at a premium of $1 if it were quoted at a price of $11. Share price discounts and premiums can at times become quite large; for example, it's not unusual for such spreads to amount to as much as 25 to 30 percent of net asset value, occasionally more. Table 13.2, on pages 564–565, lists some actively traded closed-end funds, along with prevailing premiums (+) and discounts (−).

Investment Trusts

investment trust
a type of investment vehicle whereby the trust sponsors put together a fixed/ unmanaged portfolio of securities and then sell ownership units in the portfolio to individual investors; also called a unit investment trust.

An **investment trust** (or **unit investment trust,** as it is also known) represents little more than an interest in an unmanaged pool of investments. In essence, a portfolio of securities is simply held in safekeeping for investors under conditions set down in

52 Weeks Hi	Lo	Stock	Sym	Yld Div	%	PE	Vol 100s	Hi	Lo	Close	Net Chg
				-A-A-A-							
31½	21¾	AAR	AIR	.44	1.4	20	373	31	30⅝	30⅞	...
n 10⅛	8⅜	ACM OppFd	AOF	1.01	11.1	...	103	9⅛	9	9⅛	...
11⅞	10¼	ACM Gvt Fd	ACG	1.26a	11.5	...	427	11	10⅞	11	...
n 10⅛	8½	ACM MgdIncFd	AMF	1.01	10.9	...	168	9¼	9	9¼	...
11½	10⅛	ACM SecFd	GSF	1.26	11.7	...	991	10⅞	10¾	10¾	...
x 10	8⅜	ACM SpctmFd	SI	1.01	11.4	...	x679	9	8⅞	8⅞	...
4⅜	2¾	AMCA	AIL	.12e	2.9	28	3	4⅛	4⅛	4⅛	...
6⅛	3½	AM Int	AM	...	...	...	3228	5⅞	5¾	5¾	...
23½	18⅛	AM Int pf		2.00	8.9	...	225	22½	22½	22½	...
65⅝	39	AMR	AMR	...	...	8	3903	64¼	63¼	64¼	+1⅛
27	25	ANR pf		2.67	10.4	...	230	25⅝	25⅝	25⅝	−⅜
9½	3¾	ARX	ARX	...	...	...	326	4½	4⅜	4½	...
47	35¼	ASA	ASA	3.00a	7.6	...	146	39⅝	39⅜	39⅝	...
† 22⅛	14¾	AVX	AVX	.24	1.1	11	1182	22⅜	21½	22¼	+⅝
60⅞	43	AbbotLab	ABT	1.40	2.4	17	2273	58⅞	57¾	58¾	+1
19	15⅜	Abitibi g	ABY	1.00	...	...	272	16⅝	16⅜	16⅝	+¼
12	7½	AcmeCleve	AMT	.40	3.9	...	20	10¼	10⅛	10¼	...
8	5⅞	AcmeElec	ACE	.32	4.1	18	10	8	7¾	7¾	−¼
34⅝	20¼	Acuson	ACN	...	...	27	498	34½	33⅞	34¼	+⅜
16⅞	14¼	AdamsExp	ADX	1.82e	11.7	...	149	15½	15⅜	15½	...
16⅞	7⅛	AdvMicro	AMD	...	...	...	6203	9½	9¼	9½	+⅛
43½	28¾	AdvMicro pf		3.00	9.2	...	35	32¾	32⅜	32¾	+⅜
9⅝	6½	AdobeRes	ADB	...	...	...	813	9½	9½	9½	...
21¾	19⅞	AdobeRes pf		2.40	11.6	...	1	20⅝	20⅝	20⅝	−⅛
9¾	5⅞	Advest	ADV	.12	1.7	17	107	7⅜	7¼	7¼	...
54⅞	40½	AetnaLife	AET	2.76	5.1	9	1316	53¾	53¼	53¾	+¼
s† 49	24	AffilPub	AFP	.22b	.5	...	2036	49½	47⅞	48⅞	+⅝
21	13¾	Ahmanson	AHM	.88	4.3	10	2342	20⅞	20½	20⅝	...
4⅝	2⅞	Aileen	AEE	...	...	19	20	3⅜	3¼	3⅜	+⅛
53⅜	37¾	AirProduct	APD	1.20	2.8	11	2162	43¼	42⅝	43⅛	+¼
28⅞	15½	AirbornFrght	ABF	.60	2.2	25	65	27	26¾	26¾	...
21⅛	12⅜	Airgas	ARG	...	...	13	304	20¾	20¼	20¼	−¼

FIGURE 13.4 Stock Quotations For Closed-End Investment Companies.
The quotes for closed-end investment companies are listed right along with other common stocks; and except for the lack of a P/E ratio, their quotes are no different than any other common stock. (*Source: The Wall Street Journal.*)

a trust agreement. The portfolios usually consist of corporate, government, or municipal bonds, with tax-free municipal bonds and mortgage-backed securities being the most popular type of investment vehicle. There is *no trading* in the portfolios, and as a result, the returns, or yields, are fixed and usually predictable—at least for the short run. Unit trusts are like second cousins to mutual funds: Unlike conventional mutual funds, whose securities are actively traded, a trust manager simply puts together a portfolio of securities, and that's it. After the securities are deposited with a trustee, no new securities are added and, with rare exceptions, none are sold (unless they mature or are called by the issuer).

Various sponsoring brokerage houses put these diversified pools of securities

TABLE 13.2   Some Actively Traded Closed-End Mutual Funds

Fund Name	Stock Exch.	N.A. Value*	Stock Price*	% Premium (+) or Discount (−)*
Diversified Common Stock Funds				
Adams Express	NYSE	18.29	15½	−15.25
Baker Fentress	NYSE	28.40	22⅝	−20.33
Blue Chip Value	NYSE	7.77	6⅝	−14.74
Clemente Global Gro	NYSE	9.52	7⅝	−19.91
Gemini II Capital	NYSE	18.73	15⅜	−17.91
Gemini II Income	NYSE	9.53	12¾	+33.79
General Amer Invest	NYSE	20.21	16¾	−17.12
Global Growth Capital	NYSE	9.35	8½	−9.09
Global Growth Income	NYSE	9.50	9¾	+2.63
Growth Stock Outlook	NYSE	10.04	9	−10.36
Lehman Corp.	NYSE	15.82	13⅛	−17.04
Liberty All-Star Eqty	NYSE	9.41	7¾	−17.64
Niagara Share Corp.	NYSE	16.68	13⅞	−16.82
Nicholas-Applegate	NYSE	10.66	9	−15.57
Quest For Value Cap	NYSE	15.22	11⅛	−26.91
Quest For Value Inco	NYSE	11.71	11¾	+0.34
Royce Value Trust	NYSE	10.48	9½	−9.35
Schafer Value Trust	NYSE	10.87	9¼	−14.90
Source Capital	NYSE	40.97	38⅞	−5.11
Tri-Continental Corp.	NYSE	27.29	22⅜	−18.01
Worldwide Value	NYSE	20.57	17⅜	−15.53
Zweig Fund	NYSE	11.24	11	−2.14
Closed End Bond Funds				
CIM High Yield Secs	AMEX	9.10	9	−1.10
Franklin Prin Mat Tr	NYSE	9.10	9⅝	+5.77
Franklin Universal Tr	NYSE	9.28	9¼	−0.32
Municipal High Inco	NYSE	9.56	9⅞	+3.29
Zenith Income Fund	NYSE	8.61	9⅜	+8.89
Specialized Equity and Convertible Funds				
American Capital Conv	NYSE	23.38	21⅝	−7.51
ASA Ltd	NYSE	49.51	39⅝	−19.97
Asia Pacific	NYSE	12.20	10⅞	−10.86
Bancroft Convertible	AMEX	21.47	18¾	−12.67
Bergstrom Capital	AMEX	59.61	53	−11.09
BGR Precious Metals	TOR	11.42	9⅝	−15.72
Brazil	NYSE	22.90	11⅜	−50.33
CNV Holdings Capital	NYSE	9.94	5	−49.70
CNV Holdings Income	NYSE	9.53	11½	+20.67

together and then sell units of the pool to investors (each *unit* being like a share in a mutual fund). For example, a brokerage house might put together a diversified pool of corporate bonds that amounts to, say, $10 million. The sponsoring firm would then sell units in this pool to the investing public at a price of $1,000 per unit (a common price for these securities). The sponsoring organization does little more than routine recordkeeping, and it services the investments by collecting coupons and distributing the income (often on a monthly basis) to the holders of the trust units. Figure 13.5, on page 566, depicts an announcement of a newly formed municipal bond unit trust. Like all such trusts, this one will eventually expire when

TABLE 13.2   Continued

Fund Name	Stock Exch.	N.A. Value*	Stock Price*	% Premium (+) or Discount (−)*
Specialized Equity and Convertible Funds				
Castle Convertible	AMEX	21.77	18¾	−13.87
Central Securities	AMEX	12.90	10⅛	−21.51
Duff&Phelps Sel Utils	NYSE	8.03	8⅜	+4.30
Ellsw Conv Gr&Inc	AMEX	8.73	7¾	−11.23
Engex	AMEX	12.44	8⅜	−32.68
Financ'l News Compos	NYSE	19.25	18⅜	−4.55
1stAustralia	AMEX	9.91	7⅞	−20.53
First Financial Fund	NYSE	10.34	8¾	−15.38
France Fund	NYSE	11.40	10⅝	−6.80
Gabelli Equity Trust	NYSE	13.77	13	−5.59
Germany Fund	NYSE	8.28	7⅜	−10.93
H&Q Healthcare Inv	NYSE	9.42	7¾	−17.73
Hampton Utils Tr Cap	AMEX	10.65	8⅞	−16.67
Hampton Utils Tr Pref	AMEX	49.01	47¼	−3.59
Helvetia Fund	NYSE	10.04	9	−10.36
India Growth Fund	NYSE	13.00	11⅛	−14.42
Italy Fund	NYSE	9.80	8⅛	−17.09
Korea Fund	NYSE	17.66	34⅝	+96.06
Malaysia Fund	NYSE	10.84	9	−16.97
Mexico Fund	NYSE	10.23	8⅞	−13.25
Morgan Grenf SmCap	NYSE	10.41	9¼	−11.14
Patriot Prem Div Fd	NYSE	9.30	10	+7.53
Petrol & Resources	NYSE	28.30	24¼	−14.31
Pilgrim Regional	NYSE	10.45	9	−13.88
RI Estate Sec Inco Fd	AMEX	8.73	8⅝	−1.20
Regional Fin Shrs Inv	NYSE	8.93	7½	−16.01
ROC Taiwan Fund	NYSE	14.74	18⅜	+24.66
Scudder New Asia	NYSE	12.73	10	−21.45
Spain Fund	NYSE	12.72	12⅜	−2.71
Taiwan Fund	NYSE	42.00	40⅜	−3.87
TCW Convertible Secs	NYSE	8.66	7¾	−10.51
Templeton Em Mkts	AMEX	10.77	10⅝	−1.35
Templeton Value Fund	NYSE	10.00	9	−10.00
Thai Fund	NYSE	13.05	15¼	+16.86
United Kingdom Fund	NYSE	12.18	10	−17.90
Z-Seven	OTC	14.44	14⅝	+1.28

*NAVs, stock prices, and premiums/discounts as of May 26, 1989.
Source: The Wall Street Journal.

the bonds in the portfolio mature. Trusts appeal to investors because they allow individuals with limited resources to acquire a diversified portfolio of generally high yielding securities and to earn monthly (rather than semiannual) income. But as discussed in the Investor Insights box, these investments also have their dark sides.

Load and No-Load Funds

The question of whether a fund is ''load'' or ''no-load'' is a matter of concern only to investors in *open-end* funds. (Recall from our discussion above that closed-end funds trade on listed or OTC markets and, as such, are subject to the same commis-

New Issue April 26, 1989

$10,000,000

The Municipal Investment Trust Fund

One Hundred Forty-First Insured Series

A Unit Investment Trust
A Fixed Portfolio of Insured Fixed-Rate Debt Obligations

Sponsors:

Merrill Lynch, Pierce, Fenner & Smith Incorporated

Shearson Lehman Hutton Inc.

Prudential-Bache Securities Inc.

PaineWebber Incorporated

Dean Witter Reynolds Inc.

Underwriter:

Broadcort Capital Corp.

FIGURE 13.5 A Newly Formed Bond Trust.

This is a $10 million unit investment trust that will invest in insured tax-exempt municipal bonds. Note that this issue is the 141st in a series of insured municipal bond trusts sponsored and sold by Merrill Lynch and other brokerage houses. (*Source: The Wall Street Journal,* May 3, 1989.)

sion and transaction costs as any other share of common stock.) The load charge on an open-end fund is the commission the investor pays when buying shares in a fund. Generally speaking, the term **load fund** is used to describe a mutual fund that charges a commission when shares are bought (such charges are also known as *front-end loads*); a **no-load fund,** in contrast, means no sales charges are levied. Load charges can be fairly substantial and often range from 7 to 8.5 percent of the *purchase* price of the shares. Most mutual funds, however, offer quantity discounts (which usually start with single investments of 1,000 shares or more). Although there may be little or no difference in the performance of load and no-load funds, the cost savings with no-load funds tend to give investors a real head start in achieving superior rates of return. Unfortunately, the true no-load fund may become extinct in the very near future, as more and more no-loads are becoming ''12(b)-1 funds''; although such funds do not *directly* charge commissions at the time of purchase (so they can technically call themselves no-loads), they assess what are known as 12(b)-1 charges *annually* to make up for any lost commissions (12(b)-1 charges are more fully described below).

Fortunately, it is possible to tell the players apart without a program: The quotation system used with mutual funds distinguishes the no-load from the load funds. That is, all open-end mutual funds are priced according to their net asset values, which—as we can see in Figure 13.6—are part of the standard mutual fund quotations. The NAV (Net Asset Value) column is the price the mutual fund will pay to buy back the fund shares (or, from the investor's point of view, the price at which the shares can be sold). Next to the NAV is the Offer Price, the price the investor would have to pay in order to buy the shares. Note that the Kemper Growth Fund, for example, has a higher offer price ($9.70) than net asset value ($8.88); this difference of $0.82 per share represents the load charge. For the Kemper Growth Fund, the load charge amounts to 8½ percent of the offer price. However, the load rate is actually *more* when the commission is related to a more appropriate base— the NAV of the fund. When stated as a percent of NAV, the load charge for this fund becomes 9.3 percent. Relative to what it costs to buy and sell common stocks, the costs of load funds are indeed *very high,* even after taking into account the fact that you normally don't have to pay a commission on the *sale* of most funds.

While the *maximum* load charge is 8½ percent of the purchase price, not all funds charge the maximum. Rather, some funds, like Fidelity Select-Computers, charge commissions of only 1 to 3 percent—such funds are known as **low-load funds.** There is a commission to pay on low-load funds, and as such, there will still be a difference (albeit slight) in the fund's offer price and NAV: note that it amounted to only 22 cents in the case of Fidelity Select-Computers. In contrast, note the repeated use of the letters *N.L.* in the offer price column; for example, see the Financial Program High Yield Fund in the quotes in Figure 13.6. Those letters indicate that the fund is a no-load, and as a result, the shares are bought *and* sold at the same NAV price of $7.93 a share.

Occasionally, a no-load fund will have a small **back-end load,** which amounts to a 1 to 2 percent commission on the sale of shares. In addition, a substantial (and growing) number of funds charge something called a **12(b)-1 fee**—a fee that's assessed annually for as long as you own the fund. Known appropriately as *hidden*

---

load fund
a mutual fund that charges a commission when shares are bought; also known as front-end load *fund.*

no-load fund
a mutual fund that does not charge a commission when shares are bought.

low-load fund
a mutual fund that charges a small commission (1 to 3 percent) when shares are bought.

back-end load
a 1 to 2 percent commission on the sale of shares in a mutual fund.

12(b)-1 fee
a fee levied by some mutual funds to cover management and other operating costs; amounts to as much as 1¼ percent annually on the average net assets.

Beware of Salesmen Bearing Unit Investment Trusts

I bought into unit investment trusts because I thought of them as widows-and-orphans type investments, the kind that would pay me a safe, steady return without any wild surprises,'' recalls Anita Lowe. A wealthy Los Angeles investor, Lowe was looking for a conservative counterbalance to her sizable holdings in stocks and individual bonds. UITs, with their well-balanced portfolios and regular monthly paychecks, were unquestionably the perfect answer, her broker advised.

But Lowe was in for a rude awakening. What she had believed was a fixed return on one of the trusts, Bear, Stearns' Municipal Securities Trust High Income Series 11, dropped from a current yield of 8.77% just two years ago to about 7.4%, the result of four defaults in its bond portfolio. ''I consider myself a sophisticated investor, but I never realized the yield could drop so dramatically,'' she says. In fact, of Series 11's $61 million worth of bonds, about 7% have gone into cash default, while another 40% were called or sold off early. The fact that the trust's prospectus warned investors that they must be ''able to assume the risks associated with speculative municipal bonds'' is no consolation to Lowe, who relied on the recommendation of her broker. Now she'd like to bail out. However, there is often hardly any secondary market. Bid prices have sunk from $9.61 at the March 1987 offering to only $7.85 in mid-February, with offer prices of $8.27.

Welcome to the world of unit investment trusts, an investment that has soared in popularity since Black Monday. In 1988, $12.7 billion worth were sold, up about 17% from 1987's level, according to the Investment Company Institute, the industry's trade group. Most of this money is in municipal bonds, but some UITs include flashier holdings such as real estate, zero coupon bonds, junk bonds, takeover stocks and options. All told, there is about $130 billion worth of UITs out there, compared to about $810 billion in mutual funds. But here comparisons end. Since no institutional market exists for UITs, small investors are on their own when it comes to investor safeguards, and the results are frightening. There's no independent research organization that tracks the records of individual UITs and their sponsors, the way Lipper Analytical and other groups follow mutual funds. There's no newspaper coverage of fluctuations in bid-and-ask prices. There are no regulations covering the formulas that can be used to calculate a trust's advertised yield. Worst of all, despite numerous complaints of conflicts of interest among UIT sponsors, deceptive marketing practices and other problems, there is no full-scale review of the industry scheduled by the SEC anytime soon.

Still, to hear brokerage houses tell it, UITs are the best thing for investors since Swiss bank accounts. But despite the fact that many UITs deliver basically what they promise—safety, diversification and a steady, monthly yield—the pros prefer to stay away. Says Frederick Stoever, president of Stoever Glass, which trades in both municipal bonds and UITs: ''In my 25 years in the business, I've never known any bond trader or broker who put his own money in a UIT.''

Says Steven Enright, director of financial planning at Seidman Financial Services: ''I never recommend them. If you've got $50,000 or more, you're better off buying the bonds yourself. And with less than $50,000, go with a bond mutual fund.'' Marilyn

Cohen, president of Capital Insight Brokerage, of Beverly Hills, is blunter still. "Wall Street is really pushing them. But I don't like the trusts and I wouldn't buy them myself or sell them." The reason for Wall Street's infatuation is clear: Sales commissions are fat and juicy on UITs, around 4% to 5%; compare that to a no-load mutual fund, where there is no sales fee and annual management fees average between 0.8% and 1.2%.

In theory, there's nothing wrong with the way a unit investment trust works: A brokerage house puts together a diversified portfolio, generally of bonds, and sells shares of it to investors in units of $1,000. Investors buy shares with the expectation of earning a steady, monthly income and then receiving most of their principal back when the trust expires, usually in 20 to 30 years. Once the portfolio is initially selected, it is "nonmanaged," which means that holdings change only rarely. This is a big selling point for unit trusts, since investors get the presumed benefit of holding bonds until maturity, without the volatility and risks of short-term trading.

But in today's treacherous and unpredictable financial markets, setting up a nonmanaged portfolio can be a little like declaring war without a general to direct the troops. Unlike the way mutual funds work, with unit trusts there's no active portfolio manager ready to unload bonds or stocks at the first sign of serious trouble. Worse still, there's so much competition among firms to come up with the highest returns that some have gravitated toward dicier holdings that will increase yields, at least in the short term. "If you go back years, you'll see that all the problem bonds—New York bonds, Cleveland bonds, retirement home and hospital bonds—just permeate these trusts," warns Mary Calhoun, an ex-broker. UIT sponsors do, however, have the option of selling off bonds with serious credit problems. . . .

"A lot of investors buy UITs because of the supposed management expertise that goes into the selection of their holdings," says Richard Lehmann, president of the Bond Investors Association. "But there's an inherent conflict of interest that most investors are unaware of," he warns, "because the same firms that underwrite these bonds are the ones who put together and promote the UITs." . . .

Of course, each time a bond defaults, as Anita Lowe learned the hard way, UIT yields drop and the value of shares in the secondary market declines. With trusts that invest in the most volatile investments—puts, real estate, junk bonds and the like—the roller coaster ride can be hairy. "People don't realize that regardless of what brokers tell them, unit trusts can only be as safe as their underlying investments or the underlying insurance on the unit trust, if any exists," emphasizes Michael Schwartz, manager of personal financial services at Coopers & Lybrand.

There's another risk that trust holders often ignore: bond calls. "Anytime bonds are prepaid or partially prepaid, investors' yields drop," emphasizes Cohen. Consider the case of the Bear, Stearns Series 11 trust. Anita Lowe and her fellow investors are actually receiving only 6.8% current interest, down from the original 8.77%, if one excludes a $51 return of principal from bonds that were either called or sold early. Even without defaults, the current yield on Advest's N.J. Trust Series 2 (Multistate Tax Exempt Unit Trust) dropped from 9.72% four years ago to 9.13%, thanks to early calls and the early return of a portion of the principal. "Brokers tell customers beforehand that their yields are locked in, but the truth is they can't be locked in unless every single bond is totally noncallable. And very few of them are," Cohen says. She urges investors to look for sponsors who

INVESTOR INSIGHTS (*continued*)

calculate the more realistic yield-to-call rather than yield-to-maturity on callable bonds that will probably not be held by the trust to maturity.

To be sure, some trust sponsors do a better job than others at protecting their yields, but unfortunately, there's no way for investors to track their records. "A common complaint is the lack of advertising or marketing standards," says Thomas Harman, chief counsel of the SEC's division of investment management. "Right now, everybody advertises on the basis of current yield only, rather than yield to maturity or some other, more useful statistic." The SEC says that it intends to review UIT advertising regulations, but the project has so far not been scheduled. Unfortunately, there is no independent organization that monitors yield fluctuations. "No one charts defaults, either—I don't know why not," says Matthew Fink, senior vice president and general counsel at the Investment Company Institute. "You can't even check the spread between bid and ask prices in the newspaper," adds Mary Calhoun. All this means that the only way investors can compare sponsors' records is by relying on a broker's recommendations or laboriously checking with individual sponsors.

Regrettably, with only current yields to compare, there's plenty of room for confusion. Then there's the problem of UIT prospectuses. Admittedly, most are full of legal jargon that warns investors about the prospects for rate fluctuations and bond defaults. But investors only receive prospectuses about 10 days *after* they've invested their money—a circumstance that encourages many to ignore the document entirely. Thomas Harman professes to be unconcerned. "I've been told that many sponsors allow investors to pull out within days of receiving their prospectuses if they don't like what they see." No surprise here: As with most other UIT practices, it's up to the sponsor to decide what to do.

Source: Jill Andresky, "Satanic Purses," *Financial World*, March 21, 1989, pp. 52–54.

loads, these fees have been allowed since 1980 and were originally designed to help funds (particularly the no-loads) cover their distribution and marketing costs. The 12(b)-1 fees can amount to as much as 1¼ percent *per year* of assets under management. In good markets and bad, they're paid, right off the top. And that can take its toll. Consider, for instance, $10,000 in a fund that charges a 1¼ percent 12(b)-1 fee: That translates into a charge of *$125 a year*. The figures below provide a breakdown of the types of loads and fees charged by open-end mutual funds in 1988:

LOAD CHARGE OR FEE	PERCENT OF FUNDS
Pure no-load	30.2%
Front-end load only	30.0
Front-end load + 12(b)-1 fee	19.3
12(b)-1 fee + back-end load	9.5
12(b)-1 fee only	7.4
Other combinations of loads & fees	3.6
Total	100.0%

Note that only 30 percent of the funds are pure no-loads; all the rest charge some type of load and/or fee, the most popular of which is the 12(b)-1 fee.

Other Fees and Costs

Regardless of whether a fund is load or no-load, or whether it is open-end or closed, another cost of owning mutual funds is the *management fee,* the compensation paid to the professional managers who administer the fund's portfolio. These fees generally amount to anywhere from around .50 to as much as 2.50 percent of average assets under management. (These expense ratios bear watching, since high expenses will take their toll on performance.) Unlike load charges, which are one-time costs, management fees (and 12(b)-1 charges, if imposed) are levied *annually* and are paid *regardless of the performance of the portfolio.* In addition, there are the administrative costs of operating the fund; these are fairly modest and represent the normal cost of doing business (like the commissions paid when the fund buys and sells securities).

A final cost is the taxes paid on security transactions. In order to avoid double taxation, nearly all mutual funds operate as *regulated investment companies.* This means that all (or nearly all) of the dividend and interest income is passed on to the investor, as are any capital gains realized when securities are sold. The mutual fund thus pays no taxes, but instead passes the tax liability on to its shareholders. This holds true regardless of whether such distributions are reinvested in the company (in the form of additional mutual fund shares) or paid out in cash. Mutual funds will annually provide each stockholder with a convenient summary report on the amount of dividends and capital gains received and the amount of taxable income earned (and to be reported) by the fund shareholder.

Keeping Track of Fund Fees and Loads

Critics of the mutual fund industry have come down hard on the proliferation of fund fees and charges. Indeed, some would argue that all the different kinds of charges and fees are really meant to do one thing: confuse the investor. The fact is a lot of funds were going to great lengths—lower a cost here, tack on a fee there, hide a charge somewhere else—to make themselves look like something they weren't. The funds were all following the letter of the law, and, indeed, they were fully disclosing all their expenses and fees. The trouble was that the funds were able to neatly hide all but the most conspicuous of their charges in a bunch of legalese. Fortunately, all this is beginning to change as steps have been taken to bring fund fees and loads out into the open.

For one thing, these charges are more fully reported by the financial press. You don't have to look any farther than the *mutual fund quotations* found in *The Wall Street Journal* and most other major papers. For example, refer back to the quotations in Figure 13.6; notice the use of the letters "r," "p," and "t." If you see an "r" behind a fund's name, it means the fund charges some type of *redemption fee,* or back-end load, when you sell your shares; this is the case, for example, with Fidelity Select-Computers. The use of a "p," in contrast, means the fund levies a *12(b)-1 fee,* which you'll have to pay, for example, if you invest in Flex Fund-

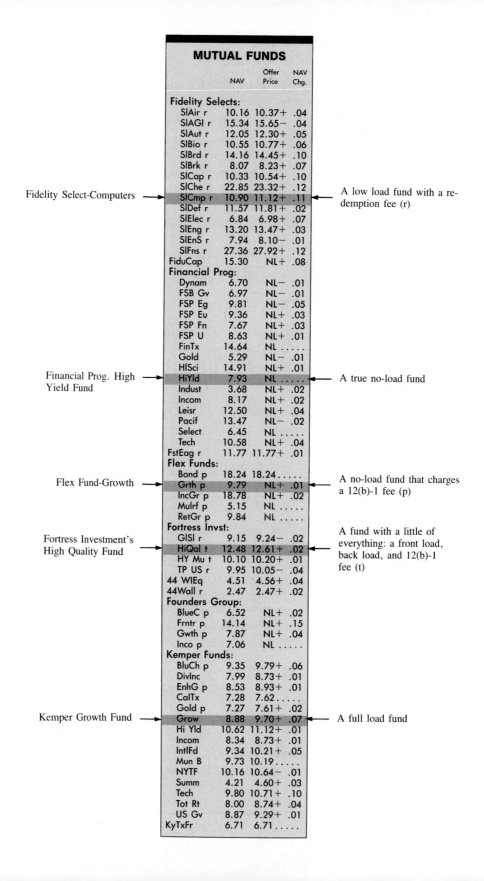

MUTUAL FUNDS

	NAV	Offer Price	NAV Chg.
Fidelity Selects:			
SlAir r	10.16	10.37+	.04
SlAGI r	15.34	15.65−	.04
SlAut r	12.05	12.30+	.05
SlBio r	10.55	10.77+	.06
SlBrd r	14.16	14.45+	.10
SlBrk r	8.07	8.23+	.07
SlCap r	10.33	10.54+	.10
SlChe r	22.85	23.32+	.12
SlCmp r	10.90	11.12+	.11
SlDef r	11.57	11.81+	.02
SlElec r	6.84	6.98+	.07
SlEng r	13.20	13.47+	.03
SlEnS r	7.94	8.10−	.01
SlFns r	27.36	27.92+	.12
FiduCap	15.30	NL+	.08
Financial Prog:			
Dynam	6.70	NL−	.01
FSB Gv	6.97	NL−	.01
FSP Eg	9.81	NL−	.05
FSP Eu	9.36	NL+	.03
FSP Fn	7.67	NL+	.03
FSP U	8.63	NL+	.01
FinTx	14.64	NL	.....
Gold	5.29	NL−	.01
HlSci	14.91	NL+	.01
HiYld	7.93	NL	.....
Indust	3.68	NL+	.02
Incom	8.17	NL+	.02
Leisr	12.50	NL+	.04
Pacif	13.47	NL−	.02
Select	6.45	NL	.....
Tech	10.58	NL+	.04
FstEag r	11.77	11.77+	.01
Flex Funds:			
Bond p	18.24	18.24	.....
Grth p	9.79	NL+	.01
IncGr p	18.78	NL+	.02
Mulrf p	5.15	NL	.....
RetGr p	9.84	NL	.....
Fortress Invst:			
GlSl r	9.15	9.24−	.02
HiQal t	12.48	12.61+	.02
HY Mu t	10.10	10.20+	.01
TP US r	9.95	10.05−	.04
44 WlEq	4.51	4.56+	.04
44Wall r	2.47	2.47+	.02
Founders Group:			
BlueC p	6.52	NL+	.02
Frntr p	14.14	NL+	.15
Gwth p	7.87	NL+	.04
Inco p	7.06	NL	.....
Kemper Funds:			
BluCh p	9.35	9.79+	.06
DivInc	7.99	8.73+	.01
EnhG p	8.53	8.93+	.01
CalTx	7.28	7.62	.....
Gold p	7.27	7.61+	.02
Grow	8.88	9.70+	.07
Hi Yld	10.62	11.12+	.01
Incom	8.34	8.73+	.01
IntlFd	9.34	10.21+	.05
Mun B	9.73	10.19	.....
NYTF	10.16	10.64−	.01
Summ	4.21	4.60+	.03
Tech	9.80	10.71+	.10
Tot Rt	8.00	8.74+	.04
US Gv	8.87	9.29+	.01
KyTxFr	6.71	6.71	.....

Fidelity Select-Computers → SlCmp r

→ A low load fund with a redemption fee (r)

Financial Prog. High Yield Fund → HiYld

→ A true no-load fund

Flex Fund-Growth → Grth p

→ A no-load fund that charges a 12(b)-1 fee (p)

Fortress Investment's High Quality Fund → HiQal t

→ A fund with a little of everything: a front load, back load, and 12(b)-1 fee (t)

Kemper Growth Fund → Grow

→ A full load fund

Growth. Finally, a "t" will appear with funds that charge *both* redemption fees and 12(b)-1 fees; notice that's what you get with Fortress Investment's High Quality Fund. In fact, if you look closely at the quotations, you'll see that Fortress High Quality not only levies redemption and 12(b)-1 fees *but also has a front-end load—* as indicated by the difference in its NAV and offer price. The point is: Don't be surprised to find load funds that also charge redemption and/or 12(b)-1 fees, and the same goes for no-load funds. The quotations, of course, tell you only the *kinds* of fees charged by the funds; they don't tell you how much is charged. To get the specifics on the amount charged, you'll have to turn to the fund itself.

All (open-end) mutual funds are required to *fully disclose* all their expenses in a standardized, easy-to-understand format. Every fund prospectus must contain, right up front, a fairly detailed *fee table,* much like the one illustrated in Figure 13.7. Notice that this table has three parts. The first specifies all *shareholder transaction costs*. In effect, this tells you what it's going to cost to buy and sell shares in the mutual fund. The next section lists all the *annual operating expenses* of the fund. Showing these expenses as a percentage of average net assets, the fund must break out management fees, those elusive 12(b)-1 fees, and any other expenses. The third section provides a rundown of the *total cost over time* of buying, selling, and owning the fund. This part of the table contains both transaction and operating expenses and shows what the total costs would be over hypothetical 1-, 3-, 5-, and 10-year holding periods. To ensure consistency and comparability, the funds have to follow a rigid set of guidelines when constructing the illustrative costs.

It's obviously in your best interest to pay close attention to the fee table whenever you're considering an investment in a mutual fund. Other things being equal, look for low initial charges as well as low expense ratios over time. As a rule, the longer you intend to hold a fund, the more willing you should be to trade a higher load charge for lower annual management and 12(b)-1 fees. That will help you keep your total holding period costs down. In the final analysis, keep in mind that costs are only one element in the decision. Another very important variable is *performance*. There may be times when higher costs are justified; there may be other times when they're not. When it comes to costs, you might want to follow these guidelines:

- Consider a *more expensive* fund if it has a better performance record (and offers more return potential) than a less expensive fund. It's all a matter of whether you'd rather own a costly performer or a low-cost "dog"!
- If there's little or no difference in performance records or return potential, go with the *less expensive* fund. In this case, lower expenses will make a difference in comparative returns.

FIGURE 13.6 (Facing Page) Mutual Funds Quotations, Showing Load and No-Load Funds.
Open-end mutual funds are listed separately from other securities and they have their own quotation system; for one thing, these securities are quoted in dollars and cents (most other securities are listed in eighths or thirty-seconds) and the type of load charge, if any, is indicated as part of the quote. (*Source: The Wall Street Journal.*)

Expenses and Costs of Investing in the Fund

The following information is provided in order to assist investors in understanding the transaction costs and annual expenses associated with investing in the Fund.

A. SHAREHOLDER TRANSACTION COSTS:

Sales Load on Purchases 2%
Sales Load on Reinvested Dividends . . . . .None
Redemption Fees or Deferred Sales Charges . . . . .None
Exchange (or Conversion) Fees . . . . .None

B. ANNUAL FUND OPERATING EXPENSES:

(as a percentage of average net assets)
Management Fees 0.40%
12(b)-1 Fees . . . . .None
Other Expenses (estimated) 0.32%

C. EXAMPLE OF FUND EXPENSES OVER TIME:

You would pay the following total expenses over time on a $1,000 investment assuming a 5% annual return, and a complete redemption of the investment at the end of each indicated time period:

1-year	3-years	5-years	10-years
$27	$43	$59	$108

FIGURE 13.7   Mutual Fund Expense Disclosure Table.
Mutual funds are now required by the SEC to make full disclosure of load charges, redemption fees, and annual expenses in a three-part table like the one shown here; the table must be conspicuously placed in the front part of the prospectus, not hidden somewhere in the back. *Source:* The prospectus of a major mutual fund; the figures used in this table are those actually incurred by a real mutual fund.

Buying and Selling Fund Shares

Buying and selling shares of *closed-end* investment companies is no different from buying shares of common stock. The transactions are executed on listed exchanges or in the OTC market through brokers or dealers who handle the orders in the normal way. They are subject to the usual transaction costs, and because they are treated like any other listed or OTC stock, the shares of closed-end funds can even be margined or sold short. The situation is considerably different, however, with *open-end* funds. There are several ways of acquiring such shares, depending on whether the fund is load or no-load. However, it should first be pointed out that regardless of whether the fund is load or no-load, it must provide you with a recent **prospectus** that describes its operations and other financial matters. A note of caution is in order here, since the prospectuses provided by many mutual funds today simply are *not* as detailed as they used to be. Many, in fact, are little more than warmed-over sales pitches—which is why many experts strongly suggest you obtain and read the fund's *Statement of Additional Information,* a publication that's far more useful than the typical prospectus.

prospectus
a document describing in varying amounts of detail the financial matters and operations of a public offering.

With load funds, investors buy the stocks from a broker or through salespeople employed by the mutual fund. Most brokerage firms are authorized to sell shares in a variety of load funds, and this is the easiest and most convenient way of buying funds for investors who have established brokerage accounts. Sometimes, however, the fund may not be sold through brokerage houses, in which case the investor would deal directly with the fund's commissioned salespeople—individuals employed by the mutual fund for the sole purpose of selling its shares.

If you happen to be interested in a no-load fund, on the other hand, you are strictly on your own. You must write or call the mutual fund directly to obtain information. You will then receive an order form from the fund and instructions on how to buy shares; no salesperson will ever call on you. To complete the transaction you simply mail your check, along with the completed order form, to the mutual fund or its designated agent. (Appendix A provides the names, addresses, telephone numbers, and purchase requirements for scores of popular no-load funds.)

Selling shares in a fund is also a do-it-yourself affair, whether the fund is load or no-load. Because commissions are usually not levied on fund sales, brokers and salespeople are of little help in selling funds. As a result, you may find that you'll have to redeem your shares by directly notifying the mutual fund (usually by mail) of your intention to sell. This can become a time-consuming process and may even involve certification of your signature. In effect, you contact the fund directly, which then buys back the shares and mails you a check. An alternative is available with funds that offer checkwriting privileges (most money funds have checkwriting privileges, as do some stock and bond funds). Using this service, it's possible to redeem shares by simply writing a check on the fund large enough to clean out the balance of the account. It is as simple as writing a check on a checking account and is obviously much easier and quicker than having to notify the fund directly. And as we noted earlier, if the fund offers conversion privileges, you can also get out by simply phoning in an order to *switch* your money from one fund to another. There are, of course, some constraints with *phone switching,* but even so, this service has made the selling of fund shares a remarkably *easy* process.

TYPES OF FUNDS AND SERVICES

Some mutual funds specialize in stocks, others in bonds; some have maximum capital gains as an investment objective, and some seek high income. Some funds will thus appeal to speculators, whereas others will be of interest primarily to income-oriented investors. Every fund has a particular investment objective, some of the more common ones being growth (or capital gains), current income, tax-exempt income, preservation of capital, or some combination thereof. Disclosure of a fund's investment objective is required by the SEC, and each fund is expected to do its best to conform to its stated investment policy and objective. Categorizing funds according to their investment policies and objectives is widely practiced in the mutual fund industry, as it tends to reflect similarities not only in how the funds manage their money, but also in their risk and return characteristics. Some of the more popular types of mutual funds include growth, aggressive growth, equity-income, balanced, growth-and-income, bond, money market, specialty, sector, and international funds. Table 13.3 lists some top-performing funds from each of these

TABLE 13.3 A Partial Menu of Mutual Funds

	Maximum Load Charge[a]	Expense Ratio[a]	5-year Performance[b] (1984–'88)
I. GROWTH FUNDS			
Fidelity Magellan	3.00%	1.14%	17.5%
Linder Fund	0, r	.89	15.0
Loomis-Sayles Cap. Dev.	0	.92	14.8
Merrill Lynch Phoenix A	6.50	1.16	17.6
Nicholas Fund	0	.86	13.3
Phoenix Growth Series	8.50	.76	15.6
II. AGGRESSIVE GROWTH FUNDS			
Dreyfus Leverage Fund	8.50%	1.23%	13.9%
Omega Fund	5.50, +, r	1.74	12.8
Oppenheimer Time Fund	8.50	.97	12.2
Phoenix Stock Fund	8.50	.76	13.2
Putnam Voyager	8.50	1.20	14.0
Quasar Associates	5.50, +	1.33	12.8
III. EQUITY-INCOME FUNDS			
Decatur Fund I	8.50%	.69%	16.0%
Fidelity Equity-Income	2.00	.66	14.3
Financial Industrial Income	0	.78	14.7
Lindner Dividend	0, r	1.04	14.2
SAFECO Income	0	.94	14.2
Stratton Monthly Dividend	0	1.21	13.0
IV. BALANCED FUNDS			
Fidelity Puritan	2.00%	.80%	14.9%
Franklin Income	4.00	.60	12.6
Income Fund of Amer.	5.75, +	.53	14.3
Mass. Financial Total Return	7.25	.63	14.2
Wellesley Income	0	.49	14.4
Wellington Fund	0	.43	14.9
V. GROWTH-AND-INCOME FUNDS			
American Leaders	4.50%, +	1.00%	14.7%
Evergreen Total Return	0	1.01	13.6
Investment Co. of America	5.75, +	.41	15.7
Merrill Lynch Capital A	6.50	.60	15.5

TABLE 13.3   (Continued)

	Maximum Load Charge[a]	Expense Ratio[a]	5-year Performance[b] (1984–'88)
V. GROWTH-AND-INCOME FUNDS			
Mutual Qualified	0	.71	18.8
Strong Total Return	1.00	1.10	15.3
VI. BOND FUNDS			
Kemper U.S. Gov. Secs.	4.50%	.51%	11.8%
Vanguard Fxd. Inc.—GNMAs	0	.35	11.3
Kemper Inc. & Capt. Preserv'n	4.50	.69	12.3
Pioneer Bond Fund	4.50	.90	10.5
SAFECO Muni Bonds	0	.61	12.8
SteinRoe Managed Munies	0	.65	13.6
VII. MONEY MARKET FUNDS			
• **General Purpose:**			
Kemper Money Mkt Fund	0	.52%	7.9%
Transamerica Cash Reserves	0	.49	7.8
Vanguard MM Reserves—Prime	0	.37	7.9
• **Government Only:**			
Cardinal Gov. Secs. Trust	0, +	.71	7.6
Fidelity U.S. Gov. Reserves	0, +	.79	7.4
Pru-Bache Govt. Secs.—MM	0, +	.63	7.6
• **Tax-Exempt:**			
Calvert Tax-free Reserves	0	.62	5.2
Dreyfus Tax-exempt Mon. Mkt	0	.57	4.8
T. Rowe Price Tax-exempt M.F.	0	.60	5.0
VIII. SPECIALTY FUNDS (EXCL'G SECTOR & INTERNAT'L FUNDS)			
Calvert Social Invsmts—Mgd. Gr.	4.50%, +	1.36%	13.2%
GIT Special Growth	0	1.50	15.2
Oppenheimer Gold & Spec. Minerals	8.50	1.22	12.1
Pru-Bache Option Growth	0, +, r	1.69	12.1
Putnam OTC Emerging Growth	6.75, +	1.49	15.1
Vanguard Index—S&P 500	0	.26	14.9
IX. SECTOR FUNDS			
Century Shares Trust	0	.81%	14.1%
Criterion Technology	4.75, +	2.50	23.3 (3 yrs)

TABLE 13.3   (Continued)

	Maximum Load Charge[a]	Expense Ratio[a]	5-year Performance[b] (1984–'88)
IX. SECTOR FUNDS			
Fidelity Select-Retailing	2.00, r	2.47	13.6 (3 yrs)
Freedom Regional Banks	0, +, r	2.24	15.9 (3 yrs)
Pru-Bache Utility Fund	0, +, r	1.63	22.4
Vanguard Spec'd—Health Care	0, r	.51	22.6 (4 yrs)
X. INTERNATIONAL FUNDS			
Fidelity Overseas	3.00%	1.61%	40.3% (4 yrs)
Merrill Lynch Pacific	6.50	.94	30.9
G.T. Japan Growth Fund	4.75, +	1.70	44.1 (3 yrs)
Paine Webber Atlas	8.50	1.24	22.7
Scudder International	0	1.21	21.7
Templeton World Fund	8.50	.67	14.9

[a] Load charges and expense ratios are as of 12/31/88; an "r" in the load column means the fund levies a redemption fee in addition to, or in place of, a front-end load; a "+" means the fund has a 12(b)-1 charge.

[b] 5-year performance figures are fully compounded returns, and assume reinvestment of all dividends and capital gains distributions; these are average annual returns and they cover the period from January 1984 through December 1988, except as noted with sector and international funds.

Source: Business Week Mutual Fund Scoreboard computer disks; and Donoghue's Mutual Funds Almanac.

ten categories, including their load charges and fees, as well as five-year performance records. Let's look now at the various types of mutual funds to see what they are and how they operate.

Types of Mutual Funds

Growth Funds

growth fund
a mutual fund whose primary goals are capital gains and long-term growth.

The objective of a **growth fund** is simple: capital appreciation. Long-term growth and capital gains are the primary goals of such funds, and as a result they invest principally in common stocks that have above-average growth potential but offer little (if anything) in the way of dividends and current income. Because of the uncertain nature of their investment income, growth funds are felt to involve a fair amount of risk exposure. They are usually viewed as long-term investment vehicles most suitable for the more aggressive investor who wants to build up capital and has little interest in current income.

Aggressive Growth Funds

Aggressive growth funds are the so-called performance (or ''go-go'') funds that tend to increase in popularity when the markets heat up. **Aggressive growth funds** are highly speculative investment vehicles that seek large profits from capital gains. In many respects, they are really an extension of the growth fund concept. Many are fairly small, and their portfolios consist mainly of high-flying common stocks. These funds often buy stocks of small, unseasoned companies, stocks with relatively high price/earnings multiples, and common stocks whose prices are highly volatile. They seem to be especially fond of turn-around situations and may even use leverage in their portfolios (that is, buy stocks on margin); they also use options very aggressively, various hedging techniques, and short selling. All this is designed, of course, to yield big returns. But aggressive funds are also highly speculative and are among the most volatile of all the types of funds. When the markets are good, aggressive growth funds do well; when the markets are bad, these funds often experience substantial losses.

Equity-Income Funds

Equity-income funds emphasize current income, and they do so by investing primarily in high-yielding common stocks. Capital preservation is also important and so is some capital gains, although capital appreciation is not a primary objective of **equity-income funds.** These funds invest heavily in high-grade common stocks, some convertible securities and preferred stocks, and occasionally even some investment-quality bonds. As far as their stock holdings are concerned, they lean heavily toward blue chips, public utilities, and financial shares. They like securities that generate hefty dividend yields but also consider potential price appreciation over the longer haul. In general, because of their emphasis on dividends and current income, these funds tend to hold higher-quality securities that are subject to less price volatility than the market as a whole. They're generally viewed as a fairly low-risk way of investing in stocks.

Balanced Funds

Balanced funds are so named because they tend to hold a balanced portfolio of both stocks and bonds, and they do so for the purpose of generating a well-balanced return of both current income and long-term capital gains. In many respects, they're a lot like equity-income funds, except that **balanced funds** usually put much more into fixed-income securities; generally, they keep at least 25 to 50 percent—and sometimes more—of their portfolios in bonds. The bonds are used principally to provide current income, and stocks are selected mainly for their long-term growth potential. The funds can, of course, shift the emphasis in their security holdings one way or the other. Clearly, the more the fund leans toward fixed-income securities, the more income-oriented it will be. For the most part, balanced funds tend to confine their investing to high-grade securities, including growth-oriented blue chip stocks, high-quality income shares, and high-yielding investment-grade bonds. As

such, they're usually considered to be a relatively safe form of investing, one where you can earn a competitive rate of return without having to endure a lot of price volatility.

Growth-and-Income Funds

growth-and-income fund
a mutual fund that seeks both long-term growth and current income, with principal emphasis on capital gains.

Growth-and-income funds also seek a balanced return made up of both current income and long-term capital gains, but they place a greater emphasis on growth of capital. Moreover, unlike balanced funds, **growth-and-income funds** put most of their money into equities—indeed, it's not unusual for these funds to have 80 to 90 percent of their capital in common stocks. They tend to confine most of their investing to quality issues, so you can expect to find a lot of growth-oriented blue chip stocks in their portfolios, along with a fair amount of high-quality income stocks. One of the big appeals of these funds is the fairly substantial returns many of them have been able to generate over the long haul. But then, these funds do involve a fair amount of risk, if for no other reason than the emphasis they place on stocks and capital gains. As such, growth and income funds are most suitable for those investors who can tolerate the risk and price volatility.

Bond Funds

bond fund
a mutual fund that invests in various kinds and grades of bonds, with income as the primary objective.

As the name implies, **bond funds** invest exclusively in various kinds and grades of bonds—from Treasury and agency bonds to corporates and municipals. Income is the primary investment objective, although capital gains is not ignored. There are two important advantages to buying shares in bond funds, rather than investing directly in bonds. First, the bond funds are generally more liquid, and second, they offer diversification. Bond funds are usually considered to be fairly conservative investment vehicles, but they are not totally without risk, since the prices of the bonds held in the fund's portfolio will fluctuate with changing interest rates. Though many of the funds are basically conservative, a growing number are becoming increasingly aggressive. In fact, much of the growth that bond funds have experienced recently can be attributed to this new investment attitude; as such, it's possible to find everything from high-grade government bond funds to highly speculative funds that invest in nothing but junk bonds. For many years, bond funds seemed to hold little appeal as investment vehicles; in the mid-1970s, however, fund managers became more aggressive and started managing their portfolios more fully. More recently, bond fund sales have been helped by the public's growing appetite for mortgage-backed securities. These funds invest primarily in government-backed mortgage securities (like GNMAs and CMOs) and in so doing, offer investors secure yet highly attractive rates of return. These funds appeal to investors not only because they provide diversification and a more affordable way to get into these securities, but also because they have a provision that allows investors (if they so choose) to reinvest the *principal* portion of the monthly cash flow, thereby enabling them to preserve, rather than consume, their capital.

As indicated by the following list, there's a full range of different types of bond funds available today:

- *Government bond funds,* which invest in U.S. Treasury and agency securities.
- *Mortgage-backed bond funds,* which put their money into various types of mortgage-backed securities of the U.S. government (like GNMA issues).
- *High-grade corporate bond funds,* which invest chiefly in investment-grade securities rated triple-B or better.
- *High-yield corporate bond funds,* which are risky investments that buy *junk bonds* for the yields they offer.
- *Municipal bond funds,* which invest in tax-exempt securities and which are suitable for investors looking for tax-free income—like their corporate counter-parts, municipals can also come out as either high-grade or high-yield funds.
- *Intermediate-term bond funds,* which invest in bonds with maturities of 7 to 10 years, or less, and offer not only attractive yields but relatively *low* price vola-tility as well.
- *International bond funds,* which center their investments in the fixed-income securities of foreign governments and companies. They seek their returns in two ways: one from the high yields available in some foreign countries and second from positive moves in foreign exchange rates.

Clearly, no matter what you're looking for in a fixed-income security, you're likely to find a bond fund that fits the bill. The number and variety of such funds has skyrocketed in the past 10 years or so; the net result was that in early 1989, there were roughly *a thousand* publicly traded bond funds that had more than $280 billion worth of bonds under management.

Money Market Funds

money market mu-tual fund
a mutual fund that pools the capital of a number of investors and uses it to invest in short-term money market instruments; also called a money fund.

The first **money market mutual fund,** or *money fund* for short, was set up in November 1972 with only $100,000 in total assets. It was a new concept that applied the mutual fund notion to the buying and selling of short-term money market instruments—such as bank certificates of deposit, U.S. Treasury bills, and the like. For the first time, money funds offered investors with modest amounts of capital access to the high-yielding money market, where many instruments require minimum investments of $100,000 or more (money funds are discussed in greater detail in Chapter 4, along with other short-term investment vehicles). The idea caught on quickly, and the growth in money funds was nothing short of phenome-nal. However, that growth temporarily peaked in 1982, as the introduction of money market deposit accounts by banks and S&Ls caused money fund assets to level off and eventually decline. However, it didn't take long for the industry to recover, and by 1989 there were 467 money funds that, together, held over $315 billion in assets—which, by the way, *accounted for about 35 percent of all the assets held by mutual funds.*

Actually, there are several different kinds of money market mutual funds:

- *General purpose money funds,* which invest in any and all types of money market investment vehicles, from Treasury bills and bank CDs to corporate

commercial paper. The vast majority of money funds are of this type: they invest their money wherever they can find attractive short-term yields.

- *Government securities money funds,* which were established as a way to meet investor concerns for safety. They effectively eliminate any risk of default by confining their investments to Treasury bills and other short-term securities of the U.S. government or its agencies (such as the Federal Farm Credit System, the Federal Home Loan Mortgage Corporation, and the Federal National Mortgage Association).

- *Tax-exempt money funds,* which limit their investing to very short (30- to 90-day) tax-exempt municipal securities. Since their income is free from federal income tax, they appeal predominantly to investors in high tax brackets. The yields on these funds are about 25 to 35 percent *below* the returns on other types of money funds, so you need to be in a high enough tax bracket to produce a competitive after-tax return. Some tax-exempt funds confine their investing to the securities of a single state, so that residents of high-tax states can enjoy income that's free from *both* federal and state tax.

Just about every major brokerage firm has at least one or two money funds of its own, and another three hundred or so are sold by independent fund distributors. Most require minimum investments of $1,000 (although $2,500 to $5,000 minimum requirements are not uncommon). Because of the nature of the securities they hold, money funds are highly liquid investment vehicles, and they're very low in risk since they are virtually immune to capital loss. However, the interest income produced by the funds is not so secure, as it tends to follow general interest rate conditions. As a result, the returns to shareholders are subject to the ups and downs of market interest rates. Even with their variability, the yields on money funds are highly competitive with other short-term securities, and with the checkwriting privileges they offer, they're just as liquid as checking or savings accounts. They are viewed by many investors as a convenient, safe, and profitable way to accumulate capital and temporarily store idle funds.

Specialty Funds

Some funds seek to achieve their investment objectives by investing within a single industry or within a specified geographical area. Others do it by confining their investments to small companies, the so-called emerging growth firms, or by setting up funds to invest in *other* mutual funds. (Actually these *fund funds* actively trade in and out of other funds as the way to generate high rates of return.) These are all examples of **specialty funds** that strive to achieve fairly attractive (and sometimes even spectacular) rates of return by adhering to unusual and, at times, unorthodox investment strategies. Specialty funds make up about 15 to 20 percent of the total *number* of mutual funds, and due to their unusual approach to investing, most are relatively small in terms of assets under management.

In addition to those noted above, there are many other types of specialty funds, including *tax-managed funds,* which seek to minimize taxes by committing funds to tax-preferred investments; *index funds,* which strive to match the return from the

specialty fund
a mutual fund that strives to achieve attractive and sometimes spectacular rates of return by adhering to unusual or unorthodox investment strategies.

stock market as a whole (as measured by an index like the S&P 500); *yield-enhanced* (or *hedge*) *funds,* which hedge their portfolios with futures and options; *socially conscious funds,* which consider morality and ethics to be the key variables in the investment decision; funds for options trading; commodity funds; and others. Due to their unusual nature, they can involve substantial risk exposure and often require specialized knowledge on the part of investors. Two of the most popular types of specialty funds are sector funds and international funds.

Sector Funds

sector fund
a mutual fund that restricts its investments to a particular segment of the market.

One of the newest products on Wall Street—and also one of the hottest—is the so-called **sector fund,** a mutual fund that restricts its investments to a particular sector, or segment, of the market. In effect, these funds concentrate their investment holdings in the one or more industries that make up the sector being aimed at. For example, a health care sector fund would confine its investments to those industries related to this segment of the market: drug companies, hospital management firms, medical suppliers, and biotech concerns. The portfolio of a sector fund would then consist of promising growth stocks from these particular industries. The underlying investment objective of a sector fund is *capital gains;* in many respects it is similar to a growth fund, and as such, should be considered speculative in nature. The idea behind the sector fund concept is that the really attractive returns come from small segments of the market, so rather than diversifying your portfolio across the market, put your money where the action is! It's an interesting notion that certainly warrants consideration by the more aggressive investor willing to take on the added risks that often accompany these funds. Among the more popular sector funds are those that concentrate their investments in aerospace and defense; energy; financial services; gold; leisure and entertainment; natural resources; electronics; chemicals; computers; telecommunications; utilities; and of course, health care—basically, all the "glamour" industries.

International Funds

international fund
a mutual fund that does all or most of its investing in foreign securities.

Another top-performing fund in the 1980s was the **international fund**—a type of mutual fund that does all or most of its investing in foreign securities. A lot of people would like to invest in foreign securities but simply don't have the experience and know-how to do so. International funds may be just the vehicle for such investors, *provided they have at least a basic appreciation of international economics.* Since these funds deal with the international economy, balance of trade positions, and currency devaluations, investors should have a fundamental understanding of what these issues are and how they can affect fund returns. Basically there are two types of international funds: (1) *global funds,* which invest primarily in foreign securities, but also in U.S. companies (usually multinational firms); and (2) *overseas funds,* which invest exclusively outside the United States, sometimes confining their activities to specific geographical regions (like Japan or Australia). As a rule, global funds provide more diversity and, with access to both the U.S. and foreign markets, can go where the action is. These funds attempt to take advantage of international economic developments not only by capitalizing on changing global

market conditions, but also by positioning themselves to benefit from the devaluation in the dollar. They do so in order to produce capital gains, which at times can be substantial. International funds are considered high-risk investments and should be used only by knowledgeable investors who are able to tolerate such risks.

Investor Services

Ask most investors why they buy a particular mutual fund and they'll probably tell you that the fund provides the kind of income and return they're looking for. Now, no one would question the importance of return in the investment decision, but there are some other reasons for investing in mutual funds, not the least of which are the services they provide. Indeed, many investors find these services so valuable that they often buy the funds as much for their services as for their returns. Some of the most sought-after *mutual fund services* include savings and reinvestment plans, regular income programs, conversion and phone-switching privileges, checkwriting privileges, and retirement programs.

Savings and Automatic Reinvestment Plans

These two very important services allow investors to adhere to a systematic and routine plan of savings and capital accumulation. Most funds offer both services, and it is possible to use one without the other, although the two usually do go together.

savings plan
a service offered by a mutual fund in which the shareholder agrees, either formally or informally, to add a certain amount of money to his/her mutual fund account on a regular basis.

Savings Plans.   In a **savings plan** an investor agrees, either formally or informally, to add a certain amount of money to his or her mutual fund account on a regular (monthly or quarterly) basis. For example, an investor might agree to add $250 to the account every quarter. The money is then used to buy additional shares in the fund. *Voluntary savings plans* are a great way to regularly add capital to an investment program.

In contrast, caution should be exercised when dealing with *contractual savings plans* that involve substantial front-end loads. These plans set up formal contractual agreements that supposedly (though *not* legally) compel the investor to a long-term investment program and then stack all the commissions that will be paid over the life of the contract onto the front end. Thus, the fund will collect all the commissions that will ever come due in the first several years of the contract and will not begin fully crediting the investor's account with share purchases until *after* these load charges have been met. For example, if an individual agrees to invest $1,000 a year for each of the next 15 years, the total size of this contractual savings plan would be $15,000. If the fund uses an 8.5 percent sales commission (and most funds that offer front-end contractual plans tend to charge the maximum), the total commission that would be paid over the life of this contract would be $1,275 (that is, .085 × $15,000). The catch is that this full commission will be deducted from the *first several payments,* whether the investor sticks with the plan for 15 years or not. Such arrangements can be very costly, since investors who drop out sacrifice some or all of the prepaid commissions and find that the number of shares that they actually own is considerably *less* than what they could have bought through regular

purchases. While the SEC requires a full refund of prepaid commissions if the investor cancels the plan within 45 days, it requires a refund of only 85 percent of prepaid loads for persons who cancel within 18 months of enrollment and no refund at all for those who cancel later. These contractual arrangements have been under considerable fire for some time and are prohibited in some states (for example, California, Illinois, Ohio, and Wisconsin).

Automatic Reinvestment Plans. This is one of the real draws of mutual funds, and it's a service that's offered by virtually every open-ended fund. A lot like the dividend reinvestment plans we looked at with stocks (in Chapter 6), the **automatic reinvestment plans** of mutual funds enable you to keep your capital fully employed. Through this service, dividend and/or capital gains income is *automatically used to buy additional shares in the fund*. Keep in mind, however, that even though an investor may reinvest all dividends and capital gains distributions, the IRS will treat them as cash receipts and as such, tax them as investment income in the year in which they were paid! Most funds deal in fractional shares, and such purchases are often commission-free.

Automatic reinvestment plans are especially attractive since they enable investors to earn fully compounded rates of return. That is, by plowing back profits (reinvested dividends and capital gains distributions), the investor essentially can put his or her profits to work in generating even more earnings. Indeed, the effects of these plans on total accumulated capital over the long haul can be substantial. Figure 13.8, on page 586, shows the long-term impact of one such plan. (These are the actual performance numbers for a *real* mutual fund—Twentieth Century Growth Investors.) In the illustration, we assume the investor starts with $10,000 and, except for the reinvestment of dividends and capital gains, adds no new capital over time. Even so, note that the initial investment of $10,000 grew to more than $380,000 over a 27-year period (which, by the way, amounts to a compounded rate of return of 14.4 percent). Of course, not all periods will match this performance, nor will all mutual funds be able to perform as well even in strong markets. The point is, as long as care is taken in selecting an appropriate fund, *attractive benefits can be derived from the systematic accumulation of capital offered by savings and/or automatic reinvestment plans.* Clearly investors should consider very seriously the idea of incorporating one or both of these plans into their mutual fund investment program.

Regular Income

Although automatic reinvestment plans are great for the long-term investor, what about the investor who's looking for a steady stream of income? Once again, mutual funds have a service to meet this kind of need. It's called a **systematic withdrawal plan,** and it's offered by most open-ended funds. Once enrolled in one of these plans, an investor will automatically receive a predetermined amount of money every month or quarter. Usually the funds require a minimum investment of $5,000 or more in order to participate in such plans, and the size of the minimum payment must normally be $50 or more per period (with no limit on the maximum). Fund

---

automatic reinvestment plan
a mutual fund service that enables shareholders to automatically buy additional shares in the fund through reinvestment of dividends and/or capital gains income.

systematic withdrawal plan
a mutual fund service that enables shareholders to automatically receive a predetermined amount of money every month or quarter.

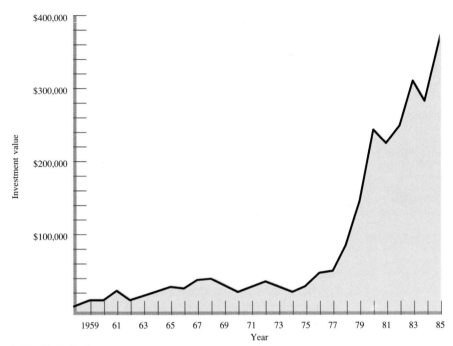

FIGURE 13.8 The Effects of Reinvesting Income.
Reinvesting dividends and/or capital gains can have tremendous effects on one's investment position. This graph shows the results of a hypothetical investor who initially invested $10,000 and for 27 years reinvested all dividends and capital gains distributions in additional fund shares. (No adjustment has been made for any income taxes payable by the shareholder—which would be appropriate so long as the fund was held in an IRA or Keogh account.) (*Source:* Twentieth Century Investors.)

managers will pay out the monthly or quarterly income first from dividends and realized capital gains; should this source prove to be inadequate and should the shareholder so authorize, the fund can then tap the principal or original paid-in capital in the account to meet the required periodic payments.

There are several types of systematic withdrawal plans, the most common of which is for the investor to specify the withdrawal of a fixed dollar amount per period. For example, an investor might choose to receive $200 every month, regardless of the source of payment. Another popular arrangement specifies a fixed number of shares to be liquidated each period. This system will result in an uneven level of income, as the price of the fund's shares will vary in the marketplace. Still another arrangement is to pay out a fixed percentage of the net asset *growth*. So long as the stated percentage value is less than 100 percent, this plan can produce a periodic, although uncertain, payout of income and still allow for some reinvestment and growth in the account. In essence, so long as the fund is profitable, the shareholder will receive some monthly or quarterly income and still have something left over to plow back into the fund itself.

Conversion Privileges and Phone Switching

conversion privilege
*feature of a mutual
fund that allows
shareholders to move
money from one fund
to another, within
the same family of
funds; also called*
exchange privilege.

fund families
*different kinds of
mutual funds all of-
fered by the same in-
vestment management
company.*

Sometimes investors find it necessary, for one reason or another, to switch out of one fund and into another. The investor's investment objectives may change, or the investment climate itself may have changed. **Conversion** (or **exchange**) **privileges** were devised to meet the needs of such investors in a convenient and economical manner. Investment management companies that offer a number of different kinds of mutual funds—these are known as **fund families**—usually provide conversion privileges that enable shareholders to easily move from one fund to another. As we saw earlier, this is usually done by phone. The only limitation is that the investor must confine the switches within the same *family* of funds. For example, an investor can switch from a Dreyfus growth fund to a Dreyfus money fund, or to its income fund, or to any other fund managed by Dreyfus. With some fund families, the alternatives open to investors seem almost without limit; indeed, some of the larger families offer 20 or 30 funds (or more). One investment company (Fidelity) has over 100 different funds in its family, as it provides everything from high-performance stock funds to bond funds, tax-exempt funds, a couple of dozen sector funds, and half a dozen money funds.

There are more than a hundred fund families in operation today. They all provide low-cost conversion/phone-switching privileges (some even *free*), although most families that offer free exchanges have limits on the number of times such switches can occur each year. Twenty of the largest fund families are listed in Table 13.4, page 588. Note that, together, these 20 families offer nearly *650* different mutual funds to the investing public. Conversion privileges are usually considered beneficial from the shareholder's point of view, since they allow investors to meet their ever-changing long-term investment goals. In addition, they permit investors to manage their mutual fund holdings more aggressively by allowing them to move in and out of funds as the investment environment changes. Unfortunately there is one major drawback: For tax purposes, the exchange of shares from one fund to another is regarded as a sale transaction followed by a subsequent purchase of a new security. As a result, if any capital gains exist at the time of the exchange, the investor is liable for the taxes on that profit even though the holdings were not truly liquidated.

Checkwriting Privileges

Checkwriting service is now available from virtually every money fund and also from a growing (although still small) number of stock and bond funds. Exactly as the name implies, shareholders are given a supply of checks that can be used to draw against the money invested in their mutual funds. These checks are like any other, except they are drawn on the fund account and paid through the fund's bank. The one catch is that the checks usually have to be written in minimum amounts ($500 or more being the most common figure). A major benefit of this privilege is that the checks, once written, continue to draw income until they actually clear. For example, if an investor has a money fund and writes a $1,000 check against that fund which takes a week to clear, the individual receives the full daily interest on that $1,000 for each of the seven days the check is in "float."

TABLE 13.4   Twenty of the Biggest Fund Families

Fund Families*	Number of Stock, Bond Funds	Number of Money Funds	Total Number of Funds
American Capital Marketing	17	1	18
Colonial Investment Services	23	1	24
Dean Witter Reynolds	19	7	26
Dreyfus Service Corp.	24	7	31
Federated Securities Corp.	17	3	20
Fidelity Distributors Corp.	96	8	104
Franklin Distributors	27	4	31
IDS Financial Services	25	3	28
Kemper Financial Services	13	5	18
Keystone Distributors	18	1	19
Mass. Financial Services	26	2	28
Merrill Lynch Funds	51	8	59
Oppenheimer Fund Mgmt	20	1	21
T. Rowe Price Assocs.	21	3	24
Prudential-Bache	35	7	42
Putnam Financial Services	33	1	34
Shearson Lehman Hutton	30	9	39
Stein Roe & Farnham	13	3	16
Vanguard Group	44	5	49
Waddell & Reed (United Fds)	15	1	16

*Number of funds in existence in late 1988; all these fund families offer conversion privileges.

Retirement Programs

As a result of government legislation, self-employed individuals are permitted to divert a portion of their pre-tax income into self-directed *retirement plans*. And all working Americans, whether they are self-employed or not, are allowed to establish individual retirement accounts. (Even after the Tax Reform Act of 1986, IRAs can still be set up by anyone who is gainfully employed, although, as noted in Chapter 4, the tax deductibility of IRA *contributions* is limited to certain individuals.) Today all mutual funds provide a special service that allows individuals to set up tax-deferred retirement programs as either IRA or Keogh accounts. The funds set up the plans and handle all the administrative details in such a way that the shareholder can easily take full advantage of available tax savings.

INVESTING IN MUTUAL FUNDS

Suppose you are confronted with the following situation: You have money to invest and are trying to select the right place to put it. You obviously want to pick a security that meets your idea of acceptable risk, but also one that will generate an attractive rate of return. The problem is you have to make the selection from a list of over 2,700 securities. Sound like a "mission impossible"? Well, that is basically

what the investor is up against when trying to select a suitable mutual fund. But perhaps if the problem is approached systematically, it may not be so formidable a task. As we will see, it is possible to whittle down the list of alternatives by matching one's investment needs with the investment objectives of the funds. However, before doing that, it might be helpful to examine more closely the various investor uses of mutual funds; with this background, we can then look at the selection process and at several measures of return that can be used to assess performance.

Investor Uses of Mutual Funds

Mutual funds can be used by individual investors in a variety of different ways. For instance, performance funds can serve as a vehicle for capital appreciation, whereas bond funds can be used to provide current income. Regardless of the kind of income a fund provides, individuals tend to use these investment vehicles for one of three reasons: (1) as a way to accumulate wealth; (2) as a speculative vehicle for achieving high rates of return; and (3) as a storehouse of value.

Accumulation of Wealth

Accumulation of wealth is probably the most common reason for using mutual funds. Basically, it involves using mutual funds over the long haul for the purpose of building up investment capital. The money accumulated is then used at some future date for retirement, to educate the children, or for some other purpose. Depending upon the investor's personality, a modest amount of risk may be acceptable, but usually preservation of capital and capital stability are considered important. Moreover, the source of return is far less important than the amount; investors are therefore just as likely to use equity-income or balanced funds for capital accumulation purposes as they are to use growth funds. The whole idea is to form a ''partnership'' with the mutual fund in building up as big a capital pool as possible: You provide the capital by systematically investing and reinvesting in the fund, and the fund provides the return by doing its best to invest your resources wisely.

Speculation and Short-Term Trading

Speculation is not a common use of mutual funds; the reason, of course, is that most mutual funds are long-term in nature and as such, are not really meant to be used as aggressive trading vehicles. However, a growing number of funds (e.g., sector funds) now cater to speculators, and some investors find that mutual funds are indeed attractive outlets for speculation and short-term trading. One way to do this is to trade in and out of funds aggressively as the investment climate changes. For example, an investor might use a performance fund when the market is strong and then switch to a money fund when it begins to soften. Load charges can be avoided (or reduced) by dealing in ''families'' of funds offering low-cost conversion privileges and/or by dealing only in no-load funds. Some investors might choose to invest in funds for the long run but still seek extraordinarily high rates of return by investing in aggressive mutual funds. There are a number of funds which follow very aggressive trading strategies and which may well appeal to investors who are willing to accept substantial risk exposure. These are usually the fairly specialized

smaller funds; sophisticated hedge funds, leverage funds, option funds, and global funds are examples, not to mention performance or sector funds. In essence, such investors are simply applying the basic mutual fund concept to their investment needs by letting professional money managers handle their accounts in a way they would like to see them handled; *aggressively*. There are also those who occasionally use mutual funds for short-term speculation. Some excellent examples are investors who use sector funds to take advantage of unusual profit opportunities in specific industries or who use selected international funds when the dollar starts to soften and/or foreign companies begin to look attractive.

Storehouse of Value

Investors may also use mutual funds as a storehouse of value. The idea here is to find a place where investment capital can be fairly secure and relatively free from deterioration yet still generate a relatively attractive rate of return. Short- and inter-mediate-term bond funds are logical choices for such purposes and so are money funds (which are rapidly becoming the most popular way of meeting this investment objective). Capital preservation and income over the long haul is very important to some investors. Still others might seek storage of value only for the short term, as a way to "sit it out" until a more attractive opportunity comes along. Money funds would be used under these circumstances by fairly aggressive investors, who would use the funds to store their money while the market is weak or until they find better investment outlets.

The Selection Process

In many respects, the mutual fund selection process is the critical dimension in defining the amount of investment success one will have with mutual funds. It means putting into action all you know about funds in order to gain as much return as possible from an acceptable level of risk. The selection process begins with an assessment of one's own investment needs; this sets the tone of the investment program. Obviously, what we want to do is select from those 2,700 or so funds the one or two (or three or four) that we feel will best meet our total investment needs. Let's now look more closely at how this might be done.

Objectives and Motives for Using Funds

Selecting the right investment means finding those funds that are most suitable to your total investment needs. *The place to start is with your own investment objectives.* In other words, why do you want to invest in a mutual fund, and what are you looking for in a fund? Obviously, an attractive rate of return would be desirable, but there is also the matter of a tolerable amount of risk exposure. Face it: Some investors are more willing to take risks than others, and this is certainly an important ingredient in the selection process. More than likely, when we look at our own risk temperament in relation to the various types of mutual funds, we will discover that certain types of funds are more appealing to us than others. For instance, aggressive growth or sector funds will probably *not* be attractive to individuals who wish to avoid high exposure to risk.

Another important factor in the selection process is the intended use of the mutual fund. That is, do we want to invest in mutual funds as a means of accumulating wealth, to speculate for high rates of return, or as a storehouse of value? This is helpful information, since it puts into clearer focus the question of exactly what we are trying to do with our investment dollars. Finally, there is the matter of the types of services provided by the fund. If there are services we are particularly interested in, we should be sure to look for them in the funds we select. All these variables (desired return performance; risk exposure; use of the fund; and services sought) are important in defining why we use funds and are vital ingredients to the selection process. Having assessed what we are looking for in a fund, we now want to look at what the funds have to offer us.

What Funds Offer

The ideal mutual fund would achieve maximum capital growth when security prices rise, provide complete protection against capital loss when prices decline, and achieve high levels of current income at all times. Unfortunately, this fund does not exist. Instead, just as each individual has a set of investment needs, each fund has its own *investment objective,* its own *manner of operation,* and its own *range of services*. These three parameters are useful in helping us to assess investment alternatives. But where does the investor look for such information? One obvious place is the fund's prospectus (or its Statement of Additional Information), where information on investment objectives, portfolio composition, management, and past performance can be obtained—the Investor Insights box on pages 592-593 offers some suggestions on what to look for in a mutual fund prospectus. In addition, publications such as *The Wall Street Journal, Barron's, Financial World,* and *Forbes* provide useful data and information concerning mutual funds. These sources provide a wealth of operating and performance statistics in a convenient and easy-to-read format. For instance, each year, *Forbes* rates nearly 1,500 mutual funds (see Figure 13.9, on page 594, for an excerpt from its 1988 report), and every quarter *Barron's* publishes an extensive mutual fund performance report. What's more, publications like *Money* and *Changing Times* produce lists of the top performing funds every month. And, of course, there are services available that provide background information and assessments on a wide variety of different kinds of funds. Among the best in this category are Morningstar's *Mutual Fund Values* (an excerpt of which is shown in Figure 13.10—page 596), Wiesenberger's *Investment Companies* (an annual publication with quarterly updates), and *Donoghue's Mutual Funds Almanac* (a low-cost, annual publication that provides a variety of operating and performance statistics). Using sources like these, investors can obtain information on such things as investment objectives, load charges and annual expense rates, summary portfolio analyses, services offered, historical statistics, and reviews of past performance. (Appendix A provides a detailed list of these mutual fund services and publications.)

Whittling Down the Alternatives

At this point, fund selection becomes a process of elimination as investor needs are weighed against the types of funds available. Large numbers of funds can be elimi-

INVESTOR INSIGHTS

What to Look for in a Mutual Fund Prospectus

The Securities and Exchange Commission requires that a mutual fund's prospectus be in your hands before the fund can accept your investment. That might seem like a cruel joke, because the typical prospectus is about as readable as the Rosetta Stone. Yet if you don't plow through this document, you lay yourself open to nasty surprises later.

Investors often complain that a lot of funds go to great lengths to camouflage important information in the prospectus. Usually it's because prospectuses are written by lawyers, whose prose can be opaque. Fortunately, more sponsors are seeing benefits in sharper writing. T. Rowe Price has shifted its prospectus-writing largely to marketing people and has attorneys review the legal points. More good news: Funds must now include a table of all fees near the front of the prospectus, followed by a hypothetical total of all fees over several years, assuming the fund earns a 5% return. This feature should end disjointed disclosure of costs.

To help you get the most out of a mutual fund prospectus, here's a guided tour through this document:

- *Investment objective.* Certain words and phrases appear regularly. Bond funds all seem to aim for "highest level of current income" that's "consistent with preservation of capital." Stock funds tell their top and secondary priorities: capital growth, dividend income, a combination of the two and, possibly, a narrow strategy, such as hunting for "special situations" or "undervalued stocks." Strategies may or may not be well-defined. If they are, the prospectus is telling you about the riskiness of the fund. For example, Fidelity Special Situations explain, "We expect to be fully invested in stocks under most market conditions." So don't cry that its manager should have been in Treasury bills if stocks crash again. The Franklin Short-Intermediate U.S. Government Securities Fund says it will maintain an average portfolio

nated from consideration simply because they fail to meet these needs. Some may be too risky; others may be unsuitable as a storehouse of value. Thus, rather than trying to evaluate 2,700 different funds, we can use a process of elimination to narrow the list down to two or three *types* of funds that best match our investment needs. From here, we can whittle the list down a bit more by introducing other constraints. For example, because of cost considerations, we may want to deal only in no-load or low-load funds, or we may be seeking certain services that are important to our investment goals. Now we introduce the final (but certainly not the least important) element in the selection process: *the fund's investment performance.* Useful information includes (1) how the fund has performed over time; (2) the type of return it has generated in good markets as well as bad; (3) the level of dividend and capital gains distributions; and (4) the type of investment stability the fund has enjoyed over time. By evaluating such information, it is possible to identify some of the more successful mutual funds—the ones that not only offer the investment objectives and services we seek but also provide the best payoffs as well. And while

maturity of two to five years. That tells you that Franklin's investments will be subject to less price volatility than an "intermediate" fund empowered to stretch to perhaps 12 years' maturity.

- *Past performance.* Established funds include five years of results—if they are that old—in a table of *per-share income and capital changes.* These condensed financial statements reveal such facts as the ratio of expenses to average net assets (over 1% is high, unless it's an international or sector fund) and the portfolio turnover rate (100% means the manager trades every stock in the portfolio every year). Many, but by no means all, prospectuses compare the fund's results to the S&P 500 or another recognized index. Total return—the measurement of price gains or losses plus dividend and interest income—is still a voluntary feature in a prospectus. . . . But you can estimate total return from the prospectus by taking the latest year-end share price, adding back all capital gains and dividends paid during the previous year and taking the percentage change from the previous year's ending price.

- *Management.* Funds don't have to tell the name and qualifications of the portfolio manager, though IDS even goes so far as to run color photos of its managers. Sometimes a fund will go out of its way to mention a resident celebrity. Dreyfus Capital Value, which performed extraordinarily well in 1987, ballyhoos in its prospectus the fund's adviser, Stanley Salvigson. . . .

- *Miscellaneous.* The back pages of the prospectus are the guts that describe such services as exchange privilege between funds in the family or signing up to a systematic withdrawal plan. If you're unfamiliar with these services, call shareholder services with questions. Ask the fund about anything you can't easily find in the prospectus. If enough investors tie up the phones to ask about what should be explained clearly in the prospectus, funds are apt to do a better job of writing them.

Source: Adapted from Jeff Kosnett, "What to Look for—and Look Out for—as You Read a Mutual Fund Prospectus," *Changing Times,* May 1988, p. 18.

you're looking at performance, it probably wouldn't hurt to check out the fund's *fee structure.* Be on guard for funds that charge abnormally high management fees, as they can really hurt your returns over time—these fees and expenses are taken out year after year, regardless of how well (or poorly) the fund does. As a point of reference, mutual funds experienced the following *median annual expense rates* in 1988: *stock funds* had median expense ratios of 1 to 1½ percent of assets under management (of course, the larger the fund, the lower the expense rate); *bond funds* had expense rates of roughly 1 percent, across the board; and for *money funds,* the median was around ¾ of 1 percent.

Note that in this investment process considerable weight is given to *past performance.* Now as a rule, the past is given little or no attention in the investment decision—after all, it's the future that matters. Although the *future performance* of a mutual fund is still the variable that holds the key to success, a good deal of time is spent on past investment results in order to get a handle on how successful the fund's investment managers have been. In essence the success of a mutual fund

1988 Fund Ratings/Stock

Performance in UP —markets—	in DOWN	Fund/distributor	Total return: Annual average 1978 to 1988	Last 12 months	Yield	Assets 6/30/88 (millions)	% change '88 vs '87	Maximum sales charge	Annual expenses per $100
		Standard & Poor's 500 stock average	16.9%	−6.9%	3.3%				
		FORBES stock fund composite	16.4%	−5.6%	2.7%				$1.49
		MFS Lifetime Emerging Growth/Mass Finl	—*	−14.1%	none	$80	58%	6.00%r	2.32
		MFS Lifetime Managed Sectors/Mass Finl	—*	−13.4%	0.7	162	125	6.00r	2.13
		MFS Managed Sectors Trust/Mass Finl	—*	−14.8	1.2	150	−25	4.75	1.48
D	B	MidAmerica High Growth Fund/MidAmerica	12.9%	−5.3	2.9	12	−10	8.50	1.00p
D	A	MidAmerica Mutual Fund/MidAmerica	14.7	−4.7	3.7	35	−8	8.50	0.91
		Midas Gold Shares & Bullion/IRI	—*	−14.3	none	17	−2	6.00	1.79p
		Mimlic Investors Fund I/Mimlic	—*	−6.5	3.1	8	5	5.00	1.00p
		Monitrend Value Fund/Pallas	—*	−3.9	2.0	19	−35	3.50	2.50p
		Morgan Grenfell SmallCap Fund/closed end	—*	0.1	none	48	0	NA	2.38
		Morgan Keegan Southern Cap/Morgan Keegan	—*	−5.9	0.1	13	35	3.00	2.00p
		Morison Asset Allocation Fund/Morison	—*	−6.5	3.1	25	38	7.25	1.72
C	B	Mutual Benefit Fund/Mutual Benefit	16.3	−1.0	2.4	20	4	8.50	1.34
D	C	Mutual of Omaha Growth/Mutual of Omaha	13.0	−5.6	0.9	40	−10	8.00	1.11
		Mutual Series Fund–Beacon[1]/Heine Secs	—*	10.3	2.3	205	82	none	0.80
D	A+	Mutual Series–Mutual Shares/Heine Secs	21.3	9.3	3.5	2,222	17	none	0.69
•C	A+	Mutual Series Fund–Qualified/Heine Secs	—*	8.8	3.7	936	23	none	0.71
C	D	National Aviation & Technology/AFA	13.4	−14.9	1.2	71	−23	4.75	1.23p
D	D	National Growth Fund/National Secs	10.3	−10.3	2.5	58	−18	7.25	0.90
D	C	National Industries Fund/Sierra	11.2	−5.1	0.8	29	−11	none	1.65
		National Real Estate–Stock/National Secs	—*	−3.4	7.8	21	8	7.75	1.43p
D	B	National Stock Fund/National Secs	15.1	−5.0	4.6	222	−3	7.25	0.74
		National Telecom & Technology/AFA	—*	−6.3	1.1	44	−24	4.75	1.63p
D	B	Nationwide Fund/Nationwide	14.2	−6.9	3.6	401	−14	7.50	0.63
C	A	Nationwide Growth Fund/Nationwide	18.8	−1.7	4.6	228	−3	7.50	0.66
•F	•D	Nautilus Fund/Eaton Vance	—*	−13.4	none	16	−25	4.75	1.78p
B	D	Neuwirth Fund/National Finl	14.8	−5.8	none	26	−16	none	1.69
		New Alternatives Fund/Accrued Eq	—*	−0.3	1.1	5	30	5.66	1.17
		New Economy Fund/American Funds	—*	−3.2	2.3	744	−23	5.75	0.73
D	A	New England Equity Income/New England	16.2	−6.0	2.3	51	6	6.50	1.52p
A	B	New England Growth Fund/New England	24.4	−7.7	none	487	3	6.50	1.28
B	B	New England Retire Equity/New England	18.5	−13.9	0.6	143	−6	6.50	1.30
A	B	New York Venture Fund/Venture	22.0	−0.9	2.7	166	−28	8.50	1.01
B	D	Newton Growth Fund/Newton	16.8	−10.6	1.3	38	−21	none	1.20
A	D	Niagara Share Corp/closed end	17.1	−6.1	2.2	193	−11	NA	1.00
		Nicholas Applegate Growth Equity/closed end	—*	−7.1	none	87	−10	NA	1.25
B	A	Nicholas Fund/Nicholas	21.6	0.6	3.2	1,148	−11	none	0.86

A stock fund is added to this list if it has at least $5 million in net assets and, if open-end, is at least 12 months old; a fund is dropped when its assets fall below $2 million. Stock funds are graded only if in operation since 7/31/82. Long-term average total return is for 2/28/78 to 6/30/88. Yield is last 12 months' income dividends divided by 6/30/88 net asset value; it may differ from "yield" as defined by the SEC. *Expense ratio is in italics if the fund has a shareholder-paid 12b-1 plan exceeding 0.1% (hidden load) pending or in force.* • Fund rated for two periods only; maximum allowable grade A. *Fund not in operation for full period. ‡Exchange fund, not currently selling new shares. p: Net of partial absorption of expenses by fund sponsor. b: Includes back-end load that reverts to fund. r: Includes back-end load that reverts to distributor. NA: Not applicable or not available. [1]Formerly Mutual Beacon Growth Fund.

rests in large part *on the investment skills of the fund managers*. Thus when investing in a mutual fund, look for consistently good performance, in up as well as down markets, over *extended* periods of time (five years or more). Most important, check to see if the same key people are still running the fund. Although past success is certainly no guarantee of future performance, a strong team of money managers can have a significant bearing on the level of fund returns.

Measuring Performance

Like any investment decision, investment performance is a major dimension in the mutual fund selection process. The level of dividends paid by the fund, its capital gains, and growth in capital are all important aspects of return. Such return information enables the investor to judge the investment behavior of the fund and to appraise its performance in relation to other funds and investment vehicles. Here, we will look at different measures that can be used by mutual fund investors to assess return; also, because risk is so important in defining the investment behavior of a fund, we will briefly review it as well.

Sources of Return

An open-end fund has three potential sources of return: (1) dividend income, (2) capital gains distribution, and (3) change in the price (or net asset value) of the fund. Depending on the type of fund, some mutual funds will derive more income from one source than another; for example, we would normally expect income-oriented funds to have much higher dividend income than capital gains distributions. Mutual funds regularly publish reports that recap investment performance. One such report is *The Summary of Income and Capital Changes,* an example of which is provided in Figure 13.11. This statement, which is found in the fund's prospectus or annual report, gives a brief overview of the fund's investment activity, including expense ratios and portfolio turnover rates. Of interest here is the top part of the report (that runs from *investment income* to *NAV at the end of the year*—lines 1 to 9); this is the part that reveals the amount of dividend income and capital gains distributed to the shareholders, along with the change in the fund's net asset value.

dividend income
income derived from the dividend and interest income earned on the security holdings of a mutual fund.

Dividend income is that derived from the dividend and interest income earned on the security holdings of the mutual fund. It's paid out of the *net investment income* that's left after all operating expenses have been met. When the fund receives dividend or interest payments, it passes these on to shareholders in the form of dividend payments. The fund accumulates all the current income it has received for the period and then pays it out on a prorated basis. If a fund earned, say, $1 million in dividends and interest in a given quarter, and if that fund had 1 million

FIGURE 13.9 (Facing Page) Performance Information About Mutual Funds.
There is a wealth of information available to investors about mutual funds; much of it, like the *Forbes* fund ratings depicted here, is in a format that allows for quick review of a large number of funds. (*Source:* Excerpted by permission of *Forbes* magazine. September 5, 1988. © Forbes Inc., 1988.)

Boston Co Cap App

Objective	Load%	Yield%	Assets $mil	N.A.V.
Growth	None	1.3	546.4	34.31

Boston Company Capital Appreciation Fund seeks long-term growth of capital. Current income is a secondary objective.

The fund invests primarily in common stocks of U.S. companies. Management continuously studies trends in the various investment criteria that it uses to select investment opportunities.

Foreign investments are limited to 10% of the fund's assets. The fund may also write covered put and call options on its securities, and purchase and write put and call options on stock indexes.

From 1947 to 1979, this fund was known as Johnston Mutual Fund.

Return Above Avg　**Risk** Below Avg

Rating ★★★★

Above Avg

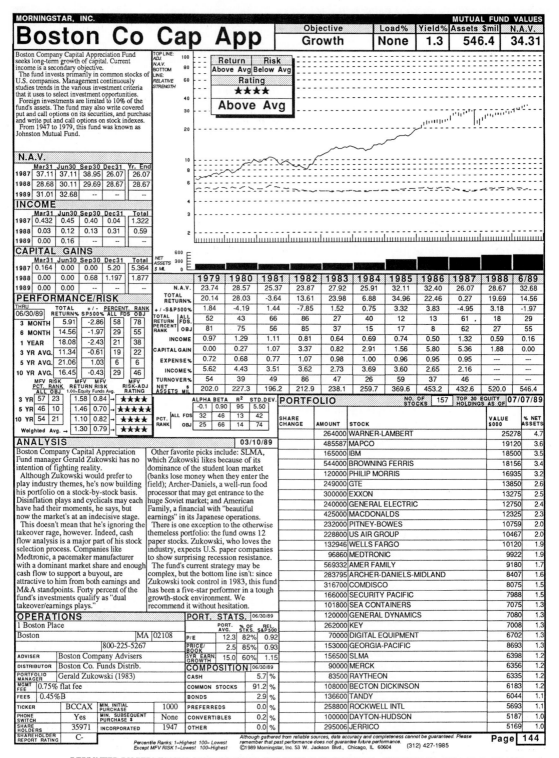

N.A.V.

	Mar31	Jun30	Sep30	Dec31	Yr. End
1987	37.11	37.11	38.95	26.07	26.07
1988	28.68	30.11	29.69	28.67	28.67
1989	31.01	32.68	--	--	--

INCOME

	Mar31	Jun30	Sep30	Dec31	Total
1987	0.432	0.45	0.40	0.04	1.322
1988	0.03	0.12	0.13	0.31	0.59
1989	0.00	0.16	--	--	--

CAPITAL GAINS

	Mar31	Jun30	Sep30	Dec31	Total
1987	0.164	0.00	0.00	5.20	5.364
1988	0.00	0.00	0.68	1.197	1.877
1989	0.00	0.00	--	--	--

PERFORMANCE/RISK

THRU 06/30/89	TOTAL RETURN%	+/- S&P500%	PERCENT. RANK ALL FDS	RANK OBJ
3 MONTH	5.91	-2.86	58	78
6 MONTH	14.56	-1.97	29	55
1 YEAR	18.08	-2.43	21	38
3 YR AVG.	11.34	-0.61	19	22
5 YR AVG.	21.06	1.03	6	6
10 YR AVG.	16.45	-0.43	29	46

	MFV RISK PCT. RANK ALL OBJ	MFV RETURN 1.00=Equity Funds Avg.	MFV RISK	RISK-ADJ RATING
3 YR	57	23	1.58	0.84 → ★★★★
5 YR	46	10	1.46	0.70 → ★★★★★
10 YR	54	21	1.10	0.82 → ★★★★
Weighted Avg.		1.30	0.79 → ★★★★

ANALYSIS
03/10/89

Boston Company Capital Appreciation Fund manager Gerald Zukowski has no intention of fighting reality.

Although Zukowski would prefer to play industry themes, he's now building his portfolio on a stock-by-stock basis. Disinflation plays and cyclicals may each have had their moments, he says, but now the market's at an indecisive stage. This doesn't mean that he's ignoring the takeover rage, however. Indeed, cash flow analysis is a major part of his stock selection process. Companies like Medtronic, a pacemaker manufacturer with a dominant market share and enough cash flow to support a buyout, are attractive to him from both earnings and M&A standpoints. Forty percent of the fund's investments qualify as "dual takeover/earnings plays."

Other favorite picks include: SLMA, which Zukowski likes because of its dominance of the student loan market (banks lose money when they enter the field); Archer-Daniels, a well-run food processor that may get entrance to the huge Soviet market; and American Family, a financial with "beautiful earnings" in its Japanese operations.

There is one exception to the otherwise themeless portfolio: the fund owns 12 paper stocks. Zukowski, who loves the industry, expects U.S. paper companies to show surprising recession resistance.

The fund's current strategy may be complex, but the bottom line isn't: since Zukowski took control in 1983, this fund has been a five-star performer in a tough growth-stock environment. We recommend it without hesitation.

OPERATIONS

1 Boston Place

Boston		MA	02108
	800-225-5267		

ADVISER	Boston Company Advisers
DISTRIBUTOR	Boston Co. Funds Distrib.
PORTFOLIO MANAGER	Gerald Zukowski (1983)
MGMT FEE	0.75% flat fee
FEES	0.45%B

TICKER	BCCAX	MIN. INITIAL PURCHASE	1000
PHONE SWITCH	Yes	MIN. SUBSEQUENT PURCHASE $	None
SHARE HOLDERS	35971	INCORPORATED	1947
SHAREHOLDER REPORT RATING	C-		

	1979	1980	1981	1982	1983	1984	1985	1986	1987	1988	6/89
N.A.V.	23.74	28.57	25.37	23.87	27.92	25.91	32.11	32.40	26.07	28.67	32.68
TOTAL RETURN%	20.14	28.03	-3.64	13.61	23.98	6.88	34.96	22.46	0.27	19.69	14.56
+/- S&P500%	1.84	-4.19	1.44	-7.85	1.52	0.75	3.32	3.83	-4.95	3.18	-1.97
TOTAL RETURN PERCENT RANK ALL FDS.	52	43	66	86	27	40	12	13	61	18	29
OBJ	81	75	56	85	37	15	17	8	62	27	55
INCOME	0.97	1.29	1.11	0.81	0.64	0.69	0.74	0.50	1.32	0.59	0.16
CAPITAL GAIN	0.00	0.27	1.07	3.37	0.82	2.91	1.56	5.80	5.36	1.88	0.00
EXPENSE%	0.72	0.68	0.77	1.07	0.98	1.00	0.96	0.95	0.95	---	---
INCOME%	5.62	4.43	3.51	3.62	2.73	3.69	3.60	2.65	2.16	---	---
TURNOVER	54	39	49	84	47	26	59	37	46	---	---
NET ASSETS MIL $	202.0	227.3	196.2	212.9	238.1	259.7	369.6	453.2	432.6	520.0	546.4

PORTFOLIO

NO. OF STOCKS 157　　TOP 30 EQUITY HOLDINGS AS OF 07/07/89

	ALPHA	BETA	R²	STD.DEV.
	-0.1	0.90	95	5.50
PCT. RANK ALL FDS	32	46	13	42
OBJ	25	66	14	74

PORT. STATS. 06/30/89

	PORT. AVG.	% OF STKS.	REL. S&P500
P/E	12.3	82%	0.92
PRICE/BOOK	2.5	85%	0.93
5YR EARN. GROWTH	15.0	60%	1.15

COMPOSITION 06/30/89

CASH	5.7 %
COMMON STOCKS	91.2 %
BONDS	2.9 %
PREFERREDS	0.0 %
CONVERTIBLES	0.2 %
OTHER	0.0 %

SHARE CHANGE	AMOUNT	STOCK	VALUE $000	% NET ASSETS
	264000	WARNER-LAMBERT	25278	4.7
	485587	MAPCO	19120	3.6
	165000	IBM	18500	3.5
	544000	BROWNING FERRIS	18156	3.4
	120000	PHILIP MORRIS	16935	3.2
	249000	GTE	13850	2.6
	300000	EXXON	13275	2.5
	240000	GENERAL ELECTRIC	12750	2.4
	425000	MACDONALDS	12325	2.3
	232000	PITNEY-BOWES	10759	2.0
	228800	US AIR GROUP	10467	2.0
	132946	WELLS FARGO	10120	1.9
	96860	MEDTRONIC	9922	1.9
	569332	AMER FAMILY	9180	1.7
	283795	ARCHER-DANIELS-MIDLAND	8407	1.6
	316700	COMDISCO	8075	1.5
	166000	SECURITY PACIFIC	7988	1.5
	101800	SEA CONTAINERS	7075	1.3
	120000	GENERAL DYNAMICS	7080	1.3
	262000	KEY	7008	1.3
	70000	DIGITAL EQUIPMENT	6702	1.3
	153000	GEORGIA-PACIFIC	8693	1.3
	156500	SLMA	6398	1.2
	90000	MERCK	6356	1.2
	83500	RAYTHEON	6335	1.2
	108000	BECTON DICKINSON	6183	1.2
	136600	TANDY	6044	1.1
	258800	ROCKWELL INTL	5693	1.1
	100000	DAYTON-HUDSON	5187	1.0
	295006	JERRICO	5169	1.0

Percentile Ranks: 1=Highest 100= Lowest
Except MFV RISK 1=Lowest 100=Highest

Although gathered from reliable sources, data accuracy and completeness cannot be guaranteed. Please remember that past performance does not guarantee future performance.
©1989 Morningstar, Inc. 53 W. Jackson Blvd., Chicago, IL 60604　(312) 427-1985

Page 144

PER SHARE INCOME AND CAPITAL CHANGES
(For a share outstanding throughout the year)

		1989	1988	1987
INCOME AND EXPENSES				
	1. Investment income	$.76	$.88	$.67
	2. Less expenses	.16	.22	.17
	3. Net investment income	.60	.66	.50
Dividend Income⟶	4. Dividends from net investment income	(.55)	(.64)	(.50)
CAPITAL CHANGES				
	5. Net realized and unrealized gains (or losses) on security transactions	6.37	(1.74)	3.79
Capital Gains Distribution⟶	6. Distributions from realized gains	(1.75)	(.84)	(1.02)
Change in NAV⟶	7. Net increase (decrease) in NAV*	4.67	(2.56)	2.77
	8. NAV at beginning of year	24.47	27.03	24.26
	9. NAV at end of year	$29.14	$24.47	$27.03
	10. Ratio of operating expenses to average net assets	1.04%	.85%	.94%
	11. Ratio of net investment income to average net assets	1.47%	2.56%	2.39%
	12. Portfolio turnover rate**	85%	144%	74%
	13. Shares outstanding at end of year (000s omitted)	10,568	6,268	4,029

*Note: *Net increase (decrease) in NAV*, line 7 = line 3 − line 4 + line 5 − line 6; for example, the 1989 net increase in NAV was found as $.60 − .55 + 6.37 − 1.75 = $4.67.

**Portfolio turnover rate* relates the number of shares bought and sold by the fund to the total number of shares held in the fund's portfolio; a high turnover rate (for example, in excess of 100 percent) would mean the fund has been doing a lot of trading.

FIGURE 13.11 A Summary of Income and Capital Changes.
The return on a mutual fund is made up of (1) the (net) investment income the fund earns from dividends and interest, and (2) the realized and unrealized capital gains the fund earns on its security transactions.

FIGURE 13.10 (Facing Page) Some Relevant Information About Specific Mutual Funds.
Investors who want in-depth information about the operating characteristics, investment holdings, and market behavior of specific mutual funds can usually find what they are looking for in periodicals like Morningstar's *Mutual Fund Values* (shown here), *Donoghue's Mutual Funds Almanac*, or Wiesenberger's *Investment Companies*. (*Source*: Morningstar, Inc., *Mutual Fund Values*, 1989.)

capital gains distributions
payments made to mutual fund shareholders that come from the profits that a fund makes from the sale of its securities.

unrealized capital gains
a capital gain made only "on paper," that is, not realized until the fund's holdings are sold; also called paper profits.

shares outstanding, each share would receive a quarterly dividend payment of $1. **Capital gains distributions** work on the same principle, except that these payments are derived from the capital gains earned by the fund. It works like this: Suppose the fund bought some stock a year ago for $50 and sold that stock in the current period for $75 per share. Clearly the fund has achieved capital gains of $25 per share. If it held 50,000 shares of this stock, it would have realized a total capital gain of $1,250,000 ($25 × 50,000 = $1,250,000). Given that the fund has 1 million shares outstanding, each share is entitled to $1.25 in the form of a capital gains distribution. Note that this capital gain distribution applies only to *realized* capital gains— that is, the security holdings were actually sold and the capital gains actually earned.

Unrealized capital gains (or paper profits) are what make up the third and final element in a mutual fund's return. When the fund's holdings go up or down in price, the net asset value of the fund moves accordingly. Suppose an investor buys into a fund at $10 per share, and some time later it is quoted at $12.50; the difference of $2.50 per share is the unrealized capital gains contained in the fund's security holdings. It represents the profit shareholders would receive (and are entitled to) if the fund were to sell its holdings. (Actually, as Figure 13.11 shows, some of the change in net asset value can also be made up of *undistributed dividends*.)

The return on *closed-end* investment companies is derived from the same three sources as that of open-end funds, and from a fourth source as well: Changes in price discounts or premiums. Because closed-end companies are traded like any common stock, they seldom trade exactly at their net asset value. Instead, they tend to trade below (at a discount) or above (at a premium) their NAV. As these discounts or premiums change over time, the return to shareholders is affected accordingly. The reason is that such changes in discount or premium actually affect the market price of the fund. Because discount or premium is already embedded in the share price of a fund, it follows that for a closed-end fund the third element of return (change in share price) is made up not only of changes in the net asset value of the fund's holdings, but also of changes in price discount or premium.

What About Future Performance?

There's no doubt that a statement like the one in Figure 13.11 provides a convenient recap of a fund's past behavior. Unfortunately, looking at past performance is one thing, but what about the future? Ideally, you want to evaluate the same three elements of return as noted above. The trouble is that when it comes to the future performance of a mutual fund, it's extremely difficult—if not impossible—to get a firm grip on what the future holds as far as dividends, capital gains, and NAV are concerned. The reason is that a mutual fund's future investment performance is directly linked to *the future makeup of its securities portfolio,* which is something that is next to impossible to get a clear reading on. It's not like evaluating the expected performance of a share of stock, in which you're keying in on one company. With mutual funds, investment performance depends on the behavior of many different stocks and bonds.

So, where do you look for insight on the future? Most market observers suggest

the first place to look is the market itself; in particular, try to get a clear fix on the *future direction of the market as a whole*. This is important because the behavior of a well-diversified mutual fund tends to reflect the general tone of the market. Thus, if the feeling is that the market is going to be drifting generally up, that should bode well for the investment performance of mutual funds. Once that's done, spend some time evaluating the *track records* of potential investment candidates. For as noted earlier, past performance has a lot to say about the investment skills of the fund's money managers. In essence, look for funds that you think will be able to capture the best of what the future market environment holds.

Measures of Return

A simple but effective measure of performance is to describe mutual fund return in terms of the three major sources noted above: dividends earned, capital gains distributions received, and change in price. These payoffs can be converted to a convenient yield figure by using the standard holding period return formula. The computations necessary can be illustrated below using the 1989 figures from Figure 13.11. Referring to the exhibit, we can see that in 1989 this hypothetical no-load fund paid 55 cents per share in dividends and another $1.75 in capital gains distributions, and that it had a price at the beginning of the year of $24.47 that rose to $29.14 by the end of the year. Thus, summarizing this investment performance, we have:

Price (NAV) at the *beginning* of the year	$24.47
Price (NAV) at the *end* of the year	29.14
Net increase	$ 4.67
Return for the year:	
Dividends received	$ .55
Capital gains distributions	1.75
Net increase in price (NAV)	4.67
Total return	$ 6.97
Holding period return	28.5%
(Total return/beginning price)	

The measure is simple to calculate and follows the standard HPR format; it not only captures all the important elements of mutual fund return but also provides a handy indication of yield. Notice that we had a total dollar return of $6.97 and, based on a beginning investment of $24.47 (the initial share price of the fund), were able to realize an annual rate of return of 28.5 percent.

But what happens if dividends and capital gains distributions are reinvested into the fund? In this case, instead of cash the investor receives additional shares of stock. Holding period return can still be used to measure return, the only modification being that the investor has to keep track of the number of shares acquired through reinvestment. To illustrate, let's continue with the example above and assume that the investor initially bought 200 shares in the mutual fund. Assume also

that the investor was able to acquire shares through the fund's reinvestment program at an average price of, say, $26.50 a share; thus the $460 in dividends and capital gains distributions [($.55 + $1.75) × 200] provided the investor with another 17.36 shares in the fund ($460/$26.50). Holding period return under these circumstances would relate the market value of the stock holdings at the beginning of the period with holdings at the end, or:

$$\text{holding period return} = \frac{\left(\begin{array}{c}\text{number of shares} \times \\ \text{ending price}\end{array}\right) - \left(\begin{array}{c}\text{number of shares} \times \\ \text{initial price}\end{array}\right)}{(\text{number of shares} \times \text{initial price})}$$

Thus, the holding period return for our hypothetical investor would be:

$$\text{holding period return} = \frac{(217.36 \times \$29.14) - (200 \times \$24.47)}{(200 \times \$24.47)}$$

$$= \frac{(\$6,333.87) - (\$4,894.00)}{(\$4,894.00)} = \underline{\underline{29.4\%}}$$

This holding period yield, like the preceding one, provides a rate of return measure that can now be used to compare the performance of this fund to that of other funds and other investment vehicles.

Rather than using one-year holding periods, it is sometimes necessary to assess the performance of mutual funds over extended periods of time. Under such circumstances, it would be *inappropriate* to employ holding period return as a measure of performance. Preferably, when faced with multiple-year investment horizons, the standard *approximate yield* measure should be used to determine the fund's average annual compound rate of return. This can be done by following established approximate yield procedures except for one slight modification: that is, *capital gains distributions should be added to dividends received to find total average annual income*. To illustrate, refer back to Figure 13.11; assume that this time we want to find the annual rate of return over the full three-year period covered (1987 through 1989). In this case, we see that the mutual fund had *average* annual dividends of 56 cents a share [(.55 + 64 + .50)/3], *average* annual capital gains distributions of $1.20 a share [(1.75 + .84 + 1.02)/3], and total *average* annual income of $1.76 a share (1.20 + .56). Given that it had a beginning price of $24.26 *in 1987* and an ending price of $29.14 *in 1989* (some 3 years later), we can find the fund's approximate yield as follows:

$$\text{approximate yield} = \frac{\begin{array}{c}\text{total average} \\ \text{annual income}\end{array} + \frac{\begin{array}{c}\text{ending} \\ \text{share price}\end{array} - \begin{array}{c}\text{beginning} \\ \text{share price}\end{array}}{\text{number of years held}}}{\frac{\begin{array}{c}\text{ending} \\ \text{share price}\end{array} + \begin{array}{c}\text{beginning} \\ \text{share price}\end{array}}{2}}$$

$$= \frac{\$1.76 + \dfrac{\$29.14 - \$24.26}{3}}{\dfrac{\$29.14 + \$24.26}{2}} = \underline{\underline{12.7\%}}$$

Thus, the mutual fund in Figure 13.11 provided its investors with an average annual rate of return of approximately 12.7 percent over the three-year period in question. Such information is helpful in assessing fund performance and in comparing the return performance of one fund to other funds and to other investment vehicles. (According to recent changes instituted by the SEC, mutual funds must now report historical return behavior in a standardized format that employs fully compounded, total return figures similar to ones obtained from the approximate yield measure. Although the funds are *not* required to report such information, if they do cite performance in their promotional material, they must follow a *full-disclosure* manner of presentation that takes into account not only dividends and capital gains distributions but also any increases or decreases in the fund's NAV that have occurred over the past 1-, 5-, and 10-year periods.)

The Matter of Risk

Because most mutual funds are so diversified, their investors, for the most part, are immune to the business and financial risks normally present with individual securities. Even with extensive diversification, however, the investment behavior of most funds is still exposed to a considerable amount of *market risk*. In fact, because mutual fund portfolios are so well diversified, they often reflect the behavior of the marketplace itself and as noted above tend to perform very much like the market. A few funds, like gold funds, tend to be defensive (or countercyclical), but for the most part, market risk is an important behavioral ingredient in a large number of mutual funds, both open- and closed-end. Investors should be aware of the effect the general market has on the investment performance of a fund and try to use such insight when formulating a mutual fund investment program. For example, if the market is trending downward and you see a continuation of such a trend, it might be best to place any new investment capital into something like a money fund until the market reverses itself. At that time, you can make a more permanent commitment.

Another important risk consideration revolves around the management practices of the fund itself. If the portfolio is managed conservatively, the risk of a loss in capital is likely to be much less than for aggressively managed funds. Obviously, the more speculative the investment goals of the fund, the greater the risk of instability in the net asset value. On the other hand, a conservatively managed portfolio does not necessarily eliminate all price volatility, since the securities in the portfolio are still subject to inflation, interest rate, and/or general market risks. But these risks will generally be reduced or minimized as the investment objectives and portfolio management practices of the fund become more and more conservative.

SUMMARY

- Mutual fund shares represent ownership in a managed portfolio of securities; many investors who lack the time, know-how, or commitment to manage their own portfolios turn to mutual funds as an investment outlet.

- Since the late 1970s mutual funds have been enjoying unprecedented (almost phenomenal) growth in number of shareholders and amount of assets under management.

- By investing in mutual funds, shareholders benefit from a level of diversification and investment performance they might otherwise find difficult to achieve; in addition, they can establish an investment program with a limited amount of capital and obtain a variety of investor services not available elsewhere.

- On the negative side, mutual fund investors may be faced with hefty load charges (commissions) as well as costly management fees and operating expenses that are paid annually, regardless of the level of investment income.

- Investors can buy either open-end funds, which have no limit on the number of shares they may issue, or closed-end funds, which have a fixed number of shares outstanding and which trade in the secondary markets like any other share of common stock. Also available are investment trusts, which consist of unmanaged pools of securities that often pay income on a monthly basis.

- Each fund has an established investment objective that determines its investment policy and identifies it as a certain type of fund; some of the more popular types of funds include growth funds, aggressive growth funds, equity-income funds, balanced funds, growth-and-income funds, bond funds, money funds, specialty funds, sector funds, and international funds. The different categories of funds have different risk-return characteristics and are important variables in the fund selection process.

- In addition to the investment returns they offer, many investors buy mutual funds to take advantage of special services, such as voluntary savings and automatic reinvestment plans, systematic withdrawal programs, low-cost conversion and phone-switching privileges, checkwriting privileges, and retirement programs.

- Investors use mutual funds to meet a variety of investment needs; that is, to build a pool of investment capital over the long haul, to speculate in order to achieve high rates of return by trading in and out of funds, and/or as a storehouse of investment value.

- The payoff from investing in a mutual fund includes dividend income, distribution of realized capital gains, and growth in capital (unrealized capital gains); holding period returns and approximate yields recognize these three elements and provide simple yet effective ways of measuring the annual rate of return from a mutual fund.

- While return is important to mutual fund investors, so is risk; and although a fund's extensive diversification may protect investors from business and financial risks, considerable market risk remains because most funds tend to perform much like the market as a whole.

REVIEW QUESTIONS AND PROBLEMS

1. What is a mutual fund? Discuss the mutual fund concept; why are diversification and professional management so important?

2. Briefly define each of the following:

    a. Closed-end investment company.

    b. Open-end investment company.

    c. Unit investment trust.

3.   What is the difference between a load fund and no-load fund? Are there some advantages to either type? What is a 12(b)-1 fund? Can such a fund operate as a no-load fund? Briefly describe a back-end load; a low load; a hidden load. How can you tell what kind of fees and charges a fund has?

4.   What are the attractions and drawbacks of mutual fund ownership?

5.   Contrast mutual fund ownership with the direct investment in common stocks and bonds. Who should own mutual funds and why?

6.   Can the shares of a mutual fund be margined or sold short? Explain.

7.   Using the mutual fund quotes in Figure 13.6, how much would you have to pay to buy each of the following funds, and how much would you pay (in dollars and percentage) in front-end load charges with each of these funds?

    a. Fidelity Select-Financial Services (SlFnS).

    b. Fiduciary Capital (FiduCap).

    c. Flexfund Retirement Growth (RetGr).

    d. Kemper Blue Chips (BluCh).

    e. Financial Program Industrial Income (Incom).

    How much would you receive if you sold these funds? Which of the five funds listed above have 12(b)-1 fees? Which ones have redemption fees? Are any of them no-loads?

8.   Briefly discuss each of the following types of mutual funds:

    a. Aggressive growth fund.

    b. Equity-income fund.

    c. Growth-and-income fund.

    d. Bond fund.

    e. Sector fund.

9.   What is so special about specialty funds? How do their investments differ from those of other types of mutual funds?

10.   For each pair of funds listed below, select the one that would likely be the *least* risky. Briefly explain your answer.

    a. Growth vs. growth-and-income.

    b. Equity-income vs. high-grade corporate bonds.

    c. Balanced vs. sector.

    d. Global vs. aggressive growth.

    e. Intermediate-term bonds vs. high-yield municipals.

11.   What are fund families? What advantages do these families offer investors? Are there any disadvantages?

12. If growth, income, and capital preservation are the primary objectives of mutual funds, why do we bother to categorize them by type? Are such classifications helpful in the fund selection process?

13. List and briefly describe several services provided by mutual funds. How important should these services be in the mutual fund selection process? How do automatic reinvestment plans work? What is phone switching, and why would an investor want to use this type of service?

14. Identify and discuss three investor uses of mutual funds.

15. How important is the general behavior of the market in affecting the price performance of mutual funds? Explain. Why is a fund's *past* performance so important to the mutual fund selection process? Does the *future* behavior of the market matter any in the selection process? Explain.

16. Identify three potential sources of return to mutual fund investors and briefly discuss how each could affect total return to shareholders; explain how the discount or premium of a closed-end fund can also be treated as a return to investors.

17. A year ago, an investor bought 200 shares of a mutual fund at $8.50 per share; over the past year the fund has paid dividends of 90 cents per share and had a capital gains distribution of 75 cents per share. Find the investor's holding period return given that this no-load fund now has a net asset value of $9.10. Find the holding period return assuming all the dividends and capital gains distributions are reinvested into additional shares of the fund at an average price of $8.75 per share.

18. Discuss the various types of risk to which mutual fund shareholders are exposed. What is the major risk exposure of mutual funds? Are all funds subject to the same level of risk? Explain.

19. A year ago, the Really Big Growth Fund was being quoted at an NAV of $21.50 and an offer price of $23.35; today it's being quoted at $23.04 (NAV) and $25.04 (offer). What is the holding period return on this load fund, given that it was purchased a year ago and its dividends and capital gains distributions over the year have totaled $1.05 per share?

20. The All State Mutual Fund has the following five-year record of performance:

	1989	1988	1987	1986	1985
Net investment income	$ .98	$ .85	$ .84	$ .75	$ .64
Dividends from net investment income	(.95)	(.85)	(.85)	(.75)	(.60)
Net realized and unrealized gains (or losses) on security transactions	4.22	5.08	(2.18)	2.65	(1.05)
Distributions from realized gains	(1.05)	(1.00)	—	(1.00)	—
Net increase (decrease) in NAV	3.20	4.08	(2.19)	1.65	(1.01)
NAV at beginning of year	12.53	8.45	10.64	8.99	10.00
NAV at end of year	15.73	12.53	8.45	10.64	8.99

Find this no-load fund's five-year (1985–1989) average annual compound rate of return; also find its three-year (1987–89) average annual compound rate of return. If an investor bought the fund in 1985 at $10.00 a share and sold it five years later (in 1989) at $15.73, how much total profit per share would she have made over the five-year holding period?

21. Using the resources available at your campus or public library, select five mutual funds—a growth fund, an equity-income fund, an international (stock) fund, a sector fund, and a

high-yield corporate bond fund—that you feel would make good investments. Briefly explain why you selected these funds; include the funds' holding period returns for the past year and their annual compound rates of return for the past three years. (Use a schedule like the one in Figure 13.11 to show relevant performance figures.)

CASE PROBLEMS

13.1 Reverend Robin Ponders Mutual Funds

Reverend Robin is the minister of a church in the Denver area. He is married with one young child, and he earns what could best be described as a "modest income." Since religious organizations are not notorious for their generous retirement programs, the Reverend has decided it would be best for him to do a little investing on his own. He would like to set up a program that enables him to supplement the church's retirement program and at the same time, provide some funds for his child's college education (which is still some 12 years away). He is not out to break any investment records, but feels that he desperately needs some backup in order to provide for the long-run needs of his family. Although his income is meager, Reverend Robin feels that with careful planning, he could probably invest about $125 a quarter (and, with luck, maybe increase this amount over time). He presently has about $2,500 in a passbook savings account which he would be willing to use to kick off this program. In view of his investment objectives, he is not interested in taking a lot of risk. Because his knowledge of investments extends to savings accounts, series EE bonds, and a little bit about mutual funds, he approaches you for some investment advice.

Questions
1. In view of the Reverend Robin's long-term investment goals, do you think mutual funds are an appropriate investment vehicle for him?
2. Do you think he should use his $2,500 savings to start off a mutual fund investment program?
3. What type of mutual fund investment program would you set up for the Reverend? Include in your answer some discussion of the types of funds you would consider, the investment objectives you would set, and any investment services (like withdrawal plans) you would seek. Would taxes be an important consideration in your investment advice? Explain.

13.2 Tom Lasnicka Seeks the Good Life

Tom Lasnicka is a widower who recently retired after a long and illustrious career with a major midwestern manufacturer. Beginning as a skilled craftsman, he worked his way up to the level of shop supervisor over a period of more than 30 years with the firm. Tom receives Social Security benefits and a generous company pension—in all, these two sources amount to over $1,500 per month (part of which is tax free, of course). The Lasnickas had no children, so he lives alone. Tom owns a two-bedroom rental house that is next to his home, with the rental income from it covering the mortgage payments for both the rental and his house. Over the years, Tom and his late wife, Camille, always tried to put a little money aside each month; the results have been nothing short of phenomenal as the value of Tom's liquid investments (all held in bank CDs and passbook savings accounts) runs well into the six figures. Up to now, Tom has just let his money grow and has not used any of his savings to supplement his social security, pension, and rental income. But things are about to change. Tom has decided, "What the heck, it's high time I start living the good life!" Tom wants to travel and do some exciting things with his life—in effect, he is determined to start reaping

the benefits of his labors. He has therefore decided to move $75,000 from one of his savings accounts to one or two high-yielding mutual funds. He would like to receive $1,000 a month from the fund(s) for as long as possible, since he plans to be around for a long time.

Questions

1.   Given Tom's financial resources and investment objectives, what kind of mutual funds do you think he should consider?
2.   Are there any factors in Tom's situation that should be taken into consideration in the fund selection process, and if so, how might these affect Tom's course of action?
3.   What types of services do you think he should look for in a mutual fund?
4.   Assume Tom invests in a mutual fund that earns about 10 percent annually from dividend income and capital gains. Given that Tom wants to receive $1,000 a month from his mutual fund, what would be the size of his investment account five years from now? How large would the account be if the fund could earn 16 percent on average and everything else remains the same? How important is the fund's rate of return to Tom's investment situation? Explain.

SELECTED READINGS

Bodnar, Janet. "Mutual Funds: How to Figure Your Real Return." *Changing Times,* April 1987, pp. 69–70.

Boroson, Warren. "The Best of Families." *Sylvia Porter's Personal Finance,* May 1989, pp. 35–41.

"A Close Look at Closed-End Funds." *Changing Times,* May 1987, pp. 87–92.

Kosnett, Jeff. "Sector Funds: How to Get a Piece of the Action." *Changing Times,* May 1987, pp. 26–32.

Schiffres, Manuel. "Loads vs. No-Loads: The Winner Is. . . . " *Changing Times,* February 1989, pp. 35–40.

Schurenberg, Eric. "When to Take the Money and Run." *Money,* November 1986, pp. 237–40.

Thomsett, Michael C. "Prospecting the Prospectus." *Sylvia Porter's Personal Finance,* June 1986, pp. 70–72.

Trotsky, Judith, and Fred W. Frailey. "A Dumb Way to Buy Mutual Funds." *Changing Times,* March 1989, pp. 59–63.

Walbert, Laura. "How to Pick a Mutual Fund." *Forbes,* September 7, 1987, pp. 162–64.

Wiener, Daniel. "The Risky Allure of Junk Funds." *U.S. News & World Report,* October 31, 1988, pp. 78–79.

14

REAL ESTATE INVESTMENTS

After studying this chapter you should be able to:

● Describe the procedures for setting real estate investment objectives, including consideration of investment characteristics, constraints and goals, and the scope of analysis.

● Explain the key determinants of value in real estate: demand, supply, the property, and the property transfer process.

● Discuss the valuation techniques commonly used to estimate the market value of real estate.

● Gain an understanding of the procedures involved in forecasting real estate investment returns.

● Apply real estate valuation techniques to a prospective real estate investment, and analyze its investment merits.

● Describe real estate investment trusts (REITs) and real estate limited partnerships (RELPs), and explain the appeal they hold for investors.

Real estate offers an attractive way to diversify an investment portfolio and also achieve favorable risk-return tradeoffs. Unlike investments in stocks, bonds, and options, managerial decisions about real estate greatly affect the returns that a property earns. In real estate you must answer questions such as: What rents should be charged? How much should be spent on maintenance and repairs? What advertising media should be selected? What purchase, lease, or sales contract provisions should be used? Along with market forces, it is the answers to these and other questions that determine whether or not you will earn the desired return on a real estate investment. Thus investing in real estate means more than just "buying right" or "selling right." It also means managing the property right! The analytical framework presented here has two purposes: (1) to help you decide what price to pay for a property and (2) to guide you through the many operating decisions you will need to make. You can maximize returns only when you consider both types of decisions. We now take up the process of real estate investment analysis, beginning with objectives.

SETTING REAL ESTATE INVESTMENT OBJECTIVES

Setting objectives involves three steps. First, you should consider how the investment characteristics of real estate differ; second, you should establish investment constraints and goals; and third, you should define the scope of analysis.

Investment Characteristics

personal residence *type of real estate that includes single-family houses, condominiums, cooperatives, and townhouses.*

Individual real estate investments differ in their characteristics even more than individual people differ in theirs. So, just as you wouldn't marry without thinking long and hard about the type of person you'd be happy with, you shouldn't select an investment property without some feeling for whether or not it is the right one for you. To select wisely, you need to consider (1) the available types of properties and (2) whether you want an equity or a debt position.

income property *type of leased-out real estate, such as apartment and office buildings and shopping centers, that provides some form of rental income to its owner.*

Types of Properties

For our purposes, we can classify real estate into three categories: personal residences, income properties, and speculative properties. **Personal residences** include single-family houses, condominiums, cooperatives, and townhouses; the **income properties** category refers to properties that are leased out, such as small apartment buildings, apartment complexes, office buildings, and shopping centers; and **speculative properties** typically include land and special-purpose buildings, such as churches, gas stations, and the like.

speculative property *type of real estate, typically including land and special-purpose buildings such as churches and gas stations, with a high degree of uncertainty for future profit.*

In terms of risk and return, personal residences generally provide the safest investment. Except in certain boom-bust markets such as the one that recently prevailed in many Texas cities, owner-occupied housing historically has offered little downside risk for loss of capital, and reasonable potential for appreciation of 3 to 8 percent per year. With respect to income properties, the chance of loss is greater than for personal residences, but so is the chance for gain. Losses can result from tenant carelessness, excessive supply of competing rental units, or poor man-

agement. On the profit side, however, income properties can provide increasing rental incomes due to a growing population, capital appreciation in the value of the property, and for certain investors, possibly even some shelter from taxes.

As the term implies, speculative properties give their buyers a chance to make a killing, but also the chance for heavy loss. This speculative characteristic usually arises from high uncertainty. For instance, rumors may start that a new multimillion dollar plant is going to be built on the edge of town. Land buyers would jump into the market, and prices soon would be bid up. The right buy-sell timing could yield returns of several hundred percent or more. But people who bought into the market late, or those who failed to sell before the market turned, might lose the major part of their investment. So you can see that before investing in real estate, you should determine the risks various types of properties present and then decide which risks you can afford to take.

Equity versus Debt

In this chapter we discuss real estate investment primarily from the standpoint of equity. It is also possible for individuals to invest in instruments of real estate debt, such as mortgages and deeds of trust. Usually these instruments provide a fairly safe rate of return if the borrowers are required to maintain at least a 20 percent equity position in the mortgaged property (no more than an 80 percent loan-to-value ratio). This owner equity position gives the real estate lender a margin of safety should foreclosure have to be initiated. Often property owners are asked to ''take back'' a debt position (owner financing) when they sell a property. Their willingness to accept this type of financing arrangement can help them get their property sold more quickly and at a higher price. However, even though owner financing can benefit sellers, they should not accept it until they determine both the buyer-borrower's ability to pay and the loan-to-value ratio necessary to provide the desired level of investment safety.

Constraints and Goals

When you decide to invest in real estate, you face a number of choices. In light of these options, you need to set financial and nonfinancial constraints and goals.

Financial Constraints and Goals

One financial constraint pertains to the risk-return relationship you find acceptable. In addition, you must consider how much money you want to allocate to the real estate portion of your portfolio. Do you want to invest $1,000, $10,000, or $50,000? Furthermore, you should define a quantifiable financial objective. Often this financial goal is stated in terms of *net present value* (also referred to as *discounted cash flows*) or approximate yield. Some investors also consider payback period, first-year cash on cash return, and tax-shelter ratios. We will show how these constraints and goals can be applied to real estate investing in the Academic Arms Apartments example later in the chapter.

In recent years, several popular ''how to get rich'' real estate books have become best sellers. Usually these books present various rule-of-thumb financial and valua-

tion guidelines. Indeed, the popularity of such books is often directly related to the simplicity of the techniques they present. One word is in order: Beware. Successful real estate investing requires you to develop your own criteria, based on your needs and the market conditions in you locality. A rule of thumb that has worked well in southern California may take a Peoria, Illinois, investor into bankruptcy.

Nonfinancial Constraints and Goals

Although you will probably want to invest in real estate for its financial rewards, you also need to consider how your technical skills, temperament, repair skills, and managerial talents fit a potential investment. Do you want a prestige, trouble-free property? Or would you prefer a fix-up special on which you can release your imagination and workmanship? Would you enjoy living in the same building as your tenants (as in a fourplex investment) or would you like as little contact with them as possible? Just as you wouldn't choose a career solely on the basis of money, neither should you buy a property just for the money.

Scope of Analysis

The framework of real estate investment analysis suggested in this chapter can aid in estimating a property's investment potential. Yet before really evaluating this potential, a scope of analysis must be established. This includes four parts: (1) identifying the physical property, (2) defining the applicable property rights, (3) deciding the time horizon for your investment, and (4) delineating a geographic area.

Physical Property

When buying real estate, make sure you are getting both the quantity and quality of property you think you are getting. Problems can arise if you fail to obtain a site survey; an accurate square-footage measurement of the buildings; or an inspection for defects, such as termite infestation, hazardous materials, dry rot, improper settling, and an inadequate electrical system. In addition, most real estate transactions do not automatically include **personal property**—which can be loosely defined as property that is not attached in a more or less permanent fashion to the real estate. So you might buy a property and think the sale includes window air-conditioning units, drapes, refrigerator, and fireplace screen and equipment. Then you discover it doesn't. When signing a contract to buy a property, make sure it accurately identifies the real estate and lists all items of personal property that you expect to receive.

personal property *property that is not attached in a more or less permanent fashion to real estate.*

Property Rights

Strange as it may seem, when buying real estate, you do not really buy the physical property. What you buy is a bundle of legal rights that not only limit the ways you can benefit from your property, but also establish certain obligations. These rights and obligations fall under concepts in law such as deeds, titles, easements, liens, and encumbrances. Too often people have bought real estate and then discovered they didn't receive good title, or they couldn't use the property the way they intended. When investing in real estate make sure that along with termite, hazardous materials, plumbing, structural, and electrical inspections, you also get a legal

inspection from a qualified attorney. Real estate sale and lease agreements should not be the work of amateurs.

Time Horizon

Like a roller coaster, real estate prices go up and down. Sometimes market forces pull them up slowly but surely; in other periods prices can fall so fast they take an investor's breath (and money) away. Before judging whether a prospective real estate investment will appreciate or depreciate, you must decide what time period is relevant. Investors who like to hold properties for the long term virtually ignore month-to-month price movements. At the other extreme are investors (speculators) who "flip" properties frequently. As soon as they sign a sales contract, they're out looking for a quick profit. Because of these various time emphases, different real estate investors weigh the specific factors that relate to demand and supply very differently. The short-term investor might count on a quick drop in mortgage interest rates and buoyant market expectations, whereas the long-term investor might look more closely at population-growth potential.

Geographic Area

Real estate is a spatial commodity, which means that its value is directly linked to what is going on around it. With some properties, the area of greatest concern consists of a few square blocks; in other instances an area of hundreds or even thousands of miles serves as the relevant market area. For example, a 7-Eleven convenience store's success is determined within a geographic area of 6 to 12 blocks. A large shopping mall, such as the Omni in Miami, Florida, or Horton Plaza in San Diego, California, brings in customers from hundreds and even thousands of miles away. As a result of these spatial differences in the market areas that apply to properties, you must delineate boundaries before you can analyze real estate demand and supply in a productive manner.

DETERMINANTS OF VALUE

In real estate investment analysis, value generally serves as the central concept. Will a property increase in value? Will it produce increasing amounts of cash flows? To address these questions intelligently, you should evaluate the four major determinants of real estate value: demand, supply, the property, and the property transfer process.

Demand

demand

in real estate, people's willingness and ability to buy or rent a given property.

Demand refers to people's willingness and ability to buy or rent a given property. Generally demand stems from a market area's economic base, the characteristics of its population, and the terms and conditions of mortgage financing.

Economic Base

In most real estate markets, the source of buying power comes from jobs. Property values follow an upward path when employment is increasing, and values typically fall when employers begin to lay off personnel. Therefore, the first question you

should ask about demand is "What is the outlook for jobs in the relevant market area?" Are schools, colleges, and universities gaining enrollment? Are major companies planning expansion? And are wholesalers, retailers, and financial institutions increasing their sales and services? Upward trends in these indicators often signal a rising demand for real estate.

Population Characteristics

All properties, however, do not benefit (or suffer) equally from changes in an area's overall growth rate. To analyze demand for a specific property, you should look at an area's population demographics and psychographics. **Demographics** refers to such things as household size, age structure, occupation, sex, and marital status. **Psychographics** are those characteristics that describe people's mental dispositions, such as personality, lifestyle, and self-concept. By comparing demographic and psychographic trends to the features of a property, you can judge whether it is likely to gain or lose favor among potential buyers or tenants.

demographics

characteristics of an area's population, such as household size, age structure, occupation, sex, and marital status; should be considered when analyzing real estate demand.

Mortgage Financing

psychographics

characteristics that describe people's mental dispositions, such as personality, lifestyle, and self-concept; should be considered when analyzing real estate demand.

Tight money can choke off the demand for real estate. As we saw in the early 1980s, rising interest rates and the relative unavailability of mortgages caused inventories of unsold properties to grow and real estate prices to fall. Conversely, as mortgage interest rates fell, beginning in late 1982 and early 1983 and continuing through 1988, real estate sales activity in many cities throughout the United States rapidly expanded.

Some good, though, came out of the topsy-turvy market for real estate financing during the past 10 years. Lenders now offer a wide range of mortgage instruments. This variety of mortgage payment plans helps lenders and borrowers meet their respective needs. The more popular and widely available plans are shown in Table 14.1.

Supply

supply analysis

study of the competition in real estate by identifying potential competitors and making an inventory of them by price and features.

Supply analysis really means sizing up the competition. Nobody wants to pay you more for a property than the price they can pay your competitor; nor when you're buying (or renting) should you pay more than the prices asked for other similar properties. As a result, an integral part of value analysis requires that you identify sources of potential competition and then inventory them by price and features.

Sources of Competition

principle of substitution

the principle that people do not buy or rent real estate per se but rather that they judge properties as different sets of benefits and costs.

In general, people in real estate think of competitors in terms of similar properties. If you are trying to sell a house, then it seems natural to see your competition as the other houses for sale in your neighborhood. For longer-term investment decisions, however, you should expand your concept of supply. That is, you should identify competitors through use of the **principle of substitution.** This principle holds that people do not really buy or rent real estate per se. Instead, they judge properties as different sets of benefits and costs. Properties fill people's needs, and it is really these needs that create demand. Thus an analysis of supply should not limit poten-

TABLE 14.1 Mortgage Payment Plans

Type of Payment Plan	Pros and Cons	Who Benefits
FIXED-RATE MORTGAGE (FRM)		
Both the interest rate and the monthly payment are fixed over the life of the mortgage. This is the traditional form of mortgage loan.	The size of the payments being fixed over the life of the loan allows the borrower to know with certainty the payment obligation. On the other hand, the plan does not offer any of the special-purpose benefits one might get from other payment plans.	No special group benefits from this traditional or most basic plan.
ADJUSTABLE-RATE MORTGAGE (ARM)		
Instead of a fixed interest rate, this loan carries an interest rate that may change within limits—up or down—from time to time during the life of the loan, reflecting changes in market rates for money. Some ARMs are convertible—they give the borrower, within a stipulated period of time, the right to convert to a fixed-rate mortgage.	Because the size of the payments in the future is uncertain, this loan is a bit of a gamble. If market rates for money go down in the future, payments will go down. But if the rates go up, so will payments.	Helps lenders keep their flow of funds in step with changing conditions, and this in turn could make loans easier to get when money is tight. Borrower may get fractionally lower interest at first or other inducements to make future uncertainties more palatable.
15-YEAR MORTGAGE (FYM)		
Typically, fixed monthly payments are made over a 15- rather than the historically more popular 30-year period. Are used primarily with fixed-rate loans, but can also be used on adjustable-rate mortgages.	Although they result in slightly higher monthly payments, the contractual interest rate is typically slightly below that on conventional 30-year loans. Result is faster equity buildup and much lower amounts paid to interest over the life of the mortgage.	Allows borrowers to more quickly build equity in their property without significantly larger monthly payments. May reduce lender's risk exposure by providing for a quicker recovery of loan principal.

TABLE 14.1 (Continued)

Type of Payment Plan	Pros and Cons	Who Benefits
BIWEEKLY MORTGAGE (BWM)		
Payments are made every two weeks rather than monthly; under this arrangement, half a normal monthly payment is made every 2 weeks. Used primarily with 30-year fixed-rate mortgages.	Total interest paid over the life of the loan is much lower than under a typical monthly payment plan. Of course, the borrower must make payments more often, which could create an "inconvenience."	Because 13 monthly payments (26 biweekly) are made within a period of a year, the mortgage is paid off well before the stated maturity date, usually after about 20 years.
GROWING-EQUITY MORTGAGE (GEM)		
Initially the monthly payments are equivalent to those on a 30-year fixed-rate mortgage, but then they rise annually by 4 to 7½ percent, causing the loan to be paid off within 12 to 15 years.	Because of the accelerated payback, most lenders are willing to give borrowers a break on the interest rate. Provides for accelerated payoff of the loan, but forces the borrower to make larger mortgage payments each year.	Both lenders and borrowers benefit, since the lender gets its money back sooner and the borrower who wishes to repay a mortgage quickly can do so at a lower and fixed interest rate.
GRADUATED-PAYMENT MORTGAGE (GPM)		
Monthly payments are arranged to start out low and get bigger later, perhaps in a series of steps at specified intervals. The term of the loan and the interest rate remain unchanged.	The object is to make buying easier in the beginning. Initial payments have to be balanced by larger payments later. One disadvantage: Possible "negative amortization" in the early years, which means that for a time the debt grows instead of diminishes.	Mainly first-time buyers, who have a hard time becoming homeowners, but can look forward to higher earnings that will enable them to afford the bigger payments later.

tial competitors to geographically and physically similar properties. In some markets, for example, low-priced single-family houses might compete with condominium units, manufactured homes (formerly called mobile homes), and even with rental apartments. So before investing in any property, you should decide what market that property appeals to, and then define its competitors as other properties that its buyers or tenants might also typically choose from.

Inventory Competitors

Real estate investment analysis requires that, after identifying all relevant competitors, you inventory these properties in terms of features and respective prices. (Many large real estate investors hire professional market consultants to do the research that the analysis of demand and supply requires.) In other words, look for the relative pros and cons of each property. With this market information, you can develop a competitive edge for your (potential) property.

The Property

Up to now we have shown that a property's sales or rental value is influenced by demand and supply. The price that people will pay is governed by their needs and the relative prices of the properties available to meet those needs. For example, as noted in the Investor Insights box, investment in a minidorm can create tax-deductible college housing for a child while acting as a real estate investment for the parents. Yet in real estate the property itself is also a key ingredient. What is the best use for a property? Which benefits should be offered? To address these issues, to try to develop a property's competitive edge, an investor should consider five items: (1) restrictions on use; (2) location; (3) site characteristics; (4) improvements; and (5) property management.

Restrictions on Use

In today's highly regulated society none of us has the right to do just as we please with a property. Both state and local laws and private contracts limit the rights of all property owners. Government restrictions derive from zoning laws, building and occupancy codes, and health and sanitation requirements. Private restrictions derive from deeds, leases, and condominium bylaws and operating rules. As a result of all these restrictions, then, you should not invest in a property until you or your lawyer determines that what you want to do with the property *fits within* applicable laws, rules, and contract provisions.

Location Analysis

You may have heard the adage, ''The three most important determinants of real estate value are location, location, and location.'' Of course, location is not the only factor that affects value; yet a good location unquestionably increases a property's investment potential. Now, with that said, you need to learn how to tell a bad location from a good location. We can add that a good location is one that meets the needs of a defined buyer (tenant) segment better than other locations. A good location rates highly on two key dimensions: convenience and environment. The

INVESTOR INSIGHTS

Minidorms: Real Estate Investments That Can Cut College Costs

In recent years, many parents looking for ways to deal with the bite of college costs have bought their children so-called kiddie condos. The child gets a place to live at school, the parents get a real-estate investment that presumably can be sold at a profit when the child graduates.

Now financial planners and accountants are recommending a wrinkle on the same idea—the minidorm. To use this tactic, says James Avedisian, a tax partner with accountants Coopers & Lybrand, "buy a house on campus for several kids to share and hire your own child as live-in rental manager."

THE MINIDORM ADVANTAGE

The minidorm has one large advantage over the kiddie condo: The child is paid a salary for finding tenants, collecting rents and the like, and uses the money to pay college expenses. But on the parents' tax return, says Mr. Avedisian, the salary is considered an expense and can be used to offset the minidorm's taxable rental income. Thus, the strategy transforms non-deductible college expenses into deductible business expenses.

Furthermore, income taxes for individuals don't kick in until earnings top $3,000. So, as long as the child's salary doesn't exceed that amount, it won't be taxed. And even if it does, it usually will be taxed only at the lowest rate of 15%.

Minidorms make especially good sense for parents with adjusted gross incomes of less than $100,000, according to Sidney Kess, a tax partner at accounting firm Peat Marwick Main & Co. That's because the Internal Revenue Service allows these people to use up to $25,000 in losses on the minidorm to offset salary or other taxable income.

---

convenience
in real estate, the accessibility of a property to the places the people in a target market frequently need to go.

esthetic environment
in real estate, neighborhoods where buildings and landscaping are well executed and well maintained and where there is no noise, sight, or air pollution nor encroaching unharmonious land uses.

analytical framework for residential location analysis briefly discussed below is depicted in Figure 14.1.

Convenience. **Convenience** refers to how accessible a property is to places the people in a target market frequently need to go. In judging the relative convenience of a residential location, for example, most tenants and home buyers try to assess the proximity of educational facilities, such as schools and colleges; recreational facilities, such as parks, swimming pools, and tennis courts; sources of employment; cultural facilities, such as churches, libraries, and museums; and shopping facilities, such as retail stores, household services, restaurants, and places of entertainment. Any selected residential or commercial market segment will have a set of preferred places its buyers or tenants will want to be close to. Another element of convenience refers to the availability of transportation facilities, such as buses, taxis, subways, and commuter trains. For example, in Piedmont, California, a suburb of San Francisco, homes close to the commuter train station and bus stops are generally preferred to similar homes located farther away.

For parents earning more than $100,000, however, the deductible amount is gradually reduced until it disappears completely at the $150,000-in-earnings mark. Still, there is a way to keep losses in the family: Put the house in the name of a grandparent making less than $100,000, suggests Mr. Kess.

Despite the minidorm's attractions, there are risks, especially since the property's manager is a youth. "He might bring in friends to share the house who don't pay rent," says Mr. Avedisian. "If they don't pay rent, it's going to be a losing proposition for Mom and Dad." What's more, he says, "if the kids trash the place, the property's value could decline."

Given those potential problems, some parents may prefer a similar, but simpler strategy. This one will work only for those with a family-owned business and calls for the parents to hire the college-age child as an employee of that business. There won't be any rental-property losses to deduct, and the child won't have a free place to live. But, as with the minidorms, the child's salary can be written off as a business expense. And, once again, the child won't pay taxes on the salary as long as it doesn't exceed $3,000.

STEERING CLEAR OF THE IRS

But be careful. Simply paying a child to clean the family pool and then calling the payments salary is not something smiled upon by the IRS. "The money has to be earned in connection with a trade or business," says Mr. Avedisian.

A child who can work in the family business only during the summer might be retained as a "consultant" the rest of the year, accountants say. "Kids who've grown up in a family business, especially retail businesses, often have some good thoughts about what kind of inventory to stock (and) what sells," Mr. Avedisian notes.

Source: Jill Bettner, "Minidorms Touted as Tactic to Cut the Costs of College," *The Wall Street Journal,* July 11, 1988, p. 19.

---

socioeconomic environment
in real estate, the demographics and lifestyles of the people who live or work near the subject property.

legal environment
in real estate, the restrictions on use that apply to properties near the subject property.

Environment. With all the public emphasis on ecology in recent years, you probably think of "the environment" in terms of trees, rivers, lakes, and air quality. But in the analysis of real estate, the term *environment* has broader meaning. When you invest in real estate, you should really consider not only the natural environment, but also the esthetic, socioeconomic, legal, and fiscal environments.

Neighborhoods with an **esthetic environment** are those where buildings and landscaping are well executed and well maintained. There is no intrusion of noise, sight, or air pollution, and encroaching unharmonious land uses are not evident. The **socioeconomic environment** refers to the demographics and lifestyles of the people who live or work in nearby properties; the **legal environment** relates to the restrictions on use that apply to nearby properties. Remember, in the absence of zoning or deed restrictions, properties near, say, a fourplex that you buy might be developed in a way that would lower your building's value. And last, you need to consider a property's **fiscal environment.** This environment refers to the amount of property taxes and municipal assessments you will be required to pay, and the government services you will be entitled to receive (police, fire, schools, parks,

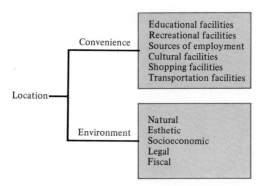

FIGURE 14.1 **Analytical Framework for Residential Location Analysis.**
This framework is useful in analyzing real estate locations; note that a good location is one
that rates highly in terms of convenience and environment—each of which involves a number
of key dimensions.

fiscal environment
in real estate, the
amount of property
taxes and municipal
assessments an
owner must pay and
the government ser-
vices to which the
owner is entitled.

water, sewers, trash collection, libraries). Property taxes are a two-sided coin. On
the one side they pose a cost, but on the other they give a property's users the right
to services that may be of substantial benefit.

Site Characteristics

One of the most important features of a property site is its size. For residential
properties, such as personal residences, condominiums, and apartments, some people want a large yard for children to play in or for a garden. Others may prefer
virtually no yard at all. With respect to commercial properties, such as office buildings and shopping centers, adequate parking space is necessary. Also, with respect
to site size, if you are planning a later addition of space, make sure the site is large
enough to accommodate it, both physically and legally. Site quality is also important, and refers to such factors as soil fertility, topography, elevation, and drainage
capacity. These features are important, for example, because grass may be difficult
to grow in certain types of soil, and sites with relatively low elevation may be
subject to flooding. (Nobody likes a basement full of water after a hard rain.) In
examining a site, you should further note any extras, such as fencing, paved drive-
way and parking areas, sewer and utility connections, landscaping, and sidewalks.
Each of these can add to the benefits a property can produce, and to its cash flows.

Improvements

improvements
in real estate, the
man-made additions
to a site, such as
buildings, sidewalks,
and various on-site
amenities.

In real estate, the term **improvements** refers to the man-made additions to a site.
Under site analysis we talked about improvements such as paved parking areas and
sidewalks. Here we are talking about the analysis of building size and quality and
on-site amenities (swimming pools, tennis courts, golf course, and so on).

Building Size and Floor Plan. Typically building size is measured and expressed
in terms of square footage. For instance, with respect to residences, and by American standards, a small house is one of less than, say, 1,400 square feet; medium-

sized houses range between 1,400 and 2,200 square feet; and to most people a house of more than 2,200 square feet would be thought of as large. Because square footage is so important in building and unit comparison, you should get accurate square footage measures on any properties you consider investing in.

Another measure of building size is room count and floor plan. For example, a well-designed 750-square-foot apartment unit might in fact be more livable than one of 850 square feet. Therefore you should determine whether the sizes of individual rooms are in proportion to their intended use. One way to check this feature is to take measurements of furniture that would be typical and see if rooms are too small, adequate, or excessively large. You should make sure that floor plans are logical, that traffic flows throughout a building will pose no inconveniences, that there is sufficient closet, cabinet, and other storage space, and that the right mix of rooms exists. For example, in an office building you should not have to cross through other offices to get to the building's only bathroom, or as an exclusive access to any other room; small merchants in a shopping center should not be placed in locations where they do not receive the pedestrian traffic generated by the larger (anchor) tenants.

Amenities, Style, Construction Quality. As another item, you should determine which amenities and personal property might be included with your potential investment properties. It is now common for houses, condominiums, and apartments to be furnished with items such as garbage disposal, refrigerator, dishwasher, and compactor. In addition, when buying an existing property, items such as window air conditioners, chandeliers, fireplace equipment, and even some furniture might be included. From shopping the market and thumbing through architectural books and magazines, you should develop a sense of style as well as some knowledge of construction materials and quality workmanship.

Property Management

In recent years real estate owners and investors have increasingly recognized that investment properties (apartments, office buildings, shopping centers, and so on) do not earn maximum cash flows by themselves. They need to be guided toward that objective. This is why skilled property management is important to property owners. Without effective property management, no real estate investment can produce maximum benefits for its users and owners. In this context we are not talking about someone who merely collects rents, calls the plumber, and hangs out vacancy signs. Today property management requires you (or a hired manager) not only to perform day-to-day chores, but also to run the entire operation. You need to segment buyers, improve a property's site and structure, keep tabs on competitors, and develop a marketing campaign. Management also assumes responsibility for the maintenance and repair of buildings and their physical systems (electrical, heating, air conditioning, and plumbing); and managers keep records to account for revenues and expenses. In addition, property managers decide the best ways to protect properties against loss from perils such as fire, flood, theft, storms, and negligence. In its broadest sense **property management** means finding the optimal level of benefits for a property, and then providing them at the lowest costs. Of course, for specula-

property management

in real estate, finding the optimal level of benefits for a property and then providing them at the lowest costs.

tive investments such as raw land, the managerial task is not so pronounced and the manager has less control over the profit picture.

The Property Transfer Process

property transfer process
the process of promotion and negotiation of real estate, which can significantly influence the cash flows a property can earn in the real estate market.

In Chapter 8 we introduced the concept of efficient markets. You may recall from that discussion that an efficient market is one in which information flows so quickly among buyers and sellers that it is virtually impossible for an investor to outperform the average systematically. As soon as something good (an exciting new product) or something bad (a multimillion-dollar product liability suit) occurs, the price of the affected company's stock adjusts to reflect its current potential for earnings or losses. Some people accept the premise that securities markets are efficient, while others do not. But one thing is sure: *No one believes real estate markets are efficient.* What this means is that real estate market research pays off. Skillfully conducted economic analysis, property type analysis (industry analysis), and property analysis (fundamental analysis) can help you beat the averages. (Note: In real estate markets, the tools of technical analysis are virtually undeveloped.) The reasons real estate markets differ from securities markets is that no good system exists for complete information exchange among buyers and sellers, and among tenants and lessors. In addition, real estate returns are partially controlled by the property owners themselves. As pointed out above, profits in real estate depend on how well you or your property manager can manage the property. In the **property transfer process** itself, the inefficiency of the market means that how you collect and disseminate information will affect your results. The cash flows a property will earn can be influenced significantly through promotion and negotiation.

Promotion

Promotion refers to the task of getting information about a property to its buyer segment. You can't sell or rent a property quickly and for top dollar unless you can reach the people you want to reach in a cost-effective way. Among the major ways to promote a property are advertising, publicity, sales gimmicks, and personal selling.

Both advertising and publicity involve media coverage for your property. In the case of advertising, you pay for this coverage; with publicity, you create a newsworthy event. For example, in Dallas a few years ago the Dondi Development Corporation used a new type of financing plan—the "Rich Uncle" program—to get good (and free) press coverage for its condominium units. A sales gimmick often relies on some type of contest or perhaps a gift of some sort. A Houston office building developer, for example, perked up demand for his project when he offered a new Mercedes to new tenants who signed a five-year lease. This sales gimmick also got the developer's project a great deal of publicity. Personal selling is often the most costly, but also the most effective way to attract buyers or tenants to a property. It places you or your sales agent in a one-on-one customer relationship.

In most instances property owners use two or more ways to promote their property. Space does not permit us to show how such an approach should be made, or to discuss the technical requirements necessary to create a promotion campaign; but at

the least, you should now see that maximizing a real estate investment's cash flows through promotion entails more than dashing off a classified newspaper advertisement.

Negotiation

Seldom does the minimum price a seller is willing to accept just equal the maximum price a buyer is willing to pay; often some overlap occurs. Also, in real estate the asking price for a property may be anywhere from 5 to 60 percent above the price that a seller (or lessor) will accept. Therefore the negotiating skills of each party determine the final transaction price.

REAL ESTATE VALUATION

market value
in real estate, the prevailing market price of a property, indicating how the market as a whole has assessed the property's worth.

In real estate the concept of **market value,** or actual worth, must be interpreted differently from its meaning in stocks and bonds. This difference arises for a number of reasons, among which are: (1) each property is unique; (2) terms and conditions of sale may vary widely; (3) market information is imperfect; (4) properties may need substantial time for market exposure, time that may not be available to any given seller; and (5) buyers too sometimes need to act quickly. All these factors mean that no one can tell for sure what a property's "true" market value is, and as a result many properties sell for prices significantly above or below their estimated (or appraised) market values. To offset such inequities, many real estate investors in addition forecast investment returns in order to evaluate potential property investments in light of their investment objectives. Here we look first at procedures for estimating the market value of a piece of real estate, and then describe methods for forecasting real estate investment returns.

Estimating Market Value

appraisal
a process for estimating the current market value of a piece of property.

In real estate, estimating the current market value of a piece of property is done through a process known as a real estate **appraisal.** Using certain techniques, an appraiser will set the value on a piece of property that he feels represents the current market value of the property. Even so, if you are told that a property has an appraised market value of, say, $150,000, you should interpret that value a little skeptically. Because of both technical and informational shortcomings, this estimate can be subject to substantial error. Although you can arrive at the market values of frequently traded stocks simply by looking at current quotes, in real estate, appraisers and investors typically must use three complex techniques and then correlate results to come up with one best estimate. These three imperfect approaches to real estate market value are (1) the cost approach; (2) the comparative sales approach; and (3) the income approach. Due to the complexity of this process, it is often helpful to use an expert.

The Cost Approach

cost approach
a real estate valuation approach based on the idea that a buyer should not pay more for a property than it would cost to rebuild it at today's prices for land, labor, and construction materials.

The **cost approach** is based on the notion that an investor should not pay more for a property than it would cost to rebuild it at today's prices for land, labor, and construction materials. This approach to estimating value generally works well for

new or relatively new buildings. Older properties, however, often suffer from wear and tear, and outdated materials or design, making the cost approach more difficult to apply. To value these older properties, you would have to subtract some amount for physical and functional depreciation from the replacement cost estimates. Most experts agree that the cost approach is a good method to use as a check against a price estimate, but rarely should it be used exclusively.

The Comparative Sales Approach

comparative sales approach
a real estate valuation approach that uses sales prices of properties that are similar to the subject property as the basic input variable.

The **comparative sales approach** uses the sales prices of properties that are similar to a subject property as the basic input variable. This method is based on the idea that the value of a given property is about the same as the prices for which other similar properties have recently sold. Of course, the catch here is that all properties are unique in some respect. Therefore the price that a subject property could be expected to bring must be adjusted upward or downward to reflect its superiority or inferiority to comparable properties. Nevertheless, because the comparable sales approach is based on *selling* prices, not asking prices, it can give you a good feel for the market. As a practical matter, if you can find at least one sold property slightly better than the one you're looking at, and one slightly worse, their recent sales prices can serve to bracket an estimated market value for a subject property.

The Income Approach

income approach
a real estate valuation approach that calculates a property's value as the present value of all its future income.

Under the **income approach** a property's value is viewed as the present value of all its future income. The most popular income approach is called *direct capitalization*. This approach is represented by the formula:

$$\text{market value } (V) = \frac{\text{annual net operating income (NOI)}}{\text{market capitalization rate } (R)}$$

$$V = \frac{\text{NOI}}{R}$$

net operating income (NOI)
the amount left after subtracting vacancy and collection losses and property operating expenses, including property insurance and taxes, from an income property's gross potential rental income.

Annual **net operating income (NOI)** is calculated by subtracting vacancy and collection losses and property operating expenses, including property insurance and property taxes, from an income property's *gross potential* rental income. An estimated **capitalization rate**—which technically means the rate used to convert an income stream to a present value—is obtained by looking at recent market sales figures and seeing what rate of return investors currently require. Then, by dividing the annual net operating income by the appropriate capitalization rate, you get an income property's estimated market value. An example of the application of the income approach is given in Table 14.2.

capitalization rate
the rate used to convert an income stream to a present value, which can be used to estimate the value of real estate under the income approach to value.

Using an Expert

Real estate valuation is a complex and technical procedure that requires reliable information about the features of comparable properties, their selling prices, and applicable terms of financing. As a result, rather than relying exclusively on their own judgment, many investors hire a real estate agent or a professional real estate

TABLE 14.2   Applying the Income Approach

Comparable Property	(1) NOI	(2) Sale Price	(3) (1) ÷ (2) Capitalization Rate (R)
2301 Maple Ave.	$16,250	$182,500	.0890
4037 Armstrong St.	15,400	167,600	.0919
8240 Ludwell St.	19,200	198,430	.0968
7392 Grant Blvd.	17,930	189,750	.0945
Subject property	$18,480	?	?

From this market-derived information, an appraiser would work through the equation:

$$V = \frac{NOI}{R}$$

$$V = \frac{\$18,480}{R}$$

$$V = \frac{\$18,480}{.093*}$$

$$V = \$198,710$$

*Based on an analysis of the relative similarities of the comparables and the subject property, the appraiser decided the appropriate R equals .093.

appraiser to advise them about the market value of a property. As a form of insurance against overpaying, the use of an expert can be well worth the cost.

Forecasting Investment Returns

Estimates of market value play an integral role in real estate decision making. Yet today more and more investors supplement their market value appraisals with investment analysis. This extension of the traditional approaches to value (cost, comparative sales, and income) gives investors a better picture of whether a selected property is likely to satisfy their investment objectives.

Market Value versus Investment Analysis

The concept of market value differs from investment analysis in four important ways: (1) retrospective versus prospective; (2) impersonal versus personal; (3) unleveraged versus leveraged; and (4) net operating income (NOI) versus after-tax cash flows.

Retrospective versus Prospective. Market value appraisals look backward; they attempt to estimate the price a property will sell for by looking at the sales prices of similar properties in the recent past. Under static market conditions such a technique can be reasonable. But if, say, interest rates, population, or buyer expectations are changing rapidly, past sales prices may not accurately indicate the current value or

the future value of a subject property. In contrast, an **investment analysis** not only considers what similar properties have sold for, but also looks at the underlying determinants of value that we have discussed. An investment analysis tries to forecast such factors as economic base, population demographics and psychographics, buying power, and potential sources of competition.

Impersonal versus Personal. As defined by the professional appraisers, a market value estimate represents the price a property will sell for under certain specified conditions—in other words, a sort of market average. But in fact each buyer and seller has a unique set of needs, and each real estate transaction can be structured to meet those needs. So an investment analysis looks beyond what may constitute a "typical" transaction and attempts to evaluate a subject property's terms and conditions of sale (or rent) as they correspond to a given investor's constraints and goals.

For example, a market value appraisal might show that with normal financing and conditions of sale, a property is worth $180,000. Yet because of personal tax consequences, it might be better for a seller to ask a higher price for the property and offer owner financing at a below-market interest rate.

Unleveraged versus Leveraged. As intimated earlier, the returns a real estate investment offers will be influenced by the amount of the purchase price that is financed. But simple income capitalization $[V = (NOI/R)]$ does not incorporate alternative financing plans that might be available. It assumes either a cash or an unleveraged purchase.

The use of financing, or **leverage,** gives differing risk-return parameters to a real estate investment. Leverage automatically increases investment risk because borrowed funds must be repaid. Failure to repay a mortgage loan results in foreclosure and possible property loss. Alternatively, leverage may also increase return. If a property can earn a return in excess of the cost of the borrowed funds, the investor's return will be increased to a level well above what could have been earned from an all-cash deal. This is known as **positive leverage.** Conversely, if return is below debt cost, the return on invested equity will be less than from an all-cash deal. This is called **negative leverage.** The following example shows how leverage affects return and provides insight into the possible associated risks.

Assume an investor purchases a parcel of land for $20,000. The investor has two financing choices. Choice A is all cash; that is, no leverage is employed. Choice B involves 80 percent financing (20 percent down payment) at 12 percent interest. With leverage (choice B), the investor signs a $16,000 note (.80 × $20,000) at 12 percent interest with the entire principal balance due and payable at the end of one year. Now suppose the land appreciates during the year to $30,000. (A comparative analysis of this occurrence is presented in Table 14.3.) Had the investor chosen the all-cash deal, the one-year return on the investor's initial equity is 50 percent. The use of leverage would have magnified that return, no matter how much the property appreciated. The leveraged alternative (choice B) involved only a $4,000 investment in personal initial equity, with the balance financed by borrowing at 12 percent interest. The property sells for $30,000, of which $4,000 represents the recovery of

TABLE 14.3 The Effect of Positive Leverage on Return: An Example*

Purchase price: $20,000
Sale price: $30,000
Holding period: one year

Item Number	Item	Choice A No Leverage	Choice B 80% Financing
1	Initial equity	$20,000	$ 4,000
2	Loan principal	0	16,000
3	Sale price	30,000	30,000
4	Capital gain [(3) − (1) − (2)]	10,000	10,000
5	Interest cost [.12 × (2)]	0	1,920
6	Net return [(4) − (5)]	10,000	8,080
	Return on investor's equity [(6) ÷ (1)]	$\frac{\$10,000}{\$20,000} = +50\%$	$\frac{\$ 8,080}{\$ 4,000} = +202\%$

*To simplify this example, all values are presented on a *before-tax* basis. To get the true return, taxes on the capital gain and the interest expense would be considered.

the initial equity investment, $16,000 goes to repay the principal balance on the debt, and another $1,920 of gain is used to pay interest ($16,000 × .12). The balance of the proceeds, $8,080, represents the investor's return. The return on the investor's initial equity is 202 percent—over four times that provided by the no-leveraged alternative, choice A.

We used 12 percent in the above example, but it is important to understand that the cost of money has surprisingly little effect on comparative (leveraged versus unleveraged) returns; for example, using 6 percent interest, the return on investor's equity rises to 226 percent, still way above the unleveraged alternative. Granted, using a lower interest cost does improve return, but, other things being equal, the thing that's really driving return on equity is the *amount* of leverage being used.

There is another side to the coin, however. For no matter what the eventual outcome, risk is *always* inherent in leverage; it can easily turn a bad deal into a disaster. Suppose the $20,000 property discussed above dropped in value by 25 percent during the one-year holding period. The comparative results are presented in Table 14.4. The unleveraged investment has resulted in a negative return of 25 percent. This is not large, however, compared to the leveraged position in which the investor loses not only the entire initial investment of $4,000, but an additional $2,920 ($1,000 additional principal on the debt + $1,920 interest). The total loss of $6,920 on the original $4,000 of equity results in a (negative) return of 173 percent. Thus the loss in the leverage case is nearly seven times the loss experienced in the unleveraged situation.

NOI versus After-Tax Cash Flows. Recall that to estimate market value, the income approach capitalizes net operating income (NOI). To most investors,

TABLE 14.4   The Effect of Negative Leverage on Return: An Example*

Purchase price: $20,000
Sale price: $15,000
Holding period: one year

Item Number	Item	Choice A No Leverage	Choice B 80% Financing
1	Initial equity	$20,000	$ 4,000
2	Loan principal	0	16,000
3	Sale price	15,000	15,000
4	Capital loss [(3) − (1) − (2)]	5,000	5,000
5	Interest cost [.12 × (2)]	0	1,920
6	Net loss [(4) − (5)]	5,000	6,920
	Return on investor's equity [(6) ÷ (1)]	$\dfrac{\$5{,}000}{\$20{,}000} = -25\%$	$\dfrac{\$6{,}920}{\$4{,}000} = -173\%$

*To simplify this example, all values are presented on a *before-tax* basis. To get the true return, taxes on the capital loss and the interest expense would be considered.

discounted cash flows
a measure of investment return, commonly used in real estate investment analysis, calculated by subtracting the original required investment from the present value of cash flows to find net present value (NPV).

though, the NOI figure holds little meaning. The reason is that, as discussed above, the majority of real estate investors finance their purchases. In addition, few investors today can ignore the effect of federal income tax law on their investment decisions. Investors want to know how much cash they will be required to put into a transaction, and how much cash they are likely to get out. The concept of NOI does not address these questions. Thus in real estate the familiar finance measure of investment return—discounted cash flow—is a prime criterion for selecting real estate investments. (Sometimes approximate yield is used instead to assess the suitability of a prospective real estate investment.)

Calculating Discounted Cash Flows

Calculating **discounted cash flows** involves the techniques of present value as discussed in Chapter 5; in addition, you need to learn how to calculate annual after-tax cash flows and the after-tax net proceeds of sale. With this knowledge you can discount the cash flows an investment is expected to earn over a specified holding period. This figure in turn gives you the present value of the cash flows. Next, you find the **net present value (NPV)**—the difference between the present value of the cash flows and the amount of equity required to make the investment. The resulting difference tells you whether the proposed investment looks good (a positive net present value) or bad (a negative net present value).

net present value (NPV)
the difference between the present value of the cash flows and the amount of equity required to make an investment.

This process of discounting cash flows to calculate the net present value (NPV) of an investment can be represented by the following equation:

$$NPV = \left[\frac{CF_1}{(1+r)^1} + \frac{CF_2}{(1+r)^2} + \cdots + \frac{CF_{n-1}}{(1+r)^{n-1}} + \frac{CF_n + CF_{R_n}}{(1+r)^n} \right] - I_0$$

where

I_0 = the original required investment

CF_i = annual after-tax cash flow for year i

CF_{R_n} = the after-tax net proceeds from sale (reversionary after-tax cash flow) occurring in year n

r = the discount rate and $[1/(1 + r)^i]$ is the present-value interest factor for $1 received in year i using an r percent discount rate.

In this equation the annual after-tax cash flows, *CF*s, may be either inflows to investors or outflows from them. Inflows would be preceded by a plus ($+$) sign, and outflows by a minus ($-$) sign.

 ### *Calculating Approximate Yield*

approximate yield procedure for assessing investment suitability by estimating the fully compounded rate of return (yield) on an investment.

An alternate way of assessing investment suitability would be to calculate the **approximate yield,** which was first presented in Chapter 5. Restating the formula in terms of the variables defined above we have:

$$\text{approximate yield} = \frac{\overline{CF} + \dfrac{CF_{R_n} - I_0}{n}}{\dfrac{CF_{R_n} + I_0}{2}}$$

where

$$\overline{CF} = \begin{array}{l}\text{average annual} \\ \text{after-tax cash} \\ \text{flow}\end{array} = \frac{CF_1 + CF_2 + \cdots + CF_{n-1} + CF_n}{n}$$

If the calculated approximate yield is greater than the discount rate appropriate for the given investment, the investment would be acceptable. In such an event, the net present value would be positive.

When consistently applied, the net present value and approximate yield approaches will always give the same recommendation for accepting or rejecting a proposed real estate investment. Now, to show how all of the elements discussed in this chapter can be applied to a real estate investment decision, let's look at an example.

THE ACADEMIC ARMS APARTMENTS

We will assume that Jack Wilson is deciding whether or not to buy the Academic Arms Apartments. Jack believes he can improve his real estate investment decision making if he follows a systematic procedure. He designs a schematic framework of analysis that corresponds closely to the topics we've discussed. Following this framework (Figure 14.2), Jack (1) sets out his investment objectives; (2) defines the scope of analysis; (3) investigates the determinants of the property's value; (4) calculates investment returns; and (5) synthesizes and interprets the results of his analysis.

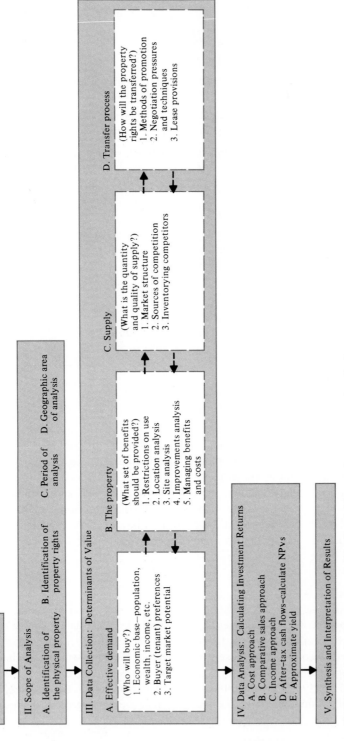

FIGURE 14.2 Framework for Real Estate Investment Analysis.

This framework depicts a logical approach for analyzing potential investment properties in order to assess whether or not they are acceptable investments that might be included in one's investment portfolio. (*Source:* Adapted from Gary W. Elred, *Real Estate: Analysis and Strategy*, New York: Harper & Row, 1987.)

Investor Objectives

Jack is a tenured associate professor of management at Finley College. He's single, age 40, and earns from salary, consulting fees, stock dividends, and book royalties an income of $65,000 per year. Jack wants to further diversify his investment portfolio. He would like to add a real estate investment that has good appreciation potential and also provides a positive yearly after-tax cash flow. For convenience Jack requires the property to be close to his office, and he feels his talents and personality suit him for ownership of apartments. Jack has $60,000 cash to invest. On this amount he would like to earn a 13 percent rate of return; toward this end, he has his eye on a small apartment complex, the Academic Arms Apartments.

Scope of Analysis

The Academic Arms building is located six blocks from the Finley College student union. The building contains eight 2-bedroom, 2-bath units of 1,100 square feet each. It was built in 1973, and all systems and building components appear to be in good condition. The present owner gave Jack an income statement reflecting the property's 1989 income and expenses. The owner has further assured Jack that no adverse easements or encumbrances affect the building's title. Of course, if Jack decides to buy Academic Arms, he would have a lawyer verify the quality of the property rights associated with the property. For now, though, he accepts the owner's word.

In this instance Jack considers a five-year holding period reasonable. At present he's happy at Finley and thinks he will stay there at least until age 45. Jack defines the market for the property as a one-mile radius from campus. He reasons that students who walk to campus (the target market) would limit their choice of apartments to those that fall within that geographic area.

Determinants of Value

Once Jack has outlined his scope of analysis, he next thinks about the factors that will determine the property's investment potential. As noted, these factors include: (1) demand; (2) the property; (3) supply; and (4) the transfer process.

Demand

The major institution, indeed the lifeblood institution in the market area, is Finley College. The base of demand for the Academic Arms Apartments will grow (or decline) with the size of the college's employment and student enrollment. On this basis, Jack judges the prospects for the area to be in the range of good to excellent. During the coming five years, major funding (due to a $25 million gift) will increase Finley's faculty by 35 percent, and expected along with faculty growth is a rise in the student population from 3,200 full-time students to 4,600 full-time students. Through further investigation Jack learns that 70 percent of the *new* students will live away from home. In the past Finley largely served the local market, but with its new affluence—and the resources this affluence can buy—the college will draw students from a wider geographic area. Furthermore, because Finley is a private

college with relatively high tuition, the majority of students come from upper-middle-income families. Parental support can thus be expected to heighten students' ability to pay. Overall, then, Jack believes the major indicators of demand for the market area look promising.

The Property

Now the question becomes, Will the Academic Arms Apartments appeal to the desired market segment? On this issue Jack concludes the answer is yes. The property already is zoned multifamily, and its present (and intended) use complies with all pertinent ordinances and housing codes. Of major importance, though, is the property's location. Not only does the site have good accessibility to the campus, but it is also three blocks from the Campus Town shopping district. In addition, the esthetic, socioeconomic, legal, and fiscal environments of the property are compatible with student preferences.

On the negative side, the on-site parking has space for only six cars. Still, the building itself is attractive, and the relatively large 2-bedroom, 2-bath units are ideal for roommates. And although Jack has no experience managing apartments, he feels that if he studies several books on property management and applies his formal business education, he can succeed.

Supply

Jack realizes that even strong demand and a good property cannot yield profits if a market suffers from oversupply. Too much competition has pushed many property owners and real estate developers into bankruptcy. Fortunately Jack thinks that Academic Arms is well insulated from competing units. Most important is the fact that the designated market area is fully built up, and as much as 80 percent of the area is zoned single-family residential. Any efforts to change the zoning would be strongly opposed by neighborhood residents. The only potential problem that Jack sees is that the college might build more student housing on campus. There has been some administrative talk about it, but as yet no funds have been allocated to such a project. In sum, Jack concludes that the risk of oversupply in the Academic Arms market area is low.

The Transfer Process

Real estate markets are inefficient. Thus before a property's sales price or rental income can reach its potential, an effective means to get information to buyers or tenants must be developed. Here, of course, Jack has great advantage. Notices on campus bulletin boards and announcements to his classes should be all he needs to keep the property rented. Although he might experience some vacancy during the summer months, Jack feels he could overcome this problem by requiring students to sign 12-month leases, but then grant them the right to sublet as long as the sublessees meet the tenant-selection criteria.

Calculating Investment Returns

Real estate cash flows depend on the underlying characteristics of the property and the market. That is why we have devoted so much attention to analyzing the deter-

TABLE 14.5   Income Statement, Academic Arms Apartments, 1989

Gross rental income		
(8 × $335 × 12)		$32,160
Operating expenses:		
Utilities	$2,830	
Trash collection	675	
Repairs and maintenance	500	
Promotion and advertising	150	
Property insurance	840	
Property taxes	3,200	
Less: Total operating expenses		8,195
Net operating income (NOI)		$23,965

minants of value. Often real estate investors lose money because they "run the numbers" without doing their homework. So as we go through our investment calculations, remember that the numbers coming out will be no better than the numbers going in.

The Numbers

At present Mrs. Bowker, the owner of Academic Arms Apartments, is asking $260,000 for the property. To assist in the sale, she is willing to offer owner financing to a qualified buyer. The terms would be 20 percent down, 11.5 percent interest, and full amortization of the outstanding mortgage balance over 30 years. The owner's income statement for 1989 is shown in Table 14.5. After talking with Mrs. Bowker, Jack believes she would probably accept an offer of $60,000 down, a price of $245,000, and a 30-year mortgage at 11 percent. On this basis Jack prepares his investment calculations.

Cash Flow Analysis

As a first step in cash flow analysis, Jack reconstructs the owner's income statement (as shown in Table 14.6). This reconstruction reflects higher rent levels, higher expenses, and a lower net operating income. Jack believes that due to poor owner management and deferred maintenance, the present owner is not getting as much in rents as the market could support. In addition, however, her expenses understate those he is likely to incur. For one thing, a management expense should be deducted. Jack wants to separate what is rightfully a return on labor from his return on capital. Also, once the property is sold, a higher property tax assessment will be levied against it. Except for promotion and advertising, other expenses have been increased to adjust for inflation and a more extensive maintenance program. With these adjustments, the expected NOI for Academic Arms during 1990 is estimated at $22,822.

after-cash tax flows (ATCFs) *the annual cash flow earned on a real estate investment, net of all expenses, taxes, and debt service.*

To move from NOI to **after-tax cash flows (ATCFs),** we need to perform the calculations shown in Table 14.7. From this table you can see that to calculate

TABLE 14.6 Reconstructed Income Statement, Academic Arms Apartments, 1990

Gross potential rental income	$37,800	
Less: Vacancy and collection losses at 4%	1,512	
Effective gross income (EGI)		$36,288
Operating expenses:		
Management at 5% of EGI	$ 1,814	
Utilities	3,100	
Trash collection	750	
Repairs and maintenance	2,400	
Promotion and advertising	150	
Property insurance	960	
Property taxes	4,292	
Less: Total operating expenses		13,466
Net operating income (NOI)		$22,822

ATCF, you must first compute the income taxes or income tax savings Jack would incur as a result of property ownership. In this case potential tax savings accrue during the first three years because the allowable tax deductions of interest and depreciation exceed the property's net operating income; in the final two years, income exceeds deductions and as such, taxes are due. The "magic" of simultaneously losing and making money is caused by **depreciation.** Tax statutes incorporate this tax deduction to reflect the declining economic life of a building. However, since this deduction does not actually require a current cash outflow by the property owner, it acts as a *noncash expenditure* which reduces taxes and increases cash flow. In other words, in the 1990–1992 period the property ownership provides Jack with a **tax shelter;** that is, Jack uses the income tax losses sustained on the property to offset the taxable income he receives from salary, consulting fees, stock dividends, and book royalties.

depreciation
in real estate investing, a tax deduction based upon the original cost of a building and used to reflect its declining economic life.

tax shelter
a form of investment that offers potential reductions of taxable income.

    Once the amount of taxes (or tax savings) is known, this amount is subtracted (or added) to the before-tax cash flow. Because Jack qualifies as an "active manager" of the property (an important provision of the Tax Reform Act of 1986 discussed more fully in Chapter 15), and since his income is low enough (also discussed in Chapter 15), he can use the real estate losses to reduce his other income. It is important to recognize that under the Tax Reform Act of 1986 the amount of tax losses that can be applied to other taxable income is limited. It is therefore important to consult a tax expert about the tax consequences of expected income tax losses when calculating ATCFs from real estate investments.

Proceeds from Sale

In this next step in his evaluation of the Academic Arms Apartments, Jack must estimate the net proceeds he will receive when he sells the property. For purposes of this analysis Jack has assumed a five-year holding period. Now he must forecast a

TABLE 14.7 Cash Flow Analysis, Academic Arms Apartments, 1990–1994

	1990	1991	1992	1993	1994
INCOME TAX COMPUTATIONS					
NOI	$22,822	$24,419	$26,128	$27,957	$29,914
− Interest*	20,350	20,259	20,146	20,022	19,877
− Depreciation**	6,545	6,545	6,545	6,545	6,545
Taxable income (loss)	($ 4,073)	($ 2,385)	($ 563)	$ 1,390	$ 3,492
Marginal tax rate	.28	.28	.28	.28	.28
Taxes (−) or tax savings (+)	+$ 1,140	+$ 668	+$ 158	−$ 389	−$ 978
AFTER-TAX CASH FLOW (ATCF) COMPUTATIONS					
NOI	$22,822	$24,419	$26,128	$27,957	$29,914
− Mortgage payment	21,280	21,280	21,280	21,280	21,280
Before-tax cash flow	$ 1,542	$ 3,139	$ 4,848	$ 6,677	$ 8,634
+ Tax savings or − taxes	+ 1,140	+ 668	+ 158	− 389	− 978
After-tax cash flow (ATCF)	$ 2,682	$ 3,807	$ 5,006	$ 6,288	$ 7,656

$$\text{Average annual after-tax cash flow } (\overline{CF}) = \frac{\$2,682 + \$3,807 + \$5,006 + \$6,288 + \$7,656}{5} = \$5,088$$

*Based on a $185,000 mortgage at 11 percent compounded annually. Some rounding has been used.

**Based on straight-line depreciation over 27.5 years and a depreciable basis of $180,000. Land value is assumed to equal $65,000.

selling price for the property; from that amount he must subtract selling expenses, the outstanding balance on the mortgage, and applicable federal income taxes. The remainder equals Jack's after-tax net proceeds from sale. These calculations are shown in Table 14.8.

Jack wants to estimate his net proceeds from sale conservatively. He believes that at a minimum, market forces will push up the selling price of the property at the rate of 5 percent per year beyond his assumed purchase price of $245,000. Thus he estimates the selling price in 5 years will be $312,620; he does this by multiplying the $245,000 by the future-value interest factor of 1.276 from Appendix B, Table B.1, for 5 percent and 5 years (that is, $245,000 × 1.276 = $312,620). Making the indicated deductions from the forecasted selling price, Jack computes an after-tax net proceeds from the sale equal to $89,514.

Discounted Cash Flow

In this step Jack discounts the projected cash flows to their present value. In making this calculation (see Table 14.9) Jack finds that at his required rate of return of 13 percent the net present value of these flows equals $5,442. Looked at another way, the present value of the amounts Jack forecasts he will receive exceeds the amount

TABLE 14.8 Estimated After-Tax Net Proceeds from Sale, Academic Arms Apartments, 1994

INCOME TAX COMPUTATIONS	
Forecasted selling price (at 5% annual appreciation)	$312,620
− Selling expenses at 7%	21,883
− Book value (purchase price less accumulated depreciation)	212,275
Gain on sale	$ 78,462
× Tax rate on gain*	28%
Taxes payable	$ 21,969

COMPUTATION OF AFTER-TAX NET PROCEEDS	
Forecasted selling price	$312,620
− Selling expenses	21,883
− Mortgage balance outstanding	179,254
Net proceeds before taxes	$111,483
− Taxes payable (calculated above)	21,969
After-tax net proceeds from sale ($CF_{R_{1994}}$)	$ 89,514

*Under the Tax Reform Act of 1986 this gain is taxed at the same 28 percent rate used to tax ordinary income.

of his initial investment by nearly $5,500. The investment therefore meets (and exceeds) his acceptance criterion.

Approximate Yield

Alternatively, the approximate yield formula could be applied using the initial equity, I_0, of $60,000, along with the average annual after-tax cash flow, $\overline{CF}$, of $5,088 (calculated at the bottom of Table 14.7), and the after-tax net proceeds from sale, $CF_{R_{1994}}$, of $89,514 (calculated in Table 14.8). Substituting these values into the approximate yield formula presented earlier gives:

$$\text{approximate yield} = \frac{\overline{CF} + \dfrac{CF_{R_n} - I_0}{n}}{\dfrac{CF_{R_n} + I_0}{2}}$$

$$= \frac{\$5,088 + \dfrac{\$89,514 - \$60,000}{5}}{\dfrac{\$89,514 + \$60,000}{2}} = \frac{\$5,088 + \$5,903}{\$74,757}$$

$$= \frac{\$10,991}{\$74,757} = 14.7\%$$

TABLE 14.9   Net Present Value, Academic Arms Apartments*

$$\text{NPV} = \left[\frac{CF_1}{(1 + r)^1} + \frac{CF_2}{(1 + r)^2} + \frac{CF_3}{(1 + r)^3} + \frac{CF_4}{(1 + r)^4} + \frac{CF_5 + CF_{R_5}}{(1 + r)^5} \right] - I_0$$

$$\text{NPV} = \left[\frac{\$2,682}{(1 + .13)^1} + \frac{\$3,807}{(1 + .13)^2} + \frac{\$5,006}{(1 + .13)^3} + \frac{\$6,288}{(1 + .13)^4} + \frac{\$97,170**}{(1 + .13)^5} \right] - \$60,000$$

$$\text{NPV}*** = \$2,374 + \$2,981 + \$3,469 + \$3,855 + \$52,763 - \$60,000$$

$$\text{NPV} = \$65,442 - \$60,000$$

$$\text{NPV} = +\ \underline{\underline{\$5,442}}$$

*All inflows are assumed to be end-of-period receipts.
**Includes both the fifth year annual after-tax cash flow of $7,656 and the after-tax net proceeds from sale of $89,514.
***Calculated using present-value interest factors from Appendix B, Table B.3.

Since the approximate yield of 14.7 percent is in excess of Jack's required rate of return of 13 percent, the investment meets (and exceeds) his acceptance criterion. Although we have merely approximated his return here, this technique, when consistently applied, should always result in the same conclusion as to acceptability as that obtained using net present value.

Synthesis and Interpretation

Now comes the time for Jack to review his work. He evaluates his market analysis, checks all the facts and figures in the investment return calculations, and then evaluates the results in light of his stated financial and nonfinancial objectives. He must ask himself: All things considered, is the expected payoff worth the risk? In this case, he decides it is. The property looks good. Even a positive finding, however, does not necessarily mean Jack should buy this property. He might still want to shop around to see if he can locate an even better investment. Furthermore, he might be wise to hire a real estate appraiser to confirm that the price he is willing to pay seems reasonable with respect to the recent sales prices of similar properties in the market area. Nevertheless, being an academic, Jack realizes that any problem can be studied to death; no one ever can obtain all the information that will bear on a decision. He gives himself a week to investigate other properties and talk to a professional appraiser. If nothing turns up to cause him second thoughts, he decides that he will offer to buy the Academic Arms Apartments. On the terms presented, he is willing to pay up to a maximum price of $245,000.

PASSIVE FORMS OF REAL ESTATE INVESTMENT

The most popular ways to invest in real estate are through individual ownership, real estate investment trusts (REITs), and real estate limited partnerships (RELPs).

Private Real Estate Partnerships for the Small Investor

What's the best way for a small investor to play Donald Trump? The answer isn't, as you might think, to put money in a real estate investment trust (REIT) or a public limited partnership, both of which pool investors' money and buy portfolios of property across the country. The best real estate investment, says Michael Sumichrast, a housing economist and publisher of the newsletter *Real Estate Perspectives,* can be found ''in your own neighborhood—a house or small commercial building, perhaps something that needs work. You're familiar with the area, you participate in the deal, you manage the property. The potential profits are really great.''

Trouble is, most people can't afford the down payment for such an investment, typically $125,000 on a property costing $500,000. But Sumichrast and other real estate experts suggest that you might consider forming a private partnership with friends or relatives. Not only will this put your share of the down payment within reach, but you'll also spread the risk among several investors and still possibly be able to write off as much as $25,000 in real estate tax losses.

Take, for example, some Denver investors. Seven and a half years ago, they chipped in $5,000 to $20,000 each for the $65,000 down payment on a $465,000 two-story commercial building on Santa Fe Drive, which was then one of the city's shabbiest neighborhoods. But the area was close to downtown and to the site of a planned convention center, and Mark Levine, the administrative partner, figured it would bounce back. He was right. Today Santa Fe Drive is being revitalized, and the convention center will open in 1990. The partnership's building houses one retail shop, six offices and a tavern.

Levine's syndicate consists of wife Ellen, a real estate consultant; Robert Pitler, his law partner; Harvey Sundel, owner of a market research firm; Andrew Selig, psychologist; and Levine's brother Kent, a real estate professor.

Mark Levine, 45, was the natural ringleader. He's a real estate specialist who wears dozens of hats, including those of attorney, accountant, author of books on real estate and professor of real estate at the University of Denver. He has also been successfully investing in property for some 20 years, which illustrates rule No. 1 of forming your own partnership: make sure you include someone who is knowledgeable about real estate—for example, a broker or an attorney.

Rule No. 2: all the partners' investment goals—and willingness to take risks—should match. What matters most, cash flow or tax benefits? Does the group want to flip the

(Due to adverse tax consequences, real estate investors typically have avoided the corporate form of ownership, although recent tax revisions may result in an increase in corporate real estate investment groups.) Individual ownership of investment real estate is most common among wealthy individuals, professional real estate investors, and financial institutions. The strongest advantage of individual ownership is

property for a fast profit or is it looking long term? In most cases, observes Levine, "real estate is cyclical—you don't come in for the quick hit."

Rule No. 3: even with ideal partners, have a lawyer draw up a formal partnership agreement. "You'll save a lot of time, money and grief later on by spending a few hundred or a few thousand on a good agreement," says Martin M. Shenkman, author of *The Total Real Estate Tax Planner* (John Wiley & Sons, $12.95). But before the lawyer's clock starts running, discuss the issues the agreement should cover. For example, will the partnership be a general one, like Levine's, in which all partners have authority and financial liability? Or will it be limited, with the general partner having most authority and every investor's liability usually no bigger than the money he or she invests? How much money will each partner put up initially and later on to carry the property if it doesn't generate enough income? What if someone wants to sell the property but the other partners don't? Levine suggests the agreement specify that the group can buy out that partner's interest.

Stay within a day's round-trip drive of home when looking for a real estate investment, and choose something you know. If the most experienced partner's expertise is limited to rental apartments, for example, don't buy a strip shopping center. Says Tom Ochsenschlager, a tax partner in the accounting firm Grant Thornton in Washington, D.C.: "There's nothing like personal experience to put you on a par with the experts." He also urges that your chief objective be profit—not tax breaks. "After tax reform," he says, "the government is no longer subsidizing real estate. Look for a property with true economics to it."

Once you find something that seems promising, Levine recommends that you make sure it meets this standard: "When you project the total annual rate of return—including appreciation, cash flow, equity buildup from paying off the loan—the return has to be at least 10% to 20%, plus tax benefits." With the Santa Fe partnership, he optimistically envisions a 40% return, even though the building is currently losing about $1,000 a month and each partner has had to kick in $100 to $200 a month to cover the shortfall. But Levine expects steady increases in the rent rolls to put the building well into the black within two years, and he feels confident that the building can be sold at a hefty profit within five years.

Why didn't Levine buy the property himself? His answer: "I wanted to diversify by owning more than one property. I wanted to cut my risk, and I wanted to get a higher-priced property." With his little syndicate, he satisfied all his goals.

Source: Robin Micheli, "To Make Big Profits, Invest with Friends in Your Own Backyard," *Money,* March 1989, pp. 177–78.

personal control, and the strongest drawback is that it requires a relatively large amount of capital. Although thus far we have emphasized active real estate investment analysis for the individual, it is likely that most readers will participate passively by investing in shares of either a real estate investment trust or a limited partnership. As noted in the accompanying Investor Insights box, small investors

may find the private partnership an ideal vehicle for obtaining needed funding, spreading risk, and receiving tax benefits from a real estate investment. Here we will examine each of these investment alternatives.

Real Estate Investment Trusts (REITs)

real estate investment trust (REIT) *a type of closed-end investment company that invests money, obtained through the sale of shares to investors, in various types of real estate and/or real estate mortgages.*

A **real estate investment trust (REIT)** is a type of closed-end investment company (see Chapter 13) that invests money, obtained through the sale of its shares to investors, in various types of real estate and/or real estate mortgages. REITs were established with the passage in 1960 of the Real Estate Investment Trust Act of 1960, which set forth requirements for forming a REIT as well as rules and procedures for making investments and distributing income. The appeal of REITs lies in their ability to allow the small investor to receive both the capital appreciation and income returns of real estate ownership without the headaches of property management. REITs were quite popular until the mid-1970s, when the bottom fell out of the real estate market as a result of many bad loans and an excess supply of property. In the early 1980s, however, both the real estate market and REITs began to make a comeback. Indeed, by 1989 there were nearly 170 such investment companies. Revived interest in REITs has been attributed not only to lower mortgage interest rates and increased real estate demand, but also to the greatly diminished appeal of real estate limited partnerships (described later) resulting from the efforts of the IRS to reduce their tax advantages. (The efforts of the IRS in fact culminated in passage of the Tax Reform Act of 1986.) As a result, REITs are popular forms of passive real estate investment that have been known to earn annual rates of return in the range of 10 to 20 percent, and for some trusts 30 percent or more.

Basic Structure

REITs sell shares of stock to the investing public and use the proceeds, along with borrowed funds, to invest in a portfolio of real estate investments. The investor, therefore, owns part of the real estate portfolio held by the real estate investment trust. Typically REITs yield a return at least 1 to 2 percentage points above money market funds and about the same return as high-grade corporate bonds. REITs are required by law to pay out 95 percent of their income as dividends, which leaves little to invest in new acquisitions. Furthermore, they must keep at least 75 percent of their assets in real estate investments and hold each investment for at least four years.

Like any investment fund, each REIT has certain stated investment objectives, which should be carefully considered before acquiring shares. Actually, there are three basic types of REITs:

- **Equity REITs:** These invest in properties such as shopping centers, hotels, apartments, and office buildings.
- **Mortgage REITs:** These make both construction and mortgage loans to real estate investors.
- **Hybrid REITs:** These invest in both properties (like equity REITs) and construction and real estate mortgage loans (like mortgage REITs).

The shares of REITs are traded on organized exchanges such as the NYSE and AMEX as well as in the over-the-counter (OTC) market. Some of the better-known REITs include Federal Realty, Pennsylvania REIT, First Union Realty, Washington Real Estate Investment Trust, ICM Property, and Mortgage Investments Plus.

Investing in REITs

REITs provide an attractive mechanism whereby an investor can make real estate property, mortgage, or both property and mortgage investments. They also provide professional management, thereby allowing the investor to assume a passive role. In addition, because their shares can be traded in the securities markets, investors can—unlike in most limited partnerships—conveniently purchase and sell shares with the assistance of a retail or discount broker. Investors in REITs can reap tax benefits by placing their shares in an individual retirement account (IRA), Keogh plan, or some other tax-deferring vehicle.

The most direct way to investigate before you buy is to get the names of REITs that interest you and then call or write the headquarters of each REIT for information on the properties and/or mortgages it holds, its management, its future plans, and its track record. Additional information on REIT investments can be obtained from the National Association of Real Estate Investment Trusts, 1129 20th Street NW, Suite 705, Washington, DC 20036 (202-785-8717).

real estate limited partnership (RELP) *a professionally managed real estate syndicate that invests in various types of real estate; the managers assume the role of general partner, whose liability is unlimited, and other (passive) investors are limited partners, whose liability is limited to the amount of their initial investment.*

The evaluation process will of course depend upon the type of REIT being considered. Equity REITs tend to be most popular since they share directly in real estate growth. If a property's rent goes up so will the dividend distribution, and share prices may also rise to reflect property appreciation. These REITs can be analyzed by applying the same basic procedures described in Chapters 7 and 8 for common stock valuation. Since mortgage REITs earn most of their income as interest on real estate loans, they tend to trade like bonds; therefore many of the techniques for analyzing bond investments presented in Chapter 9 can be used to evaluate them. Hybrid REITs have the characteristics of both property and mortgages and should therefore be evaluated accordingly. Regardless of type, you should review the REIT's investment objective and performance in a fashion similar to that used in mutual fund investing (see Chapter 13). Carefully check the types of properties and/or mortgages held by the REIT. Be sure to look at the REIT's dividend yield and capital gain potential. And above all, as with any investment, the REIT selected should be consistent with your investment risk and return objectives.

Real Estate Limited Partnerships (RELPs)

A **real estate limited partnership (RELP)** is a professionally managed real estate syndicate that invests in various types of real estate. Some RELPs are set up to speculate in raw land, others invest in income-producing properties like apartments, shopping centers, and office buildings, and still others invest in various types of mortgages (the so-called *debt partnerships* as opposed to the *equity partnerships* that own land and buildings). Managers of RELPs assume the role of general partner, which means their liability is unlimited, while other investors are limited partners, meaning they are legally liable for only the amount of their initial investment.

Most limited partnerships require a minimum investment of between $2,500 and $10,000. Because of the limited liability, along with the potentially high returns provided by these arrangements, they often appeal to the individual investor wishing to buy real estate. (A detailed discussion of the structure and operation of limited partnerships is presented in Chapter 15). Investment in a limited partnership can be made directly through ads in the financial news, through stockbrokers or financial planners, or with the assistance of a commercial real estate broker.

Types of Syndicates

single property syndicate
a type of real estate limited partnership established to raise money to purchase a specific piece (or pieces) of property.

blind pool syndicate
a type of real estate limited partnership formed by a syndicator to raise money to be invested at the syndicator's discretion.

There are two basic types of real estate limited partnerships: single property and blind pool syndicates. The **single property syndicate** is established to raise money to purchase a specific piece (or pieces) of property. For example, 50 units of a partnership can be sold at $7,500 each to buy a piece of property for $1 million. (A "unit" in a limited partnership is like a share of stock in a company and represents an ownership position in the partnership.) In this case a total of $375,000 (50 units × $7,500) would come from the partners, and the remaining $625,000 would be borrowed. The **blind pool syndicate,** on the other hand, is formed by a syndicator—often well-known—in order to raise a given amount of money to be invested at his or her discretion, though the general partner often has some or all of the properties already picked out. The blind pool syndicator takes a specified percentage of all income generated as a management fee. Large real estate brokerage firms commonly arrange these types of syndicates.

Investing in RELPs

Prior to the Tax Reform Act of 1986 much of the appeal of real estate limited partnerships came from the tax-sheltered income that these investments provided. However, that is no longer the case. Instead, like other forms of real estate, these limited partnerships are considered to be *passive* investments; and as such, the amount of write-offs that can be taken on them is limited to the amount of income they generate. This means that such write-offs cannot be used to shelter ordinary income from taxes. Although limited partnerships have lost some of their appeal, they remain a popular way to invest in real estate, especially for those with limited investment capital. The big difference is that rather than emphasizing the tax-sheltered nature of their income, many of the real estate limited partnerships of today are less leveraged (some use *no* debt at all) and are structured to provide attractive current incomes (from rents, and so on) and/or capital gains. In essence, they are now being promoted for their underlying investment merits and not on the basis of some artificial tax motive. Certainly for an individual with as little as $1,000 to $5,000 to invest, a carefully selected limited partnership may be a sensible way to invest in real estate.

The annual return on RELPs *in the past* typically ranged between 5 and 15 percent of the amount invested. (There is, of course, *no* insurance that such returns will continue to be generated in the future.) The emphasis with respect to the type of return generated differs from one syndicate to another. Most real estate limited partnerships today place major emphasis on producing attractive levels of current

income for their investors; some, however, still emphasize capital gains. Of course, the goals of the syndicate, the quality of its management, and the specific properties involved should be carefully evaluated *before* purchasing in order to estimate the expected risk and return. Information useful in analyzing RELPs can be obtained from the syndicator in the form of a *prospectus*. One of the key drawbacks of RELPs is that it's always been difficult to get out of them since there is no organized market for limited partnership units. Although a few years ago it appeared that **master limited partnerships**—partnerships that are publicly traded on major stock exchanges—would improve partnership liquidity, recent tax law changes have greatly reduced their attractiveness. Before purchasing a RELP, make sure that it is the best vehicle for meeting your investment objectives.

master limited partnership
a limited partnership that is publicly traded on a major stock exchange.

SUMMARY

- The starting point for real estate investment analysis is setting objectives. This includes considering investment characteristics, establishing investment constraints and goals, and defining the scope of analysis.

- Investment real estate includes personal residences; income properties such as apartments and office buildings; and speculative properties such as raw land. It can be extremely safe or highly speculative and can involve either an equity or a debt investment.

- To establish the scope of analysis, the physical property being considered and the quality of its associated legal rights and obligations should be accurately identified. In addition, the time period and relevant geographic area should be defined.

- The four determinants of value—demand, supply, the property, and the transfer process—form the basis for most real estate analyses. *Demand* refers to people's willingness and ability to buy or rent and *supply* includes all those properties from which potential buyers or tenants can choose.

- To analyze a property, applicable restrictions on its use, its location, site characteristics, improvements, and how the property can best be managed should all be evaluated. The transfer process includes getting information about a property to the market and negotiating the transfer contracts (sales contracts and leases).

- A market value appraisal or investment cash flow analysis can be used to estimate real estate value. Market value appraisals rely on the cost approach, the comparative sales approach, and the income approach. Some people use an expert to prepare or substantiate their market analyses.

- Investment returns can be assessed by forecasting cash flows and calculating either the net present value or the approximate yield. By applying these techniques to market-derived data, the investor can analyze a selected real estate investment.

- Risk, which can be altered depending on the degree of leverage employed in financing a real estate investment, must be considered when evaluating prospective real estate investments. Also, the quantitative analysis must be integrated with various subjective and market considerations in making the real estate investment decision.

- The real estate investment trust (REIT) is a passive form of real estate investment that allows the investor to buy publicly traded ownership shares in a professionally managed portfolio of real estate properties, mortgages, and/or both. REITs can be analyzed in light of the investor's risk-return objective in a fashion similar to that used for stocks, bonds, and mutual funds.

- Real estate limited partnerships (RELPs) provide a vehicle for buying shares in professionally managed real estate syndicates that invest in specified types of properties and/or mortgages. Their appeal today centers on the provision of attractive current income and/or capital gains rather than on tax-shelter advantages. A major drawback of RELPs is their general lack of liquidity.

REVIEW QUESTIONS AND PROBLEMS

1. Why should real estate investment analysis start with a definition of objectives?

2. How can adding real estate to your investment portfolio decrease your overall risk? Explain.

3. Define and differentiate between (a) personal residences, (b) income properties, and (c) speculative properties.

4. Which are most important when considering real estate investments, financial or nonfinancial considerations?

5. What is the difference between real estate and personal property? Discuss why this difference is important to real estate investors.

6. Demand is often shown on a graph as a downward-sloping curve. For purposes of real estate analysis, what does such a curve actually reflect?

7. Supply is often shown on a graph as an upward-sloping curve. For purposes of real estate analysis, what does such a curve actually reflect?

8. Are real estate markets efficient? Why or why not?

9. Comment on the following: Market value is always the price at which a property sells.

10. Why is property management important to a real estate investor?

11. Briefly describe each of the three approaches commonly used by real estate appraisers to estimate the market value of investment properties.

12. Real estate investments can be structured to meet a variety of investment goals. Explain various investment needs and the types of properties that best meet them.

13. Charles Cook, an investor, is considering two alternative financing plans for purchasing a parcel of real estate costing $50,000. Alternative X involves paying cash; alternative Y involves obtaining 80 percent financing at 10.5 percent interest. If the parcel of real estate appreciates in value by $7,500 in one year, calculate: (a) Charles's net return and (b) his

return on equity for each alternative. If the value dropped by $7,500, what effect would this have on your answers to (a) and (b)?

14. Define tax depreciation. Explain why it is said to offer tax shelter potential. What real estate investments provide this benefit? Explain.

15. Define: (a) net operating income (NOI) and (b) after-tax cash flow (ATCF) as they apply to income from rental properties.

16. In the coming year, Nicki Gressis expects a potential rental property investment costing $120,000 to have gross potential rental income of $20,000, vacancy and collection losses equalling 5 percent of gross income, and operating expenses of $10,000. The mortgage on the property is expected to require annual payments of $8,500. The interest portion of the mortgage payments as well as depreciation is given below for each of the next three years. Nicki is in the 28-percent marginal tax bracket.

Year	Interest	Depreciation
1	$8,300	$4,500
2	8,200	4,500
3	8,100	4,500

The net operating income is expected to increase by 6 percent each year beyond the first year.

a. Calculate the net operating income (NOI) for each of the next three years.
b. Calculate the after-tax cash flow (ATCF) for each of the next three years.

17. Walt Hubble is contemplating selling rental property originally costing $200,000. He believes that it has appreciated in value at an annual rate of 6 percent over its four-year holding period. He will have to pay a commission equal to 5 percent of the sale price to sell the property. Currently the property has a book value of $137,000. The mortgage balance outstanding at the time of sale currently is $155,000. Walt will have to pay a 28 percent tax on any capital gains.

a. Calculate the tax payable on the proposed sale.
b. Calculate the after-tax net proceeds associated with the proposed sale, CF_R.

18. Bezie Foster has estimated the annual after-tax cash flows (ATCFs) and after-tax net proceeds from sale (CF_R) of a proposed real estate investment as noted below for the planned four-year ownership period.

Year	ATCF	CF_R
1	$6,200	
2	8,000	
3	8,300	
4	8,500	
4		$59,000

The initial required investment in the property is $55,000. Bezie, at minimum, must earn 14 percent on the investment.

a. Calculate the net present value (NPV) of the proposed investment.
b. Calculate the approximate yield from the investment.
c. From your findings in a and b what recommendations would you give Bezie? Explain.

19. Explain why, in spite of being acceptable based on NPV or approximate yield, a real estate investment might still not be acceptable to a given investor.

20. Briefly describe the basic structure and investment considerations associated with the following passive forms of real estate investment:

   a. Real estate investment trusts (REITs).
   b. Real estate limited partnerships (RELPs).

CASE PROBLEMS

14.1 Gary Sofer's Appraisal of the Wabash Oaks Apartments

Gary Sofer wants to estimate the market value of the Wabash Oaks Apartments, an 18-unit building with nine 1-bedroom units and nine 2-bedroom units. The present owner of Wabash Oaks provided Gary with the following annual income statement. Today's date is March 1, 1990.

OWNER'S INCOME STATEMENT,
WABASH OAKS APARTMENTS, 1989

Gross income		$65,880
Less: Expenses		
Utilities	$14,260	
Property insurance	2,730	
Repairs and maintenance	1,390	
Property taxes	4,790	
Mortgage payments	18,380	
Total expenses		41,550
Net income		$24,330

Current rental rates of properties similar to Wabash Oaks typically run from $300 to $315 per month for 1-bedroom units and $340 to $360 per month for 2-bedroom units. From a study of the market, Gary determined that a reasonable market capitalization rate for Wabash Oaks would be 9.62 percent and that vacancy rates for comparable apartment buildings are running around 4 percent.

Questions

1. Using Figure 14.2 as a guide, discuss how you might go about evaluating the features of this property.
2. Gary has studied economics and knows all about demand and supply, yet he doesn't understand how to apply it. Advise Gary in a practical way how he might incorporate demand and supply into an investment analysis of the Wabash Oaks Apartments.
3. Should Gary accept the owner's income statement as the basis for an income appraisal of Wabash Oaks? Why or why not?
4. In your opinion, what is a reasonable estimate of the market value for the Wabash Oaks?
5. If Gary could buy Wabash Oaks for $10,000 less than its market value, would it be a good investment for him? Explain.

14.2 Analyzing Dr. Davis's Proposed Real Estate Investment

Dr. Marilyn Davis, a single, 34-year-old heart specialist, is considering the purchase of a small office building. She wants to add some diversity to her investment portfolio, which

now contains only corporate bonds and preferred stocks. In addition, because of her high tax bracket of 35 percent (federal, state, and local), Marilyn wants an investment that produces a good after-tax rate of return.

A real estate market and financial consultant has estimated that Marilyn could buy the office building for $200,000. In addition, this consultant analyzed the property's rental potential with respect to trends in demand and supply. He discussed the following items with Marilyn. (1) The office building was occupied by two tenants who each had three years remaining on their leases. (2) It was only four years old, was in excellent condition, and was located near a number of major thoroughfares. For her purposes, Marilyn decided the building should be analyzed on the basis of a three-year holding period. The gross rents in the most recent year were $32,000, and operating expenses were $15,000. The consultant pointed out that the leases had built-in 10 percent per year rent escalation clauses and that he expected operating expenses to increase by 8 percent per year. He further expected no vacancy or collection loss because both tenants were excellent credit risks.

Marilyn's accountant estimated that annual tax depreciation would be $5,100 in each of the next three years. To finance the purchase of the building Marilyn has considered a variety of alternatives, one of which would involve assuming the existing $120,000 mortgage. Upon the advice of a close friend, a finance professor at the local university, Marilyn decided to arrange a $150,000, 10.5 percent, 25-year mortgage from the bank at which she maintains her business account. The annual loan payment would total $17,000. Of this, the following breakdown between interest and principal would apply in each of the first three years:

Year	Interest	Principal	Total
1	$15,750	$1,250	$17,000
2	15,620	1,380	17,000
3	15,470	1,530	17,000

The loan balance at the end of the three years would be $145,840. The consultant expects the property to appreciate by about 9 percent per year to $260,000 at the end of three years. Marilyn will incur a 5 percent sales commission expense on this assumed sale price. The building's book value at the end of three years would be $184,700. The total gain on the sale would be taxed at Marilyn's 35 percent tax rate.

Questions

1. What is the expected annual after-tax cash flow (ATCF) for each of the three years (assuming Marilyn has other passive income that can be used to offset any losses from this property)?
2. At a 15 percent discount rate, will this investment produce a positive net present value?
3. What rate of return does the approximate yield formula show for this proposed investment?
4. Could Marilyn increase her returns by assuming the existing mortgage at a 9.75 percent interest rate, rather than arranging a new loan? What measure of return do you believe Marilyn should use to make this comparison?
5. Do you believe Marilyn has thought about her real estate investment objectives enough? Why or why not?

SELECTED READINGS

Flanigan, James. "How Safe Are Mortgage Securities?" *Financial World,* June 30, 1987, pp. 18–19.

Feder, Barnaby, Jr. ''Some Tough Challenges for Real Estate Investors.'' *New York Times Personal Investing '89,* November 13, 1988, pp. 18–19.

Haight, G. Timothy. ''Shopping for Real Estate Profits on the Stock Market.'' *Money Maker,* June/July 1988, pp. 32–35.

Kuntz, Mary. ''A Realty Fund Primer.'' *Forbes,* March 9, 1987, pp. 162–64.

Micheli, Robin. ''Tough New Rules for Rental Real Estate.'' *Money,* April 1987, pp. 193–98.

Myers, David W. ''Bricks and Mortar: Real Estate Investing After Tax Reform.'' *Personal Investor,* July 1987, pp. 26–35.

Ostler, Kevin. ''Building a Property Portfolio.'' *Personal Investor,* September 1988, pp. 18–25.

Paulson, Morton C. ''Low-Effort Real Estate Investing.'' *Changing Times,* August 1987, pp. 20–26.

Ring, Alfred, and Jerome Dasso. *Real Estate Principles and Practices,* 11th ed. (Englewood Cliffs, NJ: Prentice-Hall, Inc., 1989).

Shultz, Ellen. ''The Built-In Safety of Triple-Net Partnerships.'' *Fortune,* December 5, 1988, p. 24.

15

TAX SHELTERS AND LIMITED PARTNERSHIPS

After studying this chapter you should be able to:

● Understand what is meant by taxable income and the basic procedures involved in its calculation.

● Define tax avoidance and tax deferral and the characteristics of tax shelters under the Tax Reform Act of 1986.

● Explain how investors can earn tax-favored income, with particular emphasis on income excluded from taxation, strategies that defer tax liabilities, strategies that trade current income for capital gains, and tax swaps.

● Summarize the characteristics of deferred annuities, their use in retirement plans, fixed versus variable annuities, their appeal as investment vehicles, and understand the recently diminished popularity of single-premium life insurance as an alternative.

● Describe the tax status of limited partnerships under the Tax Reform Act of 1986, and how limited partnerships are organized and operate.

● Discuss popular forms of limited partnerships available to investors and their essential investment considerations—use of leverage, risk-return characteristics, and investment suitability.

It is often said that the necessities of life include food, clothing, and shelter. Shelter is important because it protects us from the elements—rain, wind, snow, extreme heat, or cold—in the physical environment. In a similar fashion investors need shelter from the taxes charged on income. Without adequate protection, the returns earned by an investor can be greatly reduced by the ravages of the IRS. Thus in making investment decisions we must assess not only risk and return, but also the tax effects associated with a given investment vehicle or strategy. Since the tax effects depend on one's "tax bracket," it is important to choose investment vehicles that provide the maximum after-tax return for a given risk. A common stock paying high dividends may not be appropriate for an investor in the 28 or 33 percent federal tax bracket, just as a tax-free municipal bond may be inappropriate for a person with little or no tax liability. An awareness of the various vehicles and strategies available for legally reducing one's tax liability and an understanding of the role they can play in a portfolio are fundamental to obtaining the highest after-tax returns for a given level of risk. In addition, an understanding of the role limited partnerships can play in your portfolio is important. Let us begin by looking at tax fundamentals and shelters.

TAX FUNDAMENTALS AND SHELTERS

As currently structured, federal income tax law imposes a higher tax burden on higher taxable income. This is done through a dual rate structure; there are three tax brackets. For instance, a single investor earning $16,000 in 1990 would pay additional taxes of $150 if his or her income increased by $1,000 to $17,000; but if the investor's income was initially $32,000, the additional tax would have been $280 on an additional $1,000 of income. In the first case the marginal tax rate is 15 percent ($150/$1,000); in the second it is 28 percent ($280/$1,000). Thus you pay not only more taxes as your taxable income increases, but you pay *progressively* more if your taxable income rises into a higher bracket. Table 15.1 shows the tax rates and income brackets for individual and joint returns. Notice how the tax rate increases when taxable income increases from the lower to the upper bracket (for example, at $17,850 of taxable income for a single taxpayer). To further demonstrate, notice that at $32,000 taxable income, which is twice as much as the $16,000 taxable income, a single taxpayer would pay tax of $6,640, or (.15 × $17,850) + [.28 × ($32,000 − $17,850)], versus $2,400, or (.15 × $16,000), on $16,000 of taxable income—nearly 2.8 times more.

The Tax Reform Act of 1986 provides for a phaseout of these brackets that effectively eliminates the rate graduation. This is accomplished by the 33 percent graduated rate phaseout range in Table 15.1. What this feature does is raise the effective tax rate (the rate paid as a percentage of all taxable income) so that high-income taxpayers earning in excess of the upper phaseout range bracket ($89,560 for a single taxpayer) would effectively pay a 28 percent rate on *all* taxable income. To demonstrate, a single taxpayer with taxable income of $100,000 would calculate his or her tax as follows:

$$.15 \times \$17,850 \qquad\qquad = \$\ 2,678$$
$$.28 \times (\$43,150 - \$17,850) = \quad 7,084$$

TABLE 15.1 **Tax Rates and Income Brackets for Individual and Joint Returns (1988 and later years)**

Tax Rates	Taxable Income	
	Individual Returns	Joint Returns
15%	$ 0 to $17,850	$ 0 to $29,750
28%	$17,851 to $43,150	$29,751 to $71,900
33%	$43,151 to $89,560*	$71,901 to $149,250*
28%	over $89,560*	over $149,250*

Note: In order to phase out exemptions, an additional amount equal to the lesser of (a) 5% of income in *excess of* $89,560 (for individual returns) or $149,250 (for joint returns) or (b) $546 multiplied by the number of exemptions claimed must be included in taxes due.

$$.33 \times (\$89,560 - \$43,150) = 15,315$$
$$.28 \times (\$100,000 - \$89,560) = \underline{2,923}$$
$$\text{Total tax} \qquad \underline{\$28,000}$$

Dividing the $28,000 of taxes by the $100,000 of taxable income results in an effective tax rate of 28 percent ($28,000 ÷ $100,000). It should be clear that the phaseout feature effectively causes taxpayers with high levels of taxable income to pay a flat 28 percent rate. Of course, no taxpayer's effective tax rate will ever exceed 28 percent.

tax planning
the formation of strategies that will exclude, reduce, or defer the level of taxes to be paid.

The goal of **tax planning** is to seek investment income that is not included as taxable income, or that is included at a reduced amount. An even more rewarding strategy is to find investments that actually save taxes by reducing other taxable income. For example, if the investor above in the 28 percent tax bracket could invest in a vehicle that reduces his or her taxable income by $1,000, this would offer an immediate return of $280 regardless of any other return potential it might have. Investment vehicles such as this are called *tax shelters,* and they are obviously important to investors in high tax brackets. Before examining tax shelters, however, we need to review the basic structure of the federal personal income tax.

Taxable Income

taxable income
the income to which tax rates are applied; equals adjusted gross income minus itemized deductions and exemptions.

Taxable income, as its name implies, is the income to which tax rates are applied. From an investments perspective, this includes such items as cash dividends, interest, profits from a sole proprietorship or share in a partnership, and gains from the sale of securities or other assets. The federal tax law retains an important distinction between ordinary income and capital gains (and losses).

ordinary income
any income received for labor services provided or from invested capital.

Ordinary Income

Broadly, **ordinary income** refers to any compensation received for labor services (active income) or from invested capital (portfolio or passive income). The form in

capital asset
property owned and used by the taxpayer for personal purposes, pleasure, or investment.

basis
the amount paid for a capital asset, including commissions and other costs related to the purchase.

capital gain
the amount by which the sale price of an asset exceeds its purchase price (basis); currently taxed as ordinary income.

capital loss
the amount by which the sale price of an asset is less than its purchase price (basis); a maximum of $3,000 of capital losses can be applied in any one year.

which the income is received is immaterial. For example, if you owe a debt to someone and that person forgives (excuses you from repaying) the debt, the amount could wind up as income taxable to you, depending on how the debt was initially created and treated for tax purposes in previous periods. Situations such as this sometimes arise in real estate tax shelters. As a general rule *any event that increases your net worth is income, and unless it is specifically excluded from taxable income or considered a capital gain, it is ordinary income.*

Capital Gains and Losses

The tax law as revised by the Tax Reform Act of 1986 treats gains or losses resulting from the sale of capital assets as ordinary income. A **capital asset** is defined as anything you own and use for personal purposes, pleasure, or investment. A house and a car are capital assets, so are stamp collections, bonds, and shares of common stock. Your **basis** in a capital asset usually means what you paid for it, including commissions and other costs related to the purchase. If an asset is sold for a price greater than its basis, a **capital gain** is the result; if the reverse is true, then you have a **capital loss.** All capital gains are included in full as a part of ordinary income, whereas a maximum of $3,000 of losses in excess of capital gains can be applied in any one year. Any losses that cannot be applied in the current year can be carried forward to future years and then deducted. (Timing the sale of securities to optimize the tax treatment of capital losses is an important part of tax planning and is treated more thoroughly later in the chapter.)

Determining Taxable Income

 Determining taxable income involves a series of steps. Since these are illustrated more clearly with an example, let us consider the 1988 income tax situation of the Edward and Martha Meyer family, a family of four. In 1988 the family had the following income items:

1.	Wages and salaries	
	Edward	$26,000
	Martha	12,000
2.	Interest on tax-free municipal bonds	400
3.	Interest on savings accounts	900
4.	Dividends on common stock (owned jointly)	600
5.	Capital gains on securities	1,500

The family also had the following deductions in 1988:

1.	Deductible contribution to IRA account	$1,800
2.	Charitable contributions	1,000
3.	Interest on home mortgage	6,000

TABLE 15.2   Determining 1988 Federal Income Tax Due for the Edward and Martha Meyer Family

I.	**GROSS INCOME**	
	1. Wages and salaries	
	($26,000 + $12,000)	$38,000
	2. Interest on savings accounts	900
	3. Dividends	600
	4. Capital gains	1,500
	Gross income	$41,000
II.	**ADJUSTMENTS TO GROSS INCOME**	
	Deductible IRA contribution	$ 1,800
III.	**ADJUSTED GROSS INCOME** (I − II) = ($41,000 − $1,800)	$39,200
IV.	**ITEMIZED DEDUCTIONS**	
	1. Charitable contributions	$ 1,000
	2. Mortgage interest	6,000
	Total itemized deductions	$ 7,000
V.	**EXEMPTIONS**	
	Edward, Martha, and two children (4 × $1,950)	$ 7,800
VI.	**TAXABLE INCOME**	
	(III − IV − V) = ($39,200 − $7,000 − $7,800)	$24,400
VII.	**FEDERAL INCOME TAX** (per rate schedule, Table 15.1)	
	(.15 × $24,400)	$ 3,660
VIII.	**TAX CREDITS**	$ 0
IX.	**TAX DUE** (VII − VIII) = ($3,660 − $0)	$ 3,660

The Meyers' income tax due for 1988 was $3,660, as determined in Table 15.2 and explained below.

Gross Income

Gross income begins with all includable income, but then allows certain exclusions that are provided in the tax law. Table 15.2 shows that in the Meyers' case, all income is included except interest on the tax-free municipal bonds, which is not subject to federal income tax. Notice that interest on their savings accounts and dividend income is included. In addition, all capital gains are included in gross income.

gross income
all includable income for federal income-tax purposes.

Adjustments to Gross Income

These items reflect the intent of Congress to favor certain activities. The only one shown for the Meyers (there are others) is their allowable IRA contribution of $1,800, which was determined using a formula provided under the prevailing tax

law. (See Chapter 4 for the discussion of IRAs.) You should note the tax-sheltering quality of the IRA; without it, the Meyers would have paid taxes on an additional $1,800 of income in 1988.

Adjusted Gross Income

adjusted gross income
gross income less the total allowable adjustments for tax purposes.

Subtracting the adjustments from gross income provides **adjusted gross income.** This figure is necessary in calculating certain deductions (such as medical and dental expenses, charitable contributions, job and other expenses, and the amount of allowable real estate losses) not illustrated in our example. The Meyers' adjusted gross income is $39,200.

Itemized Deductions

standard deduction
an amount, indexed to the cost of living, that taxpayers can elect to deduct from adjusted gross income without itemizing (listing) specific items.

Taxpayers can elect to take a **standard deduction** which is indexed to the cost of living. The standard deduction amounts for 1988 are noted below:

* Married taxpayers filing jointly $5,000
* Heads of households   4,400
* Single taxpayers   3,000
* Married taxpayers filing separately   2,500

If they don't wish to take the standard deduction, taxpayers can choose to itemize deductions. Taxpayers with itemized deductions in excess of the applicable standard deduction will prefer to itemize. This group will typically include those individuals owning a mortgaged primary and/or second home.

itemized deductions
personal living and family expenses, including residential mortgage interest, which can be deducted from adjusted gross income.

A number of items qualify as **itemized deductions,** the most common of which are residential mortgage interest and charitable contributions. All other things being equal, there is a tax advantage to ownership of a principal as well as a second residence, because interest on the associated mortgage loans is tax-deductible. Under the Tax Reform Act of 1986 consumer interest is *not* tax-deductible, whereas investment interest—interest paid on funds borrowed for personal investment purposes—is deductible, subject to certain limitations. Clearly, allowable interest deductions are less expensive on an after-tax basis.

Exemptions

exemption
a deduction for each qualifying dependent of a federal taxpayer.

The tax law allows a $1,950 deduction in 1988 ($2,000 in 1989, and an amount indexed to the cost of living after 1989), called an **exemption,** for each qualifying dependent. There are specific rules for determining who qualifies as a dependent, and these should be reviewed if the potential dependent is not your child or an immediate member of your family residing in your home. Table 15.2 shows that the Meyers claimed four exemptions.

Taxable Income

Deducting itemized deductions and exemptions from adjusted gross income leaves *taxable income*; in the Meyers' case, this amount is $24,400. Although the Meyers have none, certain *miscellaneous expenses*, which include union dues, safe-deposit

box rental, investment advice, membership dues for professional organizations, and business publications generally can be deducted only to the extent that they exceed 2 percent of adjusted gross income. In addition, certain *unreimbursed employee expenses* such as 80 percent of entertainment bills and 100 percent of travel expenses are deductible if substantiated by receipts.

You can use Table 15.1 to calculate the tax due for the Meyers. Their taxable income of $24,400 puts them in the 15 percent income bracket. Thus their tax, as calculated in the table, is $3,660. The Meyers pay a 15 percent **marginal tax rate,** which means the tax rate on additional income up to $29,750 is 15 percent. *It is the marginal tax rate that should be considered in evaluating the tax implications of an investment strategy.* By all means do not confuse the marginal rate with the average rate. The **average tax rate** is simply your taxes due divided by taxable income. In the Meyers' case, since they are in the lower tax bracket this rate also equals 15.0 percent ($3,660/$24,400). Of course, for taxpayers in the 28 or 33 percent tax bracket, the marginal rate will exceed the average tax rate. The average tax rate has absolutely no relevance to the Meyers' investment decision making.

marginal tax rate
the tax rate on additional income.

average tax rate
taxes due divided by taxable income; different from the marginal tax rate.

Tax Credits

A number of **tax credits** are available. These are particularly attractive since they reduce taxes on a dollar-for-dollar basis in contrast to a *deduction*, which reduces taxes only by an amount determined by the marginal tax rate. A frequently used tax credit is for child and dependent care expenses. Other common credits include the alcohol fuel credit, credit for the elderly or permanently disabled, foreign tax credit, minimum tax credit, and mortgage interest credit. The Meyers, as is true for most taxpayers under the Tax Reform Act of 1986, were not eligible for any tax credits.

tax credits
tax reductions allowed by the IRS on a dollar-for-dollar basis under certain specified conditions.

Taxes Due or Refundable

The final amount of tax due is determined by subtracting any tax credits from the income tax. The Meyers' tax due is $3,660. They now compare this amount to the total of tax withheld (indicated on their year-end withholding statements) and any estimated taxes they may have paid during 1988. If these two add up to *more* than $3,660, then they are entitled to a refund of the difference; if the total is *less* than $3,660, they must pay the difference when they file their 1988 federal income tax return.

The Alternative Minimum Tax

As a result of many taxpayers effectively using tax shelters (tax-favored investments) to reduce their taxable incomes to near zero, in 1978 Congress introduced the **alternative minimum tax (AMT).** The purpose of this measure is to raise additional revenue by making sure that all individuals, especially those with *tax preference items*—income items that receive special treatment under the tax laws— pay at least some tax. Passage of the Tax Reform Act of 1986 increased the AMT to 21 percent of the alternative minimum tax base, which is determined beginning with the individual's regular taxable income and then making a variety of adjustments to this value. The procedures for determining the alternative minimum tax base (and

alternative minimum tax (AMT)
a tax passed by Congress to ensure that all individuals, especially those using tax preference items, pay at least some federal income tax.

therefore the alternative minimum tax) are quite complicated, and a tax expert should be consulted if you feel the alternative minimum tax might apply in your situation.

Tax Avoidance and Tax Deferral

A comprehensive tax strategy attempts to maximize the total after-tax income of an investor over his or her lifetime. This objective is accomplished by either avoiding taxable income altogether or by deferring it to another period when it may receive more favorable tax treatment as a result of a lower tax rate. (Even when there is no tax reduction by deferral, it still offers the advantage of having the use of saved tax dollars over the deferral period.)

tax evasion
illegal activities designed to avoid paying taxes by omitting income or overstating deductions.

tax avoidance
reducing or eliminating taxes in legal ways that comply with the intent of Congress.

tax deferral
the strategy of delaying taxes by shifting income subject to tax into a later period.

Tax avoidance should not be confused with **tax evasion,** which consists of illegal activities such as omitting income or overstating deductions. **Tax avoidance** is concerned with reducing or eliminating taxes in legal ways and complies with the intent of Congress, which wrote the special provisions into the tax law. As we have already noted in the Meyers' example, the most popular form of tax avoidance is investing in securities offering tax-favored income (to be explained in greater detail in the next section). Another broad approach to avoiding taxes is to distribute income-producing assets to family members (usually children) who either pay no taxes at all or pay them at much lower rates. Since this is also a highly specialized area of the tax law, we do not pursue it further in this text. Again, you should seek professional counsel whenever a tax strategy of this type is contemplated.

Tax deferral deals with means of delaying taxes and can be accomplished in a number of ways. The simplest is to use those vehicles designed specifically to accomplish this end; included would be pension and retirement plans, IRAs, and annuities. The retirement vehicles were covered in Chapter 4; annuities are treated later in this chapter. Frequently taxes are deferred for only one year as part of a year-end tax strategy in order to shift income from one year to the next when it is known that taxable income or tax rates might be lower then. This latter situation existed in 1981, 1982, and 1983, when tax rates were scheduled downward beginning in 1981 and ending in 1984; and the situation again occurred in 1986, prior to the effective date of the Tax Reform Act of 1986.

Tax Shelters

tax shelter
an investment vehicle that offers potential reductions of taxable income.

A **tax shelter** refers to any investment vehicle that offers potential reductions of taxable income. Usually this means that you must be a direct—rather than an indirect—owner of the vehicle. For example, if the Meyers had a tax-deductible loss of $1,000 on investment property directly owned by them, it could have provided tax shelter; but, had they instead set up a corporation to own this property, the net loss of $1,000 would have been the corporation's, not theirs. Thus they would have lost the tax deduction (although they could have used another tax strategy— the so-called pseudo-corporation—to absorb the loss on their personal return) and the related tax savings. Similarly, when major corporations show huge losses, such as Chrysler's in the early 1980s, these are of no immediate tax benefit to the shareholders. Although the market price of the stock probably falls, which means you

could sell it at a tax loss, this is nevertheless a capital loss limited to only $3,000 a year (in excess of capital gains). From this you can see that if you owned a large amount of stock your loss might be many times that figure, and yet it may be of no immediate use in reducing your taxes.

Thus there is a tax advantage in organizing certain activities as sole proprietorships or partnerships, and even more specifically, as limited partnerships. The majority of these tax shelters are designed primarily to pass on certain deductions, such as depreciation, depletion, and amortization, directly to individuals. The specific instances in which taxes can be saved through arrangements such as these are currently limited as a result of the Tax Reform Act of 1986. The legislation specifically regulates the amount, if any, of such losses that can be deducted when calculating taxable income. The few remaining tax shelters and the structure of the limited partnership that makes them feasible will be explained later in this chapter. Now, however, let us turn our attention to those vehicles that offer tax-favored income.

TAX-FAVORED INCOME

tax-favored income

an investment return that is not taxable, that is taxed at a rate less than that on other similar investments that defer the payment of tax to a later period, or that trades current income for capital gains.

If an investment offers a return that is not taxable or is taxed at a rate less than that on other similar investments, or defers the payment of tax to a later period, or trades current for capital gain income, it is said to offer **tax-favored income.** These tax ''favors'' have been written into the tax law to foster or promote certain activities as well as to provide convenient tax-reporting procedures.

So far in this book we have examined in detail several popular tax-sheltered investments. For example, in the preceding chapter we saw how *real estate* can provide shelter from taxes for certain investors; and in Chapter 4, we saw how retirement plans, like IRAs, can provide a tax shelter to any gainfully employed individual—remember, even if your annual IRA contribution doesn't qualify as a tax deduction, the *earnings* on *any* IRA account are allowed to accumulate free of taxes. In addition to these tax shelters, there are a number of noteworthy vehicles and strategies that will be briefly examined below; later in this chapter we'll look at two other vehicles—deferred annuities and single-premium life insurance.

Income Excluded from Taxation

Some items are simply excluded from taxation, either totally or partially. These include interest earned on tax-free municipals, and Treasury and government agency issues, and certain proceeds from the sale of a personal residence. Naturally these sources of such income are particularly attractive investment vehicles.

Tax-Free Municipal Bond Interest

Municipal bonds were described in Chapter 9. All interest received from the most common form—tax-free municipals—is free of federal income tax; in fact, this income is not even reported on the return. However, any gains or losses resulting from the sale of municipal bonds must be included as capital gains or losses. In addition, interest paid on money borrowed to purchase municipal bonds is *not* tax-deductible.

Treasury and Government Agency Issues

Treasury and government agency issues were also discussed in Chapter 9. Although interest on these securities is included on the federal tax return, it is excluded for state and local income tax purposes. Since these combined income tax rates can be as high as 20 percent in some parts of the country, individuals in high tax brackets may find such exclusions worthwhile.

Sale of a Personal Residence

A capital gain results if you sell your personal residence for a price greater than its basis (the price originally paid for it). However, provisions in the tax law soften the tax impact and actually make investment in a home an excellent tax shelter. First, if a gain exists from the sale of your home, it can be deferred from taxation if you purchase another home at a price equal to or greater than the price of the home you sold—as long as you buy the other home within 24 months. The second, and more important, tax implication is that you have a one-time exclusion of $125,000 from gross income from the sale of a personal residence. On a joint return, both spouses must be age 55 or older and must meet certain other conditions to be eligible for this exclusion. This is a major tax break for most people and certainly enhances the investment appeal of the personal residence.

Strategies that Defer Tax Liabilities to the Next Year

Very often an investor may purchase securities and enjoy sizable gains within a relatively short period of time. Suppose you bought 100 shares of XYZ common stock in mid-1989; by year-end 1990 your investment would have increased in value by 50 percent, since the price of this stock increased from $30 a share to around $45 over that period. Assume that at year-end 1990 you believe the stock is fully valued in the market and wish to sell it and invest the $4,500 elsewhere. In such a case, you would be taxed on a capital gain of $1,500 ($4,500 sale price − $3,000 cost). Assuming a 28 percent tax bracket, this would lead to income taxes for 1990 of $420 on the sale. Because tax rates may be lower next year or merely to benefit from the time value of money it may be advantageous to defer the tax on this transaction to the following year (1991). Three available strategies for preserving a gain while deferring tax to the following year are (1) the short sale against the box, (2) the put hedge, and (3) the deep-in-the-money call option.

Short Sale Against the Box

shorting-against-the-box
a technique used to lock in a security profit and defer the taxes on it to the following tax year by short-selling a number of shares equal to those already owned.

The short sale against the box technique can be used to lock in a profit and defer the taxes on a profit to the next taxable year. By **shorting-against-the-box**— short-selling a number of shares equal to what you already own—you lock in an existing profit, which means you eliminate any risk of a price decline. You also give up any future increases in price, but this should not be of concern since your belief is that the current price is relatively high. For example, to lock in and defer the $1,500 capital gain on the XYZ transaction you would, prior to year-end, sell short 100 shares of XYZ. No matter what happens to the price of the stock, you are

guaranteed $1,500. You would then have two positions—one long and one short—both involving an equal number (100) of XYZ shares. After year-end you would use the 100 shares held long to close out the short position, thereby realizing the $1,500 capital gain.

 ### Put Hedge

The put hedge approach was covered in Chapter 11, where its use in locking in a profit and deferring the taxes on the profit to the next taxable year was discussed. It can be used as a technique to accomplish the same objectives as the short sale against the box without losing the potential for additional price appreciation. Essentially a **put hedge** involves buying a put option on shares currently owned. If the price of the stock falls, your losses on the shares are offset by the profit on the put option. For example, suppose when XYZ was trading at $45 you purchased a six-month put option with a striking price of $45 for $150. By doing this you locked in a price of $45, because if the price fell, say, to $40 a share your $500 loss on the stock would be offset exactly by a $500 profit on the option. However, you would still be out the $150 cost of the option. At a closing price of $40, this would be your ending after-tax position:

put hedge
the purchase of a put option on shares currently owned in order to lock in a profit and defer taxes on the profit to the next taxable year.

1.	Initial cost of 100 shares		$3,000
2.	Profit on 100 shares [100 × ($40 − $30)]		1,000
3.	Profit on the put option	$ 500	
4.	Cost of the put option	−150	
5.	Taxable gain on put option [(3) − (4)]		350
6.	Total tax on transaction		
	Profit on stock (2)	$1,000	
	Plus taxable gain on put (5)	+ 350	
	Total gain	$1,350	
	Times tax rate	× .28	
	Total tax		378
7.	After-tax position [(1) + (2) + (5) − (6)]		$3,972

deep-in-the-money call option
a tax-deferral strategy that involves selling a call option on shares currently owned, locking in a price to the extent of the amount received from the sale of the call option but giving up potential future price appreciation.

The final after-tax position here is about the same as if you had simply held the stock while its price declined to around $43.50 a share, but there are two important considerations. First, the put hedge locks in this position regardless of how low the price might fall, whereas simply holding the stock does not. Second, any price appreciation will be enjoyed with either approach. (Notice you do not give up this advantage as you do when shorting-against-the-box.)

 ### Deep-in-the-Money Call Option

Selling a **deep-in-the-money call option** is a strategy similar to the put hedge, but there are important differences. In this case you give up any potential future price increases, and you lock in a price only to the extent of the amount you receive from the sale of the call option. To illustrate, suppose call options on XYZ with a $40

striking price and six-month maturity were traded at $600 ($6 per share) when XYZ was selling for $45. If six months later XYZ closed at $40, it would result in this ending after-tax position:

1.	Initial cost of 100 shares	$3,000
2.	Profit on 100 shares [100 × ($40 − $30)]	1,000
3.	Profit on the sale of the option; since it closed at the striking price, profit is the total amount received	600
4.	Total tax on transaction	

Profit on stock (2)	$1,000	
Plus profit on option (3)	+ 600	
Total gain	$1,600	
Times tax rate	× .28	
Total tax		448

5.	After-tax position [(1) + (2) + (3) − (4)]	$4,152

This final after-tax position is better than with the put hedge, but it closes off any price appreciation. In effect, when you sell the call option you are agreeing to deliver your shares at the option's striking price; so if the price of XYZ increases to, say, $50 or beyond, you do not benefit because you have agreed to sell your shares at $40. Furthermore, your downside protection extends only to the amount received for the option—$6 per share. Therefore, if XYZ's price went to $35 you would lose $4 a share before taxes ($45 − ($35 + $6)].

Summary of the Strategies

As you can see, deferring tax liabilities to the next year is a potentially rewarding activity requiring the analysis of a number of available techniques. The choice can be simplified by considering which method works best given an expectation of the future price behavior of the stock. Table 15.3 summarizes how each strategy performs under different expectations of future price behavior. To complete the analysis you would have to consider commission costs—something we have omitted. Although these costs can be somewhat high in absolute dollars, they are usually a minor part of the total dollars involved if the potential savings is as large as the ones we have been considering in our examples. However, if the savings is relatively small—say, under $500—then commissions may be disproportionately large in relation to the tax savings and/or deferral. Clearly you need to work out the specific figures for each situation.

Strategies that Trade Current Income for Capital Gains

Whereas ordinary income is taxed in the year it's received, capital gains are not taxed until they are actually realized. This means that *unrealized* capital gains are not taxed. For example, the receipt of $100 in cash dividends on a stock in the current year would be taxed at the assumed 28 percent rate, leaving $72 of after-tax

TABLE 15.3   Ranking of Strategies to Defer Tax Liabilities to the Next Year Given Different Expectations About the Future Price of the Stock*

Strategy	Price Will Vary by a Small Amount Above or Below Current Price	Price Will Vary by a Large Amount Above or Below Current Price	Future Price Will Be Higher than Current Price	Future Price Will Be Lower than Current Price
Do nothing—hold into next tax year	2	4	1	4
Short sale against the box	3+	2+	4	1
Put hedge	3+	1	2	2
Sell deep-in-the-money call option	1	2+	3	3

*Ranking: 1, best; 4, worst.

income. On the other hand, if the price of a stock that pays no dividend rises by $100 during the current year, no tax would be due *until the stock is actually sold*— sooner or later you'll pay taxes on your income, but at least with capital gains it's deferred until the profit is actually realized, which could be years away. Therefore if the market price of the stock is stable or increasing, earning capital gains may be an attractive strategy for achieving a tax-deferred buildup of funds. From a strict tax viewpoint, investment vehicles that provide a tax-deferred buildup of value through unrealized capital gains may be more attractive than those that provide annual taxable income. Some of the more common methods for trading current income for capital gains are described below.

Growth versus Income Stocks

This is a simple yet basic way to earn capital gains income. Companies that pay out a low percentage of earnings as dividends usually reinvest the retained earnings to take advantage of growth opportunities. If you select a company that pays dividends amounting to a 10 percent current return on your investment, your after-tax return will be only 7.2 percent, assuming you are in the 28 percent tax bracket. In comparison, another company that pays no dividends but is expected to experience 10 percent annual growth in its share price from reinvestment of earnings will also offer an after-tax rate of return of 7.2 percent $[(1.0 - 0.28) \times .10]$, which will not have to be paid until the stock is actually sold and the gain realized. This deferral of tax payment is of course appealing as long as the stock price continues to increase in value.

Deep Discount Bonds

deep discount bond *a bond selling at a price far below its par value.*

Purchasing a **deep discount bond**—one that is selling at a price far below its par value—also offers a capital gain opportunity. To illustrate, suppose you have the

choice of buying ABC's bond, which has a coupon rate of 5 percent and is selling for $700 in the market. You could also buy a DEF bond with a coupon of 10 percent selling at par. Which would you prefer if both mature to a $1,000 par value at the end of 10 years? With the ABC bond, you will earn interest of $50 a year taxed as ordinary income. At the end of 10 years you will have a $300 capital gain, which will also be taxed as ordinary income. With the DEF bond, all of your return—that is, the $100 you receive each year—is ordinary income. From a strictly tax perspective, the ABC bond is clearly the better of the two, since *the portion of the return represented by the capital gain is not taxed until it's realized at maturity.* (Remember, though, that the higher-coupon bond is giving you a higher return earlier, and that adds to its attractiveness.)

To choose between the two bonds, a rate of return analysis could be performed, assuming an equal number of dollars is invested in each bond. For example, an investment of $7,000 would purchase 10 ABC bonds or 7 DEF bonds. Total annual interest on the ABC bonds would be $500, whereas on the DEF bonds it would be $700. To an investor in the 28 percent tax bracket, the after-tax advantage of the DEF bonds is $144 or $(0.72 \times \$200)$ a year. But the ABC bonds will be worth $10,000 at maturity, whereas the DEF bonds will be worth only their current value of $7,000. On an after-tax basis, the additional $3,000 is worth $2,160 or $[\$3,000 - (.28 \times \$3,000)]$. The choice boils down to whether you prefer $144 of additional income each year for the next 10 years or an additional $2,160 at the end of 10 years. Using the future value techniques developed in Chapter 5, you would arrive at the conclusion that it would take about a 9 percent rate of return to make you indifferent between the two bonds; that is, if you invest $144 a year for 10 years at 9 percent, it accumulates to around $2,160 at the end of 10 years. Interpreting this answer, if you can invest at an after-tax rate higher than 9 percent, you should select the DEF bonds; if you feel your after-tax reinvestment rate will be lower, then the ABC bonds should be selected.

Income Property Depreciation

Federal tax law, as noted in Chapter 14, permits the *depreciation* of income property such as apartment houses and similar structures. Essentially, a specified amount of annual depreciation can be deducted from ordinary pretax income. The Tax Reform Act of 1986 established depreciable lives of 27.5 years for residential rental property (apartment buildings) and 31.5 years for nonresidential property (office buildings and shopping centers). In both cases straight-line depreciation is used. When a property is sold any amount received in excess of its book value is treated as a capital gain and is taxed at the same rate as ordinary income. For example, assume you buy a 4-unit apartment building for $100,000 and hold it for three years, taking $2,900 in depreciation each year. Now suppose at the end of the third year you sell it for its original $100,000 purchase price. The depreciation you took reduced ordinary income each year by $2,900 and was worth, assuming a 28 percent tax bracket, $812, or $.28 \times \$2,900$. Your gain on the sale is $8,700, or 3 years $\times$ $2,900 per year, which results in a tax of $2,436, or $.28 \times \$8,700$. It can be seen that there is no tax savings in this situation; however, the benefit results

from the tax deferral caused by the fact that the tax savings of $812 in each of the first three years does not have to be paid back until the property is sold at the end of the third year. (Of course, if the property were sold for less than its original purchase price, full repayment would not occur.)

The ability to use the depreciation deduction (which does not actually involve any cash payment) to reduce taxes during the property's holding period, and delay the repayment of those taxes until it is sold, represents a type of interest-free loan. *This tax deferral is the primary tax benefit provided by depreciation.* In our example, the tax deferral of $812 in each of the first three years, which is repaid as $2,436 of taxes at the end of the third year, represents a loan at a zero-percent rate of interest (that is, $3 \times \$812 = \$2,436$). It is important, however, to recognize that very restrictive limits on the use of tax losses resulting from real estate investments established by the Tax Reform Act of 1986 may severely limit an investor's ability to take advantage of these depreciation tax benefits. As a result, as noted in Chapter 14, the appeal of real estate investment no longer lies in its potential tax shelter value, but rather in its ability to earn a profit from annual rents and/or price appreciation.

Tax Swaps: A Strategy that Reduces or Eliminates a Tax Liability

tax swap
selling one security that has experienced a capital loss and replacing it with another similar security in order to partially or fully offset a capital gain that has been realized in another part of the investor's portfolio.

Thus far we have considered several short-term strategies aimed at affecting an investor's tax liability in one way or another, including (1) ways to exclude income from taxation; (2) ways to defer taxes from one tax year to the next; and (3) techniques that trade current income for capital gains. We will now look at a strategy that essentially reduces or eliminates a tax liability altogether. This procedure, a so-called tax swap, is extremely popular at year-end with knowledgeable stock and bond investors. Basically, a **tax swap** is nothing more than the replacement of one security with another in order to partially or fully offset a capital gain that has been *realized* in another part of the portfolio. Of course, since we are trying to offset a gain, the security that is sold in the tax swap would be one that has performed poorly to date and, as such, has *lost* money for the investor. Since we are selling one security that has experienced a capital loss and replacing it with another similar security, the investor's stock or bond position remains essentially unchanged, although his or her tax liability has been reduced—and perhaps substantially so.

A tax swap works like this. Suppose that during the current year you realized a capital gain of $1,100 on the sale of bonds. Assume that in your portfolio you held 100 shares of International Oil Corporation common stock, purchased 20 months earlier for $38 per share and currently selling for $28 per share. Although you wish to maintain an oil stock in your portfolio, it does not matter to you whether you hold International Oil or one of the other multinational oils. To realize the $10-per-share capital loss on International Oil while not altering your portfolio, you sell the 100 shares of International Oil and buy 100 shares of World Petroleum, which is also selling for $28 per share. The result is a *realized* capital loss of $1,000 [100 × ($28 − $38)], which can be used to offset all but $100 of the $1,100 capital gain

realized on the earlier bond sale. Clearly the tax swap is an effective way of reducing and possibly eliminating a tax liability without altering one's portfolio.

Common stock swaps such as illustrated above are an important part of year-end tax planning. Even more popular are bond swaps, because it is usually far easier to find a substitute bond for the one held. Most full-service brokerage houses publish a list of recommended year-end swaps for both stocks and bonds. You might be wondering why it wouldn't make more sense just to sell the security for tax purposes and then immediately buy it back. Unfortunately this is called a **wash sale** and is disallowed under the tax law. A sold security cannot be repurchased within 30 days before or after its sale without losing the tax deduction.

wash sale
the procedure, disallowed under the tax law, of selling securities on which capital losses can be realized and then immediately buying them back.

DEFERRED ANNUITIES AND SINGLE-PREMIUM LIFE INSURANCE

annuity
a series of payments guaranteed for a number of years or over a lifetime.

single-premium annuity
a contract purchased with a single lump-sum payment.

As noted in the discussions of tax-favored income, effective tax strategy seeks to defer taxable income for extended periods of time. Although such a strategy may not reduce total taxes, the earnings on investment are not taxed when earned and are therefore available for reinvestment during the period of deferment. The additional earnings resulting from investment of pretax rather than after-tax dollars over long periods of time can be large. Put in proper perspective, a tax-deferred annuity may be worth more to an individual investor than any other single tax strategy. That is why it is important to understand the topic thoroughly. In addition, a similar product that has recently diminished in popularity is single-premium life insurance.

Annuities: An Overview

installment annuity
an annuity contract acquired by making payments over time; at a specified future date the installment payments, plus interest earned on them, are used to purchase an annuity contract.

annuitant
the person to whom the future payments on an annuity contract are directed.

immediate annuity
an annuity contract under which payments to the annuitant begin as soon as it is purchased.

An **annuity** is a series of payments guaranteed for a number of years or over a lifetime. The two types of annuities are classified by their purchase provisions. The **single-premium annuity** is a contract purchased with a single lump-sum payment. The purchaser pays a certain amount and receives a series of future payments that begins either immediately or at some future date. The second type of contract, the **installment annuity,** is acquired by making payments over time; at a specified future date the installment payments, plus interest earned on them, are used to purchase an annuity contract. The person to whom the future payments are directed is called the **annuitant.** Annuities of many types are issued by hundreds of insurance companies. One recent innovation—the finite-term annuity—described in the Investor Insights box on pages 664 and 665 has added a new wrinkle that may allow this vehicle to effectively compete with the traditional CD for investor dollars.

An **immediate annuity** is a contract under which payments to the annuitant begin as soon as it is purchased. The amount of the payment is based on statistical analyses performed by the insurance company and depends on the annuitant's sex and age; and the payment is a function of how long the insurance company expects the annuitant to live. A **deferred annuity,** in contrast, is one in which the payments to the annuitant begin at some future date. The date is specified in the contract or at the annuitant's option. The amount the annuitant will periodically receive depends on his or her contributions, the interest earned on these contributions until the annuity payments commence, the annuitant's sex, and the annuitant's age when

deferred annuity
an annuity contract in which the payments to the annuitant begin at some future date.

payments begin. The period of time between when payments are made to the insurance company and when the insurance company begins to pay the annuitant is the **accumulation period.** All interest earned on the accumulated payments during this period is tax-deferred: It stays in the account, and because it is not paid out to the purchaser no tax liability is created. The period of time over which payments are made to the annuitant is the **distribution period.** Earnings on the annuity during the accumulation and distribution periods become taxable to the annuitant when received.

Characteristics of Deferred Annuities

accumulation period
under an annuity contract, the period of time between when payments are made to the insurance company and when the insurance company begins to pay the annuitant.

The growth in popularity of deferred annuities stems from the competitive interest rates paid on these contracts. In the following discussion the contract offered and heavily promoted in early 1989 by a major life insurance company, summarized in Table 15.4 on page 666, is used as illustrative of the contracts currently being written.

Current Interest Rate

distribution period
under an annuity contract the period of time over which payments are made to an annuitant.

An annuity contract's **current interest rate** is the yearly return the insurance company is paying now on accumulated deposits. The current interest rate fluctuates with market rates over time and is not guaranteed by the insurance company. However, some contracts have a ''bailout'' provision that allows an annuity holder to withdraw the contract value—principal and all earned interest—if the insurance company fails to pay a minimum return—typically a return that is 1 percent or more below the initial rate. The sample policy offered a guaranteed one-year rate of 9.3 percent and had no bailout provision.

current interest rate
for an annuity contract, the yearly return the insurance company is currently paying on accumulated deposits.

Minimum Guaranteed Interest Rate

minimum guaranteed interest rate
for an annuity contract, the minimum interest rate on contributions that the insurance company will guarantee over the full accumulation period; usually substantially less than the current interest rate.

The deferred annuity purchase contract specifies a **minimum guaranteed interest rate** on contributions. The insurance company will guarantee this rate over the full accumulation period. The minimum rate is usually substantially less than the current interest rate. The sample policy guaranteed a rate of 4.5 percent. However, you should study a prospectus or contract and remember that *the minimum rate is all you are guaranteed*. (Very often the promotional literature provided by the company emphasizes the high *current* interest rate.)

Special Tax Features

Deferred annuities, both single-premium and installment, have several advantageous tax-shelter features. First, interest earned on the purchaser's contributions is not subject to income tax until it is actually paid to the investor by the insurance company. Suppose that $10,000 is invested in a 9.3 percent single-premium deferred annuity. During the first year the contract is in effect the account earns $930 in interest. If none of this interest is withdrawn, no income tax is due. Thus for an investor in the 28 percent tax bracket the first year's tax savings is $260. The tax-deferral privilege permits the accumulation of substantial sums of compound interest that can be used to help provide a comfortable retirement income. However,

INVESTOR INSIGHTS

The Finite-Term Annuity: New Competition for CDs?

The tax code includes few real shelters with universal appeal. Some are high risk; others place limits on how much you can shelter or how much you can earn in order to qualify.

Deferred annuities are one of the exceptions. Although many are open to anyone with as little as $1,000 to invest, they also are useful shelters for people with hundreds of thousands of dollars.

Risks are few, if you buy a fixed-rate annuity from a top-rated insurance company. Recently, the industry reduced the risks even further with a new type of instrument known as a finite-term annuity or certificate of annuity. . . .

Under the typical annuity contract, a purchaser agrees to give a sum of money to an insurer in return for a stream of income in the future. You can contribute a lump sum (single premium), as with the new certificates of annuity, to get a fully paid-up contract. Or you can make a series of payments over a period of years. Either way, taxes are deferred on earnings until withdrawal.

Your return on investment will depend upon the type of annuity you choose. In a variable annuity, you decide how your premium dollars will be allocated among a number of mutual funds, including stock funds, bond funds and money market funds. The better your investment decisions, the greater the buildup. You can suffer losses, however, and many did in the 1987 stock market crash.

Since then, most buyers have preferred less risky fixed annuities. With a fixed instrument, the insurance company guarantees a return for a given time period, which may range from a few months to 10 years. When the initial guarantee period expires, the company sets a new rate for another fixed period.

Generally, deferred annuities are used to supplement retirement income. At a certain point, you ''annuitize'' your contract—you stop paying in and start taking out. You may take a lump sum and pay all the deferred taxes at once. Or you may elect to receive periodic payments, perhaps for the rest of your life and for that of your spouse. Part of each payment will be taxed when received; part will be a tax-free return of your own contribution.

If you die while you are still in the pay-in stage, beneficiaries you name will get the cash balance of your account or your total premium payments, whichever is greater. Again, income taxes will be payable on the income but not on your original capital. Proceeds will go to your heirs without the cost and delays of probate.

With these advantages come drawbacks, chiefly the lack of liquidity. Any withdrawals you make before annuitizing the contract are fully taxed, up to the amount of the income you have earned. If you make a withdrawal before age 59½, you will also have to pay a 10 percent penalty tax on the earnings that are paid out. . . .

You may also have to pay a surrender charge to the insurer as high as 25 percent of the early withdrawals. (Some companies permit partial withdrawals without charge.)

With a fixed-rate annuity you are dependent on the insurance company to re-set your return at a competitive rate, after the guarantee period. "Some insurance companies have excellent records on renewals," said Suze Orman, president of the Suze Orman Financial Group, based in Emeryville, Calif. "Others sucker you in with a high initial rate, which they drop sharply after the guarantee period."

Consumers can seek "bailout" provisions, offering penalty-free switching to another annuity if the rate drops steeply, but annuities with such features may have lower going-in rates. Also, said Miss Orman, "bailout features won't protect you if interest rates go up and the company doesn't raise its return."

Enter the finite-term annuity. Suppose you buy a one-year, $10,000 finite-term annuity that pays 8.5 percent. (The minimum investment generally is $5,000 or $10,000 and yields now [early 1989] are about 8.5 to 8.75 percent, depending on length of maturity, a bit less than bank C.D.'s.)

After a year, you'll have $10,850 in your account. If you want, you can take the money and pay taxes on your $850 gain. There will be no surrender charge, although the 10 percent penalty tax applies if you are under 59½. But if you don't need your money right away, you can roll it over into another annuity and put off the tax bill.

Thus, you have the flexibility of C.D. investing plus the power of deciding when to pay taxes. "Anyone over 59½ is out of their mind to invest in a C.D. rather than a certificate of annuity," Miss Orman said, "because they're not subject to the 10 percent early-withdrawal tax."

Finite-term annuities, however, lack the belt-and-suspenders security of Federal deposit insurance that comes with bank C.D.'s. Each state requires insurance companies to back annuities with reserves, but problems can occur. When the annuity marketer Baldwin-United ran into financial difficulties in the early 80's, investors endured a long period of uncertainty and then got a less-than-promised return on their money.

To avoid a similar debacle, be choosy when picking a company for any type of annuity. Miss Orman recommended that investors select companies with at least a 75-year operating history, an A+ rating from A.M. Best & Company and an investment portfolio that is not top-heavy with long-term "junk bonds." And ask for the company's history of renewal rates.

Annuities are sold through many brokers as well as insurance agents. They may be billed as "no-load" even though sales commissions range from 1 to 4 percent. Insurance companies pay the commissions, then make money by investing, say, in 10 percent bonds while paying you 8 percent.

Finally, investors should understand that tax changes could affect the value of an annuity. Tax rates might rise by the time you take your money out. It does not pay to defer taxes now at the top rate of 33 percent if the top rate goes back up to 50. And a revenue-hungry Congress might specifically target annuities for cutbacks of tax benefits.

Source: Donald Jay Korn, "And Now, A Wave of Flexible Annuities," *The New York Times*, March 5, 1989, p. F-11.

TABLE 15.4   Typical Features of a Single-Premium Deferred Annuity Contract

Feature	Covered in Contract
1. Minimum contribution	Minimum single premium required is $5,000, and maximum is $500,000 without prior company approval.
2. Withdrawal privileges	After the first year, up to 10 percent of the annuity contract value can be withdrawn each year without penalty charges. This is subject to a maximum of 50 percent of premiums received. But if withdrawal decreases the contract's value to an amount below the initial premium paid, a surrender charge of 5 percent of the difference between the contract value and total premiums will be levied in the first year. The penalty declines by 1 percent each year thereafter, with no surrender charges after the fifth year. In no instance will the investor receive less than 100 percent of the original single premium, less any prior withdrawals.
3. Guaranteed rates	9.3 percent in the first year, 4.5 percent thereafter.
4. Bailout provision	None.
5. Sales charges and administration fees	None.
6. Payment options	A payout period of at least 36 months is required to avoid penalties.
7. Income tax implications	Any withdrawal of income is assessed a 10 percent penalty unless investor is over age 59½; penalty is also waived for death, disability, or hardship.
	Any withdrawal of income is taxed at the investor's tax rate in the year of withdrawal.
	The contract can be rolled over to another annuity if the registration stays the same. (A tax consultant should provide an expert opinion.)

Source: Compilation of features of a deferred annuity offered by a major life insurance company in early 1989.

tax-sheltered annuity
an annuity contract available to certain employees of institutions such as schools, governments, and not-for-profit organizations that allows them to make a tax-free contribution from current income to purchase a deferred annuity.

it is important to note that the Tax Reform Act of 1986 provides that this tax-favored treatment is available only on annuity contracts held by individuals or trusts or other entities such as a decedent's estate, a qualified employer plan, a qualified annuity plan, or an IRA. In all other cases the income on the annuity is taxed when earned.

Certain employees of institutions such as schools, universities, governments, and not-for-profit organizations may qualify for the **tax-sheltered annuity.** A special provision in the income tax laws allow these employees to make a *tax-free contribu-*

tion from current income to purchase a deferred annuity. The interest on these contributions is tax-deferred as well. For example, Professor Hector Gomez, who teaches history at Crown University in Maine, receives a pretax salary of $3,500 per month. Professor Gomez can contribute approximately $600 per month to a tax-sheltered annuity program. (Note: The maximum amount he can contribute is limited and can be determined by formula.) This $600 is excluded from current income taxation; as a result, Gomez's taxes are based on only $2,900 per month. He does not have to pay any income tax on his contributions or his interest earnings until he actually receives annuity payments in future years. When he retires, if Professor Gomez's income tax bracket is lower than his current bracket he will pay a lower income tax on his deferred income. Thus the tax-sheltered annuity is attractive because it can save income taxes today as well as provide a higher level of retirement income later.

Investment Payout

payout

the investment return provided by an annuity contract, realized when the distribution period begins.

straight annuity

an annuity contract that provides for a series of payments for the rest of the annuitant's life.

The investment return or **payout** provided by an annuity contract is realized when the distribution period begins. The annuitant can choose a **straight annuity,** which is a series of payments for the rest of his or her life. Most companies also offer a variety of other payout options, including a contract specifying payments for both annuitant and spouse for the rest of both their lives, as well as a contract specifying rapid payout of accumulated payments with interest over a short period of time. The amount an annuitant receives depends on the amount accumulated in the account and the payout plan chosen. It is important to choose the program that provides the highest return for the desired payout plan. Such a plan will probably have a relatively high interest rate and relatively low (or no) sales charges and administration fees. The contract illustrated in Table 15.4 provided an opportunity for the annuitant to select how, when, and where payments are made.

Withdrawal Provisions and Penalties

Most annuity contracts specify conditions under which accumulated contributions and interest can be withdrawn by the purchaser. These provisions should be read carefully; some insurers impose heavy penalties for premature withdrawal of funds. The sample contract has typical withdrawal provisions. Equally important is the fact that the Tax Reform Act of 1986 levied a 10 percent additional income tax on early distributions (prior to age 59½) from both deferred and tax-sheltered annuities.

Sales Charge and Administration Fees

Many annuities are sold by salespersons who must be compensated for their services. Some annuities, called "no-load," have no sales charges paid by the purchaser; in this case the insurance company pays the salesperson directly. This is the case with the sample contract. Other annuities require the purchaser to pay commissions of up to 10 percent. Administration fees for management, yearly maintenance fees, and one-time "setup charges" may also be levied. The key item for a prospective purchaser to analyze is the *actual return on investment after all sales charges and administration fees are deducted.*

TABLE 15.5 **Comparison of Two $10,000 Investments—A Deferred Annuity and a Taxable Annuity***

End of Year	Deferred Annuity					Taxable Annuity							
	Earnings	Year-end Value				Earnings	Taxes	Year-end Value					
1	$ 930	$10,000	+	$ 930	=	$ 10,930	$ 930	$260	$10,000	+	$ 930	−	$260	=	$10,670
2	1,016	10,930	+	1,016	=	11,946	992	278	10,670	+	992	−	278	=	11,384
3	1,111	11,946	+	1,111	=	13,057	1,059	297	11,384	+	1,059	−	297	=	12,146
4	1,214	13,057	+	1,214	=	14,271	1,130	316	12,146	+	1,130	−	316	=	12,960
5	1,327	14,271	+	1,327	=	15,598	1,205	337	12,960	+	1,205	−	337	=	13,828
10	—	—	+	—	=	24,333	—	—	—	+	—	−	—	=	19,120
20	—	—	+	—	=	59,211	—	—	—	+	—	−	—	=	36,556
30	—	—	+	—	=	144,080	—	—	—	+	—	−	—	=	69,895

**Assumptions:* (1) Each investment earns 9.3 percent a year, and (2) the investor is in the 28 percent tax bracket.

The Deferred Annuity: An Example

Earlier we mentioned the attractive tax-deferral features of annuities. The following example illustrates the benefits of deferring income tax on the accumulated interest in an annuity. Assume that an investor has purchased a $10,000 single-premium deferred annuity (SPDA) paying interest at an annual rate of 9.3 percent. As shown in Table 15.5, if the interest on the contract is allowed to accumulate, the investment will be worth $15,598 at the end of 5 years, $24,333 at the end of 10 years, and $144,080 at the end of 30 years. In this case the interest compounds without taxes. If the $10,000 had been placed in a taxable investment at 9.3 percent interest, the accumulated amount would have been substantially less. For example, an investor in the 28 percent bracket would have accumulated only $13,828 at the end of 5 years, $19,120 at the end of 10 years, and $69,895 at the end of 30 years. Thus the tax-deferral feature would have allowed an additional capital buildup of nearly $75,000 over the 30 years. The tax savings, coupled with more interest to compound, results in a much greater accumulation of capital. Of course, the investor will have to pay the taxes on the interest from the annuity once the payout begins. But even so, the investor has gained considerably through the tax-deferral feature; and the benefits are even greater for someone in the graduated rate phaseout range paying 33 percent taxes.

Deferred Annuities and Retirement Plans

Many investors tie the purchase of deferred annuities to their overall retirement plans. You should recall from the discussion in Chapter 4 that Keogh plans and individual retirement accounts (IRAs) are partial substitutes for deferred annuities and therefore should be evaluated with them. If you are not fully using any allowable IRA exclusion each year, you may prefer adding to it as a part of your retirement plan rather than purchasing a tax-deferred annuity. Far greater benefit results from deducting from taxable income the full amount of the allowable payment into an

IRA. With an annuity, unless you're in one of the qualified professional fields denoted above, you cannot deduct its purchase price but can only defer earned income.

While both IRA and deferred annuity withdrawals prior to age 59½ are subject to a 10 percent additional tax, it is important to recognize that income withdrawn from a deferred annuity will be taxed in the year it is withdrawn. Moreover, any annuity withdrawal is first viewed for tax purposes as income; once all income is withdrawn, subsequent withdrawals are treated as a return of principal, so any partial withdrawal will most likely be fully taxable.

Fixed Versus Variable Annuity

fixed annuity
an annuity contract with a monthly payment amount that does not change.

variable annuity
an annuity contract that adjusts the monthly payment according to the investment experience (and sometimes the mortality experience) of the insurer.

The annuity payout during the distribution period can be either fixed or variable. Most contracts are written as **fixed annuities.** This means that once a payment schedule is selected, the amount of monthly income does not change. In contrast, a growing number of annuity plans adjust the monthly income according to the actual investment experience (and sometimes the mortality experience) of the insurer. These latter contracts are called **variable annuities.** The advantage of a fixed annuity is that the dollar amount of monthly income is guaranteed to the annuitant regardless of how poorly or well the insurer's investments perform. A major disadvantage, however, is that in periods of inflation the purchasing power of the dollar erodes. For example, with a 5 percent annual inflation rate, $1 is reduced in purchasing power to 78 cents in just five years.

To overcome the lack of inflation protection provided by fixed-dollar annuities, the variable annuity was developed. With this plan annuitants face a different risk, however. They cannot be certain how well the insurer's investments—which may consist of common stocks, bonds, or money market funds—will do. Annuitants therefore take a chance that they will receive an even lower monthly income, in absolute dollars, than a fixed-dollar contract would provide. Most people who participate in variable annuity plans of course anticipate that they will at least be able to keep up with the cost of living. Unfortunately variable annuity values and inflation, often measured by the consumer price index (CPI), do not always perform the same. In spite of significant inflation evidenced by rapid increases in the CPI during the 1970s and early 1980s, a number of variable annuities during this period earned rates of return well below the rate of increase in the CPI. More recently, variable annuities were growing in popularity and experiencing rapid growth until the October 1987 market crash, which gave many investors first-hand experience with their downside risk. These experiences show that the risk of reduced benefits from variable annuities does indeed exist. (As a result of the dip in common stock values, the payments made under many variable annuity plans during the 1970s and 1980s fell below the amount paid by corresponding fixed-dollar plans.)

Although most premiums paid into variable annuities are invested in common stocks, annuitants are sometimes allowed to have their monies placed in common stocks throughout the accumulation period as well as during the distribution period. In some cases annuitants may prefer premium buildup under a variable plan and then switch to a fixed-dollar plan at retirement. In this manner they participate in the

growth of the economy over their working careers but guard against short-term recessions that may occur during retirement years.

Annuities as Investment Vehicles

Annuities have several potential uses in an investment program. An immediate annuity can provide a safe and predictable source of income for the balance of one's life. A deferred annuity offers tax shelter and safety features, and in addition can provide a convenient method for accumulating funds. When considering the purchase of a deferred annuity, the investor needs to assess its investment suitability and understand the purchase procedures.

Investment Suitability

The principal positive feature of deferred annuities is that they allow an investor to accumulate tax-deferred earnings as a source of future income. The tax-deferral feature allows interest to accumulate more quickly than would be the case if earnings were taxed. For those qualifying for a tax-sheltered annuity, current income tax on premium payments can be deferred as well. Furthermore, annuities are a low-risk type of investment.

On the negative side, deferred annuities can be faulted for two reasons: (1) lack of inflation protection and (2) high sales charges and administration fees. Most variable annuities, in spite of providing a fluctuating interest rate during the accumulation period, do not provide an annual interest rate in excess of the rate of inflation. Thus they are not an inflation hedge. The second negative aspect of annuities—relatively high sales charges and administration fees—is due largely to the fact that sales commissions, whether paid by the purchaser or the insurance company, are generous and tend to lower the purchaser's return. In addition, insurance companies have high overheads that must be met from annuity proceeds. In general, then, although annuities can play an important role in an investment portfolio, they should not be the only vehicle held. Other vehicles providing higher returns (and probably carrying higher risk) are available.

Buying Annuities

Annuities are sold by licensed salespersons and many stockbrokers. There are probably 50 or more annuity plans available through these outlets in a given community. Prior to investing in a particular annuity, you should obtain a prospectus and any other available literature on a number of them. These materials should be carefully compared, and the annuity chosen should be the one that contains features consistent with your investment objectives while at the same time offering the highest actual return on investment after all charges and fees are deducted. Just as important, since *the annuity is only as good as the insurance company that stands behind it,* check to see how the company is rated in *Best's Insurance Reports*. These ratings are much like those found in the bond market and are meant to reflect the *financial strength* of the firm. Letter grades (ranging from A+ down to C) are assigned on the principle that the stronger the company, the lower the risk of loss. Accordingly, if security is important to you, stick with insurers that carry A+ or A ratings. And if

you're considering a *variable annuity,* go over it much the same way you would a traditional mutual fund: look for superior past performance, proven management talents, moderate expenses, and the availability of attractive investment alternatives that you can switch in and out of.

Single-Premium Life Insurance (SPLI): A Popular Alternative

Since 1982, tax legislation, including the Tax Reform Act of 1986, has reduced the tax shelter appeal of single-premium deferred annuities (SPDAs). Currently a 10 percent federal tax penalty is charged on withdrawals made prior to age 59½, regardless of how long the annuity has been held. In addition, most insurers charge withdrawal penalties—typically on withdrawals of 10 percent or more during the first 7 to 10 years. Clearly these restrictions limit the tax-shelter appeal of SPDAs.

single-premium life insurance policy (SPLI)
an insurance investment vehicle for which the policyholder pays a large premium to purchase a whole life policy that provides a stated death benefit and earns a competitive interest rate on the cash value buildup, which occurs over time on a tax-free basis.

As a result of the limitations placed on single-premium deferred annuities by the Tax Reform Act of 1986, the **single-premium life insurance policy (SPLI)** emerged as a popular alternative investment vehicle. These policies, in addition to offering the features of SPDAs, provided a mechanism for making tax-sheltered withdrawals prior to age 59½. Generally the policyholder paid a large premium, often $15,000 or more, to purchase a whole life policy (see Chapter 4) that provided a stated death benefit (that passed tax-free to beneficiaries) and earned a competitive interest rate on the cash value buildup, which occurred over time on a tax-free basis. As with any whole life policy, the policyholder could cancel the policy and withdraw its cash value. In such a case taxes would be due on any gains above the amount originally invested.

The most attractive feature of SPLI policies was the ability they afforded the policyholder to *make tax-free cash withdrawals at any time using a policy loan.* Unfortunately, with passage of the *Technical and Miscellaneous Revenue Act of 1988,* Congress closed the loophole in the tax law that allowed tax-free policy loans. Prior to passage of this law in late 1988, you could borrow up to 90 percent of the cash value of your SPLI policy and not pay any taxes. Policy loans typically have a low *contractual interest rate,* most often in the range of 6 to 8 percent. Because the insurer gives the policyholder a credit for the interest rate being applied to the cash value buildup, the *net cost* of a policy loan typically is very low— between 0 and 2 percent. In other words, you could buy such a policy, get life insurance with a tax-free buildup of cash value, and make tax-free withdrawals of funds through policy loans. Not only would the policy's earnings accumulate tax free, but you could receive these funds free of taxes as well. Under the new law premiums must meet a hypothetical *7-pay net premium test*—a technical set of rules that limit the *cumulative* amount that can be paid into the policy for each of the first seven policy years. Otherwise, any cash withdrawals made before you reach age 59½ (except in the case of death, disability, or hardship) are subject to a 10 percent tax penalty. No longer can investors conveniently use policy loans to withdraw tax-free earnings from single premium policies.

Today SPLI policies have re-emerged with higher death benefits relative to the size of the premiums. These policies preserve the principal and usually guarantee

returns for the first year or so. After that, rates of return are changed periodically to reflect prevailing money market rates; however, rates normally cannot fall below a certain minimum level as specified in the policy (usually, that's around 4 to 6 percent). Single premium *variable life* policies (see Chapter 4) let policyholders put their money in a number of investment choices, ranging from stocks and bonds to mutual funds and money market instruments. However these policies *do not* guarantee preservation of principal or a minimum return. Substantial investment losses can result in these policies.

Critics of SPLI point out that although the potential tax shelter features of these policies are attractive, the rate of return on investment in these policies is frequently below the return on tax-exempt municipal bonds, and the value of SPLI as life insurance is not as great as that available from term insurance. Recent tax revisions coupled with these shortcomings have greatly diminished the tax shelter appeal of single-premium life insurance. Like all forms of whole life insurance, SPLI's only tax shelter appeals are the tax-free buildup of value and the tax-free passage of death benefits to beneficiaries. Because SPDAs are vehicles for retirement, whereas SPLI policies provide greatest benefits when held until death, interest rates on SPDAs are usually one-half percent point higher than on SPLI. (Universal and variable life insurance, as discussed in Chapter 4, also enable policyholders to accumulate earnings on a tax-free basis and as such, are also viewed—by some at least—as viable tax shelter investments. But it should be understood that these vehicles, too, often suffer from relatively low earnings rates over the long haul.) Now that Congress has closed the SPLI loophole, the tax-shelter appeal of policy loans has been virtually eliminated, thereby greatly diminishing their popularity. Despite the aggressive and often tempting sales pitches, today most experts agree that this product is *not* well suited for young, moderate-income families since it is neither a very effective form of life insurance nor an especially attractive tax shelter.

USING LIMITED PARTNERSHIPS (LPs)

limited partnership (LP)
a vehicle in which the investor can passively invest with limited liability, receive the benefit of active professional management, and apply the resulting profit or loss (subject to limits) to his or her tax liability.

passive activity
an investment in which the investor does not "materially participate" in its management or activity.

The **limited partnership (LP)** is a vehicle in which you can passively invest with limited liability, receive the benefit of active professional management, and apply the resulting profit or loss (subject to limits) to your tax liability. The Tax Reform Act of 1986 effectively eliminated the tax-sheltering appeal of LPs. It limited the tax deductions for net losses generated by passive activities to the amount of net income earned by the taxpayer on all passive activities. Generally a **passive activity** is one in which the investor does not "materially participate" in its management or activity. Rental investments involving real estate, equipment, and other property are treated as passive activities regardless of whether or not the taxpayer materially participates. An exception exists for taxpayers actively participating in real estate rental activities; in a given year they can apply up to $25,000 of net losses to other forms of income if their adjusted gross income (AGI) is less than $100,000. This exception is gradually phased out for AGI between $100,000 and $150,000, so that taxpayers with AGI above $150,000 cannot apply such losses. One other exception to the material participation rule occurs for taxpayers experiencing losses from oil and gas properties, providing the form of ownership does *not* limit their liability.

While the value of LPs for tax shelters is no longer significant, this form of ownership is widely used to structure profit-making, cash-flow-generating investments. Like any investment, limited partnerships should be purchased *on their investment merits* only after considering both risk and return. It is therefore important to first understand why LPs are used and how they work.

Pooling of Capital and Sharing of Risks

syndicate

a joint venture— general partnership, corporation, or limited partnership—in which investors pool their resources for investing.

general partnership

a joint venture in which all partners have management rights and all assume unlimited liability for any debts or obligations the partnership incurs.

corporation

a form of organization that provides limited liability benefits to shareholder investors and that has an indefinite life.

In an effort to obtain economies of scale and diversify risk, investors often pool their resources and form joint ventures. These joint ventures, frequently called **syndicates,** can take several forms: general partnerships, corporations, or limited partnerships. In a **general partnership** all partners have management rights and all assume unlimited liability for any debts or obligations the partnership incurs. Obviously the unlimited liability feature can be disadvantageous to passive investors (those who do not wish to participate actively in the partnership's operation).

The corporate form of syndication (that is, a **corporation**) provides a limited liability benefit to shareholder investors. Additionally, corporations have an indefinite life and do not cease to exist if a stockholder dies, whereas a partnership could end if a general partner dies. However, the corporate form of syndication has a significant disadvantage in that its profits and losses cannot be passed directly to its stockholders. (Note: The S corporation is a vehicle that would permit shareholders limited liability and allow profits and losses to be treated as partnership income. Due to the limitation on the number of stockholders—currently 35 or fewer—that can be owners in an S corporation, this form is not especially popular for major syndications and therefore is not discussed here.) The partnership form of syndication, on the other hand, provides for the flow-through of profits and losses. How, then, can an investor obtain the limited-liability shield of a corporation and apply profits and losses directly on his or her tax return in a fashion similar to a partnership? The solution is ingenious—the *limited partnership.* This form of syndication combines the favorable investment features of both the corporation and the general partnership to provide an investor with a limited-liability vehicle that allows profits and losses to flow through to each partner's tax return. Let us take a closer look.

How Limited Partnerships Work

Legal Structure

The limited partnership (LP) form of group investment is a legal arrangement governed principally by state law. State laws vary, of course, but typically they require that various written documents be filed with a county or state official prior to the commencement of the limited partnership's business. Additionally, the structure of the limited partnership is normally established to conform to IRS regulations; this is done to ensure that any tax benefits generated can be used by the partners. Limited partnerships can be utilized to invest in many things, and their size and scope vary widely. However, all have one common characteristic: They must have at least one general partner and at least one limited partner.

Figure 15.1 illustrates a typical limited partnership arrangement. The **general**

FIGURE 15.1 The Limited Partnership Structure.
In a limited partnership, the general partner typically provides management expertise and accepts all liability, whereas the limited partners are passive investors who supply most of the capital and accept liability limited only to the amount of their investment.

general partner
the managing partner who accepts unlimited liability and makes all decisions in a partnership.

partner, the active manager of the operation, runs the business and, in addition, assumes unlimited liability. (Often, to mitigate their unlimited liability, the general partners are corporations.) The general partner's major contribution to the enterprise is frequently in the form of management expertise, not capital, whereas most of the capital is usually supplied by the limited partners, who do little else. The latter cannot participate in the management of the enterprise, or they will lose their limited liability protection; and furthermore, a limited partner's liability normally does not exceed his or her capital contribution, an amount specified in the partnership agreement. **Limited partners,** then, are the suppliers of capital whose role in the venture is passive. Usually the only power limited partners have is to fire the general partner and/or to sell their partnership investment.

limited partners
the passive investors in a partnership, who supply most of the capital and have liability limited to the amount of their capital contributions.

The Role of the General Partner

Since, as we have already stated, the responsibility of managing the limited partnership rests on the general partner, an investor considering entering a limited partnership must carefully analyze the management capabilities of the general partner. (The limited partner's money is literally "riding on" the general partner's abilities.) The general partner may find investors, assemble the partnership, and do all the negotiating. On large ventures, the services of an investment banker may be employed. Once the necessary capital has been raised, the general partner manages the investment, and for these services he or she is paid a fee. Compensation arrangements vary widely: For example, a general partner may receive a one-time management fee when the partnership is initially set up plus a yearly management fee; or the general partner may receive a specified portion of the ongoing profits.

Return to Investors

Prior to passage of the Tax Reform Act of 1986 the primary form of return provided by LPs was tax shelter, but due to both material participation and prohibition of limited liability requirements this form of ownership can no longer be effectively used as a tax shelter. Today an investor can realize a return from a limited partnership investment in two basic ways—through cash flow and price appreciation.

Cash Flow. Investors in a successful limited partnership operation receive periodic cash payments as the investment generates income. These periodic returns are a project's *cash flow*. Limited partners receive a prorated share of the partnership's cash flow, depending on the size of their investment in the operation. Cash distributions may be made monthly, quarterly, or yearly, and these returns are taxable to the partners as ordinary income. The general partner's management fee is normally paid prior to the distribution of cash flow. However, frequently the general partner will take only a small fee until the limited partners have had their capital investment completely repaid. Once this has occurred, the general partner's share of subsequent distributions will become commensurately larger.

Price Appreciation. Another source of investment return for limited partners is *price appreciation* resulting from an increase in the value of the investment. The general partner may earn a portion of the realized price appreciation as well. Investments, such as real estate, that increase in value due to inflation and other factors are often sources of appreciated value for limited partnership investors. Like the appreciation experienced on any investment vehicle, this form of return may be realized or unrealized (as an actual return of dollars or as a "paper" return). And of course realized capital gains are taxable to the partners.

Popular Forms of Limited Partnerships

Limited partnerships have been used to invest in many different types of assets. In fact, today it is often said, "If there is an investment opportunity requiring a sizable outlay and professional management that is expected to offer attractive returns, a limited partnership will be formed to buy it." Limited partnerships vary in risk, from a conservative one formed to own a fully rented office building with long-term leases to a risky one formed to own the sperm bank of a famous trotting horse that has never sired a winning offspring. Here we focus on three principal areas: real estate, energy resources, and equipment leasing. Other popular areas include livestock feeding or breeding programs, research and development programs, major movie or play production programs, cable TV programs, and real estate mortgage programs.

Real Estate

Depending upon property type, a periodic cash flow, price appreciation, and/or tax shelter can be realized from investing in real estate. As noted earlier, limited tax shelter may be available only to those *actively* participating in real estate investment. (See Chapter 14 for a detailed discussion of real estate investment analysis.) Raw land is normally purchased for its price appreciation potential. Income property has investment appeal due to its periodic cash flow. Apartment buildings, shopping centers, office buildings, and the like can provide cash flow as well as price appreciation. Very often, these types of properties are syndicated and bought by limited partnerships. The typical real estate limited partnership consists of a general partner who manages the investment and the limited partners who provide most or all of the capital.

blind pool syndicate
a type of real estate limited partnership formed by a syndicator to raise money to be invested at the syndicator's discretion.

single-property syndicate
a type of real estate limited partnership established to purchase a specific piece of property.

exploratory programs
limited partnerships formed to drill in areas where oil or gas is believed to exist but has not yet been discovered; also known as wildcats.

developmental programs
limited partnerships that finance the drilling of oil or gas wells in areas of known and proved reserves.

income programs
limited partnerships that buy existing oil or gas wells with proven reserves.

There are two major types of real estate syndicates. The **blind pool syndicate** is formed by a syndicator—often well known—in order to raise a given amount of money to be invested at his or her discretion, though the general partner often has some or all of the properties already picked out. The **single-property syndicate,** on the other hand, is established to purchase specific properties. Very often the large, multiproperty limited partnership syndicates with many investors are blind pools. Single-property syndicates are generally smaller in scope, although many valuable parcels of property (the New York Empire State Building, for example) are owned by single-property syndicates.

Energy Resources

The United States is heavily dependent on energy for its economic well-being, so the federal government has provided various tax incentives for those who invest in the search for energy. Utilizing the limited-partnership investment vehicle, capital is pooled to finance exploration for oil, natural gas, coal, and geothermal steam. The most popular energy-related limited partnerships are oil and gas investments.

There are three basic types of oil and gas limited partnerships. **Exploratory programs,** also known as "wildcats," drill in areas where oil or gas is believed to exist but has not yet been discovered. **Developmental programs** finance the drilling of wells in areas of known and proved oil and gas reserves. (They often drill wells that are near already-producing oil or gas finds.) **Income programs** buy existing wells with proven reserves.

The oil and gas business is risky due to the high degree of uncertainty associated with it. Even the most knowledgeable geologists and petroleum engineers are never quite sure how much oil or gas is in a particular well or field. Oil and gas limited-partnership investments therefore contain risk elements as well. The degree of risk of course depends on the type of program an investor purchases. Exploratory programs carry the highest risk of the three types, and correspondingly offer the highest potential return.

Table 15.6 provides offering highlights for a typical limited partnership engaged in ownership of producing oil and gas properties—Prudential-Bache Energy Income Partnerships Series VI. In this case the smallest investment an individual can make is 20 depositary units at $250 each, a total of $5,000. This is common among most limited partnerships. Notice that this is an income program aimed at providing cash distributions from the sale of oil and gas production.

If you buy an interest in this program, how well can you expect to do with your investment? Naturally this question can't be answered until the passage of time supplies more information. However, we can ask this question: How well have prior Prudential-Bache Energy Income programs done previously? Fortunately, the advertising brochure accompanying the prospectus helps provide an answer. Table 15.7 shows annualized cash distributions for each of 21 prior Prudential-Bache–sponsored producing programs since 1983. It can be seen that past programs have consistently provided annualized cash distributions averaging around 11 percent. There is, of course, no guarantee that future programs, such as those in Series VI, will achieve those same levels of cash return. On the other hand, if anticipated

TABLE 15.6 A Public Limited Partnership—Prudential-Bache Energy Income Partnerships Series VI Offering Highlights

Name of program	Prudential-Bache Energy Income Partnerships Series VI
Who may invest	Eligible investors that have either:
	A net worth of at least $25,000 (exclusive of home, furnishings, and automobiles) and an annual gross income of at least $25,000, or
	A net worth of at least $90,000 (exclusive of home, furnishings, and automobiles)
	Investors residing in certain states will be required to represent that they satisfy different or additional suitability requirements.
How to subscribe	Investors desiring to subscribe for depositary units should contact their account executive.
Maximum offering	$500,000,000 ($250,000,000 in any one limited partnership)
Minimum per limited partnership	$20,000,000
Securities offered	Depositary units
Depositary unit size	$250
Minimum investment	$5,000, except, in most states, $1,000 for IRAs, Keogh plans, and other self-directed qualified plans and $250 for subscribers to prior oil and gas income partnerships sponsored by Energy Production
Sales commissions	7.5% of unit holders' subscriptions (subject to volume discounts)
Management	Energy Production and Graham Royalty
Primary purpose	Provide cash distributions to unit holders from the sale of oil and gas production. Partnership will not engage in any exploratory drilling.
Proposed activities	Acquisition of direct and indirect interests in producing properties located in the continental United States. An amount equal to approximately 91% of unit holders' subscriptions is anticipated to be available for the acquisition and development of producing properties.
Participation in costs and revenues	Before partnership payout, 99% to unit holders and 1% to Energy Production and Graham Royalty; thereafter, 80% to unit holders and 20% to Energy Production and Graham Royalty. All sales commissions and organization and offering costs will be borne by unit holders.
Distributions of distributable cash	Quarterly, expected to commence within approximately 90 days after closing of a partnership.
Risk factors	No assurance can be given that the income and capital growth objectives of the partnership will be attained. In addition, this offering is subject to a number of risks, including the availability and price of suitable properties, future oil and gas prices, the quantities of economically recoverable reserves, and a partnership's ability to market its oil and gas production at adequate prices.

Source: Prudential-Bache Energy Income Partnerships Series VI advertising brochure and prospectus dated August 1988.

TABLE 15.7 **Prudential-Bache–Sponsored Prior Producing Programs, As of July 20, 1988**

Partnership	Closing Date	Annualized Cash Distributions*						
		Oct. 15, 1983	July 15, 1984	July 18, 1985	July 21, 1986	July 20, 1987	July 20, 1988	Average through July 20, 1988**
P-1	9/13/83	9.70%	12.10%	15.00%	5.00%	2.40%	4.50%	8.32%
P-2	11/15/83		10.10	15.00	5.70	3.10	5.75	8.25
P-3	2/16/84		10.20	15.00	7.40	3.25	6.25	8.22
P-4	6/13/84		9.80	14.00	5.00	2.75	4.50	7.57
P-5	8/29/84			12.50	7.70	4.35	3.50	7.36
P-6	11/29/84			11.00	12.00	8.20	6.75	9.66
P-7	4/26/85			8.00	12.00	9.50	8.00	10.20
P-8	7/31/85				14.00	14.40	11.00	13.20
P-9	9/30/85				13.00	14.40	11.75	13.27
P-10	3/7/86				10.50	15.00	11.25	12.74
P-11	5/14/86				7.00	16.10	11.75	12.95
P-12	6/17/86				7.00	16.10	12.00	13.26
P-13	7/17/86					14.60	10.75	10.70
P-14	9/17/86					14.60	10.25	10.91
P-15	11/6/86					14.60	10.25	11.34
P-16	2/3/87					14.10	15.00	13.76
P-17	6/1/87					11.80	15.50	14.80
P-18	8/18/87						13.00	11.24
P-19	10/8/87						12.50	11.71
P-20	1/20/88						11.00	9.23
P-21	4/25/88						10.00	10.00

*Represents the total cash distributed to investors by a partnership for the quarter, divided by the total amount of investor funds invested in the partnership, and then multiplied by 365 days divided by the number of days during the quarter that the partnership conducted business.

**Represents total cash distributed to investors through July 20, 1988, divided by the total amount of investor funds invested in the partnership, and then annualized by dividing by the number of years (and fractions thereof) since the partnership closing date.

Source: Prudential-Bache Energy Income Partnerships Series VI advertising brochure accompanying prospectus, August 1988.

increases in oil and gas prices materialize, then even higher levels of cash distribution might result. Before investing in this or any program you should be sure that it is consistent with your risk, return, and tax objectives and that it is the best vehicle for achieving those objectives.

Equipment Leasing

Another popular limited partnership investment is the kind that deals with various types of leasable property—airplanes, railroad cars, machinery, computers, trucks, automobiles. In these types of investments the limited partnership buys the equipment, such as a computer, and then leases it to another party. As the lessor of the equipment, the partnership can depreciate the item. Additionally, the partnership may use borrowed capital to increase potential return. The business of leasing property requires a great deal of knowledge and skill. The key to investment success in leasing is a competent general partner. Computers and various types of industrial machinery, for example, often have a high obsolescence risk. For very wealthy investors, limited partnerships involving giant oil tankers are available. The tanker is leased to an oil company for a number of years, and the tanker's owners (the partners) benefit from the cash flow generated by its rental income.

Partnership Structure: Private or Public

The size and scope of limited partnerships vary considerably. For example, three friends might establish a limited partnership to buy a six-unit apartment building. In contrast, one 1988 limited partnership, Prudential-Bache Energy Income Partnership P-21, had more than 6,000 investors who contributed over $68,000,000 for use in acquiring producing oil and gas properties. There are two distinct types of limited partnerships. The **private partnership** has a limited number of investors and is not registered with a public agency such as a state securities commission or the SEC. The **public partnership** is registered with the appropriate state and/or federal regulators and usually has 35 or more limited partners. State and federal laws regulate offerings of all limited partnership programs.

private partnership
a limited partnership that has a limited number of investors and is not registered with a public agency.

public partnership
a limited partnership that is registered with state and/or federal regulators and usually has 35 or more limited partners.

offering circular
a document for a private partnership describing the property to be purchased, management fees, and other financial details; it usually also includes the limited partnership agreement.

Private Partnerships

Private limited partnerships are often assembled by a local real estate broker or an attorney; they tend to be more for the well-to-do and to *take more risks* than public partnerships. Often, the investors know one another personally. Potential investors in the partnership are commonly given an **offering circular,** a document describing the property to be purchased, management fees, and other financial details. It usually also contains the limited partnership agreement. There are several advantages to private partnerships. First, since they do not have to be registered with a public agency they usually carry lower transaction and legal costs than public partnerships. Legal fees in connection with registration of securities are costly and are paid indirectly by the limited partners. Another advantage of the private partnership is that it may be easier to obtain first-hand knowledge about the general partner. (The general partner may well be locally based, and can be investigated prior to commit-

ting any money.) A good source of information on a general partner is other limited partners who have previously invested in his or her partnerships.

Public Partnerships

Public limited partnership syndications must be registered with state and sometimes federal regulatory authorities. Interstate sales of limited-partnership interests must comply with federal as well as state laws. Offerings sold only within one state, however, need comply only with that state's laws. Public partnerships are sold by stockbrokers and other licensed securities dealers, and transaction costs are high. The brokerage commission on a typical oil and gas limited partnership is about 8 percent. Limited-partnership interests, both private and public, are relatively illiquid, and sometimes the interest cannot be sold without the approval of the state authority. A potential buyer of a public limited partnership must be given a **prospectus,** which is a detailed statement containing the financial data, management information, and transaction and legal costs associated with the offering. Most public partnerships are large in scope and usually contain over $1 million in assets. An investor in a public partnership may find that his or her shares represent an investment in a *diversified* portfolio of real estate or energy resource properties. Geographical diversity may be easier to obtain by investing in public partnerships.

prospectus
a document for a public partnership describing the financial data, management information, and transaction and legal costs associated with the offering.

Essential Investment Considerations

Limited partnerships often provide a means of earning a return that can be passed through directly to your income tax calculation; they therefore should be purchased solely on the basis of their investment merit. Limited-partnership promoters sometimes concoct unbelievable schemes for earning significant returns. They advertise that you can earn a sizable return on an investment as a result of the general partner's unique situation or expertise. Although this is possible, it is certainly not without risk, and generally the actual amount earned, if any, is far less than the amount suggested. For each potential investment in a limited partnership you should review its degree of leverage, its risk and return, and its investment suitability. The Investor Insights box on pages 682 and 683 uses some recently troubled partnerships to demonstrate the types of problems that can face limited partnership investors.

Leverage

In limited partnerships the presence of *leverage* indicates that the underlying business activity utilizes borrowed funds—perhaps in substantial amounts. An equipment-leasing venture, for example, might involve 80 to 90 percent of debt financing. This means your initial investment dollar buys more assets than would be the case if leverage were not used. For example, suppose a limited partnership raises $100,000, borrows $900,000 for which the partners have shared liability, and then buys computer equipment for $1,000,000 to lease to a business over a 10-year period. Suppose further that the partnership earns $50,000 in the first year. If you own 5 percent of the partnership (you invested $5,000), in the first year your earnings are $2,500. Your total first-year recovery is therefore equal to 50 percent

of your total investment. Had the partnership not used leverage you would have had to invest $50,000 in order to own 5 percent (.05 × $1,000,000) of the investment. In such a case, your return would have only been 5 percent on your initial investment ($2,500 ÷ $50,000). Clearly, the use of leverage enhances your return; but you must bear in mind that you are legally liable for your share of the loan, which is $45,000 or (.05 × $900,000). If the loan is with some type of captive finance company that is willing to forgive the debt in the event the partnership goes under, or if you do not have legal liability for your portion of the debt, the whole deal may (except in the case of real estate partnerships) be considered a sham by the Internal Revenue Service. In such a case, you could be subject to tax penalties. Remember that leverage can increase returns, but in order to do so it almost always carries more risk.

Risk and Return

Evaluating the risk and return of a limited partnership investment depends on the property involved, although there are two general factors to consider. First, the general partner must be carefully studied. One should investigate, for instance, whether a general partner trying to sell an interest in an exploration project has failed to discover oil in previous projects. Again, read the offering circular or prospectus carefully. Find out how much the promoters (general partner and associates) are skimming off the top in commissions, legal fees, and management fees. The more they take, the less of your money is invested in the project and the less likely it is that you will receive a high return.

A second factor to recognize is that most limited partnerships are not very liquid; in fact, depending on state law, they may not be salable prior to their disbandment. In other words, your interest may be difficult, or perhaps impossible, to resell. Recently two vehicles for enhancing the marketability of LP shares have emerged.

master limited partnership (MLP) *a limited partnership that is publicly traded on a major stock exchange.*

One is the **master limited partnership (MLP),** which is a limited partnership that is publicly traded on a major stock exchange. The stock represents a marketable claim on a group of limited partnership interests that are acquired by the MLP in any of a number of ways. Although a few years ago it appeared that the MLPs would indeed improve partnership liquidity, recent tax law changes have greatly diminished their attractiveness. The second outlet for LP shares is the emerging secondary market for them. For better-known public limited partnerships, established market makers provide quotes. (Private deals and smaller public deals remain quite illiquid, however.) Of course, sizable commissions must be paid on these LP transactions, and the general lack of LP liquidity tends to increase the risk associated with investment in them.

Investment Suitability

As you have probably concluded by now, limited partnerships are not for everyone. They tend to be risky and illiquid and thus are usually not suitable for conservative investors primarily interested in the preservation of capital. An offering circular or prospectus will often contain a statement limiting purchase to investors of at least a certain net worth (say, $100,000) and in the 28 or 33 percent tax bracket. This rule

INVESTOR INSIGHTS

A Look at Some of the Problems with Limited Partnerships

Charles Hall is worried.

Several years ago, the retired Cape Coral, Fla., executive invested about $25,000 in three limited partnerships managed by Dallas-based Southmark Corp.

Now [May 1989] the $5.3 billion real estate and financial-services concern is battling for survival. Last week, Southmark reported a $1.04 billion third-quarter loss that included a number of write-downs related to partnerships it sponsored. One of its syndication subsidiaries, Consolidated Capital Equities Corp., filed for protection from creditors under Chapter 11 of the federal Bankruptcy Code late last year.

Mr. Hall's partnerships are controlled by three of Southmark's 17 other subsidiaries. "But when you see all this trouble with Southmark, you get concerned about the condition of the other things that are under their umbrella," he says.

The 76-year old Mr. Hall isn't alone. The well-publicized troubles of some partnership sponsors are raising concern among thousands of investors who poured billions of dollars into real estate and other syndications over the past decade or so. Although many investors may fare better than they now fear, others may not even realize the extent of their problems.

Roughly 600,000 investors own interests in Southmark partnerships, and they have been jamming the company's switchboards with as many as 800 calls an hour. The Southmark syndications, known as "public" partnerships, are widely available to individuals who can invest just a few thousand dollars.

But investment advisors who follow the partnership business say most of the sponsors that have run into trouble are those involved in so-called private partnerships. These are investments designed for small groups of supposedly sophisticated individuals who can invest $25,000 or more. Before the 1986 Tax Reform Act, private partnerships were frequently sold primarily as tax shelters.

Warren Shine, a principal at New York accountants Ernst & Whinney, says he suspects problems with private-partnership sponsors are widespread. "I've seen more of this in the last few years than I wanted to in a lifetime," he says.

Just last week, Cardinal Industries Inc., Columbus, Ohio, became the latest private syndicator to file under Chapter 11. Since 1975, the company had raised about $440 million from investors in 450 real estate partnerships that bought mostly apartment complexes and motels.

In theory, a sick general partner shouldn't necessarily harm investors' chances of making money in a partnership that is itself economically sound. "If the real estate is good, the partnership should have no problem," says Peter Fass, a real estate securities attorney with Kaye, Scholer, Fierman, Hayes & Handler.

Both Southmark and Cardinal officials say their problems haven't hurt their partnership investors and that they are working hard to solve them. Cardinal immediately sent letters to its broker-dealers after filing for bankruptcy-law protection informing them that a solvent general partner would take over and that the company's property management activities are viable.

But partnership investors may not always be so lucky.

At the least, a sponsor's troubles could distract it from its role of managing the limited partnership. Real estate or some other partnership asset "may be off in some distant place and need tender loving care," says Mr. Shine. "If the general partner is on the way down, or in the tank already, there's nobody to give it that attention."

Investors in partnerships that are being kept afloat with cash infusions by a sponsor may face a more immediate problem. If that money runs out, says Mr. Shine, "Boom—all of a sudden the limited partners are on their own." In some cases, he says, the investors might not even have realized their partnerships were only limping along.

Even more ominous is the risk that a sponsor with its back to the wall could wind up using the limited partnership's funds to pay its own bills.

If a sponsor's problems do lead to trouble, an investor's first reaction may be to try to get out of the partnership. A growing number of small investment firms that purchase partnership interests for their own accounts or for resale to others are ready to help. But the prices investors receive in this unofficial secondary market are often a fraction of what they originally paid.

Limited partners in private syndications that involve payments over several years may be tempted to simply stop paying. But it's not a good idea.

Some Cardinal investors, for instance, paid for their interests over five years. If an interest cost $50,000, each investor paid $10,000 the first year and signed a note for the rest. Cardinal then borrowed against the notes, leaving investors liable to the banks.

Now, if investors stop paying on their notes, those banks can go after them for the money still due. "A partnership is a contract, and it's enforceable," says Dale Ellis, a Houston bankruptcy attorney. There may be adverse tax consequences as well.

But investment advisers say there are other options. In small private syndications, for instance, unhappy investors may be able to band together and replace the sponsor.

In larger partnerships, where organizing hundreds of investors is all but impossible, limited partners might file a class-action lawsuit against the sponsor "or anybody else within a radius of 25 miles who has money," says Robert Mills, president of a San Rafael, Calif., brokerage firm.

Some investors have received money back far more cheaply through arbitration. The option is open to anyone who buys partnership interests—in either public or private syndications—from a member of the National Association of Securities Dealers. Nearly all brokerage firms are members, as are some financial planners and partnership sponsors' sales organizations.

"If you've got a great case and rich defendants, a class-action suit is undoubtedly the way to go," says David M. Greenberg, a San Francisco lawyer formerly with the Securities and Exchange Commission. "But if you aren't in that rather narrow category, you ought to go the arbitration route."

Those proceedings, conducted by the National Association of Securities Dealers, resolve most disputes in less than a year. Investors pay filing fees ranging from $15 to a maximum of $1,000 for claims of $500,000, or more.

Source: Neil Barsky and Jill Bettner, "In Partnerships, Who Shares Problems?," *The Wall Street Journal,* May 26, 1989, p. C19.

suitability rule
*a rule excluding in-
vestors who cannot
bear a high amount
of risk from buying
limited partnership
interests.*

excluding certain types of investors is called a **suitability rule.** It's purpose is to
allow only investors who can bear a high amount of risk to participate. Additionally, there is usually a statement in the prospectus that says: ''The securities offered
herewith are very high risk.'' Believe this statement; if the regulatory authorities
require it, it must be a high-risk investment. Suitability rules vary, depending on
applicable state and federal laws. The rules are intended to prevent the sale of
high-risk projects to investors who cannot sustain the loss financially. Suitability
requirements are also usually fairly rigid for public limited partnerships (offerings
registered with securities regulators).

SUMMARY

- The federal tax law imposes higher tax burdens on higher taxable incomes.
  Taxable income can be either ordinary income—active (''earned''), portfolio,
  or passive—or capital gains or losses; both ordinary income and capital gains
  are subject to the same schedule of tax rates.

- Taxable income is calculated using a sequence of steps. First, gross income,
  which includes all forms of income with some exceptions, is calculated. After
  subtracting certain adjustments to gross income, adjusted gross income results.
  Subtracting itemized deductions and exemptions results in taxable income from
  which federal income taxes are calculated. Taxes due are found by subtracting
  any eligible tax credits from the federal income tax.

- Tax-avoidance strategies attempt to earn tax-favored income, which is essentially income not subject to taxes. Tax-deferral strategies attempt to defer taxes
  from current periods to later periods. A tax shelter is an investment vehicle that
  earns a portion of its return by offering potential offsets to the investor's other
  taxable income.

- The major forms of tax-favored income are tax-free municipal bond interest,
  Treasury and government agency issues (free of state and local income taxes),
  and the sale of a personal residence.

- Techniques often used to defer tax liabilities to the next year are (1) a short sale
  against the box, (2) a put hedge, and (3) selling a deep-in-the-money call
  option. Each of these has relative advantages and disadvantages, depending on
  the assumed future movement of the stock's price.

- Popular strategies that trade current for capital gains income are (1) buying
  growth rather than income stocks, (2) buying deep discount bonds, and (3) investing in income property. Tax swaps provide a strategy that can be used to
  reduce or eliminate a tax liability without altering the basic portfolio.

- Because they pay relatively high market rates of interest and allow for tax-free
  reinvestment, deferred annuities have some appeal as a tax-deferral vehicle.
  Their principal advantage is that income earned on them is not taxed in the year
  earned, but rather as the earnings are withdrawn from the annuity.

- Tax-sheltered annuities can be purchased by employees of certain institutions

by making limited tax-free contributions from current income. Annuity payouts can be either fixed or variable; the payouts on variable annuities depend on the insurer's investment performance.

- Deferred annuities are relatively low-risk vehicles that may not produce earnings on a par with inflation rates; therefore investors should determine by analysis whether they are suitable. The single-premium life insurance policy, in the past a popular alternative to the deferred annuity, has recently diminished in popularity due to tax law changes that virtually eliminated the ability to use policy loans to make tax-free withdrawals.

- A limited partnership is an organizational form that allows an individual to invest passively with limited liability, receiving the benefit of professional management, and apply the resulting profit or loss (subject to limits) when calculating his or her tax liability. The return from a limited partnership comes from either cash flow or price appreciation. Limited partnerships have been formed to acquire many different kinds of assets, but the most common are real estate, energy resources, and equipment for leasing purposes.

- Limited partnerships can be structured as private or public partnerships. Leverage can increase the potential earnings as well as the risk in a limited partnership. Potential investors should study the offering circular or prospectus for a limited partnership in order to carefully examine the investment's risk-return characteristics and hence its suitability. Often investors themselves must meet certain suitability rules prior to investing in a limited partnership.

REVIEW QUESTIONS AND PROBLEMS

1. Using Table 15.1, calculate Ed Robinson's income tax due on his $30,000 taxable income, assuming he files as a single taxpayer. After you make the calculation, explain to Ed what his marginal tax rate is and why it is important in making investment decisions.

2. What is a capital asset? Explain how capital asset transactions are taxed, and compare their treatment to that of ordinary income.

 3. Sheila and Jim Mendez reported the following income tax items in 1990:

Salaries and wages	$30,000
Interest on bonds	1,100*
Dividends (jointly owned stocks)	1,000
Capital gains on securities	1,500
Deductible IRA contribution	2,000
Itemized deductions	8,000

*$400 of this total was received from tax-free minicipal bonds.

If Sheila and Jim claim three dependents and file a joint return for 1990, calculate their income tax due.

4. How does tax avoidance differ from tax deferral? Explain if either of these is a form of tax evasion. Is either the same thing as a tax shelter?

5. Identify and briefly discuss sources of tax-favored income.

6. What is the tax-shelter aspect of a personal residence with respect to capital gains? Explain.

7. Explain conditions that favor the following strategies for deferring tax liabilities to the next year: (a) a short sale against the box; (b) a put hedge; and (c) selling a deep-in-the-money call option. When is it best simply to hold the stock and do nothing?

8. Shawn Healy bought 300 shares of Apple Computer common stock at $32 a share. Fifteen months later, in December, Apple was up to $47 a share and Shawn was considering selling her shares since she believed Apple's price could drop as low as $42 within the next several months. What advice would you offer Shawn for locking in the gain and deferring the tax to the following year? Explain.

9. Briefly describe each of the following strategies that trade current for capital gains income:

    a. Growth stocks.
    b. Deep discount bonds.
    c. Income property depreciation.

10. Describe how a tax swap can be used to reduce or eliminate a tax liability without significantly altering the composition of one's portfolio.

11. Define an annuity, explain the role it might play in an investment portfolio, and differentiate between:

    a. Single-premium and installment annuities.
    b. Immediate and deferred annuities.
    c. Fixed and variable annuities.

12. Define the following terms as they relate to deferred annuities: (1) current interest rate; (2) minimum guaranteed interest rate; (3) investment payout; and (4) withdrawal provisions and penalties.

13. Explain how a deferred annuity works as a tax shelter. How does a tax-sheltered annuity work, and who is eligible to purchase one? Discuss whether a deferred annuity is a better tax shelter than an IRA.

14. What is single-premium life insurance (SPLI)? Describe the basic features of SPLI, compare it to the single-premium deferred annuity (SPDA), and explain why the popularity of SPLI has recently diminished.

15. How does a limited partnership (LP) differ from a general partnership and a corporation? What are the functions of the general and limited partners? How did the Tax Reform Act of 1986 affect the popularity of LPs as tax shelters? Explain.

16. In which two ways can an investor earn a return from a limited partnership? Explain.

17. What are the popular forms of limited partnerships? Differentiate between private partnerships and public partnerships.

18. How does leverage affect the risk and return of a limited partnership? What are suitability rules, and why must they be met by limited-partnership investors?

19. A friend of yours wants you and several other individuals to invest in an equipment-leasing partnership. You and the other partners will buy a computer and then lease it to a local

concern. Explain the potential risk-return factors you would consider in your analysis of this proposed investment.

CASE PROBLEMS

15.1 Tax Planning for the Wilsons

Hal and Terri Wilson had most of their funds invested in common stock in the spring of 1989. The Wilsons didn't really do very much investment planning, and they had practically no background or understanding of how income taxes might affect their investment decisions. Their holdings consisted exclusively of common stocks selected primarily on the advice of their stockbroker, Sid Nichols. In spite of a relatively lackluster market they did experience some nice capital gains, even though several of their holdings showed losses from their original purchase prices. A summary of their holdings on December 20, 1989, appears below.

Stock	Date Purchased	Original Cost	Current Market Value
Consolidated Power and Light	2/10/87	$10,000	$16,000
Cargon Industries	7/7/89	3,000	8,000
PYT Corporation	6/29/89	7,000	6,000
Amalgamated Iron & Steel	8/9/88	8,000	5,000
Jones Building Supplies	3/6/85	4,500	4,700

Hal feels this might be a good time to revise their portfolio, and he favors selling all their holdings and reinvesting the funds in several growth-oriented mutual funds and perhaps several real estate limited partnerships. Terri agrees their portfolio could use some revision, but she is reluctant to sell everything; for one thing, she is concerned that federal income taxes might take a sizable share of their profits. In addition, she strongly believes Amalgamated Iron & Steel will make a significant recovery, as will all steel stocks, in 1990.

After some discussion, the Wilsons decided to consult their friend, Elaine Byer, who was a CPA for a major public accounting firm. Byer indicated that she was not an expert in the investment field and therefore couldn't tell the Wilsons which securities to buy or sell from that perspective. From a tax point of view, however, she did not recommend selling everything in the 1989 tax year. Instead, she said that Consolidated Power and Light, PYT Corporation, Amalgamated Iron & Steel, and Jones Building Supplies should be sold in December of 1989, but that Cargon Industries should be carried into 1990 and sold then—if that was what the Wilsons wanted to do.

Hal and Terri were grateful for Byer's advice, but they had two major concerns. First, they were a little concerned about waiting to sell Cargon Industries, since it had showed such a sizable gain and they were afraid its price might decline sharply in a stock market selloff. Secondly, they were reluctant to sell Amalgamated Iron & Steel in spite of the benefit of its tax loss, since they wanted to remain invested in the steel industry over the long run. As a final step they contacted Nichols, their stockbroker, who agreed with Byer's advice; he said not to worry about the Cargon situation. The stock was selling at $80 a share, and he would put in a short-against-the-box for them, which would enable them to deliver the shares whenever they wanted. He also explained that they could use a tax swap in order to get the tax

benefit of the loss on Amalgamated Iron & Steel while staying invested in the steel industry. He suggested United States Iron as a swap candidate since it was selling for about the same price as Amalgamated.

Questions

1. Assuming the Wilsons are in the 28 percent tax bracket, calculate the resulting federal income tax: (a) If they sold all their securities in 1989 at their current market values; and (b) if they sold Consolidated Power and Light, PYT Corporation, Amalgamated Iron & Steel, and Jones Building Supplies at their respective market values in 1989, and then sold Cargon Industries at its current market value on January 2, 1990. What do you conclude from your calculations?

2. As noted, Nichols suggested a short sale against the box for Cargon. Explain his reasoning about the future price of this stock.

3. Suppose you thought Cargon had a good possibility for further price increases in 1990, but you were equally concerned that its price could fall sharply. Would you then agree with the strategy Nichols recommended, or would you prefer a different strategy? Explain your answer.

4. Discuss the tax swap suggested by Nichols. Does this strategy allow the Wilsons to minimize taxes while retaining their position in the steel industry? Explain.

5. What overall strategies would you recommend to the Wilsons, given their investment objectives and tax status? Explain.

15.2 Do Oil and Fred Cranston Mix?

Fred Cranston, age 36, is the West Coast marketing manager and vice-president of a major auto parts supply firm. His salary reflects his success in his job: $90,000 per year. Additionally his firm provides him with a car, an excellent pension and profit-sharing plan, superior life and medical insurance coverage, and company stock options. Fred owns his home, which is located in the exclusive Marin County, California, area.

In addition to Fred's house and his pension and profit-sharing plans, he has a stock portfolio worth about $75,000, a tax-free municipal bond portfolio valued at $150,000, and about $100,000 in a highly liquid money market mutual fund. Fred would like to make some more risky investments in order to increase his returns. He is considering taking $50,000 out of the money market mutual fund and investing in some limited partnerships. His broker, Marie Bell, has proposed that he invest $50,000 divided among five oil and gas limited partnerships. Marie's specific recommendation is to buy two developmental and three income programs, each for $10,000. She explained to Fred that this $50,000 investment could potentially increase his income by $20,000 per year. Marie has also pointed out that if the expected rise in oil prices occurs, Fred could expect to receive even larger cash returns in future years. Fred meets the suitability rules required for such investments as prescribed by the securities commission of California. Being a relatively conservative individual, he is trying to justify in his mind the reasonableness of his broker's recommendations.

Questions

1. What do you think of Marie Bell's investment recommendations for Fred? Are developmental programs too risky? Should Fred buy five different oil and gas programs, or should he invest the entire $50,000 in one program? Explain.

2. How would you describe the legal structure of a limited partnership to Fred? What should Fred know about the general partner in each of these programs?

3. In general, does investment in oil and gas development and income programs make sense to you? Why, or why not?

4. What other forms of limited partnerships might you suggest that Fred consider? Discuss the leverage and risk-return tradeoffs involved in them.

SELECTED READINGS

"Annuities." *Consumer Reports,* January 1988, pp. 35–44.

Eisenberg, Richard. "Your Life as a Tax Shelter." *Money,* March 1987, pp. 153–65.

Friedman, Amy. "A New Deal for RELPs." *Financial Services Week,* April 24, 1989, pp. 25–28.

McCormally, Kevin. "Pigging Out on Tax Shelters." *Changing Times,* June 1989, pp. 45–52.

Ross, Brandon. "Annuities: A Special Supplement." *Changing Times,* March 1989.

Sachar, Laura. "Testing the Limits in Limited Partnerships." *Financial World,* July 12, 1988, pp. 30–33.

Scott, Maria Crawford. "Comparing Variable Annuities: New Fee Tables Ease the Way." *AAII Journal,* May 1989, pp. 13–15.

Topolnicki, Denise M. "How to Tell If an Immediate Annuity Makes Sense for You." *Money,* May 1989, pp. 183–84.

Trotsky, Judith. "Hooray for Hollywood?" *Changing Times,* November 1988, pp. 47–50.

Wiener, Leonard. "IRS Traps for the Unwary Home Seller." *U.S. News & World Report,* May 22, 1989, p. 79.

COMPUTER-BASED INVESTMENT MANAGEMENT: MUTUAL FUNDS AND REAL ESTATE

One of the problems initially experienced by novice investors is insufficient cash to make investments that effectively meet their risk and return criteria and contribute toward achievement of their financial goals. They could, of course, purchase a single investment vehicle, but the lack of diversification would leave them exposed to more risk than they desire. Alternatively they could simply place their money in federally insured savings accounts or certificates of deposit and forgo the potentially higher returns offered by other investment vehicles. Fortunately mutual funds, real estate investment opportunities, and various types of limited partnerships that require smaller initial cash investments and better serve the risk and return requirements of the investors are available. With these investment vehicles comes the need for more specific and better analytical tools the investor can use to select the particular vehicle that not only best fits his or her budget, but also results in the achievement of his or her personal financial goals. The programs listed below may be of help in this area.

- *Ardvark Investment Planner* (CYMA/McGraw-Hill, 1400 E. Southern Avenue, Tempe, AZ 85282; (602) 831-2607; $495.00; IBM PCs and compatibles.) Analyzes both real estate and limited partnership investments under current tax law. Can be purchased with both functions or with only limited partnership analysis. Real estate module evaluates existing and proposed real estate investments; calculates depreciation, debt amortization, net operating income, taxable income, net proceeds on sale, and rates of return. The limited partnership module analyzes projections from a prospectus and tracks the performance of currently held partnerships by combining historical with projected data. Calculations include the effect on cash flow, net present value, and rates of return.
- *Business Week Mutual Fund Scoreboard Diskettes* (Business Week Mutual Fund Scoreboard, P.O. Box 621, Elk Grove, IL 60009-0621; (800) 533-3575

or (312) 250-9292; $149.95 for either Equity Funds or Fixed-Income Funds Diskette; $293.99 for both; IBM PCs and compatibles.) Self-contained screening tools for over 700 equity and 500 fixed-income mutual funds. Menu-driven programs can be used to search and rank funds meeting specific investment objectives. Fund data, which includes name, ticker symbol, fees, objective, performance figures, portfolio data including weighted maturity in years, risk level, and beta, are updated quarterly.

- *Financial Pak* (Generic Computer Products, Inc., 190 Timber, Dept. #50-E, P.O. Box 790, Marquette, MI 49855-0790; (906) 249-9801; $149.95; IBM PCs and compatibles.) This software is for mutual fund analysis, stock investments, loan amortizations, and annuity investments. Mutual fund portion of package provides buy/sell advice on an average-cost basis. Loan amortization module handles all types of loan situations. Annuity portion provides information about lump sum and annuity investments and handles periodic savings plans, mutual funds, and IRA accounts.

- *Fundgraf* (Parsons Software, 1230 W. 6th Street, Loveland, CO 80537; (303) 669-3744; $100; IBM PCs and compatibles.) This package is for mutual fund stock investment analysis. Allows graphic and/or numerical comparisons of any stock or fund for any period up to 260 weeks. Accesses Warner Computer Systems Price Dividend (WCSPD) data for the past 5 years. Reports buy/sell signals based on relationship of moving average (user's choice of weeks used) and current price action. User can evaluate and select periods of advancing and declining prices to optimize trading profits. System consists of eight operational programs: (1) ADD-DATA; (2) GRAPHS; (3) SIGNALS; (4) RATING (calculates rating for each fund in file); (5) MOVG-AVG (calculates and prints moving average buy/sell signals); (6) PRINTOUT (creates listing of price data in files); (7) SHIFTDAT (allows user to move data from one file to another); and (8) ADD-NAME (adds, changes, or deletes names or groups of names from files).

- *The Mutual Fund Investor* (American River Software, 1523 Kingsford Drive, Carmichael, CA 95608; (916) 483-1600; $195; IBM PCs and compatibles.) This program permits the checking of a fund's progress every week or so. The program can at any time accept information on fund prices, dividends, and other distributions. Data may be entered manually, electronically via modem link to an on-line database available through CompuServe, or can be transferred to and from another program. The program can also be used to compare a fund's performance graphically with that of other funds and with the Standard & Poor's 500. It can be used to chart a simple moving average of a fund's closing prices and provides limited portfolio management capabilities.

- *Real Estate Analysis Package* (Execuware Inc., 340 Westgate Center Circle, Winston-Salem, NC 27103; (919) 760-3576; $149.95; IBM PCs and compatibles or Apple II series.) Performs income analysis for properties, calculates after-tax results, highlights tax sheltering effects, considers inflation factors, and can be used to make buy, hold, or sell decisions. Uses the Rule of 78s,

ACRS depreciation methods, and various loan scenarios to provide up to 20-year projections.

- *REMS Investor 2000* (REMS Software, 3860 159th Avenue NE, Suite 110, Redmond, WA 98052; (206) 883-7000; $395.00; IBM PCs and compatibles or Macintosh.) Performs detained multi-year analysis of the before- and after-tax cash flows and rates of return from any type of improved real estate. Offers 11 different loan types, 12 depreciation methods, and allows parameters to vary. Program computes return on investment, return on equity, internal rate of return, and financial management rate of return and has sensitivity analysis capabilities.

NOTE: The above list of programs should be viewed as illustrative in nature, and *not* interpreted as an endorsement or recommendation. Listed prices and phone numbers are the latest available and are, of course, subject to change without notice.

SIX

INVESTMENT ADMINISTRATION

THE INVESTMENT ENVIRONMENT

INVESTMENT ADMINISTRATION

INVESTING IN COMMON STOCK	INVESTING IN FIXED-INCOME SECURITIES
SPECULATIVE INVESTMENT VEHICLES	OTHER POPULAR INVESTMENT VEHICLES

16

PORTFOLIO MANAGEMENT

After studying this chapter you should be able to:

- Understand the objectives of portfolio management, including risk and diversification and the concept of an efficient portfolio.

- Discuss portfolio versus individual security risk and return, and vehicles that are candidates for inclusion in a portfolio.

- Describe the two basic approaches to portfolio management—traditional management versus the modern approach.

- Explain the relationship among investor characteristics, investor objectives, and portfolio objectives and policies.

- Summarize the motives and procedures involved in developing an asset allocation scheme consistent with the investor's portfolio objectives.

- Relate investor objectives to the risk-return profiles reflected in various types of portfolios.

In order to combine various types of investment vehicles in a fashion consistent with his or her overall disposition toward risk and return, an investor needs to understand portfolio management. The input to a portfolio is the risk-return characteristics of the individual investment vehicles, and the output is the risk-return behavior of the portfolio. Investment vehicles can be combined to create a portfolio that has a more desirable risk-return behavior than the individual securities alone. The selection of investment vehicles to be added to a portfolio in order to achieve favorable results is best accomplished using certain analytical procedures. The body of knowledge relating to the creation of portfolios that provide the best risk-return tradeoffs is quite extensive, and it is also based on complex mathematical concepts. So here we will emphasize only general principles and simple approaches that will allow an investor to develop a basic understanding of the portfolio management process. This chapter presents the basic principles and practices involved in developing and managing an investment portfolio and includes an analysis of four typical portfolios.

portfolio
a collection of investment vehicles assembled to meet a common investment goal.

growth-oriented portfolio
a portfolio whose primary objective is long-term price appreciation.

PRINCIPLES OF PORTFOLIO MANAGEMENT

income-oriented portfolio
a portfolio that stresses current dividend and interest return.

Although we have not defined it earlier, it should be clear by now that a **portfolio** is a collection of investment vehicles assembled to meet a common investment goal. Several terms regarding portfolio objectives should be clarified at this point. A **growth-oriented portfolio**'s primary orientation is long-term price appreciation. An **income-oriented portfolio** stresses current dividend and interest return.

Portfolio Objectives

The first step for the investor is to establish portfolio objectives. Setting these objectives involves definite tradeoffs between risk and return, between potential price appreciation and current income, and between varying risk levels in the portfolio. The factors involved in the portfolio objective decisions include the investor's ability to bear risk, current income needs, and income tax bracket. The key point is that the portfolio objectives must be established *before* beginning to invest. Two concepts that are especially important to successful portfolio management are the effects on risk from diversification and the concept of an efficient portfolio.

diversification
the use of a variety of noncomplementary investment vehicles for the purpose of reducing risk.

Risk and Diversification

Normally a portfolio will contain two or more investments and will strive for **diversification,** which involves the inclusion of a variety of noncomplementary investment vehicles for the purpose of reducing risk. Portfolios are diversified to reduce risk of loss while meeting the investor's return objective.

diversifiable risk
the risk unique to a particular investment vehicle, which can be eliminated through diversification.

Types of Risk. A portfolio can become a risk-reduction vehicle because any investment vehicle possesses two basic types of risk. (See Chapter 5 for a detailed discussion of risk.) When a vehicle is acquired, an investor bears both diversifiable (or unsystematic) and nondiversifiable (or systematic) risk. **Diversifiable risk** is the risk unique to a particular investment vehicle—its business and financial risk. **Nondiversifiable risk** is the risk possessed by every investment vehicle. For instance, the risk that general market movements will alter a particular security's

nondiversifiable risk
the risk possessed by every investment vehicle and therefore not capable of being eliminated through diversification.

return is nondiversifiable risk. As we will see, the investor can reduce only *diversifiable* risk through portfolio management.

A great deal of research has been conducted on the topic of risk as it relates to security investments. The results show that in general *investors earn higher rates of return by buying riskier investments;* that is, *to earn more return, one must bear more risk.* More startling, however, are research results that show that only with nondiversifiable risk is there a positive risk-return relationship. High levels of diversifiable risk do not result in correspondingly high levels of return. Because there is no reward for bearing diversifiable risk, an investor should minimize this form of risk in the portfolio. This can be done by diversifying the portfolio so that the only type of risk remaining is nondiversifiable.

Risk Diversification. Diversification minimizes diversifiable risk because of a balancing effort that tends to cause the poor return of one vehicle to be offset by the good return on another. Minimizing diversifiable risk through careful selection of investment vehicles requires that the vehicles chosen for the portfolio come from a wide range of industries. A properly diversified portfolio contains investment vehicles from two or more unrelated industries. For example, a portfolio containing only Ford, General Motors, and Chrysler stocks is obviously not well diversified, because these three companies have similar business and financial risks. In contrast, a portfolio consisting of International Business Machines, General Motors, and General Mills is diversified. (The cyclical changes in the automobile industry will probably not affect the fortunes of IBM or General Mills.) If one company in this three-stock portfolio does poorly, the other two may do well.

Given that diversification is necessary to minimize diversifiable risk, how many investment vehicles are needed in a portfolio to achieve adequate diversification? Figure 16.1 depicts the two types of risk as they relate to the number of securities in the portfolio. It can be seen that the level of nondiversifiable risk remains constant in the portfolio regardless of the number of securities. Diversifiable risk declines markedly, however, as the number of securities in the portfolio rises. If 8 to 20 securities are included, much of the diversifiable risk is eliminated. Once the number of securities in the portfolio exceeds 20, the risk-reduction effect of increasing the number of issues in the portfolio is limited. Also plotted in Figure 16.1 is **total risk,** the sum of the diversifiable and nondiversifiable risk components. Because an investor can reduce total risk by reducing diversifiable risk, the only really **relevant risk** is that which is nondiversifiable.

In choosing the ideal number of securities for a portfolio, two factors should be considered. First, somewhere between 8 and 20 issues are needed to reduce diversifiable risk substantially. Second, transaction costs must be considered if further diversification is desired. One must balance the transaction costs of a portfolio of 25 to 30 issues with the resulting risk-reduction benefits.

total risk
the sum of the diversifiable and nondiversifiable risk components of an investment vehicle.

relevant risk
risk that is nondiversifiable.

efficient portfolio
a portfolio that provides the highest return for a given level of risk, or that has the lowest risk for a given level of return.

An Efficient Portfolio

The ultimate goal of an investor is the creation of an **efficient portfolio,** one that provides the highest return for a given level of risk, or has the lowest risk for a given

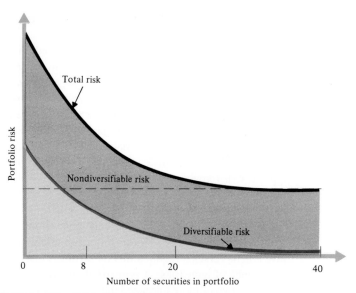

FIGURE 16.1 The Risk Diversification Process.
By including 8 to 20 securities in a portfolio, the diversifiable risk can be nearly eliminated so that the total, or relevant, risk of the portfolio is its nondiversifiable risk. The diversifiable risk can be eliminated even through the random selection of the 8 to 20 securities to be included in the portfolio.

level of return. Although it may be difficult to create such a portfolio, an investor should at least search out reasonable investment alternatives to get the best combinations of risk and return. Thus, when given the choice between two equally risky investments offering different returns, the investor would be expected to choose the alternative with the highest return; likewise, given two investment vehicles offering the same returns but differing in risk, the *risk-averse* investor would prefer the vehicle with the lower risk. In pursuing the creation of an efficient portfolio, the investor should be able to create the best portfolio possible given his or her disposition toward risk and the alternative investment vehicles available.

Portfolio versus Individual Security Risk and Return

From the preceding discussion it should be clear that the risk and return of an individual security depends upon whether or not the security is viewed in isolation or as part of a portfolio. Holding securities in a portfolio allows risk to be diversified in such a way that the greater the difference in the return behaviors of the two securities, the greater the risk-reduction achieved through diversification. For the sake of demonstration, assume that two very differently behaving but equally priced securities—A and B—having individual risk levels of 5 and 10, respectively, are combined to create portfolio AB. The risk resulting from this combination can be less than 5, and under perfect conditions it can be reduced to zero. Clearly, due to

the power of diversification the risk of securities held individually is always greater than their risk when held in a portfolio—in essence, this is a case where 2 plus 2 will amount to *less* than 4. A security's risk therefore is *always less* when viewed in a portfolio context than in isolation. In fact if the returns on two securities fluctuate by equal amounts in exactly opposite directions, the return of the portfolio created by combining them would be stable. As noted in the discussion of beta in Chapter 5, each security has its own unique risk; although the contribution of a given security to the risk of a portfolio depends on this behavior, it is *never greater* than its risk when held in isolation.

Looking at the other side of the coin, how are returns affected by viewing a security as part of a portfolio rather than in isolation? Interestingly, while risk is reduced through diversification, return is *unaffected* by this process. In other words, the return earned by a given security is the same regardless of whether it is held in isolation or in a portfolio. For example, let's assume that the returns on securities A and B are 8 percent and 12 percent, respectively. If portfolio AB is created consisting of one share of each, the return on the portfolio would be 10 percent, since the portfolio includes 50 percent of security A and 50 percent of security B: [(.50 × 8%) + (.50 × 12%) = 10%]. From this simple equation we can see that the returns of the securities are functionally unchanged whether operating individually or in a portfolio context. Thus the return of the portfolio as a whole is merely a weighted average of the returns of the securities within it. In summary, since an asset's risk in a portfolio is lower than its individual risk, while its return remains unaffected, it is apparent that risk can be reduced by portfolio diversification *without ever sacrificing return.* For this reason investors should diversify whenever possible. Diversification does not have to be limited to strictly domestic investment vehicles; global investing may be attractive for any of a number of reasons noted in the Investor Insights box on pages 700 and 701.

A Complete Investment Portfolio

Most of the discussion in this chapter centers on the management of securities portfolios; that is, the primary focus is on stock and bond investments. But true diversification would include other investment vehicles such as options, commodities and financial futures, tangibles, real estate, annuities, or limited partnerships. Table 16.1 on page 702 presents the balance sheet of Mike and Debby Grogan, a married couple with two children. Mr. and Mrs. Grogan are 34 and 30, respectively. Mike is the vice-president of a small company located in the rural farming community of Munger, Michigan, and earns $40,000 per year. Looking at their balance sheet, it can be seen that the Grogans' total asset mix consists of cash, a money market account, stocks, bonds, a land contract—a debt owed them on property they recently sold, their home, investment real estate, and the cash value of a life insurance policy. Not included in the statement are such items as automobiles and home furnishings, which are not normally considered investment assets. (Had the Grogans been antique car buffs or furniture collectors, these items would have been added to the statement.)

In the Grogan portfolio a diversity of asset holdings is found. A life insurance

INVESTOR INSIGHTS

The Case for Global Diversification

Americans marveling at the stock market's hearty climb might be surprised to learn that the U.S. was actually among the worst places to invest in stocks during the past five years. Measured by a Morgan Stanley index, the U.S. stock market has gone up about 280% since mid-1982. That's nothing to complain about, but on nearly every major exchange outside the U.S. a potent combination of low interest rates, pro-business government policies, and a declining dollar has helped lift stocks far higher: about 500% in Sweden, more than 700% in Japan, and nearly 900% in Mexico. These are the gains to U.S. investors. If you buy a foreign stock with dollars and that country's currency rises against the dollar, you get a bonus when you sell.

Until a few years ago, Americans tended to be unadventurous about investing in foreign stocks, but the big gains abroad have made them take notice. Last year [1987], according to the U.S. Treasury Department, American investors bought a record $51.7 billion of non-U.S. stocks, more than twice as much as the year before and 30 times as much as in 1975. Much of that growth has been fueled by pension funds. Their holdings of foreign stocks have vaulted from an estimated $3.3 billion in 1980 to around $45 billion by the end of last year.

Don't mortgage the house, though. With many markets now at lofty levels and interest rates edging higher in many countries, few investment pros expect big gains in the next year. Says Gilbert de Botton, chairman of Global Asset Management, a London-based mutual fund group: "This is no longer the dawn of a beautiful day. We are into the afternoon."

Still, de Botton and many other money managers say it makes sense for Americans to buy foreign stocks. Three reasons:

- You get a broader choice of securities.

policy ($100,000) on Mike Grogan is provided for the protection of the family. The children in the family are young, and this level of life insurance protection is needed to help ensure their future needs. The Grogans have wisely set aside funds in a money market account as a source of cash in case of emergency or for an attractive investment opportunity. Life insurance and a money market account provide the family with basic financial security and liquidity. The Grogans have two fixed-income investments: two tax-free municipal bonds worth $5,000 each, and a land contract worth $25,000. The municipal bonds were issued by the Munger Unified School District, and they provide the Grogans with a low-risk, tax-free investment return. This portion of their investment program, then, provides a steady source of secure income.

The Grogans own their own home, although there is a $70,000 mortgage payable on it over the next 24 years. The Grogans' investments also include a portfolio of stocks worth $40,000 and some investment real estate worth $46,000. The latter has a $30,000 mortgage on it, so the Grogans' equity in that property is $16,000. The

- You reduce risk through diversification.
- You participate in the fast growth of other economies.

These benefits are borne out by a study conducted for *Fortune* by InterSec Research Corp., a Connecticut firm that advises pension funds on foreign investing. Adding foreign stocks to a portfolio increased the return. Up to a point, it also reduced the risk, as measured by price volatility. But the portfolio with the least risk of all was a mix of 60% U.S. and 40% foreign stocks. . . .

If you are game to send capital abroad, the simplest route is a mutual fund that invests in foreign stocks. If you want to buy shares of individual companies, investment strategists suggest diversifying among at least ten stocks. But that can get expensive: Most U.S. brokers do not handle foreign-stock transactions of less than $10,000. Moreover, settling trades, getting delivery of shares, and following daily moves in prices can be considerably more difficult than with U.S. stocks.

For these reasons, the preferred securities—even among professional investors—are American Depositary Receipts. ADRs have no minimum purchase requirements. They are issued by American banks and represent actual shares held in escrow. ADRs of some 700 foreign companies from more than 15 countries trade on major U.S. exchanges and over the counter. All major brokerages follow the larger ADRs.

When it comes to picking stocks, many pros take a rifle-shot approach, trying to identify companies with particular pluses—such as a great new product. But in many foreign stock markets, where publicly available information is less plentiful than in the U.S. and insider trading is more so, an individual American investor will probably be the last to know. A "top-down" approach, which involves trying to identify the most promising national economies, may prove more successful. For those who adopt this strategy, some investment advisers recommend banks and utilities, which typically benefit from a general economic upturn. . . .

Source: John Mendes, "Are You Ready to Go Global?," *Fortune/1988 Investor's Guide,* pp. 71–78.

stock portfolio provides the Grogans with capital growth potential and is a relatively liquid asset. The investment property, a duplex rental unit, was acquired because of its long-term price appreciation potential and as a source of tax-sheltered income (since, as required, they actively manage the property). The Grogan portfolio seems to be an effective one: First, the financial foundation of life insurance and a money market account is included for basic protection; and second, the remaining assets, which consists of a diversified group of stocks, fixed-income securities, and real estate, provide investment income and the potential for capital appreciation.

TRADITIONAL PORTFOLIO MANAGEMENT VERSUS MODERN PORTFOLIO THEORY

In this section the two approaches currently in use by portfolio managers are compared and contrasted. The traditional approach refers to the methods money managers have been using since the evolution of the public securities markets. Modern portfolio theory (MPT) is a more recent development. The theory behind this ap-

TABLE 16.1 Mike and Debby Grogan's Balance Sheet

Assets		Liabilities and Net Worth	
Cash and money market account	$ 16,000	Short-term liabilities	$ 1,000
		Home mortgage	70,000
Stocks	40,000	Investment real estate mortgage	30,000
Municipal bonds (tax-free)	10,000		
Land contract	25,000	Net worth	134,000
Home	95,000	Total	$235,000
Investment real estate	46,000		
Cash value of life insurance	3,000		
Total	$235,000		

proach has been developed only over the past twenty or so years, and it continues to grow in popularity and acceptance. Some MPT concepts are indirectly used by practitioners of the traditional approach, yet there are major differences between the two.

The Traditional Approach

traditional portfolio management
an approach to portfolio management that emphasizes balancing the portfolio with a variety of stocks and/or bonds from a broad cross-section of industries.

Traditional portfolio management emphasizes "balancing" the portfolio. The traditional portfolio manager assembles a wide variety of stocks and/or bonds within the portfolio. The typical emphasis is interindustry diversification, which means that securities of companies from a broad cross-section of American industry are represented in the portfolio. Most institutional portfolio managers utilize the security analysis techniques discussed in Chapters 7 and 8 when they select individual securities for the traditional portfolio. Figure 16.2 on pages 704 and 705 presents the portfolio of a typical mutual fund that is managed by professionals using the traditional approach. This fund, the Prudential-Bache FlexiFund Aggressively Managed Portfolio, is an open-end 12(b)-1 (no initial load) mutual fund. The portfolio is valued at approximately $56 million as of July 31, 1988. Its objective is to provide investors with long-term capital growth and income by investing in high-quality stocks, debt obligations, and money market instruments. The FlexiFund Aggressively Managed Portfolio holds shares of 190 different stocks from 35 industries, 20 debt obligations, and 20 money market instruments.

Analyzing the stock portion of the FlexiFund Aggressively Managed Portfolio, which accounts for approximately 43 percent of the fund's total assets, we can observe the traditional approach to portfolio management at work. This fund holds a variety of stocks from a diverse cross-section of the total universe of available stocks. It should be noted, however, that most of the fund's stocks represent large American corporations. The fund's largest holding is IBM, the largest manufacturer of business machines. The second largest holding is Seagram Co. Ltd., a large distiller. The IBM holding represents approximately 1.6 percent of the total portfo-

lio, and the Seagram position is about 1.5 percent of the portfolio's total market value.

Traditional portfolio managers like to invest in well-known companies for three reasons. First, these companies have been and probably will continue to be successful business enterprises. Investing in the securities of large, well-known companies is perceived as less risky than investing in lesser-known firms. A second reason professional managers prefer to invest in large companies is that the securities of these firms are more liquid and are available in large quantities. Managers of large portfolios invest substantial sums of money and need to acquire securities in large quantities to achieve an efficient order size. Traditional portfolio managers also prefer well-known companies for a third reason: It is easier to convince clients to invest in well-known corporations. "Window dressing," a Wall Street cliché, refers to the practice of many investment managers of loading up portfolios with well-known stocks to make it easier to sell their management services to their clients.

modern portfolio theory
an approach to portfolio management that uses statistical measures to develop portfolio strategy.

variance
a statistical measure used to measure a security's return; calculated as the standard deviation squared.

Modern Portfolio Theory (MPT)

correlation
a statistical measure of the relationship, if any, between two series of data, such as that of an individual security's returns with the returns of the market as a whole.

positive correlation
a relationship between two series such that they move together.

negative correlation
a relationship between two series such that they move in opposite directions.

correlation coefficient
a statistical measure of the degree of correlation between two series, which ranges from +1 for perfectly positive correlation to −1 for perfectly negative correlation.

Harry Markowitz first developed the theories that form the basis of MPT during the 1950s, and many other scholars and investment experts have contributed in developing MPT to its present advanced stage. **Modern portfolio theory** utilizes several basic statistical measures to develop portfolio strategy. One such measure is the **variance** of a security's return, which is its standard deviation squared. Another is the *correlation* of an individual security's return with the return of another security or with the market as a whole. **Correlation** measures the relationship, if any, between series of numbers representing any kind of data, from sales data to security returns. If two series move in the same direction, they are **positively correlated;** if the series move in opposite directions they are **negatively correlated.** The degree of correlation is measured by the **correlation coefficient** which ranges from +1 for *perfectly positively correlated* series to −1 for *perfectly negatively correlated* series. Perfectly positively correlated series move exactly together, and perfectly negatively correlated series move in exactly opposite directions. Portfolio construction in an MPT sense places heavy emphasis on the correlation of returns from different securities.

Figure 16.3 on page 706 illustrates the relative correlation between securities' rates of returns for two portfolios (each consisting of two securities). The left graph shows the rate of return on two securities, X and Y, over time. There is obviously a strong *positive correlation* between these two securities' rates of return, since they move together. The right graph of Figure 16.3 plots the returns of securities X and Z. The rates of return of these two securities exhibit strong *negative correlation,* since they move in opposite directions. Diversification, according to MPT, is achieved by combining securities in a portfolio so that individual securities have negative (or low positive) correlations between each other's rates of return. Thus in choosing securities for an MPT portfolio, the statistical diversification—that is, negative (or low positive) return correlation—is the deciding factor. The portfolio

Prudential-Bache FlexiFund
AGGRESSIVELY MANAGED PORTFOLIO
Portfolio of Investments
July 31, 1988

Shares	Description	(Value)
	EQUITY SECURITIES—43.0%	
	Aerospace & Aircraft Mfg.—0.2%	
8,900	Avantek, Inc.*	$ 52,287
3,100	UNC Inc.	30,612
3,000	Wyman-Gordon Co.	48,000
		130,899
	Airlines—0.6%	
500	Alaska Air Group, Inc.	9,063
3,000	Delta Air Lines, Inc.	151,500
1,000	N.W.A., Inc.	46,875
3,000	USAir Group, Inc.	111,375
		318,813
	Aluminum—0.9%	
7,000	Alcan Aluminum Ltd.	215,250
5,000	Aluminum Company of America	264,375
		479,625
	Apparel—0.2%	
3,000	Angelica Corp.	76,500
1,600	Oshkosh B' Gosh, Inc.	32,800
		109,300
	Automobiles & Related—1.0%	
11,000	Echlin, Inc.	189,750
1,000	Federal-Mogul Corp.	42,750
500	General Motors Corp.	40,125
10,400	Ryder System Inc.	275,600
		548,225
	Chemicals—4.0%	
5,800	American Cyanamid Co.	292,175
200	Ausimont Compo, N.V.	7,175
2,000	Bamberger Polymers, Inc.*	25,000
7,300	Betz Laboratories, Inc.	361,350
6,000	Du Pont (E.I.) De Nemours & Co.	521,250
16,750	Learonal, Inc.	272,188
200	Loctite Corp	6,450
1,000	Morton Thiokol Inc.	40,500
16,000	Nalco Chemical Co.	592,000
100	Oakite Products, Inc.	4,125
2,300	Petrolite Corp.	57,500
400	Quaker Chemical Corp.	$ 8,400
1,000	Witco Corp.	36,000
		2,224,113
	Commercial Services—0.4%	
2,000	Nahsua Corp.	73,750
4,000	United Stationers, Inc.	84,000
4,000	Wackenhut Corp.	86,000
		243,750
	Computers & Related Equipment—2.5%	
3,000	AM International Inc.*	17,625
2,000	American Management Systems, Inc.*	29,500
300	Automatic Data Processing, Inc.	11,813
7,000	Convex Computer Corp.*	52,500
400	Duquesne Systems, Inc.*	7,100
2,000	Honeywell Inc.	128,250
7,000	International Business Machines Corp.	880,250
2,000	National Data Corp.	49,750
7,600	Seagate Technology*	84,550
5,000	Tellabs, Inc.*	73,750
13,000	Wicat Systems, Inc.*	32,500
		1,367,588

Shares	Description	(Value)
	Consumer Products—0.8%	
500	Engraph, Inc.	6,500
4,000	Gibson Greetings, Inc.	72,000
500	Helene Curtis Industries, Inc.	19,000
6,700	International Flavors & Fragrances, Inc.	339,188
		436,688
	Containers—0.2%	
2,000	Ball Corp.	59,000
2,600	Van Dorn Co.	46,150
		105,150
	Distributor/Industrial—0.2%	
4,000	Ametek, Inc.	58,000
2,625	Varlen Corp	59,719
		117,719
	Drugs & Health Care—2.6%	
2,300	Becton, Dickinson & Co.	$ 116,150
4,500	Durr-Fillauel Medical, Inc.	65,250
3,000	Johnson & Johnson	240,000
4,000	Lilly (Eli) & Co.	335,000
2,500	Medtronic, Inc.	199,375
1,000	Schering-Plough Corp.	52,875
7,000	Squibb Corp.	462,875
		1,471,525
	Electronics/Electric—4.4%	
6,500	AMP Inc.	301,438
5,500	Analog Devices, Inc.*	77,687
500	Baldor Electric Co.	12,937
1,600	CTS Corp.	41,600
4,000	Cubic Corp.	60,000
9,000	Emerson Electric Co.	274,500
1,700	Esterline Corp.*	26,350
4,100	Hewlett-Packard Co.	207,050
1,100	Insilco Corp.	21,862
5,500	Instron Corp.	70,125
200	Stocker & Yale Inc.	1,800
7,000	Tandy Corp.	305,375
3,000	Texas Instruments Inc.	130,500
6,000	Thomas & Betts Corp.	333,750
17,300	Varian Associates, Inc.	499,537
1,000	Veeco Instruments, Inc.	18,750
4,000	Zero Corp.	65,500
		2,448,761
	Energy—0.6%	
2,000	Chevron Corp.	97,000
1,500	Dresser Industries, Inc.	45,750
4,000	Questar Corp.	126,500
1,000	Texaco Inc.	47,500
500	Unocal Corp.	18,000
		334,750
	Financial Services—0.5%	
1,000	Crestar Financial Corp.	24,250
2,000	Dominion Bankshares Corp.	36,000
500	First Tennessee National Corp.	12,500
3,000	First Virginia Banks, Inc.	76,875
1,000	Marshall & Ilsley Corp.	$ 28,750
1,000	Mercantile Bankshares Corp.	37,750
1,000	Republic New York Corp.	44,875
		261,000
	Food & Beverages—3.8%	
8,000	Archer-Daniels-Midland Co.	164,000

Shares	Description	(Value)
1,500	Coca-Cola Bottling Co. Consolidated	49,125
5,000	Coca-Cola Enterprises, Inc.	70,000
1,000	Collins Foods Int'l., Inc.	14,375
4,300	Fleming Cos., Inc.	134,913
2,000	International Multifoods Corp.	65,000
2,000	Jerrico, Inc.	29,500
6,000	McCormick & Co., Inc.	149,250
2,000	Philip Morris Cos., Inc.	183,750
9,900	Pioneer Hi-Bred Int'l., Inc.	341,550
2,200	Rykoff-Sexton Inc.	62,150
15,000	Seagram Co. Ltd.	840,000
		2,103,613
	Gas Pipelines—1.0%	
3,600	Mitchell Energy & Dev. Corp.	36,450
6,100	Texas Eastern Corp.	158,600
12,000	Transco Energy Co.	382,500
		577,550
	Glass—0.7%	
4,500	Corning Glass Works	262,687
3,000	PPG Industries, Inc.	134,625
		397,312
	Hotel Management—0.3%	
4,000	Hilton Hotels Corp	191,000
	Insurance—0.3%	
45	Berkshire Hathaway Inc.*	195,750
	Leisure—0.2%	
2,000	Anthony Industries, Inc.	33,250
700	Harman International Industries, Inc.	11,462
1,400	Hasbro, Inc.	22,925
9,000	View-Master Ideal Group, Inc.*	39,375
		107,012
	Machinery & Equipment—1.8%	
2,900	Acme-Cleveland Corp.	$ 31,175
8,800	Combustion Engineering, Inc.	283,800
2,300	Cooper Industries, Inc.	128,225
13,300	Cross & Trecker Corp.*	226,100
2,500	Gorman-Rupp Co.	59,375
3,900	Goulds Pumps, Inc.	86,775
2,300	Keystone International, Inc.	49,450
3,000	United Technologies Corp.	112,875
1,800	Vermont American Corp.	40,500
		1,018,275
	Media—1.5%	
2,000	Dun & Bradstreet Corp.	100,250
11,600	Meredith Corp.	358,150
4,000	Time, Inc.	398,000
		856,400
	Mining—0.6%	
13,000	Amax, Inc.	300,625
4,000	Pittston Co.*	64,500
		365,125
	Miscellaneous Basic—2.9%	
7,300	Cabot Corp.	265,537
2,500	CBI Industries Inc.	74,375
1,000	Chicago Pacific Corp.	47,125
1,000	Core Industries, Inc.	14,500
4,000	Essef Industries Inc.*	54,000
300	General Signal Corp.	15,937
2,000	Grainger (W.W.) Inc.	119,750
3,000	Hughes Supply, Inc.	52,125
7,000	Johnson Controls, Inc.	246,750
11,125	Kuhlman Corp	134,891

Shares	Description	(Value)
1,000	Lancaster Colony Corp.	18,000
1,500	Mine Safet Applicances Co.	61,125
2,300	Modern Controls, Inc.	23,575
4,400	Sudbury Inc.*	35,200
1,000	Pittway Corp.	97,000
2,000	Rockaway Corp.	19,750
1,700	Standard Products Co.	52,062
1,000	Thomas Industries, Inc.	22,250
7,000	Waste Management, Inc.	251,125
		1,605,077
	Miscellaneous Consumer Growth Stable—0.1%	
2,000	National Presto Industries, Inc.	58,500
	Paints—0.1%	
550	Desoto Inc.	19,525
	Paper & Forest Products—2.5%	
6,000	Boise Cascade Corp. $	263,250
8,800	Champion International Corp.	304,700
200	Fibreboard Corp.	2,100
7,000	International Paper Co.	315,875
3,000	Louisiana Pacific Corp.	101,625
1,200	Potlatch Corp.	38,250
10,900	Union Camp Corp.	377,413
		1,403,213
	Petroleum & Petroleum Services—2.2%	
3,600	Baker Hughes Inc.	54,180
2,500	Cameron Iron Works, Inc.	35,312
7,000	Daniel Industries, Inc.	56,000
3,000	Halliburton Co.	87,000
3,000	Helmerich & Payne, Inc.	62,625
4,000	Louisiana Land & Exploration Co.	127,500
1,300	Mapco Inc.	73,612
2,000	Murphy Oil Corp	64,750
1,000	Noble Affiliates, Inc.	11,685
6,000	Pacific Resources, Inc.	87,750
3,800	Schlumberger Ltd	131,575
7,000	Sun Co., Inc	412,125
		1,204,114
	Retail—1.2%	
2,000	Ames Department Stores, Inc.	33,500
3,400	Best Products Co. Inc.*	46,750
800	Great Atlantic & Pacific Tea Co., Inc.	32,200
15,000	Lowe's Companies, Inc.	326,250
400	Petrie Stores Corp	7,100
5,500	Toys 'R' Us, Inc.*	208,313
		654,113
	Steel & Metals—0.3%	
5,000	Amcast Industrial Corp.	69,375
2,000	Chaparral Steel Corp.*	28,000
1,700	Copperweld Corp.*	26,350
2,000	Worthington Industries, Inc.	47,750
		171,475
	Telecommunications—0.8%	
1,600	Cincinnati Bell, Inc.	51,200
5,900	Communications Satellite Corp.	164,462
4,500	ITT Corp.	228,937
		444,599

Shares	Description	(Value)
	Textiles—0.1%	
2,200	Culp, Inc. $	17,050
	Transportation—0.7%	
5,000	Brenco, Inc.	38,750
2,500	Burlington Northern Inc.	167,813
1,000	CSX Corp.	26,750
2,900	Consolidated Rail Corp	95,338
4,800	RLC Corp	50,400
		379,051
	Utilities—2.8%	
9,000	American Electric Power Inc.	257,625
3,900	Baltimore Gas & Electric Co.	125,288
4,000	Cincinnati Gas & Electric Co.	106,500
5,000	Kansas Power & Light Co.	120,000
11,000	Northern States Power Co.	345,125
9,800	Southern California Edison Co.	311,150
10,000	Southern Co.	227,500
3,000	Southwestern Energy Co.	56,250
		1,549,438
	Total equity securities (cost $23,669,989)	23,916,098

Principal Amount (000)	Description	(Value)
	DEBT OBLIGATIONS—33.7%	
	U.S. Government and Agencies Securities—18.5%	
	United States Treasury Bonds,	
$ 500	8.875%, 8/15/93	500,000
500	8.875%, 11/15/97	491,250
2,000	9.00%, 5/15/98	1,985,000
3,500	9.125%, 5/15/18	3,465,000
		6,441,250
	Government National Mortgage Association II,	
494	9.50%, 8/15/17	476,913
1,099	9.50%, 9/15/17	1,062,112
1,832	9.50%, 10/15/17	1,768,647
565	9.50%, 11/15/17	545,048
		3,852,720
	Total U.S. Government and agencies securities (cost $10,339,123)	10,293,970
	Corporate Bonds—15.2%	
$ 500	Allied Signal Inc., 9.875%, 6/1/02 $	496,940
1,000	Austria Rep., 9.125%, 4/25/99	966,410
1,000	B.P. North America, Inc., 9.50%, 1/1/98	989,600
1,000	British Gas Finance Co., 8.75%, 3/15/98	948,410
500	Eastman Kodak Co., 9.375%, 3/15/03	475,430
500	General Telephone Co. Southwest, 8.375%, 5/1/07	424,985
1,000	New Zealand Government 8.75%, 4/1/16	876,520
1,000	Occidental Petroleum Corp., 11.75%, 3/15/11	1,036,230
500	Ohio Edison Co., 9.50%, 5/15/08	433,580
500	Pacific Gas & Electric Co., 7.75%, 6/1/05	410,765

Principal Amount (000)	Description	(Value)
500	San Diego Gas & Electric Co., 7.00%, 12/1/98	398,345
1,000	Societe-Generale, 9.875%, 7/15/03	994,240
	Total corporate bonds (cost $8,627,395)	8,451,455
	Total debt obligations	18,745,425
	MONEY MARKET INSTRUMENTS—24.1%	
	Commercial Paper—16.0%	
	Barclays American Corp.	
500	7.85%, 9/19/88	494,658
270	6.75%, 9/26/88	267,350
	Bear, Stearns & Co.,	
500	7.80%, 8/29/88	496,967
	Beneficial Corp.,	
500	7.45%, 8/12/88	498,862
	CrediThrift Financial Corp.,	
500	7.65%, 8/18/88	498,194
	Detroit Edison Co.,	
500	7.85%, 8/29/88	496,947
	General Electric Credit Corp.,	
500	7.85%, 9/6/88	496,075
	ITT Credit Corp.,	
500	7.80%, 8/30/88	496,858
	John Deere Credit Corp.,	
500	7.55%, 8/22/88 $	497,798
	Loral Corp.,	
500	7.90%, 8/19/88	498,025
	Merrill Lynch & Co.,	
500	7.80%, 8/29/88	496,967
	Pacific Enterprises Corp.,	
500	7.875%, 12/8/88	485,935
	Penny (J.C.) Financial Corp.,	
500	7.35%, 8/8/88	499,285
	Rite Aid Corp.,	
500	7.80%, 9/9/88	495,775
	Salomon Brothers Inc.,	
500	7.80%, 8/24/88	497,508
	Sears Roebuck Acceptance Corp.,	
500	7.75%, 8/24/88	497,524
	Tokai Bank, Ltd.,	
300	7.25%, 10/19/88	295,227
	Trans-American Corp.,	
400	7.40%, 9/12/88	396,457
	U.S. Leasing Corp.,	
500	7.70%, 8/10/88	499,038
	Total commercial paper (cost $8,905,540)	8,905,540
	Repurchase Agreement—8.1%	
4,538	Discount Credit Corp., 7.55%, dated 7/29/88, due 8/1/88 in the amount of $4,540,855 (cost $4,538,000; collateralized by $4,450,000 U.S. Treasury Notes, 9.625% due 11/15/90, value $4,638,807)	4,538,000
	Total money market instruments	13,443,540
	Total Investments—100.8% (cost $55,080,047; see Note 4)	56,105,063
	Liabilities in excess of other assets—(0.8%)	(434,232)
	Net Assets—100%	$ 55,670,831

FIGURE 16.2 **Portfolio of Prudential-Bache FlexiFund Aggressively Managed Portfolio, July 31, 1988.**

The Prudential-Bache FlexiFund Aggressively Managed Portfolio appears to adhere to the traditional approach to portfolio management. Its portfolio value is about $24 million in common stock; it holds 190 different stocks from 35 industry groupings, plus about $19 million in government and corporate debt obligations and $13 million in money market instruments represented by commercial paper and a repurchase agreement. (*Source:* Annual Report, Prudential-Bache FlexiFund, July 31, 1988.)

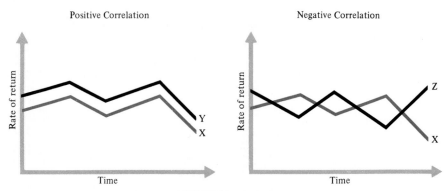

FIGURE 16.3 Correlation of Securities Returns.
The returns from securities X and Y are highly positively correlated and therefore do not offer an opportunity for diversification. The returns from securities X and Z are highly negatively correlated and therefore provide an opportunity to benefit from diversification. The less positive (or more negative) the correlation between security returns, the greater the benefit of diversification in terms of risk and return.

consisting of securities X and Y is not well diversified because each security is a near-perfect substitute for the other. The portfolio consisting of securities X and Z is much more diversified due to the strong negative correlation between their returns.

MPT has also provided an important investment tool, beta, which was first introduced in Chapter 5 and which is reviewed here.

 ## Beta

Given that a portfolio is diversified, the primary concern of the investor is with the level of nondiversifiable risk. We can measure the nondiversifiable risk of a security or a portfolio with the beta regression equation:

$$r_{i,t} = a_i + (b_i \times r_{m,t})$$

where

beta regression co-efficient
a statistical measure of the relative volatility of a security or a portfolio return as compared to a broadly derived measure of stock market return.

$r_{i,t}$ = return on security i or portfolio i over time period t

a_i = regression intercept

b_i = regression coefficient, beta

$r_{m,t}$ = return on the market portfolio over time period t

volatility
the amount of fluctuation in return exhibited by a security or portfolio.

The **beta regression coefficient** measures the relative volatility of either a security or a portfolio return as compared to a broadly derived measure of stock market return. In practice the Standard & Poor's 500 stock composite index or the New York Stock Exchange composite index are utilized as measures of return on the general market. The term **volatility** refers to the amount of fluctuation in return a security or portfolio has. Beta, in contrast, measures the *relative* fluctuation of a security or portfolio return in comparison to a market index; in essence, it indicates

the relative change in the security's or portfolio's return, as compared with the return on a market index. Stock betas are widely used in practice and are readily available from brokerage firms and investment advisory services like *Value Line*.

Uses of Beta. The usefulness of beta depends on how well the regression equation explains relative return fluctuations. The **coefficient of determination (R^2)** measures the explanatory power of a regression equation. That is, it indicates the percentage of the change in the dependent variable (the return from the individual security, $r_{i,t}$) explained by its relationship with the independent (market) variable, which is $r_{m,t}$ in our example. R^2 can range from 0 to 1.0. If a regression equation has an R^2 of 0, this means none (0 percent) of the variation in the security's return is explained by its relationship with the market. An R^2 of 1.0 indicates the existence of perfect correlation (100 percent) between a security and the market.

coefficient of determination (R^2)
a measure of the explanatory power of a regression equation; indicates the percentage of the change in the dependent variable explained by its relationship with the independent variable.

Beta is much more useful in explaining a portfolio's return fluctuations than a security's return fluctuations. A well-diversified stock portfolio will have a beta equation R^2 of around .90. This means that 90 percent of the stock portfolio's fluctuations are related to changes in the stock market as a whole. Individual security betas have a wide range of R^2s, but tend to be in the .20 to .50 range. Other factors (diversifiable risk, in particular) also cause individual security prices to fluctuate. When securities are combined in a well-diversified portfolio, most of the fluctuation in that portfolio's return is caused by the movement of the entire stock market.

Interpreting Beta. A look at the interpretation of beta may help us to understand its usefulness. If a portfolio has a beta of +1.0, the portfolio experiences changes in its rate of return equal to changes in the market's rate of return. This means the +1.0 beta portfolio would tend to experience a 10 percent increase in return if the stock market as a whole experienced a 10 percent increase in return. Conversely, if the market return fell by 6 percent, the return on the +1.0 beta portfolio would also fall by 6 percent. Table 16.2 lists the expected returns for three portfolio betas in two situations: The market experiences an increase in return of 10 percent and a decrease in return of 10 percent. The 2.0 beta portfolio is twice as volatile as the market. When the market return increases by 10 percent, the portfolio return increases by 20 percent. Conversely, the portfolio's return will fall by 20 percent when the market has a decline in return of 10 percent. This portfolio would be considered a relatively high-risk, high-return portfolio. A .5 beta portfolio is considered a relatively low-risk, low-return portfolio—a conservative portfolio for investors who wish to maintain a low-risk investment posture. The .5 beta portfolio is half as volatile as the market. A beta of −1.0 indicates that the portfolio moves in a direction opposite to that of the market. A bearish investor would probably want to own a negative beta portfolio, because this type of investment tends to rise in value when the stock market declines, and vice versa. Finding securities with negative betas is difficult, however. Most securities have positive betas, since they tend to experience return movements in the same direction as changes in the stock market.

TABLE 16.2   Portfolio Betas and Associated Changes in Returns

Portfolio Beta	Change in Return on Market	Change in Expected Return on Portfolio
+2.0	+10.0%	+20.0%
	−10.0	−20.0
+ .5	+10.0	+ 5.0
	−10.0	− 5.0
−1.0	+10.0	−10.0
	−10.0	+10.0

The Risk-Return Tradeoff: Some Closing Comments

risk-return tradeoff
the inverse relationship between the risk associated with a given investment and its expected return.

risk-free rate (R_F)
the return an investor can earn on a risk-free investment such as a T-bill or an insured money market account.

Another valuable outgrowth of modern portfolio theory is the specific delineation between nondiversifiable risk and investment return. The basic premise is that an investor must have a portfolio of relatively risky investments to earn a relatively high rate of return. That relationship is illustrated in Figure 16.4. The upward-sloping line shows the **risk-return tradeoff.** The point where the risk-return line crosses the return axis (R_F) is called the **risk-free rate.** This is the return an investor can earn on a risk-free investment such as a U.S. Treasury bill or an insured money market account. As we proceed upward along the line, portfolios of risky investments appear. For example, four investment portfolios, A through D, are depicted in Figure 16.4. Portfolios A and B are investment opportunities that provide a level of return commensurate with their respective risk levels. Portfolio C would be an excellent investment as it provides a high return at a relatively low risk level. Portfolio D, in contrast, is an investment situation that one should avoid, as it offers high risk but low return.

The Traditional Approach and MPT: A Reconciliation

We have reviewed two fairly different approaches to portfolio management—the traditional approach and MPT. The question that arises now is, Which technique should be used by the individual investor? There is no definite answer; the question must be resolved by the judgment of the investor. However, a few useful ideas can be offered. The average individual investor does not have the resources, computers, and mathematical acumen to implement an MPT portfolio strategy. Given that total MPT portfolio management is impractical for most individual investors, it follows that ideas should be drawn from *both* MPT and the traditional approach. The traditional approach stresses security selection using fundamental and technical analysis. It also emphasizes diversification of the portfolio across industry lines. MPT stresses negative correlations between securities' rates of return for the issues within the portfolio. This approach calls for diversification to minimize diversifiable risk. So, following either strategy, diversification must be accomplished in order to ensure satisfactory performance.

Beta is a useful tool for determining the level of a portfolio's nondiversifiable

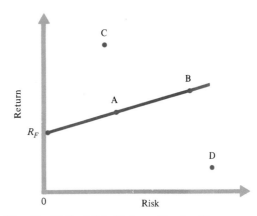

FIGURE 16.4 The Portfolio Risk-Return Tradeoff.
As the risk of an investment portfolio increases from zero, the return provided should increase above the risk-free rate, R_F. Portfolios A and B offer returns commensurate with their risk, portfolio C provides a high return at a low-risk level, and portfolio D provides a low return for high risk. Portfolio C is highly desirable; portfolio D should be avoided.

risk and should be part of the decision-making process. We recommend the following portfolio management policy:

- Determine how much risk you are willing to bear.
- Seek diversification among different types of securities and across industry lines, and pay attention to the way the return from one security is related to another.
- Consider how a security responds to the market, and use beta in diversifying your portfolio as a way to keep the portfolio in line with your acceptable level of risk.
- Evaluate alternative portfolios to make sure that the portfolio selected provides the highest return for the given level of acceptable risk.

BUILDING A PORTFOLIO USING AN ASSET ALLOCATION SCHEME

In this section we will examine the criteria that can be used to formulate an individual portfolio strategy. We will look at investor characteristics, investor objectives, and portfolio objectives and policies. These factors will then be used to develop an asset allocation scheme that provides the basic framework for selecting individual investment vehicles for inclusion in the portfolio. In attempting to weave the concepts of risk and diversification into a solid investment policy, we will rely on both traditional and modern approaches to investment management.

Investor Characteristics

An investor's personal financial and family situation are important inputs in determining portfolio policy. The following are vital determinants:

- Level and stability of income.
- Family factors.
- Net worth.
- Investor experience and age.
- Investor disposition toward risk.

The portfolio strategy of an individual investor obviously must be tailored to meet that person's needs. The types of investments in the portfolio depend upon relative income needs and ability to bear risk. The investor's income, family responsibilities, relative financial security, experience, and age all enter into the delicate equation that yields a portfolio strategy. A relatively young investor may have an aggressive investment policy, and particularly if that person's family obligations are well met. A married investor with young children would not be seeking high-risk investments until some measure of financial security has been provided for the family. On the other hand, if the married investor has ample savings and insurance protection for the family, he or she may be ready to embark on a program with risky elements. Once financial security has been provided for, more risky ventures can be undertaken. A single investor with no family responsibilities could handle risk better than an individual who has such responsibilities. Simply stated, an investor's risk exposure should not exceed that person's ability to bear risk.

The size and certainty of an investor's employment income also bear on portfolio strategy. An investor with a secure job is more likely to embark on a risk-oriented investment program than one who has a less secure position. Income taxes bear on the investment decision as well. The higher an investor's income, the more important the tax ramifications of an investment program become. For example, tax-free municipal bonds yield less in annual interest than corporate bonds because the municipal's interest income is tax-free. On an after-tax basis, however, tax-free municipal bonds may provide a superior return if an investor is in the 28 or 33 percent tax brackets. An individual's investment experience also influences the appropriate investment strategy. Normally investors assume higher levels of investment risk gradually over time. It is best to "get one's feet wet" in the investment market by slipping into it gradually rather than leaping in head first. Very often investors who make risky initial investments suffer heavy losses, damaging the long-run potential of their entire investment program. A cautiously developed investment program will likely provide more favorable long-run results than an impulsive, risky one.

Finally, investors should carefully consider risk. Much of this chapter is devoted to discussions of risk and return. High-risk investments have high-return potential and a high risk of loss. Remember, by going for a home run (a high-risk, high-return investment), the odds of striking out are much higher than in going for a base hit (a more conservative investment posture). A single is less glamorous than a home run, but it is also easier to achieve.

Specifying Investor Objectives

Once an investor has developed a personal financial profile, the next question is, "What do I want from my portfolio?" This seems like an easy one to answer. We

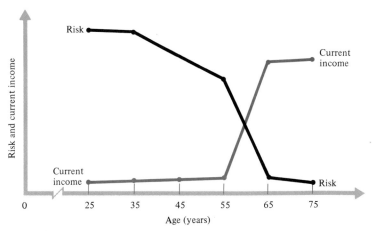

FIGURE 16.5   Investor Life Cycles: Risk and Current Income Versus Age.
A young investor tends to be more willing to take higher risks in the expectation of earning
high returns through price appreciation than the mature investor, who tends to be risk-averse
and current-income-oriented. This behavior is attributable to age-related differences in financial resources and needs.

would all like to double our money every year by making low-risk investments.
However, the realities of the highly competitive investment environment make this
outcome unlikely. The presence of risk makes the establishment of realistic goals a
basic requirement for a successful investment program. There is generally a tradeoff
between earning a high current income from an investment portfolio or obtaining
significant capital appreciation from it. An investor must usually choose one or the
other, as it is difficult to have both. The price of having high appreciation potential
in the portfolio is often low current income potential. One must balance the certainty of high current income and limited price appreciation with the uncertainty of
high future price appreciation.

The investor's needs may determine which avenue is chosen. For instance, a
retired investor whose income depends on his or her portfolio will probably choose
a lower-risk, current-income-oriented approach out of the need for financial sur-
vival. In contrast, a high-income, financially secure investor (a doctor, for instance)
may be much more willing to take on risky investments in the hope of improving net
worth. Figure 16.5 illustrates the risk-income tradeoff as compared with an investor's age. A young investor with a secure job is less concerned about current income
and is more able to bear risk. This type of investor is more appreciation oriented and
may choose speculative investments. As an investor approaches retirement, the
desired level of income rises. The aging investor is less willing to bear risk. Such an
investor wants to keep what he or she has because he or she is or will soon be
utilizing these investments as a source of retirement income. The retired 75-year-old
investor typically wants minimal risk in a portfolio because he or she needs a
dependable source of current income. Thus it should be clear that a portfolio must
be built around the individual's needs, which depend on income, responsibilities,
financial resources, age, retirement plans, and ability to bear risk.

Portfolio Objectives and Policies

Portfolio management is a very logical activity and is best implemented after careful analysis of the investor's needs and of the investment vehicles available for inclusion in the portfolio. The following objectives should be considered when structuring a portfolio:

- Current income needs.
- Capital preservation.
- Capital growth.
- Tax considerations.
- Risk.

Any one or more of these factors will play an influential role in defining the type of portfolio acquired by an investor. For convenience, these factors can be tied together as follows: the first two items, current income and capital preservation, are portfolio objectives synonymous with a low-risk, conservative investment strategy. Normally a portfolio with this orientation contains low-beta (low-risk) securities. A capital growth objective (the third item) implies increased risk and a reduced level of current income. Higher-risk growth stocks, options, commodities and financial futures, gold, real estate, and other more speculative investments may be suitable for this investor. An investor's tax bracket (the fourth item) will influence investment strategy. A high-income investor probably wishes to defer taxes and earn investment returns in the form of capital gains. This implies a strategy of higher-risk investments and a longer holding period. Lower-bracket investors are less concerned with how they earn the income, and they may wish to invest in higher current income investments. The most important item an investor must decide upon is *risk* (the final item). The risk-return tradeoff should be considered in all investment decisions.

Developing an Asset Allocation Scheme

A portfolio must be consistent with an investor's needs which depend on characteristics such as income, family responsibilities, net worth, age, and ability to bear risk. Once these needs are converted into specific portfolio objectives a portfolio can be constructed consistent with their achievement. But before buying any stocks, bonds, short-term securities, or other vehicles, an *asset allocation scheme* must be developed. **Asset allocation** involves dividing one's portfolio into various asset classes such as U.S. stocks, foreign stocks, bonds, short-term securities, and other vehicles such as tangibles—especially gold—and real estate. The emphasis of asset allocation is on *preservation of capital*—protecting against negative developments while still taking advantage of positive developments. Asset allocation is based upon the belief that the total return of a portfolio is influenced more by the way investments are allocated than by the actual investments. In fact studies have shown that as much as 90 percent or more of a portfolio's *return* comes from asset allocation, and therefore less than 10 percent can be attributed to the actual security selection. Furthermore researchers have found that asset allocation has a much

asset allocation
a scheme that involves dividing one's portfolio into various asset classes in order to preserve capital by protecting against negative developments while still taking advantage of positive developments.

greater impact on reducing total exposure to *risk* than picking an investment vehicle in any single asset category. Clearly asset allocation is an important aspect of portfolio management.

Approaches to Asset Allocation

There are three basic approaches to asset allocation. The first two—fixed weightings and flexible weightings—differ with respect to the nature of the proportions of each asset category maintained in the portfolio, whereas the third—tactical asset allocation—is a more exotic technique frequently utilized by sophisticated institutional portfolio managers.

Fixed Weightings. Under this approach a fixed percentage of the portfolio is allocated to each of the (typically 3 to 5) asset categories. Assuming only four categories—common stocks, bonds, short-term securities, and real estate—a fixed allocation might be:

Category	Allocation
Common stock	30%
Bonds	50
Short-term securities	5
Real estate	15
Total portfolio	100%

Generally with fixed weightings the weights do not change over time, hence they are *fixed*! Because of shifting market values the portfolio may have to be revised (i.e., adjusted) annually or after major market moves in order to maintain the desired fixed percentage allocations. Fixed weights may or may not represent equal percentage allocations to each category, such as 25 percent to each of the four categories above, although research has shown that over the 1967 to 1988 period equal (20%) allocations to U.S. stocks, foreign stocks, long-term bonds, cash, and real estate resulted in a portfolio that outperformed the S&P 500 both in terms of return and risk. These findings add further support to the importance of even a somewhat naive "buy and hold" asset allocation strategy.

Flexible Weightings. This approach involves the periodic adjustment of the weights for each asset category based either on market analysis or technical analysis (i.e., market timing). The use of a flexible weighting scheme is often called *strategic asset allocation*. For example the initial and new allocation based on a flexible weighting scheme may be as noted below.

Category	Initial Allocation	New Allocation
Common stock	30%	40%
Bonds	50	50
Short-term securities	5	10
Real estate	15	0
Total portfolio	100%	100%

The new allocation resulted from an expectation of lower inflation which was expected to result in increased stock and bond prices and a decline in real estate returns. The weightings were therefore changed to capture greater returns in a changing market.

Tactical Asset Allocation.   Tactical asset allocation is a sophisticated approach that uses stock index futures and bond futures (see Chapter 12) to change a portfolio's asset allocation. When stocks seem less attractive than bonds, this strategy involves selling stock index futures and buying bond futures; and, when bonds seem less attractive than stocks, the strategy results in buying stock index futures and selling bond futures. Because, to be effective, this technique relies on a large portfolio and the use of quantitative models for cues, it is generally only appropriate for large institutional investors rather than the individual investor to whom this discussion is focused.

Asset Allocation Alternatives

Assuming the use of a fixed-weight asset allocation plan and using, say, four asset categories—common stock, bonds, short-term securities, and real estate, we can demonstrate three asset allocations. Table 16.3 shows allocations in each of the categories for a conservative (low-return–low-risk), moderate (average-return–average-risk), and an aggressive (high-return–high-risk) portfolio. The conservative allocation heavily relies on bonds and short-term securities to provide predictable returns. The moderate allocation includes mostly bonds, some common stock, and more real estate than the conservative allocation. Its moderate return-risk behavior reflects a move away from safe short-term securities to a larger dose of common stock and real estate than under the conservative allocation. Finally as we move to the aggressive portfolio more dollars are allocated to common stock, less to bonds, and more to real estate, thereby generally increasing the expected portfolio return and risk.

Applying Asset Allocation

Your asset allocation plan should consider your investments, savings and spending patterns, the economic outlook, tax situation, return expectations, risk tolerance, and so forth. Age, as noted earlier, will of course have some bearing on these factors and the resulting asset allocations since younger people generally accept greater risk than those at or near retirement. Such plans must be formulated for the long run, stress capital preservation, and provide for periodic revision (see Chapter 17) in order to maintain consistency with changing investment goals.

asset allocation fund
a mutual fund that seeks to reduce volatility by investing in the right assets at the right time; emphasizes diversification and relatively consistent performance rather than spectacular gains.

Generally, to decide on the appropriate asset mix, investors must evaluate each asset category relative to: current return, growth potential, safety, liquidity, transactions costs (brokerage fees), and potential tax savings. Many investors use mutual funds (see Chapter 13) as part of their asset allocation activities. Frequently, in order to diversify within each asset category, mutual funds are employed—a family of funds can be used to permit switching among categories by phone. As an alternative to building your own portfolio you can buy shares in an **asset allocation fund**—

TABLE 16.3   Alternative Asset Allocations

Category	Allocation Alternative		
	Conservative (low-return–low-risk)	Moderate (average-return–average-risk)	Aggressive (high-return–high-risk)
Common stock	15%	30%	40%
Bonds	45	50	35
Short-term securities	35	5	0
Real estate	5	15	25
Total portfolio	100%	100%	100%

a mutual fund that seeks to reduce volatility by investing in the right assets at the right time. These funds, like all asset allocation schemes, emphasize diversification and perform at a relatively consistent level by passing up the potential for spectacular gains in favor of predictability. Some asset allocation funds such as Vanguard's Star Fund, USAA Cornerstone, and Permanent Portfolio use fixed weightings, whereas others such as Fidelity's Asset Manager, Integrated Resource's Total Return Fund, and Oppenheimer's Asset Allocation have flexible weights that change within prescribed limits. As a rule, investors with more than about $50,000 to invest and adequate time can justify do-it-yourself asset allocation. Those with between $5,000 and $50,000 and adequate time can use mutual funds to create a workable asset allocation, and those with less than $5,000 and/or limited time may find asset allocation funds most attractive.

Most important, you should recognize that to be effective an asset allocation scheme *must be designed for the long haul*. Develop an asset allocation scheme you can live with for at least 7 to 10 years, and perhaps longer. Once you have it set, stick with it. The key to success involves remaining faithful to your asset allocation. That means fighting the temptation to wander. The Investor Insights box provides additional background and some guidelines for using an asset allocation scheme for portfolio diversification.

PORTFOLIO MANAGEMENT IN ACTION

In this section, we will analyze four portfolios that have been developed to meet four different investment objectives. The principles and ideas that have been developed throughout the book will be applied to these four realistic situations.

In each of the analyses that follow, the investors' names and securities are fictitious but the objectives and the portfolios are real. Relevant income, age, net worth, and lifestyle information is provided for each investor. In addition, when possible, asset allocation weights are given. The specific reasons why a stock and/or bond is included in the portfolio are also given (the portfolios include only stocks and bonds). As a useful exercise the reader might want to consider each situation and develop his or her own recommendations utilizing current investment information.

INVESTOR INSIGHTS

Portfolio Diversification Using Asset Allocation

Many investors knew fear for the first time on Oct. 19, 1987, when the Dow Jones industrial average plunged a whopping 508 points. The magnitude of the losses suffered by millions of Americans spurred them to a new caution. Growth took second place to safety, and investors moved into more conservative investments while spreading the risk by diversifying.

As a result, a strategy long used by institutions, known as asset allocation, is suddenly enjoying widespread popularity among individual investors. Some do their own allocating; others are turning to professionals to do it for them. In either case, the rationale is to control their financial affairs better by reducing the possibility of an overwhelming setback when one or two investments go bad.

. . .

Also known as asset mixing, asset allocation is the planned process of distributing investments among available categories, either according to an established, fixed formula or with reallocations in keeping with changes in the economy. Proponents see it as a tool for limiting risk, while at the same time providing competitive returns.

"It's the buzzword of the moment," said Madeline I. Noveck, president of Novos Planning Associates of New York, and Northeast regional director of the Institute of Certified Financial Planners. "By using different categories which correlate negatively in their performance, you can plan for the unexpected."

"It's very difficult to pick winners and losers specifically," added Randy Neumann, a certified financial planner in Saddle Brook, N.J. "But if you have a diversified base of assets, and the investments are of good quality, over the long run it's hard to lose money."

Asset allocators, whether individuals or professional services, in effect create an all-weather portfolio, often in the form of mutual funds, intended to turn in good results in both bull and bear markets. The purpose is to offset declines in the value of one segment with advances in another.

The sorts of assets used in such a mix typically include domestic and international common stocks, domestic and international bonds, money market securities, precious metals and real estate. As Robert E. Lewis, managing director of the Atlanta securities firm of Marshall & Company, put it, such spreading of assets "makes an awful lot of sense."

Gerald W. Perritt, president of Investment Information Services of Chicago, said that

The four cases have divergent risk-return profiles because the investors for whom the portfolios are designed have different incomes and lifestyles. Each portfolio is constructed using the traditional approach, with the following exceptions. First, the number of securities in each portfolio is below the normal number the traditional portfolio manager would likely recommend. In line with MPT, it is assumed that the proper interindustry diversification can be achieved with the careful selection of 8 to 12 securities in a $100,000 portfolio. A larger portfolio might have slightly more securities, but it would also probably have fewer securities than a traditionalist

one way investors could do this would be by putting together a portfolio of mutual funds that could satisfy each asset class. "Five years ago, individual investors didn't have an opportunity to do this, because you didn't have international bond funds and other kinds of funds," he said.

Also bringing this technique to the investor's attention has been the increasing realization that investment results are driven primarily by the asset allocation decision. "For most portfolios, selection of the asset mix is the single most important determinant of long-term investment performance," noted William G. Droms, professor of finance at Georgetown University.

The asset allocation concept, moreover, allows for differences in the percentage devoted to the various classifications based on personal and family requirements. "Using a broad range of assets gives you more opportunity to tailor your asset mix to meet your needs," said Peter M. Hill, executive vice president of Bailard.

The way that the best asset mix can be developed is the same for everyone, regardless of the goals set. T. Rowe Price, the Baltimore-based mutual fund management company, has a worksheet that divides this process into seven steps:

- Define your financial goals clearly by outlining what you want your money to do.
- Set your time horizons as short-term (up to 2 years), mid-term (2 to 5 years) and long-term (5 years or more).
- Consider your personal risk profile as either a more conservative or less conservative investor.
- Find the investments that match your goals, taking into account the trade-offs you have to make.
- Analyze your current asset mix and see how it compares with the appropriate investments.
- Check your diversification, keeping in mind that the greater your resources, the easier it is to achieve.
- Rethink your investments periodically, since asset allocation is a lifetime process.

"This takes an awful lot of the emotion out of dealing in the marketplace," said Robert A. Leo, executive vice president of Shearson Lehman Hutton. "It makes you look at what your objectives are."

. . .

Source: Leonard Sloane, "Crash-Chastened Investors Seek to Diversify," *The New York Times Personal Investing '89,* November 13, 1988, p. 7.

might recommend. Second, beta is utilized to quantify risk in the all-equity portfolios. Thus these examples blend elements of modern portfolio theory (MPT) with the traditional approach to portfolio management.

Dara Yasakawa: Woman Wonder

At 28 Dara Yasakawa has done well for herself. She has built a $300,000 investment portfolio consisting of investment real estate in Honolulu, Hawaii, with a current market value of $240,000, and $60,000 in short-term investments. Her

current asset allocation is therefore 80 percent real estate ($240,000 ÷ $300,000) and 20 percent short-term investments. ($60,000 ÷ $300,000). Ms. Yasakawa is currently employed as the controller of Kamehameha Management, a real estate management firm in Honolulu. She is a CPA, and her income from salary and property rentals is $65,000 per year, putting her in a 35 percent marginal income tax bracket (federal and Hawaii state income tax combined). Ms. Yasakawa is single, and her only debts are secured by her properties.

Dara Yasakawa has decided to diversify her portfolio. Most of her net worth consists of rental condominiums located in the Waikiki area of Honolulu. Clearly, diversification is needed to reduce her risk exposure and to increase her overall investment return. The Hawaii real estate market is somewhat unpredictable, and Ms. Yasakawa wishes to lessen her risk exposure in that market. She asked her investment advisor, Marjorie Wong, to help her diversify into common stock. Marjorie recommended selling one of Dara's properties for $60,000 and selling $15,000 in short-term securities to obtain $75,000 to invest in common stock. The resulting asset allocation would be 60 percent real estate ($180,000 ÷ $300,000), 25 percent common stock ($75,000 ÷ $300,000), and 15 percent short-term securities ($45,000 ÷ $300,000). Because of her relatively young age and her strong future earning capacity, Ms. Yasakawa can bear the risks of a speculative investment program. Her portfolio of stocks will emphasize issues that have a strong price appreciation potential.

Ms. Yasakawa's common stock portfolio is presented in Table 16.4. It consists of eight stocks, all of which have above-average risk-return potential. The betas of the issues range from 1.13 to 2.31; the portfolio's beta is approximately 1.61, indicating an above-average risk exposure. (The beta for a portfolio can be calculated as a weighted average of the individual security betas within the portfolio.) The portfolio is diversified across industry lines, with a fairly wide mix of securities. All are selected for their above-average price appreciation potential. Altuna Airlines, an inter-island carrier in Hawaii, was chosen because of the expected increase in the number of visitors to Hawaii. Betta Computer is a fast-growing personal computer manufacturer. Easy Work is a growing retailer that services the do-it-yourself home improvement market. Gomez Industries is a rapidly expanding glass manufacturer and photo processor. Hercules is a growing brewer. Jama Motor, based in Japan, provides a measure of international diversification for the portfolio. Karl Lewis Enterprises is an expanding fast-food operator based in California. Ranch Petroleum is a small oil company with refining and oil-production interests.

Most of the securities Ms. Wong selected for Ms. Yasakawa are not "household names." Rather, they are firms with exciting growth potential. Given the portfolio's beta, Dara's holdings should fluctuate in value at a rate approximately 1.6 times greater than the stock market as a whole. The dividend yield on the portfolio is a relatively low 0.6 percent. Most of the return Ms. Yasakawa anticipates from this portfolio is in the form of price appreciation. She plans to hold the stocks for at least one to two years in order to realize this anticipated appreciation. Given Ms. Yasakawa's high marginal income tax bracket, it seems preferable for her to defer taxes and earn returns in the form of capital gains.

TABLE 16.4   Dara Yasakawa's Common Stock Portfolio

OBJECTIVE: SPECULATIVE GROWTH (HIGH-RISK, HIGH-RETURN POTENTIAL)

Number of Shares	Company	Dividend per Share	Dividend Income	Price per Share	Total Cost (including commission)	Beta	Dividend Yield
1,200	Altuna Airlines	$—	$—	$ 7	$ 8,480	1.75	—%
300	Betta Computer	—	—	30	9,090	1.87	—
400	Easy Work Tile	—	—	25	10,090	1.59	—
300	Gomez Industries	0.36	108	30	9,090	1.19	1.2
300	Hercules Brewing	0.80	240	32	9,700	1.27	2.5
300	Jama Motor ADR	0.35	105	33	10,000	1.13	1.1
500	Karl Lewis Enterprises	—	—	20	10,100	1.79	—
1,300	Ranch Petroleum	—	—	6	7,880	2.31	—
	Total		$453		$74,430		0.6%

Portfolio beta = 1.61

Bob and Gail Weiss: Lottery Winners

Bob Weiss, a professor of political science at the University of West Bay City in Michigan, and his wife, Gail, are very lucky people. After buying a $1 Michigan State Lottery ticket at a local tavern, Professor Weiss won the $275,000 prize. After paying income taxes on the prize and after spending a small amount for personal needs, Bob and Gail had $210,000 remaining. Because of their philosophy of saving any windfalls and not spending accumulated capital on day-to-day living expenses, they chose to invest these funds (in contrast with many lottery winners, who simply blow their winnings on fast living).

The Weisses have two children. Bob Weiss is 37 years of age and has a secure teaching position. His salary is approximately $40,000 per year. In addition, he earns approximately $15,000 per year from his book-publishing royalties and from several other small sources. Professor Weiss's tax bracket (federal and state) is approximately 30 percent. His life insurance protection of approximately $80,000 is provided by the university. Bob's wife, Gail, is a librarian. She currently is at home with the children and is not expected to be a source of steady income for another several years. The Weiss family owns (free and clear) their home in the Banks area of Bay City. In addition, they have about $40,000 in a money market mutual fund. Therefore their asset allocation prior to the lottery windfall was 100 percent money funds ($40,000 ÷ $40,000). They have no outstanding debts.

Professor Weiss asked his investment advisor, Gene Bowles, to develop an investment portfolio for them. Together, they decided on the following strategy. First, the professor and his wife tend to be somewhat risk-averse; that is, they do not wish to bear inordinate amounts of risk of loss. In addition, the Weisses indicated that they would welcome some increase in spendable income. Given these facts, Mr. Bowles suggested the portfolio presented in Table 16.5. With this portfolio their asset allocation would become about 84 percent common stock ($210,000 ÷

TABLE 16.5   Bob and Gail Weiss's Common Stock Portfolio

OBJECTIVE: LONG-TERM GROWTH (AVERAGE RISK, MODERATE DIVIDENDS)

Number of Shares	Company	Dividend per Share	Dividend Income	Price per Share	Total Cost (including commission)	Beta	Dividend Yield
1,000	Bancorp West, Inc.	$1.20	$ 1,200	$22	$ 22,200	.86	5.4%
600	BST, Inc.	2.80	1,680	40	24,200	1.00	6.9
1,000	Florida Southcoast Banks	1.20	1,200	23	23,200	.84	5.2
1,000	Kings	1.60	1,600	25	25,300	.88	6.3
500	Light Newspapers	0.92	460	46	23,200	1.12	2.0
600	Miller Foods	1.88	1,128	37	22,400	1.07	5.0
800	State Oil of California	1.00	800	27	21,800	1.30	3.7
600	Vornox	2.28	1,368	40	24,200	1.04	5.7
600	Woodstock	1.30	780	36	21,800	1.32	3.6
	Total		$10,216		$208,300		4.9%

Portfolio beta = 1.05

$250,000) and 16 percent money funds ($40,000 ÷ $250,000). The emphasis in the portfolio is long-term growth at an average risk level, with a moderate dividend return. The portfolio consists of nine issues, and as such, there appears to be sufficient diversification. The portfolio's beta is 1.05, indicating a level of nondiversifiable risk that approximately equals that of the stock market as a whole. The portfolio's dividend yield is about 4.9 percent, which approximates the average dividend return for the entire stock market. The betas of individual securities in the portfolio vary somewhat. However, the portfolio's overall risk is moderate.

The Weiss portfolio consists of stocks from a wide range of American business. All the companies had above-average growth potential, and none was engaged in high-risk businesses that could face technological obsolescence or heavy foreign competition. Two banking stocks were selected, Bancorp West, Inc., and Florida Southcoast Banks. The former is a well-managed bank holding company that owns the largest bank in California. The latter is a growing bank holding company located on the south coast of Florida. Both regions are experiencing rapid population and economic growth. BST, Inc., appears to be well positioned in the growing communications industry. Kings is a food processor with a solid future. Light Newspapers is a large chain with many Sunbelt papers. Miller Foods is expanding as well, helped by the 1989 acquisition of Denton Companies, a superbly managed supermarket chain. The portfolio has two natural resource stocks, State Oil and Woodstock. These companies are well positioned in their respective industries. Vornox is a major drug firm that should benefit from the aging demographic mix of America. All the stocks in the Weisses' portfolio are securities of well-managed companies; the portfolio has a moderate risk level and provides an average dividend yield. With

this portfolio, the Weisses will have potential price appreciation coupled with a steady dividend income.

Julio and Gina Vitello: Retirees

Having just sold their family business and liquidated their real estate investment property, the Vitellos are eager to begin their retirement. At age 60, both have worked hard for 35 years building the successful business they recently sold. In addition, they had made some successful real estate investments over the years. The sale of their business and real estate holdings netted them $600,000 after taxes. They wish to invest these funds and have asked their investment advisor, Jane Tuttle, to develop a portfolio for them. The relevant financial information about the Vitellos is as follows: They own their home free and clear and have a $300,000 bond portfolio that yields yearly income of $30,000. In addition, they have $100,000 in short-term securities which they wish to hold as a ready cash reserve. Their most recent asset allocation is therefore 60 percent business and real estate investments ($600,000 ÷ $1,000,000), 30 percent bonds ($300,000 ÷ $1,000,000), and 10 percent short-term securities ($100,000 ÷ $1,000,000). Mr. Vitello has a $200,000 whole life insurance policy on his life, with Mrs. Vitello the designated beneficiary.

Now that they are retired, neither of the Vitellos plans to seek employment. They do have a small pension plan that will begin paying an income of $4,000 per year in five years. However, their main source of income will be their investment portfolio. During their last few working years, their combined yearly income was approximately $90,000. Their standard of living is rather high, and they do not wish to significantly change their lifestyle. They do not plan to spend any of their investment capital on living expenses, since they wish to keep their estate intact for their two children. Thus the Vitellos' basic investment objective is current income with some capital appreciation potential. The Vitellos do not wish to reinvest in real estate, but rather have asked Ms. Tuttle to develop a $600,000 securities portfolio for them. (They will leave their $300,000 bond portfolio and $100,000 in short-term securities undisturbed.) Their resulting asset allocation would shift to 60 percent common stock, 30 percent bonds, and 10 percent short-term securities.

The portfolio developed for the Vitellos is shown in Table 16.6. It contains nine stocks with approximately $65,000 invested in each issue. The emphasis is on quality, with low-risk, high-yield issues, and diversification. The portfolio's beta is approximately .80—a risk level that is below that of the general stock market. It is expected that a large portion of the portfolio's total return (dividends plus price appreciation) will be in the form of dividend income. The portfolio has a current dividend yield of approximately 8.7 percent, an above-average dividend yield. Dividend income totals over $52,000, which added to the bond income and the short-term securities' interest will provide the Vitellos with a gross income of about $90,000. The Vitellos' after-tax income will equal their working years' income; thus they will not have to alter their lifestyle.

Analyzing the individual issues in the Vitellos' portfolio, we can see that four public utility stocks are included. Utility stocks are often suitable for low-risk,

TABLE 16.6   Julio and Gina Vitello's Common Stock Portfolio

OBJECTIVE: CURRENT INCOME (LOW-RISK, HIGH-YIELD)

Number of Shares	Company	Dividend per Share	Dividend Income	Price per Share	Total Cost (including commission)	Beta	Dividend Yield
3,000	Alaska Bancorp, Inc.	$1.20	$ 3,600	$22	$ 66,600	.86	5.4%
2,000	Dallas National Corporation	2.40	4,800	30	60,600	.81	7.9
2,500	Energon	3.00	7,500	27	68,100	1.01	11.0
2,000	Findly Power and Light	3.36	6,720	32	64,600	.63	10.4
2,000	Geoco	2.80	5,600	35	70,700	1.13	7.9
2,500	Gulf Gas and Electric	3.00	7,500	28	70,700	.53	10.6
4,000	Public Power Company	1.76	7,040	16	64,600	.72	10.9
2,500	Smith, Roberts and Company	1.36	3,400	27	68,100	.92	5.0
3,000	Southwest Utilities	2.04	6,120	21	63,600	.60	9.6
	Total		$52,280		$597,600		8.7%

Portfolio beta = .80

current-income–oriented portfolios. High-quality electric and natural gas concerns tend to have moderate growth in earnings and dividends. The four issues in the portfolio, Findly Power and Light, Gulf Gas and Electric, Public Power Company, and Southwest Utilities, have growing service areas and records of profit and dividend increases. The stocks of two very large American companies, Energon and Smith, Roberts and Company, are included in the portfolio. Energon is a large U.S. energy company that offers a high dividend yield. Smith, Roberts is one of the largest retailers, and the company is now diversifying into financial services. Two bank holding company stocks were also selected, Alaska Bancorp and Dallas National. Alaska Bancorp offers a top-quality vehicle to participate in Alaska's growth. Dallas National was selected for its above-average dividend yield and because the firm is well positioned in the Dallas market. Additionally, the company has raised its dividend several times in recent years, and future dividend increases are expected. Geoco is a large company with chemical and other diversified operations. All the issues in the Vitello's portfolio are well-known, relatively large corporations. Stability, low risk, and a relatively high dividend yield with some potential for increase characterize the stocks in this portfolio.

Lucille Hatch: Widow

In the preceding example, a portfolio was developed for a fairly affluent retired couple. Most retirees are less fortunate than the Vitellos; they have less funds to invest. Lucille Hatch, age 70, was recently widowed. Between the estate of her late husband, her personal assets, and their jointly owned assets, Lucille has approximately $350,000 in liquid assets, all of it in savings and money market accounts (short-term investments). Her current asset allocation is therefore 100 percent short-

TABLE 16.7   Lucille Hatch's Bond Portfolio

	OBJECTIVE: MAXIMIZE CURRENT INCOME (MINIMAL RISK)						
Par Value	Issue	Standard & Poor's Bond Rating	Interest Income	Price	Total Cost	Yield to Maturity	Current Yield
$50,000	Boise Northern 12⅞% due 2011	A	$ 6,437.50	100	$ 50,000	12.875%	12.875%
50,000	Dalston and Company 11½% due 1995	A	5,750.00	98	49,000	11.900	11.700
50,000	Maryland-Pacific 10.70% due 1993	A	5,350.00	97	48,500	11.600	11.000
50,000	Pacific Utilities 12⅞% due 2019	AA	6,437.50	100	50,000	12.875	12.875
50,000	Trans-States Telephone 12.70% due 2025	A	6,350.00	97	48,500	13.200	13.100
50,000	Urban Life 12½% due 1996	AA	6,250.00	100	50,000	12.500	12.500
	Total		$36,575.00		$296,000	12.500%	12.400%

term investments ($350,000 ÷ $350,000). Lucille owns her home free and clear. Other than the interest on her savings, her income consists of $600 per month from social security. Unfortunately, her husband's employer did not have a pension plan. She has turned to her investment advisor, Charles Puckett, to discuss strategy and to develop an investment policy.

Between social security and interest earned on her short-term investments, Mrs. Hatch's current income is approximately $35,000 annually. She wishes to increase that income, if possible, while only minimally raising her risk exposure. Mr. Puckett recommended the investment portfolio presented in Table 16.7. The portfolio's objective is to maximize current income while keeping risk at a low level. As seen, all the money was invested in fixed-income securities, with approximately $296,000 going to high-quality corporate bonds and the balance (of $54,000) retained in short-term investments in order to provide a substantial contingency reserve. The resulting asset allocation is about 85 percent bonds ($296,000 ÷ $350,000) and 15 percent short-term investments ($54,000 ÷ $350,000). By investing in the bond portfolio, Mrs. Hatch's yearly income will rise from approximately $35,000 to about $47,800 ($7,200 social security, $4,000 earnings on short-term investments, and $36,600 bond interest). This puts Mrs. Hatch in a 30 percent marginal tax bracket (federal and state tax combined). Taxable corporate bonds were recommended over tax-free municipal bonds because her after-tax rate of return would be greater with the former.

Turning to the portfolio, we see that there are six corporate bond issues that cost about $50,000 each. Each issuer is a high-quality company with a very low risk of default. Mrs. Hatch's portfolio is diversified in several ways. First, it contains a mix

of industrial, utility, railroad, and financial issues. The two utility bond issues are Pacific Utilities and Trans-States Telephone. Both companies are quite large and financially secure. The two industrial concerns, Dalston and Maryland-Pacific, are very large as well. Boise Northern is a financially solid railroad, and Urban Life is a large, secure insurance company. A second added measure of diversification is attained by staggering the bonds' maturities. They mature in six different years: 1993, 1995, 1996, 2011, 2019, and 2025. The shorter-term bonds will provide ready cash when they mature, and they generally will fluctuate less in price than the longer-term ones. The portfolio has been diversified to keep the risk of loss very low. By switching funds out of her short-term investments into bonds, Mrs. Hatch was able to increase her current income substantially while experiencing only a minimal increase in risk.

SUMMARY

- A portfolio is a collection of investment vehicles assembled to achieve a common investment goal. To develop an efficient portfolio, an investor should establish a list of objectives; portfolios may be growth-oriented or income-oriented. A portfolio may contain one type of investment vehicle or many.

- Diversification involves the inclusion of various noncomplementary investment vehicles in a portfolio in order to minimize risk, which may be diversifiable or nondiversifiable. An investor is rewarded only for taking nondiversifiable risk.

- A security's risk in a portfolio is lower than its risk individually, whereas its return is unaffected by the form in which it is held. The investment portfolio can include not only stocks and bonds, but options, commodities and financial futures, tangibles, real estate, annuities, or limited partnerships.

- Under the traditional approach portfolios are constructed by selecting securities issued by companies from a broad cross-section of industries. Traditional portfolio managers often invest in a large number of companies.

- Modern portfolio theory (MPT) utilizes statistical measures such as the correlation of a security's return with the return of another security or with the market as a whole. In choosing securities for a MPT portfolio, statistical diversification—that is, negative return correlation—is a key factor.

- The nondiversifiable risk of a security or a portfolio can be measured with the beta coefficient. Beta measures the relative volatility, or change, in the security's or portfolio's return as compared to the return on a broad market index.

- A valuable outgrowth of modern portfolio theory is the establishment of a specific relationship between nondiversifiable risk and investment return. As the risk of an investment portfolio increases, the return provided should also increase.

- The individual investor should determine the risk he or she is willing to bear, use beta to assemble a diversified portfolio reflecting an acceptable level of

risk, and evaluate alternative portfolios to make sure that the portfolio selected provides the highest return for the given level of acceptable risk.

- To formulate a portfolio management strategy, the investor should consider characteristics such as level and stability of income, family factors, net worth, experience and age, and disposition toward risk.

- After an investor has developed a personal financial profile, he or she should specify desired portfolio objectives: current income, capital preservation, capital growth, tax considerations, and level of risk. These objectives should act as a guide in structuring the portfolio.

- Before buying specific investment vehicles to be included in a portfolio, the investor should develop an asset allocation scheme that divides the portfolio into various asset classes, such as common stock, bonds, short-term securities, and real estate, consistent with his or her portfolio objectives.

REVIEW QUESTIONS AND PROBLEMS

1. What is a portfolio? Explain the first step an investor should take in developing a viable portfolio.

2. Define diversification and explain the motive behind the diversification of a portfolio.

3. Identify and differentiate between the two types of portfolio risk. What is the total risk of a portfolio? Explain.

4. Graphically relate the number of securities in a portfolio to the level of (a) diversifiable, (b) nondiversifiable, and (c) total risk. Explain the significance of this graph in the portfolio management process.

5. What factors should be considered when choosing the ideal number of securities for a portfolio? Explain.

6. Define an efficient portfolio. As an investor, discuss how you would go about creating an efficient portfolio.

7. Compare and contrast a security held in isolation and the same security held as part of a portfolio in terms of (a) risk and (b) return. What effect, if any, does diversification have on risk and return?

8. Compare and contrast traditional portfolio management with modern portfolio theory (MPT).

9. Give three reasons why traditional portfolio managers like to invest in well-established companies. Explain each reason.

10. Define beta. Explain how the nondiversifiable risk of a security or portfolio can be measured by beta. Use examples.

11. If portfolio A has a beta of $+1.5$ and portfolio Z has a beta of -1.5, what do the two values indicate? If the return on the market rises by 20 percent, what impact, if any, would this have on the return from portfolios A and Z? Explain.

12. Are there any particular techniques an investor can use as part of a portfolio strategy? Explain how traditional and modern portfolio approaches can be reconciled.

13. What role, if any, do an investor's personal characteristics play in establishing investment policies? Explain.

14. It is often said that a portfolio must be built around an individual's needs. Do you agree or disagree with this statement? Explain.

15. Describe the risk-income tradeoff as it relates to an investor's age. Compare and contrast the expected portfolios of: (a) a retired investor in need of income; (b) a high-income, financially secure investor; (c) a young investor with a secure job and no dependents.

16. Briefly discuss the possible investment objectives one might consider when formulating portfolio objectives and policies.

17. What is an asset allocation scheme? What role does it play in building an investment portfolio?

18. Briefly describe the three approaches to asset allocation—(a) fixed weightings, (b) flexible weightings, and (c) tactical asset allocation.

19. Describe the procedures used to apply asset allocation. What role could an asset allocation fund play in this process?

CASE PROBLEMS

16.1 Traditional Versus Modern Portfolio Theory: Who's Right?

Walt Davies and Shane O'Brien are district managers for Lee, Inc. Over the years as they moved through the firm's sales organization they became, and still remain, close friends. Walt, who is 33 years old, currently lives in Newark, New Jersey; Shane, who is 35, lives in Houston, Texas. Recently at the national sales meeting they were discussing various company matters, as well as bringing each other up to date on their families, when the subject of investments came up. Each of them had always been fascinated by the stock market, and now that they had achieved some degree of financial success, they had begun actively investing. As they discussed their investments, Walt indicated that he felt the only way an individual who did not have hundreds of thousands of dollars can invest safely is to buy mutual fund shares, since they contain a large number of securities representing the stocks of the leading firms in a broad cross-section of industries. Walt emphasized that in order to be safe, a person needs to hold a broadly diversified portfolio and that only those with a lot of money and time can achieve the needed diversification that can be readily obtained by purchasing mutual fund shares.

Shane totally disagreed. He said, "Diversification! Who needs it?" He felt that what you must do is to look carefully at stocks possessing desired risk-return characteristics and then invest all your money in that one best stock. Walt told him he was crazy. He said, "There is no way to conveniently measure risk—you're just gambling." Shane disagreed. He explained how his stockbroker had acquainted him with beta, which is a measure of risk. Shane said that the higher the beta, the more risky the stock, and therefore the higher its return. By looking up the betas for potential stock investments in his broker's beta book, he can pick stocks having an acceptable risk level for him. Shane explained that with beta one does not need to diversify; one merely needs to be willing to accept the risk reflected by beta and then hope for the best. The conversation continued, with Walt indicating that although he knew nothing about beta, he didn't believe you could safely invest in a single stock. Shane continued to argue that his broker had explained to him that betas can be calculated not just for a

single stock, but also for a portfolio of stocks such as a mutual fund. He said, ''What's the difference between a stock with a beta, of say, 1.20 and a mutual fund with a beta of 1.20? They both have the same risk and should therefore provide similar returns.''

As Walt and Shane continued to discuss their differing opinions relative to investment strategy, they began to get angry with each other. Neither was able to convince the other that he was right. The level of their voices now raised, they attracted the attention of the company vice-president of finance, Elmer Green, who was standing nearby. He came over to Walt and Shane and indicated he had overheard their argument about investments and thought that, given his expertise on financial matters, he might be able to resolve their disagreement. He asked them to explain the crux of their disagreement, and each reviewed his own viewpoint. After hearing their views, Elmer responded: ''I have some good news and some bad news for each of you. There is some validity to what each of you says, but there also are some errors in each of your explanations. Walt tends to support the traditional approach to portfolio management; Shane's views are more supportive of modern portfolio theory.'' Just then, the company president interrupted them, indicating that he must talk to Elmer immediately. Elmer apologized for having to leave and made an arrangement to continue their discussion later that evening.

Questions

1. Analyze Walt's argument and explain to him why a mutual fund investment may be over-diversified and that one does not necessarily have to have hundreds of thousands of dollars in order to diversify adequately.
2. Analyze Shane's argument and explain the major error in his logic relative to the use of beta as a substitute for diversification. Explain the key assumption underlying the use of beta as a risk measure.
3. Briefly describe the traditional approach to portfolio management and relate it to the approaches supported by Walt and Shane.
4. Briefly describe modern portfolio theory (MPT) and relate it to the approaches supported by Walt and Shane. Be sure to mention diversifiable, nondiversifiable, and total risk along with the role of beta.
5. Explain how the traditional approach and modern portfolio theory can be blended into an approach to portfolio management that might prove useful to the individual investor. Relate this to reconciling Walt's and Shane's differing points of view.

16.2 Susan Lussier's Inherited Portfolio: Does It Meet Her Needs?

Susan Lussier is a 35-year-old divorcee currently employed as a tax attorney for a major oil and gas exploration company. She has no children and earns nearly $70,000 per year from her salary as well as through participation in the company's drilling activities. Divorced only one year, Susan has found being single quite exciting. An expert on oil and gas taxation, Susan does not concern herself with job security—she is content with her income and finds it adequate to allow her to buy and do whatever she wishes. Her current philosophy is to live each day to its fullest, not concerning herself with retirement, which is too far in the future to require her current attention.

A month ago Susan's only surviving parent, her father, was killed in a sailing accident. He had retired in La Jolla, California, two years earlier and had spent most of his time sailing. Prior to retirement he owned a children's clothing manufacturing firm in South Carolina, which he sold. He invested the proceeds in a security portfolio that provided him with retirement income of over $30,000 per year. In his will, which incidentally had been drafted by Susan a number of years earlier, he left his entire estate to her. The estate had been

CASE 16.2   Susan Lussier's Inherited Securities Portfolio

BONDS

Par Value	Issue	S&P Rating	Interest Income	Price	Total Cost	Current Yield
$40,000	Delta Power and Light 10⅛% due 2008	AA	$4,050	$ 98	$39,200	10.33%
30,000	Mountain Water 9¾% due 2001	A	2,925	102	30,600	9.56
50,000	California Gas 9½% due 1995	AAA	4,750	97	48,500	9.79
20,000	Trans-Pacific Gas 10% due 2006	AAA	2,000	99	19,800	10.10
20,000	Public Service 9⅞% due 1996	AA	1,975	100	20,000	9.88

COMMON STOCKS

Number of Shares	Company	Dividend per Share	Dividend Income	Price per Share	Total Cost	Beta	Dividend Yield
2,000	International Supply	$2.40	$4,800	$ 22	$44,900	.97	10.91%
3,000	Black Motor	1.50	4,500	17	52,000	.85	8.82

MUTUAL FUNDS

Number of Shares	Issue	Dividend per Share	Dividend Income	Price per Share	Total Cost	Beta	Dividend Yield
2,000	International Capital Income A Fund	$ .80	$ 1,600	$ 10	$ 20,000	1.02	8.00%
1,000	Grimner Special Income Fund	2.00	2,000	15	15,000	1.10	7.50
4,000	Ellis Diversified Income Fund	1.20	4,800	12	48,000	.90	10.00
	Total annual income:		$33,400	Portfolio value:	$338,000	Portfolio current yield:	9.88%

structured in such a way that, in addition to a few family heirlooms, Susan received a security portfolio having a market value of nearly $350,000 and about $10,000 in cash. The portfolio contained 10 securities—5 bonds, 2 common stocks, and 3 mutual funds. A table listing the securities and key characteristics is given above. The two common stocks were issued by large, mature, well-known firms that had exhibited continuing patterns of dividend payment over the past five years. The stocks offered only moderate growth potential—probably no more than 2 to 3 percent appreciation per year. The three mutual funds in the portfolio were income funds invested in diversified portfolios of income-oriented stocks and bonds. They provided stable streams of dividend income but little opportunity for capital appreciation.

Now that Susan owns the portfolio, she wishes to determine whether or not it is suitable for her situation. She realizes that the high level of income provided by the portfolio will be taxed at a rate (federal and state) in excess of 35 percent. Since she does not currently need it, Susan plans to invest the after-tax income in tax-deferred real estate, oil and gas partnerships, and/or in common stocks offering high capital gain potential. She clearly needs to shelter

taxable income. (Susan is already paying out a sizable portion of her current income in taxes.) She feels fortunate to have received the portfolio and wants to make certain that it provides her the maximum benefits, given her financial situation. The $10,000 cash left to her will be especially useful in paying broker's commissions associated with making portfolio adjustments.

Questions
1. Briefly assess Susan's financial situation, and develop a portfolio objective for her that's consistent with her needs.
2. Evaluate the portfolio left to Susan by her father. Assess its apparent objective, and evaluate how well it may be doing in fulfilling this objective. Use the total cost values to describe the asset allocation scheme reflected in the portfolio. Comment on the risk, return, and tax impact of this portfolio.
3. If Susan decided to invest in a security portfolio consistent with her needs (indicated in response to question 1), describe the nature and mix, if any, of securities you would recommend she purchase. What asset allocation scheme would result from your recommendation? Discuss the risk, return, and tax implications of such a portfolio.
4. Compare the nature of the security portfolio inherited by Susan (from the response to question 2) with what you believe would be an appropriate security portfolio for her (from the response to question 3).
5. What recommendations would you give Susan about the inherited portfolio? Explain the steps she should take to adjust the portfolio to her needs.

SELECTED READINGS

Dame, Mark, and Stephen L. Kessler. ''Portfolio Power.'' *Financial Planning,* May 1989, pp. 78–85.

Gannes, Stuart. ''How You Can Future-Proof Your Nest Egg.'' *Fortune/1988 Investor's Guide,* pp. 31–38.

Goldinger, Jay. ''The Portfolio Pros.'' *USAir,* November 1988, pp. 18–26.

Hedberg, Augustin. ''Diversification: The Proven Way to Cut Risk and Protect Profits.'' *Money,* September 1988, pp. 62–72.

''How to Beat the Pros.'' *Changing Times,* May 1989, pp. 32–34.

Jacob, Rahul. ''Five Investment Portfolios.'' *Fortune/1989 Investor's Guide,* pp. 104–14.

Maturi, Richard J. ''Add International Flair to Portfolio.'' New York Time News Service, reprinted in *Dayton, Inc., Dayton Daily News,* July 11, 1988, p. 14.

Reid, Jeanne L. ''Choosing Tactics in the War Against Risk.'' *Money,* September 1988, pp. 83–88.

Wiles, Russ. ''Birth of a Planned Portfolio.'' *Personal Investor,* January 1988, pp. 23–28.

———. ''Pillars of Strength,'' *Personal Investor,* July 1988, pp. 46–53.

17

MONITORING YOUR INVESTMENT PORTFOLIO

After studying this chapter you should be able to:

● Discuss sources of needed data, indexes of investment performance, and techniques for measuring the performance of investment vehicles.

● Describe the methods used to compare investment performance to investment goals.

● Understand the techniques used to measure current income, appreciation in value, and total portfolio return relative to the amount of money actually invested in the portfolio.

● Summarize the methods used to evaluate portfolio performance relative to certain standards, the importance of portfolio revision, and the role of personal computers.

● Describe the role of formula plans and the logic of dollar cost averaging, constant dollar plans, constant ratio plans, and variable ratio plans.

● Explain the role of limit and stop-loss orders in investment timing, the warehousing of liquidity, and the key factors in timing investment sales in order to achieve maximum benefits.

Imagine that one of your most important personal goals is to accumulate savings of $15,000 three years from now in order to have enough money to purchase your first home. Based on your projections, the desired home will cost $100,000, and the $15,000 will be sufficient to make a 10 percent down payment and pay the associated closing costs. Your calculations indicate that this goal can be achieved by investing existing savings plus an additional $200 per month over the next three years in a vehicle earning 12 percent per year. Projections of your earnings over the three-year period indicate that you should just be able to set aside the needed $200 per month. Consultation with an investment advisor, Cliff Orbit, leads you to believe that under his management the 12 percent return can be achieved.

It seems simple: Give Cliff your existing savings and send him $200 each month over the next 36 months, and at the end of that period you will have the $15,000 needed to purchase the home. Of course, there are many uncertainties involved in this decision. For example, What if your income proves inadequate to set aside $200 each month? What if Cliff fails to earn the needed 12 percent annual return? What if the desired house costs more than $100,000 in three years? and so on. Clearly one must do more than simply devise what appears to be a feasible plan for achieving a future goal. By periodically assessing progress toward the goal, one can improve the chances that it will be met. For example, had you found that your earnings were not adequate to permit the $200 per month investment, you might have found a new, higher-paying job; or if the required 12 percent return was not being earned on your funds, you might have sought a new investment advisor. As *actual* outcomes occur, one must compare them to the *planned* outcomes in order to make any necessary alterations in one's plans. If such changes do not permit goal achievement, the goal and/or its timing may have to be adjusted.

The final, and most important, aspect of the personal investment process involves continuously monitoring and periodically adjusting the portfolio as needed in order to keep moving toward the achievement of financial goals. The monitoring process involves assessing actual performance, comparing it to planned performance, revising and making needed adjustments, and timing these adjustments to achieve maximum benefit. Let us see how this is done.

EVALUATING THE PERFORMANCE OF INDIVIDUAL INVESTMENTS

Investment vehicles are typically selected for inclusion in a portfolio on the basis of expected returns, associated risks, and certain tax considerations that may affect the returns. Since the actual outcomes may not necessarily coincide with those expected, we must measure and compare actual performance with anticipated performance. Here we will emphasize developing measures suitable for analyzing investment performance. We begin with sources of data.

Obtaining Needed Data

The first step in analyzing investment returns is gathering data that reflect the actual performance of each investment owned. As pointed out in Chapter 3, a broad range of sources of investment information is available. *The Wall Street Journal* and

Barron's, for example, contain numerous items of information useful in assessing the performance of securities. The same type of information used when making an investment decision is used to monitor the performance of investments held as part of an investment portfolio. Two key areas one must keep abreast of are returns on owned investments, and economic and market activity.

Return Data

The basic ingredient in the analysis of investment returns is current market information. Many publications provide daily price quotations for securities such as stocks and bonds. Investors often maintain logs that contain the cost of each investment, as well as dividends, interest, and other sources of income received. By regularly recording price and return data, an investor can create an ongoing record of price fluctuations and cumulative returns that can be used in monitoring performance. The investor should also monitor corporate earnings and dividends, since a company's earnings and dividends will affect its stock price. The two sources of investment return—current income and capital appreciation—of course must be combined to determine total return. The combination of components using the techniques presented in Chapter 5 will be illustrated for some of the more popular investment vehicles later in this chapter.

Economic and Market Activity

Changes in the economy and market will affect returns—both the level of current income and the market value of an investment vehicle. The astute investor will keep abreast of both national and local economic and market developments. By following economic and market changes, an investor should be able to assess their potential impact on individual investment returns and on the portfolio's return. For example, local real estate prices are affected by such regional indicators as home construction, local income and unemployment, and local zoning law changes. Furthermore, the prices of real estate are more commonly affected by local developments than by national policy changes. The astute real estate investor therefore should keep abreast of local as well as national developments.

Stock prices are affected by the national economy. As we pointed out in Chapter 3, national economic analyses are often available at local banks and are published by many investment services. An investor should relate macroeconomic developments to the returns on securities held in a portfolio. As economic and market conditions change, an investor must be prepared to make revisions in the portfolio to respond to new developments. In essence, a knowledgeable investor is in a much better position to generate a profit (or avoid a loss).

Indexes of Investment Performance

In measuring investment performance, it is often worthwhile to compare the investor's returns with appropriate broad-based market measures. Let us look briefly at several indexes against which an investor can compare the results of his or her investment strategies. (Detailed discussions of these averages and indexes were included in Chapter 3.) Indexes useful for the analysis of common stock include the

Dow Jones industrial average (DJIA), the Standard & Poor's 500 stock composite index (S&P 500), and the New York Stock Exchange composite index (NYSE index).

Despite the widespread use of the Dow Jones industrial average by the news media, it is *not* considered the most appropriate comparative gauge of stock price movement. This is due to its narrow coverage and because it excludes many types of stocks from its scope. For example, companies like CBS, Dow Chemical, K-Mart, and Quaker Oats are not included in the DJIA. If an investor's portfolio is composed of a broad range of common stocks, the NYSE composite index is probably a more appropriate tool. This index consists of stocks that constitute more than 50 percent of all publicly traded stocks, based upon dollar market value. The scope of coverage as measured by market value is three times that of the DJIA.

A number of bond market indicators are also available for assessing the general behavior of these markets. These indicators consider either bond price behavior or bond yield. The Dow Jones composite bond average is a popular measure of bond price behavior and is based on the closing prices of 10 utility and 10 industrial bonds. Like bond quotations, this average reflects the average percentage of face value at which the bonds sell. A variety of sources of bond yield data, which reflect the rate of return one would earn on a bond purchased today and held to maturity, is also available. *Barron's,* for example, quotes these yields for the Dow Jones composite bond average. Other sources are Standard & Poor's, Moody's Investor Services, and the Federal Reserve. Indexes of bond price and bond yield performance can be obtained for specific types of bonds (industrial, utility, and municipal), as well as on a composite basis. In addition, these and other indexes are sometimes reported in terms of *total returns*—that is, price behavior (capital gain or loss) is combined with dividend/interest income to reflect total return. Such indexes are available for both stocks and bonds.

There are a few other indexes that cover listed options and futures, although there are no widely publicized indexes/averages for tangibles, mutual funds, and so on. Nor is there a broad index of real estate returns. Such returns tend to be localized; that is, they vary widely from area to area. And different types of property investments yield widely varying returns. For example, farmland moves in value in relation to farm product prices and to foreign investment in farmland. Thus real estate investors should compare their returns with those earned by other local real estate investors. In addition, it might be wise to compare the investor's real estate returns with the Consumer Price Index and with the NYSE composite index. The former will serve as a useful comparative measure of its effectiveness as an inflation hedge. The latter is useful in comparing the relative return on a diversified stock portfolio with that from real estate investment. Similar approaches can be used in assessing other forms of property investment.

Measuring Investment Performance

 Reliable techniques for consistently measuring the performance of each investment vehicle are needed to monitor an investment portfolio. In particular, the holding period return (HPR) measure first presented in Chapter 5 (and used in one form or

another throughout most of this book to measure an investment's *expected* return) is also used to determine *actual* return performance from stocks, bonds, tangibles, mutual funds, real estate, and other investments. Investment holdings need to be evaluated periodically over time—at least once a year. HPR is an excellent way to assess actual return behavior, since it captures *total return* performance and is most appropriate for holding or assessment periods of one year or less. Total return, in this context, includes the periodic cash income from the investment as well as price appreciation or loss, whether realized or unrealized. Clearly the calculation of returns for periods of more than a year should, as noted in Chapter 5, be made using *yield* (internal rate of return) since it recognizes the time value of money; yield can easily be estimated with the *approximate yield formula*. Since the following discussions center on the annual assessment of return, HPR will be used as the measure of return. The formula for HPR, presented in Chapter 5 and applied throughout this chapter, is restated below:

$$\text{HPR} = \frac{\text{current income} + \text{capital gain (or loss)}}{\text{beginning investment value}}$$

Stocks and Bonds

There are several measures of investment return for stocks and bonds. The dividend yield, for instance, measures the current yearly dividend return earned from a stock investment. It is calculated by dividing a stock's yearly cash dividend by its price. This measure of investment return was discussed in Chapter 6. The current yield and promised yield (yield to maturity) for bonds were analyzed in Chapter 9. These measures of investment return capture various components of an investor's return, but do not reflect actual total return. To provide a measure of total return, the holding period return method is applied. The total return on an investment in stocks or bonds consists of two components: current income (dividends or interest), plus any capital gain or loss. *Holding period return (HPR) measures the total return (income plus change in value) actually earned on an investment over a given investment period.* We will use a holding period of approximately one year in the illustrations that follow.

Stocks. The HPR for common and preferred stocks includes both cash dividends received as well as any price change in the security during the period of ownership. Table 17.1 illustrates the HPR calculation as applied to the actual performance of a common stock. This investor purchased 1,000 shares of Dallas National Corporation in May 1989 at a cost of $27,312 (including commissions). After holding the stock for just over one year, the stock was sold with proceeds to the investor of $32,040. The investor received $2,000 in cash dividends during the period of ownership. In addition, a $4,728 capital gain was realized on the sale. Thus the calculated HPR is 24.63 percent.

The HPR found above was calculated without consideration for income taxes paid on the dividends and capital gain. Because many investors are concerned with both pretax and after-tax rates of return, it is useful to calculate an after-tax HPR.

TABLE 17.1   Calculation of Pretax HPR on a Common Stock

Security: Dallas National Corporation common stock
Date of purchase: May 1, 1989
Purchase cost: $27,312
Date of sale: May 7, 1990
Sale proceeds: $32,040
Dividends received (May 1989 to May 1990): $2,000

$$\text{holding period return} = \frac{\$2,000 + (\$32,040 - \$27,312)}{\$27,312}$$

$$= +24.63\%$$

We assume, for simplicity, that the investor in this example is in the 30 percent tax bracket (federal and state combined); we also assume that like the federal tax code, the state also taxes capital gains at the full marginal tax rate. Thus, dividend and capital gain income to this investor is taxed at a 30 percent rate. Income taxes reduce the after-tax dividend income to $1,400 [(1 − .30) × $2,000] and the after-tax capital gain to $3,310 [(1 − .30) × ($32,040 − $27,312)]. The after-tax HPR, therefore, is 17.25 percent, a reduction of 7.38 percent. It should be clear that both the pretax and after-tax HPR are useful gauges of return.

Bonds.   The HPR for a bond investment is similar to that for stocks. The calculation holds for both straight debt and convertible issues, and includes the two components of a bond investor's return: interest income and capital gain or loss. Calculation of the HPR on a bond investment is illustrated in Table 17.2. The investor purchased the Phoenix Brewing Company bonds for $10,000, held them for just over one year, and then realized $9,704 at sale. In addition, the investor earned $1,000 in interest during the period of ownership. Thus the HPR of this investment is 7.04 percent. The HPR is lower than the bond's current yield of 10 percent ($1,000 interest ÷ $10,000 purchase price) because the bonds were sold at a capital loss. Assuming a 30 percent tax bracket, the after-tax HPR is 4.93 percent: [[(1 − .30) × $1,000] + [(1 − .30) × ($9,704 − $10,000)]] ÷ $10,000—about 2 percent less than the pretax HPR.

Mutual Funds

There are two basic components of return from a mutual fund investment: dividend income (including any capital gains distribution) plus any change in value. Again, the basic HPR equation for mutual funds is identical to that for stocks. Table 17.3 presents a holding period return calculation for a no-load mutual fund. The investor purchased 1,000 shares of the fund in July 1989 at an NAV of $10.40 per share. Because it is a no-load fund, no commission was charged, so the investor's cost was $10,400. During the one-year period of ownership, the Pebble Falls Mutual Fund

---

TABLE 17.2   Calculation of Pretax HPR on a Bond

Security: Phoenix Brewing Company 10% bonds
Date of purchase: June 2, 1989
Purchase cost: $10,000
Date of sale: June 5, 1990
Sale proceeds: $9,704
Interest earned (June 1989 to June 1990): $1,000

$$\text{holding period return} = \frac{\$1,000 + (\$9,704 - \$10,000)}{\$10,000}$$

$$= \underline{\underline{+7.04\%}}$$

---

distributed investment income dividends totaling $270 and capital gains dividends of $320. The investor redeemed (sold) this fund at an NAV of $10.79 per share, thereby realizing $10,790. As seen in Table 17.3, the pretax holding period return on this investment is 9.42 percent. Assuming a 30 percent tax bracket, the after-tax HPR for the fund is 6.60 percent [[(1 − .30) × ($270 + $320)] + [(1 − .30) × ($10,790 − $10,400)]] ÷ $10,400—nearly 3 percent below the pretax return.

Real Estate

The two basic components of an investor's return from real estate are the yearly after-tax cash flow and the change in property value that is likely to occur. (For a more expanded analysis of real estate investments, see Chapter 14.)

An investor who purchases raw land is interested only in capital appreciation because there is normally no positive cash flow from such an investment. Carrying costs associated with a raw land investment may include property taxes, special assessments, and interest costs if financing is used. An investor's return from a raw land investment is normally realized on its disposition. **Reversion,** the after-tax net proceeds received upon disposition of property, is calculated by subtracting from the property's realized selling price all selling costs (commissions plus closing costs), plus any mortgage principal balances that are paid upon sale, and income taxes paid on realized capital gains from the sale. Reversion, then, represents the after-tax dollars an investor puts in his or her pocket when the property is sold. An income property investment provides return in two forms: yearly after-tax cash flow and reversion. A property's yearly after-tax cash flow is basically its rental income minus operating expenses, mortgage payments, and income taxes. In other words, after-tax cash flow is the yearly net cash return an investor receives from rental properties. When calculating an investor's total return from a rental property, both yearly after-tax cash flow and reversion are included.

To provide some insight into the calculation of real estate investment returns, the calculation of the after-tax holding period return on an apartment property is demonstrated in Table 17.4 on page 740. (Note: Due to the more complex nature of real estate taxation, only the after-tax HPR calculation is illustrated.) The Maitland

reversion
the after-tax net proceeds received upon disposition of property; calculated by subtracting selling costs, mortgage repayment, and taxes from the realized selling price.

TABLE 17.3 Calculation of Pretax HPR on a Mutual Fund

Security: Pebble Falls Mutual Fund
Date of purchase: July 1, 1989
Purchase cost: $10,400
Date of redemption: July 3, 1990
Sale proceeds: $10,790
Distributions received (July 1989 to July 1990):
  Investment income dividends: $270
  Capital gains dividends: $320

$$\text{holding period return} = \frac{(\$270 + \$320) + (\$10{,}790 - \$10{,}400)}{\$10{,}400}$$

$$= \underline{+9.42\%}$$

Apartments were acquired one year ago with a $100,000 equity investment by Prudence Zwick, who is in the 30 percent tax bracket. If Prudence sold the property today she would realize reversion of $110,000 after all sales expenses, mortgage repayments, and taxes. The holding period return analysis (Table 17.4) contains the proper real estate cash flow statement, owner's tax statement for the past year of ownership, and the HPR calculation. Ms. Zwick received $6,750 in after-tax cash flow plus $10,000 ($110,000 − $100,000) in after-tax capital appreciation, resulting in an after-tax HPR of 16.75 percent. An investor seeking to compare a security's return with real estate or other property investments' return should find the HPR calculation illustrated above a useful analytical tool.

Other Investment Vehicles

The only source of return on other investment vehicles (like options, commodities, financial futures, and tangibles) is capital appreciation. As noted in the Investor Insights box on pages 738 and 739, portfolios may be diversified by including nontraditional investments along with traditional vehicles such as stocks, bonds, mutual funds, and real estate. To calculate a holding period return for an investment in gold, for instance, the basic HPR formula is used (excluding current income, of course). If an investor purchased 10 ounces of gold for $425 per ounce and sold the gold one year later for $500 per ounce, the pretax holding period return would be 17.65 percent. This is simply sales proceeds ($5,000) minus cost ($4,250) divided by cost. Assuming a 30 percent tax rate, the after-tax HPR would be 12.35 percent, which is the after-tax gain of $525 [$750 − (.30 × $750)] divided by cost ($4,250). Options, commodities, and financial futures' HPRs are calculated in a similar fashion. Because the return is in the form of capital gains only, the HPR analysis can be applied to any investment on a pretax or an after-tax basis. (The same basic procedure would be used for securities that are sold short.)

INVESTOR INSIGHTS

Portfolio Diversification into Nontraditional Investments

A few money managers have decided that if a little diversification is a good thing, a lot is great.

Not for these managers the timeworn routine of shuffling money back and forth among the traditional arenas of stocks, bond and cash. They are spewing clients' investment dollars in a dozen different directions, dabbling in everything from takeover stocks to foreign currencies and commodity futures contracts.

The managers say they are only trying to reduce investors' risk. But critics contend they are running amok.

"This kind of diversification is the wave of the future," says an admiring Mort Baratz, editor of Managed Account Reports, a Columbia, Md., publication.

"It's a great marketing idea that probably has a life of about 18 months," scoffs Robert Stovall, president of Stovall/Twenty-First Advisers Inc., a New York money-management firm.

There now are several limited partnerships open to wealthy investors—and at least one offshore mutual fund—that employ a host of nontraditional investments, each of which is managed by a specialist in the area.

The theory is simple: By reducing the potential impact of a setback in any one particular investment segment, investors should be able to gain a given return with less risk.

Some call it a natural progression. First, research showed years ago that having both stocks and bonds in a portfolio reduced risk. Then, the more defensive managers added cash equivalents such as Treasury bills. And about five years ago the late John Lintner, a Harvard University finance professor, asserted that a portfolio could reap a higher overall return for the same amount of risk by adding a segment devoted to trading futures, which are contracts to buy or sell a specific commodity.

Some nontraditional portfolios now engage in "convertible hedging," which may involve trading stock, convertible bonds and warrants of the same company; short selling, in which borrowed stock is sold in hopes that the price will drop; and trading high-yield "junk" bonds and securities of companies in bankruptcy proceedings.

Mr. Stovall is skeptical. The thirst for asset diversification, he says, reminds him of the 1960s conglomerates built by the likes of Jimmy Ling, which were all but impossible to manage because of their heterogeneity.

But two gung-ho practitioners are Henry Swieca and Glenn Dubin, of Shearson Lehman Hutton Inc. in New York. Both 31 years old, they grew up together in the Washing-

Comparing Performance to Investment Goals

After computing an HPR (or yield) on an investment, the investor must compare it to his or her investment goal. Keeping track of an investment's performance by periodically computing its return will help you decide which investments you should continue to hold and which have become possible sales candidates. Clearly an investment holding would be a candidate for sale if: (1) it failed to perform up to

ton Heights section of upper Manhattan. Both now are senior vice presidents at Shearson, where they have set up a consulting unit that seeks out managers and scrutinizes portfolios for investors wanting to get a finger into many pies.

The two men start with some assumptions: A particular investment adviser will thrive only in certain types of markets. No single adviser will do well in all markets. A manager should have a strong track record in a particular area of investment, much like a specialist in a doctor's office.

According to Mr. Swieca, he and his colleague look for investment sectors and managers whose returns aren't "correlated" with each other. When one sector is doing well, the others might be flat or eroding. Hence the overall risk is reduced.

The two men in August [1988] launched an offshore mutual fund called the Overlook Performance Fund, which isn't available to U.S. investors. It's in 12 different sectors, and it has 52% of its more than $55 million of assets invested in the futures and options markets. The fund through the end of March was up about 10.7% from its inception, after subtracting all fees, while the S&P 500 index advanced 12.3%.

"While our return is about the same as the S&P during this period," Mr. Dubin notes, "our volatility was about one-third of that of the S&P." Because the first six months of the fund's life have been a period of rising securities prices, though, they don't provide a good test of diversification.

The fund was set up offshore because of the regulatory complications of getting approval for a fund that trades both equities and futures contracts.

Messrs. Dubin and Swieca keep a close eye on their managers' performance. If the value of the trading portfolio drops by a predetermined percentage, they cut off the trading immediately. In March, for example, they dismissed a commodity trading adviser. He had presided over a 20% shrinkage in his segment while engaging in what Messrs. Dubin and Swieca viewed as unduly risky trading, by concentrating his efforts in too few commodities.

Of course, such services don't come free. The Overlook fund charges a management fee of 2% of net assets a year. In addition the trading managers receive an incentive fee that ranges between zero and 33% of trading profits. Some of the fixed-income managers receive no incentive fee but do receive an additional asset-management fee.

Robert Gordon, president of Twenty-First Securities Corp., says, "Tactical allocation of funds to highly diverse sectors will probably not ever result in major losses to an investor. But by the same token, such a strategy is highly unlikely to be very profitable either."

Source: Stanley W. Angrist, "Variety Spices up More Portfolios," *The Wall Street Journal,* May 2, 1989, p. C1.

expectations and no real change in performance is anticipated; (2) it has met the original investment objective; or (3) more attractive uses of your funds (better investment outlets) are currently available.

Comparing Risk and Return

In this book, we have frequently discussed the basic tradeoff between investment risk and return. The relationship is fundamentally as follows: To earn more return,

TABLE 17.4   Cash Flow, Tax Statement, and After-Tax HPR Calculation for Maitland Apartments (Past Year)

REAL ESTATE CASH FLOW STATEMENT	
Gross potential rental income	$51,000
Less: Vacancy and collection losses	− 1,500
Effective gross income (EGI)	$49,500
Less: Total operating expenses	− 20,000
Net operating income (NOI)	$29,500
Less: Mortgage payment	− 20,500
Before-tax cash flow	$ 9,000
Less: Owner's income tax (from below)	− 2,250
After-tax cash flow (ATCF)	$ 6,750

OWNER'S INCOME TAX STATEMENT	
Net operating income	$29,500
Less: Interest	− 17,000
Less: Depreciation	− 5,000
Taxable income	$ 7,500
Owner's income tax (tax rate = .30)	$ 2,250

AFTER-TAX HPR CALCULATION

$$\text{after-tax HPR} = \frac{\$6,750 + (\$110,000 - \$100,000)}{\$100,000}$$

$$= +16.75\%$$

you must take more risk. Risk is the chance that the actual investment return will be less than expected. In analyzing an investment, the key question is, "Am I getting the proper return for the amount of investment risk that I am taking?"

Nongovernment security and property investments are by nature riskier than U.S. government bonds or insured money market accounts. This implies that a rational investor should invest in risky situations *only when the expected rate of return is well in excess of what could have been earned from a low-risk investment.* Thus when analyzing investment returns, one benchmark against which to compare them is the rate of return on low-risk investments. If one's risky investments failed to outperform low-risk investments, a careful examination of the investment strategy is in order. The fact that one's investments are outperforming low-risk investments is an indication that they are obtaining extra return for taking extra risk.

Isolating Problem Investments

problem investment
*an investment that
has not lived up to
expectations.*

A **problem investment** is one that has not lived up to expectations. It may be a loss situation or an investment that has provided a return less than the investor expected. Many investors try to forget about problem situations, hoping the problem will go away or the investment will turn around by itself. This is obviously a mistake. Problem investments require immediate attention, not neglect. In studying a problem investment, an investor must make the basic decision whether or not to continue to hold it. Should I take my loss and get out, or should I hang on and hope it turns around? That's the key question. Some investors do not like to realize losses on their investments. They hold on to mediocre ones in hope that they will turn around and can eventually be sold for a profit. Such a strategy can result in a portfolio of poorly performing investments.

It is best to periodically analyze each investment in a portfolio. For each, two questions should be considered. First, has it performed in a manner that could reasonably be expected? Second, if the investment were not currently in the portfolio, would you buy it for the portfolio today? If the answers to both are negative, then the investment probably should be sold. A negative answer to one of the questions qualifies the investment for the "problem list." It should be watched closely. In general, maintaining a portfolio of investments requires constant attention and analysis to ensure the best chance of satisfactory returns. Problem investments need special attention and work.

A Risk-Adjusted, Market-Adjusted
Measure of Return

 So far our discussion has focused on computing the rate of return on each of a variety of investment vehicles. Now we look at a risk-adjusted, market-adjusted return measure. This method of gauging investment performance is most suitable for common stocks and for portfolios of common stocks.

The Risk-Adjusted, Market-Adjusted Rate of Return (RAR)

This measure, called RAR for short, is similar to the capital asset pricing model (CAPM) we looked at in Chapter 5, as it too utilizes beta and a broadly based market index. The measure provides an investor with a tool to gauge investment performance that factors out the influences of general market movements on the portfolio. For instance, if an investor has a portfolio that earned a rate of return of +15 percent over the past year, that return in and of itself does not provide a true comparative measure of portfolio return. The raw return figure alone requires further analysis because an investor needs to know how the portfolio has performed *in relation to other portfolios of similar risk* and *in relation to the market in general.*

To develop a comparative portfolio return measurement, a risk- and market-adjusted rate of return (RAR) needs to be calculated. The formula for the RAR for a given period is:

$$\text{RAR} = \begin{array}{c}\text{return on}\\\text{security or}\\\text{portfolio}\end{array} - \left[\begin{array}{c}\text{risk-free}\\\text{rate}\end{array} + \left[\begin{array}{c}\text{beta of}\\\text{security}\\\text{or portfolio}\end{array} \times \left(\begin{array}{c}\text{return on}\\\text{broad}\\\text{market index}\end{array} - \begin{array}{c}\text{risk-free}\\\text{rate}\end{array} \right) \right] \right]$$

(*Note:* all variables are measured at the same point in time.)

The return on a security or portfolio is its holding period return. The beta of the security or portfolio is computed (or found) according to the method previously discussed. The return on the broad market index is the total return (dividends plus price change) an investor could have earned in the given period if he or she had invested in the market portfolio. The Standard & Poor's 500 stock composite index or the New York Stock Exchange composite index are often used to represent the market portfolio.

risk-adjusted, market-adjusted rate of return (RAR)
the return a security or portfolio has earned after the effects of risk and market movements have been factored out.

Basically the **risk-adjusted, market-adjusted rate of return (RAR)** is the return a security or portfolio has earned after the effects of risk and market movements have been factored out. For example, if a portfolio earned a 16 percent return when the risk-free rate was 7 percent, its beta was 1.5, and the market return was 13 percent, then its RAR is zero percent: $[16\% - [7\% + [1.5 \times (13\% - 7\%)]] = 0\%]$. From these results we can see that the portfolio performed exactly as it was expected to. If a stock or a portfolio has a positive RAR, it can be said that it has outperformed the market in general. Conversely, a negative RAR indicates an inferior performance relative to the market. Thus RAR is a useful tool to gauge a security's or a portfolio's *relative* performance.

A Stock Example

Table 17.5 presents an RAR analysis for an individual stock. The stock, which had a beta of .93, was in the portfolio for one year and yielded a holding period return of 16.63 percent. In comparison, a portfolio composed of securities assembled in a manner similar to the securities in the NYSE composite index would have earned a return of 18.76 percent over the same time period. Utilizing the RAR equation, the stock's risk-adjusted, market-adjusted rate of return for the holding period is -1.52 percent. This security performed worse than the market, earning a return approximately 1.5 percent below that expected during the period of the analysis. Clearly this stock is a candidate for replacement.

A Portfolio Example

In Chapter 16 we said that beta is more useful for portfolio investment strategy decisions than for individual stocks. This is because a smaller portion of a stock's volatility is related to nondiversifiable risk. Typically, approximately 90 percent of a diversified portfolio's volatility is due to general stock market fluctuations. Thus the RAR analysis, while useful for individual stocks, is much more beneficial in the study of portfolio returns. Mutual funds are, of course, portfolios of stocks and bonds, so RAR analysis is particularly useful in the study of mutual fund returns. The beta and the returns on a mutual fund are easy to find and to calculate. Several publications periodically list both the relative fluctuations of fund NAVs as well as fund dividend distributions. Using this raw data, RAR analysis can be utilized to

TABLE 17.5   Risk-Adjusted, Market-Adjusted Rate of Return (RAR) Analysis on a Common Stock

Security: Generous Motors common stock
Holding period: June 20, 1989 to July 1, 1990
Holding period return: +16.63%
Risk-free rate: 10%
Stock beta (May 1, 1989):   .93
Return on the NYSE composite index (July 1, 1989 to June 30, 1990):   18.76%

$$RAR = 16.63\% - [10\% + [.93 \times (18.76\% - 10\%)]]$$
$$= 16.63\% - 18.15\%$$
$$= \underline{\underline{-1.52\%}}$$

rank the relative performance of mutual fund investment managers. An example of mutual fund RAR analysis is presented in Table 17.6.

This fund, the no-load Maize and Blue Mutual Fund, is growth-oriented and riskier than average, as its beta of 1.33 indicates. The period of analysis is slightly over one year, from May 1, 1989, through May 4, 1990. During that time span, the fund paid $.40 per share in investment income dividends and $1.40 per share in capital gains dividends. The fund's NAV rose from $24.12 per share to $26.41 per share. The pretax holding period return for the fund is 16.96 percent. In the RAR analysis it is found that the fund's risk-adjusted, market-adjusted rate of return equals 2.59 percent. The fund's positive RAR indicates a better-than-expected return performance. A mutual fund whose management has consistently earned positive RARs would be an excellent investment indeed.

ASSESSING PORTFOLIO PERFORMANCE

The procedures used to assess portfolio performance are based on many of the concepts presented earlier in the chapter. Here we will look at the portfolio performance assessment process, using a hypothetical securities portfolio over a one-year holding period. The holding period return method is an important part of this assessment process.

Measuring Portfolio Return

Table 17.7 presents the investment portfolio of Robert K. Hathaway, as of January 1, 1990. Mr. Hathaway is 50 years old, a widower, and his children are married. His income is $60,000 per year. His primary investment objective is long-term growth with a moderate dividend return. He selects stocks with two criteria in mind: quality and growth potential. On January 1, 1990, his portfolio consisted of 10 issues, all of good quality. Mr. Hathaway has been fortunate in his selection process in that he has approximately $74,000 in unrealized price appreciation in his portfolio. During 1990 he decided to make a change in his portfolio. On May 7, he sold 1,000 shares of Dallas National for $32,040. Mr. Hathaway's holding period return

TABLE 17.6   RAR Analysis on a Mutual Fund Portfolio

Security: Maize and Blue Mutual Fund
Holding period: May 1, 1989, to May 4, 1990
NAV, May 1, 1989: $24.12
NAV, May 4, 1990: $26.41
Distributions paid out (May 1989 to May 1990):
    Investment income dividends: $.40 per share
    Capital gains dividends: $1.40 per share
Risk-free rate: 8%
Fund beta (May 1, 1989):   1.33
Return on NYSE composite index (May 1, 1989 to April 30, 1990):   12.79%

HOLDING PERIOD RETURN

$$\text{HPR} = \frac{(\$.40 + \$1.40) + (\$26.41 - \$24.12)}{\$24.12}$$

$$= +16.96\%$$

RISK-ADJUSTED, MARKET-ADJUSTED RATE OF RETURN

$$\text{RAR} = 16.96\% - [8\% + [1.33 \times (12.79\% - 8\%)]]$$

$$= 16.96\% - 14.37\%$$

$$= +2.59\%$$

---

for that issue was discussed earlier in this chapter (see Table 17.1). Using funds from the Dallas National sale, he acquired an additional 1,000 shares of Florida Southcoast Banks on May 10. He decided to make the switch because he believed the prospects for the Florida bank holding company were better than those of Dallas National, a Texas-based bank holding company. Florida Southcoast is based in one of the fastest-growing counties in the country.

Measuring the Amount Invested

Every investor would be well advised to periodically list his or her holdings, as done in Table 17.7. The table lists number of shares, acquisition date, cost, and current value for each issue. These data aid in continually formulating strategy decisions; the cost data, for example, is used to determine the amount invested. Mr. Hathaway's portfolio does not utilize the leverage of a margin account. If leverage were present, all return calculations would be based on the investor's equity in the account. (Recall from Chapter 2 that an investor's equity in a margin account equals the total value of all the securities in the account minus any margin debt.)

To measure Mr. Hathaway's return on his invested capital we need to perform a one-year holding period return analysis. His invested capital as of January 1, 1990,

TABLE 17.7   Robert K. Hathaway's Portfolio (January 1, 1990)

Number of Shares	Company	Date Acquired	Cost (including commissions)	Cost per Share	Current Price per Share	Current Value
1,000	Bancorp West, Inc.	1/16/88	$ 21,610	$21.61	$30	$ 30,000
1,000	Dallas National Corporation	5/ 1/89	27,312	27.31	29	29,000
1,000	Dator Companies, Inc.	4/13/84	13,704	13.70	27	27,000
500	Excelsior Industries	8/16/87	40,571	81.14	54	27,000
1,000	Florida Southcoast Banks	12/16/87	17,460	17.46	30	30,000
1,000	Maryland-Pacific	9/27/87	22,540	22.54	26	26,000
1,000	Moronson	2/27/87	19,100	19.10	47	47,000
500	Northwest Mining and Mfg.	4/17/88	25,504	51.00	62	31,000
1,000	Rawland Petroleum	3/12/88	24,903	24.90	30	30,000
1,000	Vornox	4/16/88	37,120	37.12	47	47,000
	Total		$249,824			$324,000

is $324,000. No new additions of capital were made in the portfolio during 1990, although he sold one stock, Dallas National, and used the proceeds to buy another, Florida Southcoast Banks.

Measuring Income

There are two sources of return from a portfolio of common stocks: income and capital appreciation. Current income is realized from dividends. Current income from a portfolio of bonds is earned in the form of interest. Investors must report taxable dividends and interest on federal and state income tax returns. Companies are required to furnish income reports (Form 1099-DIV for dividends and Form 1099-INT for interest) to stockholders and bondholders. Many investors maintain logs to keep track of dividend and interest income as received. Table 17.8 lists Mr. Hathaway's dividends for 1990. He received two quarterly dividends of $.45 per share before he sold the Dallas stock, and he received two $.32 per share quarterly dividends on the additional Florida Southcoast Banks shares he acquired. His total dividend income for 1990 was $10,935.

Measuring Appreciation in Value

An analysis of the unrealized appreciation in value for each of the issues in the Hathaway portfolio is contained in Table 17.9. For each issue except the additional shares of Florida Southcoast Banks, the January 1, 1990, and December 31, 1990, values are listed. The amounts listed for Florida Southcoast Banks reflect the fact that 1,000 additional shares of the stock were acquired on May 10, 1990, at a cost of $32,040. It can be seen that Mr. Hathaway's current holdings had beginning-of-the-year values of $327,040 (including the additional Florida Southcoast Banks shares at the date of purchase) and are worth $356,000 at year-end. During 1990 the portfolio increased in value by 8.9 percent, or $28,960, in unrealized capital appre-

TABLE 17.8   Dividend Income on Hathaway's Portfolio (Calendar Year 1990)

Number of Shares	Company	Annual Dividend per Share	Dividends Received
1,000	Bancorp West, Inc.	$1.20	$ 1,200
1,000	Dallas National Corporation*	1.80	900
1,000	Dator Companies, Inc.	1.12	1,120
500	Excelsior Industries	2.00	1,000
2,000	Florida Southcoast Banks**	1.28	1,920
1,000	Maryland-Pacific	1.10	1,100
1,000	Moronson	—	—
500	Northwest Mining and Mfg.	2.05	1,025
1,000	Rawland Petroleum	1.20	1,200
1,000	Vornox	1.47	1,470
	Total		$10,935

*Sold May 7, 1990.
**1,000 shares acquired on May 10, 1990.

ciation. In addition, Mr. Hathaway realized a capital gain in 1990, by selling his Dallas National holding. From January 1, 1990, until its sale on May 7, 1990, the Dallas holding rose in value from $29,000 to $32,040. This was the only sale in 1990; thus total *realized* appreciation was $3,040. During 1990 the portfolio had both realized appreciation of $3,040 and unrealized appreciation of $28,960. The total increment in value equals the sum of the two: $32,000. Put another way, since no capital was added to or withdrawn from the portfolio over the year, total capital appreciation is simply the difference between the year-end market value (of $356,000, from Table 17.9) and the value on January 1 (of $324,000, from Table 17.7). This, of course, amounts to $32,000, of which only $3,040 is considered realized for tax purposes.

Measuring the Portfolio's Holding Period Return

To measure the total return on the Hathaway portfolio during 1990, the HPR measurement is used. The basic one-year HPR formula for portfolios is:

$$\text{HPR for a portfolio} = \frac{\begin{array}{c}\text{dividends and} \\ \text{interest} \\ \text{received}\end{array} + \begin{array}{c}\text{realized} \\ \text{appreciation}\end{array} + \begin{array}{c}\text{unrealized} \\ \text{appreciation}\end{array}}{\begin{array}{c}\text{initial} \\ \text{equity} \\ \text{investment}\end{array} + \left(\begin{array}{c}\text{new} \\ \text{funds}\end{array} \times \dfrac{\begin{array}{c}\text{number of} \\ \text{months in} \\ \text{portfolio}\end{array}}{12}\right) - \left(\begin{array}{c}\text{withdrawn} \\ \text{funds}\end{array} \times \dfrac{\begin{array}{c}\text{number of months} \\ \text{withdrawn} \\ \text{from portfolio}\end{array}}{12}\right)}$$

This formula includes both realized return (income plus appreciation) and unrealized yearly appreciation of the portfolio. Portfolio additions and deletions are time-weighted for the number of months they are in the portfolio.

TABLE 17.9   **Unrealized Appreciation in Value of Hathaway's Portfolio (January 1, 1990, to December 31, 1990)**

Number of Shares	Company	Market Value (1/1/90)	Market Price (12/31/90)	Market Value (12/31/90)	Unrealized Appreciation (Loss)	Percentage Change
1,000	Bancorp West, Inc.	$ 30,000	$27	$ 27,000	$(3,000)	−10.0%
1,000	Dator Companies, Inc.	27,000	36	36,000	9,000	+33.3
500	Excelsior Industries	27,000	66	33,000	6,000	+22.2
2,000	Florida Southcoast Banks*	62,040	35	70,000	7,960	+12.8
1,000	Maryland-Pacific	26,000	26	26,000	—	—
1,000	Moronson	47,000	55	55,000	8,000	+17.0
500	Northwest Mining and Mfg.	31,000	60	30,000	(1,000)	− 3.2
1,000	Rawland Petroleum	30,000	36	36,000	6,000	+20.0
1,000	Vornox	47,000	43	43,000	(4,000)	− 8.5
	Total	$327,040**		$356,000	$28,960	+ 8.9%

* 1,000 additional shares acquired on May 10, 1990, at a cost of $32,040. The value listed is the cost plus the market value of the previously owned shares as of January 1, 1990.

** This total includes the $324,000 market value of the portfolio on January 1, 1990 (from Table 17.7) plus the $3,040 *realized* gain on the sale of the Dallas National Corporation Stock on May 7, 1990. The inclusion of the realized gain in this total is necessary in order to calculate the *unrealized* gain on the portfolio during 1990.

A detailed change in value analysis is contained in Table 17.9, in which all the issues that are in the portfolio as of December 31, 1990, are listed and the unrealized appreciation during the year is calculated. The beginning and year-end values are included for comparison purposes. The crux of the analysis is the HPR calculation for the year presented in Table 17.10. All the elements of a portfolio's return are included. Dividends total $10,935 from Table 17.8. The realized appreciation figure of $3,040 represents the increment in value of the Dallas National holding from January 1, 1990, until its sale. During 1990 the portfolio had $28,960 of unrealized appreciation (from Table 17.9). There were no additions of new funds and no funds were withdrawn. Utilizing the formula for HPR, we find that the portfolio had a total return of 13.25 percent in 1990.

Comparison of Return with Overall Market Measures

The HPR figure derived from the calculation above should be utilized in a risk-adjusted, market-adjusted rate of return (RAR) analysis. This type of comparative study is useful because it can provide some idea of how your portfolio is doing in comparison to the stock market as a whole. The Standard & Poor's 500 stock composite index or the New York Stock Exchange composite index are acceptable indexes for this type of analysis because they are broadly based and appear to represent the stock market as a whole. Assume that during 1990 the return on the S&P 500 index was +10.75 percent; this return includes both dividends and price appreciation. The return from Mr. Hathaway's portfolio, as calculated above, was +13.25 percent. This compares very favorably with the broadly based index: The

---

TABLE 17.10   Holding Period Return Calculation on Hathaway's Portfolio (January 1, 1990, to December 31, 1990, Holding Period)

DATA

Portfolio value (1/1/90): $324,000
Portfolio value (12/31/90): $356,000
Realized appreciation: $3,040 (1/1/90 to 5/7/90 when Dallas National was sold)
Unrealized appreciation (1/1/90 to 12/31/90): $28,960
Dividends received: $10,935
New funds invested or withdrawn: None

PORTFOLIO HPR CALCULATION

$$\text{HPR} = \frac{\$10,935 + 3,040 + \$28,960}{\$324,000}$$

$$= \underline{\underline{+13.25\%}}$$

Hathaway portfolio performed about 23 percent better than this broad indicator of stock market return.

As discussed earlier in the chapter, meaningful return comparisons must consider risk. In this case, Mr. Hathaway should determine the risk-adjusted, market-adjusted return (RAR). If the RAR is positive, the portfolio performance would be superior (above average), whereas a negative RAR indicates an inferior (below-average) performance. Assuming the risk-free rate is 7.50 percent, the beta of Mr. Hathaway's portfolio is 1.20, and the market return is 10.75 percent, the RAR would be:

$$\text{RAR} = 13.25\% - [7.50\% + [1.20 \times (10.75\% - 7.50\%)]]$$

$$= 13.25\% - 11.40\%$$

$$= \underline{\underline{+1.85\%}}$$

Thus during 1990 Mr. Hathaway's portfolio earned an above-average rate of return.

Portfolio Revision

In the example presented above, one transaction occurred during the year under consideration. The reason for this transaction was that Mr. Hathaway believed the Florida Southcoast Banks stock had more return potential than the Dallas National stock. An investor should periodically analyze the portfolio with one basic question in mind: "Does this portfolio continue to meet my needs?" In other words, does the portfolio contain those issues that are best suited to the investor's risk-return needs? Investors who systematically study the issues in their portfolios will find an occasional need to sell certain issues and to purchase new securities. This process is commonly called **portfolio revision.** As the economy evolves, certain industries

portfolio revision
the process of selling certain issues in a portfolio and of purchasing new ones.

and stocks become either more or less attractive as investments. And in today's stock market, timeliness is the essence of profitability.

Given the dynamics of the investment world, periodic reallocation and rebalancing of the portfolio are a necessity. There are many circumstances when such movements or changes are required. In Chapter 16 we discussed the effect of lifecycle changes on investment strategy. Basically, as an investor nears retirement, the portfolio's emphasis normally evolves from a growth/capital appreciation orientation to a more conservative preservation of capital strategy. For an investor approaching retirement, an appropriate strategy might be to switch gradually from growth issues into low-risk, high-yield securities. Changing a portfolio's emphasis normally involves an evolutionary process rather than an overnight switch. Individual issues in the portfolio often change in risk-return characteristics. As this occurs, an investor would be wise to eliminate those issues that do not meet his or her objectives. In addition, the need for diversification is a constant one. As issues rise or fall in value, their diversification effect may be lessened. Thus portfolio revision may be needed to maintain diversification in the portfolio.

The Role of Personal Computers

As noted in earlier chapters, many investors own personal computers (PCs). These small computers can be programmed to perform many useful functions, including portfolio management and investment performance monitoring. Over the past few years institutional investors and some individual investors have begun using computers to monitor securities prices based upon certain decision-rules that trigger the purchase or sale of securities. This approach, called **program trading,** has had a major impact on securities markets as a result of institutional investors quickly making large trades in order to revise their portfolios in response to computer-generated instructions.

program trading
the use of computers to monitor securities prices based upon certain decision-rules that trigger the purchase or sale of securities.

In addition, software programs are available that enable an investor to do analyses such as those we have just completed. Many investors are now acquiring software packages useful for fundamental and technical security analysis, bond analysis, and real estate investment analysis. During the next few years many more investors are expected to realize that a personal computer is a relatively inexpensive aid in streamlining the investment administration process, as well as for providing database access and performing numerous other investment-related functions. (See Chapter 3 for a description of some of the popular PC hardware, software, and news/retrieval and database capabilities currently available.)

TIMING TRANSACTIONS

The essence of timing is to "buy low and sell high." This is the dream of all investors. Although there is no tried and true way for achieving such a goal, there are several methods you can utilize to time purchase and sale actions. For one thing, there are formula plans, discussed below. Investors can also use limit and stop-loss orders as a timing aid, follow procedures for warehousing liquidity, and take into consideration other aspects of timing when selling investments. Of course, as noted in the Investor Insights box, although buying investment vehicles is generally easy,

INVESTOR INSIGHTS

"Always Sell What Shows You a Loss" . . . Easier Said than Done

Buying is easy. People often accumulate things without having the money to pay for them. They won't travel across the street without a Visa.

The purchase mentality is not limited to sweaters and Volvos; it extends to investments, be they houses, paintings or stocks and bonds.

But selling is another matter. Many people find it hard to unload.

. . .

Of course, selling securities does not generally involve a financial Armageddon. People buy a stock, it goes up or down 10, 15 or 20 percent, and they face a decision.

"Always sell what shows you a loss and always keep what shows you a profit," said Jessee Livermore, a famous stock speculator of the 1920's.

That may have worked for Mr. Livermore, but it is not quite that simple any more. Letting one's profits "run" is harder to do in today's volatile markets, where a hard-won gain can evaporate overnight. All it takes is one rotten trade figure. (The new tax code has encouraged the hit-and-run school of investing by eliminating preferential treatment for long-term gains.)

But if investors are probably more inclined to get out early, most still agonize about abandoning a losing position.

"It's a blow to their ego, if they buy a stock and it goes down," Bernard Herold, who owns a small Manhattan brokerage house, noted. "People hate to take losses."

But with rare exceptions, clinging irrationally to an investment that has collapsed can be disastrous. A small loss can quickly turn into a financial catastrophe.

And opportunity losses can be even more debilitating. Being stuck in the "nonperforming asset" when other investors are making hay elsewhere is the stuff of ulcers.

"A small loss, when realized, becomes an opportunity for profit elsewhere," says Martin Zweig, in his book, *Winning on Wall Street* (Warner Books, 1986). "It gives you the chance to turn a liability into an asset instead of just sitting there praying."

. . .

Unfortunately, neither Mr. Livermore nor anyone else has provided any hard-and-fast rules that tell investors when to sell.

Individual investors may tailor their own guidelines. Some sell when an investment goes up or down a certain percentage; many such people use stop orders with stocks. Some use time frames; they are out by a certain date, no matter what the investment does. Others give their brokers discretion over their accounts; they just don't want to know.

But few people are so disciplined or so disinterested, and selling remains a skill that consists of equal parts of financial need, intuition, luck and grit.

There are lessons to be learned from people who have had to sell under pressure.

Lesson No. 1: When an investment has reached the point the investor had hoped it would, it should probably be sold—especially if it "feels" like it is the right time to sell. First inclinations are often the best.

On Memorial Day in 1984, Richard T. Santulli, chairman of RTS Capital Inc., a Manhattan-based aircraft leasing company, was faced with a decision most investors only dream about. Convinced that interest rates had peaked, he had, over the previous six weeks, built up a huge position in United States Treasury bond futures.

"As a fundamentalist, I believed interest rates were too high," he said. "I made a bet." Some bet. His broker recalls that Mr. Santulli laid out $3 million to control $20 million worth of bonds.

Mr. Santulli was right. Interest rates plunged; Treasury bond prices soared. He sat on a paper profit of $1 million. And although he was pretty sure rates would continue to fall, and his profits mount, he took the $1 million, much to relief of his broker.

"I didn't sell because I had made so much money," Mr. Santulli said. "I never do that. I sold because I felt that interest rates had reached a reasonable level. It was a fundamental decision."

Lesson No. 2: The crowd is usually wrong. When everyone loves an investment, maybe that is the time to head for the exit. The corollary is: load up when everyone else is selling.

Most successful investments are not home runs like Mr. Santulli's; they are more likely to be a series of singles. What does one do with the stock that has gone up steadily but unspectacularly? Mr. Herold, the broker, has a tale:

In 1964 or '65, Chrysler was at 65 a share, give or take an ⅛. And the head of one of the great chart services—I don't want to mention his name—told me it was going to be 71 within a week, based on his charts. The news was all great. The company was going to make zillions. I bet him a nickel that the stock was going to sell at 10 before it sold at 70. I framed that nickel."

Mr. Herold explained that everyone—the chartist, the media, the financial analysts had all jumped on the Chrysler bandwagon. He jumped off. The rest is history. Not only did Chrysler fall below 10, but the company almost went out of business before Lee Iacocca engineered a spectacular government-aided recovery and became a best-selling author and an American icon (as opposed to a Carl Icahn).

Nevertheless, sometimes buy-and-hold is the right tactic. Not too long ago, I ran into a client from my stockbroking years. The lady, whom I had not seen in more than a decade, spotted me in a restaurant and darted over. Given my previous stock-selection record, I could not rule out an assassination attempt.

But she smiled—and thanked me for putting her into the stock of Ralston Purina in 1979 at $12 a share.

"You must have made a nice profit," I said, relieved that she wasn't the one I had put into the company that made asbestos-lined cigarette filters. Profit, what profit, she said, "I still own it! It's at 80 a share."

And she wouldn't dream of selling.

Source: Lawrence J. DeMaria, "When Investors Won't Let Go—No Sale," *The New York Times Personal Investing '89,* November 13, 1988, p. 31.

many people for a variety of reasons find it hard to sell them—especially when they will realize a loss.

Formula Plans

formula plans
mechanical methods of portfolio management used to try to take advantage of price changes in securities that result from cyclical price movements.

Formula plans are mechanical methods of portfolio management used to try to take advantage of price changes in securities that result from cyclical price movements. Formula plans are not set up to provide unusually high returns; rather, they are conservative strategies that are primarily oriented toward investors who do not wish to bear a high level of risk. Four formula plans are discussed here: dollar cost averaging; the constant dollar plan; the constant ratio plan; and the variable ratio plan.

 ## *Dollar Cost Averaging*

dollar cost averaging
a formula plan for timing investment transactions, in which a fixed dollar amount is invested in a security at fixed intervals; a passive buy-and-hold strategy.

Dollar cost averaging is a basic type of formula plan. In this strategy, a fixed dollar amount is invested in a security at fixed intervals. This is a passive buy-and-hold strategy in which a periodic dollar investment is held constant. The investor must have the discipline to invest on a regular basis in order to make the plan work. The hoped-for outcome of a dollar cost averaging program is growth in the value of the security to which the funds are allocated. The price of the investment security will probably fluctuate over time. If the price declines, more shares are purchased per period; conversely, if the price rises, fewer shares are purchased per period. Table 17.11 presents an example of dollar cost averaging. The investor is investing $500 per month in the Wolverine Mutual Fund, a growth-oriented, no-load mutual fund.

In the illustration, during one year's time the investor has placed $6,000 in the mutual fund shares. This is a no-load fund, so shares are purchased at net asset value. Purchases were made at NAVs ranging from a low of $24.16 to a high of $30.19. At year-end, the investor's holdings in the fund were valued at slightly less than $6,900. Whereas dollar cost averaging is a passive strategy, other formula plans have a more active posture.

Constant Dollar Plan

constant dollar plan
a formula plan for timing investment transactions, in which the investor establishes a target dollar amount for the speculative portion of the portfolio and transfers funds to or from the conservative portion as needed to maintain the target dollar amount.

A **constant dollar plan** consists of a portfolio that is divided into two parts. The speculative portion is invested in securities having high promise of capital appreciation. The conservative portion consists of low-risk investments such as bonds or a money market account. The constant dollar plan basically skims off profits from the speculative portion of the portfolio if it rises a certain percentage or amount in value. These funds are then added to the conservative portion of the portfolio. If the speculative portion of the portfolio declines by a specific percentage or amount, then funds are added to it from the conservative portion. The target dollar amount for the speculative portion is constant, and the investor establishes trigger points (upward or downward movement in the speculative portion) where funds are removed from or added to that portion.

Table 17.12 is an illustration of a constant dollar plan over time. The beginning $20,000 portfolio consists of a $10,000 portion invested in a high-beta no-load mutual fund and $10,000 deposited in a money market account. The investor has

TABLE 17.11 **Dollar Cost Averaging ($500 per Month, Wolverine Mutual Fund Shares)**

	TRANSACTIONS	
Month	Net Asset Value (NAV), Month End	Number of Shares Purchased
January	$26.00	19.23
February	27.46	18.21
March	27.02	18.50
April	24.19	20.67
May	26.99	18.53
June	25.63	19.51
July	24.70	20.24
August	24.16	20.70
September	25.27	19.79
October	26.15	19.12
November	29.60	16.89
December	30.19	16.56

ANNUAL SUMMARY
Total investment: $6,000.00
Total number of shares purchased: 227.95
Average cost per share: $26.32
Year-end portfolio value: $6,881.81

decided to rebalance the portfolio every time the speculative portion is worth $2,000 more or $2,000 less than its initial value of $10,000. If the speculative portion of the portfolio equals or exceeds $12,000, sufficient shares of the fund are sold to bring its value down to $10,000. The proceeds from the sale are added to the conservative portion. If the speculative portion declines in value to $8,000 or less, funds are taken from the conservative portion and used to purchase sufficient shares to raise the value of the speculative portion to $10,000.

Two portfolio rebalancing actions are taken in the time sequence illustrated in Table 17.12. Initially $10,000 is allocated to each portion of the portfolio. Then, when the mutual fund's NAV rises to $12.00 so that the speculative portion is worth $12,000, the investor sells 166.67 shares valued at $2,000 and the proceeds are added to the money market account. Later the mutual fund's NAV declines to $9.50 per share, causing the value of the speculative portion to drop below $8,000. This triggers the purchase of sufficient shares to raise the value of the speculative portion to $10,000. Over the long run, if the speculative investment of the constant dollar plan rises in value, the conservative component of the portfolio will increase in dollar value as profits are transferred into it. The next formula plan, constant ratio, relies on the ratio between the speculative and the conservative portions as a rebalancing trigger.

TABLE 17.12   **Constant Dollar Plan**

Mutual Fund NAV	Value of Speculative Portion	Value of Conservative Portion	Total Portfolio Value	Transactions	Number of Shares in Speculative Portion
$10.00	$10,000.00	$10,000.00	$20,000.00		1,000
11.00	11,000.00	10,000.00	21,000.00		1,000
12.00	12,000.00	10,000.00	22,000.00		1,000
→12.00	10,000.00	12,000.00	22,000.00	Sold 166.67 shares	833.33
11.00	9,166.63	12,000.00	21,166.63		833.33
9.50	7,916.64	12,000.00	19,916.64		833.33
→ 9.50	10,000.00	9,916.64	19,916.64	Purchased 219.30 shares	1,052.63
10.00	10,526.30	9,916.64	20,442.94		1,052.63

Constant Ratio Plan

constant ratio plan
a formula plan for timing investment transactions, in which a desired fixed ratio of the speculative to the conservative portion of the portfolio is established; when the actual ratio differs by a predetermined amount from the desired ratio, transactions are made to bring the actual ratio back to the desired amount.

The **constant ratio plan** establishes a desired fixed ratio of the speculative to the conservative portion of the portfolio. When the actual ratio of the two differs by a predetermined amount from the desired ratio, rebalancing occurs. That is, at that point transactions are made in order to bring the actual ratio back to the desired amount. An investor using the constant ratio plan must decide on the appropriate apportionment of the portfolio between speculative and conservative investments. Then, a decision must be made regarding the ratio trigger point at which transactions occur.

A constant ratio plan for an initial portfolio of $20,000 is illustrated in Table 17.13. The investor has decided to allocate 50 percent of the portfolio to the speculative high-beta mutual fund and 50 percent to a money market account. Rebalancing will occur when the ratio of the speculative portion to the conservative portion is greater than or equal to 1.20 or less than or equal to .80. A sequence of net asset value changes is listed in Table 17.13. Initially $10,000 is allocated to each portion of the portfolio. When the fund NAV reaches $12, the 1.20 ratio triggers the sale of 83.33 shares. Then, the portfolio is back to its desired 50-50 ratio. Later, the fund NAV declines to $9, lowering the value of the speculative portion to $8,250. The ratio of the speculative portion to the conservative portion is then .75, which is below the .80 trigger point. A total of 152.78 shares is purchased to bring the desired ratio back up to the 50-50 level.

The long-run expectation under a constant ratio plan is that the speculative security or securities will rise in value. When this occurs, sales of the security will be undertaken to reapportion the portfolio and increase the value of the conservative portion. This philosophy is similar to the constant dollar plan, except that a *ratio* is utilized as a trigger point. The last plan presented below is a variable ratio plan. It could be said that this is the most aggressive of these four fairly passive investment strategies.

TABLE 17.13 Constant Ratio Plan

Mutual Fund NAV	Value of Speculative Portion	Value of Conservative Portion	Total Portfolio Value	Ratio of Speculative Portion to Conservative Portion	Transactions	Number of Shares in Speculative Portion
$10.00	$10,000.00	$10,000.00	$20,000.00	1.000		1,000
11.00	11,000.00	10,000.00	21,000.00	1.100		1,000
12.00	12,000.00	10,000.00	22,000.00	1.200		1,000
→12.00	11,000.00	11,000.00	22,000.00	1.000	Sold 83.33 shares	916.67
11.00	10,083.00	11,000.00	21,083.00	0.917		916.67
10.00	9,166.70	11,000.00	20,166.70	0.833		916.67
9.00	8,250.00	11,000.00	19,250.00	0.750		916.67
→ 9.00	9,625.00	9,625.00	19,250.00	1.000	Purchased 152.78 shares	1,069.44
10.00	10,694.40	9,625.00	20,319.40	1.110		1,069.44

Variable Ratio Plan

variable ratio plan
a formula plan for timing investment transactions, in which the ratio of the speculative portion to the total portfolio varies depending on the movement in the value of the speculative securities; when the ratio rises or falls by a predetermined amount, the amount committed to the speculative portion of the portfolio is reduced or increased, respectively.

The **variable ratio plan** attempts to more aggressively capture stock market movements to the investor's advantage. It is another plan aimed at timing the market; that is, it tries to "buy low and sell high." The ratio of the speculative portion to the total portfolio varies depending upon the movement in value of the speculative securities. When the ratio rises a certain predetermined amount, the amount committed to the speculative segment of the portfolio is reduced. Conversely, if the value of the speculative portion declines such that it drops significantly in proportion to the whole portfolio, the percentage of commitment in the speculative vehicle is increased. In implementing the variable ratio plan, an investor has several decisions to make. First, one has to determine the initial allocation between the speculative and conservative portions of the portfolio. Next, trigger points to initiate buy or sell activity are chosen. These points are a function of the ratio between the value of the speculative portion and the value of the *total* portfolio. Finally, the adjustments in that ratio at each trigger point are set.

An example of a variable ratio plan is shown in Table 17.14. Initially the portfolio is divided equally between the speculative and the conservative portions. The former consists of a high-beta (around 2.0) mutual fund, and the latter is a money market account. It was decided that when the speculative portion is 60 percent of the total portfolio, its proportion would be reduced to 45 percent. If the speculative portion of the portfolio dropped to 40 percent of the total portfolio, then its proportion would be raised to 55 percent. The theory behind this strategy is an attempt to time the cyclical movements in the mutual fund's value. When the fund moves up in value, profits are taken and the proportion invested in the no-risk money market account is increased. When the fund declines markedly in value, the proportion of capital committed to it is increased.

TABLE 17.14   Variable Ratio Plan

Mutual Fund NAV	Value of Speculative Portion	Value of Conservative Portion	Total Portfolio Value	Ratio of Speculative Portion to Total Portfolio	Transactions	Number of Shares in Speculative Portion
$10.00	$10,000.00	$10,000.00	$20,000.00	0.50		1,000
15.00	15,000.00	10,000.00	25,000.00	0.60		1,000
→15.00	11,250.00	13,750.00	25,000.00	0.45	Sold 250 shares	750
10.00	7,500.00	13,750.00	21,250.00	0.35		750
→10.00	11,687.50	9,562.50	21,250.00	0.55	Purchased 418.75 shares	1,168.75
12.00	14,025.00	9,562.50	23,587.50	0.41		1,168.75

A sequence of transactions is depicted in Table 17.14. When the fund NAV climbs to $15, the 60 percent ratio trigger point is reached and 250 shares of the fund are sold. The proceeds are placed in the money market account, which then represents 45 percent of the value of the portfolio. Later the fund NAV declines to $10, causing the speculative portion of the portfolio to drop to 35 percent. This triggers a portfolio rebalancing, and 418.75 shares are purchased, moving the speculative portion to 55 percent. When the fund NAV then moves to $12, the total portfolio is worth in excess of $23,500. In comparison, if the initial investment of $20,000 had been allocated equally and no rebalancing had been done between the mutual fund and the money market account, the portfolio's value at this time would be only $22,000: ($12 × 1,000 = $12,000 in the speculative portion plus $10,000 in a money market account).

Using Limit and Stop-Loss Orders

In Chapter 2 we discussed the market order, the limit order, and the stop-loss order. Here we will see how the limit and stop-loss orders are employed to rebalance a portfolio. These types of security orders, if properly used, can increase an investor's return by lowering transaction costs.

Limit Order

market order
an order to buy or sell securities at the best price available.

limit order
an order that specifies the investor's minimum sell price or the maximum price the investor will pay to buy a security.

In review, there are two basic types of security transaction orders. The **market order** instructs the broker to buy or sell securities at the best price available. This often means that buy orders are executed at the market maker's "ask" price and sell orders at the market maker's "bid" price. Limit orders constrain the broker as to the price and the time limit until canceled if unexecuted. A **limit order** specifies the investor's minimum sell price or the maximum price he or she will pay to buy a security. For example, if an order to sell 100 shares of Full Curve Contact Lens at 18 was placed with a broker, the broker would sell those shares only if a price of $18 per share or higher was obtained. Conversely, if a buy order for that security was placed, the order would be executed only if the broker could buy the stock for

good 'til canceled (GTC)
an order to buy or sell securities that remains in effect for six months unless executed, canceled, or renewed.

day order
an order to buy or sell securities that expires at the end of the trading day it was entered, if not executed that day.

the customer at $18 per share or less. In addition to the price constraint, a limit order can have a time duration of one day or longer or can be **good 'til canceled (GTC).** A GTC order, often called an ''open order,'' remains in effect for six months unless executed, canceled, or renewed. In contrast, a **day order** expires at the end of the trading day it was entered, if it was not executed that day.

There are many ways an investor can use limit orders when securities are bought or sold. For instance, if an investor has decided to add a stock to the portfolio, a limit buy order will ensure that the investor buys only at the desired purchase price or below. An investor using a limit GTC order to buy has the broker trying to buy stock until the entire order is filled. The primary risk in using limit instead of market orders is that the order may not be executed. For example, if an investor placed a GTC order to buy 100 shares of State Oil of California at $27 per share and the stock never traded at $27 per share or less, the order would never be executed. Thus an investor must weigh the need for immediate execution (market order) versus the possibility of a better price with a limit order. Limit orders, of course, can increase an investor's return if they enable the investor to buy a security at a lower cost or sell at a higher price. During a typical trading day a stock will fluctuate up and down over a normal trading range. For example, suppose the common shares of Jama Motor traded ten times in the following sequence: 36, 35⅞, 35¾, 35⅞, 35½, 35⅝, 35¾, 36, 36⅛, 36. A market order to sell could have been executed at somewhere between 35½ (the low) and 36⅛ (the high). A limit order to sell at 36 would have been executed at 36. Thus, a half-point per share (50 cents) might have been gained by using a limit order.

Stop-Loss Order

stop-loss order
a type of suspended order that requests the broker to sell a security at the best available price only if it trades at a specific price or lower.

The **stop-loss order** is a type of suspended order that requests the broker to sell a security at the best available price only if it trades at a specific price or lower. In essence a stop-loss order becomes a market order to sell if a stock trades at the trigger price or lower. The order can be used to limit the downside loss exposure of an investment. For example, an investor purchases 500 shares of Easy Work at 26. The investor has set a specific goal to sell the stock if it reaches 32 or drops to 23. To implement this goal, a GTC stop order to sell is entered with a price limit of 32, and another stop order is entered at a price of 23. If the issue trades at 23 or less, the stop-loss order becomes a market order, and the stock is sold at the best price available. Conversely, if the issue trades at 32 or higher, the broker will sell the stock. In the first situation, the investor is trying to reduce his losses, and in the second, he's trying to protect a profit.

whipsawing
the situation in which a stock drops in price and then bounces back upward; a principal risk associated with the use of stop-loss orders.

The principal risk in using stop-loss orders is **whipsawing,** which refers to a situation where a stock temporarily drops in price and then bounces back upward. If Easy Work dropped to 23, then 22½, and then rallied back to 26, the investor who placed the stop-loss at 23 would have been sold out at 22½. For this reason limit orders, including stop-loss orders, require careful analysis before they are placed. An investor must consider the stock's probable fluctuations as well as the need to purchase or sell the stock when choosing between a market, a limit, and a stop-loss order.

Warehousing Liquidity

One recommendation for an efficient portfolio is to keep a portion of it in a low-risk, highly liquid investment. Let us see why and how this works.

A Buffer

Investing in risky stocks or in property offers probable returns in excess of money market accounts or bonds. However, stocks and property are risky investments. So, one reason to invest a portion of a portfolio in a low-risk asset is to protect against total loss. The low-risk asset acts as a buffer against possible investment adversity. A second reason for maintaining funds in a low-risk asset is the possibility of future opportunities. When opportunity strikes, an investor who has the extra cash available will be able to take advantage of the situation. A sudden market dip, an attractive real estate deal, or a valuable painting available at a low price are all examples of situations where an investor with cash to invest immediately may benefit. An investor who has set aside funds in a highly liquid investment need not disturb the existing portfolio.

Choosing a Liquid Investment

There are two primary media for warehousing liquidity: money market accounts at financial institutions and money market mutual funds. The money market as well as some NOW accounts at banks and savings and loan associations provide relatively easy access to funds and provide returns competitive with (but somewhat lower than) money market mutual funds. With time the products offered by financial institutions are expected to become more competitive with those offered by mutual funds and stock brokerage firms. (See Chapter 4 for a detailed discussion of the role and vehicles available for warehousing liquidity.)

Timing Investment Sales

One of the more difficult decisions an investor must make concerns the appropriate time to sell an investment. Periodically an investor must review the portfolio and consider possible sales and new purchases. Two items relevant to the sales decision are discussed here: tax consequences and achieving investment goals.

Tax Consequences

The coverage of the major tax laws and strategies in Chapter 15 makes it clear that taxes, although often complicated and affecting large investors more, affect nearly all investment actions. There are certain basics that all investors can and should understand. The treatment of capital losses is important; a maximum of $3,000 of losses in excess of capital gains can be applied in any one year. If an investor has a loss position in an investment and has concluded it would be wise to sell it, the best time to sell is when a capital gain against which the loss can be applied is available. Clearly the tax consequences of investment sales should be carefully considered prior to taking action.

Achieving Investment Goals

Every investor would enjoy buying an investment at its lowest price and selling it at its top price. At a more practical level, an investment should be sold when it no longer meets the needs of the portfolio's owner. In particular, if an investment has become either more or less risky than is desired, or if it has not met its return objective, it should be sold. The tax consequences mentioned above help to determine the appropriate time to sell. However, taxes are not the foremost consideration in a sale decision: the dual concepts of risk and return should be the overriding concerns.

Each investment should be examined periodically in light of its return performance and relative risk. If the investment no longer belongs in the portfolio, the investor should sell it and buy vehicles that are more suitable. And finally, an investor should not hold out for every nickel of profit. Very often, those who hold out for the top price watch the value of their holdings plummet downward. If an investment looks ripe to sell, an investor should sell it, take the profit, reinvest it in an appropriate vehicle, and enjoy his or her good fortune. An investor, in sum, should set realistic goals and criteria, and stick with them.

SUMMARY

- Portfolios should contain investment vehicles selected on the basis of expected returns, associated risks, and certain tax considerations. To analyze investment returns, the investor must gather data reflecting the financial performance of each investment.

- Investment performance can be assessed using an index such as the Dow Jones industrial average (DJIA). Bond market indicators are also available for assessing the general behavior of these markets. Because broad indexes are unavailable for assessing real estate returns, investors can compare their returns to those of other local real estate investors.

- Investment returns can be measured on both a pretax and an after-tax basis. Holding period return (HPR) can be used to measure the total return earned on a stock, a bond, a mutual fund, real estate, and other investment vehicles (options, futures, tangibles).

- If one's investments are outperforming low-risk investments, they are earning extra return for taking extra risk. If the opposite occurs, an investor should closely examine the portfolio to isolate problem investments.

- A risk-adjusted, market-adjusted rate of return (RAR) utilizes beta and a broadly based market index to gauge the investment performance of common stocks and portfolios of common stocks. A positive RAR indicates an excess return, whereas a negative RAR indicates an inferior performance.

- Portfolio revision is the systematic study by investors of issues in their portfolios that need to be sold and other new ones that need to be purchased. Periodic

reallocation and rebalancing helps eliminate issues that do not meet the portfolio's objectives.

- Formula plans are used to time purchase and sales decisions. The four commonly used formula plans are dollar cost averaging; the constant dollar plan; the constant ratio plan; and the variable ratio plan.

- The limit order specifies the investor's minimum selling price or the maximum price he or she will pay to buy a security; it can have a time duration of one day or until canceled. The stop-loss order is a suspended order that requests the broker to sell a security at the best available price only if a security trades at a specific price.

- A portion of a portfolio can be held in low-risk investment vehicles in order to protect against total loss and to be prepared to take advantage of future opportunities. The two primary media for warehousing liquidity are money market accounts (and some NOWs) and money market mutual funds.

- An investor who has decided to sell an investment vehicle must consider both the tax consequences and investment goals. Realized capital losses can, up to a limit, be used to reduce taxes. Investments should be sold when they no longer meet the needs of the investor.

REVIEW QUESTIONS AND PROBLEMS

1. Why is it important for an investor to continuously monitor and periodically adjust his or her portfolio? Explain.

2. How do changes in economic and market activity affect investment returns? Explain.

3. Which indexes can an investor use to assess the results of his or her investment portfolio? Briefly explain each of these indexes.

4. What are bond market indicators and how are they different from stock market indicators? Name three sources of bond yield data.

5. Aside from comparing returns on real estate investment with those of local real estate investors, why would a real estate investor also compare returns with the Consumer Price Index and with the New York Stock Exchange composite index? Explain.

6. Briefly discuss dividend yield and holding period return (HPR) as measures of investment return. Are they equivalent? Explain.

7. Mark Smith purchased 100 shares of the Tomco Corporation in December 1989, at a total cost of $1,762. He held the shares for 15 months and then sold them, netting $2,500. During the period he held the stock, the company paid him $200 in cash dividends. How much, if any, was the capital gain realized upon the sale of stock? Calculate Mark's pretax HPR.

8. Joe Clark invested $25,000 in the bonds of Industrial Aromatics, Inc. He held them for 13 months, at the end of which he sold them for $26,746. During the period of ownership he earned $2,000 interest. Calculate the before- and after-tax HPR on Joe's investment. Assume he is in the 33 percent tax bracket.

9. Distinguish between the types of dividend distributions mutual funds make. Are these dividends the only source of return from a mutual fund? Explain.

10. What are the two basic components of an investor's return from real estate investment? What is meant by the term *reversion,* and how is it calculated? Explain.

 11. Describe the holding period return calculation for real estate. Peter Hancock bought a parcel of land in the Red Woods area one year ago for $35,000. He sold the property this year for $42,000, and his reversion from the sale was $40,000 after deducting $2,000 in closing costs and income taxes. Estimate Peter's after-tax holding period return on the investment.

12. What is a problem investment? What two questions should be considered when analyzing an investment portfolio? Explain.

13. Discuss the risk-adjusted, market-adjusted rate of return (RAR) measure. How is it calculated? How can it be used to assess portfolio performance? Explain.

14. Describe the steps involved in measuring portfolio performance. Explain the role of the portfolio's HPR in this process, and explain why one must differentiate between realized and unrealized appreciation.

15. Briefly define and discuss portfolio revision. Explain its role in the process of monitoring a portfolio.

16. Explain the role formula plans can play in timing security transactions. Describe the logic underlying the use of these plans.

17. Briefly describe and differentiate among each of the following plans.

a. Dollar cost averaging.
b. Constant dollar plan.
c. Constant ratio plan.
d. Variable ratio plan.

18. Define and differentiate among each of the following types of orders.

a. Market order.
b. Limit order.
c. Good 'til canceled (GTC)
d. Day order.
e. Stop-loss order.

19. Give two reasons why an investor might want to maintain funds in a low-risk, highly liquid investment. Explain.

20. Describe the two items an investor should consider before reaching a decision to sell an investment vehicle. Explain.

CASE PROBLEMS

17.1 Assessing the Stalchecks' Portfolio Performance

The Stalchecks, Mary and Nick, have an investment portfolio containing four vehicles. It was developed in order to provide them with a balance between current income and capital appreciation. Rather than acquire mutual fund shares or diversify within a given class of investment vehicle, they developed their portfolio with the idea of diversifying across various types of vehicles. The portfolio currently contains common stock, industrial bonds, mutual fund shares, and a real estate investment. They acquired each of these vehicles during the past three years, and they plan to invest in gold and other vehicles sometime in the future.

Currently the Stalchecks are interested in measuring the return on their investment and

assessing how well they have done relative to the market. They are hopeful that the return earned over the past calendar year is in excess of what they would have earned by investing in a portfolio consisting of the Standard & Poor's 500 stock composite index. Their investigation indicates that the risk-free rate was 7.2 percent and the (before-tax) return on the S&P stock portfolio was 10.1 percent during the past year. With the aid of a friend, they were able to estimate the beta of their portfolio, which was 1.20. In their analysis they planned to ignore taxes, since they felt their earnings were adequately sheltered. Since they did not make any portfolio transactions during the past year, the Stalchecks would have to consider only unrealized capital gains, if any. In order to make the necessary calculations, the Stalchecks gathered the following information on each of the four vehicles in their portfolio:

> *Common stock.* They own 400 shares of KJ Enterprises common stock. KJ is a diversified manufacturer of metal pipe and is known for its unbroken stream of dividends. Over the past few years it has entered new markets and as a result has offered moderate capital appreciation potential. Its share price has risen from 17¼ at the start of last calendar year to 18¾ at the end of the year. During the year, quarterly cash dividends of $.20, $.20, $.25, and $.25 were paid.
>
> *Industrial bonds.* The Stalchecks own 8 Cal Industries bonds. The bonds have a $1,000 par value, a 9¾ percent coupon, and are due in 2000. They are A-rated by Moody's. The bond was quoted at 97 at the beginning of the year and ended the calendar year at 96⅜.
>
> *Mutual fund.* They hold 500 shares in the Holt Fund, a balanced, no-load mutual fund. The dividend distributions on the fund during the year consisted of $.60 in investment income and $.50 in capital gains. The fund's NAV at the beginning of the calendar year was $19.45, and it ended the year at $20.02.
>
> *Real estate.* They own a parcel of raw land that had an appraised value of $26,000 at the beginning of the calendar year, and although they did not have it appraised at year-end, they were offered $30,500 for it at that time. Since the offer was made through a realtor, they would have had to pay nearly $1,500 in order to make the sale at that price.

Questions

1. Calculate the holding period return on a before-tax basis for each of the four investment vehicles described above.

2. Assuming that the Stalchecks' ordinary income is currently being taxed at a combined (state and federal) tax rate of 38 percent, determine the after-tax HPR for each of their four investment vehicles.

3. Recognizing that all gains on the Stalchecks' investments were unrealized, calculate the (before-tax) portfolio HPR for their four-vehicle portfolio during the past calendar year. Evaluate this return relative to its current income and capital gain components.

4. Perform a risk-adjusted, market-adjusted rate of return (RAR) analysis on the Stalchecks' portfolio, using your HPR findings from question 3. Assess their portfolio's performance. Also comment on the reasonableness of applying the RAR analysis to a four-vehicle portfolio.

5. Based upon your analysis in questions 1, 3, and 4, what, if any, recommendations might you offer the Stalchecks relative to the revision of their portfolio? Explain your recommendations.

17.2 Evaluating Formula Plans: Charles Schultz's Approach

Charles Schultz, a mathematician with Ansco Petroleum Company, wishes to develop a rational basis for timing his portfolio transactions. He currently holds a security portfolio with a market value of nearly $100,000, divided equally between a very conservative low-beta common stock, ConCam United, and a highly speculative high-beta stock, Fleck Enterprises. Based upon his reading of the investments literature, Charles does not believe it is necessary to diversify one's portfolio across 8 to 20 securities. His own feeling, based on his independent mathematical analysis, is that one can achieve the same results by holding a two-security portfolio in which one security is very conservative and the other is highly speculative. Clearly his feelings on this point will not be altered; he plans to continue to hold such a two-security portfolio until he finds that his theory does not work. During the past couple of years, he has earned a rate of return in excess of the risk-adjusted, market-adjusted rate expected on such a portfolio.

Charles's current interest centers on investigating and possibly developing his own formula plan for timing portfolio transactions. The current stage of his analysis centers on the evaluation of four commonly used formula plans in order to isolate the desirable features of each. The four plans being considered are (1) dollar cost averaging, (2) the constant dollar plan, (3) the constant ratio plan, and (4) the variable ratio plan. Charles's analysis of the plans will involve the use of two types of data. Since dollar cost averaging is a passive buy-and-hold strategy in which the periodic investment is held constant, whereas the other plans are more active in that they involve periodic purchases and sales within the portfolio, differing data are needed to evaluate each of them.

For evaluating the dollar cost averaging plan, Charles decided he would assume the investment of $500 at the end of each 45-day period. He chose to use 45-day time intervals in order to achieve certain brokerage fee savings that would be available by making larger transactions. The $500 per 45 days totaled $4,000 for the year and equaled the total amount Charles invested during the past year. In evaluating this plan, he would assume that half ($250) was invested in the conservative stock (ConCam United) and the other half in the speculative stock (Fleck Enterprises). The share prices for each of the stocks at the end of the eight 45-day periods when purchases were to be made are given below.

	Price per Share	
Period	ConCam	Fleck
1	22⅛	22⅛
2	21⅞	24½
3	21⅞	25⅜
4	22	28½
5	22¼	21⅞
6	22⅛	19¼
7	22	21½
8	22¼	23⅝

In order to evaluate the other three plans, Charles planned to begin with a $4,000 portfolio evenly split between the two stocks. He chose to use $4,000, since that amount would correspond to the total amount invested in the two stocks over one year using dollar cost averaging. He planned to use the same eight points in time given earlier in order to assess and

make, if required, transfers within the portfolio. For each of the three plans evaluated using these data, he established the triggering points given below.

> *Constant dollar plan.* Each time the speculative portion of the portfolio is worth 13 percent more or less than its initial value of $2,000, the portfolio is rebalanced in order to bring the speculative portion back to its initial $2,000 value.
>
> *Constant ratio plan.* Each time the ratio of the value of the speculative portion of the portfolio to the value of the conservative portion is greater than or equal to 1.15 or less than or equal to .84, the portfolio is rebalanced through sale or purchase, respectively, in order to bring the ratio back to its initial value of 1.0.
>
> *Variable ratio plan.* Each time the value of the speculative portion of the portfolio rises above 54 percent of the total value of the portfolio, its proportion would be reduced to 46 percent; and each time the value of the speculative portion of the portfolio drops below 38 percent of the total value of the portfolio, its proportion would be raised to 50 percent of the portfolio value.

Questions

1. Under the dollar cost averaging plan, determine (a) the total number of shares purchased, (b) the average cost per share, and (c) the year-end portfolio value expressed both in dollars and as a percentage of the amount invested for (1) the conservative stock, (2) the speculative stock, and (3) the total portfolio.
2. Using the constant dollar plan, determine the year-end portfolio value expressed both in dollars and as a percentage of the amount initially invested for (1) the conservative portion, (2) the speculative portion, and (3) the total portfolio.
3. Repeat question 2 for the constant ratio plan. Be sure to answer all parts.
4. Repeat question 2 for the variable ratio plan. Be sure to answer all parts.
5. Compare and contrast your results from questions 1 through 4. You may want to summarize them in tabular form. Which plan would appear to have been most beneficial in timing Charles's portfolio activities during the past year? Explain.

SELECTED READINGS

Anrig, Greg, Jr. "Figuring Your Own Fund's Performance," *Money,* June 1986, p. 113.

Boroson, Warren. "Stop That Loss!" *Sylvia Porter's Personal Finance,* November 1986, pp. 83–84.

Edleson, Michael E. "Value Averaging: A New Approach to Accumulation." *AAII Journal,* August 1988, pp. 11–14.

Giese, William. "7 Deadly Investment Sins and How to Avoid Them." *Changing Times,* July 1989, pp. 54–58.

Gottschalk, Earl C., Jr. "Investors Turn to Stop and Limit Orders to Guard Against Stock Market Savings." *The Wall Street Journal,* February 24, 1988, p. 27.

Jacob, Nancy, and R. Richardson Pettit. *Investments,* 2nd edition. (Homewood, IL: Richard D. Irwin, 1988), Chapter 22.

Radcliffe, Robert C. *Investment: Concept, Analysis, and Strategy,* 2nd edition. (Glenview, IL: Scott, Foresman and Company, 1987), Chapter 21.

Sivy, Michael. "Putting Together a Portfolio with a 10% Yield." *Money,* July 1989, pp. 7–14.

Updegrove, Walter L. "To Keep Profits on a Roll, Stay Tuned to the Business Cycle." *Money,* May 1989, pp. 169–72.

Wiener, Daniel P. "When It's Right to Sell a Stock." *U.S. News & World Report,* October 24, 1988, pp. 74–75.

PART SIX

COMPUTER-BASED INVESTMENT MANAGEMENT: PORTFOLIO MANAGEMENT

First the investor must spend considerable time and effort evaluating her or his personal financial position, determining financial goals and investment objectives, researching financial markets and investment vehicles, and finally, over time, developing an investment portfolio that conforms to his or her strategies and contributes toward achievement of investment goals. Then, however, the task shifts from one of development to one of management. Like financial markets themselves, a portfolio is not a static creation. If the portfolio is to continuously meet the investor's expectations, it must be constantly monitored to identify and adjust for weaknesses developed as a consequence of changes in the markets as well as the world's economy. The management and monitoring of a successful investment portfolio can be tedious and is time-consuming. Even though the portfolio is an important part of the investor's wealth, not every individual has sufficient time to commit to these activities, and most people cannot afford the services of a professional portfolio manager. Therefore, the individual investor must do the best she or he can with the time available. The availability of computer software programs specifically for portfolio management and monitoring provides vehicles for efficiently carrying out this process. Listed below are some of these programs.

- *Computer Portfolio Manager* (Dynacomp, Inc., The Dynacomp Office Building, 178 Phillips Rd., Webster, NY 14580; (716) 671-6160 or (800) 828-6772; $79.95; Apple II series.) A portfolio management program that includes all essential portfolio accounting features. Generates a variety of professional reports. User may define investment categories. Does not provide for automatic portfolio updating via the telephone.
- *Portfolio Manager* (Walton Group, 12 Chestnut Street, Boston, MA 02108; (617) 720–4996; $195; IBM PC or compatible.) Uses analytical techniques to measure and report investment performance. Generates five reports which provide information on all aspects of the portfolio. Uses stock betas and beta-adjusted returns to quantify risk in all calculations. Includes a number of mini

programs that allow users to review, correct, and rearrange their security data. System enables users to update prices through Dow Jones New/Retrieval and other data systems and interfaces with spreadsheets such as Lotus 1-2-3.

- *Portfolio Pro* (Personal Micro Services, 1758 Deerpath Court, Suite 1018, Naperville, IL 60565; (312) 420-7108; $69.95; Apple II, IBM PC or compatible.) A portfolio management package that can be used to track stocks, bonds, precious metals, IRAs, and other security investments. Can be used to create portfolios, update prices, record dividends and interest, and make other data entries. The program will generate a current portfolio position, relevant tax schedules, closed-out positions, and an investment summary showing realized and unrealized gains and losses. Program also calculates holding period return, annualized return, and months held for each security.

- *Rory Tycoon Portfolio Manager* (Coherent Software Systems, 771 Antony Road, Portsmouth, RI 02871; (401) 683-5886; $49.95 basic, $99.95 advanced; IBM PC or compatible.) Organizes, tracks, and reports on up to 2,500 investments in stocks, bonds, options, cash accounts, CDs, precious metals, etc. Program calculates net worth, profit/loss, yield-to-maturity, asset distribution, margin, brokerage costs, and much more. Calculations can be displayed for individual investments, categories of investments, or the entire portfolio. Program generates 19 printed reports including certain tax schedules. Can capture security prices from various on-line quote services.

- *Stock Portfolio Allocator* (Portfolio Software, Inc., 14 Lincoln Avenue, Quincy, MA 02170; (617) 328-8248; $35; IBM PC or compatible.) Helps investors minimize investment risk by automatically generating portfolio allocations that have the least possible risk for a specified rate of return. Incorporates the mathematical techniques of modern portfolio theory to tell investors how many shares of each stock to buy for their portfolio. Program includes a built-in database capability for maintaining stock prices, dividends, and rates of return.

- *Stock Portfolio System* (Smith Micro Software, Inc., P.O. Box 7137, Huntington Beach, CA 92615; (714) 964-0412; IBM PC, XT, AT, jr., and compatibles and Macintosh: $225, Apple II series: $185.) This software provides a portfolio valuation report, profit and loss statement, automatic update via Dow Jones News/Retrieval, as well as manual update. It tracks cash investments; generates dividend and interest income reports, expense reports; incorporates current tax law; and provides timing notices (securities going long-term, dividends/bond interest due, options expiring). The program also does margin accounting, option writing, return on investment calculations, position averaging, save/recall historical quotes, and computations of net worth. Expandable for direct access to financial news.

NOTE: The above list of programs should be viewed as illustrative in nature, and *not* interpreted as an endorsement or recommendation. Listed prices and phone numbers are the latest available and are, of course, subject to change without notice.

APPENDIXES

SOURCES OF FINANCIAL INFORMATION

Financial Publications, Journals, and Newspapers

Books for Investors

Information Sources

Commercial Bank Letters and Reports

Professional Journals and Publications

Academic Journals

Institutional Publications

Investors' Subscription Services

Mutual Fund Directories

Investment Advisories and Newsletters

No-Load Mutual Funds

Load Funds

Prominent Independent Mutual Fund Organizations and Their Switching Policies

Financial Publications, Journals, and Newspapers

PUBLICATION	FREQUENCY OF PUBLICATION	YEARLY SUBSCRIPTION RATE	PUBLISHER	TYPE OF INFORMATION
The Wall Street Journal	Daily	$129.00	Dow Jones & Co., Inc. 200 Liberty St. New York, NY 10281 (800) 841-8000	General business, financial and world news, with market quotations.
American Stock Exchange Weekly Bulletin	Weekly	$ 20.00	American Stock Exchange 86 Trinity Place Registration Dept. New York, NY 10006 (212) 306-1445	Summation of exchange activity on a weekly basis.
Barron's	Weekly	$ 96.00	Dow Jones & Co., Inc. 200 Liberty St. New York, NY 10281 (413) 592-7761	Financial and investment news; information on commodities, international trading; numerous weekly market quotation data and summaries.
Comex Weekly Market Report; for Copper, Silver & Gold	Weekly	$ 35.00	Comex 4 World Trade Center Room 9108 New York, NY 10048 (212) 938-2900	Trading activity and trends in metals, futures markets; statistics.
Economist	Weekly	$ 75.00	Economist Newspaper, Ltd. 25 St. James Street London, SWIA IHG England	Economic and political news and trends. European perspective on U.S. business and political developments.
Media General Financial Weekly; Market Digest	Weekly	$108.00	Media General Financial Weekly Box C-32333 Richmond, VA 23293 (804) 649-6000	A statistical wonderland, publishing exhaustive numbers on thousands of stocks and scores of stock groups and subgroups. Also follows mutual funds and prints detailed excerpts from brokerage firms' research reports, market commentaries, and investment advisory newsletters.
Investor's Daily	Daily	$94	Investor's Daily P.O. Box 25970 Los Angeles, CA 90025-9970 (800) 223-1673	Similar to *The Wall Street Journal*, but with more statistics and fewer articles.

PUBLICATION	FREQUENCY OF PUBLICATION	YEARLY SUBSCRIPTION RATE	PUBLISHER	TYPE OF INFORMATION
National OTC Stock Journal	Weekly	$ 89.00	OTC Stock J., Inc. 1780 S. Bellaire St. Suite 400 Denver, CO 80222 (303) 758-9131	Calls itself "America's Financial Weekly for Over-the-Counter Stocks." Often described as a penny-stock publication, but covers many investing subjects, such as financial planning and investor protection. A comprehensive paper in a risk-loaded environment.
Fortune	Biweekly	$ 47.97	Time, Inc. Time & Life Building Rockefeller Center New York, NY 10020	Business and economic developments; evaluates specific industries and corporations; notes banking and energy news.
Financial World	Fortnightly	$ 39.00	Financial World Partners 1450 Broadway New York, NY 10018 (212) 869-1616	Investment analysis and forecasts for specific companies and industries as a whole.
Forbes	Fortnightly	$ 48.00	Forbes, Inc. 60 Fifth Avenue New York, NY 10011 (212) 620-2200	General economic and financial news; reports on various corporations, executives, stocks, and industries. August issue: Annual Performance Review of Mutual Funds.
Changing Times	Monthly	$ 18.00	Kiplinger Washington Editors, Inc. 1729 H Street, NW Washington, DC 20006 (202) 887-6400	Articles of general consumer interest, tax and personal financial planning.
Futures	Monthly	$ 34.00	Futures Magazine, Inc. 219 Parkade Cedar Falls, IA 50613 (800) 221-4352	Charts, illustrations, statistics, articles in the areas of commodities and futures trading and markets.
Inc.	Monthly	$ 25.00	Inc. Publishing Corp. P.O. Box 2607 Boulder, CO 80322 (800) 234-0999	Stresses how-to aspects of financial management, marketing, sales, administration, and operations for small growing companies.
Money	Monthly	$ 33.95	Time, Inc. Box 2500 Boulder, CO 80302 (800) 621-8200	Reports on personal finance: stock market trends, estate planning, taxes, tax shelters, and consumer affairs.

Title	Frequency	Price	Source	Description
National Real Estate Investor	Monthly	$59.00	Communication Channels Inc. 6255 Barfield Road Atlanta, GA 30328 (404) 256-9800	Articles, book reviews, current topics in real estate financing, marketing, partnership offerings and taxation for professionals and serious real estate investors.
Nation's Business	Monthly	$22.00	Chamber of Commerce of the United States 1615 H Street NW Washington, DC 20062 (202) 659-6000	Forecasts, analyzes, and interprets trends and developments in business and government.
New York Stock Exchange Statistical Highlights	Monthly	Free	New York Stock Exchange 11 Wall Street New York, NY 10005 (212) 656-3000	Updates on New York Stock Exchange activity.
Open Outcry	Monthly	Free	Chicago Mercantile Exchange 30 Wacker Drive Chicago, IL 60606 (312) 930-1000	Report on activities of the Chicago Mercantile Exchange.
Personal Investor	Bimonthly	$7.87	Plaza Communications Inc. 18818 Teller Avenue Irvine, CA 92715 (714) 851-2220	Features practical information for investors on everything from mutual funds to how to invest in thoroughbreds. Organized by "Outlook" sections, interest rates, futures, collectibles, and personal finances.
American Stock Exchange Quarterly Report	Quarterly	Free	American Stock Exchange 86 Trinity Place New York, NY 10006 (212) 306-1386	Reports of American Stock Exchange activity on a quarterly basis.
Everybody's Money	Quarterly	$3.00	Credit Union National Association Box 431–B Madison, WI 53701 (608) 231-4000	A guide to family finance and consumer action.
Journal of Financial Planning Today	Quarterly	$60.00	New Directions Publications, Inc. Box 5359 Lake Worth, FL 33461 (407) 964-8727	Articles on personal financial management; estate planning, taxes, tax shelters, mutual funds, commodities, stocks and bonds.

PUBLICATION	FREQUENCY OF PUBLICATION	YEARLY SUBSCRIPTION RATE	PUBLISHER	TYPE OF INFORMATION
Action in The Marketplace: Trading Commodity Futures	Updated Annually	Free	Chicago Board of Trade Literature Section 141 W. Jackson St. Suite 2210 Chicago, IL 60606 (312) 435-7217	Describes activities of the Chicago Board of Trade and the operation of commodity markets.
New York Stock Exchange Fact Book	Annual	$ 10.00	New York Stock Exchange Publications, 18th Floor 11 Wall Street New York, NY 10005 (212) 656-5029	Description of the New York Stock Exchange activity.

Books for Investors

TITLE AND AUTHOR(S)	PUBLISHER	PRICE	TYPE OF INFORMATION
Barron's Finance and Investment Handbook	Barron's Education Series, Inc. 250 Wireless Blvd. Hauppauge, NY 11788 (516) 434-3311	$21.95	Provides an analysis of investment fundamentals and discusses personal investment alternatives. Explains how to read annual reports and financial news and contains a dictionary of 2,500 key terms. Includes listings and addresses of NYSE, AMEX, and NASDAQ (NMS) stocks, as well as directories, with current and historical data, of mutual funds, investment newsletters, and financial institutions.
How to Buy Stocks Brendan Boyd and Louis Engel	Little, Brown Publishers, Inc. 200 W St. Waltham, MA 02154 (7th revision) (800) 343-9204/(617) 227-0730	$17.45	A classic guide to how the market works and how to deal with brokers and securities firms.
Intelligent Investor Benjamin Graham with Warren Buffet	Harper & Row Publishers, Inc. Keystone Industrial Park Scranton, PA 18512 (1973; 4th revision) (212) 207-7000	$21.45	The late Benjamin Graham was the father of modern security analysis. Stock-picking systems come and go, but Graham's fundamental theories, first published in 1949 and revised several times, are still applicable.

PUBLICATION	PUBLISHER	PRICE	TYPE OF INFORMATION
Investment Fundamentals: A Guide to Becoming a Knowledgeable Investor Lawrence J. Gitman and Michael D. Joehnk	Harper & Row Publishers, Inc. Keystone Industrial Park Scranton, PA 18512 (1988) (212) 207-7000	$24.45	An easy-to-understand primer that takes investors by the hand, explains investment vehicles, and shows them how they can "do the numbers" themselves to decide if an investment is worthwhile for their personal financial situation.
Random Walk Down Wall Street Burton G. Malkiel	Norton, W.W. & Co., Inc. 500 Fifth Avenue New York, NY 10110 (1985; 4th revision) (212) 354-5500	$11.95	Presents observations on mortgage securities, zero-coupon bonds, and other investment vehicles available in the contemporary markets. Also includes Malkiel's now classic examination of why stock prices are unpredictable.

Information Sources

PUBLICATION	PUBLISHER	PRICE	TYPE OF INFORMATION
Broker-Dealer Directory	Reference Services Center for Electronic Records National Archives and Records Admin. Washington, DC 20408 (202) 523-3267	$ 16.80	Listing of all broker-dealers registered with the Securities and Exchange Commission.
Business Information Sources. Rev. ed.	University of California 2120 Berkeley Way Berkeley, CA 94720 (800) 822-6657	$ 40.00	Guide to selected business books and reference sources with a section on investment sources.
Encyclopedia of Business Information Services	Gale Research Company Dept. 77748 Book Tower Detroit, MI 48277-0748 (313) 961-2242	$220.00	Comprehensive listings and description of business and investment information sources.
The Fortune Investment Information Directory	The Dushkin Publishing Group Sluice Dock Guilford, CT 06437 (800) 243-6532/(203) 453-4351	$ 8.25	Guide to investing information sources: periodicals, books, courses, recordings, broadcasts, software and databases, and group activities.

PUBLICATION	PUBLISHER	PRICE	TYPE OF INFORMATION
Directory of Investment Advisors	McGraw-Hill Publishing Money Market Directories, Inc. P.O. Box 1608 Charlottesville, VA 22901 (800) 446-2810	$225.00	List of investment advisors registered with the Securities and Exchange Commission.
Money Market Directory	Money Market Directories, Inc. Box 1608 Charlottesville, VA 22901 (800) 446-2810	$685.00	Information on investment management, including tax-exempt funds, investment services, and research departments of brokerage firms.
SIE Catalog	Select Information Exchange 2095 Broadway New York, NY 10023 (212) 874-6408	Free	Irregularly issued catalog providing a directory to publications and services concerned with business and investment in the United States and abroad.
Ulrich's International Periodicals Directory	R.R. Bowker Company Order Dept. Box 762 New York, NY 10011 (27th edition) (800) 521-8110	$279.95	Comprehensive directory of all periodicals published in the United States and abroad.

Commercial Bank Letters and Reports

Most large commercial banks publish regular reports, often free of charge, covering various aspects of the economy, business, and the financial markets. A quarterly index to articles and reports found in 50 U.S. and Canadian bank publications is available as a reference in most business school libraries.

SOME MAJOR BANK NEWSLETTERS AND REPORTS

PERIODICAL	FREQUENCY OF PUBLICATION	YEARLY SUBSCRIPTION RATE	PUBLISHER	TYPE OF INFORMATION
Economic Week	Weekly	$225.00	Citibank Economics Dept. 43rd Floor 55 Order St. New York, NY 10043 (212) 825-5553	Weekly newsletter on U.S. economic trends, consumer prices, construction activity, exchange rates, and inventories.

Title	Frequency	Cost	Address	Description
Financial Digest	Biweekly	Free	Manufacturers Hanover Trust Company, 270 Park Avenue, New York, NY 10022, (212) 286-7342	Selected Federal Reserve data, bank loan figures, business indicators, securities market, New York and international money markets, etc.
Wells Fargo Economic Monitor	Monthly	$ 85.00	Wells Fargo Bank Economics Division No. 0188-057, 111 Sutter Street, San Francisco, CA 94194, (415) 399-7351	A special series of publications on business and finance. Up-to-minute reports on: 1. The Nation, providing analysis of current U.S. and international business conditions and trends, along with a forecast of key economic indicators; 2. California, providing analysis similar to the national report, applying to California only; and 3. money and credit markets, covering Federal Reserve and administrative policies, interest rate movements, and prime rate projections. Also, subscribers may phone members of the Wells Fargo economic department directly to answer questions on business and finance.
Business Review	Bimonthly	Free	Wells Fargo Bank Publications Dept. Box 44000, San Francisco, CA 94144, (415) 396-3000	Review of general business conditions in the Western United States.
Economic Report	Bimonthly	Free	Manufacturers Hanover Trust Company, 270 Park Avenue, New York, NY 10022, (212) 286-7342	Covers the world economy, including foreign trade.
Financial Talk	Bimonthly	Free	Harris Bank, 111 W. Monroe Street, Chicago, IL 60603, (312) 461-2121	Consumer-oriented newsletter on financial products and services.
Economic Outlook	Annual	Free	Bank of America Economics Dept. Box 37000, San Francisco, CA 94137, (415) 962-2060	Three separate reports on world, U.S., and California economic growth. Evaluates future growth, inflation, capital investment, financial market trends, regional growth, and key industrial sectors.

Professional Journals and Publications

Many journals are directed primarily toward the needs of the professional broker, analyst, portfolio manager, and planner but have articles and features which may be of interest to investors generally. These journals are available in most public and college libraries. Some which may be of most interest to investors include:

PROFESSIONAL PUBLICATION	FREQUENCY OF PUBLICATION	YEARLY SUBSCRIPTION RATE	PUBLISHER	TYPE OF INFORMATION
Bond Buyer	Daily	$1,480.00	Bond Buyer One State Street Plaza New York, NY 10004 (212) 943-8200	Newspaper interprets international financial and economic news, covers money markets, government and corporate bond markets, and stock market.
Financial Services Times	Weekly	$ 29.95	M&S Communications, Inc. 437 Newtonville Avenue Newton, MA 02160	Newspaper for financial planners with articles on insurance products, investments, banking, mutual funds, etc.
National Underwriter: Life and Health Insurance	Weekly	$ 60.00	National Underwriter Customer Service 420 E. 4th St. Cincinnati, OH 45202-3396 (513) 721-2140	Weekly newspaper with articles on insurance products, marketing, regulation, taxation, and related issues. Interviews with prominent insurance executives, company news, trends in the industry, statistics, and special issues and inserts devoted to major insurance events.
Property & Casualty Insurance	Weekly	$ 63.00	National Underwriter Customer Service 420 E. 4th St. Cincinnati, OH 45202-3396 (513) 721-2140	Similar to Life and Health edition, but related to property and casualty insurance.
Wall Street Transcript	Weekly	$1,440.00	Wall Street Transcript Corp. 120 Wall Street New York, NY 10005 (212) 747-9500	A professional publication for the business and financial community; reproduces the text of selected brokerage house reports, speeches, and interviews by leading investment managers, and other useful items on companies, mergers, and new issues.
Successful Estate Planning Ideas & Methods	Biweekly	$ 432.00	235 French Court Paramus, NJ 07652 (800) 562-0245	Practical, tested, workable ideas and methods currently used in estate planning.

Title	Frequency	Price	Publisher	Description
Bests Review: Life/Health Insurance Edition	Monthly	$ 15.00	A.M. Best Co. 1 Ambest Road Oldwick, NJ 08858 (201) 439-2200	Articles, columns, and features concerning the life/health insurance industry. Book reviews.
Financial & Estate Planning	Monthly	$ 615.00	Commerce Clearing House 4025 W. Peterson Avenue Chicago, IL 60646 (312) 583-8500	Four volumes for the professional, providing strategies, forms, planning aids, and a newsletter of current articles concerning financial and estate planning.
Institutional Investor	Monthly	$ 195.00	Institutional Investor Systems, Inc. 488 Madison Avenue New York, NY 10022 (212) 303-3300	Articles of particular interest to managers of large institutional investment portfolios.
Journal of Taxation	Monthly	$ 125.00	Warren, Gorham & Lamont, Inc. 210 South Street Boston, MA 02111 (617) 432-2020	A national professional journal of current news and comment for tax practitioners with many articles and regular departments related to tax tips and planning ideas of interest to sophisticated investors.
National Real Estate Investor	Monthly	$ 59.00	Communication Channels, Inc. 6255 Banfield Road Atlanta, GA 30328 (404) 256-9800	An important magazine for news about real estate developments, finance, investment, and management. Each issue includes articles discussing real estate developments in about five different cities or areas.
The Practical Accountant	Monthly	$ 60.00	Warren, Gorham & Lamont, Inc. 210 South Street Boston, MA 02111 (800) 922-0066	Magazine with tax saving and tax planning tips as well as other accounting-related articles. Generally, articles are of interest to practicing accountants, but many articles may be of interest to sophisticated investors.
Property/Casualty Insurance Edition	Monthly	$ 15.00	A.M. Best Co. 1 Ambest Road Oldwick, NJ 08858 (201) 439-2200	Articles, columns, and features concerning the property/casualty insurance industry. Book reviews.
Taxation for Accountants	Monthly	$ 89.00	Warren, Gorham & Lamont, Inc. 210 South Street Boston, MA 02111 (617) 423-2020	A national monthly professional tax magazine for the accountant in general practice, with articles, notes, and comments that often provide relevant tax planning ideas of interest to sophisticated investors.

PROFESSIONAL PUBLICATION	FREQUENCY OF PUBLICATION	YEARLY SUBSCRIPTION RATE	PUBLISHER	TYPE OF INFORMATION
Taxes: The Tax Magazine	Monthly	$ 90.00	Commerce Clearing House, Inc. 4025 W. Peterson Chicago, IL 60646 (312) 583-8500	Published to promote sound thought in economic, legal, and accounting principles relating to all federal and state taxation. Contains articles on tax subjects of current interest and reports on recent federal and state tax matters.
The Tax Advisor	Monthly	$ 85.00	American Institute of Certified Public Accountants 1211 Ave. of the Americas New York, NY 10019 (212) 575-6200	Published by the American Institute of Certified Public Accountants for accountants, but with many practical and informative tax tips for sophisticated investors. Includes notes on relevant current cases, tax legislation, and trends in tax and tax planning.
Practical Lawyer	8/year	$ 20.00	American Law Institute-American Bar Assoc. Committee on Continuing Professional Education 4025 Chestnut Street Philadelphia, PA 19104 (215) 243-1600	A non-technical magazine for practicing lawyers with many tax and legal planning ideas that would benefit sophisticated investors.
Estate Planning	Bimonthly	$ 88.00	Warren, Gorham & Lamont, Inc. 210 South Street Boston, MA 02111 (800) 922-0066	National professional journal for lawyers, accountants, and insurance, trust, and investment practitioners concerned with estate planning, family asset management, trust and estate administration.
Estates, Gifts & Trusts	Bimonthly	$ 529.00	Bureau of National Affairs Tax Management, Inc. 1231 25th Street, NW Washington, DC 20037 (202) 452-4200	How-to-do-it guidance and current developments for informed estate planning.
Financial Analysts Journal	Bimonthly	$ 48.00	Financial Analysts Journal Publications Dept. 5 Boarshead Lane Charlottesville, VA 22903 (804) 977-8977	Articles and transcripts of interest to securities analysts.

Publication	Frequency	Price	Source	Description
Journal of the American Society CLU & ChFC	Bimonthly	$ 24.00	American Society of Chartered Life Underwriters—ChFC P.O. Box 59 270 Bryn Mawr Ave. Bryn Mawr, PA 19010 (215) 526-2500	Insurance education, estate and tax planning, business insurance.
Benefits Quarterly	Quarterly	$ 58.00 (Student $ 40.00)	International Society of Certified Employee Benefit Specialists (ISCEBS) 18700 W. Bluemond Road P.O. Box 209 Brookfield, WI 53008-0209	Objective is to keep employee benefits specialists well informed concerning new developments, trends, problems, issues, and tax and legislative changes in employee benefits field.
CFA Digest	Quarterly	$ 20.00	Institute of Chartered Financial Analysts P.O. Box 3668 Charlottesville, VA 22903 (804) 977-6600	Abstracts of articles in academic and professional journals having particular relevance to investment community.
Institute of Certified Financial Planners	Quarterly	$ 45.00	Institute of Certified Financial Planners 3443 S. Galena, Suite 190 Denver, CO 80231 (303) 751-7600	Articles of importance relating to financial planning profession.
Journal of Real Estate Taxation	Quarterly	$ 98.00	Warren, Gorham & Lamont, Inc. 210 South Street Boston, MA 02111 (617) 423-2200	For professionals and sophisticated investors, articles addressing current tax issues, pending legislation, recent court cases, tax strategies and tactics associated with real estate investing.
Practical Tax Lawyer	Quarterly	$ 25.00	ALI-ABA Committee on Continuing Professional Education 4025 Chestnut Street Philadelphia, PA 19104 (215) 243-1600	Published with the cooperation of the Section of Taxation of the ABA. This journal focuses on the practical aspects of tax law.
Real Estate Review	Quarterly	$ 69.50	Warren, Gorham & Lamont, Inc. 210 South Street Boston, MA 02111 (800) 922-9966	This quarterly is sponsored by the Real Estate Institute, New York University. It contains practical articles on all aspects of real estate and related subjects, written by real estate, legal, and accounting experts. Good book review section.

PROFESSIONAL PUBLICATION	FREQUENCY OF PUBLICATION	YEARLY SUBSCRIPTION RATE	PUBLISHER	TYPE OF INFORMATION
The Review of Taxation of Individuals	Quarterly	$ 88.00	Warren, Gorham & Lamont, Inc. 210 South Street Boston, MA 02111 (617) 423-2200	Articles, essays, decisions, planning ideas, other items of interest to practicing tax attorneys, accountants, estate planners, corporate counsel, executives, and high-income individuals.
Bests' Flitcraft Compend	Annual	$ 35.00	A.M. Best Co. 1 Ambest Road Oldwick, NJ 08858 (201) 439-2200	Gives information on the policies, rates, values, and dividends of most U.S. life insurance companies. At the end are annuity data on over 50 companies; settlement options, cash value tables, mortality tables, compound interest tables, mortgage amortization tables, text of the Social Security Act, analysis of Medicare.
Bests' Insurance Reports Life-Health (Property-Casualty)	Annual	$ 460.00	A.M. Best Co. 1 Ambest Road Oldwick, NJ 08858 (201) 439-2200	Canadian life/health, property/casualty companies listed; usually giving for each a brief corporate history, management and operation, assets and liabilities; investment data, operating comment; statistics on growth of company, insurance in force, new business issued. Rates each company for financial soundness.
Insurance Facts	Annual	$ 15.00	Insurance Information Institute 110 William St. New York, NY 10038 (212) 669-9200	Provides basic facts relating to property/casualty insurance business for editors, writers, students, and insurance people.
Life Insurance Fact Book	Annual	Free	American Council of Life Insurance 1001 Pennsylvania Ave., NW Washington, DC 20004-2599 (202) 624-2000	Offers statistical tables, charts, and interprets text on the life insurance business in the United States. Includes brief historical information and a glossary/index.
REIT Fact Book	Annual	$ 40.00	National Association of Real Estate Investment Trusts 1129 20th St., NW Suite 705 Washington, DC 20036 (202) 785-8717	Provides an overview of 25 years of the REIT industry: who, when, how. Includes historical and year-end statistics and current industry information.

Academic Journals

These journals will be of interest to sophisticated investors who wish to keep abreast of the most recent advances in financial and investment theory and application.

PUBLICATION	FREQUENCY OF PUBLICATION	YEARLY SUBSCRIPTION RATE	PUBLISHER	TYPE OF INFORMATION
Journal of Finance	5 per year	$ 39.00	The Journal of Finance American Finance Association 100 Trinity Place New York, NY 10006	Academic articles on finance, including investments.
Journal of Financial and Quantitative Analysis	4 per year	$ 30.00	JFQA Graduate School of Business University of Washington Seattle, WA 98195 (206) 543-4598	Academic articles on finance, including investments.
Financial Management	Quarterly	$ 30.00 (Student $ 15.00)	Financial Management Assoc. College of Business Adm. Univ. of South Florida P.O. Box 1379 Tampa, FL 33620 (813) 974-2084	Academic articles with an applications orientation, emphasizing both financial management and investments.
Journal of Business	Quarterly	$ 22.00	University of Chicago Press 5801 Ellis Avenue Chicago, IL 60637 (312) 702-7600	Sophisticated academic articles on business and investments.
Journal of Financial Economics	Quarterly	$142.50	Elsevier Sequoia S.A. P.O.B. 564 CH-1001 Lausanne 1 Switzerland	Highly technical/mathematical academic articles on investments, pricing of securities, portfolio analysis, and behavior of speculative markets.
Journal of Portfolio Management	Quarterly	$175.00	Institutional Investor Systems, Inc. 488 Madison Avenue New York, NY 10022 (212) 303-3300	Trends and developments in the management of large portfolios, both theoretical and applied.

PUBLICATION	FREQUENCY OF PUBLICATION	YEARLY SUBSCRIPTION RATE	PUBLISHER	TYPE OF INFORMATION
Journal of Financial Research	Quarterly	$18 (SFA) $19 (SWFA)	Journal of Financial Research Dept. of Finance College of Business Arizona State University Tempe, AZ 85287-3906	Academic articles on finance, including financial management, investments, financial institutions, capital market theory, and portfolio theory.
Journal of Risk and Insurance	Quarterly	$ 40.00	American Risk and Ins. Association c/o Dr. David Klock Executive Director Dept. of Finance College of Business University of Central Florida Orlando, FL 32816 (407) 275-2525	Academic articles in insurance-related areas.

Institutional Publications

GOVERNMENT PUBLICATIONS

Various agencies of the government publish documents that give detailed statistics on virtually all aspects of business, finance, and the economy. The major publications are available for reference in most public and university libraries. These include:

Business Conditions Digest (monthly)
Business Statistics (biennial)
Economic Indicators (monthly)
Long Term Economic Growth (book)
Statistical Abstract of U.S. (annual)
Survey of Current Business (monthly)
U.S. Industrial Outlook (annual)

Information about these publications, including prices and content description, may be obtained by writing to:

Superintendent of Documents
U.S. Government Printing Office
Washington, DC 20402

Federal Reserve Bulletin — Monthly — $25.00

Federal Reserve System
Board of Governors
Publications Dept.
MS 138
Washington, DC 20551
(202) 452-3000

Covers the U.S. Federal Reserve system and its activities.

FEDERAL RESERVE DISTRICT BANKS

Each of the twelve district banks provides various weekly, monthly, quarterly, and yearly reports focusing on current economic issues, monetary policy, recent business activity, money and bond markets, and banking and finance. Most reports are offered free of charge. A list of publications offered may be acquired by writing to the addresses below.

Federal Reserve Bank of Atlanta
104 Marietta St.
Atlanta, GA 30303

Federal Reserve Bank of Boston
600 Atlantic Ave.
Boston, MA 02106

Federal Reserve Bank of Cleveland
East 6th St. and Superior Ave.
Cleveland, OH 44101

Federal Reserve Bank of Chicago
Box 834
Chicago, IL 60690

Federal Reserve Bank of Dallas
Station K
Dallas, TX 75222

Federal Reserve Bank of Kansas City
Federal Reserve Station
Kansas City, MO 64198

Federal Reserve Bank of Minneapolis
250 Marquette Ave.
Minneapolis, MN 55480

Federal Reserve Bank of New York
33 Liberty St.
New York, NY 10045

Federal Reserve Bank of Philadelphia
Box 66—Public Services
Philadelphia, PA 19105

Federal Reserve Bank of Richmond
Box 27622
Richmond, VA 23261

Federal Reserve Bank of St. Louis
Box 442
St. Louis, MO 63166

Federal Reserve Bank of San Francisco
Box 7702
San Francisco, CA 94120

NONGOVERNMENT PUBLICATIONS

American Council of Life Insurance
1850 K Street
Washington, DC 20006
A Life Insurance Fact Book (free)
A List of Worthwhile Life and
Health Insurance Books (free)

The American Economic Foundation
51 East 42 St.
New York, NY 10017
Sample packet of materials (free)

Chamber of Commerce of the United States
1615 H Street NW
Washington, DC 20062
Publications directory (free)

Chicago Board of Trade
Literature Services
141 W. Jackson Blvd.
Chicago, IL 60604

Dun & Bradstreet, Inc.
Public Relations Dept.
99 Church St.
New York, NY 10007
Reports and reference books (free)

New York Stock Exchange
Information Bureau
Box 252 Wall Street Station
New York, NY 10005

NONGOVERNMENT PUBLICATIONS

American Stock Exchange, Inc.
86 Trinity Place
New York, NY 10006
Publications catalog (free)

Chicago Mercantile Exchange
444 W. Jackson Blvd.
Chicago, IL 60606
Bibliography and information source list (free)

Dow Jones & Company, Inc.
The Educational Service Bureau
Box 300, Princeton, NJ 08540
Programs, services, and materials (free)

Tax Foundation, Inc.
Publications Catalog
50 Rockefeller Plaza
New York, NY 10020

Investors' Subscription Services

Once one is comfortable with the fundamentals of investing and possibly, after evaluating personal finances and establishing investment goals, has taken the plunge, so to speak, it is time to monitor one's investments to ensure they are performing as intended. If they are not, it may be advantageous to adjust one's portfolio.

Effective monitoring requires current information. Unfortunately, obtaining needed resources usually requires considerable time and effort, both of which most people do not normally have. There are, however, subscription services which present current, needed information in a concise and timely fashion. The services are not cheap, but they do perform necessary research and present important information. The services reduce the time and effort required for proper monitoring of an investment portfolio.

Two of the better known are Standard and Poor's and Moody's Investors Services. Products these two organizations offer are presented in the following listings.

STANDARD AND POOR'S: 345 HUDSON STREET, NEW YORK, NEW YORK 10014

PUBLICATION	FREQUENCY OF PUBLICATION	SUBSCRIPTION PRICE	TYPE OF INFORMATION
Corporation Records	Daily revisions	$2,136.00	Comprehensive reference library on corporations in 6 loose-leaf binders.
Dividend Record	Daily Weekly Quarterly	$ 610.00 $ 305.00 $ 120.00	Authority on dividend details.
Called Bond Record	Semiweekly	$ 800.00	Reports calls and tenders, sinking-fund proposals, defaulted issues, forthcoming redemptions, etc.
Creditweek	Weekly	$1,238.00	Comments on trends and outlook for fixed-income securities, including money-market instruments and corporate and government bonds. Money market rates, bond yields, federal figures, new offerings, credit analyses.

Title	Frequency	Price	Description
Daily Action Stock Charts	Weekly	$ 447.00	Numerous stocks plotted on a daily basis.
Registered Bond Interest Record	Weekly	$1,900.00	Weekly cumulative record of information relating to interest payment on registered bonds.
The Outlook	Weekly	219.00	Specific advice on individual stocks. Analyzes and projects business trends. Advice and articles on special situations, stock groups, economics, industries, options, and subjects of concern to investors.
Review of Financial Services Regulation	Semi-monthly	$1,900.00	Practical analysis of regulation affecting the banking and insurance industries. Covers a broad spectrum—banks offering brokerage services; financial planning; insurance companies offering financial services; consumer credit.
Bond Guide	Monthly	$ 145.00	Descriptive and statistical data on 3,000 corporate bonds. Nearly 10,000 state, municipal, general obligation, and revenue bonds, over 650 convertibles, and more than 200 foreign bonds.
Current Market Perspectives	Monthly	$ 157.00	Books of charts on 100 issues shows Hi-Lo-Close, for five years.
Stock Guide	Monthly	$ 88.000	Data and reviews on over 5,100 common and preferred stocks listed and OTC. Also, special section on performance of over 380 mutual funds.
OTC Chart Manual	Bimonthly	$ 129.00	Charts the most active over-the-counter stocks.
Daily Stock Price Record	Quarterly	$ 268.00 ASE 282.00 NYSE 340.00 OTC	Three sets of volumes, each set devoted to one market—NYSE, ASE, or OTC. NYSE volumes cover over 2,400 issues; ASE volumes cover more than 1,000; OTC volumes cover over 4,000 issues, including more than 500 mutual funds and 3,500 NASDAQ bank, insurance, and industrial companies.
Growth Stocks Handbook	Semiannual update	$ 57.00	Facts and figures on over 300 stocks with accelerated earnings growth over the past 5 years.
Oil and Gas Stocks Handbook	Semiannual update	$ 57.00	Over 250 stock reports on international and domestic oil companies; crude oil and gas producers; coal companies; refining companies, exploration and gathering companies; oil-well service companies; off-shore drilling companies; and marine construction companies. Special editorial appraising energy situation.

PUBLICATION	FREQUENCY OF PUBLICATION	SUBSCRIPTION PRICE	TYPE OF INFORMATION
OTC Handbook	Semiannual update	$ 57.00	Individual stock reports on over 526 important OTC stocks; the biggest, most actively traded; the fastest growing OTC stocks; low-priced stocks, and selected banks and insurance companies.
Analysts Handbook	Annual (monthly updates)	$ 605.00	Per-share data on various industries and S&P's Industrials.
Register of Corporate Directors and Executives	Annual (with supplements)	$ 425.00	Directory of executive personnel.
Industry Surveys	Annual (with 2 supplements)	$ 995.00	Surveys 65 leading industries under 32 headings. Trend and projections. Letter that forecasts industry and economic trends; earnings supplement.
Stock Summary	Annual	$ 43.50	Condensed information on widely traded stocks, editorial features highlighting industries of current interest to investors and S&Ps. Rapid growth stocks feature focusing on companies with high 5-year growth rates.
ASE Stock Reports	Periodically revised	$ 660.00	Data on American Exchange issues, financial aspects, current items, etc.
NYSE Stock Reports	Periodically revised	$ 820.00	Data on numerous NYSE issues, including financial data, latest developments, etc.
OTC Stock Reports	Periodically revised	$ 660.00	Regional and over-the-counter stocks surveyed.

MOODY'S INVESTORS SERVICES, INC. 99 CHURCH STREET, NEW YORK, NEW YORK 10007

PUBLICATION	FREQUENCY OF PUBLICATION	SUBSCRIPTION PRICE	TYPE OF INFORMATION
Dividend Record	Twice weekly and annual year-end issue	345.00	Dividend information on various issues.
Bond Survey	Weekly	$ 895.00	Comments and recommendations on issues in various bond categories
International Manual	Biweekly	$1,280.00	Business/financial information on over 3,000 major corporations and multinational institutions in 95 countries.
Bond Record	Monthly	$ 125.00	Issues, current prices, call prices, ratings, and other statistics on numerous bonds.

Handbook of Common Stocks	Quarterly	$ 145.00	Statistics and background on common stocks.
Moody's Bank and Finance News Reports	Yearly (supplement twice weekly)	$ 895.00	Facts and figures on financial enterprises.
Moody's Industrial Manual	Yearly (supplement twice weekly)	$ 895.00	Information on industrial stocks, history, management, financial data.
Moody's Municipal and Governments Manual	Yearly (supplement twice weekly)	$1,175.00	Information and ratings on governments, municipals, foreign bonds.
Moody's Public Utility Manual	Yearly (supplement twice weekly)	$ 780.00	Information on public utilities, plus special studies on market areas.
Moody's Transportation Manual	Yearly (supplement twice weekly)	$ 750.00	Information on transportation companies such as air, rail, bus, oil pipelines, tunnel and bridge companies, trucking.
OTC Industrial Manual	Yearly (supplement twice weekly)	$ 815.00	Reference source for over 2,700 OTC issues.
OTC Unlisted Manual	Yearly (supplement weekly)	$ 750.00	Detailed information on 2,000 hard-to-find, emerging companies not listed on any of the major or regional exchanges and not reported on the NASDAQ National Market System.

Mutual Fund Directories

PUBLICATION	FREQUENCY OF PUBLICATION	YEARLY SUBSCRIPTION RATE	PUBLISHER	TYPE OF INFORMATION
Mutual Fund Guide	Biweekly	$500.00	Commerce Clearing House Inc. 4025 W. Petersen Ave. Chicago, IL 60646 (312) 583-8500	Covers federal and state rules governing mutual funds.
United Mutual Fund Selector	Semi-monthly	$110.00	United Business Service Company 210 Newbury Street Boston, MA 02116 (617) 267-8855	This report evaluates mutual funds, including bond and municipal bond funds. Reports industry developments; includes tables and charts.
Fundline	Monthly	$127.00	Fundline Box 663 Woodland Hills, CA 91365 (818) 346-5637	Monthly report on no-load mutual funds with buy-sell recommendations.

PUBLICATION	FREQUENCY OF PUBLICATION	YEARLY SUBSCRIPTION RATE	PUBLISHER	TYPE OF INFORMATION
Growth Fund Guide	Monthly	$ 89.00	Growth Fund Research Box 6600 Rapid City, SD 57709 (605) 341-1971	Twenty-four page publication tracking solidly proven funds. Ranks funds by the volatility of stock portfolio.
Mutual Fund Trends	Monthly	$119.00	Growth Fund Research Box 6600 Rapid City, SD 57709 (605) 341-1971	Chart book for no-load and low-load fund investors.
Mutual Fund Forecaster	Monthly	$ 49.00	Institute for Econometric Research 3471 N. Federal Hwy. Fort Lauderdale, FL 33306 (305) 563-9000	Forecasts performance for more than 300 mutual funds and rates best buys. A Directory of Mutual Funds is included in which performance data, one-year profit projections, and risk ratings are presented.
No-load Fund X	Monthly	$100.00	No-Load Fund X 235 Montgomery St. Suite 662 San Francisco, CA 94104 (415) 866-7979	Monthly publication ranking over 300 no-load funds. Provides switching advice for movement of investments among fund families.
Telephone Switch	Monthly	$117.00	Telephone Switch Newsletter 5772 Bolsa Avenue Suite 100 Huntington Beach, CA 92647 (714) 898-2588	Monthly report providing specific market timing investment funding switching advice. Includes a telephone hot line to inform subscribers of changes in recommendations.
Wiesenberger's Current Performance	Monthly	$175.00	Warren, Gorham & Lamont, Inc. 210 South Street Boston, MA 02111 (617) 423-2020	A supplement to Wiesenberger Services, Inc., *Investment Companies*, providing detailed monthly data on mutual fund performance.
Donoghue's Money Letter	Bimonthly	$ 87.00	Box 6640 Holliston, MA 01746 (508) 429-5930	Reports exclusively on money market mutual funds: performance, portfolio composition, management, current yields.
Donoghue's Mutual Fund Almanac	Annual	$ 26.00	Box 6640 Holliston, MA 01746 (508) 429-5930	Statistical review of 10-year performance of over 850 mutual funds.

	FREQUENCY OF PUBLICATION	YEARLY SUBSCRIPTION RATE	PUBLISHER	TYPE OF INFORMATION
Morningstar's Mutual Fund Values	Biweekly	$295.00	Morningstar, Inc. 53 W. Jackson Blvd. Chicago, IL 60604 (800) 876-5005	Provides a thorough, in-depth analysis of the investment behavior and market performance of nearly 1,000 mutual funds; looks at both risk and return characteristics.
Mutual Fund Investing	Annual	$ 99.00	Phillips Publishing Co. 7811 Montrose Road Potomac, MD 20854 (301) 340-2100	Investment advice designed for investor's investment goals.
Wiesenberger Services, Inc. Investment Companies	Annual	$395.00	Warren, Gorham & Lamont, Inc. 210 South Street Boston, MA 02111 (617) 423-2020	The publication considered by many in the investment community to be the bible on mutual funds and investment companies. Gives background, management policy, and financial record for all leading U.S. and Canadian investment companies. Published annually with quarterly updatings. This publication is available for reference in most public and college libraries.

Investment Advisories and Newsletters

PUBLICATION	FREQUENCY OF PUBLICATION	YEARLY SUBSCRIPTION RATE	PUBLISHER	TYPE OF INFORMATION
American Banker	Daily	$555.00	American Banker/Bond Buyer 1 State St. Plaza New York, NY 10004 (800) 221-1800	Daily news and features to meet the working needs of bankers in the United States.
Commodity Service	Weekly	$245.00	Dunn & Hargitt, Inc. 22 N. 2nd Street Box 1100 Lafayette, IN 47902 (317) 423-2624	The service charts 34 of the most actively traded commodities. Includes buy and sell recommendations.
Dow Theory Forecasts	Weekly	$198.00	Dow Theory Forecasts, Inc. 7412 Calumet Avenue Hammond, IN 46324-2692 (219) 931-6480	Forecasts of stock market based on Dow theory. List of their stock choices, generally blue chips.

PUBLICATION	FREQUENCY OF PUBLICATION	YEARLY SUBSCRIPTION RATE	PUBLISHER	TYPE OF INFORMATION
RHM Survey of Warrants, Options & Low-Price Stocks	Weekly	$185.00	RHM Associates, Inc. 172 Forest Avenue Glen Cove, NY 11542 (516) 759-2904	Investment advice on warrants, call and put options, and low-priced stocks. Tables and charts.
The Kiplinger Washington Letter	Weekly	$ 58.00	Kiplinger Washington Editors, Inc. 1729 H Street, NW Washington, DC 20006 (202) 887-6400	Newsletter with briefings on business trends, pertinent government policies, and information on employment, investments, and interest rates.
United Business & Investment Report	Weekly	$215.00	United Business Service Company 210 Newbury Street Boston, MA 02116 (617) 267-8855	Weekly newsletter evaluates stock market and other investment trends. Notes related federal developments, tables.
Value Line Investment Survey	Weekly	$495.00	Value Line, Inc. 711 Third Avenue New York, NY 10017 (212) 687-3965	Weekly loose-leaf booklet covering the business activities of about 1,700 major corporations in a variety of industries. Charts and graphs.
Value Line Options & Convertibles	Weekly	$750.00	Value Line Options & Convertibles Value Line, Inc. 711 Third Avenue New York, NY 10017 (212) 687-3965	Evaluation and analysis of hundreds of convertible bonds, warrants, and options. Most probably the preeminent source of this information for active investors.
Weekly Insider Report	Weekly	$152.00	Vickers Stock Research 226 New York Avenue Huntington, NY 11743 (516) 423-7710	Information on stock transactions of 500 or more shares by corporate officers, directors, and 10% holders who buy or sell shares in their own companies.
Contrary Investor	Fortnightly	$ 85.00	Fraser Mgmt. Assoc. Box 494 Burlington, VT 05402 (802) 658-0322	Newsletter espousing the "contrary opinion" theory of investing that reviews and comments on recommendations and trends in the traditional investment community. Broad market timing recommendations.

Name	Frequency	Price	Address	Description
Value Line OTC Special Situations Service	Fortnightly	$390.00	Value Line, Inc. / 711 Third Avenue / New York, NY 10017 / (212) 687-3965	Loose-leaf newsletter contains information for investors on stocks traded over-the-counter.
Grant's Interest Rate Observer	Every two weeks	$375.00	Grant's Interest Rate Observer / 233 Broadway / Suite 4008 / New York, NY 10279 / (212) 608-7994	In this literary magazine of financial comings and goings, former *Barron's* writer James Grant presents wonderfully creative indexes and statistics and gives pithy advice on fixed-income investments.
Holt Investment Advisory	Semimonthly	$ 89.00	Holt Advisory / P.O. Box 2923 / West Palm Beach, FL 33402 / (800) 274-8911	Discusses the economy and stock market for investors concerned with long-term capital growth.
InvesTech Market Letter	Twice a month	$165.00	InvesTech / 2472 Birch Glen / Whitefish, MT 59937 / (406) 862-7777	Summaries and reactions to other letter editors' views, clear technical analysis, and stock and mutual fund choices.
Investment Horizons	Twice a month	$250.00	Investment Horizons / Investment Information Services / 205 W. Wacker Drive / Chicago, IL 60606 / (312) 750-9300	Gerald Perritt follows small companies that aren't extensively watched by professional analysts. For example, one issue explained why small Utilities can be better buys than large ones. A well-done letter for intellectual investors.
Market Logic	Twice a month	$200.00	Market Logic / The Institute for Econometric Research / 3471 N. Federal Hwy. / Fort Lauderdale, FL 33306 / (305) 563-9000	The flagship publication of the institute, this is a concise, thorough, and multifaceted stock market guide. Predicts market movements and recommends trades. Full of indicators and other research tools.
Realty Stock Review	Twice a month	$288.00	Realty Stock Review / Audit Investments, Inc. / 136 Summit Ave., Suite 200 / Montvale, NJ 07645 / (212) 661-1710	The authority on real estate investment trusts and other real estate stocks. Securities are rated and there's plenty of company news.
The Cabot Market Letter	Twice a month	$195.00	The Cabot Market Letter / Cabot Farm/Orange St. / P.O. Box 3044 / Salem, MA 01970 / (617) 745-5532	Model portfolios, trend lines, recommended stocks, and market commentary in a concise and readable form. Also discusses mutual funds.

PUBLICATION	FREQUENCY OF PUBLICATION	YEARLY SUBSCRIPTION RATE	PUBLISHER	TYPE OF INFORMATION
The Babson Staff Letter	Twice a month	$ 16.00	David L. Babson & Co. One Memorial Drive Cambridge, MA 02142 (617) 225-3800	From one of the nation's oldest money-management firms comes an attractively presented, educational essay on some facet of the market, whether it be how high is high or confusion in the computer industry.
The Insiders	Twice a month	$100.00	The Insiders The Institute for Econometric Research 3471 N. Federal Hwy. Fort Lauderdale, FL 33306 (305) 563-9000	Another publication based on the idea that company officials and directors who trade in their own stock know something. Collects and translates SEC data on buying and selling by insiders and makes recommendations.
Technical Digest	20 per year (plus twice weekly *HOTLINE*)	$125.00	Technical Digest Woodland Road New Vernon, NJ 07976 (201) 822-3315	A regular stock and bond market letter for investors; includes commentary, charts, statistics, recommendations, and summaries of other major market letters.
The Asute Insiders	Every three weeks	$247.00	Investor's Analysis, Inc. P.O. Box 988 Paoli, PA 19301 (215) 296-2411	Robert Nurock, of Wall Street Week, writes about the stock market, covering both technical and fundamental developments. One of the best letters for intellectually minded stock market fans.
Alan Shawn Feinstein Insiders Report	Monthly	$ 90.00	Alan Shawn Feinstein and Associates 41 Alhambra Circle Cranston, RI 02905 (401) 467-5155	Reports on special investment opportunities, inside tips, new or unusual opportunities.
America's Fastest Growing Companies	Monthly	$185.00	Financial Data Systems 38 E. 29th St. New York, NY 10016 (212) 689-2777	A useful agglomeration of model portfolios, company profiles, ratings and statistics on small companies and emerging industries. Does not make specific buy-and-sell calls.
Better Investing Magazine	Monthly	$ 17.00	National Association of Investors Corporation 1515 E. 11 Mile Road Royal Oak, MI 48067 (313) 543-0612	Guidelines and advice on investment techniques for investment clubs. Investment education: one company analyzed each month. General articles on investment topics.

Name	Frequency	Price	Address	Description
Dines Letter	Monthly	$195.00	James Dine & Company Box 22 Belvedere, CA 94920 (415) 435-5458	Combines important technical, psychological, and business indicators concerning the markets.
Forbes Special Situation Survey	Monthly	$395.00	Forbes Investors Advisory Institute, Inc. 60 Fifth Avenue New York, NY 10011 (212) 620-2200	Monthly loose-leaf report discusses and recommends the purchase of one speculative equity security in each issue.
Forecasts & Strategies	Monthly	$ 99.00	Forecasts & Strategies Phillips Publishing, Inc. 7811 Montrose Road Potomac, MD 20854 (301) 340-2100	Mark Skousen's common sense on investment, taxes, and "financial privacy," with an emphasis on tax avoidance and keeping the government and others out of your financial affairs. Analyses of new products, such as single-premium variable life insurance.
Income & Safety	Monthly	$ 49.00	Income & Safety The Institute for Econometric Research 3471 N. Federal Hwy. Fort Lauderdale, FL 33306 (305) 563-9000	A guide to safe places to save and invest for income, concentrating on money-market funds, bank accounts, and tax-free income funds.
Real Estate Investing Letter	Monthly	$ 84.00	Real Estate Investing Letter 379 W. Broadway New York, NY 10012 (212) 966-8822	Monthly newsletter covers real estate investments, including tax strategies, depreciation, and real estate syndication.
Robert Kinsman's Low-Risk Growth Letter	Monthly	$139.00	Robert Kinsman's Low-Risk Growth Letter 4340 Redwood Highway Suite 150 San Rafael, CA 94903 (415) 479-3209	Recommended investments and model portfolios for income-oriented readers. A lot of common-sense educational materials as well.
Stanger Register— Partnership Profiles	Monthly	$245.00	Robert A. Stanger and Company P.O. Box 7490 1129 Broad Street Shrewsbury, NJ 07701 (201) 389-3600	Investment information, listings, and ranking on public and private partnerships; financial planning ideas, investment product ideas, and articles and features on various investment products, concepts, and strategies.

PUBLICATION	FREQUENCY OF PUBLICATION	YEARLY SUBSCRIPTION RATE	PUBLISHER	TYPE OF INFORMATION
The Gourgues Report	Monthly	$125.00	Harold Gourgues Co., Inc. Suite 300 3155 Roswell Road Atlanta, GA 30305	Practical investment advice and information directed toward non-institutional investors.
The Investor's Guide to Closed-End Funds	Monthly	$275.00	The Investor's Guide to Closed-End Funds Thomas J. Herzfeld Advisors, Inc. P.O. Box 161465 Miami, FL 33116 (305) 271-1900	From the only brokerage firm specializing in closed-end investment companies comes an update and recommendation on these overlooked funds, including foreign ones.
The McKeever Strategy Letter	Monthly	$195.00	The McKeever Strategy Letter P.O. Box 4130 Medford, OR 97501 (503) 826-9279	James McKeever is one of the more respected letter writers, and he leads off his longer-than-average letters with essays on economic or market topics, before giving advice on stocks, bonds, metals, and currencies.
The Stanger Report: A Guide to Partnership Investing	Monthly	$345.00	Robert A. Stanger and Company P.O. Box 7490 1129 Broad Street Shrewsbury, NJ 07702-7490	Ten-page monthly newsletter with topics of interest, tax planning ideas, news and views related to limited partnership ventures, and other tax shelter investments.
AARP Bulletin	11 per year	Included in AARP membership fee (Nonmember $5.00)	AARP Bulletin 1909 K St., NW Washington, DC 20049 (202) 662-4842	To stimulate persons 50 years old or older, retired or otherwise, toward active retirement, independence, and purpose, improving every aspect of living for older people—health, community service, travel articles.
Growth Stock Outlook	Semi-monthly	$175.00	Growth Stock Outlook, Inc. P.O. Box 15381 Chevy Chase, MD 20815 (301) 654-5205	Reports on selected stocks with vigorous growth. The growth stock outlook gives specific buy-sell recommendations. (The "Junior Growth Stock Outlook" was deleted.)
MMI Memo	Semiannual	Free	Household Finance Corporation Money Management Institute 2700 Sanders Road Prospect Heights, IL 60070 (312) 564-5000, Ext. 5368	Newsletter on consumer and personal fiance topics.

Moody's Manuals and Financial Guides	—	Free	Moody's Investors Services, Inc. 99 Church Street New York, NY 10007 (212) 553-0300	Brochure listing and describing Moody's various services and publications and providing price information.
Source Book of Health Insurance Data	—	Free	Health Insurance Association of America 1025 Connecticut Ave., NW Washington, DC 20036 (202) 223-7806	Compilation and documentation of data on health insurance industry.
Standard and Poor's Catalog of Services and Publications	—	Free	Standard and Poor's 25 Broadway New York, NY 10004 (212) 208-8000	Brochure listing and describing Standard and Poor's various services and publications, with price information. Also, lists addresses of S&P's branch and foreign offices.

No-Load Mutual Funds

The following is a list of no-load mutual funds. The list is not all-inclusive but does contain pertinent information (addresses, telephone numbers, and purchase requirements) for nearly 150 of the more prominent funds. The funds are also grouped by type, such as growth funds, funds that seek maximum capital gains, income funds, balanced funds, municipal bond funds, money funds, and specialty funds. (Addresses, telephone numbers, and purchase requirements are correct as of the date of publication but are subject to change without notice.)

GROWTH FUNDS

FUND	PURCHASE REQUIREMENTS	
	INITIAL	SUBSEQUENT
American Investors Income Box 2500 Greenwich, CT 06836 (800) 243-5353/(203) 531-5000	$ 500	$ 100
Boston Company Capital Appreciation One Boston Place Boston, MA 02106 (800) 225-5267	$ 1,000	$ 0
Bull and Bear Capital Growth 11 Hanover Square New York, NY 10005 (800) 847-4200/(212) 785-0900	$ 1,000	$ 100

FUND	PURCHASE REQUIREMENTS	
	INITIAL	SUBSEQUENT
Fidelity Trend 82 Devonshire St. Boston, MA 02109 (800) 544-6666/(617) 523-1919	$ 1,000	$ 250
Founders Growth 3033 E. First Avenue Suite 810 Denver, CO 80206 (800) 525-2440/(800) 874-6301	$ 1,000	$ 100
Gradison Established Growth 580 Walnut Street Cincinnati, OH 45202 (800) 543-1818/(800) 582-7062	$ 1,000	$ 50

FUND	PURCHASE REQUIREMENTS	
	INITIAL	SUBSEQUENT
Fidelity Contrafund 82 Devonshire St. Boston, MA 02109 (800) 544-6666/(617) 523-1919	$ 1,000	$ 250
Ivy Fund 40 Industrial Park Road Hingham, MA 02043 (800) 235-3322	$ 1,000	$ 0
Lehman Opportunity American Express Towers New York, NY 10285 (800) 221-5350/(212) 668-8578	$ 1,000	$ 100
Lindner Fund P.O. Box 11208 St. Louis, MO 63105 (314) 727-5305	$ 2,000	$ 100
Mathers Fund 100 Corporate North Suite 201 Bannockburn, IL 60015 (800) 962-3863/(312) 295-7400	$ 1,000	$ 200
W.L. Morgan Growth Box 2600 Valley Forge, PA 19482 (800) 662-7447	$ 1,500	$ 100
Mutual Shares Corporation 51 John F. Kennedy Avenue Short Hills, NJ 07078 (800) 858-3013/(800) 553-3014	$ 1,000	$ 100
Nicholas Fund 700 N. Water Street, #1010 Milwaukee, WI 53202 (800) 227-5987/(414) 272-6133	$ 500	$ 100

FUND	PURCHASE REQUIREMENTS	
	INITIAL	SUBSEQUENT
Partners Fund 342 Madison Avenue New York, NY 10173 (800) 848-0920/(212) 850-8300	$ 1,000	$ 100
Penn Square Mutual 2650 Westview Drive Wyomissing, PA 19610 (800) 523-8440/(800) 222-7506	$ 500	$ 100
T. Rowe Price Growth Stock 100 E. Pratt St. Baltimore, MD 21202 (800) 638-5660/(301) 547-2308	$ 1,000	$ 100
T. Rowe Price New Era 100 E. Pratt St. Baltimore, MD 21202 (800) 638-5660/(301) 547-2308	$ 1,000	$ 100
Scudder Capital Growth 160 Federal Street Boston, MA 02110 (800) 225-2470	$ 1,000	$ 0
Scudder Common Stock 160 Federal Street Boston, MA 02110 (800) 225-2470	$ 1,000	$ 0
Steinroe and Farnham Capital Opportunities P.O. Box 1162 Chicago, IL 60690 (800) 338-2550	$ 1,000	$ 100
Steinroe and Farnham Stock P.O. Box 1162 Chicago, IL 60690 (800) 338-2550	$ 1,000	$ 0

FUND	PURCHASE REQUIREMENTS	
	INITIAL	SUBSEQUENT
Steinroe Universe P.O. Box 1162 Chicago, IL 60690 (800) 338-2550	$1,000	$100
Twentieth Century Select 4500 Main St. Kansas City, MO 64111 (800) 345-2021/(816) 531-5575	$0	$0
USAA Mutual Growth USAA Building San Antonio, TX 78288 (800) 531-8000/(512) 498-8000	$1,000	$25

FUNDS THAT SEEK MAXIMUM CAPITAL GAINS

FUND	PURCHASE REQUIREMENTS		FUND	PURCHASE REQUIREMENTS	
	INITIAL	SUBSEQUENT		INITIAL	SUBSEQUENT
Acorn Fund 2 N. LaSalle St. Suite 500 Chicago, IL 60602-3790 (312) 621-0630	$4,000	$1,000	Founders Special 3033 E. First Avenue Suite 810 Denver, CO 80206 (800) 525-2440/(303) 874-6301	$1,000	$100
Bruce Fund 20 N. Wacker Drive Suite 1425 Chicago, IL 60606 (312) 236-9160	$1,000	$500	GIT Equity Trust-Special Growth 1655 N. Fort Myer Drive Arlington, VA 22209 (800) 336-3063/(800) 368-3133	$1,000	$0
Explorer Box 2600 Valley Forge, PA 19482 (800) 662-7447	$3,000	$100	Janus Value 100 Fillmore St., Suite 300 Denver, CO 80206 (800) 525-3713/(303) 333-3863	$1,000	$50
Financial Dynamics Box 2040 Denver, CO 80201 (800) 525-8085/(800) 525-9769	$250	$50	Northeast Investors Growth 50 Congress Street Boston, MA 02109 (800) 225-6704/(617) 523-3588	$1,000	$0
44 Wall Street Fund 630 Third Ave. New York, NY 10017 (800) 221-7836/(212) 808-5220	$1,000	$100	T. Rowe Price New Horizons 100 E. Pratt St. Baltimore, MD 21202 (800) 638-5660/(301) 547-2308	$1,000	$100

FUND	PURCHASE REQUIREMENTS	
	INITIAL	SUBSEQUENT
Scudder Development 160 Federal Street Boston, MA 02110 (800) 225-2470	$ 1,000	$ 0
Steinroe Special Fund P.O. Box 1162 Chicago, IL 60690 (800) 338-2550	$ 1,000	$ 100
Tudor One New York Plaza New York, NY 10004 (800) 223-3332/(212) 908-9582	$ 1,000	$ 50
Twentieth Century Growth 4500 Main St. Kansas City, MO 64141 (800) 345-2021/(816) 531-5575	$ 0	$ 0
Twentieth Century Ultra 4500 Main St. Kansas City, MO 64111 (800) 345-2021/(816) 531-5575	$ 0	$ 0
USAA Sunbelt Era USAA Building San Antonio, TX 78288 (800) 531-8000/(512) 498-8000	$ 1,000	$ 25
UMB Stock 2440 Pershing Road Kansas City, MO 64108 (800) 821-5591/(816) 471-5200	$ 1,000	$ 100
Value Line Leveraged Growth 711 Third Avenue New York, NY 10017 (800) 223-0818	$ 1,000	$ 100
Value Line Special Situations 711 Third Avenue New York, NY 10017 (800) 223-0818	$ 1,000	$ 100

INCOME FUNDS

FUND	PURCHASE REQUIREMENTS	
	INITIAL	SUBSEQUENT
Babson Bond Trust 2440 Pershing Road Kansas City, MO 64108 (800) 821-5591/(816) 471-5200	$ 500	$ 50
Boston Co. GNMA Fund One Boston Place Boston, MA 02106 (800) 225-5267	$ 1,000	$ 0
Dreyfus A Bonds Plus 600 Madison Avenue New York, NY 10022 (800) 645-6561/(718) 895-1206	$ 2,500	$ 100
Dreyfus Convertible Securities 600 Madison Avenue New York, NY 10022 (800) 645-6561/(718) 895-1206	$ 2,500	$ 100

Fund	Minimum	Subsequent
Evergreen Total Return 550 Mamaroneck Avenue Harrison, NY 10528 (800) 235-0064	$ 2,000	$ 0
Financial Industrial Income Box 2040 Denver, CO 80201 (800) 525-8085/(800) 525-9769	$ 250	$ 50
Mutual Qualified Income 51 John F. Kennedy Pkwy. Short Hills, NJ 07078 (800) 858-3013/(800) 553-3014	$ 1,000	$ 50
Northeast Investors Trust 50 Congress Street Boston, MA 02109 (800) 225-6704/(617) 523-3588	$ 1,000	$ 0
One Hundred & One 899 Logan Street, #211 Denver, CO 80203 (800) 333-1101/(303) 837-1020	$ 250	$ 50
T. Rowe Price New Income 100 E. Pratt Street Baltimore, MD 21202 (800) 638-5660/(301) 547-2308	$ 2,000	$ 100
Pine Street 140 Broadway New York, NY 10005 (800) 225-8011	$ 1,000	$ 100
Safeco Equity P.O. Box 34890 Seattle, WA 98124 (800) 426-6730/(800) 562-6810	$ 1,000	$ 100
Scudder Income 160 Federal Street Boston, MA 02110 (800) 225-2470	$ 1,000	$ 0
Selected American Shares 230 W. Monroe Street Chicago, IL 60606 (800) 553-5533/(312) 641-7862	$ 1,000	$ 100
Steadman Associated 1730 K Street NW Washington, DC 20006 (800) 424-8570/(202) 223-1000	$ 500	$ 25
Steinroe Managed Bond P.O. Box 1162 Chicago, IL 60690 (800) 338-2550	$ 1,000	$ 100
Value Line Income 711 Third Avenue New York, NY 10017 (800) 223-0818	$ 1,000	$ 100
Vanguard GNMA Portfolio Box 2600 Valley Forge, PA 19482 (800) 662-7447	$ 3,000	$ 100
Vanguard High Yield Bond Box 2600 Valley Forge, PA 19482 (800) 662-7447	$ 3,000	$ 100
Wellesley Income Box 2600 Valley Forge, PA 19482 (800) 662-7447	$ 1,500	$ 100

BALANCED FUNDS

FUND	PURCHASE REQUIREMENTS	
	INITIAL	SUBSEQUENT
Axe-Houghton Fund B 400 Benedict Avenue Tarrytown, NY 10591 (800) 431-1030/(914) 631-8131	$ 1,000	$ 0
Babson Value Fund 2440 Pershing Road Kansas City, MO 64108 (800) 821-5591/(816) 471-5200	$ 1,000	$ 100
Dodge & Cox Balanced Fund One Post Street, 35th Floor San Francisco, CA 94104 (415) 434-0311	$ 1,000	$ 100
Fidelity Fund 82 Devonshire Street Boston, MA 02109 (800) 544-6666/(617) 523-1919	$ 1,000	$ 250
Financial Industrial Fund Box 2040 Denver, CO 80201 (800) 525-8085/(800) 525-9769	$ 250	$ 50
Guardian Mutual 342 Madison Avenue New York, NY 10173 (800) 848-0920/(212) 850-8300	$ 1,000	$ 100
Loomis-Sayles Mutual 399 Boylston Street Boston, MA 02117 (800) 343-7104/(617) 267-6600	$ 250	$ 50
Mairs & Power Income Fund W-2062 First Bank Building St. Paul, MN 55101 (612) 222-8478	$ 1,000	$ 100

FUND	PURCHASE REQUIREMENTS	
	INITIAL	SUBSEQUENT
Pax World Fund 224 State Street Portsmouth, NH 03801 (603) 431-8022	$ 250	$ 50
T. Rowe Price Growth and Income 100 E. Pratt Street Baltimore, MD 21202 (800) 638-5660/(301) 547-2308	$ 1,000	$ 100
Steinroe Total Return P.O. Box 1162 Chicago, IL 60690 (800) 338-2550	$ 1,000	$ 500
Value Line Fund 711 Third Avenue New York, NY 10017 (800) 223-0818	$ 1,000	$ 100
Vanguard Index Trust Box 2600 Valley Forge, PA 19482 (800) 662-7447	$ 1,500	$ 100
Wellington Fund Box 2600 Valley Forge, PA 19482 (800) 662-7447	$ 1,500	$ 100
Windsor Fund Box 2600 Valley Forge, PA 19482 (800) 662-7447	$ 1,500	$ 100

MUNICIPAL BOND FUNDS

FUND	PURCHASE REQUIREMENTS	
	INITIAL	SUBSEQUENT
Babson Tax-Free Fund— Long Term 2440 Pershing Road Kansas City, MO 64108 (800) 821-5591/(816) 471-5200	$ 1,000	$ 100
Dreyfus Tax-Exempt Bond Fund 600 Madison Avenue New York, NY 10022 (800) 645-6561/(718) 895-1206	$ 2,500	$ 100
Federated Short-Intermediate Muni Trust Federated Tower Pittsburgh, PA 15222-3779 (800) 245-2423/(412) 288-1900	$25,000	$ 0
Fidelity High Yield Municipal 82 Devonshire Street Boston, MA 02109 (800) 544-6666/(617) 523-1919	$ 2,500	$ 250
Fidelity Municipal Bond Fund 82 Devonshire Street Boston, MA 02109 (800) 544-6666/(617) 523-1919	$ 2,500	$ 250
T. Rowe Price Tax-Free Income Fund 100 E. Pratt Street Baltimore, MD 21202 (800) 638-5660/(301) 547-2308	$ 2,000	$ 100
Safeco Municipal Bond Fund Safeco Plaza Seattle, WA 98185 (800) 426-6730/(206) 545-5530	$ 1,000	$ 100
Scudder Managed Municipal Bonds 160 Federal Street Boston, MA 02110 (800) 225-2470	$ 1,000	$ 0
State Farm Muni Bond Fund One State Farm Plaza Bloomington, IL 61710 (309) 766-2029	$ 1,000	$ 500
Steinroe Managed Municipals P.O. Box 1162 Chicago, IL 60690 (800) 338-2550	$ 1,000	$ 100
Vanguard Municipal Bond— Intermediate Box 2600 Valley Forge, PA 19482 (800) 662-7447	$ 3,000	$ 100
Vanguard Municipal Bond— Long Term Box 2600 Valley Forge, PA 19482 (800) 662-7447	$ 3,000	$ 100

MONEY MARKET FUNDS

FUND	PURCHASE REQUIREMENTS	
	INITIAL	SUBSEQUENT
Cash Equivalent Fund—MM Portfolio 120 S. LaSalle Street Chicago, IL 60603 (800) 621-1048/(312) 781-1121	$ 1,000	$ 100
Current Investment Fund 1000 Louisiana Houston, TX 77002-5098 (800) 231-4645/(800) 999-3863	$ 1,000	$ 50
Daily Cash Accumulation Fund 3410 S. Galena Street Denver, CO 80231 (800) 525-7048/(800) 356-3556	$ 500	$ 25
DBL Cash Fund—MM Portfolio 60 Broad Street New York, NY 10004 (800) 221-3290/(212) 480-6000	$ 1,000	$ 100
Delaware Cash Reserve Fund 10 Penn Center Plaza Philadelphia, PA 19103 (800) 523-4640/(215) 988-1333	$ 1,000	$ 25
Dreyfus Liquid Assets 600 Madison Avenue New York, NY 10022 (800) 645-0561/(718) 895-1206	$ 2,500	$ 100
Fidelity Cash Reserves 82 Devonshire Street Boston, MA 02109 (800) 544-6666/(617) 523-1919	$ 1,000	$ 250

FUND	PURCHASE REQUIREMENTS	
	INITIAL	SUBSEQUENT
IDS Cash Management Fund P.O. Box 534 Minneapolis, MN 55440 (800) 222-9700/(612) 372-3733	$ 2,000	$ 100
Kemper Money Market Fund 120 S. LaSalle Street Chicago, IL 60603 (800) 621-1048/(312) 781-1121	$ 1,000	$ 100
Liquid Capital Income Fund 100 The Hale Building 1228 Euclid Avenue Cleveland, OH 44115 (800) 231-2322/(216) 781-4440	$ 1,000	$ 250
Merrill Lynch Ready Assets P.O. Box 9011 Princeton, NJ 08543 (609) 282-2800	$ 5,000	$1,000
National Liquid Reserves 1345 Avenue of the Americas New York, NY 10105 (212) 698-6000	$ 1,500	$ 100
Paine Webber Cash Fund 1285 Avenue of the Americas New York, NY 10019 (800) 544-9300	$ 5,000	$ 500
Reserve Fund—Primary Portfolio 810 Seventh Avenue New York, NY 10019 (800) 223-5547/(212) 977-9880	$ 1,000	$1,000

FUND	PURCHASE REQUIREMENTS	
	INITIAL	SUBSEQUENT
T. Rowe Price Prime Reserves Fund 100 E. Pratt Street Baltimore, MD 21202 (800) 638-5660/(301) 547-2308	$ 2,000	$ 100
Scudder Cash Investment Trust 160 Federal Street Boston, MA 02110 (800) 225-2470	$ 1,000	$ 0
Shearson Daily Dividend One Western Union Plaza 15th Floor New York, NY 10004 (212) 825-3115	$ 2,500	$1,000
Vanguard Money Market Trust—Prime Portfolio Box 2600 Valley Forge, PA 19482 (800) 662-7447	$ 1,000	$ 100
Washington Square Cash Fund 20 Washington Avenue, South Minneapolis, MN 55401 (612) 372-5507	$ 1,000	$ 50
Webster Cash Reserve 20 Exchange Place New York, NY 10005 (212) 510-5351	$ 1,500	$ 100

MONEY MARKET FUNDS—U.S. GOVERNMENT SECURITIES ONLY

FUND	PURCHASE REQUIREMENTS	
	INITIAL	SUBSEQUENT
Capital Preservation Fund I 755 Page Mill Road Palo Alto, CA 94304 (800) 472-3389/(800) 982-6150	$ 1,000	$ 100
Capital Preservation Fund II 755 Page Mill Road Palo Alto, CA 94304 (800) 472-3389/(800) 982-6150	$ 1,000	$ 100
Dreyfus Money Market Instruments—Gov't. Series 600 Madison Avenue New York, NY 10022 (800) 645-6561/(718) 895-1206	$ 2,500	$ 100
Fund for Government Investors 4922 Fairmont Avenue 3rd Floor Bethesda, MD 20814 (800) 343-3355/(301) 657-1510	$ 2,500	$ 0
Merrill Lynch Government Fund P.O. Box 9011 Princeton, NJ 08543 (609) 282-2800	$ 5,000	$1,000
Shearson Government and Agencies Fund One Western Union Plaza 15th Floor New York, NY 10004 (212) 825-3115	$ 2,500	$1,000

FUND	PURCHASE REQUIREMENTS	
	INITIAL	SUBSEQUENT
TrustFunds Cash Plus— Fed. Securities 680 E. Swedesford Road Wayne, PA 19087 (800) 345-1151	$ 0	$ 0
U.S. Treasury Securities Fund—MM P.O. Box 29467 San Antonio, TX 78229 (800) 873-8637/(512) 523-2453	$ 100	$ 50

TAX-EXEMPT MONEY MARKET FUNDS

FUND	PURCHASE REQUIREMENTS	
	INITIAL	SUBSEQUENT
Calvert Tax-Free Reserve —MM Portfolio 1700 Pennsylvania Ave. NW Washington, DC 20006 (800) 368-2748/(301) 951-4800	$ 2,000	$ 250
Carnegie Tax-Free Income Trust 1100 The Hale Building 1228 Euclid Avenue Cleveland, OH 44115 (800) 321-2322/(216) 781-4440	$ 1,000	$ 250
Daily Tax-Free Income Fund 100 Park Avenue New York, NY 10017 (800) 221-3079/(212) 370-1110	$ 5,000	$ 100
Fidelty Tax-Exempt Money Market Trust 82 Devonshire Street Boston, MA 02109 (800) 544-5666/(617) 523-1919	$10,000	$ 500
Municipal Working Capital Trust 200 Berkeley Street Boston, MA 02116 (617) 423-3500	$ 1,000	$ 0
Nuveen Tax-Free Reserves 333 W. Wacker Drive Chicago, IL 60606 (800) 621-7210	$ 1,000	$ 100
T. Rowe Price Tax-Exempt Money Fund 100 E. Pratt Street Baltimore, MD 21202 (800) 638-5660/(301) 547-2308	$ 2,000	$ 100
Scudder Tax-Free Money 160 Federal Street Boston, MA 02110 (800) 225-2470	$ 1,000	$ 0
Tax-Exempt CA Money Market Fund 120 S. LaSalle Street Chicago, IL 60603 (800) 621-1048/(312) 781-1121	$ 1,000	$ 100
Tax-Free Money Fund 1345 Avenue of the Americas New York, NY 10105 (212) 698-6000	$ 7,500	$ 100

SPECIALTY FUNDS

FUND	PURCHASE REQUIREMENTS	
	INITIAL	SUBSEQUENT
Analytic Optioned Equity 2222 Martin St., Suite 230 Irvine, CA 92715 (714) 833-0294	$ 5,000	$ 500
Bull & Bear Gold Investors Ltd. 11 Hanover Square New York, NY 10005 (800) 847-4200/(212) 363-1100	$ 1,000	$ 100
Century Shares Trust One Liberty Square Boston, MA 02109 (800) 321-1928/(617) 482-3060	$ 500	$ 25
Energy Fund 342 Madison Avenue New York, NY 10173 (800) 367-0770/(212) 850-8300	$ 1,000	$ 100
Gateway Option Income 400 TechneCenter Drive Suite 220 Milford, OH 45150 (800) 354-6339/(513) 248-2700	$ 500	$ 100

FUND	PURCHASE REQUIREMENTS	
	INITIAL	SUBSEQUENT
Lexington Goldfund P.O. Box 1515 Saddle Brook, NJ 07662 (800) 526-0056	$ 1,000	$ 50
T. Rowe Price International 100 E. Pratt Street Baltimore, MD 21202 (800) 638-5660/(301) 547-2308	$ 2,000	$ 100
Scudder International 160 Federal Street Boston, MA 02110 (800) 225-2470	$ 1,000	$ 0
United Services Gold Shares P.O. Box 29467 San Antonio, TX 78229-0467 (800) 873-8637/(512) 696-1234	$ 100	$ 50

Load Funds

Some investment professionals believe load funds present greater returns on an investment than no-loads. Their contention is that because of the load, load funds often have lower management and operational charges. It is their belief that when all charges are totaled and compared to those involved with a no-load fund, the load fund has lower overall costs, therefore returning a greater portion of its earnings to the investor. This is, of course, a matter of discussion and disagreement among individuals involved in the investment community. And there does not appear to be the possibility of a final resolution in the near future.

The following pages present listings of some of the more prominent load funds. Both equity and debt-instrument funds are listed. The lists include telephone numbers, initial and subsequent purchase requirements, and the applied loads. The funds are also grouped by type. For example, the equity funds are categorized as maximum capital gains funds, growth funds, growth and income funds, equity income funds, and balanced funds, to name just a few. Bond funds include high-yield corporate funds, high-grade corporate funds, U.S. government securities, mortgage-backed securities funds, high-yield tax-exempt bond funds, etc. (Addresses, telephone numbers, and purchase requirements are correct as of the date of publication but are subject to change without notice.)

Equity Funds

MAXIMUM CAPITAL GAINS FUNDS

FUND	PURCHASE REQUIREMENTS		LOAD*
	INITIAL	SUBSEQUENT	
ABT Emerging Growth 700 Dixie Terminal Bldg. Cincinnati, OH 45202 (800) 354-0436/(800) 582-7396	$1,000	$ 50	4¾
Constellation Growth Fund 11 Greenway Plaza Suite 1919 Houston, TX 77046 (800) 392-9681/(800) 231-0803	$1,000	$ 100	4¾
Pacific Horizon Aggregate 156 W. 56th Street New York, NY 10119 (800) 367-6075/(212) 492-1600	$1,000	$100	4½
Putnam Voyager One Post Office Square Boston, MA 02109 (800) 225-1581	$ 500	$ 50	8½
Weingarten Equity Fund 11 Greenway Plaza Suite 1919 Houston, TX 77046 (800) 392-9681/(800) 231-0803	$1,000	$100	4¾

*Stated as a percentage of investment

GROWTH FUNDS

FUND	PURCHASE REQUIREMENTS		LOAD*
	INITIAL	SUBSEQUENT	
Fidelity Magellan 82 Devonshire Street Boston, MA 02109 (800) 544-6666/(617) 523-1919	$1,000	$250	3
Franklin Equity 777 Mariner Island Blvd. San Mateo, CA 94404 (800) 342-5236	$ 100	$ 25	4
Guardian Park Ave. 201 Park Ave. South New York, NY 10003 (800) 522-7800/(800) 221-3253	$ 300	$ 50	8½
IDS New Dimensions P.O. Box 534 Minneapolis, MN 55440 (800) 222-9700/(612) 372-3733	$2,000	$100	5
Lehman Capital American Express Towers New York, NY 10285 (800) 221-5350/(212) 668-8578	$1,000	$100	5
New England Life Growth Fund 399 Boylston Street Boston, MA 02117 (800) 343-7104/(617) 267-6600	$ 250	$ 25	6½

GROWTH AND INCOME FUNDS

FUND	PURCHASE REQUIREMENTS		LOAD*
	INITIAL	SUBSEQUENT	
Eaton Vance Total Return 24 Federal Street Boston, MA 02110 (800) 225-6265	$1,000	$ 50	4¾
Fundamental Investors 135 S. State College Blvd. Brea, CA 92621 (800) 421-9900/(714) 671-7000	$ 250	$ 50	5¾
Investment Co. of America 135 S. State College Blvd. Brea, CA 92621 (800) 421-9900/(714) 671-7000	$ 250	$ 50	5¾
Seligmann Common Stock One Banker Trust Plaza New York, NY 10006 (800) 221-2450/(800) 522-6869	0	0	4¾
Sentinel Common Stock National Life Drive Montpelier, VA 05604 (802) 229-7274	$ 250	$ 25	8½

EQUITY INCOME FUNDS

FUND	PURCHASE REQUIREMENTS		LOAD*
	INITIAL	SUBSEQUENT	
Colonial Equity Income One Financial Center Boston, MA 02111 (800) 426-3750/(800) 248-2828	$ 250	$ 25	6¾
Fidelity Equity Income 82 Devonshire Street Boston, MA 02109 (800) 544-6666/(617) 523-1919	$1,000	$250	2
National Total Income 605 Third Avenue New York, NY 10158 (800) 223-7757/(212) 661-3000	$ 250	$ 25	7¼
Seligman Income One Bankers Trust Plaza New York, NY 10006 (800) 221-2450/(800) 522-6869	$ 0	$ 0	4¾
United Income Fund P.O. Box 418343 Kansas City, MO 64141 (800) 842-1075	$ 500	$ 0	8½

BALANCED FUNDS

FUND	PURCHASE REQUIREMENTS		LOAD*
	INITIAL	SUBSEQUENT	
Alliance Balanced Shares 500 Plaza Drive, 3rd Floor Secaucus, NJ 07094 (800) 221-5672/(800) 523-5695	$ 250	$ 50	5½
Drexel Burnham Fund 60 Broad Street New York, NY 10004 (800) 221-3290/(212) 480-6000	$1,000	$250	5
Dreyfus Fund 600 Madison Avenue New York, NY 10022 (800) 645-6561/(718) 895-1206	$2,500	$100	8½
IDS Mutual Fund P.O. Box 534 Minneapolis, MN 55440 (800) 222-9700/(612) 372-3733	$2,000	$100	5
Kemper Total Return 120 S. LaSalle Street Chicago, IL 60603 (800) 621-1048/(312) 781-1121	$1,000	$100	8½
Phoenix Balanced Fund One American Row Hartford, CT 06115 (800) 243-4361	$ 500	$ 25	8½
United Continental Income P.O. Box 418343 Kansas City, MO 64141 (800) 842-1075	$ 500	$ 0	8½

*Stated as a percentage of investment

SMALL COMPANY GROWTH FUNDS

FUND	PURCHASE REQUIREMENTS		LOAD*
	INITIAL	SUBSEQUENT	
Fairfield Fund 605 Third Avenue New York, NY 10158 (800) 223-7757/(212) 661-3000	$ 500	$ 50	8½
Nicholas II 700 N. Water St., #1010 Milwaukee, WI 53202 (800) 227-5987/(412) 272-6133	$1,000	$100	1**
OTC Securities Fund 275 Commerce Drive Suite 228 Ft. Washington, PA 19034 (800) 523-2578/(215) 643-2510	$ 500	$ 25	4½
Putnam OTC Emerging Growth Fund One Post Office Square Boston, MA 02109 (800) 225-1581	$ 500	$ 50	6¾
United New Concepts P.O. Box 418343 Kansas City, MO 64141 (800) 842-1075	$ 500	$ 0	8½

SECTOR FUNDS

FUND	PURCHASE REQUIREMENTS		LOAD*
	INITIAL	SUBSEQUENT	
Alliance Technology 500 Plaza Drive, 3rd Floor Secaucus, NJ 07094 (800) 523-5695	$ 250	$ 50	5½
Fidelity Select— Financial Services 82 Devonshire Street Boston, MA 02109 (800) 544-6666/(617) 523-1919	$1,000	$250	2 & 1**
Fidelity Select—Health Care 82 Devonshire Street Boston, MA 02109 (800) 544-6666/(617) 523-1919	$1,000	$250	2 & 1**
G.T. Pacific 50 California Street Suite 2700 San Francisco, CA 94111-4624 (800) 824-1580/(415) 392-6181	$ 500	$100	4¾
Medical Technology Fund P.O. Box 1111 Blue Bell, PA 19422 (800) 262-3863/(215) 825-0400	$1,000	$ 0	4¾
National Aviation and Tech. Corp. 50 Broad Street New York, NY 10004 (800) 654-0001/(212) 482-8100	$1,000	$100	4¾
Pru-Bache—Utilities One Seaport Plaza New York, NY 10292 (800) 225-1852	$1,000	$100	5**
Putnam Health Sciences Trust One Post Office Square Boston, MA 02109 (800) 225-1581	$ 500	$ 50	8½

*Stated as a percentage of investment
**Back-end Load

GOLD AND PRECIOUS METALS FUNDS

FUND	PURCHASE REQUIREMENTS		LOAD*
	INITIAL	SUBSEQUENT	
IDS Precious Metals P.O. Box 534 Minneapolis, MN 55440 (800) 222-9700/(612) 372-3733	$2,000	$100	5
International Investors 122 E. 42nd Street, 42nd Floor New York, NY 10168 (800) 221-2220/(212) 687-5201	$1,000	$100	8½
Keystone Precious Metals 99 High Street Boston, MA 02110 (800) 633-4900/(617) 338-3400	$ 250	$ 0	4**
Oppenheimer Gold and Special Metals Two World Trade Center New York, NY 10048 (800) 525-7048/(212) 323-0200	$1,000	$ 25	8½

FUND	PURCHASE REQUIREMENTS		LOAD*
	INITIAL	SUBSEQUENT	
Strategic Investments 2030 Royal Lane Dallas, TX 75229 (800) 527-5027/(214) 484-1326	$ 500	$100	8½

GLOBAL FUNDS

FUND	PURCHASE REQUIREMENTS		LOAD*	FUND	PURCHASE REQUIREMENTS		LOAD*
	INITIAL	SUBSEQUENT			INITIAL	SUBSEQUENT	
New Perspective Fund 135 S. State College Blvd. Brea, CA 92621 (800) 421-9900/(714) 671-7000	$ 250	$ 50	5¾	Paine Webber Atlas 1285 Avenue of the Americas New York, NY 10019 (800) 762-1000	$1,000	$100	8½
Oppenheimer Global Two World Trade Center New York, NY 10048 (800) 525-7048/(212) 323-0200	$1,000	$ 25	8½	Putnam International Equities One Post Office Square Boston, MA 02109 (800) 225-1581	$ 500	$ 50	8½

*Stated as a percentage of investment
**Back-end Load

INTERNATIONAL FUNDS

FUND	PURCHASE REQUIREMENTS		LOAD*	FUND	PURCHASE REQUIREMENTS		LOAD*
	INITIAL	SUBSEQUENT			INITIAL	SUBSEQUENT	
IDS International P.O. Box 534 Minneapolis, MN 55440 (800) 222-9700/(612) 372-3733	$2,000	$100	5	Templeton World Fund P.O. Box 33030 St. Petersburg, FL 33733 (800) 237-0738	$ 500	$ 25	8½
Kemper International 120 S. LaSalle Street Chicago, IL 60603 (800) 621-1048/(312) 781-1121	$1,000	$100	8½	United International Growth Fund P.O. Box 418343 Kansas City, MO 64141 (800) 842-1075	$ 500	$ 0	8½
Merrill Lynch Pacific P.O. Box 9011 Princeton, NJ 08543 (609) 282-2800	$ 250	$ 50	6½				

Bond Funds

HIGH-YIELD CORPORATE BOND FUNDS

FUND	PURCHASE REQUIREMENTS		LOAD*
	INITIAL	SUBSEQUENT	
Cigna High Yield Fund, Inc. 900 Cottage Grove Road Bloomfield, CT 06002 (800) 562-4462	$ 500	$ 50	5
Colonial High Yield Securities One Financial Center Boston, MA 02111 (800) 426-3750/(800) 248-2828	$ 250	$ 25	4¾
Kemper High Yield Fund 120 S. LaSalle Street Chicago, IL 60603 (800) 621-1048/(312) 781-1121	$1,000	$100	4½
Pilgrim High Yield Fund 10100 Santa Monica Blvd. Los Angeles, CA 90067 (800) 334-3444	$1,000	$100	4¾
Shearson High Yield Fund Two World Trade Center New York, NY 10048 (212) 321-7155	$ 500	$200	5

*Stated as a percentage of investment

HIGH-GRADE CORPORATE BOND FUNDS

FUND	PURCHASE REQUIREMENTS		LOAD*
	INITIAL	SUBSEQUENT	
Bond Fund of America 135 S. State College Blvd. Brea, CA 92621 (800) 421-9900/(714) 671-7000	$1,000	$ 50	4¾
Hutton Investment Series— Bond and Income One Battery Park Plaza New York, NY 10004 (800) 447-7757	$ 500	$250	5**
Pioneer Bond Fund 60 State Street Boston, MA 02109 (800) 622-0181/(800) 622-0180	$1,000	$100	6
Sigma Income Shares 3801 Kennett Pike, C-200 Greenville, DE 19807 (800) 441-9490/(302) 652-3091	$ 0	$ 0	8½
United Bond Fund P.O. Box 418343 Kansas City, MO 64141 (800) 842-1075	$ 500	$ 0	8½

U.S. GOVERNMENT SECURITIES FUNDS

FUND	PURCHASE REQUIREMENTS		
	INITIAL	SUBSEQUENT	LOAD*
AMEV U.S. Gov't. Fund Box 64284 St. Paul, MN 55164 (800) 872-2638/(800) 328-1001	$ 500	$ 50	4½
Carnegie Gov't. Securities —High Yield 1228 Euclid Avenue Cleveland, OH 44115 (800) 321-2322/(216) 781-4440	$1,000	$250	4¾
Hancock (John) U.S. Gov't. Security Fund John Hancock Place P.O. Box 21 Boston, MA 02117 (800) 225-5291	$ 500	$ 25	8½
Lord Abbett U.S. Gov't. Securities 767 Fifth Avenue New York, NY 10153 (212) 848-1800	$ 500	$ 0	4¾
U.S. Gov't. Guaranteed Securities 135 S. State College Blvd. Brea, CA 92621 (800) 421-9900/(714) 671-7000	$1,000	$ 50	4¾

*Stated as a percentage of investment
**Back-end Load

MORTGAGE-BACKED SECURITIES FUNDS

FUND	PURCHASE REQUIREMENTS		
	INITIAL	SUBSEQUENT	LOAD*
Alliance Mortgage Securities, Inc. 500 Plaza Drive, 3rd Floor Secaucus, NJ 07094 (800) 221-5672/(800) 523-5695	$ 250	$ 50	5½
Franklin U.S. Gov't. Series 777 Mariner Island Blvd. San Mateo, CA 94401 (800) 342-5236	$ 100	$ 25	4
Kemper U.S. Gov't. Securities 120 S. LaSalle Street Chicago, IL 60603 (800) 621-1048/(312) 781-1121	$1,000	$100	4½
Seligman High Income— Sec. Mort. Income One Bankers Trust Plaza New York, NY 10006 (800) 221-2450/(800) 522-6869	$ 0	$ 0	4¾
United Gov't. Securities P.O. Box 418343 Kansas City, MO 64141 (800) 842-1075	$ 500	$ 0	4¼

HIGH-YIELD TAX-EXEMPT BOND FUNDS

FUND	PURCHASE REQUIREMENTS		LOAD*
	INITIAL	SUBSEQUENT	
IDS High Yield Tax Exempts P.O. Box 534 Minneapolis, MN 55440 (800) 222-9700/(612) 372-3733	$2,000	$100	5
Merrill Lynch Muni Fund Bond P.O. Box 9011 Princeton, NJ 08543 (609) 282-2800	$1,000	$100	4
MFS Managed High Yield 200 Berkeley Street Boston, MA 02116 (617) 423-3500	$ 250	$ 25	4¾
Putnam TF High Yield Fund One Post Office Square Boston, MA 02109 (800) 225-1581	$ 500	$ 50	5
Seligmann California Tax-Exempt—High Yield One Banker Trust Plaza New York, NY 10006 (800) 221-2450/(800) 522-6869	$ 0	$ 0	4½

HIGH-GRADE TAX-EXEMPT BOND FUNDS

FUND	PURCHASE REQUIREMENTS		LOAD*
	INITIAL	SUBSEQUENT	
Calvert Tax-Free Reserve— Ltd. Term Port. 1700 Pennsylvania Ave., NW Washington, DC 20006 (800) 368-2748/(301) 951-4800	$2,000	$250	2
Composite Tax-Exempt Bond Fund W. 601 Riverside Avenue Spokane, WA 99201 (800) 541-0830/(509) 624-4101	$1,000	$100	4
DMC Tax-Free Trust—PA Series Ten Penn Center Plaza Philadelphia, PA 19103 (800) 523-4640/(215) 988-1333	$1,000	$ 25	4¾
Hutton AZ Muni Bond One Battery Park New York, NY 10004 (800) 447-7757	$ 500	$250	4
Kemper Muni Bond Fund 120 S. LaSalle Street Chicago, IL 60603 (800) 621-1048/(312) 781-1121	$1,000	$100	4½
Mutual of Omaha Tax-Free, Inc. 10235 Regency Circle Omaha, NE 68114 (800) 228-9011/(800) 642-8112	$1,000	$ 50	8

*Stated as a percentage of investment

FUND	PURCHASE REQUIREMENTS		LOAD*
	INITIAL	SUBSEQUENT	
Nuveen Municipal Bond Fund 333 W. Wacker Drive Chicago, IL 60606 (312) 621-7210	$1,000	$100	4
United Municipal Bond Fund P.O. Box 418343 Kansas City, MO 64141 (800) 842-1075	$ 500	$ 0	4¼

*Stated as a percentage of investment

Prominent Independent Mutual Fund Organizations and Their Switching Policies*

COMPANY NAME	HEADQUARTERS	TELEPHONE	FUNDS MANAGED	SWITCHING POLICIES
Alliance	Secaucus, NJ	(800) 221-5672	26	Switching available; there may be charges on some funds.
American Capital	Houston, TX	(800) 231-3638	18	There is no limit. The load is applied if a switch is made from a no-load to a load fund, or the load is charged if switching is made among load funds.
American Funds	Brea, CA	(800) 421-9900	23	Switching available; there may be charges on some funds.
Calvert	Washington, DC	(800) 368-2748	16	Switching available; there may be charges on some funds.
Carnegie Capital	Cleveland, OH	(800) 321-2322	16	Switching available; there may be charges on some funds.
Colonial Investment	Boston, MA	(800) 426-3750	24	Switching available; there may be charges on some funds.
Criterion Distributors	Houston, TX	(713) 751-2400	22	Switching available; there may be charges on some funds.
Dreyfus	New York, NY	(800) 242-8671	31	No limit or fee is applied.
Eaton Vance	Boston, MA	(800) 225-6265	21	Switching available; there may be charges on some funds.
Federated	Pittsburgh, PA	(800) 245-0242	20	No limits to switching are in effect.
Fidelity	Boston, MA	(800) 544-6666	104	There are charges on select funds, and only five switches per year are permitted.
Financial Programs	Denver, CO	(800) 525-8085	19	Switching available; there may be charges on some funds.
Franklin	San Mateo, CA	(800) 342-5236	31	No switching limit is in effect, but a $5 fee is applied.
IDS	Minneapolis, MN	(800) 222-9700	28	No limit or fee is applied.
Jones & Babson	Kansas City, MO	(800) 422-2766	16	Switching available; there may be charges on some funds.
Kemper	Chicago, IL	(800) 621-1148	18	No change is permitted after having been involved with any given fund for six months or more.

Keystone	Boston, MA	(800) 633-4900	19	Five switches per year are permitted with a $5 fee.
Lord Abbett	New York, NY	(212) 848-1800	11	Switching available; there may be charges on some funds.
Massachusetts Financial Service	Boston, MA	(617) 423-3500	28	No switching limit is in effect, but a $5 fee may be charged.
Nuveen	Chicago, IL	(312) 917-8200	14	Switching available; there may be charges on some funds.
Oppenheimer	New York, NY	(800) 525-7048	22	Switching available; there may be charges on some funds.
Putnam	Boston, MA	(800) 225-1581	34	No switching limit is in effect but a $5 fee may be charged.
Scudder	Boston, MA	(800) 225-2470	32	No switching limit has been established.
Seligman	New York, NY	(800) 221-2450	30	Switching available; there may be charges on some funds.
SteinRoe	Chicago, IL	(800) 338-2550	16	No switching limit has been established.
Templeton	St. Petersburg, FL	(800) 237-0738	6	Switching permitted among the funds.
T. Rowe Price	Baltimore, MD	(800) 638-5660	24	Limited switching among stock funds is permitted.
Twentieth Century	Kansas City, MO	(800) 345-2021	11	Switching available; there may be charges on some funds.
Vanguard Group	Valley Forge, PA	(800) 662-7447	49	No charge is applied, but frequent switching is discouraged.
Waddell and Reed	Kansas City, MO	(800) 842-1075	16	Generally, switching is permitted, but certain funds are excluded.

*This information current as of the date of publication.

FINANCIAL TABLES

Table B.1 Future-Value Interest Factors for One Dollar, CVIF

					INTEREST RATE					
Year	1%	2%	3%	4%	5%	6%	7%	8%	9%	10%
1	1.010	1.020	1.030	1.040	1.050	1.060	1.070	1.080	1.090	1.100
2	1.020	1.040	1.061	1.082	1.102	1.124	1.145	1.166	1.188	1.210
3	1.030	1.061	1.093	1.125	1.158	1.191	1.225	1.260	1.295	1.331
4	1.041	1.082	1.126	1.170	1.216	1.262	1.311	1.360	1.412	1.464
5	1.051	1.104	1.159	1.217	1.276	1.338	1.403	1.469	1.539	1.611
6	1.062	1.126	1.194	1.265	1.340	1.419	1.501	1.587	1.677	1.772
7	1.072	1.149	1.230	1.316	1.407	1.504	1.606	1.714	1.828	1.949
8	1.083	1.172	1.267	1.369	1.477	1.594	1.718	1.851	1.993	2.144
9	1.094	1.195	1.305	1.423	1.551	1.689	1.838	1.999	2.172	2.358
10	1.105	1.219	1.344	1.480	1.629	1.791	1.967	2.159	2.367	2.594
11	1.116	1.243	1.384	1.539	1.710	1.898	2.105	2.332	2.580	2.853
12	1.127	1.268	1.426	1.601	1.796	2.012	2.252	2.518	2.813	3.138
13	1.138	1.294	1.469	1.665	1.886	2.133	2.410	2.720	3.066	3.452
14	1.149	1.319	1.513	1.732	1.980	2.261	2.579	2.937	3.342	3.797
15	1.161	1.346	1.558	1.801	2.079	2.397	2.759	3.172	3.642	4.177
16	1.173	1.373	1.605	1.873	2.183	2.540	2.952	3.426	3.970	4.595
17	1.184	1.400	1.653	1.948	2.292	2.693	3.159	3.700	4.328	5.054
18	1.196	1.428	1.702	2.026	2.407	2.854	3.380	3.996	4.717	5.560
19	1.208	1.457	1.753	2.107	2.527	3.026	3.616	4.316	5.142	6.116
20	1.220	1.486	1.806	2.191	2.653	3.207	3.870	4.661	5.604	6.727
21	1.232	1.516	1.860	2.279	2.786	3.399	4.140	5.034	6.109	7.400
22	1.245	1.546	1.916	2.370	2.925	3.603	4.430	5.436	6.658	8.140
23	1.257	1.577	1.974	2.465	3.071	3.820	4.740	5.871	7.258	8.954
24	1.270	1.608	2.033	2.563	3.225	4.049	5.072	6.341	7.911	9.850
25	1.282	1.641	2.094	2.666	3.386	4.292	5.427	6.848	8.623	10.834
30	1.348	1.811	2.427	3.243	4.322	5.743	7.612	10.062	13.267	17.449
35	1.417	2.000	2.814	3.946	5.516	7.686	10.676	14.785	20.413	28.102
40	1.489	2.208	3.262	4.801	7.040	10.285	14.974	21.724	31.408	45.258
45	1.565	2.438	3.781	5.841	8.985	13.764	21.002	31.920	48.325	72.888
50	1.645	2.691	4.384	7.106	11.467	18.419	29.456	46.900	74.354	117.386

Table B.1   Future-Value Interest Factors for One Dollar, CVIF (Continued)

INTEREST RATE

Year	11%	12%	13%	14%	15%	16%	17%	18%	19%	20%
1	1.110	1.120	1.130	1.140	1.150	1.160	1.170	1.180	1.190	1.200
2	1.232	1.254	1.277	1.300	1.322	1.346	1.369	1.392	1.416	1.440
3	1.368	1.405	1.443	1.482	1.521	1.561	1.602	1.643	1.685	1.728
4	1.518	1.574	1.630	1.689	1.749	1.811	1.874	1.939	2.005	2.074
5	1.685	1.762	1.842	1.925	2.011	2.100	2.192	2.288	2.386	2.488
6	1.870	1.974	2.082	2.195	2.313	2.436	2.565	2.700	2.840	2.986
7	2.076	2.211	2.353	2.502	2.660	2.826	3.001	3.185	3.379	3.583
8	2.305	2.476	2.658	2.853	3.059	3.278	3.511	3.759	4.021	4.300
9	2.558	2.773	3.004	3.252	3.518	3.803	4.108	4.435	4.785	5.160
10	2.839	3.106	3.395	3.707	4.046	4.411	4.807	5.234	5.695	6.192
11	3.152	3.479	3.836	4.226	4.652	5.117	5.624	6.176	6.777	7.430
12	3.498	3.896	4.334	4.818	5.350	5.936	6.580	7.288	8.064	8.916
13	3.883	4.363	4.898	5.492	6.153	6.886	7.699	8.599	9.596	10.699
14	4.310	4.887	5.535	6.261	7.076	7.987	9.007	10.147	11.420	12.839
15	4.785	5.474	6.254	7.138	8.137	9.265	10.539	11.974	13.589	15.407
16	5.311	6.130	7.067	8.137	9.358	10.748	12.330	14.129	16.171	18.488
17	5.895	6.866	7.986	9.276	10.761	12.468	14.426	16.672	19.244	22.186
18	6.543	7.690	9.024	10.575	12.375	14.462	16.879	19.673	22.900	26.623
19	7.263	8.613	10.197	12.055	14.232	16.776	19.748	23.214	27.251	31.948
20	8.062	9.646	11.523	13.743	16.366	19.461	23.105	27.393	32.429	38.337
21	8.949	10.804	13.021	15.667	18.821	22.574	27.033	32.323	38.591	46.005
22	9.933	12.100	14.713	17.861	21.644	26.186	31.629	38.141	45.923	55.205
23	11.026	13.552	16.626	20.361	24.891	30.376	37.005	45.007	54.648	66.247
24	12.239	15.178	18.788	23.212	28.625	35.236	43.296	53.108	65.031	79.496
25	13.585	17.000	21.230	26.461	32.918	40.874	50.656	62.667	77.387	95.395
30	22.892	29.960	39.115	50.949	66.210	85.849	111.061	143.367	184.672	237.373
35	38.574	52.799	72.066	98.097	133.172	180.311	243.495	327.988	440.691	590.657
40	64.999	93.049	132.776	188.876	267.856	378.715	533.846	750.353	1051.642	1469.740
45	109.527	163.985	244.629	363.662	538.752	795.429	1170.425	1716.619	2509.583	3657.176
50	184.559	288.996	450.711	700.197	1083.619	1670.669	2566.080	3927.189	5988.730	9100.191

Table B.1 Future-Value Interest Factors for One Dollar, CVIF *(Continued)*

INTEREST RATE

Year	21%	22%	23%	24%	25%	26%	27%	28%	29%	30%
1	1.210	1.220	1.230	1.240	1.250	1.260	1.270	1.280	1.290	1.300
2	1.464	1.488	1.513	1.538	1.562	1.588	1.613	1.638	1.664	1.690
3	1.772	1.816	1.861	1.907	1.953	2.000	2.048	2.097	2.147	2.197
4	2.144	2.215	2.289	2.364	2.441	2.520	2.601	2.684	2.769	2.856
5	2.594	2.703	2.815	2.932	3.052	3.176	3.304	3.436	3.572	3.713
6	3.138	3.297	3.463	3.635	3.815	4.001	4.196	4.398	4.608	4.827
7	3.797	4.023	4.259	4.508	4.768	5.042	5.329	5.629	5.945	6.275
8	4.595	4.908	5.239	5.589	5.960	6.353	6.767	7.206	7.669	8.157
9	5.560	5.987	6.444	6.931	7.451	8.004	8.595	9.223	9.893	10.604
10	6.727	7.305	7.926	8.594	9.313	10.086	10.915	11.806	12.761	13.786
11	8.140	8.912	9.749	10.657	11.642	12.708	13.862	15.112	16.462	17.921
12	9.850	10.872	11.991	13.215	14.552	16.012	17.605	19.343	21.236	23.298
13	11.918	13.264	14.749	16.386	18.190	20.175	22.359	24.759	27.395	30.287
14	14.421	16.182	18.141	20.319	22.737	25.420	28.395	31.691	35.339	39.373
15	17.449	19.742	22.314	25.195	28.422	32.030	36.062	40.565	45.587	51.185
16	21.113	24.085	27.446	31.242	35.527	40.357	45.799	51.923	58.808	66.541
17	25.547	29.384	33.758	38.740	44.409	50.850	58.165	66.461	75.862	86.503
18	30.912	35.848	41.523	48.038	55.511	64.071	73.869	85.070	97.862	112.454
19	37.404	43.735	51.073	59.567	69.389	80.730	93.813	108.890	126.242	146.190
20	45.258	53.357	62.820	73.863	86.736	101.720	119.143	139.379	162.852	190.047
21	54.762	65.095	77.268	91.591	108.420	128.167	151.312	178.405	210.079	247.061
22	66.262	79.416	95.040	113.572	135.525	161.490	192.165	228.358	271.002	321.178
23	80.178	96.887	116.899	140.829	169.407	203.477	244.050	292.298	349.592	417.531
24	97.015	118.203	143.786	174.628	211.758	256.381	309.943	374.141	450.974	542.791
25	117.388	144.207	176.857	216.539	264.698	323.040	393.628	478.901	581.756	705.627
30	304.471	389.748	497.904	634.810	807.793	1025.904	1300.477	1645.488	2078.208	2619.936
35	789.716	1053.370	1401.749	1861.020	2465.189	3258.053	4296.547	5653.840	7423.988	9727.598
40	2048.309	2846.941	3946.340	5455.797	7523.156	10346.879	14195.051	19426.418	26520.723	36117.754
45	5312.758	7694.418	11110.121	15994.316	22958.844	32859.457	46897.973	66748.500	94739.937	134102.187
50	13779.844	20795.680	31278.301	46889.207	70064.812	104354.562	154942.687	229345.875	338440.000	497910.125

Table B.1 Future-Value Interest Factors for One Dollar, CVIF (Continued)

					INTEREST RATE					
Year	31%	32%	33%	34%	35%	36%	37%	38%	39%	40%
1	1.310	1.320	1.330	1.340	1.350	1.360	1.370	1.380	1.390	1.400
2	1.716	1.742	1.769	1.796	1.822	1.850	1.877	1.904	1.932	1.960
3	2.248	2.300	2.353	2.406	2.460	2.515	2.571	2.628	2.686	2.744
4	2.945	3.036	3.129	3.224	3.321	3.421	3.523	3.627	3.733	3.842
5	3.858	4.007	4.162	4.320	4.484	4.653	4.826	5.005	5.189	5.378
6	5.054	5.290	5.535	5.789	6.053	6.328	6.612	6.907	7.213	7.530
7	6.621	6.983	7.361	7.758	8.172	8.605	9.058	9.531	10.025	10.541
8	8.673	9.217	9.791	10.395	11.032	11.703	12.410	13.153	13.935	14.758
9	11.362	12.166	13.022	13.930	14.894	15.917	17.001	18.151	19.370	20.661
10	14.884	16.060	17.319	18.666	20.106	21.646	23.292	25.049	26.924	28.925
11	19.498	21.199	23.034	25.012	27.144	29.439	31.910	34.567	37.425	40.495
12	25.542	27.982	30.635	33.516	36.644	40.037	43.716	47.703	52.020	56.694
13	33.460	36.937	40.745	44.912	49.469	54.451	59.892	65.830	72.308	79.371
14	43.832	48.756	54.190	60.181	66.784	74.053	82.051	90.845	100.509	111.119
15	57.420	64.358	72.073	80.643	90.158	100.712	112.410	125.366	139.707	155.567
16	75.220	84.953	95.857	108.061	121.713	136.968	154.002	173.005	194.192	217.793
17	98.539	112.138	127.490	144.802	164.312	186.277	210.983	238.747	269.927	304.911
18	129.086	148.022	169.561	194.035	221.822	253.337	289.046	329.471	375.198	426.875
19	169.102	195.389	225.517	260.006	299.459	344.537	395.993	454.669	521.525	597.625
20	221.523	257.913	299.937	348.408	404.270	468.571	542.511	627.443	724.919	836.674
21	290.196	340.446	398.916	466.867	545.764	637.256	743.240	865.871	1007.637	1171.343
22	380.156	449.388	530.558	625.601	736.781	866.668	1018.238	1194.900	1400.615	1639.878
23	498.004	593.192	705.642	838.305	994.653	1178.668	1394.986	1648.961	1946.854	2295.829
24	652.385	783.013	938.504	1123.328	1342.781	1602.988	1911.129	2275.564	2706.125	3214.158
25	854.623	1033.577	1248.210	1505.258	1812.754	2180.063	2618.245	3140.275	3761.511	4499.816
30	3297.081	4142.008	5194.516	6503.285	8128.426	10142.914	12636.086	15716.703	19517.969	24201.043
35	12719.918	16598.906	21617.363	28096.695	36448.051	47190.727	60983.836	78660.188	101276.125	130158.687
40	49072.621	66519.313	89962.188	121388.437	163433.875	219558.625	294317.937	393684.687	525508.312	700022.688

Table B.2 Future-Value Interest Factors for a One-Dollar Annuity, CVIFA

INTEREST RATE

Year	1%	2%	3%	4%	5%	6%	7%	8%	9%	10%
1	1.000	1.000	1.000	1.000	1.000	1.000	1.000	1.000	1.000	1.000
2	2.010	2.020	2.030	2.040	2.050	2.060	2.070	2.080	2.090	2.100
3	3.030	3.060	3.091	3.122	3.152	3.184	3.215	3.246	3.278	3.310
4	4.060	4.122	4.184	4.246	4.310	4.375	4.440	4.506	4.573	4.641
5	5.101	5.204	5.309	5.416	5.526	5.637	5.751	5.867	5.985	6.105
6	6.152	6.308	6.468	6.633	6.802	6.975	7.153	7.336	7.523	7.716
7	7.214	7.434	7.662	7.898	8.142	8.394	8.654	8.923	9.200	9.487
8	8.286	8.583	8.892	9.214	9.549	9.897	10.260	10.637	11.028	11.436
9	9.368	9.755	10.159	10.583	11.027	11.491	11.978	12.488	13.021	13.579
10	10.462	10.950	11.464	12.006	12.578	13.181	13.816	14.487	15.193	15.937
11	11.567	12.169	12.808	13.486	14.207	14.972	15.784	16.645	17.560	18.531
12	12.682	13.412	14.192	15.026	15.917	16.870	17.888	18.977	20.141	21.384
13	13.809	14.680	15.618	16.627	17.713	18.882	20.141	21.495	22.953	24.523
14	14.947	15.974	17.086	18.292	19.598	21.015	22.550	24.215	26.019	27.975
15	16.097	17.293	18.599	20.023	21.578	23.276	25.129	27.152	29.361	31.772
16	17.258	18.639	20.157	21.824	23.657	25.672	27.888	30.324	33.003	35.949
17	18.430	20.012	21.761	23.697	25.840	28.213	30.840	33.750	36.973	40.544
18	19.614	21.412	23.414	25.645	28.132	30.905	33.999	37.450	41.301	45.599
19	20.811	22.840	25.117	27.671	30.539	33.760	37.379	41.446	46.018	51.158
20	22.019	24.297	26.870	29.778	33.066	36.785	40.995	45.762	51.159	57.274
21	23.239	25.783	28.676	31.969	35.719	39.992	44.865	50.422	56.764	64.002
22	24.471	27.299	30.536	34.248	38.505	43.392	49.005	55.456	62.872	71.402
23	25.716	28.845	32.452	36.618	41.430	46.995	53.435	60.893	69.531	79.542
24	26.973	30.421	34.426	39.082	44.501	50.815	58.176	66.764	76.789	88.496
25	28.243	32.030	36.459	41.645	47.726	54.864	63.248	73.105	84.699	98.346
30	34.784	40.567	47.575	56.084	66.438	79.057	94.459	113.282	136.305	164.491
35	41.659	49.994	60.461	73.651	90.318	111.432	138.234	172.314	215.705	271.018
40	48.885	60.401	75.400	95.024	120.797	154.758	199.630	259.052	337.872	442.580
45	56.479	71.891	92.718	121.027	159.695	212.737	285.741	386.497	525.840	718.881
50	64.461	84.577	112.794	152.664	209.341	290.325	406.516	573.756	815.051	1163.865

Table B.2   Future-Value Interest Factors for a One-Dollar Annuity, CVIFA *(Continued)*

INTEREST RATE

Year	11%	12%	13%	14%	15%	16%	17%	18%	19%	20%
1	1.000	1.000	1.000	1.000	1.000	1.000	1.000	1.000	1.000	1.000
2	2.110	2.120	2.130	2.140	2.150	2.160	2.170	2.180	2.190	2.200
3	3.342	3.374	3.407	3.440	3.472	3.506	3.539	3.572	3.606	3.640
4	4.710	4.779	4.850	4.921	4.993	5.066	5.141	5.215	5.291	5.368
5	6.228	6.353	6.480	6.610	6.742	6.877	7.014	7.154	7.297	7.442
6	7.913	8.115	8.323	8.535	8.754	8.977	9.207	9.442	9.683	9.930
7	9.783	10.089	10.405	10.730	11.067	11.414	11.772	12.141	12.523	12.916
8	11.859	12.300	12.757	13.233	13.727	14.240	14.773	15.327	15.902	16.499
9	14.164	14.776	15.416	16.085	16.786	17.518	18.285	19.086	19.923	20.799
10	16.722	17.549	18.420	19.337	20.304	21.321	22.393	23.521	24.709	25.959
11	19.561	20.655	21.814	23.044	24.349	25.733	27.200	28.755	30.403	32.150
12	22.713	24.133	25.650	27.271	29.001	30.850	32.824	34.931	37.180	39.580
13	26.211	28.029	29.984	32.088	34.352	36.786	39.404	42.218	45.244	48.496
14	30.095	32.392	34.882	37.581	40.504	43.672	47.102	50.818	54.841	59.196
15	34.405	37.280	40.417	43.842	47.580	51.659	56.109	60.965	66.260	72.035
16	39.190	42.753	46.671	50.980	55.717	60.925	66.648	72.938	79.850	87.442
17	44.500	48.883	53.738	59.117	65.075	71.673	78.978	87.067	96.021	105.930
18	50.396	55.749	61.724	68.393	75.836	84.140	93.404	103.739	115.265	128.116
19	56.939	63.439	70.748	78.968	88.211	98.603	110.283	123.412	138.165	154.739
20	64.202	72.052	80.946	91.024	102.443	115.379	130.031	146.626	165.417	186.687
21	72.264	81.698	92.468	104.767	118.809	134.840	153.136	174.019	197.846	225.024
22	81.213	92.502	105.489	120.434	137.630	157.414	180.169	206.342	236.436	271.028
23	91.147	104.602	120.203	138.295	159.274	183.600	211.798	244.483	282.359	326.234
24	102.173	118.154	136.829	158.656	184.166	213.976	248.803	289.490	337.007	392.480
25	114.412	133.333	155.616	181.867	212.790	249.212	292.099	342.598	402.038	471.976
30	199.018	241.330	293.192	356.778	434.738	530.306	647.423	790.932	966.698	1181.865
35	341.583	431.658	546.663	693.552	881.152	1120.699	1426.448	1816.607	2314.173	2948.294
40	581.812	767.080	1013.667	1341.979	1779.048	2360.724	3134.412	4163.094	5529.711	7343.715
45	986.613	1358.208	1874.086	2590.464	3585.031	4965.191	6879.008	9531.258	13203.105	18280.914
50	1668.723	2399.975	3459.344	4994.301	7217.488	10435.449	15088.805	21812.273	31514.492	45496.094

Table B.2 Future-Value Interest Factors for a One-Dollar Annuity, CVIFA (Continued)

Year	21%	22%	23%	24%	25%	26%	27%	28%	29%	30%
1	1.000	1.000	1.000	1.000	1.000	1.000	1.000	1.000	1.000	1.000
2	2.210	2.220	2.230	2.240	2.250	2.260	2.270	2.280	2.290	2.300
3	3.674	3.708	3.743	3.778	3.813	3.848	3.883	3.918	3.954	3.990
4	5.446	5.524	5.604	5.684	5.766	5.848	5.931	6.016	6.101	6.187
5	7.589	7.740	7.893	8.048	8.207	8.368	8.533	8.700	8.870	9.043
6	10.183	10.442	10.708	10.980	11.259	11.544	11.837	12.136	12.442	12.756
7	13.321	13.740	14.171	14.615	15.073	15.546	16.032	16.534	17.051	17.583
8	17.119	17.762	18.430	19.123	19.842	20.588	21.361	22.163	22.995	23.858
9	21.714	22.670	23.669	24.712	25.802	26.940	28.129	29.369	30.664	32.015
10	27.274	28.657	30.113	31.643	33.253	34.945	36.723	38.592	40.556	42.619
11	34.001	35.962	38.039	40.238	42.566	45.030	47.639	50.398	53.318	56.405
12	42.141	44.873	47.787	50.895	54.208	57.738	61.501	65.510	69.780	74.326
13	51.991	55.745	59.778	64.109	68.760	73.750	79.106	84.853	91.016	97.624
14	63.909	69.009	74.528	80.496	86.949	93.925	101.465	109.611	118.411	127.912
15	78.330	85.191	92.669	100.815	109.687	119.346	129.860	141.302	153.750	167.285
16	95.779	104.933	114.983	126.010	138.109	151.375	165.922	181.867	199.337	218.470
17	116.892	129.019	142.428	157.252	173.636	191.733	211.721	233.790	258.145	285.011
18	142.439	158.403	176.187	195.993	218.045	242.583	269.885	300.250	334.006	371.514
19	173.351	194.251	217.710	244.031	273.556	306.654	343.754	385.321	431.868	483.968
20	210.755	237.986	268.783	303.598	342.945	387.384	437.568	494.210	558.110	630.157
21	256.013	291.343	331.603	377.461	429.681	489.104	556.710	633.589	720.962	820.204
22	310.775	356.438	408.871	469.052	538.101	617.270	708.022	811.993	931.040	1067.265
23	377.038	435.854	503.911	582.624	673.626	778.760	900.187	1040.351	1202.042	1388.443
24	457.215	532.741	620.810	723.453	843.032	982.237	1144.237	1332.649	1551.634	1805.975
25	554.230	650.944	764.596	898.082	1054.791	1238.617	1454.180	1706.790	2002.608	2348.765
30	1445.111	1767.044	2160.459	2640.881	3227.172	3941.953	4812.891	5873.172	7162.785	8729.805
35	3755.814	4783.520	6090.227	7750.094	9856.746	12527.160	15909.480	20188.742	25596.512	32422.090
40	9749.141	12936.141	17153.691	22728.367	30088.621	39791.957	52570.707	69376.562	91447.375	120389.375
45	25294.223	34970.230	48300.660	66638.937	91831.312	126378.937	173692.875	238384.312	326686.375	447005.062

Table B.2   Future-Value Interest Factors for a One-Dollar Annuity, CVIFA *(Continued)*

INTEREST RATE

Year	31%	32%	33%	34%	35%	36%	37%	38%	39%	40%
1	1.000	1.000	1.000	1.000	1.000	1.000	1.000	1.000	1.000	1.000
2	2.310	2.320	2.330	2.340	2.350	2.360	2.370	2.380	2.390	2.400
3	4.026	4.062	4.099	4.136	4.172	4.210	4.247	4.284	4.322	4.360
4	6.274	6.362	6.452	6.542	6.633	6.725	6.818	6.912	7.008	7.104
5	9.219	9.398	9.581	9.766	9.954	10.146	10.341	10.539	10.741	10.946
6	13.077	13.406	13.742	14.086	14.438	14.799	15.167	15.544	15.930	16.324
7	18.131	18.696	19.277	19.876	20.492	21.126	21.779	22.451	23.142	23.853
8	24.752	25.678	26.638	27.633	28.664	29.732	30.837	31.982	33.167	34.395
9	33.425	34.895	36.429	38.028	39.696	41.435	43.247	45.135	47.103	49.152
10	44.786	47.062	49.451	51.958	54.590	57.351	60.248	63.287	66.473	69.813
11	59.670	63.121	66.769	70.624	74.696	78.998	83.540	88.335	93.397	98.739
12	79.167	84.320	89.803	95.636	101.840	108.437	115.450	122.903	130.822	139.234
13	104.709	112.302	120.438	129.152	138.484	148.474	159.166	170.606	182.842	195.928
14	138.169	149.239	161.183	174.063	187.953	202.925	219.058	236.435	255.151	275.299
15	182.001	197.996	215.373	234.245	254.737	276.978	301.109	327.281	355.659	386.418
16	239.421	262.354	287.446	314.888	344.895	377.690	413.520	452.647	495.366	541.985
17	314.642	347.307	383.303	422.949	466.608	514.658	567.521	625.652	689.558	759.778
18	413.180	459.445	510.792	567.751	630.920	700.935	778.504	864.399	959.485	1064.689
19	542.266	607.467	680.354	761.786	852.741	954.271	1067.551	1193.870	1334.683	1491.563
20	711.368	802.856	905.870	1021.792	1152.200	1298.809	1463.544	1648.539	1856.208	2089.188
21	932.891	1060.769	1205.807	1370.201	1556.470	1767.380	2006.055	2275.982	2581.128	2925.862
22	1223.087	1401.215	1604.724	1837.068	2102.234	2404.636	2749.294	3141.852	3588.765	4097.203
23	1603.243	1850.603	2135.282	2462.669	2839.014	3271.304	3767.532	4336.750	4989.379	5737.078
24	2101.247	2443.795	2840.924	3300.974	3833.667	4449.969	5162.516	5985.711	6936.230	8032.906
25	2753.631	3226.808	3779.428	4424.301	5176.445	6052.957	7073.645	8261.273	9642.352	11247.062
30	10632.543	12940.672	15737.945	19124.434	23221.258	28172.016	34148.906	41357.227	50043.625	60500.207

Table B.3 Present-Value Interest Factors for One Dollar, PVIF

Year	\multicolumn{10}{c}{DISCOUNT (INTEREST) RATE}
	1%	2%	3%	4%	5%	6%	7%	8%	9%	10%
1	.990	.980	.971	.962	.952	.943	.935	.926	.917	.909
2	.980	.961	.943	.925	.907	.890	.873	.857	.842	.826
3	.971	.942	.915	.889	.864	.840	.816	.794	.772	.751
4	.961	.924	.888	.855	.823	.792	.763	.735	.708	.683
5	.951	.906	.863	.822	.784	.747	.713	.681	.650	.621
6	.942	.888	.837	.790	.746	.705	.666	.630	.596	.564
7	.933	.871	.813	.760	.711	.665	.623	.583	.547	.513
8	.923	.853	.789	.731	.677	.627	.582	.540	.502	.467
9	.914	.837	.766	.703	.645	.592	.544	.500	.460	.424
10	.905	.820	.744	.676	.614	.558	.508	.463	.422	.386
11	.896	.804	.722	.650	.585	.527	.475	.429	.388	.350
12	.887	.789	.701	.625	.557	.497	.444	.397	.356	.319
13	.879	.773	.681	.601	.530	.469	.415	.368	.326	.290
14	.870	.758	.661	.577	.505	.442	.388	.340	.299	.263
15	.861	.743	.642	.555	.481	.417	.362	.315	.275	.239
16	.853	.728	.623	.534	.458	.394	.339	.292	.252	.218
17	.844	.714	.605	.513	.436	.371	.317	.270	.231	.198
18	.836	.700	.587	.494	.416	.350	.296	.250	.212	.180
19	.828	.686	.570	.475	.396	.331	.277	.232	.194	.164
20	.820	.673	.554	.456	.377	.312	.258	.215	.178	.149
21	.811	.660	.538	.439	.359	.294	.242	.199	.164	.135
22	.803	.647	.522	.422	.342	.278	.226	.184	.150	.123
23	.795	.634	.507	.406	.326	.262	.211	.170	.138	.112
24	.788	.622	.492	.390	.310	.247	.197	.158	.126	.102
25	.780	.610	.478	.375	.295	.233	.184	.146	.116	.092
30	.742	.552	.412	.308	.231	.174	.131	.099	.075	.057
35	.706	.500	.355	.253	.181	.130	.094	.068	.049	.036
40	.672	.453	.307	.208	.142	.097	.067	.046	.032	.022
45	.639	.410	.264	.171	.111	.073	.048	.031	.021	.014
50	.608	.372	.228	.141	.087	.054	.034	.021	.013	.009

Table B.3　Present-Value Interest Factors for One Dollar, PVIF (*Continued*)

Year	DISCOUNT (INTEREST) RATE									
	11%	12%	13%	14%	15%	16%	17%	18%	19%	20%
1	.901	.893	.885	.877	.870	.862	.855	.847	.840	.833
2	.812	.797	.783	.769	.756	.743	.731	.718	.706	.694
3	.731	.712	.693	.675	.658	.641	.624	.609	.593	.579
4	.659	.636	.613	.592	.572	.552	.534	.516	.499	.482
5	.593	.567	.543	.519	.497	.476	.456	.437	.419	.402
6	.535	.507	.480	.456	.432	.410	.390	.370	.352	.335
7	.482	.452	.425	.400	.376	.354	.333	.314	.296	.279
8	.434	.404	.376	.351	.327	.305	.285	.266	.249	.233
9	.391	.361	.333	.308	.284	.263	.243	.225	.209	.194
10	.352	.322	.295	.270	.247	.227	.208	.191	.176	.162
11	.317	.287	.261	.237	.215	.195	.178	.162	.148	.135
12	.286	.257	.231	.208	.187	.168	.152	.137	.124	.112
13	.258	.229	.204	.182	.163	.145	.130	.116	.104	.093
14	.232	.205	.181	.160	.141	.125	.111	.099	.088	.078
15	.209	.183	.160	.140	.123	.108	.095	.084	.074	.065
16	.188	.163	.141	.123	.107	.093	.081	.071	.062	.054
17	.170	.146	.125	.108	.093	.080	.069	.060	.052	.045
18	.153	.130	.111	.095	.081	.069	.059	.051	.044	.038
19	.138	.116	.098	.083	.070	.060	.051	.043	.037	.031
20	.124	.104	.087	.073	.061	.051	.043	.037	.031	.026
21	.112	.093	.077	.064	.053	.044	.037	.031	.026	.022
22	.101	.083	.068	.056	.046	.038	.032	.026	.022	.018
23	.091	.074	.060	.049	.040	.033	.027	.022	.018	.015
24	.082	.066	.053	.043	.035	.028	.023	.019	.015	.013
25	.074	.059	.047	.038	.030	.024	.020	.016	.013	.010
30	.044	.033	.026	.020	.015	.012	.009	.007	.005	.004
35	.026	.019	.014	.010	.008	.006	.004	.003	.002	.002
40	.015	.011	.008	.005	.004	.003	.002	.001	.001	.001
45	.009	.006	.004	.003	.002	.001	.001	.001	.000	.000
50	.005	.003	.002	.001	.001	.001	.000	.000	.000	.000

Table B.3 Present-Value Interest Factors for One Dollar, PVIF (Continued)

Year	DISCOUNT (INTEREST) RATE									
	21%	22%	23%	24%	25%	26%	27%	28%	29%	30%
1	.826	.820	.813	.806	.800	.794	.787	.781	.775	.769
2	.683	.672	.661	.650	.640	.630	.620	.610	.601	.592
3	.564	.551	.537	.524	.512	.500	.488	.477	.466	.455
4	.467	.451	.437	.423	.410	.397	.384	.373	.361	.350
5	.386	.370	.355	.341	.328	.315	.303	.291	.280	.269
6	.319	.303	.289	.275	.262	.250	.238	.227	.217	.207
7	.263	.249	.235	.222	.210	.198	.188	.178	.168	.159
8	.218	.204	.191	.179	.168	.157	.148	.139	.130	.123
9	.180	.167	.155	.144	.134	.125	.116	.108	.101	.094
10	.149	.137	.126	.116	.107	.099	.092	.085	.078	.073
11	.123	.112	.103	.094	.086	.079	.072	.066	.061	.056
12	.102	.092	.083	.076	.069	.062	.057	.052	.047	.043
13	.084	.075	.068	.061	.055	.050	.045	.040	.037	.033
14	.069	.062	.055	.049	.044	.039	.035	.032	.028	.025
15	.057	.051	.045	.040	.035	.031	.028	.025	.022	.020
16	.047	.042	.036	.032	.028	.025	.022	.019	.017	.015
17	.039	.034	.030	.026	.023	.020	.017	.015	.013	.012
18	.032	.028	.024	.021	.018	.016	.014	.012	.010	.009
19	.027	.023	.020	.017	.014	.012	.011	.009	.008	.007
20	.022	.019	.016	.014	.012	.010	.008	.007	.006	.005
21	.018	.015	.013	.011	.009	.008	.007	.006	.005	.004
22	.015	.013	.011	.009	.007	.006	.005	.004	.004	.003
23	.012	.010	.009	.007	.006	.005	.004	.003	.003	.002
24	.010	.008	.007	.006	.005	.004	.003	.003	.002	.002
25	.009	.007	.006	.005	.004	.003	.003	.002	.002	.001
30	.003	.003	.002	.002	.001	.001	.001	.001	.000	.000
35	.001	.001	.001	.001	.000	.000	.000	.000	.000	.000
40	.000	.000	.000	.000	.000	.000	.000	.000	.000	.000
45	.000	.000	.000	.000	.000	.000	.000	.000	.000	.000
50	.000	.000	.000	.000	.000	.000	.000	.000	.000	.000

Table B.3   Present-Value Interest Factors for One Dollar, PVIF (Continued)

					DISCOUNT (INTEREST) RATE					
Year	31%	32%	33%	34%	35%	36%	37%	38%	39%	40%
1	.763	.758	.752	.746	.741	.735	.730	.725	.719	.714
2	.583	.574	.565	.557	.549	.541	.533	.525	.518	.510
3	.445	.435	.425	.416	.406	.398	.389	.381	.372	.364
4	.340	.329	.320	.310	.301	.292	.284	.276	.268	.260
5	.259	.250	.240	.231	.223	.215	.207	.200	.193	.186
6	.198	.189	.181	.173	.165	.158	.151	.145	.139	.133
7	.151	.143	.136	.129	.122	.116	.110	.105	.100	.095
8	.115	.108	.102	.096	.091	.085	.081	.076	.072	.068
9	.088	.082	.077	.072	.067	.063	.059	.055	.052	.048
10	.067	.062	.058	.054	.050	.046	.043	.040	.037	.035
11	.051	.047	.043	.040	.037	.034	.031	.029	.027	.025
12	.039	.036	.033	.030	.027	.025	.023	.021	.019	.018
13	.030	.027	.025	.022	.020	.018	.017	.015	.014	.013
14	.023	.021	.018	.017	.015	.014	.012	.011	.010	.009
15	.017	.016	.014	.012	.011	.010	.009	.008	.007	.006
16	.013	.012	.010	.009	.008	.007	.006	.006	.005	.005
17	.010	.009	.008	.007	.006	.005	.005	.004	.004	.003
18	.008	.007	.006	.005	.005	.004	.003	.003	.003	.002
19	.006	.005	.004	.004	.003	.003	.003	.002	.002	.002
20	.005	.004	.003	.003	.002	.002	.002	.002	.001	.001
21	.003	.003	.003	.002	.002	.002	.001	.001	.001	.001
22	.003	.002	.002	.002	.001	.001	.001	.001	.001	.001
23	.002	.002	.001	.001	.001	.001	.001	.001	.001	.000
24	.002	.001	.001	.001	.001	.001	.001	.000	.000	.000
25	.001	.001	.001	.001	.001	.000	.000	.000	.000	.000
30	.000	.000	.000	.000	.000	.000	.000	.000	.000	.000
35	.000	.000	.000	.000	.000	.000	.000	.000	.000	.000
40	.000	.000	.000	.000	.000	.000	.000	.000	.000	.000
45	.000	.000	.000	.000	.000	.000	.000	.000	.000	.000
50	.000	.000	.000	.000	.000	.000	.000	.000	.000	.000

Table B.4 Present-Value Interest Factors for a One-Dollar Annuity, PVIFA

Year	

Year	1%	2%	3%	4%	5%	6%	7%	8%	9%	10%
					DISCOUNT (INTEREST) RATE					
1	.990	.980	.971	.962	.952	.943	.935	.926	.917	.909
2	1.970	1.942	1.913	1.886	1.859	1.833	1.808	1.783	1.759	1.736
3	2.941	2.884	2.829	2.775	2.723	2.673	2.624	2.577	2.531	2.487
4	3.902	3.808	3.717	3.630	3.546	3.465	3.387	3.312	3.240	3.170
5	4.853	4.713	4.580	4.452	4.329	4.212	4.100	3.993	3.890	3.791
6	5.795	5.601	5.417	5.242	5.076	4.917	4.767	4.623	4.486	4.355
7	6.728	6.472	6.230	6.002	5.786	5.582	5.389	5.206	5.033	4.868
8	7.652	7.326	7.020	6.733	6.463	6.210	5.971	5.747	5.535	5.335
9	8.566	8.162	7.786	7.435	7.108	6.802	6.515	6.247	5.995	5.759
10	9.471	8.983	8.530	8.111	7.722	7.360	7.024	6.710	6.418	6.145
11	10.368	9.787	9.253	8.760	8.306	7.887	7.499	7.139	6.805	6.495
12	11.255	10.575	9.954	9.385	8.863	8.384	7.943	7.536	7.161	6.814
13	12.134	11.348	10.635	9.986	9.394	8.853	8.358	7.904	7.487	7.103
14	13.004	12.106	11.296	10.563	9.899	9.295	8.746	8.244	7.786	7.367
15	13.865	12.849	11.938	11.118	10.380	9.712	9.108	8.560	8.061	7.606
16	14.718	13.578	12.561	11.652	10.838	10.106	9.447	8.851	8.313	7.824
17	15.562	14.292	13.166	12.166	11.274	10.477	9.763	9.122	8.544	8.022
18	16.398	14.992	13.754	12.659	11.690	10.828	10.059	9.372	8.756	8.201
19	17.226	15.679	14.324	13.134	12.085	11.158	10.336	9.604	8.950	8.365
20	18.046	16.352	14.878	13.590	12.462	11.470	10.594	9.818	9.129	8.514
21	18.857	17.011	15.415	14.029	12.821	11.764	10.836	10.017	9.292	8.649
22	19.661	17.658	15.937	14.451	13.163	12.042	11.061	10.201	9.442	8.772
23	20.456	18.292	16.444	14.857	13.489	12.303	11.272	10.371	9.580	8.883
24	21.244	18.914	16.936	15.247	13.799	12.550	11.469	10.529	9.707	8.985
25	22.023	19.524	17.413	15.622	14.094	12.783	11.654	10.675	9.823	9.077
30	25.808	22.397	19.601	17.292	15.373	13.765	12.409	11.258	10.274	9.427
35	29.409	24.999	21.487	18.665	16.374	14.498	12.948	11.655	10.567	9.644
40	32.835	27.356	23.115	19.793	17.159	15.046	13.332	11.925	10.757	9.779
45	36.095	29.490	24.519	20.720	17.774	15.456	13.606	12.108	10.881	9.863
50	39.197	31.424	25.730	21.482	18.256	15.762	13.801	12.234	10.962	9.915

Table B.4   Present-Value Interest Factors for a One-Dollar Annuity, PVIFA (Continued)

DISCOUNT (INTEREST) RATE

Year	11%	12%	13%	14%	15%	16%	17%	18%	19%	20%
1	.901	.893	.885	.877	.870	.862	.855	.847	.840	.833
2	1.713	1.690	1.668	1.647	1.626	1.605	1.585	1.566	1.547	1.528
3	2.444	2.402	2.361	2.322	2.283	2.246	2.210	2.174	2.140	2.106
4	3.102	3.037	2.974	2.914	2.855	2.798	2.743	2.690	2.639	2.589
5	3.696	3.605	3.517	3.433	3.352	3.274	3.199	3.127	3.058	2.991
6	4.231	4.111	3.998	3.889	3.784	3.685	3.589	3.498	3.410	3.326
7	4.712	4.564	4.423	4.288	4.160	4.039	3.922	3.812	3.706	3.605
8	5.146	4.968	4.799	4.639	4.487	4.344	4.207	4.078	3.954	3.837
9	5.537	5.328	5.132	4.946	4.772	4.607	4.451	4.303	4.163	4.031
10	5.889	5.650	5.426	5.216	5.019	4.833	4.659	4.494	4.339	4.192
11	6.207	5.938	5.687	5.453	5.234	5.029	4.836	4.656	4.487	4.327
12	6.492	6.194	5.918	5.660	5.421	5.197	4.988	4.793	4.611	4.439
13	6.750	6.424	6.122	5.842	5.583	5.342	5.118	4.910	4.715	4.533
14	6.982	6.628	6.303	6.002	5.724	5.468	5.229	5.008	4.802	4.611
15	7.191	6.811	6.462	6.142	5.847	5.575	5.324	5.092	4.876	4.675
16	7.379	6.974	6.604	6.265	5.954	5.669	5.405	5.162	4.938	4.730
17	7.549	7.120	6.729	6.373	6.047	5.749	5.475	5.222	4.990	4.775
18	7.702	7.250	6.840	6.467	6.128	5.818	5.534	5.273	5.033	4.812
19	7.839	7.366	6.938	6.550	6.198	5.877	5.585	5.316	5.070	4.843
20	7.963	7.469	7.025	6.623	6.259	5.929	5.628	5.353	5.101	4.870
21	8.075	7.562	7.102	6.687	6.312	5.973	5.665	5.384	5.127	4.891
22	8.176	7.645	7.170	6.743	6.359	6.011	5.696	5.410	5.149	4.909
23	8.266	7.718	7.230	6.792	6.399	6.044	5.723	5.432	5.167	4.925
24	8.348	7.784	7.283	6.835	6.434	6.073	5.747	5.451	5.182	4.937
25	8.422	7.843	7.330	6.873	6.464	6.097	5.766	5.467	5.195	4.948
30	8.694	8.055	7.496	7.003	6.566	6.177	5.829	5.517	5.235	4.979
35	8.855	8.176	7.586	7.070	6.617	6.215	5.858	5.539	5.251	4.992
40	8.951	8.244	7.634	7.105	6.642	6.233	5.871	5.548	5.258	4.997
45	9.008	8.283	7.661	7.123	6.654	6.242	5.877	5.552	5.261	4.999
50	9.042	8.305	7.675	7.133	6.661	6.246	5.880	5.554	5.262	4.999

Table B.4 Present-Value Interest Factors for a One-Dollar Annuity, PVIFA (Continued)

Year	DISCOUNT (INTEREST) RATE									
	21%	22%	23%	24%	25%	26%	27%	28%	29%	30%
1	.826	.820	.813	.806	.800	.794	.787	.781	.775	.769
2	1.509	1.492	1.474	1.457	1.440	1.424	1.407	1.392	1.376	1.361
3	2.074	2.042	2.011	1.981	1.952	1.923	1.896	1.868	1.842	1.816
4	2.540	2.494	2.448	2.404	2.362	2.320	2.280	2.241	2.203	2.166
5	2.926	2.864	2.803	2.745	2.689	2.635	2.583	2.532	2.483	2.436
6	3.245	3.167	3.092	3.020	2.951	2.885	2.821	2.759	2.700	2.643
7	3.508	3.416	3.327	3.242	3.161	3.083	3.009	2.937	2.868	2.802
8	3.726	3.619	3.518	3.421	3.329	3.241	3.156	3.076	2.999	2.925
9	3.905	3.786	3.673	3.566	3.463	3.366	3.273	3.184	3.100	3.019
10	4.054	3.923	3.799	3.682	3.570	3.465	3.364	3.269	3.178	3.092
11	4.177	4.035	3.902	3.776	3.656	3.544	3.437	3.335	3.239	3.147
12	4.278	4.127	3.985	3.851	3.725	3.606	3.493	3.387	3.286	3.190
13	4.362	4.203	4.053	3.912	3.780	3.656	3.538	3.427	3.322	3.223
14	4.432	4.265	4.108	3.962	3.824	3.695	3.573	3.459	3.351	3.249
15	4.489	4.315	4.153	4.001	3.859	3.726	3.601	3.483	3.373	3.268
16	4.536	4.357	4.189	4.033	3.887	3.751	3.623	3.503	3.390	3.283
17	4.576	4.391	4.219	4.059	3.910	3.771	3.640	3.518	3.403	3.295
18	4.608	4.419	4.243	4.080	3.928	3.786	3.654	3.529	3.413	3.304
19	4.635	4.442	4.263	4.097	3.942	3.799	3.664	3.539	3.421	3.311
20	4.657	4.460	4.279	4.110	3.954	3.808	3.673	3.546	3.427	3.316
21	4.675	4.476	4.292	4.121	3.963	3.816	3.679	3.551	3.432	3.320
22	4.690	4.488	4.302	4.130	3.970	3.822	3.684	3.556	3.436	3.323
23	4.703	4.499	4.311	4.137	3.976	3.827	3.689	3.559	3.438	3.325
24	4.713	4.507	4.318	4.143	3.981	3.831	3.692	3.562	3.441	3.327
25	4.721	4.514	4.323	4.147	3.985	3.834	3.694	3.564	3.442	3.329
30	4.746	4.534	4.339	4.160	3.995	3.842	3.701	3.569	3.447	3.332
35	4.756	4.541	4.345	4.164	3.998	3.845	3.703	3.571	3.448	3.333
40	4.760	4.544	4.347	4.166	3.999	3.846	3.703	3.571	3.448	3.333
45	4.761	4.545	4.347	4.166	4.000	3.846	3.704	3.571	3.448	3.333
50	4.762	4.545	4.348	4.167	4.000	3.846	3.704	3.571	3.448	3.333

Table B.4   Present-Value Interest Factors for a One-Dollar Annuity, PVIFA *(Continued)*

DISCOUNT (INTEREST) RATE

Year	31%	32%	33%	34%	35%	36%	37%	38%	39%	40%
1	.763	.758	.752	.746	.741	.735	.730	.725	.719	.714
2	1.346	1.331	1.317	1.303	1.289	1.276	1.263	1.250	1.237	1.224
3	1.791	1.766	1.742	1.719	1.696	1.673	1.652	1.630	1.609	1.589
4	2.130	2.096	2.062	2.029	1.997	1.966	1.935	1.906	1.877	1.849
5	2.390	2.345	2.302	2.260	2.220	2.181	2.143	2.106	2.070	2.035
6	2.588	2.534	2.483	2.433	2.385	2.339	2.294	2.251	2.209	2.168
7	2.739	2.677	2.619	2.562	2.508	2.455	2.404	2.355	2.308	2.263
8	2.854	2.786	2.721	2.658	2.598	2.540	2.485	2.432	2.380	2.331
9	2.942	2.868	2.798	2.730	2.665	2.603	2.544	2.487	2.432	2.379
10	3.009	2.930	2.855	2.784	2.715	2.649	2.587	2.527	2.469	2.414
11	3.060	2.978	2.899	2.824	2.752	2.683	2.618	2.555	2.496	2.438
12	3.100	3.013	2.931	2.853	2.779	2.708	2.641	2.576	2.515	2.456
13	3.129	3.040	2.956	2.876	2.799	2.727	2.658	2.592	2.529	2.469
14	3.152	3.061	2.974	2.892	2.814	2.740	2.670	2.603	2.539	2.477
15	3.170	3.076	2.988	2.905	2.825	2.750	2.679	2.611	2.546	2.484
16	3.183	3.088	2.999	2.914	2.834	2.757	2.685	2.616	2.551	2.489
17	3.193	3.097	3.007	2.921	2.840	2.763	2.690	2.621	2.555	2.492
18	3.201	3.104	3.012	2.926	2.844	2.767	2.693	2.624	2.557	2.494
19	3.207	3.109	3.017	2.930	2.848	2.770	2.696	2.626	2.559	2.496
20	3.211	3.113	3.020	2.933	2.850	2.772	2.698	2.627	2.561	2.497
21	3.215	3.116	3.023	2.935	2.852	2.773	2.699	2.629	2.562	2.498
22	3.217	3.118	3.025	2.936	2.853	2.775	2.700	2.629	2.562	2.498
23	3.219	3.120	3.026	2.938	2.854	2.775	2.701	2.630	2.563	2.499
24	3.221	3.121	3.027	2.939	2.855	2.776	2.701	2.630	2.563	2.499
25	3.222	3.122	3.028	2.939	2.856	2.776	2.702	2.631	2.563	2.499
30	3.225	3.124	3.030	2.941	2.857	2.777	2.702	2.631	2.564	2.500
35	3.226	3.125	3.030	2.941	2.857	2.778	2.703	2.632	2.564	2.500
40	3.226	3.125	3.030	2.941	2.857	2.778	2.703	2.632	2.564	2.500
45	3.226	3.125	3.030	2.941	2.857	2.778	2.703	2.632	2.564	2.500
50	3.226	3.125	3.030	2.941	2.857	2.778	2.703	2.632	2.564	2.500

A GUIDE TO PROFESSIONAL CERTIFICATION PROGRAMS

INTRODUCTION

The financial services industry has undergone, and continues to undergo, rapid and dynamic transition and growth. More people with greater incomes and a more sophisticated awareness of and demand for financial security currently participate in the financial markets than ever before. This has presented tremendous opportunities for the financial services sector. As well, it has presented an increased need for well-educated, knowledgeable, and qualified professionals who possess high standards of personal integrity. One result of this need has been an increased emphasis on the importance of professional associations or societies and their attendant designations. Candidates for or current holders of the various designations must meet not only certain academic qualifications but must also possess specified professional experience and conform to standards of performance and ethics. The following discussion provides a brief overview of the major professional designations.

DESIGNATIONS

Chartered Financial Analyst—CFA

The Chartered Financial Analyst (CFA) designation is conferred by The Institute of Chartered Financial Analysts. The Institute was formed in 1959, receiving its initial support from The Financial Analysts Federation, with the conviction that investors as well as the public would receive maximum service only from financial analysts who continuously work to meet reasonable professional and personal standards. These standards are set through the consensus and conscientious efforts of the Institute's membership, and they are met by completion of several programs designed and implemented by the Institute.

A financial analyst seeking membership to the Institute of Chartered Financial Analysts must: (1) meet eligibility requirements; (2) fully comply with the CFA Code of Ethics and Standards of Professional Conduct; (3) study books, journal articles, and other readings designated by the Institute; and (4) successfully pass three examinations, each approximately six hours in length and administered by the Institute.

The candidate for the CFA designation must have at least a single current and principal engagement:

- in financial analysis of securities investment for a bank, investment company, insurance company, or other financial services or investment management firm.
- as an assistant, associate, or full professor or dean of a college or university and who teaches and/or researches securities investments.
- as an economist involved in financial analysis of securities investment.
- as a portfolio manager.
- as a financial analyst of securities investment within a public agency.
- as a financial analyst of securities investment for a corporate pension, profit sharing, or other retirement fund.
- as a manager of financial analysts or portfolio managers involved with securities investment and who, before assumption of management obligations, was a financial analyst or portfolio manager.

Financial analytical tools and techniques are constantly improving and changing to meet the demands of a dynamic investment environment. Therefore, the course and examination contents are continuously changing to remain current with the latest in analytical theory. Once an applicant has been accepted for candidacy for the CFA, he or she will be sent a Study Guide listing a detailed reading list. The entire program is based on home study, and no formal classroom instruction is presented by the Institute. The Institute does, however, organize study groups in cooperation with CFA educational coordinators of local analyst societies or colleges and universities. There are also study guides, textbooks, and reading lists published periodically by the Institute to assist candidates in their study.

The CFA is awarded to candidates who have passed the examinations and met the other requirements specified by The Institute of Chartered Financial Analysts. The examinations, which are given the first Saturday in June each year and are offered worldwide, are: Examination I—Investment Principles; Examination II—Applied Financial Analysis; and Examination III—Investment Management.

To register, a detailed application form and supporting documents must be submitted by the applicant no later than July 15 of the year immediately prior to the date on which the applicant expects to take Examination I. There is a $50 fee which must accompany the registration form. Late registrations between July 15 and October 1 are accepted but are charged an additional late fee of $50, making a total of $100. No applications are accepted after October 1. Registration fees are non-refundable. Fees for admission to take the examinations vary and depend on the time of payments and the examination for which the candidate registers.

More information can be obtained by contacting:

The Institute of Chartered Financial Analysts
P.O. Box 3668
Charlottesville, Virginia 22903

Telephone No.: (804) 977-6600

Chartered Investment Counselor—CIC

This designation is relatively new to the financial services industry and is a rather specialized credential. It is given only to an individual specifically working as an investment counselor.

The person can be employed by a financial services organization, a private or public corporation or institution, or be an independent consultant. But he or she must be functioning as a counselor of investments.

Individuals seeking the CIC must already hold the Chartered Financial Analyst (CFA) designation and at the time of application be an associate with a member firm of the Investment Counselor's Association of America. Professional references from a number of holders of the CIC must also be submitted with the application.

There is no ancillary course of study nor examinations required for acquiring the CIC designation. Cost of the CIC, which is often paid by the sponsoring member firm with which the applicant is associated, is $25. Once the CIC has been conferred, its holder retains it wherever he or she might move or advance, as long as the designate remains a member in good standing of the Investment Counselor's Association of America and continues to function as an investment counselor.

More information can be obtained by contacting:

Investment Counselor's Association of America
20 Exchange Place
New York, New York 10005

Telephone No.: (212) 344-0999

Chartered Financial Consultant—ChFC

The Chartered Financial Consultant (ChFC) is a designation developed to expand the knowledge and professional skills of financial planners and life insurance agents. It is conferred upon successful completion of a ten-part course of study covering the fundamentals of financial counseling, investment management, and personal financial management. The course of study can be completed through home study or by attending classes offered by either a branch of the American Society of Chartered Financial Consultants or an affiliated college or university.

Enrollment in the course of study requires three years of professional experience in the insurance, investment, or financial management environments. No specific academic degree is required, but a high school diploma is normally requested. Personal and professional references are also required.

The course of study consists of ten college-level courses, each lasting approximately 15 weeks. A three-hour examination taken at the conclusion of each course must be passed to successfully complete the program. Frequency and time of course and examination offerings as well as costs vary with location as well as sponsoring society or institution.

More information can be obtained by contacting:

The American College
270 Bryn Mawr Avenue
Bryn Mawr, Pennsylvania 19010

Telephone No.: (215) 896-4500

Chartered Life Underwriter—CLU

The Chartered Life Underwriter (CLU) credential is specifically designed to enhance the knowledge of people employed in the life insurance industry. Most, but not all, individuals who seek or have earned this designation are also licensed insurance agents or brokers. The CLU is conferred only upon successful completion of a ten-part course of study which covers

fundamentals of economics, finance, taxation, investments, and other areas of risk management as they apply to life insurance. The course of study can be completed through home study or by attendance of courses offered by either a branch of the American Society of Chartered Life Underwriters or an affiliated college or university.

Enrollment in the CLU program requires an individual have at least three years of professional experience in the insurance industry, preferably in life insurance. There are no degree requirements, although a high school diploma is strongly suggested. Three recommendations from clients and/or professional colleagues are also requested.

The course of study consists of ten college-level courses, each lasting approximately 15 weeks. A three-hour examination taken at the conclusion of each course must be passed to successfully complete the program. Frequency and time of course and examination offerings as well as costs vary with location as well as sponsoring society or institution.

More information can be obtained by contacting:

The American College
270 Bryn Mawr Avenue
Bryn Mawr, Pennsylvania 19010

Telephone No.: (215) 896-4300

Certified Financial Planner—CFP

The Certified Financial Planner designation is awarded after successful completion of a six-part course of study. A three-hour examination must be passed after completion of each section, totaling 18 hours of testing. Historically the CFP has been conferred only by the College for Financial Planning located in Denver, Colorado. The college recently relinquished control of the designation to the International Board of Standards and Practices for Certified Financial Planners.

Enrollment in the CFP program requires an individual to have at least three years of professional experience in the investment, personal finance, or financial management arena. There are no degree requirements, although a high school diploma is strongly suggested. The six-part course of study consists of: (1) introduction to financial planning; (2) risk management; (3) investments; (4) tax planning; (5) retirement planning and employee benefits; and (6) estate planning. Examinations are given three times a year.

More information can be obtained by contacting:

International Board of Certified Financial Planners
5445 DPC Parkway, Suite 1
Englewood, CO 80111

Telephone No.: (303) 850-0333

Certified Public Accountant—CPA

Accountants compile and analyze financial and business data and records. From such information they prepare profit and loss statements, balance sheets, cost studies, tax reports, and various other documents pertaining to the firm or organization by whom they are employed or consulted. Accountants may specialize in such areas as auditing, taxation, cost accounting, budgeting and control, or systems and procedures. As well, they may concentrate on a particular segment of the business environment, such as agricultural accounting or corporate taxation. Accountants work in both the public as well as private sectors.

To acquire the CPA designation in most states an individual must pass a qualifying examination prepared and presented by the American Institute of Certified Public Accountants. The four-part examination tests a candidate's knowledge of the theory and practice of accountancy which the AICPA considers necessary for the licensure and practice of public accounting. The examination, which takes three days to complete, is normally administered on the first Wednesday, Thursday, and Friday of May and November. Actual certification, however, depends on each state's regulations and varies among the states. Some states require nothing more than the CPA and have no further certifying requirements. Nearly all states, however, require a candidate to have at least two years of public accounting experience or its equivalent before being permitted to sit for the examination.

Each state operates its own certifying agency, but more information can be obtained by contacting:

American Institute of Certified Public Accountants
1211 Avenue of the Americas
New York, New York 10036

Telephone No.: (212) 575-6200

GLOSSARY

Numbers in parentheses indicate the chapter in which the term is first discussed in detail.

accrual-type securities (4)   securities for which interest is paid upon surrender, at or before maturity, rather than periodically over the life of the bond.

accumulation period (15)   under an annuity contract, the period of time between when payments are made to the insurance company and when the insurance company begins to pay the annuitant.

activity ratios (7)   financial ratios that are used to measure how well a firm is managing its assets.

adjustable rate preferreds (10)   preferred stock whose dividends are adjusted periodically in line with yields on Treasury issues; also called *floating rate preferreds.*

adjusted gross income (15)   gross income less the total allowable adjustments for tax purposes.

after-cash tax flows (ACTFs) (14)   the annual cash flow earned on a real estate investment, net of all expenses, taxes, and debt service.

agency bonds (9)   debt securities issued by various agencies and organizations of the U.S. government, such as the Tennessee Valley Authority.

aggressive growth fund (13)   a highly speculative mutual fund that seeks large profits from capital gains.

alternative minimum tax (AMT) (15)   a tax passed by Congress to ensure that all individuals, especially those using tax preference items, pay at least some federal income tax.

American Depositary Receipts (ADRs) (2)   the security through which foreign stocks are traded in American markets; these negotiable instruments are like common stock, as each one represents a specific number of shares in a specific foreign company; may be company sponsored or unsponsored; traded on the NYSE, AMEX, and OTC markets.

AMEX index (3)   measure of the current price behavior of stocks listed on the AMEX, relative to a base of 100, set 8/31/73.

analytical information (3)   available current data in conjunction with projections and recommendations about potential investments.

annual stockholders' meeting (6)   yearly meeting of a firm's stockholders at which time the annual report is presented, board members are elected, and other special business transacted.

annuitant (15)   the person to whom the future payments on an annuity contract are directed.

annuity (5)   a series of equal payments that occur in equal intervals over time, guaranteed for a number of years or over a lifetime.

appraisal (14)   a process for estimating the current market value of a piece of property.

approximate yield (14)   procedure for assessing investment suitability by estimating the fully compounded rate of return (yield) on an investment.

arbitration (2)   a dispute process in which a broker and customer present their cases before a panel which then makes a decision to resolve the dispute.

ask price (2)   the lowest price at which a dealer is willing to sell a given security.

asset allocation (16)   a scheme that involves dividing one's portfolio into various asset classes in order to preserve capital by protecting against negative developments while still taking advantage of positive developments.

asset allocation fund (16) a mutual fund that seeks to reduce volatility by investing in the right assets at the right time; emphasizes diversification and relatively consistent performance rather than spectacular gains.

automatic reinvestment plan (13) a mutual fund service that enables shareholders to automatically buy additional shares in the fund through reinvestment of dividends and/or capital gains income.

average tax rate (15) taxes due divided by taxable income; different from the *marginal tax rate*.

averages (3) numbers used to measure the general behavior of stock prices by reflecting the arithmetic average price behavior of a representative group of stocks at a given point in time.

back-end load (13) a 1 to 2 percent commission on the sale of shares in a mutual fund.

back-office research reports (3) analyses of and recommendations on current and future investment opportunities; published by and made available to clients of brokerage firms.

balance sheet (7) a financial summary of a firm's assets, liabilities, and shareholder's equity at a single point in time.

balanced fund (13) a mutual fund whose objective is to generate a balanced return of both current income and long-term capital gains.

bar chart (8) the simplest kind of chart on which share price is plotted on the vertical axis and time on the horizontal axis; stock prices are recorded as vertical bars showing high, low, and closing prices.

Barron's **(3)** a weekly publication by Dow Jones; the second most popular source of financial news.

basis (15) the amount paid for a capital asset, including commissions and other costs related to the purchase.

basis points (12) an amount equal to 1/100 of 1 percent, used to quote T-bill and Eurodollar contracts.

bear markets (2) unfavorable markets associated with investor pessimism, economic slowdowns, and government restraint.

bearer bonds (9) bonds whose holders are considered to be their owners; there is no official record of ownership kept by the issuer.

bellwether stocks (8) stocks that are believed to consistently reflect the state of the market; watched by technical analysts for shifts in market behavior.

beta (5) a measure of nondiversifiable risk, which shows how the price of a security responds to market forces; found by relating the historical returns on a security with the historical returns for the market; in general, the higher the beta, the riskier the security.

beta regression coefficient (16) a statistical measure of the relative volatility of a security or a portfolio return as compared to a broadly derived measure of stock market return.

bid price (2) the highest price offered by a dealer to purchase a given security.

blind pool syndicate (14) a type of real estate limited partnership formed by a syndicator to raise money to be invested at the syndicator's discretion.

bond fund (13) a mutual fund that invests in various kinds and grades of bonds, with income as the primary objective.

bond ladders (9) a bond investment strategy wherein an equal amount of money is invested in a series of bonds with staggered maturities—for example, an equal amount is invested in notes and bonds with maturities of 3, 6, 9, 12, and 15 years.

bond ratings (9) letter grades that designate investment quality, assigned to a bond issue on the basis of extensive financial analysis.

bond swap (9) an investment strategy wherein an investor liquidates one of his or her current bond holdings and simultaneously buys a different issue in its place.

bond yields (3) summary measures of the return an investor would receive on a bond if it were held to maturity; reported as an annual rate of return.

bonds (1) publicly traded long-term debt securities, whereby the issuer agrees to pay a fixed amount of interest over a specified period of time and to repay a fixed amount of principal at maturity.

book value (6) the amount of stockholders' equity in a firm; equals the amount of the firm's assets minus the firm's liabilities and preferred stock.

book value (of preferred stock) (10) a measure of the amount of debt-free assets supporting each share of preferred stock; equals the total assets of a firm minus its liabilities; also called *net asset value*.

brokered CDs (4) certificates of deposit sold by stockbrokers; offer slightly higher interest rates than other CDs and no penalty for sale prior to maturity.

bull markets (2) favorable markets associated with investor optimism, economic recovery, and governmental stimulus.

business cycle (7) an indication of the current state of the economy, it reflects change in total economic activity over time.

business risk (5) the degree of uncertainty associated with an investment's earnings and the investment's ability to pay investors the returns owed them.

call (9) a negotiable instrument that gives the holder the right to buy shares of common stock at a stated price on or before some future date.

call feature (9) feature that specifies whether, and under what conditions, the issuer can retire a bond prior to maturity.

call premium (9) the amount added to a bond's par value and paid to investors when a bond is retired prematurely.

call price (9) the price the issuer must pay to retire a bond prematurely; equal to par value plus the call premium.

capital asset (4) property owned and used by the taxpayer for personal reasons, pleasure, or investment.

capital asset pricing model (CAPM) (5) model that helps investors evaluate risk-return tradeoffs in investment decisions; uses beta and market return to find required return for securities.

capital gain (1) the amount by which the proceeds from the sale of a capital asset exceed its purchase price (basis); currently taxed as ordinary income.

capital gains distributions (13) payments made to mutual fund shareholders that come from the profits that a fund makes from the sale of its securities.

capital loss (4) the amount by which the proceeds from the sale of a capital asset are less than its purchase price (basis); a maximum of $3,000 of capital losses can be applied in any one year.

capital market (1) the long-term financial market, dominated by various securities exchanges, in which long-term securities such as stocks and bonds are bought and sold.

capitalization rate (14) the rate used to convert an income stream to a present value, which can be used to estimate the value of real estate under the income approach to value.

cash account (2) a brokerage account in which a customer can make only cash transactions.

cash dividend (6) payment of a dividend in the form of cash.

cash market (12) a market in which a product or commodity changes hands in exchange for a cash price paid at the time the transaction is completed.

cash value (4) the amount of money set aside by an insurer to provide for the payment of a death benefit.

central asset account a comprehensive deposit account that combines checking, investing, and borrowing activities and that automatically sweeps excess balances into short-term investments.

certificates of deposit (CDs) (4) savings instruments in which funds must remain on deposit for a specified period; premature withdrawals incur interest penalties.

charting (8) the activity of charting price behavior and other market information, and then using the patterns that these charts form to make investment decisions.

classified common stock (6) common stock issued in different classes, each of which offers different privileges and benefits to its holders.

closed-end investment companies (2) a type of investment company that operates with a fixed number of shares outstanding.

coefficient of determination (R^2) (16) a measure of the explanatory power of a regression equation; indicates the percentage of the change in the dependent variable explained by its relationship with the independent variable.

collateral trust bonds (9) senior bonds backed by securities owned by the issuer but held in trust by a third party.

collateralized mortgage obligation (CMO) (9) a type of mortgage-backed bond whose holders are divided into classes based on the length of investment desired; then, principal is channeled to short-term investors first, intermediate-term investors next, and long-term investors last.

collectibles (12) items that have value because of their attractiveness to collectors and because of their relative scarcity and historical significance.

commercial paper a short-term, unsecured promissory note issued by corporations with high credit standing.

commodities and financial futures contracts obligations that the sellers of the contracts will make delivery and the buyers will take delivery of a specified commodity, foreign currency, or financial instrument at some specific date in the future.

common stock (1) equity investment representing ownership in a corporation; each share of common stock represents a fractional ownership interest in the firm.

company-sponsored ADRs (2) ADRs that meet certain government registration requirements and are listed and traded on the New York or American stock exchange.

comparative sales approach (14) a real estate valuation approach that uses sales prices of properties that are similar to the subject property as the basic input variable.

compound interest (5) interest paid not only on the initial deposit but also on any interest accumulated from one period to the next.

confidence index (8) a ratio of the average yield on high-grade corporate bonds to the average yield on low-grade corporate bonds; a technical indicator based on the theory that market trends usually appear in the bond market before they do in the stock market.

constant dollar plan (17) a formula plan for timing investment transactions, in which the investor establishes a target dollar amount for the speculative portion of the portfolio and transfers funds to or from the conservative portion as needed to maintain the target dollar amount.

constant ratio plan (17) a formula plan for timing transactions, in which a desired fixed ratio of the speculative to the conservative portion of the portfolio is established; when the ratio differs by a predetermined amount, transactions are made to bring the ratio back into balance.

continuous compounding (5) interest calculation in which interest is compounded over the smallest interval of time possible; results in the maximum rate of return that can be achieved with a stated interest rate.

contributory plan (4) retirement plan partially funded by the employee, whose contributions usually amount to 3–10 percent of wages.

convenience (14) in real estate, the accessibility of a property to the places the people in a target market frequently need to go.

conventional options (11) put and call options sold over the counter.

conversion equivalent (10) the price at which the common stock would have to sell in order to make the convertible security worth its present market price; also called *conversion parity*.

conversion feature (10) allows the holder of a convertible preferred to convert to a specified number of shares of the issuing company's common stock; a feature that is more commonly found on bonds (as in convertible bonds).

conversion period (10) the time period during which a convertible issue can be converted.

conversion premium (10) the amount by which the market price of a convertible exceeds its conversion value.

conversion price (10) the stated price per share at which common stock will be delivered to the investor in exchange for a convertible issue.

conversion privilege (10) feature of a mutual fund that allows shareholders to move money from one fund to another, within the same family of funds; also called *exchange privilege*.

conversion ratio (10) the number of shares of common stock into which a convertible issue can be converted.

conversion value (10) an indication of what a convertible issue should trade for if it were priced to sell on the basis of its stock value; equals the conversion ratio of the issue times the current market price of the underlying common stock.

convertible securities (1) fixed-income obligations with a feature permitting the holder to convert the security into a specified number of shares of the issuing company's common stock.

corporation (15) a form of organization that provides limited liability benefits to shareholder investors and that has an indefinite life.

correlation (16) a statistical measure of the relationship, if any, between two series of data, such as that of an individual security's returns with the returns of the market as a whole.

correlation coefficient (16) a statistical measure of the degree of correlation between two series, which ranges from $+1$ for perfectly positive correlation to -1 for perfectly negative correlation.

cost approach (14) a real estate valuation approach based on the idea that a buyer should not pay more for a property than it would cost to rebuild it at today's prices for land, labor, and construction materials.

coupon (9) the feature on a bond that defines the amount of annual interest income.

covered options (11) options written against stock owned (or sold short) by the writer.

cumulative provision (10) a provision on preferred stock requiring that any preferred dividends that have been passed must be paid in full before dividends can be restored to common stockholders.

cumulative voting (6) a system of stockholder voting, in which shareholders cast all their combined votes in any manner they wish.

currency futures (12) futures contracts on foreign currencies, traded much like commodities.

currency options (11) put and call options written on foreign currencies.

current income (5)   cash or near-cash that is periodically received as a result of owning an investment.

current interest rate (15)   for an annuity contract, the yearly return the insurance company is currently paying on accumulated deposits.

current yield (9)   the measure of the amount of current income a bond provides relative to its prevailing market price.

custodial account (2)   the brokerage account of a minor, in which a parent or guardian is part of all transactions.

daily price limit (12)   restriction on the day-to-day change in the price of an underlying commodity.

databases (3)   organized collections of information, both historical and current.

date of record (6)   the date on which an investor must be a registered shareholder of a firm to be entitled to receive a dividend.

day order (2)   an order to buy or sell securities that if not executed is automatically cancelled at the end of the business day.

dealers (2)   traders who make markets by offering to buy or sell certain over-the-counter securities at stated prices.

debenture (9)   an unsecured (junior) bond.

debit balance (2)   the amount of money being borrowed; the size of a margin loan.

debt (1)   funds loaned in exchange for the receipt of interest income and the promised repayment of the loan at a given future date.

deep discount bond (15)   a bond selling at a price far below its par value.

deep-in-the-money call option (15)   a tax-deferral strategy that involves selling a call option on shares currently owned, locking in a price to the extent of the amount received from the sale of the call option but giving up potential future price appreciation.

deferred annuity (15)   an annuity contract in which the payments to the annuitant begin at some future date.

deferred equity securities (6)   securities initially issued in one form (warrants or convertibles) and later redeemed or converted into shares of common stock.

defined benefit plan (4)   retirement plan that links benefits to a formula that is generally based on level of earnings and length of service.

defined contribution plan (4)   retirement plan that defines precisely the amounts employer and employee contribute to the plan, but does not specify the retirement income.

de-listed (2)   to be removed from one's listing on an organized stock exchange for failure to meet specified listing requirements.

delivery month (12)   the time when a commodity must be delivered; defines the life of a futures contract.

demand (14)   in real estate, people's willingness and ability to buy or rent a given property.

demographics (14)   characteristics of an area's population, such as household size, age structure, occupation, sex, and marital status; should be considered when analyzing real estate demand.

denominations (9)   standard principal amounts into which a bond issue is broken to facilitate its sale to the public.

depreciation (14)   in real estate investing, a tax deduction based upon the original cost of a building and used to reflect its declining economic life.

derivative securities (11)   securities, such as puts and calls and other options, whose value is derived from the price behavior of an underlying financial asset.

descriptive information (3) factual data on the past behavior of the economy, the stock market, or a given investment vehicle.

developmental programs (15) limited partnerships that finance the drilling of oil or gas wells in areas of known and proved reserves.

direct investment (1) investment in which an investor directly acquires a claim on a security or property.

discount basis a method of earning interest on short-term investments by selling a security for a price less than its redemption value, the difference being the interest earned.

discount bond (9) a bond with a market value lower than par; occurs when market rates are greater than the coupon rate.

discount brokers (2) security brokers who execute orders for clients at substantially reduced commissions.

discount rate (5) the annual rate of return that could be earned currently on a similar investment; used when finding present value; also called *opportunity cost.*

discounted cash flows (14) a measure of investment return, commonly used in real estate investment analysis, calculated by subtracting the original required investment from the present value of cash flows to find net present value (NPV).

discretionary account (2) an account in which a broker can use his or her discretion to buy or sell stock on behalf of the customer.

distribution period (15) under an annuity contract, the period of time over which payments are made to an annuitant.

diversifiable risk (5) the portion of an investment's risk resulting from uncontrollable or random events, that can be eliminated through diversification; also called *unsystematic risk.*

diversification (1) the inclusion of a number of different investment vehicles in a portfolio, in order to increase returns or be exposed to less risk; may be random or purposive.

dividend income (13) income derived from the dividend and interest income earned on the security holdings of a mutual fund.

dividend reinvestment plans (DRPs) (6) plans in which shareholders have cash dividends automatically reinvested in additional shares of the firm's common stock.

dividend valuation model (8) model that values a share of stock on the basis of the future dividend stream it is expected to produce.

dividend yield (6) a measure of the amount of return earned on dividend income; relates dividends to share price and in so doing puts common stock dividends on a relative (percent) rather than absolute (dollar) basis; equals annual dividend income divided by the price of the stock.

dividends (1) periodic payments made by firms to their stockholders.

dollar cost averaging (17) a formula plan for timing investment transactions, in which a fixed dollar amount is invested in a security at fixed intervals; a passive buy-and-hold strategy.

Dow Jones bond averages (3) mathematical averages of closing prices for groups of utility, industrial, and composite bonds.

Dow Jones Industrial Average (DJIA) (3) a stock average made up of 30 high-quality industrial stocks selected for total market value and broad public ownership and believed to reflect overall market activity.

Dow theory (8) a technical approach based on the idea that the market's performance can be described by the long-term price trend in the DJIA, as confirmed by the Dow transportation average.

downtick (2) the decrease in the price of a stock issue since its last transaction.

dual listing (2) a listing of a firm's shares on more than one exchange.

earnings per share (EPS) (6) the amount of annual earnings available to common stock-holders, as stated on a per share basis.

economic analysis (7) a study of general economic conditions that is used in the valuation of common stock.

efficient markets (8) the theory that the market price of securities always fully reflects available information and therefore it is difficult, if not impossible, to consistently outperform the market by picking ''undervalued'' stocks.

efficient portfolio (16) a portfolio that provides the highest return for a given level of risk, or that has the lowest risk for a given level of return.

equipment trust certificates (9) senior bonds secured by specific pieces of equipment; popular with railroads, airlines, and other transportation companies.

equity (1) an ongoing ownership interest in a specific business or property.

equity capital (6) evidence of ownership position in a firm, in the form of shares of common stock.

equity-income fund (13) a mutual fund that emphasizes current income and capital preservations and thereby invest primarily in high-yielding common stocks.

equity kicker (10) the tendency for the market price of convertible issues to behave much like the common stock into which they can be converted.

esthetic environment (14) in real estate, neighborhoods where buildings and landscaping are well executed and well maintained and where there is no noise, sight, or air pollution nor encroaching unharmonious land uses.

ethics (1) standards of conduct or moral judgment.

event risk (5) risk that comes from a largely or totally unexpected event which has a significant and usually immediate effect on the underlying value of an investment.

excess margin (2) more equity than is required in a margin account.

ex-dividend date (6) the date four business days before the date of record, which determines whether one is an official shareholder of a firm and thus eligible to receive a declared dividend.

exemption (15) a deduction for each qualifying dependent of a federal taxpayer.

exercise price (11) the price at which a share of stock can be purchased, as specified on a warrant; the price at which a new share of common stock will be sold, as specified on a right; also called *subscription price*.

expiration date (11) the date at which the life of a warrant or an option expires.

exploratory programs (15) limited partnerships formed to drill in areas where oil or gas is believed to exist but has not yet been discovered; also known as *wildcats*.

extendable notes (9) a specialty issue, typically with short maturities (1–5 years), which can be redeemed or renewed for the same period at a new interest rate.

extra dividends (6) additional dividend declared when the level of earnings is higher than expected; usually paid in the final quarter of the year.

fill-or-kill order (2) an order that if not immediately executed is cancelled.

financial futures (12) a type of futures contract in which the underlying ''commodity'' consists of a certain amount of some type of financial asset, such as debt securities, foreign currencies, or market baskets of common stocks.

financial institutions (1) organizations that typically accept deposits and then lend or invest them.

financial markets (1) forums in which suppliers and demanders of funds are brought together to make transactions.

financial planner (3) a professional advisor who works with a client to develop a financial plan or strategy.

financial risk (5)   the degree of uncertainty associated with the mix of debt and equity used to finance a firm or property; the larger the proportion of debt used, the greater the financial risk.

financial supermarket (1)   a financial institution at which customers can obtain a full array of financial services.

first and refunding bonds (9)   a bond that is secured in part with first and secured mortgages.

fiscal environment (14)   in real estate, the amount of property taxes and municipal assessments an owner must pay and the government services to which the owner is entitled.

fixed annuity (15)   an annuity contract with a monthly payment amount that does not change.

fixed charge coverage (10)   a measure of how well a firm is able to cover its preferred stock dividends.

fixed-commission schedules (2)   fixed brokerage charges applicable to small transactions.

fixed-income securities (1)   investment vehicles that offer a fixed periodic return.

fixed payout ratio (6)   dividend policy that pays to owners a percentage of each dollar earned in the form of a cash dividend.

flower bonds (9)   older government bonds issued at a discount and used at par to pay federal estate taxes.

forced conversion (10)   the calling in of convertible bonds by the issuing firm.

Form 10-K (3)   a statement filed with the SEC by all firms listed on a securities exchange or traded in the national OTC market.

formula plans (17)   mechanical methods of portfolio management used to try to take advantage of price changes in securities that result from cyclical price movements.

401(k) plan (4)   a retirement plan that allows employees to divert a portion of salary to a company-sponsored tax-sheltered savings account, thus deferring taxes until retirement.

fourth market (2)   transactions made directly between large institutional buyers and sellers.

fully taxable equivalent yield (9)   the return a fully taxable bond would have to provide to match the after-tax return of a lower-yielding, tax-free municipal bond.

fund families (13)   different kinds of mutual funds all offered by the same investment management company.

fundamental analysis (7)   the in-depth study of the financial condition and operating results of a firm.

future value (5)   the amount to which a current deposit will grow over a period of time when it is placed in an account paying compound interest.

futures contract (12)   a commitment to deliver a certain amount of some specified item at some specified date in the future.

futures market (12)   the organized market for the trading of futures contracts.

futures options (12)   options that give the holders the right to buy or sell a single standardized futures contract for a specified period of time at a specified striking price; the ultimate leverage vehicle.

gemstones (12)   diamonds and colored precious stones (rubies, sapphires, and emeralds).

general obligation bonds (9)   municipal bonds backed by the full faith and credit, and taxing power, of the issuer.

general partner (15)   the managing partner who accepts unlimited liability and makes all decisions in a partnership.

general partnership (15)   a joint venture in which all partners have management rights and all assume unlimited liability for any debts or obligations the partnership incurs.

globalization (financial markets) (1) the access of investors to financial markets around the world.

good 'til canceled (GTC) (2) an order to buy or sell securities that remains in effect for six months unless executed, canceled, or renewed.

government securities money fund (4) a money market mutual fund that limits its investments to Treasury bills and other short-term securities of the U.S. government and its agencies.

gross income (15) all includable income for federal income-tax purposes.

gross national product (GNP) (7) estimate of the total dollar value of the nation's output of goods and services.

growth-and-income fund (13) a mutual fund that seeks both long-term growth and current income, with principal emphasis on capital gains.

growth cycle (7) a reflection of the amount of business vitality that occurs within an industry over time.

growth fund (13) a mutual fund whose primary goals are capital gains and long-term growth.

growth-oriented portfolio (16) a portfolio whose primary objective is long-term price appreciation.

hardware (3) the mechanical components of a computer system.

hedge (11) a combination of two or more securities into a single investment position for the purpose of reducing or eliminating risk.

hedgers (12) the producers and processors who use futures contracts as a way to protect their interest in an underlying commodity or financial instrument.

high liquidity (4) the ability to convert an asset into cash quickly and with little or no loss in value.

high-risk investments (1) investments considered speculative with regard to the receipt of a positive return.

holding period (5) the relevant period of time over which one wishes to measure the return on any investment vehicle.

holding period return (HPR) (5) the total return earned from holding an investment for a specified holding period (usually one year or less); the sum of current income and capital gains (or losses) achieved over the holding period, divided by the beginning investment value.

immediate annuity (15) an annuity contract under which payments to the annuitant begin as soon as it is purchased.

improvements (14) in real estate, the man-made additions to a site, such as buildings, sidewalks, and various on-site amenities.

in arrears (10) having outstanding unfulfilled preferred-dividend obligations.

income approach (14) a real estate valuation approach that calculates a property's value as the present value of all its future income.

income bonds (9) unsecured bonds that require that interest be paid only if a specified amount of income is earned.

income programs (15) limited partnerships that buy existing oil or gas wells with proven reserves.

income property (14) type of leased-out real estate, such as apartment and office buildings and shopping centers, that provides some form of rental income to its owner.

income statement (7) a financial summary of the operating results of a firm covering a specified period of time, usually one year.

income-oriented portfolio (16) a portfolio that stresses current dividend and interest return.

index price (12) technique used to price T-bill (and other short-term securities) futures contracts, which reflects the actual price movements of these futures contracts.

indexes (3) numbers used to measure the general behavior of stock prices by measuring the current price behavior of a representative group of stocks in relation to a base value set at an earlier point in time.

indirect investment (1) investment made in a portfolio or group of securities or properties.

individual investors (1) investors who manage their own funds.

individual retirement account (IRA) (4) a self-directed, tax-deferred retirement plan, in which gainfully employed persons may contribute annually up to $2,000 for an individual or $2,250 for an individual and non-working spouse.

industry analysis (7) study of industry groupings, by looking at the competitive position of a particular industry in relation to others and by identifying companies within an industry that hold particular promise.

industry option (11) a put or call option written on a portfolio of stocks from a specific industry segment of the market; also called a *sub-index option*.

inflation (5) a period of rising price levels.

initial deposit (12) the amount of investor capital that must be deposited with a broker at the time of a commodity transaction.

initial margin (2) the minimum amount of money (or equity) that must be provided by a margin investor at the time of purchase.

initial public offering (IPO) (6) a special category of common stocks issued by (relatively) new firms going public for the first time.

insider trading (1) the illegal use of non-public information about a company to make profitable securities transactions.

installment annuity (15) an annuity contract acquired by making payments over time; at a specified future date the installment payments, plus interest earned on them, are used to purchase an annuity contract.

institutional investors (1) investment professionals paid to manage other people's money.

insurance (4) a mechanism that allows people to reduce financial risk by sharing in the losses associated with the occurrence of uncertain events.

insurance policy (4) a contract between the insured and the insurer that requires the insured to make periodic premium payments in exchange for the insurer's promise to pay for losses according to specified terms.

interest rate futures (12) futures contracts on debt securities, traded much like commodities.

interest rate options (11) put and call options written on fixed-income (debt) securities.

interest rate risk (5) the degree of uncertainty in the prices of securities associated with changes in interest rates; as interest rates rise, the prices of securities––particularly fixed-income securities—decline, and vice versa.

international fund (13) a mutual fund that does all or most of its investing in foreign securities.

in-the-money (11) a call option with a striking price less than the market price of the underlying security; a put option with a striking price greater than the market price of the underlying security.

intrinsic value (7) the underlying or inherent value of a stock, as determined through fundamental analysis.

investing (1) the process of placing funds in selected investment vehicles with the expectation of increasing their value and/or earning a positive return.

investment (1) a vehicle for funds, expected to maintain or increase its value and/or generate positive returns.

investment advisors (3) individuals or firms that provide investment advice, usually for a fee.

investment analysis (14) real estate analysis that considers not only what similar properties have sold for, but also looks at the underlying determinants of value, and tries to forecast such factors as economic base, population demographics and psychographics, buying power, and potential sources of competition.

investment banking firm (2) organization that specializes in selling new security issues.

investment club (3) a legal partnership through which a group of investors is bound to an organizational structure, operating procedures, and purpose—typically making moderate-risk investments to earn favorable long-run returns.

investment company (13) a firm, such as a mutual fund, that combines the investment capital of many people with similar investment goals and invests the funds in a wide variety of securities.

investment goals (1) the financial objectives that one wishes to achieve by investing in potential investment vehicles; includes statements of the timing, magnitude, form, and risks associated with a desired return.

investment letters (3) provide, on a subscription basis, the analyses, conclusions, and recommendations of various experts in different aspects of securities investment.

investment plan (4) a written document describing financial goals, how funds will be invested, the target date for the accomplishment of goals, and the amount of tolerable risk.

investment premium (11) the difference between the market value of an option and its true value; indicates the amount of excess value embedded in the quoted price of a put or call.

investment trust (13) a type of investment vehicle whereby the trust sponsors put together a fixed/unmanaged portfolio of securities and then sell ownership units in the portfolio to individual investors; also called a *unit investment trust.*

investment value (6) the amount that investors believe a security should be trading for, or what they think it is worth; the price at which a convertible would trade if it were nonconvertible and if it were priced at or near the prevailing market yields of comparable nonconvertible issues.

itemized deductions (15) personal living and family expenses, including residential mortgage interest, which can be deducted from adjusted gross income.

junior bonds (9) debt obligations backed only by the promise of the issuer to pay interest and principal on a timely basis.

junk bonds (9) high risk securities that have received low ratings and as such, produce high yields so long as they don't go into default.

Keogh plan (4) a retirement plan that allows self-employed individuals to establish tax-deferred retirement plans for themselves and their employees.

legal environment (14) in real estate, the restrictions on use that apply to properties near the subject property.

leverage (11) a concept whereby debt is used to reduce the level of required capital in a given investment position, thereby magnifying returns; in *real estate,* the use of financing to purchase a piece of property and thereby affect its risk-return parameters.

leverage measures (7) financial ratios that measure the amount of debt being used to support operations, and the ability of the firm to service its debt.

life insurance (4) a mechanism that can provide financial protection for a family if the primary breadwinner or other family member dies prematurely.

limit order (2) an order to buy securities at or below a specified price, or to sell at or above a specified price.

limited partners (15) the passive investors in a partnership, who supply most of the capital and have liability limited to the amount of their capital contributions.

limited partnership (LP) (15) a vehicle in which the investor can passively invest with limited liability, receive the benefit of active professional management, and apply the resulting profit or loss (subject to limits) to his or her tax liability.

liquidation value (6) the amount left if a firm's assets were sold or auctioned off and the liabilities and preferred stockholders paid off.

liquidity (4) the ability to convert an investment into cash quickly and with little or no loss in value.

liquidity measures (7) financial ratios concerned with the firm's ability to meet its day-to-day operating expenses and satisfy its short-term obligations as they come due.

liquidity risk (5) the risk of not being able to liquidate an investment conveniently and at a reasonable price.

listed options (11) put and call options listed and traded on organized securities exchanges such as the CBOE.

load fund (13) a mutual fund that charges a commission when shares are bought; also known as *front-end load fund*.

long purchase (2) a transaction in which investors buy securities in the hope that they will increase in value and can be sold for profit at a later date.

long-term investments (1) investments with maturities of longer than a year, or with no maturity at all.

low-load fund (13) a mutual fund that charges a small commission (1 to 3 percent) when shares are bought.

low-risk investments (1) investments considered safe with regard to the receipt of a positive return.

maintenance deposit (12) the minimum amount of margin that must be kept in a margin account at all times.

maintenance margin (2) the minimum amount of equity that investors must carry in their margin accounts at all times.

majority voting (6) the most common system of stockholder voting, in which each shareholder is entitled to one vote per share of stock owned and may cast that number of votes for each position on the board.

management fee (13) a fee levied annually for professional mutual fund services provided; paid regardless of the performance of the portfolio.

margin account (2) a brokerage account in which the customer has borrowing privileges.

margin call (2) notification of the need to bring the equity of an undermargined account up to the required level or have margined holdings sold to reach this point.

margin deposit (12) amount deposited with a broker to cover any loss in the market value of a futures contract that may result from adverse price movements.

margin loan (2) vehicle through which borrowed funds are made available, at a stated interest rate, in a margin transaction.

margin trading (2) the use of borrowed funds to purchase securities; magnifies returns by reducing the amount of capital that must be put up by the investor.

marginal tax rate (15) the tax rate on additional income.

market order (2) an order to buy or sell securities at the best price available.

market price (1) the point of equilibrium between the forces of supply and demand.

market return (5) the average return on all, or a large sample of, stocks, such as those in the Standard & Poor's 500 stock composite index.

market risk (5) risk of changes in investment returns that result from factors independent of the given security or property investment, such as political, economic, and social events, or changes in investor tastes and preferences.

market value (6) the prevailing market price of a security; in real estate, the prevailing market price of a property, indicating how the market as a whole has assessed the property's worth.

mark-to-the-market (12) a daily check of an investor's margin position; the gain or loss in a contract's value is determined at the end of each session, at which time the broker debits or credits the account as needed.

master limited partnership (MLP) (14) a limited partnership that is publicly traded on a major stock exchange.

maturity date (9) the date on which a bond matures and the principal must be repaid.

maximum daily price range (12) the amount a commodity price can change during a day; usually equal to twice the daily price limit.

minimum guaranteed interest rate (15) for an annuity contract, the minimum interest rate on contributions that the insurance company will guarantee over the full accumulation period; usually substantially less than the current interest rate.

mixed stream (5) a stream of returns that, unlike an annuity, exhibits no special pattern.

modern portfolio theory (16) an approach to portfolio management that uses statistical measures to develop portfolio strategy.

money market (1) market in which short-term securities are bought and sold.

money market deposit accounts (MMDAs) (4) a bank account with features similar to money market mutual funds; has no legal minimum balance but many banks impose their own.

money market mutual fund (MMMF) (4) a mutual fund that pools the capital of a large number of investors and uses it to invest in high-yielding, short-term money market instruments; also called a *money fund*.

Moody's Investors Services (3) publisher of a variety of financial reference manuals, including *Moody's Manuals*.

mortgage-backed bond (9) a debt issue secured by a pool of home mortgages; issued primarily by federal agencies.

mortgage bonds (9) senior bonds secured by real estate.

municipal bonds (9) debt securities issued by states, counties, cities, and other political subdivisions, like school districts; most of these bonds are tax-exempt, meaning that there is no federal income tax on interest income.

municipal bond guarantees (9) guarantees from a party other than the issuer that principal and interest payments will be made in a prompt and timely manner.

municipal bonds (9) debt securities issued by states, counties, cities, and other political subdivisions; in most cases, interest income on municipals is free from federal taxation.

mutual fund (1) a company that invests in a diversified portfolio of securities and sells shares to investors who thus obtain an interest in the portfolio.

naked options (11) options written on securities not owned by the writer.

NASDAQ indexes (3) measures of current price behavior of securities sold OTC, relative to a base of 100, set 2/5/71.

NASDAQ/National Market System (NASDAQ/NMS) (2) a list of NASDAQ stocks

meeting certain qualification standards relative to financial size, performance, and trading activity.

National Association of Securities Dealers Automated Quotation (NASDAQ) System (2) an automated system that provides up-to-date bid and ask prices on certain selected, highly active OTC securities.

negative correlation (16) a relationship between two series such that they move in opposite directions.

negative leverage (14) a position in which, if a property's return is below its debt cost, the investor's return will be less than from an all-cash deal.

negotiated commissions (2) transactions costs for the sale and purchase of securities that are negotiated between brokers and institutional investors or individuals with large accounts.

net asset value (NAV) (13) the underlying value of a share of stock in a particular mutual fund; represents the net market value of the securities held by a mutual fund.

net operating income (NOI) (14) the amount left after subtracting vacancy and collection losses and property operating expenses, including property insurance and taxes, from an income property's gross potential rental income.

net present value (NPV) (14) the difference between the present value of the cash flows and the amount of equity required to make an investment.

no-load fund (13) a mutual fund that does not charge a commission when shares are bought.

noncontributory plan (4) retirement plan completely funded by the employer.

noncumulative provision (10) a provision found on some preferred stocks excusing the issuing firm from having to make up any passed dividends.

nondiversifiable risk (5) the risk possessed by every investment vehicle and therefore not capable of being eliminated through diversification; see also called *systematic risk*.

note (9) a debt security originally issued with a maturity of from 2 to 10 years.

NOW (Negotiated Order of Withdrawal) account (4) a checking account that pays interest; has no legal minimum balance but many banks impose their own.

NYSE index (3) measure of the current price behavior of the stocks listed on the NYSE in relation to a base of 50, set 12/31/65.

odd lots (2) an amount of stock less than 100 shares.

offering circular (15) a document for a private partnership describing the property to be purchased, management fees, and other financial details: it usually also includes the limited partnership agreement.

open-end investment company (2) a type of investment company in which investors buy shares from, and sell them back to, the mutual fund itself; there is no limit on the number of shares the fund can issue.

open interest (12) the number of contracts presently outstanding on a commodity or financial future.

open outcry auction (12) in futures trading, auction in which trading is done through a series of shouts, body motions, and hand signals.

option (1) a type of security that gives the holder the right to buy or sell a certain amount of an underlying financial asset at a specified price for a specified period of time.

option maker (11) the individual or institution that writes put and call options; also called *option writer*.

option premium (11) the listed purchase price of a put or call option.

option straddle (11) the simultaneous purchase (or sale) of a put and a call on the same underlying common stock.

options spreading (11)   combining two or more options with different strike prices and/or expiration dates into a single transaction.

ordinary income (15)   any income received for labor services provided or from invested capital.

organized securities exchanges (2)   centralized institutions in which transactions are made in already outstanding securities.

out-of-the-money (11)   a call option with no real value because the striking price exceeds the market price of the stock; a put option whose market price exceeds the striking price.

over-the-counter (OTC) market (2)   widely scattered telecommunications network through which buyers and sellers of certain securities can be brought together; also the primary market in which public issues are sold.

paper profits   see *unrealized capital gain*.

paper return (5)   a capital gain return that has been achieved, but not yet realized from the sale of an investment vehicle.

par value (6)   the stated, or face, value of a stock.

participating provision (10)   a provision on some preferred stocks giving preferred stockholders additional dividends when and if payments to common stockholders exceed a certain amount.

passbook savings account (4)   a savings vehicle, generally paying a low rate of interest, having no minimum balance, and few or no restrictions on withdrawal.

passive activity (15)   an investment in which the investor does not "materially participate" in its management or activity.

payout (15)   the investment return provided by an annuity contract, realized when the distribution period begins.

personal computer (PC) (1)   a relatively inexpensive but powerful home computer.

personal financial planning (3)   the process by which a person's assets, liabilities, and sources of income are so arranged as to maximize the achievement of their financial goals and objectives.

personal property (14)   property that is not attached in a more or less permanent fashion to real estate.

personal residence (14)   type of real estate that includes single-family houses, condominiums, cooperatives, and townhouses.

point-and-figure charts (8)   charts used to keep track of emerging price patterns by plotting significant price changes with Xs and Os but with no time dimension used.

pooled diversification (13)   a process used to spread the risk of securities' ownership whereby investors buy into a diversified portfolio of securities, which is held for the collective benefit of the individual investors.

portfolio (1)   a collection of investment vehicles assembled to meet one or more investment goals.

portfolio revision (17)   the process of selling certain issues in a portfolio and of purchasing new ones.

positive correlation (16)   a relationship between two series such that they move together.

positive leverage (14)   a position in which, if a property's return is in excess of its debt cost, the investor's return will be increased to a level well above what could have been earned from an all-cash deal.

precious metals (12)   tangible assets, like gold, silver, and platinum, that concentrate a great deal of value in a small amount of weight and volume.

precious metals (12)   tangible assets, like gold, silver, and platinum, that concentrate a great deal of value in a small amount of weight and volume.

preemptive right (11) the right of existing stockholders to maintain their proportionate share of ownership in a firm.

preference preferreds (10) a type of preferred that has seniority over other preferred stock in its right to receive dividends and in its claim on assets; also called *prior preferred stock*.

preferred stock (1) a stock that has a prior claim (ahead of common) on the income and assets of the issuing firm.

premium bond (9) a bond that has a market value in excess of par; occurs when interest rates drop below the coupon rate.

present value (5) the current value of a future sum; the inverse of *future value*.

primary market (2) market in which new issues of securities are brought to the public.

prime rate (2) the lowest interest rate charged the best business borrowers.

principal (9) on a bond, the amount of capital that must be paid at maturity.

principle of substitution (14) the principle that people do not buy or rent real estate per se but rather that they judge properties as different sets of benefits and costs.

private partnership (15) a limited partnership that has a limited number of investors and is not registered with a public agency.

problem investment (17) an investment that has not lived up to expectations.

profitability measures (7) financial ratios that measure the returns of a company by relating relative success of a firm through comparison of profits to sales, assets, or equity.

program trading (3) use of a computer to monitor price and trading volume of securities and to apply various rules to initiate trades and create or revise portfolios; widely used by brokerage houses and other Wall Street firms to make money when the futures and stock markets get out of balance, it has led to violent swings in stock prices.

promised yield (9) considers both interest income and price appreciation and measures the fully compounded rate of return, assuming a bond is held to maturity.

property (1) investments in real property or in tangible personal property.

property management (14) in real estate, finding the optimal level of benefits for a property and then providing them at the lowest costs.

property transfer process (14) the process of promotion and negotiation of real estate, which can significantly influence the cash flows a property can earn in the real estate market.

prospectus (2) a document describing in varying amounts of detail the key aspects of new security issues, the issuer, and its management and financial position.

psychographics (14) characteristics that describe people's mental dispositions, such as personality, lifestyle, and self-concept; should be considered when analyzing real estate demand.

public offering (6) an offering to sell to the investing public a set number of shares of a firm's stock at a specified price.

public partnership (15) a limited partnership that is registered with state and/or federal regulators and usually has 35 or more limited partners.

publicly traded issues (6) shares of stock readily available to the general public, which are bought and sold in the open market.

purchasing power (5) the amount of some commodity that can be bought with a given amount of a currency, such as one dollar.

purposive diversification (1) selecting investment vehicles to achieve a stated portfolio objective.

put (10) a negotiable instrument that enables the holder to sell the underlying security at a specified price on or before some future date.

put bond (9) a type of speciality bond that gives the holder the right to redeem the bonds at certain specified times before maturity.

put hedge (15)   the purchase of a put option on shares currently owned in order to lock in a profit and defer taxes on the profit to the next taxable year.

pyramiding (2)   the technique of using paper profits in margin accounts to partly or fully finance the acquisition of additional securities.

quotations (3)   price information about various types of securities, including current price data and statistics on recent price behavior.

random diversification (1)   selecting investment vehicles at random.

random walk hypothesis (8)   the theory that stock price movements are unpredictable and thus, there's really little way of knowing where future prices are headed.

ratio analysis (7)   the study of the relationships among and between various financial statement accounts.

real estate (1)   property such as residential homes, raw land, and income property (warehouses, apartment buildings, cooperatives, and condominiums).

real estate investment trust (REIT) (14)   a type of closed-end investment company that invests money, obtained through the sale of shares to investors, in various types of real estate and/or real estate mortgages.

real estate limited partnership (RELP) (14)   a professionally managed real estate syndicate that invests in various types of real estate; the managers assume the role of general partner, whose liability is unlimited, and other (passive) investors are limited partners, whose liability is limited to the amount of their initial investment.

real property (1)   land, buildings, and that which is permanently affixed to the land.

realized gain (4)   a capital gain realized upon the sale of a capital asset.

realized return (5)   return received by an investor during the period.

realized yield (9)   the rate of return earned by an investor over a period of time that is less than the life of the issue.

red herring (2)   a preliminary statement available to prospective investors after a registration statement has been filed but before its approval.

refunding provision (9)   a provision similar to a call feature except that it prohibits the premature retirement of an issue from the proceeds of a lower-coupon refunding bond.

registered bonds (9)   bonds issued to specific owners, whose names are formally registered with the issuer.

relative P/E multiple (8)   the measure of how a stock's P/E behaves relative to the average market multiple.

relevant risk (16)   risk that is nondiversifiable.

required (or desired) rate of return (8)   the return necessary to compensate an investor for the risk that is involved in an investment.

residual owners (6)   owners/stockholders of a firm, who are entitled to dividend income and a prorated share of the firm's earnings only after all the firm's other obligations have been met.

restricted account (2)   a margin account whose equity is less than the initial margin requirement and from which the amount that can be withdrawn is restricted until the account is restored to initial margin levels.

return (5)   the expected level of profit from an investment; the reward for investing.

return on invested capital (12)   return to investors based on the amount of money actually invested in a security, rather than the value of the contract itself.

revenue bonds (9)   municipal bonds backed by the revenue-generating capacity of the issuer; requires that principal and interest be paid only if a sufficient level of revenue is generated.

reverse stock split (6)   a maneuver in which a company reduces the number of shares outstanding by exchanging a fractional amount of a new share for each outstanding share of stock.

reversion (17)   the after-tax net proceeds received upon disposition of property, calculated by subtracting selling costs, mortgage repayment, and taxes from the realized selling price.

right (1)   an option to buy shares of a new issue of common stock at a specified price below the current market price, over a specified (fairly short) period of time.

rights-off (11)   condition when a firm's common stock and its rights are trading in separate markets, separate from each other; also called *ex-rights*.

rights offering (6)   an offering of a new issue of stock to existing stockholders who may purchase new shares in proportion to their current ownership position.

rights-on (11)   condition when a firm's common stock is trading with the right attached to it.

risk (4)   the chance that the actual return from an investment may differ from what is expected; the more variable, or broader, the range of possible returns, the greater the risk, and vice versa; in insurance, the uncertainty related to economic loss.

risk-adjusted, market-adjusted rate of return (RAR) (17)   the return a security or portfolio has earned after the effects of risk and market movements have been factored out.

risk-averse (5)   describes an investor who requires greater return in exchange for greater risk.

risk-free rate (R_F) (16)   the return an investor can earn on a risk-free investment such as a T-bill or an insured money market account.

risk-indifferent (5)   describes an investor who does not require greater return in exchange for greater risk.

risk-return tradeoff (5)   the inverse relationship between risk and return, in which investments with more risk should provide higher returns, and vice versa.

risk-taking (5)   describes an investor who will accept a lower return in exchange for greater risk.

round lots (2)   100-share units of stock, or multiples thereof.

round trip commissions (12)   the commission costs on both ends (buying and selling) of a securities transaction.

savings plan (13)   a service offered by a mutual fund in which the shareholder agrees, either formally or informally, to add a certain amount of money to his/her mutual fund account on a regular basis.

secondary market (2)   the market in which securities are traded after they have been issued; also called the *aftermarket*.

sector fund (13)   a mutual fund that restricts its investments to a particular segment of the market.

securities (1)   investments that represent debt, business ownership, or the legal right to acquire or sell a business ownership interest.

Securities Investor Protection Corporation (SIPC) (2)   an agency of the federal government that insures each customer's account for up to $500,000.

securities markets (2)   markets allowing suppliers and demanders of funds to make transactions; may provide trading in either money or capital.

securitization (9)   market technology whereby various types of bank lending vehicles are transformed into marketable securities much like mortgage-backed securities.

security analysis (7)   the process of gathering and organizing information and then using it to determine the value of a share of common stock.

security market line (SML) (5) the graphic depiction of the capital asset pricing model; for each level of nondiversifiable risk, measured by beta, reflects the investor's required return.

selling group (2) a large number of brokerage firms that join to accept responsibility for selling a certain portion of the issue of a new security.

senior bonds (9) secured debt obligations, backed by a legal claim on specific property of the issuer.

serial bond (9) a bond that has a series of different maturity dates.

Series EE savings bonds (4) savings bonds issued by the U.S. Treasury and sold at banks and through payroll deductions, in varying denominations, at 50% of face value; they pay a variable rate of interest depending on the length of time held.

settle price (12) the closing price (last price of the day) for commodities and financial futures.

short interest (8) the number of stocks sold short in the market at any given time; a technical indicator believed to indicate future market demand.

short selling (2) the sale of borrowed securities, their eventual repurchase by the short seller at a (hopefully) lower price, and their return to the lender.

shorting-against-the-box (2) a technique used to lock in a security profit and defer the taxes on it to the following tax year by short-selling a number of shares equal to those already owned.

short-term investments (1) investments that typically mature within one year.

short-term vehicles (1) savings instruments that usually have lives of one year or less.

simple interest (5) interest paid only on the actual balance for the actual amount of time it is on deposit.

single-premium annuity (15) a contract purchased with a single lump-sum payment.

single-premium life insurance policy (SPLI) (15) an insurance investment vehicle for which the policyholder pays a large premium to purchase a whole life policy that provides a stated death benefit and earns a competitive interest rate on the cash value buildup, which occurs over time on a tax-free basis.

single-property syndicate (14) a type of real estate limited partnership established to purchase a specific piece of property.

sinking fund (9) a provision that stipulates the amount of principal that will be retired annually over the life of a bond.

Small Investor Index (3) an index that measures gains and losses of the average investor, relative to a base of 100 set on 12/31/87; based on a portfolio including types of investments held by average small investors.

social security (4) Federal government income program for retired or disabled persons, to which individuals contribute over their working lifetimes, and with benefits and conditions set by law.

socioeconomic environment (14) in real estate, the demographics and lifestyles of the people who live or work near the subject property.

software (3) the programs that instruct a computer which functions to perform.

specialists (2) stock exchange members who specialize in one or more stocks and make odd-lot transactions for exchange members.

specialty fund (13) a mutual fund that strives to achieve attractive and sometimes spectacular rates of return by adhering to unusual or unorthodox investment strategies.

speculation (1) the process of buying investment vehicles in which the future value and level of expected earnings are uncertain.

speculative investment vehicles (1) investment vehicles with high levels of risk.

speculative property (14) type of real estate, typically including land and special-purpose

buildings such as churches and gas stations, with a high degree of uncertainty for future profit.

split ratings (9)   different ratings given to a bond issue by the two major rating agencies.

Standard & Poor's Corp. (S&P) (3)   publisher of a variety of financial reports and services, including *Corporation Records* and *Stock Reports*.

Standard & Poor's indexes (3)   true indexes that measure the current price of a group of stocks relative to a base established for the 1941–1943 period, which has an index value of 10.

standard deduction (15)   an amount, indexed to the cost of living, that taxpayers can elect to deduct from adjusted gross income without itemizing (listing) specific items.

statement of cash flows (7)   a financial summary of a firm's cash flow and other events that caused changes in the company's cash position.

statement of changes in stockholders' equity (7)   a financial summary of the amount of profits reinvested in the business, the amount of dividends paid out to investors, and other changes in a firm's equity position.

stock (1)   securities that give the purchaser an equity interest in a business.

stock dividend (6)   payment of a dividend in the form of additional shares of stock.

stock index futures (12)   futures contracts written on broad-based measures of stock market performance like the S&P 500 Stock Index; traded much like commodities, allowing investors to participate in the general movements of the stock market.

stock index option (11)   a put or call option written on a specific stock market index such as the S&P 500.

stock split (6)   a maneuver in which a company increases the number of shares outstanding by exchanging a specified number of new shares of stock for each outstanding share.

stock valuation (8)   the process by which the underlying value of a stock is established, as based on future risk and return performance of the security.

stockbrokers (2)   individuals licensed by stock exchanges to enable investors to buy and sell securities; also called *account executives*.

stockholder's (annual) report (3)   a report published yearly by every publicly held firm; contains a wide range of information including financial statements for the most recent fiscal year.

stop-loss order (2)   an order to sell a stock when its market price reaches or drops below a specified level; also called a *stop order*.

straight annuity (15)   an annuity contract that provides for a series of payments for the rest of the annuitant's life.

strategic metals (12)   non-U.S.-mined metals, such as cobalt, chromium, and magnesium, vital to the production of many U.S.-made goods.

street name (2)   stock certificates issued in the brokerage house's names but held in trust for their customers who actually own them.

striking price (11)   the price contract between the buyer of an option and the writer, it's the stated price at which you can buy a security with a call, or sell a security with a put.

stripped Treasuries (9)   zero-coupon bonds sold by the U.S. Treasury; created by stripping the coupons from a Treasury bond and selling them separately from the principal.

sub-index option (11)   see *industry option*.

subordinated debentures (9)   unsecured bonds that have a claim that is secondary to other debentures.

subscription price (11)   see *exercise price*.

suitability rule (15)   a rule excluding investors who cannot bear a high amount of risk from buying limited partnership interests.

supply analysis (14) study of the competition in real estate by identifying potential competitors and making an inventory of them by price and features.

syndicate (15) a joint venture—general partnership, corporation, or limited partnership—in which investors pool their resources for investing.

systematic risk same as *nondiversifiable risk*.

systematic withdrawal plan (13) a mutual fund service that enables shareholders to automatically receive a predetermined amount of money every month or quarter.

tangible investments (12) investments that have an actual form or substance, such as precious metals, stamps, or works of art; assets which are held, in part, for their investment merits.

tangible personal property (1) property such as gold, antiques, art, and other collectibles.

tax avoidance (15) reducing or eliminating taxes in legal ways that comply with the intent of Congress.

tax credits (15) tax reductions allowed by the IRS on a dollar-for-dollar basis under certain specified conditions.

tax deferral (15) the strategy of delaying taxes by shifting income subject to tax into a later period.

tax evasion (15) illegal activities designed to avoid paying taxes by omitting income or overstating deductions.

tax planning (4) the formation of strategies that will exclude, reduce, or defer the level of taxes to be paid.

tax shelter (4) an investment vehicle that offers potential reductions of taxable income.

tax swap (4) selling one security that has experienced a capital loss and replacing it with another similar security in order to partially or fully offset a capital gain that has been realized in another part of the investor's portfolio; used to avoid IRS regulations against wash sales.

taxable income (15) the income to which tax rates are applied; equals adjusted gross income minus itemized deductions and exemptions.

taxable munis (9) municipal bonds, used to finance projects considered nonessential, whose interest income is fully taxable by the federal government.

tax-exempt money fund (4) a money market mutual fund that limits its investments to tax-exempt municipal securities with very short maturities.

tax-favored income (15) an investment return that is not taxable, that is taxed at a rate less than that on other similar investments that defer the payment of tax to a later period, or that trades current income for capital gains.

tax-sheltered annuity (15) an annuity contract available to certain employees of institutions such as schools, governments, and not-for-profit organizations that allows them to make a tax-free contribution from current income to purchase a deferred annuity.

technical analysis (8) the study of the various forces at work in the marketplace and their effect on stock prices.

term bond (9) a bond that has a single, fairly lengthy maturity date.

term life insurance (4) form of life insurance in which the insurer agrees pay a specified amount if the insured dies within the policy period; the least expensive form of life insurance.

***The Wall Street Journal* (3)** a daily newspaper, published regionally by Dow Jones; the most popular source of financial news.

theory of contrary opinion (8) a technical indicator that uses the amount and type of odd-lot trading as an indicator of the current state of the market and pending changes.

third market (2) over-the-counter transactions made in securities listed on the NYSE, AMEX, or other organized exchanges.

time value of money (5) the principle that as long as an opportunity exists to earn interest, the value of money is affected by the point in time when it is expected to be received.

total return (5) the sum of the current income and the capital gains (or losses) earned on an investment over a specified period of time.

total risk (16) the sum of the diversifiable and nondiversifiable risk components of an investment vehicle.

traditional portfolio management (16) an approach to portfolio management that emphasizes balancing the portfolio with a variety of stocks and/or bonds from a broad cross-section of industries.

Treasury bonds (9) U.S. Treasury debt securities that are issued with maturities of more than 10 years—usually 25 years or more.

Treasury notes (9) U.S. Treasury debt securities that are issued with maturities of 10 years or less.

treasury stock (6) shares of stock that have been issued and subsequently repurchased (and held) by the issuing firm.

12(b)-1 fee (13) a fee levied by some mutual funds to cover management and other operating costs; amounts to as much as 1¼ percent annually on the average net assets.

undermargined (2) the condition of a margin account whose equity is less than the maintenance margin level.

underwriting (2) the guarantee of an investment banker that a firm issuing a new security will receive a specified minimum amount for the issue.

underwriting syndicate (2) a group formed to spread the financial risk associated with the selling of new securities.

unit investment trust (13) see *investment trust*.

unrealized capital gain (4) a capital gain made only ''on paper,'' that is, not realized until the fund's holdings are sold; also called *paper profit* or *paper gain*.

unsponsored ADRs (2) ADRs that are not registered with the U.S. government and therefore are traded over the counter.

unsystematic risk same as *diversifiable risk*.

uptick (2) the increase in the price of a stock issue since its last transaction.

U.S. Treasury bills (T-bills) (4) obligations of the U.S. Treasury, sold on a discount basis, and having varying short-term maturities and virtually no risk.

valuation (1) process by which an investor determines the perceived worth of a security using risk, return, and valuation concepts.

Value Line composite average (3) a stock average, published by Value Line, that reflects the percentage changes in share price of about 1,700 stocks traded on the NYSE, AMEX, and OTC market, relative to a base of 100, set 6/30/61.

Value Line Investment Survey (3) a weekly subscription service covering about 1,700 of the most widely held stocks and their industries; popular among individual investors.

variable annuity (15) an annuity contract that adjusts the monthly payment according to the investment experience (and sometimes the mortality experience) of the insurer.

variable life insurance (4) form of life insurance that offers insurance coverage with a savings feature that allows the insured to decide how the cash value is invested; the amount of insurance coverage varies with the policy's investment returns.

variable-rate note (9) a speciality bond issue with two unique features: (1) after a specified

period of time (6–18 months), the coupon "floats" at a certain amount above T-bill or T-note rates, and (2) every year or so the notes are redeemable at par, at the bondholder's option.

variable ratio plan (17)   a formula plan for timing investment transactions, in which the ratio of the speculative portion to the total portfolio varies depending on the movement in the value of the speculative securities; when the ratio rises or falls by a predetermined amount, the amount committed to the speculative portion of the portfolio is reduced or increases, respectively.

variance (16)   a statistical measure used to measure a security's return; calculated as the standard deviation squared.

vested (rights) (4)   benefits, accumulated under a pension plan, that have become the employee's nonforfeitable rights.

volatility (16)   the amount of fluctuation in return exhibited by a security or portfolio.

warrant (1)   a long-lived option that gives the holder the right to buy stock in a company at a price as specified in the warrant itself.

warrant premium (11)   the difference between the true value of a warrant and its market price.

wash sale (4)   the procedure, disallowed under the tax law, of selling securities on which capital losses can be realized and then immediately buying them back.

whipsawing (17)   the situation in which a stock drops in price and then bounces back upward; a principal risk associated with the use of *stop-loss orders*.

whole life insurance (4)   form of life insurance that provides coverage over the entire life of the insured; offers a savings benefit.

Wilshire 5000 Index (3)   measure of the total dollar value (in billions) of 5,000 actively traded stocks, including all those on the NYSE and the AMEX, plus active OTC stocks.

wrap account (2)   an account in which customers with large portfolios pay to a brokerage firm a flat annual fee that covers the cost of a money manager's services and the cost of commissions.

yield (5)   the actual rate of return earned by a long-term investment; it considers the time value of money; also called the *internal rate of return*.

yield curve (9)   graphic representation of the relationship between a bond's term to maturity and its yield at a given point in time.

yield pickup swap (9)   replacement of a low-coupon bond for a comparable higher-coupon bond in order to realize an increase in current yield and yield to maturity.

yield spreads (9)   differences in interest rates that exist in various sections of the market.

yield to maturity (9)   another name for *promised yield*.

zero-coupon bonds (9)   bonds with no coupons that are sold at a deep discount from par value; they increase in value over time at a compound rate of return so that at maturity they are worth considerably more than their initial cost.

INDEX

ACKNOWLEDGMENTS: We wish to thank the following copyright holders who granted permission to reprint the material listed: ASSOCIATE CLUBS PUBLICATIONS *For* "Scams, Dupes, Grafts, and Goldbricks," *Private Clubs,* © 1989 Associate Clubs Publications, Inc. BARRON'S *For* "Market Laboratory Stocks." © Dow Jones & Company, 1989. All rights reserved. *For* Edward A. Wyatt, "Program Trading: Gosh, Here It Comes Again." © Dow Jones & Company, 1989. All rights reserved. BUSINESS WEEK *For* Business Week Index, reprinted from July 24, 1989, issue of *Business Week,* by special permission, copyright © 1989 by McGraw-Hill, Inc. CHANGING TIMES *For* Dan Moreau, "Changing Agents: Money-Market Funds Didn't Seem Such a Good Idea in 1970," *Changing Times,* March 1989, © Kiplinger Washington Editors, Inc., 1989. *For* Manuel Schiffres, "The Federal Reserve Walks Quietly, But It Affects the Economy with a Big Stick," *Changing Times,* October 1988, © Kiplinger Washington Editors, Inc., 1988. *For* "When to Sell That Stock," *Changing Times,* April 1986, © Kiplinger Washington Editors, Inc., 1986. *For* Jeff Kosnett, "What to Look For—and Look Out For—As You Read a Mutual Fund Prospectus," *Changing Times,* May 1988, © Kiplinger Washington Editors, Inc., 1988. All material reprinted with permission from *Changing Times* Magazine. These reprints are not to be altered in any way, except with permission from *Changing Times.* COMMODITY PRICE CHARTS *For* "CRB Futures Index," 1988. Courtesy of Commodity Price Charts, 219 Parkade, Cedar Falls, IA 50613. CONSUMERS UNION *For* table from "Comparison of Universal vs. Traditional Life Insurance," *Consumer Reports,* January 1982. THE DONOGHUE ORGANIZATION, INC. *For* data from *Donoghue's Mutual Funds Almanac* ($26, P.O. Box 6640, Holliston, MA 01746). DOW JONES & COMPANY For the following material from *The Wall Street Journal: For* Matthew Winkler, Michael W. Miller, and Steve Schwartz, "Big Board Considers Trading Electronically During Off-Hours." © Dow Jones & Company, 1989. All rights reserved. *For* Sonja Steptoe, "Many States Are Nixing Brothel Stock." © Dow Jones & Company, 1989. All rights reserved. *For* adaptation from Robert L. Rose, "Compounding: It's Boring But a Wonder." © Dow Jones & Company, 1985. All rights reserved. *For* Dean Rotbart, "Price-to-Sales Ratios Are Gaining Prominence as a Handy Tool to Avoid Poor Investments." © Dow Jones & Company, 1984. All rights reserved. *For* Earl C. Gottschalk, Jr., "Picking Stocks by the Book Is A Standby Some Swear By." © Dow Jones & Company, 1988. All rights reserved. *For* Tom Herman & Rick Stine, "New 52-Week T-Bills Are Extremely Popular, Bonds Stage Biggest One-Day Rally of the Year." © Dow Jones & Company, 1989. All rights reserved. *For* George Anders, "Picking a Peck of PIK-Preferreds Can Be Precarious." © Dow Jones & Company, 1988. All rights reserved. *For* Jill Bettner, "Convertible Bonds May Be Right for the Times, But Do Some Figuring Before You Buy Them." © Dow Jones & Company, 1982. All rights reserved. *For* Stanley W. Angrist, "Put Options Can Help Protect Portfolios." © Dow Jones & Company, 1989. All rights reserved. *For* Jill Bettner, "Minidorms Touted as Tactics to Cut the Costs of College." © Dow Jones & Company, 1988. All rights reserved. *For* Neil Barsky and Jill Bettner, "In Partnership, Who Shares Problems?" © Dow Jones & Company, 1989. All rights reserved. *For* Stanley W. Angrist, "Variety Spices Up More Portfolios." © Dow Jones & Company, 1989. All rights reserved. *For* graph of the Dow Jones Averages, April 28, 1989. © Dow Jones & Company, 1989. All rights reserved. And for quotations and prices from *The Wall Street Journal* shown throughout the book, © Dow Jones & Company. All rights reserved.

For Dow Jones News/Retrieval *Summary of Information Services,* May 1989. © Dow Jones & Company, 1989. All rights reserved. EASTMAN KODAK COMPANY *For* Summary of the Year in Figures from the 1988 Stockholder's Report. Reprinted courtesy of Eastman Kodak Company. FIDELITY INVESTMENTS *For* partial list of portfolio holdings, 1988. FINANCIAL WORLD *For* Jill Andresky, "Satanic Purses," *Financial World* Magazine, March 21, 1989, 52–54. FORBES *For* Gail Eisenstodt, "Apparel, Shoes and Textiles." Reprinted by permission of *Forbes* magazine, January 9, 1989. © Forbes Inc., 1989. *For* page from the 1988 Forbes Fund Ratings/Stock. Excerpted by permission of *Forbes* magazine, September 5, 1988. © Forbes Inc., 1988. FORTUNE *For* "Inflation Will Speed Up, But It Won't Start Running Away," *Fortune,* © 1988 Time Inc. All rights reserved. *For* Joshua Mendes, "Are You Ready to Go Global?" *Fortune,* 1988 Investor's Guide, © 1988 Time Inc. All rights reserved. GREYHOUND *For* use of stock certificate and 1988 proxy statement. INVESTMENT COMPANY INSTITUTE *For* data from *Mutual Fund Fact Book,* 1984 and 1989, published by Investment Company Institute, Washington, D.C. MONEY *For* Malcolm N. Carter, "How Much Do You Really Need?", *Money,* © 1982 Time Inc. All rights reserved. *For* adaptation from Gretchen Morgenson, "Options," *Money,* © 1984 Time Inc. All rights reserved. *For* an adaptation from David S. Krause, "Baseball Cards Bat .425," *Money,* © 1988 Time Inc. All rights reserved. *For* Robin Mitchell, "To Make Big Profits, Invest with Friends in Your Own Backyard," *Money,* © 1989 Time Inc. All rights reserved. MONEY MAKER *For* Dan Ruck, "The Hidden Stock Market," *Money Maker* Magazine, December/January 1989, pp. 46–48. MOODY'S INVESTOR'S SERVICES, INC. *For* ratings from Moody's *Bond Record* and from Moody's *Preferred Stock Rating.* MORNINGSTAR, INC. *For* "Boston Company Capital Appreciation Fund," *Mutual Fund Values.* Reprinted by permission of Morningstar Inc., 53 W. Jackson Blvd., Chicago, IL 60604. PRUDENTIAL-BACHE SECURITIES *For* excerpts from advertising brochure and prospectus, Prudential-Bache Energy Income Partnerships, Series VI, August 1988. *For* excerpts from listing of Prudential-Bache Flexi-Fund, Portfolio of Investments, July 31, 1988. READER'S DIGEST *For* "Meltdown Monday—The Day the Market Crashed." Reprinted with permission from the February 1988 Reader's Digest. And for permission from the following original sources for that article: Dow Jones & Co., Inc.; The New York Times Co.; Time Inc.; and News Group Publications, Inc., New York, N.Y. SILK GREENHOUSE For page from 1989 prospectus. Reprinted by permission. STANDARD & POOR'S CORPORATION *For* illustrations and data from S & P's *Standard NYSE Stock Reports,* from S & P's *Stock Guide,* from S & P's *1988 Analyst's Handbook,* from S & P's *Statistical Service—Security Price Index Record,* from S & P's *Trade and Securities Statistics,* and from S & P's *Bond Guide.*

THE NEW YORK TIMES *For* Richard T. Maturi, "Taking Stock of Investment Clubs." Copyright © 1988 by The New York Times Company. *For* Donald Jay Korn, "And Now, a Wave of Flexible Annuities." Copyright © 1989 by The New York Times Company. *For* Leonard Sloane, "Crash-Chastened Investors Seek to Diversify." Copyright © 1989 by The New York Times Company. *For* Lawrence J. DeMaria, "When Investors Won't Let Go—No Sale," Copyright © 1989 by The New York Times Company. All material reproduced by permission. THE ORLANDO SENTINEL *For* Lisa M. Keefe, "Going for Brokers—Check It Out," published in *The Orlando Sentinel.* TIME *For* illustration, "A Leveraged Buyout in Action." Copyright 1988 Time Inc. Reprinted by permission. VALUE LINE *For* Value Line Investment Survey Report on Eastman Kodak, March 24, 1989. Copyright © 1989 by Value Line, Inc.; used by permission.

THE INVESTMENT MANAGEMENT DISK (IMD)

SYSTEM REQUIREMENTS

- Any IBM or IBM compatible PC
- DOS Version 2.1 or higher
- 512K of memory or more
- Dual (floppy) disk drives a minimum. Program will also run on a system with one floppy disk drive and a hard disk.
- Printer recommended, but not required.

USER INSTRUCTIONS

1. Insert your DOS disk into drive A (the one on the left, or top, of the dual disk drive). Always insert disks with the label side up.
2. Turn on the computer; after a short period of time the computer will request the current date (e.g., 09/16/88) and time (e.g., 15:45—in a 24-hour format).
3. The computer will then display a "prompt": A>.
4. At this point, remove the DOS disk and insert the IMD Program disk into drive A.
5. Insert the IMD Overlay disk into drive B.
6. Now type in START, and press the <Enter> key.
7. The IMD is now being loaded. In a few moments a title screen will appear, followed by the main menu.
8. Your IMD program is now running. The program is menu driven, which means you select the routines you want directly from the menu.
9. To select a chapter or routine from the menu use the cursor keys (the four keys with arrows on them) to move the highlight bar up or down. When you have the desired menu selection highlighted, press the <Enter> key and your desired selection will appear.
10. Now run the program by providing the requested information.
11. All routines in the IMD are keyed to pages in this book for reference purposes.

THE INVESTMENT MANAGEMENT DISK MENU

Chapter 1   The Role and Scope of Investments (No Routines)

Chapter 2   Investment Markets and Transactions
Margin Position
Return on Invested Capital from a Margin Transaction
Margin on a Short Sale
Return on Invested Capital from a Short Sale

Chapter 3   Sources of Investment Information and Advice
   (No Routines)

Chapter 4   Developing Investment Strategies
Annual Rate of Return on a Discount Security

Chapter 5   Measuring Investment Return and Risk
Future Value of a Single Cash Flow
Future Value of a Mixed Stream
Future Value of an Annuity
Present Value of a Single Cash Flow
Present Value of a Mixed Stream
Present Value of an Annuity
Holding Period Return (HPR)
Yield (or Internal Rate of Return) for a Mixed Stream of Income
Yield (or Internal Rate of Return) for a Stream of Income
Yield (or Internal Rate of Return) for an Annuity
Approximate Yield (or Internal Rate of Return)
Capital Asset Pricing Model (CAPM)

Chapter 6   Common Stock Investments
Book Value/B.V. per Share
Earnings per Share
Dividend Yield

Chapter 7   Common Stock Analysis
Current Ratio
Net Working Capital
Accounts Receivable Turnover
Inventory Turnover
Total Asset Turnover
Debt-Equity Ratio
Times Interest Earned
Operating Ratio
Net Profit Margin
Return on Assets
Return on Equity